A HISTORICAL GRAMMAR OF
BIBLICAL HEBREW

A HISTORICAL GRAMMAR OF BIBLICAL HEBREW

A PRESENTATION OF PROBLEMS WITH SUGGESTIONS TO THEIR SOLUTION

BY

ALEXANDER SPERBER

THE JEWISH THEOLOGICAL SEMINARY OF AMERICA

LEIDEN

E. J. BRILL

1966

CONTENTS

CONTENT

FOREWORD

In September 1934 I joined the Faculty of the *Jewish Theological Seminary of America*, and thus the treasures of its famous Library became easily accessible to me. This resulted in an almost complete re-orientation in my Biblical studies. For up till then, while in Bonn, my research was based upon the well-known printed Bibles, which were in general use at that time, as e.g. those prepared by Chr. D. Ginsburg and Rudolf Kittel, and which claimed to be faithful reproductions of Jacob ben Chayim's First Masoretic Bible. The mere application of the term "Masoretic" to characterize their text endowed these Bibles with an aura of antiquity and authority.

But upon coming to America, I could fill the shelves of my study— thanks to the liberality of the Seminary's Library—with all the genuine, old Bible editions, both Hebrew and polyglot, such as e.g. Felix Pratensis, Jacob ben Chayim, etc. And so these editions and not their later follow-ups became now the basis of my daily Bible reading. The first result was utter confusion on my part! I saw the cherished rules of Hebrew grammar crumble, one after the other, since the actual facts as exhibited in these Bibles did not uphold them. I then tried to concentrate on the re-examination of specific, individual problems according to the new findings, and to present the outcome of such studies in separate monographs, whenever I felt that the material which I had assembled, allowed for the formulation of definite conclusions.

These monographs appeared in the *Hebrew Union College Annual* (volumes XII/XIII, XIV, XVI and XVII), the *Journal of Biblical Literature* (1940, 1943 and 1945), the *Proceedings of the American Academy for Jewish Research* (vol. XVIII), *Miscellanea Giovanni Mercati* (1946) and the *Alexander Marx Jubilee Volume* (1950).

At that time I did not yet realize the existence of an interrelation between these problems, which I had investigated. All I could see then, were isolated trees, plenty of them; but I failed to see the forest, which they formed, provided they were methodically combined into an entity.

In the ensuing years since these monographs were first published, certain developments have taken place, which helped to broaden my outlook and thus *make a new, revised and augmented publication of these studies, from a general viewpoint, possible and imperative.* For the phenomena, which were treated disjointedly when first published, now appear to me in a new light as the interconnected links of a grammatical system, reflecting the historical development of Hebrew grammar from an earlier traceable period until the ultimate emergence of what is known to us as Masoretic Hebrew.

And while continuing with my daily reading of the Bible, I found additional evidence of new grammatical phenomena, which I had failed to observe before, and which may substantially contribute to getting a clearer picture of the historical background of the present-day grammatical outlook. Hence, the *Historical Grammar of Biblical Hebrew* deals with the problems of Hebrew Grammar in a logical arrangement and presents them in a substantially more elaborate way. I suggest that the reader first acquaints himself with the "Index of Subject Matters", which appears at the end of the book and thus realizes the "Plan" and "Aufbau" of this grammar.

Thus, the fundamental difference of this *new approach* in treating the respective problems of Hebrew grammar, from the way they have hitherto been dealt with—if treated they were at all and not completely overlooked—, will at once become evident and—I hope I may also add— convincing.

As a follow-up of these studies I strongly recommend a careful examination of my *Grammar of Masoretic Hebrew* (Copenhagen 1959).

In conclusion may I be permitted to add a few remarks of a more personal nature. Before elaborating on my own theories and method of approach, I had first to demonstrate the weakness, inner contradictions and finally the utter untenability of the current theories and approaches. This negative part of my task had to be done forcefully so as to be accomplished at all. Of course, this refers only to my arguments and my way of reasoning, and not to the kind of language I used, which—I do hope—reflects the high esteem in which I hold these very scholars, whose viewpoints I so strongly oppose. I feel the greatest respect for these scholars, whose names I mention and whose works I quote in order to refute them. I consider myself a pupil of theirs, even though I feel I have outgrown their teaching. No author, nor book, mentioned here has failed to teach me much. And I could not possibly pay my respect to them in a more appropriate way than by a careful and detailed perusal of their works. When in the course of preparing the manuscript for my *Grammar of Masoretic Hebrew* I wrote to Robert H. Pfeiffer that I quote him there (pp. 89 ff.) in order to refute him, he immediately replied: "Tear me to pieces—but quote me"!

When I said before that I feel I have outgrown the teaching of my teachers, I did not mean to claim any credit for it for myself. Because in our Seminary Library I had an advantage over my teachers, the extent of which only he will realize, who has ever enjoyed the privileges I had. I can express my indebtedness to our Seminary in no better way than by quoting the Bible (I Chron. 29, 14): כִּי מִמְּךָ הַכֹּל וּמִיָּדְךָ נָתַנּוּ לָךְ: "For all things come of Thee, And of Thine own have we given Thee".

SIGLA, SYMBOLS AND ABBREVIATIONS

Q = Qere
K = Ketib
Ma = Ma'arbae
Md = Madinḥae
Seb = Sebirin

This Masoretic material is derived from Ch. D. Ginsburg's *The Massorah* compiled from Manuscripts, I, London 1880, pp. 591-9; II, London 1883, pp. 55-93 and 324-9. In indicating the vowel signs I follow MT, irrespective of whether Ginsburg assigns the word thus vocalized to the Q or K, Ma or Md.

VarK = Variant reading according to Kennicott, *Vetus Testamentum cum variis lectionibus*, 2 vols., Oxford 1776 and 1780
BHK = Biblia Hebraica ed. Kittel, Leipzig 1913
BHKK = Biblia Hebraica... ed. Rud. Kittel... P. Kahle, Stuttgart 1937
B-L = Hans Bauer und Pontus Leander, *Historische Grammatik der hebräischen Sprache des Alten Testaments*, Halle (Saale) 1918 seq.
Bergst. = G. Bergsträsser, *Hebräische Grammatik*, Leipzig 1918 seq.
    Part II is indicated by a 2 before the paragraph quoted

Both B-L and Bergstr. are quoted merely in order to bring into sharp relief the difference between the current explanation of these grammatical phenomena as offered by them and the new approach as elaborated here.

Frequent reference is made to readings of the first Biblia Rabbinica, Venice 1515-17 and its marginal notes; they are quoted as: Venice 1515 and: marg. respectively. All Bible quotations refer—unless another source is mentioned—to the first Masoretic Bible, Venice 1524/5.

Due to technical difficulties, the *dagesh* had often to be omitted, where it was not essential to the understanding of the problems under investigation. Similarly, the inferior dot (like ḳ in ḳal) could not be consistently applied.

Quite frequently I have retained here the use of the established terminology of Hebrew grammar (e.g. perfect, imperfect, consecutive *waw*, verbs *mediae waw*), though I prove that these terms are based on misconceptions and outright mistakes. In doing so, I was guided by my desire to make myself better understood by the student of Hebrew philology, to whom my own terminology as proposed here is still new and therefore less familiar.

AV = The Authorized Version
RV = The Revised Version
JPS = The Holy Scriptures (Jewish Publication Society, Philadelphia
    1917)

Two vertical strokes (//) separate the two components of a doublet.
The English translations, when within "quotation marks", are taken
from JPS; but when in Italics, they represent my own interpretation of
the passage.

In Chapter Two:

A stands for Codex A of the Septuagint; B for Codex B; where
both codices agree in their reading, I put G
O indicates the Second Column of Origen's Hexapla
H-R refers to the Septuagint Concordance by Hatch and Redpath
Quotations in Latin Alphabet originate from Jerome: On after
such a citation indicates, that it is taken from his Onomastica Sacra;
J gives his commentaries as the source

MT = The Hebrew Masoretic Text, according to Kittel's *Biblia Hebraica*,
    Leipzig 1905
MdO = P. Kahle, *Masoreten des Ostens*, Leipzig 1913

The sigla used in connection with Hebrew words in Babylonian
vocalization (f.i. Ec 1) refer to Professor Kahle's "Catalogue of Hebrew
Bible Mss. from Babylon," published in the *ZAW* 1928, pp. 113-137.
A continuation of this Catalogue appeared in a leaflet headed: "Sigla
für die hebräischen Bibelhandschriften aus Babylonien," which is included
in the edition of Numeri and Deuteronomium of Kittel's *Biblia Hebraica*,
Stuttgart 1935.

MTK = Paul Kahle, *Der masoretische Text des Alten Testaments nach
    der Überlieferung der babylonischen Juden*, Leipzig 1902. The basis of
    this monograph is the Ms. or. qu. 680 of the Berlin State Library,
    which is called "Ec 1" in the above cited Catalogue.
MdW I   = Paul Kahle, *Masoreten des Westens* I, Stuttgart 1927
MdW II = id., II, Stuttgart 1930
Bar = Falk Bar, *Liturgische Dichtungen von Jannai und Samuel*, Bonn
    1936
Edelmann = Rafael Edelmann, *Zur Frühgeschichte des Maḥzor*,
    Stuttgart 1934
Ms. 105 JThS = A Bible Ms. with the Babylonian vocalization contain-
    ing most of the former prophets with Targum, in the Library of the
    Jewish Theological Seminary of America
HUCA = *Hebrew Union College Annual*

JBL   = *Journal of Biblical Literature*
PAAJR = *Proceedings of the American Academy for Jewish Research*
ZAW   = *Zeitschrift für die Alttestamentliche Wissenschaft*
BV   = Babylonian vocalization
PV   = Palestinian vocalization
S or Sam. = Hebrew Pentateuch of the Samaritans
Mayser = E. Mayser, *Grammatik der griechischen Papyri aus der Ptole-mäerzeit*, Leipzig 1906
Thompson = E. M. Thompson, *An Introduction to Greek and Latin Palaeography*, Oxford 1912
Th   = Theodoret of Kyros (*vol. 81*), *Patrologia Graeca* ed. Migne
Cy   = Cyril of Alexandria (*vols. 71, 72*), *Patrologia Graeca* ed. Migne
MH = A. Sperber, *A Grammar of Masoretic Hebrew* (Copenhagen 1959)
OT   = Old Testament
NT   = New Testament
LXX or G = Septuagint according to Codex B or, where missing, Codex A
O' = *Origenis Hexaplorum quae supersunt* ed. Fridericus Field; 2 vols. Oxford 1875
al. ex. = *alia exemplaria* (quoted by Field)

ABBREVIATIONS IN THE MASORA
QUOTED ON PP. 490-553

K = כתיב; Q = קרי

אֹב = אלפא ביתא		לֹ = לית
אור = אוריתא		לֹק = לא קרי
אמֹצ = אמצע		ליֹש = לישנא; לישני
אֹסֹפ = אתנח סוף פסוק		מלֹ = מלא
ביֹנ = ביניהון		מלֹי = מלין
בֹמֹב = בר מן ב (= two)		מסֹה = מסורה הגדולה
בֹר = בראשית רבה		מצֹע = מצעות
בתֹר = בתריה; בתראה; בתרין		נבֹי = נביאים
דסֹמ = דסמיכין		נמֹס = נמסר
זֹק = זקף		נֹס = נסיב
חֹס = חסר		סֹ = סוף; ספר
טֹע = טעותא; טעמא		סֹא = ספר אחד (אחר :or)
יֹס = יש ספרים		סֹפֹ = סוף פסוק
כֹת = כתיב		סֹפ = ספרא
כֹכֹ = כתיב כן		סֹת = ספר תורה

רפ̇	= ריש פסוקא		פֹּס	=	פסוקא; פסוקין
רפֿ	= רפה		פֹּת	=	פתח; פתחין
תוֹ	= תורה		ק	=	קרינן
תיֹ	= תיבותא		קֹד	=	קדמאה
תֹני	= תניינא		קֹמ	=	קמץ; קמצין
תרֹג	= תרגום		קרֹי	=	קריא; קרינן

A dotted letter (e. g. בֹ or הֹ) indicates: that the word referred to occurs either so many times (twice, or five times), or is spelled in such a way (with ב or ה).

To the memory of my brother

Dr. Jakob Sperber נ״ע

(b. Dec. 30, 1890 — d. Oct. 23, 1918)

Dozent at the Rabbiner-Seminar in Berlin

וְאָמְרוּ כִּי קְבָרוּהוּ בְּעָפָר וּבֵין הַלֵּב וּמוֹרָשָׁיו קְבַרְתִּיו

(cf. שירי החל׃ משה אבן עזרא editio Brody, p. 248)

CHAPTER ONE

HEBREW PHILOLOGY IN REVIEW

I. GRAMMAR

A. GRAMMATICAL THEORIES

§ 1.   Hebrew philology deals mainly with three aspects of the Hebrew Bible: 1) the Bible text; 2) its grammar; 3) its dictionary. They are dependent on one another in exactly the same order as we listed them here.

§ 2.   In establishing the Bible text, we must follow up the textual tradition as far back as possible. Only a Bible text, which is edited on the basis of manuscript evidence alone, without editorial interference (cf. p. 418, § 7 and p. 548, §§ 18-22) can be regarded a solid foundation of Hebrew philology. We are not at liberty to deviate from this basis in order to make the text conform to our own theories about the grammatical structure of the language. For all our theories are merely explanations of the facts and are derived from the observation of the details of the text; the Bible text ranks first, the grammar being merely the outcome of a study of the Bible; cf. p. 553, § 23, and p. 576, § 28.

§ 3.   The grammar consists of three parts: 1) morphology; 2) phonology; 3) syntax. In the morphology, the words found in the Bible are grouped and classified according to certain functions and features. A separate treatment is accorded to the different parts of speech, each of which is further divided and subdivided into smaller groups of words. The sole purpose of this progressing division is to bring into sharp relief the characteristics of each group as compared to those of another group. This leads the grammarian to the formulation of general rules concerning the phonology. Thus, phonology is the outgrowth of morphology and dependent on it. It is quite conceivable that one and the same word (e.g., a segolate) be listed by one grammarian in one group, and by another grammarian in another group. As a result, their theories with regard to Hebrew phonology will show corresponding differences (cf. B-L § 61j′, where בֶּטֶן, שֶׁמֶשׁ; ib. l′: קָמָה, שֶׁבַע are listed as ḳatl-forms); cf. here § 12.

§ 4.   It must be emphasized that in order to edit the Bible text so as

to meet with our expectations as outlined in § 2, the editor must be guided
solely by objective facts, to the absolute exclusion of his personal preferences. But the grammarian, on the other hand, is perfectly free to impress
his personality upon his grammatical theories. Grammar is a commentary
of the text, from a linguistic point of view; and just as there can be more
than one commentary on the Bible, so there is room, too, for more than
one grammar. To some of us, the theories of one grammar may appear
convincing; to some others, those of another grammar. The theories,
which are not palatable to us, must not be styled as incorrect; they
merely fail to convince us, but may convince others. Grammatical
theories may be accepted or rejected without ceasing to be correct, if
they are based upon the observation of facts. In the course of time, a
grammar becomes outdated; but it still retains a certain historic value
as reflecting the standard and method of its epoch. In this connection
it will be of interest to quote Saadia's (892-942) introductory discussion
of inflection in Hebrew, the earliest known attempt of its kind in Hebrew
philology: "We have separated the letters prefixed to nouns and found
them to be eleven; seven of these prefixes, viz., שמלכוהב, do not
change the vocalization (grammatical form) of the noun to which they
are added, as שדבר, מדבר, לדבר, כדבר, וְדָבָר, הַדָּבָר, בְּדָבָר, where the noun
retains its vocalization of two Ḳameṣes. The other four, viz., תניא,
necessarily change the vocalization of the noun [!] to which they are
prefixed, as תדבר, נדבר, יְדַבֵּר, אֲדַבֵּר, where the vowels change to Pataḥ
and Ṣere with a Dagesh. Instances of ש serving as prefix: אשרי העם שככה
כי לאדם שטוב לפניו (Ps. 144.15), לו אשרי העם שיי״י אלהיו (Eccl. 2.26) and
their like." (Solomon L. Skoss in JQR, N.S. XXXIII, 1942/3, p. 177).
Saadia's explanation of denominative verbs does not sound convincing
to us; we are struck by the apparent absence of all those essential qualities,
which make any theory acceptable to us. But with his contemporaries
this explanation must have carried weight. In the thousand years that have
passed since Saadia formulated his grammatical interpretation of Hebrew,
it has lost its appeal to the reader; but it remained "correct" in a sense.

B.   They Explain Facts

§ 5.   The purpose of the grammar is to account for the facts: why is a
given word formed thus, conjugated or declined in such and such a way?

Why e.g. do we find as absolute noun the form בֶּטֶן, in pausa בָּטֶן, and with suffixes בִּטְנִי? The explanation is given by way of formulating a theory. But an indispensable prerequisite is that the theory or grammatical law be based upon the observation of all the facts available. The grammarian must have at his disposal a complete collection of the material, derived from a careful perusal of the Bible itself. Any grammatical theories which are built up on an arbitrary collection of evidence, or second-hand evidence, is valueless from the beginning. G. Bergsträsser's admission is his doom: "Für die Sammlung des Sprachmaterials haben über Gesenius-Kautzsch hinaus in der Formenlehre Böttcher und König, in der Syntax König—zu dem ich mich in fast ständigem wissenschaftlichen Gegensatz befinde—als Hauptquelle gedient; doch bedurften auch sie oft der Ergänzung. So musste ich für viele Paragraphen—in vorliegendem Teil grosse Stücke von §§ 14-20 sowie die §§ 21-31—das Material aus Konkordanz und Lexikon neu ausgehoben werden" (*Hebräische Grammatik*, 2. Teil, Verbum, I. Hälfte, Leipzig 1926, Vorwort, p. iv). One cannot but wonder over the naiveté of this confession. Not only did he base his theories upon second-hand collections of material, but he even made use of the Concordance and the dictionary in order to complete these collections. Little did he realize that both, concordance and dictionary, are dependent on and based upon the grammar (cf. § 15). What, then, shall we think of a grammar which is based upon such a foundation?

C. Must be in Accord with Facts

§ 6. Bergsträsser was outspoken enough to admit how and where he obtained his material; other grammarians procured their material in a similar way, but did not disclose their sources. A few examples will illustrate this procedure: Bauer-Leander state: "מִן (=arab.) behält diese Form: 1. vor dem Artikel, § 15k: מִן הָאָרֶץ 'aus dem Lande'; Ausnahmen sind selten: מֵהַבְּהֵמָה 'einen Teil vom Vieh' 1 Reg. 18.5, מֵהַבַּיִת 'aus dem Hause' Ezek. 43. 6, מֵהֶעָרִים 'aus den Städten' Jud. 20.15 (neben מִן הֶעָרִים Jud. 20.14)" (B-L § 81p', p. 642). Against the three instances of "exceptions" which B-L list, saying that such exceptions are "rare," I herewith submit, as a result of my study of the Bible, a list of occurrences of this grammatical phenomenon: the preposition מ before the noun with the article. My list contains 57 nouns in this position (not occurrences; these are even more numerous!). I wonder whether in the light of this evidence this phenomenon can still be termed "a rare exception" (cf. p. 284, § 70 for our explanation of this grammatical phenomenon as reflecting a dialectic difference).

מֵהָאוֹרֵב: Josh. 8.7

מֵהָאֹכֵל: Jud. 14.14

מֵהָאֱלֹהִים: 1 Chron. 5.22; 2 Chron. 25.20

מֵהָאֲנָשִׁים: 1 Sam. 30.22

מֵהָאָרֶץ: 1 Sam. 28.3, 23; 2 Sam. 12.20; Ezek. 41.20; 42.6—(also: מִן הָאָרֶץ)

מֵהָאֵשׁ: Ezek. 15.7—(also: מִן הָאֵשׁ)

מֵהַבְּאֵר: 2 Sam. 17.21—(also: מִן הַבְּאֵר)

מֵהַבְּהֵמָה: 1 Ki. 18.5—(also: מִן הַבְּהֵמָה)

מֵהַבַּיִת: Ezek. 40.7, 8, 9; 43.6—(also: מִן הַבַּיִת)

מֵהַבָּמָה: 1 Sam 9.25; 10.5

מֵהַבֹּקֶר: 2 Sam. 2.27; 24.15; 1 Ki. 18.26—(also: מִן הַבֹּקֶר)

מֵהַגְּבָעוֹת: Zeph. 1.10

מֵהַגְּדוּד: 2 Sam. 3.22

מֵהַגּוֹלָה: Ezra 6.21

מֵהַגַּנּוֹת: Isa. 1.29

וּמֵהַגֵּר: Ezek. 14.7—(also: וּמִן הַגֵּר)

וּמֵהַגְּשָׁמִים: Ezra 10.9

מֵהָהָר: Josh. 2.23—(also: מִן הָהָר)

מֵהַחוּץ: Ezek. 41.25—(also: מִן הַחוּץ)

מֵהֶחָצֵר: Ezek. 42.9

מֵהַיּוֹם: 1 Sam. 16.13; 18.9; 30.25—(also: מִן הַיּוֹם)

מֵהַיָּם: Isa. 19.5—(also: מִן הַיָּם)

מֵהַכֹּהֲנִים: 2 Ki. 17.27, 28; Ezra 3.12; 2 Chron. 29.34—(also: מִן הַכֹּהֲנִים)

מֵהַלְּבָנוֹן: 2 Chron. 2.7—(also: מִן הַלְּבָנוֹן)

וּמֵהַלְוִיִּם: 2 Chron. 34.13—(also: מִן הַלְוִיִּם)

מֵהַמִּדְבָּר: Josh. 1.4; 1 Sam. 25.14—(also: מִן הַמִּדְבָּר)

מֵהַמֶּלֶךְ: 2 Sam. 3.37—(also: מִן הַמֶּלֶךְ)

מֵהַמְּעָרָה: 1 Sam. 24.7—(also: מִן הַמְּעָרָה)

מֵהַמַּעֲרָכָה: 1 Sam. 4.12—(also: מִן הַמַּעֲרָכָה)

מֵהַגְּבִיאִים: 1 Ki. 20.41

מֵהַנָּוִיד: 2 Ki. 4.40

מֵהַנַּחַל: 1 Ki. 17.4—(also: מִן הַנַּחַל)

מֵהַנְּעָרִים: 1 Sam. 9.3; 16.18; 25.14; 26.22; 2 Sam. 1.15; 2.21—(also: מִן הַנְּעָרִים)

מֵהַנֶּשֶׁף: 1 Sam. 30.17

מֵהַסֶּלַע: Judg. 1.36—(also: מִן הַסֶּלַע)

מֵהָעֵבֶר: 1 Sam. 14.4 (bis)

מֵהָעֵדֶר: 1 Sam. 17.34

מֵהָעוֹלָם: Ps. 41.14—(also: מִן הָעוֹלָם)

מֵהָעוֹף: Gen. 6.20—(also: מִן הָעוֹף)

וּמֵהָעֲזָרָה: Ezek. 43.14

מֵהָעִיר: Judg. 17.8; Jer. 33.5; 52.7—(also: מִן הָעִיר)

מֵהָעָם: 1 Sam. 14.28—(also: מִן הָעָם)

מֵהָעַמּוֹנִיב: 2 Chron. 20.1

מֵהֶעָרִים: Josh. 20.4; Judg. 20.15, 42; Ezek. 25.9—(also: מִן הֶעָרִים)

מֵהַקְּדִים: Ezek. 42.9

מֵהַקֹּדֶשׁ: Ezek. 42.14—(also: מִן הַקֹּדֶשׁ)

מֵהַקַּרְקַע: 1 Ki. 7.7—(also: מִן הַקַּרְקַע)

מֵהָרֹאשׁ: 2 Sam. 16. 1

מֵהַשְּׂמֹאול: Ezek. 1.10; 2 Chron. 3.17

מֵהַשְּׁבִי: Ezra 3.8; 8.35—(also: מִן הַשְּׁבִי)

מֵהַשִּׁטִּים: Josh. 3.1—(also: מִן הַשִּׁטִּים)

מֵהַשָּׁלָל: 1 Sam. 15.21; 30.22, 26—(also: מִן הַשָּׁלָל)

מֵהַשְּׁלִשִׁים: 2 Sam. 23.13—(also: מִן הַשְּׁלִשִׁים)

מֵהַשָּׁמַיִם: 2 Chron. 7.1—(also: מִן הַשָּׁמַיִם)

מֵהַתַּחְתֹּנוֹת: Ezek. 42.5, 6

וּמֵהַתִּיכֹונוֹת: Ezek. 42.5, 6

מֵהַתֹּפֶת: Jer. 19.14

D. DERIVED STEMS

§ 7. In § 38 of their grammar, Bauer-Leander deal with the so-called derived stems: "Schon in protosemitischer Zeit sind im Verb zum Ausdruck verschiedener Modifikationen eine Reihe von Stammformen (hebräisch בִּנְיָנִים 'formationes') herausgebildet worden (§ 38a). Aus dem Grundstamm (scil. *Ḳal*) haben sich ferner *Intensivstämme* herausgebildet, d.h. Formen, die eine grössere Intensität, Energie bei der Ausführung der

Handlung ausdrücken [referring to *pi'el* and its derivatives; ib. § 38g].
Zum Grundstamm bildete sich noch ein Stamm heraus, das *Kausativ*, zum
Ausdruck der Veranlassung einer Handlung oder eines Zustandes [referring
to *hiph'il* and its derivatives; ib. § 38w]. Nur bei wenigen Verben sind die
sieben gewöhnlichen Stammformen sämtlich belegt [ib. § 38f']''. In other
words, according to Bauer-Leander (this is merely a *terminus ad quem* and
by no means a *terminus a quo*, for this is one of the most ancient misconceptions of Hebrew grammar), Hebrew actually used every verbal root in
seven derived stems; and it is only due to our limited literary heritage,
limited to the Hebrew Bible, that we are unable to prove the existence of
these forms—but exist they did. Hence B-L compiled "mit besonderer
Sorgfalt Paradigmentafeln, ... um die wirklich belegten Formen als
solche zu kennzeichnen" (p. vi). Here, B-L are caught in a significant
contradiction: for in § 38l'-r' they deal with the so-called *passive Kal* and
list the verbal forms supposedly belonging to this group. Now, the very
term *passive Kal* is based on the presupposition that the verbs in question
do not occur in the *Intensiv-Stamm*, and must, therefore, be considered
as *Kal* formations. But according to the foregoing quotation from B-L,
the fact that a certain *Stammform* does not occur, is no proof whatsoever
that it did not once exist; thus, the fundation upon which the term *passive
Kal* rests, is withdrawn. Cf. also p. 252, note 3 and p. 254, note 1. But
quite apart from this difficulty, there are other considerations, too. For
I must confess to utter ignorance of Hebrew; for these 91 pages of verbal
forms, which were allegedly "Hebrew" while the language of the Bible
was a living tongue, are as many pages of mysteries and unsurmountable
difficulties to me. How my forebears could have mastered them is to me
a real miracle! But apart from this common-sense consideration against
this "reconstruction" of forms which in reality never existed, there is
factual proof against any assumption of the former existence of seven
derived stems for each verb, with each stem indicating a difference in the
shade of the meaning (intensity or causation, respectively). I am going
to disprove this notion by demonstrating that the so-called verbal stems
were interchangeably used in order to indicate one and the same meaning,
without implying the slighest differentiation.

a)   *Ḳal* and *hiph'il* interchangeably used:

אהל: Gen. 13.18: וַיֶּאֱהַל
Isa. 13.20: יַהֵל (ולא)

אור: 1 Sam. 14.29: אֹרוּ (עיני)
Ezek. 43.2: הָאִירָה (מכבודו) (והארץ)

אטם: Isa. 33.15: אֹטֵם (אזנו)
Ps. 58.5: יַאְטֵם (אזנו)

ארך: Ezek. 12.22: יַאַרְכוּ (הימים)
Deut. 25.15: יַאֲרִיכוּ (ימיך)

באש: Ex. 7.18: וּבָאַשׁ (היאר)
Ex. 16.24: הִבְאִישׁ (ולא)

בוש: Jer. 48.13: וּבֹשׁ (מואב)
Jer. 48.20: הֹבִישׁ (מואב)

בזה: Prov. 15.20: בּוֹזֶה (אמו)
Esth. 1.17: לְהַבְזוֹת (בעליהן)

בין: Deut. 32.7: בִּינוּ (שנות דור ודור)
Prov. 8.5: הָבִינוּ (לב) (וכסילים)

גלה: Am. 1.5: וְגָלוּ (עם ארם)
2 Ki. 17.33: הַגְלוּ (אתם משם) (אשר)

גנן: Isa. 37.35: וְגַנּוֹתִי (על העיר הזאת)
Isa. 31.5: יָגֵן · · · על (ירושלם)

דקק: Isa. 41.15: וְתָדֹק (תדוש הרים)
2 Ki. 23.15: הָדַק (לעפר)

חוש: Hab. 1.8: חָשׁ (לאכול) (כנשר)
Judg. 20.37: הֵחִישׁוּ (והארב)

חלה: Jer. 5.3: חָלוּ (ולא)
Hos. 7.5: הֶחֱלוּ (שרים)

חלם: Gen. 42.9: חָלַם (את החלמות אשר)
Jer. 29.8: מַחְלְמִים (את חלמתיכם אשר אתם)

חסר: Jer. 44.18: חָסַרְנוּ (ומן אז חדלנו · · ·)
Ex. 16.18: הֶחְסִיר (והממעיט לא)

חפר: Mic. 3.7: וְחָפְרוּ (הקסמים)
Isa. 33.9: הֶחְפִּיר (לבנון)

חרש : Ps. 35.22: (אל) תֶּחֱרַשׁ
Num. 30.15: (כי) הֶחֱרִישׁ (לה)

Prov. 6.14: חֹרֵשׁ (רע)
1 Sam. 23.9: מַחֲרִישׁ (הרעה)

חשה : Isa. 65.6: (לֹא) אֶחֱשֶׂה (כי אם שלמתי)
Isa. 42.14: הֶחֱשֵׁיתִי (מעולם)

חשך : Isa. 13.10: חָשַׁךְ (השמש)
Jer. 13.16: (בטרם) יַחְשִׁךְ

טמן : Gen. 35.4: וַיִּטְמֹן (אתם יעקב)
2 Ki. 7.8: (וילכו) וַיַּטְמִנוּ

יבש : Isa. 40.7: יָבֵשׁ (חציר נבל ציץ)
Joel 1.10: הוֹבִישׁ (תירוש אמלל יצהר)

ילד : Gen. 25.3: (ויקשן) יָלַד (את שבא)
Gen. 25.19: (אברהם) הוֹלִיד (את יצחק)

יסף : Gen. 38.26: (ולֹא) יָסַף (עוד לדעתה)
2 Ki. 24.7: (ולֹא) הֹסִיף (עוד · · · לצאת)

יעד : Ex. 21.9: (ואם לבנו) יִעָדֶנָּה
Jer. 50.44: (כי מי כמוני ומי) יוֹעִדֶנִּי

יקץ : 1 Ki. 18.27: (אולי ישן הוא) וְיָקֵץ
2 Ki. 4.31: (לֹא) הֵקִיץ (הנער)

ירש : Deut. 6.18: וְיָרַשְׁתָּ (את הארץ)
Num. 33.53: וְהוֹרַשְׁתֶּם (את הארץ)

לוז : Prov. 3.21: (אל) יָלֻזוּ (מעיניך)
Prov. 4.21: (אל) יַלִּיזוּ (מעיניך)

לעג : Ps. 80.7: יִלְעֲגוּ (למו)
Ps. 22.8: יַלְעִגוּ (לי)

מרה : Isa. 63.10: מָרוּ (ועצבו את רוח)
Ps. 106.33: הִמְרוּ (את רוחו)

משש : Gen. 27.21: (גשה נא) וַאֲמֻשְׁךָ
Ps. 115.7: (ידיהם ולֹא) יְמִישׁוּן

נזה : Lev. 6.20: (אשר) יִזֶּה (עליה)
Lev. 16.14: (ולפני הכפרת) יַזֶּה

נטה:	Isa. 23.11:	(ידו) נָטָה (על הים)
	Jer. 6.12:	אַטֶּה (את ידי)
נטף:	Joel 4.18:	יִטְּפוּ (ההרים עסיס)
	Am. 9.13:	וְהִטִּיפוּ (ההרים עסיס)
נסך:	Ex. 30.9:	(ונסך לא) תִסְכוּ (עליו)
	Gen. 35.14:	וַיַּסֵּךְ (עליה נסך)
נשה:	Jer. 15.16:	(ולא) נָשׁוּ (בי)
	Deut. 15.2:	(אשר) יַשֶּׁה (ברעהו)
סגר:	Ezek. 46.12:	וְסָגַר (את השער)
	Lev. 14.38:	וְהִסְגִּיר (את הבית)
עוה:	Dan. 9.5:	(חטאנו) וְעָוִינוּ (והרשענו)
	1 Ki. 8.47:	(חטאנו) וְהֶעֱוִינוּ (רשענו)
עצב:	1 Ki. 1.6:	(ולא) עֲצָבוֹ (אביו מימיו)
	Ps. 78.40:	יַעֲצִיבוּהוּ (בישימון)
ערץ:	Deut. 1.29:	(לא) תַעַרְצוּן (ולא תיראון)
	Isa. 8.12:	(לא תיראו ולא) תַעֲרִיצוּ
עשר:	Hos. 12.9:	(אך) עָשַׁרְתִּי
	Prov. 23.4:	(אל תיגע) לְהַעֲשִׁיר
פנה:	1 Ki. 8.28:	וּפָנִיתָ (אל תפלת)
	Jer. 47.3:	(לא) הִפְנוּ (אבות אל בנים)
פקד:	Deut. 20.9:	וּפָקְדוּ (שרי צבאות בראש העם)
	Gen. 39.5:	הִפְקִיד (אתו בביתו)
פרח:	Ps. 72.7:	יִפְרַח (בימיו צדיק)
	Ps. 92.14:	(בחצרות אלהינו) יַפְרִיחוּ
פשט:	Lev. 6.4:	וּפָשַׁט (את בגדיו)
	Job 19.9:	(כבודי מעלי) הִפְשִׁיט
צלח:	Jer. 22.30:	(לא) יִצְלַח (מזרעו איש)
	Gen. 39.2:	(ויהי איש) מַצְלִיחַ
צמח:	Ps. 85.12:	(אמת מארץ) תִּצְמָח
	Isa. 45.8:	(וצדקה) תַצְמִיחַ
צפן:	Ex. 2.2:	וַתִּצְפְּנֵהוּ (שלשה ירחים)
	Ex. 2.3:	(ולא יכלה עוד) הַצְּפִינוֹ
קרב:	Ex. 32.19:	(כאשר) קָרַב (אל המחנה)
	Gen. 12.11:	(כאשר) הִקְרִיב (לבוא מצרימה)

קשב: Isa. 32.3:   (ואזני שמעים) תִּקְשַׁבְנָה

Jer. 6.10:   (ערלה אזנם ולא יוכלו) לְהַקְשִׁיב

רבץ: Ezek. 34.14:   (שם) תִּרְבַּצְנָה (בנוה טוב)

Cant. 1.7:   (איכה) תַּרְבִּיץ (בצהרים)

שכל: I Sam. 18.30:   שָׂכֵל (דוד מכל עבדי שאול)

I Sam. 18.14:   (ויהי דוד לכל דרכו) מַשְׂכִּיל

passive:

חבא: Josh. 10.27:   (אל המערה אשר) נֶחְבְּאוּ (שם)

Isa. 42.22:   (ובבתי כלאים) הָחְבָּאוּ

b) *Kal* and *pi'el* interchangeably used:

אהב: Prov. 8.21:   (להנחיל) אֹהֲבַי

Hos. 2.7:   (אלכה אחרי) מְאַהֲבַי

אזר: I Sam. 2.4:   אָזְרוּ (חיל)

Ps. 18.40:   וַתְּאַזְּרֵנִי (חיל)

אחר: Gen. 32.5:   וָאֵחַר (עד עתה)

Hab. 2.3:   (בא יבא לא) יְאַחֵר

אמץ: Gen. 25.23:   (ולאם מלאם) יֶאֱמָץ

Ps. 31.25:   (חזקו) וְיַאֲמֵץ (לבבכם)

ארב: Judg. 20.29:   (וישם ישראל) אֹרְבִים

Judg. 9.25:   (וישימו ...) מְאָרְבִים

בכה: 2 Sam. 19.2:   בֹּכֶה (ויתאבל)

Jer. 31.14:   מְבַכָּה (על בניה)

בלע: Num. 16.30:   (ופצתה האדמה את פיה) וּבָלְעָה

Isa. 25.8:   בִּלַּע (המות)

בקע: Isa. 48.21:   וַיִּבְקַע (צור ויזבו מים)

Ps. 78.15:   יְבַקַּע (צרים במדבר)

Am. 1.13:   (על) בִּקְעָם (הרות הגלעד)

2 Ki. 15.16:   (את כל ההרותיה) בִּקֵּעַ

ברה: 2 Sam. 12.17:   (ולא) בָּרָה (אתם לחם)

Lam. 4.10:   (היו) לְבָרוֹת (למו)

בתר: Gen. 15.10:   (ואת הצפר לא) בָתָר

Gen. 15.10:   וַיְבַתֵּר (אתם בתוך)

גדע :	I Sam. 2.31 :	וְגָדַעְתִּי (אֶת זְרֹעֲךָ)
	Deut. 12. 3 :	(וּפְסִילֵיהֶם) תְּגַדֵּעוּן
גלה :	Prov. 20.19 :	גּוֹלֶה (סוֹד הוֹלֵךְ רָכִיל)
	Prov. 11.13 :	(הוֹלֵךְ רָכִיל) מְגַלֶּה (סוֹד)
גנב :	Gen. 31.26 :	וַתִּגְנֹב (אֶת לְבָבִי)
	2 Sam. 15.6 :	וַיְגַנֵּב (· · · אֶת לֵב)
גרש :	Ex. 34.11 :	(הִנְנִי) גֹרֵשׁ (מִפָּנֶיךָ אֶת הָאֱמֹרִי)
	Ex. 33.2 :	וְגֵרַשְׁתִּי (אֶת הַכְּנַעֲנִי הָאֱמֹרִי)
דבר :	Num. 36.5 :	(כֵּן מַטֵּה בְנֵי יוֹסֵף) דֹּבְרִים
	Isa. 65.24 :	(עוֹד הֵם) מְדַבְּרִים
זבח :	Lev. 17.5 :	וְזָבְחוּ (זִבְחֵי שְׁלָמִים)
	I Ki. 8.5 :	מְזַבְּחִים (צֹאן וּבָקָר)
זרה :	Jer. 15.7 :	וָאֶזְרֵם (בְּמִזְרֶה בְּשַׁעֲרֵי הָאָרֶץ)
	Ezek. 12.15 :	וְזֵרִיתִי (אוֹתָם בָּאֲרָצוֹת)
חבק :	Eccl. 3.5 :	(עֵת) לַחֲבוֹק
	Eccl. 3.5 :	(וְעֵת לִרְחֹק) מֵחַבֵּק
חבר :	Ex. 26.3 :	חֹבְרֹת (אִשָּׁה אֶל אֲחֹתָהּ)
	Ex. 26.6 :	וְחִבַּרְתָּ (· · · אִשָּׁה אֶל אֲחֹתָהּ)
חבש :	Isa. 30.26 :	(בְּיוֹם) חֲבֹשׁ (· · · אֶת שֶׁבֶר עַמּוֹ)
	Ps. 147.3 :	וּמְחַבֵּשׁ (לְעַצְּבוֹתָם)
חכה :	Isa. 30.18 :	(אַשְׁרֵי כָּל) חוֹכֵי (לוֹ)
	Isa. 64.3 :	לִמְחַכֵּה (לוֹ)
חמד :	Mic. 2.2 :	וְחָמְדוּ (שָׂדוֹת)
	Cant. 2.3 :	(בְּצִלּוֹ) חִמַּדְתִּי
חפש :	Prov. 2.4 :	(וְכַמַּטְמוֹנִים) תַּחְפְּשֶׂנָּה
	2 Ki. 20.6 :	וְחִפְּשׂוּ (אֶת בֵּיתֶךָ)
חשב :	Mic. 2.3 :	חֹשֵׁב (עַל · · · רָעָה)
	Prov. 24.8 :	מְחַשֵּׁב (לְהָרֵעַ)
ידה :	Jer. 50.14 :	(כָּל דֹּרְכֵי קֶשֶׁת) יְדוּ (אֵלֶיהָ)
	Lam. 3.53 :	וַיַּדּוּ (אֶבֶן בִּי)
יסד :	Ps. 104.5 :	יָסַד (אֶרֶץ עַל מְכוֹנֶיהָ)
	Isa. 14.32 :	(כִּי יְהוָה) יִסַּד (צִיּוֹן)
יסר :	Prov. 9.7 :	יֹסֵר (לֵץ לֹקֵחַ לוֹ קָלוֹן)
	Deut. 8.5 :	(יְהוָה אֱלֹהֶיךָ) מְיַסְּרֶךָּ

כבש: Jer. 34.16: (וַתִּכְבְּשׁוּ (אתם · · · לעבדים

2 Sam. 8.11: (מכל הגוים אשר) כִּבֵּשׁ

כסה: Prov. 12.16: (וְכֹסֶה (קלון ערום

Prov. 17.9: (מְכַסֶּה (פשע מבקש אהבה

כעס: Eccl. 5.16: (וְכָעַס (הרבה

Deut. 32.21: (כִּעֲסוּנִי (בהבליהם

לקט: Ruth 2.8: (לִלְקֹט (בשדה אחר

2 Ki. 4.39: (ויצא אחד אל השדה) לְלַקֵּט

לקק: Judg. 7.5: (כל אשר) יָלֹק (בלשונו

Judg. 7.6: (ויהי מספר) הַמְלַקְקִים

מדד: Ezek. 40.20: (מָדַד (ארכו ורחבו

Ps. 60.8: (ועמק סכות) אֲמַדֵּד

משל: Ezek. 18.2: (אתם) מֹשְׁלִים (את המשל הזה

Ezek. 21.5: (הלא) מְמַשֵּׁל (משלים הוא

נאף: Lev. 20.10: (אשר) יִנְאַף (את אשת רעהו

Jer. 29.23: (וַיְנַאֲפוּ (את נשי רעיהם

נאץ: Ps. 107.11: (ועצת עליון) נָאָצוּ

Isa. 1.4: (נִאֲצוּ (את קדוש ישראל

נהג: Isa. 20.4: (יִנְהַג (· · · את שבי מצרים

Isa. 63.14: (נְהַגְתָּ (עמך

נקר: 1 Sam. 11.2: (בִּנְקוֹר (לכם כל עין ימין

Judg. 16.21: (וַיְנַקְּרוּ (את עיניו

סקל: 1 Ki. 21.13: (וַיִּסְקְלֻהוּ (באבנים

2 Sam. 16.6: (וַיְסַקֵּל (באבנים את דוד

סתם: 2 Ki. 3.25: (וכל מעין מים) יִסְתֹּמוּ

Gen. 26.15: (וכל הבארת · ·) סִתְּמוּם

עטר: Ps. 5.13: (כצנה רצון) תַּעְטְרֶנּוּ

Ps. 8.6: (וכבוד והדר) תְּעַטְּרֵהוּ

פזר: Jer. 50.17: (שה) פְזוּרָה

Esth. 3.8: (מְפֻזָּר (ומפרד

פרש: Lam. 1.10: (ידו) פָּרַשׂ (צר

Isa. 25.11: (וּפֵרַשׂ (ידו

פתח: Isa. 14.17: (אסיריו לא) פָתַח (ביתה

Ps. 116.16: (פִּתַּחְתָּ (למוסרי

צעק: 1 Ki. 20.39: (והוא) צָעַק (אֶל הַמֶּלֶךְ)
2 Ki. 2.12: (והוא) מְצַעֵק

קבץ: Ezek. 22.19: (הִנְנִי) קֹבֵץ (אֶתְכֶם אֶל תּוֹךְ)
Isa. 56.8: מְקַבֵּץ (נִדְחֵי יִשְׂרָאֵל)

קבר: Jer. 19.11: (מֵאֵין מָקוֹם) לִקְבּוֹר
1 Ki. 11.15: לְקַבֵּר (אֶת הַחֲלָלִים)

רדף: Deut. 16.20: (צֶדֶק צֶדֶק) תִּרְדֹּף
Prov. 15.9: וּמְרַדֵּף (צְדָקָה)

רחק: Isa. 59.9: רָחַק (מִשְׁפָּט מִמֶּנּוּ)
Isa. 29.13: (וְלִבּוֹ) רִחַק (מִמֶּנִּי)

שנא: Ps. 86.17: (וְיִרְאוּ) שֹׂנְאַי (וְיֵבֹשׁוּ)
Prov. 8.36: (כָּל) מְשַׂנְאַי (אָהֲבוּ מָוֶת)

שבר: Jer. 48.38: שָׁבַרְתִּי (אֶת מוֹאָב)
Ex. 9.25: (וְאֵת כָּל עֵץ הַשָּׂדֶה) שִׁבֵּר

שלח: Ex. 3.20: וְשָׁלַחְתִּי (אֶת יָדִי וְהִכֵּיתִי)
Lev. 26.25: וְשִׁלַּחְתִּי (דֶּבֶר בְּתוֹכְכֶם)

passive:

אכל: Zech. 9.4: (בָּאֵשׁ) תֵּאָכֵל
Neh. 2.3: אֻכְּלוּ (בָאֵשׁ)

בהל: Ps. 30.8: (הִסְתַּרְתָּ פָנֶיךָ הָיִיתִי) נִבְהָל
Esth. 8.14: (יָצְאוּ) מְבֹהָלִים

בזז: Am. 3.11: וְנָבֹזּוּ (אַרְמְנוֹתָיִךְ)
Jer. 50.37: (חֶרֶב עַל אוֹצְרֹתֶיהָ) וּבֻזָּזוּ

גרש: Jonah 2.5: נִגְרַשְׁתִּי (מִנֶּגֶד עֵינֶיךָ)
Ex. 12.39: (כִּי) גֹרְשׁוּ (מִמִּצְרַיִם)

דבר: Ezek. 33.30: (בְּנֵי עַמְּךָ) הַנִּדְבָּרִים (בְּךָ)
Ps. 87.3: (נִכְבָּדוֹת) מְדֻבָּר (בָּךְ)

יסד: Ex. 9.18: (לְמִן הַיּוֹם) הִוָּסְדָה
Hag. 2.18: לְמִן הַיּוֹם אֲשֶׁר) יֻסַּד (הֵיכַל יְהוָה)

אסף: 2 Sam. 17.11: הֵאָסֹף (יֵאָסֵף עָלֶיךָ כָל יִשְׂרָאֵל)
Deut. 33.5: בְּהִתְאַסֵּף (רָאשֵׁי עָם)

באש: 2 Sam. 10.6: נִבְאֲשׁוּ (בְדָוִד)
1 Chron. 19.6: הִתְבָּאֲשׁוּ (עִם דָּוִד)

c)   *Pi'el* and *hiph'il* interchangeably used:

אבד: 2 Ki. 13.7:   (כי) אִבְּדָם (מלך ארם)
Deut. 28.63:   לְהַאֲבִיד (אתכם)

יחל: Ps. 119.74:   (לדברך) יִחָלְתִּי
Ps. 130.5:   (ולדברו) הוֹחָלְתִּי

מלט: Ezek. 33.5:   (נפשו) מִלֵּט
Isa. 31.5:   (גנון והציל פסוח) וְהִמְלִיט

סגר: 2 Sam. 18.28:   (אשר) סִגַּר (את האנשים)
Deut. 32.30:   (צורם מכרם ויהוה) הִסְגִּירָם

עצב: Isa. 63.10:   וְעִצְּבוּ (את רוח קדשו)
Ps. 78.40:   (ימרוהו במדבר) יַעֲצִיבוּהוּ (בישימון)

קדש: Ex. 40.10:   וְקִדַּשְׁתָּ (את המזבח)
1 Ki. 9.3:   הִקְדַּשְׁתִּי (את הבית)

קטר: 1 Ki. 22.44:   (מזבחים) וּמְקַטְּרִים (בבמות)
1 Ki. 3.3:   (רק בבמות הוא מזבח) וּמַקְטִיר

קנא: Deut. 32.21:   (הם) קִנְאוּנִי (בלא אל)
Deut. 32.21:   (ואני) אַקְנִיאֵם (בלא עם)

שחת: 2 Ki. 19.12:   (אשר) שִׁחֲתוּ (אבותי)
Isa. 37.12:   (אשר) הִשְׁחִיתוּ (אבותי)

שכל: Ezek. 36.13:   וּמְשַׁכֶּלֶת (גויך היית)
Jer. 50.9:   (חציו כגבור) מַשְׁכִּיל

שכן: Jer. 7.3:   וַאֲשַׁכְּנָה (אתכם במקום הזה)
Ezek. 32.4:   וְהִשְׁכַּנְתִּי (עליך כל עוף השמים)

שכר: Jer. 51.7:   מְשַׁכֶּרֶת (כל הארץ)
Jer. 51.57:   וְהִשְׁכַּרְתִּי (שריה וחכמיה)

passive:

טבע: Ex. 15.4:   (ומבחר שלשיו) טֻבְּעוּ (בים סוף)
Jer. 38.22:   הָטְבְּעוּ (בבץ רגלך)

It thus becomes clear that the so-called derived stems are not verbal stems, but verbal conjugations; and it is in the main due to the schematizing efforts of the grammarians, eager to bring all verbs down to the common denominator of a triliteral root, that these conjugations were misunderstood as stems derived from the *kal*.

E. Hebrew Grammar Basically Medieval

§ 8. Hebrew grammar was and still basically is a medieval structure; cf. p. 420, § 8. Of course, the grammarians wish to make us believe that with the publication of the first edition of Wilhelm Gesenius' Hebrew Grammar in 1813, a new era began in the grammatical interpretation of the language of the Bible (B-L § 3i). G. Bergsträsser, whose grammar was published as the 29th edition of Gesenius' work, makes this break with the medievalism plain by saying: "Die jüdischen Grammatiker [scil. of the middle ages] sind nur berücksichtigt in Dingen, für die sie als Vertreter einer noch lebendigen Tradition gelten können, d.h. vor allem für Orthographie und Aussprache; eine Neubearbeitung würde wohl auch sonst aus den jüdischen Grammatikern und Kommentatoren einzelne wertvolle Bemerkungen gewinnen können" (2. Teil, Vorwort, p. iv). This presumptuous language and condescending attitude towards the Fathers of Hebrew grammar contrasts strangely with the actual presentation of the various grammars. Take for instance the case of the prepositions ל כ ב: "Das *h* des Artikels fiel nach den proklitischen בְּ 'in,' לְ 'zu,' und כְּ 'wie,' wobei auch das Schwa der Proklitika elidiert wurde: *bᵉhaiiŏm* > בַּיּוֹם 'am Tage,' *lᵉhaʿʿăm* > *laʿʿăm* > לָעָם 'dem Volke,' *kᵉhaddabăr* > כַּדָּבָר 'wie das Wort'" (B-L § 25w; but cf. our new interpretation based on the facts as found in the Bible, p. 625, §§ 99 ff.). As far as I can see, we have here the old theory in a modernized garb and a new terminology, in accordance with Western philology.

F. Latin and Greek Terminology Misleading

§ 9. In the chapter *Adverbia*, this book says: "*Negationen*: אַל lateinisch 'ne,' griechisch 'μή'; לֹא lateinisch 'non,' griechisch 'οὐ'" (B-L § 80c). But a careful examination of the use of אַל and לֹא in the Bible reveals that they are indiscriminately used (cf. p. 284, § 71).

a) Ex. 12.9, 10: אַל תֹּאכְלוּ · · · וְלֹא תוֹתִירוּ

  Ex. 23.1: לֹא תִהְיֶה · · · אַל תָּשֶׁת

  Ex. 34.3: וְאִישׁ לֹא יַעֲלֶה · · · וְגַם אִישׁ אַל יֵרָא

  Lev. 10.6: אַל תִּפְרָעוּ · · · לֹא תִפְרֹמוּ

  Lev. 19.4: אַל תִּפְנוּ · · · לֹא תַעֲשׂוּ

  Judg. 13.14: לֹא תֹאכַל · · · אַל תֵּשְׁתְּ

  1 Ki. 20.8: אַל תִּשְׁמַע וְלוֹא תֹאבֶה

	Jer. 7.6:	לֹא תַעֲשֹׁקוּ · · · אַל תִּשְׁפֹּכוּ
	Jer. 25.6:	וְאַל תֵּלְכוּ · · · וְלֹא תַכְעִיסוּ
	Am. 5.5:	וְאַל תִּדְרֹשׁוּ · · · לֹא תָבֹאוּ
	Prov. 27.2:	וְלֹא פִיךָ · · · וְאַל שְׂפָתֶיךָ
b)	Lev. 25.14:	אַל תּוֹנוּ אִישׁ אֶת אָחִיו
	Lev. 25.17:	וְלֹא תוֹנוּ אִישׁ אֶת עֲמִיתוֹ
	Num. 14.42:	אַל תַּעֲלוּ
	Deut. 1.42:	לֹא תַעֲלוּ; narrating the identical event
	Deut. 1.21:	אַל תִּירָא וְאַל תֵּחָת
	Deut. 31.8:	לֹא תִירָא וְלֹא תֵחָת
	1 Sam. 12.20:	אַל תָּסוּרוּ
	1 Sam. 12.21:	וְלֹא תָסוּרוּ
	1 Ki. 3.26:	וְהָמֵת אַל תְּמִיתֻהוּ
	1 Ki. 3.27:	וְהָמֵת לֹא תְמִיתֻהוּ
	1 Ki. 13.17:	לֹא תֹאכַל לֶחֶם וְלֹא תִשְׁתֶּה · · · מָיִם
	1 Ki. 13.22:	אַל תֹּאכַל לֶחֶם וְאַל תֵּשְׁתְּ מָיִם
	Jer. 16.5:	אַל תָּבוֹא בֵּית מַרְזֵחַ
	Jer. 16.8:	וּבֵית מִשְׁתֶּה לֹא תָבוֹא
	Jer. 42.19:	אַל תָּבֹאוּ מִצְרָיִם
	Jer. 43.2:	לֹא תָבֹאוּ מִצְרָיִם

§ 10. We now ask: what good do these references to Latin and Greek words do us, if they convey an erroneous definition of the supposedly corresponding Hebrew words? To put it quite bluntly: to our mind, modern Hebrew grammar gained little if anything by substituting Latin or Greek terms for the original Hebrew (or Arabic) ones. On the contrary, this only led to more confusion; cf. our refutation of the term "particle" on p. 600, § 60. For not only do we apply Western terminology, but we even find ourselves treating Hebrew as a Western language. So, e.g., Bauer-Leander call the first noun in a construct state formation the *regens* (B-L § 64g), because in Western languages it remains unchanged and in the nominative, and causes the second noun to be put in the genetive; cf. their example "der Zorn deines Bruders." But according to the Hebrew way of thinking it is exactly *vice versa*: the second noun remains unchanged and even gets the article if determined, and causes the first noun to undergo certain changes.

An even cursory examination of the *Verbparadigmen* (Anhang, B-L) proves that schematization still is a very prominent feature of Hebrew grammar. There, B-L offer on 91 pages their own fancy under the guise of Hebrew verbal forms.

G. PRESENT-DAY PRONUNCIATION MISLEADING (Cf. MH §§ 58 ff.)

§ 11. The grammar follows blindly our present-day pronunciation of Hebrew and thus identifies it as *the* pronunciation of Hebrew, without even realizing that this in itself represents a problem of the utmost gravity. Let us demonstrate this on one example. The vowel *o* was originally indicated by a *waw* (cf. below p. 566 ff. passim); after the invention of the vowel points, a *holem* or a *kames* (according to the Masoretic laws concerning open and closed syllables, long and short vowels, and stress; cf. p. 414, § 1, law V) took the place of the *waw*. In such cases, the *kames* is termed *kames hatuf*; on the interrelation between *kames hatuf* and *hatef kames*, cf. p. 442, § 73. The Tiberian vocalization thus exhibits the sign of ֭, which as regular *kames* was pronounced *a* (cf. p. 434, § 48), but as *kames hatuf o* (cf. p. 444, § 74). This resulted in confusion: the tendency arose to pronounce every ֭ as *o*, in the so-called ashkenazic pronunciation. But even in many separate instances the ֭ was erroneously pronounced *o*, as can be seen in cases of inflected verbal forms: cf. imperative forms like מָלְכָה‎, מָלְכִי‎ (p. 249, § 16d) or construct infinitive with suffix פָּקְדִי‎ (ib. § 16e). We pronounce the ֭ of the first syllable in forms like these as *o*, and the grammarians are hard put to explain this vowel *o*. But in the parallel (unvocalized) sources of p. 235 ff., these forms are spelled as מלוכה‎, פקודי‎, מלוכי‎ respectively. If we be permitted to apply Tiberian vowel-signs to these forms, they would be: פָּקוּדִי*‎, מָלוּכִי*‎, מָלוּכָה*‎. But according to a Masoretic law (cf. p. 415, § 2c), there can be no long vowel in an open syllable two syllables removed from the stress; either the first or the second vowel must be reduced to *sheva*; cf. e.g., שָׁמַר‎ — plural שָׁמְרוּ*‎ — שָׁמְרוּ‎. In the very same manner we explain: מָלְכִי* — מָלְכִי‎; מָלְכָה — מָלְכָה*‎; פָּקְדִי* — פָּקְדִי‎. Hence the ֭ in the first syllable is not *o*, but corresponds to *a*; why should this ֭ suddenly become *o*, while in the parallel case of שָׁמְרוּ‎ it remained *a*? Similarly: In the fragments from the Geniza in Cairo with the Palestinian vocalization, published by Paul Kahle in his *Masoreten des Westens*, we find the following cases of a Tiberian *kames hatuf* or *ḥatef ḳameṣ* indicated by the signs ˈ or ˉ, both of which are even elsewhere indiscriminately used to indicate the vowel *a* (cf. p. 432, § 41): Jonah 1.5: MT: בָּאֳנִיָּה—Kahle p. יח: באניה; Ezek. 27.29: MT: מֵאֳנִיּוֹתֵיהֶם— Kahle p. יח: מֵאֳנִיּוֹתִיהֶם; Jer. 30.18: MT: אָהֳלֵי—Kahle p. א: אהלי; Nah. 2.2: MT: מָתְנַיִם—Kahle p. כ: מתנים. In these cases, the Palestinian vocalization is proof that the vowel which now is pronounced *o*, was originally pronounced *a*, contrary to our present-day pronunciation which the grammar has unquestioningly adopted, but—strangely enough—in accord with the way these words are pronounced in Arabic.

H.   *Ḳatl-* AND *ḳitl-*FORMATIONS

§ 12.   Incidentally, the basic inconsistency of the current Hebrew grammar reveals itself herein, too: while e.g., בֶּטֶן, שֶׁמֶשׁ (B-L § 61j′), שֶׁבַע, קֶמַח (ib. l′), נֹאד, צֹאן, רֹאשׁ (ib. m′) are classed as *ḳatl*-forms on the strength of their equivalents in cognate languages (monosyllabic nouns with the vowel *a*), the nouns mentioned at the end of the preceding paragraph: אֹהֶל, אֳנִיָּה and מָתְנַיִם, are grouped with the *ḳutl*-forms (ib. h″), although their equivalents in Arabic exhibit the characteristic vowel *a*. B-L mention these equivalents, introducing each of these references with "aber," thus indicating that in these instances the nominal form in Arabic carries no weight in the classification of the respective Hebrew noun. The evidence from cognate languages is similarly brushed away ib. q′, where B-L list as *ḳatl*-forms "Ursprüngliche *ḳitl*-Formen" like: מֶלַח, זֶפֶת, קֶרֶב, תֶּבֶן, בֶּרֶךְ, רֶגֶל. Their equivalents in Arabic or Accadian, which are quoted there for each of these nouns, offer *i* as characteristic vowel; and so does even Hebrew, with the sole exception or רֶגֶל, which in the Tiberian vocalization only exhibits *a* instead, while the transliteration as well as the Babylonian vocalization have even here an *i*; cf. ch. o s.v. The reason for which B-L treat these nouns as *ḳatl*-forms, is obviously the *Law of Philippi* (B-L § 14z): "*i* in *geschlossener Haupt—oder Nebendrucksilbe* wurde zu *ă*." If we were guided by the objective facts, and grouped these nouns as *ḳitl*-forms, then they might be brought up as proofs against the validity of this phonetic law. It thus becomes evident that B-L prefer it to leave Philippi's law unchallenged, and to declare instead these nouns as *ḳatl*-forms, though all the evidence—including that from cognate languages—is against it. They are thus caught in a trap:

they give the preference to phonology against morphology, and fail to realize that the morphology is based on solid facts, while the phonology is merely a theory to explain—but not to do away with—these facts: cf. § 3.

I. Cognate Languages

§ 13. And this brings us back to the problem of the advisability of writing a comparative Hebrew grammar at the present time. The modern Hebrew grammars which claim to apply the method of comparative philology, are in reality nothing but plain ''Hebrew'' grammars (with all the shortcomings outlined above), based almost solely on the Tiberian vocalization, to the exclusion of non-Masoretic evidence (cf. p. 228/9), with occasional references to cognate languages (cf. the preceding paragraph), whenever such references seemed opportune to the author. So we are told, for instance, that the ה with subsequent *dagesh* as sign of the article in Hebrew corresponds to ال in Arabic, the *dagesh* indicating the missing letter ל. But how about the ה *interrogativum*? Here the grammars prefer an eloquent silence. For if reference were made to Arabic هل, then the Masoretic vocalization of this ה with ־ֲ could not be accounted for, since we would expect a subsequent *dagesh* in lieu of the missing ל. Similarly, phenomena of such outstanding importance in the current Hebrew grammar as the *waw consecutivum* or verbs *primae nun*, have no equivalents in cognate languages. Our attitude, therefore, is not to single out grammatical phenomena and compare them with corresponding features of related languages; but to examine thoroughly the phenomena in Hebrew according to all the material available, both Masoretic and non-Masoretic alike, and only then compare the final result with the outcome of a similar investigation of cognate languages.

§ 14. In this grammar we shall limit ourselves to an examination of the Hebrew Bible, and exclude from our observations any reference to similar phenomena in cognate languages. The time is not yet ripe for a comparative grammar of Hebrew. We must first establish what is genuine Hebrew by eliminating the medieval Masoretic schematizations, and by freeing ourselves from the present-day pronunciation of Hebrew, which is the result of an inner development in the course of the last millenium.

II. DICTIONARY

A. DEPENDS ON GRAMMAR

§ 15.   The dictionary (cf. § 1) is dependent on the grammar. It lists
the words found in the Bible text under their respective root, which has
previously been established by the grammarian. Thus, e.g. לָדַעַת, לָטַעַת
and לָקַחַת are listed s.v. ידע, נטע and לקח, in accordance with the grammatical theories of verbs *primae yod* and *primae nun*, the latter to include
also the verb לקח (cf. B-L § 52p). Consequently, the dictionary stands and
falls with the grammatical theories upon which it is based. If we explain
in a new way the derivation of nominal and verbal forms offered in the
Bible text, then the dictionary has to rearrange its material and list these
forms under the roots, which the grammar has established anew. Thus,
e.g. the difference between the various editions of Gesenius' Hebrew
Dictionary reflects corresponding differences in the grammatical treatment of the language in the respective editions of Gesenius' Hebrew
grammar.

B. CURRENT DICTIONARY LACKS METHOD

§ 16.   The Hebrew dictionary as it presents itself to us in its most
up-to-date form in the Gesenius-Buhl edition, is the result of the labors
of generations of scholars. Monographs, articles, and stray notes in the
field of Hebrew lexicography were all carefully collected and are referred
to in the proper rubric of this dictionary. Buhl thus gives us a fair report
on what has been written with regard to each separate item in his dictionary, and is our standard work of reference for lexicographical bibliography.
But such a collection of materials is not a dictionary: We are presented
with bricks, and not with the finished building, which has been left to our
own abilities or fancies. The accumulation of hundreds of individual
catchwords does not relieve the editor of his duty to introduce system
and method in their selection and arrangement. This may seem a harsh
judgment to Biblical scholars, who generally regard with deepest respect
each latest edition of the Gesenius dictionary as the last word in scholarship; I shall therefore substantiate my statement.

C. NOUNS AND VERBS

§ 17.   Generally speaking, a different treatment is accorded to nouns and verbs, respectively. In instances like טָרֹף טֹרַף יִטְרַף (Gen. 37.33), (Ex. 22.12), בָּרוֹךְ בֵּרַךְ וַיְבָרֶךְ (Josh. 24.10), קַטֵּר יַקְטִירוּן (1 Sam. 2.16) we have cases of a finite verb with the infinitive absolute. For obvious reasons, we would hardly look for them in the dictionary under the same stem, but rather under *ḳal* and *puʿal*, *ḳal* and *niphʿal* etc., although these infinitives are used to stress the meaning of their finite verbs and should by right be of the same stem. However, we are saved from any such errors by the fact that verbal forms which occur in the Bible, are grouped (whatever their root) under their stem, as complementing one another. Only very few verbs occur in the Bible in all the so-called stems (cf. § 7 end of paragraph); the vast majority of verbal roots occur only in one stem (active and passive formations I do not count as different stems), and in a limited number of forms. Forms are assigned to their respective stems: קַטֵּר is *piʿel*, and its finite verb יַקְטִירוּן is *hiphʿil*, because we know from analogous forms of other verbs that these are the characteristics of the vocalization of these stems.

The nouns, however, are treated each as an individual, with no regard for similar formations, and without allowing for conclusions on the basis of analogies. Various nominal forms, which happen to occur in the Bible, are listed under one and the same catchword, merely because they show striking resemblance in spelling and in meaning. But let it be emphasized right now: striking though their resemblance may be, it is not more striking than that of the verbal forms which we have just discussed; the same is true of the identity of the meaning. Thus, e.g. יוֹנִים is listed as plural to יוֹנָה, קוֹלוֹת as plural to קוֹל, although, were we to judge from analogies in the formation of the plural, we would say that יוֹנִים belongs ot יוֹן*, and קוֹלוֹת to קוֹלָה*.

D. Masculine and Feminine Formations (Cf. MH § 188)

§ 18. But here, grammarians may raise the objection that it is a familiar fact that singular-forms ending in a ה reflect a distinct difference in meaning from the otherwise identical forms ending in a consonant, while no such difference exists between יוֹנִים and יוֹנָה, or between קוֹלוֹת and קוֹל: "Als Feminina wurden auch aufgefasst: 1. *Nomina unitatis*, ursprünglich wohl mit der Endung *-tū* (vielleicht < *tauu, vgl. arabisch *tauu* 'Einzelding,' 'einzelnes Stück'): אֳנִיָּה 'Schiff,' von אֳנִי 'Flotte'; שַׂעֲרָה*

'einzelnes Haar,' von שֵׂעָר 'Haar'; שִׁירָה 'Lied,' von שִׁיר 'Gesang' '' (B-L
§ 62z).

§ 19.   This statement of Bauer-Leander represents an effort to project
an Arabic characteristic upon Biblical Hebrew. It is superficial, since it is
based solely upon the external resemblance of the spelling, and pays no
attention at all to the actual facts. In fact, the dictionary and the grammar are here at odds with one another. Gesenius-Buhl stresses that אָרְזָה,
דָּגָה, עֵצָה (see later s.v.) are *nomina collectiva*, thus upsetting B-L's statement that forms ending in ה are *nomina unitatis*. Bauer-Leander sensed
in one case the difficulty in the application of their theory: ''אֲרָיִים
'Löwen'; אֲרָיוֹת 'Löwenbilder' '' (B-L § 63r). On the other hand, Gesenius-
Buhl lists both אֲרָיִים and אֲרָיוֹת under one catchword: אֲרִי. Both overlook
the facts: against B-L see p. 294, § 83, the example 1 Ki. 10.20 as compared
with 2 Chron. 9.19, and also 2 Ki. 17.25, 26 where אֲרָיִים and אֲרָיוֹת are used
with the identical connotation; against Gesenius-Buhl cf. Judg. 14.5:
כְּפִיר אֲרָיוֹת, referred to in v. 8 as: הָאַרְיֵה. These instances show how unreliable the current Hebrew grammars are in certain matters (cf. § 5 ff.).

§ 20.   As a matter of fact, a considerable number of nouns occur in the
Bible both in masculine and feminine forms (cf. p. 294, § 83). The following tentative (and decidedly incomplete) list of such nouns proves that
the pairs were used in the identical meaning. If the catchword occurs in
the absolute state, then it is vocalized here accordingly. The examples
were chosen to make it clear that masculine and feminine forms were used
in identical, or at least similar phrases.

אָבָק:	Deut. 28.24:	יתן · · · מטר ארצך אָבָק
אבקה:	Cant. 3.6:	אַבְקַת רוכל
אֵבֶר:	Isa. 40.31:	יעלו אֵבֶר כנשרים
אֶבְרָה:	Job 39.13:	אם אֶבְרָה חסידה
אהב:	Hos. 8.9:	התנו אֲהָבִים
אַהֲבָה:	Jer. 2.33:	לבקש אַהֲבָה
אהל:	Prov. 7.17:	מר אֲהָלִים
אהלה:	Ps. 45.9:	מר וַאֲהָלוֹת
אוֹר:	Isa. 9.1:	אוֹר נגה עליהם
אוֹרָה:	Esth. 8.16:	ליהודים היתה אוֹרָה

אֹכֶל: Gen. 43.4: ונשברה לך אֹכֶל

אָכְלָה: Gen. 1.29: לכם יהיה לְאָכְלָה

אֻם: Ps. 117.2: שבחוהו כל הָאֻמִּים

אֻמָּה: Num. 25.15: ראש אֻמּוֹת

אֹמֶן: Isa. 26.2: שמר אֱמֻנִים

אֱמוּנָה: Prov. 28.20: איש אֱמוּנוֹת

אֵמֶר: Num. 24.4: אִמְרֵי אל

אִמְרָה: Ps. 12.7: אִמְרוֹת יהוה

אֳנִי: 1 Ki. 10.22: תבוא אֳנִי תרשיש

אֳנִיָּה: Jonah 1.3: אֳנִיָּה באה תרשיש

אֹפֶל: Ps. 11.2: לירות במו אֹפֶל

אֲפֵלָה: Deut. 28.29: כאשר ימשש העור בָּאֲפֵלָה

אָצִיל: Ezek. 13.18: על כל אַצִּילֵי ידי

אַצִּילָה: Jer. 38.12: תחת אַצִּילוֹת ידיך

אֶרֶז: Isa. 41.19: אתן במדבר אֶרֶז

אַרְזָה: Zeph. 2.14: כי אַרְזָה ערה

אֲרִי: Ezek. 22.25: כַּאֲרִי שואג

אַרְיֵה: Am. 3.8: אַרְיֵה שאג

אִשִׁישׁ: Hos. 3.1: ואהבי אֲשִׁישֵׁי ענבים

אֲשִׁישָׁה: Cant. 2.5: סמכוני בָּאֲשִׁישׁוֹת

אָשָׁם: Jer. 51.5: כי ארצם מלאה אָשָׁם

אַשְׁמָה: 2 Chron. 28.13: כי רבה אַשְׁמָה לנו

אשר: Isa. 27.9: לא יקמו אֲשֵׁרִים

אֲשֵׁרָה: 2 Chron. 33.3: ויעש אֲשֵׁרוֹת

בוז: Gen. 38.23: פן נהיה לָבוּז

בּוּזָה: Neh. 3.36: כי היינו בוּזָה

בַּז: Isa. 33.23: בזזו בַז

בִּזָּה: 2 Chron. 25.13: ויבזו בִּזָּה רבה

בֶּטַח: Isa. 32.17: השקט וָבֶטַח

בִּטְחָה: Isa. 30.15: בהשקט וּבְבִטְחָה

בְּכוֹר: Neh. 10.37: בְּכוֹרֵי בקרינו

בְּכֹרָה: Deut. 12.6: וּבְכֹרֹת בקרך

גְּבוּל: Deut. 19.14: לא תסיג גְּבוּל רעך

גְּבוּלָה: Deut. 32.8: יצב גְּבֻלֹת עמים

גֶּבַע: ‎1 Sam. 13.16: ‎בְּגֶבַע בְּנִימָן

גִּבְעָה: ‎1 Sam. 13.2: ‎בְּגִבְעַת בְּנִימִין

גֵּז: Ps. 72.6: ‎ירד כמטר על גֵּז

גִּזָּה: Judg. 6.39: ‎יהי נא חרב על הַגִּזָּה

גֵּזֶל: Ezek. 22.29: ‎וגזל גֵּזֶל

גְּזֵלָה: Ezek. 18.7: ‎גְּזֵלָה לא יגזל

גִּיל: Joel 1.16: ‎שמחה וָגִיל

גִּילָה: Isa. 65.18: ‎הנני בורא · · · גִּילָה

גְּמוּל: Isa. 66.6: ‎יהוה משלם גְּמוּל לאיביו

גְּמוּלָה: Jer. 51.56: ‎אל גְּמֻלוֹת יהוה שלם ישלם

גַּן: Gen. 3.2: ‎מפרי עץ הַגַּן נאכל

גַּנָּה: Jer. 29.28: ‎ונטעו גַנּוֹת ואכלו את פריהן

דָּבָר: Gen. 20.18: ‎על דְּבַר שרה

דברה: Eccl. 3.18: ‎על דִּבְרַת בני אדם

דָּג: Jonah 2.1: ‎ויהי יונה במעי הַדָּג

דָּגָה: Jonah 2.2: ‎ויתפלל יונה · · · ממעי הַדָּגָה

דּוֹר: Isa. 51.8: ‎וישועתי לדור דּוֹרִים

דּוֹרָה: Isa. 51.9: ‎דּוֹרוֹת עולמים

דֵּע: Job 32.6: ‎ואירא מחות דֵּעִי

דֵּעָה: Isa. 28.9: ‎את מי יורה דֵּעָה

הֶדֶר: Dan. 11.20: ‎הֶדֶר מלכות

הדרה: Prov. 14.28: ‎הַדְרַת מלך

הֵיכָל: Isa. 13.22: ‎ותנים בְּהֵיכְלֵי ענג

היכלה: Hos. 8.14: ‎ויבן הֵיכָלוֹת

הֶרֶג: Isa. 30.25: ‎ביום הֶרֶג רב

הֲרֵגָה: Jer. 12.3: ‎והקדשם ליום הֲרֵגָה

זעק: Isa. 30.19: ‎חנון יחנך לקול זַעֲקֶךָ

זְעָקָה: Isa. 65.19: ‎קול בכי וקול זְעָקָה

זָקֵן: Gen. 48.10: ‎ועיני ישראל כבדו מִזֹּקֶן

זִקְנָה: Ps. 71.18: ‎עד זִקְנָה ושיבה

זְרֹעַ: Gen. 49.24: ‎זְרֹעֵי ידיו

זרועה: Ezek. 30.24: ‎זְרֹעוֹת פרעה

חֲבֹל: Ezek. 33.15: חֲבֹל יָשִׁיב רָשָׁע

חֲבֹלָה: Ezek. 18.7: חֲבֹלָתוֹ חוֹב יָשִׁיב

חֲגוֹר: Prov. 31.24: וַחֲגוֹר נָתְנָה לַכְּנַעֲנִי

חֲגוֹרָה: 2 Ki. 3.21: מִכֹּל חֹגֵר חֲגֹרָה

חֹזֶק: Am. 6.13: הֲלֹא בְחָזְקֵנוּ לָקַחְנוּ

חָזְקָה: 2 Sam. 2.16: וְאִם לֹא לָקַחְתִּי בְּחָזְקָה

חֵטְא: Deut. 19.15: בְּכָל חֵטְא אֲשֶׁר יֶחֱטָא

חֲטָאָה: Ex. 32.31: חָטָא הָעָם הַזֶּה חֲטָאָה

חִיל: Ex. 15.14: חִיל אָחַז יֹשְׁבֵי פְּלָשֶׁת

חִילָה: Job 6.10: וַאֲסַלְּדָה בְחִילָה

חֲלִי: Prov. 25.12: נֶזֶם זָהָב וַחֲלִי כָתֶם

חֶלְיָה: Hos. 2.15: וַתַּעַד נִזְמָהּ וְחֶלְיָתָהּ

חַלּוֹן: Ezek. 40.25: וְחַלּוֹנִים לוֹ וּלְאֵילַמּוֹ סָבִיב סָבִיב

חַלּוֹנָה: Ezek. 40.29: וְחַלּוֹנוֹת לוֹ וּלְאֵילַמּוֹ סָבִיב סָבִיב

חֵלֶק: Deut. 12.12: כִּי אֵין לוֹ חֵלֶק וְנַחֲלָה

חֶלְקָה: 2 Ki. 3.25: וְכָל חֶלְקָה טוֹבָה

חֶמֶד: Isa. 32.12: שְׂדֵי חֶמֶד

חֶמְדָּה: Nah. 2.10: כְּלֵי חֶמְדָּה

חֲנִית: 2 Chron. 23.9: אֶת הַחֲנִיתִים

חֲנִיתָה: Isa. 2.4: וַחֲנִיתוֹתֵיהֶם לְמַזְמֵרוֹת

חֹנֶף: Isa. 32.6: לַעֲשׂוֹת חֹנֶף

חֲנֻפָּה: Jer. 23.15: יָצְאָה חֲנֻפָּה

חֹק: Ex. 15.25: שָׂם שָׂם לוֹ חֹק וּמִשְׁפָּט

חֻקָּה: Num. 9.14: כְּחֻקַּת הַפֶּסַח וּכְמִשְׁפָּטוֹ

חֹרֶב: Jer. 49.13: לְחֶרְפָּה לְחֹרֶב

חָרְבָּה: Ezek. 5.14: לְחָרְבָּה וּלְחֶרְפָּה

חֶרֶס: Job 9.7: הָאֹמֵר לַחֶרֶס וְלֹא יִזְרָח

חַרְסָה: Judg. 14.18: בְּטֶרֶם יָבֹא הַחַרְסָה

חֹשֶׁךְ: Isa. 45.7: יוֹצֵר אוֹר וּבוֹרֵא חֹשֶׁךְ

חֲשֵׁכָה: Ps. 139.12: כַּחֲשֵׁכָה כָּאוֹרָה

טֶבַח: Prov. 7.22: כְּשׁוֹר אֶל טֶבַח יָבוֹא

טִבְחָה: Ps. 44.23: נֶחְשַׁבְנוּ כְּצֹאן טִבְחָה

טֹהַר: Ex. 24.10: וּכְעֶצֶם הַשָּׁמַיִם לָטֹהַר

טָהֳרָה: 2 Chron. 30.19: כְּטָהֳרַת הַקֹּדֶשׁ

טֶרֶף: Num. 23.24: עַד יֹאכַל טֶרֶף

טְרֵפָה: Ex. 22.30: טְרֵפָה לֹא תֹאכֵלוּ

יְגִיעַ: Gen. 31.42: יְגִיעַ כַּפַּי

יְגִיעָה: Eccl. 12.12: יְגִעַת בָּשָׂר

יְלֵל: Deut. 32.10: יְלֵל יְשִׁמֹן

יְלָלָה: Isa. 15.8: עַל אֲגְלַיִם יִלְלָתָהּ

יְסוֹד: Mic. 1.6: וִיסֹדֶיהָ אֲגַלֶּה

יְסוֹדָה: Ezek. 30.4: וְנֶהֶרְסוּ יְסֹדוֹתֶיהָ

יֹשֶׁר: Ps. 119.7: בְּיֹשֶׁר לֵבָב

יִשְׁרָה: 1 Ki. 3.6: וּבְיִשְׁרַת לֵבָב

יֶתֶר: Ex. 23.11: וְיִתְרָם תֹּאכַל חַיַּת הַשָּׂדֶה

יִתְרָה: Isa. 15.7: עַל כֵּן יִתְרָה עָשָׂה

כֶּסֶל: Ps. 78.7: וְיָשִׂימוּ בֵאלֹהִים כִּסְלָם

כִּסְלָה: Job 4.6: הֲלֹא יִרְאָתְךָ כִּסְלָתֶךָ

לַהַב: Isa. 29.6: וְלַהַב אֵשׁ אוֹכֵלָה

לֶהָבָה: Isa. 4.5: וְנֹגַהּ אֵשׁ לֶהָבָה

לֵיל: Isa. 21.11: שֹׁמֵר מַה מִּלֵּיל

לַיְלָה: Isa. 21.11: שֹׁמֵר מַה מִּלַּיְלָה

מִבְצָר: Dan. 11.24: וְעַל מִבְצָרִים יְחַשֵּׁב מַחְשְׁבֹתָיו

מִבְצָרָה: Dan. 11.15: וְלָכַד עִיר מִבְצָרוֹת

מִגְדָּל: 2 Chron. 26.15: עַל הַמִּגְדָּלִים וְעַל הַפִּנּוֹת

מִגְדָּלָה: 2 Chron. 32.5: וַיַּעַל עַל הַמִּגְדָּלוֹת

מָגֵן: Neh. 4.10: הַמָּגִנִּים וְהַקְּשָׁתוֹת

מָגֵנָה: 2 Chron. 23.9: וְאֶת הַמָּגִנּוֹת וְאֶת הַשְּׁלָטִים

מוֹעֵד: Neh. 10.34: הַשַּׁבָּתוֹת הֶחֳדָשִׁים לַמּוֹעֲדִים

מוֹעֵדָה: 2 Chron. 8.13: לַשַּׁבָּתוֹת וְלֶחֳדָשִׁים וְלַמּוֹעֲדוֹת

מָחוֹל: Jer. 31.4: וְיָצָאת בִּמְחוֹל מְשַׂחֲקִים

מְחוֹלָה: Cant. 7.1: כִּמְחֹלַת הַמַּחֲנָיִם

מָנוֹחַ: Isa. 34.14: וּמָצְאָה לָהּ מָנוֹחַ

מְנוּחָה: Jer. 45.3: וּמְנוּחָה לֹא מָצָאתִי

מסמר	Isa. 41.7:	ויחזקהו בְּמַסְמְרִים
מסמרה	Jer. 10.4:	בְּמַסְמְרוֹת ··· יְחַזְּקוּם
מַצָּב	1 Sam. 14.11:	ויגלו שניהם אל מַצַּב פלשתים
מַצָּבָה	1 Sam. 14.12:	ויענו אנשי הַמַּצָּבָה
מָצוֹק	Ps. 119.143:	צר וּמָצוֹק מצאוני
מְצוּקָה	Zeph. 1.15:	יום צרה וּמְצוּקָה
מָצוֹר	Ps. 60.11:	עיר מָצוֹר
מְצוּרָה	2 Chron. 14.5:	ערי מְצוּרָה
מַשְׁעֵן / מַשְׁעֵנָה	Isa. 3.1:	מַשְׁעֵן וּמַשְׁעֵנָה
מַתָּן	Prov. 21.14:	מַתָּן בסתר יכפה אָף
מַתָּנָה	Ezek. 46.17:	וכי יתן מַתָּנָה
נָחוּשׁ	Job 6.12:	אם בשרי נָחוּשׁ
נְחוּשָׁה	Isa. 48.4:	ומצחך נְחוּשָׁה
נָקָם	Isa. 34.8:	יום נָקָם
נְקָמָה	Jer. 46.10:	יום נְקָמָה
נָתִיב	Ps. 119.35:	הדריכני בִּנְתִיב מצותיך
נְתִיבָה	Prov. 12.28:	ודרך נְתִיבָה אל מות
סָבִיב	Jer. 32.44:	וּבִסְבִיבֵי ירושלם
סביבה	Ps. 79.3:	סְבִיבוֹת ירושלם
סֵבֶל	Ps. 81.7:	הסירותי מִסֵּבֶל שכמו
סבלה	Ex. 6.6:	והוצאתי ··· מתחת סִבְלֹת מצרים
סַעַר	Am. 1.14:	בְּסַעַר ביום סופה
סְעָרָה	Isa. 29.6:	סופה וּסְעָרָה
סַף	Jer. 52.19:	ואת הַסִּפִּים
ספה	1 Ki. 7.50:	וְהַסִּפּוֹת
סֵפֶר	Ex. 32.32:	מחני נא מִסִּפְרְךָ
ספרה	Ps. 56.9:	שימה דמעתי ··· בְּסִפְרָתֶךָ
סֵתֶר	Isa. 16.4:	הוי סֵתֶר למו מפני שודד
סִתְרָה	Deut. 32.38:	יהי עליכם סִתְרָה
עָב	1 Ki. 18.45:	והשמים התקדרו עָבִים
עבה	2 Sam. 23.4:	בקר לא עָבוֹת

עָוֶל:	Ezek. 33.13:	והוא בטח על צדקתו ועשה עָוֶל
עַוְלָה:	Zeph. 3.5:	יהוה צדיק בקרבה לא יעשה עַוְלָה
עֵזֶר:	Deut. 33.7:	וְעֵזֶר מצריו תהיה
עֶזְרָה:	Ps. 46.2:	עֶזְרָה בצרות נמצא מאד
עָנָן:	Ex. 40.35:	כי שכן עליו הֶעָנָן
עֲנָנָה:	Job 3.5:	תשכן עליו עֲנָנָה
עֵץ:	Deut. 19.5:	לכרת הָעֵץ
עֵצָה:	Jer. 6.6:	כרתו עֵצָה
עֹצֶם:	Deut. 8.17:	כחי וְעֹצֶם ידי
עָצְמָה:	Isa. 40.29:	ולאין אונים עָצְמָה ירבה
עֶצֶם } עצמה { :	Ezek. 37.7:	ותקרבו עֲצָמוֹת עֶצֶם אל עצמו
פֶּטֶר:	Ex. 13.2:	פֶּטֶר כל רחם
פטרה:	Num. 8.16:	פִּטְרַת כל רחם
פֹּעַל:	Isa. 59.6:	וּפֹעַל חמס בכפיהם
פעלה:	Prov. 11.18:	רשע עשה פְעֻלַּת שקר
פֶּרֶץ:	Am. 4.3:	וּפְרָצִים תצאנה
פרצה:	Ezek. 13.5:	לא עליתם בַּפְּרָצוֹת
פשת:	Hos. 2.7:	צמרי וּפִשְׁתִּי
פִּשְׁתָּה:	Ex. 9.31:	וְהַפִּשְׁתָּה גבעל
צֹאן:	Ps. 78.70:	ויקחהו ממכלאת צֹאן
צֹנֶה:	Ps. 8.8:	צֹנֶה ואלפים כלם
צֶדֶק:	Ps. 119.121:	עשיתי משפט וָצֶדֶק
צְדָקָה:	Gen. 18.19:	לעשות צְדָקָה ומשפט
צַוָּאר:	Jer. 27.12:	הביאו את צַוְּארֵיכֶם בעל
צוארה:	Mic. 2.3:	לא תמישו משם צַוְּארֹתֵיכֶם
צִיץ:	Isa. 28.1:	וְצִיץ נבל צבי תפארתו
ציצה:	Isa. 28.4:	והיתה צִיצַת נבל צבי תפארתו
צָמֵא:	Hos. 2.5:	והמתיה בַּצָּמָא
צִמְאָה:	Jer. 2.25:	מנעי · · · וגרונך מִצִּמְאָה
צַעַד:	Prov. 30.29:	מיטיבי צָעַד
צְעָדָה:	2 Sam. 5.24:	ויהי בשמעך · · · צְעָדָה

צָר :	Ps. 119.143:	צַר וּמָצוֹק מְצָאוּנִי
צָרָה :	Ps. 116.3:	צָרָה וְיָגוֹן אֶמְצָא
צַר :	Isa. 5.30:	חֹשֶׁךְ צַר
צָרָה :	Isa. 8.22:	צָרָה וַחֲשֵׁכָה
קֶלֶס :	Jer. 20.8:	לְחֶרְפָּה וּלְקֶלֶס
קַלָּסָה :	Ezek. 22.4:	חרפה ··· וְקַלָּסָה
קֹר :	Gen. 8.22:	וְקֹר וָחֹם
קָרָה :	Nah. 3.17:	בְּיוֹם קָרָה
רֹגֶז :	Job 3.26:	לא שלותי ··· וַיָּבֹא רֹגֶז
רָגְזָה :	Ezek. 12.18:	בְּרָגְזָה וּבִדְאָגָה
רַעַד :	Ex. 15.15:	יֹאחֲזֵמוֹ רָעַד
רְעָדָה :	Ps. 48.7:	רְעָדָה אֲחָזָתַם
רֵעַ :	2 Sam. 13.3:	וּלְאַמְנוֹן רֵעַ
רֵעֶה :	2 Sam. 15.37:	רֵעֶה דָוִד
רֶשַׁע :	Prov. 16.12:	עֲשׂוֹת רֶשַׁע
רִשְׁעָה :	Mal. 3.15:	עֹשֵׂי רִשְׁעָה
סְבַךְ :	Gen. 22.13:	נֶאֱחַז בַּסְּבַךְ
שְׂבָכָה :	Job 18.8:	וְעַל שְׂבָכָה יִתְהַלָּךְ
שֹׂבַע :	Lev. 26.5:	וַאֲכַלְתֶּם לַחְמְכֶם לָשֹׂבַע
שָׂבְעָה :	Ezek. 39.19:	וַאֲכַלְתֶּם חֵלֶב לְשָׂבְעָה
שִׂיחַ :	Ps. 64.2:	שמע אלהים קולי בְּשִׂיחִי
שִׂיחָה :	Ps. 119.57:	כל היום היא שִׂיחָתִי
שֵׂעָר :	Num. 6.5:	שְׂעַר ראשו
שערה :	1 Sam. 14.45:	מִשַּׂעֲרַת ראשו
שׁוֹשָׁן :	1 Ki. 7.26:	כמעשה שפת כוס פרח שׁוֹשָׁן
שׁוֹשַׁנָּה :	2 Chron. 4.5:	כמעשה שפת כוס פרח שׁוֹשַׁנָּה
שִׁיר :	Isa. 26.1:	יושר הַשִּׁיר הזה
שִׁירָה :	Ex. 15.1:	ישיר ··· הַשִּׁירָה הזאת
שָׁלוֹם :	Hos. 9.7:	ימי הפקדה ··· ימי הַשִּׁלֻּם
שלמה :	Ps. 91.8:	וְשִׁלֻּמַת רשעים תראה
שֶׁפַע :	Deut. 33.19:	כי שֶׁפַע ימים יינקו
שפעה :	Isa. 60.6:	שִׁפְעַת גמלים תכסך
תֹּפֶת :	Jer. 7.32:	וקברו בְּתֹפֶת
תָּפְתֶּה :	Isa. 30.33:	כי ערוך מאתמול תָּפְתֶּה

The inconsistency of Gesenius-Buhl's dictionary is manifest when it lists all the following roots—no matter whether they be masculine or feminine formations—under one catchword for each: אציל, אמה, אהל, מגדל, מבצר, לילה, חנית, חרס, חלון, זרע, היכל, דור, בכור, אשרה, אשישה, שושנה, צואר, פרץ, עצם, עב, סף, סביב, מסמר, מועד, מגן. But the other words listed above appear under the masculine and the feminine forms.

E. Nomina Segolata

§ 21. A similar case of inconsistency in the treatment of nouns occurs in the listing of the inflected forms of the so-called segolates. The following is a tentative (and incomplete) list of segolates and similar nominal formations, which vary in the vocalization of their absolute and inflected forms: cf. p. 194, § 83, p. 198, § 88; p. 454, "General Conclusions" XIb and XII. In Gesenius-Buhl's dictionary, the roots בסר and נכח occur only once as catchwords, vocalized with *holem* on the first radical; and we are made to believe that the forms בסרו and נכחו belong, as inflected forms, to these so-called *kutl*-forms. Buhl was obviously unconscious of the fact that the ten other cases representing the identical linguistic phenomenon, are listed under *two* catchwords each in his dictionary. Cf. also MH § 19.

אֹמֶר:	Ps. 68.12:	אדני יתן אֹמֶר
אמר:	Ps. 107.11:	כי המרו אִמְרֵי אל
אֹרֶךְ:	Prov. 25.15:	בְּאֹרֶךְ אפים יפתה קצין
אֶרֶךְ:	Prov. 15.18:	וְאֶרֶךְ אפים ישקיט ריב
בֹּסֶר:	Isa. 18.5:	וּבֹסֶר גמל יהיה נצה
בסר:	Job 15.33:	יחמס כגפן בִּסְרוֹ
בֹּשֶׂם:	Ex. 30.23:	וקנה בֹּשֶׂם
בֶּשֶׂם:	Ex. 30.23:	וקנמן בֶּשֶׂם
חֹזֶק:	Hag. 2.22:	והשמדתי חֹזֶק ממלכות הגוים
חזק:	Ps. 18.2:	ארממך יהוה חִזְקִי
חֹסֶר:	Am. 4.6:	וְחֹסֶר לחם
חֶסֶר:	Prov. 28.22:	ולא ידע כי חֶסֶר יבאנו
חֹצֶן:	Isa. 49.22:	בְּחֹצֶן · · · עַל כָּתֵף
חצן:	Ps. 129.7:	כַּפּוֹ · · · וְחִצְנוֹ
טֹפַח:	Ex. 25.25:	ועשית לו מסגרת טֹפַח סביב
טֶפַח:	1 Ki. 7.26:	ועביו טֶפַח

נֹכַח: I Ki. 20.29: ויחנו אלה נכח אלה

נִכְח: Ex. 14.2: נכחו תחנו על הים

עֹצֶב: Isa. 48.5: עָצְבִּי עשם ופסלי ··· צום

עֶצֶב: Jer. 22.28: הָעֶצֶב נבזה האיש הזה

רֹבַע: Num. 23.10: ומספר את רֹבַע ישראל

רבע: Ps. 139.3: ארחי וְרִבְעִי זרית

שֹמע: Esth. 9.4: וְשָׁמְעוֹ הולך בכל המדינות

שֵׁמַע: Isa. 66.19: אשר לא שמעו את שִׁמְעִי

שֹׁד: Isa. 60.16: וְשֹׁד מלכים תינקי

שַׁד: Lam. 4.3: גם תנין חלצו שַׁד

אֹסֶף: Isa. 32.10: כלה בציר אֹסֶף בלי יבוא

אָסִיף: Ex. 23.16: וחג הָאָסִף ··· באספך את מעשיך

עֹמֶר: Deut. 24.19: ושכחת עֹמֶר בשדה

עָמִיר: Am. 2.13: העגלה המלאה לה עָמִיר

שֹׂבַע: Lev. 25.19: ואכלתם לָשֹׂבַע

שָׂבָע: Gen. 41.30: ונשכח כל הַשָׂבָע

תֹּמֶר: Judg. 4.5: והיא יושבת תחת תֹּמֶר

תָּמָר: Cant. 7.8: קומתך דמתה לְתָמָר

§ 22. In summing up my observations, I would say that the Gesenius-Buhl dictionary offers great help to the student of Hebrew philology, by providing a selected bibliography which presents the present state of research. But we miss a carefully thought over master-plan combining the individual entries into a complete system: Buhl thus failed to perfect into a dictionary of real help to the exegete of the Bible this repository of lexicographical notes.

III. EXEGESIS

A. BASED UPON GRAMMAR AND DICTIONARY

§ 23. The study of Hebrew philology (cf. § 1) leads up to and climaxes in the understanding of the Hebrew Bible. This fact finds its expression either in Biblical commentaries, or—more comprehensively—in Bible translations. For a translation of the Bible is at the same time a running commentary to the text, provided that the translator is successful in surmounting the difficulties which the Eastern way of thinking and speaking offers to the Western mind (cf. above, § 9, and especially p. 600, § 60) and thus presents to the reader an intelligible text in his own language. Biblical commentaries and translations may be joined under the general term of Biblical Exegesis.

§ 24.   Our understanding of the Bible thus rests on our knowledge of Hebrew grammar and our ability to make good use of the Hebrew diction- ary. Thus e.g. S. R. Driver in his *Notes on the Hebrew Text of the Books of Samuel* remarks on 1 Sam. 14.29 s.v. "הזה [מעט דבש הזה] הזה does not belong to דבש (as accents)—for it could not in that case have the article—but to the definite מעט דבש 'this little honey.' " The sentence in full is: רְאוּ נָא כִּי אֹרוּ עֵינַי כִּי טָעַמְתִּי (מעט דבש הזה) "See, I pray you, how mine eyes are brightened because I tasted...." הזה is a demonstrative pronoun. This term is based on the fact that it is used in connection with something near you, to which you can point with your finger, saying: *this here*! Now, how could Jonathan possibly have said: (because I tasted) *this* little honey, when some time had already elapsed since he partook of it, so that the honey which he had eaten could no longer be produced in order to point a finger at it and say: "*this* (here) little honey!" Common sense necessitates our connecting הזה with דבש (cf. p. 603, § 68, 2) and consequently our translating: "(because I tasted) a little of this (here) honey." This example demonstrates that grammar itself must follow the dictates of common sense in order to be acceptable to us and applicable to the interpretation of a given Biblical passage (cf. p. 597, § 57a).

§ 25.   The same holds true of the Hebrew dictionary. We read in Jer. 13.16: "Give glory to the Lord your God, Before it grow dark, And before your feet stumble, Upon the mountains of twilight." What are "mountains of twilight"? To have witnessed the twilight high up in the mountains, either at sunrise or sunset, is certainly a unique experience of unforgettable beauty to every enthusiast of the grandeur of nature. But "mountains of twilight" cannot be identified with sunrise or sunset *in* the higher mountainous regions. Furthermore: the context "before it grow dark and before your feet stumble upon the mountains of twilight" does not at all fit into the gay picture of a tourist mountain-climber, with a keen perception for the scenic beauty of his surroundings. Thus, "mountains of twilight," although a literal translation of הָרֵי נָשֶׁף, defies common sense, and is, therefore, no translation at all. A rendition of a

Biblical passage, which merely offers the equivalents of each individual Hebrew word without shaping them into a sentence which yields sense, cannot be regarded as a translation (cf. § 23). We shall. therefore, conclude that both the Hebrew grammar and the Hebrew dictionary must conform to the demands of common sense, if they are to serve as bases for Biblical Exegesis.

B. TRANSLATION REFLECTS EXEGESIS

§ 26. In 1917, the Jewish Publication Society of America published a volume under the title *The Holy Scriptures according to the Masoretic Text. A New Translation* (Philadelphia). In the *Preface*, mention is made of already existing English translations of the Hebrew Bible with a brief evaluation of their respective merits. But in conclusion, the need for this *New Translation* is stressed: "The most popular, however, among these translations (scil. among English-speaking Jews) was that of Leeser, which was ... the accepted version in all the synagogues of the United States. ... With the advance of time and the progress made in almost all departments of Bible study, it was found that Leeser's translation would bear improvement and recasting." (*Preface*, p. v). Though speaking only of "improving on" and "recasting" the work of Leeser, the editors offer a virtually new translation. Of course, the works of its forerunners were made use of. Already the title-page indicates that this new venture was performed "with the aid of previous versions"; and in the *Preface* the editors are even more outspoken and explicit: "In preparing the manuscript ... Professor Margolis took into account the existing English versions" (ib., p. vi). "We are ... deeply grateful for ... the Authorized Version with its admirable diction ... as well as for the Revised Version with its ample learning. ... The editors have ... used these famous English versions." (ib., p. viii).

The aim of this new translation being to "give to the Jewish world a translation of the Scriptures done by men imbued with the Jewish consciousness" (ib., p. vii), it is only natural that "as to the text and order of the biblical books, ... it follows Jewish tradition" (ib., p. viii). "Even with regard to the latest book of the Scriptures, we read its text substantially in the form in which the great Rabbi Akiba read it. ... In that system (scil. 'by which the sacred text was guarded'), the letters were actually counted, ... to the end that no alterations should creep in. ... Not only does the text known as the masoretic represent the text current in the Synagogue with regard to consonants, but also with regard to its signs standing for vowels and accents. ... A translation must naturally follow the guide of the latter" (ib., p. ix). "A translation ... can follow only one text, and that must be the traditional" (ib., p. x).

With a program as indicated above to guide the various translators of the respective Biblical books, the publishers were justified in adding *according to the Masoretic Text* as a subtitle in order to characterize this work.

C. Translation Deviates from MT

§ 27. But the question may be asked: And was this program really put into practice? Do the actual facts substantiate the claim laid down in the program? I am afraid, the answer must be in the negative. For even a cursory examination of certain Isaiah-passages, picked at random, will reveal a strikingly different attitude towards the Masoretic Text: there is apparent a disregard for the consonants and their vocalization, as established in the Masoretic Text:

Isa. 13.20: יַרְבִּצוּ: "make their fold"=יִרְבְּצוּ; elsewhere the *hiph'il* is translated as causative, cf. Jer. 33.12: מַרְבִּצִים: "causing ... to lie down," Ezek. 34. 15: אַרְבִּיצֵם: "I will cause them to lie down."

Isa. 14.30: יַהֲרֹג: "shall be slain"=יֵהָרֵג.

Isa. 17.5: קָצִיר: "the harvestman"=קֹצֵר.

Isa. 28.18: וְכֻפַּר: "shall be disannulled"=וְתֻפַר.

Isa. 28.25: שׂוֹרָה: "in rows"=שׁוּרָה.

Isa. 29.5: זָרָיִךְ: "thy foes"=צָרַיִךְ.

Isa. 30.19: יֵשֵׁב: "that dwellest"=יֹשֵׁב.

Isa. 30.21: תַּאֲמִינוּ: "ye turn to the right hand"=תֵּימִינוּ.

Isa. 34.13: חָצִיר: "an enclosure"=חָצֵר.

Isa. 40.10: בְּחָזָק: "as a Mighty One"=כְּחָזָק.

Isa. 40.17: מֵאֶפֶס: "as things of nought"=כְּאֶפֶס; cf. parallel כְּאַיִן: "as nothing."

Isa. 42.4: יָרוּץ: "he shall (not...) be crushed"=יֵרוֹץ.

Isa. 56.5: לוֹ: "(I will give) them"=לָהֶם.

Isa. 57.3: וַתִּזְנֶה: "and the harlot"=וְזֹנָה.

For additional instances cf. §§ 36 f., p. 606, § 73b and p. 607, § 75b *passim*.
All these emended readings can be found listed in Kittel's *Biblia Hebraica*
as corrections of the Masoretic Bible Text, suggested by modern Biblical
scholars. Instances of disagreement in the person, the gender or the number
between subject and predicate, or between several closely connected verbs,
the adjustment of which forms a very substantial part of the activites of
the Textual Criticism of the Bible, were disregarded here, since the English
language does not lend itself to an imitation of these characteristics of the
Hebrew style; the translators simply had to follow the rules of English
syntax.

D. Interrelation between Translations

§ 28.   We should not be hasty in our judgment, but take the history
of the genesis of the JPS translation into consideration: it might be—
theoretically reasoning—that translations like those noted above were
taken over from the previously existing English translations, thus at-
testing, it is true, to the new translator's neglect of duty in failing to check
up on them, but not implying his disregard for the very task which he was
supposed to perform: the preserving of the Masoretic Text. But a comparison of JPS with AV and RV reveals that though a translation of the
passages under scrutiny according to the Masoretic Text did exist, the
editor of the JPS nevertheless preferred a rendition, which involved a
break with the Masoretic tradition and with their own program:

Isa. 13.20: יַרְבִּצוּ: RV: make teir flocks to lie down there
AV: make their fold there=JPS

Isa. 14.30: יַהֲרֹג: AV: and he shall slay
RV: shall be slain=JPS

Isa. 29.5: זָרָיִךְ: AV: thy strangers
RV: thy foes=JPS

Isa. 30.19: יֵשֵׁב: AV and RV: shall dwell
JPS: "that dwellest"

Isa. 40.10: בְּחָזָק: AV: with strong (hand)
RV: As a mighty one=JPS

Isa. 40.17: מֵאֶפֶס: AV and RV: less than nothing
RV *marginalis*: as a thing of nought=JPS

Isa. 56.5:   לוֹ:   RV *marginalis*: Heb. him
                        AV and RV: them=JPS

E. EXPLANATORY NOTES

§ 29. There exists, as we have seen, a discrepancy between the JPS translation's claim to be *according to the Masoretic Text* (with the definition of this term as given in the *Preface*) and the actual facts. With a scholar of rank like the late Professor Max L. Margolis heading the editorial board as editor-in-chief, it would be ridiculous to assume their unawareness of this discrepancy. Those interested in the JPS translation are acquainted with the huge volume of *Notes on The New Translation of the Holy Scriptures, prepared by the Former Editor-in-Chief Dr. Max L. Margolis (For Private Circulation Only)*, which gives eloquent evidence of the penetrating and painstaking endeavors of Margolis. I have, therefore, not the slightest doubt that these observations did not simply escape his attention. And nevertheless, not one of these or other deviations from the Masoretic Text that are reflected in JPS, is discussed or even mentioned in the *Notes*. The only explanation of this puzzling situation I can think of is: American Israel needed an English Bible to comply with its religious needs; consequently, the translation had to emphasize its being based strictly upon the Hebrew Bible of the Synagogue, i.e. the Masoretic Text. But as a scholar, Margolis had to comply "with the advance of time and the progress made in almost all departments of Bible study." He thus— unwittingly, perhaps—proved that a strict adherence to all the *minutiae* concerning the consonants and the vocalization, as embodied in the Masoretic Text, can no longer be made a *conditio sine qua non* for a Jewish Bible translation.

In fairness to Professor Margolis and his work I had to use the terminology of those days and speak of *the* Masoretic Text, in the singular. This, of course, can no longer be regarded as correct; for on pp. 520-548, I demonstrated after examining three independent Masoras that they all disagree with one another and even contradict their own respective texts. Now. the fact alone that one of these Masoras (in *Biblia Rabbinica*, Bomberg, Venice 1524/5) by virtue of its being repeatedly reproduced in print, has become more widely known, does not entitle us to regard it as *the* Masora κατ᾽ ἐξοχήν. And even Jacob ben Chayim, the editor of this

Masora, often explicitly calls attention to the self-contradictory character of the Masoretic tradition; cf. especially pp. 548 ff.

F. Translation and Grammar

§ 30. But Hebrew consonants and their vocalization are merely like clay in the hands of the interpreter of the Bible; and it is the grammarian with his theories concerning phonology, morphology and syntax, which puts the spirit of life into these otherwise disjointed words and shapes them into a sentence. Hebrew grammar, on the other hand, is based upon the observation and classification of the many philological phenomena of the language of the Bible. And who is in a better position to notice these phenomena, than the translator of the Bible himself, he who has to find a suitable exegesis for every passage in the Scriptures. We must not expect him to adhere strictly to the grammatical theories of his day; for such theories, while quite fitting to explain certain Biblical passages, may prove inadequate if applied to others. In such cases the translator could actually prepare the ground for the coming grammarian by calling attention to his observations, which however, he never does. I shall demonstrate this on a few examples.

G. Verbal Tenses

§ 31. The verbal tenses (again speaking in the terminology of forty years ago) were known as perfect and imperfect. As a matter of fact, JPS does its best to translate a Hebrew verb in the perfect with the corresponding English verb in the past tense, and an imperfect with a future tense. But this method cannot be applied consistently. For "a translator is not a transcriber of the text. His principal function is to make the Hebrew intelligible" (*Preface*, p. x):

Hos. 2.1:   יֵאָמֵר · · · · יֹאמַר: "(that which) was said ... (it) shall be said." .

Zech. 8.14, 15: זָמַמְתִּי : · · · · זָמַמְתִּי: "I purposed...: ...do I purpose."

Hos. 6.1:   יַךְ · · · · טָרָף: "He hath torn ... He hath smitten."

Hos. 8.7:   יִקְצֹרוּ · · · · יִזְרָעוּ: "thy sow ... they shall reap."

These problems are now dealt with pp. 587 ff.

H. CONSECUTIVE WAW

§ 32.   "The principal peculiarity of the Hebrew verbal system is the construction with consecutive *waw*. ... Thus the tenses seem to be inverted" (G. R. Driver: *Problems of the Hebrew Verbal System*, p. 85). JPS are at pains to translate verbal forms with consecutive *waw* with the inverted English tense. But here, too, consistency was unattainable, as the following examples will show. They are the result of a collation of 2 Sam. 22 with Ps. 18. The verbs in question appear in both these parallel sources in the identical form (tense, number and gender), the sole difference being that in one source a consecutive *waw* is prefixed. This should lead to the inverting of the tense of the English verb in the translation. But such a procedure was rejected by JPS, obviously due to their effort "to make the Hebrew intelligible"; and the *waw* was rendered by merely "and" or "also" like any ordinary conjunctive *waw*. Thus JPS offer additional proof for the correctness of my theories on p. 586, § 38 ff. and p. 591, § 47 ff.

Ps. 18.7:   יִשְׁמַע (מהיכלו קולי): "(Out of His temple) He heard my voice."

2 Sam. 22.7:   וַיִּשְׁמַע (מהיכלו קולי): "And (out of His temple) He heard my voice."

Ps. 18.12:   יָשֶׁת (חשך): "He made (darkness)."

2 Sam. 22.12:   וַיָּשֶׁת (חשך): "And He made (darkness)."

2 Sam. 22.14:   יַרְעֵם (מן שמים יהוה): "(The Lord) thundered (from heaven)."

Ps. 18.14:   וַיַּרְעֵם (בשמים יהוה): "(The Lord) also thundered (in the heavens)."

2 Sam. 22.16:   יִגָּלוּ (מסדות תבל): "(The foundations of the world) were laid bare."

Ps. 18.16:   וַיִּגָּלוּ (מוסדות תבל): "And (the foundations of the world) were laid bare."

Ps. 18.39:   אֶמְחָצֵם (ולא יכלו קום): "I have smitten them through."

2 Sam. 22.39:   וָאֲמְחָצֵם (ולא יקומון): "(I have ...) and smitten them through."

Ps. 18.39:   יִפְּלוּ (תחת רגלי): "They are fallen (under my feet)."

2 Sam. 22.39:   וַיִּפְּלוּ (תחת רגלי): "Yea, they are fallen (under my feet)."

Ps. 18.44:　(מריבי עם) תְּפַלְּטֵנִי: "Thou hast delivered me."

2 Sam. 22.44:　(מריבי עמי) וַתְּפַלְּטֵנִי: "Thou also hast delivered me."

I. Our Western Way of Thinking

§ 33.　In the instances discussed in the preceding §§ 31 and 32, JPS sensed the impossibility of applying certain rules laid down by the grammarians and preferred to disregard them there. But they did not consider these rules to be invalidated altogether by such a procedure; on the contrary: wherever only feasible, they followed them. We, thus, have instances for the applicability of a rule, and again instances of exceptions to this rule. And here we find ourselves confronted with a new aspect to this problem: How to draw the dividing line between the instances for and against a given grammatical rule? Just how far are we to go with the application of the rule and when are we to deviate from it? In other words: When does a rendering cease to "make the Hebrew intelligible" and impresses the reader as merely a grammatical twist? Here, much depends on personal taste and preferences; and I will frankly admit that my own taste and preferences are considerably different from those of the editors of the JPS translation as exhibited in their work.

J. Formation of Plural

§ 34.　It is well known that the absolute form of the masculine noun in the plural ends in ־ים. The ending in ־י on the other hand may indicate, according to the preceding vowel, one of the following three forms: a) the construct state of the plural (if vocalized ־ֵי); b) the pronominal suffix of the first person of the plural (if vocalized ־ַי or ־ָי), or c) of the singular (if vocalized ־ִי). But, still, in order to discharge their task conscienciously, JPS had to treat forms ending in ־י variously vocalized as *pluralis absolutus*:

a)　Am. 6.6:　(ביין) בְּמִזְרְקֵי (השתים): "(That drink wine) in bowls."

b)　Isa. 19.9:　חוֹרָי (וארגים): "(they that weave) cotton."

　　Jer. 22.14:　חַלּוֹנָי (וקרע לו): "(And cutteth him out) windows."

　　Ezek. 13.18:　יָדָי (אצילי): "elbows."

　　Am. 7.1:　גֹּבָי (והנה יוצר): "(and behold, He formed) locusts."

c)　Isa. 38.12:　רֹעִי (כאהל): "(As) a shepherd's (tent)."

§ 35.   Now this rule can no longer claim general applicability. So, why limit the exceptions to the instances listed above, and why not re-examine other nominal forms ending in ־ִי as to whether their context does not advocate an interpretation as absolute plural?

2 Sam. 22.24: מֵעֲוֹנִי:
   N o t : "from mine iniquity."
   B u t : *from iniquity.*

2 Sam. 22.34: בָּמוֹתַי:
   N o t : "my high places."
   B u t : *high places*; on this unusual plural formation cf. for the time being 2 Ki. 25.4: הַחֹמֹתַיִם.

Isa. 7.13: אֱלֹהָי:
   N o t : "my God."
   B u t : *God*; cf. parallel אֲנָשִׁים.

Isa. 16.4: נִדָּחַי
   N o t : "mine outcasts."
   B u t : *the outcasts*; cf. v. 3: נִדָּחִים.

Isa. 37.29: חַחִי · · · · וּמִתְגִּי:
   N o t : "My hook. ... And My bridle."
   B u t : *hooks ... And bridles.*

Isa. 49.11: הָרַי . . . וּמְסִלֹּתַי:
   N o t : "My mountains. ... And My highways."
   B u t : *the mountains. ... And the highways.*

Isa. 51.4: עַמִּי וּלְאוּמִּי:
   N o t : "O My people..., O My nation."
   B u t : *peoples..., nations.*

Jer. 49.25: מְשׂוֹשִׂי (קְרִית):
   N o t : "(The city of) my joy."
   B u t : (The city of) *joy.*

Hab. 3.19: בָּמוֹתַי; cf. on 2 Sam. 22.34.

Zech. 1.17: עָרַי:
   N o t : "My cities."
   B u t : *cities.*

K. Pronominal Suffixes with י

§ 36. In the days of the JPS it was considered characteristic for nominal forms with pronominal suffixes to exhibit the letter י between the noun and the suffix, in order to indicate that the noun is in the plural. This *yod*, thus, was indicative of the number of the noun. (Now cf. p. 261 ff., and p. 575, § 26, where I proved that this *yod* is merely a *mater lectionis*). The translator was often enough faced with the fact that the verb or adjective, closely connected with such a supposedly plural-form of a noun, was used in the singular. Here, too, JPS silently admitted the existence of exceptions to this rule by disregarding the implication of this *yod* on the number of the noun:

Deut. 28.48: אֹיְבֶיךָ . . יְשַׁלְּחֶנּוּ: "thine enemy whom . . . shall send."
1 Sam. 19.4: מַעֲשָׂיו טוֹב (לְךָ): "his work hath been very good."
Judg. 13.12: יָבֹא דְבָרֶיךָ: "thy word cometh to pass."
Mic. 4.11: וְתַחַז · · · · עֵינֵינוּ: "let our eye gaze."

§ 37. But unfortunately JPS overlooked numerous other instances of the same nature, while in some of them they even apparently emended the obviously singular-form of the predicate into the plural, in order to coordinate their number with what they considered to be a plural-form of the subject:

Deut. 21.10: (עַל) אֹיְבֶיךָ וּנְתָנוֹ:
   N o t : "thine enemies, and . . . delivereth them" (=וּנְתָנָם).
   B u t : *thine enemy, and . . . delivereth him.*

Judg. 19.19: עֲבָדֶיךָ:
   N o t : "thy servants."
   B u t : *thy servant* (referring to himself).

2 Sam. 24.13: (לִפְנֵי) צָרֶיךָ וְהוּא (רֹדְפֶךָ):
   N o t : "thy foes while they" (=וְהֵם).
   B u t : *thy foe while he.*

Isa. 10.15: מְרִימָיו:
   N o t : "them that lift it up."
   B u t : *him that lifts it up*; cf. parallel מְנִיפוֹ.

Isa. 64.10: מַחֲמַדֵּינוּ הָיָה:

  N o t : "our pleasant things are" (=הָיוּ).

  B u t : *our delight is.*

Ps. 37.31: (לֹא) תִמְעַד אֲשֻׁרָיו:

  N o t : "None of his steps slide" (= תִמְעַדְנָה).

  B u t : *His step doth not slide.*

Ps. 44.19: וַתֵּט אֲשֻׁרֵינוּ:

  N o t : "Neither have our steps declined."

  B u t : *Neither hath our step declined.*

Prov. 16.7: אוֹיְבָיו יַשְׁלִם:

  N o t : "He maketh (even) his enemies to be at peace."

  B u t : *(Even) his enemy maketh peace.*

L. Nominal Forms Ending in יִם‑

§ 38. As a *tertium comparationis* in advancing a new method of interpreting the Hebrew Bible text, I have chosen *The Holy Scriptures, according to the Masoretic Text* (Philadelphia 1917). The reason for it is
obvious: I also interpret the Masoretic text, and avoid as far as possible
emending it. I do not intend to "correct" the text to conform with our
way of thinking, but would rather adjust my way of thinking to the text
of the Bible in order to reach at a better understanding thereof (cf. § 102).
The translators of *The Holy Scriptures* considered it their duty to indicate
as far as feasible in their translation the exact *nuance* of the Hebrew word
and its grammatical form. So e.g. רַחֲמָתַיִם (Judg. 5.10) is rendered: "two
damsels," רִקְמָתַיִם (ib.): "two dyed garments," נַעֲלָיִם (Am. 2.6): "a pair
of shoes," הַמַּחֲנָיִם (Cant. 7.1): "two companies"; for these forms end in
יִם‑ (or יָם‑), and according to the grammar this indicates a dual. Of
course, there are common-sense objections (cf. §§ 24 and 25); one might ask,
in connection with the example mentioned last: what is so particular in
"a dance of two companies?" Is there any difference in the way barrack
dances are performed, if the participants belong to one company only,
or to two companies?

§ 39. But apart from these considerations, there are also weighty
reasons against the term "dual" and its implication from a purely grammatical point of view. Human speech consists of sentences, and not of
unrelated words. Now, sentences for the most part have a subject and a

predicate, which are supposed to conform with one another in the person, gender and number. The number of the predicate, which in the majority of cases is a verb, is twofold: singular and plural; but the number of the subject, which is a noun (cf. p. 601, § 62), is threefold: singular, dual and plural. How, then, shall a verb conform to a subject in the dual? Is the dual of the noun considered a singular or a plural, as far as the predicate is concerned? Since the dual represents more than a single unit, we would have to class it as a plural in this respect. Hence we would have to say: The number of noun and verb alike is twofold: singular and plural. With nouns, however, the plural is subdivided into dual and plural, the first form being used in order to indicate that the noun mentioned refers to a pair. This is logically correct; but do the actual facts of the Bible corroborate these theoretic conclusions?

§ 40.   There are, it is true, a few nominal forms ending in םִ‎יַ֫‎־, which may well be considered as duals: not only קַרְנַ֫יִם‎, עֵינַ֫יִם‎, רַגְלַ֫יִם‎, יָדַ֫יִם‎, but also forms like כִּלְאַ֫יִם‎ Lev. 19.19, וְהַמֶּלְקָחַ֫יִם‎ 2 Ki. 7.49. But these forms constitute only a negligible minority against the considerable number of instances, where the ending םִ‎יַ֫‎־ can hardly indicate a dual. Apart from well-known and frequently occurring nouns like: מִצְרַ֫יִם‎, אֶפְרַ֫יִם‎, שָׁמַ֫יִם‎, מַ֫יִם‎; (בֵּין‎) הָעַרְבַּ֫יִם‎, צָהֳרַ֫יִם‎, note אֲפָסַ֫יִם‎ (מֵי‎) Ezek. 47.3 and בַּעֲצַלְתַּ֫יִם‎ Eccl. 10.18. The latter is translated in Gesenius-Buhl's dictionary: "die beiden faulen Hände," in order to get out a dual-meaning. But why limit the term "laziness" to manual labor? In the case of a messenger, for instance, בַּעֲצַלְתַּ֫יִם‎ according to Gesenius-Buhl would have to be rendered: "die beiden faulen Füsse." There is a word in German indicating laziness with regard to thinking: "denkfaul"; I wonder if בַּעֲצַלְתַּ֫יִם‎ in connection with a "denkfaul" man should be translated "the two lazy brains!" It is absurd to force preconceived grammatical notions upon the Bible text.

§ 41.   The following examples of nouns ending in םִ‎יַ֫‎־ will, we hope, finally dispel the current explanation of the grammars that this ending implies the meaning of a dual.

a)   אַרְבַּעְתַּ֫יִם‎: 2 Sam. 12.6   שִׁבְעָתַ֫יִם‎: Gen. 4.15
       אַרְבַּע רַגְלָיִם‎: Lev. 11.23   מַרְבֵּה רַגְלַ֫יִם‎: Lev. 11.42
       וְאַרְבַּע כְּנָפַ֫יִם‎: Ezek. 1.6   שֵׁשׁ כְּנָפַ֫יִם‎: Isa. 6.2
       שִׁבְעָה עֵינַ֫יִם‎: Zech. 3.9   שְׁלֹשׁ הַשִּׁנַּ֫יִם‎: 1 Sam. 2.13

b) In order to indicate a pair (dual), the Bible uses the proper form of
שְׁתַּיִם or שְׁנַיִם.

שְׁתֵּי כְרָעַיִם: Am. 3.12   שְׁתֵּי הַכְּלָיֹת: Ex. 29.13

וּשְׁתֵּי כַפּוֹת יָדָיו: 1 Sam. 5.4   שְׁתֵּי כְתֵפוֹת: Ex. 28.7

דְּלָתַיִם: Deut. 3.5; but וּשְׁתַּיִם דְּלָתוֹת: Ezek. 41.23, and וּשְׁתֵּי דְלָתוֹת:
Ezek. 41.24

דְּרָכַיִם: Prov. 28.6; but שְׁנַיִם דְּרָכִים: Ezek. 21.24, and שְׁנֵי הַדְּרָכִים:
Ezek. 21.26

לֻחֹתַיִם: Ezek. 27.5; but שְׁנֵי לֻחֹת (הָעֵדֻת): Ex. 31.18

c) Note also:

אַפַּיִם: Gen. 19.1; הַחֹמֹתַיִם: 2 Ki. 25.4; חֲמֹרָתַיִם: Judg. 15.16; בִּנְחֻשְׁתַּיִם:
Judg. 16.21; הַמִּשְׁפְּתָיִם: Judg. 5.16; שְׁפַתַּיִם: Ps. 68.14; רִבֹּתַיִם: Ps. 68.18.

M. Syntactic Position Decisive

§ 42. Consequently, the instances mentioned at the beginning of § 40
(רַגְלִים, יָדַיִם, etc.), as well as some others like יוֹמַיִם, פַּעֲמַיִם which have to
be explained as indicating a dual, should not be termed *dual-forms* on the
basis of their ending in ־יִם, but rather *interpreted syntactically as dual-
forms* in view of their context. Further proof for the fact that "dual"
(in case we wish to continue this misleading term at all) refers only to
the meaning which our exegesis attaches to the word, but is entirely
divorced from its vocalization as provided by the grammarians, can be
seen in חֲבָלִים Ezek. 47.13, which clearly means *two* parts. Compare also:
נַעֲלַיִם Am. 2.6 but בַּנְּעָלִים Cant. 7.2; נַחֲלַיִם Ezek. 47.9 but נְחָלִים Isa. 11.15;
הַמַּחֲנָיִם Cant. 7.1 but הַבַּמַּחֲנִים Num. 13.19; שְׂפַתַּיִם Ex. 6.30 but וְשִׂפְתוֹת
Eccl. 10.12.

N. Diphthong *ai* and Vowel *i*

§ 43. How, then, are we to explain grammatically nominal forms
ending in ־יִם? First we wish to establish that ־יִם is one syllable only,
since the vocalization by ־ֽ is meant to indicate the diphthong *ai*. For
had the Tiberian vocalizers intended it to be *two* vowels, *a* and *i*, then a
dagesh in the yod would have been required so as to close the preceding
open syllable with the short vowel ־ (cf. p. 414, § 1, Rules V and VIβ);
cf. e.g. חַיִּים. Now it is noteworthy that in the Palestinian vocalization

the ending ‎יִם‏- in forms like those listed in the foregoing paragraphs is vocalized by the simple vowel *i*; cf. ‎לִירוֹשְׁלִם‏ Isa. 44.26; ‎וִירוֹשְׁלִם‏ Joel 4.20; ‎אֶפְרִים‏ Jer. 31.6; ‎מִצְרִים‏ Hos. 2.17; ‎בִּשְׁמִי‏ Ps. 119.89; ‎הַשָּׁמִים‏ Deut. 26.15; ‎שִׁבְעָתִים‏ Ps. 12.7; ‎מָתְנִים‏ Nah. 2.2 (taken from P. Kahle, *Masoreten des Westens*, Stuttgart 1927). We will, therefore, say that Hebrew as reflected in the Palestinian vocalization apparently had no diphthong *ai*. But even our Tiberian vocalization offers evidence of an existing uncertainty as to whether the diphthong *ai* of the simple vowel *i* should be employed in a given case; cf. ‎בֵּית‏ (‎לָהּ‏) Ezek. 1.27 (usually: ‎בַּיִת‏) (‎כָּבֵד‏); ‎בְּחֵיל‏ (‎כָּבֵד‏) Isa. 36.2 (usually: ‎חַיִל‏); cf. also ‎שְׁבִי‏ Ezra 2.42 with ‎וְשֹׁבַי‏ 2 Chron. 17.27 and ‎חוֹרִי‏ 1 Chron. 11.32 with ‎חוֹרַי‏ 2 Chron. 5.14. In thus combining the simple vowel *i* with the diphthong *ai* in the vocalization of these identical forms, our Tiberian vocalization represents a mixed type; cf. p. 457, paragraph XII.

§ 44. Let us now compare inflected forms like: ‎דֶּרֶךְ‏: ‎דַּרְכַּיִם‏: ‎דְּרָכִים‏ and ‎דְּרָכִים‏; ‎פַּעַם‏: ‎פְּעָלִים‏; ‎נַעַל‏: ‎נְעָלַיִם‏: ‎נְעָלִים‏ and ‎נְעָלִים‏; ‎נַחַל‏: ‎נְחָלַיִם‏ and ‎נְחָלִים‏; ‎נָהָר‏: ‎נְהָרַיִם‏ and ‎נְהָרִים‏; ‎פַּעֲמַיִם‏ and ‎פְּעָמִים‏. Their origin has to be explained in the following manner: ‎פַּעַם‏ became *‎פַּעֲמִים‏, with preservation of its original vowels, cf. p. 215, sub a. But according to a basic law of the Masoretic Hebrew grammar (cf. p. 415, § 2c), no vowel could remain in an open syllable which was two syllables removed from the stress; either the first or the second vowel was reduced to *shewâ*. We thus get as the two possibilities ‎פְּעָמִים‏ and ‎פַּעֲמִים‏; subsequently, the ◌ַ in the open syllable was changed to ◌ָ (‎פְּעָמִים‏), and the ‎עָ‏ vocalized ‎עֲ‏ (cf. p. 428, § 37 f.). One of these forms received the simple vowel *i* for the plural ending ‎יִם‏-, while the other got the diphthong *ai*. It is quite reasonable to see in this difference in the vocalization evidence for the fact that the two possibilities of reducing the first or the second vowel to *shewâ*, go back to original differences in the pronunciation of Hebrew.

O. *Hiph'il* A DENOMINATIVE FORMATION (Cf. MH §§ 152-155)

§ 45. In the case of another linguistic phenonemom, the term by which it is known in Hebrew grammars has obviously misled the translators. The so-called *hiph'il* is also known as the "causative stem," and the translators of *The Holy Scriptures* (cf. § 38) seem to have given the preference to verbs which indicate causation. Thus, e.g., Gen. 2.5 ‎כִּי לֹא‏

הִמְטִיר יהוה אֱלֹהִים "for the Lord God had not caused it to rain"; 19.24: וַיהוה הִמְטִיר "Then the Lord caused to rain"; 7.4: אָנֹכִי מַמְטִיר "I will cause it to rain"; Job 38.26: לְהַמְטִיר "to cause it to rain." In § 7 we have demonstrated "that the so-called derived stems are not verbal stems, but verbal conjugations." They shed light on the important problem of the interrelation between verb and noun of the identical root, namely: which one is genuine, and which is only a derivation (B-L § 26h mentions it as a problem, but does not even attempt to solve it). We wish to suggest a solution on the basis of a differentiation between the simple verb and the derived stems, with the understanding that passive formations are not to be considered as "stems" (e.g. *niph'al*), but belong to their respective active stem. We are of the opinion that the verb in the *kal* led to the formation of derived nominal forms (e.g.: זָכַר – זֵכֶר, שָׁפַט – מִשְׁפָּט), while the so-called derived stems (*pi'el* and *hiph'il*) are in the main denominative verbs. Note, e.g., Gen. 22.2: (לְעֹלָה) ··· וְהַעֲלֵהוּ; Ex. 26.28: (··· וְהַבְּרִיחַ); 17.15: (··· נְסְכּוֹ) הַקְדָּשִׁים); 16.13: (··· נְסְכּוֹ) וַיַּסֵּךְ; 2 Ki. 12.19: (··· הִקְדִּישׁוּ) מַבְרִחַ; Num. 25.18: (··· הַכְּעָסִים); 23.26: (הַכְעִיסוּ ···) (עֵדֹותָיו ···) הֵעִיד; (בְּנִכְלֵיהֶם ···) נִכְּלוּ. Similarly, קַטֵּר and הִקְטִיר are denominative verbs from קְטֹרֶת; הִשְׁקָה from שֹׁקֶת (Gen. 24.20); הֵשִׁירוּ (Hos. 8.4) from שָׁר; and הִמְטִיר from מָטָר, meaning "to rain" (and not "to cause to rain"). Hence Jer. 14.22: (הֲיֵשׁ בְּהַבְלֵי הַגּוֹיִם) מַגְשִׁמִים is not to be translated: "that can cause rain" but: *that do rain* (מַגְשִׁמִים denominative, from גֶּשֶׁם); cf. Am. 4.7: וְגַם אָנֹכִי מָנַעְתִּי מִכֶּם אֶת הַגֶּשֶׁם "And I also have withholden the rain from you," followed by וְהִמְטַרְתִּי ··· לֹא אַמְטִיר (not "caused it ..." but *And I shall rain upon one city, And not rain upon another city*). The Lord not merely "causes" the rain, but he actually rains, just as in Ps. 29.3: אֵל הַכָּבוֹד הִרְעִים "The God of glory thundereth" (הִרְעִים being a denominative verb from רַעַם).

IV. TEXTUAL CRITICISM

I. *Textual Criticism in Theory*

A. THE BIBLE IS IN DISSONANCE WITH THE GRAMMAR

§ 46. In 1902 Rudolf Kittel, the noted Leipzig theologian, published a monograph with the somewhat lengthy title: *Über die Notwendigkeit und Möglichkeit einer neuen Ausgabe der Hebräischen Bibel* (Leipzig). Judging by this title, the reader might have expected to find the problems of editing the Hebrew Bible discussed therein from two main points of view: first to see the "Notwendigkeit" of such a project established, and only then the "Möglichkeit" of seeing it practically through made plausible. But as matters stand, the need for a critical edition of the Hebrew Bible text is dealt with only in the briefest manner in the short introduction; for, according to the author, this "Notwendigkeit" is a reality too keenly felt by everyone who ever was seriously engaged in studying and teaching the Bible to require lengthy explanations: "Besonders die ... Lektüre historischer Bücher wie Richter, Samuel, Könige lässt ... den Übelstand empfindlich fühlen, dass uns in der gedruckten hebräischen Bibel auf Schritt und Tritt Wörter und Wortgruppen aufstossen, die so, wie sie dastehen, nur mit Mühe und *unter Verleugnung oder Beugung der ... grammatischen Regeln übersetzt werden können*" (ib., p. 1). In other words: there exists a deplorable incongruity between the various stages of our teaching of Hebrew in the academic institutions. The student is taught first Hebrew grammar, a subject, which is intended to prepare him for the study of the Hebrew Bible proper. But when we take up the reading and interpretation of the Bible text, beginning of course with the so-called Former Prophets, due to the fact that here the sentences are of a comparatively simple grammatical structure, we find ourselves handicapped by the results of our own teaching efforts: It becomes apparent to both student and teacher that the course in Hebrew Grammar was decidedly an inadequate step preparatory to the study of the Bible text, which it had preceded. For to our amazement we find a discrepancy between Hebrew morphology and syntax as taught in the grammar course and as reflected in these unpretentious narratives. Faced with this dilemma, Kittel sees its solution in a revision of the Bible text so as to conform with the rules laid down by the grammarians: "Man wird es daher verstehen, dass auch dem Schreiber dieser Zeilen (scil. Rud. Kittel) schon vor Jahren das Bedürfnis einer von *augenscheinlichen Irrtümern, Schreibfehlern und Verstössen aller Art gereinigten Textausgabe* des Alten Testaments ... entgegentrat" (ib., p. 2).

B. THE GRAMMAR RANKS FIRST

A. A CRITICAL BIBLE EDITION TO ACHIEVE HARMONY

§ 47. Thus, the "Notwendigkeit" of a New Edition of the Hebrew

Bible is proven. In parenthesis I should like to add: according to the way of thinking and reasoning prevalent at the beginning of this century. And now Kittel devotes himself to the task of discussing the "Möglichkeit" of such a Bible Edition, in order to establish just what is "Das Erreichbare Ziel." In keeping with his *Weltanschauung* in general, Kittel shows even in this respect his innate conservatism and is inclined to proceed only with great caution: Though "Das Ideal" would be the restauration of the "Autographon," he demonstrates the unsurmountable difficulties, which stand in the way of achieving this goal; he, therefore, limits himself to "Das Wirkliche Ziel," which might be within reach: "Unser wirkliches Ziel kann, so wie die Dinge liegen, nicht kurzweg die Urschrift selber sein, sondern die Gestalt des Textes zu einer bestimmten Zeit vor seiner Fixierung durch die Massora, unsere Aufgabe also die Fortbildung, genauer die Rückbildung des massoretischen Textes in der Richtung auf die Urschrift bis zu einem bestimmten, zwischen der Urschrift und der Massora liegenden, Punkte" (ib., p. 36).

§ 48. The Hebrew Bible text—being a Semitic text—consists of a consonantal text only, the vowels of which are indicated by an independent system with a tradition of its own. How about this vocalization? Shall we retain it in the new edition, or hadn't we better do away with it, since available evidence (please remember that this monograph was published in 1902!) from ancient sources does not seem to support the pronunciation, which these vowel-signs imply? Kittel is outspoken in favor of their retention, out of practical considerations: "... was können wir mit Mesa (i.e. the Mesha Stone) und den phönizischen Inschriften anfangen ..., wenn wir nicht stillschweigend die massoretische Vokalization ... ihnen unterlegen könnten? Stillschweigend operieren wir, wenn wir Mesa oder den Siloastein lesen, im grossen Ganzen mit den uns bekannten hebräischen Vokalen des Massoretentextes, wohl wissend, dass es sich hier um einen Notbehelf handelt, ... der streng genommen wissenschaftlich unzulässig wäre" (ib., p. 34).

§ 49. Needless to say, the Bible text itself should be presented in a *critical* edition. This means that not only should readings from ancient sources (manuscripts of the Hebrew Bible as well as Bible translations), which differ from the basic text, be listed in an *apparatus criticus*; but even emendations as suggested by modern Bible scholars would have to find their place in these critical notes. Of course, not everything that has been said and written deserved being perpetuated in the contemplated critical Bible edition: "Eine Textausgabe würde ... sorgfältig zu sichten haben. Ohne selbst den subjektiven Charakter jeder Konjektur zu verleugnen, müsste sie doch bemüht sein, nur das Probehaltige und Wahrscheinliche festzuhalten. ... Auch was etwa der Kommentar als Möglichkeit andeuten mag, ist noch lange nicht reif für eine Ausgabe des Textes" (ib., p. 42). Here the ground under the prospective editor's feet becomes somewhat slippery. Kittel finds himself in complete accord with Theodor Nöldeke, who had raised his voice in warning: "Die Einführung einzelner mehr oder weniger sicherer Verbesserungen in einen zusammenhängenden Text späterer Rezension ergibt unter allen Umständen eine buntscheckige Gestalt, welche so nie auch nur annähernd existiert hat und welche meinem philologischen Sinn einen gelinden Schauer erregt" (Theodor Nöldeke in his review of Wellhausen's *Text der Bücher Samuel,* in *Zeitschrift für wissenschaftliche Theologie,* 1873, p. 118; quoted by Kittel, op. cit., p. 34). Kittel must thus have been fully aware of the difficulties involved in such an endeavor to combine theoretical reasoning with practical feasibility. The outcome of these investigations and researches is embodied in his well-known *Biblia Hebraica.*

B. BIBLIA HEBRAICA IN THREE EDITIONS

§ 50.   It is of the utmost interest to the student of the Bible to get a clear picture of the form into which Kittel's academic reasoning has been finally cristallized. A few statements quoted from the introductory remarks to the various editions of his *Biblia Hebraica* will suffice for the present. As basic text he retained the text of Jacob ben Chayim's First Masoretic Bible (cf. on it pp. 537 ff.):

"Editionem B, quam egregiis virtutibus praestare ceteris nemo negat, supposui. Sed quo diutius hunc laborem subibam, eo saepius commovebar, ut lectiones minus probatas, quae etiam in codice a me supposito opinione frequentiores inveniebantur, secundum certissimos testes, in quibus inprimis Baer et Ginsburg numerandi sunt, mutarem. Quae methodus ab eclectica ratione non longe distat: hinc textus a me propositus fere ex toto cum codicis B congruit, illinc multae et minus probatae lectiones dispersis locis sublatae sunt, id quod plerumque silentio factum est. Nam ne apparatus nimis oneraretur, solum gravissimae allatae sunt." (*Biblia Hebraica*, edidit Rud. Kittel, Leipzig 1913; Prolegomena § 2).

§ 51.   While generally following this text, Kittel allowed himself certain arbitrary deviations in details of the vocalization and accentuation, on the basis of preconceived rules of grammatical theories. "Quod attinet ad *Meteg* scribendum, codex B (i.e. the basic text) saepe indiligenter et ex libidine se gerit. Quae cum ita sint, in omnibus partibus textus—in notis ut hac in re omnia congruerent fieri non potuit—editor principia a Baer et Merx, *Archiv für wissenschaftliche Erforschung des Alten Testaments*, I, 1867 deposita secutus est. Interdum—sed raro—insuper Meteg, si certissima testificatione nitebatur, receptum est" (Prolegomena, 4). "Item *Chateph Qamez* illud omisi, quod a Baer saepe pro *Qamez chatuph* scribitur ita, ut errare haud difficile sit, quodque saepius, sed nulla ratione constanti ... etiam in codice B legitur." (ib., 2e).

§ 52.   The third edition of the *Biblia Hebraica* (Stuttgart 1937) was completed only after Kittel's death. In the *Vorwort*, which first was printed together with the book of Isaiah, the first of a series of Biblical books, which was published in his lifetime (Stuttgart 1929), Kittel stated that Jacob ben Chayim's text no longer served as the basic text, and that a Leningrad manuscript was used instead, which he designated with the *siglum* L. It is now of interest to note his remarks on the selfsame subject of *Meteg* with regard to this new basic text: "Die Metegsetzung (deren grosse Sparsamkeit wiederum L mit zahlreichen der ältesten HSS gemein hat, während C [=ms. Cairo] darin wesentlich freigebiger ist) weist in L —wie auch in C—starke Inkonsequenzen auf. ... Ich habe ... Meteg überall da gesetzt oder weggelassen, wo der Schreiber von L besondere Gründe zur Setzung oder Weglassung zu haben schien. ... Konsequent dagegen habe ich in Übereinstimmung mit den *diqdūqē hate'amim* ... Meteg gesetzt, ausserdem ... aus pädagogischen Gründen, ... um minder Geübten die Unterscheidung zwischen *ā* und *ŏ* zu erleichtern." (Vorworte, I, § 3d). Similarly independent was Kittel's action with regard to "Das Zeichen *Raphe*, das L fast durchweg, aber ohne strenge Folgerichtigkeit setzt, ist, wie schon früher, auch jetzt beiseite gelassen" (ib., I § 3c). The critical apparatus itself underwent a change in the arrangement of the material presented therein: "Blosse Varianten und minder wichtige Mitteilungen sind in dem oberen, ... die wirklichen Textänderungen und das sonst Bedeutsamere sind im untern Apparat ... verzeichnet" (ib., I, § 2).

C. EMENDATIONS SELECTED AND APPROVED OF

§ 53. I wish to emphasize the terminology, which Kittel used in order to indicate the relative importance of the material listed in the upper and lower critical apparatus respectively: evidence from ancient sources (both genuine Hebrew manuscripts and Old Bible Versions) are termed *"blosse"* (merely) *Varianten*, while emendations suggested by modern scholars are referred to as *"die wirklichen Textänderungen."* These emendations listed by *Biblia Hebraica* do not include every emendation put forward by any scholar; cf. Kittel's directive quoted in § 49. They are the result of a "careful selection" made by the respective editor of each Biblical book. To a very large extent they also carry a mark of approval, indicating as to what degree the editor in question associated his personal linguistic taste with that of the originator of the emendation under scrutiny. I noted the use of the following terms:

melius: 1 Sam. 8.5; Ps. 4.5; 7.10; 8.3; 19.5; 37.16, 39; 38.14, 17; 44.5; 55.18, 24; 59.5, 10.

frt. melius: Ps. 8.3.

potius: Gen. 2.4; 1 Sam. 14.32; 25.29; 2 Sam. 3.36; 2 Ki. 23.5; Isa. 10.13; 17.11; 19.3; 30.31.

recte: Num. 3.32; 6.3; Jer. 23.23; Ps. 16.2.

frt. recte: Gen. 12.4; Ex. 2.25; Num. 25.4; Judg. 18.22; 20.18; 1 Ki. 2.3, 29; 10.15; Isa. 55.10; Ps. 41.2; 43.4; 48.8; 50.21.

prb. recte: Ps. 17.2; 27.7; 64.6; 67.3.

minus recte: Judg. 5.26; 1 Sam. 14.19; Isa. 14.17, 18.

vix recte: 2 Sam. 1.12; Isa. 66.17; Ps. 35.15.

rectius: 1 Sam. 31.10; Isa. 23.1; Jer. 4.20.

frt. rectius: Gen. 35.1; Isa. 22.3; 24.23; 30.6; 36.13.

prb. rectius: Isa. 36.10.

By using frt. (=fortasse) or prb. (=probabiliter) the editors merely meant to avoid a monotony of style in the notes; these words do not indicate any corresponding difference of certainty in his assertion on behalf of the editor; cf. here throughout in almost every paragraph.

The editor's preference is indicated by the way how he arranged the notes; e.g.:

Gen. 48.20: בך יְבָרֵךְ ישראל BHKK GS al יְבָרֵךְ vel potius יִתְבָּרֵךְ, frt. recte.

Ps. 4.5:   אִמְרוּ בלבבכם BHKK prps. מְרוּ vel הַמְרוּ vel melius הָמֵרוּ (a מרר).

Job. 12.2:   אמנם כי אתם עם BHKK 1 הָעָם vel frt. melius הַיֹּדְעִים.

§ 54. For the sake of brevity I shall henceforth refer to *Biblia Hebraica* as an entity and to Rudolf Kittel as *the* editor, instead of treating each Biblical book with its respective editor as a separate unit. After all, both credit and blame must needs go back to the editor-in-chief, who conceived the plan and supervised its realization.

C. THE BIBLE RANKS FIRST

A. OUR GRAMMAR IN NEED OF REVISION

§ 55. In case one wonders just upon what principle (or principles) the selection of emendations embodied in *Biblia Hebraica* (but by no means originating in *Biblia Hebraica*; they are only a collection and compilation of the results of the ingenuity of generations of scholars) was made, I think we shouldn't have to look very far for an answer. It is contained in the preliminary statement of Kittel's monograph (cf. p. 46 towards the end of the pg.): to purge the Bible text of "obvious mistakes and errors of any kind." In the light of Kittel's remarks quoted at the beginning of p. 46, there can be no doubt at all as to the meaning implied by the words "obvious mistakes and errors." They refer to any deviation from the rules and laws of Hebrew grammar. And it is just this attitude towards the Hebrew Bible, to give the right of priority to *The Grammar* and to make the Scriptures conform with it, which I refuted by saying: "Whether he admits it or not, the exegete assumes that the laws of the Hebrew language, as laid down in the Hebrew grammar, are binding for the Bible. Whenever a discrepancy is discovered between the Bible and these "established" grammatical laws, the Bible is the loser: the text is "emended" so as to conform with the grammar . . . . It is high time that Bible scholars ... approach the Bible not as schoolmasters teaching the prophets how Hebrew sentences should be formed and Hebrew words spelled, but as humble students of these great masters of Hebrew" (cf. § 102).

§ 56. I have no doubt that neither the original authors of textual emendations of the Bible as characterized above, nor their collectors and compilers in the *Biblia Hebraica* ever viewed their activities in such a light. On the contrary, they all were—and still are—convinced of performing the praiseworthy task of restoring the genuine text of the Hebrew Bible by erasing everything which runs counter to the grammatical laws of Biblical Hebrew. While grouping and classifying the notes of the critical apparatus in *Biblia Hebraica*, I gradually got a fairly clear picture of the grammatical structure of Biblical Hebrew as seen through *their* eyes.

§ 57. My own method of approach is fundamentally different from that indicated by Kittel. I am not studying the Bible in the light of Hebrew Grammar (the authority of which neither Kittel nor anyone else engaged in textual criticism of the Bible ever dared to challenge, though, it is true, they were none of them ever embarrassed by having this problem put squarely before them as I do it!), but in its own light. I discard with Biblical commentaries and look nowhere else for help and assistance in explaining the grammatical structure of the Bible, but try to get everything out of the Bible itself. Thus, I am approaching the Bible just as one might approach the interpretation of a newly unearthed ancient document; I let the Bible speak for itself and tell me, what Biblical Hebrew is like. It goes without saying that due allowance must be made to the history of the Bible text. It would never occur to me to deny the existence of "augenscheinliche Irrtümer, Schreibfehler und Verstösse aller Art." But these terms according to my conception refer solely to spellings, which are obviously erroneous (as, e.g., the cases discussed on pp. 476 ff., §§ 35-71), and most certainly not to passages, which are perfectly clear and yield good sense, and the only fault of which merely is that they "so, wie sie dastehen, nur mit Mühe und unter Verleugnung oder Beugung der im Schweiss des Angesichts eingeübten grammatischen Regeln übersetzt werden können." In such cases I must regretfully state that the "Schweiss des Angesichts" was an effort in vain. I shall cheerfully deny ("verleugnen") any grammatical rule, if the Biblical text denies it. It is the Bible, upon which the authority for all Hebrew grammar rests. And whenever and wherever the facts in the Bible do not uphold a grammatical law, this law has no leg to stand on and becomes immediately null and void.

B.   OBJECTION REFUTED

§ 58.   I put the utmost emphasis on this declaration of my attitude· In theory, I feel sure, there will be no gainsaying it. But when it becomes a question of applying it in praxis, here and there a voice may be heard expressing doubts as to its applicability. Even as enlightened a scholar as Paul Kahle seems to hesitate to give up the "established" grammatical laws in the light of my evidence, and prefers to consider this material brought in evidence merely as "irregularities of the Masoretes" (cf. Paul E. Kahle, *The Cairo Geniza*, London 1947, p. 109). Do I have to tell a scholar of his rank that evidence is weighed and not counted? And furthermore: there is no such thing as "established" grammar, which in turn could be "disestablished" only under very extraordinary circumstances. A grammatical law is only as long "established," as it offers a satisfactory explanation of all the given facts, which come under that category. As soon as this ceases to be the case, we are accustomed to consider the law still as valid and to list any contradictory evidence merely as "exceptions" or "irregularities." I, on the other hand, prefer to see in these divergent forms evidence for a corresponding new law, and re-phrase or re-formulate the old law accordingly. What I was and still am trying to demonstrate, is: that it is futile to attempt to bring the grammatical phenomena of the language of the Bible under one common denominator. The silent presupposition of any endeavor of such a nature (and this refers almost to all grammatical theories concerning Biblical Hebrew, which have ever been advanced) is that one single set of grammatical laws is valid for the whole Bible; and no matter how numerous the contradictions thereto found in the Bible, they must be viewed as "irregularities." But mightn't one argue: and why these "irregularities"? What causes them? Why should the very same Biblical book so often exhibit evidence for the "rule" *and* the "irregularities," with no apparent reason for this backsliding into poor grammar or spelling? And finally: What does "irregularities of the Masoretes" mean? According to Kahle's interpretation of the activities of the Masoretes (there is no need for me

to go back to his *Cairo Geniza* for this purpose; I still remember it from
my student days in Bonn!), the Masoretes were anxious to shape the Bible
text (i.e. in its grammatical aspect, as e.g. the vocalization) after a single
pattern of their own devicing. Hence, "irregularities of the Masoretes"
must refer to those passages, which for one reason or another escaped
their levelling activities and thus retained (and this is most important!)
their old or (to use a favorite term of Kahle's) pre-Masoretic form. And
now I wish to ask: are we interested in continuing the Masoretic activities
by pointing to the results, which they achieved as *the* Hebrew grammar
κατ᾽ ἐξοχήν; or shouldn't we rather pay the utmost of attention to each
remaining evidence of Hebrew grammar prior to these Masoretic activities,
as reflected in such "irregularities"? For they are not "irregularities *of the*
Masoretes," but only "irregularities" *from the point of view of the Masoretes*.
And I am sure that Kahle does not identify his viewpoint of Hebrew
grammar with that of the Masoretes (according to his own interpretation).

II. *Textual Criticism in Praxis*

A. BIBLIA HEBRAICA IS INADEQUATE

A. GENERAL REMARKS

§ 59. Before proceeding with a detailed examination of such "irregularities," as defined above, in order to establish what really is Biblical
Hebrew, a few remarks will be in place so as to clear up some aspects of
a more technical nature. I derive my material from BHKK, because here
we have a depository of all those textual emendations, which in the
opinion of competent Bible scholars deserved to be perpetuated (cf. § 49).

In its effort to make the fullest possible use of the comparatively short
space allotted to the critical apparatus, BHKK often limits the spelling
or vocalization of a word to the letter or letters, which are indicative of
the suggested emendation. I on the other hand considered it advisable
to add the consonants and vocalization, which BHKK omitted as non-
essential, thus quoting every word in full, in order to achieve utmost
clarity on each subject under discussion.

§ 60. While quoting BHKK, reference is made here throughout only
to the notes of the lower critical apparatus; for they are intended to
suggest to the reader an emendation of the Biblical text; cf. the intro-

ductory "l" (=lege) or "prps" (=propositum). The notes in the upper
apparatus mainly record readings or spellings from manuscripts; they
cannot be considered as reflecting the editor's view-point, except in cases,
where these recorded readings are based upon Old Bible Versions and
not upon genuine Hebrew manuscripts. Such readings are oftentimes a
criterion of the editor's ability to render into Biblical Hebrew selected
passages from these Ancient Versions; cf. דֹּדָיךְ in Cant. 1.2, 4 BHKK
G L V דַּדָּיךְ. Now, the word according to this suggested vocalization
(with ‿) indicated a part of the female anatomy, and its connection with
the suffix of the 2nd pers. *masc.* is a monstrosity! But we shall not concern
ourselves here with problems of this kind.

Wherever the editor believes that support for his emendation may be
found in an Old Version, he indicates it by listing the respective siglum
after the introductory "l" or "prps."; e.g. "l c G S". Such references
I omit here as irrelevant, and indicate this omission by the insertion of
dots; e.g. "l . . .". It will be noted that such dots appear quite inconsistently, when we compare BHKK's notes to some words or phrases, which
occur more than once in the Bible and, consequently, in this study.
This inconsistency reveals the haphazard way the editors used in getting
their material from the Old Versions. We shall, therefore, henceforth
regard with suspicion any "evidence" for variant readings from the Old
Versions, as long as they are not the result of a thorough investigation of
their own rextual tradition, coupled with a methodical comparison of
their entire text (and not merely of selected passages, picked at random)
with the Hebrew Bible.

§ 61.   In presenting the material in this study, I adopted from §§ 68-89
the following method: Each subject matter is dealt with in two main
separate parts. I list first evidence for a certain Biblical usage in order to
establish the validity of the grammatical rule and then I adduce such
Biblical passages, which, though exhibiting the identical grammatical
phenomenon, have been subjected to textual emendations in the notes
of the lower apparatus of BHKK. By this procedure I achieve a twofold
purpose: I hereby demonstrate that the editors of BHKK not only failed
to realize the existence of the grammatical phenomenon under discussion,
but also showed a regrettable lack of method in performing their task,
by the very fact that they accorded different treatment to the Biblical

passages quoted here in the two parts: some were "corrected," while
others apparently escaped their attention. The ways, by means of which
such "corrections" were brought about, are interesting, too. They leave
no doubt in our mind that the "corrections" were motivated solely by
the intention to force upon the Bible text a compliance with preconceived
grammatical rules. For full evidence I refer the reader to the various
headings, under which the respective paragraphs are further subdivided
(cf. § 86).

B. GRAMMATICAL RULE MISLEADING

§ 62. I shall begin with a few examples, which I have carefully selected
in order to prove these assertions. In Ezek. 40-43 the word חצר is frequently mentioned. Referring to the "inner court," חצר is used as a masculine
noun, while when denoting the "outer court" it is apparently feminine.
BHKK consequently corrects the masculine form of the adjective meaning
"inner" into its feminine equivalent, or even changes the entire phrase,
in an obvious attempt to improve on the prophet's poor grammar:

Ezek. 40.17: הֶחָצֵר הַחִיצוֹנָה

Ezek. 40.19: הֶחָצֵר הַפְּנִימִי BHKK l הַפְּנִימִית

Ezek. 40.20: לֶחָצֵר הַחִיצוֹנָה

Ezek. 40.23: לֶחָצֵר הַפְּנִימִי BHKK frt. l הַפְּנִימִית

Ezek. 40.27: לֶחָצֵר הַפְּנִימִי BHKK frt. l הַפְּנִימִית

Ezek. 40.28: חָצֵר הַפְּנִימִי BHKK frt. l הַפְּנִימִית

Ezek. 40.31: חָצֵר הַחצוֹנָה

Ezek. 40.32: הֶחָצֵר הַפְּנִימִי BHKK l . . . · · · · הַשַּׁעַר הַפֹּנֶה

Ezek. 40.34: לֶחָצֵר הַחִיצוֹנָה

Ezek. 40.37: לֶחָצֵר הַחִיצוֹנָה

Ezek. 40.44: בֶּחָצֵר הַפְּנִימִי BHKK prb. l . . . הַפְּנִימִית

Ezek. 42.1: הֶחָצֵר הַחִיצוֹנָה

Ezek. 42.3: לֶחָצֵר הַפְּנִימִי BHKK frt. l הַפְּנִימִית

Ezek. 42.3: לֶחָצֵר הַחִיצוֹנָה

Ezek. 42.7: הֶחָצֵר הַחצוֹנָה

Ezek. 42.8: לֶחָצֵר הַחצוֹנָה

Ezek. 42.9: מֵהֶחָצֵר הַחצֹנָה

Ezek. 42.14: הֶחָצֵר הַחִיצוֹנָה

Ezek. 43.5: הֶחָצֵר הַפְּנִימִי BHKK frt. l הַפְּנִימִית

It seems to me to be a rather strange coincidence that one and the same mistake should have occurred no less than 8 times and in such close propinquity to the apparently correct feminine form for "outer court." Now, there can be no question as to the gender of פְנִימִי; it is masculine. But is חצונה necessarily feminine? True, it ends in ‑ָה and The Grammar sees therein an indication of the feminine; but is it really so? There are right here in Ezek. 40, as well as elsewhere, similar cases, and no one would assign these words to the feminine gender, merely because they end in ‑ָה:

Ezek 40.35: שַׁעַר הַצָּפוֹן   Ezek 40.10: דֶּרֶךְ הַקָּדִים

Ezek 40.40: הַשַּׁעַר הַצָּפוֹנָה   Ezek 40.6 : דֶּרֶךְ הַקְּדִימָה

Ezek 40.19: הַשַּׁעַר הַתַּחְתּוֹנָה BHKK 1 הַתַּחְתּוֹן

1 Ki 6.30 : לִפְנִימָה וְלַחִיצוֹן

2 Ki 16.18 : מְבוֹא הַמֶּלֶךְ הַחִיצוֹנָה BHKK 1 הַחִיצוֹן

In suchlike instances I explain the ending as "euphonic" (cf. p. 277 ff.), and it is only logical to see in the ‑ה of החצונה in the cases listed above further evidence for a "euphonic ה," leaving the gender of the word unchanged as masculine. Consequently we will say that חצר is used here as a masculine noun in all the occurrences cited above, and there is no justification whatsoever for "corrections," by forcing upon the Biblical text a misunderstood grammatical law that the ending in ה signifies the feminine.

C.   CONSISTENCY AND INCONSISTENCY BOTH LEAD AD ABSURDUM

i. אל AND על

§ 63.   The reproof of inconsistency, which I raised against BHKK (cf. § 61), will be substantiated later (cf. §§ 66 ff.) and very amply, too. But even consistency, if wrongly applied, may disclose a lack of grammatical (i.e. logical) thinking. Grammars and dictionaries alike teach us to differentiate between אל and על. The Bible itself obviously is ignorant of any difference between אל and על and uses them indiscriminately; cf. ch. o, § ooo. Especially the books of Jeremiah and Ezekiel abound in such "irregularities": we find על, where according to grammar and dictionary we would expect אל, and *vice versa*. This fact is taken cognizance of differently by the respective editors of these books in BHKK. The editor of Jeremiah remarks on Jer. 1.1: "in toto libro עַל־ et אֶל־ saepe permutantur." I cannot let this note pass without vigorously taking exception to it. To say that עַל and אַל are being confused with one another (or: exchanged for one another) presupposes that we know the exact meaning of each one of these words, and find that they are used in the wrong places here. But where from do we derive our knowledge? From the Bible! Hence, the Bible does not "confuse" them, but uses them in the identical meaning, because they obviously *are* identical in their connotation. The editor of Ezekiel, however, chose a different procedure. He consistently annotated every occurrence of עַל and אַל, where the meaning (according to grammar and dictionary) is "confused," obviously hoping thus to "restore" Biblical Hebrew in its original purity, as is the purpose of *Biblia Hebraica* (cf. p. 47).

a. Biblical אל

Ezek. 2.6:	וְאֶל עקרבים אתה יושב BHKK 1	וְעַל
Ezek. 6.9:	אֶל הרעות אשר עשו BHKK 1	עַל
Ezek. 6.11:	אֶל כל תועבות רעות BHKK 1	עַל
Ezek. 6.13:	אֶל כל גבעה רמה BHKK 1	עַל
Ezek. 7.14:	כי חרוני אֶל כל המונה BHKK 1	עַל
Ezek. 7.18:	וְאֶל כל פנים בושה BHKK 1	וְעַל
Ezek. 7.26:	ושמעה אֶל שמועה תהיה BHKK 1	עַל
Ezek. 10.1:	ואראה והנה אֶל הרקיע BHKK 1	עַל
Ezek. 11.11:	אֶל גבול ישראל אשפט אתכם BHKK 1	עַל
Ezek. 12.12:	אֶל כתף ישא BHKK 1...	עַל
Ezek. 12.19:	ואמרת אֶל עם הארץ BHKK 1	עַל
Ezek. 13.2:	הנבא אֶל נביאי ישראל BHKK 1...	עַל
Ezek. 13.9:	והיתה ידי אֶל הנביאים BHKK 1	עַל
Ezek. 13.20:	הנני אֶל כסתותיכנה BHKK 1	עַל
Ezek. 14.4:	אשר יעלה את גלוליו אֶל לבו BHKK 1	עַל
Eezk. 14.7:	ויעל גלוליו אֶל לבו BHKK 1	עַל
Ezek. 14.19:	או דבר אשלח אֶל הארץ ההיא BHKK 1...	עַל
Ezek. 14.21:	שלחתי אֶל ירושלם BHKK 1	עַל
Ezek. 16.5:	ותשלחי אֶל פני השדה BHKK 1	עַל
Ezek. 16.25:	אֶל כל ראש דרך בנית BHKK 1	עַל
Ezek. 17.8:	אֶל מים רבים היא שתולה BHKK 1	עַל

Ezek. 18.6:   עַל BHKK 1   אֶל ההרים לא אכל

Ezek. 18.11:   עַל BHKK 1   כי גם אֶל ההרים אכל

Ezek. 19.1:   עַל ...1 BHKK   שא קינה אֶל נשיאי ישראל

Ezek. 19.9:   עַל BHKK 1   לא ישמע קולו עוד אֶל הרי ישראל

Ezek. 21.2:   עַל BHKK 1   והנבא אֶל יער השדה נגב

Ezek. 21.7:   עַל BHKK 1   שים פניך אֶל ירושלם

Ezek. 21.9:   עַל BHKK 1   תצא חרבי··· אֶל כל בשר

Ezek. 21.12:   עַל BHKK 1   אֶל שמועה כי באה

Ezek. 21.17:   עַל BHKK 1   לכן ספק אֶל ירך

Ezek. 21.19:   עַל ...1 BHKK   והך כף אֶל כף

Ezek. 21.22:   עַל BHKK 1   וגם אני אכה כפי אֶל כפי

Ezek. 21.26:   עַל BHKK 1   כי עמד מלך בבל אֶל אם הדרך

Ezek. 21.33:   וְעַל 1 ;עַל BHKK 1   כה אמר··· אֶל בני עמון וְאֶל חרפתם על

Ezek. 21.34:   עַל BHKK 1   אֶל צוארי חללי רשעים

Ezek. 22.9:   וְעַל BHKK 1   וְאֶל ההרים אכלו בך

Ezek. 22.13:   עַל ...1 BHKK   הכיתי כפי אֶל בצעך

Ezek. 23.5:   עַל BHKK 1   אֶל אשור קרובים

Ezek. 23.12:   עַל BHKK 1   אֶל בני אשור עגבה

Ezek. 23.42:   עַל ...1 BHKK   ויתנו צמידים אֶל ידיהן

Ezek. 24.2:   עַל ...1 BHKK   ממך מלך בבל אֶל ירושלם

Ezek. 25.3:   וְעַל 1 ;עַל BHKK 1   יען אמרך האח אֶל מקדשי··· וְאֶל

Ezek. 25.6:   עַל BHKK 1   אֶל אדמת ישראל

Ezek. 26.7:   עַל BHKK 1   הנני מביא אֶל צר

Ezek. 29.10:   וְעַל BHKK 1   לכן הנני··· וְאֶל יאריך

Ezek. 29.18:   עַל BHKK 1   העביד את חילו··· אֶל צר

Ezek. 30.22:   עַל BHKK 1   הנני אֶל פרעה מלך מצרים

Ezek. 30.25:   עַל ...1 BHKK   ונטה אותה אֶל ארץ מצרים

Ezek. 31.7:   עַל BHKK 1   כי היה שרשו אֶל מים רבים

Ezek. 31.12:   עַל BHKK 1   ויטשהו אֶל ההרים

Ezek. 31.13:   וְעַל BHKK 1   וְאֶל פארתיו היו כל חית

Ezek. 32.6:   עַל BHKK 1   אֶל ההרים

Ezek. 34.10:   עַל BHKK 1   הנני אֶל הרעים

Ezek. 34.13:   עַל BHKK 1   ורעיתים אֶל הרי ישראל

Ezek. 34.14:   עַל BHKK 1   אֶל הרי ישראל

Ezek. 36.1:   עַל ...1 BHKK   הנבא אֶל הרי ישראל

Ezek. 38.12:   וְעַל BHKK 1   וְאֶל עם מאסף מגוים

Ezek. 40.2:   עַל BHKK 1   וַיְנִיחֵנִי אֶל הר גבה מאד

Ezek. 40.16:   וְעַל BHKK 1   וְאֶל איל תמרים

Ezek. 40.17:   עַל BHKK 1   שלשים לשכות אֶל הרצפה

Ezek. 40.26:   עַל BHKK 1   אֶל איליו

Ezek. 40.43:   וְעַל BHKK 1   וְאֶל השלחנות

Ezek. 40.49:   עַל BHKK 1   ועמדים אֶל האילים

Ezek. 41.4:   עַל BHKK 1   אֶל פני ההיכל

Ezek. 41.6:   עַל BHKK 1   צלע אֶל צלע

Ezek. 41.12:   עַל BHKK 1...   אֶל פני הגזרה

Ezek. 41.15:   עַל BHKK 1   אֶל פני הגזרה

Ezek. 41.17:   וְעַל BHKK 1   וְאֶל כל הקיר סביב

Ezek. 41.19:   עַל BHKK 1   אֶל כל הבית סביב סביב

Ezek. 41.25:   עַל BHKK 1   אֶל פני האולם מהחוץ

Ezek. 41.26:   עַל BHKK 1   אֶל כתפות האולם

Ezek. 42.7:   עַל BHKK 1   אֶל פני הלשכות

Ezek. 42.10:   וְעַל 1 ;עַל BHKK 1   אֶל פני הגזרה וְאֶל פני הבנין

Ezek. 42.13:   עַל BHKK 1...   אשר אֶל פני הגזרה

Ezek. 43.3:   עַל 1... ;עַל BHKK 1...   אשר ראיתי אֶל נהר כבר ואפל אֶל פני

Ezek. 43.13:   עַל BHKK 1   אֶל שפתה סביב

Ezek. 43.16:   עַל BHKK 1   אֶל ארבעת רבעיו

Ezek. 43.17:   עַל BHKK 1...   אֶל ארבעת רבעיה

Ezek. 43.20:   וְעַל BHKK 1   וְאֶל ארבע פנות העזרה

Ezek. 44.4:   עַל BHKK 1   אֶל פני הבית

Ezek. 44.7:   עַל BHKK 1   אֶל כל תועבותיכם

Ezek. 44.11:   עַל BHKK 1   פקדות אֶל שערי הבית

Ezek. 44.30:   עַל BHKK 1   להניח ברכה אֶל ביתך

Ezek. 45.7:   וְעַל 1 ;עַל BHKK 1   אֶל פני תרומת הקדש וְאֶל פני אחזת

Ezek. 45.19:   וְעַל 1 ;עַל BHKK 1...   ונתן אֶל מזוזת הבית וְאֶל ארבע פנות

Ezek. 47.7:   עַל BHKK 1...   והנה אֶל שפת הנחל עץ

Ezek. 47.16:   עַל BHKK 1   אשר אֶל גבול חורן

Ezek. 48.1:   עַל BHKK 1   אֶל יד דרך חתלן

Ezek. 48.12:   עַל BHKK 1   אֶל גבול הלוים

Ezek. 48.20:   עַל BHKK 1   אֶל אחזת העיר

Ezek. 48.21:   עַל BHKK 1   אֶל פני חמשה ועשרים אלף

b.   Biblical אל *with suffixes*

Ezek. 33.22:   עָלַי   BHKK 1   ויד יהוה היתה אֵלַי

Ezek. 7.7:   עָלֶיךָ   BHKK 1   באה הצפירה אֵלֶיךָ

Ezek. 29.10:   עָלֶיךָ   BHKK 1   לכן הנני־אֵלֶיךָ

Ezek. 35.3:   עָלֶיךָ ...   BHKK 1   הנני אֵלֶיךָ הר שעיר

Ezek. 38.3:   עָלֶיךָ   BHKK 1   הנני אֵלֶיךָ גוג

Ezek. 39.1:   עָלֶיךָ   BHKK 1   הנני אֵלֶיךָ גוג

Ezek. 7.6:   עָלָיִךְ   BHKK 1   הקיץ אֵלָיִךְ

Ezek. 21.8:   עָלָיִךְ   BHKK 1   הנני אֵלָיִךְ

Ezek. 27.31:   עָלָיִךְ   BHKK 1   והקריחו אֵלָיִךְ קרחה

Ezek. 27.32:   עָלָיִךְ   BHKK 1   ונשאו אֵלָיִךְ ... קינה

Ezek. 36.15:   עָלָיִךְ   BHKK 1   ולא אשמיע אֵלָיִךְ עוד

Ezek. 19.4:   עָלָיו   BHKK 1 ...   וישמעו אֵלָיו גוים

Ezek. 2.10:   עָלֶיהָ   BHKK 1   וכתוב אֵלֶיהָ קנים

Ezek. 13.8:   עֲלֵיכֶם   BHKK 1   הנני אֲלֵיכֶם

Ezek. 6.2:   עֲלֵיהֶם   BHKK 1 ...   והנבא אֲלֵיהֶם

Ezek. 40.39:   עֲלֵיהֶם   BHKK 1   לשחוט אֲלֵיהֶם העולה

Ezek. 41.25:   עֲלֵיהֶן   BHKK 1   ועשויה אֲלֵיהֶן

c.   Biblical על

Ezek. 1.17:   אֶל   BHKK 1   עַל ארבעת רבעיהן

Ezek. 1.20:   אֶל   BHKK 1   עַל אשר יהיה שם הרוח ללכת

Ezek. 10.4:   אֶל   BHKK 1 ...   וירם כבוד יהוה ... עַל מפתן הבית

Ezek. 16.36:   וְאֶל אֶל et   BHKK 1   עַל מאהביך וְעַל כל גלולי תועבותיך

Ezek. 19.11:   אֶל   BHKK 1 ...   ותגבה קומתו עַל בין עבתים

Ezek. 29.2:   אֶל   BHKK 1 ...   שים פניך עַל פרעה

Ezek. 29.14:   אֶל   BHKK 1   והשבתי אתם ... עַל ארץ

Ezek. 32.9:   אֶל   BHKK 1   בהביאי שברך ... עַל ארצות

Ezek. 35.2:   אֶל   BHKK 1 ...   שים פניך עַל הר שעיר

Ezek. 41.7:   אֶל   BHKK 1   יעלה עַל העליונה

Ezek. 44.13:   אֶל   BHKK 1 ...   ולגשת עַל כל קדשי

Ezek. 47.18:   אֶל   BHKK 1   מגבול עַל הים ... תמדו

Ezek. 48.28:   אֶל   BHKK 1 ...   נחלה עַל הים הגדול

d. Biblical על with suffixes

Ezek. 38.7 : אֵלֶיךָ BHKK 1 וכל קהלך הנקהלים עָלֶיךָ

Ezek. 17.7 : אֵלָיו BHKK 1 כפנה שרשיה עָלָיו

The result is quite a showy one: 130 "Corrections" in *one* Biblical book! Is this proof of the existence of a corresponding grammatical law that אל and על were identical in meaning (cf. p. 631, § 106) at that time and at that place, or should we go on with our old praxis and see therein "irregularities"?

ii. אֹתִי AND אִתִּי

§ 64. A similar case is the differentiation in meaning between את, with suffixes אִתִּי etc. and את, with suffixes אֹתִי etc. I counted 44 passages, spread all over the Bible, where BHKK "corrects" the text. I arranged them here according to the verb or the phrase, with which they are connected. But first I wish to list as exceptions the few instances, which though exhibiting the identical characteristics, were not "corrected": Lev. 15.18, 24 : ישכב איש אֹתָה (cf. here under *a*); Gen. 21.2 : דבר אֹתוֹ; Jer. 4.12 : אוֹתָם · · · · אדבר; Jer. 5.5 : ואדברה אוֹתָם; Jer. 12.1 : אדבר אוֹתְךָ (cf. here under *b*).

a. In connection with שכב

Num. 5.19 :	שָׁכַב איש אתָךְ	BHKK=אתָךְ
Gen. 34.2 :	וישכב אתָה	BHKK 1... אתָה
Num. 5.13 :	ישכב אתָה	BHKK=אתָה
2 Sam. 13.14 :	וישכב אתָה	BHKK 1? אתָה
Ezek. 23.8 :	אותָה שכבו	BHKK 1 אתָה

b. In connection with דבר

1 Ki. 22.24 :	לדבר אותָךְ	BHKK 1 אתָךְ
Ezek. 2.1 :	ואדבר אתָךְ	BHKK 1 אתָךְ
Ezek. 3.22 :	אדבר אותָךְ	BHKK 1 אתָךְ
Ezek. 3.24 :	וידבר אתִי	BHKK 1 אתִי
Ezek. 3.27 :	ובדברי אותְךָ	BHKK 1 אתְךָ
Ezek. 14.4 :	דבר אותָם	BHKK 1 אתָם
Ezek. 44.5 :	מדבר אתָךְ	BHKK 1 אתָךְ
2 Chron. 18.23 :	לדבר אתָךְ	BHKK 1... אתָךְ

c. In connection with עשה

Jer. 21.2:	אֶתְּנוּ=BHKK יעשה יהוה אוֹתָנוּ
Ezek. 16.59:	אֹתָךְ BHKK 1 ועשיתי אוֹתָךְ
Ezek. 20.17:	אֹתָם BHKK 1 עשיתי אוֹתָם
Ezek. 22.14:	אֹתָךְ BHKK 1 אני עשה אוֹתָךְ
Ezek. 23.25:	אֹתָךְ BHKK 1 ועשו אוֹתָךְ
Ezek. 23.29:	אֹתָךְ BHKK 1 ועשו אוֹתָךְ
Ezek. 39.24:	אֹתָם BHKK 1 עשיתי אֹתָם

d. In connection with דרש

1 Ki. 22.7:	מֵאֹתוֹ BHKK 1... ונדרשה מֵאֹתוֹ
1 Ki. 22.8:	מֵאֹתוֹ BHKK 1... לדרש··· מֵאֹתוֹ
2 Ki. 3.11:	מֵאֹתוֹ BHKK 1... ונדרשה··· מֵאוֹתוֹ
2 Ki. 8.8:	מֵאֹתוֹ BHKK 1... ודרש··· מֵאוֹתוֹ

e. In connection with הלחם

Josh. 10.25:	אֹתָם BHKK 1 נלחמים אוֹתָם
1 Ki. 20.25:	אֹתָם BHKK 1 ונלחמה אוֹתָם

f. In connection with ברית

Isa. 59.21:	אֹתָם BHKK 1 בריתי אוֹתָם
Ezek. 16.8:	אֹתָךְ BHKK 1 ואבוא בברית אֹתָךְ
Ezek. 16.60:	אֹתָךְ BHKK 1 בריתי אוֹתָךְ
Ezek. 37.26:	אֹתָם BHKK 1... ברית עולם יהיה אוֹתָם

g. Various other usages

1)	Josh 14.12:	אֹתִי BHKK 1... אולי יהוה אוֹתִי
	Jer. 10.5:	אֹתָם=BHKK היטיב אין אוֹתָם
	Jer. 20.11:	אֹתִי=BHKK ויהוה אוֹתִי
2)	2 Ki. 1.15:	אֹתוֹ BHKK 1... רד אוֹתוֹ
	2 Ki. 1.15:	אֹתוֹ BHKK 1... וירד אוֹתוֹ
	Ezek. 10.17:	אֹתָם BHKK prb. 1 ירומו אוֹתָם
3)	Gen. 34.9:	אֹתָנוּ BHKK 1 והתחתנו אֹתָנוּ
	2 Sam. 24.24:	מֵאֹתָךְ=BHKK אקנה מֵאוֹתָךְ
4)	2 Ki. 3.12:	אֹתוֹ BHKK 1... יש אוֹתוֹ
	2 Ki. 3.26:	אֹתוֹ BHKK 1... ויקח אוֹתוֹ

2 Ki. 6.16:	אַתָּם ...1 BHKK אשר אתנו מאשר אותָם
Ezek. 23.23:	אַתָּם BHKK 1 כל בני אשור אותָם
Ezek. 38.9:	אַתָּךְ ...1 BHKK ועמים רבים אותָךְ
Job 32.6:	אִתְּכֶם BHKK 1 frt. מֵחַוֹּת דֵּעִי אֶתְכֶם

I hope there can be no difference of opinion on this point: such a treatment of the Hebrew Bible under the pretense of "correcting obvious mistakes" is utterly injustifiable.

iii. ראה IN *kal* AND *niph'al*

§ 65. The aim of *Biblia Hebraica* avowedly is "not to restore the *Urschrift*" (this being beyond the limits of our power), but to establish that form which the Bible text had prior to Masoretic activities thereon. How are we now reconcile with this policy the fact that whenever the verb ראה with a Divine Name as an object in the accusative is used in the *niph'al*, that *niph'al* form is consistently changed into the corresponding *qal* form?

Ex. 23.15:	תִּרְאֶה vel תֵּרָאוּ frt. BHKK 1 ולא יֵרָאוּ פני ריקם
Ex. 23.17:	יֵרָאֶה BHKK 1 פני האדן יהוה · · ·
Ex. 34.20:	תִּרְאֶה vel תֵּרָאוּ frt. BHKK 1 ולא יֵרָאוּ פני ריקם
Ex. 34.23:	יֵרָאֶה BHKK 1 פני האדן יהוה · · ·
Ex. 34.24:	לִרְאוֹת BHKK 1 לֵרָאוֹת את פני יהוה
Deut. 16.16:	יֵרָאֶה 1° BHKK 1 את פני יהוה · · ·
Deut. 16.16:	יֵרָאֶה BHKK 1 ולא יֵרָאֶה את פני יהוה ריקם
Deut. 31.11:	לִרְאוֹת BHKK 1 לֵרָאוֹת את פני יהוה
I Sam. 1.22:	וְרָאָה frt. BHKK 1 וְנִרְאָה את פני יהוה
Isa. 1.12:	לִרְאוֹת ...?1 BHKK לֵרָאוֹת פני
Ps. 42.3:	וְאֵרָאֶה ...1 BHKK וְאֶרְאֶה פני אלהים
Ps. 84.8:	יֵרָאוּ prb. BHKK 1 יֵרָאֶה אל אלהים

I do not enter here into a discussion of the underlying theological implications. I merely wish to point out that at the period preceding the Rise of the Masora (no matter how early we fix that date) the supposedly original conception of "seeing the Lord" was long superseded by the view expressed by the *niph'al*. In including in its notes reference to that presumed early stage of theological development, BHKK committed that

very grave mistake, against which Nöldeke and even Kittel himself had
warned (cf. § 49).

B. THE VERB

A. THE TENSES (Cf. p. 591, § 48)

i. INDISCRIMINATELY USED

§ 66. The Hebrew verbal tenses may indiscriminately be used to indicate any time: present, past and future (cf. p. 591, § 47). On p. 591, § 46
I listed a few examples from the Pentateuch, where the so-called perfect
(which I myself term: suffix tense) has the meaning of a future tense;
on p. 589, § 45 I brought instances (again from the Pentateuch only) for
the so-called imperfect (which I term: prefix tense) having the meaning
of a past tense. That the Hebrew tenses are in reality timeless, has been
recognized by Biblical scholars long ago. And still, in complete disregard
of this basic truth, we find numerous cases of "corrections" listed in
BHKK, as if the Hebrew tenses had the same implications of time as
the English or German verbs have.

a. *Suffix tense changed into prefix tense*

Gen. 11.6:	כל אשר יָזמו לעשות BHKK 1? יָזמּו
Gen. 24.15:	טרם כִּלָּה BHKK 1 frt. יְכַלֶּה
1 Sam. 3.7:	טרם יָדַע BHKK 1 יֵדַע
1 Sam. 17.26:	חֵרֵף מערכות אלהים חיים BHKK 1? יְחָרֵף
2 Sam. 14.21:	עָשִׂיתִי את הדבר הזה BHKK prps. אֶעֱשֶׂה
2 Sam. 20.6:	פן מָצָא לו ערים BHKK 1 יִמְצָא
Hos. 10.5:	כי אָבַל עליו עמו BHKK prps. יֶאֱבַל
Ps. 11.3:	צדיק מה פָּעָל BHKK prps. יִפְעָל
Ps. 19.5:	בכל הארץ יָצָא קום BHKK melius יֵצֵא
Ps. 38.17:	פן··· במוט רגלי עלי הִגְדִּילוּ BHKK melius יַגְדִּילוּ
Ps. 46.10:	וְקִצֵּץ חנית BHKK 1 prb. יְקַצֵּץ

b. *Suffix tense changed into participle*

Num. 23.23:	מה פָּעַל אל BHKK 1 prb. פֹּעֵל
1 Sam. 10.2:	והנה נטש··· וְדָאַג לכם BHKK 1 וְדֹאֵג
2 Sam. 13.35:	הנה בני המלך בָּאוּ BHKK 1? בָּאִים
Hos. 7.1:	פָּשַׁט גדוד בחוץ BHKK 1 פֹּשֵׁט
Eccl. 1.5:	וְזָרַח השמש BHKK 1 וְזֹרֵחַ

c. Prefix tense changed into suffix tense

Num. 9.15: הָיָה BHKK 1?... וּבָעֶרֶב יִהְיֶה עַל הַמִּשְׁכָּן
(cf. v. 16: כֵּן יִהְיֶה תָמִיד BHKK no emendation)

2 Sam. 2.28: רָדְפוּ BHKK 1? וְלֹא יָרְדְּפוּ עוֹד אַחֲרֵי יִשְׂרָאֵל

1 Ki. 20.33: נַחֲשׁוּ BHKK 1 frt. וְהָאֲנָשִׁים יְנַחֲשׁוּ

Isa. 63.16: הִכִּירָנוּ BHKK 1? וְיִשְׂרָאֵל לֹא יַכִּירָנוּ

Jer. 2.15: שָׁאֲגוּ BHKK 1 עָלָיו יִשְׁאֲגוּ כְפִרִים

Jer. 2.17: עָשָׂה BHKK 1 הֲלוֹא זֹאת תַּעֲשֶׂה לָּךְ

Nah. 3.10: רֻטְּשׁוּ BHKK 1 גַּם עֹלָלֶיהָ יְרֻטְּשׁוּ

Ps. 9.8: יָשַׁב BHKK frt. 1 וַיהוה לְעוֹלָם יֵשֵׁב

Ps. 40.4 רָאוּ BHKK 1 prb. יִרְאוּ רַבִּים וְיִירָאוּ

Ps. 67.7: בֵּרְכָנוּ BHKK prps. יְבָרְכֵנוּ אֱלֹהִים אֱלֹהֵינוּ

Job 2.10: דִּבַּרְתְּ BHKK 1 כְּדַבֵּר אַחַת הַנְּבָלוֹת תְּדַבֵּרִי

d. Participle changed into suffix or prefix tense

1 Sam. 15.12: הַצִּיב BHKK 1 frt.... וְהִנֵּה מַצִּיב לוֹ יָד

1 Sam. 17.20: יָצָא BHKK 1... וְהַחַיִל הַיֹּצֵא

Isa. 9.19: וַיִּרְעַב BHKK 1? וַיִּגְזֹר עַל יָמִין וְרָעֵב

Ps. 19.5: יָצָא BHKK melius וְהוּא כְּחָתָן יֹצֵא מֵחֻפָּתוֹ

Ps. 81.14: שָׁמַע BHKK 1 prb. יִשְׁמַע vel לוּ עַמִּי שֹׁמֵעַ לִי

Ps. 84.7: יַעְבְּרוּ BHKK prps. עָבְרוּ vel עֹבְרֵי בְּעֵמֶק הַבָּכָא

ii. TENSE USED IN NOMINAL AND VERBAL CLAUSES

§ 67. I must preface the coming investigations with a few remarks of a more general nature; they will help us better to understand the subsequent criticism:

I. Hebrew clauses are either:

a) nominal clauses; e.g. 2 Sam. 11.2: וְהָאִשָּׁה טוֹבַת מַרְאֶה מְאֹד; ib. v. 9: הֲיַד יוֹאָב אִתָּךְ; ib. v. 19: וְהַמֶּלֶךְ וְכִסְאוֹ נָקִי; ib. 14.9: וְהוּא פִסֵּחַ שְׁתֵּי רַגְלָיו; or בְּכָל זֹאת; or

b) verbal clauses; e.g. Gen. 25.34: וַיֹּאכַל וַיֵּשְׁתְּ וַיָּקָם וַיֵּלַךְ; ib. 43.31: וַיֵּצֵא וַיִּשְׂרְצוּ וַיִּרְבּוּ וַיַּעַצְמוּ (פָּרוּ); Ex. 1.7: וַיִּתְאַפַּק וַיֹּאמֶר; 1 Sam. 19.12: וַיֵּלֶךְ וַיִּבְרַח וַיִּמָּלֵט; 1 Ki. 19.6: וַיֹּאכַל וַיֵּשְׁתְּ וַיָּשָׁב וַיִּשְׁכָּב; Ruth 2.3: וַתֵּלֶךְ וַתָּבוֹא וַתְּלַקֵּט. The verb represents both subject *and* predicate. Similarly, in amplified verbal clauses, e.g. Gen. 25.34: וַיִּבֶן עֵשָׂו אֶת

הַבְּכֹרָה, subject *and* predicate are indicated by the verb וַיִּבֶז, while
עֵשָׂו is an apposition and הַבְּכֹרָה an object.

II. The Biblical text is subdivided in such a manner that verses some-
    times do not meet with the requirements of even one clause; e.g.
    Lev. 4.11; 9.19; 11.14-19; 14.55, 56; 22.19.

III. In narratives each clause as a rule begins with an introductory *waw*.
     Asyndetic connection is comparatively very rare.

IV. In amplified verbal clauses the verb can be either a) in initial, or
    b) in medial position.

 V. Referring to past events, the tense predominantly used is:
    a) in initial position: the prefix tense (cf. p. 591, § 48); e.g. Gen. 7.18:
       וַיִּגְבְּרוּ המים; ib. 11.13: וַיְחִי ארפכשד; and
    b) in medial position: the suffix tense; e.g. Gen. 7.19; והמים גָּבְרוּ;
       ib. 11.12: וארפכשד חַי.

VI. Referring to future happenings, the tense predominantly used is:
    c) in initial position: the suffix tense; e.g. Lev. 14.12: וְלָקַח הכהן;
       ib. v. 13: וְשָׁחַט את הכבש; and
    d) in medial position: the prefix tense; e.g. Lev. 14.19: ואחר יִשְׁחַט;
       ib. v. 26: ומן השמן יִצֹק.

§ 68.   In using the word "predominantly" I merely indicate the frequency with which we meet a certain tense in a given meaning in the
Bible. It implies the occurrence of the respective opposite tense in the
identical meaning, though to a lesser extent. Frequency of use is important
only, when we analyze the composite character of our Bible (cf. p. 298 ff.)
so as to establish the approximate share of each component source
in the shaping of its present form.

§ 69.   The suffix tense can be used in initial position to indicate past
events (cf. § 67 Va):

   a.   With introductory waw (cf. § 67 III)

Gen. 38.9:   וְהָיָה אם בא אל אשת אחיו
Ex. 36.1:   וְעָשָׂה בצלאל
Num. 11.8:   וְהָיָה טעמו כטעם לשד השמן

1 Ki. 9.25:	וְהֶעֱלָה שלמה · · · עלות ושלמים
1 Ki. 12.32:	וְהֶעֱמִיד בבית אל כהני הבמות
2 Ki. 12.12:	וְנָתְנוּ את הכסף
2 Ki. 21.6:	וְהֶעֱבִיר את בנו באש
2 Ki. 22.17:	וְנִצְּתָה חמתי במקום הזה
2 Ki. 23.10:	וְטִמֵּא את התפת
2 Ki. 23.14:	וְשִׁבַּר את המצבות
2 Ki. 24.14:	וְהִגְלָה את כל ירושלם
Jer. 18.12:	וְאָמְרוּ נואש כי · · · נלך
Jer. 25.4:	וְשָׁלַח יהוה אליכם
Ezek. 9.7:	וְיָצְאוּ והכו בעיר
Ezek. 37.7:	וְנִבֵּאתִי כאשר צויתי
Ezek. 37.8:	וְרָאִיתִי והנה עליהם גדים
Job 1.1:	וְהָיָה האיש ההוא תם וישר
Ezra 8.30:	וְקִבְּלוּ הכהנים והלוים משקל הכסף
Ezra 8.36:	וְנִשְׂאוּ את העם ואת בית האלהים
Neh. 10.33:	וְהֶעֱמַדְנוּ עלינו מצות
2 Chron. 33.4:	וּבָנָה מזבחות בבית יהוה

b. In asyndetic connection

Gen. 14.2:	עָשׂוּ מלחמה את ברע
Num. 11.8:	שָׁטוּ הָעָם ולקטו
Judg. 20.43:	כִּתְּרוּ את בנימן

§ 70. BHKK arbitrarily "corrects" such cases, so as to conform with the predominant usage (cf. § 67 Va).

Gen. 15.6:	וְהֶאֱמִן ביהוה BHKK 1 frt. וַיַּאֲמֵן
Gen. 34.5:	וְהֶחֱרֵשׁ יעקב עד באם BHKK... וַיַּחֲרֵשׁ?
Gen. 21.25:	וְהוֹכִחַ אברהם את אבימלך BHKK 1 frt. וַיּוֹכַח
Gen. 38.5:	וְהָיָה בכזיב בלדתה אתו BHKK 1... וְהִיא
Ex. 36.29:	וְהָיוּ תואמם מלמטה BHKK 1 וַיִּהְיוּ
Num. 27.11:	וְהָיְתָה לבני ישראל לחקת משפט BHKK 1? וַתְּהִי
Judg. 16.18:	וְעָלוּ אליה סרני פלשתים BHKK 1... וַיַּעֲלוּ
Judg. 19.8:	וְהִתְמַהְמְהוּ עד נטות היום BHKK 1 וַיִּתְמַהְמְהוּ
1 Sam. 1.12:	וְהָיָה כי הרבתה להתפלל BHKK 1 וַיְהִי
1 Sam. 13.22:	וְהָיָה ביום מלחמת BHKK 1... וַיְהִי

1 Sam. 25.20:   וְהָיָה הִיא רכבת   BHKK 1   וַיְהִי

2 Sam. 6.16:   וְהָיָה ארון יהוה בא   BHKK 1...   וַיְהִי

2 Sam. 16.5:   וּבָא המלך   BHKK 1?   וַיָּבֹא

2 Ki. 14.14:   וְלָקַח את כל הזהב   BHKK prps.   וַיִּקַּח

2 Ki. 18.7:   וְהָיָה יהוה עמו   BHKK prps.   ויהוה היה

2 Ki. 18.36:   וְהֶחֱרִישׁוּ העם   BHKK 1...   וַיַּחֲרִישׁוּ

2 Ki. 21.4:   וּבָנָה מזבחת בבית יהוה   BHKK prps.   וּבָנֹה

Isa. 9.8:   וְיָדְעוּ העם כלו   BHKK 1   וַיֵּדְעוּ

Jer. 7.31:   וּבָנוּ במות התפת   BHKK 1?   וַיִּבְנוּ

Jer. 19.5:   וּבָנוּ את במות הבעל   BHKK 1?   וַיִּבְנוּ

Jer. 37.11:   וְהָיָה בהעלות חיל הכשדים   BHKK 1?   וַיְהִי

Jer. 38.28:   וְהָיָה כאשר נלכדה ירושלם   BHKK 1?...   וַיְהִי

Ezek. 41.3:   וּבָא לפנימה   BHKK 1?   וַיָּבֹא

Ezra 3.10:   וְיִסְּדוּ הבנים את היכל יהוה   BHKK prps.   וַיְיַסְּדוּ

Neh. 4.16:   וְהָיוּ לנו הלילה משמר   BHKK prps.   וַיְהִי

iii.   NO *consecutio temporum* IN HEBREW

§ 71.   I stated in § 67 Ib) that a verbal clause consists of the verb only, which represents both subject *and* predicate. Consequently, there is no *consecutio temporum* in Biblical Hebrew, for each verb means a new and independent clause. Neither the preceding, nor the following verb, nor even the fact of their being used with or without the introductory *waw* (cf. § 67 III) can influence the tense of a given verb.

I)   The preceding verb is in the suffix tense (cf. § 69).

a.   With introductory waw

Gen. 30.41:   וְהָיָה בכל יחם הצאן · · · וְשָׂם יעקב

Num. 21.8:   וְהָיָה כל הנשוך וְרָאָה אתו

Judg. 19.30:   וְהָיָה כל הראה וְאָמַר

1 Sam. 16.23:   וְהָיָה בהיות רוח אלהים · · · וְלָקַח דוד

1 Sam. 7.16:   וְהָלַךְ מדי שנה בשנה וְסָבַב בית־אל

Jer. 20.9:   וְאָמַרְתִּי לא אזכרנו · · · וְהָיָה בלבי

b.   In asyndetic connection

Gen. 26.10:   שָׁכַב · · · וְהֵבֵאתָ

Gen. 38.9:   אם בָּא · · · וְשִׁחֵת

I Sam. 2.22: זָקֵן · · · וְשָׁמַע

Jer. 28.12: מטות עץ שָׁבָרְתָּ וְעָשִׂיתָ · · ·

2 Chron. 29.6: כי מָעֲלוּ אבתינו וְעָשׂוּ הרע

c. BHKK "corrects" such cases (cf. § 67 Va)

Gen. 28.6: וְשָׁלַח · · · בֵּרַךְ BHKK 1? וַיִּשְׁלַח

Gen. 31.7: הֵתֶל בי וְהֶחֱלִף BHKK 1 frt.... וַיַּחֲלֵף

Gen. 37.3: אָהַב · · · וְעָשָׂה BHKK 1 frt. וַיַּעַשׂ

I Ki. 21.12: קָרְאוּ צום וְהֹשִׁיבוּ BHKK 1 frt. וַיֹּשִׁיבוּ

2 Ki. 14.7: הוא הִכָּה · · · וְתָפַשׂ BHKK 1? וַיִּתְפֹּשׂ

It is interesting to note that the reverse case occurs, too, in BHKK:
Num. 25.13: קִנֵּא לאלהיו וַיְכַפֵּר על בני ישראל BHKK prps. וְכִפֶּר. Here
BHKK contradicts its own "correcting" efforts listed above! For a
similar case, cf. § 74, 4).

2) The preceding verb is in the prefix tense (cf. § 67 Va).

a. Passages apparently overlooked by BHKK

I Sam. 1.4: וַיִּזְבַּח · · · וְנָתַן

I Sam. 7.15-16: וַיִּשְׁפֹּט · · · וְהָלַךְ

2 Sam. 12.16: וַיָּצֶם · · · וּבָא

2 Ki. 17.21: וַיַּדַּח · · · את ישראל וְהֶחֱטִיאָם

2 Ki. 23.4: וַיִּשְׂרְפֵם · · · וְנָשָׂא את עפרם

2 Ki. 23.8: וַיְטַמֵּא · · · וְנָתַץ

2 Ki. 23.12: וַיָּרָץ משם וְהִשְׁלִיךְ את עפרם

2 Ki. 23.15: וַיִּשְׂרֹף את הבמה · · · וְשָׂרַף אשרה

b. BHKK "corrects" such cases

Gen. 49.23: וַיָּרֹבּוּ וַיְמָרֲרֻהוּ וָרֹבּוּ BHKK 1

Judg. 3.23: וַיִּנְעֹל · · · וַיִּסְגֹּר BHKK 1? וְנָעַל

I Sam. 5.7: וַיֹּאמְרוּ · · · וַיִּרְאוּ BHKK 1 וְאָמְרוּ

I Sam. 17.35: וָקָם BHKK 1 וַיָּקָם עלי וְהֶחֱזַקְתִּי בזקנו

I Sam. 17.38: וַיִּתֵּן BHKK 1 frt. וַיַּלְבֵּשׁ · · · וְנָתַן

2 Sam. 13.18: וַיִּנְעֹל BHKK 1? וַיֵּצֵא אותה · · · וְנָעַל הדלת

I Ki. 14.27: וַיַּפְקִדוּ BHKK 1? וַיַּעַשׂ המלך · · · וְהִפְקִיד על יד

I Ki. 18.4: וַיְכַלְכְּלֵם BHKK 1? וַיַּחְבִּיאֵם · · · וְכִלְכְּלָם לחם ומים

I Ki. 20.21: וַיַּךְ BHKK 1 וְהִכָּה · · · וַיַּךְ

3)   The following verb is in the prefix tense (cf. § 67 Va and § 69).

a.   *Passages apparently overlooked by BHKK*

Judg. 12.5:   וְהָיָה כִּי יאמרו · · · · וַיֹּאמְרוּ לוֹ

Isa. 44.15:   וְהָיָה לְאָדָם לְבָעֵר וַיִּקַּח מֵהֶם

Jer. 3.9:   וְהָיָה מִקֹּל זְנוּתָהּ וַתֶּחֱנַף אֶת הארץ

b.   *BHKK "corrects" such cases*

1 Sam. 10.9:   וַיְהִי BHKK 1   וְהָיָה כהפנתו · · · · וַיַּהֲפָךְ

1 Sam. 17.48:   וַיְהִי BHKK 1   וְהָיָה כִּי קָם הפלשתי וַיֵּלֶךְ

2 Ki. 3.15:   וַיְהִי BHKK frt. 1   וְהָיָה כנגן המנגן וַתְּהִי עליו

Jer. 37.11, 12:   וַיְהִי BHKK 1?   וְהָיָה בהעלות חיל · · · · וַיֵּצֵא

4)   The preceding verb is a participle.

BHKK "corrects" such cases

1 Sam. 17.20:   וַיָּרִיעוּ BHKK 1   וְהַחַיִל הַיֹּצֵא · · · · וְהֵרֵעוּ

2 Sam. 20.12:   עֹמֵד BHKK 1 frt.   כל הַבָּא עליו וְעָמָד

1 Ki. 11.9, 10:   וּמְצַוֶּה BHKK prps.   יהוה · · · · הַנִּרְאָה אליו · · · · וְצִוָּה אליו

§ 72.   In § 71 I asserted that Biblical Hebrew has no *consecutio temporum* to go by. BHKK does not seem to have realized that. The following instances are in accord with my rule formulated in § 67 VI. The first clause in each of these examples has the verb in medial position (cf. VId); in the second it is in initial position (cf. VIc). Thus the transition from prefix to suffix tense (with the implication of a future tense unchanged) is accounted for:

Gen. 32.12:   פֶּן יָבוֹא וְהִכַּנִי אם על בנים

Gen. 12.12:   כי יִרְאוּ אתך המצרים וְאָמְרוּ

Gen. 46.33:   כי יִקְרָא לכם פרעה וְאָמַר

Gen. 50.24:   יִפְקֹד אתכם וְהֶעֱלָה אתכם

Num. 20.26:   ואהרן יֵאָסֵף וּמֵת שם

Num. 27.21:   ולפני אלעזר · · · · יַעֲמֹד וְשָׁאַל לו

Deut. 1.41:   אנחנו נַעֲלֶה וְנִלְחַמְנוּ

Deut. 6.15:   פֶּן יֶחֱרֶה אף יהוה · · · · וְהִשְׁמִידָךְ

Deut. 7.25:   לא תַחְמֹד כסף וזהב · · · · וְלָקַחְתָּ

Deut. 31.12:   למען יִלְמְדוּ וְיָרְאוּ את יהוה

1 Ki. 9.8:   כל עבר עליו יִשֹּׁם וְשָׁרָק

2 Ki. 19.4:   יִשְׁמַע יהוה · · · וְהוֹכִיחַ בדברים אשר שמע

Isa. 19.5:   ונהר יֶחֱרַב וְיָבֵשׁ

Jer. 17.21:   ואל תִּשְׂאוּ משא · · · וַהֲבֵאתֶם

Jer. 22.10:   לא יָשׁוּב עוד וְרָאָה את ארץ

2 Chron. 7.21:   לכל עבר עליו יִשֹּׁם וְאָמַר

In complete disregard of this fact is the following suggestion listed in
BHKK, in an apparent attempt to harmonize the tenses:

Ex. 5.7:   וַיְקֹשְׁשׁוּ   הם יֵלְכוּ וְקֹשְׁשׁוּ להם תבן   BHKK 1...

B.   THE ABSOLUTE INFINITIVE

§ 73. Finite verbs are often continued by an absolute infinitive
(cf. p. 276, § 58).

1) The finite verb is in the prefix tense, implying a past event (cf.
§ 67 Va):

Gen. 41.43:   וַיַּרְכֵּב אתו במרכבת המשנה · · · וְנָתוֹן אתו על

Judg. 7.19:   וַיִּתְקְעוּ בשופרות וְנָפוֹץ הכדים

Jer. 37.21:   וַיַּפְקִדוּ את ירמיהו · · · וְנָתֹן לו ככר לחם

2 Chron. 7.3:   · · · וַיִּשְׁתַּחֲווּ וְהוֹדוֹת ליהוה כי טוב

2) The finite verb is in the prefix tense, implying a future happening
(cf. § 67 VId):

Josh. 9.20:   זאת נַעֲשֶׂה להם וְהַחֲיֵה אותם

Jer. 32.44:   שדות בכסף יִקְנוּ וְכָתוֹב בספר

Jer. 36.23:   יִקְרָעֶהָ בתער הספר וְהַשְׁלֵךְ אל האש

Ezek. 23.36:   הֲתִשְׁפּוֹט את אהלה · · · וְהַגֵּד להן

Esth. 6.8, 9:   יָבִיאוּ לבוש · · · וְנָתוֹן הלבוש

Neh. 7.3:   יָגִיפוּ הדלתות · · · וְהַעֲמִיד משמרות

3) The finite verb is in the suffix tense, implying a past event (cf. § 69).

a.   In asyndetic connection

1 Sam. 2.27, 28: הנגלה נִגְלֵיתִי אל בית אביך · · · וּבָחֹר אתו

Isa. 8.6:   יען כי מָאַס העם הזה את מי השלח ... וּמְשׂוֹשׂ את

Isa. 37.18, 19:   הֶחֱרִיבוּ מלכי אשור · · · וְנָתֹן את אליהם באש

Jer. 14.5:   כי גם אילת בשדה יָלְדָה וְעָזוֹב כי לא היה דשא

Jer. 19.13: אשר קִטְּרוּ עַל גגתיהם · · · וְהַסֵּךְ נסכים

Hag. 1.6: זְרַעְתֶּם הרבה וְהָבֵא מעט

Zech. 3.4: הֶעֱבַרְתִּי מעליך עונך וְהַלְבֵּשׁ אתך

Zech. 7.5: כי צַמְתֶּם וְסָפוֹד בחמישי ובשביעי

Eccl. 8.9: את כל זה רָאִיתִי וְנָתוֹן את לבי לכל

Esth. 9.16: ושאר היהודים · · · נִקְהֲלוּ וְעָמֹד עַל נפשם

Neh. 9.13: ועל הר סיני יָרַדְתָּ וְדַבֵּר עמהם משמים

b. With introductory waw

1 Ki. 9.25: וְהֶעֱלָה שלמה · · · עלות ושלמים · · · וְהַקְטֵיר אתו

Zech. 12.10: וְסָפְדוּ עליו · · · וְהָמֵר עליו

Dan. 9.5: הרשענו וּמָרָדְנוּ וְסוֹר ממצותך

Neh. 9.8: וּמָצָאתָ את לבבו נאמן לפניך וְכָרוֹת עמו הברית

§ 74.   BHKK "corrects" such cases.

1)   The finite verb is in the prefix tense, implying a past event.

Gen. 42.25: לְמַלֵּא BHKK 1 frt. וַיְמַלְאוּ את כליהם בר וּלְהָשִׁיב כספיהם

Ex. 8.11: וַיַּכְבֵּד BHKK 1 prb... וַיַּרְא פרעה · · · וְהַכְבֵּד את לבו

2)   The finite verb is in the prefix tense, implying a future happening.

Ex. 18.22: וְיֵקַלּוּ BHKK... יִשְׁפְּטוּ הם וְהָקֵל מעליך

Num. 30.3: יִשָּׁבֵע BHKK 1? איש כי יִדֹּר נדר · · · · או הִשָּׁבַע שבעה

Obad. 4: תָּשִׂים BHKK 1 אם תַּגְבִּיהַּ כנשר ואם בין כוכבים שִׂים קנך

1 Chron. 21.24: לְהַעֲלוֹת BHKK 1... כי לא אֶשָּׂא אשר לך ליהוה וְהַעֲלוֹת עולה

3)   The finite verb is in the suffix tense, implying a past event.

a.   In asyndetic connection

Eccl. 9.11: וָאֶרְאֶה BHKK 1 שַׁבְתִּי וְרָאֹה תחת השמש

Esth. 8.8: וְנֶחְתָּם BHKK 1 כי כתב אשר נכתב · · · · וְנַחְתּוֹם בטבעת

b.   With introductory waw

Ezek. 4.2: וְשַׂמְתָּ BHKK frt. 1 וְנָתַתָּה עליה מחנות וְשִׂים עליה

4)   BHKK contradicts its own "correcting" efforts by listing the following emendation.

2 Ki. 19.17, 18: וְנָתֹן BHKK 1... הֶחֱרִיבוּ מלכי אשור · · · וְנָתְנוּ את

For a similar case, cf. § 71 1c.

5) *Absolute infinitive* continued by a finite verb.

a. Suffix tense

2 Sam. 13.19: וַתֵּלֶךְ הָלוֹךְ וְזָעָקָה BHKK... potius וְזָעֹק

Josh. 6.13: הַכֹּהֲנִים ··· הֹלְכִים הָלוֹךְ וְתָקְעוּ BHKK 1 וְתָקוֹעַ

Isa. 31.5: יָגֵן ··· גָּנוֹן וְהִצִּיל פָּסוֹחַ וְהִמְלִיט BHKK 1 וְהַצֵּיל et וְהַמְלֵיט

b. Prefix tense

2 Sam. 16.13: הָלֹךְ ··· הָלוֹךְ וַיְקַלֵּל BHKK 1 וְקַלֵּל

I Sam. 19.23: וַיֵּלֶךְ הָלוֹךְ וַיִּתְנַבֵּא BHKK 1 וְהִתְנַבֵּא (inf.)

Isa. 57.17: קָצַפְתִּי ··· הַסְתֵּר וָאֶקְצֹף BHKK 1 וְקָצֹף

c. Participle

2 Sam. 16.5: יֹצֵא יָצוֹא וּמְקַלֵּל

2 Sam. 18.25: וַיֵּלֶךְ הָלוֹךְ וְקָרֵב

Gen. 26.13: וַיֵּלֶךְ הָלוֹךְ וְגָדֵל BHKK 1? וְגָדֵל (inf.)

Jer. 41.6: הֹלֵךְ הָלֹךְ וּבֹכֶה BHKK... וּבָכֹה

C. Noun and Verb

A. THE GENDER

§ 75. The problem of the gender of the Hebrew noun is a very difficult one. The pertinent statements found in B-L are so evasive that not only are they of no avail in our search for a solution, but even add to our own confusion and perplexities by the sheer vagueness of their assertions.

"Für einen ursprünglichen deteriorativen Charakter des Femininums scheint zwar die Tatsache zu sprechen, dass im Hebräischen vielfach solche Tiergattungen, die sich stark und mutig zeigen, als Maskulina, solche, die für schwach und furchtsam gelten, als Feminina gedacht werden." (B-L § 62c).

As examples are listed:

"Mask.: אַלּוּף Rind, דֹּב Bär, זְאֵב Wolf, כֶּלֶב Hund; Fem.: אַרְנֶבֶת Hase, חֲסִידָה Storch, יוֹנָה Taube, נְמָלָה Ameise." (ib.).

But the learned authors overlooked the obvious fact that by these words he- and she-animals, respectively, are indicated. Thus, the difference of sex is reflected in their different gender.

"Sie [scil. many feminine nouns] zeigen sich als Feminina nur dadurch, dass ihre Attribute und Pronomina sowie, unter gewissen Bedingungen (!; they are nowhere indicated!] die mit ihnen als Subjekten verbundenen Prädikate feminine Formen haben." (B-L § 62d).

In order to demonstrate the untenability of these statements, I shall limit myself to pointing out the manner, in which the Bible applies the different genders.

§ 76. How can we possibly take a "deteriorative character of the feminine gender" into consideration, when the Bible frequently treats the *nomina propria* of nations as *feminina*?

אדום:	Jer. 49.17:	וְהָיְתָה אֱדוֹם לְשַׁמָּה
	Mal. 1.4:	כִּי תֹאמַר אֱדוֹם
	Ezek. 35.15:	וְכָל אֱדוֹם כֻּלָּהּ
ארם:	2 Sam. 8.6:	וַתְּהִי אֲרָם
	2 Sam. 10.11:	אִם תֶּחֱזַק אֲרָם
אשור:	Num. 24.22:	עַד מָה אַשּׁוּר תִּשְׁבֶּךָּ
יהודה:	Jer. 3.8:	בָּגְדָה יְהוּדָה
	Jer. 23.6:	בִּימָיו תִּוָּשַׁע יְהוּדָה
	Mal. 2.11:	בָּגְדָה יְהוּדָה
	Ps. 114.2:	הָיְתָה יְהוּדָה
	Lam. 1.3:	גָּלְתָה יְהוּדָה
	Zech. 14.14:	וְגַם יְהוּדָה תִּלָּחֵם
	Jer. 13.19:	הָגְלָת יְהוּדָה כֻּלָּהּ
	Jer. 14.2:	אָבְלָה יְהוּדָה וּשְׁעָרֶיהָ אֻמְלָלוּ
ישראל:	1 Sam. 17.21:	וַתַּעֲרֹךְ יִשְׂרָאֵל
	2 Sam. 24.9:	וַתְּהִי יִשְׂרָאֵל
	Jer. 3.6:	עָשְׂתָה מְשֻׁבָה יִשְׂרָאֵל
מואב:	Judg. 3.30:	וַתִּכָּנַע מוֹאָב
	2 Sam. 8.2:	וַתְּהִי מוֹאָב
	Jer. 48.4:	נִשְׁבְּרָה מוֹאָב
מצרים:	Ex. 12.33:	וַתֶּחֱזַק מִצְרַיִם
שבא:	Job 1.15:	וַתִּפֹּל שְׁבָא

It will be sufficient proof to refute the second statement, which I had quoted from B-L in § 75, if I list here some of the very many instances, where neither "ihre Attribute und Pronomina," nor "die Prädikate" agree with the gender, which grammar and dictionary in common accord assign to these nouns.

§ 77.   The substantive precedes the predicate or attribute.

Gen. 15.17:   וַעֲלָטָה הָיָה

Gen. 20.17:   אִשְׁתּוֹ וְאַמְהֹתָיו וַיֵּלֵדוּ

Gen. 27.15:   בִּגְדֵי עשו · · · · הַחֲמֻדֹת; cf. Lev. 6.20:   הַבֶּגֶד אשר יזה עָלֶיהָ

Ex. 12.16:   כל מְלָאכָה לא יֵעָשֶׂה

Ex. 13.7:   מַצּוֹת יֵאָכֵל; id. Num. 28.17; Ezek. 45.21

Ex. 13.12:   בְּהֵמָה אשר יִהְיֶה לך; cf. Zech. 14.15

Ex. 17.12:   וִידֵי משה כְּבֵדִים

Ex. 28.32:   שָׂפָה יִהְיֶה לפיו

Lev. 2.1:   סֹלֶת יִהְיֶה קרבנו

Lev. 2.8:   הַמִּנְחָה אשר יֵעָשֶׂה

Lev. 26.33:   וְעָרֵיכֶם יִהְיוּ

Num. 16.29:   וּפְקֻדַּת · · · · יִפָּקֵד

Deut. 18.2:   וְנַחֲלָה לא יִהְיֶה לו

Josh. 24.33:   בְּגִבְעַת פינחס בנו אשר נִתַּן לו

Isa. 8.22:   וַאֲפֵלָה מְנֻדָּח

Isa. 44.28:   וְהֵיכָל תִּוָּסֵד

Isa. 59.7:   רַגְלֵיהֶם · · · · יָרֻצוּ

Zech. 4.10:   עֵינֵי יהוה הֵמָּה מְשׁוֹטְטִים; cf. Prov. 23.33

Zech. 13.8:   וְהַשְּׁלִשִׁית יִוָּתֶר

Zech. 14.15:   וכל הַבְּהֵמָה אשר יִהְיֶה; cf. Ex. 13.12

Mal. 2.6:   וְעַוְלָה לא נִמְצָא

Ps. 124.4:   נַחֲלָה עָבַר

Prov. 23.33:   עֵינֶיךָ יִרְאוּ; cf. Zech. 4.10

Cant. 6.9:   ראוה בָנוֹת וַיְאַשְּׁרוּהָ מְלָכוֹת · · · · וַיְהַלְלוּהָ

Eccl. 10.5:   כִּשְׁגָגָה שֶׁיֹּצָא

The uncertainty of the Bible in the gender to be applied becomes even more obvious, when we consider these following instances:

1) Num. 15.6:   סֹלֶת שני עשרנים בְּלוּלָה

   Num. 15.9:   סֹלֶת שני עשרנים בָּלוּל

2) I Ki. 17.14:   וְצַפַּחַת הַשֶּׁמֶן לֹא תֶחְסָר

    I Ki. 17.16:   וְצַפַּחַת הַשֶּׁמֶן לֹא חָסֵר

3) I Ki. 10.22:   תָּבוֹא אֲנִי · · · נֹשְׂאֵת

    I Ki. 10.11:   אֳנִי חִירָם · · · נָשָׂא · · · הֵבִיא

4) Neh. 10.35:   לְעִתִּים מְזֻמָּנִים

    Neh. 13.31:   בְּעִתִּים מְזֻמָּנוֹת

BHKK "corrects" such cases:

Gen. 4.7:   חַטָּאת רֹבֵץ   BHKK l?   תִּרְבָּץ
Gen. 49.15:   מְנוּחָה כִּי טוֹב   BHKK l?   טוֹבָה
Josh. 2.17:   מִשְּׁבֻעָתֵךְ הַזֶּה   BHKK l frt.   הַזֶּה
Judg. 16.28:   הַפַּעַם הַזֶּה   BHKK l frt.   יהוה
I Sam. 10.18:   הַמַּמְלָכוֹת הַלֹּחֲצִים   BHKK?   הַמְּלָכִים
2 Sam. 1.22:   קֶשֶׁת · · · נָשׂוֹג אָחוֹר   BHKK l   נָשׂוֹגָה vel תָּשׂוּג
Isa. 32.12:   עַל שָׁדַיִם סֹפְדִים   BHKK l   סֹפְדָה
Jer. 22.14:   וַעֲלִיּוֹת מְרֻוָּחִים   BHKK prp.*   מְרֻוָּחִים
Ezek. 1.16:   וּדְמוּת אֶחָד   BHKK l   אַחַת
Ezek. 7.25:   קְפָדָה בָא   BHKK l   תָּבֹא
Ezek. 10.10:   דְּמוּת אֶחָד   BHKK l   אַחַת
Ezek. 21.24:   מֵאֶרֶץ אֶחָד   BHKK l...   אַחַת
Ezek. 40.17:   וְרִצְפָה עָשׂוּי   BHKK prb. l   עֲשׂוּיָה
Hos. 14.1:   וְהָרִיּוֹתָיו יְבֻקָּעוּ   BHKK l frt.   תְּבַקֵּעְנָה
Hab. 1.16:   וּמַאֲכָלוֹ בְּרִאָה   BHKK l   בָּרָא
Hab. 3.4:   וְנֹגַהּ כָּאוֹר תִּהְיֶה   BHKK l   יִהְיֶה
Ps. 42.2:   כְּמוֹ אַיֶּלֶת תַּעֲרֹג   BHKK l frt.   כְּאַיָּל תַּעֲרֹג
Job 1.14:   הַבָּקָר הָיוּ חֹרְשׁוֹת   BHKK l   חֹרְשִׁים
Job 8.7:   וְאַחֲרִיתְךָ יִשְׂגֶּה מְאֹד   BHKK l   תִּשְׂגֶּה
Job 20.26:   אֵשׁ לֹא נֻפָּח   BHKK l   נֻפָּחָה vel נֻפָּחָה
Job 27.4:   וּלְשׁוֹנִי אִם יֶהְגֶּה רְמִיָּה   BHKK l...   תֶהְגֶּה
2 Chron. 3.13: כַּנְפֵי הַכְּרוּבִים הָאֵלֶּה פֹּרְשִׂים   BHKK l   פֹּרְשִׂים, rectius   פְּרֻשׂוֹת

A case of a substantive with two verbs, one preceding it and the other following it, is dealt with in BHKK in the same fashion:

Jer. 48.1:   הֹבִישָׁה הַמִּשְׂגָּב וָחָתָּה   BHKK l   הֹבִישׁ ;l   וָחַת

§ 78. The predicate or attribute precedes the substantive:

Gen. 35.5:   וַיְהִי חִתַּת אֱלֹהִים

Gen. 35.16:   וַיְהִי עוֹד כִּבְרַת הָאָרֶץ

Gen. 39.5:   וַיְהִי בִּרְכַּת יהוה

Gen. 49.20:   שְׁמֵנָה לַחְמוֹ

Ex. 17.12:   וַיְהִי יָדָיו אֱמוּנָה; cf. Zeph. 3.16; Eccl. 7.26

Ex. 31.15:   יֵעָשֶׂה מְלָאכָה; idem Lev. 11.32

Num. 18.27:   וְנֶחְשַׁב לכם תְּרוּמַתְכֶם

Num. 26.54:   יֻתַּן נַחֲלָתוֹ; cf. v. 62; 36.4

Num. 26.55:   יֵחָלֵק אֶת הָאָרֶץ; cf. 32.5

Num. 26.62:   לֹא נִתַּן להם נַחֲלָה; cf. v. 54; 36.4

Num. 32.5:   יֻתַּן אֶת הָאָרֶץ; cf. 26.55

Num. 36.4:   יִגָּרַע נַחֲלָתָן; but preceding וְנוֹסְפָה נַחֲלָתָן; cf. 26.54, 62

Deut. 25.13:   לֹא יִהְיֶה · · · אֶבֶן

Deut. 25.14:   לֹא יִהְיֶה · · · אֵיפָה

Judg. 14.18:   בטרם יָבֹא הַחַרְסָה

1 Ki. 22.36:   וַיַּעֲבֹר הָרִנָּה

Isa. 2.17:   וְשַׁח גַּבְהוּת האדם

Isa. 17.9:   יִהְיוּ עָרֵי מָעֻזּוֹ

Isa. 47.11:   וּבָא עליך רָעָה

Jer. 13.18:   יָרַד · · · עֲטֶרֶת תפארתכם

Jer. 29.22:   וְלֻקַּח מהם קְלָלָה

Zeph. 3.12:   ולא יִמָּצֵא · · · לְשׁוֹן תרמית

Zeph. 3.16:   אַל יִרְפּוּ יָדָיִךְ; cf. Ex. 17.12

Zech. 3.9:   שִׁבְעָה עֵינָיִם

Zech. 5.10:   הֵמָּה מוֹלִכוֹת

Ps. 109.13:   יְהִי אַחֲרִיתוֹ

Job 1.4:   וקראו לִשְׁלֹשֶׁת אַחְיֹתֵיהֶם

Eccl. 7.26:   אֲסוּרִים יָדֶיהָ; cf. Ex. 17.12

Neh. 3.34:   וְהֵמָּה שְׂרוּפוֹת

1 Sam. 2.34:   וְזֶה לְךָ הָאוֹת

Jer. 44.29:   וְזֹאת לכם הָאוֹת

BHKK "corrects" such cases:

Gen. 38.24:   כְּמִשְׁלֹשֶׁת ויהי כְּמִשְׁלֹשׁ חֳדָשִׁים BHKK 1...

Gen. 13.6:   נָשָׂאָה ולא נָשָׂא אֹתָם הָאָרֶץ BHKK 1...

Judg. 14.18:　　הַחַדְרָה　　BHKK 1　בטרם יָבֹא הַחַרְסָה

Num. 31.28:　　אֶחָד נֶפֶשׁ　　BHKK prb. נפש dl

1 Sam. 10.3:　　שָׁלֹשׁ　　BHKK 1　שְׁלֹשֶׁת כִּכְּרוֹת לֶחֶם

1 Sam. 10.4:　　שְׁנֵי　　BHKK 1 frt.　שְׁתֵּי לֶחֶם

1 Sam. 25.27:　　הֵבִיאָה　　BHKK 1...　אשר הֵבִיא שִׁפְחָתְךָ

2 Ki. 3.26:　　חָזְקָה　　BHKK 1 prb.　כי חָזַק ממנו הַמִּלְחָמָה

Isa. 32.11:　　חֲרָדָה　　BHKK 1 frt.　חִרְדוּ שַׁאֲנַנּוֹת　(imp. aram, 2 fem. pl.)

Jer. 30.19:　　וְיָצְאָה　　BHKK 1　וְיָצָא · · · תּוֹדָה

Ezek. 23.29:　　וְנִגְלְתָה　　BHKK 1　וְגִלָּה עֶרְוַת זְנוּנָיִךְ

Ezek. 28.15:　　עָוֶל　　BHKK prb. 1　עד נִמְצָא עַוְלָתָה

Am. 5.12:　　חַטָּאיכֶם　　BHKK prps.　וַעֲצֻמִים חַטֹּאתֵיכֶם

Zeph. 2.6:　　וְהָיְתָה　　BHKK 1　וְהָיְתָה חֶבֶל הִים

Job 20.9:　　יְשׁוּרֶנּוּ　　BHKK 1　ולא עוד תְּשׁוּרֶנּוּ מְקוֹמוֹ

§ 79.　The substantive is used as being of both genders in one and the same phrase.

Gen. 28.22:　　וְהָאֶבֶן הַזֹּאת · · · יִהְיֶה

Gen. 29.20:　　שֶׁבַע שָׁנִים וַיִּהְיוּ בעיניו

Gen. 41.27:　　וְשֶׁבַע הַשִּׁבֳּלִים הָרֵקוֹת · · · יִהְיוּ

Gen. 47.24:　　וְאַרְבַּע הַיָּדֹת יִהְיֶה

Ex. 12.49:　　תּוֹרָה אַחַת יִהְיֶה

Ex. 28.7:　　שְׁתֵּי כְתֵפֹת חֹבְרֹת יִהְיֶה

Lev. 24.5:　　יִהְיֶה הַחַלָּה הָאֶחָת

Num. 9.14:　　חֻקָּה אַחַת יִהְיֶה

Num. 15.29:　　תּוֹרָה אַחַת יִהְיֶה לכם

Num. 36.3:　　וְנִגְרְעָה נַחֲלָתָן · · · וְנוֹסַף

Deut. 25.15:　　אֶבֶן שְׁלֵמָה וָצֶדֶק יִהְיֶה

Deut. 25.15:　　אֵיפָה שְׁלֵמָה וָצֶדֶק יִהְיֶה

1 Sam. 13.22:　　ולֹא נִמְצָא חֶרֶב · · · וַתִּמָּצֵא

Isa. 14.31:　　נָמוֹג פְּלֶשֶׁת כֻּלֵּךְ

Isa. 19.18:　　יִהְיוּ חָמֵשׁ עָרִים · · · מְדַבְּרוֹת

Isa. 21.2:　　חָזוּת קָשָׁה הֻגַּד לִי

Jer. 4.30:　　וְאַתְּ שָׁדוּד מַה תַּעֲשִׂי

Jer. 31.9:　　בְּדֶרֶךְ יָשָׁר · · · בָּהּ

Jer. 36.23:　　שָׁלֹשׁ דְּלָתוֹת וְאַרְבָּעָה

Ezek. 8.3:　　שַׁעַר הַפְּנִימִית הַפּוֹנֶה

Ezek. 23.32:   תִּשְׁתִּי · · · תִּהְיֶה

Ezek. 47.9:   נֶפֶשׁ חַיָּה אשר יִשְׁרֹץ

Ezek. 47.9:   וְהָיָה הַדָּגָה רַבָּה

Mic. 1.9:   אנושה מכותיה כי בָאָה · · · נָגַע

Zech. 6.7:   לכו התהלכו · · · וַתִּתְהַלַּכְנָה

Mal. 2.11:   בָּגְדָה יהודה · · · כי חִלֵּל יהודה

Ps. 120.3:   יִתֵּן · · · יֹסִיף · · · לָשׁוֹן רְמִיָּה

Prov. 14.12:   יש דֶּרֶךְ יָשָׁר · · · וְאַחֲרִיתָהּ ; idem 16.25

Dan. 8.9:   יָצָא קֶרֶן אַחַת

2 Chron. 7.15:   עתה עֵינַי יִהְיוּ פְתֻחוֹת

BHKK "corrects" such cases:

Gen. 32.9:   הָאֶחָד   BHKK 1... הַמַּחֲנֶה הָאַחַת וְהִכָּהוּ

Gen. 49.21:   נֹתְנָה BHKK 1?   אַיָּלָה שְׁלֻחָה הַנֹּתֵן

Judg. 4.20:   עֲמֹד   BHKK 1 frt.... וַיֹּאמֶר אֵלֶיהָ עֲמֹד

1 Ki. 13.10:   בָּהּ ? BHKK 1   בְּדֶרֶךְ אַחֵר · · · אשר בא בָהּ

Isa. 17.1:   מוּסָרָה   BHKK 1 דַּמֶּשֶׂק מוּסָר מֵעִיר וְהָיְתָה

Isa. 33.9:   אָבְלָה   BHKK 1 אָבַל אֻמְלְלָה אָרֶץ

Jer. 48.20:   חַת (ה dittogr.)   BHKK 1 הֵבִישׁ מוֹאָב כי חַתָּה

Jer. 48.39:   חַת   BHKK 1 חַתָּה · · · הִפְנָה · · · מוֹאָב

Ezek. 13.14:   וְנָפַל   BHKK 1 וְנִגְלָה יְסֹדוֹ וְנָפְלָה

Job 1.19:   תִּגַּע   BHKK 1... רוּחַ גְּדוֹלָה בָּאָה · · · וַיִּגַּע

2 Chron. 3.11:   מַגַּעַת   BHKK 1 וְהַכָּנָף הָאַחֶרֶת מַגִּיעַ · · ·

2 Chron. 17.13:   הָיְתָה   BHKK 1... וּמְלָאכָה רַבָּה הָיָה לוֹ

§ 80.   But in its own critical notes BHKK reveals its lack of decision as to which gender should be used. The learned editors overlooked that one note may sometimes affect the grammatical structure of an entire phrase, and thus created a discrepancy of their own:

Gen. 33.7:   רָחֵל וְיוֹסֵף   BHKK 1... ואחר נִגַּשׁ יוֹסֵף וְרָחֵל (n o t : נִגְּשָׁה!)

Judg. 1.20:   וַיּוֹרֶשׁ   BHKK ins. אֶת שְׁלֹשֶׁת הֶעָרִים וַיְּגָרֶשׁ (n o t : שָׁלֹשׁ!)

2 Sam. 20.8:   חָגוּר   BHKK 1... ועליו חֲגוֹר חֶרֶב מְצֻמֶּדֶת (n o t : חֲגוֹרָה!)

1 Ki. 10.22:   אֳנִיּוֹת   BHKK prps. תָּבוֹא אֲנִי תַרְשִׁישׁ נֹשֵׂאת (n o t : תָּבֹאנָה נֹשְׂאֹת · · ·!)

Ezek. 1.6:   מֵהֶם   BHKK 1... לְאַחַת לָהֶם (n o t : מֵהֶן!)

Ps. 73.9:   מִתְהַלֵּךְ   BHKK frt. וּלְשׁוֹנָם תִּהֲלַךְ בארץ (n o t : מִתְהַלֶּכֶת!)

Job 28.2:   יוּצָק   BHKK 1 וְאֶבֶן יָצוּק נחושה (n o t : תּוּצָק!)

Of course, I am not going to hold these instances against BHKK as evidence that its editors were not so firm in Hebrew grammar, either. But I hope this will help to demonstrate the fallacy of applying the yard-stick of ill conceived grammatical laws to the language of the Bible (cf. also § 86 2d).

§ 81. The gender of the substantive as reflected in the *pronomen suffixum*.

Gen. 26.15:	הַבְּאֵרֹת · · · סִתְּמוּם · · · וַיְמַלְאוּם
Gen. 26.18:	בְּאֵרֹת · · · וַיְסַתְּמוּם · · · לָהֶן
Gen. 33.13:	עָלוֹת · · · וּדְפָקוּם
Gen. 41.23:	שֶׁבַע שִׁבֳּלִים · · · אַחֲרֵיהֶם
Ex. 2.17:	(בָּנוֹת · · · :) וַיְגָרְשׁוּם · · · וַיּוֹשִׁעָן · · · צֹאנָם
Ex. 25.29:	יֻסַּךְ בָּהֵן · · · אֹתָם
Ex. 28. 9:	שְׁתֵּי אַבְנֵי שֹׁהַם · · · עֲלֵיהֶם
Ex. 35.17:	קַלְעֵי הֶחָצֵר · · · עַמֻּדָיו · · · אֲדָנֶיהָ
Lev. 26.3:	ואת מצותי תשמרו ועשיתם אתם
Num. 36.6:	לבנות צלפחד · · · לטוב בעיניהם תהיינה
Num. 36.6:	מטה אביהם תהיינה לנשים
Deut. 17.19:	וְהָיְתָה עמו וקרא בו
Deut. 27.2:	אבנים גדלות ושדת אתם
2 Sam. 1.24:	בנות ישראל · · · הַמַּלְבִּשְׁכֶם · · · לְבוּשְׁכֶן
2 Ki. 18.13:	עָרֵי יהודה הַבְּצֻרוֹת וַיִּתְפְּשֵׂם
Isa. 3.16:	וּבְרַגְלֵיהֶם תְּעַכַּסְנָה
Isa. 10.10:	לְמַמְלְכֹת הָאֱלִיל וּפְסִילֵיהֶם
Isa. 36.1:	עָרֵי יהודה הַבְּצֻרוֹת וַיִּתְפְּשֵׂם
Isa. 37.11:	לכל הָאֲרָצוֹת לְהַחֲרִימָם
Isa. 60.8:	וְכַיּוֹנִים אל אֲרֻבֹּתֵיהֶם
Jer. 29.17:	כַּתְּאֵנִים הַשֹּׁעָרִים אשר לא תֵאָכַלְנָה
Jer. 33.24:	הַמִּשְׁפָּחוֹת · · · בָּהֶם וַיִּמְאָסֵם
Jer. 43.9:	אבנים גדלות וּטְמַנְתָּם
Jer. 44.2:	עָרֵי יהודה וְהִנָּם · · · בָּהֶם
Jer. 50.37:	סוּסָיו · · · רִכְבּוֹ · · · בְּתוֹכָהּ
Ezek. 1.9:	לא יִסַּבּוּ בְּלֶכְתָּן
Ezek. 1.10:	לְאַרְבַּעְתָּם · · · לְאַרְבַּעְתָּן
Ezek. 1.18:	וְגַבֵּיהֶן וגבה לָהֶם

Ezek. 1.19:	הַחַיּוֹת · · · אֶצְלָם
Ezek. 1.24:	בְּעָמְדָם תְּרַפֶּינָה כַנְפֵיהֶן
Ezek. 5.6:	וְחֻקּוֹתַי לֹא הָלְכוּ בָהֶם
Ezek. 13.20:	אַתֶּם מְצֹדְדוֹת
Mic. 2.1:	אָוֶן · · · רָע · · · יַעֲשׂוּהָ
Zech. 5.9:	שְׁתַּיִם נָשִׁים יוֹצְאוֹת · · · בְּכַנְפֵיהֶם וְלָהֵנָּה
Zech. 5.10:	הֵמָּה מוֹלִכוֹת
Zech. 11.9:	לֹא אֶרְעֶה אֶתְכֶם הַמֵּתָה תָמוּת וְהַנִּכְחֶדֶת
Zech. 12.12:	מִשְׁפַּחַת · · · וּנְשֵׁיהֶם
Ps. 34.20:	רַבּוֹת רָעוֹת · · · וּמִכֻּלָּם
Ruth 1.9:	יִתֵּן יְהוָה לָכֶם וּמְצֶאןָ מְנוּחָה
Cant. 2.7:	הִשְׁבַּעְתִּי אֶתְכֶם בְּנוֹת יְרוּשָׁלַ͏ִם
Cant. 4.2:	שֶׁכֻּלָּם מַתְאִימוֹת וְשַׁכֻּלָה אֵין בָּהֶם
Cant. 6.5:	עֵינַיִךְ · · · שֶׁהֵם הִרְהִיבֻנִי
Gen. 19.8:	בָּנוֹת · · · אֶתְהֶן · · · לָהֶן
Judg. 19.24:	בִּתִּי · · · וּפִילַגְשֵׁהוּ · · · אוֹתָם · · · לָהֶם
Num. 16.6, 7:	מַחְתּוֹת · · · וּתְנוּ בָהֵן · · · עֲלֵיהֶן
Num. 16.18:	מַחְתָּתוֹ וַיִּתְּנוּ עֲלֵיהֶם · · · עֲלֵיהֶם
Gen. 31.52:	עֵד הַגַּל הַזֶּה וְעֵדָה הַמַּצֵּבָה
Gen. 21.30:	בַּעֲבוּר תִּהְיֶה לִּי לְעֵדָה
Deut. 21.19:	לְמַעַן תִּהְיֶה לִּי הַשִּׁירָה הַזֹּאת לְעֵד

BHKK "corrects" such cases:

Gen. 18.24:	בְּקִרְבָּהּ BHKK 1 וְלֹא תִשָּׂא לַמָּקוֹם · · · אֲשֶׁר בְּקִרְבָּהּ
Gen. 19.13:	לְשַׁחֲתָם BHKK 1? אֶת הַמָּקוֹם הַזֶּה · · · לְשַׁחֲתָהּ
Gen. 32.16:	וּבְנֵיהֶן BHKK 1? גְּמַלִּים מֵינִיקוֹת וּבְנֵיהֶם
Josh. 17.4:	לָהֶן BHKK 1... וַיִּתֵּן לָהֶם · · · אֲחֵי אֲבִיהֶן
Isa. 15.3:	וּבְרְחֹבֹתָיו ;גַּגּוֹתָיו BHKK 1 בְּחוּצֹתָיו · · · גַּגֹּתֶיהָ וּבִרְחֹבֹתֶיהָ
Isa. 51.12:	אַתָּה וַתִּירְאִי et מְנַחֶמְךָ BHKK 1 אָנֹכִי מְנַחֶמְכֶם מִי אַתְּ · · · וַתִּירְאִי
Jer. 11.16:	בְּעָלֶיהוּ BHKK 1 prb. הִצִּית אֵשׁ עָלֶיהָ · · · דָּלִיּוֹתָיו
Jer. 30.15:	תִּזְעָקִי ,BHKK=תִּזְעַק sic 1? מַה תִּזְעַק עַל שִׁבְרֵךְ
Ezek. 1.13:	מַרְאֵה BHKK 1 וּדְמוּת הַחַיּוֹת מַרְאֵיהֶם
Ezek. 2.9:	וְהִנֵּה בָהּ BHKK 1 יָד שְׁלוּחָה אֵלָי וְהִנֵּה בוֹ
Ezek. 42.14:	הֵמָּה ;בָהֶם · · · בָּהֶן · · · הֵנָּה BHKK 1... בִּגְדֵיהֶם · · · בָהֶם
Am. 4.1:	לַאֲדֹנֵיהֶן BHKK prps. הָאֹמְרֹת לַאֲדֹנֵיהֶם
Am. 4.2:	אַפְּכֶן BHKK prps. וְנִשָּׂא אֶתְכֶם · · · וְאַחֲרִיתְכֶן

Am. 9.11: אֶת פְּרָצֶיהָ וַהֲרִסֹתֶיהָ BHKK 1 וגדרתי את פרציהן וַהֲרִסֹתָיו אקים

Nah. 2.5: מַרְאֵיהֶם BHKK 1 יִתְהוֹלְלוּ הרכב · · · מַרְאֵיהֶן

Hab. 1.10: וַיִּלְכְּדֵהוּ BHKK prps. מִבְצָר · · · וַיִּלְכְּדָהּ

Lam. 2.5: אַרְמְנוֹתָיו BHKK 1 בלע כל אַרְמְנוֹתֶיהָ שחת מִבְצָרָיו

Ruth 1.19: שְׁתֵּיהֶן BHKK 1... וַתֵּלַכְנָה שְׁתֵּיהֶם

Ruth 4.11: שְׁתֵּיהֶן BHKK... כרחל וכלאה אשר בנו שְׁתֵּיהֶם

1 Chron. 23.22: אֲחֵיהֶן ;1 וַיִּשָּׂאוּם BHKK 1 בָּנוֹת וַיִּשָּׂאוּם בני קיש אֲחֵיהֶם

B. THE NUMBER

§ 82. Just as indefinite as Biblical Hebrew is with regard to the use of the gender of a substantive, so it is also concerning the application of the number with substantives and verbs alike.

a. The number of the verb

1) The predicate preceding.

a. One subject (cf. p. 271, § 49α)

2 Sam. 10.15:	וַיַּרְא אֲרָם		
1 Ki. 20.20:	וַיָּנֻס BHKK 1... וַיָּנֻס		
1 Ki. 12.16:	וַיֵּלֶךְ יִשְׂרָאֵל	Ex. 14.25:	וַיֹּאמֶר מִצְרַיִם
1 Ki. 12.19:	וַיִּפְשְׁעוּ יִשְׂרָאֵל	Ex. 14.10:	וַיִּרְדְּפוּ מִצְרַיִם
Gen. 44.13:	וַיַּעֲמֹס אִישׁ	Ex. 14.23:	מִצְרַיִם נֹסֵעַ
Gen. 44.11:	וַיּוֹרִדוּ אִישׁ	Ex. 14.27:	וּמִצְרַיִם נָסִים
1 Sam. 14.45:	וַיֹּאמֶר הָעָם	1 Sam. 13.16:	וְהָעָם הַנִּמְצָא עמם
Judg. 9.36:	וַיֹּאמְרוּ הָעָם	1 Sam. 13.15:	הָעָם הַנִּמְצָאִים עמו
1 Sam. 14.40:	הנה עם יוֹרֵד	Obad. 18:	וְהָיָה בֵית יַעֲקֹב
Judg. 9.37:	הנה עם יוֹרְדִים	Obad. 17:	וְיָרְשׁוּ בֵית יַעֲקֹב
Josh. 6.20:	וַיָּרַע הָעָם · · · וַיָּרִיעוּ הָעָם	Num. 31.31:	וַיַּעַשׂ משה ואלעזר הכהן
Lev. 9.24:	וַיַּרְא כל הָעָם וַיָּרֹנּוּ	Num. 31.13:	וַיֵּצְאוּ משה ואלעזר הכהן

b. Two subjects (cf. p. 271, § 49)

Ex. 4.29:	וַיֵּלֶךְ משה ואהרן	Ex. 29.19:	וְסָמַךְ אהרן ובניו
Ex. 5.1:	בָּאוּ משה ואהרן	Ex. 29.15:	וְסָמְכוּ אהרן ובניו
Judg. 8.2:	וַיֹּאמֶר זבח וצלמנע	Judg. 14.3:	וַיֹּאמֶר לו אביו ואמו
Judg. 8.12:	וַיָּנֻסוּ זבח וצלמנע	Deut. 21.19:	וְתָפְשׂוּ בו אביו ואמו

2)   The predicate following, with two subjects preceding:

1 Sam. 18.16:   וכל ישראל ויהודה אֹהֵב

1 Ki. 4.20:   יהודה וישראל רַבִּים

Num. 11.22:   הצאן ובקר יִשָּׁחֵט   Ex. 9.31:   והפשתה והשערה נֻכָּתָה

Ex. 34.3:   הצאן והבקר אל יִרְעוּ   Ex. 9.32:   והחטה והכסמת לֹא נֻכּוּ

3)   The subject is a collective noun.

Jer. 31.7:   קָהָל גָּדוֹל   Deut. 23.9:   דּוֹר שְׁלִישִׁי יָבֹא

Num. 22.4:   יְלַחֲכוּ הַקָּהָל   Gen. 15.16:   וְדוֹר רְבִיעִי יָשׁוּבוּ

BHKK unnecessarily "corrects":

Obad. 6:   נֶחְפַּשׂ   BHKK 1 נֶחְפְּשׂוּ עשׂו

4)   Both numbers are used in connection with one substantive in one
and the same phrase:

עם :   2 Sam. 13.34:   עַם רַב הֹלְכִים
       1 Ki. 18.37:   וְיֵדְעוּ הָעָם הַזֶּה
       Isa. 65.2:   עַם סוֹרֵר הַהֹלְכִים
       Jer. 13.10:   הָעָם הַזֶּה הָרָע הַמֵּאֲנִים
       Hag. 1.2:   הָעָם הַזֶּה אָמְרוּ

עדה :   Num. 14.35:   הָעֵדָה הָרָעָה הַזֹּאת הַנּוֹעָדִים

קהל :   1 Sam. 17.47:   וְיֵדְעוּ כל הַקָּהָל הַזֶּה

דור :   Gen. 15.16:   וְדוֹר רְבִיעִי יָשׁוּבוּ

b.   The number of the substantive (cf. p. 269, § 48)

§ 83.   The examples, which I list here, reflect almost every degree of
possible mix-up in the use of the number, and in a variety of phrases. We
shall see phrases of one substantive only, and others of a small and even
large group of substantives. They all have one feature in common: No
matter whether they are all used in the singular or plural, or some of them
in one number and the rest of the phrase in the other, this change of the
number cannot be explained as affecting a corresponding change in their
respective meaning. Whether they are meant to indicate one single item
or a plurality of items of the thing, which the respective word denotes,
can be established solely by consulting their context; for they are not
detached grammatical forms, but part of a coherent narrative or poetic

portion; and it is the meaning of the entire context which determines the exact implication of the various parts of each phrase. I begin with abstract nouns; they cannot be translated with a corresponding English plural form and are, therefore, best suited to prove the point to the way of thinking, to which we are used.

1) Isa. 4.5:   אֵשׁ לֶהָבָה   Prov. 6.19:   עֵד שָׁקֶר

     Ps. 105.32:   אֵשׁ לֶהָבוֹת   Prov. 19.9:   עֵד שְׁקָרִים

     Ps. 140.12:   אִישׁ חָמָס   Prov. 19.22:   מֵאִישׁ כָּזָב

     Ps. 140.5:   מֵאִישׁ חֲמָסִים   Prov. 21.18:   עֵד כְּזָבִים

     Prov. 17.27:   אִישׁ תְּבוּנָה   Ps. 106.3:   עֹשֵׂה צְדָקָה

     Prov. 11.12:   וְאִישׁ תְּבוּנוֹת   Ps. 103.6:   עֹשֵׂה צְדָקוֹת

     Prov. 14.25:   עֵד אֱמֶת)
     Prov. 14.5:   עֵד אֱמוּנִים)   cf. Jer. 42.5:   לְעֵד אֱמֶת וְנֶאֱמָן

     Jer. 6.20:   מֵאֶרֶץ מֶרְחָק

     Jer. 8.19:   מֵאֶרֶץ מַרְחַקִּים

     2 Chron. 14.5:   עָרֵי מְצוּרָה

     2 Chron. 11.10:   עָרֵי מְצֻרוֹת

     1 Ki. 15.30:   בְּכַעְסוֹ אשר הכעיס

     2 Ki. 23.26:   על כל הכעסים אשר הכעיסו

     Num. 6.6:   על נפש מת לא יבא

     Lev. 21.11:   ועל כל נפשת מת לא יבא

     Ps. 14.7:   מי יתן מציון ישועת ישראל

     Ps. 53.7:   מי יתן מציון ישעות ישראל

     2 Chron. 24.23:   לתקופת השנה

     1 Sam. 1.20:   לתקפות הימים

     Neh. 10.1:   ועל החתום

     Neh. 10.2:   ועל החתומים

     1 Chron. 22.9:   אִישׁ מְנוּחָה

     Ps. 23.2:   מֵי מְנֻחוֹת

2) 1 Ki. 10.2:   וְאֶבֶן יְקָרָה

     1 Ki. 7.11:   אֲבָנִים יְקָרוֹת

     Josh. 7.25:   וַיִּסְקְלוּ אֹתוֹ ··· אֶבֶן   cf. following: וַיִּסְקְלוּ אֹתָם בָּאֲבָנִים

     Deut. 21.21:   בָּאֲבָנִים ··· ירגמהו

Ps. 85.6:   הַלְעוֹלָם תֶּאֱנַף בָּנוּ

Ps. 77.8:   הַלְעוֹלָמִים יִזְנַח אֲדֹנָי

Joel 1.11:   עַל חִטָּה וְעַל שְׂעֹרָה

2 Sam. 17.28:   וְחִטִּים וּשְׂעֹרִים

Ex. 15.25:   שָׂם שָׂם לוֹ חֹק וּמִשְׁפָּט

Deut. 4.5:   לִמַּדְתִּי אֶתְכֶם חֻקִּים וּמִשְׁפָּטִים

3) 1 Chron. 22.8:   דָּם לָרֹב שָׁפַכְתָּ · · · דָּמִים רַבִּים שָׁפַכְתָּ

Deut. 17.16:   לֹא יַרְבֶּה לּוֹ סוּסִים · · · לְמַעַן הַרְבּוֹת סוּס

1 Ki. 10.10:   וּבְשָׂמִים הַרְבֵּה · · · כַּבֹּשֶׂם הַהוּא

Gen. 30.37:   מַקַּל לִבְנֶה לַח וְלוּז וְעַרְמוֹן · · · הַמַּקְלוֹת

Ex. 9.31:   וְהַפִּשְׁתָּה

Jer. 13.1:   פִּשְׁתִּים

4) Gen. 47.29:   וְעָשִׂיתָ עִמָּדִי חֶסֶד וֶאֱמֶת

Gen. 32.11:   מִכֹּל הַחֲסָדִים וּמִכָּל הָאֱמֶת אֲשֶׁר עָשִׂיתָ

Gen. 17.27:   יְלִיד בֵּיתוֹ וּמִקְנַת כֶּסֶף

Gen. 17.23:   יְלִידֵי בֵיתוֹ · · · מִקְנַת כַּסְפּוֹ

5) Josh. 22.29:   לְעֹלָה לְמִנְחָה וּלְזָבַח

Gen. 7.21:   בָּעוֹף וּבַבְּהֵמָה וּבַחַיָּה וּבְכָל הַשֶּׁרֶץ

Gen. 7.23:   מֵאָדָם עַד בְּהֵמָה עַד רֶמֶשׂ וְעַד עוֹף

Hag. 2.19:   הַגֶּפֶן וְהַתְּאֵנָה וְהָרִמּוֹן וְעֵץ הַזַּיִת

Zech. 14.15:   הַסּוּס הַפֶּרֶד הַגָּמָל וְהַחֲמוֹר וְכָל הַבְּהֵמָה

6) Gen. 32.6:   וַיְהִי לִי שׁוֹר וַחֲמוֹר צֹאן וְעֶבֶד וְשִׁפְחָה

Gen. 12.16:   וַיְהִי לוֹ צֹאן וּבָקָר וַחֲמֹרִים וַעֲבָדִים וּשְׁפָחֹת

2 Ki. 3.25:   וְכָל חֶלְקָה · · · וְכָל מַעְיַן מַיִם · · · וְכָל עֵץ

2 Ki. 3.19:   וְכָל עֵץ · · · וְכָל מַעְיְנֵי מַיִם · · · וְכָל הַחֶלְקָה

Deut. 4.17, 18:   צִפּוֹר · · · · רֶמֶשׂ · · · דָּגָה

1 Ki. 5.13:   וְעַל הָעוֹף וְעַל הָרֶמֶשׂ וְעַל הַדָּגִים

Ps. 150.4:   (הַלְלוּהוּ) בְּתֹף וּמָחוֹל

Ex. 15.20:   בְּתֻפִּים וּבִמְחֹלֹת

2 Ki. 6.15:   חַיִל · · · וְסוּס וָרֶכֶב

2 Ki. 6.14:   סוּסִים וָרֶכֶב וְחַיִל

7) Lev. 20.27:   אוֹב אוֹ יִדְּעֹנִי (sing.)

Deut. 18.11:   אוֹב וְיִדְּעֹנִי (plur.)

2 Ki. 21.6:   אוֹב וְיִדְּעֹנִים

1 Sam. 28.9:   אֶת הָאֹבוֹת וְאֶת הַיִּדְּעֹנִים

2 Ki. 23.24:   אֶת הָאֹבוֹת וְאֶת הַיִּדְּעֹנִי

2 Sam. 6.18:   מֵהַעֲלוֹת הָעוֹלָה וְהַשְּׁלָמִים

2 Sam. 24.25:   וַיַּעַל עֹלוֹת וּשְׁלָמִים

Ezek. 26.7:   בְּסוּס וּבְרֶכֶב וּבְפָרָשִׁים

Ezek. 27.14:   סוּסִים וּפָרָשִׁים

8) 1 Ki. 5.3:   לבד מֵאַיָּל וּצְבִי וְיַחְמוּר וּבַרְבֻּרִים

Zeph. 1.3:   אָדָם וּבְהֵמָה · · · עוֹף הַשָּׁמַיִם וּדְגֵי הַיָּם

Jer. 51.21-23:   סוּס וְרֹכְבוֹ · · · : · · · אִישׁ וְאִשָּׁה · · · זָקֵן וָנָעַר · · · בָּחוּר וּבְתוּלָה · · ·

· · · רֹעֶה וְעֶדְרוֹ · · · אִכָּר וְצִמְדּוֹ · · · פַּחוֹת וּסְגָנִים

Gen. 9.2:   חַיַּת הָאָרֶץ · · · עוֹף הַשָּׁמַיִם · · · דְּגֵי הַיָּם

9) Gen. 11.1:   שָׂפָה אַחַת וּדְבָרִים אֲחָדִים

Ezek. 14.8:   לְאָתוֹת וּלְמוֹפְתִים cf. Isa. 8.18:   וַהֲשִׁמֹּתִיהוּ לְאוֹת וְלִמְשָׁלִים

Jer. 51.26:   אֶבֶן לְפִנָּה וְאֶבֶן לְמוֹסָדוֹת

1 Ki. 5.8:   וְהַשְּׂעֹרִים וְהַתֶּבֶן

1 Ki. 6.7:   וּמַקָּבוֹת וְהַגַּרְזֶן

Hab. 3.17:   גָּזַר מִמִּכְלָה צֹאן וְאֵין בָּקָר בָּרְפָתִים

2 Ki. 12.17:   כֶּסֶף אָשָׁם וְכֶסֶף חַטָּאוֹת

10) Deut. 12.18:   אַתָּה וּבִנְךָ וּבִתֶּךָ וְעַבְדְּךָ וַאֲמָתֶךָ

Deut. 12.12:   אַתֶּם וּבְנֵיכֶם וּבְנֹתֵיכֶם וְעַבְדֵיכֶם וְאַמְהֹתֵיכֶם

§ 84.   BHKK "corrects" the number of substantives:

Num. 28.2:   אֶת קָרְבָּנִי לַחְמִי לְאִשַּׁי   BHKK 1 prb.   לַחְמִי

Deut. 5.5:   לְהַגִּיד לָכֶם אֵת דְּבַר יהוה   BHKK . . .   דְּבָרֵי

Judg. 2.22:   הֲשֹׁמְרִים הֵם אֶת דֶּרֶךְ יהוה   BHKK 1   דַּרְכֵי

1 Sam. 14.45:   אִם יִפֹּל מִשַּׂעֲרַת רֹאשׁוֹ אַרְצָה   ?1 BHKK   מִשַּׂעֲרַת

1 Ki. 5.12:   וַיְהִי שִׁירוֹ חֲמִשָּׁה וָאָלֶף   BHKK prps.   וַיִּהְיוּ שִׁירָיו

1 Ki. 10.22:   אֳנִי תַרְשִׁישׁ לַמֶּלֶךְ בַּיָּם   BHKK prps.   אֳנִיּוֹת

Isa. 10.19:   וּשְׁאָר עֵץ יַעְרוֹ   BHKK 1   עֲצֵי

Isa. 16.4:   תַּמּוּ רֹמֵס מִן הָאָרֶץ   BHKK 1   רֹמְסִים

Jer. 12.16:   אִם לָמֹד יִלְמְדוּ אֶת דַּרְכֵי עַמִּי   . . .1 BHKK   דֶּרֶךְ

Ezek. 8.12:   זִקְנֵי בֵית יִשְׂרָאֵל עֹשִׂים · · · · אִישׁ בְּחַדְרֵי מַשְׂכִּיתוֹ   . . .1BHKK   בַּחֲדַר

Ezek. 16.38:   וּשְׁפַטְתִּיךְ מִשְׁפְּטֵי נֹאֲפוֹת   . . .1 BHKK   מִשְׁפַּט

Hos. 10.5:   לְעֶגְלוֹת בֵּית אָוֶן יָגוּרוּ שְׁכַן שֹׁמְרוֹן · · · ·   BHKK 1   לְעֵגֶל

Am. 8.11: ‏דְּבַר‎ ··· BHKK 1 ‏לשמע את דִּבְרֵי יהוה‎

Mic. 1.14: ‏לְמֶלֶךְ‎ prps. BHKK ‏בתי אכזיב לאכזב לְמַלְכֵי ישראל‎

§ 85. The Bible abounds in instances, where the verb and the substantive, which belongs to it, do not agree with one another concerning
their number. Now it does not matter, whether we term this substantive
a subject or, as I suggested (cf. § 67 Ib) an apposition. To our way of
thinking, they must be of the same number. This not being the case, as
I am going to show, we have herein additional evidence for the difference
between our Western way of thinking and that of the Bible (cf. p. 600,
§ 60 f., and here § 93).

1) The subject precedes the verb (cf. p. 269, § 47b).

Gen. 27.39: ‏מִשְׁמַנֵּי הארץ יִהְיֶה מושבך‎

Gen. 35.11: ‏גּוֹי וּקְהַל גּוֹיִם יִהְיֶה ממך‎

Ex. 9.31: ‏וְהַפִּשְׁתָּה וְהַשְּׂעֹרָה נֻכָּתָה‎; but v. 32: ‏וְהַחִטָּה וְהַכֻּסֶּמֶת לא נֻכּוּ‎

Num. 19.20: ‏וַיֵּצְאוּ מַיִם רַבִּים‎; cf. 20.11: ‏מֵי נדה לא זֹרַק עליו‎

Lev. 25.31: ‏וּבָתֵּי החצרים‎ ··· ‏יֵחָשֵׁב‎

Num. 18.13: ‏בִּכּוּרֵי כל אשר‎ ··· ‏לך יִהְיֶה‎

2 Sam. 20.10: ‏וְיוֹאָב וַאֲבִישַׁי אחיו רָדַף‎

1 Ki. 5.17: ‏מפני הַמִּלְחָמָה אשר סְבָבֻהוּ‎

Jer. 51.58: ‏חֹמוֹת בבל הָרְחָבָה‎

2) The verb precedes the subject (cf. p. 269, § 47a).

Gen. 10.25: ‏ולעבר יֻלַּד שְׁנֵי בָנִים‎

Ex. 7.25: ‏וַיִּמָּלֵא שִׁבְעַת יָמִים‎

Ex. 20.3: ‏לא יִהְיֶה לך אֱלֹהִים אֲחֵרִים‎; idem Deut. 5.7

Num. 35.5: ‏זֶה יִהְיֶה להם מִגְרְשֵׁי הערים‎

Josh. 11.22: ‏לא נוֹתַר עֲנָקִים‎

Judg. 8.2: ‏הֲלֹא טוֹב עֹלְלוֹת אפרים‎

Isa. 17.6: ‏וְנִשְׁאַר בו עֹלֵלֹת‎

Jer. 36.32: ‏ועוד וֹוסַף עליהם דְּבָרִים‎

Prov. 4.4: ‏יִתְמָךְ דְּבָרַי לבך‎

Num. 20.2: ‏וַיֵּצְאוּ מַיִם רַבִּים‎; cf. v. 11: ‏ולא הָיָה מַיִם‎

1 Chron. 26.6: ‏ולשמעיה בנו נוֹלַד בָּנִים‎

1 Chron. 26.31: ‏וַיִּמָּצֵא בהם גִּבּוֹרֵי חיל‎

§ 86.   BHKK "corrects" such cases.

1)   The subject precedes the verb.

a.   The verb is "corrected"

Gen. 35.26:   יֻלְּדוּ ...1 BHKK   בְּנֵי יעקב אשר יֻלַּד לו

Gen. 46.22:   יֻלְּדָה ...1 BHKK   בְּנֵי רחל אשר יֻלַּד ליעקב

Num. 30.6:   יָקוּמוּ ...1 BHKK   כל נְדָרֶיהָ וֶאֱסָרֶיהָ · · · לא יָקוּם

Deut. 30.10:   הַכְּתוּבוֹת frt. 1 BHKK   מִצְוֹתָיו וְחֻקֹּתָיו הַכְּתוּבָה

Judg. 5.26:   תִּשְׁלַחְנָה prps..., תִּשְׁלַח ,...1 BHKK   יָדָהּ ליתד תִּשְׁלַחְנָה

Isa. 40.15:   יִטּוֹלוּ 1 BHKK   הן איים כדק יִטּוֹל

Jer. 31.15:   אֵינָם ...?1 BHKK   להנחם על בָּנֶיהָ כי אֵינֶנּוּ

Jer. 48.41:   נִתְפָּשׂוּ ...1 BHKK   וְהַמְּצָדוֹת נִתְפָּשָׂה

Ezek. 18.30:   יִהְיוּ prb. 1 BHKK   מכל פִּשְׁעֵיכֶם ולא יִהְיֶה לכם

Ezek. 26.11:   יוֹרִידוּ ...1 BHKK   וּמַצְּבוֹת עזך · · · תֵּרֵד

Ezek. 40.21:   הָיוּ prb. 1 BHKK   וְאֵילָו וְאֵלַמָּו הָיָה

Hos. 8.4:   יִכָּרֵתוּ ...BHKK   עָשׂוּ להם עֲצַבִּים למען יִכָּרֵת

Hos. 10.14:   יוּשַׁדּוּ prps. BHKK   וכל מִבְצָרֶיךָ יוּשַׁד

Zech. 11.5:   יֹאמְרוּ 1 BHKK   וּמֹכְרֵיהֶן יֹאמַר

Zech. 11.5:   יַחְמְלוּ 1 BHKK   וְרֹעֵיהֶם לא יַחְמוֹל

Ps. 58.9:   חָזוּ prps. BHKK   נֵפֶל אשת בל חָזוּ שמש

Prov. 3.18:   מְאֻשָּׁרִים 1 BHKK   וְתֹמְכֶיהָ מְאֻשָּׁר

Prov. 18.21:   יֹאכְלוּ ...1 BHKK   וְאֹהֲבֶיהָ יֹאכַל פריה

b.   The subject is "corrected"

Isa. 59.10:   וְחַטָּאתֵנוּ עָנְתָה 1 BHKK   וְחַטֹּאותֵינוּ עָנְתָה

Ezek. 22.13:   דָּמֵיךְ 1 BHKK   ועל דָּמֵךְ אשר הָיוּ בתוכֵך

Joel 1.20:   בֶּהֱמַת 1 BHKK   בַּהֲמוֹת שדה תַּעֲרוֹג

Zech. 6.14:   הָעֲטֶרֶת 1 BHKK · · ·   וְהָעֲטָרֹת תִּהְיֶה

c.   BHKK "corrects" the pronomen suffixum

2 Ki. 3.3:   בְּחַטֹּאות ירבעם · · · דבק לא סר מִמֶּנָּה BHKK 1... sing. (cf. מִמֶּנָּה)

2 Ki. 13.2:   וילך אחר חַטֹּאת ירבעם · · · לא סר מִמֶּנָּה BHKK 1 חַטַּאת, cf. מִמֶּנָּה

2 Ki. 13.6:   אך לא סרו מֵחַטֹּאות בית ירבעם · · · בָּהּ הלך BHKK 1... בָּהּ, cf. מֵחַטַּאת

2 Ki. 13.11: חַטֵּאת ‎ ...1 BHKK‏ לא סר מכל חטאות ירבעם ··· בָּהּ הלך
(cf. בָּהּ)

2 Ki. 17.22: ‎...1 BHKK‏ וילכו ··· בכל חטאות ירבעם ··· לא סרו מִמֶּנָּה
חַטַּאת (cf. ממנה)

2) The verb precedes the subject.

a. The verb is "corrected"

Gen. 5.23: ‎...1 BHKK‏ וַיְהִי כל יְמֵי חנוך
Ex. 1.10: (תִּקְרֶנוּ pro) תִּקְרֶאנָּה ‎...1 BHKK‏ כִּי תִקְרֶאנָה מִלְחָמָה
Josh. 17.9: וְהָיָה ‎...prb 1 BHKK‏ וַיְהִי תֹצְאֹתָיו
Judg. 8.6: ‎...1 BHKK‏ וַיֹּאמֶר שָׂרֵי סכות
2 Ki. 7.11: plur. ...1 (on ויקרא) BHKK‏ וַיִּקְרָא הַשֹּׁעֲרִים
Isa. 44.18: ‎1 BHKK‏ כי טַח מראות עֵינֵיהֶם
Jer. 49.36: ‎...1 BHKK‏ לא יָבוֹא שם נִדְחֵי עילם
Jer. 51.48: ‎...1 BHKK‏ כי מִצָּפוֹן יָבוֹא לה הַשּׁוֹדְדִים
Ezek. 14.1: ‎...1 BHKK‏ וַיָּבוֹא אלי אֲנָשִׁים-
Obad. 6: ‎1 BHKK‏ איך נֶחְפְּשׂוּ עֵשָׂו ···
Ps. 57.2: ‎1? BHKK‏ עד יַעֲבֹר הַוֹּת
Ps. 124.5: הֲמוֹן הַזֵּדִים ‎prps BHKK‏ עָבַר על נפשנו הַמַּיִם הַזֵּידוֹנִים
Job 42.15: ‎...1 BHKK‏ ולא נמצא נָשִׁים יָפוֹת
1 Chron. 24.28: ‎...1 BHKK‏ ולא הָיָה לו בָּנִים

b. The subject is "corrected"

Lev. 19.23: עָרֵל ‎frt 1 BHKK‏ יִהְיֶה לכם עֲרֵלִים
Ezek. 26.2: דֶּלֶת ‎prb 1 BHKK‏ נִשְׁבְּרָה דַּלְתוֹת העמים
Mic. 1.9: מַכָּתָהּ ‎1 BHKK‏ אֲנוּשָׁה מַכּוֹתֶיהָ
Hag. 2.7: חֲמָדוֹת ‎1 BHKK‏ וּבָאוּ חֶמְדַּת כל הגוים

c. BHKK leaves the reader the choice (cf. § 53)

Isa. 28.3: תֵּרָמֵס ‎1 BHKK‏ vel תֵּרָמַסְנָה עֲטֶרֶת גֵּאוּת

d. BHKK itself commits a grammatical error (cf. § 80)

Num. 17.25: (וַתְּכַלֶּינָה :not) וְתֵכַל ‎prb 1 BHKK‏ וּתְכַל תְּלוּנֹתָם

§ 87. The subject is used as being of both numbers (sing. *and* plur.) in one and the same phrase:

Gen. 15.16:   וְדוֹר רְבִיעִי יָשׁוּבוּ

Ex. 16.4:   וְיָצָא הָעָם וְלָקְטוּ

Ex. 22.24:   תַּלְוֶה · · · תִּהְיֶה · · · תְשִׂימוּן

Josh. 24.19:   כִּי אֱלֹהִים קְדֹשִׁים הוּא

2 Sam. 1.4:   הַרְבֵּה נָפַל מִן הָעָם וַיָּמֻתוּ

Isa. 9.8:   וְיָדְעוּ הָעָם כֻּלּוֹ

Isa. 9.12:   והעם לא שָׁב · · · לא דָרָשׁוּ

Isa. 14.1:   וְנִלְוָה הַגֵּר עֲלֵיהֶם וְנִסְפְּחוּ

Isa. 54.3:   וְזַרְעֵךְ · · · יִירָשׁ · · · יוֹשִׁיבוּ

Jer. 41.2:   וַיַּכּוּ אֶת גדליהו · · · וַיָּמֶת אֹתוֹ

Hos. 9.3:   וְשָׁב אפרים · · · טמא יֹאכֵלוּ

Hos. 9.16:   הֻכָּה אפרים שָׁרְשָׁם יָבֵשׁ

Hos. 10.1:   כְּטוֹב לְאַרְצוֹ הֵיטִיבוּ מצבות ;but preceding: · · · כֶּרֶב לְפִרְיוֹ הִרְבָּה

Hos. 10.9:   חָטָאתָ ישראל שָׁם עָמָדוּ

Hos. 10.13:   חֲרַשְׁתֶּם · · · קְצַרְתֶּם אֲכַלְתֶּם · · · בָּטַחְתָּ בְדַרְכְּךָ

Hos. 12.2:   אפרים רֹעֶה רוּחַ וְרֹדֵף קָדִים · · · יִכְרֹתוּ

Joel 2.4:   כְּמַרְאֵה סוּסִים מַרְאֵהוּ · · · יְרוּצוּן

Mic. 5.5:   וְרָעוּ אֶת אֶרֶץ אַשּׁוּר · · · וְהִצִּיל מֵאַשּׁוּר

Zech. 13.9:   וּצְרַפְתִּים · · · וּבְחַנְתִּים · · · הוּא יִקְרָא

Judg. 20.25:   כל אֵלֶּה שֹׁלְפֵי חרב

Judg. 20.35:   כל אֵלֶּה שֹׁלֵךְ חרב

Num. 10.28:   אֵלֶּה מַסְעֵי בני ישראל

Num. 4.15:   אֵלֶּה מַשָּׂא בני קהת

Lev. 11.11:   וכל אשר אין לו סנפיר וקשקשת · · · שקץ הֵם לכם

Lev. 11.12:   כל אשר אין לו סנפיר וקשקשת · · · שקץ הוּא לכם

1 Chron. 29.4:   { שלשת אלפים כִּכְּרֵי זהב · · ·
          { ושבעת אלפים כִּכַּר כסף

Ex. 30.14:   כל הָעֹבֵר עַל הפקדים · · · יִתֵּן

Ex. 30.13:   זֶה יִתְּנוּ כל הָעֹבֵר עַל הפקדים

§ 88.   BHKK "corrects" such cases.

2 Ki. 12.17:   כֶּסֶף אָשָׁם · · · לא יוּבָא · · · לַכֹּהֲנִים יִהְיוּ ....prb 1 BHKK יִהְיֶה

1 Sam. 13.6:   וְאִישׁ יִשְׂרָאֵל רָאוּ כִּי צַר לוֹ   BHKK 1 רָאָה

Ex. 20.18:   וכל הָעָם רֹאִים · · · וַיַּרְא הָעָם   ...1 BHKK וַיִּרְאוּ

Josh. 5.4:   הָעָם הַיֹּצֵא ממצרים הַזְּכָרִים   frt. 1 BHKK הַיֹּצְאִים

I Sam. 13.6: כִּי נִגַּשׂ הָעָם וַיִּתְחַבְּאוּ הָעָם   BHKK dl הָעָם (1°)

Isa. 2.8: יִשְׁתַּחֲוֶה   למעשה יָדָיו יִשְׁתַּחֲווּ   BHKK 1 frt.

Jer. 16.6: יָקְרֵחַ··· יִתְגֹּדֵד··· יִסָּפְדוּ   BHKK G··· יִתְגֹּדְדוּ; Vrs. יָקְרְחוּ

Jer. 22.4: הֵמָּה   מְלָכִים יֹשְׁבִים··· רֹכְבִים··· הוּא וַעֲבָדָיו וְעַמּוֹ   BHKK GV;
וְעַמָּם; GV וְעַבְדֵיהֶם G

Hos. 11.4: וָאֹט אֲכָלְם··· וָאֶהְיֶה לָהֶם··· וָאֹט אֵלָיו   BHKK 1 frt.

Hos. 41.1: הָרִיוֹתָם··· עֲלֵיהֶם··· שֹׁמְרוֹן··· וְהָרִיוֹתָיו   BHKK 1 frt.

Hab. 2.6: וַיֹּאמַר··· מָשָׁל יִשָּׂאוּ   BHKK (on וַיֹּאמַר) add.

Ps. 104.12: יִשְׁכֹּנוּ   עוֹף הַשָּׁמַיִם יִשְׁכּוֹן··· יִתְּנוּ קוֹל   BHKK frt. 1

Ps. 107.43: וְיִתְבּוֹנֵן   מִי חָכָם וְיִשְׁמָר אֵלֶּה וְיִתְבּוֹנְנוּ   BHKK 1...

§ 89. The *pronomen suffixum* referring to one and the same substantive is being used in both numbers in the indentical phrase:

Ex. 20.25: אֲבָנִים··· אֶתְהֶן··· עָלֶיהָ וַתְּחַלְלֶהָ

Ex. 23.31: גְּבֻלְךָ··· בְּיֶדְכֶם··· וְגֵרַשְׁתָּמוֹ

Ex. 28.3: חַכְמֵי לֵב··· מִלֵּאתִיו

I Ki. 18.18: בַּעֲזָבְכֶם··· וַתֵּלֶךְ

Isa. 59.8: נְתִיבוֹתֵיהֶם··· כֹּל דֹּרֵךְ בָּהּ

Jer. 33.9: אנכי עשה אוֹתָם··· אנכי עשה לָהּ

BHKK "corrects" such cases:

Isa. 56.5: לָמוֹ   1...(on לוֹ) BHKK··· וְנָתַתִּי לָהֶם··· אתן לו

Jer. 16.7: אוֹתוֹ   1... BHKK··· לְנַחֲמוֹ··· ולא ישקו אותם··· על אָבִיו

Mic. 2.9: עוֹלְלֵיהֶן··· תַּעֲנֻגֶיהָ··· עֲלֶיהָ   BHKK 1 תַּעֲנֻגֵיהֶן et נְשֵׁי עמי··· תַּעֲנֻגֶיהָ

Ps. 62.5: בְּפִימוֹ   1... BHKK··· בְּפִיו יְבָרֵכוּ

D. Miscellaneous Problems

A. Verbal Forms

§ 90. The phenomena, which I am going to discuss in the following paragraphs, icnlude such aspects of the Hebrew language, which do not recur very frequently. Consequently, the material, which I was able to collect, is comparatively more limited than has hitherto been the case. For practical considerations I shall, therefore, discontinue dividing the material into "rule" and "correction" by BHKK, but arrange all the instances that came to my knowledge under one and the same heading. All quotations from BHKK are to be understood as "corrections."

§ 91.   The *pronomen suffixum* to verbal forms does not necessarily imply an object in the accusative; BHKK's "corrections" are motivated by this erroneous assumption.

Gen. 37.4:   ולא יכלו דַּבְּרוֹ לשלם   BHKK 1 ... (לְ)דַבֵּר לוֹ

Num. 11.23:   הֲיִקְרְךָ דברי אם לא   BHKK prps. הֲיָקוּם

1 Sam. 2.25:   אם יחטא איש לאיש וּפִלְלוֹ אלהים   BHKK 1 וּפִלֵּל לוֹ

Isa. 22.3:   כל נִמְצָאַיִךְ אסרו יחדו   BHKK 1 prb. כל אַמִּיצַיִךְ

Isa. 28.15:   שוט שוטף כי יעבר לא יְבוֹאֵנוּ

Jer. 9.1:   מי יִתְּנֵנִי במדבר מלון ארחים

Jer. 10.20:   בני יְצָאֻנִי ואינם   BHKK 1 prb. . . . . בני   וְצֹאנִי et dl

Jer. 20.7:   פתיתני · · · · ואפת חֲזַקְתַּנִי ותוכל

Zech. 7.5:   הצום צַמְתֻּנִי אני

Ps. 5.5:   לא יְגֻרְךָ רע

Ps. 13.5:   פן יאמר איבי יְכָלְתִּיו   BHKK frt. 1 יָכֹלְתִּי לוֹ

Ps. 44.18:   כל זאת בָּאַתְנוּ

Ps. 85.5:   שׁוּבֵנוּ אלהי ישענו   BHKK prps. שׁוּב נָא

Prov. 2.19:   כל בָּאֶיהָ לא ישובון

Neh. 9.28:   וישובו וַיִּזְעָקוּךָ

§ 92.   The participle with the article may also carry a *pronomen suffixum.*

Deut. 8.14:   הַמּוֹצִיאֲךָ מארץ מצרים

Deut. 8.15:   הַמּוֹלִיכְךָ במדבר הגדל

Deut. 8.16:   הַמַּאֲכִלְךָ מן במדבר

Deut. 13.6:   וְהַפֹּדְךָ מבית עבדים

Deut. 20.1:   הַמַּעַלְךָ מארץ מצרים

2 Sam. 1.24:   הַמַּלְבִּשְׁכֶם שני

Isa. 9.12:   והעם לא שב עד הַמַּכֵּהוּ   BHKK 1 frt. . . . . הַמַּכֶּה (al. מַכֵּהוּ)

Isa. 63.11:   איה הַמַּעֲלֵם מים   BHKK 1 prb. . . . . הַמַּעֲלֶה

§ 93.   Hebrew has an active and a passive participle. However, in applying the one or the other, the Bible followed its own way of thinking, which differs from ours (cf. § 85).

   1)   The passive participle.

1 Ki. 12.6:   איך אתם נוֹעָצִים   "What counsel give ye me"

Isa. 60.11:   ומלכיהם נְהוּגִים   BHKK 1 נֹהֲגִים

Zech. 9.9: (צדיק) וְנוֹשָׁע הוּא "and victorious"

Ps. 37.22: וּמְקַלְלָיו 1 ;מְבָרְכָיו‏ BHKK 1...כי מְבֹרָכָיו···וּמְקֻלָּלָיו

Ps. 103.14: זָכוּר כי עפר אנחנו "He remembereth"

Ps. 112.7: בָּטֹחַ‏ BHKK G נכון לבו בָּטֻחַ ביהוה ?

Ps. 137.8: הַשָּׁדוּדָה‏ BHKK 1...בת בבל הַשְּׁדוּדָה

Job 35.9: עֲשׁוּקִים‏ BHKK 1...מרב עֲשׁוּקִים יזעיקו

Cant. 3.8: אֲחֻזֵי‏ BHKK prps.כלם אֲחֻזֵי חרב

2) The active participle:

1 Sam. 28.14: עֹטֶה מעיל "and he is covered"

Isa. 21.2: בָּגוּד‏ BHKK prps. et שָׁדוּד הבוגד בּוֹגֵד והשודד שׁוֹדֵד

Isa. 49.7: לִמְתָעֵב 1 ;לִבְזוּי‏ BHKK 1 לבזה נפש לְמְתָעֵב גוי

Obad. 21: נוֹשָׁעִים‏ BHKK 1 ועלו מוֹשִׁעִים בהר ציון

2 Chron. 3.13: פְּרֻשׂוֹת rectius פֹּרְשִׂים‏ BHKK 1 כנפי הכרובים···פֹּרְשִׂים

2 Chron. 18.34: מָעֳמָד‏ BHKK melius... ומלך ישראל היה מַעֲמִיד במרכבה

2 Chron. 32.31: הַמְשֻׁלָּחִים‏ BHKK 1...במליצי שרי בבל הַמְשַׁלְּחִים עליו לדרש

3) The following instances exhibit the same characteristics:

Num. 9.17: ולפי הֵעָלוֹת הענן

Num. 9.21: וְנַעֲלָה הענן ונסעו

Ezra 1.11: הַעֲלוֹת‏ BHKK prps. עם הֵעָלוֹת הגולה

§ 94. As a rule, the participle of *pi'el*-forms have a preformative מ.
I noted, however, these divergent formations:

Ex. 7.27: ואם מָאֵן אתה

Jer. 13.10: העם הזה הרע הַמֵּאֲנִים

Zeph. 1.14: וּמִמַּהֵר vel וּמְהַר‏ BHKK 1 קרוב וּמַהֵר מאד

Eccl. 4.2: וְשִׁבֵּחַ‏ BHKK 1 trt. וְשַׁבֵּחַ אני את המתים

These forms, and those listed in the paragraphs to follow, appear to be
exceptions to their respective grammatical rule. But it is wrong to force
them to comply with the rule by an otherwise unjustifiable emendation.
The future grammarian will be more methodical in his work, if he will
correct his views according to the text, and not *vice versa*.

B. PREFIXES

§ 95. The various meanings, which the prefix *waw* implies, have not
been fully recognized by the editors of BHKK.

1)   The prefix *waw* indicates conditional "if".

Judg. 6.11:   וְיֵשׁ יהוה עמנו ולמה מצאתנו כל זאת

2 Ki. 7.9:   וְחִכִּינוּ עד אור הבקר ומצאנו עוון

1 Sam. 25.31:   וְהֵיטִיב יהוה לאדני וזכרת את אמתך

Ezek. 33.5:   וְהוּא נזהר נפשו מלט   (BHKK 1 הַזְהִיר misunderstood the passage!)

Prov. 6.31:   וְנִמְצָא ישלם שבעתים

2)   The prefix *waw* indicates a question.

1 Sam. 20.9:   וְלֹא אתה אגיד לך   BHKK prps. הֲלֹא

Ezek. 15.5:   וְנַעֲשָׂה עוד למלאכה   BHKK... הֲיֵעָשֶׂה

Ezek. 17.15:   והפר ברית וְנִמְלָט   BHKK... הֲיִמָּלֵט

Ezek. 18.13:   ותרבית לקח וָחָי

Ezek. 18.24:   ככל התועבות · · · יעשה וָחָי

Ezek. 20.3:   וַאֲנִי אדרש לכם

Ezek. 33.25:   ודם תשפכו וְהָאָרֶץ תירשו

Prov. 30.3:   וְדַעַת קדשים אדע   BHKK 1 frt. הֲדַעַת

2 Ki. 19.11:   וְאַתָּה תנצל

3)   In this connection I also wish to list a few instances of questions without an introductory interrogative preposition (cf. p. 622, § 93 ff.), and which BHKK has "corrected" unnecessarily:

Gen. 3.1:   אַף כי אמר אלהים   BHKK 1? הַאַף

1 Sam. 14.30:   כי עתה לא רבתה מכה   BHKK 1 הֲלֹא

1 Sam. 30.8:   אֶרְדֹּף אחרי הגדוד   BHKK 1 prb. הַאֶרְדֹּף

Ezek. 11.13:   כָּלָה אתה עשה   BHKK 1 הֲכָלָה

Ezek. 17.9:   כה אמר אדני יהוה תִּצְלָח   BHKK 1... הֲתִצְלָח

Cant. 8.7:   בּוֹז יבוזו לו   BHKK prps. הֲבוֹז

C.   VOCALIZATION

§ 96.   Unusually vocalized nominal and verbal forms.

1) Gen. 9.2:   וּמוֹרַאֲכֶם

   Gen. 32.20:   בְּמִצְאֲכֶם BHKK pro בְּמָצְאֲכֶם

   Ex. 23.5:   שֹׂנַאֲךָ

   Lev. 18.24:   בְּטַמַּאֲכֶם

Num. 32.24:   לְצֹנַאֲכֶם   BHKK 1... לְצֹאנְכֶם (but cf. Ps. 8.8: צֹנֶה)

Isa. 43.1:   בֹּרַאֲךָ

Ezek. 28.13:   הִבָּרַאֲךָ

Deut. 1.12:   וּמַשַּׂאֲכֶם

2) (cf. § 7c)

I Sam. 15.4:   וַיְשַׁמַּע שאול את העם   BHKK 1

I Sam. 23.8:   וַיְשַׁמַּע שאול את כל העם   BHKK 1

Lev. 27.2:   איש כי יַפְלִא נדר   BHKK prps. יְפַלֵּא

Num. 6.2:   איש··· כי יַפְלִא לנדר נדר   BHKK prps. יְפַלֵּא

Mic. 6.14:   ולא תַפְלִיט ואשר תְּפַלֵּט   BHKK 1

Ex. 8.17:   כי אם אינך מְשַׁלֵּחַ את עמי הנני מַשְׁלִיחַ בך

Gen. 19.13:   כי מַשְׁחִתִים אנחנו··· וישלחנו יהוה לְשַׁחֲתָהּ

Ezek. 27.9:   מְחַזְּקֵי בדקך   BHKK 1

Ezek. 27.27:   מְחַזְּקֵי בדקך   BHKK 1

Isa. 41.13:   יהוה··· מַחֲזִיק יְמִינֶךָ

2 Ki. 15.19:   לְהַחֲזִיק הממלכה בידו

2 Sam. 2.15:   יַקְטְרוּן   BHKK

2 Sam. 2.16:   יַקְטִירוּן   BHKK 1 frt.

2 Sam. 2.28:   לְקַטֵּר   BHKK 1 לְהַקְטִיר

Hos. 2.15:   תְּקַטֵּר   BHKK 1 תַּקְטִיר

Num. 7.2:   וַיַּקְרִיבוּ נשיאי ישראל   BHKK prps. וַיַּקְרְבוּ (but cf. Gen. 12.11: הִקְרִיב)

3) Josh. 6.17:   הֶחְבֵּאַתָה   BHKK 1 הָחְבִּיאָה

2 Sam. 1.26:   נִפְלְאַתָה   BHKK 1 נִפְלְאָה

4) Ex. 20.5:   ולא תָעָבְדֵם

Deut. 5.9:   ולא תָעָבְדֵם   BHKK 1 prb. תַעַבְדֵם

Deut. 13.3:   וְנָעָבְדֵם   BHKK prb. 1 וְנַעַבְדֵם

5) Josh. 2.17:   הִשְׁבַּעְתָּנוּ   BHKK 1 frt. הִשְׁבַּעְתָּנוּ

Josh. 2.20:   הִשְׁבַּעְתָּנוּ   BHKK 1 frt. הִשְׁבַּעְתָּנוּ

Cant. 5.9:   הִשְׁבַּעְתָּנוּ   BHKK 1 הִשְׁבַּעְתָּנוּ

6) 2 Sam. 6.16:   וַתִּבֶז לו בלבה   BHKK 1 וַתָּבָז

Esth. 3.6:   וַיִּבֶז בעיניו   BHKK 1 וַיָּבָז

7) Gen. 8.10:   וַיָּ֫חֶל BHKK 1 וַיָּ֫חֶל
   Gen. 8.12:   וַיִּיָּ֫חֶל BHKK 1 וַיִּיָּ֫חֶל
   Judg. 3.25:   וַיָּחִ֫ילוּ BHKK 1 וַיָּחִ֫ילוּ

8) Gen. 16.11:   הנך הרה וְיֹלַדְתְּ BHKK 1 frt. וְיֹלַדְתְּ
   Judg. 13.5:   הנך הרה וְיֹלַדְתְּ BHKK 1 frt. וְיֹלַדְתְּ
   Judg. 13.7:   הנך הרה וְיֹלַדְתְּ BHKK 1 frt. וְיֹלַדְתְּ

9) Gen. 45.11:   (רוש a) תּוּרֵשׁ BHKK 1? פֶּן תִּוָּרֵשׁ
   Prov. 20.13:   פֶּן תִּוָּרֵשׁ
   Prov. 23.21:   וְזוֹלֵל יִוָּרֵשׁ
   Prov. 30.9:   וּפֶן אִוָּרֵשׁ

10) Esth. 3.8:   יֶשְׁנוֹ BHKK melius יֶשְׁנוֹ
   Deut. 29.14:   יֶשְׁנוֹ
   1 Sam. 14.39:   יֶשְׁנוֹ
   1 Sam. 23.23:   יֶשְׁנוֹ

11) 2 Ki. 1.2:   מֵחֳלִי זֶה BHKK 1...
   2 Ki. 8.8:   מֵחֳלִי זֶה BHKK 1...
   2 Ki. 8.9:   מֵחֳלִי זֶה BHKK 1...

12) Zech. 9.5:   הביש מִבְטָחָהּ BHKK prps. מִבְטָחָה (!)
   Isa. 20.5:   ובשו מכוש מַבָּטָם
   Isa. 20.6:   הנה כה מַבָּטֵנוּ

13) Jer. 44.21:   הַקֵּטֶר אשר קטרתם BHKK prps. הַקְּטֹרֶת
   Jer. 23.17:   דִּבֵּר יהוה שלום יהיה BHKK 1... דִּבֶּר
   Jer. 42.19:   דִּבֶּר יהוה עליכם BHKK prps. זֶה דָּבָר
   Jer. 5.13:   וְהַדִּבֵּר אין בהם
   Hos. 1.2:   תחלת דִּבֶּר יהוה בהושע

14) Josh. 5.5:   וכל העם הַיְלֹדִים במדבר BHKK prps. הַיְלָדִים
   2 Sam. 5.14:   ואלה שמות הַיְלֹדִים לו
   Jer. 16.3:   על הבנים ועל הבנות הַיִּלּוֹדִים

15) Josh. 18.4:   וְיָבֹאוּ אלי BHKK 1 frt. וְיָבֹאוּ
   Josh. 18.9:   וַיָּבֹאוּ אל יהושע BHKK 1 prb.... וַיָּבֹאוּ

16) 2 Sam. 19.32:   וַיַּעֲבֹר··· הירדן BHKK 1 וַיַּעֲבֹר
   2 Sam. 19.37:   יַעֲבָר··· את הירדן BHKK 1 יַעֲבֹר

Note the following cases of an insistence on the change of the *hiphʿil*-form into the corresponding *qal*.

17) Ezek. 12.5:   וְהוֹצֵאתָ   BHKK 1...
    Ezek. 12.6:   תֵצֵא   BHKK 1...
    Ezek. 12.7:   יָצָאתִי   (2°) BHKK 1... הוֹצֵאתִי
    Ezek. 12.12:   לָצֵאת   BHKK GS לְהוֹצִיא

18) Cant. 3.11:   צְאֶנָה   BHKK 1 (וּרְאֶינָה)
        (But Ex. 2.20: קְרֶאןָ BHKK not קְרֶאן,)
    Hos. 7.9:   זָרְקָה   BHKK 1 prb.
        (But Nah. 3.7: שָׁדְדָה BHKK not שָׁדְדָה)

19) Judg. 13.21:   לְהֵרָאֹה   BHKK 1? ולא יסף···לְהֵרָאֹת
    1 Sam. 3.21:   ויסף יהוה לְהֵרָאֹה

§ 97.   The following instances of an ־ (or its derivatives) being "corrected" in ־ will be understood in the light of the material, which I listed
on p. 224, A 5; p. 248 § 16 and p. 275, § 56.

 1) Deut. 28.48:   עד הִשְׁמִידוֹ אתך
    1 Ki. 15.29:   הַשְׁמִדוֹ   BHKK 1? עד הִשְׁמִדוֹ
    2 Ki. 10.17:   הִשְׁמִידוֹ   BHKK 1 prb. עד הִשְׁמִידוֹ
    Deut. 7.24:   עד הִשְׁמִדְךָ אתם
    Josh. 11.14:   הִשְׁמִדָם   BHKK 1 עד הִשְׁמִדָם אותם
    2 Ki. 24.20:   הִשְׁלִיכוֹ   BHKK 1 prb. עד הִשְׁלִיכוֹ אתם
    Jer. 52.3:   הִשְׁלִיכוֹ   BHKK= עד הִשְׁלִיכוֹ אותם
        Similarly: 2 Ki. 13.23: (ולא אבה הַשְׁחִיתָם) ולא הִשְׁלִיכָם
        וְלֹא אָבָה מעל פניו is infinitive with suffix, implying:
        השליכם

 2) Lev. 7.35:   ביום הַקְרִיב אתם
    Jer. 31.32:   ביום הֶחֱזִיקִי בידם
    Ps. 18.1:   ביום הַצִּיל יהוה אותו
    Lev. 14.46:   כל ימי הַסְגִּיר אתו
    2 Sam. 3.13:   (לַהֲבִיאֲךָ (but Deut. 4.31: לִפני הֲבִיאֲךָ)
    2 Sam. 5.6:   (לַהֲסִירָה (but cf. Jer. 32.31: כי אם הֲסִירֶךָ)
    1 Sam. 25.15:   כל ימי הִתְהַלַּכְנוּ אתם

 3) Jer. 51.33:   הַדְרִיכָהּ   BHKK= עת הַדְרִיכָהּ
    Lev. 14.43:   חִלֵּץ   BHKK 1 prb.... אחר חִלֵּץ
    Lev. 14.43:   הַקְצִיעַ   BHKK 1 prb. ואחרי הַקְצוֹת
    2 Chron. 29.27:   הָחֵל   BHKK...= ובעת הֵחֵל העולה

4) Jer. 50.34:   וְהִרְגִּיז ... וְהַרְגִּיעַ   BHKK=הַרְגִּיעַ‎, וְהִרְגִּיז

5) Deut. 28.55:   מבלי הַשְׁאִיר לו
   Gen. 31.20:   על בלי הַגִּיד לו
   2 Ki. 3.25:   עד הִשְׁאִיר אבניה
   1 Ki. 11.16:   עד הִכְרִית כל זכר באדום

6) Num. 21.35:   עד בלתי הִשְׁאִיר לו שריד   BHKK=הִשְׁאִיר
   Deut. 3.3:   עד בלתי הִשְׁאִיר לו שריד
   Josh. 8.22:   עד בלתי הִשְׁאִיר להם שריד   BHKK 1 frt. הִשְׁאִיר
   Josh. 10.33:   עד בלתי הִשְׁאִיר לו שריד   BHKK 1 הִשְׁאִיר
   Josh. 11.8:   עד בלתי הִשְׁאִיר להם שריד   BHKK 1 prb. הִשְׁאִיר
   2 Ki. 10.11:   עד בלתי הִשְׁאִיר לו שריד

7) Josh. 10.28:   הֶחֱרֵם אותם   BHKK prps. הַחֲרֵם
   Josh. 11.12:   הֶחֱרִים אותם   BHKK prps. הַחֲרִים
   Prov. 19.11:   הֶאֱרִיךְ אפו   BHKK 1... הַאֲרִיךְ
   Ps. 77.2:   וְהַאֲזֵין אלי   (=Deut. 1.45: וְהֶאֱזִין)

8) Jer. 49.8:   נסו הפנו הֶעְמִיקוּ לשבת   BHKK=הֶעֱמִיקוּ
   Ezek. 20.9, 14, 22:   לבלתי הֵחֵל   BHKK frt. 1 הָחֵל
   Deut. 1.5:   הואיל משה בֵּאֵר את התורה
   Jer. 23.14:   לבלתי שָׁבוּ איש מרעתו   BHKK 1... שׁוּב
   Jer. 27.18:   לבלתי בָּאוּ הכלים   BHKK 1 יָבֹאוּ vel... בֹּא

§ 98.   The stress laid by BHKK in the following cases on a certain type of the various shades of the vowel *i* is unwarranted by the Bible; cf. p. 434, § 49 ff.

1) Eccl. 10.20:   יַגִּיד דבר   BHKK 1 יַגֵּיד
   Ezek. 5.16:   ורעב אֹסֵף   BHKK 1 אֹסִף
   Hos. 9.15:   לא אוֹסֵף   BHKK 1 אוֹסִף
   Joel 2.2:   לא יוֹסֵף
   Deut. 18.16:   לא אֹסֵף   BHKK 1... אֹסִף
   Job 33.11:   יָשֵׂם בסד רגלי   BHKK 1 יָשִׂם
   Num. 22.19:   מה יֹסֵף יהוה דבר

2) 1 Ki. 14.4:   כי קמו עיניו מִשֵּׂיבוֹ   BHKK prps. מִשִּׂיבוֹ
   Ezek. 9.1:   ואיש כלי מַשְׁחֵתוֹ בידו   BHKK 1 מַשְׁחִתוֹ

3) Ezek. 17.19:   ובריתי אשר הֵפִיר   BHKK 1 הֵפֵר
   Ps. 89.34:   וחסדי לא אָפִיר   BHKK melius אָפֵר

57 45ה

Prov. 23.1:   תֶּבֶן   BHKK 1   בִּין תָּבִין אֵת אֲשֶׁר לְפָנֶיךָ

Ps. 16.5:   תּוֹמֵךְ   BHKK prb. 1   אַתָּה תּוֹמִיךְ גּוֹרָלִי

Isa. 29.14:   יוֹסֵף ?1   BHKK   הִנְנִי יוֹסִף לְהַפְלִיא אֶת הָעָם

Eccl. 1.18:   וְיוֹסֵף   BHKK 1   וְיוֹסִיף דַּעַת יוֹסִיף מַכְאוֹב

4) Isa. 43.8:   הוֹצִיא   BHKK 1   הוֹצִיא עַם עִוֵּר

Ezek. 21.31:   הָסֵר   BHKK 1   הָסִיר הַמִּצְנֶפֶת

Ezek. 21.31:   וְהָרֵם   BHKK 1   וְהָרִים הָעֲטָרָה

Ezek. 21.31:   הַשְׁפֵּל   BHKK 1   וְהַגְבֵהַ הַשְׁפִּיל

5) 2 Ki. 10.30:   רְבֵעִים   BHKK 1 frt.   בְּנֵי רְבִעִים

2 Ki. 15.12:   רְבֵעִים   BHKK prps.   בְּנֵי רְבִיעִים

§ 99. In the following instances BHKK "corrects" under the silent presupposition that ו and וֹ represent long vowels and must not be followed by a *aagesh* (cf. p. 414, § 1 V), since the syllable has to remain open; against this attitude cf. p. 455 ff. (General Conclusions, especially III).

1) Judg. 18.21:   הָעֲבֻדָּה   BHKK 1   הַכְּבוּדָּה

Ezek. 23.41:   כְּבוּדָּה   BHKK 1...   רְבוּדָה

Ps. 45.14:   כְּבֻדָּה   BHKK...   כְּבוּדָה

2 Sam. 7.21:   הַגְּדוּלָה   BHKK 1 frt.   הַגְּדוּלָה

2 Sam. 7.23:   הַגְּדוּלָה   BHKK 1   גְּדֻלּוֹת

1 Chron. 17.19:   הַגְּדוּלָה

Jer. 11.16:   הֲמוּלָה

Ex. 16.12:   תְּלֻנּוֹת

Num. 17.25:   תְּלֻנּוֹתָם

Isa. 5.5:   מְשׁוּכָּתוֹ

Isa. 16.8:   שְׁרוּקֶיהָ

2) Isa. 28.16:   מוּסָד   BHKK frt. dl

Ezek. 27.19:   מְאוּזָל   BHKK frt. 1...   מֵאוּזָל

3) Jer. 31.34:   כֻּלָּם

Ezek. 20.18:   בְּחֻקֵּי

4) Ezek. 10.17:   יָרוּמוּ   BHKK prb. 1   יָרֹמּוּ

Ezek. 10.19:   וַיֵּרוּמוּ   BHKK prb. 1   וַיֵּרֹמּוּ

Ps. 94.21:   יָגוֹדּוּ   BHKK 1 prb...   יָגֹדּוּ

Ps. 107.27:   יָחוּגּוּ   BHKK 1 frt.   יָחֹגּוּ

Job 24.24:   רֹומוּ   BHKK 1 רָמּוּ
Ps. 62.6:   דֹומִּי

5) Ps. 31.5:   מָעוּזִּי   BHKK prb. 1... מָעֹוזִי
   Ps. 37.39: מָעוּזָּם   BHKK melius מָעֹוזָם
   Ps. 43.2:   מָעוּזִּי   BHKK melius... מָעֹוזִי
   Ps. 52.9:   מָעוּזֹּו   BHKK melius מָעֹוזֹו
   Ps. 81.2:   עוּזֵּנּו   BHKK melius עֹוזֵנּו
   2 Sam. 22.33: מָעוּזִּי
   Isa. 17.9: מָעוּזֹּו
   Isa. 27.5: בְּמָעוּזִּי
   Dan. 11.19: לְמָעוּזֵּי

6) Job 5.6:   יוּלָּד   BHKK 1 יֹולָד
   1 Chron. 3.5: נוּלְּדוּ BHKK... נֹולְדוּ
   Judg. 13.8: הַיּוּלָּד
   Judg. 18.29: יוּלָּד
   1 Chron. 20.8: נוּלְּדוּ
   Ezek. 16.4: הֻולֶּדֶת

7) Hos. 10.14: יוּשַּׁד   BHKK prps. יֻושְּׁדוּ
   Ps. 49.6:   יְסוּבֵּנִי BHKK... יְסֻובֵּנִי
   Isa. 28.27: יוּסַּב
   Ezek. 16.34: זוּנָּה
   Ps. 78.63: הוּלָּלוּ
   Ps. 102.5: הוּכָּה

8) Isa. 55.4: לְאוּמִּים BHKK 1... לְאֻמִּים
   Isa. 51.4: וּלְאוּמִּי BHKK 1... וּלְאֻמִּים (thus retaining the *dagesh*!)
   Job 22.6:   עֲרוּמִּים

D.   THE MEANING OF A WORD

§ 100.   BHKK sometimes insists on the substitution of another word for that used by the Bible, a procedure, for which I can see no other explanation than the dictate of the Hebrew dictionaries (which should be corrected, and not the Bible!).

2 Ki. 11.14:   עמד על הָעַמּוּד   BHKK 1 frt. הָעֹמֵד
2 Ki. 23.3:   ויעמד ... על הָעַמּוּד   BHKK 1 frt. הָעֹמֵד
2 Chron. 23.13: עומד על עַמּוּדֹו   BHKK 1? עָמְדֹו

2 Sam. 15.18: עֹמְדִים BHKK 1 וכל עבדיו עֹבְרִים

2 Sam. 15.23: עֹמֵד BHKK 1 והמלך עֹבֵר

2 Ki. 6.30: עֹמֵד BHKK 1 frt. עֹבֵר על החמה

2 Sam. 6.8: וַיִּצֶר BHKK 1? וַיִּחַר לדוד

2 Sam. 13.21: וַיֵּצֶר BHKK prps. וַיִּחַר לו

Num. 11.24: וַיֵּצֵא BHKK 1? וַיֵּצֵא משה

Num. 12.5: וַיֵּצְאוּ BHKK 1? וַיֵּצְאוּ שניהם

E. Conclusion

§ 101. In summing up the result of the foregoing investigations it may—I hope—be said with no hesitation that Biblical criticism as embodied in *Biblia Hebraica* is based to a very large extent on the erroneous assumption expressed by Kittel in the introduction of his programmatic monograph (cf. § 46) and is consequently lacking in value as a scholarly achievement. The Bible scholar, who proudly showed off his mastery of the rules of Hebrew Grammar by applying them to the Bible and emending it accordingly at will, should become a thing of the past. A re-orientation is imperative! Of course, I don't mean to say that we have to give up our critical approach to the Bible. I only advocate a change in the method of our critical approach. There is no denying that the Bible text has "augenscheinliche Irrtümer, Schreibfehler und Verstösse aller Art" (cf. § 46). But by changing our approach I mean that henceforth we shall not define them as mistakes and errors in the light of a preconceived Hebrew grammar.

§ 102. The dependence of the exegete upon the grammarian and the lexicographer implies that any change in the grammatical or lexicographical treatment of the language of the Bible necessarily results in a corresponding change in the exegete's approach to the Bible. For whether he admits it or not, the exegete assumes that the laws of the Hebrew language, as laid down in the Hebrew grammar, are binding for the Bible. Wherever a discrepancy is discovered between the Bible and these "established" grammatical laws, the Bible is the loser: the text is "emended" so as to conform with the grammar. Kittel's *Biblia Hebraica*, a repository of corrections and emendations suggested by scholars through many generations, reminds me of a schoolboy's composition, with the

teacher's corrections of faulty grammar and spelling. It is high time that
Bible scholars outgrow this attitude of superiority, and approach the
Bible not as schoolmasters teaching the prophets how Hebrew sentences
should be formed and Hebrew words spelled; but as humble students of
these great masters of Hebrew, anxious to learn from them. By a very
conservative estimate I should say that about two thirds of the emendations listed in Kittel's *Biblia Hebraica* go back to such a schoolmasterly
attitude.

TWO HEBREW DIALECTS COMBINED FORM BIBLICAL HEBREW

I. PRE-MASORETIC PRONUNCIATION OF HEBREW

A. THE BASIC SOURCES

A. THE SOURCES

The material upon which this investigation is based, is to be found in three sources: 1) the transliterations of proper names in the *Septuagint*; 2) the material preserved from the *Second Column of Origen's Hexapla*; and 3) the transliterations of *St. Jerome*.

B. HEBREW PROPER NAMES IN THE SEPTUAGINT

In the first chapter of my *Septuagintaprobleme* (Kohlhammer, Stuttgart 1929) I dealt only with such forms of transliterated proper names which indicated an accumulating corruption in the Greek spelling in the various Mss. The thesis was there advanced that the growing inaccuracies in such spellings were proofs of the later date of the more corrupt Ms. At the present time however we are concerned only with those transliterations which accurately reproduce the Hebrew consonants. This consideration applies only to the consonants, since the vocalization of the Tiberian Grammarians is irrelevant to a study of the systems of vocalization used by the transliterators. Thus, to give an instance, if the Masoretic text reads צְלָפְחָד and the Septuagint renders it Σαλπααδ, then the only possible conclusion is that in the time of the Septuagint the name was still pronounced צלֹפְחֹד, which corresponds to צְלָפַחד in the Tiberian system (cf. B-L § 14z and g'), or even צְלָפַחד, cf. the form בְּצַלְאֵל. Thus the name צלפחד proves to be a theophorous name-form, meaning "the shadow of פַּחַד"; cf. Gen. 31.53, where פחד is referred to as the God of Isaac.

Hebrew proper names are for the most part either α) nominative or β) verbal forms; sometimes γ) a combination of both; cf. f.i. α) אבימלך, אבשלום‎ ,β) יבחר ,יזרח ;γ) פדהאל ,ראובן. The study of the transliterations, may, therefore, indicate how any given noun or verb was pronounced in that particular period.

Of Septuagint Mss. I have selected for this study the codices B and A (according to Henry B. Swete, *The Old Testament in Greek*, 3 vols., Cambridge 1901 sq.), since they contain the most characteristic grammatical tendencies. In codex B there are preserved the oldest transliterated forms known to us, whereas in codex A we have the transition to the period of the Second Column (see next paragraph). It is well to note the frequent rendering of ח by χ (cf. חבר χαβερ in B and αβερ in A, חפה χοφφα in B and οφφα in A), of ז by σ (cf. אחז αχας in B and αχαζ in A, יזרע ισρα in B and ιζρα in A), of long ־ִי by ει (cf. אבי αβει in B and αβι in A, אחי αχει in B and αχι in A) in codex B; cf. also paragraph od on the Article. This estimate of the comparative age of the basic texts of these two codices is valid only if they are considered in their totality, but is no indication of the age of any particular transliteration. There are any number of forms in codex B which are late (cf. חפצי αψει and חריף αρειφ; זכרי ζεχρει and זמה ζεμμα; אהלי οολι), and correspondingly there are forms in codex A which are early (cf. חותם χωθαμ and חלק χελεχ; יריב ιαρειβ and ישׁיב ιασειβ) (cf. p. 227 f.). I have arranged my material in such a way that this is obvious in any particular instance. We can, therefore, apply here the statement which is elaborated in my *Septuagintaprobleme* (p. 46) to the effect that the uniformity of a given Ms. indicates nothing as to the uniformity of the Ms. from which it is derived, nor is there any possibility of determining the age of the basic text by ascribing the Ms. to any particular period.

C.   ORIGEN'S HEXAPLA

For the Second Column of the Hexapla I used the citations in Fridericus Field, *Origenis Hexaplorum quae supersunt* (2 vols., Oxford 1875) and the fragments discovered by *Mercati* (cf. Alfred Rahlfs, *Verzeichnis der griechischen Handschriften des Alten Testaments*, Berlin 1914, p. 130 sq., under the symbol O. 39 sup.). These fragments have first been printed by Franz X. Wutz in his commentary *Die Psalmen* (Munich 1925), but without any comment on them or even the slightest attempt to compare them with the corresponding text in Hebrew characters for the sake of mere textual criticism; cf. the final remarks in paragraph P on p. 118/9.

Fortunately I could verify his indications by reference to Hatch and Redpath, *A Concordance to the Septuagint* (Supplement, Oxford 1906, pp. 199-216). These fragments have been posthumously published under the title *Psalterii Hexapli Reliquiae* Cura et Studio Iohannis Card. Mercati editae. In Bibliotheca Vaticana 1958. I have revised my material according to this edition.

The understanding of these transliterations is made more difficult by the fact that very often words are rendered in forms that differ from those of the Masora; cf. Ps. 18.48: MT: וַיְדַבֵּר Origen: ουιεδαββερ=וַיְּדַבֵּר; ib. 46.6: MT: יַעְזְרֶהָ Origen: ουεζρα=וְעֶזְרָה. In regard to the method of rendering Hebrew words, the transliterations of the Second Column agree for the most part with the system of codex A of the Septuagint, but not infrequently they agree with codex B. This leads to the conclusion that the Second Column is very definitely not a uniform text. In this connection compare the subdivisions a and b of the respective paragraphs in the section dealing with the verb, f.i. § 3a and b, § 27a and b, § 53a and b for the perfect; § 7a and b, § 10a and b, § 31a and b for the imperfect; § 15a and b for the participle; § 78 and § 79 for the waw as waw conjunctivum and waw consecutivum; cf. similarly the paragraphs headed "Nouns with varying vocalization" in the section dealing with the noun, f.i. § 83 and § 88 for the formation of the noun; § 115 and § 116 for the article and § 117 sq. for the inseparable prepositions בכלם. I had, therefore, originally attempted to arrange the material from the Hexapla in such a way as to enable me to assign the various fragments which have been discovered by Mercati to different textual types; f.i. s.v. בקר as a qutl-form (to use the Tiberian terminology) בקר βοκρ in Ps. 46.6 and as a qitl-form לבקר λαβεκρ in Ps. 49.15; s.v. דרך as a qitl-form דרך δερχ in Ps. 89.42 and as a qatl-form דרכם δαρχαμ in Ps. 49.14; s.v. קרב as a qutl-form בקרב βεκορβ in Ps. 36.2; as a qitl-form בקרבה βκερβα in Ps. 46.6 and as a qatl-form קרבם καρβαμ in Ps. 49.12. But as a result of this investigation I realized that any such attempt must finally prove to be a failure, since the fragments represent already a mixed type. Compare, f.i., s.v. חפץ: the participle forms החפץ ααφης and חפצי ωφση, both occurring in the same verse (Ps. 35.27); s.v. יד: מיד μειεδ and ידו ιαδω, both in the same chapter (Ps. 89); cf. further the paragraphs cited above which deal with the different ways of verbal formations, the examples for which are taken in large part from the very same Biblical chapter.

D.   JEROME'S ROLE

Numerically considered, the overwhelming majority of transliterated words is taken from St. Jerome. A glance at the arrangement of this study, in which instances are brought from Jerome for almost every subdivision of every paragraph, makes it evident that his transliterations must be based upon *Vorlagen* (originals) belonging to different periods. By merely external evidence, there are two main sources to which his references can be traced, namely the *Onomastica Sacra* which are merely a Latin transliteration of Greek texts, and his large Commentary to the various Biblical books, where Jerome's own pronunciation of Hebrew or rather that of his Jewish teachers is given.

E.   THE ONOMASTICA SACRA GO BACK TO GREEK 'VORLAGEN'

The Onomastica Sacra I have worked through in the edition of Lagarde (Göttingen 1887). When I had finished collecting my material from this source and sat down to classify it and to distribute the quotations to the various paragraphs where they belonged, I arrived at the conclusion that they are not genuine transliterations of Hebrew *Vorlagen*, but unquestionably go back to originals in Greek characters. How else could one account for the fact that he himself points out the divergencies between his transliteration and the corresponding Hebrew word? Cf. his remarks to עמרה, צער and חם on p. 109. I discussed this problem with a scholarly friend and he raised objections against my conclusion. To meet his objections I once again took up the study of the Onomastica Sacra, and this time I found there a plain statement of Jerome to this effect, which must have escaped my attention on previous occasions. This statement reads as follows (editio Lagarde, p. 26): "Philo, uir disertissimus Iudaeorum, Origenis quoque testimonio conprobatur edidisse librum hebraicorum nominum eorumque etymologias iuxta ordinem litterarum e latere copulasse, qui cum uulgo habeatur a Graecis, et bibliothecas orbis impleuerit, studii mihi fuit in latinam eum linguam uertere." Cf. also the headline on p. 156 of *Philonis Iudaei Alexandrini omnes quae apud Graecos et Latinos extant libri* (Basileae, per Henricum Petrum, 1538) reading: "Divi Hieronymi Presbyteri in librum Philonis Iudaei de nominibus Hebraicis praefatio." This work, thus ascribed to Philo, is only

Pseudo-Philonic; cf. Leopold Cohn, *Einteilung und Chronologie der Schriften Philos*, VII. Supplementband des *Philologus* (Leipzig 1899, p. 426) and at full length Franz Wutz, *Onomastica Sacra*, I, Leipzig 1914, § 2.

F.   THE PRONUNCIATION OF ח AND ע HAD CHANGED

The transliteration of the Greek *Vorlagen* of the Onomastica Sacra into Latin characters is the best indication of the exactness and puncti-liousness of Jerome. In spite of the fact that the pronunciation of Hebrew had changed materially between the time of the writing of the Greek originals and the period of Jerome, and despite the fact that Jerome himself was fully aware of the incongruities between the transliteration and the contemporary pronunciation of Hebrew, he made no attempt to avoid these discrepancies by means of corrections, but rather reproduced his originals faithfully and limited himself to mere glosses. Thus he remarks while explaining the name עֲמֹרָה (ed. Lagarde, p. 33): "Gomorra populi timor (this would mean: עַם and מוֹרָא) siue seditio (probably: עַם and מוֹרֶה, cf. Deut. 21.18: וּמוֹרֶה), sciendum quod G litteram in hebraico non habet, sed scribitur per uocalem ע." Similarly he notes to צֹעַר (ib. in the Genesis list of names beginning with S): "Segor parua (cf. Gen. 19.20). ipsa est quae et supra Seor. sed sciendum quia G litteram in medio non habet, scribaturque apud Hebraeos per uocalem ain." As regards this inconsistency in transliterating Hebrew words (Segor and Seor) cf. Jerome's preface (ed. Lagarde, p. 26). "uerum tam dissona inter se exemplaria repperi et sic confusum ordinem, ut tacere melius indi-cauerim quam reprehensione quid dignum scribere."

On the name חָם Jerome remarks (ib., p. 30): "Cham calidus. sed sciendum quod in hebraeo χ (this corresponds to 'ch' in Jerome's trans-literation; cf. p. 111) litteram non habeat, scribitur autem per ח, quae duplici adspiratione profertur." He speaks at greater length concerning the question of transliterating the ח in his *Quaestiones hebraicae in libro Geneseos* to Gen. 9.18: "frequenter LXX interpretes, non ualentes heth literam quae duplicem aspirationem sonat, in graecum sermonem uertere, chi graecam literam addiderunt, ut nos docerent in istius modi uocabulis aspirare debere: unde et in praesenti loco Cham transtulerunt, pro eo quod est Ham, a quo et Aegyptus usque hodie Aegyptiorum lingua dicitur."

This manifests what Jerome understood by the duplex aspiratio: an

H. His explanation of the fact that ה is transliterated in the older texts by χ, is hardly correct. On the contrary, such transliterations clearly indicate that ח had then the consonantal value of χ. But when in the period of the Second Column ח became merely a vowel, no change was made in the transliterations of proper names which were utilized in the current texts. That Jerome's explanation is not based upon any well founded tradition, but rather upon his own fancy, is demonstrated by the inconsistent manner in which he himself transliterates ח one time with an h and another time simply as a vowel; cf. for instance: חדלו hedalu, חדש hodes as compared with: חלד eled, חנף oneph; even the same Hebrew word is transliterated in different places in different ways, cf. חמר omer and homer, חרב areb and hareb, חרוץ arus and harus. Moreover, even his transliteration of ח by h fails to satisfy completely his own demands for a double aspirate, since h according to him is only a simple aspirate; cf. Onomastica Sacra, p. 51: "H autem a plerisque adspiratio putatur esse, non littera." Accordingly Jerome transliterates the ה—in so far as he deals with it not simply as a vowel—equally by h; so for instance in his Questiones on Gen. 14.5: "porro BAHEM, pro quo dixerunt (namely: the Septuagint) μετ' αὐτοῖς (hoc est cum eis) putauerunt scribi per ה, ducti elementi similitudine, cum per heth scriptum sit. BAHEM enim cum per tres literas scribitur, si mediam he habet, interpretatur in eis, si autem heth (ut in praesenti) locum significat, id est Hom." As to the fact that Jerome read בהם here instead of the Masoretic spelling בהם, cf. p. 114.

G.   THE 'VORLAGEN' BELONG TO DIFFERENT TYPES

It is, therefore, explicable that Jerome sometimes renders the same Hebrew name forms, occurring in the various Biblical books or even in the same book, differently; f.i. אחי achi and ahi, זבדי zabdi and zebdi, זמרי zamri and zemeri, מלכי melchi and malchi. It is obvious that his *Vorlagen* could not have been parts of a uniform tradition. This fact was naturally taken into consideration in the arrangement of the material utilized in this study; note for instance the order in which the transliterations are cited for אחז: αχαζ, achaz - ααζ, aaz; or for מעון: μαων, maon - μεων, meon. Jerome himself definitely indicates these various possibilities of pronunciation (editio Vallarsi, vol. VI, p. 24c on Hos. 2.18):

"בעלי. inter Beth et Lamed literas consonantes Ain uocalis litera ponitur, quae iuxta linguae illius proprietatem nunc BEEL, nunc BAAL legitur."

H.   HOW TO RECONSTRUCT THE ORIGINAL GREEK

One can reconstruct without any difficulty the Greek originals of Jerome's rendering of the Hebrew name lists in the Onomastica Sacra, when we keep in mind that the following are the Greek equivalents of his Latin characters: a=α, b=β, c=χ, ch=χ, d=δ, e=ε or η, f=φ, g=γ, i and j=ι, l=λ, m=μ, n=ν, o=o or ω, p=π, ph=φ, r=ρ, s=σ, t=τ, th=θ, u=ου, z=ζ. If our conjecture be correct, Jerome has permitted himself only one major deviation from the normal Greek spelling; that is between two vowels immediately following one another he inserts an h to indicate that they are to be pronounced separately; so for instance (in the name lists of the Genesis and of Exodus in the Onomastica Sacra): ישראל Israhel, בצלאל Beselehel, ימואל Iamuhel, מישאל Misahel, רעואל Raguhel, בעל פעור Behelfegor, בעל צפון Behelsefon, בעל מעון Bahalmeon. Compare also the passage in *Quaestiones* on Gen. 17.3, cited in paragraph oo, which states that by adding an a to the name Abram it became Abraham; the h inserted between the two a's does not count. Cases like אחר aher (cf. αερ B), נחלה nehela (cf. νεελαθαχ O), מרחם merehem (cf. μηρεμ O) have, therefore, to be treated similarly; an assumption that the h here corresponds to the Hebrew ה, would be unjustified.

I.   JEROME'S COMMENTARIES ARE BASED UPON THE HEBREW TEXT

Jerome's Commentaries I have gone through in the edition of Vallarsi (Venice 1767 sq.); for the *Quaestiones hebraicae in libro Geneseos* I used also Lagarde's edition (Leipzig 1868). Whereas the Onomastica Sacra, considered as a unit, undoubtedly render Hebrew pronunciations as they were known before the time of Jerome, since they agree for the most part with codex A and frequently even with codex B, in the transliterations which appear in his commentaries we have a mixtum compositum, which includes, it is true, old material but at the same time a great deal that is purely contemporary; cf. f.i., ברורה barura (§ 19a) against דרושה drusa (§ 19c); בת bath and beth (§ 83); שרף saraph and seraph (§ 93); הרס ares and heres; (§ 96); עגור agor and agur (§ 109); הצדק asedec and השדמות asademoth (§ 115) against הגוי aggoi and המלך ammelech (§ 116);

מבטן mebeten and מקדם mecedem (§ 121a) against מבית mebbeth and
מכנף mecchenaph (§ 122); בסופה basupha and בקרב bacereb (§ 117a)
against בגוים baggoim and בפוך baphphuch (§ 120). This results from
the fact that Jerome in his commentaries has not limited himself to a
mere explanation of the text offered by the Septuagint but has consulted
the Hebrew text in every instance. This Hebrew text which he utilized
must have consisted of unvocalized consonants (as was already pointed
out by Wilhelm Nowack, *Die Bedeutung des Hieronymus für die alttestamentliche Textkritik*, Göttingen 1875, p. 55), since he frequently calls
attention to the various possibilities for the pronunciation of the consonantal word; so for instance (editio Vallarsi, vol. IV, p. 856E): "רעים.
Verbum enim REIM, quod quattuor literis scribitur RES, AIN, JOD,
MEM, et amatores et pastores utrumque significat. Et si legamus REIM,
amatores significat; si ROIM, pastores;" this means: רֵעִים and רֹעִים.
He has also noticed that various Hebrew characters are sufficiently
similar to be confused; note for instance his remark (ib., vol. VI, p.
818AB): "oculum eorum, quod Hebraice dicitur ENAM, et scribitur per
AIN, JOD, NUN, MEM. Sive iniquitatem eorum; quae si per VAV
literam scripta esset, recte legeretur ONAM, ut LXX putaverunt;"
the two words referred to are: עֵינָם and עֲוֹנָם.

In basing his work upon the original Hebrew text of the Bible, Jerome
must have performed a task, which in his time was a mark of unusual
scholarly achievement. Otherwise he would not have called special
attention to this fact (ib., vol. V, p. 239): "Accedit ad hanc dictandi
difficultatem, quod caligantibus oculis senectute et aliquid sustinentibus
beati Isaac, ad nocturnum lumen nequaquam valeamus Hebraeorum
volumina relegere, quae etiam ad solis dieique fulgorum literarum nobis
parvitate caecantur." In instances, where Jerome felt doubtful as to his
conception of the meaning of particular passages of the Bible, he followed
the practice of turning to a Jew for advice and guidance; and in his
explanations he calls attention to this procedure; so for instance (ib.,
vol. IV, p. 172A): "Hebraeus, quo ego praeceptore usus sum," or (ib.,
vol. VI, p. 288D; cf. also ib. pp. 383C, 550A, 570A, 637D): "Hebraeus
autem, qui nos in Scripturis sanctis erudivit." In particularly difficult
passages he was not satisfied with one such consultation, but would
seek the advice of several Jews; note the plural for instance in the

remark (ib., vol. VI, p. 808AB): "quid videatur Hebraeis, a quibus in veteri Testamento eruditi sumus."

J.   UNCERTAINTY OF ETYMOLOGY

These Jews who served as sources of information for Jerome and whom he so respectfully calls his teachers, must have been considered in their time authorities in matters of Biblical exegesis; otherwise he would not have turned particularly to them for instruction. Consequently it is all the more interesting to read an answer like the following to one of his questions (ib., vol. VI, p. 834BC on Zech. 14.20 מְצִלּוֹת): "Verbum Hebraicum MESULOTH (this question implies that Jerome vocalized the word as מְצֻלּוֹת; cf. ib. 10.11), Aquila et Theodotio βυθόν interpretati sunt, id est profundum; Symmachus περίπατον σύσκιον, id est incessum umbrosum. Soli Septuaginta χάλινον, id est frenum, transtulerunt; quos et nos in hoc loco sequuti sumus, ne novum aliquid in quaestione vulgata videremus afferre. Quod quum ab Hebraeo quaererem quid significaret, ait mihi, non debere nos legere MESULOTH sed MESALOTH (i.e. מְצֻהֲלוֹת; cf. Jer. 8.16; 13.27—the word is, therefore, not a ἅπαξ λεγόμενον, as Jerome says), quod significat phaleras equorum et ornatum bellicum et excepto hoc loco, in nullo penitus sanctarum Scripturarum volumine hoc verbum reperiri."

Such suggestions indicate clearly that the Hebrew text of the Bible itself, even in passages where Jerome's consonantal text is identical with our *textus receptus*, could at that time be read very differently from the vocalization to which we are accustomed as a result of the activities of the Tiberian school of grammarians. Both the pronunciation and the etymological derivation of Hebrew words were at that time to a large extent decidedly uncertain, as Jerome himself frequently remarks; for instance in *Quaestiones* to Gen. 48.2: "ipsum uerbum METTA, quod hic in lectulum transtulerunt, supra . . . uirgam potius quam lectulum nominauerunt"; i.e. מַטֶּה and מִטָּה. Similarly to Gen. 21.31: "septem enim dicuntur SABEE . . . et iuramentum SABEE similiter appellatur," as compared with his assertion to Gen. 41.29: "uerbum hebraicum SABEE . . . abundantiam siue satietatum . . . interpretati sumus," i.e. שָׂבַע, שְׂבוּעָה and שָׁבַע. This explanation Jerome repeats in his commentary (editio Vallarsi, vol. IV, pp. 64E and 945E): "licet iuxta Hebraei sermonis ambiguitatem, qui verbum SABA, nunc septem, nunc plures, nunc iuramentum, interpretantur."

K. VARIANTS AGAINST MT

But even in respect to the consonantal text the tradition was fluctuating and uncertain, a fact which did not escape the attention of Jerome. Thus he remarks on Hab. 2.19 (ib., vol. VI, p. 630BC): "וכל־רוח. Unde et Aquila significantius vertit Hebraicum dicens: Et spiritus eius non est in visceribus sive in medio eius. Propterea sciendum in quibusdam Hebraicis voluminibus non esse additum omnis, sed absolute spiritum legi"; these Mss. had, according to this statement, the reading: ורוח. In this connection it is interesting to indicate the fact that in the large collections of textual variations by Kennicott (*Vetus Testamentum cum variis lectionibus*, 2 vols., Oxford 1776 and 1780), de Rossi (*Variae lectiones Veteris Testamenti*, 4 vols., Parma 1784-88), and Ginsburg (*The Old Testament ... with the various readings from Mss.*, London 1926) there are still evidences for such non-Masoretic readings of Jerome:

Gen. 14.5:   בְּהָם; Jerome: בְּחָם (cf. p. 110); 7 Mss. de Rossi.

Isa. 29.4:   כְּאוֹב; Jerome: כְּאָב; 2 Mss. Kennicott.

Ezek. 29.10: מִגְדֹּל; Jerome: מִגְדָּל; 5 Mss. Ginsburg

Ezek. 46.23: טִירוֹת; Jerome: טוּרוֹת; 1 Ms. Kennicott

Mic. 5.3:   יָשֻׁבוּ; Jerome: יָשׁוּבוּ; 1 Ms. Kennicott, 2 Mss. de Rossi,
                                                                 1 Ms. Ginsburg

Zech. 12.5:   אַמְצָה; Jerome: אֶמְצָא; 2 Mss. de Rossi

L. ORIGEN'S HEBREW TEXT DIFFERS FROM MT, TOO

A further indication of the importance of these collections of variants is the fact that they frequently substantiate the deviations from Masoretic readings which are already found in the Second Column of Origen's Hexapla:

Ps. 30.4:   מִן שְׁאוֹל; Origen: מִשְּׁאוֹל; 4 Mss. Kennicott, 2 Mss. Ginsburg

Ps. 31.25: חִזְקוּ; Origen: חֲזַק; 1 Ms. Kennicott

Ps. 31.25: הַמְיַחֲלִים; Origen: הַמְּיחלִים; 2 Mss. Ginsburg

Ps. 35.1:   לְחַם; Origen: לְחֹם; 1 Ms. Kennicott

Ps. 35.25: בִּלְבָם; Origen: בְּלְבָם; 4 Mss. Kennicott

Ps. 36.2: לְבִּי; Origen: לִבּוֹ; 2 Mss. Kennicott, 4 Mss. de Rossi, 1 Ms. Ginsburg

Ps. 76.10: עַנְוֵי; Origen: עֲנִי; 1 Ms. Kennicott

Ps. 89.36: בְּקָדְשִׁי; Origen: בְּקָדֶשׁ; 1 Ms. Kennicott

Ps. 89.47: תִּסָּתֵר; Origen: תַּסְתִּיר; 5 Mss. Kennicott

The establishment of this fact is all the more important, since these collections are based on relatively late Hebrew Bible Mss. which otherwise follow almost entirely the Tiberian school. How numerous and widespread must have been such variae lectiones in the time of the transliterations, if in spite of the unifying activities of the Masoretes of Tiberias, remnants of such readings could have been preserved in Mss. dating from a period possibly a thousand years later than that of the transliterations.

M.   JEROME TRANSLATES WORDS, REGARDLESS OF THE CONTEXT

Attention has already been called to Jerome's commentary on Zech. 14.20 (p. 114), where the explanation of the difficult word מצלות was referred to a Jew, who indicated the various possibilities of reading it. It is interesting that no attempt was made to explain this word so as to fit in its context. It was sufficient that the single word should be explained. This is not the only instance for such a procedure in Jerome. On the contrary, it is obvious from the manner both of the question and the answer that only single words and not the sense of the passages were the subjects of his inquiry. It made little difference at that time whether the words so explained fitted into the passages or not. We are thus in a position to understand how it could come about that sometimes the Septuagint offers translations of separate words based upon a vocalization of the Hebrew consonants, which in itself is quite possible, but which fails to make sense in the context. I have already brought instances of such renderings (see my articles *Das Alphabet der Septuaginta-Vorlage*, OLZ 1929, p. 533 f. and *The Problems of the Septuagint Recensions*, JBL 1935, p. 82, paragraph II), and may I at this point add the following:

1 Sam. 11.5:   הַבָּקָר; LXX: τὸ πρωί = הַבֹּקֶר

Isa. 26.14:   זֵכֶר; LXX: ἄρσεν = זָכָר

Isa. 55.1:   וְחָלָב; LXX: στέαρ = וְחֵלֶב

Jer. 6.23:   כְּאִישׁ; LXX: ὡς πῦρ = כָּאֵשׁ

Jer. 6.23:   וְאָנֹשׁ; LXX: ἄνθρωπος = וֶאֱנוֹשׁ

Jer. 18.14:   שָׁדַי; LXX: μαστοί = שָׁדַי

Ezek. 16.30:   לִבָּתֵךְ; LXX: τὴν θυγατέρα σου = לְבִתֵּךְ

Ezek. 24.17:   דֹּם; LXX: αἵματος = דָּם

Ezek. 26.10:   מִבְקָעָה; LXX: ἐκ πεδίου = מִבִּקְעָה

Ezek. 34.3:   הַחֵלֶב; LXX: τὸ γάλα = הֶחָלָב

Translations of this kind are generally referred to a obvious misconceptions; and there can hardly be any disagreement on this point. But it is a very important problem, whether they really originate in erroneous readings of the then undoubtedly unvocalized text. Going through the few instances which we have just listed, we note that in Isa. 55.1 the Septuagint misunderstood וְחָלָב as וְחֵלֶב, while in Ezek. 34.3 vice versa הַחֵלֶב was misconceived as הֶחָלָב. These two facts combined advocate the assumption that in that early period חָלָב milk and חֵלֶב fat were similarly pronounced and could thus be confused with each other. The same may have been the case with זֵכֶר and זָכָר (Isa. 26.14); cf., f.i., our remarks on רָשָׁע and רֶשַׁע on p. 214/5; and in regard to שָׁדַי and שָׁדַי (Jer. 18.14), the explanation offered on p. 172 is of a similar nature. These considerations lead us to the conclusion that mistranslations of this kind may largely be due not so much to a mistaken reading of the word in question as to a faulty etymology; cf. the similar case from b. Sanh. 5b, dealt with on p. 226/7. Bearing this in mind we may now try to solve some similar vexing problems: The word רְפָאִים is rendered by the Septuagint with γιγάντες; cf. Isa. 14.9; Job 26.5. However, in two passages, namely Isa. 26.14 and Ps. 88.11 they translate it: ἰατροί; this would correspond to a vocalization of the word as רֹפְאִים. Needles to emphasize that a meaning "healers" is quite out of place in these two verses. It is, therefore, all the more interesting to note that Jerome in the Deuteronomy Name List of his Onomastica Sacra (p. 51) remarks: "Raphaim medici uel gigantes." We have now to dispense with any attempt to explain the translation ἰατροί as based upon a mere mistake in the pronunciation, but have to admit that, speaking in the terms of the Tiberian Hebrew grammar, רְפָאִים shades and רֹפְאִים healers were similarly pronounced at least until Jerome's days. With the results of this study in mind we can easily account for it: 1) רפאים raphaim meaning: shades. The Tiberian nominal plural form רְפָאִים presupposes a singular רְפָא, just as דְּבָרִים is the plural of דָּבָר. In paragraph oo we will show that according to the system of the transliterations, the plur. masc. is formed by merely adding *im* to the noun without its undergoing any phonetic change as is the case in the Tiberian system. Thus, f.i., תמר θαμαρ is in the plural: thamarim; accordingly, to the sing. רְפָא rapha, shade, corresponds a plural רפאים raphaim.   2) רפאים raphaim meaning: healers. The Tiberian Hebrew grammar vocalizes רֹפֵא healer as a participle to רפא. But there is no reason why it should not be pronounced as a nominal form רַפָּא like f.i. גַּנָּב (from גנב) or רַכָּב (from רכב). Now, in the Tiberian grammar, *paṭaḥ* is a short vowel and can not stand in an open syllable; the *dagesh* is therefore put in the immediately following consonant (נ and כ respectively) to close the preceding syllable with the *paṭaḥ*. But this rule does not hold true for the transliteration system; cf. f.i., in § 80 the following plural forms without the gemination of the second radical, as required by the Tiberian grammar: s.v. גל: γαλειμ; s.v. ים: ιαμιμ; s.v. רב: ραβιμ; s.v. עם: αμιμ. We may thus assume a nominal singular form רפא rapha healer, to which the plural according to paragraph oo would be: rapahim. On the Tiberian pluralis fractus רְפָאִים or דְּבָרִים see the discussion of שרפים on p. 216, and of subdivision n.

N.   BEGINNINGS OF ETYMOLOGICAL CONSIDERATION

The variants on the Masoretic text as found in the transliterations belong to a certain extent to this category of words, being theoretically possible, but out of context in their particular passage. Such renderings are, therefore, impossible, not only because they fail to make sense in the context, which in those days was a matter of little importance as evidenced by the examples brought from the Septuagint, but also because they are etymologically unsound. However, an etymological sense was foreign to the contemporaries of Jerome; cf. his statement in Quaestiones on Gen. 17.16: "quidam pessime suspicantur ante eam lepram fuisse uocitatam et postea principem: cum lepra SARATH dicatur, quae in nostra quidem lingua uidetur aliquam habere similitudinem, in hebraeo autem penitus est diuersa. scribitur enim per SADE et AIN et RES et THAU: quod multum a superioribus tribus literis, id est SIN, RES et HE, quibus SARAA scribitur, discrepare manifestum est." If one could think of an etymological connection between צרעת and שרה, so that Jerome found it necessary to call attention to the different spelling of the two words in order to refute such an interpretation, it must be readily admitted that at that time etymological considerations played a very small role, indeed, in Biblical exegesis.

O. TRACING BACK JEROME'S MISTAKES

The evidence for the variant readings of the transliterations, which was brought from Tiberian Bible Mss., indicates how long such variants were still current. On the other hand we can see from the agreement of the Septuagint with some of these variants that such texts are much older than the time when they were committed to writing by Origen and Jerome, since they served in part as *Vorlagen* for the Septuaginta itself. For instance:

Gen. 26.12:	שְׂעָרִים;	Jerome:	שְׂעָרִים;	LXX:	κριθήν
Jer. 18.3:	אָבְנָיִם;	Jerome:	אֲבָנִים;	LXX:	τῶν λίθων
Ezek. 23.23:	פְּקוֹד;	Jerome:	פְּקוּד;	LXX (3 Mss.):	Φακουδ
Ezek. 40.21:	תָּאָו;	Jerome:	תָּאֵי;	LXX:	θεέ
Am. 5.26:	סִכּוּת;	Jerome:	סָכּוֹת;	LXX:	τὴν σκηνήν
Hag. 1.11:	חֹרֶב;	Jerome:	חֶרֶב;	LXX:	ῥομφαίαν
Zech. 2.7:	יֹצֵא;	Jerome:	יָצָא;	LXX:	ἱστήκει (tempus!)
Zech. 12.5:	אַמְצָה;	Jerome:	אָמְצָא;	LXX:	εὑρήσομεν
Mal. 2.13:	מִיֶּדְכֶם;	Origen:	מִידֵיכֶם;	LXX:	ἐκ τῶν χειρῶν ὑμῶν
Ps. 18.37:	צַעֲדִי;	Origen:	צְעָדַי;	LXX:	τὰ διαβήματά μου
Ps. 36.2:	לִבִּי;	Origen:	לִבּוֹ;	LXX:	ἐν ἑαυτῷ
Ps. 46.3:	אֶרֶץ;	Origen:	הָאָרֶץ;	LXX:	τὴν γῆν

P. VARIAE LECTIONES OF ORIGEN AND JEROME

For the benefit of the Biblical scholar who is interested in textual criticism, I consider it worth while to give here a full list of the variae lectiones of Origen and Jerome as compared with the Masoretic Hebrew text, based upon their transliterations of the words in question. These transliterations are scattered all over the Dictionary, and can be looked up there sub voce. Here I arrange them according to the order of the Biblical books. Those variants, which have been dealt with in the preceding paragraphs, will be noted with a reference to the respective paragraph. The variants from the Septuagint and the Onomastica Sacra referring to the pronunciation of Hebrew Proper Names, will easily be found with the help of the Alphabetical Index on pp. 166 ff.

Gen. 14.5: בְּהָם; cf. p. 114

Gen. 26.12: שְׁעָרִים; cf. p. 118

2 Ki. 23.7: הַקְּדֵשִׁים; Origen: הַקְּדֵשִׁים

Isa. 7.14: קָרָאת; Jerome: קָרָאתִי

Isa. 8.21: וּבֵאלֹהָיו; Origen: בֵּאלֹהָיו

Isa. 24.16: זְמָרֹת; Jerome: זְמָרֹת

Isa. 26.3: יֵצֶר; Origen: יִצְרוֹ

Isa. 26.10: רָשָׁע; Jerome: רֶשַׁע; cf. p. 214/5

Isa. 29.4: כְּאוֹב; cf. p. 114

Isa. 38.10: דְּמִי; Jerome: דְּמִי

Isa. 46.3: מִנִּי בֶטֶן; Jerome: מִבֶּטֶן

Isa. 46.3: מִנִּי רָחַם; Jerome: מֵרֶחֶם

Isa. 62.4: שְׁמֵמָה; Jerome: שְׁמָמָה

Jer. 4.19: הֹמֶה; Jerome: הֹמָה

Jer. 5.8: מַשְׁכִּים; Jerome: מַשְׁכִים

Jer. 5.26: יָשׁוּר; Jerome: יָשִׁיר

Jer. 13.16: נֶשֶׁף; Jerome: נִשְׁפָּה

Jer. 18.3: אָבְנָיִם; cf. p. 118

Jer. 23.6: צִדְקֵנוּ; Jerome: צִדְקֵנוּ

Ezek. 1.14: בָּזָק; Jerome בָּזָק

Ezek. 7.23: הָרַתּוּק; Jerome: הָרַתּוּק

Ezek. 23.23: פְּקוֹד; cf. p. 118

Ezek. 29.10: מִגְדֹּל; cf. p. 114

Ezek. 30.17: אָוֶן; Jerome: אוֹן

Ezek. 40.16: תִּמֹרִים; Jerome: תִּמָרִים

Ezek. 40.16: אַטֻמוֹת; Jerome: אַטֻמוֹת

Ezek. 40.21: תָּאָו; cf. p. 118

Ezek. 40.24: אֵילָם; Jerome: אוּלָם

Ezek. 46.23: טִירוֹת; cf. p. 114

Hos. 9.7: יָדְעוּ; Jerome: יָדְעוּ

Hos. 11.1: וָאֹהֲבֵהוּ; Origen: וָאֹהֲבֵהוּ

Hos. 12.5: וַיָּשַׂר; Jerome: יֵשַׁר

Am. 4.12: הִכּוֹן; Jerome: הֵכִין

Am. 5.26: סִכּוּת; cf. p. 118

Am. 7.1: גֹּבַי; Jerome: גֹּבַי

Mic. 5.3: יֵשְׁבוּ; cf. p. 114

Hab. 1.5: רְאוּ; Jerome: רָאוּ

Hab. 1.11: וְאָשֵׁם; Jerome: וְאָשֵׁם

Hab. 3.13: לְיֵשַׁע; Jerome: לִישׁוּעָה

Zeph. 1.5: מַלְכָּם; Jerome: מִלְכֹם

Hag. 1.11: חֹרֶב; cf. p. 118

Zech. 2.7: יֹצֵא; cf. p. 118

Zech. 8.14: נִחַמְתִּי; Jerome: נֶחָמְתִּי

Zech. 12.5: אַמְצָה; cf. pp. 114 and 118

Zech. 14.20: מְצֻלּוֹת; Jerome: מְצִלּוֹת and מְצֹהֲלוֹת; cf. p. 113

Mal. 2.13: פָּנוֹת; Origen: פָּנוֹת

Mal. 2.13: מִיֶּדְכֶם; cf. p. 118

Ps. 1.1: רְשָׁעִים; Origen: הָרְשָׁעִים

Ps. 7.15: יְחַבֵּל; Origen: יְחַבֵּל

Ps. 9.1: לַבֵּן Origen: בֵּן

Ps. 9.1: עַל מוּת; Jerome: עַלְמוּת

Ps. 9.7: חֳרָבוֹת; Origen: חָרְבוֹת

Ps. 9.7: הֵמָּה; Origen: הֵם

Ps. 12.9: כְּרֻם; Origen: כֶּרֶם

Ps. 18.32: מִבַּלְעֲדֵי; Origen: מִבַּלְעֲדֵי

Ps. 18.33: הַמְאַזְּרֵנִי; Origen: הַמְאַזרני

Ps. 18.35: וְנִחֲתָה; Origen: וְנִחֲתָה

Ps. 18.35: זֵרוֹעֹתַי; Origen: זְרוֹעֹתַי

Ps. 18.37: צְעָדִי; cf. p. 118

Ps. 18.37: תַּחְתָּי; Origen: תַּחְתִּי

Ps. 18.40: וַתְּאַזְּרֵנִי; Origen: וּתְאַזְרֵנִי

Ps. 18.41: וּמְשַׂנְּאַי; Origen: וּמְשַׂנְאַי

Ps. 18.48: וַיַּדְבֵּר; Origen: וַיַּדְבֵּר

Ps. 28.6: שְׁמַע; Origen: שְׁמַע

Ps. 28.9: וְרַעֵם; Origen: וְהָרֵם

Ps. 30.4: מִן שְׁאוֹל; cf. p. 114

Ps. 30.13: יִדֹּם; Origen: יָדֹם

Ps. 30.13: אוֹדְךָ; Origen: אוֹדְךָ

Ps. 31.8: וְאֶשְׂמְחָה; Origen: וְאֶשְׂמַח

Ps. 31.21: מֵרִיב; Origen: מֵרִיבֵי

Ps. 31.24: וּמְשַׁלֵּם; Origen: וְשָׁלֵם

Ps. 31.25: חִזְקוּ; cf. p. 114

Ps. 31.25: הַמְיַחֲלִים; cf. p. 114

Ps. 35.1: לְחַם; cf. p. 114

Ps. 35.2: וְקוּמָה; Origen: וְקוּם

Ps. 35.14: כְּאָבֵל; Origen: כְּאָבֵל

Ps. 35.19: שֹׂנְאַי; Origen: שֹׂנְאַי

Ps. 35.19: אֹיְבַי; Origen: אֹיְבֵי

Ps. 35.22: תֶּחֱרַשׁ; Origen: תַּחֲרֵשׁ

Ps. 35.25: בִּלַּעֲנוּם; cf. p. 115

Ps. 35.27: חֲפֵצֵי; Origen: חֹפְצֵי

Ps. 36.2: לָרָשָׁע; Origen: לְרֶשַׁע; cf. p. 214/5

Ps. 36.2: לִבִּי; cf. pp. 115 and 118

Ps. 46.1: עֲלָמוֹת; Origen: עֲלָמוֹת

Ps. 46.2: עֶזְרָה; Origen: עֵזֶר

Ps. 46.3: אָרֶץ; cf. p. 118

Ps. 46.5: יְשַׂמְּחוּ; Origen: יִשְׂמְחוּ

Ps. 46.6: וְעֶזְרֶהָ; Origen: וְעֶזְרָה

Ps. 46.9: שַׁמּוֹת; Origen: שֵׁמוֹת

Ps. 46.10: יְשַׁבֵּר; Origen: יִשָּׁבֵר

Ps. 48.3: צָפוֹן; Origen: צָפוֹן

Ps. 49.4: וְהָגוּת; Origen: וְהָגִית

Ps. 49.4: חָכְמוֹת; Origen: חָכְמוֹת

Ps. 49.6: יְסֻבֵּנִי; Origen: יְסַבְּנִי

Ps. 49.6: עֲקֵבַי; Origen: עֲקֵבַי

Ps. 49.9: וְחָדַל; Origen: יֶחְדַּל

Ps. 49.12: קָרְאוּ; Origen: קָרְאוּ

Ps. 49.12: בְּתִימוֹ; Origen: בֵּיתָמוֹ

Ps. 49.14: יִרְצוּ; Origen: יָרֹצוּ

Ps. 49.15: וַיִּרְדּוּ; Origen: וְיִרְדוּ

Ps. 75.4: עַמּוּדֶיהָ; Origen: עַמּוּדָה

Ps. 76.10: עַנְוֵי; cf. p. 115

Ps. 89.31: וּבְמִשְׁפָּטַי; Origen: וּבְמִשְׁפָּטִי

Ps. 89.31: יֵלְכוּן; Origen: יְהַלֵּכוּן

Ps. 89.36: בְּקָדְשִׁי; cf. p. 115

Ps. 89.45: מִגַּרְתָּה; Origen: מָגְרַתָּה

Ps. 89.47: תִּסָּתֵר; cf. p. 115

Ps. 89.51: זְכֹר; Origen: אֶזְכֹּר

Ps. 92.7: יֵדַע; Origen: יָדַע

Ps. 110.3: מִשְׁחָר; Origen: מְשַׁחֵר

Ps. 127.2: הָעֲצָבִים; Origen: עֲצָבִים

When I had, then assistant editor in charge of the Ancient Bible Versions of Rudolf Kittel's *Biblia Hebraica* (third edition), to revise Frants Buhl's manuscript on the book of the Psalms for this edition, I embodied

in it the variants from Origen's Hexapla, as far as they seemed to me to fit
into the plans of the *Biblia Hebraica*; as a siglum I chose the sign "ﬡ°,"
which means: the Hebrew of Origen. By an oversight, due to the death
of Professor Rudolf Kittel and my subsequent resignation from the
Biblia Hebraica, this sign is not contained in the explanatory list of that
edition. The same is true of the siglum "ℭᵖ," which I had chosen for
variants from the Palestinian Targum on the Pentateuch; cf. MdW I,
p. 11*, note 1.

B. OUR APPROACH TO THE PROBLEMS

A. HOW TO USE THE SOURCE-MATERIAL

We wish to give here, as fully as our sources permit, an outline of a
Hebrew Grammar and Dictionary based upon the Greek and Latin
transliterations of Hebrew words and their respective derivatives. The
sources of these transliterations date from the third century B.C.E. to
the beginning of the fifth century C.E. Thus the end of this period antedates by several centuries the beginnings of the activities of the Masoretic
school of Tiberias. Because of this, while arranging the transliterations,
I did not consider the vocalization which the Masoretes of Tiberias gave
to the Hebrew words in question. For the better understanding of the
transliteration I had put in juxtaposition merely the Hebrew consonants
of the word to which the transliteration referred, without originally
vocalizing these consonants, since the transliteration was meant to indicate how these consonants should be vocalized and read; for instance:
מבלעדי μεββελαδη would mean that the word has to be read as מִבְּלְעֲדֵי,
and not מִבַּלְעֲדֵי as the Masoretes vocalized it; יחבל ιεβαλ would be יְחֲבֵּל,
as against יְחַבֵּל of the Masoretes. But for reasons of practical utility, in
the course of my work, I abandoned this method of leaving the Hebrew
equivalents of the transliterations unvocalized, and I vocalized them
with Tiberian vowel signs. Although these vowel signs, which I added
to the Hebrew consonants, are Tiberian, I did not always follow the
Tiberian rules in applying them. Sometimes I used the Tiberian signs
to indicate the vowels which are presupposed by the transliterated text;
for instance: חֹפְצִי, יְדְלַף instead of the Tiberian way of vocalizing these
forms as חֲפֵצִי, יִדְלֹף. This method I followed in the relatively numerous

cases, where the transliteration presupposes a word, different from that found in the Masoretic text; for instance: צָפוֹן, רֶשַׁע as compared with their corresponding Masoretic forms צָפוֹן, רֶשַׁע. Of course this method could not be followed throughout, since I could not vocalize a word like חֲלוֹם to read חֵלֶם, thus following the transliteration *helem*, although this form has its parallel in the Aramaic חילמא, since such a procedure would definitely diminish the intelligibility and practical utility of this study.

The necessity for vocalizing the Hebrew consonants first arose while dealing with those words, in which the transliteration yielded forms differing not only in pronunciation from the Masoretic reading, but actually changing the meaning of the Hebrew word as intended by the Masoretes; for instance: מִשְׂכִּים instead of מַשְׂכִּים, or שְׂעֹרִים instead of שְׂעָרִים. In order to bring into sharp relief the distinction between the Masoretic and the transliterated word, it was necessary to vocalize the Masoretic word too. The Tiberian system was used for this purpose, since this system covers— unlike the Babylonian or Palestinian system—the entire Biblical Hebrew vocabulary. The Tiberian vocalization, therefore, serves only a practical end and is irrelevant for an appreciation of the problems dealt with in this investigation. Cf. also pages 214 and 220.

B.   CURRENT APPROACHES REFUTED

Each of the sources has already been dealt with in special monographs; so for instance the Septuagint by Cl. Könnecke in his paper *Die Behandlung der hebräischen Namen in der Septuaginta*, Stargard 1885; the Hexaplaric material more recently by O. Pretzl in "Biblische Zeitschrift" 1932, pp. 4-32; and Jerome by C. Siegfried in ZAW, IV, 1884, pp. 34-83. But all of them missed the point; for they considered the Masoretic textus receptus with its Tiberian vocalization as the Hebrew text which served as the basis for the Septuagint, Origen and St. Jerome respectively for their transliterations. In the early days of Könnecke and Siegfried one could hardly expect a more critical standpoint as regards the Masoretic text; and when we find that for instance Siegfried went sometimes even so far as to "correct," according to the Masoretic text, Jerome's spelling of a Hebrew word in his transliteration without noting down, that his citation is based upon such a "correction"

—e.g. דעה deah instead of dea; רוח ruah instead of rua; מלככם malche-
chem instead of melchechem—we may excuse it out of this consideration.
But even Pretzl, who criticizes Max L. Margolis' approach to the problem
(in the latters paper *The pronunciation of* שוא *according to new Hexaplaric
material*, AJSL, XXVI, p. 62 f.), shows just the same misconception;
cf. f.i. p. 8 in his paper, § I 3β where he advances a theory that the
Greek ε was pronounced like "a" since it is used to indicate a *patah*, as
f.i. in δερχω for דַרכו, δερχι for דַרכי, ρεγλαι for רַגלי. I am rather doubtful
as to whether such a procedure is methodically justifiable. For I think
that Pretzl would first have to prove from purely Greek sources that ε
could have had the phonetic value of an α. But even then, a mere comparison of the words in question with their equivalent forms in the
Babylonian vocalization would have taught him that according to this
system דרך and רגל belong to the *qitl*-class, cf. דרכּם Prov. 1.31; דרכֹּי
ib. 3.17; דרכֹּו ib. 11.5 (in Ms. Ec 1); further רגלֹי Ps. 40.3 (in Ms. Ec 1)
and רגליֹו Ex. 25.26 (in Ms. Ea 5). In these cases the Greek transliteration
and the Babylonian vocalization of Hebrew are in full agreement between
themselves and both presuppose a pronunciation of Hebrew, different
from what the Tiberian Masoretes offer us. This most essential point
Pretzl failed to see. I deal with these details at length so as to show that
all the reasearch that has been done in this field until now could not
spare me the trouble of starting my own investigation from the very
beginning, i.e. to go through the sources indicated above for collecting
my material. And may I be permitted here to say that it was not an easy
task at all to find the proper method for arranging and classifying the
large amount of material, which first seemed to contradict itself in nearly
every detail. I did my best to present the results of long years of conti-
nuous study in such a form, as may interest the serious minded student
of Hebrew Grammar, without making him aware of the uncountable
difficulties which I had to overcome before I found my way out of this
labyrinth.

Five years after these researches were published in their first edition
(under the title *Hebrew based upon Greek and Latin Transliterations*,
HUCA, 1937/8), there appeared Einar Brónno's *Studien über Hebräische
Morphologie und Vokalismus auf Grund der Mercatischen Fragmente der
zweiten Kolumne der Hexapla des Origenes* as volume 28 of the *Abhand-*

lungen für die Kunde des Morgenlandes, Leipzig 1943. I know of no more impartial way to describe the author's approach to the grammatical problems involved than by quoting him. According to him, Greek EPSILON occurs 471 times and indicates: 1) *Sere* (34 times); 2) *Chirez* in geschlossener, druckloser Silbe (107 times); 3) *Segol* in ursprünglich geschlossener, druckloser Silbe (45 times); 4) *Patach* in ursprünglich geschlossener, druckloser Silbe (69 times); 5) *Patach* in ursprünglich geschlossener Drucksilbe (17 times); 6) *Segol* in Drucksilben (57 times); 7) *Schewa Quiescens* (5 times); 8) *Schewa Mobile* (33 times); 9) *Chateph-Segol* (25 times); 10) *Chapeth-Patach* (16 times); 12) *Jod* oder *langes Chirez* (4 times); 13) *Qames* (7 times).—Greek ALPHA occurs 804 times and indicates: 1) *Chirez* (24 times); 2) *Segol* (42 times); 3) *Patach* (212 times); 4) *Chateph-Segol* (twice); 5) *Chateph-Patach* (33 times); 6) *Schewa Mobile* (44 times); 7) *Qames Antetonicum* (146 times); 8) *Qames non-Antetonicum* (216 times); 9) Abweichende Formenbildungen (19 cases). Thus, the author's contention is that in all instances the transliteration reflects the Masoretic form with all the *minutiae* of its Tiberian vocalization (cf. MH §§ 84 and 85). According to the author, any Greek vowel-letter can indicate any Hebrew vowel. I hope I'll be forgiven if I refuse to take such an attitude seriously enough to deserve a more detailed refutation. Cf. also MH §§ 5-7.

C. HEBREW DICTIONARY

The subdivisions (a, b, c) indicate that these transliterations are evidence of different pronunciations, as dealt with in the respective paragraphs of the Grammar p. 178 ff.; for nominal forms cf. d 3) General Observations 2a (classifications of מֶלֶךְ). As a rule, differences in the rendering of Hebrew consonants (cf. d 1) 5)) are hereby *not* considered.

א

אָב αβ G in Ελιαβ, Ex. 31.6; ab On in Eliab ib.

אָבִי αβει B in Αβειηλ, 1 Sam. 9.1; αβι A in Αβιηλ, ib.; O Ps. 89.27; abi J in Abimelech, Gen. 20.2.

אֲבוֹתָם abotham J Isa. 14.21.

אֹבֹת אבת ωβωθ G Num. 21.10.

יֹאבְדוּ אבד ιοβαδου O Ps. 49.11; cf. BV Prov. 19.9: יֹאבַד in Ms. Ec 1 for MT יֹאבֵד.

אָבִיב abib J Ezek. 3.15.

אֶבְיוֹן ebion J Isa. 25.4.

וְאֶבְיוֹן ουεβιων O Ps. 49.3.

אֶבְיוֹנִים ebionim J Jer. 5.28.

אֲבִיוֹנָה abiona J Eccl. 12.5.

אָבֵל αβελ G 2 Sam. 20.14; abel On in Abelsattim, Num. 33.49.

אָבֵל a) כְּאָבֵל χεεβλ O Ps. 35.14; MT: כַּאֲבֵל; cf. BV ib. אָבֵל in Ms. Ec 1.

b) אָבֵל εβελ B in Εβελχαρμειν, Ju. 11.33; MT: אָבֵל.

אֶבֶן a) אֲבָנִים abanim J Jer. 18.3; MT: אֲבָנִים.

b) אֶבֶן αβεν G in Αβενεζερ, 1 Sam. 7.12; aben J Zech. 5.7.

אַבְרֵךְ abrech J Gen. 41.43.

אַגְמוֹן agmon J Isa. 19.15.

אַגָּן אַגָּנוֹת aganoth J Isa. 22.24.

אָדוֹן אֲדוֹנִי αδωνει B in Αδωνειραμ, 1 Ki. 4.6; αδωνι A in Αδωνιραμ, ib.; adoni On in Adoniram, ib.

אֲדֹנָי αδωναι O Ps. 30.9.

אָדָם αδαμ A Gen. 3.21; O Ps. 31.20; adam On Gen. 3.21.

הָאָדָם aadam J Isa. 2.22.

אֲדָמִים אדם adamim J Zech. 6.2; cf. s.v. אמץ.

אֲדָמָה αδαμα G Deut. 29.23; MT: אֲדָמָה; adama On ib.

אֲדָמוֹת αδαμωθ O Ps. 49.12.

וָאֹהֲבֵהוּ אהב ουεαβηου O Hos. 11.1; MT: וָאֹהֲבֵהוּ; cf. אָהַב Prov. 8.17; cf. B-L § 53r, u.

אֶהֱבוּ αβου O Ps. 31.24.

אהל a) אָהֳלִי ολι A in Ολιβα, Ezek. 23.4; oli On in Olibama, Gen. 36.2; cf. in BV monosyllabic nominal forms like: כָּאֹהֳלֵי Cant. 1.5; בְּאָהֳלֶךָ Ps. 91.10; בְּאָהֳלֵיהֶם Ps. 106.25 (Ms. Ec 1).

b) אֹהֶל οολ A 1 Chron. 3.20: OOA lege: OOΛ. אָהֳלִי οολι B in Οολιβα, Ezek. 23.4; ooli On in Ooliba, ib.

אוֹי oi J Isa. 24.16.

אוֹיֵב a) ωιηβ O Ps. 31.9. אֹיְבִי ωιεβη O Ps. 35.19: ωεβη lege: ωιεβη; cf. Thompson Facs. 6 (I-E); MT: אֹיְבִי. אֹיְבִי οιεβαι O Ps. 18.38; οιεββαι O Ps. 30.2.

b) אֹיְבֶיךָ οιβαχ O Ps. 89.52. אֹיְבָיו οιβαυ O Ps. 89. 43.

אוּלָם ουλαμ G 1 Chron. 7.16; ulam J Ezek. 40.24; MT: אֵילָם.

אָוֶן aven J Am. 1.5; aben On in Bethaben, Hos. 4.15; for the interchange of v and b, cf. Josh. 3.10: הַחִוִּי Codex B: ευαιον, Codex n: εβαιον (the Hebrew ו rendered as: υ-β); the reverse cf. ib.: וְהַיְבוּסִי Codex B: ιεβουσαιον, Codex b: ιευουσαιον (the Hebrew ב rendered as: β-υ); cf. *The Old Testament in Greek*, edited by A. E. Brooke and N. Mc Lean, Vol. I, Part IV, Cambridge 1917.

אוֹן a) αυν B Num. 16.1; aun On Ezek. 30.17; MT: אֹן; cf. B-L § 17b; cf. s.v. מות sub a.

אוֹנָן αυναν A Gen. 38.9.

b) אוֹן ων G Hos. 4.15; MT: אָוֶן; on On, ib.; cf. in the PV הָאוֹן, (MdWI, p. ?, line 5), וּמֵאוֹן (ib., line 6).
אוֹנִי oni On in Benoni, Gen. 35.18.
אוֹנוֹ ωνω G Neh. 7.37.
אוֹנָם ωναμ A 1 Chron. 1.40.
אוֹנָן ωναν B 1 Chron. 1.40; MT: אוֹנָם; onan On Gen. 38.9.

אוֹר or J Isa. 31.9.
אוֹרֹת oroth J Isa. 26.19.

אוּר ουρ G in Cεδιουρ, Num. 1.5; ur J Isa. 31.9.
אוּרִי ουρει B 1 Chron. 2.20; ουρι A, ib.

אוֹר יָאִיר ιαειρ G Deut. 3.14; iair On Num. 32.41.
תָּאִיר θαειρ O Ps. 18.29.

אוֹן אָזְנִי οζνι O Ps. 49.5; ozni On Num. 26.16.
אָזְנֶךָ οζναχ O Ps. 31.3.

אזן הַאֲזִינוּ eezinu J Joel 1.2.
אזר וְתְּאַזְּרֵנִי ουθεζορηνι O Ps. 18.40; MT: וַתְּאַזְּרֵנִי.
וַתְּאַזְּרֵנִי ουεθαζερηνι O Ps. 30.12; without gemination of the 2nd radical; cf. on אָכְזָב.
הַמְאַזְּרֵנִי αμμααζερηνι O Ps. 18.33; MT: הַמְאַ'.

אָח a) αχ G in Αχααβ, 2 Ki. 1.1.
אָחִי αχει B in Αχεινααν, 1 Sam. 25.43; αχι A in Αχινααμ, ib.; achi On in Achisamech, Ex. 31.6.
b) אָח α O Ps. 49.8; cf. p. 175 sub ה.
כְּאָח χαα O Ps. 35.14.
אָחִי ahi On in Ahihod,

Num. 34.27; for the insertion of the h between a and i, cf. p. 111.
אח אֹחִים oiim J Isa. 13.21; p. 245C; ohim J ib., p. 174E; for the insertion of h between o and i, cf. p. 111.
אַחַד aad J Gen. 48.22.
אָחוּ ahu J Gen. 41.2; cf. p. 111 and p. 175 sub ה.
אָחָז αχας B in Ιωαχας, 2 Ki. 10.35; cf. p. 175 sub ז and ה.
αχαζ A in Ιωαχαζ, ib.; achaz On Mic. 1.1.
ααζ A in Ααζια, 2 Ki. 14.13; aaz On 2 Ki. 15.38.
אַחַר αερ B 1 Chron. 7.12; aher J Isa. 42.8; cf. p. 111 and p. 175 sub ה.
לַאֲחֵרִים λαηριμ O Ps. 49.11; for the change of ε in the singular to η in the plural, see our remarks on p. 215/6.
אַחֲרֵי וְאַחֲרֵיהָם ουααρηεμ O Ps. 49.14: OYΔAPHEM, lege A pro Δ; cf. Thompson Facs. 4 and 5.
אַחַת ααθ O Ps. 89.36.
אָטָד αταδ G Gen. 50.10; atad On, ib.
אטם אֲטֻמוֹת atemoth J Ezek. 40.16; MT: אֲטֻמוֹת.
אי אִיִּים iim J Isa. 13.22.
אַיֵּה αιη O Ps. 89.50.
אַיִל el J Ezek. 40.14.
אֵלִים elim J Ezek. 40.14.
אֵלִי ele J Isa. 61.3.
אֵלָו elau J Ezek. 40.21.
אַיָּלָה aiala J Gen. 49.21.
כְּאַיָּלוֹת χαιαλωθ O Ps. 18.34.
אִין אֵין ην O Ps. 32.9.

וְאֵין ουην O Ps. 18.42.

מֵאֵין μηην O Mal. 2.13.

אֵיפָה epha J Isa. 5.10.

אִישׁ εις B in Ειστωβ, 2 Sam. 10.6;
O Ps. 31.21; eis J Gen.
32.29.

ις A in Ιστωβ, 2 Sam. 10.6;
O Ps. 92.7; is J Jer. 1.11.
his On in Histob, 2 Sam. 10.6.

הָאִישׁ αεις O Ps. 1.1.

אִישִׁי issi J Hos. 2.18; cf. in
the BV אִשִׁי 2 Sam. 14.5 in
Ms. 105 JThS; the omis-
sion of the ' after א necessitates a gemination of the
שׁ according to the rules of
the Tiberian Grammar.

אֵיתָן a) αιθαν G 1 Chron. 15.17;
cf. s.v. בית and חִיל sub a.

b) ethan J Jer. 5.15

אֵתָנִים ethanim J Mic. 6.2.

אַךְ ach J Jer. 32.30.

אָכֵן αχην O Ps. 31.23.

אַל ελ O Gen. 49.4; Ps. 31.2; cf.
in the BV אַל 2 Sam. 1.21
in Ms. 105 JThS.

אֵל a) al J in alechcha: אֵל־חִכְּךָ
Hos. 8.1; cf. in the BV
אֵל 2 Sam. 14.8 in Ms. 105
JThS.

b) ελ O Mal. 2.13.

וְאֵל ουελ O Ps. 30.9.

אֵלַי ηλαι O Gen. 43.23; elai
J Isa. 21.11.

ιλει O Ps. 31.3; cf. in the BV
אֵל 2 Sam. 3.8 in Ms. 105
JThS.

אֵלֶיךָ ηλαχ O Ps. 30.9.

אֵלָיו ηλαυ O Ps. 32.6.

אֵל ηλ G in Αβειηλ, 1 Sam. 9.1;
O Ps. 29.3; ελ G in Ελκα-
να, Ex. 6.24; el J Isa. 9.15.

הָאֵל αηλ O Ps. 18.31.

אֵלִי ηλει B in Μελλιηλει, Num.
26.45; ηλι O Ps. 89.27;
ελι G in Ελιαβ, Num. 1.9;
eli On in Eliezer, Ex. 18.4.

אֵלִים ηλιμ O Ps. 29.1.

אֱלֹהִים ελωειμ O Ps. 36.2; eloim J
Gen. 6.2.

מֵאֱלֹהִים μηελωειμ O Ps. 8.6.

אֱלֹהֵי ελωη O Ps. 18.47;
ελωει O Ps. 72.15; ελωι
O Ps. 47.10; to the He-
brew ending in ־ִ, ren-
dered by η, ει and ι respectively, cf. p. 175 sub י.

אֱלֹהַי ελωαι O Ps. 18.29.

וּבֵאלֹהַי ουβελωαι O Ps. 18.30.

אֱלֹהֶיךָ ελωαχ O Ps. 45.8;
eloach J Am. 4.12:
ELOAH is a misprint for:
ELOACH.

בֵּאלֹהָיו βελοαυ O Isa. 8.21;
MT: וּבֵאלֹהָיו.

אֱלֹהֵינוּ ελωηνου O Ps. 18.32:
ΕΛΩΝΝΟΥ lege ΕΛΩΗ-
ΝΟΥ; cf. Thompson Facs.
5 (N-H).

אֱלוֹהַּ ελω O Ps. 18.32; cf. in the BV
אֱלוֹהַ Job 3.23: in Ms. Ec1.

אֵלֶּה ella J Jer. 2.34.

אֵלֶּה ela On Gen. 36.41.

אֵלְמוֹת אלם elamoth J Ezek.
40.16.

אֵם εμ O Ps. 35.14.

אִם εμ O Ps. 89.31.

אַמָּה αμμα G 2 Sam. 2.24 (B:
AMMAN is a scribe's
mistake); amma On ib.

אֱמוּנִים אמון

a) εμουνιμ O Ps. 31.24.

b) εμμουνειμ O Isa. 26.2;
emmunim J ib.

אֱמוּנָה emuna J Jer. 5.3.

בֶּאֱמוּנָתִי βαεμουναθι O Ps. 89.34.

בֶּאֱמוּנָתֶךָ βαεμουναθαχ O Ps. 89.50.

בֶּאֱמוּנָתוֹ baemunatho J Hab. 2.4.

אָמִיר amir J Isa. 17.9.

אָמֵן αμην O Ps. 89.53; amen J Isa. 65.16.

וְאָמֵן ουαμην O Ps. 89.53.

אמן נֶאֱמָן νεεμαν O Ps. 89.38.

נֶאֱמְנָת νεεμαναθ O Ps. 89.29.

נֶאֱמָנִים neemanim J Isa. 17.11.

אמץ אֹמְצִים amasim J Zech. 6.3; cf. s.v. אדם.

אָמַר αμαρ G in Αμαρεια, 1 Chron. 5.33.

אָמַרְתִּי αμαρθι O Ps. 30.7.

אָמְרוּ αμρου O Ps. 35.21.

יֹאמְרוּ ιωμρου O Ps. 35.25.

אָמַר εμμηρ G Jer. 20.1; emmer J ib.

אמרה אִמְרַת εμαραθ O Ps. 18.31.

אֱמֶת ημεθ O Ps. 31.6; cf. in the BV אֹמֶת Prov. 11.18 in Ms. Ec 1, and in the PV אֹמֶת Prov. 22.21 (MdWl, p. יה).

אֲמִתֶּךָ εμεθθαχ O Ps. 30.10; on the change of η in ημεθ to ε in εμεθθαχ, see our remarks in p. 215/6.

אָנָּא αννα O Ps. 118.25.

אָנָּה anna J Jon. 4.2.

אֱנוֹשׁ ενως A Gen. 4.26; enos On ib.

אָנוּשׁ anus J Isa. 17.11.

אֲנִי ανι O Ps. 89.48.

וַאֲנִי ουανι O Ps. 30.7.

אֲנָךְ enach J Am. 7.7.

אָנֹכִי ανωχ O Ps. 46.11.

אנקה וַאֲנָקה ουανακα O Mal. 2.13.

אָסִיר ασειρ B Ex. 6.4.; MT: אַסִּיר; ασηρ A ib.; asir On ib.; cf. our note on אֱלֹהַי.

אָסָף ασαφ G Isa. 36.3; asaf On ib.

וְנֶאֱסְפוּ ουνεεσαφου O Ps. 35.15: ΟΥΝΕССΑΦΟΥ lege E for first C; cf. s.v. אמן; cf. Thompson Facs. 5 (E-C).

אסר אֲסוּרִים assurim J Eccl. 7.26.

אַף αφ O Ps. 89.28.

אף אַפּוֹ aphpho J Am. 1.11.

בְּאַפּוֹ βααφφω O Ps. 30.6; baaphpho J Isa. 2.22.

אֵפוֹד ephod J Zech. 12.10.

אֶפְעֶה ephee J Isa. 59.5; the second e is probably the transliteration of the ע; cf. p. 176 sub ע.

אֵפֶר כָּאֵפֶר χαεφηρ O Ps. 147.16.

אֵצֶל asel J Zech. 14.5; cf. MT אָצֵל 1 Chron. 8.37.

אֵצֶל asel J Mic. 1.11.

אֹצֶר ωσαρ B 1 Chron. 1.42; MT: אֹצֶר.

אֶקְדָּח ecda J Isa. 54.12.

אַרְבֶּה arbe J Hos. 13.3.

אַרְבָּה a) orobba J Hos. 13.3.

b) אֲרֻבּוֹת arobboth On 1 Ki. 4.10.

אַרְבַּע arbee On Gen. 23.2; on the second e cf. p. 176 sub ע.

אַרְבָּעִים αρβαειμ O 1 Sam. 4.18; arbaim J Jon. 3.4.

ארג אֲרָגִים ωργειμ G 2 Sam. 21.19.

אַרְגָּמָן argaman J Ezek. 27.16.

אֶרֶז araz J Jer. 22.15.

ארח אָרְחֶךָ ορχ O Ps. 44.19.

אֲרִי αρι G in Αριηλ, Isa. 29.1; ari J in ariel, ib.

אַרְיֵה a) αρεια B 2 Ki. 15.25; aria J Isa. 21.8 (IV, p. 216A).

b) αριε A 2 Ki. 15.25; arie Isa. 21.8 (IV, p. 305A).

אֹרֶךְ ορεχ A Gen. 10.10; MT: אֶרֶךְ; orech On ib.

ארמון אַרְמְנוֹת armanoth J Jer. 17.27; cf. B-L § 67f and § 26 o'.

אֶרֶץ αρς O Ps. 35.20.

הָאָרֶץ ααρς O Ps. 46.3; MT: אָרֶץ

בָּאָרֶץ βααρς O Ps. 46.9, 11.

לָאָרֶץ λααρς O Ps. 89.40, 45.

אֵשׁ ες O Ps. 89.47.

בָּאֵשׁ βαες O Ps. 46.10.

אִשָּׁה issa J Jer. 1.11; hissa J Gen. 2.23; cf. s.v. אִישׁ.

נָשִׁים nasim J Isa. 3.12.

נְשֵׁי nese J Zech. 12.12.

אשור אֲשׁוּרֵינוּ ασουρενου O Ps. 44.19.

אשם וְאָשַׁם vasam J Hab. 1.11; MT: וְאָשֵׁם; cf. in the BV כָּאֹשֶׁם 2 Sam. 14.13 in Ms. 105 JThS for MT כְּאֶשֶׁם; וּיֹבֵשׁ Job 14.11 in Ms. Ec 1 for MT וְיָבֵשׁ; כֹּבֵד Gen. 13.2 and שֹׁלֵם ib. 15.16, both instances in Ms. Ka 2, for MT כָּבֵד and שָׁלֵם respectively. The spelling of the transliteration has to be corrected to: uasam; cf. p. 175 sub ו.

אשמה אַשְׁמַת asamath J Am. 8.14.

אֲשֶׁר a) ασερ O Ps. 1.1.; aser J Isa. 2.22.

b) εσερ O Ps. 31.8; eser J Ezek. 40.49.

אָשֵׁר ασηρ G Ex. 1.4; aser On ib.

אַשְׁרֵי εσρη O Ps. 1.1.

אֲשִׁישֵׁי asise J Hos. 3.1.

אֵת εθ O Mal. 2.13; Ps. 28.9; eth J Hab. 3.13.

אוֹתִי ωθι O Ps. 31.6.

אַתָּה a) αθθα O Ps. 18.28.

b) וְאַתָּה ουαθ O Ps. 89.39.

ב

בְּךָ— בָּךְ βαχ O Isa. 26.3.

בּוֹ βω O Ps. 18.31.

בָּהּ βα G in Οψειβα, 2 Ki. 21.1; ba On in Ooliba, Ezek. 23.4.

בָּהֶם bahem J Gen. 14.5; MT: בְּהָם.

בָּם βαμ O Ps. 49.15.

בְּאֵר a) בְּאֵר βηρ G in Βηρσαβεε, 1 Chron. 21.2; cf. Sam. Gen. 24.20: הביר (MT: הבאר). ber On in Bersabee, ib.

בְּאֵרֹת βηρωθ G Deut. 10.6; beroth On ib.

b) בְּאֵר βεηρ B in Βηρσαβεε, 2 Chron. 19.4.

בְּאֵרִי beeri On Gen. 26.34.

באש בְּאָשִׁים busim J Isa. 5.2.

בַּד bad J Zech. 12.12.

בַּדִּים baddim J Ezek. 9.2.

בַּדָּיו baddau J Hos. 11.6.

בהל נִבְהָל νεβαλ O Ps. 30.8.

בהלה לְבֶּהָלָה labala J Isa. 65.23.

בהמה a) כַּבְּהֵמוֹת χαβημωθ O Ps. 49.13.

b) בַּהֲמוֹת beemoth J Isa. 30.6.

בוא בָּא βα O Gen. 43.23.

בָּאוּ bau J Jer. 32.29.

וְיָבוֹא ουιαβω O Isa. 26.2.

לָבוֹא λαβω B Ju. 3.3.; cf. MT Jer. 46.13: לָבוֹא.

הַבָּא αββα O Ps. 118.26.

בּוּז buz On Gen. 22.21.

בּוּזִי βουζει G Ezek. 1.3; buzi On ib.

בּוּץ bus J Ezek. 27.16.

בּוֹר βωρ O Ps. 30.4; bor J Jer. 6.7.

בּוֹשׁ יֵבוֹשׁוּ ιηβωσου O Ps. 35.26.

בּוּשָׁה βωσα O Ps. 89.46.

בֶּזֶק βεζεκ B Ju. 1.4; bezec J Ezek. 1.14; MT: בָּזָק.

בָּחוּר בַּחוּרִים βαουρειμ G 2 Sam. 19.17; baurim On ib.

בחר יִבְחַר a) ιβααρ B 1 Chron. 3.6: βααρ lege ιβααρ; haplography.

b) ιεβααρ A ib.

בֶּטַח bete J Gen. 34.25.

בָּטַח βατε O Ps. 28.7.

בָּטַחְתִּי βαταθι O Ps. 31.7.

וְהַבּוֹטֵחַ ουαββωτη O Ps. 32.10.

הַבֹּטְחִים αββωτεειμ O Ps. 49.7.

בְּטֻחוּ βετου O Isa. 26.4.

בֶּטֶן a) בֶּטֶן βατνε A Josh. 19.25; cf. in the BV בֹטְנֵי Prov. 31.2; בֹטְנֵךְ Cant. 7.3 in Ms. Ec 1.

b) בֶּטֶן beten On Josh. 19.25; מִבֶּטֶן mebeten J Isa. 46.3; MT: מִנִּי־בֶטֶן.

בִין יָבִין ιαβειν B Ju. 4.2; ιαβιν O Ps. 92.7; iabin On Ju. 4.2.

הָבִין αβιν O Ps. 32.9.

בית a) הַבַּיִת αββαιθ O Ps. 30.1.

בֵּית βαιθ B in Βαιθηλ, Josh. 7.2.; cf. s.v. חִיל sub a.

b) בֵּית βηθ A in Βηθαυν Josh.

7.2; βεθ A in Βεθθαπφουε, Josh. 15.53; beth On in Bethel, Gen. 12.8.

לְבֵית λβηθ O Ps. 31.3.

מְבֵית mebbeth J Am. 1.5.

בֵּיתִי bethi J Gen. 15.2.

בֵּיתָמוֹ βηθαμου O Ps. 49.12; MT: בָּתֵּימוֹ.

בְּכוֹר a) βχωρ O Ps. 89.28.

b) bechor On Gen. 46.21; MT: בֶּכֶר.

בכורה בְּכוֹרַת βεχωραθ A 1 Sam. 9.1.

בְּכוּרָה bechchora J Mic. 7.1.

בְּכִי βεχι O Mal. 2.13; Ps. 30.6.

בֵּל bel J Hos. 2.18.

בַּל βαλ O Ps. 30.7.

בלה יִבְלוּ ιεβλου O Ps. 18.46: IEBAOY lege Λ for A.

לְבַלּוֹת λαβαλωθ O Ps. 49.15.

בְּלִיַּעַל βελιαλ O Prov. 16.27; cf. in the BV בְּלִיַּעַל ib. 6.12: in Ms. Ec 1; belial J Isa. 27.1.

בלם לִבְלוֹם λαβλωμ O Ps. 32.9.

בָּלַע βαλα A Gen. 46.21; MT: בָּלַע.

בִּלְעָם βαλααμ G Num. 22.5; MT: בִּלְעָם; balaam On ib.

יִבְלַע ιεβλα G in Ιεβλααμ, Ju. 1.27; iebla On in Ieblaam 2 Ki. 9.27.

בִּלְעֲנוּהוּ βελλενουου O Ps. 35.25.

בלעדי מִבִּלְעֲדִי μεββελαδη O Ps. 18.32; MT: מִבַּלְעֲדִי.

בָּמָה βαμα G 1 Sam. 9.12; bama On ib.

בָּמוֹת βαμωθ G Num. 21.19; bamoth On ib.

בֵּן a) βεν A 1 Ki. 4.8; O Ps. 9.1; MT: לַבֵּן; ben On in Ruben, Gen. 29.32.

וּבֵן uben J Gen. 15.2.

בֵּן baben J Gen. 1.1.

בָּנַיִךְ benaich J Ezek. 27.4;
cf. in the PV בְּנֵ (Edelmann, p. ד, line 15); בְּנֵי
Ex. 13.18 (ib., line 7).

b) לִבְנֵי λαβανι O Hos. 11.1.

בְּנֵי βαναι B in Βαναιβακατ,
Josh. 19.45.
βανη A in Βανηβαρακ, ib.;
O Ps. 18.46; bane On in
Banebarac, Josh. 19.45.

בָּנָיו βαναυ O Ps. 89.31.

c) בְּנֵי βνη O Ps. 29.1.
לִבְנֵי λαβνη O Ps. 49.1; Ps.
46.1.
λεβνη O Ps. 12.9.

בנה בָּנַיִךְ bonaich J Ezek. 27.4.

בַּעַל βααλ G in Βααλβεριθ, Ju. 9.4.;
baal On in Baalberith,
Num. 33.7.

בַּעֲלִי baali J Hos. 2.18.

בְּעָלִים βααλειμ G 1 Sam. 7.4;
baalim On ib.

בעל בְּעוּלָה bula J Isa. 62.4.

בַּעֲלָה a) בְּעָלוֹת βαλωθ A Josh.
15.24.

b) בַּעֲלָה βααλα A Josh.
15.29; baala On ib.

בְּעָלוֹת baaloth On Josh.
15.24.

בַּעַר a) בַּעַר βαρ O Ps. 92.7.

b) וְבַעַר ουβααρ O Ps. 49.11.

בער תִּבְעַר θεβαρ O Ps. 89.47.

בֶּצַע βεσε O in μεββεσε, Ps. 30.10.

בַּקְבּוּק a) bocboc J Jer. 19.1.

b) βαϰβουϰ A Ezra 2.51.

בֶּקַע bace J Gen. 24.22.

בֹּקֶר a) לַבֹּקֶר λαβεϰρ O Ps. 49.15.

b) בֹּקֶר βοϰρ O Ps. 46.6.

בקר בּוֹקֵר bocer J Am. 7.14.

בַּר bar J Zech. 12.12.

ברא בְּרָאתָ βαραθα O Ps. 89.48.

בָּרָד βαραδ A Gen. 16.14; MT:
בָּרָד; barad On ib.

ברד בְּרֻדִּים borodim J Zech. 6.3.

בָּרִיחַ bari J Isa. 27.1.

בְּרִיחִים barihim J Isa. 43.14;
cf. p. 111 and 175 sub ח.

בְּרִית a) βεριθ B in Βααλβεριθ, Ju.
9.4; berith On Ju. 9.46.

b) βριθ O Ps. 89.40; brith
J Mal. 2.4.

בְּרִיתִי βριθι O Ps. 89.35.

וּבְרִיתִי ουβριθι O Ps. 89.29.

בֹּרִית borith J Jer. 2.22.

בָּרֵךְ βαραχ G in Βαραχιηλ, Job
32.2; barach On in Ba-
rachel, ib.

בָּרוּךְ βαρουχ G Jer. 32.12;
O Ps. 118.26; baruch On
Jer. 32.12.

וּבָרֵךְ ουβαρεχ O Ps. 28.9.

בָּרָק βαραϰ B Ju. 4.6; barac On ib.

ברר בְּרוּרָה barura J Zeph. 3.9.

תִּתְבָּרָר θεθβαραρ O Ps. 18.
27: ΘΕΘΒΑΡΑΒ lege P
for second B.

בָּשָׂר a) basar J Ezek. 10.12.

בְּשָׂרִי basari J Hos. 8.12; cf.
B-L § 26s'.

b) בָּשָׂר bosor J Isa. 34.6;
cf. s.v. זָכָר; cf. also the
following spellings in Sam:
Gen. 11.31: כלותו (MT:
כַּלָּתוֹ); ib. 18.33: שוב
(MT: שָׁב); Ex. 32.25:
בקומיהם (MT: בְּקֻמֵיהֶם);
Lev. 26.26: במשקול (MT:
בַּמִּשְׁקָל).

בֹּשֶׁת a) βοσθε B in Ισβοσθε, 2
Sam. 2.8.

b) boseth On in Hisboseth,
ib.

בַּת a) bath J Ezek. 45.11; Mic. 4.14.

b) beth J Isa. 5.10.

בְּתוּלָה bethula J Isa. 7.14.

ג

גַּאֲוָה a) γαυα O Ps. 31.24: ραυα lege γ for ρ; phonetic mistake: γ before an α and o sounded like ρ.

b) בְּגַאֲוָתוֹ βγηουαθω O Ps. 46.4.

גָּאוֹן גאון gaon J Hos. 5.5.

גָּאַל גאל a) ιγααλ B Num. 13.7: ΙΛΑΑΛ lege: ΙΓΑΑΛ; cf. Thompson Facs. 6 (Λ-Γ).

b) ιγαλ A ib.

c) iegal On ib.

גּוֹאֵל goel J Isa. 59.20.

גְּאָלְתֶךָ גאלה goolathach J Ezek. 11.15.

גַּב a) gab J Ezek. 43.13.

b) gob J Ezek. 16.24.

גֵּבִים גב gebim J Isa. 10.31.

גְּבוּל gebul J Obad. 20.

גְּבוּלַיִךְ gebulaich J Ezek. 27.4: gebulaic lege -aich; cf. p. 176 sub כ.

גִּבּוֹר a) γιββωρ O Isa. 9.5; gibbor J ib.

b) גִּבּוֹרִים geborim J Isa. 13.3.

גְּבוּרוֹת גבורה geburoth J Jer. 13.18; cf. in the PV גְּבוֹרְתָךְ Ps. 71.18 (MdWII, p. 86).

בִּגְבוּרֹתָיו βεγεβουροθαυ O Ps. 150.2.

גְּבִירָה gebira J Jer. 13.18.

גִּבְעָה γαβαα G Josh. 15.57; gabaa On 1 Sam. 10.26.

גִּבְעַת γαβααθ A Josh. 18.28;

gabaath On Josh. 24.33.

גִּבְעוֹת γαβαωθ B Josh. 18.28; MT: גִּבְעַת.

גֶּבֶר a) גֶּבֶר γαβρ O Ps. 89.49.

גַּבְרִי γαβρι G in Γαβριηλ, Dan. 8.16.

b) גֶּבֶר geber J Isa. 22.17.

c) גֶּבֶר γαβερ G Num. 33.35.

גֶּבֶר γαβρ O Ps. 18.26.

גְּדוּד γεδουδ O Ps. 18.30; gedud J Mic. 4.14.

גָּדוֹל gadol J Jon. 2.1.

גְּדוּפָה geddupha J Ezek. 5.15.

גִּדַּל גדל ιεγδελ O Ps. 35.27.

גְּדֵּל γεδδηλ A Ezra 2.47.

גִּדַּלְתִּי γεδδελθι A 1 Chron. 25.29.

הַמַּגְדִּילִים [αμ]μαγδιλιμ O Ps. 35.26.

גָּדֵר γαδερ A Josh. 12.13; MT: גָּדֵר; gader J Ezek. 42.7.

גְּדֵר גדר goder J Isa. 58.12.

גְּדֵרָה a) γαδηρα G Josh. 15.36; gadera On ib.

גְּדֵרוֹת γαδηρωθ A Josh. 15.41; gaderoth On ib.

b) גְּדֵרֹתָיו γαδρωθαυ O Ps. 89.41: ΓΑΔΡΩΘΑΣ, lege Y for C.

וַיְגֹהַר גהר ουιεγαρ O 2 Ki. 4.35.

גּוֹי γωι O Isa. 26.2; goi J Zeph. 2.5.

הַגּוֹי aggoi J Mal. 3.9.

גּוֹיִם γωειμ A Josh. 12.23; γωιμ O Ps. 46.7.

בַּגּוֹיִם baggoim J Hab. 1.5.

גּוּר גור ιαγουρ A Josh. 15.21; iagur On ib.

גָּר gar J Zeph. 2.5.

גֹּזִי גזז gozi J Am. 7.1; MT: גֹּזִּי; cf. Ps. 71.6.

גֶּזֶם gezem J Joel 1.4; MT: גָּזָם.

גֶּזַע geza J Isa. 11.1.

גֶּזֶר γαζερ G Josh. 12.12; gazer On ib.

גְּזְרָה gazera J Ezek. 42.10.

גַּיְא γαι G Deut. 34.6; gai On ib.
גֵּיא ge J Isa. 28.1.

גִיל אֲגִילָה αγιλα O Ps. 31.8.
וְגִילוּ ουγιλου O Ps. 32.11.

גַּל gal J Gen. 31.46.

גַּלִּים a) γαλειμ B Isa. 10. 30.

b) γαλλειμ A ib.; gallim J ib.

גַּלְגַּל γελγελ G Ezek. 10.13; gelgel J Ib.; cf. MT: גַּלְגַּל Isa. 28.28 and וְנַלְגַּלָיו ib. 5.28.

גְּלוּלֵי גלולים gelule J Ezek. 20.7.

גְּלִילָה galila J Ezek. 47.8; cf. MT: גְּלִילָה 2 Ki. 15.29.

גְּלִילוֹת γαλιλωθ A Josh. 22. 10; B Josh. 18.17: ΓΑΛΙ-ΑΩΘ lege Λ for the second A; galiloth J Joel 4.4.

גָּלְמִי גלם γολμη O Ps. 92.7.

גַּם γαμ O Ps. 49.3.

גְּמַלִי גמל γαμαλι A Num. 13.12; cf. B-L § 24g; B ib.: ΓΑΜΑΙ lege ΓΑΜΑΛΙ.

גָּמוּל גמל γαμουλ B 1 Chron. 24.17.

גַּן γαν A in Βαιατγαν, 2 Ki. 9.27; gan J Gen. 2.2.

הַגַּן agan On in Bethagan, 2 Ki. 9.27.

גַּנִּים γαννιμ A in Ηγαννιμ, Josh. 19.21; gannim On in Engannim, ib.

גֵּר γηρ G in Γηρσαμ, Ex. 2.22; ger On in Gersom, ib.

נִגְרַזְתִּי גרז νεγρεσθι O Ps. 31.23.

גֶּשֶׁם gesem J Zech. 14.17.

גַּת γεθ G 1 Sam. 6.17; geth On Josh. 11.22; cf. B-L § 14c'.

ד

דֹּאג דאג δωηγ A 1 Sam. 22.9; δωηκ B ib.; doec On ib.

דְּבִיר δαβειρ G Josh. 11.21; δαβιρ O Ps. 28.2; dabir On Josh. 11.21.

דְּבוֹרָה δεββωρα G Ju. 4.4.; debbora On ib.

דָּבָר a) דִּבְרֵי δαβρη O Ps. 35.20; dabre J in Dabrejamim, 1 Chron. 1.1.

b) דְּבָר δαβαρ G in Λωδαβαρ, 2 Sam. 17.27; dabar On in Lodabar, ib.

דְּבָרֶיךָ dabarach J Hos. 13.14; cf. B-L § 2w and § 26c'.

יְדַבֵּר דבר ιδαββερ O Ps. 49.4; idabber J Isa. 32.6.

וַיְדַבֵּר ουιεδαββερ O Ps. 18.48; MT: וַיְדַבֵּר.

יְדַבְּרוּ ιδαββηρου O Ps. 35.20.

דֶּבֶר deber J Hab. 3.4.

דַּבֶּשֶׁת dabbasth On Josh. 19.11; cf. similarly in the PV וּדְבַשׁ Deut. 26.15 (MdWI, p. ז); cf. also s.v. חרשׁת.

דָּג dag J Jon. 2.1.

הַדָּגִים adagim J Zeph. 1.10.

דֹּדִים dodim J Ezek. 16.8.

דּוֹדִי דוד dodi J Jer. 32.8.

דֹּדְךָ dodach J Jer. 32.7.

דָּן דון δαν A Gen. 14.14; dan On ib.

דּוֹר δωρ G in Αελδωρ, 1 Sam. 28.7; dor On in Aendor, ib.

לְדוֹר λδωρ O Ps. 49.12: ΑΔΩΡ lege ΛΔΩΡ (Λ for

A) or ΛΑΔΩΡ (Λ before A, haplography).

וָדוֹר ουαδωρ O Ps. 49.12; cf. in the PV וְדוֹר (Bar, p. 22).

דיה דִּיּוֹת dajoth J Isa. 34.15.

דלג אֶדְלֵג εδαλλεγ O Ps. 18.30.

דלה דִּלִּיתָנִי δελλιθανη O Ps. 30.2.

דלף יִדְלַף ιεδλαφ A Gen. 22.22: ΙΕΛΔΑΦ lege: ΙΕΔΛΑΦ; cf. in the BV יִדְלֹף Eccl. 10.18 in Ms. Ec 1; iedlaf On Gen. 22.22.

דם בְּדָמִי βδαμι O Ps. 30.10.

דְּמֵי dame J Isa. 38.10; MT: דְּמִי.

דמה דְּמִינוּ δεμμηνου O Ps. 48.10.

נִדְמוּ νεδμου O Ps. 49.13.

דמם דָּמוּ δαμμου O Ps. 35.15.

יָדֹם ιαδομ O Ps. 30.13; MT: יִדֹּם.

דִּמְעָה δεμα O Mal. 2.13.

דֵּעָה dea J Isa. 28.9.

דַּעַת daath J Eccl. 8.6.

דֹּק doc J Isa. 40.22.

דקר דָּקָרוּ dacaru J Zech. 12.10.

דְּרוֹר deror J Ezek. 46.17.

דֶּרֶךְ a) דֶּרֶךְ δερχ O Ps. 89.42.

בַּדֶּרֶךְ βδερχ O Ps. 32.8.

דַּרְכִּי δερχι O Ps. 18.33; cf. in the BV דַרְכֶם Prov. 1.31; דַּרְכֵּי ib. 3.17: in Ms. Ec 1.

דַּרְכּוֹ δερχω O Ps. 18.31; cf. in the BV דַרְכּוֹ Prov. 11.5: in Ms. Ec 1.

b) דַּרְכָּם δαρχαμ O Ps. 49.14.

דרש דְּרוּשָׁה drusa J Isa. 62.12.

ה

הָאָח αα O Ps. 35.21.

הבל a) הַבְלִי αβλη O Ps. 31.7.

b) הֶבֶל abal J Eccl. 1.2; cf. in the BV הֶבֶל ib. in Ms. Ec 1.

הֲבָלִים abalim J Eccl. 1.2.

c) הֶבֶל αβελ A Gen. 4.2; abel On ib.

הגה תֶּהְגֶּה θααγε O Ps. 35.28: ΘΑΑΓΣ, lege E for C.

הָגָּיוֹן a) εγαων O Ps. 92.4: ΕΙΑΩΝ lege Γ for Ι; cf. Thompson Facs. 3.

b) εγγαων O Ps. 9.17.

הגית וְהָגִית ουαγιθ O Ps. 49.4; MT: וְהָגוּת.

הַד ad J in adarim, Ezek. 7.7.

הדרה בְּהַדְרַת βααδαρεθ O Ps. 29.2.

הוּא ου O Ps. 18.31; hu On Ex. 16.15 s.v. man.

הוֹד ωδ A 1 Chron. 8.6; MT: אֵחוּד; hod J Zech. 6.13.

הוֹי oi J Isa. 29.1.

הָיָה αεα O Ps. 89.42; haja J Zeph. 3.18.

הָיִיתִי αιθι O Ps. 30.8.

יִהְיֶה ιειε O Ps. 89.37; cf. in the PV יֹהִי Ps. 69.23; תֹּהִי ib., 26 (MdWII, p. 84).

תִּהְיוּ θου O Ps. 32.9.

הֶיֵה αιη O Ps. 30.11.

היכל הֵיכָלֵךְ ηχαλαχ O Ps. 48.10.

הֵילֵל elil J Isa. 14.12.

הִין hin J Ezek. 4.11.

הָלַךְ αλαχ O Ps. 1.1.

תֵּלֶךְ θηληχ O Ps. 32.8.

לְכוּ λχου O Ps. 46.9.

יְהַלְּכוּן ιαλληχουν O Ps. 89. 31; MT: יֵלְכוּן.

הִתְהַלַּכְתִּי εθαλλαχθι O Ps. 35.14.

הלל הֵלֵל ελληλ B Jud. 12.13.

יְהַלֵּל ιαλλελ A in Ιαλλεληλ, 1 Chron. 4.16.

אֲהַלְלֶךָ εελλελεχ O Ps. 35.18.
הַלְלוּ allelu J in alleluia, Isa. 26.4.
מְהוֹלָל molal J Eccl. 2.2.
יִתְהַלְלוּ ιθαλλαλου O Ps. 49.7.
הֵם εμ O Ps. 9.7; MT: הֵמָּה.
הֵמָה
הֵמוּ αμου O Ps. 46.7.
יֶהֱמוּ ιεεμου O Ps. 46.6.
הֹמֶה homa J Jer. 4.19; MT: הֹמֶה.
הָמוֹן a) amun J Isa. 33.3.
  b) αμων G in Βεεθλαμων, Cant. 8.11.
הַמוֹנָה amona J Ezek. 7.13.
הַמֹנִים amonim J Joel 4.14.
הַמָסִים amasim J Isa. 64.1.
הָפַךְ הָפַכְתָּ αφαχθ O Ps. 30.12.
הַר αρ A in Αρσαφαρ, Num. 33.23; O Ps. 48.3.
הָרִים αριμ O Ps. 46.3; arim J Am. 4.13.
לְהַרְרִי λααραρι O Ps. 30.8.
הֶרֶס a) ares J Isa. 19.18.
  b) heres J Isa. 24.23.

ז

זְאָב ζηβ G Jud. 7.25; zeb On ib.
זֹאת ζωθ O Ps. 49.2.
וְזֹאת ουζωθ O Mal. 2.13.
זבד a) זַבְדִי ζαβδει G 1 Chron. 8.19; zabdi On Josh. 7.1.
  b) זַבְדִי zebdi On Josh. 7.1.
  c) זֶבֶד ζαβεδ G 1 Chron. 2.36; MT: זָבָד.
זבוד זבד a) ζαβουθ B 1 Ki. 4.5.
  b) ζαββουθ A ib.
זבוב zebub On in Baalzebub, 2 Ki. 1.2.
זְבוּל ζεβουλ G Jud. 9.28; zebul On ib.
זֶבַח a) ζεβεε G Jud. 8.5; the last ε is the transliteration of

the ח; cf. p. 175 sub ח; cf. in the PV זֹבַח (Bar, p. 20).
b) zeba J Ezek. 46.20.
זבל יִזְבְּלֵנִי iezbuleni J Gen. 30.20.
זֶה ζε O Ps. 49.14.
זָהָב a) ζοοβ A in Μεζοοβ, Gen. 36.39.
  b) zaab On in Mezaab, ib.
זֹהַר zor J Ezek. 8.2.
זוּ a) ζου O Ps. 32.8.
  b) zo J Hag. 1.1.
זוּז זוּז יָזִיז ιαζειζ B 1 Chron. 27.31.
זוּלָתִי ζουλαθι O Ps. 18.32.
זחל זֹחֶלֶת ζωελεθ A 1 Ki. 1.9.; zoeleth On ib.
זִיז ziz J Isa. 66.11.
זָכַר zochor J Isa. 26.14; cf. s.v. בָּשָׂר sub b.
זֵכֶר a) לְזֵכֶר λζεχρ O Ps. 30.5: AZEXP lege ΛZEXP or ΛΛZEXP.
  זִכְרִי ζεχρει B Ex. 6.21; zechri On ib.
  b) זֶכֶר zachar J Isa. 26.14.
זָכַר ζαχαρ A in Ιωζαχαρ, 2 Ki. 12.22; zachar On in Iozachar, ib.
אֶזְכֹּר ηζχορ O Ps. 89.51; MT: זְכֹר
זֵכֶר ζχορ O Ps. 89.48.
זִמָּה ζεμμα B 1 Chron. 6.5; zemma J Ezek. 16.27.
זמר a) זִמְרִי ζαμβρει B Num. 25.14; the Septuagint frequently renders the letters מר by μβρ; f.i.: Gen. 46.13; שמרן ζαμβραμ; Ex. 6.18: עמרם αμβραμ; Num. 32.3: נמרה ναμβρα.
ζαμβρι A Num. 25.14.
zamri On ib.

b) זִמְרִי zemeri On Num. 25.14.

זמר זַמְּרֶךָ ιζαμμερεχ O Ps. 30.13.

זַמְּרוּ ζωημερου O Ps. 30.5.

זמרה זִמְרָת zemroth J Isa. 24.16; MT: זִמְרָת; cf. the relation of MT בְּנִקְרַת in Ex. 33.22 to the form בנקירות in the Sam.; Gen. 4.23; MT: אָמַרְתִּי and Sam. אמירתי.

זְנוּנִים zanunim J Hos. 1.2.

זנח זָנַחְתָּ ζαναθ O Ps. 89.39.

זָנוֹחַ ζανω A Josh. 15.34; zanoe On ib.; cf. p. 175 sub ח.

זְעֵיר zer J Isa. 28.10.

זֶרַח a) ζαρα G Num. 26.20.

זַרְחִי ζαραει B Num. 26.20; ζαραι A ib.

b) זֶרַח zare On Num. 26.20.

זֶרַח ζαρα A 1 Chron. 6.6; zara On Gen. 36.13.

ζαραε A 1 Chron. 4.24; cf. p. 175 sub ח.

ζαρε B in Ζαρεια, Ezra 8.4.

יִזְרַח ιεσραε B 1 Chron. 27.8: ECPAE lege IECPAE, haplogr.; cf. Thompson Facs. 6 (I-E); also p. 175 sub ח.

זֶרַע a) zera J Isa. 1.4.

b) zara J Ezek. 31.17.

זַרְעוֹ ζαρω O Ps. 89.30.

זרע יִזְרַע a) ισρα B in Ισραηλ, 1 Sam. 29.1.

ιζρα A in Ιζραηλ A, ib.

b) ιεζρα A in Ιεζραελ, Josh. 17.16; iezra On in Iezrahel, ib.

זְרֻעֹתַי ζερουωθαι O Ps. 18.35; MT: זְרוֹעֹתַי.

ח

חבל יְחַבֵּל ιεβαλ O Ps. 7.15; MT: יְחַבֵּל.

חָבֵר χαβερ B Jud. 4.11; chaber On Gen. 46.17.

αβερ A 1 Chron. 4.18; aber On Num. 26.45; MT: חֶבֶר.

חבר חָבוֹר αβωρ G 2 Ki. 17.6.

חג חַגִּי αγγει B Num. 26.15; αγγι A ib.; aggi On ib.

חָגָּא agga J Isa. 19.17.

חָגָב αγαβ G Ezra 2.46.

הֶחָגָב aagab J Eccl. 12.5.

חד חַדָּה αδδα A in Ηναδδα, Josh. 19.21; adda On in Enadda, ib.

חָדֵל edel J Isa. 38.11.

חדל יֶחְדָּל ιεδαλ O Ps. 49.9; MT: וְחָדָל.

חָדְלוּ hedalu J Isa. 2.22; with retention of the 2nd vowel (against B-L § 26d'').

חדש חֲדָשָׁה αδασα A Josh. 15.37; adasa On ib.

חֹדֶשׁ a) hodes J Hos. 4.6.

b) חָדְשֵׁי odsi On 2 Sam. 24.6.

חוֹבָה choba On Gen. 14.15.

חוּל ουλ A Gen. 10.23; ul On ib.

חוֹמָה homa J Isa. 24.23.

חוֹתָם χωθαμ A 1 Chron. 7.32.

חָזָה αζα G in Αζαηλ, 1 Ki. 19.15; aza On in Azahel, ib.

חָזוּ εεζου O Ps. 46.9; cf. p. 175 sub ח.

חָזוֹן hazon J Hab. 2.2.

חִנָּיוֹן ezzahon On 1 Ki. 15.18; MT: חֶזְיוֹן.

חזיז חֲזִיזִים azizim J Zech. 10.1.

חזק חָזַק εζαχ O Ps. 31.25: εζαχ

lege εζακ; MT: חִזְקוּ. The ε may be considered as a transliteration of the ח; cf. p. 175 sub ח; or otherwise cf. in the BV the corresponding vocalization with אָ in forms like אֹור Job 38.3 in Ms. Ec 5; אֹמֶר Ezek. 33.10 in Ms. Eb 10.

הֶחָזָק εεζεκ O Ps. 35.2.

חטא   חַטָּאִים ατταειμ O Ps. 1.1.

חטאת   attath J Gen. 4.7; hatath J ib. (editio Lagarde).

חַי αι O Ps. 18.47.

חידה   חִידָתִי ιδαθι O Ps. 49.5.

חיה   יְחְיֶה ιειε O Ps. 89.37.

יְחְיוּ jeju J Isa. 26.19.

חִיִּיתַנִי ιιθανι O Ps. 30.4: ιθανι lege ιιθανι.

חַיֵּהוּ heieu J Hab. 3.2.

חַיִל   a) χαιλ G in Αβειχαιλ, Num. 3.35.

αιλ O Ps. 18.40; O Ps. 18.33: ΑΙΔ lege ΑΙΛ.

חֵילָם αιλαμ G 2 Sam. 10.16; cf. s.v. איתן sub a.

b) חֵילָם ηλαμ O Ps. 49.7; cf. MT: בְּחֵיל 2 Ki. 18.17.

חַיִּים αιιμ O Ps. 30.6.

חִיץ his J Ezek. 13.10.

חֵיק   חִיקִי ηκι O Ps. 35.13.

בְּחֵיקִי βηηκι O Ps. 89.51.

חך   חִכְּךָ echcha J in alechcha, Hos. 8.1.

חכם   חֲכָמִים αχαμιμ O Ps. 49.11.

חכמה   חֲכָמוֹת αχαμωθ O Ps. 49.4; MT: חָכְמוֹת.

חֶלֶד eled J Isa. 38.11.

חֶלֶד   a) ολδ O Ps. 49.2; MT: חֶלֶד.

b) holed J Isa. 38.11.

חלה   בַּחֲלוֹתָם βααλωθαμ O Ps. 35.13.

חֲלוֹם helem J Zech. 6.10.

חֳלִי oli On Josh. 19.25; MT: חֳלִי.

חלל   חִלַּלְתָּ ελλελθ O Ps. 89.40.

אֲחַלֵּל ααλλελ O Ps. 89.35.

יְחַלֵּלוּ ιαλληλου O Ps. 89.32.

חלם   כְּחֹלְמִים χαωλεμιμ O Ps. 126.1.

חלץ   חֲלָצֵי eluse J Isa. 15.4.

חָלָק αλακ A Josh. 11.17; alac On ib.

חֵלֶק χελεκ A Num. 26.30.

חֶלְקִי χελεκι A ib.

חֵלֶק elec On Josh. 17.2.

חלק   הֶחֱלִיק εελικ O Ps. 36.3; cf. p. 175 sub ח.

חלקה   חֶלְקַת χελκαθ A Josh. 19.25.

elcath On ib.

חָם   χαμ A Gen. 10.1; cham On ib.

חַמָּה hamma J Isa. 24.23.

חמה   a) חֲמָתָךְ εμαθαχ O Ps. 89.47.

b) חֲמָתִי αμαθι A Gen. 10.18; amathi On ib.

חֲמוֹר εμμωρ G Jud. 9.28; cf. in the BV לַחֲמֹרֵנוּ Ju. 19.19; וַחֲמֹרִים 1 Sam. 27.9 in Ms. 105 JThS; this vocalization (חֲ) would imply a gemination of the following מ according to the rules of the Masoretic Grammar; cf. MTK, p. 27.

emor On Gen. 33.19.

חמל   חָמוּל amul On Gen. 46.12.

חֹמֶר   a) וְחֹמֶר ουομρ O Hos. 3.2.

b) חֹמֶר omer J Hos. 3.2.

homer J Ezek. 45.13.

חמר   יַחְמְרוּ ιεμρου O Ps. 46.6.

חֵן hen J Jer. 31.2.

חָנָה hana J Isa. 29.1.

חֲנִית ανιθ O Ps. 46.10.

חנכה חֲנֻכַּת οννεχαθ O Ps. 30.1.

חִנָּם ενναμ O Ps. 35.19.

חָנַן αναν G in Ελεαναν, 2 Sam. 21.19; anan On in Elia-nan, ib.

חָנֻן ανουν G Neh. 3.13.

אֶתְחַנַּן εθανναν O Ps. 30.9.

בְּחַנְפֵי βαανφη O Ps. 35.16.

חֹנֶף oneph J Isa. 32.6.

חֶסֶד εσδ A 1 Ki. 4.10; O Ps. 32.10.

חַסְדִּי εσδι O Ps. 89.29; cf. in the BV חֹסְדִּי Ps. 107.43 in Ms. Ec 1.

בְּחַסְדֶּךָ βεεζδαξ O Ps. 31.8.

חַסְדּוֹ εσδω O Ps. 31.22; cf. in the BV חֹסְדּוֹ Ps. 100.5 in Ms. Ec 1.

חֲסָדֶיךָ εσδαχ O Ps. 89.50.

חסה חָסִיתִי ασιθι O Ps. 31.2.

הַחֹסִים αωσιμ O Ps. 18.31.

לַחֹסִים λαωσιμ O Ps. 31.20.

חָסִיד ασιδ O Ps. 18.26.

חֲסִידָיו ασιδαυ O Ps. 31.24: ACIΛAY lege ACIΔAY.

חֲסִידָה asida J Jer. 8.7.

חָסִיל hasil J Joel 1.4.

חָפָּה χοφφα B in Οχχοφφα, 1 Chron. 24.13.
οφφα A ib.

בְּחִפְזִי βααφζι O Ps. 31.23.

חֶפְצִי חפץ a) αψει B in Αψειβα, 2 Ki. 21.1.

b) οφσι A in Οφσιβα ib.

c) ephsi J Isa. 62.4; ebsi On in Ebsiba, 2 Ki. 21.1.

d) ephesi J in epesiba lege ephesiba, Isa. 62.4.

הֶחָפֵץ ααφης O Ps. 35.27: ΑΛΦΗΣ lege A for Λ.

חֶפְצֵי ωφση O Ps. 35.27; MT חֲפֵצֵי.

וַיֶּחְפְּרוּ ουιφφρου O Ps. 35.26; cf. in the BV וִיחְפְּרוּ Ps. 35.4 in Ms. Ec 1.

חֲפַרְפָּרוֹת pharpharoth J Isa. 2.20.

חֲצִי εσει A 1 Chron. 2.52.

חָצֵר a) ασρ B in Αρσεναειμ, Num. 34.9 lege Ασρεναειμ.

b) ασαρ A in Ασαρμωθ, Gen. 10.26; asar On in Asar-moth, ib.

c) ασερ A in Ασερναιν, Num. 34.9; aser On in Asergad-da, Josh. 15.27.

חֲצֵרוֹת ασηρωθ G Num. 11.35; aseroth On ib.

חֶרֶב areb J Zech. 13.7.
hareb J Zeph. 2.14; Hag. 1.11; MT: חֹרֶב.

חרב חוֹרֵב χωρηβ G Ex. 3.1.
oreb On ib.

חרבה חָרְבוֹת αρβωθ O Ps. 9.7; MT: חֳרָבוֹת.

חרג וַיַּחְרְגוּ ουιεργου O Ps. 18.46.

חרד וַיֶּחְרְדוּ ουιχαρδου O Ps. 49.15; MT: וַיֶּחֶרְדוּ.

חֲרָדָה arada On Num. 33.24.

חָרָה ara J Jon. 4.4.

חָרִיף αρειφ B Neh. 7.24.

חֵרֶם herem J Ezek. 44.29.

חֶרֶס αρες G Ju. 8.13; MT: חָרֶס; ares On ib.

חַרְסִית harsith J Jer. 19.2.

חֵרְפוּ ηρφου O Ps. 89.52.

חֶרְפָּה αρφ O Ps. 89.42.

חֶרְפַּת αρφαθ O Ps. 89.51.

חָרוּץ αρους G Ki. 21.19; arus On ib.
harus On Joel 4.14.

חֲרָצוֹת arsoth J Am. 1.3.

חָרֹק חרק αρωκ O Ps. 35.16.

חֶרֶשׂ ares J Isa. 19.18.

חֶרֶשׂ αρες A 1 Chron. 9.15.

חֹרֶשׁ hores J Isa. 17.9.

חרש חֲרַשְׁתֶּם arasthem J Hos. 10.13.

יַחֲרֹשׁ jeros J Hos. 10.11; cf. in the BV יֶחֱרֹשׁ Prov. 20.4 in Ms. Ec 1.

תַּחֲרֹשׁ θαρες O Ps. 35.22; MT: תֶּחֱרַשׁ.

חֲרֹשֶׁת arasth On Ju. 4.2; MT: חֲרֹשֶׁת; cf. s.v. דַּבֶּשֶׁת dab-basth.

חָשַׁב ασαβ G in Ασαβια, 1 Chron. 9.14.

חֲשֻׁבָה ασουβε B 1 Chron. 3.20.

נֶחְשָׁב nesab J Isa. 2.22.

חֶשְׁבּוֹן εσεβων G Num. 21.25; esebon On ib.

חָשְׁכִּי οσχι O Ps. 18.29. חשך

חָשְׁקִי esci J Isa. 21.4. חשק

ט

טֶבַח tabech On Gen. 22.24; cf. MT in pausa טָבַח: Isa. 34.2.

טַבָּעוֹת טַבַּעַת a) ταβαωθ B Neh. 7.46: ΓΑΒΑΩΘ lege T for cf. Γ; cf. Thompson Facs. 3.

b) ταββαωθ A ib.

טֵבֵת tebeth J Ezek. 29.1; cf. Esth. 2.16.

טוֹב τωβ G Ju. 11.3; tob On in Achitob, 1 Sam. 14.3.

טוֹבִים tobim J Zech. 8.19.

טוּבְךָ τουβαχ O Ps. 31.20. טוב

טוּרוֹת turoth J Ezek. 46.23; MT: טִירוֹת. טור

טָמְנוּ ταμνου O Ps. 31.5. טמן

י

יוֹאֵל יאל ιωηλ G 1 Sam. 8.2; iohel On ib.; cf. p. 111 (insertion of h).

יְאֹר ior J Isa. 23.10.

יוּבַל יבל ιουβαλ A Gen. 4.21; iubal On ib.

יָבֵשׁ ιαβεις G Ju. 21.8; iabes On ib.; elsewhere ει and ι of the Septuagint correspond to i in the Onomastica.

יד a) בְּיָדְךָ βιαδαχ O Ps. 31.6: ΒΙΑΔΑΘ lege ΒΙΑΔΑΧ.

יָדוֹ ιαδω O Ps. 89.26; jado J Hab. 3.4.

יָדִי ιαδαι O Ps. 18.35.

b) בְּיָד βιεδ O Ps. 31.9.

מִיָּד μειεδ O Ps. 89.49.

c) מִיָּדֵיכֶם μειδηχεμ O Mal. 2.13; MT: מִיֶּדְכֶם; cf. in the BV יְדֵיהֶם Lev. 8.18 in Ms. Ea 11.

הַיּוֹדְךָ αιωδεχχα O Ps. 30.10.

אוֹדְךָ ωδεχ O Ps. 35.18; 30.13; MT: אוֹדְךָ.

אֲהוֹדֶנּוּ αωδεννου O Ps. 28.7.

וְהוֹדוּ ουωδου O Ps. 30.5.

יָדִיד ιδεδ B in Ιδεδει, 2 Sam. 12.25; idid On in Ididia, ib.

יְדִידֹת ιδιδωθ O Ps. 45.1.

יָדַע ιαδα A in Βαλλιαδα, 1 Chron. 14.7.

ιαδαε B in Ελιαδαε, 1 Ki. 11.14; O Ps. 92.7; MT: יֵדַע; cf. p. 176 sub ע; iadahe On in Ioiadahe, 2 Sam. 23.20; cf. p. 111.

יָדַעְתָּ ιαδαθ O Ps. 31.8.

יָדְעוּ jadau J Hos. 9.7; MT: יֵדְעוּ; cf. B-L § 2w.

וְדְעוּ ουαδου O Ps. 46.11.

יָהּ ia J Isa. 26.4.

בְּיַה βαια O Isa. 26.4.

הָבוּ αβου O Ps. 29.1.

יהוה αδωναι O Ps. 118.25; adonai J Isa. 7.12.

בַּיהוה βαδωναι O Isa. 26.4.

בְּיוֹם יום biom J Isa. 17.11.

הַיּוֹם αιωμ O Ps. 35.28.

יָמִים iamim J Gen. 35.18.

יְמֵי ιμη O Ps. 89.46.

בִּימֵי βιμη O Ps. 49.6.

כִּימֵי χιμη O Ps. 89.30.

יוֹנָה ιωνα G 2 Ki. 14.25; iona On ib.

יֵזַע jeze J Ezek. 44.18.

יַחַד ιααδ O Ps. 49.3; ιααδε O Ps. 49.11; I find this form inexplicable, unless by assuming that ε is the scribe's suggestion for the second α: ιαεδ; cf. p. 175 sub ח.

יַחְדָּו ιαδαυ O Ps. 35.26: ΙΔΑΥ lege ΙΑΔΑΥ, haplography A before Δ.

יָחִיד jaid J Jer. 6.26.

יְחִידָתִי ιιδαθι O Ps. 35.17; cf. in the BV יְחִידָךְ Gen. 22.2 in Ms. Ea 1.

הַמְיַחֲלִים αμμηαλιμ O Ps. 31.25; MT: הַמְ'.

יָכְלוּ ιουχαλευ O Ps. 18.39.

יָם iam J Isa. 2.16.

מִיָּם mejam J Hos. 11.10.

יַמִּים ιαμιμ O Ps. 46.3.

יָמִין a) ιαμειν A Gen. 46.10; iamin On ib.

b) יְמִין ιμιν O Ps. 89.43.

וִּימִינְךָ ουιμιναχ O Ps. 18.36: OYEMINAX, lege I for E; cf. Thompson Facs. 6.

יְמִינוֹ ιμινω O Ps. 89.26.

c) יְמִינִי ιεμενει B Ps. 7.1;

ιεμενι A ib.; iemini On ib.

מֵינִיקָה ינק meneca J Gen. 35.8 (editio Lagarde): menecha is a misprint; MT: מֵינֶקֶת.

מֵינֶקֶת meneceth J Gen. 35.8.

יוֹסֵף יסף ιωσηφ G Gen. 30.24; ioseph On ib.

נוֹעַד יעד νωαδ A in Νωαδα, Ezra 8.33.

יוֹעֵץ יעץ ioes J Isa. 9.5.

יַעַר a) יַעַר ιαρ A 1 Sam. 14.25; jar J Hos. 2.15; cf. in the PV לַיַּעַר Isa. 32.15 (MdWI, p. יב).

יְעָרִים ιαρειμ B Josh. 15.9; ιαριμ A ib.; iarim On in Cariathiarim, ib.

b) יַעַר ιααρ B 1 Sam. 14.25: Ιααλ lege ρ for λ.

יָצָא jasa J Zech. 2.7; MT: יָצָא.

תּוֹצִיאֵנִי θωσιηνι O Ps. 31.5: ΘΟΩCIHNI dele O; dittography; cf. Thompson Facs. 3 and 5 (Θ-Ο).

יצר a) יִצְרִי ιεσρι A Num. 26.49.

יִצְרוֹ ιεσρο O Isa. 26.3; MT: יֵצֶר.

b) יֵצֶר ιεσερ B Num. 26.49; ieser On inb.

יִצְרִי ιεσερει B ib.

יוֹצֵר יצר joser J Zech. 11.12.

בִּיקָר יקר βιακαρ O Ps. 49.13: BAKAP lege BIAKAP; cf. in the PV וּקָר (MdWI, p. יו, line 3).

וַיֵּקֶר יקר ουικαρ O Ps. 49.9; cf. MT וַיִּיקַר 1 Sam. 18.30.

אִירָא ירא ιρα O Ps. 49.7.

נִירָא νιρα O Ps. 46.3.

יָרֵא ιαρη O Ps. 112.1: APH lege IAPH.

לְירֵאֶיךָ λιριαχ O Ps. 31.20.

ירד יֵרֶד jered J Jon. 1.3.

מִיּוֹרְדֵי μειωρδη O Ps. 30.4.

בְּרִדְתִּי βρεδεθι O Ps. 30.10; the addition of the suffix does thus not result in a change of the vocalization of the verb; cf. in the Sam. Ex. 32.34: פְּקוּדִי as compared with the Masoretic form פָּקְדִי.

ירה וְאוֹרְךָ ουωρεχ O Ps. 32.8: ουωρεκ lege ουωρεχ.

יְרוּשָׁה ιερουσα A 2 Chron. 27.1. ιερουσσα B ib.

יָרֵחַ iare J Am. 4.7; iaree On Gen. 20.16; MT: יָרֵחַ; cf. p. 175 sub ח.

כְּיָרֵחַ χιαρη O Ps. 89.38.

יריב יְרִיבַי ιριβιαι O Ps. 35.1; perhaps to be explained as an amalgamation of the two readings: יְרִיבִי ιριβι and יְרִיבַי ιριβαι: cf. on מֵעִמּוֹ.

ירכה יַרְכְּתֵי ιερχθη O Ps. 48.3; cf. in the BV יִרְכָּתִי Ju. 19.18 in Ms. 105 JThS.

יֵשׁ is J Gen. 30.18.

יָשַׁב ιασαβ O Ps. 29.10.

יֵשֶׁב ιησηβ O Ps. 9.8.

יוֹשֶׁבֶת josebeth J Mic. 1.11.

ישועה a) יְשׁוּעָתִי ιασουαθι O Ps. 89.27.

b) לִישׁוּעָה lajesua J Hab. 3.13; MT: לְיֵשַׁע; cf. in the PV יְשׁוּעָתֶךָ Ps. 69.30 (MdWII, p. 85).

c) יְשׁוּעוֹת ισουωθ O Ps. 28.8.

יֵשַׁן ιασαν G 2 Sam. 23.32: ασαν lege ιασαν, haplography; MT: יָשֵׁן; iasan On ib.

הַיְשָׁנָה αισανα G Neh. 3.6.

ישע יִשְׁעִי ιεσει A 1 Chron. 2.31; O Ps. 18.47: IECCI is to be emended in IECEI, the second ε corresponding to the ע, cf. p. 176 sub ע, or in IECI; dittography.

יִשְׁעֲךָ ιεσαχα O Ps. 18.36.

ישע תּוֹשִׁיעַ θωσι O Ps. 18.28: ΘΩΕΙ lege C for E.

מוֹשִׁיעַ μωσι O Ps. 18.42.

מוֹשִׁיעִים mosim J Obad. 21.

הוֹשִׁיעָה ωσια O Ps. 28.9: ΙΩCΙΑ lege ΩCΙΑ.

הוֹשִׁיעָה נָא ωσιεννα O Ps. 118.25.

לְהוֹשִׁיעֵנִי λωσιηνι O Ps. 31.3.

ישר יִשְׁרֵי ισρη O Ps. 32.11.

ישר יֵשַׁר isar J Hos. 12.5; cf. וַיִּקַר s.v. יקר; MT: וַיָּשַׁר.

יָתֵד jathed J Isa. 22.25.

יתר a) יִתְרוֹ iethro On Ex. 3.1.

b) יֶתֶר ιεθερ O Ps. 31.24.

יתר תּוֹתַר θωθαρ O Gen. 49.4.

כ

כְּאֵב cheb J Isa. 29.4; MT: כְּאוֹב.

כָּבוֹד χαβωδ O Ps. 29.1; chabod J Isa. 11.10.

χαβωθ G in Βαρχαβωθ, 1 Sam. 4.21.

caboth On in Escaboth, 1 Sam. 14.3.

הַכָּבוֹד αχχαβωδ O Ps. 29.3.

כָּבוֹד χαβωδ O Ps. 29.2.

כברה כִּבְרַת chabratha On 2 Ki. 5.19.

כַּדְכֹּד chodchod J Isa. 54.12.

כּוֹכָב chocab J Am. 5.26.

כון יָכוֹן ιεχχον O Ps. 89.38.

חָכִין hechin J Am. 4.12; MT: הַכּוֹן.

יָכִין ιαχειν G Num. 26.12; iachin On Gen. 46.10.

כַּנֻּנִים chauonim J Jer. 7.18.

כָּזָב chasab J Isa. 28.17.

כזב אַכַזֵב εχαζεβ O Ps. 89.36; without gemination of the second radical; cf. וַתְּאַוְּרֵנִי, שְׂמַחְתָּ, פִּתַּחְתָּ, פַּלֵּט, under their respective headings.

כחש כָּחֲשׁוּ chaesu J Zech. 13.4; the e=ח, cf. p. 175.

כִּי χι O Ps. 18.28; chi J Isa. 2.22.

כִּידוֹן chidon On Josh. 8.18.

כִּיּוּן chion J Am. 5.26.

כִּימָה chima J Am. 5.8.

כִּכָּר chachar J Zech. 5.7; cf. in the BV כְּכָרֵי 2 Chron. 9.13 in MS. Ec. 1.

κεχαρ B 2 Sam. 18.23.

כָּל a) χωλ A in Εσχωλ, Gen. 14.24; χολ O Ps. 31.24; chol On in Fichol, Gen. 21.22.

χολ A in Φικολ, Gen. 21.22.

לְכָל λαχολ O Ps. 18.31.

כֻּלֹּה chollo J Ezek. 11.15; cf. in the BV כֻּלָּם Berakot 6,2 (Kahle, "The Mishna Text in Babylonia", HUCA, Cincinnati, 1935).

b) chullo J ib.

כלה כַּלּוֹתָם χελλωθαμ O Ps. 18.38.

כְּלוּב chelub J Am. 8.2.

כִּלְיוֹן κελαιων B Ruth 1.2; MT: כִּלְיוֹן; cf. in the PV כְּלֹי

(=כליון) Isa. 10.22 (Kahle in ZAW 1901, p. 282).

כַּמָּה χαμμα O Ps. 35.17.

כְּמוֹ χαμω O Ps. 89.47.

כמר a) כְּמָרִים χωμαρειμ G 2 Ki. 23.5; chomarim On ib.

b) הַכְּמָרִים acchumarim J Zeph. 1.4.

כֵּן χεν O Ps. 46.3; chen J Zech. 11.11.

כִּנּוֹר chennor On Ezek. 26.13.

בְּכִנּוֹר βχεννωρ O Ps. 49.5.

כְּנַעֲנִי chanani On Ex. 3.8.

כנף מִכְּנַף mecchenaph J Isa. 24.16; cf. in the PV כֹּנְפִי Ezek. 16.12 (MdWII, p. 70).

כסא וְכִסְאוֹ ουχεσσω O Ps. 89.30.

כסה כַּסּוֹת χεσσουθ O Mal. 2.13.

כְּסִיל a) chasil J Am. 5.8.

b) כְּסִילִי chisile J Isa. 13.10.
כְּסִילֵיהֶם chisileem J Isa. 13.10.

c) כְּסִיל χσιλ O Ps. 49.11: ΧΕΙΛ lege C for E.
וּכְסִיל ουχσιλ O Ps. 92.7.

כֶּסֶל χεσλ O Ps. 49.14.

כִּסְלֵו chasleu J Zech. 7.1.

כָּסָמִים chasamim J Isa. 28.17.

כעס בְּכַעַס βαχας O Ps. 31.10.

כַּפָּה chaphphe J Isa. 19.25.

כְּפוֹר χεφορ O Ps. 147.16.

כָּפִיס chaphis J Hab. 2.11.

כְּפִיר a) chaphir J Ezek. 38.13. caphir J ib.

b) מִכְּפִירִים μεχφεριμ O Ps. 35.17.

כפר כָּפְרוּ χοφρω O Ps. 49.8.

כפתור כַּפְתּוֹרִים caphthorim J Am. 9.1, 7.

כֹּר χορ G in Βαιθχορ, 1 Sam. 7.11.

כְּרוּב a) χαρουβ B Neh. 7.61.

b) χερουβ A Neh. 7.61; cherub J Ezek. 9.3.

כְּרוּבִים χερουβειμ G Ex. 25.18; cherubim Ezek. 9.3.

הַכְּרוּבִים accherubim On Ex. 25.20: accherubin lege m for n.

כֶּרֶם χαρμ O Ps. 12.9; MT: כָּרֶם. χαρμα B in Βαιθαχαρμα, Jer. 6.1; charma On in Beth-acharma, ib.

כַּרְמִי χαρμει B Ex. 6.14; χαρμι A ib.; charmi On ib.

כַּרְמִים χαρμειμ B in Εβελ-χαρμειν lege -ειμ, Jud. 11.33.

כשף כַּשָּׁפֵי cassaphe J Jer. 27.9.

ל

ל־ לִי λι O Ps. 18.36; li J Isa. 24.16.

לְךָ λαχ O Ps. 110.3; lac J Jon. 4.4.

לוֹ λω O Ps. 89.29.

לָנוּ λανου O Ps. 46.8; lanu J Isa. 6.8.

לָכֶם lachem J Isa. 2.22.

לָהֶם laem J Mic. 7.13; lahem J Isa. 33.7; cf. p. 111 and p. 174 sub ה.

לָמוֹ λαμου O Ps. 28.8.

לֹא λω G in Λωδαβαρ, 2 Sam. 17.27; O Ps. 32.6; lo On in Lodabar, 2 Sam. 9.4.

וְלֹא ulo J Isa. 7.12.

לֵב λεβ O Ps. 32.11.

בְּלֵב βλεβ O Ps. 46.3.

לִבִּי λεββι O Ps. 28.7.

לִבּוֹ λεββαυ O Ps. 36.2; MT: לִבִּי.

לבב a) לְבַבְכֶם λεββαβεχεμ O Ps. 31.25.

b) בִּלְבָבָם βαλβαβαμ O Ps. 35.25; MT: בִּלְבָּם; cf. Gen. 18.5: MT: לִבְּכֶם Sam. לבבכם.

לְבוֹנָה λεβωνα G Jud. 21.19.

לבוש לְבוּשִׁי λεβουσι O Ps. 35.13.

לביא לְבָאוֹת labaoth On in Beth-labaoth, Josh. 19.6.

לָבָן λαβαν A Gen. 24.29; laban On ib.

לְבָנָה λαβανα G Neh. 7.48; MT: לְבָנָא; labana J Isa. 24.23.

לְבֵנָה lebena J Isa. 24.23.

לְהָבִים להב לָהֲבִים laabim On Gen. 10.13.

לוה יִלְוֶה illaue J Gen. 30.34 (editio Lagarde).

לִוְיָתָן leviathan J Isa. 27.1.

לוח הַלְּחוֹת alluoth J Hab. 2.2.

לֶחֶם a) לֶחֶם λαεμ B in Βαιθαλαεμ, 1 Chron. 2.51; the ε=ח, cf. p. 175 sub ח.

b) לֶחֶם λεεμ G in Βαιθλεεμ, Jud. 12.10; the second ε=ח; cf. p. 175 sub ח.

לַחְמִי λεεμει A 1 Chron. 20.5; see the note on לחם.

לחם לַחֲמַי λωαμαι O Ps. 35.1.

לָחֹם λοομ O Ps. 35.1; MT: לְחָם; cf. in the BV לֹחֲמוּ Prov. 9.5 in Ms. Ec 1, for MT לַחֲמוּ.

לחש הַלּוֹחֵשׁ a) αλωης B Neh. 10.25.

b) αλλωης A Neh. 3.12.

לטש לְטוּשִׁים λατουσιειμ A Gen. 25.3. latusim On ib.

לילית lilith J Isa. 34.14.

לין יָלִין ιαλιν O Ps. 30.6.

תָּלִינוּ thalinu J Isa. 21.13.

לַיְשׁ a) λαεις B 1 Sam. 25.44: AMEIC lege ΛΑΕΙC; cf. Thompson Facs. 3; λαις A ib.

b) leis J Isa. 30.6.

למד מְלַמֵּד μαλαμμεδ O Ps. 18.35.

לָמָה λαμα O Ps. 49.6.

לְמַעַן λαμαν O Ps. 30.13.

וּלְמַעַן ουλμαν O Ps. 31.4.

לעג לַעֲגֵי λαγη O Ps. 35.16.

לַפִּידוֹת λαφειδωθ B Jud. 4.4; λαφιδωθ A ib.; lapidoth On ib.

לץ לֵצִים ληςιμ O Ps. 1.1.

לְקְרַאת lacerath J Am. 4.12.

לשון וּלְשׁוֹנִי ουαλσωνι O Ps. 35.28.

לְשֹׁנוֹת λσχνωθ O Ps. 31.21; λσ*νωθ, lege λσωνωθ.

לְתֶךְ a) וְלֶתֶךְ ουλεθχ O Hos. 3.2.

b) לֶתֶךְ lethech J Hos. 3.2.

מ

מְאֹד μωδ O Ps. 46.2.

מאה מְאַת maath J Eccl. 8.12.

מָאוֹר maor J Isa. 24.23.

מאזנים מֹאזְנֵי mozene J Ezek. 45.10.

מַאֲכָל machal J Ezek. 47.12; cf. in the BV מָאֹכָל Ps. 44.12 in Ms. Ec 1.

מאס וַתְּמְאַס ουαθθεμας O Ps. 89.39.

מְבוּכָה mabucha J Mic. 7.4.

מִבְחָר μαβαρ A 1 Chron. 11.38.

מִבְצָר μαψαρ G 2 Sam. 24.7; μαβσαρ A 1 Chron. 1.53; mabsar On Gen. 36.42; cf. in the BV הַמִּבְצָר 2 Chron. 17.19 in Ms. Ec 1.

מִבְצָרָיו μαβσαραυι O Ps. 89.41.

מִבְשָׂם μαβσαμ A 1 Chron. 1.29:

Μαβσαν lege μ for ν; cf. in the BV מִבְשָׂם 1 Chron. 4.25 in Ms. Ec 1; mabsam On Gen. 25.13.

מָג mag On in Rabmag, Jer. 39.3. μακ A in Ραβμακ, ib.

מִגְדָּל μαγδαλ A Josh. 15.37; cf. in the BV מִגְדָּל Prov. 18.10 in Ms. Ec 1; magdal On in Magdalgad, Josh. 15.37; J Ezek. 29.10; MT: מִגְדָּל.

מָגוֹר magur J Jer. 20.3.

מְגִלָּה megella J Zech. 5.1.

מָגֵן μαγεν O Ps. 18.31.

וּמָגִנִּי ουμαγεννι O Ps. 28.7; cf. in the BV מִגִּנּוֹ Job 15.26 in Ms. Ec 1.

מגן אֲמַגֶּנְךָ amaggenach J Hos. 11.8.

מגר מָגַרְתָּה μαγαρθ O Ps. 89.45; MT: מִגַּרְתָּה.

מִגְרָשׁ magras J Ezek. 48.17; cf. in the BV מִגְרָשֶׁיהָ 1 Chron. 6.43 in Ms. Ec 1.

מִדְבָּר μαδβαρ B in Μαδβαρειτιδι, Josh. 5.5; cf. in the BV מִדְבַּר Prov. 21.19 in Ms. Ec 1.

מדד תָּמֹדּוּ thamoddu J Ezek. 47.18.

מָדוֹן μαδων A Josh. 11.1; madon On ib.

מה a) μα O Ps. 89.47; MT: מָה; ma J Am. 4.13.

בַּמָּה bama J Isa. 2.22; bamma J ib.

b) מַה με O in μεββεσε, Ps. 30.10.

מֶה μη O Ps. 89.48.

מְהֵרָה μηηρα O Ps. 31.3.

מוג תָּמוּג θαμουγ O Ps. 46.7.

מוֹט מָטוּ ματου O Ps. 46.7.

תְּמוֹט θεμμοτ O Ps. 46.6: ΘΕΜΜΟΥ lege ΘΕΜ-MOT; cf. Thompson Facs. 5 and 6 (Y-T).

וּבְמוֹט ουβαμωτ O Ps. 46.3.

מוֹטָה a) mota J Isa. 58.6.
b) מוֹטֹת mutoth J Jer. 28.13.

מוּל mul J Mic. 2.8.

מוֹצָא וּמוֹצָא ουμωσα O Ps. 89.35.

מוֹקֵשׁ moces J Am. 8.2.

מוֹר בְּהָמִיר βααμιρ O Ps. 46.3.

מוֹרָשָׁה מֹרֶשֶׁת maraseth J Mic. 1.14.

מָוֶת a) μαυθ O Ps. 89.49; cf. B-L § 17b'; cf. s.v. און sub a.
b) μωθ B in Βηθασμωθ, Neh. 7.28; A in Ασαρμωθ. Gen. 10.26; O Ps. 49.15; moth On in Asarmoth Gen. 10.26.

מות יָמוּתוּ ιαμωθου O Ps. 49.11: ιαμουθω lege ιαμωθου.

מִזְבֵּחַ מזבח μασβηη O Mal. 2.13; cf. in the BV מִזְבֵּחַ 2 Sam. 24.21 in Ms. Eb 12; stat. constr. מִזְבַּח Ps. 43.4 in Ms. Ec 1.

מָזוֹר a) mezur J Hos. 5.13.
b) mezor J ib.

מִזְמוֹר μαζμωρ O Ps. 29.1.

מִזְרָח מִמִּזְרָח mimizra J Gen. 2.8.

מָחוֹל a) μαουλ A 1 Ki. 5.11.
b) maol On ib.

לִמְחוֹל λμαωλ O Ps. 30.12.

מַחֲלָה a) μαλα G Num. 26.33; MT: מַחְלָה, here and in the following instances.
μαελα B 1 Chron. 7.18; ε corresponds to ח, cf. p. 175 sub ח.
b) μααλα G Num. 36.11;

maala On Num. 26.33.

מַחְמָד mamad J Hos. 9.6.

מַחֲנֶה מחנה manaim On Josh. 13.26.

מַחֲסֶה μασε O Ps. 46.2.

מַחַץ אֶמְחָצֶם εμωσημ O Ps. 18.39.

מְחִתָּה μεεθθα O Ps. 89.41.

מַטָּה a) meta J Gen. 48.2.
b) metta J ib., editio Lagarde.

מַטֶּה mate J Ezek. 4.16.

מְטַהֲרוֹ מטהר ματαρω O Ps. 89.45; MT מְטַהֲרוֹ is an erroneous dagesh in the ט; cf. MH § 12.

מִי μι O Ps. 18.32.

מַיִם μαειμ A in Μασρεφωθμαειμ, Josh. 11.8; μαιμ A in Αβελμαιν, lege μ for ν, 2 Chron. 16.4; maim J Hos. 11.10.

הַמַּיִם αμμαιμ O Ps. 29.3.

מֵימָיו μημαυ O Ps. 46.4.

מִישׁוֹר μεισωρ G Deut. 3.10; misor On ib.

מִישָׁר מֵישָׁרִים messarim J Isa. 26.7.

מַכְאוֹב מַכְאוֹבִים μαχωβιμ O Ps. 32.10.

מְכוֹנָה מכונה μεχωνωθ G 1 Ki. 7.27; mechonoth On ib.

מִכְתָּב machthab J Isa. 38.9; cf. in the BV מִכְתָּב Deut. 10.4 in Ms. Ka 19.

מַכְתֵּשׁ machthes J Zeph. 1.11.

מְלֵאָה malea J Nah. 3.1.

יִמְלָא מלא ιεμλα A 2 Chron. 18.7; iemla On 1 Ki. 22.8; MT: יִמְלָה.

מְלִיתִי μελληθι A 1 Chron. 25.26; MT: מַלּוֹתִי.

מַלְאָךְ malach J Hag. 1.13.

מַלְאָכִי malachi J Mal. 1.1.

מַלְאֲכֵי malache J Isa. 14.32.

מִלּוֹא a) μελω A 1 Ki. 9.15.

b) mello J Isa. 38.8.

מֶלַח a) μελε B in Ρεμελε, 2 Ki. 14.7; the second ε is the transliteration of the ח, cf. p. 175 sub ח; this is, therefore, a qitlform; cf. in the PV מֶלַח (MdWI, p. ט, line 13).

b) μελα A in Γαιμελα, 2 Ki. 14.7.

מלחמה וּמִלְחָמָה ουμαλαμα O Ps. 76.4; cf. in the BV מִלְחָמֹה Prov. 20.18 in Ms. Ec 1.

בַּמִּלְחָמָה βαμμαλαμα O Ps. 89.44; cf. in the BV בְּמִלְחָמֹה 1 Chron. 7.40 in Ms. Ec 1.

לַמִּלְחָמָה λαμαλαμα O Ps. 18.35.

מִלְחָמוֹת μαλαμωθ O Ps. 46.10; cf. in the BV מִלְחָמֹות 1 Chron. 16.9 in Ms. Ec 1.

מלט יְמַלֵּט ιμαλλετ O Ps. 89.49.

מלך a) מַלְכִּי malchi On in Mal-chihel, Num. 26.45.

לְמַלְכֵּי λαμαλχη O Ps. 89.28.

b) מַלְכִּי μελχει B in Μελ-χειηλ, Num. 26.45; cf. in the BV מַלְכִיה 1 Chron. 9.12 in Ms. Ec 1 for MT מַלְכִּיָה; μελχι A in Μελ-χιηλ, Num. 26.45; melchi On in Melchisedec, Gen. 14.18; cf. B-L § 14c'.

מַלְכְּכֶם melchechem J Am. 5.26.

מַלְכָּם μελχαμ A 1 Chron. 8.9.

c) מֶלֶךְ μελεχ B in Αδραμε-λεχ, 2 Ki. 17.31; melech On in Adramelech, ib.

μελεχ A in Αδραμελεχ, ib.

הַמֶּלֶךְ ammelech J Zech. 14.10.

מִלְכֹּם melchom J Zeph. 1.5; MT: מַלְכָּם.

מַלְקֹחַיִם malcaim J Isa. 6.6.

מַמְזֵר mamzer J Zech. 9.6.

ממלכה מַמְלָכוֹת μαμλαχωθ O Ps. 46.7: ΜΑΛΛΑΧΩΘ lege M for first Λ; cf. Thompson Facs. 3.

ממשק מִמְשַׁק mamasac J Zeph. 2.9.

מָן man On Ex. 16.15.

מִן men J Isa. 2.22.

מִמֶּנִּי a) μιμμενι O Ps. 35.22.

b) memmenni J 2 Ki. 4.27.

מנה יִמְנָה ιεμνα A Gen. 46.17; MT: יִמְנָה; iemna On ib.

תִּמְנָה θαμνα A Josh. 15.57; thamna On ib.

מִנִּי a) μενι O Ps. 44.19.

b) menni J Isa. 46.3.

מנוד מָנוֹד μανουδ O Ps. 44.15.

מָנוֹחַ a) manue On Ju. 13.2.

b) μανωε G ib.

מנוחה מְנוּחָתוֹ mnuatho J Jer. 11.10.

מנחה a) הַמִּנְחָה αμμανα O Mal. 2.13.

b) מִנְחָה manaa J Jer. 17.26.

מנע יִמְנָע ιμνα G 1 Chron. 7.35: IMANA lege IMNA; cf. Thompson Facs. 3 (M-A).

תִּמְנָע θαμνα A Gen. 36.12; thamna On ib.

מסגרת מִמִּסְגְּרוֹתֵיהֶם μεμασγωρω-θεειμ O Ps. 18.46: ΜΕ-ΜΑΣΤΩΡΩΘΕΕΙΜ lege Γ for T; cf. Thompson Facs. 3.

מִסְפָּר μασφαρ G Neh. 7.7.; cf in the BV מִסֹּפֵר Job 5.9. in Ms. Ec 1.

מֵעַד מָעֲדוּ μααδου O Ps. 18.37.

מָעוֹג μαωγ O Ps. 35.16.

מָעוֹז μαοζ O Ps. 31.3; maoz J Isa. 30.3.

מָעוּזִּי μαοζι O Ps. 31.5; cf. in the BV מֵעוֹזִי ib.; מָעוֹם ib. 37.39 in Ms. Ec 1; cf. B-L § 14q.

מָעוֹן μαων A 1 Chron. 2.45; maon On Josh. 15.55.

μεων B 1 Chron. 2.45; the ε may be considered as the rendering of the ע, cf. p. 176 sub ע; meon On in Bahalmeon, Num. 32.38.

מְעַט ματ O Ps. 8.6; cf. the bi-syllabic form in the PV מֵעַט and מֵעַט Job 10.20 (MdWI, p. יב); cf. s.v. שְׁאָר.

מְעִיל mail J Isa. 61.10.

מִמַּעַל memmal J Isa. 6.2.

מִפְעָל מִפְעָלוֹת μαφαλωθ O Ps. 46.9; cf. in the BV מִפְעָלִין Prov. 8.22 in Ms. Ec 1.

מִפְקָד μαφεκαδ G Neh. 3.31.

מֹצָא אֶמְצָא emsa J Zech. 12.5; MT: אֶמְצָה.

לִמְצֹא λαμσω O Ps. 36.3.

נִמְצָא νεμσα O Ps. 46.2.

מַצָּב μεσσαβ G 1 Sam. 14.1.

מְצוּדָה וּמְצוּדָתִי ουμσουδαθι O Ps. 31.4.

מְצוּדוֹת μσουδωθ O Ps. 31.3.

מִצְוָה וּמִצְוֹתַי ουμασωθαι O Ps. 89.32: OYMCΩΘAI lege OY-MACΩΘAI; cf. Thompson Facs. 3 (M-A); in the BV מִצְוֹתַי Lev. 26.15 in Ms. Ea 13.

מָצוֹר a) masur J Hab. 2.1.

b) μασωρ O Ps. 31.22; masor J Mic. 7.12.

מְצַהֲלוֹת mesaloth J Zech. 14.20; MT: מְצִלּוֹת.

מְצוּלָה מְצוּלוֹת mesuloth J Zech. 14.20; MT: מְצֻלּוֹת.

מִצְרַיִם mezraim J Isa. 19.1.

וּמִמִּצְרַיִם ουμεμμισραιμ O Hos. 11.1.

מַקְהֵלָה μακηλωθ G Num. 33.25; maceloth On ib.

מָקוֹם macoma J Nah. 1.8.

מַקֵּל מַקְלוֹת macaloth J Zech. 11.7; cf. B-L § 14a'.

מִקְנֶה macne J Jer. 9.9.; cf. in the BV מִקְנֹה Eccl. 2.7 in Ms. Ec 1.

מַר מָרָה mara On Ex. 15.23.

מָרוֹת maroth J Mic. 1.12.

מֶרְחָב בַּמֶּרְחָב βαμμαρ[αβ] O Ps. 31.9.

מֶרְכָּבָה מַרְכָּבוֹת μαρχαβωθ A in Βαιθμαρχαβωθ, 1 Chron. 4.31; marchaboth On Josh. 19.5.

מִרְמָה μαρμα A 1 Chron. 8.10; cf. in the BV מִרְמֹה Prov. 11. 1 in Ms. Ec 1.

מִרְמוֹת μαρμωθ O Ps. 35.20; cf. in the BV וּמִרְמוֹת Ps. 38.13 in Ms. Ec 1.

מְרֵעִים mrim J Isa. 1.4. mereim J ib.

מַרְפֵּא marphe J Eccl. 10.4.

מֶרֶץ נִמְרֶצֶת nimrezeth J 1 Ki. 2.8.

מַשָּׂא μασση A Gen. 25.14. massa On ib.; J Isa. 19.1. messa J Isa. 13.1.

מִשְׁאָל μασααλ A Josh. 21.30.

מִשְׂגָּב μισγαβ O Ps. 46.8.

מֶשִׁי a) mesi J Ezek. 16.13.

b) messe J Ezek. 16.10.

משיח a) מְשִׁיחֲךָ μσιαχ O Ps. 89.52; but perhaps should MCIAX be corrected to MECIAX? haplography: E before C; cf. Thompson Facs. 9.

μεσιαχ O Ps. 89.39.

מְשִׁיחוֹ μεσιω O Ps. 28.8.

b) מְשִׁיחֲךָ messiach J Hab. 3.13.

מְשִׁיחוֹ messio J Am. 4.13.

משך מֹשְׁכִים mosechim J Jer. 5.8; MT: מַשְׁכִים.

מֹשְׁכֵי mosche J Isa. 66.19.

משכן מִשְׁכְּנֵי μεσχνη O Ps. 46.5: MCXNH lege MECXNH.

מִשְׁכְּנֹתָם μισχνωθαμ O Ps. 49.12.

מָשָׁל μασαλ A 1 Chron. 6.59 masal J Isa. 14.4.

לְמָשָׁל λαμεσαλ O Ps. 49.5.

משל נִמְשָׁל νεμσαλ O Ps. 49.13.

מִשְׁמָע μασμα A Gen. 25.14; cf. in the BV מִשְׁמָע 1 Chron. 4.25 in Ms. Ec 1; masma On Gen. 25.14.

מִשְׁפָּח mesphaa J Isa. 5.7.

מִשְׁפָּט mesphat J Isa. 5.7.

לְמִשְׁפָּטִי λαμεσφατι O Ps. 35.23.

וּבְמִשְׁפָּטִי ουβμεσφατι O Ps. 89.31; MT: וּבְמִשְׁפָּטַי.

מֶשֶׁק masec On Gen. 15.2.

mesec J ib.; mesech is a mistake, dele h; cf. p. 177 sub ק.

משקה מִמַּשְׁקֵה memmasce J Ezek. 45.15.

מִשְׁרָה mesra J Isa. 9.6.

משרפת מִשְׂרְפוֹת μασρεφωθ A in Μασρεφωθμαειμ, Josh. 11.8.

masarfoth On ib.

מת מְתֶיךָ methecha J Isa. 26.19: metheca is a mistake, cf. p. 176 sub כ.

מתג בְּמֶתֶג βαμεθγε O Ps. 32.9.

מַתָּן μαθθαν B 2 Ki. 24.17; MT: מַתַּנְיָה; ματθαν A 2 Chron. 23.17; matthan On 2 Ki. 11.18.

מַתָּנָה mathana On Num. 21.18.

matthana J Eccl. 7.7.

נ

נָאוֹת naoth J Joel 1.20.

נְאָם νουμ O Ps. 36.2.

נאר נֶאְרְתָה νηερθ O Ps. 89.40.

נָבִיא nebia J Jer. 28.1.

נְבִיאִים nebim J Zech. 13.2.

nebeim J Jer. 28.1.

נֵבֶל a) νεβλ O Ps. 92.4; MT: נָבֶל.

b) nebel J Jer. 13.12.

נָבָל ναβαλ G 1 Sam. 25.3; nabal On ib.

נְבָלָה nabala J Isa. 32.6.

נָבָר ναβαρ O Ps. 18.27.

נֶגֶב negeb J Isa. 30.6.

נֶגֶד νεγδ O Ps. 31.20.

לְנֶגֶד λανεγδ O Ps. 36.2.

מִנֶּגֶד μενεγδ O Ps. 31.23.

נֶגְדִּי νεγδι O Ps. 89.37.

נגד הַגִּיד αιεγγιθ O Ps. 30.10: ΑΙΕΓΓΙΘΙ lege ΑΙΕΓΓΙΘ.

נֹּגַהּ a) ναγαι B 1 Chron. 3.7.

b) ναγε A ib.

נגה יַגִּיהַּ [ι]αγι O Ps. 18.29.

נגע וּבְנְגָעִים ουβανγαιμ O Ps. 89.33.

נגע יַגִּיעוּ ιγγιου O Ps. 32.6.

נגש נֹוגֵשׂ noges J Zech. 10.4.

נָדָב ναδαβ G Ex. 6.23; MT: נָדָב; nadab On ib.

נְדֻבה נְדֻבוֹת nadaboth J Am. 4.5.

נהל וּתְנַהֲלֵנִי ουθνεελητι O Ps. 31.4.

נהר a) וּבַגְּהָרוֹת ουβαναρωθ O Ps. 89.26.

b) נָהָר νααρ O Ps. 46.5.

נום יָנוּם יָנוּם ιανουμ A Josh. 15.53; ianum On ib.

נֶזֶם nezem J Ezek. 16.12.

נזר נִזְרוֹ νεζρω O Ps. 89.40.

נחה תַּנְחֵנִי θενηνι O Ps. 31.4.

נַחַל nehel J Ezek. 47.7; cf. p. 111 and 175 sub ח.

נַחֲלָה nehela J Isa. 17.11; see the note on נַחַל.

נַחֲלָתְךָ νεελαθαχ O Ps. 28.9.

נחם מְנַחֵם μαναημ G 2 Ki. 15.17; manaem On ib.

נחמה נִחָמְתִי naamathi J Zech. 8.14; MT: נִחַמְתִי.

נָחָשׁ ναας G 2 Sam. 17.25; naas On ib.

נחש נְחוּשָׁה νεουσα O Ps. 18.35.

נַחַת naath On Gen. 36.13.

נחת וְנָחֲתָה ουνααθα O Ps. 18.35; MT: וְנִחֲתָה.

נטה וַתֵּט ουαθετ O Ps. 44.19.

אַטֶּה αττε O Ps. 49.5.

הַטֵּה εττη O Ps. 31.3.

נְכֹאת nechotha J Gen. 43.11.

נְכֹתה nechotha J Isa. 39.2.

נָכוֹן ναχων A 2 Sam. 6.6.

נְכִים νηχιμ O Ps. 35.15.

נֵכָר νηχαρ O Ps. 18.46.

נָמֵר nemer J Jer. 5.6.

נסה אֲנַסֶּה enasse J Isa. 7.12.

נְסִיכֵי nesiche J Mic. 5.4.

נסס מְתְנוֹסְסוֹת methnosasoth J Zech. 9.16.

נעמן נַעֲמָנִים neamenim J Isa. 17.10.

נֹעַם a) νεεμ G in Αβεινεεμ, Jud.

4.6; the second ε is a transliteration of the ע; cf. p. 176 sub ע.

b) noem On in Abinoem, ib.; see the preceding note.

נַעֲצוּץ nesus J Isa. 55.13.

נַעַר νερ O Hos. 11.4.

נְפִילִים a) nifilim J Gen. 6.4 (editio Lagarde).

b) הַנְּפִילִים annaphilim J Gen. 6.4.

נפל תֵּפֹל thephphol J Ezek. 8.1.

יִפְּלוּ ιεφφολου O Ps. 18.39.

נפתול נַפְתּוּלֵי nephthule J Gen. 30.8; neptule J ib. (ed. Lagarde).

נפש נַפְשִׁי νεφσι O Ps. 30.4.

נַפְשׁוֹ νεφσω O Ps. 89.49.

נַפְשֵׁנוּ νεφσινου O Ps. 35.25.

נצח לָנֶצַח λανες O Ps. 49.10.

נצח לַמְנַצֵּחַ λαμανασση O Ps. 31.1; lamanasse J praefatio in Dan.

נְצִיב a) νασειβ B Josh. 15.43; nasib On ib.

b) νεσιβ A ib.

נצל הַצִּילֵנִי εσιληνι O Ps. 31.3.

נֵצֶר neser J Isa. 11.1.

כִּנֵצֶר chaneser J Isa. 14.19.

נצר תִּצֹּר θεσαρ O Isa. 26.3.

תִּצְּרֵנִי θεσσερηνι O Ps. 32.7.

נֹצֵר νωσηρ O Ps. 31.24.

נְצוּרֵי nesure J Isa. 49.6.

נֶקֶב ναχεβ A Josh. 19.33.

נקד נֹקְדִים nocedim J Am. 1.1.

נקמה נְקָמוֹת νακαμωθ O Ps. 18.48.

נֵר νηρ G 2 Sam. 14.51; ner On ib.

נשא שָׂאתִי σαθι O Ps. 89.51.

וְנִשָּׂאם ουνεσσημ O Ps. 28.9.

נשג וְאַשִּׂיגֵם ουεσιγημ O Ps. 18.38.

נשה מְנַשֶּׁה a) μανασση B Gen. 41.51; manasse On ib.

b) μαννασση A ib.

נָשִׂיא nasi J Ezek. 46.12.

נְשָׁמָה nasama J Isa. 2.22.

נִשְׁמוֹת nasamoth J Isa. 57.16.

נֶשֶׁף neseph J Isa. 21.4.

נִשְׁפָּה nesepha J Jer. 13.16; MT: נֶשֶׁף.

נְתִינִים ναθινειμ A Ezra 2.58.

הַנְּתִינִים αννατινιμ A in Βηθ-αννατινιμ, Neh. 3.31.

נָתַן ναθαν G Ezra 8.16; O Ps. 46.7; nathan On in Jonathan, Jud. 18.30.

נָתַתָּה ναθαθ O Ps. 18.41.

וַיִּתֵּן ουιεθθεν O Ps. 18.33.

וַתִּתֵּן ουθεθθεν O Ps. 18.36.

אֶתְּנֵהוּ εθνηου O Ps. 89.28.

הַנּוֹתֵן αννωθην O Ps. 18.48.

ס

סבב יְסוֹבְבֶנּוּ ισωβαβενηου O Ps. 32.10.

תְּסוֹבְבֵנִי θσωβαβηνι O Ps. 32.7.

יְסֻבֵּנִי ισαββουνι O Ps. 49.6; MT: יְסֻבֵּנִי.

סְבָךְ a) sabac On Gen. 22.13.

b) σαβεκ A ib.; sabech J ib.

סְגֻלָּה sgolla J Mal. 3.17.

סְגַר הִסְגַּרְתַּנִי εσγερθανι O Ps. 31.9.

סוֹד a) בְּסוֹד βασωδ A in Βασω-δια, Neh. 3.6; basod J Jer. 23.18.

סוֹדִי sodi On Num. 13.10.

b) σουδει B ib.; σουδι A ib.

סוּס sus J Isa. 38.14.

כְּסוּס χισους O Ps. 32.9.

סוּסִי σουσει B Num. 13.11; σουσι A ib.; susi On ib.

סוּפָה בְּסוּפָה basupha J Nah. 1.3.

סִיג sig J Ezek. 22.18.

סִיגִים sigim J Isa. 1.22.

סִינִים sinim J Isa. 49.12.

סִיס sis J Isa. 38.14.

סכה סֻכֹּת σοκχωθ G Num. 33.5; socchoth On Ex. 12.37. socoth On Gen. 33.17; sochoth J ib.; Am. 5.26; MT: סֻכּוֹת.

סֹכֵן socen J Isa. 22.15.

סכן הַמְסֻכָּן amsuchan J Isa. 40.20.

סֶלָה a) σελα O Ps. 32.7; sela J Hab. 3.3.

b) σελ O Ps. 3.3.

סלע סַלְעִי σελει O Ps. 31.4; cf. in the BV סֹלְעִי ib. 42.10 in Ms. Ec 1.

סָמָךְ σαμαχ A in Αχισαμαχ, Ex. 35.34; σαμακ B in Αχι-σαμακ, ib.

סָמוּךְ samuch J Isa. 26.3.

סְנָא הַסְּנָאָה ασανουα A 1 Chron. 9.7.

סעד תִּסְעָדֵנִי θεσαδηνι O Ps. 18.36: ΘΕΣ*ΔΗΝΙ lege ΘΕΣΑ-ΔΗΝΙ.

סַף seph J Ezek. 40.6.

סֹפֵר sopher J Isa. 36.3.

סְפָרַד sapharad J Obad 20.

סָרִיס σαρεις A in Ραβσαρεις, 2 Ki. 18.17; saris On in Rab-saris, ib.

סַרְפַּד sarphod J Isa. 55.13.

סֵתֶר σεθρ O Ps. 32.7.

בְּסֵתֶר βσεθρ O Ps. 31.21.

סִתְרִי σεθρι A Ex. 6.22; sethri On ib.

σετρι B ib.: ΣΕΓΡΙ lege

T for Γ; cf. Thompson Facs. 3.

סתר הִסְתַּרְתָּ εσθερθα O Ps. 30.8.

תַּסְתִּיר θεσθερ O Ps. 89.47; MT: תַּסְתֵּר.

תַּסְתִּירֵם θεσθιρημ O Ps. 31.21.

סָתוּר σαθουρ G Num. 13.13; MT: סָתוּר.

ע

עֶבֶד a) αβδ G in Αβδεμελεχ, Jer. 38.7.

לְעֶבֶד λααβδ O Ps. 36.1.

עַבְדִי αβδει B 1 Chron. 6.29; αβδι A ib.

עַבְדְּךָ αβδαχ O Ps. 89.40.

עַבְדּוֹ αβδω O Ps. 35.27.

עַבְדִי αβδη A in Αβδησελμα, Ezra 2.58; O Ps. 113.1.

עֲבָדֶיךָ αβδαχ O Ps. 89.51; cf. in the PV עבדיך Ps. 90.13 (MdWI, p. א).

b) עבד αβεδ A Jud. 9.26; abed On ib.; cf. B-L § 20m.

עבד עוֹבֵד ωβηδ G Ruth 4.17; obeth On ib.

עֵבֶר a) εβερ A Gen. 10.21; eber On ib.

b) עֲבָרִים αβαρειμ G Num. 33.47; abarim On ib.

מֵעֲבָרִים meabarim J Jer. 22.20.

עבר עָבַרְתִּי abarthi J Hos. 10.11.

אֶעֱבָר eebor J Am. 5.17.

עֶבְרִי ωβρη O Ps. 89.42.

הִתְעַבַּרְתָּ εθαββαρθ O Ps. 89.39.

עברה עֶבְרַת ebrath J Am. 1.11.

עברה בְּעַבְרוֹת βεγαβρωθ O Ps. 7.7.

עִבְרִי ibri J Gen. 14.13.

הָעִבְרִים ahebrim On Ex. 2.6; on the h see p. 111.

עִבְרִיּוֹת ebrioth On Ex. 1.16.

עָגוּר a) agor J Isa. 38.14.

b) agur J ib.

עֶגְלָה a) αγλα A 1 Chron. 3.3.

b) egla J Hos. 10.11.

עגלה עֲגָלוֹת αγαλωθ O Ps. 46.10.

עַד αδ O Ps. 89.47; O Ps. 18.38: *Δ, lege ΑΔ.

לָעַד laed J Mic. 7.18.

עד וָעֶד ουηδ O Ps. 89.38.

עדד עוֹדֵד ωδηδ B 2 Chron. 15.1.

עָדִים eddim J Isa. 64.5.

עֶדְיוֹ αδιω O Ps. 32.9.

עֵדֶן εδεν A Gen. 2.8; eden On ib.

עֵדֶר a) εδερ A 1 Chron. 23.23.

b) ader On Gen. 35.21.

עוֹד ωδ O Ps. 49.10.

עולם a) לְעוֹלָם λωλαμ O Ps. 30.7; lolam J Ezek. 26.21.

הָעוֹלָם αωλαμ O Ps. 28.9.

b) עוֹלָמִים ωλεμειμ O Isa. 26.4.

עון עָוֹן αων O Ps. 49.6.

עֲוֹנָם αυωναν O Ps. 89.33; perhaps to be explained as an amalgamation of two readings: αυναν (cf. אוֹנָן αυναν)+ωναν; cf. on מעמו; onam J Zech. 5.6.

עור הָעִירָה αιρα O Ps. 35.23.

עוֹרֵב ωρηβ G Ju. 7.25; oreb On ib.

עוֹרְבִים orbim J Isa. 15.7.

עֹז οζ O Ps. 28.8.

עֻזִּי οζει G in Οζειηλ, Ex. 6.18; O Ps. 28.7; cf. עָזִּי Ex. 15.2; further in the BV: עֹזְךָ Ps. 63.3; עֹזוֹ Prov. 10.15 in Ms. Ec 1; ozi On in Ozihel, Ex. 6.18.

עָז   ας B in Ασγαδ, Ezra 2.12; αζ A in Αζγαδ, Ezra 8.12.

עזב   וְעָזְבוּ ουαζβου O Ps. 49.11.
יַעַזְבוּ ιεζεβου O Ps. 89.31.
עֲזוּבָה αζουβα A 1 Ki. 22.42; azuba On ib.

עֵזֶר   a) εζρ O Ps. 46.2; MT: עֶזְרָה.
עֶזְרִי εζρι A Ju. 6.11; ezri On ib.; εσδρει B ib.
וְעֶזְרָה ουεζρα O Ps. 46.6; MT: יַעְזְרָה.
b) עֵזֶר εζερ G in Αβιεζερ, Ju. 6.34.

עָזַר   αζαρ G in Ελεαζαρ, Ex. 6.23; azar On in Eleazar, ib.
עֹזֵר ωζηρ O Ps. 30.11.
עָזוּר azur On Ezek. 11.1; MT: עַזֻּר.
וְנֶעֱזָרְתִּי ουνεζαρθι O Ps. 28.7; ουναζερθι lege ουνεζαρθι.

עזרה   בְּעֶזְרָתִי βαεζραθι O Ps. 35.2.
עֶזְרָה azara J Ezek. 43.17.
עטה   הֶעֱטִיתָ εετηθ O Ps. 89.46.
עֲטָרָה   αταρα B 1 Chron. 2.26.
עֲטָרוֹת αταρωθ G Num. 32.3; ataroth On ib.

עַיִן   a) αιν A Josh. 19.7; O Ps. 35.9; ain On Num. 34.11.
b) עֵין ην A in Ηναδδα, Josh. 19.21; en On in Enadda, ib.
עֵינִי ηνι O Ps. 31.10.
עֵינֵנוּ ηνηνου O Ps. 35.21.
עֵינָם enam J Zech. 5.6.
עֵינַיִם enaim On Gen. 38.21.
וְעֵינַיִם ουηναιμ O Ps. 18.28: OYNNAIM lege H for the first N; cf. Thompson Facs. 5.
עֵינֶיךָ ηναχ O Ps. 31.23.
עֵינָיו ηναυ O Ps. 36.2.
בְּעֵינָיו βεηναυ O Ps. 36.3;

B*NNAY lege H for the first N; cf. Thompson Facs. 5.

עִיר   ιρ O Ps. 46.5; ir J Isa. 26.5.
בְּעִיר βεειρ O Ps. 31.22.
הָעִיר αειρ O Gen. 28.19.
עִירָם iram On Gen. 36.43.
עָרִים arim J Isa. 14.21.

עַל   αλ O Ps. 8.1; al J Hab. 3.1.
וְעַל ουαλ O Ps. 18.34.
עָלַי αλαι O Ps. 35.21.
עָלֶיךָ αλαχ O Ps. 32.28.
עָלָיו αλαυι O Ps. 89.46.
וְעָלֶיהָ ουαλεα O Ps. 7.8.
עֲלֵיהֶם alehem J Zech. 14.17.

עלה   הֶעֱלִיתָ εελθ O Ps. 30.4: perhaps to be corrected to εεληθ; cf. § 53aβ.

עלז   וַיַּעֲלֹז ουαιαλεζ O Ps 28.7.
עֲלִי   αλη O Ps. 49.12; αλε O Ps. 92.4 (1°).
וַעֲלִי ουαλε O Ps. 92.4.
עֲלֵה   ale J Ezek. 47.12.
עלומים   עֲלוּמָיו αλουμαυ O Ps. 89.46.
עֶלְיוֹן ελιων O Ps. 46.5; elion J Isa. 2.22.
עליל   בַּעֲלִיל βααλιλ O Ps. 12.7.
עלם   נֶעֶלְמָה naalma J Job 28.21.
הָעֵלִים eelim J 2 Ki. 4.27 (vol. IV, p. 109B).
עַלְמָה   alma J Isa. 7.14.
עֲלָמוֹת alamoth J Ps. 9.1 (on Isa. 7.14); MT: עַל מוּת.
עֲלָמוֹת   αλμωθ O Ps. 46.1; MT: עֲלָמוֹת.
עָם   εμ O Ps. 18.26.
מֵעִמּוֹ μηεμμωαυ O Ps. 89.34; perhaps originating in the combination of two separate readings: μηεμμω + μηεμμαυ; cf. on יְרִיבִי and on עֲוֺנָם.

עִמָּנוּ εμμανου G in Εμμανου-
ηλ, Isa. 7.14; O Ps. 46.8;
emmanu On in Emma-
nuhel, Isa. 7.14.

עם a) αμ O Ps. 18.28; am On in
Amram, Ex. 6.18.

בְּעַם βααμ O Ps. 35.18.

עַמִּי αμει B in Αμειναδαβ,
Num. 1.7; αμι A in Αμι-
ναδαβ, ib.; ami On in
Aminadab, ib.

עַמִּים αμιμ O Ps. 89.51.

הָעַמִּים ααμιμ O Ps. 49.2:
AAMIN lege M for N.

b) עַמִּי ammi On in Am-
miod, 2 Sam. 13.37.

עַמְּךָ αμμαχ O Ps. 28.9.

עַמִּים αμμιμ O Ps. 18.48:
AMIMIM lege AMMIM.

עמד הֶעֱמַדְתָּ εεμεδεθ O Ps. 31.9.

יַעֲמִידֵנִי ιεμιδηνι O Ps.
18.34. (ICMIANNI lege
IEMIΔHNI).

עמוד עֲמוּדָה αμουδα O Ps. 75.4;
MT: עַמּוּדֶיהָ.

עמית עֲמִיתִי amithi J Zech. 13.7.

עֵמֶק emec On Josh. 17.16.

הָעֵמֶק αεμεκ A in Βηθαεμεκ,
Josh. 19.27.

עָנָה ανα A Gen. 36.14; MT: עֲנָה;
ana On ib.

עָנָם αναμ O Ps. 18.42.

עֲנָתָה anatha J Hos. 2.17.

עֲנִיתִי εννηθι O Ps. 35.13.

מְעוֹנִים μοουνειμ A Ezra 2.50.

ענוה וְעֲנַוְתְּךָ ουαναυαθαχ O Ps. 18.
36; perhaps to be cor-
rected to: ουανουαθαχ.

עָנִי ανι O Ps. 18.28.

עֲנִיִּי ανιη O Ps. 76.10; MT:
עֶנְוִי; anie J Zech. 11.11.

עני עֲנִיִּי ονι O Ps. 31.8; perhaps to

be corrected to ονι; ha-
plography; the following
word ιαδαθ begins with ι,
too.

עִנְיָן anian J Eccl. 1.13.

עֹנֶה onena J Isa. 57.3.

עֲנָק ενακ A Num. 13.22; εναχ
B ib.

עֲנָקִים ενακειμ G Deut. 2.10.
anacim On ib.: anacin, lege
m for the second n.

עפף מְעוֹפֵף mopheph J Isa. 14.
29.

עָפָר αφαρ O Ps. 30.10; aphar J
Gen. 3.14; afar J ib., ed.
Lagarde.

כְּעָפָר χααφαρ O Ps. 18.43.

עָפְרָה afara On Josh. 18.23;
MT: עָפְרָה.

עֲצַבִּים ασεβειν O Ps. 127.2; MT:
הָעֲצַבִּים.

עצה בַּעֲצַת βησαθ O Ps. 1.1; cf.
in the PV וְעֻצַת Isa. 44.26
(MdWI, p. ד).

עצם עָצוּם ασουμ O Ps. 35.18.

עֲצָרָה asara J Joel 1.14.

עֵקֶב a) עֲקֻבוֹת εκβωθ O Ps. 89.52.
b) עֵקֶב eceb J Am. 4.12.

עקב יַעֲקֹב ιακωβ G Gen. 25.26;
·iacob On ib.

עֲקֻבַּי ακοββαι O Ps. 49.6;
MT: עֲקֻבִּי; cf. Hos. 6.8.

עקרב עַקְרַבִּים a) ακραβειμ B Josh.
15.3: Ακραβειν lege μ for ν.
b) ακραββειμ A ib.; acrab-
bim On ib.

עֵקֶשׁ εκκης O Ps. 18.27; A 1 Chron.
11.28.

עֵר ηρ A Gen. 38.3; er On ib.

ערב a) בְּעָרֶב βααρβ O Ps. 30.6.
b) עֶרֶב arab J Isa. 21.13.

עֲרָבָה αραβα B in Βαιθαραβα, Josh.

15.6; araba On Deut.
1.7.

עֲרָבוֹת αραβωθ G Num. 26.
63; araboth On ib.

עֲרָבִי arabe J Jer. 3.2.

עֲרָבִים arabim J Isa. 15.7.

עָרוּם arom J Gen. 3.1.

עֲרִירִי ariri J Jer. 22.29.

עֹרֶף ορφ O Ps. 18.41.

אֶרֶשׂ ares J Am. 3.12.

עָשׁ as J Hos. 5.12.

עָשָׂה ασα G in Ασαηλ, 2 Sam. 23.
24; asa On in Asahel, ib.

תַּעֲשׂוּ θεσου O Mal. 2.13.

עֹשֶׂה ωση O Ps. 31.24.

עָשׂוֹר ασωρ O Ps. 92.4.

עָשִׂיר ασιρ O Ps. 49.3: CIP lege
ACIP; haplography
(IAAΔ CIP; Δ-A).

עָשָׁן ασαν A I Sam. 30.30; asan
On Josh. 19.7.

עשר עֲשָׂרָם οσραμ O Ps. 49.7.

עֶשְׂרֵה esre J Ezek. 40.49.

עשש עֲשָׁשָׁה ασσα O Ps. 31.10.

עַשְׁתֵּי aste J Ezek. 40.49.

פ

פאה פְּאַת fath On Lev. 19.9.

פְּארָה phura J Isa. 10.33.

פגר פְּגָרִים phagarim J Jer. 31.
40; cf. in the BV גֹּנְרִי Lev.
26.30 in Ms. Ea 13.

פָּדָה φαδα G in Φαδαηλ, Num. 34.
28; fada On in Fadaia,
2 Ki. 23.36.

פָּדִיתָ φαδιθ O Ps. 31.6: ΦΑ-
ΛΙΘ, lege Δ for Λ.

יִפְדֶּה ιεφδε O Ps. 49.8: ΙΕ-
ΦΑΕ, lege Δ for A.

פָּדָה φαδω O Ps. 49.8.

פִּדְיוֹן φεδιων O Ps. 49.9.

פה st. constr. פִּי φι A in Φιχολ,

Gen. 21.22; fi On in
Fichol. ib.

פִּי φι O Ps. 49.4.

פִּיהֶם φιεμ O Ps. 35.21.

בְּפִיהֶם βαφιεμ O Ps. 49.14.

פוך בַּפּוּךְ baphphuch J Isa.
54.11.

פוע יָפִיעַ ιαφιε A Josh. 10.3; ε is
the transliteration of the
ע, cf. p. 176 sub ע; iafie
On ib.

פור אָפִיר αφιρ O Ps. 89.34.

פוּרָה phura J Isa. 63.3.

פז φας B in Ελειφας, 1 Chron.
1.35.

φαζ A in Ελιφαζ, ib.; phaz
J Isa. 13.12; faz On in
Elifaz, Gen. 36.4.

פחד πααδ G in Σαλπααδ, Num.
26.33.

φααδ O Ps. 36.2; faath On
in Salfaath, Num. 26.33.

פחה פַּחַת φααθ A in Φααθμωαβ,
Ezra 10.30.

φααδ B in Φααδμωαβ, ib.

פחז פּוֹחֲזִים phoezim J Zeph. 3.4.

פֶּלֶא phele J Isa. 9.5.

הַפְלִיא εφλι O Ps. 31.22.

פֶּלֶג a) faleg On Gen. 10.25;
φαλεκ A ib.; φαλεχ B
1 Chron. 1.25.

b) פִּלַגְיוֹ φλαγαυ O Ps. 46.5.

פֶּלֶט φαλητ O Ps. 32.7; without
gemination of the 2nd
radical; cf. on אַכְזָב.

פַּלְטֵנִי φελλετηνι O Ps. 31.2.

פְּלֵיטָה a) phaleta J Joel 3.5.

b) פְּלֵיטִים pheletim J Obad
17.

פֶּנַּג phanag J Ezek. 27.17.

פנה לִפְנוֹת λαφνωθ O Ps. 46.6:
ΛΦΝΩΘ lege ΛΑΦΝΩΘ.

פֻּנּוֹת φεννωθ O Mal. 2.13; MT: פֻנוֹת.

יָקְנֶה ιεφοννη G Num. 13.7.

פָּנִים פְּנֵי φανη O Ps. 18.43.

פָּנֶיךָ φαναχ O Ps. 30.8.

פָּנָיו phanau J Isa. 6.2.

פֶּסֹח phase J Ezek. 25.15.

תִּפְסַּח θαψα A I Ki. 5.4.

פֶּעַל פָּעָלְךָ phalach J Hab. 3.2.

פָּעַל φααλ A in Ελφααλ, I Chron. 8.18.

פָּעָלְתָ φααλθα O Ps. 31.20.

פקד וּפְקַדְתִּי ουφακαδθι O Ps. 89.33: ουφαδθι lege ουφακαδθι.

פָּקוּד phacud J Ezek. 23.23; MT: פְּקוֹד.

אַפְקִיד εφικιδ O Ps. 31.6.

פַּר phar J Ezek. 43.23.

פָּרִים pharim J Hos. 14.3.

פֶּרֶא phara J Gen. 16.12; fara J ib., ed. Lagarde.

פרד כְּפֶרֶד χφαρδ O Ps. 32.9.

פָּרָה φαρα B Josh. 18.23.

הַפָּרָה affara On ib.

פרח פָּרוּחַ φαρρου A I Ki. 4.17.

פְּרִי pheri J Hos. 14.3.

פָּרִיץ pharis J Ezek. 18.10.

פֶּרֶץ a) φαρες A Gen. 38.29; fares On ib.

b) pheres J Isa. 58.12.

c) פְּרָצִים φαρασειμ A in Βααλφαρασειν, lege μ for ν, I Chron. 14.11; pharasim J Isa. 28.27.

פרץ פָּרְצְתָ φαρασθ O Ps. 89.41.

פֶּרֶק pherec J Nah. 3.1.

פֶּרֶשׁ phares J Mal. 2.3.

פֶּשַׁע φεσα O Ps. 36.2.

פִּשְׁעָם φεσαμ O Ps. 89.33: ΦCAM lege ΦECAM.

פּוֹתָה photha J Mic. 7.11.

פתח בִּפְתָחֶיהָ baphethee J Mic. 5.5.

פתוח פְּתוּחָה phetee J Zech. 3.9.

פָּתַח παθα B in παθαια, Neh. 11.24. φαθα A in φαθαια, ib.

יִפְתַּח ιεφθα A Josh. 15.43; ιεφθαε G Ju. 11.14; the second ε = ח, cf. p. 175 sub ח; iepte On Josh. 15.43.

אֶפְתַּח εφθα O Ps. 49.5.

מִפְתַּח maphate J Zech. 3.9.

פִּתְחָ φεθεθα O Ps. 30.12; without gemination of the 2nd radical; cf. on אָכֻב.

פְּתִיגִיל phthigal J Isa. 3.24.

פתל נִפְתַּלְתִּי nephthalethi J Gen. 30.8; neptalti J ib., ed. Lagarde.

תִּתְפַּתָּל θεθφαθθαλ O Ps. 18.27.

צ

צֹאָה soa J in cisoa, Isa. 28.8.

צֹאן כַּצֹּאן χασων O Ps. 49.15.

צֶאֱצָאִים sasaim J Isa. 22.24.

צְבָאוֹת σαβαωθ G I Sam. 1.3; O Ps. 46.8; sabaoth On I Sam. 1.3.

צְבִי sabai J Dan. 11.41.

צֵדָה seda J Gen. 45.21.

צַדִּיק a) σαδικ O Isa. 26.2.

b) צַדִּיקִים σαδδικιμ O Ps. 32.11.

צדק a) צִדְקִי σεδκι O Ps. 35.27.

צִדְקֶךָ σεδκαχ O Ps. 35.28.

כְּצִדְקֶךָ χσεδκαχ O Ps. 35.24: XCEΔKAΔ lege X for second Δ; for some resemblance cf. Thompson Facs. 18.

b) צֶדֶק σεδεκ A in Μελχι-

σεδεκ, Gen. 14.18; sedec
On in Melchidesec, ib.

הַצֶּדֶק asedec J Isa. 19.18.

צדק צִדְקֵנוּ sadecenu J Jer. 23.6;
MT: צִדְקֵנוּ; cf. in the
BV צִדְקִי Job 35.2 in Ms.
Ec 1, for MT צִדְקִי.

צדקה a) בְּצִדְקָתֶךָ βσεδκαθαχ O
Ps. 31.2.

b) צְדָקָה sadaca J Isa. 5.7.

צהר יִצְהָר ισααρ A Ex. 6.18; MT:
יִצְהָר; isaar J Zech. 4.14.
iessaar On Ex. 6.18.

צָו sau J Isa. 28.10; cf. B-L § 17z.
לָצָו lasau J ib.

צוד sud J Hos. 9.13.

צום בַּצּוֹם βασωμ O Ps. 35.13.

צוף σουφ G 1 Chron. 6.20.

צור a) σουρ G Num. 25.15; O
Ps. 18.32; sur J Isa. 10.
26.
לְצוּר ασουρ lege λασουρ vel
λασουρ; O Ps. 31.3.

צוּרִי σουρει B in Σουρεισαδαι,
Num. 1.6; σουρι A in
Σουρισαδαι, ib.; O Ps. 18.
47; suri On in Surisaddai,
Num. 1.6.
וְצוּרָם ουσουραμ O Ps. 49.15.

b) צוּר σωρ O Isa. 26.4.

צוּרִי sori On in Sorihel, Num.
3.35.

צחק יִצְחַק ισαακ G Gen. 21.3;
isaac On ib.; MT: יִצְחָק.

צַחַר soor J Ezek. 27.18.

צִי צִיִּים siim J Isa. 13.21.

ציון בְּצִיּוֹן basaion J Isa. 25.5.

ציון צִיִּנִים sionim J Jer. 31.21.

צִינק sinac J Jer. 29.26.

צִיר sir J Obad 1.

צֵל a) σαλ G in Σαλπααδ, Num.
26.33; cf. in the BV צֵל

Job 8.9 in Ms. Ec 1; sal
On in Salfaath, Num.
26.33; cf. B-L § 14z and
g'.

b) בְּצֵל βεσελ G in Βεσελεηλ,
Ex. 31.2; besel On in
Beselehel, ib.

צְלָה sela On Gen. 4.19; MT:
צִלָּה; cf. Jerome's explanation: umbra eius.

σελλα A ib.

צלח הַצְלִיחָה נָא ασλιαννα O Ps.
118.25.

צלע וּבְצַלְעִי ουβσαλη O Ps. 35.15.

צִלְצָל selsel J Isa. 18.1.

צמה צַמָּתֵךְ semmathech J Isa.
47.2.
samthech J ib.

צֶמַח sema J Zech. 6.12.

צמת אַצְמִיתֵם ασμιθαυμ O Ps.
18.41.

צִנָּה a) σενα A Josh. 15.3.
b) σεννα B ib.: CENNAK
dele K, dittography.
וְצִנָּה ουσεννα O Ps. 35.2.
c) צִנּוֹת sannoth J Am. 4.2.

צָנִיף saniph J Zech. 8.5.

צנע הַצְנֵעַ esne J Mic. 6.8.

צנתר צַנְתְּרוֹת sinthoroth J Zech.
4.12.

צעד צְעָדַי σααδαι O Ps. 18.37;
MT: צַעֲדִי.

צְעָקָה saaca J Isa. 5.7.

צפה צוֹפִים σωφιμ A 1 Sam. 1.1;
sofim On ib.

צָפוֹן σαφων B Num. 26.15; MT:
צָפוֹן; saphon J Jer.
25.26.

צְפוֹנִי σαφωνει B Num. 26.15;
σαφωνι A ib.

צְפוֹר σεπφωρ G Num. 22.2; sefor
On ib.

צְפִיעוֹת sephoth J Isa. 22.24.

צְפִירָה sephphira J Ezek. 7.10.

צָפָן σαφαν G in Ελεισαφαν, Num. 3.30.

צָפַנְתָּ σαφανθα O Ps. 31.20.

תִּצְפְּנֵם θισφνημ O Ps. 31.21.

צָפוּן σαφουν O Ps. 48.3; MT: צָפוֹן.

צפען צִפְעֹנִים saphphonim J Jer. 8.17.

צַר σαρ O Ps. 31.10; sar J Am. 3.11.

מֵצַר μεσσαρ O Ps. 32.7.

צָרָיו σαραυι O Ps. 89.43.

צרה בְּצָרוֹת βσαρωθ O Ps. 31.8; 46.2.

צרע צָרוּעָה σαρουα A 1 Ki. 11.26.

צָרַעַת sarath J Gen. 17.16.

צרף צְרוּפָה σερουφα O Ps. 18.31.

ק

קבע חַיְקָבַּע hajecba J Mal. 3.8.

קָדִים cadim J Ezek. 27.26.

קֶדֶם κεδεμ G Ezek. 25.4; cedem J ib.

מִקֶּדֶם mecedem J Gen. 2.8.

קֵדְמָה κεδμα A Gen. 25.15; cedma On ib.

קדש קֹדֶשׁ κοδς O Ps. 46.5.

קֹדֶשׁ a) κοδς O Ps. 29.2.

בְּקֹדֶשׁ βεκοδς O Ps. 89.36; MT: בְּקָדְשִׁי.

קָדְשׁוֹ κοδσω O Ps. 30.5: ΚΟΔΕΩ lege C for E.

קָדְשָׁה codsa J Isa. 40.13.

b) קֹדֶשׁ codes J Isa. 52.1.

קָדְשׁוֹ cadeso J Isa. 63.10; cf. in the PV קָדְשׁוֹ Ps. 105.42 (Edelmann, p. ד, line 8).

c) הַקְּדֵשִׁים ακκοδασιμ O 2 Ki. 23.7; MT: הַקְּדֵשִׁים.

קָדֵשׁ καδης A Gen. 14.7; cades On ib.

קָדֵשִׁים καδησειμ B 2 Ki. 23.7; καδησιμ A ib.: καδησιν lege μ for ν; cadesim On ib.

קָדֵשָׁה cadesa J Isa. 27.1.

קָדֵשׁוֹת cadesoth J Hos. 4.14.

קהל בְּקָהָל βακααλ O Ps. 35.18.

קהל קֹהֶלֶת coeleth J Eccl. 1.1.

קַו cau J Isa. 28.10; cf. B-L § 17z.

לָקַו lacau J ib.

קוֹל κωλ A in Κωλεια, Neh. 11.7; O Ps. 28.6.

בְּקוֹלוֹ βκωλω O Ps. 46.7.

קום קָם καμ G in Αδανεικαμ, Ezra 8.13; cam On in Ahicam, 2 Ki. 22.12.

יָקוּם jaccum J Nah. 1.6.

קָמַי καμαι O Ps. 18.40.

וָקוּם ουκουμ O Ps. 35.2; MT: וְקוּמָה.

קוּם κουμ O Ps. 18.39.

הֲקִמֹתוֹ ακιμωθω O Ps. 89.44.

יָקִים ιακειμ G 1 Chron. 8.19; iacim On in Eliacim 2 Ki. 18.18.

קוֹץ κως G 1 Chron. 24.10.

הַקּוֹץ a) ακως B Neh. 3.4.

b) ακκως A ib.

קוֹץ וְהַקּוֹצָה ουακισα O Ps. 35.23.

קטן הַקָּטָן a) ακαταν B Ezra 8.12.

b) ακκαταν A ib.

קיא ci J in cisoa, Isa. 28.8.

קִיטֹר citor J Gen. 19.28.

קִינָה κινα A Josh. 15.22.

קִיקָיוֹן ciceion J Jonah 4.6.

קִיר cir J Isa. 38.2.

קלל קַלּוֹת calloth J Nah. 1.14.

קלע קוֹלֵעַ colea J Jer. 10.18.

קִנְאָה cena J Ezek. 8.3.

קָנֶה cane J Jer. 6.20.

קָנָה κανα G in Ελκανα, Ex. 6.24; cana On in Elcana, ib.

קָנְנִי canani J Prov. 8.22.

קָנִיתִי canithi J Gen. 4.1.

קֶסֶת cesath J Ezek. 9.2.

קצה קָצֶה κασε O Ps. 46.9.

קָצִין κασιν A Josh. 19.13: κασιμ lege ν for μ; casin On ib.: casim lege n for m.

קצץ וְקָצֵץ ουκεσσες O Ps. 46.10: OYK.CCEC lege OY-KECCEC.

קצר הִקְצַרְתָּ εκσερθ O Ps. 89.46.

קרא קָרָאת carath J Jer. 3.12.

קְרָאתִי καραθι O Hos. 11.1; carathi J Isa. 7.14; MT: קָרָאת.

וַיִּקְרָא ουικρα O Lev. 1.1.

יִקְרָאֵנִי ικραηνι O Ps. 89.27.

אֶקְרָא εκρα O Ps. 30.9. εεκρα lege εκρα.

קוֹרֵא κωρη G 2 Chron. 31.14.

קְרָאוּ κερου O Ps. 49.12; MT: קָרָאוּ.

קרב a) בְּקֶרֶב βεκορβ O Ps. 36.2.

b) בְּקִרְבָּהּ βκερβα O Ps. 46.6.

c) קָרְבָּם καρβαμ O Ps. 49.12.

d) בְּקֶרֶב bacereb J Hab. 3.2.

קרב קָרֹב καρωβ O Ps. 32.9: ΚΑΡΩΘ lege B for Θ; MT: קָרֹב.

קְרִיָה caria J Isa. 26.5.

קִרְיַת καριαθ G in Καριαθ-βααλ, Josh. 15.60; cariath J Hos. 2.15.

קִרְיָתַיִם καριαθαιμ A Jer. 48.1; cariathaim On Num. 32.37.

קְרִיּוֹת carioth On Jer. 48.24.

הַקְּרִיּוֹת ακκαριωθ A Jer. 48.41.

קרן קַרְנַיִם καρναιμ A Gen. 14.5: καρναιν lege μ for second ν; carnaim On ib.

קרסלים קַרְסֻלַּי χορσελαι O Ps. 18.37: ΧΟΡΣΕΛΑΙ kege K for X; cf. Thompson Facs. 7.

קרץ יְקַרְצוּ ικερσου O Ps. 35.19; cf. in the BV ישמעו 1 Sam. 13.3; יקראו Jer. 23.6 in MdO, p. 185; cf. also Sam. Ex. 21.35: יחיצון for MT: יֶחֱצוּן.

קשה קָשָׁה casa J Isa. 27.1.

קֶשֶׁת a) κασθ O Ps. 46.10.

b) κεσθ O Ps. 18.35.

c) ceseth J Isa. 66.19.

ר

רָאָה raa J Gen. 32.29; raha J ib., ed. Lagarde.

רָאֲתָה ρααθα O Ps. 35.21.

רָאִיתָ ραιθ O Ps. 31.8.

רָאִיתָה ραειθα O Ps. 35.22: PACIxx lege E for C and add ΘΑ.

וְרָאִיתִי uraithi J Ezek. 41.8.

רָאוּ rau J Hab. 1.5; MT: רָאוּ.

יִרְאֶה ιερε O Ps. 89.49.

תִּרְאֶה θερε O Ps. 35.17: ΘΕΡC lege E for C.

רָאוּ ρου A in Ρουβην, Gen. 29.32; ru On in Ruben, ib.

רָאמוֹת ramoth J Ezek. 27.16.

רֹאשׁ a) ρως G Ezek. 38.3; ros J ib.

הָרֹאשׁ αρως A 1 Chron. 24.31.

b) רֹאשׁ rus On Gen. 46.21.

רֵאשִׁית בְּרֵאשִׁית βρησιθ O Gen. 1.1; bresith J ib.

ראשון הָרָאשֹׁנִים αρισωνιμ O Ps. 89.50.

רַב a) ραβ A in Ραβσαρεις, 2 Ki. 18.17; O Ps. 31.20; rab On in Rabsaris, 2 Ki. 18. 17.

רַבִּים ραβιμ O Ps. 32.6.

b) רַבָּה ραββα A Josh. 13.25.

רַבַּת rabbath On Deut. 3.11.

רַבִּים ραββιμ O Ps. 32.10.

רַבּוֹת rabboth On Josh. 19.20; MT: רַבִּית.

רב וּבְרֹב ουεβροβ O Ps. 49.7.

רבה תַּרְבֵּנִי θερβηνι O Ps. 18.36.

רגל רַגְלַי ρεγλαι O Ps. 18.34; ib. 31.9: εργλαι lege ρεγλαι; cf. in the BV רַגְלִי Ps. 40.3 in Ms. Ec 1.

רַגְלָיו reglau J Isa. 6.2; cf. in the BV רַגְלָיו Ex. 25.26 in Ms. Ea 5.

רגל רֶגֶל ρωγηλ G Josh. 18.16.

רֹגְלִים a) ρωγελειμ A 2 Sam. 17.27.

b) ρωγελλειμ B ib.

רֶגַע ρεγε O Ps. 30.6.

רגע רִגְעֵי ρεγη O Ps. 35.20.

רדידים הָרְדִידִים ardidim J Isa. 3.23.

רדף אֶרְדּוֹף ερδοφ O Ps. 18.38.

רַהַב reeb J Isa. 30.7.

רוד רָד rad J Hos. 12.1.

רוּחַ a) rua J Isa. 40.13. ruha J Eccl. 6.9.

בְּרוּחַ barua J Gen. 3.8; ed. Lagarde; MT: לָרוּחַ.

b) לָרוּחַ larue J Gen. 3.8; on the e cf. p. 175 sub ח.

רוּחִי ρουη O Ps. 31.6. ruhi J Ezek. 39.29.

רום וְיָרוּם ουιαρουμ O Ps. 18.47.

אָרוּם αρουμ O Ps. 46.11.

רָם ραμ G 1 Chron. 2.9.

רָמָה ραμα G Josh. 18.25; rama On ib.

רָמוֹת ραμωθ A 1 Ki. 4.13; O Ps. 18.28; ramoth On 1 Ki. 4.13.

הָרִימוֹת αρημωθ O Ps. 89.43.

וְהָרֵם ουαρημ O Ps. 28.9; MT: וּרְעֵם.

רוץ אֶרֶץ αρους O Ps. 18.30.

רָצִים ρασειμ A 2 Ki. 11.4.

רָזוֹן ραζων A 1 Ki. 11.23; MT: רָזוֹן; razon On ib.

רחב וְרֹחַב urob J Ezek. 40.49.

רחב תַּרְחִיב θεριβ O Ps. 18.37.

וַיַּרְחִיבוּ ουειεριβου O Ps. 35.21.

רחוב רְחֹבֹת rooboth On Gen. 10. 11.

רַחוּם ραουμ A Neh. 3.17; MT: רָחוּם.

רָחֵל ραχηλ A Gen. 29.6; rachel On ib.

רחם a) מֵרֶחֶם μηρεμ O Ps. 110.3.

b) רֶחֶם rehem J Am. 1.11. מֵרֶחֶם merehem J Isa. 46.3; MT: מִנִּי רָחַם.

רחם יְרֹחָם ιεροαμ A 1 Sam. 1.1; ieroam On ib.

רחף מְרַחֶפֶת marahaefeth J Gen. 1.2, ed. Lagarde. merefeth J ib.

רחק תִּרְחַק θαραχ O Ps. 35.22.

ריב רִיבָה ριβα O Ps. 35.1.

יָרִיב ιαρειβ A 1 Chron. 4.24; ιαριβ A in Ιωιαριβ, Neh. 11.5; jarib J Hos. 5.13; MT: יָרֵב.

ריב לְרִיבִי λεριβι O Ps. 35.23: ΛΕΡΒΙ lege ΛΕΡΙΒΙ; ha-plography I-P; cf. Thompson Facs. 6 and 9.

מְרִיבֵי μριβη O Ps. 31.21; MT: מְרִיב.

רָכִיל rachil J Ezek. 22.9.

רְכוּשׁ rachus J Gen. 14.16.

מֶרְכָּסִי רכסי μερυχση O Ps. 31.21.

רָם ραμ G I Chron. 2.9.

רָמָה ραμα G Josh. 18.25; rama On ib.

רָמַת ραμαθ A Josh. 19.21; MT: רֶמֶת; ramath On ib.

רָמָתַיִם ramathaim On I Sam. 1.1.

רָמֹת ραμωθ G Josh. 21.38; O Ps. 18.28; ramoth On Josh. 21.38.

רִמּוֹן ρεμμων G in Γεθερεμμων, Josh. 21.24; remmon On in Remmonfares, Num. 33.19.

אֲרוֹמִמְךָ רמם ερωμεμεχ O Ps. 30.2.

רֶמֶשׂ remes J Hab. 1.14.

רַנֵּי ραννη O Ps. 32.7.

רֹן רַנּוּ ιαροννου O Ps. 35.27.

וְהַרְנִינוּ ουερνινου O Ps. 32.11.

רֶסֶן a) וְרֶסֶן ουαρεσν O Ps. 32.9.

b) רֶסֶן resen J Zech. 14.20.

רֵעַ ρε G in Αχειρε, Num. 1.15; re J Hos. 3.1.

ree J Gen. 38.12; on the second e (=ע) cf. p. 176 sub ע.

כְּרֵעַ χρηε O Ps. 35.14.

רֵעִים reim J Jer. 3.1.

רַע ρα O Ps. 49.6.

רָעִים raim J Isa. 56.11.

רָעָה רָעַת raath J Eccl. 8.6.

רָעָתִי ρααθι O Ps. 35.26.

רעה יְרֵעֶם ιερημ O Ps. 48.15.

וּרְעֵם ουαρημ O Ps. 28.9.

רֹעֶה roe J Gen. 38.12.

רֹעִים roim J Isa. 56.11.

רֹעִי roi J Isa. 44.28.

רְעוּת rooth J Eccl. 1.14.

רַעַם reem J in banereem, Isa. 62.4.

רעם הָרְעִים ερειμ O Ps. 29.3.

רעע רֹעוּ rou J Isa. 8.9.

רעש יִרְעֲשׁוּ ιερασουι O Ps. 46.4.

רפא יִרְפָּא ιερφα A in Ιερφαηλ, Josh. 18.27.

רוֹפְאִים rophaim J Isa. 26.19.

רָפוּא ραφου G Num. 13.9.

רְפָאִים raphaim J Isa. 26.19.

רפה הַרְפוּ αρφου O Ps. 46.11.

רצה תִּרְצָה θαρσα B Josh. 12.24; MT: תִּרְצָה. θερσα G Num. 26.33; MT: תִּרְצָה; thersa On ib.

רָצוֹן ρασων O Mal. 2.13.

בִּרְצוֹנְךָ βαρσωναχ O Ps. 30.8.

בִּרְצוֹנוֹ βαρσωνω O Ps. 30.6.

רִצְפָּה ρεσφα G 2 Sam. 3.7; respha On ib.

רצץ יָרֹצּוּ ιαροσου O Ps. 49.14; MT: יָרֹצּוּ.

רַק ρεχ O Ps. 32.6.

רָקָב recob J Hos. 5.12.

רשע לָרָשָׁע λαρασα O Ps. 32.10.

הָרְשָׁעִים αρσαειμ O Ps. 1.1; MT: רְשָׁעִים.

רֶשַׁע resa J Isa. 26.10; MT: רָשָׁע.

לָרָשָׁע λαρεσα O Ps. 36.2; MT: לָרָשָׁע.

רֶשֶׁף reseph J Hab. 3.5.

מֶרֶשֶׁת μερεσθ O Ps. 31.5.

רתיק הָרַתִּיק arethic J Ezek. 7.23; MT: הָרַתּוּק.

רָתֵת rathath J Hos. 13.1.

שׁ

(cf. p. 172/3)

שאג יִשְׁאַג jesag J Am. 1.2.

שָׁאוֹל σωλ O Ps. 89.49.

לִשְׁאוֹל λασωλ O Ps. 49.15.

מִשְׁאוֹל μεσσω O Ps. 30.4: lege: μεσσωλ; MT: מִן שְׁאוֹל.

שָׁאוֹן σαων G Jer. 46.17; saon J Hos. 10.14.

שאל שָׁאוּל σαουλ A Gen. 36.37; saul On ib.

שאף שׁוֹאֵף soeph J Eccl. 1.5.

שְׁאָר sar J Isa. 10.21; cf. the bi-syllabic form in the PV שְׁאָר (MdWI, p. ב, line 15); cf. s.v. מֵעַט.

שְׁכָבִים sababim J Hos. 8.6.

שְׁבוּעָה sabaa J Isa. 65.15.

שְׁבָעֹת sabaoth J Jer. 5.24.

שבט בְּשֵׁבֶט βσαβτ O Ps. 89.33.

שֵׁבֶט sabat J Zech. 1.7.

שֶׁבַע a) sabe On Josh. 19.2.
σαβεε G in Βηρσαβεε, Josh. 19.2; on the second ε (=ע) cf. p. 176 sub ע; sabee On in Bersabee, 1 Sam. 3.20.
b) saba J Isa. 4.1.

שבע נִשְׁבַּעְתָּ νεσβαθ O Ps. 89.50.
נִשְׁבַּעְתִּי νεσβαθ[ι] O Ps. 89.36.

שִׁבְעָה saba J Jer. 15.9; cf. in the BV שֶׁבַעֹה 1 Chron. 5.13 in Ms. Ec 1.

שבק יִשְׁבֹּק ιεσβοκ A Gen. 25.2; iesboc On ib.
שׁוֹבֵק σωβηκ G Neh. 10.24.

שֶׁבֶר a) σεβερ A 1 Chron. 2.48.
b) σαβερ B ib.

שבר תְּשַׁבֵּר θεσσαβερ O Ps. 48.8; with gemination of the f'rst radical; cf. on וּמִשְׁנָאֵי.
יְשַׁבֵּר ισουβερ O Ps. 46.10; MT: יְשַׁבֵּר; without gemi-nation, cf. on אָכֵב. But the reading is doubtful.

שַׁבָּת sabat On 2 Ki. 4.23.

שבת הַשַּׁבָּת εσβεθ O Ps. 89.45.

מַשְׁבִּית μισβιθ O Ps. 46.9; cf. in the BV forms like מֵצִיל Job 5.4; מֵצִיב 1 Sam. 15. 12 in MdO, p. 193.

שְׁגָגָה segaga J Eccl. 5.5.

שִׁגְיֹנוֹת segionoth J Hab. 3.1.

שֹׁד sod J Isa. 16.4.

שדד שָׁדוּד sadud J Jer. 4.30.

שָׂדֶה sade J Ezek. 21.2.

שָׂדוֹת sadoth J Am. 3.10.

שָׂדַי sadai J Ps. 80.14.

שָׂדֶה sadda J Eccl. 2.8.

שְׂדוֹת saddoth J ib.

שַׁדַּי σαδδαι G Ezek. 10.5; saddai J Ezek. 1.24.

שְׁדֵמָה הַשְּׁדֵמוֹת asademoth J Jer. 31.39.

שְׁדֵמוֹת σαδημωθ A 2 Ki. 23.4; sademoth On ib.

שָׁוְא σαυ O Ps. 31.7; cf. B-L § 17z.

שוב יָשׁוּב ιασουβ G Num. 26.24; iasub On ib.

תָּשׁוּב θασουβ O Ps. 35.13.

אָשׁוּב ασουβ O Ps. 18.38.

יָשׁוּבוּ jasubu J Mic. 5.3; MT: יָשֻׁבוּ.

יָשִׁיב ιασειβ A in Ελιασειβ, 1 Chron. 3.24.

תָּשִׁיב θασιβ O Ps. 89.44.

הָשִׁיבָה ασιβα O Ps. 35.17.

שָׁוֶה σαυη A Gen. 14.5; sau siue sauhe On ib.

שוה מְשֻׁוֶּה μοσαυε O Ps. 18.34.

שוח σουε A Gen. 25.2: Σωυε lege σουε or σωε cf. p. 175 sub ו; sue On ib.

שׁוֹט sot J Isa. 28.15.

שׁוּעַ sue J Ezek. 23.23.

שוע יְשַׁוְּעוּ ιεσαυου O Ps. 18.42; cf. B-L § 17z and d'.

בְּשׁוּעִי βεσαυει O Ps. 31.23.

שׁוּעָל σουαλ A 1 Chron. 7.36.

שׁוּעָלִים sualim On in Asar-sualim, Josh. 19.3.

שׁוֹפָר sophar J Isa. 58.1.

שׁוֹר שֹׁרִים surim J Hos. 12.12.

שׁוּר σουρ G Ex. 15.22; O Ps. 18.30; sur On Gen. 20.1.

שׁוֹר בְּשׁוּרִי basori J Hos. 9.12.

יָשִׁיר jasir J Jer. 5.26.

שׁחה הִשְׁתַּחֲוּוּ εσθαυου O Ps. 29.2.

שׁחח שַׁחוֹתִי σεωθι O Ps. 35.14; ε is possibly the transliteration of ח; cf. p. 175 sub ח.

שְׁחִין siin J Isa. 38.21.

שַׁחַל a) sohol J Hos. 5.14.
b) sohel J ib.

שׁחק בְּשַׁחַק βσακ O Ps. 89.38.

שׁחק יִשְׂחַק isaac J Am. 7.16; MT: יִשְׂחָק.

שׁחק וְאֶשְׁחָקֵם ουεσοκημ O Ps. 18.43.

שַׁחַר σααρ A in Αχισααρ, 1 Chron. 7.10.

מִשְׁחָר μεσσααρ O Ps. 110.3; MT: מִשְׁחָר.

שַׁחַת σααθ O Ps. 30.10.

הַשַּׁחַת ασσααθ O Ps. 49.10; MT: הַשָּׁחַת.

שָׂטָה setta J Isa. 41.19.

שִׂטִּים settim On Ex. 25.5.

שָׂטָן σαταν G 1 Ki. 11.14; satan On ib.

שִׂטְנָה satana J Gen. 26.21.

שׁטף לְשֵׁטֶף λσετφ O Ps. 32.6.

שַׁי σαι A in Αβισαι, 1 Sam. 26.6; sai On in Abisai, 1 Ki. 1.3.

שִׂיחַ sia J Am. 4.13.

שֵׂחוֹ sio J in masio, Am. 4.13.

שׂים שָׂם σαμ O Ps. 46.9.

שַׂמְתָּ σαμθ O Ps. 89.41.

וְשַׂמְתִּי ουσαμθι O Ps. 89.30.

שׂימה שָׂמוֹת σιμωθ O Ps. 46.9 (from the root שׂים); MT: שָׂמוֹת.

שִׁיר σιρ O Ps. 30.1.

וּמְשִׁירִי ουμεσσιρι O Ps. 28.7.

שַׁיִת saith J Isa. 5.6.

שׂכל אַשְׂכִּילְךָ εσχιλεχ O Ps. 32.8.

שֶׁכֶם σεχεμ A Josh. 17.2.

שָׁכֵן לִשְׁכֵנָיו λσαχηναυ O Ps. 89.42.

שָׂכָר σαχαρ A in Ισσαχαρ, Gen. 30.18; sachar On in Issachar, ib.

שִׂכּוֹרֵי sacchore J Isa. 28.3.

שָׁלוּ בְּשַׁלְוִי βσαλουι O Ps. 30.7.

שָׁלוֹם σαλωμ G in Αβεσσαλωμ, 2 Sam. 3.3.; O Ps. 35.20.

שָׁלוֹם σαλωμ O Ps. 35.27.

שָׁלַח a) sale On in Mathusale, Gen. 5.21; on e (=ח) cf. p. 175 sub ח.

b) σαλα A Gen. 10.24; sala J Joel 2.8.

שלח שְׁלָחָה a) salua J Gen. 49.21: sluaa is a misprint.

b) selua J ib., ed. Lagarde.

שָׁלִישׁ salis J Isa. 40.12.

שָׁלֵם a) σαλημ A Gen. 33.18; salem On ib.

b) שְׁלֵמָה salma J Am. 1.9.

c) שְׁלָמִים salamim J Gen. 34.21.

שלם וְשָׁלֵם ουσαλημ O Ps. 31.24 (cf. s.v. חָפֵץ); MT: וּמְשַׁלֵּם.

שָׁלֵם σελλημ A Num. 26.49.

מְשֻׁלָּם μεσουλαμ G Neh. 6.18.

שַׂלְמָה σαλαμα G Gen. 36.36; salama On ib.; MT: שַׂמְלָה; cf. Ex. 22.8: MT: שלמה, Sam. שמלה.

שְׁלָמִים salamim J Ezek. 46.12.

שָׁלֹשׁ salos J Jonah 3.4.

שְׁלִישִׁיָּה a) σαλασεια B Jer. 48.34.

b) σαλισια A ib.; cf. in the
BV שְׁלִשִׁים 1 Sam. 19.21
in Ms. 105 JThS.

שָׁם σαμ O Isa. 28.13; sam J Isa.
28.10.

שָׁמָּה sama J Ezek. 48.34.

שֵׁם σημ A Gen. 6.10; σεμ O Gen.
28.19; sem On Gen. 6.10.

שִׁמְךָ σεμαχ O Ps. 31.4.

שְׁמוֹ σεμω O Ps. 29.2.

בָּשְׂמַת basemoth On Gen.
26.34; MT: בָּשְׂמַת; cf. our
remark on שַׂר.

שְׁמוֹת semoth On Ezek. 48.1.

בִּשְׁמוֹתָם βσεμωθαμ O Ps.
49.12: BCEBΩΘAM lege
M for the second B.

שַׁמָּה a) σαμα B 1 Sam. 16.9.

שָׁמוֹת σαμωθ A 1 Chron. 11.27.

b) שַׁמָּה σαμμα A 1 Sam.
16.9; samma On Gen.
36.13.

שָׁמוֹת σαμμωθ B 1 Chron.
11.27: CAMAΩΘ lege M
for the second A.

שׂמח שָׂמְחוּ σαμου O Ps. 35.15.

וְאֶשְׂמַח ουεσμα O Ps. 31.8:
OYCEMA lege OYEC-
MA; MT: וְאֶשְׂמְחָה.

שְׂמֵחִי: σμην lege σμηη, O Ps.
35.26.

יִשְׂמְחוּ ιεσμου O Ps. 46.5; MT:
יִשְׂמְחוּ.

ισουμοχ O Ps. 35.19.

ιεσεμου O Ps. 35.24; cf.
on יָקְרְצוּ.

וְיִשְׂמְחוּ ουειεσαμου O Ps.
35.27.

שָׂמְחוּ σεμου O Ps. 32.11:
cf. IEMOY lege CEMOY;
Thompson Facs. 6 (I-C).

שְׂמַחְתָּ σεμεθ O Ps. 30.2; with-

out gemination of the
second radical; cf. on
אָכֵֽב.

הַשְּׂמַחְתָּ εσμεθ O Ps. 89.43.

שִׂמְחָה σεμα O Ps. 30.12.

שָׁמַיִם a) samaim J Isa. 1.2.

b) σαμμαιμ O Ps. 89.30.

c) σουμην O Gen. 1.8.

הַשְּׁמִינִית ασεμινιθ O Ps.
שמיני 12.1.

שָׁמִיר σαμειρ B Josh. 15.48; samir
On Jud. 10.1.

שמם שְׁמָמָה semema J Isa. 62.4;
MT: שְׁמָמָה.

שמם מַשְׁמִים masmim J Ezek. 3.15.

שְׁמֵנִים semanim J Isa. 28.1.

שמע שִׁמְעִי σεμεει B Ex. 6.17; on
the second ε (=ע) cf.
p. 176 sub. ע; σεμει
A ib.; semei On ib.

שָׁמַע σαμα G in Ελεισαμα, Num.
1.10; O Ps. 28.6.

σαμαε B in Ελεισαμαε, 1
Chron. 14.7; cf. p. 176
sub ע.

same On in Elisame, Num.
1.10; ε=ע; cf. p. 176
sub ע.

שָׁמַעְתָּ σαμαθ O Ps. 31.23.

יִשְׁמַע ισμα A in Ισμαηλ, Gen.
16.11; isma On in Is-
mahel, ib.

שָׁמַע σμα O Ps. 30.11.

σμαε O Ps. 28.6: CMAC
lege CMAE; MT: שָׁמַע.

שִׁמְעוּ σιμου O Ps. 49.2;
semu J Isa. 1.2.

שמר אֶשְׁמוֹר εσμωρ O Ps. 89.29.

יִשְׁמְרוּ ιεσμωρου O Ps. 89.32.

שׁוֹמֵר σωμηρ G 1 Chron. 7.32;
O Isa. 26.2; somer On
1 Ki. 16.24; MT: שֹׁמֵר.

הַשֹּׁמְרִים ασσωμριμ O Ps. 31. 7.

שמש a) כַּשֶּׁמֶשׁ χασαμς O Ps. 89. 37.

b) שִׁמְשִׁי semsi On 1 Sam. 6.18.

c) שֶׁמֶשׁ σαμες A Josh. 19.41; sames On ib.

d) semes J Isa. 24.23.

שן שְׁנֵּימוֹ σεννημω O Ps. 35.16.

שנא שָׂנֵאתִי σανηθι O Ps. 31.7.

שֹׂנְאַי σωνη O Ps. 35.19; MT: שֹׂנְאַי.

וּמְשַׂנְּאַי ουμασανναι O Ps. 18.41; MT: וּמְשֹׂנְ'.

שנה אֶשְׁנֶה ασσανε O Ps. 89.35.

שני שֵׁנִית σηνιθ O Mal. 2.13.

שנים שְׁנֵי sene J Ezek. 15.4.

שָׁנִים sanim J Hab. 3.2.

שְׁנֵי sane J Ezek. 15.4.

שסס שַׂסָהוּ σασουου O Ps. 89.42.

שְׂעִירִים sirim J Isa. 13.21.

שען אֶשְׁעַן εσαν A Josh. 15.52.

שער שְׁעָרִים σααρειμ O Isa. 26.2; saarim On Josh. 15.36; MT: שַׁעֲרַיִם; cf. in PV שֹׁעֲרִים (MdWI, p. יו, 22).

שערה שֹׁעֲרִים a) σεωρειμ B 1Chron. 24.8; σεωριμ A ib.: σεωριν lege μ for ν; O Hos. 3.2; seorim J ib.

b) sorim J Gen. 26.12; MT: שְׁעָרִים.

שֹׁעָרִים suarim J Jer. 29.17.

שפה הַשְּׂפָתַיִם asephathaim J Ezek. 40.43.

שְׂפָתַי σφωθαι O Ps. 89.35; MT: שְׂפָתַי.

שפה נִשְׁפֶּה nesphe J Isa. 13.2.

שָׁפָט σαφατ G Num. 13.5; safat On ib.; saphat On in Josaphat, 1 Ki. 22.2.

שָׁפְטֵנִי σεφθηνι O Ps. 35.24: ΕΦΘΗΝΙ lege ΣΕΦΘΗΝΙ.

שפך אֶשְׁפּוֹךְ esphoch J Joel 3.1.

שפל תַּשְׁפִּיל θεσφιλ O Ps. 18.28: ΘΕΟΦΙΛ lege C for O; cf. Thompson Facs. 4 and 7.

שְׁפֵלָה σεφηλα G Jer. 33.13; sefela On ib.; sephela J Jer. 17.26.

שָׁפָן σαφαν G Jer. 39.14; safan On ib.

שפק יַשְׂפִּיקוּ jesphicu J Isa. 2.6.

שַׂק σεκ O Ps. 35.13.

שַׂקִּי σεκκι O Ps. 30.12.

שָׁקֵד seced J Jer. 1.11.

שקד שָׁקֵד soced J Eccl. 12.5.

שקוץ שִׁקּוּצֵי secuse J Ezek. 20.7.

שֶׁקֶל secel J Gen. 23.15.

שֶׁקֶר σεκρ O Ps. 35.19.

שקר אֲשַׁקֵּר ασσακερ O Ps. 89.34.

שׁר σαρ A in Αχισαρ, 1 Ki. 4.6; sar On in Ahisar, ib.; שׁ for Masoretic שׂ; cf. the reverse case s.v. שם בְּשֵׂמֹת for Masoretic בְּשֵׁמַת (שׂ for שׁ).

שָׂרִים sarim J Hos. 12.12.

שָׂרֵי sare J Ezek. 21.2.

שרה שָׂרִיתָ sarith J Gen. 32.29.

שָׂרִיגִים a) sarigim J Gen. 4.10.

b) sariagim J ib., ed. Lagarde.

שָׂרִיד σαριδ A Josh. 19.12; sarid J Obad 18; sarith On Josh. 19.12.

שְׂרִידִים saridim J Joel 3.5.

שָׂרָף a) σαραφ A 1 Chron. 4.22; saraph J Isa. 14.29.

b) seraph J Isa. 6.6.

שְׂרָפִים seraphim J Isa. 6.6.

שרף יִשְׂרֹף ισροφ O Ps. 46.10.

שֶׁרֶק σωρηκ G Isa. 5.2; sorec On ib.

שָׂשׂוֹן σασων O Ps. 45.9.

שֹׁשַׁנִּים σωσανειμ O Ps. 45.1.

שתת שַׁתּוּ σαθου O Ps. 49.15.

ת

תא תָּאִים theim J Ezek. 40.16.

תָּאֵי thee J Ezek. 40.21; MT: תָּאָו.

תבונה תְּבוּנוֹת θβουνωθ O Ps. 49.4.

תֵּבֵל thebel J Isa. 13.11.

תהלה תְּהִלָּתֶךָ θελαθαχ O Ps. 35.28.

תָּו thav J Isa. 59.20.

תּוֹא tho J Isa. 51.20.

תּוֹדָה thoda J Jer. 17.26.

תּוֹלַעַת tholath J Isa. 41.14.

תּוֹרָה thora J Ezek. 9.4.

בְּתוֹרַת βθωραθ O Ps. 1.2; ΒΟΩΡΑΘ lege Θ for O; cf. Thompson Facs. 1-5.

תּוֹרָתִי θωραθι O Ps. 89.31.

תחנון תַּחֲנוּנַי θανουναι O Ps. 28.6.

תַּחַשׁ thas J Ezek. 16.10.

תַּחַת a) θεθ O Ps. 18.39.

תַּחְתִּי θεθι O Ps. 18.37; MT: תַּחְתָּי.

תַּחְתָּי θεθαι O Ps. 18.48.

b) תַּחַת theeth On Num. 33.26.

c) θααθ G 1 Chron. 6.22.

תחתי תַּחְתִּים theethim On 2 Sam. 24.6.

תֵּימָן theman J Hab. 3.3.

תִּירוֹשׁ thiros J Zech. 9.17.

תֵּל θελ G in Θελμελεθ, Neh. 7.61.

תלה יִתְלֶה ιεθλα A Josh. 19.42; MT: יִתְלֶה.

תמה יִתְמָהוּ jethmau J Jer. 4.9.

תַּמּוּז thamuz J Ezek. 8.14.

תָּמִיד θαμιδ O Ps. 35.27.

תָּמִים a) θαμιμ O Ps. 18.26; thamim J Ezek. 46.13.

b) θαμμιμ O Ps. 18.33; ib. 18.31: ΘΑΜΜΙΝ lege M for N.

תמם תְּתַמָּם θεθαμμαμ O Ps. 18.26: ΘΕΜΑΜΜΑΜ lege Θ for the first M.

תָּמָר θαμαρ G Ruth 4.12; thamar On Gen. 14.7.

תְּמָרִים thamarim J Ezek. 40.16; MT: תִּמֹרִים.

תַּמְרוּרִים themrurim J Jer. 31.21.

תַּנִּים a) thennin J Jer. 13.22.

b) thannim J ib.

תַּנִּין thannin J Isa. 27.1.

תעב נִתְעָב nethab J Isa. 14.19.

תַּעֲלוּלִים thalulim J Isa. 3.4.

תַּעֲלוּלַי thalule J Isa. 66.4.

תִּפְאֶרֶת thophert J Ezek. 16.12.

תַּפּוּחַ a) θαφου B in Βαιθαχου lege Βαιθθαφου, Josh. 15.53; ταφου B Josh. 16.8. thafue On in Beththafue, Josh. 15.53.

b) θαπφουε A in Βεθθαπφουε, Josh. 15.53; cf. p. 175 sub ח; thaffue On Josh. 12.17; cf. p. 177 sub פ.

תָּפֵל thaphel J Ezek. 13.10.

תפלה תְּפִלַּת thephellath J Isa. 38.5.

וּתְפִלָּתִי ουθφελλαθι O Ps. 35.13.

תֹּפֶת thophet J Jer. 19.6; tophet J Jer. 7.31.

תַּרְדֵּמָה thardema J Isa. 29.10; tardema J Gen. 15.12.

תְּרוּעָה therua J Am. 2.2.

תְּרָפִים therafim J Gen. 31.19.

Alphabetical Index of Hebrew Proper Names occuring in the Dictionary in the Transliteration of the Septuagint or of the Onomastica.

(Only the consonants matter; the matres lectionis and the Masoretic vocalization are immaterial; cf. p. 105)

כל	אֶשְׁכֹּל	קום	אֲחִיקָם	אב, אל	אֲבִיאֵל
שען	אֶשְׁעָן	רע	אֲחִירַע	חיל	אֲבִיחַיִל
אשר	אָשֵׁר	שחר	אֲחִישָׁחַר	אב	אֲבִימֶלֶךְ
		שר	אֲחִישַׁר	נעם	אֲבִינֹעַם
באר	בְּאֵרוֹת		אַחֵר	עזר	אֲבִיעֶזֶר
באר	בְּאֵרִי		אָטָד	שי	אֲבִישַׁי
באר, שבע	בְּאֵר שֶׁבַע	כבוד	אִי כָבוֹד		אָבֵל
	בּוּז	אולם	אֵילָם	אבל	אָבֵל הַשִּׁטִּים
בוז	בּוּזִי	בשת	אִישׁ בֹּשֶׁת	אבל, כרם	אָבֵל כְּרָמִים
בזק	בֶּזֶק	איש	אִישׁ טוֹב	מים	אָבֵל מַיִם
בחור	בַּחוּרִים		אֵיתָן	אבן	אֶבֶן הָעֶזֶר
בטן	בֶּטֶן		אֵלָה	שלום	אַבְשָׁלוֹם
און, בית	בֵּית אָוֶן	חנן	אֶלְחָנָן	אב	אֹבֹת
בית	בֵּית אֵל	אב, אל	אֱלִיאָב		אָדָם
גן	בֵּית הַגָּן	ידע	אֶלְיָדָע		אַדְמָה
כרם	בֵּית הַכֶּרֶם	אל	אֱלִיעֶזֶר	קום	אֲדֹנִיקָם
נתינים	בֵּית הַנְּתִינִים	פז	אֱלִיפַז	אדון	אֲדֹנִירָם
עמק	בֵּית הָעֵמֶק	צפן	אֱלִיצָפָן	מלך	אֲדַרְמֶלֶךְ
ערבה	בֵּית הָעֲרָבָה	קום	אֶלְיָקִים		אֹהֶל
כר	בֵּית כָּר	שוב	אֶלְיָשִׁיב	אהל, ב—	אָהֳלִיבָה
לביא	בֵּית לְבָאוֹת	שמע	אֱלִישָׁמָע	אהל	אָהֳלִיבָמָה
לחם	בֵּית לֶחֶם	עזר	אֶלְעָזָר		אוֹן
מרכבת	בֵּית מַרְכָּבוֹת	פעל	אֶלְפַּעַל		אָוֶן
מו	בֵּית עַזְמָוֶת	אל, קנה	אֶלְקָנָה		אוֹנוֹ
בית, תפוח	בֵּית תַּפּוּחַ		אַמָּה	און	אוֹנָם
בכורה	בְּכוֹרַת		אִמֵּר	און	אוֹנָן
בכור	בֶּכֶר	אמר	אֲמַרְיָה	אור	אוּרִי
	בֶּלַע		אֱנוֹשׁ	אזן	אָזְנִי
בלע	בִּלְעָם		אַסִּיר	אח	אַחְאָב
	בָּמָה		אָסָף	הוד	אֵחוּד
במה	בָּמוֹת		אֵצֶר		אָחָז
	בֵּן	ארבה	אַרְבּוֹת	אחז	אֲחַזְיָהוּ
און	בֶּן אוֹנִי	ארג	אַרְגִּים	טוב	אֲחִטוּב
בן	בְּנֵי בְרַק	ארי	אֲרִיאֵל	אח	אֲחִיהוּד
סוד	בְּסוֹדְיָה		אַרְיֵה	אח	אֲחִינֹעַם
בעל, ברית	בַּעַל בְּרִית		אֶרֶךְ	אח, סמך	אֲחִיסָמָךְ

חרב	חוֹרֵב		דַּבֶּשֶׁת		בַּעֲלָה
	חוֹתָם	דון	דָּן	המון	בַּעַל הָמוֹן
חזה	חֲזָאֵל		הֶבֶל	בעלה	בְּעָלוֹת
	חֶזְיוֹן		הוֹד	זבוב	בַּעַל זְבוּב
חיל	חֵילָם	ישן	הַיְשָׁנָה	ידע	בְּעֶלְיָדָע
	חֲלִי	כרוב	הַכְּרֻבִים	בעל	בְּעָלִים
	חָלָק	לחש	הַלּוֹחֵשׁ	מעון	בַּעַל מְעוֹן
	חֵלֶק		הָלֵל	פרץ	בַּעַל פְּרָצִים
חלק	חֶלְקִי	סנא	הַסְּנוּאָה	צל	בְּצַלְאֵל
חלקה	חֶלְקַת	עברי	הָעִבְרִים		בַּקְבּוּק
	חָם	פרה	הַפָּרָה		בָּרֶד
חמל	חָמוּל	קוץ	הַקּוֹץ		בָּרוּךְ
	חֲמוֹר	קטן	הַקָּטָן		בְּרִית
חמה	חֲמָתִי	קריה	הַקְּרִיּוֹת	ברך	בְּרַכָאֵל
חנן	חָנוּן	ראש	הָרֹאשׁ		בָּרָק
	חֶסֶד	הר	הַר שָׁפֵר	שם	בָּשְׂמַת
	חֻפָּה	שמש	הַשִּׁמְשִׁי		
ב־, חפץ	חֶפְצִי בָהּ		זְאֵב		גִּבְעָה
	חֲצִי		זָבָד	גבעה	גִּבְעַת
חצר	חֲצַר גַּדָּה	זבד	זַבְדִּי		גֶּבֶר
חצר	חֲצֵרוֹת	זבד	זָבוּד	גבר	גַּבְרִיאֵל
חצר, מות	חֲצַר מָוֶת		זֶבַח		גָּדֵל
חצר	חֲצַר עֵינָן		זְבֻל	גדל	גִּדַּלְתִּי
שועל	חֲצַר שׁוּעָל	זחל	זֹחֶלֶת		גֶּדֶר
	חֲרָדָה	זכר	זִכְרִי		גְּדֵרָה
חרץ	חָרוּץ		זִמָּה	גדרה	גְּדֵרוֹת
	חָרִיף	זמר	זִמְרִי	גוי	גּוֹיִם
	חֶרֶס	זנח	זָנוֹחַ		גֵּר
	חֶרֶשׁ		זֶרַח		גֵּיא
	חֲרֹשֶׁת	זרח	זַרְחִי	מלח	גֵּיא מֶלַח
חשב	חֶשְׁבָּה	זרח	זַרְחִיָּה		גַּלְגַּל
	חֶשְׁבּוֹן			גלילה	גְּלִילוֹת
חשב	חֲשַׁבְיָה			גל	גַּלִּים
		חבר	חָבוֹר	גמל	גָּמוּל
	טֶבַח		חֵבֶר	גמל	גְּמַלִּי
טבעת	טַבָּעוֹת		חֶבֶר	גר	גֵּרְשֹׁם
	טוֹב		חָגָב		גַּת
		חג	חַגִּי	רמון	גַּת רִמּוֹן
אור	יָאִיר	חדש	חֲדָשָׁה		דָּאֵג
בחר	יִבְחָר	חדש	חָדָשִׁי		דְּבוֹרָה
בלע	יִבְלְעָם		חוֹבָה		דְּבִיר
בין	יָבִין		חוּל		

מלא	מַלּוֹתִי	שוב	יָשׁוּב	גאל	יָבֵשׁ
מלך	מַלְכִּיאֵל	שמע	יִשְׁמָעֵאל	גור	יִגְאָל
אל	מַלְכִּיאֵלִי		יֶשֶׁן	ידיד	יָגוּר
מלך, צדק	מַלְכִּי צֶדֶק		יִשְׁעִי	דלף	יְדִידְיָה
מלך	מַלְכָּם	שכר	יִשָּׂשכָר	ידע	יִדְלֹף
	מָן	תלה	יִתְלָה	נתן	יְהוֹיָדָע
	מָנוֹחַ	יתר	יִתְרוֹ	שפט	יְהוֹנָתָן
נחם	מְנַחֵם			הלל	יְהוֹשָׁפָט
נשה	מְנַשֶּׁה	כברה	כִּבְרַת	יאל	יְהַלְלְאֵל
	מִסְפָּר		כִּידוֹן	יבל	יוֹאֵל
	מָעוֹן		כִּכָּר	זכר	יוּבָל
ענה	מְעוּנִים		כִּלְיוֹן	ריב	יוֹזָכָר
	מִפְקָד	כמר	כְּמָרִים		יוֹיָרִיב
	מַצָּב		כִּנּוֹר		יוֹנָה
מקהלה	מַקְהֵלֹת		כְּנַעֲנִי	יסף	יוֹסֵף
מר	מָרָה		כְּרוּב	זוז	יָזִיז
	מִרְמָה	כרוב	כְּרֻבִים	זרח	יִזְרַח
	מַשָּׂא	כרם	כַּרְמִי	זרע	יִזְרְעֵאל
	מִשְׁאָל	דבר, לא	לֹא דָבָר	כון	יָכִין
	מָשָׁל	בוא	לָבוֹא		יָמִין
שלם	מְשֻׁלָּם		לְבוֹנָה	ימין	יְמִינִי
	מִשְׁמָע		לָבָן	מלא	יִמְלָא
	מֶשֶׁק	לבן	לְבֵנָא	מנה	יִמְנָה
מים, משרפת	מִשְׂרְפוֹת מַיִם	להב	לְהָבִים	מנע	יִמְנָע
שלח	מְתוּשֶׁלַח	לחם	לַחְמִי	נום	יָנוּם
	מַתָּן	לטש	לְטוּשִׁים	עקב	יַעֲקֹב
	מַתָּנָה		לַיִשׁ		יָעַר
מתן	מַתַּנְיָה		לַפִּידוֹת	יער	יְעָרִים
	נָבָל			פוע	יָפִיעַ
	נֹגַהּ		מִבְחָר	פנה	יִפְנֶה
	נָדָב		מִבְצָר	פתח	יִפְתָּח
יעד	נוֹעַדְיָה		מִבְשָׂם	צהר	יִצְהָר
	נָחָשׁ	מגדל	מִגְדָּל גָּד	צחק	יִצְחָק
	נַחַת		מִדְבָּר		יֵצֶר
	נָכוֹן		מָדוֹן	יצר	יִצְרִי
	נָצִיב		מָחוֹל	קום	יָקִים
	נֶקֶב		מַחְלָה		יְרוּשָׁה
מחנה	נֵר	מחנה	מַחֲנַיִם		יָרַח
	נְתִינִים	זהב	מֵי זָהָב	רחם	יְרֹחָם
	נָתָן		מִישׁוֹר	ריב	יָרִיב
		מכונה	מְכֹנוֹת	רפא	יִרְפָּאֵל
			מִלּוֹא	שבק	יִשָׁבָּק

Form	Root
סְבַךְ	
סוֹדִי	סוד
סוּסִי	סוס
סֻכּוֹת	סכה
סְתוּר	סתר
סִתְרִי	סתר
עֶבֶד	
עַבְדִּי	עבד
עֶבֶד מֶלֶךְ	עבד
עַבְדֵי שְׁלֹמֹה	עבד
עֵבֶר	
עֲבָרִים	עבר
עֶבְרִיּוֹת	עברי
עֶגְלָה	
עֵדֶן	
עֵדֶר	
עוֹבֵד	עבד
עוֹדֵד	עדד
עוֹרֵב	
עַזְגָּד	עז
עֲזוּבָה	עזב
עַזּוּר	עזר
עֲזִיאֵל	עז
עֶזְרִי	עזר
עֲטָרָה	
עֲטָרוֹת	עטרה
עַיִן	
עֵין גַּנִּים	גן
עֵין דּוֹר	דור
עֵין חַדָּה	חד, עין
עֵינַיִם	עין
עִירָם	עיר
עַמִּיהוּד	עם
עַמִּינָדָב	עם
עִמָּנוּאֵל	עם
עֵמֶק	
עַמְרָם	עם
עֲנָה	
עֲנָק	
עֲנָקִים	ענק
עָפְרָה	עפר

Form	Root
עַקְרַבִּים	עקרב
עֹקֶשׁ	
עֵר	
עֲרֻבּוֹת	ערבה
עֲשָׂהאֵל	עשה
עָשָׁן	
פָּאת	פאה
פְּדַהאֵל	פדה
פְּדָיָה	פדה
פַּחַת מוֹאָב	פחה
פִּיכֹל	כל, פה
פֶּלֶג	עבר
פְּקוֹד	פקד
פָּרָה	
פָּרוּחַ	פרח
פֶּרֶץ	
פְּתַחְיָה	פתח
צְבָאוֹת	
צוּף	
צוֹפִים	צפה
צוּר	
צוּרִיאֵל	צור
צוּרִישַׁדָּי	צור
צִלָּה	צל
צְלָפְחָד	פחד, צל
צִנָּה	
צָפוֹן	
צְפוֹנִי	צפון
צִפּוֹר	
צְרוּעָה	צרע
קֶדֶם	
קֵדְמָה	
קָדֵשׁ	
קְדֵשִׁים	קדש
קֹהֶלֶת	קהל
קוֹלָיָה	קול
קוֹץ	
קוֹרֵא	קרא
קִנָה	
קָצִין	

Form	Root
קִרְיַת אַרְבַּע	ארבע
קִרְיַת בַּעַל	קריה
קִרְיָתַיִם	קריה
קִרְיַת יְעָרִים	יער
קַרְנַיִם	קרן
רְאוּבֵן	בן, ראה
רֹאשׁ	
רַבָּה	רב
רַבּוֹת	רב
רַבִּית	רב
רַב מָג	מג
רַב סָרִיס	סריס, רב
רַבַּת	רב
רֶגֶל	
רְגָלִים	רגל
רָצוֹן	
רְחֹבֹת	רחוב
רְחוּם	
רָחֵל	
רָם	רום, רם
רָמָה	רום, רם
רָמוֹת	רום, רם
רָמַת	רם
רָמָתַיִם	רם
רִמּוֹן פֶּרֶץ	רמון
רְפוּא	רפא
רָצִים	רוץ
רִצְפָה	
שָׁאוּל	שאל
שָׁאוֹן	
שֶׁבַע	
שֶׁבֶר	
שַׁבָּת	
שַׁדַּי	
שְׁדֵיאוּר	אור
שַׁדְמוֹת	שדמה
שׁוֹבֵק	שבק
שָׁוֵה	
שׁוּחַ	
שׁוֹמֵר	שמר

שׁוּעָל		שָׁמוֹת	שמה	שָׁרָף	
שׁוּר		שָׁמִיר		שָׁרַק	
שִׁטִּים	שׁטה	שַׂמְלָה	שלמה		
שָׁטָן		שִׁמְעִי	שמע	תַּחַת	
שֶׁכֶם		שֶׁמֶר		תַּחְתִּים	תחתי
שֶׁלַח		שֶׁמֶשׁ		תֵּל מֶלַח	תל
שְׁלִישִׁיָּה		שַׁעֲרַיִם	שער	תִּמְנָה	מנה
שָׁלֵם		שְׂעָרִים	שערה	תִּמְנָע	מנע
שִׁלֵּם		שָׁפָט		תָּמָר	
שֵׁם		שְׁפֵלָה		תַּפּוּחַ	
שַׁמָּה		שָׁפָן		תִּפְסַח	פסח
שְׁמוֹת	שׁם	שָׂרִיד		תִּרְצָה	רצה

D. GRAMMAR

1. PHONOLOGY

A.   THE GRECO-LATIN ALPHABETS INADEQUATE FOR TRANSLITERATION

Jerome was quite aware of the incompatability of the Latin and Greek alphabets for rendering Hebrew sounds, insofar as the Greco-Latin alphabets have for one thing no exact equivalents for Semitic Gutturals or Sybillants. So he prefaces the list from Genesis with the following remark (p. 27): "Non statim, ubicumque ex A littera, quae apud Hebraeos dicitur aleph, ponuntur nomina, aestimandum est ipsam esse solam quae ponitur. nam interdum ex ain, saepe ex he, non numquam ex heth litteris, quae adspirationes suas uocesque commutant, habent exordium. sciendum igitur quod tam in Genesi quam ceteris in libris, ubi a uocali littera nomen incipit, apud Hebraeos a diuersis (ut supra diximus) incohetur elementis, sed quia apud nos non est uocum tanta diuersitas, simplici sumus elatione contenti. unde accidit ut eadem uocabula, quae apud illos non similiter scripta sunt, nobis uideantur in interpretatione uariari." This general statement Jerome further elucidates in discussing the changes in the name forms of אברהם–אברם and שרה–שרי in *Quaestiones* on Gen. 17.3: "dicunt autem Hebraei quod ex nomine suo deus, quod apud illos tetragrammum est, he literam Abrahae et Sarae addiderit: dicebatur enim primum Abram, quod interpretatur pater excelsus (this means: composed of אָב and רָם) et postea uocatus est

Abraham, quod transfertur pater multarum (i.e. אָב and הָמוֹן): nam quod sequitur, gentium, non habetur in nomine, sed subauditur. nec mirandum quare, cum apud Graecos et nos A litera uideatur addita, nos he literam hebraeam additam dixerimus: idioma enim linguae illius est, per E quidem scribere, sed per A legere: sicut e contrario A literam saepe per E pronuntiant." This conception is rounded out in his explanation to Gen. 17.15: "Sarai igitur primum uocata est per sin res ioth: sublata ergo ioth, id est I elemento, addita est he litera, quae per A legitur, et uocata est Saraa. causa autem ita nominis immutati haec est, quod antea dicebatur princeps mea, unius tantum modo domus mater familiae, postea uero dicitur absolute princeps, id est ἄρχουσα."

B. GUTTURALS

Gutturals have, therefore, no independent consonantal value, but serve merely to carry the vowel sign. This yields a double conclusion: when two different Gutturals bear the same vowel signs we can have the result that two entirely distinct words may be pronounced identically and consequently be identical in transliteration. An example for such a case we find in *Quaestiones* to Gen. 30.13: "Aser ergo non diuitiae, sed beatus dicitur, dum taxat in praesenti loco. nam in aliis secundum ambiguitatem uerbi possunt et diuitiae sic uocari." The two Hebrew words Jerome refers to here, are: אָשֵׁר and עָשִׁיר. Similarly he explains in his Onomastica Sacra (p. 36) רעמה Gen. 10.7: "Rama tonans uel excelsa," i.e. רעמה (from רעם thunder) and ראמה (from רום cf. Zech. 14.10: וראמה). But on the other hand, when the same Guttural appears in two etymologically different words with identical spelling, and the Guttural has different vowels, then the transliterations fail to indicate the identical consonantal spelling in the original Hebrew. So Jerome remarks in *Quaestiones* on Gen. 26.12: "licet enim eiusdem literis et aestimatio scribatur et hordeum, tamen aestimationes SAARIM leguntur, hordea uero SORIM," Jerome thinks here of שְׁעָרִים and שְׂעֹרִים.

C. SYBILLANTS

Concerning the difficulty of rendering Hebrew Sybillants, Jerome discourses in his introduction to those explanations coming under the letter S (Onomastica, p. 36): "Quod in principio dixeramus in uocalibus

litteris obseruandum eo, quod apud nos una sit interdum littera et apud
Hebraeos uariis uocibus proferatur, hoc nunc quoque in S littera sciendum est. siquidem apud Hebraeos tres S sunt litterae: una, quae dicitur
samech, et simpliciter legitur quasi per S nostram litteram describatur:
alia sin, in qua stridor quidam non nostri sermonis interstrepit: tertia
sade, quam aures nostrae penitus reformidant. sicubi ergo euenerit ut
eadem nomina aliter atque aliter interpretentur, illud in causa est quod
diuersis scripta sunt litteris." In another place (editio Vallarsi, vol. IV,
p. 155E) Jerome nevertheless attempts to explain the pronunciation of
the צ: "נצר. Sed sciendum quod hic NESER per SADE literam scribatur:
cuius proprietatem et sonum inter Z et S Latinus sermo non exprimit.
Est enim stridulus et strictis dentibus vix linguae impressione profertur."

Due to the circumstance that in the Greek and Latin alphabets the
three Hebrew letters ס, צ and שׂ can be rendered only by one character
(σ, s), there results the situation in which two entirely different words
are identical in transliteration. When the opportunity presents itself,
Jerome himself indicates this; so for instance (Onomastica, p. 53):
"Aser beatus, si per aleph et sin litteram scribitur; sin autem per heth
et sade, atrium interpretatur." Jerome has in mind: אָשֵׁר and חָצֵר.

D.   שׁ AND שׂ

From the passages of the Onomastica Sacra cited above and from all
those other passages in which Jerome attempts to explain the pronunciation and transliteration of Semitic Sybillants (cf. especially *Quaestiones*
on Gen. 26.12; 41.29), it is obvious that for him the שׂ had but one sound:
sin. He is unfamiliar with the differentiation between שׂ and שׁ. In this
connection cf. Jud. 12.6: in Ephraim (i.e. the kingdom of Israel) the שׁ
had the same consonantal value as שׂ. Later on, maybe due to the inclusion of parts of Israel into the kingdom of Judah after the destruction
of Samaria (cf. Rudolf Kittel, *Geschichte des Volkes Israel*, 5. Auflage,
Gotha 1922, p. 473 note 1 and p. 482 note 2, also the references cited
there), we meet with this phenomenon even in Judah; cf., f.i., Jer. 23.38,
39: וְאִם מַשָּׂא יהוה תֹּאמְרוּ··· וְנָשִׁיתִי אֶתְכֶם נָשֹׁא: a play on words: משא from
the root נָשָׂא, with the verb נָשָׁה to forget, cf. Lam. 3.17 (tertiae ה and א
are interchangeably used; cf. p. 595, § 55). Cf. also Talmud babli
Sabbat 9a: הלא פרוש לרעב לחמך בשי"ן כתיב (Isa. 58.7) as compared with

the spelling of the Masoretic text: פָּרֹס, and with Rabbi Akiba Eger's remark (ib. 55b) on the passage: ובספרים שלנו כתיב ב סין. Cf. also p. 230 sub 2. In the alphabetical arrangement of the word list beginning with שׁ I have therefore not considered the fact, whether according to the Tiberian grammatical system this sign is pronounced שׁ or שׂ, but have followed the conception of Jerome. Cf. also MH §§ 41-44.

E.   THE PRONUNCIATION OF THE HEBREW ALPHABET

In the fall of 1927 I began to study the Greek transliterations of Hebrew proper names contained in the Septuagint, which served as the starting point for this investigation. I soon realized the necessity to extend my investigation to include also to the material from the Second Column of the Hexapla of Origen. In my paper *Das Alphabet der Septua-ginta-Vorlage*, OLZ, 1929, p. 533-40, I summed up the results which I had arrived at then in the following sentences: "Zwischen der Abfassungszeit der Septuaginta und der der Hexapla des Origenes liegen vier bis fünf Jahrhunderte; trotzdem glaube ich im Rechte zu sein, wenn ich die Transkriptionen der Septuaginta und die der zweiten Kolumne der Hexapla *zusammen* behandelt wissen möchte. Denn weder ist—wie schon Wutz richtig erkannt hat—die zweite Kolumne eine erst ad hoc ange-fertigte Transkription, noch können wir in den Transkriptionen der frühestens aus dem vierten nachchristlichen Jahrhundert stammenden ältesten Septuaginta-Handschrift die Aussprache des Hebräischen im 3.-2. vorchristlichen Jahrhundert wiedererkennen. Hier wie dort ist das Material verschiedener Epochen in buntem Durcheinander und man kann ebensowenig eine Grammatik des Hebräischen im 2. nachchristlichen Jahrhundert auf Grund der Transkriptionen der 2. Kolumne schreiben, wie eine Grammatik des Hebräischen im 3.-2. vorchristlichen Jahrhundert auf Grund der Transkriptionen der Septuaginta; denn es handelt sich dabei nicht um einheitliche Formen, die sich in *eine* Grammatik zusam-menfassen lassen. Dagegen ist es unter Benutzung des gesamten Trans-kriptionsmaterials, das aus diesen zwei Quellen stammt, bis zu einem gewissen Grade wohl möglich, den *Wandel* in der Aussprache des He-bräischen vom 3. vorchristlichen bis zum 2. nachchristlichen Jahrhundert zu verfolgen." The subsequent years of study since the publication of the paper cited here, leading to the inclusion of Jerome's transliterations, only confirmed me in my conviction of the correctness of that statement. Consequently, only inner criteria were used in the arrangement of the material, and the relatively higher or lower age of the respective sources has been entirely disregarded; cf. p. 227 ff.

Originally I had in mind to write only an essay on the pronunciation of the Hebrew consonants in the period of the Septuagint. By means of the alphabetical arrangement of the source material in the Dictionary, this problem is for the most part solved of its own accord and I can limit myself to brief explanatory notes:

א has no consonantal value of its own, but serves only to carry a vowel sign; cf. p. 170/71 f.

ב is always β. For later Greek confusion with ου cf. Dictionary s.v. אָמֵן.

ג is γ; the gemination of ג is transliterated by γγ, f.i. חני αγγει; at the end of the word ג is sometimes rendered by κ, as f.i. in דאג δωηκ, פלג φαλεκ; (cf. Mayser, § 36 I, 1).

ד is δ; at the end of the word it is not infrequently θ, f.i. זבוד ζαβουθ, כבוד χαβωθ, עובד obeth; see also: היגיד αιεγγιθ and פחד faath; cf. Mayser, § 36 III, 1).

ה is without consonantal value, like א; at the beginning of the word Jerome nevertheless often transliterates it by h; cf., f.i., הוד hod, המה homa, as compared with הבל abal, הרים arim; cf. also in his Onomastica: הוא hu. Since the Onomastica go back to a *Vorlage* in Greek characters (see p. 108), which have no equivalent for an h in their alphabet and considered the ה merely as the bearer of the respective vowel (see Jerome's general statement on p. 170), we are lead to the conclusion that Jerome added here the h upon his own responsibility, probably after having consulted the Hebrew text. It is worth while noting that this is—as far as I can see—the only case of transliterating an ה by an h in the Onomastica (cases like Ahihod for אחיהוד in Num. 34.27 are explained on p. 111) and it does not concern a real proper name, but the Hebrew phrase מן־הוא in Ex. 16.15.

ו at the beginning of the word is mostly ου; cf. the cases of waw conjunctivum and waw consecutivum, as dealt with in § 78 and § 79; otherwise it is ου or ω; cf. Jerome's statement (editio Vallarsi, vol. VI, p. 366C): "vau quippe litera et pro u, et pro o, eorum lingua accipitur." The same

uncertainty as to whether to vocalize a given word with u or with o can
be noted in BV also, cf., f.i., in Ms. Ec 1 בְּטוֹב Ps. 27.13 and בְּטֻוֹב ib. 65.5;
מוּתָר Prov. 14.23 and וּמוֹתָר ib. 21.5; בְּעֻזֶּךָ Ps. 21.2 and עֻזֶּךָ ib. 63.3; עָמְקָה
Prov. 22.14 and עֻמְקָה ib. 23.27; תְּבוּאַת Prov. 10.16 and תְּבֻאַת ib. 18.20.
To illustrate Jerome's assertion, cf. f.i., sub סוד: βασωδ and σουδει; sub
צור: σουρ and σωρ; sub המון: αμων and amun; sub כמר: χωμαρειμ and
acchumarim; sub עגור: agor and agur. This statement of Jerome may
also be applied to those transliterations, where ου and ω are promiscuously used to indicate the vowel, which is represented in Hebrew by
another mater lectionis; f.i. ראש: ρως and rus. B-L § 14q has to be corrected accordingly: it is not so, that the o in מָנוֹחַ changed into u in מְנוּחָה;
but מְנוּחָה is a further development of the feminine formation to מנוח as
manue (with u), cf. the Dictionary s.v. Originally this form must have
been pronounced מנוחה manua, with retention of the first vowel a; cf.
p. 215 sub a; cf. similarly מחולה (אבל) rendered as μαουλα in 1 K. 4.12
and μεουλα in Jud. 7.22 (both in Cod. B); for the change of α into ε cf.
p. 215/6 sub b.

ז in the earlier period corresponds to σ, f.i.: אחז αχας, יזרע ισρα, יזרח
ιεσραε, גרזתי νεγρεσθι, כזב chasab, מזבח μασβηη; later it was transliterated
by ζ; cf. in the Dictionary the list of words beginning with ז; cf. Mayser,
§ 46 I.

ח in the earlier period equals χ; cf. the characteristics of codex B and
A on p. 106 and our discussion of Jerome's remark on חָם p. 109.
In the later period ח lost its consonantal value and like א served
merely for carrying the vowel. We may assume that the transition
from the earlier to the later period is marked by those transliterations,
where ח is rendered by ε; note f.i. at the beginning of the word: חזו εεζου,
החזק εεζεχ, החליק εελικ; in the middle of the word: כחשו chaesu, לחם
λαεμ, מחלה μαελα; at the end of the word: זרח ζαρας, יזרח ιεσραε, יפתח
ιεφθαε, זנוח zanoe, מנוח μανωε, מזבח μασβηη. These transliterations can,
therefore, not be used as evidence for the existence of a pataḥ furtivum,
as B-L § 18j would make us believe. The only cases of pataḥ furtivum
in transliterations are קולע colea, רוח rua. In this connection I wish to
point out, that B-L § 14f is likewise incorrect: ח was never transliterated
as χ; but according to Greek phonetics, χ at the end of a wo d could
phonetically and, consequently graphically, be confused with κ, cf. to כ.

The transliteration of טבח as ταβεκ, which B-L quote as a proof for their assertion, is therefore to be explained as a further inner Greek development of the form tabech (= ταβεχ, cf. p. 111), as represented by Jerome in his Onomastica; cf. the Dictionary s.v.

ט is τ.

י is ι and its phonetic derivations: ε, η, αι, ει; note f.i. in § 55α: תַּסְתִּיר θεσθερ, with ε, but תַּסְתִּירֵם θεσθιρημ with ι; also the transliteration of the suffix in חייתני ιιθανι as compared with דליתני δελλιθανη (§ 73b), and the examples listed in § 123 1) 2) 4). Note further בית βαιθ (§ 138a) as compared with βηθ (§ 138b) and s.v. בן: βαναι as compared with βανη; cf. also the helping vowels (ε, ι, η) in § 127.

כ is χ; as exceptions, which are most likely due to the phonetic interchange of χ and κ (cf. Mayser, § 36, I, 2), I note: כבוד caboth; ככר κεχαρ B; כל κολ A; כליון κελαιων B; כפיר caphir; כפתורים caphthorim. The gemination is indicated in the Septuagint by κχ, in Origen by χχ; cf. f.i.: sub סכה σοκχωθ (G) and σοχχα (O). At the end of the word it is sometimes rendered by κ; f.i.: סבך σαβεκ, סמך σαμακ, מלך μελεκ.

ל is λ.

מ is μ.

נ is ν.

ס is σ.

ע is not a consonant, but a vowel; cf. on א, and Jerome's assertions in paragraph oo. In the middle and at the end of the word it was sometimes transliterated by ε (cf. on ה); f.i. in the middle of the word: נעם νεεμ, רעם reem; see also Jerome's statement on בעלי on p. 111; at the end of the word: שמע σαμαε, ידע ιαδαε, יפיע ιαφιε, רע ρηε, שוע sue; cf. similar forms in BV: Job 15.8: תִּשְׁמָע, ib. 13.19: וְאֶגְוָע; see MTK, p. 31. Against the assumption in B-L § 18j, cf. on ה.—In the Septuagint and accordingly in Jerome's Onomastica cases are still recorded, where an ע, corresponding to an Arabic غ, is transliterated by γ; cf. f.i. Jerome's statements on עמרה and on צער on p. 109.

פ is rendered in almost all the instances by φ. Jerome even makes a general statement to the effect that no equivalent for the Latin character P can be found in the Hebrew alphabet (editio Vallarsi, vol. V, p. 724C):

"אפדנו APEDNO. Notandum autem, quod P literam Hebraeus sermo non habeat, sed pro ipsa utatur PHE, cuius vim Graecum φ sonat. In isto tantum loco apud Hebraeos scribatur quidem PHE, sed legatur P." As exceptions I would like to note: פחד πααδ and פתח παθα (cf. Mayser, § 36, II, 1); the spelling iepte for יפתח and neptalti for נפתלתי may originate in printers (or even copyists) mistakes, instead of iephthe and nephthalthi. The gemination of פ is indicated in the Septuagint by πφ and in Origen by φφ; cf. f.i.: s.v. תפוח: θαπφουε (A) and thaffue, s.v. צפור: σεπφωρ (G), s.v. אף: βααφφω (O), s.v. נפל: ιεφφολου (O). Forms like חפה χοφφα (B) would prove the late date, when this transliteration originated; but on the other hand, the rendering of ח by χ is old, cf. on ח.

צ is σ; cf. Jerome's statements on p. 172.

ק is κ.

ר is ρ.

שׁ and שׂ are σ; cf. Jerome's assertions quoted on p. 172 and our conclusions on p. 172/3.

ת is θ; gemination: τθ (in the Septuagint) and θθ (in Origen); cf. f.i.: מתן ματθαν (G), אתה αθθα (O), s.v. נתן: ουιεθθεν (O).

This list together with the list given on p. 111 will be sufficient to clarify the problem of the phonetic value of the letters of the Greek and Latin alphabets respectively, too. Only one letter remains, which requires a special discussion: ε (e). Does this letter indicate a full vowel or only a murmuring vowel? We are anxious not to introduce here the terminology of the Tiberian grammar: otherwise we would formulate our problem thus: does ε stand for a vowel or for a שוא? The cases dealt with in § 19b as differentiated from c might suggest an answer that ε could very well be thought of as indicating a mere murmuring vowel. But these three instances are, as far as I can see, the only possible proofs for such an assumption, since elsewhere ε stands for a short i sound (cf. Mayser, § 11, I); cf. f.i. § 23α and β. On the other hand it seems to me that the murmuring vowel or שוא of the Tiberian grammar has no equivalent in the pronunciation underlying the transliterations; cf. § 22: זכר ζχορ, שמע σμα; § 23: לכו λχου. It is practically impossible to pronounce these words, without inserting some kind of a helping vowel between the two subsequent consonants. And yet the transliterator saw no need to indicate it. Consequently, if we find an ε, we have to consider it as representing a full vowel. But how then can we account for the cases listed in § 19b? The form נחושה νεουσα can be eliminated, since ε may be considered as the consonantal equivalent of ה (cf. above sub ה) and not as a vowel; thus this form belongs to the subdivision c, being like דרושה drusa. Otherwise § 19b corresponds exactly to the nominative forms listed in § 103 (as compared with § 102). The close phonetic relationship between ε and ι may also be realized from the transliterations in § 55α, where ε and ι are used promiscuously; cf. especially the change of ε into ι from the absolute form תסתיר θεσθερ to the corresponding conjugated form תסתירם θεσθιρημ, while תשפיל θεσφιλ has the ι even in the absolute form.

II. MORPHOLOGY

The subdivisions (α, β, γ or 1, 2, 3 respectively) separate the sound roots from the various types of weak stems, where one consonant of the stem is apparently missing in the transliteration, as expounded pp. 174 f., sub א, ה, ח and ע.

THE VERB

i. Ḳal

a. Perfect

§ 1. 3. pers. sing. masc.

a) Sound Verbs.

בָּרַךְ βαραχ G	נָדַב ναδαβ G	צָפַן σαφαν G
זָכַר ζαχαρ A	נָתַן ναθαν G	שָׁפַט σαφατ G
יָשַׁב ιασαβ O	סָמַךְ σαμαχ A, σαμακ B	

b) Verbs with a Guttural.

α)	אָחַז αχας B,	אָסַף ασαφ G		חָשַׁב ασαβ G
	αχαζ G,	אָשַׁם asam		עָזַר αζαρ G
	ααζ A	הָלַךְ αλαχ O	β)	יָצָא jasa
	אָמַר αμαρ G	חָנַן αναν G		פָּדָה φαδα G

קָנָה κανα G	חָזָה αζα G	עָנָם αναμ O
קְנָנִי canani	חָנָה hana	עָשָׂה ασα G
γ) פָּעַל φααλ A	חָרָה ara	רָאָה raha
δ) הָיָה αεα O, haja	עָנָה ανα A	

c)   Verba med. ו and י.

בָּא βα O	קָם καμ G	שָׂם σαμ O
דָּן δαν A	רָד rad	

d)   Verba tertiae ה and ע.

α) בָּלַע βαλα A	יָדַע ιαδα A		שָׁמַע σαμαε B
בִּלְעָם βαλααμ G	שָׁמַע σαμα G	γ) בָּטַח βατε O
זָרַח ζαρα A β)	זָרַח ζαραε A		זָרַח ζαρε B
פָּתַח παθα B, φαθα A	יָדַע ιαδαε B		שָׁמַע same

§ 2.   3. pers. sing. fem.

a)   With retention of the second vowel.

נֶחְתָּה νααθα O	עָנְתָה anatha	רָאֲתָה ρααθα O

b)   With loss of the second vowel.

עָשְׂשָׂה ασσα O

§ 3.   2. pers. sing. masc.

a)   Ending in a Consonant.

α₁) הָפַכְתָּ αφαχθ O	α₂) וְנִחְתָּ ζαναθ O	β₁) פָּדִיתָ φαδιθ O
מָגַרְתָּה μαγαρθ O	יָדַעְתָּ ιαδαθ O	שָׂרִיתָ sarith
נָתַתָּה ναθαθ O	קָרָאתָ carath	β₂) רָאִיתָ ραιθ O
פָּרַצְתָּ φαρασθ O	שָׁמַעְתָּ σαμαθ O	γ) שַׁמְתָּ σαμθ O
		δ) קַלּוֹת calloth

b)   Ending in a Vowel.

α) בָּרָאתָ βαραθα O	צָפַנְתָּ σαφανθα O	β) רָאִיתָה ραειθα O
פָּעַלְתָּ φααλθα O		

§ 4.   1. pers. sing.

α) אָמַרְתִּי   αμαρθι O   קְרָאתִי καραθι O   רָאִיתִי raithi

בָּטַחְתִּי   βαταθι O   β) הָיִיתִי αιθι O   γ) שָׂנֵאתִי σανηθι O

עָבַרְתִּי   abarthi   חָסִיתִי ασιθι O   δ) שָׁחוֹתִי σεωθι O

פָּקַדְתִּי   φακαδθι O   קָנִיתִי canithi   ε) שַׂמְתִּי σαμθι O

§ 5.   3. pers. plur.

   a) With retention of the second vowel (cf. B-L § 2w).

דָּקְרוּ dacaru   יָדְעוּ jadau   מָעֲדוּ μααδου O

   b) With loss of the second vowel.

אָמְרוּ αμρου O   כָּחֲשׁוּ chaesu   עָזְבוּ αζβου O

טָמְנוּ ταμνου O

   c) Defective verbs.

α) בָּאוּ bau   רָאוּ rau   β) דָּמוּ δαμμου O

הָמוּ αμου O   שָׂמְחוּ σαμου O   γ) שַׂסָּהוּ σασουου O

מָטוּ ματου O   שָׁתוּ σαθου O

§ 6.   2. pers. plur. masc.

חֲרַשְׁתֶּם arasthem

b. Imperfect

§ 7.   3. pers. sing. masc.

   a) With vocalic prefix.

α) יִזְרַע ισρα B, ιζρα A   β) יִבְחַר ιβααρ B   γ) יֵקַר ικαρ O

יִמְנַע ιμνα G   יִגְאַל ιγααλ B   יֵשַׁר isar

יִקְרָא ικρα O   יִצְהַר ισααρ A   δ) יִשְׂרֹף ισροφ O

יִקְרָאֵנִי ικραηνι O   יִצְחַק ισαακ G   יְסוֹבְבֶנּוּ ισωβαβεννου

יִשְׁמַע ισμα A   יִשְׂחָק isaac   O

   b) With consonantal prefix.

α) יִבְלַע ιεβλα G   יִמְנֶה ιεμνα A   β) יֶחְבַּל ιεβαλ O

יִגְדַּל iegdal   יִפְתַּח ιεφθα A   יֶחְדַּל ιεδαλ O

יִדְלַף ιεδλαφ A   יִקְבַּע jecba   γ₁) יִגְאַל iegal

יִזְרַע ιεζρα A   יִרְפָּא ιερφα A   יִגְהַר ιεγαρ O

יִמְלָא ιεμλα A   יִתְלֶה ιεθλα A   יִשְׁאַג jesag

γ₂) יִבְחַר ιεβααρ A   יָרוּם ιαρουμ O   η₂) יִפְתַּח iepte
יִצְהַר iessaar   יָשׁוּב ιασουβ G   יִפְדֶּה ιεφδε O
δ₁) יִשְׁבֹּק ιεσβοκ A   ζ) יָבוֹא ιαβω O   η₃) יֵרֵד jered
δ₂) יִזְבְּלֵנִי iezbuleni   יָדוֹם ιαδομ O   יֵשֵׁב ιησηβ O
δ₃) יַחֲרֹשׁ jeros   יִכּוֹן ιεχχον O   η₄) יִגְדִּל ιεγδελ O
δ₄) יַעֲקֹב ιακωβ G   η₁) יִהְיֶה ιειε O   יִתֵּן ιεθθεν O
ε) יָגוּר ιαγουρ A   יִחְיֶה ιειε O   θ) יִזְרַח ιεσραε B
יָנוּם ιανουμ A   יִרְאֶה ιερε O   יִפְתַּח ιεφθαε G
יָקוּם jaccum   יִרְעַם ιερημ O

§ 8.   3. pers. sing. fem.=2. pers. sing. masc.

a)   With α in the first syllable.

α) תִּמְנֶה θαμνα A   תִּרְצֶה θαρσα B   תָּשׁוּב θασουβ O
תִּמְנַע θαμνα A   β) תִּרְחַק θαρακ O   δ) תֶּהְגֶּה θααγε O
תִּפְסַח θαψα A   γ) תָּמוּג θαμουγ O

b)   With ε in the first syllable.

α) תִּרְצֶה θερσα G   γ) תִּרְאֶה θερε O   ε) תִּפֹּל thephphol
β) תִּבְעַר θεβαρ O   תֵּלֵךְ θηληχ O   תְּאַזְּרֵנִי θεζορηνι O
תִּמְאַס θεμας O   δ) תִּתֵּן θεθθεν O   תִּצְפְּנֵם θισφνημ O
תִּסְעָדֵנִי θεσαδηνι O   תִּצְרֵנִי θεσσερηνι O
β₁) תְּצֻר θεσαρ O   תָּמוֹט θεμμοτ O

c)   Miscellaneous forms.

וַתֵּט ουθετ O   תְּסוֹבְבֵנִי θσωβαβηνι O

§ 9.   1. pers. sing.

α) אֶמְצָא emsa   אֶרְדּוֹף ερδοφ O   אֶרֶץ αρους O
אֶפְתַּח εφθα O   אֶשְׁמוֹר εσμωρ O   אָשׁוּב ασουβ O
אֶקְרָא εκρα O   אֶשְׁפּוֹךְ esphoch   ε) אִירָא ιρα O
אֶשְׂמַח εσμα O   γ¹) אֱעֱבֹר eebor   אֲגִילָה αγιλα O
β) אֶשְׁעַן εσαν A   אֶמְחָצֵם εμωσημ O   ζ) אַרְמְמָךְ ερωμεμεχ O
אֲהַבֵּהוּ εαβηου O   אֶשְׁחָקֵם εσοκημ O   אֶתְנֵהוּ εθνηου O
γ) אֶזְכֹּר ηζχορ O   δ) אָרוּם αρουμ O

§ 10.   3. pers. plur. masc.

a)   With vocalic prefix.

| יַחְפְּרוּ ιφρου O | יְסַבְּנִי ισαββουνι O | יַקְרְצוּ ιχερσου O |
| יַחְרְדוּ ιχαρδου O | | |

b)   With consonantal prefix.

| α) | יֵבֹשׁוּ ιηβωσου O | β₁) יָשׁוּבוּ jasubu | | יֶהֱמוּ ιεεμου O |

α) יֵבֹשׁוּ ιηβωσου O	β₁) יָשׁוּבוּ jasubu	יֶהֱמוּ ιεεμου O
יַחְרְגוּ ιερογου O	γ) יְחְיוּ jeju	ε) יִרְעֲשׁוּ ιερασουι O
יִפְּלוּ ιεφφολου O	יַחְמְרוּ ιεμρου O	יִתְמְהוּ jethmau
יִשְׁמֹרוּ ιεσμωρου O	יִבְלוּ ιεβλου O	ζ) יֹאבְדוּ ιοβαδου O
β) יָמוּתוּ ιαμωθου O	יִשְׂמְחוּ ιεσμου O	ζ₁) יֹאמְרוּ ιωμρου O
יָרֹצוּ ιαροσου O	δ) יַעֲזְבוּ ιεζεβου O	
יָרֹנּוּ ιαροννου O	יִשְׂמְחוּ ιεσεμου O	

§ 11.   2. pers. plur. masc.

| תִּהְיוּ θου O | תָּמֹדוּ thamoddu | תַּעֲשׂוּ θεσου O |

§ 12.   1. pers. plur.

| נִירָא νιρα O |

c.   Participle

§ 13.   ptc. act. sing. masc.

α) בּוֹטֵחַ βωτη O	נֹגֵשׂ noges	רֹגֵל ρωγηλ G
בּוֹקֵר bocer	עוֹבֵד ωβηδ G,	רֹעֶה roe
גּוֹאֵל goel	obeth	שׁוֹאֵף soeph
גֹּדֵר goder	עוֹדֵד ωδηδ B	שׁוֹבֵק σωβηκ G
דֹּאֵג δωηγ A,	נֹצֵר νωσηρ O	שׁוֹמֵר σωμηρ G
δωηκ B	נוֹתֵן νωθην O	שֹׁקֵד soced
חוֹרֵב χωρηβ G,	סֹפֵר sopher	β) חָפֵץ αφης O
oreb	עֹזֵר ωζηρ O	יָרֵא ιαρη O
יוֹעֵץ ioes	עֹשֶׂה ωση O	שָׁלֵם σαλημ O
יוֹצֵר joser	קוֹלֵעַ colea	γ) גֵּר gar
לוֹחֵשׁ λωης G	קוֹרֵא κωρη G	רָם ραμ G

§ 14.   ptc. act. sing. fem.

| α) זֹחֶלֶת ζωελεθ A | קֹהֶלֶת coeleth | γ) רָמָה ραμα G |
| יוֹשֶׁבֶת josebeth | β) הֹמָה homa | |

§ 15.   ptc. act. plur. masc. (cf. B-L § 26t).

   a)   With retention of the second vowel (cf. B-L § 14f′).

בֹּטְחִים βωτεειμ O   מֹשְׁכִים mosechim   פּוֹחֲזִים phoezim
חֹלְמִים ωλεμιμ O   נֹקְדִים nocedim   גֹּלִים ρωγελειμ A

   b)   With loss of the second vowel (cf. B-L § 26t).

α) אֹרְגִים ωργειμ G   β) חֹסִים ωσιμ O   רֹעִים roim
שֹׁמְרִים σωμριμ O   צֹפִים σωφιμ A   γ) רָצִים ρασειμ A

§ 16.   ptc. act. plur. fem.

רָמוֹת ραμωθ A

§ 17.   Inflected forms of the act. ptc.

α) גֹּזִי gozi   γ) יוֹרְדִי ιωδρη O   שֹׂנְאִי σωνη O
רֹעִי roi   מֹשְׁכֵי mosche   δ) בֹּנַיִךְ bonaich
β) לֹחֲמַי λωαμαι O   חֹפְצֵי ωφση O   לִירֵאֶיךָ λιριαχ O
קָמַי καμαι O   עֹבְרֵי ωβρη O

§ 18.   pass. ptc. sing. masc.

בָּרוּךְ βαρουχ G   סָמוּךְ samuch   צָפוּן σαφουν O
גָּמוּל γαμουλ B   סָתוּר σαθουρ G   רָפוּא ραφου G
זָבוּד ζαβουθ B   עָזוּר azur   שָׁאוּל σαουλ A
חָמוּל amul ·   עָצוּם ασουμ O   שָׁדוּד sadud
חָנוּן ανουν G   פָּקוּד phacud
חָרוּץ αρους G   פָּרוּחַ φαρρου A

§ 19.   pass. ptc. sing. fem.

   a)   With retention of the vowel after the first radical.

בְּרוּרָה barura   סְנָאָה σανουα A   צְרוּעָה σαρουα A
חֲשָׁבָה ασουβε B   עֲזוּבָה αζουβα A   שְׁלָחָה salua

   b)   With ε after the first radical.

נְחוּשָׁה νεουσα O   צְרוּפָה σερουφα O   שְׁלָחָה selua

   c)   With elision of the first vowel.

בְּעוּלָה bula   דְּרוּשָׁה drusa

§ 20.   pass. ptc. plur. masc.

   a)   With retention of the vowel after the first radical.

אֲסוּרִים assurim   לְטֻשִׁים latusim

   b)   With ε after the first radical.

אֲמוּנִים εμουνιμ O

§ 21.   Inflected forms of the pass. ptc.

α) חֲלָצֵי eluse   β) עֲקֻבֵּי ακοββαι O   זְרוּעֹתָי ζερουωθαι O
   נְצוּרֵי nesure

d.   Imperative

§ 22.   impv. sing. masc.

α)   זְכָר ζχορ O   שְׁמַע σμα O,   δ) רִיבָה ριβα O
     לְחֹם λοομ O   σμαε O   ε) הֱיֵה αιη O
β)   חֲזַק εζαχ O   γ) קוּם κουμ O

§ 23.   impv. plur. masc.

α) בִּטְחוּ βετου O   β) גִּילוּ γιλου O   רְאוּ ρου A
   חֲזוּ εεζου O   שִׁמְעוּ σιμου O   דְעוּ δου O
   קִרְאוּ κερου O   γ) אֶהֱבוּ αβου O   ε) רְעוּ rou
   שִׁמְחוּ σεμου O   הָבוּ αβου O   ζ) חֶדְלוּ hedalu
   שִׁמְעוּ semu   δ) לְכוּ λχου O

e.   Infinitive

§ 24.   inf. abs.

α)   זָנֹחַ ζανω A,   פָּדֹה φαδω O   צוּד sud
     zanoe   קָרֹב καρωβ O   קוּם κουμ O
     חָבוֹר αβωρ G   β) בּוּז buz
     חָרֹק αρωχ O   חוּל ουλ A

§ 25.   inf. constr.

   a)   With prefix.

α) לִבְלוֹם λαβλωμ O   לִפְנוֹת λαφνωθ O   בְּמוֹט βαμωτ O
   לִמְצֹא λαμσω O   β) לָבוֹא λαβω B

b)   With suffix.

α)   בּוּזִי   βουζει G   β)   בְּשׁוֹרִי   basori   בְּרָדְתִּי   βρεδεθι O

שְׁאֵתִי   σαθι O   בְּחָפְזִי   βααφζι O   γ)   בַּחֲלוֹתָם   βααλωθαμ O

ii.   Pi'el

a.   Perfect

§ 26.   3. pers. sing. masc.

אָמֵר   εμμηρ G   הִלֵּל   ελληλ B   קִצֵּץ   κεσσης O

גִּדֵּל   γεδδηλ A   עִקֵּשׁ   εκκης A   שִׁלֵּם   σελλημ A

§ 27.   2. pers. sing. masc.

a)   Ending in a consonant.

חִלַּלְתָּ   ελλελθ O   נֵאַרְתָּה   νηερθ O   שִׂמַּחְתָּ   σεμεθ O

b)   Ending in a vowel.

פִּתַּחְתָּ   φεθεθα O   דִּלִּיתָנִי   δελλιθανη O   חִיִּיתַנִי   ιιθανι O

§ 28.   1. pers. sing.

גִּדַּלְתִּי   γεδδελθι A   מִלֵּיתִי   μελληθι A   עִנֵּיתִי   εννηθι O

§ 29.   3. pers. plur.

חֵרְפוּ   ηρφου O

§ 30.   1. pers. plur.

דִּמִּינוּ   δεμμηυου O   בִּלַּעֲנוּהוּ   βελλενουου O

b.   Imperfect

§ 31.   3. pers. sing. masc.

a)   With vocalic prefix.

יְדַבֵּר   ιδαββερ O   יְזַמְּרֶךָ   ιζαμμερεχ O   יְמַלֵּט   ιμαλλετ O

b)   With consonantal prefix.

יְדַבֵּר   ιεδαββερ O   יְהַלֵּל   ιαλλελ A

§ 32.   2. pers. sing. masc.

α)   וַתְּאַזְּרֵנִי   ουεθαζερηνι O   וּתְנַהֲלֵנִי   ουθνεελνι O   β)   תְּשַׁבֵּר   θεσσαβερ O

§ 33.   1. pers. sing.

α) אֶדְלֶג εδαλλεγ O   אֲמַגֶּנְךָ amaggenach   אֲשַׁקֵּר ασσακερ O

     אֲנַסֶּה enasse   γ) אֲהַלְּלָךְ εελλελεχ O   ε) אֲכַזֵּב εχαζεβ O

β) אֲחַלֵּל ααλλελ O   δ) אֲשַׁנֶּה ασσανε O

§ 34.   3. pers. plur. masc.

        a)   With vocalic prefix.

     יְדַבְּרוּ ιδαββηρου O

        b)   With consonantal prefix.

     יְהַלְּכוּן ιαλληχουν O   יְחַלְּלוּ ιαλληλου O   יְשַׁוְּעוּ ιεσαυου O

c.   Participle

§ 35.   ptc. act. sing. masc.

α) מְלַמֵּד μαλαμμεδ O   β) מְנַחֵם μαναημ G   γ) מְשַׁוֶּה μοσαυε O

    מְנַצֵּחַ μανασση O   מְפַתֵּחַ maphate   מְעוֹפֵף mopheph

    מְנַשֶּׁה μανασση B;   הַמְּאַזְּרֵנִי αμμααζερηνι

                μαννασση A   O

§ 36.   ptc. act. sing. fem.

     מְרַחֶפֶת marahaefeth

§ 37.   ptc. act. plur. masc.

     הַמְיַחֲלִים αμμηαλιμ O   וּמְשַׁנְּאַי ουμασσανεαι O

d.   Imperative

§ 38.   impv. sing. masc.

α) נַשֵּׂאם νεσσημ O   β) בָּרֵךְ βαρεχ O   γ) חַיֵּידוּ heieu

    פַּלְּטֵנִי φελλετηνι O   צַדְּקֵנוּ sadecenu

§ 39.   impv. plur. masc.

     הַלְּלוּ allelu   זַמְּרוּ ζωημερου O

e.   Infinitive

§ 40.   inf. constr.

α) פַּנּוֹת φεννωθ O   β) כַּסּוֹת χεσσουθ O   לְבַלּוֹת λαβαλωθ O

    כַּלּוֹתָם χελλωθαμ O   γ) פַּלֵּט φαλητ O   בְּשַׁוְּעִי βασαυει O

iii.   Niph'al

a.   Perfect

§ 41.   3. pers. sing. masc.

נִמְשַׁל νεμσαλ O   נוֹעַד νωαδ A

§ 42.   2. pers. sing. masc.

נִשְׁבַּעְתָּ νεσβαθ O

§ 43.   1. pers. sing.

α) נֶעֱזַרְתִּי νεζαρθι O   נִשְׁבַּעְתִּי νεσβαθι O   β) נִגְרַזְתִּי νεγρεσθι O
נִפְתַּלְתִּי neptalti

§ 44.   3. pers. plur.

נֶאֶסְפוּ νεεσαφου O   נִדְמוּ νεδμου O

b.   Imperfect

§ 45.   3. pers. sing. masc.

יִלָּוֶה illaue

c.   Participle

§ 46.   ptc. sing. masc.

α) נִבְהָל νεβαλ O   נִתְעָב nethab   γ) נִמְצָא νεμσα O
נֶחְשָׁב nesab   β) נֶאֱמָן νεεμαν O   δ) נִשְׁפֶּה nesphe

§ 47.   ptc. sing. fem.

נֶאֱמֶנֶת νεεμαναθ O   נֶעְלָמָה naalma   נִמְרֶצֶת nimrezeth

§ 48.   ptc. plur. masc.

נֶאֱמָנִים neemanim

iv.   Pu'al

a.   Imperfect

§ 49.   3. pers. sing. masc.

a)   With vocalic prefix.

יְשֻׁבַּר ισουβερ O

b)   With consonantal prefix.

יִרֹחַם ιεροαμ A   יָפֻנֶּה ιεφοννη G

b.   Participle

§ 50.   ptc. sing. masc.

מְהוֹלָל molal   מְשָׁלָם μεσουλαμ G   הַמְּסָכָן amsuchan

§ 51.   ptc. plur. masc.

מְעוּנִים μοουνειμ A

v.   Hiph'il

a.   Perfect

§ 52.   3. pers. sing. masc.

α) הֵכִין hechin   הִרְעִים εριμ O   הֶעֱלִים eelim
    הִפְלִיא εφλι O   β) הֶחֱלִיק εελιχ O

§ 53.   2. pers. sing. masc.

a)   Ending in a consonant.

α) הִקְצַרְתָּ εκσερθ O   β) הֶעֱטִיתָ εετηθ O   γ) הֲרִימוֹתָ αρημωθ O
    הִשְׁבַּתָּ εσβεθ O   β₁) הֶעֱלִיתָ εελθ O   γ₁) הֲקֵמֹתוֹ ακιμωθωO
    הִשְׂמַחְתָּ εσμεθ O   β₂) הֶעֱמַדְתָּ εεμεδεθ O

b)   Ending in a vowel.

הִסְתַּרְתָּ εσθερθα O   הִסְגַּרְתַּנִי εσγερθανι

b.   Imperfect

§ 54.   3. pers. sing. masc.

a)   Verba mediae ו and י.

α) יָאִיר ιαειρ G   יָרִיב ιαρειβ A   יָרִיב ιαριβ A
    יָבִין ιαβειν B   יָשִׁיב ιασειβ A   γ) יָאִיר iair
    יָזִיז ιαζειζ B   β) יָבִין ιαβιν O   יָכִין iachin
    יָכִין ιαχειν G   יָלִין ιαλιν O   יָקִים iacim
    יָקִים ιακειμ G   יָפִיעַ ιαφιε A   יָשִׁיר jasir

b)   Miscellaneous forms.

α)   יוֹאֵל ιωηλ G   α₁)   יוֹדְךָ ιωδεχχα O   β₁)   יַעֲמִידֵנִי ιεμιδηνι O

יוֹסֵף ιωσηφ G   β)   יַגִּיד ιεγγιθ O   γ)   יַגִּיהַ ιαγι O

§ 55.   2. pers. sing. masc.

α)   תַּשְׁפִּיל θεσφιλ O   β)   תּוֹשִׁיעַ θωσι O   δ)   תַּנְחֵנִי θενηνι O

תַּסְתִּיר θεσθερ O   תּוֹצִיאֵנִי θωσιηνι O   תַּרְבֵּנִי θερβηνι O

תַּסְתִּירֵם θεσθιρημ O   γ)   תָּאִיר θαειρ O   ε)   תַּחֲרֵשׁ θαρες O

α₁)   תַּרְחִיב θεριβ O   תָּשִׁיב θασιβ O   ζ)   תּוֹתַר θωθαρ O

§ 56.   1. pers. sing.

α)   אָפִיר αφιρ O   אַשִּׁיגֵם εσιγημ O   δ)   אֲהוֹדֶנּוּ αωδεννου O

אַצְמִיתֵם ασμιθαυμ O   γ)   אוֹדְךָ ωδεχ O   ε)   אַטֶּה αττε O

β)   אַשְׂכִּילְךָ εσχιλεχ O   אוֹרְךָ ωρεχ O

§ 57.   3. pers. plur. masc.

יַגִּיעוּ ιγγιου O   יַרְחִיבוּ ιεριβου O   יַשְׂפִּיקוּ jesphicu

§ 58.   2. pers. plur. masc.

תָּלִינוּ thalinu

c.   Participle

§ 59.   ptc. sing. masc.

מַשְׁמִים masmim   מַשְׁבִּית μισβιθ O   מוֹשִׁיעַ μωσι O

§ 60.   ptc. sing. fem.

מֵינִיקָה meneca   מֵינֶקֶת meneceth

§ 61.   ptc. plur. masc.

מַגְדִּילִים μαγδιλιμ O   מוֹשִׁיעִים mosim

d.   Imperative

§ 62.   impv. sing. masc.

α)   הָקִיצָה ακισα O   α₁)   הָרֵם αρημ O   β₁)   הַצִּילֵנִי εσιληνι O

הָשִׁיבָה ασιβα O   β)   הַטֵּה εττη O   γ)   הוֹשִׁיעָה ωσια O

הַצְלִיחָה נָא ασλιαννα O   הַחֲזֵק εεζεχ O   γ₁)   הוֹשִׁיעָה נָא ωσιεννα O

הָעִירָה αιρα O

§ 63.   impv. plur. masc.

α) הַרְנִינוּ εϱνινου O   β) הַרְפּוּ αϱφου O   γ) הוֹדוּ ωδου O
הַאֲזִינוּ eezinu

e.   Infinitive

§ 64.   a)   inf. abs.

הָבִין αβιν O   הַצְנֵעַ esne

b)   inf. constr.

בְּהָמִיר βααμιϱ O   לְהוֹשִׁיעֵנִי λωσιηνι O

vi.   Hophʻal
Imperfect

§ 65.   3. pers. sing. masc.

יוּבַל ιουβαλ A

vii.   Hithpaʻel
a.   Perfect

§ 66.   2. pers. sing. masc.

הִתְעַבַּרְתָּ εθαββαϱθ O

§ 67.   1. pers. sing.

הִתְהַלָּכְתִּי εθαλλαχθι O

b.   Imperfect

§ 68.   2. pers. sing. masc.

תִּתְבָּרַר θεθβαϱαϱ O   תִּתְפַּתָּל θεθφαθθαλ O   תִּתַּמָּם θεθαμμαμ O

§ 69.   1. pers. sing.

אֶתְחַנַּן εθανναν O

§ 70.   3. pers. plur. masc.

יִתְהַלָּלוּ ιθαλλαλου O

c.   Participle

§ 71.   ptc. plur. fem.

מִתְנוֹסְסוֹת methnosasoth

d. Imperative

§ 72. impv. plur. masc.

הִשְׁתַּחֲווּ εσθανου O

viii. Verbal forms with suffixes

§ 73. Suffix of the 1. pers. sing.: νι.

a) With helping vowel η.

α) זְבֻלֵנִי iezbuleni   הַמְאַוְּרֵנִי αμμααζερηνι   הַצִּילֵנִי εσιληνι O

תְּסָעָדֵנִי θεσαδηνι O   O   β) יְקָרָאֵנִי ικραηνι O

תְּצָרֵנִי θεσσερηνι O   פַּלְּטֵנִי φελλετηνι O   תּוֹצִיאָנִי θωσινηνι O

תְּאַזְרֵנִי θεζορηνι O   יַעֲמִדֵנִי ιεμιδηνι O   לְהוֹשִׁיעֵנִי λωσιηνι O

תְּסוֹבְבֵנִי θσωβαβηνι O   תַּנְחֵנִי θενηνι O

וַתְּאַזְּרֵנִי ουεθαζερηνιO   תַּרְבֵּנִי θερβηνι O

b) Without a helping vowel.

α) יִסַבְּנִי ισαββουνι O   β) חִיִּיתַנִי ιιθανι O   β₁) דְּלִיתָנִי δελλιθανη O

קָנָנִי canani   הִסְגַּרְתַּנִי εσγερθανι O

§ 74. Suffix of the 2. pers. sing masc.: εχ, ach (cf. p. 218 f 3), χα.

α) אֲרוֹמִמְךָ ερωμεμεχ O   אַשְׂכִּילְךָ εσχιλεχ O   β) אֲמַגֶּנְךָ amaggenach

יְזַמֶּרְךָ ιζαμμερεχ O   אוֹדְךָ ωδεχ O   γ) יוֹדְךָ ιωδεχχα O

אֲהַלְלֶךָ εελλελεχ O   אוֹרְךָ ωρεχ O

§ 75. Suffix of the 3. pers. sing. masc.: ου, ω.

α) יְסוֹבְבֶנּוּ ισωβαβεννου   β) אֶתְנֶהוּ εθνηου O   γ) שָׁסָהוּ σασουου O

O   אֲהַבְהוּ εαβηου O   בִּלְעֲנוּהוּ βελλενουου O

אֲהוֹדֶנּוּ αωδεννου O   חַיֵּהוּ heieu   δ) הֲקִמֹתוֹ ακιμωθω

§ 76. Suffix of the 1. pers. plur.: ενου.

צִדְקֵנוּ sadecenu

§ 77. Suffix of the 3. pers. plur. masc.: ημ, αμ.

α) אֲמִחָצֵם εμωσημ O   יִרְעֵם ιερημ O   בִּלְעָם βαλααμ G

אֶשְׁחָקֵם εσοκημ O   נַשָּׁאֵם νεσσημ O   אַצְמִיתֵם ασμιθαυμ O

תַּסְתִּירֵם θεσθιρημ O   אַשִּׂיגֵם εσιγημ O

תִּצְפְּנֵם θισφνημ O   β) עֲנֵם αναμ O

ix.   Waw conjunctivum and waw consecutivum

§ 78.   Transliterated as ου (cf. p. 219 3).

a)   Before a consonant.

וְנֶחְתָה	ουναασθα O	וְתֶאֱזְרֵנִי	ουθεζορηνι O	וּבָרֵךְ	ουβαρεχ O
וּפָקַדְתִּי	ουφακαδθι O	וְקוּם	ουκουμ O	וְנַשְׁאַם	ουνεσσημ O
וְרָאִיתִי	uraithi	וְגִילוּ	ουγιλου O	וְנֶעֱזַרְתִּי	ουνεζαρθι O
וְשָׁמְתִּי	ουσαμθι O	וְקֵץ	ουκεσσης O	וְנֶאֶסְפוּ	ουνεεσαφου O
וַתִּתֵּן	ουθεθθεν O	וּתְנַחֲלֵנִי	ουθνεελνι O		

b)   Before a vowel.

וְאֶשְׁחָקֵם	ουεσοκημ O	וְעָזְבוּ	ουαζβου O	וַיֶּקֶר	ουικαρ O
וְאֶשְׂמַח	ουεσμα O	וְהָקִיצָה	ουακισα O	וַיִּקְרָא	ουικρα O
וְאַשִּׂיגֵם	ουεσιγημ O	וְהָרֵם	ουαρημ O	וַיַּחְרְדוּ	ουιχαρδου O
וְהַרְנִינוּ	ουερνινου O	וְהוֹדוּ	ουωδου O	וַיַּחְפְּרוּ	ουιφρου O
וְאָהֵבֵהוּ	ουεαβηου O	וְאוֹרֵךְ	ουωρεχ O		

c)   Before a consonantal ι.

וַיִּתֵּן	ουιεθθεν O	וַיְדַבֵּר	ουιεδαββερ O	וְיָרוּם	ουιαρουμ O
וַיִּגְהַר	ουιεγαρ O	וְיַחְרְגוּ	ουιερογου O	וְיָבֹא	ουιαβω O

§ 79.   Transliterated as ου plus helping vowel.

α)	וַתֶּאֱזְרֵנִי	ουεθαζερηνι O	וַיַּרְחִיבוּ	ουειεριβου O	וַתְּמָאֵס	ουαθθεμας O
			β)	וּדְעוּ	ουαδου O	וַתֵּט	ουαθετ O

THE NOUN

(Derived Forms are given in Parentheses)

x.   Monosyllabic biconsonantal nouns

§ 80.   The a-class (α, a).

1)	בר bar	דם (δαμι O;	פז φας B
	בת bath	dame)	פר phar
	גב gab	יד (ιαδαχ, ιαδω,	(pharim)
	גל gal	ιαδαι O)	צל σαλ G
	(γαλειμ B)	ים iam	צר σαρ O
	דג dag (dagim)	(ιαμιμ O)	(σαραυι O)

רב ραβ A   2) אב αβ G   עז ας B
  (ραβιμ O)   (αβει B)   עם αμ O (αμει
רם ραμ G   אח αχ G   B, αμιμ O)
שי σαι A   (αχει B)   עש as
שר σαρ A   הד ad   רע ρα O (raim)
  (sarim, sare)   הר αρ A (αριμ O)

a) Feminine forms.

1) במה βαμα G   (ραμαθ A;   מאה (maath)
   (βαμωθ G)   ramathaim;   פחה (φααθ A)
פרה φαρα B   ραμωθ G)   רעה (raath;
צרה (σαρωθ O)   2) אב (abotham)   ρααθι O)
רמה ραμα G   דעה (daath)   חמה (αμαθι A)

b) With geminated 2nd radical.

1) בד bad (baddim,   (γαννιμ A)   עם αμ O
   baddau)   רב ραβ A   (ammi;
גל gal   (ραββιμ O)   αμμαχ,
   (γαλλειμ A)   2) אף (αφφω O)   αμμιμ O)
גן γαν A   חג (αγγει B)

c) Feminine forms.

1) רבה ραββα A   rabboth)   2) אמה αμμα G
   (rabbath,

§ 81.   The i-class (ε, η, e).

1) בל bel   נכים (νηχινμ O)   אם εμ O
   בן βεν A   נר νηρ G   אש ες O
   בת beth   סף seph   חך (echcha)
   גב (gebim)   צל σελ G (sela)   עד ηδ O
   גר γηρ G   שם σημ A   ער ηρ A
   גת γεθ G   (σεμαχ,   רע ρε G (reim)
   חן hen   σεμω O)   תא (theim)
   יד ιεδ O   תל θελ G
   לץ (λησιμ) O   2) אל ηλ G (ηλει B)

a)   Feminine forms.

1)   שם (semoth;   2)   דעה dea   עצה (ησαθ O)
      σεμωθαμ O)   חמה (εμαθαχ O)

b)   With geminated 2nd radical.

1)   לב λεβ O   צל σελ G   2)   איש ις A (issi)
      (λεββι,   (σελλα A)   עד (eddim)
      λεββαυ O)   שק σεκ O (σεκκι O)

c)   Feminine form.

זמה ζεμμα B

d)   Reduplicated forms.

גלגל γελγελ G   צלצל selsel

§ 82.   The o-class (o, ω, o).

1)   גב gob   רב ροβ O   עז οζ O (οζει
      דק doc   שד sod   O)
      כר χορ G   2)   אח (oiim)

a)   Feminine form.

אב (ωβωθ G)

b)   With geminated 2nd radical.

כל χωλ A (chollo)

c)   Feminine forms.

חפה χοφφα B   סכה σοχχα O

d)   Reduplicated forms.

בקבוק bocboc   כדכד chodchod

§ 83.   Nouns with varying vocalization.

1)   Change of α and ε (cf. B-L § 14z).

בת bath—beth   צל σαλ G—   חמה (αμαθι A)—
יד (ιαδαχ O)—   σελ G   (εμαθαχ O)
ιεδ O

2) Change of α and o.

גב gab—gob

xi. Monosyllabic triconsonantal nouns

§ 84.   The a-class (α, a).

1) גבר γαβρ O   מלך (malchi;   2) ארץ αρς O

    (γαβρι G)   μαλχη O)   חפץ (αψει B)

דרך (δαρχαμ O)   פרד φαρδ O   חצר ασρ B

זבד (ζαβδει G)   קרב (καρβαμ O)   עבד αβδ G

זמר (ζαμβρει B)   קרן (καρναιν A)   (αβδει B;

כרם χαρμ O   קשת κασθ O   αβδαχ,

    (χαρμει,   שבט σαβτ O   αβδω O)

    χαρμειμ B)   שמש σαμς O   ערב αρβ O

a)   Feminine forms.

חרפה αρφα O   עגלה αγλα A   עלמה alma

  (αρφαθ O)

b)   With weak 2nd radical.

בער βαρ O   לעג (λαγη O)   שחק σαχ O

יער ιαρ A   מעט ματ O   תחש thas

  (ιαρειμ B)   פעל (phalach)

כעס χας O   שאר sar

c)   Feminine forms.

בהלה bala   בעלה (βαλωθ A)   נהר (ναρωθ O)

§ 85.   The i-class.

a)   With the vowel ε or η.

1) בקר βεχρ O   יצר (ιεσρι A;   μελχαμ A)

דרך δερχ O   ιεσρο O)   נגד νεγδ O

  (δεχρι,   יתר (iethro)   (νεγδι O)

  δεχρω O)   כסל χεσλ O   נזר (νεζρω O)

זבד (zebdi)   לתך λεθχ O   נפש (νεφσι,

זכר ζεχρ O   מלך (μελχει B;   νεφσω,

  (ζεχρει B)   melchechem;   νεφσινου O)

סתר σεθρ O   רסן ρεσυ O   εσδαχ O)
(σεθρει A)   רשת ρεσθ O   חפץ (ephsi)
צדק (σεδκι,   שטף σετφ O   חשק (esci)
σεδκαχ O)   שמש (semsi)   עזר εζρ O
קרב (κερβα O)   שקר σεκρ O   (εζρι A;
קשת κεσθ O   2) אבל εβλ O   εζρα O)
רגל (ρεγλαι O;   חסד εσδ A   שמע (σεμει A)
reglau)   (εσδι, εσδω,

a)   Feminine forms.

1) חלקה (χελκαθ A)   2) דמעה δεμα O   עגלה egla
צדקה (σεδκαθαχ O)   עברה (ebrath)   עקב (εκβωθ O)
רצפה ρεσφα G   עזרה (εζραθι O)   שמחה σεμα O

b)   With weak 2nd radical.

איל el (elim,   זאב ζηβ G   נער νερ O
ele, elau)   זעיר zer   רחם ρεμ O
באר βηρ G   כאב cheb   תחת θεθ O

c)   Feminine forms.

באר (βηρωθ G)   בהמה (βημωθ O)

b)   With the vowel ι.

a)   With weak 2nd radical.

זיז ziz   סיס sis   קיר cir
חיץ his   עיר ειρ O   שיר σιρ O (σιρι O)
סיג sig (sigim)   ציר sir   שעיר (sirim)

b)   Feminine form.

קינה κινα A

§ 86.   The o-class.

a)   With the vowel o or ω.

1) בקר βοκρ O   קדש κοδς O   קרב κορβ O
גלם (γολμη O)   (κοδσω O;   2) אזן (οζνι,
כפר (χοφρω O)   codsa)   οζναχ O)

חדש (odsi)   חפץ (οφσι A)   ערף ορφ O
חלד ολδ O   חשך (οσχι O)   עשר (οσραμ O)
חמר ομρ O

a) With weak 2nd radical.

און ων G   זהר zor   צום σωμ O
(oni; ωνω,   טוב τωβ G   צור σωρ O (sori)
G; ωναμ,   (tobim)   קול κωλ A
ωναν A)   יאר ior   (κωλω O)
אור or   יום iom   קוץ κως G
בור βωρ O   מאד μωδ O   ראש ρως G
דוד (dodi, dodach)   מות μωθ B   רחב rob
דור δωρ G   סוד σωδ A (sodi)   שאול σωλ O
הוד ωδ A   צאן σων O   שוט sot

b) Feminine forms.

אור (oroth)   חומה homa   פותה photha
בושה βωσα O   יונה ιωνα G
חובה choba   מוטה mota

b) With the vowel ου.

a) With weak 2nd radical.

אור ουρ G   נאם νουμ O   (σουρει B;
(ουρει B)   סוד (σουδει B)   σουραμ O)
באש (busim)   סוס sus (σουσει B)   ראש rus
בוץ bus   צוף σουφ G   שור (surim)
טוב (τουβαχ O)   צור σουρ G   שור σουρ G

b) Feminine forms.

טור (turoth)   פארה phura   פורה phura
סופה supha

§ 87. Monosyllabic Nouns with affixed helping vowel.

בטן βατνε A   כרם χαρμα B   מתג μεθγε O
בשת βοσθε B

§ 88.   Nouns with varying vocalization.

1)   Change of α and ε.

דרך (δαρχαμ O)—δερχ O	מלך (malchi)—(μελχει B)	שמש σαμς O—(semsi)
זבד (ζαβδει G)—(zebdi)	קרב (καρβαμ O)—(κερβα O)	עגלה αγλα A—egla
חפץ (αψει B)—(ephsi)	קשת κασθ O—κεσθ O	

2)   Change of α and o.

חפץ (αψει B)—(οφσι A)	קרב (καρβαμ O)—κορβ O

3)   With weak 2nd radical: change of o and ου (cf. p. 175 sub ו).

סוד (sodi)—(σουδι A)	צור σωρ O—σουρ G	ראש ρως G—rus

xii.   Triconsonantal nouns, which appear as monosyllabic or bisyllabic forms

§ 89.   Insertion of ε as second vowel.

1)   Nouns of the a-class.

גבר γαβρ O—γαβερ G	עבד αβδ G—αβεδ A	שמש σαμς O—σαμες A
חצר ασρ B—aser		

2)   Nouns of the i-class.

חפץ (ephsi)—(ephesi)	עזר εζρ O—εζερ G	רסן ρεσν O—resen
לתך λεθχ O—lethech	קשת κεσθ O—ceseth	

3)   Nouns of the o-class.

בשת βοσθε B—boseth	חמר ομρ O—homer	קדש κοδς O—codes
חלד ολδ O—holed		

§ 90.   Reiteration of the vowel. Nouns with weak 2nd radical.

1)   Nouns of the a-class.

בער βαρ O—   יער ιαρ A—   נהר (ναρωθ O)—
     βααρ O   ιααρ B   νααρ O

a)   Feminine form.

בעלה (βαλωθ A)—(baaloth)

2)   Nouns of the i-class.

באר βηρ G—   רחם ρεμ O—   תחת θεθ O—
     βεηρ B   rehem   teeth

a)   Feminine form.

בהמה (βημωθ O)—(beemoth)

3)   Nouns of the o-class.

אהל (ολι) A—(οολι B)

xiii.   Bisyllabic triconsonantal nouns

1.   *With the characteristic vowel in the second syllable*

(cf. p. 216/7)

a.   The a-class

§ 91.   With α in the first syllable.

1)	ברד βαραδ A	נבל ναβαλ G		אדם αδαμ A	
	ברק βαρακ B	נבר ναβαρ O		אדם (adamim)	
	בשר basar	סבך sabac		אטד αταδ G	
	(basari)	פגר (phagarim)		אמץ (amasim)	
	גמל (γαμαλι A)	פרץ (φαρασειμ A)		ארז araz	
	דבר δαβαρ G	קטן καταν G		הבל (abal,	
	(dabarach)	שטן σαταν G		abalim)	
	ישן ιασαν G	שכר σαχαρ A		המסים (amasim)	
	כזב chasab	שפן σαφαν G		חגב αγαβ G	
	ככר chachar	שרף σαραφ A		חכם (αχαμιμ O)	
	כסמים (chasamim)	תמר θαμαρ G		חלק αλακ A	
	לבן λαβαν A		(thamarim)		חצר ασαρ A
	משל μασαλ A	2)	אבן (abanim)		עבר (αβαρειμ G)

ענק anacim	עשן ασαν A	רפאים (raphaim)
עפר αφαρ O (afara)	3) זרח ζαρα G (ζαραει B)	שלח σαλα A
ערב arab	פרא phara	

a) Feminine forms.

1) לבנה λαβανα G	אילה aiala	עלמה (alamoth)
מקל (macaloth)	(αιαλωθ O)	עצרה asara
נבלה nabala	אנקה ανακα O	ערבה αραβα G
נדבה (nadaboth)	אשמה (asamath)	(αραβωθ G)
נקמה (νακαμωθ O)	חדשה αδασα A	3) גבעה γαβαα G
נשמה nasama (nasamoth)	חכמה (αχαμωθ O)	(γαβααθ A; γαβαωθ B)
	חרדה arada	
צדקה sadaca	עגלה (αγαλωθ O)	לביא (labaoth)
שלמה σαλαμα G	עזרה azara	צבאות (σαβαωθ G)
2) אדמה αδαμα G (αδαμωθ O)	עטרה ατατα B (αταρωθ G)	

b) With weak 2nd radical.

אחד aad	יחד ιααδ O	צעד (σααδαι O)
בעל βααλ G (baali; βααλειμ G)	יער ιααρ B	קהל κααλ O
	להב (laabim)	שחר σααρ A
	נהר νααρ O	שחת σααθ O
בער βααρ O	נחש νααϛ G	שער (σααρειμ O)
דעת daath	נחת naath	תחת θααθ G
זהב zaab	פחד πααδ G	

c) Feminine forms.

בעלה βααλα A (baaloth)	נחמה (naamathi)	צעקה saaca

d) With geminated 2nd radical.

חגא agga	חטא (ατταειμ O)	כשף (cassaphe)

§ 92. With ε in the first syllable.

1) ככר κεχαρ B	נכר νηχαρ O	שלמים (selamim)
כנף chenaph	קסת cesath	שמנים (semanim)

שרף seraph   2) אנך enach   ענק εναχ A
(seraphim)   (εναχειμ G)

a) Feminine forms.

אלם (elamoth)   אמרה (εμαραθ O)   שגגה segaga

b) Tertiae ה and ע.

גזע geza   פשע φεσα O   רשע ρεσα O
זבח zeba   (φεσαμ O)
זרע zera   צמח sema

§ 93. With α and ε respectively in the first syllable.

זרע zara—zera   ככר chachar—   שרף saraph—
                    κεχαρ B   seraph

b. The i-class

α. With the vowel ε

§ 94. With α in the first syllable.

1) גבר γαβερ G	קדש καδης A	חצר ασερ A
גדר γαδερ A	(καδησειμ B)	חרב areb
גזר γαζερ G	שבר σαβερ B	חרס αρες G
זבד ζαβεδ G	שכן (σαχηναυ O)	חרש ares
חבר χαβερ B	שמש σαμες A	עבד αβεδ A
טבח tabech 2)	אבל αβελ G	עדר ader
יתד jathed	אבן αβεν G	עצבים (ασεβειν O)
משק masec	און aven	ערש ares
נקב νακεβ A	אחר αερ B 3)	בקע bace
סבך σαβεχ A	(αηριμ O)	זרח zare
פלג φαλεχ A	אצל asel	ירח ιαρη O
פרץ φαρες A	הבל αβελ A	קצה κασε O
פרש phares	הרס ares	שלח sale

a) Feminine forms.

1) גדרה γαδηρα G	קדשה cadesa	חצר (ασηρωθ G)
(γαδηρωθ A)	(cadesoth)	מלא malea
גזרה gazera	שדמה (σαδημωθ A)	
פליטה phaleta 2)	אטם (atemoth)	

§ 95.   With ε in the first syllable.

1)   בזק βεζεκ B   נזם nezem   אמת ημεθ O
      בטן beten   נמר nemer   (εμεθθαχ O)
      גבר geber   נצר neser   אפר εφηρ O
      גזם gezem   נשף neseph   חפץ (ephesi)
      גשם gesem   פרץ pheres   חדל edel
      דבר deber   פרק pherec   חלד eled
      הרס heres   צדק σεδεκ A   עבר εβερ A
      זמר (zemeri)   קדם cedem   עדן εδεν A
      חלום helem   קרב cereb   עדר εδερ A
      חלק χελεκ A   קשת ceseth   עזר εζερ G
      (χελεκι A)   רמש remes   עמק εμεκ A
      חרם herem   רסן resen   עקב eceb
      יצר ιεσερ B   רשף reseph   3)   בטח bete
      (ιεσερει B)   שבר σεβερ A   בצע βεσε O
      יתר ιεθερ O   שכם σεχεμ A   זבח ζεβεε G
      לתך lethech   שמש semes   יוע jeze
      מלך μελεχ B   שקד seced   מלח μελε B
      משק mesec   שקל secel   פלא phele
      נבל nebel   תבל thebel   שמע (σεμεει B)
      נגב negeb   2)   אבל εβελ B

    a)   Feminine forms.

לבנה lebena   נשפה nesepha

    b)   With weak 2nd radical.

באר βεηρ B   לחם λεεμ G   נעם νεεμ G
    (beeri)   (λεεμει A)   רהב reeb
בעל βεελ G   נחל nehel   רחם rehem
                                               רעם reem

    c)   Feminine forms.

בהמה (beemoth)   נחלה nehela (νεελαθαχ O)

§ 96.   With α and ε respectively in the first syllable.

    גבר γαβερ G—   הרס ares—heres   עדר ader—
        geber   משק masec—mesec   εδερ A

פרץ φαρες A—   שבר σαβερ B—   שמש σαμες A—
    pheres   σεβερ A   semes

β.   With the vowel ι

§ 97.   With α in the first syllable.

1) דביר δαβειρ G   קדים cadim   חזיז (azizim)
    חסיל hasil   קצין κασιν A   חסיד ασιδ O
    יבש ιαβεις G   רכיל rachil   (ασιδαυ O)
    ימין ιαμειν A   שליש salis   חריף αρειφ B
    כסיל chasil   שמיר σαμειρ B   עליל αλιλ O
    כפיס chaphis   שריד σαριδ A   עמית (amithi)
    כפיר chaphir   (saridim)   עשיר ασιρ O
    נפילים (naphilim)   תמיד θαμιδ O   3) בריח bari
    נציב νασειβ B   תמים θαμιμ O   נשיא nasi
    נתינים (ναθινειμ A) 2) אביב abib   4) יחיד jaid
    סריס σαρεις A   אמיר amir   ליש λαεις B
    פריץ pharis   אסיר ασειρ B   מעיל mail
    צניף saniph   אשישי (asise)

    a)   Feminine forms.

גלילה galila   לפידות (λαφειδωθ B)   καριαθαιμ A;
    (γαλιλωθ A)   קריה caria   καριωθ A)
חסידה asida   (καριαθ G;

§ 98.   With ε in the first syllable.

1) ברית βεριθ B   רתיק rethic   פרי pheri
    נסיך (nesiche)   2) בכי βεχι O
    נציב νεσιβ A   חצי εσει A

    a)   Feminine form.

גבירה gebira

§ 99.   With α and ε respectively in the first syllable.

    נציב νασειβ B— νεσειβ A

c.   The o-class

α.   With the vowel o

§ 100.   With α in the first syllable.

1) גדול gadol   רזון ραζων A   (amona,
    חזון hazon   רצון ρασων O   amonim)
    כבוד χαβωδ O   שלום σαλωμ G   עגור agor
    נכון ναχων A   ששון σασων O   ערום arom
    ציון saion   2) אדון (αδωνει B;   עשור ασωρ O
    צפון σαφων B   αδωναι O)   3) גאון (gaon)
    (σαφωνει B)   המון αμων G   שאון σαων G

§ 101.   With ε in the first syllable.

1) בכור bechor   2) אנוש ενως A   3) אלוה ελω O
    דרור deror   אפוד ephod   מלוא μελω A
    כפור χεφορ O   חמור emor

    a)   Feminine forms.

בכורה (βεχωραθ A)   לבונה λεβωνα G

    b)   With geminated 2nd radical.

חמור εμμωρ G   מלוא mello   רמון ρεμμων G
כנור χεννωρ O

    c)   Feminine forms.

בכורה bechchora   דבורה δεββωρα G

β.   With the vowel ου

§ 102.   With α in the first syllable.

1) זנונים (zanunim)   אשור (ασουρενου O)   עמוד (αμουδα o)
    כרוב χαρουβ B   המון amun   3) תפוח θαφου B
    רכוש rachus   עגור agur   4) בחור (βαουρειμ G)
2) אנוש anus   עלומים (αλουμαυ O)   רחום ραουμ A

    a)   Feminine form.

ישועה (ιασουαθι O)

§ 103.   With ε in the first syllable.

אמון (εμουνιμ O)	גלולים (gelule)	כרוב χερουβ A
גבול gebul	זבוב zebub	(χερουβειμG)
(gebulaic)	זבול ζεβουλ G	לבוש (λεβουσι O)
גדוד γεδουδ O	כלוב chelub	שקוץ (secuse)

a)   Feminine forms:

אמונה emuna	בתולה bethula	ירושה ιερουσα A
(εμουναθαχ O;	גבורה (geburoth;	ישועה jesua
emunatho)	γεβουροθαυ O)	

§ 104.   With α and ε respectively in the first syllable.

כרוב χαρουβ B—χερουβ A

2.   *With the characteristic vowel in the first syllable*

a.   The a-class

§ 105.   With α and ε respectively in the second syllable.

חצר ασαρ A—	סבך sabac—	פרץ (pharasim)
ασερ A	σαβεχ A	—φαρες A

b.   The o-class

§ 106.   With α in the second syllable.

1) חותם χωθαμ A		שופר sophar	3) מטה mota
כמר (χωμαρειμ	2)	אצר ωσαρ B	מוצא μωσα O
G)		עולם ωλαμ O	

§ 107.   With ε in the second syllable.

1) בשת boseth		חרש hores	תפת thophet
חדש hodes		סכן socen	2) ארך ορεχ A
חלד holed		קדש codes	חנף oneph
חמר homer		שחל sohel	

a)   Feminine form.

עננה onena

§ 108.   With o in the second syllable.

    a)   Nouns with weak 2nd radical.

אהל ooλ A (ooλι B)   צהר soor   שהל sohol

זהב ζooβ A   רעות rooth

    b)   Feminine forms.

גאלה (goolathach)   רחוב (rooboth)

3.   *Nouns with varying vocalization*

§ 109.   Change of o and ου (cf. p. 174 sub ו).

המון αμων G—   כמר (χωμαρειμ   עגור agor—agur
     amun   G)—(chumarim)

§ 110.   Nomina tertiae ה.

זבח ζεβεε G—zeba   זרח zare—zara

xiv.   Nouns with prefixed מ

Vocalized as μα (cf. p. 217 sub c)

§ 111.   The a-class.

1) מבצר μαβσαρ A		מטהר (ματαρω O)		משמע μασμα A
(μαβσαραυι O)		מכתב machthab	4)	מבחר μαβαρ A
מבשם μαβσαμ A		מספר μασφαρ G		מרחב μαραβ O
מגדל μαγδαλ A	2)	מאכל machal		מלאך malach,
מגרש magras		מחמד mamad		(malachi,
מדבר μαδβαρ B	3) מלקחים	(malcaim)		malache)

    a)   Feminine forms.

1) ממלכה (μαμλα-	2)	מחלה μαλα G		מפעל (μαφαλωθ O)
χωθ O)	3) מלחמה	μαλαμα O	4)	מרמה μαρμα A
מרכבת (μαρχα-		(μαλα-		(μαρμωθ O)
βωθ A)		μωθ O)	5)	מנחה μανα O

§ 112.   The i-class. With the vowel e, η.

מזבח μασβη O   ממזר mamzer   מרפא marphe

מכתש machthes   מקנה macne   משא μασση A

    a)   Feminine form.

מקהלה (μακηλωθ G)

§ 113.   The o-class.

1)   With the vowel o, ω.

מזמור μαζμωρ O   מכאוב (μαχωβιμ O)

a)   Mediae ו.

מאור	maor	מעוג μαωγ O	מצור μασωρ O
מדון	μαδων A	מעוז μαοζ O	מקום (macoma)
מחול	μαωλ O	(μαοζι O)	
מנוח	μανωε G	מעון μαων A	

2)   With the vowel ου. Nomina mediae ו.

מגור	magur	מנוד μανουδ O	מצור masur
מחול	μαουλ A	מנוח manue	

a)   Feminine form.

מבוכה mabucha

xv.   The article

The article is always transliterated as α (cf. p. 217d)

§ 114.   Before a vowel.

1) האדם	aadam		הארץ ααρς O		החסים αωσιμ O
האיש	αεις O	2)	החגב aagab	3)	העיר αειρ O
האל	αηλ O		החפץ ααφης O		העמק αεμεκ A

§ 115.   Before a consonant.

הגן	agan	הצדק	asedec	הרשעים	αρσαειμ O
הדגים	adagim	הקוץ	ακως B	השדמות	asademoth
היום	αιωμ O	הקטן	ακαταν B	השמינית	ασεμινιθ O
הלוחש	αλωης B	הראש	αρως A	השפתים	asephathaim
הסנאה	ασανουα A	הרדידים	ardidim		

§ 116.   With gemination of the following consonant.

הבא	αββα O	הכבוד	αχχαβωδ O	המאזרני	αμμααζερηνι
הבוטה	αββωτη O	הכמרים	acchumarim		O
הבוטחים	αββωτεειμ O	הכרובים	accherubim	המיחלים	αμμηαλιμ O
הבית	αββαιθ O	הלוחש	αλλωης A	המים	αμμαιμ O
הגוי	aggoi	הלחות	alluoth	המלך	ammelech

המנחה	αμμανα Ο	הפרה	affara	הקריות	αχχαριωθ Α
הנותן	αννωθην Ο	הקוץ	αχχως Α	השחת	ασσααθ Ο
הנתינים	ανναθινιμ Α	הקטן	αχχαταν Α	השמרים	ασσωμριμ Ο

xvi.   The inseparable prepositions בכלם

a.   The prepositions בכל

§ 117.   Transliterated as βα, χα, λα respectively.

a)   Before a consonant.

1)	בבן	baben	בציון	basaion	לכל	λαχολ Ο
	ביה	βαια Ο	בקרב	bacereb	למלחמה	λαμαλαμα Ο
	בכעס	βαχας Ο	ברוח	barua	למשל	λαμασαλ Ο
	בלבבם	βαλβαβαμ Ο	ברצונך	βαρσωναχ Ο	למשפטי	λαμεσφατι Ο
	בגעים	βανγαιμ Ο	ברצונו	βαρσωνω Ο	לנגד	λανεγδ Ο
	בנהרות	βαναρωθ Ο	בשמות	basemoth	לצו	lasau
	בסוד	βασωδ Α	2) כבהמות	χαβημωθ Ο	לקו	lacau
	בסופה	basupha	כנצר	chaneser	לרשע	λαρασα Ο
	בפיהם	βαφιεμ Ο	כצאן	χασων Ο	לרשע	λαρεσα Ο
	בפתחיה	baphethee	כשמש	χασαμς Ο	לשאול	λασωλ Ο
	בצום	βασωμ Ο	3) לבקר	λαβεκρ Ο		

b)   Before the vowel α:

1)	באפו	βααφφω Ο	בעליל	βααλιλ Ο		כעפר	χααφαρ Ο
	בארץ	βααρς Ο	בעם	βααμ Ο	3)	לארץ	λααρς Ο
	בהדרת	βααδαρεθ Ο	בערב	βααρβ		להררי	λααραρι Ο
	בחנפי	βαανφη Ο	2) כאח	χαα Ο		לעבד	λααβδ Ο

c)   Before the vowel ε.

באמונתך	βαεμουναθαχ	באמונתו	baemunatho	בעזרתי	βαεζραθι Ο
	Ο	באש	βαες Ο	לעד	laed

§ 118.   Transliterated as βε, χε, λε respectively.

a)   Before the vowel ε.

בחיקי	βηηχι Ο	בעיר	βεειρ Ο	כאבל	χεεβλ Ο
בחסדך	βεεζδαχ Ο				

b)   Before a consonant.

בגבורתיו	βεγεβουροθαυ O	בעברות βεγαβρωθ O	לבני λεβνη O

§ 119.   Transliterated merely as β, χ, λ respectively.

a)   Before a consonant.

בגאותו 1)	βγηουαθω O	בצדקתך βσεδκαθαχ O	בתורת βθωραθ O
בדמי	βδαμι O	בצלעי βσαλη O	2) כירח χιαρη O
בדרך	βδερχ O	בצרות βσαρωθ O	כפרד χφαρδ O
ביד	βιεδ O	בקולו βκωλω O	כצדקך χσεδκαχ O
בידך	βιαδαχ O	בקרבה βκερβα O	כרע χρηε O
ביום	biom	בראשית βρησιθ O	3) לבית λβηθ O
בכנור	βχεννωρ O	ברבת βροβ O	למחול λμαωλ O
בלב	βλεβ O	בשבט βσαβτ O	לשטף λσετφ O
במשפטי	βμεσφατι O	בשחק βσακ O	לשכניו λσαχηναυ O
בסכה	βσοχχα O	בשלוי βσαλουι O	
בסתר	βσεθρ O	בשמותם βσεμωθαμ O	

b)   Before a vowel.

באלהי 1)	βελωαι O	בימי βιμη O	כימי χιμη O
באלהיו	βελοαυ O	בעצת βησαθ O	3) לאחרים λαηριμ O
ביהוה	βαδωναι O	2) כאילות χαιαλωθ O	לעולם λωλαμ O

§ 120.   Transliterated as βα, with gemination of the following consonant.

בגוים	baggoim	במרחב βαμμαραβ O	בפוך baphphuch
במלחמה	βαμμαλαμα O		

b.   The preposition מ

§ 121.   Transliterated as μ plus helping vowel ε.

a)   Before a consonant.

מבטן	mebeten	ממסגרותיהם μεμχσγρω-	מרחם μηρεμ O
מיד	μειεδ O	θεειμ O	מרכסי μερυχση O
מים	mejam	מנגד μενεγδ O	מרשת μερεσθ O
מכפירים	μεχφεριμ O	מקדם mecedem	

b)   Before a vowel.

מאין μηην O   מידיכם μειδηχεμ O   מעברים meabarim

§ 122.   With gemination of the following consonant.

מבית mebbeth   ממצרים μεμμισραιμ O   משחר μεσσααρ O
מבלעדי μεββελαδη O   ממשקה memmasce   משירי μεσσιρι O
מכנף mecchenaph   משאול μεσσωλ O

xvii.   Nouns with personal suffixes

a.   The singular noun

§ 123.   The suffix of the 1. pers. sing.: ει, ι, η.

1)	אבי αβει B		דרבי δερχι O		מגני μαγεννι O
	אחי αχει B		יצרי ιεσρι A	3)	אוני oni
	אלי ηλει B		מלכי μελχι A		חדשי odsi
	אורי ουρει B		נגדי νεγδι O		חשקי esci
	אדוני αδωνει B		כרמי χαρμι A		בשרי basari
	חגי αγγει B		מעוזי μαοζι O		אישי issi
	לחמי λεεμει A		גמלי γαμαλι G	4)	גלמי γολμη O
	יצרי ιεσερει B		חלקי χελεκι A		צלעי σαλη O
2)	אהלי οολι B		לבושי λεβουσι O		רוחי ρουη O
	חשכי οσχι O		משפטי μεσφατι O		
	אזני οζνι O		לבי λεββι O		

§ 124.   The suffix of the 2. pers. sing. masc.: αχ (cf. p. 224B 1), χα.

1)	אזנך οζναχ O		היכלך ηχαλαχ O		גאלתך goolathach
	ארחך οραχ O		חמתך εμαθαχ O		משיחך μεσιαχ O
	דודך dodach		נחלתך νεελαθαχ O	2)	ישעך ιεσαχα O
	עבדך αβδαχ O		אמתך εμεθθαχ O		חכך echcha
	טובך τουβαχ O		אמונתך εμουναθαχ O		

§ 125.   The suffix of the 3. pers. sing. masc.: ω, ο.

אונו ωνω G		יתרו iethro		ימינו ιμινω O
ידו jado		נזרו νεζρω O		משיחו μεσιω O
דרכו δερχω O		כפרו χοφρω O		מנוחתו mnuatho
חסדו εσδω O		אפו αφφω O		אמונתו emunatho
יצרו ιεσρο O		כסאו χεσσω O		

§ 126.   The suffix of the 3. pers. sing. fem.: α.

עזרה εζρα O   המונה amona   עמודה αμουδα O

קדשה codsa   מקומה macoma   עפרה afara

§ 127.   The suffix of the 1. pers. plur.: ενου, ινου, ηνου.

אשורנו ασουρενου O   נפשנו νεφσινου O   עיננו ηνηνου O

§ 128.   The suffix of the 2. pers. plur. masc.: εχεμ (cf. p. 218 f 2).

לבבכם λεββαβεχεμ O   מלככם melchechem

§ 129.   The suffix of the 3. pers. plur. masc.: αμ, εμ.

1) דרכם δαρχαμ O   עינם enam   אונם ωναμ A

חילם αιλαμ G   עשרם οσραμ O   פשעם φεσαμ O

מלכם μελχαμ A   לבבם λβαβαμ O   2) פיהם φιεμ O

b.   The plural noun

§ 130.   The suffix of the 1. pers. sing.: αι.

אדוני αδωναι O   ידי ιαδαι O   שפתי σφωθαι O

אלהי ελωαι O   צעדי σααδαι O   תחנוני θανουναι O

איבי οιεβαι O   מצותי μσωθαι O

§ 131.   The suffix of the 2. pers. sing. masc.: αχ (cf. on § 128), cha.

1) איביך οιβαχ O   חסדיך εσδαχ O   2) מתיך methecha

אלהיך ελωαχ O   עבדיך αβδαχ O

דבריך dabarach   עיניך ηναχ O

§ 132.   The suffix of the 2. pers. sing. fem.: aich.

בניך benaich   גבוליך gebulaich

§ 133.   The suffix of the 3. pers. sing. masc.: αυ, αυι.

1) איביו οιβαυ O   מימיו μημαυ O   בדיו baddau

איליו elau   חסידיו ασιδαυ O   2) מבצריו μαβσαραυι O

אלהיו ελοαυ O   עלומיו αλουμαυ O   צריו σαραυι O

בניו βαναυ O   שכניו σαχηναυ O   עליו αλαυι O

עיניו ηναυ O   גבורתיו γεβουροθαυ O

§ 134.   The suffix of the 2. pers. plur. masc.: χεμ.

ידיכם ιδηχεμ O

§ 135.   The suffix of the 3. pers. plur. masc.: εμ, αμ, ημω.

1) אחריהם αρηεμ O   2) משכנותם μισχνωθαμ   אבותם abotham
   כסיליהם chisileem   O   3) שנימו σεννημω O

xviii.   The formation of the plural

§ 136.   Masculine forms.

a)   By adding ειμ, ιμ to the noun.

אביון ebion—	המון αμων G—	כרם χαρμ O—
ebionim	amonim	χαρμειμ B
איתן ethan—	הר αρ O—	קדש καδης A—
ethanim	αριμ O	καδησειμ B
אחר αερ B—	טוב τωβ G—	רע ρα O—raim
αηριμ O	tobim	שועל σουαλ A—
איל el—elim	ים iam—	sualim
אל ηλ G—ηλιμ	ιαμιμ O	שטה setta—
O	כרוב χερουβ A—	settim
בעל βααλ G—	χερουβειμ G	שריד σαριδ A—
βααλειμ G	סיג sig—sigim	saridim
בריח bari—	עם αμ G—	שרף seraph—
barihim	αμιμ O	seraphim
גל gal—	פר phar—	תמר θαμαρ G—
γαλειμ B	pharim	thamarim

b)   With gemination of the 2nd radical.

גל gal—	גן γαν A—	עם αμ G—
γαλλειμ A	γαννιμ A	αμμιμ O

§ 137.   Feminine forms: by adding ωθ.

a)   The noun ending in a consonant.

אור or—oroth	באר βηρ G—	חצר ασερ A—
	βηρωθ G	ασηρωθ G

b)   The noun ending in a vowel (α, ε), and dropping it:

אדמה αδαμα G—	אילה aiala—	במה βαμα G—
αδαμωθ O	αιαλωθ O	βαμωθ G

בעלה	βααλα A— baaloth	נשמה	nasama— nasamoth	שבועה	sabaa— sabaoth
גבעה	γαβαα G— γαβαωθ B	סכה	σοχχα O— σοκχωθ G	שדה	sade— sadoth
גדרה	γαδηρα G— γαδηρωθ A	עטרה	αταρα B— αταρωθ G	שדה	sadda— saddoth
גלילה	galila— γαλιλωθ A	קדשה	cadesa— cadesoth	שמה	σαμα B— σαμωθ A
מלחמה	μαλαμα O— μαλαμωθ O	קריה	caria— carioth	שמה	σαμμα A— σαμμωθ B
מרמה	μαρμα A— μαρμωθ O	רמה	ραμα G— ραμωθ G		

xix.   The construct state

a.   Masculine forms

§ 138.   stat. constr. masc. sing.

a)   Equals the absolute state.

בית	βαιθ B	מזבח	μασβηη O	מנוד	μανουδ O
כבוד	χαβωθ O	שלום	σαλωμ O		
גאון	gaon	הבל	abal		

b)   With a change in the vowel.

אין	ην O	בית	βηθ O	גיא	ge
עין	ην A				

§ 139.   stat. constr. masc. plur. (cf. p. 217c).

1)	בן	βανη A	הבל	αβλη O	רגע	ρεγη O
	דם	dame	חנף	ανφη O	4) גלולים	gelule
	פנים	φανη O	לעג	λαγη O	מלאך	malache
	שנים	sane	מלך	μαλχη O	נסיך	nesiche
	שר	sare	עבד	αβδη A	תעלולים	thalule
2)	דבר	δαβρη O	3)	ישר	ισρη O		

b. Feminine forms

§ 140.   stat. constr. fem. sing.

   a)   Monosyllabic nouns.

1) חלקה χελκαθ A   רבה rabbath   פחה φααθ A

   חרפה αρφαθ O   רמה ραμαθ A   רעה raath

   עברה ebrath   תורה θωραθ O

   עצה ησαθ O   2) מאה maath

   b)   Bisyllabic nouns.

אמרה εμαραθ O   בכורה βεχωραθ A   קריה καριαθ G

אשמה asamath   גבעה γαβααθ A   הדרה αδαρεθ O

§ 141.   stat. constr. fem. plur.

ארמון armanoth   משרפת μασρεφωθ A   שדמה σαδημωθ A

מפעל μαφαλωθ O   ערבה αραβωθ G   שם semoth

§ 142.   Dual-forms.

מחנה manaim   קריה καριαθαιμ A   שפה asephathaim

מלקחים malcaim   קרן καρναιμ A

עין enaim   רמה ramathaim

III.   General Observations

A.   Method Applied

I put myself to pains to explain every form in transliteration from the standpoint of the text as it is found, without attempting to make arbitrary corrections in conformity with the Masoretic text. The temptation to such a procedure was frequently very great, particularly in those passages, where the different reading of Origen's Hexapla, as compared with the corresponding Hebrew word, did not seem to fit in the context; cf. f.i. Mal. 2.13: MT: פְּנוֹת (Kal), Origen: פַּנּוֹת (Pi'el). According to the usage of Biblical Hebrew, the verb פנה in the Ḳal means "to turn somewhere," and in the Pi'el "to remove something." It is obvious that Origen, although he read here the verb in the Pi'el, must have connected with it the meaning of the Ḳal; for otherwise the sentence is senseless. A similar case is Ps. 36.2: MT: לָרָשָׁע, Origen לָרָשָׁע. The Masoretic vocalizations indicates a person who sins, whilst the transliteration would mean the abstractum, the sin. But the personal suffix in the following word לְבִי clearly refers to a person. Whether Origen has been misled by the rhythm: φεσα . . . ρεσα, or whether in his days רָשָׁע and רֵשַׁע could be used promiscuously to indicate the same meaning, is hard to decide; cf. also Isa. 26.10, where Jerome reads רֵשַׁע for the Masoretic רָשָׁע.

I was saved from any such treatment of the transliterations as based upon subjective corrections by the methodology indicated by Bergsträsser as fundamental to all scholarly activity of this type (*Hebräische Grammatik*, II. Teil, I. C. Hinrichs, Leipzig 1929, p. v): "Zu beachten ist, dass ein in seinem Aufbau gestörter, im ganzen sinnloser Satz sehr wohl einwandfreie Einzelworte und -formen enthalten, dass umgekehrt aus zum Teil unmöglichen Einzelformen ein syntaktisch möglicher Satz aufgebaut sein, ja dass innerhalb des Einzelwortes Sinnvolles und Sinnloses sich mischen kann, dass also die Frage der grammatischen Verwertbarkeit von Fall zu Fall mit Rücksicht auf die zur Erörterung stehende grammatische Erscheinung erwogen werden muss." As an example of the possibilities last referred to by Bergsträsser I should like to cite the word בְּחַסְדְּךָ in Ps. 31.8 which according to Wutz and Mercati is rendered by Origen: βεεζδαχ, and according to H-R: βεελδαχ. Both transliterations are open to suspicion. Even the rendering of a ס by ζ (according to Wutz) would constitute a ἅπαξ λεγόμενον; but its transliteration into λ (according to H-R) is completely inexplicable. Yet in § 118a I have included the word, since there the prepositions are discussed and in that connection the rendering of בְּ in בחסדך is a matter not open to doubt.

B.   GENERAL RESULTS: THE NOUN

a)   I am inclined to consider as the most characteristic feature of the pronunciation of Hebrew, as reflected in the transliterations, the fact that the vocalization of the noun does not undergo any changes—except in the latter period—when suffixes are added to it (as for instance: the personal pronoun, the feminine ending), or when the noun is being put in the plural. To illustrate this fact, I bring a selection of examples in the same order as they are listed in the Grammar, always referring to the paragraph, where they can be found: § 15a; the singular-forms, which have to be presupposed, can be seen in § 13. It will be noted that the second vowel in the singular-forms is an η (f.i. בטח βωτη), whilst in the plural-forms the spelling is with an ε (f.i. בטחים βωτεειμ). Whether this is only accidental, since ε and η were at the time of the transliterations no longer differentiated (cf. f.i. אמת ημεθ and אמתך εμεθθαχ; גדר γαδερ and גדרה γαδηρα), or whether this change in spelling was meant to indicate that the accent does not rest any longer on this syllable, this I must leave open.—§ 19a; in § 20a note לטושים latusim.—§ 82b: כל χωλ and chollo.—§ 91a: לבנה λαβανα; נבלה nabala; נדבה nadaboth; נקמה νακαμωθ; נשמה nasama, nasamoth; צדקה sadaca.—§ 94a: גדרה γαδηρα and קדשה cadesa, as compared with the corresponding forms in § 94: גדר γαδερ and קדש καδης.—§ 123: יצרי ιεσερει; חלקי χελεκι; מעוזי μαοζι; בשרי basari. —§ 126: מקומה macoma.—§ 131: דבריך dabarach.—§ 133: שכניו σαχηναυ. —§ 136a: קדש κσδης, καδησειμ; שריד σαριδ, saridim; תמר θαμαρ, thamarim.—§ 137b: גבעה γαβαα, γαβαωθ; גדרה γαδηρα, γαδηρωθ; גלילה γαλιλα, γαλιλωθ. This grammatical rule can be traced even in the Babylonian and Palestinian systems; cf. לִבְקָרִים Lam. 3.23; Ps. 101.8; Job 7.18 in Ms. Ec 1 (MTK, p. 71) בְּרֹאשִׁנוּ 1 Ki. 20.32 in Ms. 105 JThS; cf. also p. 224 B 6.—In this connection I wish to point out that originally even the Construct State did not imply a change or a dropping of a vowel; cf. f.i. § 138a and § 139; also in § 140b forms like: אמרה εμαραθ; אשמה asamath; גבעה γαβααθ; in § 141: ארמן armanoth and שדמה σαδημωθ; cf. p. 224 sub B 8. Cf. also MH §§ 197/8 and 212.

Consequently, if we find the following forms in transliteration for the Hebrew root מלך: מלך μελεχ; המלך ammelech; מלכי μελχει, malchi; מלככם melchechem; מלכם μελχαμ; למלכי λαμαλχη—they go back to the following different ways of pronouncing this triconsonantal noun, and have to be arranged accordingly: מלך: a) (cf. § 84) מלכי malchi, למלכי λαμαλχη; b) (cf. § 85) מלכי μελχει, מלככם melchechem, מלכם μελχαμ; c) (cf. § 95) מלך μελεχ, המלך ammelech. Similarly, שְׂרָפִים seraphim must not be regarded as a pluralis fractus to שָׂרָף saraph—to which the plural could only be saraphim, cf. תמר θαμαρ, plur. thamarim—, but is the regularly built plural to שרף seraph.

b)   Generally speaking, all nouns can be divided into three main groups according to their characteristic vowel: the a-class, the i-class and the o-class. Further phonetic development results in the partition of the i-class into an ε-group and an ι-group (cf. p. 176 sub י),

and similarly in a subdivision of the o-class into an o-group and an
ου-group (cf. ib. sub ו). This observation furnished us with the key for
the systematical arrangement of the various nominal formations. While
applying this system to the Bisyllabic Triconsonantal Nouns (p. 199 ff.)
we noticed, much to our own surprise, that it was the *second* syllable
that mostly had the characteristic vowel, the first syllable varying in
every group between α and ε. This would suggest a supposition that in
these cases the second syllable had the stressed vowel, a rather startling
assertion; for these nouns generally coincide with nominal formations
called in the Tiberian grammar nomina segolata, whose characteristic
feature it is that their second vowel is grammatically considered as a
mere helping vowel, the first vowel being the stressed one. We confine
ourselves here to merely noting this amazing fact without commenting
upon it; cf. the explanation of this attitude of ours in paragraph oo.
The variation between α and ε as first vowel we would attribute to dialectical differences; cf. p. 229 ff. The same variation occurs also in
§ 19a compared with b, and in § 117 compared with § 118; cf. here
subdivision e near the end.

c)   Nearly all the cases of nominal formations with prefixed מ, which
can be found in transliteration, have the vowel *a* in the first syllable;
they are listed and classified on p. 206/7. But still the following few
forms remain to be mentioned, where the prefix has the vowel *i*: s.v.
מזרח: mimizra; s.v. מצהלה: mesaloth; s.v. משגב μισγαβ O; s.v. משכן:
μεσχνη O; s.v. משפט: mesphat, μεσφατι O; s.v. משרה mesra.

In this connection I wish to call attention to a similar fact: According
to § 139, the formation of the stat. constr. masc. plur. does not involve
any change of a vowel in the transliteration. The only exception I am
aware of is: s.v. בן βνη O (as compared with βανη in codex A).

d)   Paragraphs 114 ff. (on p. 207 ff.) prove that the article has always
been pronounced as α, even—if we be permitted to point to a differentiation
in the Tiberian Grammar—before a הָ (cf. B-L § 31k); cf. in § 114: החפץ
ααφης and החגב aagab.—It seems that only from the period of the
Second Column on, which coincides, as we said on p· 106 f., with Codex A
of the Septuagint, the article was followed by gemination of the immediately subsequent consonant; cf. f.i. הקוץ ακως, הלוחש αλωης, and הקטן
ακαταν, all three in codex B (§ 115), as compared with their spelling

αxxως, αλλωης, and αxxαταν in codex A (§ 116). The period of the Second Column marks the beginning, and not the final accomplishment of this development. So it is explicable that in even as late a period as Jerome's days this rule was not yet strictly observed; note f.i. forms like: הדגים adagim, הצדק asedec (§ 115), taken from his Commentaries.

e)   A careful examination of the examples listed and arranged on p. 208 f. will prove that the transliteration of the Inseparable Pre-positions בכל as βα, χα, λα respectively (in § 117), does not coincide with the cases, when according to the Tiberian grammar (cf. B-L § 25w), they carry this vowel to indicate the article; note f.i. cases like בְיָה βαια, בְכַעַס βαχας, בִּלְבָבָם βαλβαβαμ; the context (construct state or noun with personal suffixes) excludes any possibility of vocalizing these words as with an article; cf. p. 224 B 5.

f)   1) The pronunciation of the nominal suffix of the 2. pers. sing. masc. as αχ, as expounded in § 124 subdivision 1, is upheld by the spelling יחידאך in Sam. Gen. 22.2, 13, 16 for יְחִידְךָ of the Masoretic Text. The א is in these cases mater lectionis for a; cf. in Sam. forms like Gen. 42.38; 44.32 ביאגון (MT בְּיָגוֹן); Ex. 23.31 ושאתי (MT וְשַׁתִּי); Num. 5.18 המארים (MT הַמָּרִים); Deut. 28.7 הקאמים (MT הַקָּמִים); cf. also p. 224 B 1 — 2) According to § 128, between the noun in the singular and the suffix of the 2. pers. plur. masc. χεμ, a helping vowel ε is inserted; cf. corresponding forms in the Sam. Lev. 26.19 עזיכם (MT עֻזְּכֶם); Ex. 12.11 ומקליכם (MT וּמַקֶּלְכֶם); Lev. 1.2 קרבניכם (MT קָרְבַּנְכֶם). In these instances the noun is undoubtedly in the sing.; for the plural formations of the cited nouns would be ומקלותיכם and קרבנותיכם respectively; cf. also Sam. Gen. 45.20 ועיניכם (MT וְעֵינְכֶם), which is a sing. form, according to the verb תחוס; cf. also p. 225 sub 16).— 3) The vocalization of the suffix of the 2. pers. sing. masc. with verbal forms as *ach* (cf. § 74β) has its parallel in the spelling with Sam. Num. 11.23 היקראך (MT הֲיִקְרְךָ).

It is very regrettable that we could not rely on the text of the Samaritan Pentateuch, which Gall used as the basis for his edition (*Der hebräische Pentateuch der Samaritaner*, Giessen 1914-18), but had to consult his apparatus criticus in nearly all the instances, where reference is made throughout here to Sam.

C.   THE VERB

1)   Verbal forms (and nominal forms just the same) I have arranged according to the criterion of similar vocalization in the spelling of the transliteration, without paying too much attention as to whether this treatment is justified by their place in the Hebrew conjugations. Take for instance § 54: The common element in the forms discussed there is their vocalization α-ι. For this reason I have listed the forms of Imperfect Ḳal of the verba mediae י together with the Imperfect Hiphʻil forms of the verba mediae ו, since they belong to that category by virtue of their vocalization (α-ι).

2)   The verb is dealt with in the Grammar exhaustively; at least I endeavoured, and I may hope that I succeeded in listing there every form which occurs in transliteration. I originally tried to reach the same degree of completeness even in the second part of the Grammar, dealing with the nominal forms: but experience taught me the impossibility of attaining that goal, and practical considerations proved that it may not even be desirable to overload the lists, which are sometimes long enough anyhow.

3)   Paragraph 78 shows that in the earlier period the waw, both as waw conjunctivum and as waw consecutivum, was similarly transliterated merely as ου; cf. p. 230 subdivision 3; cf. also in the MT forms like: וְאֶכְרֹת and וְאָבוֹא (Isa. 37.24), וְאַחְרִב (ib., 25), וּתְהִי (ib., 26). There can be no doubt at all, that the waws in these verbal forms are consecutive waws; note the perfect עָלִיתִי in verse 24, marking the beginning of this poem. B-L § 24d are therefore wrong in stating that "die ursprüngliche Form dieser Konjunktion (scil. the waw consecutivum) ist ụa (mit kurzem freiem ă)"; similarly, the *Biblia Hebraica* editio R. Kittel (Liber Jesaiae, Stuttgart 1929) had no right to emend these forms into: וָאֶכְרֹת, וָאָבוֹא, וָאַחְרֵב and וַתְּהִי. Here again, as in the case of the article (cf. p. 217 sub d and p. 221 sub 4), the Second Column marks the beginning of a new method; cf. § 79. But forms like וַתִּתֵּן ουθεθθεν (§ 78a), וַיִּקְרָא ουικρα (§ 78b), וַיַּגֵּר ουιεγαρ (§ 78c) prove that here, too, this development had just begun and the goal was still far from being reached.

D.   RELATION TO THE TIBERIAN SYSTEM

I purposely avoided referring to the rules of Hebrew Grammar according to the Tiberian School. The problem as to whether the Tiberian system can be linked to the non-Masoretic systems (I emphasize the plural!), has to be investigated very carefully, and I would consider it poor method, if I were to pick out the raisins from the cake, instead of paying similar attention to all the grammatical and lexical phenomena. Nevertheless, here and there I pointed out a few striking proofs of divergencies in the development of the two systems in question (i.e. the Tiberian system and the transliterations),—cf. f.i. our remarks on וַתְּאַזְרֵנִי (s.v. אזר), אֲכַזֵּב (s.v. כזב), אוֹן, דְּבָרֶיךָ (s.v. דבר), as well as § 5a, § 15—by merely citing the corresponding paragraph in B-L.

By this procedure I merely wish to indicate what a new approach to so many problems of Hebrew grammar we may arrive at by freeing ourselves of the traditional grammatical conception. Instead of fixing rules and noting exceptions to these rules, a practice adopted by all Hebrew grammars, we do better to realize that the cases listed as mere exceptions form also rules, and are evidence of an otherwise forgotten different pronunciation of certain grammatical formations. To this conclusion we are lead by projecting the results of our investigation upon the Tiberian vocalization. I would rather have any more detailed discussion of these problems postponed until later when the presentation of my researches in this field is advanced enough to permit the formulation of more or less definite conclusions. Only this I wish to make clear right now that instead of speaking of the Tiberian system (in the singular!) I would consider it more appropriate to differentiate between the *various ways of pronouncing Hebrew, by the combination of which the so-called Tiberian system arose.* This statement, if proven to be correct, will result, I am sure, in an essentially new explanation of very many grmmatical phenomena thus leading towards the establishment of dialectical differences in the pronunciation of Hebrew between the two kingdoms of Israel and Judah, cf. pp. 229 ff. To substantiate it I wish to bring a few instances of rather general importance: 1) In the Tiberian grammar the gutturals are treated sometimes as full and sometimes as weak consonants; cf. s.v. אסר the forms: וַיֶּאְסֹר Gen. 46.29 and וַיַּאְסֹר ib. 42.24; לְאָסֹר Ps. 105.22 and לֶאְסֹר Num. 30.3.—

s.v. חבל the forms: תַּחְבֹּל Ex. 22.25 and יַחֲבֹל Deut. 24.6.—s.v. הפך the forms: נֶהְפְּכוּ Ps. 78.57 and נֶהְפְּכוּ 1 Sam. 4.19.—s.v. חזק the forms: יֶחְזְקוּ Isa. 28.22 and יֶחֱזְקוּ 2 Sam. 10.11.—s.v. חרד the forms: יֶחֶרְדוּ Ezek. 26.18 and יֶחֶרְדוּ Hos. 11.11. — 2) The current Hebrew grammar invented the term "virtual lengthening," to explain away some of the cases, where a guttural is treated as a full consonant; cf. s.v. בער the forms: לְבַעֵר Neh. 10.35 and לְבָעֵר Isa. 44.15. — 3) We leave the question open as to whether nominal and verbal forms in pausa represent a lengthening of the context forms or the original forms; but there can be doubt about it that both, the context form and its pausal form, belong to the same respective grammatical scheme (qatl, qitl, qutl or with a, i, u in the perfect respectively, to give an instance); how can we now account for instance for the following pausal forms: s.v. בטן: Num. 5.21: בִּטְנֵךְ a qitl-form, but in pausa: Gen. 30.2: בָּטֶן a qatl-form; s.v. שבט: Prov. 13.24: שִׁבְטוֹ a qitl-form, but in pausa: Ex. 28.21: שָׁבֶט a qatl-form; s.v. שמש: Jer. 15.9: שְׁמִשָׁה a qitl-form, but in pausa: Eccl. 1.3: הַשָּׁמֶשׁ a qatl-form. Or verbal forms: Gen. 37.3: אָהַב and ib. 27.14: אָהֵב; Gen. 2.24: דָּבַק and 2 Ki. 3.3: דָּבֵק. The usual explanation that these pausal forms are built on the analogy of the other respective group of nominal or verbal forms, does not suffice at all; for, strangely enough, the three nouns cited here are vocalized with an *a* (i.e., as qatl-forms, to use the Tiberian terminology) in the Babylonian vocalization, and in the transliterations, and even their equivalent in Arabic is vocalized with an *a*. Consequently, instead of considering the Tiberian pausal forms as exceptions which require explanation, we find that the respective context-forms fall out of the regular qatl-scheme and belong to a different tradition, which served as one of the basic sources for the Tiberian vocalization. — 4) A similar development we can notice with certain forms with waw consecutivum, like: s.v. בנה the forms: Gen. 2.22: וַיִּבֶן and Josh. 19.50: וַיִּבְנֶה; s.v. נכה the forms: Jer. 52.27: וַיַּכֶּה and 2 Ki. 25.21: וַיַּךְ; s.v. אוה the forms: 2 Sam. 23.15: וַיִּתְאַוֶּה and 1 Chron. 14.17: וַיִּתְאָו; further s.v. אסף the forms: Num. 11.30: וַיֵּאָסֵף and Gen. 49.33: וַיֵּאָסֶף; s.v. בער the forms: Judg. 15.5: וַיַּבְעֶר and וַיַּבְעֵר; s.v. ישב the forms: Gen. 47.11: וַיּוֹשֵׁב and Ps. 107.36: וַיּוֹשֶׁב. — 5) To explain away the inconsistency in applying the dagesh lene to the בגדכפת, the grammarians invented the term "שוא medium," the apparent fallacy of which may be demonstrated by a few instances:

s.v. ברכה the forms: Gen. 49.26: בִּרְכֹת and ib. 28.4: בִּרְכַּת; further Jer. 17.2: כְּזִכֹּר and 2 Sam. 17.9: כִּנְפֹל; s.v. הפך the forms: Gen. 19.21: הָפְכִּי and 2 Sam. 10.3: וּלְהָפְכָה. These and many other similar observations induced me to refrain here as far as possible from referring to any parallel phenomena as might otherwise have been pointed out in the course of this study.

E.   RELATION TO THE BABYLONIAN AND PALESTINIAN SYSTEM

Entirely different is my attitude towards the non-Masoretic systems of vocalization, namely the Babylonian and the Palestinian system. I went carefully through all the material I could get hold of (cf. the list of abbreviations) and made as profuse a use of it as possible. The references to words with the Babylonian vocalization in most cases go back to manuscripts and Geniza fragments, which have not been published until now anywhere else; these texts have been made available to me by the courtesy of my late friends Professors Kahle and Marx. But although the references with the Palestinian vocalization appeared already in print in various text publications, I still venture to say that *my evaluation* of these cited forms is *entirely new,* since I abandon the prevalent standpoint, as adopted in the text publications from which I derived my references, namely not to consider these forms as units in themselves, but always to discuss merely their single vowel points in connection with and as equivalents of the corresponding Tiberian punctuation; cf. f.i. MdW II, p. 17*: "Dies Zeichen (i.e. ֵ) steht auch da, wo in tiberischer Punktation ein defektiv geschriebenes kurzes u steht. . . . Von den beiden Zeichen für e (ֵ und ֶ) entspricht im allgemeinen das erstere tiberischem Ṣere, das letztere tiberischen Segol und Šwa mobile; jedoch findet sich das erstere Zeichen häufig auch da, wo wir Šwa mobile erwarten würden. . . . ; das Zeichen entspricht auch öfters tiberischem Segol. . . . Andererseits entspricht das Zeichen ֵ gelegentlich auch tiberischem Ṣere," etc. Bar p. 19: "Ein Schwa kennt die Handschrift nicht. Stets ist ein bei uns mit שוא versehener Buchstabe mit Vokal versehen. Am häufigsten mit einem a Vokal."

By these explanations the learned editors of the texts referred to presuppose—though perhaps without being aware of it themselves—

that the Palestinian vocalization represents merely a new possibility of
expressing Tiberian Hebrew vowels. To disprove any assumption of this
kind, we wish to point out two examples: In the forms בְּמִקְּהֹ (for במלקחים,
cf. further down sub B 11), and יֹדְעִי (cf. ib. 8) we would have to explain
the first ˒ as corresponding to a שוא, and the immediately following same
vowel sign as a Ṣere or Segol respectively. The aim of the vocalization
was surely not to confuse the reader, who would thus be at a perfect loss
in his endeavors to identify the ˒ with one of the corresponding Tiberian
vowels. Similarly we would consider it utterly illogical to state that "in
the PV the שוא is replaced by a vowel, mostly by a." We are entitled to
expect an explanation as to when this שוא is replaced by an a and when
and under what phonetic conditions by another vowel; furthermore:
how do we know that a שוא was originally there; and why was a full
vowel substituted for it? Cf. our refutation of O. Pretzl on p. 123.—
Pontus Leander's *Bemerkungen zur palästinischen Überlieferung des Hebräischen*, ZAW 1936, pp. 91-99, deal with the subject from an entirely
different angle.

In dealing with these non-Masoretic texts, I on the other hand paid
no attention whatsoever to the Tiberian system, but was anxious to
explain every *grammatical phenomenon* apart from any outside consideration, startling though the results may have seemed at first to a man
who has been thoroughly trained in the Masoretic Grammar. I thus hope
to have paved the way also for a real grammatical appreciation of Hebrew
according to these two non-Masoretic vocalization systems.

A.   1) As a parallel phenomenon to the cases of preservation of the
second vowel in verbal forms, as dealt with in § 5a and elsewhere (f.i. in
§ 10bα the forms: יחרגו ιερογου, יפלו ιεφφολου, ישמרו ιεσμωρου), I should
like to mention the Babylonian vocalization, where we meet similar
forms, like: Job 6.17: יֹזֹרְבֿוּ; ib. 6.25: נִמְרְצוּ; Ps. 106.28: וַיִּצְמְֿדֹוּ; all these
instances are taken from the Ms. Ec 1; cf. also sub B 7. — 2) The formations discussed in the §§ 7a, 31a and 49a have parallels in the Babylonian system, too, in forms like: יָבְֿרְֿכֶךָ, יֶּחֱֿלֹון and others, cf. MdO, p. 165.
— 3) The preservation of the second vowel in verbal forms with personal
suffixes, as f.i. תאזרני θεζορηνι, תסובבני θσωβαβηνι, יסובבנו ισωβαβεννου
(cf. § 73 f.), can be proved in the Babylonian system as well, cf. forms
like: Prov. 29.4: יֶהֶרְֿסֶֿנָּה; ib. 1.32: תְּהֶרְֿגֵֿם; Job 29.16: אֶחְֿקְֿרֵֿהֹו; Ps. 37.33:

יֵעָזְבֶֽנּוּ; ib. 27.9: תֵּעָזְבֶּֽנּוּ; Job 21.15: נִעֶבְדֶֽנּוּ; all these examples originate in the Ms. Ec 1; cf. also MdO, p. 185, and similarly here sub B 10. — 4) To the transliteration of the imperative of the pi‘el with ε in the first syllable (§ 38α) cf. כֶּבְדוּהוּ. Ps. 22.24 in MS. Ec 1 (MTK, p. 79); זֵעֹֽוּ Jud. 19.24 in Ms. 105 JThS. — 5) To the transliteration of the imperative of the hiph‘il with ε in the first syllable (§ 36α) cf. הֵסִירוֹ 1 Sam. 7.3; הֵצִּיתֹהַ 2 Sam. 14.30; הֵכּוּ 2 Sam. 13.28; all three instances in Ms. 105 JThS. — 6) Parallel forms to § 59, cf. p. 161 s.v. שבת.

B.   In his *Masoreten des Westens* I, p. 46, Paul Kahle notes as a result of an evaluation of the Hebrew texts with the Palestinian vocalization, which he published there, three major deviations of general importance from the established rules of the Tiberian Hebrew Grammar; two of them have their parallel phenomena in the transliterations: 1) The nominal suffix of the 2. pers. sing. masc. is -*ak* (and not -*ka*), cf. § 124 subdivision 1; under subdivision 2 only two cases could be listed of an ending in -*ka*; cf. also p. 218 sub f 1. — 2) The verbal forms of the 2. pers. sing. masc. of the perfect are vocalized according to a pronunciation *qatalt* (and not *qatalta*); cf. the §§ 3a, 27a, 42, 53a and 66.—At this occasion I wish to point out some more parallel developments of general importance between these two systems, which have not been noticed until now in the respective publications of Hebrew texts with PV. — 3) To the cases dealt with in the §§ 2a and 5a, namely: the retention of the second vowel in verbal formations, cf. וּנִיבְנֵתָה Jer. 30.18 (MdWI, p. א), וִיפֹרָחוּ Hos. 14.8 (ib. p. ט); נֻקָּשׁ, abbreviated for וְנוּקְשׁוּ Isa. 8.15 (Kahle in ZAW 1901, p. 281. — 4) To the respective §§ on p. 213 f: the noun remains unchanged in the construct state, cf. שְׁבוּת Jer. 30.18 (ib., p. א), דְּבַר Isa. 44.26 (ib. p. ד), וּמְקוֹם Ps. 26.8 (ib., p. ז) and בִּמְחַשְּׁבֹת (ib., p. ג, line 2). — 5) To § 117 (cf. also p. 218 sub e), cf. forms like: בְּבוֹא (ib., p. יח, line 16), בָּטֵל and בָּשִׁיר (Bar, p. 19); לְ, abbreviated for לְמִשְׁלֹח Isa. 7.25 (Kahle in ZAW 1901, p. 280). — 6) To the cases dealt with on p. 215 sub a: retention of the original vowels in derived nominal forms, cf. וּתְמִימָה (MdWI, p. יז, line 12); גְּלוֹיִים (Edelmann, p. יא, line 23; three times!). — 7) To § 10bα (and similarly in the Babylonian system, cf. above under subdivision A1), cf. יַעֲמֹֽדוֹ Dan. 11.14 (MdWII, p. 75). — 8) To § 15a (cf. also p. 215 sub a), cf. forms like: יֵדְעֵי Dan. 11.32 (ib., p. 76), עֹמְדִים Dan. 12.5 (ib., p. 77), הַצָּֽץ (= הַמְצַפְצְפִים) Isa. 8.19

(Kahle in ZAW 1901, p. 281). — 9) To § 35: the prefix מ vocalized with *a*, cf. מָא, an abbreviation for מאחרי, Isa. 5.11 (Kahle in ZAW 1901, p. 277). — 10) To § 73 f. (and similarly in the Babylonian system, cf. above under subdivision A3), cf. נֹתתִיך Jer. 1.5 (MdWII, p. 78). — 11) To § 118 cf. forms like כֹּד, an abbreviation for כדברם, Isa. 5.17; בְּמֹקָה, an abbreviation for במלקחים, Isa. 6.6; לֹמ, an abbreviation for למר, Isa. 5.20; all three instances from Kahle, ZAW 1901. — 12) The forms listed in § 79α need not necessarily be considered as waw consectivum; cf. וּרִיב Ps. 55.10 (MdWII), p. 84), וּבאָף Ps. 55.4 (ib., p. 83), וּצֹהרֹים Ps. 55.18 (ib., p. 84). — 13) To § 23α: impv. forms with ε in the first syllable, cf. חִשׁוֹב (Edelmann, p. ח, line 1). — 14) To § 55α, δ and § 57: imperfect forms of the hiph'il with ε in the first syllable, cf. וִיּסֹב Ex. 13.18 (Edelmann, p. ד, line 6). — 15) To § 7bδ3: 3. pers. sing. masc. of the imperfect of verba primae gutturalis, with ε in the first syllable, cf. יֶעזוֹּב Isa. 55.7 (Edelmann, p. יד, line 4). — 16) To § 128: the suffix of the 2. pers. plur. masc. as εχεμ, cf. רֹצ, abbreviated for מעריצכם Isa. 8.13 (Kahle in ZAW 1901, p. 281); cf. also p. 218 f 2.

The parallels to the transliterations of *single words* in their various derivations, which can be found in Hebrew Bible texts with Babylonian or Palestinian vocalization, as differing from the Tiberian way of vocalizing these words, I have noted at the proper places in the Dictionary.

F.   FORMATION OF THE NOUN

Nouns I have treated separately according to their masculine or feminine formation; not according to their grammatical gender, but rather according to the external criterion of their endings. Thus for instance שם σημ (σεμαχ, σεμω)—the derivatives of a noun I bring in parenthesis—in § 81 is listed as a masculine, whereas שם (semoth, σεμωθαμ) in § 81a is given as a feminine *form* (not feminine noun!). This classification has a pragmatic sanction and may also be theoretically justified by the generalization of Jerome (editio Vallarsi, vol. IV, p. 10C): "Estque Hebraici characteris idioma, ut omnia, quae in syllabam finiuntur IM masculina sint, et pluralia, ut CHERUBIM et SERAPHIM. Et quae in OTH, feminina et pluralia, ut SABAOTH;" cf. similarly p. 172 f. (end of paragraph).

G.   TRANSLITERATIONS AND RABBINIC STATEMENTS

In paragraph E (p. 221 ff.) we believe to have established beyond any doubt the interrelation between the various non-Masoretic systems of pronunciation of Hebrew words. By applying the term "non-Masoretic" to these systems, we are afraid we might create the impression that they are thus discriminated against, denying them, so to say, the right of existence as compared with the authorised Masoretic system. We, therefore, wish to emphasize that the traditional terminology is wrong in both directions: The term Tiberian or Masoretic system is misleading, since it represents a combination of at least two different systems, as we have shown on pp. 220 ff.; and the classification of the non-Tiberian systems as non-Masoretic is incorrect, too; for there are quite a number of Rabbinic passages which can not be understood unless we refer to these non-Tiberian systems as the basic pronunciation of Hebrew of their days. I wish to illustrate this thesis by one example for each: the transliteration system and the Babylonian system: 1) In מדרש בראשית רבה editio Theodor (Berlin 1903 f.) p. 70 on the verse: וירא אלהים את כל אשר עשה והנה טוב מאד (Gen. 1.31) we read: בתורתו של רבי מאיר מצאו כתוב והנה טוב מאד והנה טוב מות. This statement requires such a pronunciation of the two words מאד and מות, that they could phonetically be misunderstood for each other; the Tiberian vocalization as מְאֹד and מָוֶת excludes any such chance. But in the transliteration of the Second Column of the Hexapla מאד is rendered μωδ (Ps. 46.2) and μωθ מות (Ps. 49.15). The only difference between μωδ and μωθ, namely δ-θ, does not count; cf. p. 174 sub ד, where 5 instances are brought to prove that ד at the end of the world was sometimes rendered by θ, so that even מאד could very likely have been pronounced as: μωθ; cf. A. Marx in JQR, N.S. XIII (1923), p. 358. — 2) In the Babylonian Talmud, Sanhedrin fol. 5b we read: פעם אחת הלך רבי למקום אחד וראה בני אדם שמגבלים עיסותיהם בטומאה: אמר להם: מפני מה אתם מגבלים עיסותיכם בטומאה? אמרו לו: תלמיד אחד בא לכאן והורה לנו: מי בצעים אין מכשירין: והוא מי ביצים דרש להו, ואינהו סבור מי בצעים קאמר "Once Rabbi came to a certain place and saw people kneading their dough in a state of impurity. Said he to them: Wherefore do ye knead your dough in impurity? They replied: A certain scholar came here and taught us: Water of the pond (מי בצעים) does not make fit for impurity. But he had

really taught them: the liquid of eggs (מי ביצים) and they misunderstood
him to say: water of the pond." On this passage Tossafoth remark:
תוספות ד״ה ואינהו סבור מי בצעים, תימא: דהיאך טעו בין ביצים לבצעים? וארׄת
דאינהו סבור דמי ביצים דקאמר· דהיינו מי בצים· דכתיב היגאה גמא בלי בצה· (Job 8.11):
מי ביצים וטעו בין בצים לביצים: "It is surprising that they could err between מי ביצים
and מי בצעים? Said R. Tam: They thought that by saying מי ביצים
he meant water of the pond, referring to the verse Job 8.11; they thus
confused בצים (ponds) and ביצים (eggs)." R. Tam thus deviates from the
wording of the Talmud by declaring a confusion of ביצים (eggs) and
בצעים (ponds) too far fetched; he therefore substitutes the Hebrew word
בצים for its Aramaic equivalent בצעים and finds a confusion between
ביצים (eggs) and בצים (ponds) quite possible. According to the Tiberian
system, they are vocalized בֵּיצִים (eggs) and בִּצִּים (ponds); there does,
therefore, still exist a difference in the pronunciation of these two words.
Fortunately, the verse Job 8.11 referred to by R. Tam is preserved in
the Babylonian vocalization in Ms. Ec 1 and the word in question is
vocalized here as בֹּצָּה (MTK, p. 71), which corresponds exactly to the
pronunciation of this word in the meaning: eggs. We now interpret the
Talmudical passage thus: The scholar had taught: מי ביצים meaning: the
liquid of eggs; his audience heard him very well, but misunderstood the
etymology of his decision מי ביצים as meaning: water of the pond, having
in mind the verse Job 8.11; cf. p. 117/8.

H.   TRANSLITERATIONS AND THE SEPTUAGINT

By applying the results of this study, as worked out especially on
p. 174 ff., to the Septuagint, we are in a position to differentiate
between the various sources, by the combination of which an apparently uniform Septuagint text arose. Since this criterion had entirely been overlooked until now, I wish to substantiate my assertion by pointing out a few instances: Codex A of the Septuagint is
composed of different portions, each of them belonging to different
periods; cf. f.i. the transliteration of חבר in 1 Chron. 7.31 as χαβερ and
ib. 4.18 as αβερ; the explanation may be found on p. 175 sub ח. —
עזר is rendered in 1 Chron. 7.21 as εζερ (cf. § 95) and ib. 12.9 as αζερ
(cf. § 94). — חרן is in Gen. 29.4: χαρραν and ib. 11.27: αρραν (cf. p. 175
sub ח). These examples are sufficient to prove that codex A, not only

when considered as an entity covering the entire Bible, but even on the single Biblical books, goes back to different sources. The same is true of Codex B also, as may be seen from these examples: the word מחולה (in the connection אבל מחולה) is transliterated in 1 Ki. 4.12 as μαωλα; ib. 19.16 as μαουλα and Judg. 7.22 as μεουλα. For explanation cf. p. 175 sub ו (ω-ου) and sub ח (rendered as ε). — 2 Chron. 8.18: אוֹפִירָה is rendered: εἰς Σωφειρα (read: εἰς Ωφειρα) and ib. 9.10: מֵאוֹפִיר: ἐκ Σουφειρ (read: ἐξ Ουφειρ); cf. p. 175 sub ו. It may be of interest to refer here to the similar conclusions we arrived at concerning the Hexapla of Origen (cf. p. 107) and the transliterations of Jerome (cf. p. 110 ff.). We thus realize that *one of the most significant criteria of the works of those early centuries is their mixed type.* And why should we blame those pious compilers or copyists for having overlooked apparent discrepancies, if these inner contradictions escaped the attention of the scholars until to-day, as is the case with the transliterations of the Septuagint and Origen; and as to Jerome, all we have until now is the general statement, unaccompanied by any evidence at all, which Franz X. Wutz makes in his book: *Die Transkriptionen von der Septuaginta bis zu Hieronymus* (Kohlhammer, Stuttgart 1925, p. 3): "Hieronymus ist nur mit grösster Vorsicht zu benützen, da er ein gewaltiges Sammelsurium von Formen aus allen Jahrhunderten eines Zeitraumes von 7-800 Jahren bot. Da Hieronymus trotz aller Gelehrsamkeit der historisch-kritische Blick für die Divergenz seiner Materialien fehlte, so häufte er Material auf Material ohne zu ahnen, um was es ging; ja er nahm oft Stellung gegen alte Formen, ohne zu wissen, wie sehr sie durch die alte Orthographie berechtigt waren." I do hope that the scholarly reader of this study will not find himself at a loss as Dr. Wutz did; but I am not so sure of it that it is entirely the fault of Jerome that Dr. Wutz could not find the key to an understanding of the systems underlying his transliterations. And as to Jerome's lack of a historical-critical sense—what an absurdity to expect it from an author of the beginning of the fifth century!

The mixed type as a characteristic feature we could also see, though in general outline only, in the Tiberian system; cf. p. 220 f.; the non-Masoretic systems represent it likewise, as became clear to me while going through the entire material to look out for parallel grammatical developments. In future, the *Hebrew Grammar* and the *Hebrew Dictionary* will have to take these facts into account and to broaden their basis so as to *include all the material available*, without discriminating between Masoretic forms as authoritative and non-Masoretic forms merely to frame the work up scientifically; cf. the statement made in OLZ 1929, quoted on p. 173.

E.   Judaean and Israelitish Hebrew (Cf. MH p. 135 f.)

TWO DIALECTS OF BIBLICAL HEBREW

1)   Throughout this study we laid the main emphasis upon recording grammatical facts as preserved in these non-Masoretic evidences of pronunciation, and upon arranging and classifying them according to their own laws, the basis for which had to be found through inner criteria. No serious attempt has been made to explain the phenomena; the limited material at our disposal does not seem to be encouraging for any attempt of this kind. But there is even another consideration, which has to be taken into account and which directly excludes the possibility of phonetic connections and interdependance of the variously pronounced grammatical forms.

While merely noting facts, we had to record a great many nominal and verbal forms, which belong to different formations according to the different systems of vocalization; f.i. שבט and שמש are qitl-forms in the Tiberian system, but qatl-forms in the transliteration; vice versa דרך and נפש are qatl-forms in the Tiberian system, but qitl-forms in the transliteration; the imperative to לחם is in the Tiberian system לְחַם (i.e. an imperfect with a), but λοομ in the transliteration (i.e. imperfect with o); the participle plur. of חפץ is חֲפֵצִי in the Tiberian system, but ωφση in the transliteration. These and similar observations suggest the explanation that the two systems involved can not be considered as directly connected with each other, or one to be a later phonetic development of the other, but that they most definitely reflect a twofold way of pronouncing Hebrew. Both of them may go back to a common ancestor, which we would call *Original Hebrew* (Urhebräisch); they represent two separate branches of this original, each one of them with a further phonetic development of its own.

And now the problem arises: can we account, in the historical development of Hebrew during the Biblical period, for such an assumption of two
independent pronunciations or dialects? I am inclined to answer this
question in the affirmative and to regard the kingdoms of Israel and
Judah respectively as the homelands of these dialectical differences.

2)   On p. 172/3 we saw that the practice of the transliterations
to make no differentiation between שׂ and שׁ (note especially the citations
from Jerome referred to: Quaestiones on Gen. 26.12; 41.29) agrees with
what we know as an Ephraimitic peculiarity of pronunciation; cf. Jud.
12.6. We, therefore, believe we are justified in ascribing the Tiberian
way of differentiating between שׂ and שׁ to the Judaean dialect. We hereby
do not mean to generalize, stating that the transliterations as an entirety
reflect the Israelitish pronunciation, while the Tiberian system in the
same way follows the Judaean dialect. Neither of these systems can be
regarded as a whole, since they are lacking in the first prerequisite:
consistency; cf. the paragraphs on Origen, Jerome and the Tiberian
System. My assertion, therefore, is that by collecting all available
evidences for the pronunciation of Hebrew, from Tiberian as well as from
non-Tiberian sources, and by systematically arranging them according
to the lines set up here, we may be able to arrive at conclusions concerning
the most important characteristic features of the two dialects of Hebrew
as a spoken language, namely the Israelitish and the Judaean dialect.

3)   To meet a possible argument that the mere fact that שׂ and שׁ
were or were not differentiated can not be considered a solid basis for the
assumption of dialectical differences between Israel and Judah in general,
we wish to avail ourselves of this opportunity to point out that a comparison between the Hebrew Pentateuch in its Masoretic form with
Sam. will furnish us with a great many further differences of general
importance. A few instances will suffice: To the inconsistency of the
Tiberian system as discussed on p. 221 subdivision 4, cf. the following similar differences between MT and Sam.: Gen. 31.10: MT:
וָאֵרֶא Sam. ואראה; Deut. 2.33: MT: וַנַּךְ Sam. ונכה; ib. 3.18: MT: וָאֲצַו
Sam. ואצוה. Similarly without shortening of the last syllable: Gen. 5.3:
MT: וַיּוֹלֶד Sam. ויוליד; ib. 24.28: MT: וַתַּגֵּד Sam. ותגיד; ib. 31.42: MT:
וַיּוֹכַח Sam. ויוכיח. Formulating a rule based upon these facts we will say
that according to the Samaritan usage the waw consecutivum does not

at all affect the structure of the respective verbal form. At the very same conclusion we arrived while discussing the transliterations; cf. § 78 and p. 219 subdivision 3. We are thus led to the assumption that, generally speaking, the Samaritan Pentateuch represents the Hebrew Pentateuch in the Israelitish or *Samaritan recension,* while in the Masoretic text the Judaean recension is mainly preserved.

4)   We wish to emphasize that we are far from *identifying* the MT with the Judaean, or Sam. with the Israelitish recension of the Hebrew Bible. Neither of them can be regarded now as representing its prototype in its original dialectical purity. The textual changes which they underwent in the various stages of their redaction may have been instrumental, too, in eliminating here and there characteristic dialectic idioms. We can not even tell, when this process was finished; apparently at a somewhat late century; for we can prove that at least in one important passage Sam. offered as late as in the days of Jerome an entirely different reading from what we now have in all the manuscripts of this text.

5a)   I should like to demonstrate the correctness of this assertion by referring to a statement made by Jerome in his *Quaestiones Hebraicae in libro Geneseos* (editio Lagarde, Leipzig 1868). To Gen. 5.25-27 Jerome remarks: *"Et uixit Mathusalam annis CLXVII et genuit Lamech. et uixit Mathusala, postquam genuit Lamech, annos DCCCII et genuit filios et filias. et fuerunt omnes dies Mathusalae, quos uixit, anni DCCCCLXVIIII et mortuus est.* famosa quaestio et disputatione omnium ecclesiarum uentilata quod iuxta diligentem subputationem XIIII annos post diluuium Mathusala uixisse referatur. etenim cum esset Mathusala annorum CLXVII, genuit Lamech. rursum Lamech, cum esset annorum CLXXXVIII, genuit Noe. et fiunt usque ad diem natiuitatis Noe anni uitae Mathusalae CCCLV. sexcentesimo autem anno uitae Noe diluuium factum est. ac per hoc habita subputatione per partes DCCCCLV anno Mathusalae diluuium fuisse conuincitur. cum autem supra DCCCCLXVIIII annis uixisse sit dictus, nulli dubium est XIIII eum annos uixisse post diluuium. et quo modo uerum est quod octo tantum animae in arca saluae factae sunt? restat ergo ut quomodo in plerisque, ita et in hoc sit error in numero. siquidem et in hebraeis et Samaritanorum libris ita scriptum repperi *et uixit Mathusala CLXXXVII annis et genuit Lamech. et uixit Mathusala, postquam genuit Lamech DCCLXXXII annos, et genuit filios et filias. et fuerunt omnes dies Mathusalae anni DCCCCLXVIIII et mortuus est. et uixit Lamech CLXXXII annos et genuit Noe.* a die ergo natiuitatis Mathusalae usque ad diem natiuitatis Noe sunt anni CCCLXIX: his adde DC annos Noe, quia in sexcentesimo uitae eius anno diluuium factum est: atque ita fit, ut DCCCCLXIX anno uitae suae Mathusala mortuus sit, eo anno quo coepit esse diluuium.''

In short: according to Jerome, the Septuagint records that Methuselah was 167 years old, when he begat Lamech, and that he lived afterwards 802 years, so that all his days were 969 years. Now Lamech was 188 years of age, when he begat Noah. Methuselah, therefore, was 355 years old, when Noah was born. When Noah was 600 years old, the flood came. How old was then Methuselah? 355+600=955 years. But since Methuselah lived 969 years, it would mean, that he survived the flood for 14 years, in contradiction to the Biblical narrative, which does not include him amongst the persons saved in Noah's ark. The solution of this problem Jerome finds in the data given in the Hebrew and in the Samaritan Bible. Both texts are referred to as stating that Methuselah was 187 years old when he begat Lamech, while Lamech was 182 years of age when he begat Noah. Methuselah, therefore, was 369 years old at Noah's birth. Adding to it 600 years—for Noah was 600 years old when the flood came —we find, that the flood began, when Methuselah was 969 years of age; this means, that Methuselah died, when the flood came.

b)   Let us now test Jerome's assertions: The Septuagint reads: Verse 25: καὶ ἔζησεν Μαθουσαλα ἑκατὸν καὶ ὀγδοήκοντα ἑπτὰ ἔτη, καὶ ἐγέννησεν τὸν Λαμεχ. Methuselah lived 187 years, and he begat Lamech. This reading agrees exactly with the Masoretic Hebrew text in the most essential point, which gave rise to Jerome's question. The original reading of the Septuagint, as presupposed by Jerome, is still to be found in a quotation of a Church Father in Field's *Origenis Hexaplorum quae supersunt* (Oxford 1875) and in some Septuagint Mss. of the cursive type, as quoted in the Cambridge edition of the Septuagint. This is a further instance for the importance of this group of Septuagint Mss.; cf. my *Septuagintaprobleme* (Stuttgart 1929, p. 56). As to the Samaritan Pentateuch, it offers in verse 25 and verse 28, where the ages of Methuselah and Lamech are recorded at the time of birth of Lamech and Noah respectively, readings which have nothing in common with the entire numerical system of the Masoretic Hebrew text.

c) We have seen, that in the passage in question Jerome had in the Septuagint and in the Samaritan Pentateuch readings before him, which differ materially from those readings, which we find there now. It is only logical to assume, that just as these particular verses have undergone such important changes in these Non-Masoretic Bible texts, in the same way many other passages may have shared this fate, although that for the time being we are lacking evidence from old sources such as Jerome to prove it. The present agreement in the reading of a certain Biblical passage between the Masoretic Text and any of the Non-Masoretic texts is, therefore, no proof whatsoever, that this passage always read in this way. On the contrary, it may very often be assumed, that this agreement is only the result of the harmonizing efforts of later scribes.

d) Keeping this in mind, we realize to what an extent the original text of Sam. may have been changed and modelled; a glimpse into the critical apparatus of Kennicott's *Vetus Testamentum Hebraicum cum variis lectionibus* (Oxford 1776-80) will convince us that the MT shared the same fate. And still I venture to say that by carefully comparing these two textual forms of the Hebrew Pentateuch we may arrive at definite conclusions as to the characteristic features of the two Hebrew dialects which they mainly represent. I should like to demonstrate this on a few examples; for the practical benefit of the reader I vocalize some of the Samaritan readings, too, according to the Tiberian system: 1) Gen. 8.3: MT: וָשׁוֹב ···הָלוֹךְ, Sam. וישבו הָלֹכְוּ וְשָׁבוּ; ib., 5: וְחָסוֹר הָלוֹךְ, הָיוּ ··· Sam.: הָלְכוּ וְחָסְרוּ; ib., 7: יָצוֹא וָשׁוֹב···ויצא, Sam. וְשָׁב יָצָא; ib. 12.9: הָלַךְ וְנָסַע. In MT a verbum finitum is continued וַיִּסַּע ··· הָלוֹךְ וְנָסוֹעַ, Sam.: by an infinitivus absolutus, while in the Samaritan Pentateuch it is followed by a verb in the very same tempus. — 2) Gen. 3.13: MT: עָשִׂית, Sam.: עשיתי; ib. 12.11: אַתְּ, Sam.: אתי; ib. 16.8: בָּאת, Sam. באתי; ib. 16.11: וְקָרָאת···וְיָלַדְתְּ, Sam.: וקראתי···וילדתי; ib. 18.15: צָחַקְתְּ, Sam.: צחקתי. The suffix of the 2. pers. fem. of the perfect is in MT: תְּ, but תי according to the Sam. — 3) Gen. 12.5: MT: אַרְצָה, Sam.: ארץ; ib. 24.16: הָעַיְנָה, Sam.: העין; ib. 28.2: בֵּיתָה, Sam.: בית; Deut. 4.19: הַשָּׁמַיְמָה, Sam.: השמים. The MT has a locative with the ending in הָ,

while in the Sam. the absolute form is used in this meaning. — 4) Gen. 6.17: MT: לְשַׁחֵת, Sam.: להשחית; cf. 9.11, 15; ib. 19.13: MT: לְשַׁחֲתָהּ, Sam.: להשחיתה; ib. 19.29: MT: בְּשַׁחֵת, Sam. בהשחית; ib. 7.3: MT: לְחַיּוֹת, Sam.: להחיות; Deut. 6.19: לַהֲדֹף, Sam.: להדיף; ib. 9.4: בַּהֲדֹף, Sam.: בהדיף. The Sam. shows a preference for the respective hiph'il forms of the verb.

In the following chapter we present a detailed evaluation of the Sam. from this point of view, and this approach will result — we are sure— in a new appreciation of the philology of the Bible in its various aspects.

Just a few instances to indicate what we have in mind: On p. 173 we could show the influence of the Israelitish dialect upon the language of Jeremiah; in addition to the proof of the pronunciation of שׁ and שׂ, which we discussed there, cf. forms like: לִמַּדְתִּי Jer. 2.33; קְרָאתִי ib. 3.4; דִּבַּרְתִּי ib. 3.5, which belong to the group of verbal formations listed above under subdivision 2 as a characteristic of Sam. The same holds true of verbal forms with waw consecutivum like וָאַשְׁקֶה Jer. 25.17; וַיַּכֶּה ib. 20.2; cf. above sub 3, near the beginning of the paragraph.

II. GRAMMATICAL PHENOMENA IN TWOFOLD FORMATION

PREFATORY REMARKS: THE SOURCES

I derive the material from three sources, each of them representing *one and the same* historic narrative, legal text or prophetic vision in two recensions: 1) the Hebrew Pentateuch as represented by the Masoretic Text and the Samaritan Bible; 2) Parallel passages in the Hebrew Bible, mainly Sam.-Kings as compared with Chronicles; and 3) textual variants recorded by the Masora as Ketib-Qere, Ma'arbae-Madinhae, Sebirin. Thus, the very nature of my source material marks this research as a comparative study: each example consists of two readings of *the same* passage, demonstrating the two possibilities of morphology (§§ 1-44), syntax (§§ 45-81) or vocabulary (§§ 82-88). It is, therefore, essential to emphasize right at the outset that in all instances the two quotations forming one example are taken from the *very same text*, which has been handed down to us in two recensions, the variants of which are grouped and classified herein.

A. The Verb

§ 1. 2. pers. masc. sing. perf. ending in תה or ת.¹

1) The personal pronoun (B-L § 28 l).

Num. 11.15	MT	אַתְּ (עֹשֶׂה)
	S	אתה
Deut. 5.24	MT	וְאַתְּ (תדבר)
	S	ואתה
Job 1.10	K	את
	Q	אַתָּה ²
1 Sam. 24.19	K	ואת
	Q	וְאַתָּה ³

2) The verb (Bergstr. 2, § 4a).

a) Ḳal.

Gen. 21.23	MT	גַּרְתָּה
	S	גרת
2 Sam. 7.27		גָּלִיתָה
1 Chron. 17.25		גָּלִיתָ
2 Sam. 10.11		וְהָיִיתָה
1 Chron. 19.12		וְהָיִיתָ
Josh. 13.1	Ma	זָקַנְתָּה
	Md	זקנת
Jer. 38.17	K	וְהָיִיתָה
	Q	וחיית
Deut. 23.14	MT	וְחָפַרְתָּה
	S	וחפרת
Deut. 17.14	MT	וְיָשַׁבְתָּה
	S	וישבת

Ex. 12.44	MT	וּמַלְתָּה
	S	ומלת
2 Ki. 14.10		וְנָפַלְתָּה
2 Chron. 25.19		וְנָפַלְתָּ
Num. 14.19	MT	נָשָׂאתָה
	S	נשאת
2 Chron. 6.30		וְנָתַתָּה
1 Ki. 8.39		וְנָתַתָּ
Deut. 25.12	MT	וְקַצֹּתָה
	S	וקצת
Num. 27.13	MT	וְרָאִיתָה
	S	וראית
Ps. 90.8	Q	שַׁתָּה
	K	שת

b) Pi'el.

| Num. 27.19 | MT | וְצִוִּיתָה |
| | S | וצוית |

c) Niph'al.

| Gen. 31.30 | MT | נִכְסַפְתָּה |
| | S | נכספת |

d) Hiph'il.⁴

Ex. 18.20	MT	וְהִזְהַרְתָּה
	S	והזהרת
Num. 14.15	MT	וְהֵמַתָּה
	S	והמת

---

¹ Cf. p. 224B, subdivision 2; also Paul Kahle in ZAW 1921, p. 234: "Nur wo in diesen Formen (scil. 2. pers. sing. masc. perf.) ausdrücklich ein ה am Ende steht, wird das a ge-schrieben und also auch gelesen." Cf. also here § 41α.

² Cf. similarly Eccl. 7.22.
³ Cf. also Jer. 18.23; Ps. 6.4.
⁴ Cf. Mic. 4.13: וְהַדִקוֹת; Venice 1515 marg.: וַהֲדִקוֹת.

Ex. 19.23	MT	הָעֵדֹתָה	Ex. 5.22	MT	הֲרֵעֹתָה
	S	העדת		S	הרעת
Isa. 37.23		הֲרִימֹותָה			
2 Ki. 19.22		הֲרִימֹותָ			

§ 2.   2. pers. fem. sing. perf. ending in ת or תי (B-L § 42k, l).[1] (Cf. MH § 181).

1) The personal pronoun (B-L § 28m; Bergstr. 2, § 4a).

Gen. 12.11	MT	אַתְּ
	S	אתי [2]
1 Ki. 14.2	Q	אַתְּ
	K	אתי [3]

Gen. 18.15	MT	צָחַקְתְּ
	S	צחקתי
Gen. 16.11	MT	וְקָרָאת
	S	וקראתי [6]
Ruth 3.4	Q	וְשָׁכַבְתְּ
	K	ושכבתי
Jer. 4.19	Q	שָׁמַעַתְּ
	K	שמעתי
Gen. 30.15	MT	וְלָקַחַת [7]
	S	ולקחתי

2) The verb.

A) Ḳal.

a) Regular verbs.

Isa. 47.10	Ma	אָמַרְתְּ
	Md	אמרתי [4]
Ezek. 16.13	Q	אָכָלְתְּ
	K	אכלתי
Jer. 31.21	Q	הָלָכְתְּ
	K	הלכתי [5]
Ezek. 16.22, 43	Q	זָכָרְתְּ
	K	זכרתי
Ezek. 16.20	Q	יָלָדְתְּ
	K	ילדתי
Ruth 3.3	Q	וְיָרַדְתְּ
	K	וירדתי

b) Weak verbs.

α) Tertiae ה.

Ezek. 16.31	Q	הָיִית
	K	הייתי
Gen. 3.13	MT	עָשִׂית
	S	עשיתי [8]
Num. 5.19, 20	MT	שָׂטִית
	S	שטיתי

β) Mediae ו or י.

Gen. 16.8	MT	בָאת
	S	באתי

---

[1] Cf. Jud. 5.7: שַׁקַּמְתִּי, mistaken for 1. pers. (B-L § 56u″ s.v. קוּם). Cf. also שָׁבַרְתִּי and נִתַּקְתִּי in Jer. 2.20, followed by 2. pers. וַתֹּאמְרִי. See also p. 233, subdivision d, sub 2.

[2] Cf. also ib. v. 13; 24.23; 47.60 etc.

[3] Cf. similarly 2 Ki. 4.16, 23 etc.

[4] Cf. similarly Isa. 57.10.

[5] Cf. similarly Ezek. 16.47.

[6] Cf. similarly Q-K on Jer. 3.4.

[7] This form is a perf. = ולקחת, and not an inf.; cf. Ezek. 16.4: הָמְלַחַת, Venice 1515 marg.: הָמְלַחְתְּ; see also our note 4, on page 265.

[8] Cf. Q-K on Ezek. 16.31.

Ruth 3.3	Q	וְשָׂמְתְּ
	K	ושמתי

γ) נתן.

Ezek. 16.18, 36	Q	נָתַתְּ
	K	נתתי

B) Pi'el.

Jer. 3.5	Q	דִּבַּרְתְּ
	K	דברתי
Jer. 2.33	Q	לִמַּדְתְּ
	K	למדתי [1]

C) Niph'al.

Jer. 22.23	Q	נֶחַנְתְּ
	K	נחנתי
Num. 5.20	MT	נִטְמֵאת
	S	נטמאתי

D) Hiph'il.

Jer. 46.11	Q	הִרְבֵּית
	K	הרביתי

E) Hithpa'el.

Num. 22.29	MT	הִתְעַלַּלְתְּ
	S	התעללתי
I Ki. 14.2	Q	וְהִשְׁתַּנִּית
	K	והשתניתי

3) Participle fem.

Hos. 10.11	Q	אהבת
	K	אֹהַבְתִּי
2 Ki. 4.23	Q	הֹלֶכֶת
	K	הלכתי
Gen. 16.11	MT	וְיֹלַדְתְּ
	S	וילדתי
Jer. 10.17	Q	יוֹשֶׁבֶת
	K	יושבתי [2]
Jer. 22.23	Q	יֹשַׁבְתְּ
	K	ישבתי
Jer. 51.13	Q	שֹׁכַנְתְּ
	K	שכנתי
Jer. 22.23	Q	מְקֻנֶּנְתְּ
	K	מקננתי

§ 3.   3. pers. fem. plur. perf. ending in ו or ה [3] (Bergstr. 2, § 4b).

a) Kal.

Num. 34.5	MT	וְהָיוּ
	S	והיה [4]
Gen. 48.10	MT	כָּבְדוּ
	S	כבדה
I Sam. 4.15	Q	קָמוּ
	K	קמה
Deut. 21.7	Q	שָׁפְכוּ
	K	שפכה

b) Niph'al.

Jer. 22.6	Q	נוֹשֵׁבוּ
	K	נושבה
Jer. 2.15	Q	נִצְּתוּ
	K	נצתה
Gen. 7.11	MT	נִפְתָּחוּ
	S	נפתחה
I Ki. 22.49	Q	נִשְׁבְּרוּ
	K	נשברה

[1] Cf. also 13.21.
[2] Cf. similarly Lam. 4.21; Ezek. 27.3.
[3] Indicating u (cf. p. 565 § 3c) and a (cf. p. 563 § 1b), respectively.
[4] Cf. Q-K on Josh. 8.12.

| Jer. 48.41 | Q | נתפשו |
| | K | נתְפָּשָׂה |

c) Reduplicated stem.

| Job 16.16 | Q | חֳמַרְמְרוּ |
| | K | חמרמרה |

§ 4.   3. pers. fem. plur. imperf.

a)   Ending in ן or נה (Bergstr. 2, § 5a).

α)   Ḳal. [1]

Ex. 2.19	MT	וַתֹּאמַרְן,
	S	ותאמרנה
Gen. 41.24	MT	וַתִּבְלַעְןָ,
	S	ותבלענה
Ex. 27.2	MT	תִּהְיֶיןָ,
	S	תהיינה
Gen. 19.36	MT	וַתַּהֲרֶיןָ,
	S	ותהרנה
Gen. 30.39	MT	וַתֵּלַדְןָ,
	S	ותלדנה
Ex. 15.20	MT	וַתֵּצֶאןָ,
	S	ותצאנה
Ex. 1.17	MT	וַתִּירֶאןָ,
	S	ותיראנה
Gen. 27.1	MT	וַתִּכְהֶיןָ,
	S	ותכהינה
Deut. 31.21	MT	תִמְצֶאןָ,
	S	תמצאנה
Gen. 33.6	MT	וַתִּגַּשְׁן,
	S	ותגשנה

| Num. 25.2 | MT | וַתִּקְרֶאןָ, |
| | S | ותקראנה |

similarly:

| Ruth 1.12 | K | לכן |
| | Q | לֵכְנָה |

β)   Derived stems.

Ex. 1.17	MT	וַתְּחַיֶּיןָ,
	S	ותחינה
Gen. 33.6	MT	וַתִּשְׁתַּחֲוֶיןָ,
	S	ותשתחוינה

b)   Ending in ן or הן. [2]

Gen. 30.38	MT	תָּבֹאןָ,
	S	תבאהן
Gen. 19.33	MT	וַתַּשְׁקֶיןָ,
	S	ותשקיהן

c)   Ending in נה or הן. [3]

Gen. 41.21	MT	וַתָּבֹאנָה
	S	ותבאהן
Deut. 1.44	MT	תַּעֲשֶׂינָה
	S	תעשיהן

---

[1] Cf.
Gen. 41.7:   ותבלענה השבלים הדקות
Gen. 41.24:   .ותבלען השבלים הדקות
[2] Cf. similar nominal forms: Ex. 35.
26: MT לבן — S לבהן; Gen. 30.38:
MT בבאן — S בבאהן.

[3] Cf. similar nominal forms: Ex. 35.
26: MT אתהן — S אתהן; 21.29: MT
קרבנה — S לבדנה; 41.21: MT לבדהן —
S קרבהן (B-L § 29p, p').

§ 5.   Jussive or shortened forms (B-L § 26b; Bergstr. § 2 l).

1) With preservation of the ׳ of
the hiph'il.

a) Imperfect.

Num. 6.25	MT	יָאֵר
	S	יאיר
Eccl. 10.20	Q	יגד
	K	יַגֵּיד
Ps. 21.2	Q	יָגֵל
	K	יגיל
Num. 30.13, 16	MT	יָפֵר
	S	יפיר
Gen. 24.8	MT	תָּשֵׁב
	S	תשיב
Gen. 19.9	MT	נָרַע
	S	נריע

b) Perfect.

Ezek. 17.16	Q	הֵפֵר
	K	הפיר

c) Infinitive.

α) Regular verbs.

Deut. 7.2	MT	הַחֲרֵם
	S	החרים [1]
Deut. 32.8	MT	בְּהַנְחֵל
	S	בהנחיל
Deut. 15.8	MT	וְהַעֲבֵט
	S	והעביט
Lev. 9.2	MT	וְהַקְרֵב
	S	והקריב

Am. 9.8	Q	השמד
	K	הַשְׁמֵיד

β) Weak verbs.

Jer. 36.16	Q	הגד
	K	הַגֵּיד
Jer. 44.17	Q	וְהַסֵּךְ
	K	והסיך
Deut. 22.4	MT	הָקֵם
	S	הקים [2]

d) Imperative.

Ex. 16.33	MT	וְהַנַּח
	S	והניח
2 Ki. 8.6	Q	השב
	K	הָשֵׁיב
Gen. 19.12	MT	הוֹצֵא
	S	הוציא [3]
Ex. 33.5	MT	הוֹרֵד
	S	הוריד

2) With preservation of the ה
of verbs tertiae ה. [4] (Cf. MH
§ 184).

a) 3. pers. masc. sing. imperf.

Gen. 30.34	MT	יְהִי
	S	יהיה [5]
Ex. 32.11	S	יחר [6]
	MT	יֶחֱרֶה
Gen. 44.33	MT	יַעַל
	S	יעלה

---

¹ Cf. similarly ib. 13.16; 20.17.
² Cf. also Q-K on Jer. 44.25.
³ Cf. similarly Lev. 24.14.
⁴ Cf. § 10β.

⁵ Cf. Ezek. 45.10: יְהִי, Venice 1515
marg.: יְהְיֶה.
⁶ Cf. also Deut. 6.15.

Ruth 1.8	Q	יַעַשׂ	Deut. 9.14	MT	הֶרֶף
	K	יעשה		S	הרפה
Gen. 41.33	MT	יֵרֶא			
	S	יראה [1]			

3) Jussive forms with אל.

a) with preservation of the י of the hiph'il.

Gen. 1.22	MT	יֶרֶב	Ex. 23.1	MT	תָּשֵׁת
	S	ירבה		S	תשית

α) Derived stems.

Deut. 28.8	MT	יְצַו	Deut. 9.26	MT	תַּשְׁחֵת
	S	יצוה		S	תשחית
Lev. 9.6	MT	וְיֵרָא	Gen. 49.4	MT	תּוֹתַר
	S	ויראה		S	תותיר

b) 3. pers. fem. sing. imperf.

			Ex. 16.19	MT	יוֹתַר
				S	יותיר
Gen. 26.28	MT	תְּהִי			
	S	תהיה			

b) with preservation of the ה of verbs tertiae ה.

c) 1. pers. plur. imperf.

			Gen. 37.27	MT	תְּהִי
Gen. 38.23	S	נהי		S	תהיה
	MT	נִהְיֶה [2]	Jer. 40.16	K	תעש
Isa. 41.23	K	ונרא		Q	תַּעֲשֶׂה [3]
	Q	וְנִרְאֶה	Lev. 10.9	MT	תֵּשְׁתְּ

d) Imperative.

				S	תשתה
Ps. 51.4	Q	הֶרֶב	Ex. 34.3	MT	יֵרָא
	K	הרבה		S	יראה

§ 6. Imperfect with consecutive waw and preservation of the final vowel.

1) Hiph'il with preservation of the י (Bergstr. 2, § 5d).

			Lev. 9.20	MT	וַיַּקְטֵר
				S	ויקטיר
			Num. 16.10	MT	וַיַּקְרֵב

a) 3. pers. masc. sing.[4]

				S	ויקריב
Gen. 2.9	MT	וַיַּצְמַח	Gen. 50.25	MT	וַיַּשְׁבַּע
	S	ויצמיח		S	וישביע

---

[1] Cf. similarly K-Q on Jer. 17.8.
[2] Cf. also Gen. 47.19.
[3] Cf. similarly MT-S on Gen. 22.12.
[4] Cf. p. 219, subdivision 3.

α) weak verbs.

Gen. 31.42	MT	וַיּוֹכַח
	S	וייכיח
Gen. 6.10	MT	וַיּוֹלֶד
	S	וייליד
Ex. 14.21	MT	וַיּוֹלֶךְ
	S	וייליך
Ex. 14.30	MT	וַיּוֹשַׁע
	S	ויושיע
Gen. 8.21	MT	וַיָּרַח
	S	ויריח

b) 3. pers. fem. sing.

Gen. 21.15	MT	וַתַּשְׁלֵךְ
	S	ותשליך
Gen. 24.28	MT	וַתַּגַּד
	S	ותגיד
Lev. 18.25	MT	וַתָּקֵא
	S	ותקיא

c) 1. pers. plur.

Num. 31.50	MT	וַנַּקְרֵב
	S	ונקריב
Gen. 43.7	MT	וַנַּגֶּד
	S	ונגיד
Gen. 43.21	MT	וַנָּשֶׁב
	S	ונשיב

2) Mediae ו Ḳal with preservation of the ו.

Judg. 19.21	Q	וַיָּבָל
	K	ויבול
Gen. 25.17	MT	וַיָּמָת
	S	וימות

Num. 17.15	MT	וַיָּשָׁב
	S	וישוב [1]
2 Sam. 13.8	Q	וַתָּלָשׁ
	K	ותלוש [2]

3) Tertiae ה with preservation of the ה.[3] (Cf. MH §§ 184 and 207)

A) Ḳal.

a) 3. pers. masc. sing.

Num. 3.43	MT	וַיְהִי
	S	ויהיה
Job 42.16	K	וירא
	Q	וַיִּרְאֶה

b) 3. pers. fem. sing. = 2. pers. masc. sing.

Lev. 15.24	MT	וַתְּהִי
	S	ותהיה
2 Chron. 34.27		וַתִּבֵּךְ
2 Ki. 22.19		וַתִּבְכֶּה
2 Chron. 18.34		וַתַּעַל
1 Ki. 22.35		וַתַּעֲלֶה
Jer. 3.7	Q	וַתֵּרֶא
	K	ותראה

c) 1. pers. sing.

Ps. 18.24		וָאֱהִי
2 Sam. 22.24		וָאֶהְיֶה
Deut. 10.3	MT	וָאַעַשׂ ··· וָאַעַל
	S	ואעשה ··· ואעלה
Gen. 41.22	MT	וָאֵרֶא
	S	ואראה [4]
Gen. 24.46	MT	וָאֵשְׁתְּ
	S	ואשתה

---

[1] Cf. Q-K on Ezek. 18.28.
[2] Cf. Ruth 1.6: Venice 1515: ותקום, marg.: ותקם.

[3] Cf. § 10β.
[4] Cf. Q-K on Josh. 7.21.

d) I. pers. plur.

Deut. 3.1   MT   וַנֵּפֶן וַנַּעַל
               S   ונפנה ונעלה

B) Hiph'il.

e) 3. pers. masc. sing.

2 Chron. 18.23   וַיַּךְ
I Ki. 22.24   וַיַּכֶּה [1]

f) 3. pers. fem. sing.

Gen. 35.16   MT   וַתֵּקֶשׁ
               S   ותקשה

Ezek. 23.19   K   ותרב
               Q   וַתַּרְבֶּה

g) I. pers. sing.

Ex. 9.15   MT   וָאַךְ
               S   ואכה

Num. 23.4   MT   וָאַעַל
               S   ואעלה

Josh. 24.3   K   וארב
               Q   וָאַרְבֶּה

h) I. pers. plur.

Deut. 2.33   MT   וַנַּךְ
               S   ונכה

C) Niph'al.

i) 3. pers. masc. sing.

Lev. 9.23   MT   וַיֵּרָא
               S   ויראה

j) I. pers. sing.

Ex. 6.3   MT   וָאֵרָא
               S   וארא

D) Pi'el.

k) 3. pers. masc. sing.

Ex. 1.22   MT   וַיְצַו
               S   ויצוה

l) I. pers. sing.

Deut. 3.18   MT   וָאֲצַו
               S   ואצוה

E) Hithpa'el.

m) 3. pers. masc. sing.

I Chron. 11.17   וַיִּתְאָו
2 Sam. 23.15   וַיִּתְאַוֶּה

§ 7.   The i-imperfect ḳal (Bergstr. 2, § 14h).[2]

a) Imperf. with second vowel i.

Ex. 35.3   MT   תְּבַעֲרוּ   Ex. 34.19   MT   תִּזְכָּר
               S   תבעירו   S   תזכיר

Num. 35.20   MT   יֶהְדְּפֶנּוּ   Deut. 29.22   MT   תִּזְרַע
               S   יהדיפנו   S   תזריע

Ps. 77.12   Q   אֶזְכּוֹר   Ex. 21.35   MT   יֶחֱצוּן
               K   אזכיר   S   יחיצון

---

[1] Cf. similarly 2 Chron. 18.33 — I Ki. 22.34; 2 Chron. 21.9 — 2 Ki. 8.21.

[2] Cf. H. Yalon in לשוננו, II (Tel-Aviv תר"ץ), p. 113 f.; cf. also here § 20.

Deut. 22.10	MT	תַּחֲרֹשׁ		Gen. 41.56	MT	וַיִּשְׁבֹּר
	S	תחריש			S	וישביר
Jer. 34.11	Q	וַיִּכְבְּשׁוּם		Deut. 2.6	MT	תִּשְׁבְּרוּ
	K	ויכבישום			S	תשבירו
Deut. 2.6	MT	תִּכְרוּ		Lev. 23.32	MT	תִּשְׁבְּתוּ
	S	תכירו			S	תשביתו
Deut. 20.19	MT	תִּכְרֹת				
	S	תכרית				

b) Infinitive with second vowel i.

Gen. 4.14	MT	אֶסָּתֵר	
	S	אסתיר [1]	

α) Inf. absol.

Lev. 25.46	MT	תַּעֲבֹדוּ		Isa. 22.18	Q	צָנוֹף
	S	תעבידו			K	צניף
Num. 14.41	MT	תִּצְלָח [2]				
	S	תצליח		β)	Inf. constr.	
Ps. 56.7	Q	יִצְפּוֹנוּ		Deut. 9.4	MT	בַּהֲדֹף
	K	יצפינו [3]			S	בהדיף
Deut. 22.9	MT	תִּקְדַּשׁ		Deut. 6.19	MT	לַהֲדֹף
	S	תקדיש			S	להדיף
Job 24.6	Q	יִקְצוֹרוּ		2 Sam. 18.3	Q	לַעֲזוֹר
	K	יקצירו			K	לעזיר

§ 8.   Verbs primae ו or י.

a) Kal.[5]

1 Sam. 13.8	Q	וַיּוֹחֶל [6]		Ezek. 16.13	K	ותופי
	K	וייחל [7]			Q	וַתִּיפִי
2 Sam. 20.5	Q	וַיּוֹחֶר		Jer. 17.4	Q	תּוּקַד [8]
	K	וייחר			K	תיקד [9]

---

[1] Cf. Ps. 89.47: MT תִּסָּתֵר, Origen: Θεσθερ; cf. p. 151, s.v. סתר.

[2] The a-imperf. has no consistent laws; cf. Jer. 5.7: Q אֶסְלַח, K אסלוח; 1 Ki. 22.30: לְבֹשׁ, Venice 1515 marg.: לביש; see also p. 124 ff., s.v. חלם —Ps. 35.1: MT לָחַם —O: לְחֹם; further: Ps. 10.2: MT יִדְלַק. — Var K ידלוק.

[3] Cf. in § 16b the instance MT-S on Ex. 2.2.   [4] Cf. § 21.

[5] The context excludes the explana- tion of these forms as hoph'al.

[6] Cf. the derivative תּוֹחֶלֶת.

[7] Cf. יָחִיל.

[8] Cf. the derivative מוֹקֵד.

[9] Cf. יָקֹד and יָקוּד.

Num. 21.32	Q	וַיּוֹרֶשׁ [1]	Gen. 8.17	K	הוצא [4]
	K	ויירש [2]		Q	הַיְצֵא [5]
Gen. 24.33	Q	וַיּוּשַׂם	Ps. 5.9	K	הושר
	K	ויישם [3]		Q	הַיְשַׁר

b) Derived stems.

| Isa. 45.2 | K | אושר |
| | Q | אֲיַשֵּׁר |

§ 9.   Verbs mediae ו or י.[6]

a) Imperf. ḳal.

Deut. 31.7	MT	תָּבוֹא [7]	Prov. 17.13	Q	תָּמוּשׁ
	S	תביא [8]		K	תמיש
Prov. 23.24	K	יגול	Num. 32.7	K	תנואון
	Q	יָגִיל		Q	תְנִיאוּן
Ezek. 30.16	Q	תָּחוּל	Ps. 72.17	Q	יָנוֹן
	K	תחיל		K	ינין
Ex. 16.2	Q	וַיִּלוֹנוּ·	Judg. 7.21	Q	וַיָּנֻסוּ
	K	וילינו		K	ויניסו
Num. 16.11	K	תלונו	2 Sam. 15.20	K	אנוּעֵךְ
	Q	תַּלִּינוּ		Q	אֲנִיעֶךָ
Num. 14.36	K	וילונו	Ps. 59.16	K	יְנוּעוּן
	Q	וַיַּלִּינוּ		Q	יְנִיעוּן
Ezek. 45.3	Q	תָּמוֹד	Lam. 2.13	K	אעודך [9]
	K	תמיד		Q	אֲעִידֵךְ [10]
Ps. 140.11	Q	יָמוֹטוּ	Prov. 23.5	K	התעוף
	K	ימיטו		Q	הֲתָעִיף
Ezek. 48.14	Q	ימור	Job 41.2	Q	יְעוּרֶנּוּ
	K	יָמֵר		K	יעירנו
Ex. 13.22;	S	ימוש	Prov. 3.30	K	תרוב
33.11	MT	יָמִישׁ		Q	תָּרִיב

[1] Cf. מוֹרֶשֶׁת.
[2] Cf. יְרֵשָׁה.
[3] On the interchange of the weak roots ישׁם—שׂים, cf. § 14.
[4] Cf. מוֹצָא.   [5] Cf. יְצִיא.

[6] Cf. § 22.
[7] Cf. the derivative מָבוֹא.
[8] Cf. בָּאָה.
[9] Cf. the derivative תְּעוּדָה.
[10] Cf. עֵדָה.

Ps. 89.18	Q	תָּרוּם ¹		Deut. 17.15	MT	שׂום
	K	תרים ²			S	שִׂים ⁹
Ps. 66.7	Q	יְרוּמוּ		Ps. 71.12	Q	חוּשָׁה
	K	יְרימו			K	חישה
Jer. 50.44	K	ארוצם				
	Q	אֲרִיצֵם				

c) Inf. constr.

Joel 4.1	K	אשוב ³		Hos. 10.11	Q	לָדוּשׁ ¹⁰
	Q	אָשִׁיב ⁴			K	לדיש ¹¹
Ps. 54.7	K	ישוב		Gen. 24.25	MT	לָלוּן
	Q	יָשִׁיב ⁵			S	ללין
2 Sam. 15.8	Q	יָשׁוּב		Judg. 21.22	K	לרוב
	K	ישיב ⁶			Q	לָרִיב
Ezek. 16.55	Q	תְּשׁוּבֶנָה		Ps. 119.148	K	לשוח
	K	תשיבנה			Q	לָשִׂיחַ
Lam. 3.20	Q	וְתָשׁוּחַ ⁷		Gen. 45.7	MT	לָשׂום
	K	ותשיח ⁸			S	לשים ¹²
Ex. 4.11	MT	יָשׂוּם		Isa. 10.6	Q	וּלְשׂוּמוֹ
	S	ישים			K	ולשימו
				1 Sam. 18.6	K	לשור
					Q	לָשִׁיר

b) Inf. absol.

Prov. 23.24	K	גול
	Q	גיל

§ 10.   Verbs tertiae ה with interchange between ה and י.¹³ (Cf. MH p. 164)

α) Full forms.

Num. 24.4	MT	יֶחֱזֶה		Gen. 30.31	MT	אֶרְעֶה
	S.	יחזי			S	ארעי
Gen. 29.35	MT	אוֹדֶה		Gen. 24.48	MT	וָאֶשְׁתַּחֲוֶה
	S	אודי			S	ואשתחוי
Gen. 29.34	MT	יִלָּוֶה		Deut. 5.9	MT	תִּשְׁתַּחֲוֶה
	S	ילוי			S	תשתחוי

¹ Cf. תְּרוּמָה.
² Cf. יְרימֹות.
³ Cf. שׁוּבָה.
⁴ Cf. שִׁיבָה; cf. similarly Jer. 33.26.
⁵ Cf. similarly Prov. 12.14; Job 39.12.
⁶ Cf. also Ps. 73.10.

⁷ Cf. שׁוּחָה.   ⁸ Cf. שִׁיחָה.
⁹ Cf. K-Q on 2 Sam. 14.7.
¹⁰ Cf. מְדוּשָׁה.   ¹¹ Cf. דִּישׁ.
¹² Cf. also Num. 11.11; Deut. 12.5.
¹³ Cf. p. 486, § 65; see further § 25 and note 2, on p. 256.

Gen. 22.5	MT	וְנִשְׁתַּחֲוֶה	Gen. 7.23	MT	וַיִּמַח
	S	ונשתחוי		S	וימחי
Gen. 6.14	MT	עֲשֵׂה	Num. 20.11	MT	וַתֵּשְׁתְּ
	S	עשי		S	ותשתי
Num. 8.7	MT	הַזֵּה	Ex. 18.7	MT	וַיִּשְׁתַּחוּ
	S	הזי		S	וישתחוי

β) Shortened forms.[1]

| Lev. 24.2 | MT | צַו |
| | S | צוי |

§ 11.   Verbs tertiae ו or ה (Bergstr. § 17c, r).[2]

a) Inf. absol. kal.

Hos. 4.2	Q	אלו	Ex. 17.14	Q	מָחֹו
	K	אָלֹה		K	מחה
Ex. 15.1	Q	גָּאֹו[3]	Jer. 49.12	Q	נקו
	K	גאה[4]		K	נָקֹה
Am. 5.5	Q	גלו[5]	2 Sam. 24.24		קָנֹו
	K	גָּלֹה[6]	1 Chron. 21.24		קָנֹה
Ex. 2.19	Q	דָּלֹו	Ex. 3.7	MT	רָאֹה[8]
	K	דלה		S	ראו[9]
Hos. 1.2	Q	זנו	Jer. 49.12	Q	שתו(2°)
	K	זָנֹה		K	שָׁתֹה
Ezek. 18.9	Q	חיו			
	K	חָיֹה[7]	b) Perfect kal.		
Ex. 19.13	Q	יָרֹו	Ezek. 26.4	K	וסחותי
	K	ירה		Q	וְסָחֵיתִי[10]

§ 12.   Verbs tertiae א or ה. [11]

| Job 19.2 | K | תְּדַכְּאוּנֵנִי[12] | 2 Chron. 18.24 | | לְהֵחָבֵא[14] |
| | Q | תדכוני[13] | 1 Ki. 22.25 | | לְהֵחָבֵה[15] |

[1] Cf. § 5 2 and § 6 3.
[2] ה stands for י, cf. § 10; cf. also § 23.
[3] Cf. the derivative גַּאֲוָה.
[4] Cf. גָּאָה.   [5] Cf. גָּלוּת.
[6] Cf. גּוֹלָה.   [7] Cf. also ib. 33.16.
[8] Cf. מַרְאֶה.   [9] Cf. רָאֲה.

[10] סחה—סחו, with the final ה changed into י, cf. § 10.
[11] Cf. §§ 35 on p. 476 and 1b on p. 563; also p. 147, s.v. מצא: Zech. 12.5: MT אמצה — J אמצא. דְּכִי.   [12] Cf. דְּכָּא.   [13] Cf. מַחֲבֵא.   [14] Cf. חֶבְיוֹן.   [15] Cf.

Job 1.21	Q	יָצָאתִי	Gen. 24.12	S	הקרא
	K	יצתי		MT	הַקְרֵה
Ex. 15.25	S	ויראהו	Jer. 51.9	K	רפאנו
	MT	וַיּוֹרֵהוּ		Q	רְפִינוּ
2 Sam. 11.24	K	ויראו המוראים	Hos. 11.3	K	רְפָאתִים
	Q	וַיֹּרוּ הַמּוֹרִים ¹		Q	רפתים
Jer. 26.9	Q	נִבֵּאתָ	Ezek. 47.8	K	ונרפאו
	K	נבית		Q	וְנִרְפּוּ
Zech. 5.9	Q	ותשאנה	2 Ki. 25.29		וְשָׁנָא
	K	וַתִּשֶּׂנָה	Jer. 52.33		וְשָׁנָה
Ex. 9.4	S	והפלא	2 Sam. 21.12	Q	תְּלָאוּם
	MT	וְהִפְלָה		K	תלום
Gen. 27.20	S	הקרא	Isa. 37.26		לְהַשְׁאוֹת ³
	MT	הִקְרָה	2 Ki. 19.25		לַהְשׁוֹת
Ex. 3.18	S	נקרא			
	MT	נִקְרָה ²			

§ 13.   Inf. constr. of verbs tertiae ה (B-L § 2v; Bergstr. § 2g).⁴

Ex. 2.4	MT	לְדֵעָה	Ex. 18.18	MT	עֲשֹׂהוּ
	S	לדעת		S	עשותו
Gen. 50.20	MT	עֲשֹׂה	Gen. 46.3	MT	מֵרְדָה
	S	עשות		S	מרדת

§ 14.   Verbs of weak roots.

Judg. 12.3	K	ואישמה ⁵	1 Ki. 12.2		וַיֵּשֶׁב
	Q	וְאָשִׂימָה ⁶	2 Chron. 10.2		וַיָּשָׁב
Ezek. 35.9	K	תישבנה	Prov. 23.26	K	תרצנה
	Q	תָּשׁוֹבְנָה ⁷		Q	תִּצְּרְנָה ⁸

¹ Verb and noun from the root
ירה—ירא.
² Cf. 2 Sam. 1.6: נקרא נקריתי.
³ This form is a combination of tertiae ה and א.
⁴ Cf. the following paragraph; I,
therefore, assume here an interchange

between primae י and tertiae ה: ידע—
רדה—ירד; דעה.
⁵ Root ישם; cf. on § 8a.
⁶ Root שים.
⁷ שיב—ישב.
⁸ נצר—רצה (or metathesis? cf. § 70
on p. 489).

2 Sam. 14.30	K	וְהוֹצִיתִיהָ	Isa. 30.5	K	הבאיש
	Q	וְהַצִּיתוּהָ [1]		Q	הֹבִישׁ [7]
1 Sam. 14.27	K	ותראנה	α)	Mediae geminatae (B-L	
	Q	וַתָּאֹרְנָה [2]		§ 21r, s).[8]	
1 Ki. 10.26		וַיַּנְחֵם	Deut. 3.7	MT	בְּזֹונוּ
2 Chron. 1.14		וַיַּנִּיחֵם [3]		S	בזזנו
Jer. 30.16	K	שאסיך [4]	Gen. 31.19	S	לגז
	Q	שֹׁסַיִךְ [5]		MT	לִגְזֹז
1 Sam. 18.29	K	ויאסף	2 Sam. 22.6		סַבֻּנִי
	Q	וַיּוֹסֶף [6]	Ps. 18.6		סְבָבוּנִי

§ 15.   Assimilation of the ת in the hithpaʻel (B-L § 15e-g; Bergstr. § 19b).[9]

Num. 21.27	MT	וְתִכּוֹנֵן	Num. 24.7	MT	וְתִנַּשֵּׂא
	S	ותתכונן		S	ותתנשא
Ps. 18.45		יְכַחֲשׁוּ	Isa. 66.17	K	המקדשים
2 Sam. 22.45		יִתְכַּחֲשׁוּ		Q	הַמִּתְקַדְּשִׁים
Gen. 38.14	MT	וַתְּכַס	similarly:		
	S	ותתכס	2 Sam. 10.6		נִבְאֲשׁוּ
Num. 26.55	MT	יִנָּחֲלוּ	1 Chron. 19.6		הִתְבָּאֲשׁוּ
	S	יתנחלו			

§ 16.   Preservation of the second vowel in inflected verbal forms.[10]
(Cf. MH § 189)

a) Inflected forms of the participle (B-L § 26t).[11]			Num. 5.15	MT	מַזְכֶּרֶת
				S	מזכירת
α) Part. fem. sing.			Lev. 11.3	MT	מַפְרֶסֶת
Deut. 22.6	MT	רֹבֶצֶת		S	מפריסת
	S	רביצת			

---

[1] נצת—יצת; cf. Ex. 2.4: MT וַתֵּצֶב —
S וַתִּתְיַצֵּב (יצב—נצב); and similarly Gen.
42.1: MT תֵּרָאוּ — S תִּתְרָאוּ (ירא—ראה).
[2] אור—ראה.   [3] נוח—נחה.
[4] On the א, cf. p. 562, § 1a; consequently, this form is a participle with
suffix of the root שוס.
[5] שסה—שוס.   [6] יסף—אסף.
[7] יבש—באש.

[8] Cf. MT לֵב – S לבב: Gen. 18.5; Ex.
4.14; Deut. 4.11; also 2 Chron. 6.38 —
1 Ki. 8.48; Isa. 38.3 — 2 Ki. 20.3; note
further זַמֹּתִי Zech. 8.14 and זַמֹּתִי Jer.
4.28; יֶחֱנַן Am. 5.15 and יָחֹן Deut. 28.50.
[9] Cf. H. Yalon in Tarbiz, III (Jerusalem תרצא), p. 99 f.
[10] Cf. § 33; also p. 215 sub a and
p. 224B 8.   [11] Cf. p. 183, § 15 a.

β)　Part. masc. plur.

Gen. 40.6	MT	זֹעֲפִים
	S	זעיפים
Ex. 5.6	MT	הַנֹּגְשִׂים
	S	הנגישים
Num. 3.46	MT	הָעֹדְפִים
	S	העודפים
Gen. 29.2	MT	רֹבְצִים
	S	רביצים
Gen. 47.14	MT	שֹׁבְרִים
	S	שבירים

b)　Imperfect forms.[1]

Isa. 18.4	Q	אֶשְׁקֳטָה
	K	אשקוטה
Jer. 32.9	Q	וָאֶשְׁקֳלָה
	K	ואשקולה
Deut. 32.7	MT	וְיַגֵּדְךָ
	S	ויגידך
Jer. 1.5	Q	אֶצָּרְךָ
	K	אצורך
Ex. 2.2	MT	וַתִּצְפְּנֵהוּ
	S	ותצפינהו [2]
Jer. 5.6	Q	יְשָׁדְדֵם
	K	ישודדם

c)　Perfect forms.[3]

Lev. 20.24	MT	הִבְדַּלְתִּי
	S	הבדילתי
Num. 10.29	MT	וְהֵטַבְנוּ
	S	והיטיבנו
Deut. 2.34	MT	הִשְׁאַרְנוּ
	S	השאירנו
Num. 36.4	MT	וְנֹוסְפָה
	S	ונוסיפה

d)　Imperative (Bergstr. 2, § 14k).

Judg. 9.8	Q	מָלְכָה
	K	מלוכה
Ps. 26.2	Q	צָרְפָה
	K	צרופה
Judg. 9.12	Q	מָלְכִי
	K	מלוכי
1 Sam. 28.8	Q	קָסֳמִי
	K	קסומי
Num. 31.3	MT	הֵחָלְצוּ
	S	החליצו
Gen. 18.4	MT	וְהִשָּׁעֵנוּ
	S	והשעינו
Deut. 3.28	MT	וְאַמְּצֵהוּ
	S	ואמיצהו
Deut. 3.28	MT	וְחַזְּקֵהוּ
	S	וחזיקהו

---

[1] Some of these formations might be explained as "pausal forms"; but since no rules exist, when context forms should be used, and when the corresponding pausal forms, I introduced the new terminology: Preservation of the 2nd vowel (p. 223 A1). Cf. f.i. Job 19.24: Ma יַחֲצֹבוּן — Md יַחְצְבוּן; Ps. 50.3: נִשְׂעֲרָה, Venice 1515 marg.: נשערה; Josh. 24.15: תַּעֲבֹדוּן, Venice 1515 marg.: תַּעֲבְדוּן; p. 139, s.v. ידה: Ps. 35.18: MT אֹודְךָ — O אֹודֶךָ. Cf. also here § 35 A a (note 1, page 261).

[2] Cf. in § 7a the instance Q-K on Ps. 56.7.

[3] Cf. 1 Chron. 4.10: וְהִרְבִּית; Venice 1515 marg.: וְהַרְבִּית: preservation of the vowel a in the first syllable.

e) Inf. constr. (Bergstr. 2, § 14n [f]).

Ex. 32.34	MT	פְּקֹדִי
	S	פקודי
Ps. 38.21	Q	רָדְפִי
	K	רדופי

f) The verb in Sandhi.

α) Imperfect.

Josh. 9.7	Q	אֶכְרָת
	K	אכרות ¹
Hos. 8.12	Q	אֶכְתָב
	K	אכתוב
Ps. 89.29	Q	אֶשְׁמָר
	K	אשמור
Ps. 10.15	Q	תדרש
	K	תִּדְרוֹשׁ
Isa. 44.17	Q	יִסְגָּד
	K	יסגוד
Isa. 26.20	Q	יַעֲבָר
	K	יעבור
Prov. 22.14	Q	יִפָּל
	K	יפול

Prov. 22.8	Q	יִקְצָר
	K	יקצור

β) Imperative.²

Ezek. 24.2	Q	כְּתָב
	K	כתוב

γ) Inf. constr.

Am. 7.8	Q	עבר
	K	עֲבוֹר
Ezek. 21.28	Q	כְּקְסָם
	K	כקסום
Ezek. 44.3	Q	לֶאֱכָל
	K	לאכול
Ruth 4.6	Q	לִגְאָל
	K	לגאול
Isa. 44.14	Q	לִכְרָת
	K	לכרות
Nah. 2.1	Q	לַעֲבָר
	K	לעבור
1 Sam. 8.10		לִשְׁאָל
2 Chron. 18.10		לִשְׁאָוֹל
1 Sam. 25.31	Q	וְלִשְׁפָּךְ
	K	ולשפוך ³

§ 17.   The use of the tenses.⁴

a) Perfect or imperfect.

Deut. 30.1	MT	הֱדִיחֲךָ
	S .	ידיחך
2 Chron. 22.6		הִכָּהוּ
2 Ki. 8.29		יַכָּהוּ

Isa. 37.34		בָּא
2 Ki. 19.33		יָבֹא
Isa. 1.11	Seb	אמר
	MT	יֹאמַר

¹ Cf. Venice 1515 marg.: אכרת.

² Cf. Ps. 119.49: זְכָר; Venice 1515 marg.: זְכֹר.

³ Cf. Ezek. 22.27: לִשְׁפָּךְ, Venice 1515 marg.: לִשְׁפֹּךְ.

⁴ Cf. Hos. 7.14: זְעָקוּ; Venice 1515 marg.: יְזְעָקוּ; cf. also Lev. 17.4: וְאֶל פתח אהל מועד לא הֱבִיאוֹ Lev. 17.9: ואל פתח אהל מועד לא יְבִיאֶנּוּ

b) Participle or imperfect (Bergstr. § 2i).[1]

Gen. 15.3	MT	יוֹרֵשׁ
	S	יירש
2 Chron. 18.7		מִתְנַבֵּא
1 Ki. 22.8		יִתְנַבֵּא

1 Ki. 10.1	שָׁמַעַת
2 Chron. 9.1	שָׁמְעָה

d) Imperative or imperfect.

Ex. 17.5	MT	קַח
	S	תקח
2 Ki. 11.15		הָמֵת
2 Chron. 23.14		יוּמַת

c) Participle or perfect.[2]

1 Sam. 31.1	נִלְחָמִים
1 Chron. 10.1	נִלְחָמוּ

§ 18.   Active or passive construction (Cf. MH § 192).

a) Niph'al or ḳal.[3]

α) Imperfect.

Num. 28.17	MT	יֵאָכֵל
	S	תאכלו
Lev. 11.13	MT	יֵאָכְלוּ
	S	תאכלו
Lev. 25.34	MT	יִמָּכֵר
	S	ימכרו
Num. 28.15	MT	יֵעָשֶׂה
	S	יעשו
2 Ki. 16.20		וַיִּקָּבֵר [4]
2 Chron. 28.27		וַיִּקְבְּרֻהוּ
Deut. 16.16	MT	יֵרָאֶה
	S	יראו

β) Perfect.

Lev. 13.25	MT	נֶהְפַּךְ
	S	הפך
1 Chron. 14.8		נִמְשַׁח
2 Sam. 5.17		מָשְׁחוּ
Ex. 25.28	MT	וְנִשָּׂא
	S	ונשאו
Gen. 9.2	MT	נִתָּנוּ
	S	נתתיו

b) Niph'al or hiph'il.[5]

Gen. 10.1	MT	וַיִּוָּלְדוּ
	S	ויולידו
2 Sam. 5.13		וַיִּוָּלְדוּ
1 Chron. 14.3		וַיּוֹלֶד

---

[1] Cf. also § 72α (Lev. 17.10).

[2] Cf. also § 72α (Deut. 6.12).

[3] Cf. 1 Sam. 25.12: וַיַּהֲפְכוּ; Venice 1515 marg.: וַיֵּהָפְכוּ; Nah. 3.3: Venice 1515: יְכָשְׁלוּ; marg.: יִכָּשְׁלוּ; 1 Chron. 11.1: Venice 1515: וַיִּקְבְּצוּ; marg.: וַיִּקָּבְצוּ.

[4] Cf. similarly: 2 Ki. 21.18 — 2 Chron. 33.20; 1 Ki. 11.43 — 2 Chron. 9.31; cf. further in conjunction with § 59: 2 Ki. 14.20 — 2 Chron. 25.28 and 2 Ki. 15.38 — 2 Chron. 27.9.

[5] Cf. p. 151, s.v. סתר: Ps. 89.47: MT תַּסְתִּיר — O תִּסָּתֵר.

c)   Pu‘al or pi‘el.¹

Ex. 34.34	MT	יְצֻוֶּה
	S	יצוהו
Num. 3.16	MT	צֻוָּה
	S	צוהו

d)   Hoph‘al or ḳal.

Lev. 6.23	MT	יוּבָא
	S	יבוא
Num. 35.17	MT	יוּמַת ²
	S	ימות
2 Ki. 14.6		יוּמְתוּ
2 Chron. 25.4		יָמוּתוּ
Lev. 11.35	MT	יֻתָּץ ³
	S	יתצו

e)   Hoph‘al or hiph‘il.

α)   Imperfect.

2 Ki. 11.15		תּוּמַת
2 Chron. 23.14		תְּמִיתֻהָ
2 Ki. 11.16		וַתּוּמַת
2 Chron. 23.15		וַיְמִיתֻהָ
Lev. 4.35	MT	יוּסַר
	S	יסיר

β)   Perfect.

Ex. 27.7	MT	וְהוּבָא
	S	והבאת
Deut. 17.4	MT	וְהֻגַּד
	S	והגידו
Lev. 4.31	MT	הוּסַר
	S	יסיר

§ 19.   The use of the derived stems.

a)   Ḳal or hiph‘il.⁴

2 Ki. 22.9		וַיָּבֹא
2 Chron. 34.16		וַיָּבֵא
1 Sam. 31.12		וַיָּבֹאוּ
1 Chron. 10.12		וַיְבִיאֻם
Lev. 20.5	MT	לִזְנוֹת
	S	להזנות ⁵

Gen. 21.18	S	וחזקי
	MT	וְהַחֲזִיקִי ⁶
Num. 1.51	MT	וּבַחֲנֹת
	S	ובהחנת
Ex. 21.35	MT	וְחָצוּ
	S	והחצו

---

¹ Cf. 2 Chron. 15.6: וְכִתְּתוּ, Venice 1515 marg.; וְכִתְּתוּ; p. 161, s.v.; שבר: Ps. 46.10: MT יְשַׁבֵּר — O יְשַׁבֵּר.

² Cf. K-Q on Prov. 19.16; Q-K on 2 Ki. 14.6 and S-MT on Num. 35.12.

³ Cf. § 19c; the term "Passive Ḳal" (B-L § 38 l'-r') will have to be discarded as a mere invention of the grammarians. This term is based upon the assumption that the verbs in question either do not occur in the pi‘el at all, or if they do, at least in a different connotation. Thus, the MT is the sole basis for this grammatical phenomenon; cf. p. 214 on פנה, where I showed that the change in the stem does not involve a change in the meaning, as intended by the Masoretes. Cf. also here note 1, p. 254.

⁴ Cf. 2 Chron. 16.2: וַיֵּצֵא, Venice 1515 marg.: וַיֵּצֵא; 2 Chron. 21.13: Venice 1515: וַתַּזְנֶה; marg. וַתַּזְנֶה.

⁵ Cf. Lev. 20.6; 21.9; Num. 25.1; Deut. 22.21.

⁶ Cf. Lev. 25.35: MT וְהֶחֱזַקְתָּ — S וחזקת.

Num. 21.2	S	וְחֵרַמְתִּי
	MT	וְהַחֲרַמְתִּי
Num. 30.5	S	וְחֵרִישׁ
	MT	וְהֶחֱרִישׁ [1]
Gen. 22.23	MT	יָלַד
	S	הוֹלִיד [2]
1 Sam. 27.4	Q	יָסַף
	K	יוסף
Deut. 20.8	MT	וְיָסְפוּ
	S	ויוסיפו
2 Sam. 7.15		יָסוּר
1 Chron. 17.13		אָסִיר
2 Sam. 22.23		אָסוּר
Ps. 18.23		אָסִיר
Ex. 12.12	MT	וְעָבַרְתִּי
	S	והעברתי
Deut. 29.11	MT	לְעָבְרְךָ
	S	להעברך
1 Ki. 10.29		וַתַּעֲלֶה וַתֵּצֵא
2 Chron. 1.17		וַיַּעֲלוּ וַיּוֹצִיאוּ
Gen. 34.1	MT	לִרְאוֹת
	S	להראות
Lev. 26.22	S	ושלחתי
	MT	וְהִשְׁלַחְתִּי

b)   Pi'el or hiph'il.

Num. 33.52	MT	תְּאַבְּדוּ
	S	תאבידו

Deut. 7.24	S	וְאָבַדְתָּ
	MT	וְהַאֲבַדְתָּ [3]
Gen. 12.2	MT	וַאֲגַדְּלָה
	S	ואגדילה
Ex. 14.4	MT	וְחִזַּקְתִּי
	S	והחזקתי
Gen. 7.3	MT	לְחַיּוֹת
	S	להחיות [4]
1 Chron. 11.18		וַיְנַסֵּךְ
2 Sam. 23.16		וַיַּסֵּךְ
2 Chron. 34.25	Q	וַיְקַטְּרוּ [5]
	K	ויקטירו
2 Sam. 24.16		לְשַׁחֲתָהּ
1 Chron. 21.15		לְהַשְׁחִיתָהּ [6]
2 Ki. 19.12		שִׁחֲתוּ
Isa. 37.12		הִשְׁחִתוּ

c)   Pu'al or niph'al (B-L § 38m'-r').[7]

Gen. 40.15	MT	גֻּנֹּבְתִּי
	S	נגנבתי
Ex. 22.6	MT	וְגֻנַּב
	S	ונגנב
Lev. 11.38	MT	יֻתַּן
	S	ינתן [8]
2 Sam. 21.20		יֻלַּד
1 Chron. 20.6		נוֹלַד
2 Sam. 21.22		יֻלְּדוּ
1 Chron. 20.8		נוֹלְדוּ [9]

---

[1] Cf. Num. 30.15.
[2] Cf. Gen. 6.4; 10.8; 25.3.
[3] Cf. Lev. 23.30; Deut. 9.3.
[4] Cf. Deut. 6.24.
[5] Cf. 2 Ki. 22.17.
[6] Cf. Gen. 19.13; further Gen. 6.17;

9.11, 15; 19.29 in conjunction with § 53d.
[7] Cf. our note 3 on page 252.
[8] Cf. Q-K on 2 Sam. 21.6.
[9] Cf. Venice 1515 marg.: נוֹלְדוּ; similarly in 1 Chron. 3.5.

d) Pi'el or kal.[1]

α) Active.			β) Passive.		
Gen. 22.17	MT	בֵּרַךְ	Gen. 25.10	MT	קָבַר
	S	ברוך		S	קבור
Isa. 14.23	Q	וְטֵאטֵיתִיהָ	Lev. 10.16	MT	שָׂרַף
	K	וטאטאתיה [2]		S	שרוף

B. The Noun

§ 20.   Substantives derived from verbs with imperf. in o or i.[3]

Isa. 23.13	Q	בַּחוּנָיו	Ezek. 4.15	K	צפועי
	K	בחיניו		Q	צְפִיעֵי
Zech. 11.2	K	הבצור	1 Ki. 6.21	Q	בְּרַתּוּקוֹת
	Q	הַבָּצִיר		K	ברתיקות
Nah. 2.6	K	בהלוכתם	Jer. 18.15	K	שבולי
	Q	בַּהֲלִיכָתָם		Q	שְׁבִילֵי
Jer. 37.4	Q	הַכְּלוּא			
	K	הכליא			
Judg. 7.13	K	צלול			

α) Substantives with preformative (ת, שׁ).

Judg. 7.13	Q	צְלִיל			
Isa. 62.3	K	וצנוף	Jer. 5.30	Q	וְשַׁעֲרוּרָה
	Q	וּצְנִיף		K	ושערירה
Ps. 17.14	Q	וּצְפוּנְךָ	Jer. 43.10	K	שפרורו
	K	וצפינך		Q	שַׁפְרִירוֹ
			Prov. 20.30	Q	תַּמְרוּק
				K	תמריק

§ 21.   Substantives derived from verbs primae ו or י. [4]

Gen. 11.30	MT	וָלָד [5]	Ruth 2.1	Q	מוֹדַע
	S	ילד [6]		K	מידע

---

[1] Cf. p. 214 on פנה; further p. 124 ff.: s.v. חבל: Ps. 7.15: MT יְחַבֶּל — O ; s.v. מגר: Ps. 89.45: MT מִגַּרְתָּ — O ; s.v. נחת: Ps. 18.35: וְנִחֲתָה מְגַּרְתָּ ; — O וְנִחַתָה; s.v. שלם: Ps. 31.24: MT וְשַׁלֵּם — O וּמְשַׁלֵּם; s.v. שמח: Ps. 46.5: MT יִשְׂמְחוּ — O יְשַׂמְּחוּ. Cf. also Jer. 51.36: Venice 1515: וְנָקַמְתִּי; marg.: Prov. 28.8: Venice 1515: יַקְבְּצֶנּוּ; marg.:

יַקְבְּצֶנּוּ; 2 Chron. 33.3: Venice 1515: נָתַץ; marg.: נִתַּץ; 1 Ki. 20.27: Venice 1515: מָלְאוּ; marg.: מִלְאוּ; Ezek. 34.4: חִזַּקְתֶּם; Venice 1515 marg.: חֲזַקְתֶּם.

[2] Cf. p. 562, § 1a.

[3] Cf. § 7.

[4] Cf. § 8.

[5] Cf. מוֹלֶדֶת.

[6] Cf. יָלִיד; cf. also Q-K on 1 Sam. 6.23.

2 Ki. 16.18	Q	מוּסַךְ	Ezek. 41.8	Q	מוּסְדוֹת
	K	מיסך		K	מיסדות

§ 22. Substantives derived from verbs mediae ו of י.[1]

Jer. 6.7	K	בּוֹר	Isa. 30.6	K	עורים
	Q	בַּיִר [2]		Q	עֲיָרִים
Deut. 6.11	MT	וּבֹרֹת	Ps. 49.15	Q	וְצוּרָם
	S	בירות		K	וצירם
Ezek. 47.10	K	דוגים	Jer. 18.22	Q	שׁוּחָה
	Q	דַּיָּגִים		K	שיחה
Job 6.2	Q	וְהַוָּתִי	Isa. 28.15	Q	שׁוֹט
	K	והיתי		K	שיט
Ps. 74.11	K	חוקך			
	Q	חֵיקְךָ			

α) Substantives with preformative (ת, מ, י).

Prov. 23.31	Q	בַּכּוֹס	1 Ki. 6.5	K	יצוע
	K	בכיס		Q	יָצִיעַ
2 Sam. 3.15	K	לוש	Isa. 11.8	Q	מְאוּרַת
	Q	לַיִשׁ		K	מארת
Isa. 57.19	K	נוב	Prov. 18.19	K	ומדונים
	Q	ניב		Q	וּמִדְיָנִים
Ezek. 22.18	K	לסוג	Prov. 18.20	Q	תְּבוּאַת
	Q	לְסִיג		K	תביאת

§ 23. Substantives derived from verbs tertiae ו or י.[3]

2 Ki. 23.12	K	עלות			
	Q	עֲלִיַּת			

α) Substantives with performative (ת, מ).

Ps. 9.13	Q	עֲנָוִים	Ps. 129.3	K	למעונתם
	K	עֲנִיִּים [4]		Q	לְמַעֲנִיתָם
Eccl. 5.10	Q	רְאוּת	Jer. 14.14	K	ותרמות
	K	ראית		Q	וְתַרְמִית
Jer. 30.3	Q	שְׁבוּת			
	K	שבית			

---

[1] Cf. § 9.   [2] Cf. ch. 129, s.v. בּאר.   [4] Cf. p. 153, s.v. עני; Ps. 76.10: MT
[3] Cf. § 11; the ה there is equivalent עֲנָוֵי — O עֲנָוִי.
to a י; cf. § 10.

§ 24.   Substantives derived from verbs tertiae א or ה.[1]

| 2 Chron. 9.18 | לִכְסֵא | 2 Chron. 1.16 | מִקְוֵא |
| 1 Ki. 10.19 | לִכְסֵה | 1 Ki. 10.28 | מִקְוֵה |

§ 25.   Substantives derived from verbs tertiae ה, with interchange between ה and י.[2]

Deut. 18.1	S	אשה	Gen. 47.4	MT	מִרְעֶה
	MT	אשֵּׁי		S	מרעי
Deut. 28.60	MT	מַדְוֶה	Lev. 26.36	MT	עָלֶה
	S	מדוי		S	עלי
Num. 19.21	MT	וּמַזֵּה	2 Chron. 34.10		עֹשֵׂה
	S	ומזי	2 Ki. 22.5		עֹשֵׂי
Num. 24.16	MT	מַחֲזֵה	Ex. 25.32	S	קנה
	S	מחזי		MT	קְנֵי
Mal. 3.5	Q	ומטה	Deut. 9.13	MT	קְשֵׁה
	K	וּמַטֵּי		S	קשי [4]
2 Ki. 22.17		מַעֲשֵׂה	Gen. 21.20	MT	רֹבֶה
2 Chron. 34.25		מַעֲשֵׂי		S	רבי
1 Ki. 7.46		בְּמַעֲבֵה	Gen. 47.3	MT	רֹעֵה
2 Chron. 4.17		בַּעֲבִי [3]		S	רעי
Deut. 23.11	MT	מִקְרֵה	Deut. 22.1	S	שהו
	S	מקרי		MT	שֵׂיוֹ
Eccl. 11.9	Q	וּבְמַרְאֶה			
	K	ובמראי			

§ 26.   Substantives derived from verbs of weak roots.

2 Sam. 3.25	Q	מוֹבָאֶךָ	1 Ki. 12.15		סִבָּה
	K	מבואך [5]	2 Chron. 10.15		נְסִבָּה [7]
Deut. 26.8	MT	וּבְמֹרָא			
	S	ובמראה [6]			

---

[1] Cf. § 12; also note 11 on p. 246.

[2] Cf. § 10; the context of these forms makes it evident that neither does the ending in ה indicate a sing., nor the י a plural; cf. § 35 f., and especially § 38 f.

[3] On the difference in the nominal formation: with or without prefix מ,

cf. § 85a.   [4] Cf. K-Q on Ezek. 2.4.

[5] בוא—יבא.

[6] ראה—ירא; cf. similarly Gen. 9.2; Deut. 4.34; 11.25; 34.12.

[7] נסב—סבב; cf. Gen. 19.4: נָסַבּוּ: Ḳal with preservation of the second vowel; cf. p. 224 B 3.

§ 27. Substantives of which the second radical is vocalized i.[1]

Ex. 2.6	MT	הַיֶּלֶד	Num. 32.16	MT	גדרת
	S	הילֶיד		S	גדירות 4
Ex. 1.17	MT	הַיְלָדִים	Prov. 31.27	K	הילכות
	S	הילידים		Q	הֲלִיכוֹת
Ex. 2.6	MT	מֵיַלְדֵי	Gen. 34.4	MT	הַיַּלְדָּה
	S	מילידי		S	הילידה
Gen. 30.26	MT	יְלָדַי	Lev. 5.2	MT	בְּנִבְלַת
	S	ילידי		S	בנבילת
Gen. 33.7	MT	וִילָדֶיהָ	Ex. 33.22	MT	בְּנִקְרַת
	S	ווילידיה		S	בנקירות
Gen. 32.23	MT	יְלָדָיו	Lev. 23.21	MT	עֲבֹדָה
	S	ילידיו		S	עבידה
Gen. 33.2	MT	יַלְדֵיהֶן	Ex. 5.9	MT	הָעֲבֹדָה
	S	ילידיהן		S	העבידה
Ezek. 4.6	Q	הַיְמָנִי	Num. 7.5	MT	עֲבֹדָתוֹ
	K	הימיני		S	עבידתו
Num. 23.10	MT	יְשָׁרִים	Num. 7.7	MT	עֲבֹדָתָם
	S	ישירים		S	עבידתם
Num. 16.27	MT	נִצָּבִים	Num. 32.3	MT	עֲטָרוֹת
	S	נציבים 2		S	עטירות
Deut. 12.5	MT	לְשִׁכְנוֹ	Gen. 15.6	MT	צְדָקָה
	S	לשכינו		S	צדיקה
			Deut. 33.21	MT	צִדְקַת
α) Feminine forms. 3				S	צדיקת
Deut. 32.11	MT	אֶבְרָתוֹ	Gen. 30.33	MT	צִדְקָתִי
	S	אבירתו		S	צדיקתי
Gen. 4.23	MT	אִמְרָתִי	Lev. 27.10	MT	וּתְמוּרָתוֹ
	S	אמירתי		S	ותמירתו
Deut. 33.9	MT	אִמְרָתֶךָ			
	S	אמירתך			

---

[1] Cf. Jer. 11.20: צֶדֶק, Venice 1515 marg.: נִצָּבִים; cf. further: Q-K on 2 marg.: צַדִּיק; Ezek. 17.24: Venice 1515: Chron. 8.10.
שָׁפֵל; marg.: שָׁפָל.   [3] Cf. p. 136, s.v. זמרה.
[2] Cf. 1 Ki. 4.7: נִצָּבִים; Venice 1515   [4] Cf. p. 132, s.v. גדרה.

β) Substantives with preform-   Num. 13.19   MT   בְּמִבְצָרִים
ative מ.   S   מבצירים

Num. 32.36   MT   מִבְצָר   Lev. 6.2   MT   מוֹקְדָה
              S   מבציר   S   המוקידה ¹

§ 28. Substantives of which the first radical is vocalized i.

Deut. 28.65   MT   וְדַאֲבוֹן   Deut. 17.12   MT   בְּזָדוֹן
               S   ודיבון   S   בזידון

Gen. 27.37   MT   וְדָגָן
              S   ודיגן

§ 29. Miḳtal or miḳtol forms.

Isa. 37.24   מִבְחַר   Lev. 26.26   MT   בַּמִּשְׁקָל
2 Ki. 19.23   מִבְחוֹר   S   במשקול
Lam. 1.11   Q   מַחֲמַדֵּיהֶם
             K   מחמודיהם

§ 30. Substantives of which the second radical is vocalized o or i.

Gen. 43.33   MT   הַבְּכוֹר   Num. 15.40   MT   קֲדֹשִׁים ²
              S   הבכיר   S   קדישים
Jer. 50.45   K   צעורי   Ex. 32.27   MT   קֵרְבוֹ
              Q   צְעִירֵי   S   קריבו
Jer. 48.4   K   צעוריה   Lev. 10.3   MT   בִּקְרֹבַי
             Q   צְעִירֶיהָ   S   בקריבי
Jer. 14.3   K   צעוריהם
             Q   צְעִירֵיהֶם

§ 31. The absolute state ending in ה or ת (B-L § 25i'-l').

Jer. 52.4   בַּשָּׁנָה   Jer. 49.25   K   תהלה
2 Ki. 25.1   בִּשְׁנַת ³   Q   תְּהִלַּת

§ 32. Formation of the plur. masc.

α) Ending in ים or ין (B-L § 63t).

Job 32.11   Md   מִלִּים   2 Chron. 23.12   הָרָצִים
             Ma   מלין   2 Ki. 11.13   הָרָצִין

---

¹ On the Article in S, cf. § 50b.   21.6; 24.9; Num. 5.17; 16.3.
² Cf. Lev. 11.44, 45; 19.2; 20.7, 26;   ³ Cf. Q-K on Jer. 28.1; 32.1; 51.59.

| Lam. 4.3 | Q | תַּנִּים |
| | K | תנין |

γ) Substantives with masc. or fem. ending (B-L § 63p).[3]

β) Ending in ם or ים.[1]

Ezek. 29.4	Q	חַחִים
	K	חחיים
Ezek. 23.14	Q	כַּשְׂדִּים
	K	כשדיים
Isa. 23.12	Q	כִּתִּים
	K	כתיים [2]
Gen. 10.13		לוּדִים
I Chron. 1.12		לוּדִיּים

Num. 13.20	MT	בְּכוּרֵי
	S	בכרות
Gen. 25.16	MT	בְּחַצְרֵיהֶם
	S	בחצרותם
Ex. 28.12	MT	כְּתֵפָיו
	S	כתפתיו
Ps. 18.8		וּמוֹסְדֵי
2 Sam. 22.8		מוֹסְדוֹת

§ 33. Inflected nominal forms with preservation of the second vowel.[4]

Ex. 17.6	MT	זְקֵנִי
	S	זקיני
Lev. 8.21	MT	וְהַכְּרָעַיִם
	S	והכורעים
Lev. 4.11	MT	כְּרָעָיו
	S	כורעיו
Ex. 36.32	MT	לַיַּרְכָתַיִם
	S	לירכותים
Num. 6.3	MT	מִשְׁרַת
	S	משארת
Deut. 7.13	MT	וְעַשְׁתְּרֹת
	S	ועשתארות
Lev. 14.4	MT	צִפֳּרִים
	S	צפורים

α) The substantive in Sandhi.

Nah. 1.3	Q	וּגְדָל
	K	וגדול [5]
Prov. 22.11	Q	טְהָר
	K	טהור

β) Construct state fem. plur. (B-L § 63q).

Deut. 33.13	Q	בָּמֳתֵי
	K	במותי
Ex. 26.22	MT	וּלְיַרְכְּתֵי
	S	ולירכותי
I Ki. 6.16	Q	מִיַּרְכְּתֵי
	K	מירכותי

[1] Cf. Josh. 2.17, 20: נְקִיִּם; Venice 1515 marg.: נקיים; on the letter י as an indicator of the vowel i, cf. p. 564 § 2a.

[2] Cf. K-Q on Ezek. 27.6.

[3] Cf. § 83.

[4] Cf. § 16; also p. 215, sub a and p. 224 B 6.

[5] Cf. Ps. 145.8.

§ 34.   The substantive unchanged in the construct state.[1]

a) Dual forms.

Deut. 33.11	MT	מָתְנַיִם קָמָיו
	S	מתני ⋯⋯
2 Chron. 4.3		שְׁנַיִם טוּרִים
1 Ki. 7.24		שְׁנֵי ⋯⋯ [2]
Lev. 24.6	MT	שְׁתַיִם מַעֲרָכוֹת
	S	שתי ⋯⋯

b) Plural forms.

Num. 13.32	S	אנשים מדות
	MT	אַנְשֵׁי ⋯⋯
Ex. 32.28	S	אלפים איש
	MT	אַלְפֵי ⋯⋯
Num. 3.38	MT	שֹׁמְרִים מִשְׁמֶרֶת [3]
	S	שמרי ⋯⋯

c) Fem. sing.

Deut. 21.11	S	אשה יְפַת תֹאַר
	MT	אֵשֶׁת ⋯⋯
Gen. 17.17	MT	מֵאָה שָׁנָה
	S	מאת ⋯⋯ [4]
Num. 28.3	MT	עֹלָה תָמִיד
	S	עלת ⋯⋯
Jer. 52.21	K	קומה הָעַמֻד
	Q	קוֹמַת ⋯⋯

d) Cardinals

Lev. 27.7	MT	עֲשָׂרָה שְׁקָלִים
	S	עשרת ⋯⋯
1 Ki. 12.5		שְׁלֹשָׁה יָמִים
2 Chron. 10.5		שְׁלֹשֶׁת ⋯⋯
Ezek. 46.6	K	וששה כְבָשִׂים
	Q	וְשֵׁשֶׁת ⋯⋯
Lev. 32.18	S	שבעה כבשים
	MT	שִׁבְעַת ⋯⋯

e) The substantive taking the article.

1 Sam. 26.22	K	החנית הַמֶּלֶךְ
	Q	חֲנִית ⋯⋯
2 Ki. 7.13	K	ההמון יִשְׂרָאֵל
	Q	הֲמוֹן ⋯⋯
Jer. 32.12	K	הַסֵּפֶר הַמִּקְנֶה [5]
	Q	ספר ⋯⋯
2 Sam. 10.7		הַצָּבָא הַגִּבּוֹרִים
1 Chron. 19.8		צָבָא ⋯⋯ [6]
Isa. 36.16		הַמֶּלֶךְ אַשּׁוּר [7]
2 Ki. 18.31		מֶלֶךְ ⋯⋯
Isa. 39.2		הַשֶּׁמֶן הַטּוֹב
2 Ki. 20.13		שֶׁמֶן ⋯⋯
Num. 34.2	MT	הָאָרֶץ כְּנַעַן
	Seb	ארץ ⋯⋯

[1] Cf. p. 217 sub c, p. 224 B 4, and p, 213 § 138 f.

[2] Cf. MT-S on Ex. 25.18 and Deut. 17.6; also: 2 Chron. 4.13 — 1 Ki. 7.42: further K-Q on Jud. 11.38; 2 Ki. 17.16.

[3] Cf. Ex. 26.26: בְּרִיחִם עֲצֵי שִׁטִּים חֲמִשָּׁה
Ex. 36.31: בְּרִיחֵי עֲצֵי שִׁטִּים חֲמִשָּׁה.

[4] Cf. Gen. 23.1.

[5] Cf. Ex. 28.24: שתי עֲבֹתֹת הזהב
Ex. 39.17: שתי הָעֲבֹתֹת הזהב.

[6] Cf. Venice 1515 marg.: צָבָא.

[7] Cf. 2 Ki. 25.11: ואת הנפלים אשר נפלו על הַמֶּלֶךְ בבל
Jer. 52.15: ואת הנפלים אשר נפלו על מֶלֶךְ בבל.

C. Nominal and Verbal Suffixes

A. The helping vowel ' in connection with the suffixes

The pronominal suffixes to the noun in the sing. and in the plur. are the same; ' is merely a helping vowel and does not indicate the number of the noun; cf. the number of the respective predicates in the instances listed in this chapter. Cf. also MH p. 184 f.

§ 35.   The pronominal suffix of the 2. pers. masc. sing. (B-L § 29r).

A) The masculine noun.

a) MT vocalizes pausal form sing.[1]

Deut. 20.1	MT	אֹיִבְךָ
	S	איביך
Gen. 30.34	MT	כִּדְבָרֶךָ
	S	כדבריך [2]
Ex. 33.13	MT	דָּרְכֶּךָ
	S	דרכיך
Deut. 2.7	MT	יָדֶךָ
	S	ידיך [3]
Ruth 3.9	Ma	כְּנָפֵךְ
	Md	כנפיך
Lev. 25.5	MT	נְזִירֶךָ
	S	נזיריך
Isa. 37.17		עֵינֶךָ
2 Ki. 19.16		עֵינֶיךָ

b) MT vocalizes context form sing.

Prov. 24.17	Q	אֹיִבְךָ
	K	איביך [4]
Deut. 24.14	MT	מִגְרֶךָ
	S	מגריך
Ex. 8.6	MT	כִּדְבָרְךָ
	S	כדבריך [5]
2 Sam. 1.16	Q	דָּמְךָ
	K	דמיך
Ps. 16.10	Q	חֲסִידְךָ
	K	חסידיך
Gen. 49.8	MT	יָדְךָ
	S	ידיך [6]
Ex. 9.19	MT	מִקְנְךָ
	S	מקניך [7]
1 Ki. 1.27	Q	עַבְדְּךָ
	K	עבדיך

---

[1] The pausal-form is an arbitrary vocalization; cf. Ps. 143.10: Venice 1515: רְצוֹנְךָ; marg.: רְצוֹנֶךָ; Ps. 68.30: מֵהֵיכָלֶךָ; Venice 1515 marg.: מהיכלך; Ezek. 4.8: צַדֶּךָ; Venice 1515 marg.: צדך; Ps. 79.6: חֲמָתְךָ; Venice 1515 marg.: חֲמָתֶךָ; cf. also § 16b note 1.

[2] Cf. Gen. 47.30; Num. 14.20.

[3] Cf. Deut. 6.8.

[4] Cf. 1 Sam. 24.5; 26.8.

[5] Cf. Q-K: Jud. 13.12, 17; 1 Ki. 8.26; 18.36; 22.13; Jer. 15.16; Ps. 119.147, 161.

[6] Cf. Q-K: Josh. 10.8; 1 Ki. 22.34; Prov. 3.7.

[7] Cf. Gen. 30.29; Ex. 9.3; 34.19.

Lev. 2.13	MT	קָרְבָּנָךְ	Num. 23.3	MT	עֹלָתֶךָ
	S	קרבניך		S	עלתיך

Deut. 4.4 — MT וְרַגְלָךְ / S ורגליך [1]

d) MT vocalizes context form
   sing.

Prov. 3.28 — Q לְרֵעֶךָ / K לרעיך

Isa. 26.20 — Q דְּלָתְךָ / K דלתיך

Ps. 77.20 — Q וּשְׁבִילָךְ / K ושביליך

Lev. 2.13 — MT (1°) מִנְחָתְךָ / S מנחתיך

B) The feminine noun.

c) MT vocalizes pausal form
   sing.[2]

Lev. 2.13 — MT (2°) מִנְחָתָךְ / S מנחתיך

§ 36.   The pronominal suffix of the 2. pers. fem. sing.

A) The masculine noun.

Gen. 12.12 — MT אֹתָךְ / S אתיך

a) MT vocalizes the noun as
   sing. (B-L § 29b').

Gen. 20.16 — MT לָךְ / S ליך

Gen. 20.13 — MT חַסְדֵּךְ / S חסדיך

Gen. 12.13 — MT בִּגְלָלֵךְ / S בגליך

Ezek. 23.29 — Q יְגִיעֵךְ / K יגיעיך

Gen. 12.13 — MT בַּעֲבוּרֵךְ / S בעבוריך

Gen. 21.18 — MT יָדֵךְ / S ידיך

b) MT vocalizes the noun as plur.

Gen. 24.14 — MT כַּדֵּךְ / S כדיך [3]

Ezek. 36.13 — K גוֹיֵךְ / Q גּוֹיַיִךְ

Cant. 2.14 — Q וּמַרְאַיִךְ / K ומראיך

Ezek. 27.12 — K עזבונך / Q עִזְבוֹנָיִךְ

Ex. 2.9 — MT שְׂכָרֵךְ / S שכריך

B) The feminine noun.

α) Particles.

c) MT vocalizes the noun as
   sing.

Gen. 20.16 — MT אִתָּךְ / S אתיך

Ezek. 16.26 — Q תַּזְנוּתֵךְ / K תזנותיך

---

[1] Cf. Q-K: Eccl. 4.17.
[2] The inconsistency of the pausal vocalization is shown in our note 1 on page 261.   [3] Cf. Gen. 24.43.

d) MT vocalizes the noun as plur.

| | | | | Ezek. 16.25 | K | תזנותך |
| | | | | | Q | תַזְנוּתָיִךְ |

| Ezek. 16.57 | K | אחותך | | Ruth 3.3 | K | שמלתך |
| | Q | אֲחוֹתַיִךְ | | | Q | שִׂמְלֹתַיִךְ |

§ 37.   The pronominal suffix of the 3. pers. masc. sing.[1]

a) The masculine noun (B-L § 29s).

Prov. 30.10	K	אדנו
	Q	אֲדֹנָיו
2 Sam. 18.17	K	לאהלו
	Q	לְאֹהָלָיו [2]
1 Ki. 8.37		אִיבוֹ
2 Chron. 6.28		אֹיְבָיו
Lev. 17.14	S	אכלו
	MT	אֹכְלָיו [3]
1 Sam. 23.5	K	ואנשו
	Q	וַאֲנָשָׁיו
2 Ki. 21.6		בְנוֹ
2 Chron. 33.6		בָנָיו [4]
Ps. 10.5	K	דרכו
	Q	דְּרָכָיו [5]
1 Ki. 8.15		וּבְיָדוֹ
2 Chron. 6.4		וּבְיָדָיו [6]
Job 38.41	K	ילדו
	Q	יְלָדָיו

| Eccl. 4.8 | Q | עינו |
| | K | עיניו [7] |

α) Particles.

2 Sam. 23.9	K	ואחרו
	Q	וְאַחֲרָיו
1 Sam. 22.13	K	אלו
	Q	אֵלָיו [8]
Josh. 8.11	K	בינו
	Q	בֵּינָיו [9]
1 Sam. 2.10	K	עלו
	Q	עָלָיו [10]
2 Sam. 3.12	K	תחתו
	Q	תַּחְתָּיו [11]

b) The feminine noun.

Jer. 15.8	K	אלמנותו
	Q	אַלְמְנוֹתָיו
Prov. 6.13	K	באצבעתו
	Q	בְּאֶצְבְּעֹתָיו

---

[1] Cf. p. 565, § 4a.

[2] Cf. 2 Sam. 20.22; 2 Ki. 14.12.

[3] Cf. Lev. 19.8.

[4] Cf. K-Q on Deut. 2.33; 33.9; 1 Sam. 30.6.

[5] Cf. 1 Sam. 8.3; 18.14; Jer. 17.10; Ezek. 18.23; Job 26.14.

[6] Cf. MT-S on Ex. 17.11; also K-Q on Ex. 32.19; Lev. 9.23; 16.21; Isa. 25.11; Ezek. 43.26; Job 5.18.

[7] Cf. MT-S on Lev. 13.55; 21.20; also K-Q on 1 Sam. 3.2, 18; 2 Sam. 10.12; 12.9; 13.34; 19.19; 24.22; Jer. 32.4; Job 21.20.

[8] Cf. Ezek. 9.4; Zech. 2.8.

[9] Cf. Josh. 3.4.

[10] Cf. 2 Sam. 20.8.

[11] Cf. 2 Sam. 2.23; 16.8; Job 9.13.

Prov. 22.25	K	אֲרחֹתו	Ezek. 40.26	K	עֲלוֹתו
	Q	אֹרְחֹתָיו		Q	עֲלוֹתָיו [1]
2 Ki. 11.18	K	מזבחתו	Ezek. 3.20	K	צדקתו
	Q	מִזְבְּחֹתָיו		Q	צִדְקוֹתָיו [2]

§ 38.   The pronominal suffix of the 1. pers. plur.[3]

Isa. 53.4	Ma	וּמַכְאֹבנוּ	Num. 32.16	MT	לְמִקְנֵנוּ
	Md	וּמַכְאֹבֵינוּ		S	למקנינו
Gen. 5.29	MT	מִמַּעֲשֵׂנוּ	Ex. 34.9	MT	לַעֲוֺנֵנוּ
	S	ממעשינו		S	לעונינו

§ 39.   The pronominal suffix of the 2. pers. masc. plur.

a) The masculine noun.[4] ### b) The feminine noun.

Ex. 12.11	MT	וּמַקֶּלְכֶם	Gen. 47.23	MT	אַדְמַתְכֶם
	S	ומקליכם		S	אדמתיכם
Gen. 45.20	MT	וְעֵינְכֶם	Ex. 32.30	MT	חֲטָאתְכֶם
	S	ועיניכם [5]		S	חטאתיכם [6]
Lev. 26.19	MT	עֻזְּכֶם	Num. 18.26	MT	בְּנַחֲלַתְכֶם
	S	עזיכם		S	בנחלתיכם
Lev. 1.2	MT	קָרְבַּנְכֶם	Num. 10.10	MT	שִׂמְחַתְכֶם
	S	קרבניכם		S	שמחתיכם

§ 40.   The pronominal suffix of the 3. pers. fem. plur.[7]

Num. 27.5	MT	מִשְׁפָּטָן	α) Lev. 8.16	MT	חֶלְבְּהֶן
	S	משפטין		S	חלביהן
Num. 36.12	MT	נַחֲלָתָן	β) Num. 31.9	MT	מִקְנֵהֶם
	S	נחלתין		S	מקניהם
Lev. 18.10	MT	עֶרְוָתָן			
	S	ערותין			

---

[1] Cf. MT-S on Num. 23.6, 17.

[2] Cf. Ezek. 18.24; 33.13.

[3] Cf. Josh. 2.20: דִּבַּרְנוּ זֶה; Venice 1515 marg.: דברינו.

[4] Cf. p. 218 f 2 and p. 225 B 16; also p. 139 s.v. יד: Mal. 2.13: MT מִיֶּדְכֶם — O מִיֶּדְכֶם; cf. further: Jer. 44.25: Venice 1515: וּבְיֶדְכֶם, marg.: וּבִידְכֶם.

[5] Cf. Q-K on Ezek. 9.5; also K-Q on Ezek. 33.25.

[6] Cf. Num. 32.23; Deut. 9.18, 21.

[7] Cf. also p. 564, § 2b.

B.   THE SUFFIXES

§ 41.   2. pers. masc. sing. ‎ךְ‎ or ‎אךְ‎ (B-L § 29i, j, f').[1]

Gen. 22.2	MT	יְחִידְךָ		2 Sam. 22.30		בְּכָה
	S	יחידאך		Ps. 18.30		בְּךָ
Hos. 4.6	Q	וְאֶמְאָסְךָ		Ex. 15.11	MT	כָּמֹכָה
	K	ואמאסאך			S	כמוך
Deut. 32.6	MT	קֹנֶךָ		Gen. 3.9	MT	אַיֶּכָּה
	S	קנאך			S	איך
Deut. 25.18	MT	קָרְךָ		Deut. 28.22	MT	יַכְּכָה
	S	קראך			S	יכך
Num. 11.23	MT	הֲיִקְרְךָ				
	S	היקראך				

β)   ‎יךְ‎ or ‎(ךְ)כה‎ (B-L § 29i).[3]

α)   ‎כה‎ or ‎ךְ‎.[2]

				Ex. 13.16	MT	יָדְכָה
					S	ידיך
Num. 22.33	MT	אֹתְכָה		Gen. 48.4	MT	מַפְרְךָ
	S	אתך			S	מפריך

§ 42.   2. pers. fem. sing. ‎ךְ‎ or ‎כִי‎. (Cf. MH § 185).

2 Ki. 4.7	Q	וּבָנַיִךְ		2 Ki. 4.3	Q	שְׁכֵנָיִךְ
	K	בניכי			K	שכניכי
2 Ki. 4.7	Q	נִשְׁיֵךְ		1 Ki. 17.13	Q	וְלָךְ
	K	נשיכי			K	ולכי

§ 43.   3. pers. masc. sing.

a)   ‎ו‎ or ‎ה‎ (B-L § 29k).[4]

α)   Nouns.

Ex. 22.4	Q	בְּעִירוֹ		Gen. 49.11	Q	עִירוֹ
	K	בעירה			K	עירה
Ex. 22.26	Q	כְּסוּתוֹ		Isa. 37.24		קִצּוֹ
	K	כסותה		2 Ki. 19.23		קִצֹּה
				Lev. 23.13	Q	וְנִסְכּוֹ
					K	ונסכה

---

[1] Cf. p. 224 B 1; cf. also 1 Sam. 13.13: ‎צִוְּךָ‎; Venice 1515 marg.: ‎צֻוְּךָ‎.

[2] Cf. note 1 on page 235.

[3] Cf. p. 210, § 124, subdivision 2, and § 74α on p. 191.

[4] Hence, passages like: Gen. 24.36: MT ‎זָקְנָתָה‎ — S ‎זקנתו‎; Num. 30.16: MT ‎עֹנָה‎ — S ‎עונו‎; Gen. 50.11: MT ‎שָׁמָּה‎ — S ‎שמו‎, according to the interpretation of S, will have to be vocalized as ‎זקנתה‎, ‎עונה‎ and ‎שמה‎ respectively. Cf. note 7, page 236 and note 1, page 266.

β)   Verbal forms.

2 Ki. 6.10	Q	וְהִזְהִירוֹ
	K	והזהירה
Num. 10.36	Q	וּבְנֻחֹה
	K	ובנחה
Ex. 32.25	Q	פְּרָעוֹ
	K	פרעה
Num. 23.8	Q	קַבּוֹ
	K	קבה
Ex. 32.17	Q	בְּרֵעוֹ
	K	ברעה

b)   Of forms ending in a consonant ו or הו.[1]

Gen. 27.27	MT	בֵּרֲכוֹ
	S	ברכהו
Deut. 34.10	MT	יְדָעוֹ
	S	ידעהו
Deut. 33.8	MT	נִסִּיתוֹ
	S	נסיתהו

Ex. 2.3	MT	הַצְּפִינוֹ
	S	הצפינהו
Ex. 20.8	MT	לְקַדְּשׁוֹ
	S	לקדשהו
Ex. 4.28	MT	שְׁלָחוֹ
	S	שלחהו
1 Sam. 18.1	K	ויאהבו
	Q	וַיֶּאֱהָבֵהוּ

c)   Of forms ending in a vowel ו or הו.

Num. 11.12	MT	יְלִדְתִּיהוּ
	S	ילדתיו
Ex. 2.10	MT	מְשִׁיתִהוּ
	S	משיתיו
1 Chron. 17.9		וּנְטַעְתִּיהוּ
2 Sam. 7.10		וּנְטַעְתִּיו
1 Chron. 16.12		פִּיהוּ
Ps. 105.5		פִּיו [2]

§ 44.   3. pers. masc. plur. ם or הם (B-L § 29e, q, s).

1 Ki. 8.34		לַאֲבוֹתָם	Ex. 34.13	MT	מַצֵּבֹתָם
2 Chron. 6.25		וְלַאֲבֹתֵיהֶם		S	מצבתיהם [4]
Ex. 36.34	MT	טַבְעֹתָם	2 Chron. 6.37		שָׁבְיָם
	S	טבעתיהם	1 Ki. 8.47		שֹׁבֵיהֶם [5]
Ex. 34.13	MT	מִזְבְּחֹתָם	1 Ki. 8.49		תְּחִנָּתָם [6]
	S	מזבחתיהם [3]	2 Chron. 6.39		תְּחִנֹּתֵיהֶם
2 Sam. 22.46		מִמִּסְגְּרוֹתָם	1 Ki. 14.27		תַּחְתָּם
Ps. 18.46		מִמִּסְגְּרוֹתֵיהֶם	2 Chron. 12.10		תַּחְתֵּיהֶם [7]

[1] Consequently, in instances like: Ex. 18.7: MT וַיָּבֹא — S ויבאהו; Num. 20.27: MT וַיַּעֲלוּ — S ויעלהו; Ex. 15.22: MT וַיֵּצֵא — S ויוצאהו, the MT will have to be understood as וַיַּעֲלוּ; וַיֹּצֵא and וַיָּבֹא respectively; cf. note 4, page 265.

[2] Cf. MT-S on Ex. 4.15.

[3] Cf. Deut. 12.3.

[4] Cf. Deut. 12.3.

[5] Lege שֹׁבֵיהֶם?   [6] Lege תְּחִנֹתָם?

[7] Cf. MT-S on Deut. 2.12, 21, 22, 23.

Ex. 32.12	MT	הוֹצִיאָם		I Chron. 16.6		בָּהֶם
	S	הוציאהם		I Ki. 15.22		בָּם ²
				Num. 22.12	MT	עִמָּהֶם
α) Particles.					S	עמם ³
Gen. 32.1	MT	אֶתְהֶם				
	S	אתם ¹				

D. Syntax

A. SUBJECT AND PREDICATE

§ 45. The gender of the noun (B-L § 62c').

Gen. 13.6	MT	נָשָׂא ···· הָאָרֶץ		Num. 31.28	MT	אֶחָד נֶפֶשׁ ·
	S	···· נשאה			S	אחת ···· ⁸
Jer. 48.45	MT	אֵשׁ יָצָא		Cant. 4.9	K	בְּאֶחָד מֵעֵינַיִךְ
	Seb	···· יצאה			Q	···· בְּאַחַת
I Ki. 22.43		דֶּרֶךְ ···· מִמֶּנּוּ		I Sam. 31.7		הֶעָרִים ···· בָּהֵן
2 Chron. 20.32		···· מִמֶּנָּה ⁴		I Chron. 10.7		בָּהֶם ····
Ex. 38.24	MT	תֵּשַׁע ···· כִּכָּר		2 Sam. 23.8	K	בְּפַעַם אֶחָד
	S	···· תשעה			Q	אַחַת ····
Gen. 49.20	MT	שְׁמֵנָה לַחְמוֹ		Gen. 30.39	MT	וַיֵּחַמוּ הַצֹּאן
	S	···· שמן			S	···· ויחמנה ⁹
2 Sam. 5.12		נָשָׂא מַמְלַכְתּוֹ		Ex. 37.3	MT	צַלְעוֹ הַשֵּׁנִית
I Chron. 14.2		···· נִשֵּׂאת			S	···· השני
Gen. 49.15	MT	מְנוּחָה ···· טוֹב		Ex. 11.6		
	S	טובה ···· ⁵			MT	צְעָקָה ··· כָּמֹהוּ ··· וְכָמֹהוּ
Judg. 19.13	K	בְּאַחַד הַמְּקֹמוֹת			S	···· כמוה ···· וכמוה
	Q	···· בְּאַחַת ⁶				
Ex. 37.22	MT	מִקְשָׁה אַחַת		Dan. 8.9	MT	יָצָא קֶרֶן אַחַת
	S	אחד ···· ⁷			Seb	···· יצאה

¹ Cf. Ex. 18.20; Num. 21.3.

² Cf. MT-S on Ex. 19.22; 29.29, 33; 32.10; also S-MT on Ex. 25.28; Lev. 15.27; Num. 4.12.

³ Cf. S-MT on Deut. 29.24.

⁴ Cf. MT-S on Deut. 28.7, 25; also MT-Seb on Jud. 2.22: Isa. 30.21.

⁵ Cf. MT-Seb on Lev. 6.8.

⁶ Cf. Q-K: 2 Sam. 17.9, 12.

⁷ Cf. Ex. 25.36.

⁸ Cf. Gen. 46.22, 25; Lev. 20.6; also Md-Ma on Jer. 38.16.

⁹ Cf. S-MT on Ex. 21.37; Num. 31.37; also: I Ki. 22.17 — 2 Chron. 18.16.

Ex. 10.13	MT	וְרוּחַ ⋯⋯ נָשָׂא
	S	⋯⋯ נשאה
1 Ki. 19.4	K	רֹתֶם אַחַת
	Q	⋯⋯ אֶחָד
Gen. 48.22	MT	שְׁכֶם אֶחָד
	S	⋯⋯ אחת
Gen. 19.23	MT	הַשֶּׁמֶשׁ יָצָא
	S	⋯⋯ יצאה [1]
Deut. 23.17	MT	בְּאַחַד שְׁעָרֶיךָ
	S	⋯⋯ באחת [2]
1 Ki. 8.38		תְּחִנָּה ⋯⋯ תִהְיֶה
2 Chron. 6.29		⋯⋯ יְהְיֶה

α) Adjustment in gender.

Ex. 1.16	MT	בַּת ⋯⋯ וְחָיָה
	S	⋯⋯ וחיתה
2 Sam. 24.12		אַחַת מֵהֶם
1 Chron. 21.10		מֵהֵנָּה ⋯⋯

β) The nomen regens a construct state.[3]

Jer. 17.24	Q	יוֹם הַשַּׁבָּת ⋯⋯ בּוֹ
	K	⋯⋯ בה
Num. 7.61	MT	קַעֲרַת כֶּסֶף אַחַת
	S	⋯⋯ אחד
Gen. 47.26	MT	אַדְמַת הַכֹּהֲנִים לְבַדָּם
	S	⋯⋯ לבדה
Num. 28.31	MT	עֹלַת הַתָּמִיד וּמִנְחָתוֹ
	S	⋯⋯ ומנחתה

γ) Names of nations.

2 Sam. 8.5	וַתָּבֹא אֲרָם
1 Chron. 18.5	⋯⋯ וַיָּבֹא [4]
2 Sam. 24.9	וַתְּהִי יִשְׂרָאֵל
1 Chron. 21.5	⋯⋯ וַיְהִי

§ 46.   Agreement in number between subject and predicate.

a) The verb precedes the noun.

Gen. 9.29	MT	וַיְהִי כָּל יְמֵי
	S	⋯⋯ ויהיו [5]
Num. 9.6	MT	וַיְהִי אֲנָשִׁים
	S	⋯⋯ ויהיו
Gen. 30.42	MT	וְהָיָה הָעֲטֻפִים
	S	⋯⋯ והיו
Num. 32.25	MT	וַיֹּאמֶר בְּנֵי גָד
	S	⋯⋯ ויאמרו
Ex. 4.29	MT	וַיֵּלֶךְ מֹשֶׁה וְאַהֲרֹן [6]
	S	⋯⋯ וילכו

Gen. 10.25	MT	יֻלַּד שְׁנֵי בָנִים
	S	⋯⋯ ילדו [7]
Deut. 21.19	S	וְתָפַשׂ בּוֹ אָבִיו וְאִמּוֹ
	MT	⋯⋯ וְתָפְשׂוּ [8]

b) The verb follows the noun.

Gen. 46.27	MT	וּבְנֵי יוֹסֵף אֲשֶׁר יֻלַּד
	S	⋯⋯ ילדו [9]
Lev. 25.31	MT	וּבָתֵּי הַחֲצֵרִים ⋯⋯ יֵחָשֵׁב
	S	⋯⋯ יחשבו

---

[1] Cf. Ex. 16.21; also Q-K: Jer. 15.9.
[2] Cf. Deut. 15.7; 16.5; 17.2; 18.6.
[3] Cf. Deut. 28.61: בספר התורה הַזֹּאת
   Deut. 29.20: בספר התורה הַזֶּה.
[4] Cf. 2 Sam. 8.6 — 1 Chron. 18.6.
[5] Cf. Gen. 5.23, 31.

[6] Cf. Ex. 29.10, 19: וְסָמַךְ אהרן ובניו
   Ex. 29.15: וְסָמְכוּ אהרן ובניו.
[7] Cf. Gen. 41.50; Num. 26.33.
[8] Cf. Lev. 8.14.
[9] Cf. Gen. 35.26.

Gen. 13.7			2 Ki. 9.11		
MT	וְהַכְּנַעֲנִי וְהַפְּרִזִּי אָז יֹשֵׁב		MT	עֲבָדָיו אֵלָיו וַיֹּאמֶר לוֹ	
S	ישבים ····		Seb	···· ויאמרו ···· [1]	
			Num. 27.3 S	וּבָנִים לֹא הָיָה לוֹ	
			MT	···· הָיוּ ····	

§ 47. Agreement in number between several verbs.

a) Adjustment to the preceding verb.		b) Adjustment to the following verb.	
Ex. 39.3 MT	וַיְרַקְּעוּ ···· וְקִצֵּץ	Ex. 10.17 MT	שָׂא ···· וְהַעְתִּירוּ
S	וקצצו ····	S	שאו ···· [2]
Lev. 14.42		Ex. 12.46	
MT וְלָקְחוּ ···· וְהֵבִיאוּ ···· יִקַּח וְטָח		MT	לֹא תוֹצִיא ···· לֹא תִשְׁבְּרוּ
S יקחו וטחו ····		S	תוציאו ····
Lev. 19.27		Num. 31.29 MT	תִּקְחוּ וְנָתַתָּה
MT לֹא תַקִּפוּ ···· וְלֹא תַשְׁחִית		S	תקח ····
S תשחיתו ····		Num. 33.54 MT	תַּרְבּוּ ···· תַּמְעִיט
Num. 13.2 MT	שְׁלַח ···· תִּשְׁלָחוּ	S	תרבה ····
S	תשלח ····	Deut. 4.25	
Num. 21.32 MT	וַיִּלְכְּדוּ ···· וַיּוֹרֶשׁ	MT כִּי תוֹלִיד ···· וְנוֹשַׁנְתֶּם ···· וְהִשְׁחַתֶּם	
S	ויורישו ····	S תולידו ····	
Deut. 12.5 MT	תִדְרְשׁוּ וּבָאתָ	Deut. 12.16	
S	ובאתם ····	MT	לֹא תֹאכְלוּ ···· תִּשְׁפְּכֶנּוּ
		S	תאכל ····
		Isa. 36.7	תֹּאמַר ···· בָּטָחְנוּ
		2 Ki. 18.22	תֹאמְרוּן ····

§ 48. Collective nouns used in the sing. or plur. (B-L § 63x).

Lev. 20.27	MT	בָּאֶבֶן	1 Chron. 10.7		אִישׁ
	S	באבנים	1 Sam. 31.7		אַנְשֵׁי [3]
Lev. 8.13	MT	אַבְנֵט	2 Ki. 25.17	K	אמה
	S	אבניטים		Q	אַמּוֹת

[1] Cf. Josh. 6.19; Jud. 11.15; 1 Ki. 20.3; Ezek. 44.9.

[2] Cf. Jud. 18.9: קומה ונעלה, Venice 1515 marg.: קומו ונעלה.

[3] Cf. 1 Chron. 10.1 — 1 Sam. 31.1.

Reference		Hebrew		Reference		Hebrew
1 Ki. 10.22		אֲנִי (1°)		Gen. 17.13	MT	יָלִיד
2 Chron. 9.21		אֳנִיּוֹת			S	ילידי ⁴
Gen. 41.57	MT	הָאָרֶץ		1 Ki. 10.14		כִּכָּר
	S	הארצות		2 Chron. 9.13		כִּכְּרֵי
2 Ki. 21.3		אֲשֵׁרָה		2 Chron. 9.19		(כָל) מַמְלָכָה
2 Chron. 33.3		אֲשֵׁרוֹת		1 Ki. 10.20		מַמְלָכוֹת
1 Chron. 19.10		בָּחוּר		Num. 4.15	MT	מַשָּׂא
2 Sam. 10.9		בְּחוּרֵי			S	משאי
Num. 3.50	MT	בְּכוֹר		Lev. 25.5	MT	סָפִיחַ
	S	בכורי ¹			S	ספיחי
2 Ki. 21.3		לַבַּעַל		Deut. 32.14	MT	עֵנָב
2 Chron. 33.3		לַבְּעָלִים			S	ענבים
Ex. 35.28	MT	הַבֹּשֶׂם		Lev. 23.40	MT	וַעֲנַף
	S	הבשמים			S	וענפי
1 Ki. 12.24		דְּבַר		2 Sam. 5.11		עֵץ ⁵
2 Chron. 11.4		דִּבְרֵי ²		1 Chron. 14.1		עֵצִים
Ex. 22.1	S	דם		1 Chron. 6.45		עִיר
	MT	דָּמִים		Josh. 21.19		עָרִים
2 Ki. 16.3		בְּדֶרֶךְ		Num. 15.38	MT	צִיצִת
2 Chron. 28.2		בְּדַרְכֵי ³			S	ציציות
Ps. 18.49		חָמָס		Gen. 15.10	MT	הַצִּפֹּר
2 Sam. 22.49		חֲמָסִים			S	הצפרים
2 Ki. 11.10		הַחֲנִית		Ex. 26.20	MT	קֶרֶשׁ
2 Chron. 23.9		הַחֲנִיתִים			S	קרשים
1 Sam. 20.38	K	החצי		Num. 11.31	S	שלוי
	Q	הַחִצִּים			MT	שַׂלְוִים
2 Ki. 12.12	K	יד		2 Ki. 22.1		שָׁנָה
	Q	יְדֵי		2 Chron. 34.1		שָׁנִים ⁶

¹ Cf. Num. 3.46.

² Cf. MT-S on Deut. 5.5.

³ Cf. 2 Ki. 8.27 — 2 Chron. 22.3; 2 Ki. 22.2 — 2 Chron. 34.2; also 2 Chron. 21.13: בְּדֶרֶךְ, Venice 1515 marg.: בְּדַרְכֵי.

⁴ Cf. Lev. 22.11.

⁵ Cf. Ezek. 15.6: בְּעֵץ, Venice 1515 marg.: בַּעֲצֵי.

⁶ Cf. MT-S on Gen. 17.24; K-Q on 2 Ki. 8.17; and 2 Ki. 24.8 — 2 Chron. 36.9; cf. also 2 Sam. 2.10: שנים (ושתים), Venice 1515 marg.: שָׁנָה.

§ 49.   The subject: a collective noun—the predicate: in the plur. or sing.

Josh. 9.7	Q	וַיֹּאמֶר אִישׁ יִשְׂרָאֵל [1]
	K	וַיֹּאמְרוּ ....
Ex. 15.24	MT	וַיִּלֹּנוּ הָעָם
	S	וַיָּלֶן .... [2]
1 Chron. 11.13		וְהָעָם נָסוּ
2 Sam. 23.11		נָס .... [3]
2 Chron. 36.1		וַיִּקְחוּ עַם הָאָרֶץ
2 Ki. 23.30		וַיִּקַּח .... [4]
Gen. 15.16	MT	וְדוֹר רְבִיעִי יָשׁוּבוּ
	S	יָשׁוּב ....
2 Chron. 18.18		צָבָא .... עֹמְדִים
1 Ki. 22.19		עֹמֵד ....
Num. 22.4	MT	יְלַחֲכוּ הַקָּהָל
	S	יְלַחֵךְ ....

α)   Names of nations.

1 Chron. 18.13		וַיִּהְיוּ כָל אֱדוֹם
2 Sam. 8.14		וַיְהִי ....
Hos. 12.9	Seb	וַיֹּאמְרוּ אֶפְרַיִם
	MT	וַיֹּאמֶר ....
1 Chron. 19.16		אֲרָם .... נִגְּפוּ
2 Sam. 10.15		נִגַּף ....
1 Chron. 11.4		הַיְבוּסִי יֹשְׁבֵי הָאָרֶץ
2 Sam. 5.6		יוֹשֵׁב .... [5]
2 Chron. 10.1		בָּאוּ כָל יִשְׂרָאֵל
1 Ki. 12.1		בָּא ....
1 Chron. 18.2		וַיִּהְיוּ מוֹאָב
2 Sam. 8.2		וַתְּהִי .... [6]
Ex. 14.10	MT	מִצְרַיִם נֹסֵעַ
	S	נֹסְעִים .... [7]

B.   THE ARTICLE

§ 50.   The article is used (Bergstr. § 2 l).

a)   In a construct state form-
      ation.[8]

1 Chron. 8.28	רָאשֵׁי אָבוֹת
1 Chron. 9.34	הָאָבוֹת ....
Ps. 96.12	עֲצֵי יַעַר
1 Chron. 16.33	הַיַּעַר ....
2 Sam. 8.13	בְּגֵיא מֶלַח
1 Chron. 18.12	הַמֶּלַח ....

2 Sam. 7.2		בְּבֵית אֲרָזִים
1 Chron. 17.1		הָאֲרָזִים ....
2 Sam. 5.24		קוֹל צְעָדָה
1 Chron. 14.15		הַצְּעָדָה ....
Jer. 17.19	K	בְּנֵי עם
	Q	הָעָם ....
Jer. 32.19	K	בְּנֵי אדם
	Q	הָאָדָם ....

---

1 Cf. Jud. 18.11: שֵׁשׁ מֵאוֹת אִישׁ חָגוּר כְּלִי מִלְחָמָה

Jud. 18.16: שֵׁשׁ מֵאוֹת אִישׁ חֲגוּרִים כְּלֵי מִלְחָמָה.

2 Cf. Num. 14.1; Ex. 16.30; also 1 Ki. 12.5 — 2 Chron. 10.5.

3 Cf. MT-S on Ex. 24.2; also S-MT on Num. 12.15.

4 Cf. 2 Chron. 23.21 — 2 Ki. 11.20; 2 Chron. 33.25 — 2 Ki. 21.24.

5 Cf. Md-Ma on Jud. 1.21.

6 On the difference in the gender of the verb, cf. § 45γ.   7 Cf. Ex. 14.25.

8 Cf. p. 160, s.v. רשע: Ps. 1.1: MT הרשעים; p. 153 s.v. רשעים (בעצת) O— עצבים: Ps. 127.2: MT העצבים (לחם) —O עצבים.

Ezek. 18.2	K	וְשֵׁנֵי בנים
	Q	.... הַבָּנִים
2 Ki. 15.25	K	בֵּית מלך
	Q	1 .... הַמֶּלֶךְ
2 Ki. 25.28	K	כִּסֵּא מלכים
	Q	2 .... הַמְּלָכִים
Eccl. 7.2	Ma	בֵּית מִשְׁתֶּה
	Md	.... המשתה
2 Ki. 11.20	K	עַם ארץ
	Q	3 .... הָאָרֶץ
2 Chron. 4.1	Ma	מִזְבַּח נְחֹשֶׁת
	Md	.... הנחשת
2 Chron. 8.9		אַנְשֵׁי מִלְחָמָה
1 Ki. 9.22		.... הַמִּלְחָמָה
2 Chron. 9.14		מַלְכֵי עֶרֶב
1 Ki. 10.15		.... הָעֶרֶב
Jer. 38.11	Q	בְּלוֹי סְחָבוֹת
	K	.... הסחבות

b) In connection with a preposition.

1 Sam. 14.32	K	אֶל שלל
	Q	.... הַשָּׁלָל
1 Ki. 22.31		אֶת קָטֹן וְאֶת גָּדוֹל
2 Chron. 18.30		הַקָּטֹן .... הַגָּדוֹל
2 Sam. 23.21		אֶת אִישׁ מִצְרִי
1 Chron. 11.23		הָאִישׁ הַמִּצְרִי

2 Ki. 15.25	K	וְאֶת אריה
	Q	.... הָאַרְיֵה
Lam. 1.18	K	4 כָּל עמים
	Q	.... הָעַמִּים
1 Ki. 7.21	K	לְעֵבֶר שבכה
	Q	.... הַשְּׂבָכָה
2 Sam. 5.23		מִמּוּל בְּכָאִים
1 Chron. 14.14		.... הַבְּכָאִים
2 Sam. 7.16	(1°)	עַד עוֹלָם
1 Chron. 17.14		.... הָעוֹלָם
1 Ki. 4.7	K	עַל אחד
	Q	.... הָאֶחָד

c) When the noun is rendered emphatic in other ways.[5]

Jer. 40.3	K	דבר הַזֶּה
	Q	הַדָּבָר ....
Jer. 27.3	K	מַלְאָכִים הַבָּאִים
	Q	הַמלאכים ....
2 Sam. 23.30		בְּנָיָהוּ פִּרְעָתֹנִי
1 Chron. 11.31		.... הַפִּרְעָתֹנִי
1 Ki. 9.17		בֵּית חֹרֹן תַּחְתּוֹן
2 Chron. 8.5		.... הַתַּחְתּוֹן

d) When the noun is otherwise undetermined.[6]

2 Sam. 7.5		תִּבְנֶה לִּי בַיִת
1 Chron. 17.4		.... הַבַּיִת

---

[1] Cf. 2 Ki. 11.20; 15.18.
[2] Cf. Jer. 52.32.
[3] Cf. Jer. 10.13.
[4] Cf. Deut. 11.24: כל הַמָּקוֹם אשר תדרך כף רגלכם בו
Josh. 1.3: כל מָקוֹם אשר תדרך כף רגלכם בו.
[5] Cf. Ex. 29.39: את הכבש הָאֶחָד תעשה בבקר

Num. 28.4: את הכבש אֶחָד תעשה בבקר; cf. also Ezek. 40.31: חָצֵר הַחִצוֹנָה;
Venice 1515 marg.: הֶחָצֵר.
[6] Cf. Josh. 15.18: ויהי בבואה ותסיתהו לשאול מאת אביה שָׂדֶה
Jud. 1.14: ויהי בבואה ותסיתהו; cf. also p. 129, לשאול מאת אביה הַשָּׂדֶה
s.v. ארץ: Ps. 46.3: MT ארץ (בהמיר) הָאָרֶץ — O.

2 Chron. 9.6	לֹא הֻגַּד לִי חֲצִי	1 Chron. 20.5	וַתְּהִי עוֹד מִלְחָמָה
1 Ki. 10.7	הַחֵצִי ….	2 Sam. 21.19	הַמִּלְחָמָה ….

§ 51.   The emphatic state is indicated by the article or suffix.

Gen. 38.21	MT	מְקֹמָה
	S	הַמָּקוֹם

α)   The article is assimilated to an inseparable preposition.

Lev. 3.8	MT	דָּמוֹ [1]
	S	הַדָּם

2 Sam. 24.13	בְּאַרְצֶךָ
1 Chron. 21.12	בָּאָרֶץ
2 Chron. 9.6	לְדִבְרֵיהֶם
1 Ki. 10.7	לַדְּבָרִים
1 Ki. 22.34	לְרַכְּבוֹ
2 Chron. 18.33	לָרֶכֶב
Ezek. 29.7 K	בכפך
Q	בַּכַּף

1 Chron. 10.7	עָרֵיהֶם
2 Sam. 31.7	הֶעָרִים
2 Chron. 23.13	עַמּוּדוֹ
2 Ki. 11.14	הָעַמּוּד [2]
2 Sam. 10.18	צְבָאוֹ
1 Chron. 19.18	הַצָּבָא
1 Sam. 31.5	חַרְבוֹ
1 Chron. 10.5	הַחֶרֶב

§ 52.   The article includes the meaning of a demonstrative pronoun (B-L § 30i).[3]

α)   Masc. sing.

Gen. 3.3	MT	הָעֵץ
	S	העץ הזה
Gen. 19.12	MT	הַמָּקוֹם
	S	המקום הזה
Num. 22.4	MT	הַקָּהָל
	S	הקהל הזה
Num. 29.12	MT	לַחֹדֶשׁ הַשְּׁבִיעִי
	S	לחדש השביעי הזה
2 Ki. 20.9		אֶת הַדָּבָר
Isa. 38.7		אֶת הַדָּבָר הַזֶּה
2 Chron. 10.10		לָעָם
1 Ki. 12.10		לָעָם הַזֶּה [4]

β)   Fem. sing.

Gen. 21.13	MT	הָאָמָה
	S	האמה הזאת
1 Ki. 8.44		הָעִיר
2 Chron. 6.34		הָעִיר הַזֹּאת

γ)   Plural.

Gen. 48.16	MT	אֶת הַנְּעָרִים
	S	את הנערים האלה
2 Ki. 18.35		הָאֲרָצוֹת
Isa. 36.20		הָאֲרָצוֹת הָאֵלֶּה

[1] Cf. Lev. 1.11: וְזָרְקוּ בְּנֵי אַהֲרֹן הַכֹּהֲנִים
אֶת דָּמוֹ
Lev. 3.2: וְזָרְקוּ בְּנֵי אַהֲרֹן הַכֹּהֲנִים
אֶת הַדָּם.

[2] Cf. 2 Chron. 34.31 — 2 Ki. 23.3.
[3] Cf. MGWJ 1937, p. 64, on Ruth 3.13.
[4] Cf. MT-S on Deut. 10.11.

§ 53. Preservation of the article with an inseparable preposition (B-L § 25w, x; Bergstr. § 16b).[1]

a) With the preposition בְ.

Deut. 21.1	MT	בָּאֲדָמָה
	S	בהאדמה
Gen. 8.5	MT	בָּעֲשִׂירִי
	S	בהעשירי
2 Ki. 7.12	Q	בַּשָּׂדֶה
	K	בהשדה

b) With the preposition כְ.

Gen. 3.5	MT	כֵּאלֹהִים
	S	כהאלהים
Deut. 6.24	S	כיום הזה
	MT	כְּהַיּוֹם הַזֶּה

c) With the preposition לְ.

| Gen. 1.5 | MT | לָאוֹר |
| | S | להאור |

Ex. 1.20	MT	לַמְיַלְּדֹת
	S	להמילדות
1 Ki. 12.7		לָעָם הַזֶּה
2 Chron. 10.7		לְהָעָם הַזֶּה

d) The prefixed ה in verbal formations.

Deut. 1.33	MT	לַחֲנֹתְכֶם
	S	להחנותכם
Ex. 13.21	MT	לַנְחֹתָם
	S	להנחתם
Deut. 1.33	MT	לַרְאֹתְכֶם
	S	להראותכם
2 Ki. 9.15	K	לגיד [2]
	Q	לְהַגִּיד
2 Ki. 7.15	Q	בְּחָפְזָם
	K	בהחפזם

C.   THE VERB

§ 54. The use of the consecutive waw (Bergstr. § 2i).

a) With the perfect.

Ex. 8.12	MT	וְהָיָה
	S	ויהי
Josh. 19.29	Q	וְהָיוּ
	K	ויהיו [3]

Gen. 27.4	S	והבאת
	MT	וְהֵבֵיאָה
Ex. 3.10	S	והוצאת
	MT	וְהוֹצֵא [4]

---

[1] The vocalization of the בכל with a pataḥ does not necessarily imply the assimilation of the Article; cf. p. 218 e. Similarly, no consistent rules can be established for their vocalization with pataḥ or ḳameẓ (Bergstr. § 28p); cf. 1 Ki. 8.12: בָּעֲרָפֶל — 2 Chron. 6.1: בָּעֲרָפֶל; 2 Chron. 1.15: כָּאֲבָנִים —

1 Ki. 10.27: כָּאֲבָנִים; Ezek. 7.19: בְּחֻצוֹת, Venice 1515 marg.: בָּחֻצוֹת.

[2] Cf. Jer. 39.7: MT לְבִיא for לְהָבִיא.

[3] Cf. K-Q on Jer. 18.23.

[4] On the difference between this example and the preceding one, cf. § 63c.

2 Chron. 18.33		וְהוֹצֵאתַנִי	2 Sam. 19.41	K	וַיַּעֲבִרוּ
1 Ki. 22.34		וְהוֹצִיאֵנִי		Q	הֶעֱבִירוּ
Ex. 8.23	MT	וְזָבַחְנוּ	Prov. 22.3	K	רָאָה ··· וַיִּסָּתֵר
	S	ונזבחה		Q	וְנִסְתָּר ····
1 Chron. 14.10		הַאֶעֱלֶה ··· וּנְתַתָּם	1 Ki. 12.16		וַיַּרְא כָּל יִשְׂרָאֵל
2 Sam. 5.19		הַאֶעֱלֶה ··· הַתִּתְּנֵם	2 Chron. 10.16		וְכָל יִשְׂרָאֵל רָאוּ
Lev. 26.43	S	והרצתה [1]	2 Ki. 19.26		וַיֵּבֹשׁוּ
	MT	וְתִרֶץ	Isa. 37.27		וָבֹשׁוּ

b)   With the imperfect.

Gen. 27.22	MT	וַיְמֻשֵּׁהוּ	1 Chron. 15.29		וַיְהִי
	S	והמשהו	2 Sam. 6.16		וְהָיָה
Isa. 36.21		וַיַּחֲרִישׁוּ	Gen. 37.3	S	ויעש
2 Ki. 18.36		וְהֶחֱרִישׁוּ		MT	וְעָשָׂה

§ 55.   The use of the inf. absol. or imperative (Bergstr. 2, § 12k).

Deut. 31.26	MT	לָקֹחַ	Deut. 27.1	MT	שָׁמֹר
	S	לקחו [2]		S	שמרו
Num. 25.17	MT	צָרוֹר	2 Sam. 24.12		הָלוֹךְ
	S	צררו	1 Chron. 21.10		לֵךְ
Num. 15.35	MT	רָגוֹם	Ps. 105.8		זָכֹר [3]
	S	רגמו	1 Chron. 16.15		זִכְרוּ [4]
Deut. 1.16	MT	שָׁמֹעַ			
	S	שמעו			

§ 56.   Particle and verb: the verb in the inf. constr. or finite tense (Bergstr. 2, § 11).

a)   אחרי.   b)   לבלתי; למען.

Gen. 46.30	MT	אַחֲרֵי רְאוֹתִי	Deut. 17.20	MT	לְבִלְתִּי רוּם
	S	ראיתי ····		S	ראם ···· [5]
Deut. 12.30	MT	אַחֲרֵי הִשָּׁמֶדָם	Jer. 17.23	Q	לְבִלְתִּי שָׁמוֹעַ
	S	השמידם ····		K	שומע ····
			Jer. 25.7	Q	לְמַעַן הַכְעִיסֵנִי
				K	הכעסוני ····

---

[1] On this form, cf. Lev. 26.34: MT וְהִרְצָת — S והרתצה; 25.21: MT וְעָשָׂת — S ועשתה; 2 Ki. 9.37: K והית — Q וְהָיְתָה.

[2] Cf. Ex. 29.1: לְקַח; 1 Ki. 17.11: לָקְחִי.   [3] Lege זָכֹר.   [4] Cf. MT–S on Ex. 13.3.   [5] Cf. p. 562, § 1a.

c) עד.

Gen. 39.16	MT	עד בוא
	S	1 .... בא
Gen. 27.45	MT	עד שוב
	S	.... שב
Num. 32.18	MT	עד התנחל
	S	התנחלו ....

Deut. 28.20

	MT	עַד הִשָּׁמֶדְךָ וְעַד אֲבָדְךָ
	S	2 .... השמידוך ... האבידוך

d) ביום.

Num. 3.13	MT	בְּיוֹם הַכֹּתִי
	S	.... הכיתי
Num. 9.15	MT	וּבְיוֹם הָקִים
	S	3 .... הוקם

§ 57. Inf. constr. with בכלם and pronominal suffixes.

a) With the preposition ב.

Gen. 19.29	MT	בַּהֲפֹךְ
	S	בהפכו

b) With the preposition כ.

Gen. 33.10	MT	כִּרְאֹת
	S	כראותי
Gen. 24.30	MT	כִּרְאֹת
	S	כראותו

c) With the preposition ל.

Gen. 28.4	S	לרשת
	MT	לְרִשְׁתְּךָ

Ex. 28.1	S	לכהן
	MT	לְכַהֲנוֹ
Deut. 21.5	S	לשרת
	MT	לְשָׁרְתוֹ
1 Chron. 17.4		לָשֶׁבֶת
2 Sam. 7.5		לְשִׁבְתִּי
2 Ki. 21.6		לְהַכְעִיס
2 Chron. 33.6		לְהַכְעִיסוֹ

d) With the preposition מ.

Deut. 16.9	MT	מֵהָחֵל
	S	מהחלך
1 Chron. 11.19		מֵעֲשׂוֹת
2 Sam. 23.17		מֵעֲשֹׂתִי

§ 58. Finite verb continued by inf. absol. or finite tense (B-L § 36e', h'; Bergstr. 2, § 12h).[4]

Gen. 8.3	MT	וַיָּשֻׁבוּ .... הָלוֹךְ וָשׁוֹב
	S	.... הלכו ושבו
Gen. 8.5	MT	הָיוּ הָלוֹךְ וְחָסוֹר
	S	.... הלכו וחסרו

Gen. 8.7	MT	וַיֵּצֵא יָצוֹא וָשׁוֹב
	S	.... יצא ושב
Gen. 12.9	MT	וַיִּסַּע .... הָלוֹךְ וְנָסוֹעַ
	S	.... הלך ונסע

---

[1] Cf. Gen. 43.24.
[2] Cf. Deut. 7.23; further: Jer. 52.3: הַשְׁלִיכוֹ (עד)(הַשְׁלִיכוּ), Venice 1515 marg.
[3] On the change from *hiph'il* to *hoph'al* cf. § 18e.
[4] Cf. p. 233, subdivision d sub 1.

Ex. 8.11	MT	וַיַּרְא ⋯⋯ וְהַכְבֵּד	Isa. 37.30	
	S	⋯⋯ ויכבד	K	זְרְעוּ וְקִצְרוּ וְנִטְעוּ ⋯⋯ ואכול
Isa. 37.18, 19		הֶחֱרִיבוּ ⋯⋯ וְנָתֹן	Q	⋯⋯ וְאִכְלוּ [1]
2 Ki. 19.17, 18		וְנָתְנוּ ⋯⋯		

§ 59. Verbal forms with pronominal suffixes (Bergstr. § 2i).[2] The pronominal suffix is added to the verb or to the particle את (cf. § 00).

Lev. 10.5	MT	וַיִּשָּׂאֵם	Num. 24.10	MT	קְרָאתִיךָ
	S	וישאו אתם		S	קראתי לך
Deut. 9.28	MT	לַהֲבִיאָם	1 Chron. 19.12		וְהוֹשַׁעְתִּיךָ
	S	להביא אתם	2 Sam. 10.11		לְהוֹשִׁיעַ לָךְ
2 Chron. 25.28		וַיִּשָּׂאֻהוּ	Ps. 18.20		וַיּוֹצִיאֵנִי
2 Ki. 14.20		וַיִּשְׂאוּ אֹתוֹ	2 Sam. 22.20		וַיֹּצֵא ⋯⋯ אֹתִי
2 Chron. 36.1		וַיַּמְלִיכֻהוּ	2 Chron. 10.13		וַיַּעֲנֵם
2 Ki. 23.30		וַיַּמְלִיכוּ אֹתוֹ	1 Ki. 12.13		וַיַּעַן ⋯⋯ אֶת הָעָם
2 Chron. 23.14		הוֹצִיאוּהָ	1 Ki. 10.1		לְנַסֹּתוֹ
2 Ki. 11.15		הוֹצִיאוּ אֹתָהּ	2 Chron. 9.1		לְנַסּוֹת אֶת שְׁלֹמֹה

D.   THE ה EUPHONICUM

a.   With verbal forms

§ 60.   Ḳal.

a)   1. pers. sing. imperf.

1)   The regular verb.

α)   Imperfect in o.

			Ps. 18.38	אֶרְדּוֹף
			2 Sam. 22.38	אֶרְדְּפָה
			Ex. 6.5	MT	וָאֶזְכֹּר
				S	ואזכרה
Gen. 30.32	MT	אֶעֱבֹר	Deut. 10.2	MT	וָאֶכְתֹּב
	S	אעברה		S	ואכתבה

---

[1] =2 Ki. 19.29. Cf. likewise 2 Ki. 21. 13: כַּאֲשֶׁר יִמְחֶה ⋯⋯ מָחָה וְהָפַךְ ⋯; the proposed correction in מחה והפך (BHKK) is, therefore, basically erroneous.

[2] Cf. Lev. 6.22: כל זכר בכהנים יאכל אתה; Lev. 7.6: כל זכר בכהנים יאכלנו;

Num. 18.11: כל טהור בביתך יאכל אתו
Num. 18.13: כל טהור בביתך יאכלנו. Consequently, readings like: Ex. 2.6: MT ותראהו את הילד (cf. S ותרא); ib. 35.5: יביאה את תרומת יהוה (cf. S יביא) represent doublets; cf. our note 5 on p. 293.

Deut. 10.3	MT	וָאֶפְסֹל
	S	ואפסלה
Lev. 26.13	MT	וָאֶשְׁבֹּר
	S	ואשברה
Deut. 9.21	MT	וָאֶשְׂרֹף
	S	ואשרפה
Deut. 9.17	MT	וָאֶתְפֹּשׂ
	S	ואתפשה

β) Imperfect in a.[1]

Deut. 22.14	MT	וָאֶקְרַב
	S	ואקרבה
Deut. 2.26	MT	וָאֶשְׁלַח
	S	ואשלחה
Jer. 8.6	K	וָאֶשְׁמָע
	Q	ואשמעה

2) Weak verbs.

γ) Imperfect in i.

Ex. 3.8	MT	וָאֵרֵד
	S	וארדה
Gen. 34.12	S	ואתן
	MT	וָאֶתְּנָה

δ) Imperfect in a.

Gen. 18.5	S	ואקח
	MT	וָאֶקְחָה
Num. 22.19	S	ואדע
	MT	וָאֵדְעָה ²

ε) Primae א.

Ex. 3.17	MT	וָאֹמַר
	S	ואמרה
Gen. 27.25	S	ואכל
	MT	וָאֹכְלָה

ζ) Primae נ.

Deut. 9.21	MT	וָאֶכֹּת
	S	ואכתה
1 Chron. 21.13		אֶפֹּל
2 Sam. 24.14		אֶפְּלָה

η) Mediae ו and י.

Isa. 37.24		וָאָבוֹא
2 Ki. 19.23		וְאָבוֹאָה
Ex. 3.3	S	אסור
	MT	אָסֻרָה
Deut. 10.5	MT	וָאָשִׂם
	S	ואשימה

b) 1. pers. plur. imperf.

1) The regular verb.

α) Imperfect in o.

Gen. 41.11	S	ונחלם
	MT	וַנַּחְלְמָה
Deut. 3.4	MT	וַנִּלְכֹּד
	S	ונלכדה
Deut. 2.13	MT	וַנַּעֲבֹר
	S	ונעברה

β) Imperfect in a.[3]

Ex. 8.22	MT	נִזְבַּח
	S	נזבחה
Gen. 43.21	S	ונפתח
	MT	וַנִּפְתְּחָה
Gen. 24.57	S	ונשאל
	MT	וְנִשְׁאֲלָה

---

[1] Cf. p. 163, s.v. שמח: Ps. 31.8: MT וָאֶשְׂמְחָה — O וְאֶשְׂמְחָה.

[2] Cf. K-Q on Ruth 4.4.

[3] Cf. in § 7a the instance from Num. 14.41, and our note 2, page 243.

2) Weak verbs.

γ) Imperfect in i.

Ex. 8.23	MT	נֵלֵךְ
	S	נלכה
Num. 14.4	S	נתן
	MT	נִתְּנָה

δ) Imperfect in a.

Gen. 19.5	S	ונדע
	MT	וְנֵדְעָה
Deut. 1.19	MT	וַנִּסַע
	S	ונסעה

ε) Primae א.

Num. 11.13	S	ונאכל
	MT	וְנֹאכְלָה
Gen. 34.23	S	נאות
	MT	נֵאוֹתָה

ζ) Mediae ו.

Gen. 35.3	S	ונקום
	MT	וְנָקוּמָה
Num. 14.4	S	ונשוב
	MT	וְנָשׁוּבָה¹

c) Imperative (Bergstr. 2 § 5f).

α) Imperfect in o.

Num. 21.16	MT	אֱסֹף
	S	אספה

§ 61. Pi'el.

a) 1. pers. sing. imperf.

Gen. 12.3	S	ואברך
	MT	וַאֲבָרְכָה

β) Imperfect in a.

Isa. 37.17	Q	פְּקַח
	K	פקחה
Gen. 15.9	S	קח
	MT	קְחָה
Gen. 43.8	S	שלח
	MT	שִׁלְחָה
Num. 23.18	MT	וּשְׁמַע
	S	ושמעה

γ) Imperfect in i.

Gen. 19.9	MT	גֶּשׁ
	S	גשה
2 Chron. 25.17		לְךְ
2 Ki. 14.8		לְכָה
2 Ki. 14.10		וְשֵׁב
2 Chron. 25.19		שְׁבָה
Gen. 14.21	MT	תֶּן
	S	תנה

δ) Mediae ו.²

Num. 23.18	MT	קוּם
	S	קומה
Gen. 27.3	S	וצוד
	MT	וְצוּדָה

d) Infinitive.

Ex. 36.2	S	לקרב
	MT	לְקָרְבָה
Gen. 1.30	S	לאכל
	MT	לְאָכְלָה

Num. 24.13	MT	אֲדַבֵּר
	S	אדברה

¹ Cf. K-Q on Lam. 5.21.

² Cf. p. 157, s.v. קוּם: Ps. 35.2: MT וְקוּם O — וְקוּמָה.

2 Sam. 22.50		אֹמַר
Ps. 18.50		אֲזַמְּרָה
Ex. 32.30	S	אכפר
	MT	אֲכַפְּרָה
Ex. 9.28	S	ואשלח
	MT	וַאֲשַׁלְּחָה

b) 3. pers. fem. sing. imperf.

Ezek. 23.16	K	ותעגב
	Q	וַתַּעְגְּבָה

c) Imperative.

2 Chron. 18.8	מַהֵר
1 Ki. 22.9	מַהֲרָה

§ 62. Niph'al.

a) 1. pers. sing. imperf.

Gen. 19.20	S	אמלט
	MT	אִמָּלְטָה
Hag. 1.8	K	ואכבד
	Q	וְאִכָּבְדָה

b) Imperative.

Gen. 25.33	S	השבע
	MT	הִשָּׁבְעָה

c) Infinitive.

Num. 12.15	MT	הֵאָסֵף
	S	האספה

§ 63. Hiph'il.

a) 1. pers. sing. imperf.

1 Chron. 17.8		וָאַכְרִית
2 Sam. 7.9		וָאַכְרִתָה
Deut. 32.20	S	אסתיר
	MT	אַסְתִּירָה
Deut. 32.26	S	אשבית
	MT	אַשְׁבִּיתָה
Deut. 9.21	MT	וָאַשְׁלֵךְ
	S	ואשליכה

α) Primae י.

Gen. 32.10	S	ואיטיב
	MT	וְאֵיטִיבָה
Gen. 19.8	S	אוצא
	MT	אוֹצִיאָה

β) Mediae ו.

Josh. 24.8	Q	וָאָבִיא
	K	ואביאה

b) 1. pers. plur. imperf.

Deut. 3.6	MT	וַנַּחֲרֵם
	S	ונחרימה

c) Imperative.

Gen. 27.7	S	הבא
	MT	הָבִיאָה
Lam. 5.1	K	הבט
	Q	הַבִּיטָה
2 Chron. 16.3		הָפֵר
1 Ki. 15.19		הָפֵרָה
Deut. 26.15	S	השקף
	MT	הַשְׁקִיפָה

§ 64. Hithpaʿel.

a) 1. pers. sing. imperf.

Deut. 9.18	MT	וָאֶתְנַפַּל
	S	ואתנפלה
Deut. 9.20	MT	וָאֶתְפַּלֵּל
	S	ואתפללה
Ps. 18.24		וָאֶשְׁתַּמֵּר
2 Sam. 22.24		וָאֶשְׁתַּמְּרָה

b) 1. pers. plur. imperf.

2 Sam. 10.12		וְנִתְחַזֵּק
1 Chron. 19.13		וְנִתְחַזְּקָה
Ex. 1.10	S	נתחכם
	MT	נִתְחַכְּמָה

b.   With nouns and particles

§ 65.   The so-called ה locativum.

a) The noun in the construct state (B-L § 65n).[1]

Gen. 12.5	MT	אַרְצָה כְּנָעַן
	S	.... ארץ [2]
Ex. 34.26	S	ביתה יהוה
	MT	.... בֵּית
Ex. 10.19	MT	יָמָּה סוּף
	S	.... ים
Num. 34.5	MT	נַחְלָה מִצְרָיִם
	S	.... נחל

b) The noun in the emphatic state.

Ex. 33.9	MT	הָאֹהֱלָה
	S	האהל
Gen. 37.24	MT	הַבֹּרָה
	S	הבור

1 Sam. 9.26	Q	הַגָּגָה
	K	הגג
Ex. 1.22	MT	הַיְאֹרָה
	S	היאר
Num. 14.25	S	המדברה
	MT	הַמִּדְבָּר
Lev. 5.12	MT	הַמִּזְבֵּחָה
	S	המזבח
Ex. 7.15	MT	הַמַּיְמָה
	S	המים
Gen. 24.16	MT	הָעַיְנָה
	S	העין
1 Chron. 19.15		הָעִירָה
2 Sam. 10.14		הָעִיר
Gen. 19.16	MT	הַפֶּתְחָה
	S	הפתח
2 Chron. 6.13		הַשָּׁמַיְמָה
1 Ki. 8.22		הַשָּׁמַיִם [3]

---

[1] Cf. Deut. 4.41: בעבר הירדן מִזְרָחָה שמש; Deut. 4.47: בעבר הירדן מִזְרַח שמש. See also p. 234, subdivision d, sub 3.

[2] Cf. similarly Gen. 20.1; 29.1; 32.4; 46.28; Ex. 4.20.

[3] Cf. similarly MT-S on Gen. 15.5; 28.12; Ex. 9.8, 10; Deut. 4.19; 30.12.

c) Proper names.

Ex. 15.27	MT	אֵילִמָה
	S	אילים
2 Ki. 20.17		בָּבֶלָה
Isa. 39.6		בָּבֶל
Gen. 46.1	MT	בְּאֵרָה שָׁבַע
	S	באר ••••
Num. 13.21	S	חמתה
	MT	חֲמָת
Isa. 36.2		יְרוּשָׁלַמָה
2 Ki. 18.17		יְרוּשָׁלָם
2 Chron. 36.4		מִצְרָיְמָה
2 Ki. 23.34		מִצְרָיִם
Gen. 13.10	S	צערה
	MT	צֹעַר
2 Chron. 10.1		שְׁכֶמָה
1 Ki. 12.1		שְׁכֶם
2 Ki. 14.14		שֹׁמְרוֹנָה
2 Chron. 25.24		שֹׁמְרֹן

d) The ה clearly a euphonic ending only.

Deut. 3.17	MT	וְהָעֲרָבָה וְהַיַּרְדֵּן
	S	והירדנה ••••
Deut. 23.14	MT	בְּשִׁבְתְּךָ חוּץ
	S	החוצה ••••
Gen. 10.4		וְתַרְשִׁישׁ
1 Chron. 1.7		וְתַרְשִׁישָׁה
1 Chron. 10.12		בְיָבֵשׁ
1 Sam. 31.13		בְיָבֵשָׁה
Ex. 38.12	MT	וְלִפְאַת יָם
	S	ימה •••• [1]
Num. 34.3	MT	גְּבוּל נֶגֶב
	S	נגבה •••• [2]
Ex. 36.25	MT	לִפְאַת צָפוֹן
	S	צפונה •••• [3]
Gen. 50.3	MT	וַיִּבְכּוּ אֹתוֹ מִצְרַיִם
	S	מצרימה ••••

§ 66.   Particles and pronouns (B-L § 28p, q; § 65x).

Deut. 7.17	MT	אֵיכָה
	S	איך [4]
Gen. 27.39	MT	הִנֵּה
	S	הן [5]
Gen. 43.30	MT	שָׁמָּה
	S	שם [6]

Num. 17.11	MT	מְהֵרָה
	S	מהר [7]
Gen. 31.6	MT	וְאַתֵּנָה
	S	ואתין
2 Chron. 8.9		הֵמָּה [8]
1 Ki. 9.22		הֵם

[1] Cf. Ex. 27.12.

[2] Cf. Ex. 27.9; 36.23; 38.9.

[3] Cf. Ex. 26.20, 35; 27.10; 38.11; cf. also Jer. 23.8: (מארץ) צפונה), Venice 1515 marg.: צפון.

[4] Cf. Deut. 12.30; 18.20; 32.30; also Q-K on Jer. 48.17.

[5] Cf. Ex. 1.9; Num. 22.5, 10; 23.20; also Q-K: Isa. 54.16.

[6] Cf. also K-Q: Joel 4.7; and Md-Ma on 1 Ki. 17.4.

[7] Cf. Deut. 11.17.

[8] Cf. p. 135, s.v. הם: Ps. 9.7: MT הֵמָּה — O הם; further Deut. 3.20: עד אשר יניח יהוה לאחיכם ככם וירשו גם הֵם את הארץ
Josh. 1.15: עד אשר יניח יהוה לאחיכם ככם וירשו גם הֵמָּה את הארץ.

Num. 9.7	MT	הָהֵמָּה		Gen. 41.19	MT	כָהֵנָּה
	S	ההם [1]			S	כהן
Ex. 36.1	MT	בָהֵמָּה [2]		Lev. 4.2	MT	מֵהֵנָּה
	S	בהם			S	מהן
Lev. 5.22	MT	בָהֵנָּה				
	S	בהן [3]				

E. PREPOSITIONS AND PARTICLES

§ 67.   The prepositions ב and כ.

Est. 3.4	K	באמרם		Judg. 19.25	K	בעלות
	Q	כְּאָמְרָם			Q	כַּעֲלוֹת [4]
1 Sam. 11.9	K	בחם		Jer. 36.23	K	בקרוא
	Q	כְּחֹם			Q	כִּקְרוֹא
Jer. 44.23	K	ביום		Josh. 6.5	K	בשמעכם
	Q	כַּיּוֹם			Q	כִּשְׁמֹעֲכֶם [5]

§ 68.   The locative preposition ב (B-L § 22a; Bergstr. § 20e[e]).

Gen. 24.23	MT	בֵּית [6]		1 Ki. 7.40	בֵּית
	S	בבית [7]		2 Chron. 4.11	בְּבֵית [9]
2 Chron. 23.9		בֵּית			
2 Ki. 11.10		בְּבֵית [8]			

§ 69.   The ל finalis (Bergstr. 2, § 11i-p).

a)   In connection with היה.

2 Sam. 5.2	תִהְיֶה לְנָגִיד		Ps. 18.19	וַיְהִי .... לְמִשְׁעָן
1 Chron. 11.2	.... נָגִיד		2 Sam. 22.19	.... מִשְׁעָן
2 Sam. 8.2	וַתְּהִי .... לַעֲבָדִים		2 Chron. 18.21	וְהָיִיתִי לְרוּחַ
1 Chron. 18.2	.... עֲבָדִים [10]		1 Ki. 22.22	.... רוּחַ

---

[1] Cf. Md-Ma on Jer. 50.20.

[2] Cf. Ex. 30.4: לָשֵׂאת אֹתוֹ בָּהֵמָּה
Ex. 37.27: לָשֵׂאת אֹתוֹ בָּהֶם.

[3] Cf. Num. 13.19.

[4] Cf. Josh. 4.18; 6.15; 1 Sam. 9.26.

[5] Cf. 1 Sam. 11.6; 2 Sam. 5.24.

[6] Cf. Num. 20.17: דֶּרֶךְ הַמֶּלֶךְ נֵלֵךְ
Num. 21.22: בְּדֶרֶךְ הַמֶּלֶךְ נֵלֵךְ.

[7] Cf. Num. 30.7; also Q-K: 2 Ki. 22.5;

Jer. 52.11; further: MT-Seb on Ex. 8.20; 2 Ki. 2.3; 10.29.

[8] Cf. 2 Chron. 26.21 — 2 Ki. 15.5; 2 Chron. 34.30 — 2 Ki. 23.2.

[9] Cf. 2 Sam. 23.14 — 1 Chron. 11.16; 1 Ki. 10.17 — 2 Chron. 9.16; 2 Ki. 11.3 — 2 Chron. 22.12; 2 Ki. 14.14 — 2 Chron. 25.24; also S-MT on Gen. 39.2.

[10] Cf. 2 Sam. 8.6 — 1 Chron. 18.6.

b) In connection with other
   verbs.

Gen. 22.2   MT   וְהַעֲלֵהוּ ··· לְעֹלָה
             S   ··· עלה

2 Chron. 18.7

             מִתְנַבֵּא לְטוֹבָה ··· לְרָעָה

1 Ki. 22.8   ¹ ··· טוֹב ···· רָע

2 Chron. 5.1   עָשָׂה ···· לְבֵית

1 Ki. 7.51   ··· בֵּית

2 Chron. 18.12   לִקְרֹא לְמִיכָיְהוּ

1 Ki. 22.13   ··· מִיכָיְהוּ

2 Sam. 7.23   לִפְדוֹת לוֹ לְעָם

1 Chron. 7.21   ··· עָם

c) In connection with a particle.

Num. 32.19 MT   מֵעֵבֶר הַיַּרְדֵּן
             S   ² ··· לירדן

2 Sam. 10.3   בַּעֲבוּר חֲקֹר

1 Chron. 19.3   ··· לַחְקֹר

§ 70.   The use of מִן or מ (B-L § 81p′ f.; § 15k; Bergstr. § 19a).³

2 Sam. 23.13   מֵהַשְּׁלֹשִׁים

1 Chron. 11.15   מִן הַשְּׁלוֹשִׁים

2 Sam. 23.20   מִקַּבְצְאֵל

1 Chron. 11.22   מִן קַבְצְאֵל

1 Ki. 9.22   וּמִבְּנֵי

2 Chron. 8.9   ⁴ וּמִן בְּנֵי

2 Ki. 15.2   מִירוּשָׁלָם

2 Chron. 26.3   ⁵ מִן יְרוּשָׁלָם

1 Sam. 24.8 Q   מֵהַמְּעָרָה

             K   ⁶ מִן המערה

Num. 23.7   MT   מִן אֲרָם
             S   מארם

§ 71.   Imperfect with אַל or לֹא.⁷

Gen. 3.17   MT   לֹא תֹאכַל
              S   ··· אל

Ex. 12.22   MT   לֹא תֵצְאוּ
              S   ··· אל

Ex. 23.7   MT   לֹא תִקַּח
              S   ··· אל

Lev. 19.17   MT   וְלֹא תִשָּׂא
              S   ··· אל

---

¹ On the difference between רעה,
טובה (fem.) and רע, טוב (masc.), cf.
§ 83.

² Cf. 1 Ki. 14.15: (מעבר) לנהר, Venice 1515 marg.: הנהר.

³ Cf. p. 124 ff., s.v. שאול: Ps. 30.4: MT
משאול — O מן שאול; s.v. בטן: Isa. 46.3:
MT מבטן; J — מני בטן; s.v. רחם: Isa.
46.3: MT מרחם; J — מני רחם; cf. also
1 Ki. 18.5: Venice 1515: מן בהמה,
marg.: מהבהמה.

⁴ Cf. S-MT on Lev. 1.14; 14.30; Ex.
9.18.

⁵ Cf. 2 Chron. 25.1 — 2 Ki. 14.2; Isa.
36.2 — 2 Ki. 18.17.

⁶ Cf. 1 Ki. 18.5; Joel 1.12; Lam. 1.6;
also 2 Chron. 7.1: מהשמים, Venice 1515
marg.: מן השמם.

⁷ Cf. Num. 13.2: תִּשְׁלָחוּ; here the Masora parva in the edition Venice 1524-5
reads: ב ויאמר אל תשלחו. But the passage 2 Ki. 2.16 referred to, has: ויאמר
לֹא תשלחו.

2 Ki. 11.15	אַל (תוּמַת) ¹	Ex. 5.9	MT	וְאַל יָשֻׁעוּ
2 Chron. 23.14	לֹא		S	ולא ....

§ 72. The use of אשר (Bergstr. § 2 l).²

Gen. 39.4	MT	וְכָל .... יֶשׁ־לוֹ	2 Sam. 10.5		עַד .... יְצַמַּח
	S	.... אשר	1 Chron. 19.5		.... אֲשֶׁר

Ex. 13.20 MT .... בִּקְצֵה הַמִּדְבָּר
S אשר ....

α) The use of the article or אשר.³

Ex. 18.20 MT הַדֶּרֶךְ .... יֵלְכוּ בָהּ
S .... אשר

2 Ki. 22.13 הַנִּמְצָא
2 Chron. 34.21 אֲשֶׁר נִמְצָא

Lev. 17.6 MT .... פֶּתַח אֹהֶל מוֹעֵד
S אשר ....

Deut. 6.12 S הַמּוֹצִיאֲךָ
MT אֲשֶׁר הוֹצִיאֲךָ ⁴

Isa. 36.2 בִּמְסִלַּת
2 Ki. 18.17 .... אֲשֶׁר

Lev. 17.10 MT הַגָּר
S אשר יגור ⁵

§ 73. The direction is indicated by the accusative or אֶל, לְ.

2 Sam. 10.2	וַיָּבֹאוּ .... אֶרֶץ	2 Sam. 24.16	וַיִּשְׁלַח .... יְרוּשָׁלַם
1 Chron. 19.2	.... אֶל אֶרֶץ	1 Chron. 21.15	.... לִירוּשָׁלַם
2 Sam. 6.10	וַיַּטֵּהוּ בֵית	Ex. 17.10 MT	עֲלוֹ רֹאשׁ
1 Chron. 13.13	.... אֶל בֵּית	S	אל ראש .... ⁶
1 Ki. 22.29	וַיַּעַל .... רָמֹת		
2 Chron. 18.28	.... אֶל רָמֹת		

§ 74. The use of אֶל or לְ.

a) With verbs of speech.⁷

Gen. 19.5	MT	וַיֹּאמְרוּ לוֹ	Ex. 10.17	MT	וְהַעְתִּירוּ לַיהוָה
	S	אֵלָיו .... ⁸		S	אל יהוה .... ⁹

---

¹ Cf. 1 Ki. 3.26: תְּנוּ לָהּ אֶת הַיָּלוּד הַחַי וְהָמֵת אַל תְּמִיתֻהוּ

1 Ki. 3.27: תְּנוּ לָהּ אֶת הַיָּלוּד הַחַי וְהָמֵת לֹא תְמִיתֻהוּ.

² Cf. Judg. 6.26: בְּמַעַרְכָה, Venice 1515 marg.: אֲשֶׁר בְּמַעַרְכָה; 1 Sam. 26.3: Venice 1515: עַל פְּנֵי הַיְשִׁימֹן; MT praemittit: אֲשֶׁר.

³ Cf. 2 Chron. 10.8: הָעֹמְדִים — 1 Ki. 12.8: אֲשֶׁר הָעֹמְדִים; the passage in Kings thus represents a doublet; cf. B-L § 32a

and e. See also our note 5 on page 293. 1 Ki. 21.11: אֲשֶׁר הַיֹּשְׁבִים is a doublet, too.

⁴ On the difference in the tense cf. § 17c.

⁵ On the difference in the tense cf. § 17b. ⁶ Cf. Deut. 3.27.

⁷ Cf. Judg. 21.22: (וְאָמַרְנוּ) אֲלֵיהֶם, Venice 1515 marg.: לָהֶם; 1 Ki. 18.44: (אֱמֹר) אֶל אַחְאָב, Venice 1515 marg.: לְאַחְאָב. ⁸ Cf. Gen. 27.32; 42.1; Ex. 3.14; 8.5; Num. 21.16; 22.28; 23.3, 17.

⁹ Cf. Gen. 25.21.

Ex. 19.20	MT	וַיִּקְרָא ‥‥ לְמֹשֶׁה
	S	‥‥¹ אל משה
2 Chron. 34.23		וַתֹּאמֶר לָהֶם
2 Ki. 22.5		‥‥² אֲלֵיהֶם
1 Chron. 19.3		וַיֹּאמְרוּ ‥‥ לְחָנוּן
2 Sam. 10.3		‥‥ אֶל חָנוּן
1 Sam. 31.4		וַיֹּאמֶר ‥‥ לְנֹשֵׂא
1 Chron. 10.4		‥‥³ אֶל נֹשֵׂא

b) With other verbs.

Gen. 24.56	MT	וְאֵלְכָה לַאדֹנִי
	S	‥‥ אל אדני
Num. 31.47	MT	וַיִּתֵּן ‥‥ לַלְוִיִּם
	S	‥‥ אל הלוים
Num. 36.9	MT	וְלֹא תִסֹּב‥לְמַטֶּה
	S	‥‥ אל מטה
Gen. 32.10	MT	שׁוּב לְאַרְצְךָ
	S	אל ארצך
2 Ki. 19.7		וְשָׁב לְאַרְצוֹ
Isa. 37.7		‥‥ אֶל אַרְצוֹ

2 Chron. 10.16		לֹא שָׁמַע ‥‥ לָהֶם
1 Ki. 12.16		‥‥ אֲלֵהֶם
Ps. 96.2		בַּשְּׂרוּ מִיּוֹם לְיוֹם
1 Chron. 16.23		‥‥ אֶל יוֹם

c)　Addition of אל or לְ.

Gen. 18.29	MT	וַיֹּאמֶר
	S	‥‥⁴ אֵלָיו
2 Chron. 18.13		יֹאמַר
1 Ki. 22.14		‥‥⁵ אֵלַי
Isa. 36.12		וַיֹּאמֶר
2 Ki. 18.27		‥‥ אֲלֵיהֶם
Gen. 29.7	MT	וַיֹּאמֶר
	S	‥‥⁶ להם
2 Ki. 20.14		בָּאוּ
Isa. 39.3		‥‥ אֵלַי
Ex. 34.32	MT	נִגְּשׁוּ
	S	‥‥ אֵלָיו
1 Chron. 10.11		וַיִּשְׁמְעוּ
1 Sam. 31.11		‥‥ אֵלָיו

§ 75.　The government of prepositions (Bergstr. § 2 l).

a)　Preposition אל.

Gen. 30.25	MT	אֶל מְקוֹמִי וּלְאַרְצִי
	S	‥‥ ואל ארצי
Gen. 31.3		
	MT	אֶל אֶרֶץ אֲבוֹתֶיךָ וּלְמוֹלַדְתֶּךָ
	S	‥‥ ואל מולדתך
Lev. 10.6		
	MT	אֶל אַהֲרֹן וּלְאֶלְעָזָר וּלְאִיתָמָר
	S	‥‥ ואל אלעזר ואל איתמר

Ex. 12.43	MT	אֶל מֹשֶׁה וְאַהֲרֹן
	S	‥‥ ואל אהרן
1 Chron. 17.4		אֶל דָּוִיד עַבְדִּי
2 Sam. 7.5		אֶל עַבְדִּי אֶל דָּוִד

b)　Preposition את.

Ex. 12.28	MT	אֶת מֹשֶׁה וְאַהֲרֹן
	S	‥‥ ואת אהרן

---

¹ Cf. Ex. 8.21.
² Cf. 1 Chron. 21.24 — 2 Sam. 24.24.
³ Cf. S-MT on Gen. 21.29; 24.58; 37.9;
Ex. 18.6; 35.30; also 2 Ki. 19.6 — Isa. 37.6.

⁴ Cf. Gen. 47.1; also 2 Chron. 18.14 —
1 Ki. 22.15.
⁵ Cf. MT-S on Num. 24.13; also K-Q: Ruth 3.5.
⁶ Cf. Gen. 12.7; Num. 13.30

Num. 22.6

MT   אֵת אֲשֶׁר תְּבָרֵךְ ⋯ וַאֲשֶׁר תָּאֹר

S   ⋯⋯ וְאֵת אשר ⋯⋯

Deut. 22.4

MT   אֶת חֲמוֹר אָחִיךָ אוֹ שׁוֹרוֹ

S   ⋯⋯ אוֹ אֵת ⋯⋯

Num. 15.31

MT   כִּי דְבַר ⋯⋯ וְאֶת מִצְוָתוֹ

S   ⋯⋯ כִּי אֵת ⋯⋯

2 Chron. 11.1

אֶת (בֵּית יְהוּדָה) וּבִנְיָמִן

1 Ki. 12.21   ¹ ⋯⋯ וְאֶת (שֵׁבֶט בִּנְיָמִן)

c)   Preposition עַל.

1 Chron. 17.7   עַל עַמִּי יִשְׂרָאֵל

2 Sam. 7.8   עַל עַמִּי עַל יִשְׂרָאֵל

d)   Preposition בּ.

Josh. 8.17   MT   בָּעַי וּבֵית אֵל

    Seb   ⋯⋯ וּבֵית ⋯⋯

Jer. 52.3   בִּירוּשָׁלַם וִיהוּדָה

2 Ki. 24.20   ⋯⋯ וּבִיהוּדָה

Prov. 28.8   Q   בְּנֶשֶׁךְ וְתַרְבִּית

    K   ⋯⋯ וּבְתַרְבִּית

e)   Preposition כּ.

Gen. 48.5   MT   כִּרְאוּבֵן וְשִׁמְעוֹן

    S   ⋯⋯ וְכַשִּׁמְעוֹן

1 Chron. 17.21   כְּעַמְּךָ יִשְׂרָאֵל

2 Sam. 7.23   כְּיִשְׂרָאֵל ⋯⋯

f)   Preposition לְ.

Ex. 2.14   MT   לְאִישׁ שַׂר וְשֹׁפֵט

    S   ⋯⋯ וּלְשֹׁפֵט

1 Chron. 17.9   לְעַמִּי יִשְׂרָאֵל

2 Sam. 7.10   ⋯⋯ לְיִשְׂרָאֵל

2 Chron. 9.22   לְעֹשֶׁר וְחָכְמָה

1 Ki. 10.23   ⋯⋯ וּלְחָכְמָה

g)   Preposition מ.

Num. 29.39

MT   ² מִנִּדְרֵיכֶם וְנִדְבֹתֵיכֶם

S   ⋯⋯ וּמִנְּדָבֹתֵיכֶם

2 Ki. 17.24

K   וּמֵעַוָּא וּמֵחֲמָת וּספּרוים

Q   ⋯⋯ וּמִסְפַרְוַיִם

Gen. 7.8 MT   וּמִן הָעוֹף וְכֹל אֲשֶׁר

    S   ⋯⋯ וּמִכֹּל ⋯⋯

h)   Nouns and phrases.

2 Chron. 35.18   מִימֵי ⋯⋯ וְכָל מַלְכֵי

2 Ki. 23.22   ⋯⋯ וְכֹל יְמֵי

2 Chron. 10.11, 14

אָבִי יִסַּר אֶתְכֶם ⋯⋯ וַאֲנִי

1 Ki. 12.11, 14   ⋯⋯ וַאֲנִי אֲיַסֵּר אֶתְכֶם

Deut. 17.6   MT   עַל פִּי ⋯⋯ אוֹ

    S   ⋯⋯ אוֹ עַל פִּי

Ps. 18.1   מִכַּף ⋯⋯ וּמִיַּד

2 Sam. 22.1   ⋯⋯ וּמִכַּף

Ps. 18.32   מִבַּלְעֲדֵי ⋯ זוּלָתִי

2 Sam. 22.32   ⋯⋯ מִבַּלְעֲדֵי

---

¹ On the insertion of שבט here, cf. § 80c.

² Cf. Zech. 1.4: מִדַּרְכֵיכֶם ⋯ וּמַעַלְלֵיכֶם; Venice 1515 marg.: וּמִמַּעַלְלֵיכֶם.

³ Cf. Ezek. 19.2: בֵּין אֲרָיוֹת בְּתוֹךְ כְּפִירִים; Venice 1515 marg.: בֵּין ⋯ בֵּין.

§ 76.   The use of the particle את (Bergstr. § 2 l).[1]

Gen. 44.26 MT   לִרְאוֹת פְּנֵי הָאִישׁ
S   .... את ....

Deut. 26.2 MT   לְשַׁכֵּן שְׁמוֹ שָׁם
S   .... את ....

Ex. 2.9   MT   הַיֶּלֶד וַתִּקַּח הָאִשָּׁה
S   .... את ....

1 Chron. 17.26
וַתְּדַבֵּר (עַל עַבְדְּךָ) הַטּוֹבָה הַזֹּאת
2 Sam. 7.28   .... אֶת ....

Lev. 4.17
MT   וְטָבַל הַכֹּהֵן אֶצְבָּעוֹ
S   .... את ....

1 Chron. 19.17 הַיַּרְדֵּן וַיַּעֲבֹר
2 Sam. 10.17   .... אֶת ....

2 Chron. 18.26 זֶה שִׂימוּ
1 Ki. 22.27   .... אֶת ....

Num. 22.41
MT   וַיַּרְא מִשָּׁם קְצֵה הָעָם
S   .... את ....

2 Sam. 24.13 שְׁלָחִי מָה אָשִׁיב
1 Chron. 21.12   .... אֶת ....

§ 77.   The prepositions אל and על.

1) Gen. 50.21 MT   וַיְדַבֵּר עַל לִבָּם
S   .... אל ....

2 Chron. 34.24
מֵבִיא רָעָה עַל הַמָּקוֹם
2 Ki. 22.16   .... אֶל ....

Ex. 40.23
MT   וַיַּעֲרֹךְ עָלָיו עֵרֶךְ לֶחֶם
S   .... אליו ....

2) Num. 13.30
וַיַּהַס כָּלֵב אֶת הָעָם אֶל מֹשֶׁה MT
S   .... עַל ....

Lev. 16.14
MT   וְהִזָּה ... עַל פְּנֵי הַכַּפֹּרֶת
S   .... אל ....

Ex. 32.34
נְחֵה אֶת הָעָם אֶל אֲשֶׁר דִּבַּרְתִּי MT
S   .... עַל ....

1 Chron. 10.3
וַתִּכְבַּד הַמִּלְחָמָה עַל
1 Sam. 31.3   .... אֶל

Deut. 30.1 MT וַהֲשֵׁבֹתָ אֶל לְבָבֶךָ
S   .... עַל ....

1 Chron. 19.2 לְנַחֲמוֹ עַל אָבִיו
2 Sam. 10.2   ... אֶל ....

2 Chron. 16.4 אֶל עָרֵי ... וַיִּשְׁלַח
1 Ki. 15.20   ... עַל ....

1 Chron. 18.7 אֲשֶׁר הָיוּ עַל עַבְדֵי
2 Sam. 8.7   ... אֶל ....

2 Chron. 34.28 אֶל אֲבֹתֶיךָ אֹסִפְךָ
2 Ki. 22.20   .... עַל ....

2 Chron. 18.16 נְפוֹצִים עַל הֶהָרִים
1 Ki. 22.17   ... אֶל ....

2 Chron. 34.15 שָׁפָן אֶל וַיֹּאמֶר
2 Ki. 22.8   ... עַל ....

---

[1] On את with the pronomen sufifxum, cf § 59.

§ 78.   The word-order in the sentence.

1)   Inseparable prepositions.

Ex. 40.38 MT   וְאֵשׁ תִּהְיֶה לַיְלָה בּוֹ
S   בִּי לילה ....

Lev. 18.23
MT   לֹא תִתֵּן שְׁכָבְתְּךָ לְטָמְאָה בָהּ
S   בת לטמאה ....

Gen. 50.12 MT   וַיַּעֲשׂוּ בָנָיו לוֹ
S   לו בניו ....

Ex. 30.19
MT   וְרָחֲצוּ אַהֲרֹן וּבָנָיו מִמֶּנּוּ
S   ממנו אהרן ובניו ....

2)   Particle אל.

Gen. 31.16 MT   אָמַר אֱלֹהִים אֵלֶיךָ [1]
S   אליך אלהים ....

Ex. 3.2 MT   וַיֵּרָא מַלְאַךְ יהוה אֵלָיו
S   אליו מלאך יהוה ....

1 Chron. 19.10
כִּי הָיְתָה פְנֵי הַמִּלְחָמָה אֵלָיו
2 Sam. 10.9   אֵלָיו פְּנֵי הַמִּלְחָמָה ....

3)   Particle את.

Ex. 35.29 MT   אֲשֶׁר נָדַב לִבָּם אֹתָם
S   אתם לבם .... [2]

Lev. 13.27 MT   וְטִמֵּא הַכֹּהֵן אֹתוֹ
S   אתו הכהן ....

4)   Preposition כל.

Gen. 19.28 MT   וְעַל כָּל פְּנֵי אֶרֶץ
S   פני כל ....

Gen. 41.56 MT   עַל כָּל פְּנֵי הָאָרֶץ
S   פני כל ....

Num. 8.16
MT   תַּחַת פִּטְרַת כָּל רֶחֶם בְּכוֹר
S   כל בכור פטר רחם ....

Num. 1.20
MT   בְּמִסְפַּר שֵׁמוֹת לְגֻלְגְּלֹתָם כָּל זָכָר
S   כל זכר לגלגלתם ....

5)   Particle עוד.

Gen. 8.21 MT   לֹא אֹסִף לְקַלֵּל עוֹד
S   עוד לקלל ....

Gen. 35.10 MT   לֹא יִקָּרֵא שִׁמְךָ עוֹד
S   עוד שמך ....

Deut. 34.10 MT   וְלֹא קָם נָבִיא עוֹד
S   עוד נביא .... [3]

1 Chron. 14.3   וַיּוֹלֶד דָּוִיד עוֹד
2 Sam. 5.13   עוד לְדָוִד ....

1 Chron. 19.19
לְהוֹשִׁיעַ אֶת בְּנֵי עַמּוֹן עוֹד
2 Sam. 10.19   עוד אֶת בְּנֵי עַמּוֹן ....

6)   Particle על.

Ex. 19.18 MT   אֲשֶׁר יָרַד עָלָיו יהוה
S   יהוה עליו ....

7)   Personal pronouns.

Gen. 20.12 MT   אֲחֹתִי בַת אָבִי הִוא
S   היא בת אבי ....

Ex. 29.18 MT   אִשֶּׁה לַיהוה הוּא
S   הוא ליהוה ....

Gen. 42.32
S   שְׁנֵים עָשָׂר אַחִים אֲנַחְנוּ
MT   אֲנַחְנוּ אַחִים ....

---

[1] Cf. Lev. 9.12: וימצאו בני אהרן אליו
את הדם
Lev. 9.18: וימצאו בני אהרן את
הדם אליו.

[2] Cf. Lev. 18.28: ולא תקיא הארץ אתכם
Lev. 20.22: ולא תקיא אתכם
הארץ.

[3] Cf. similarly Gen. 9.11; Deut. 19.20.

8) Verb and object.

Lev. 21.21

אֶת לֶחֶם אֱלֹהָיו לֹא יִגַּשׁ לְהַקְרִיב MT

לא יגש להקריב לחם אלהיו S

1 Chron. 17.18

וְאַתָּה אֶת עַבְדְּךָ יָדַעְתָּ

2 Sam. 7.20   יָדַעְתָּ אֶת עַבְדְּךָ ····

1 Chron. 19.13   הַטּוֹב בְּעֵינָיו יַעֲשֶׂה

2 Sam. 10.12   יַעֲשֶׂה הַטּוֹב בְּעֵינָיו

Deut. 12.22 MT   יַחְדָּו יֹאכְלֶנּוּ

S   יאכלנו יחדו

9) Noun and apposition.

2 Chron. 16.6   וְאָסָא הַמֶּלֶךְ

1 Ki. 15.22   וְהַמֶּלֶךְ אָסָא

1 Chron. 17.24   דָּוִיד עַבְדְּךָ

2 2 Sam. 7.26   עַבְדְּךָ דָּוִד ¹

10) The accusative-object.

2 Chron. 15.16

עָשְׂתָה לַאֲשֵׁרָה מִפְלָצֶת

1 Ki. 15.13   מִפְלֶצֶת לַאֲשֵׁרָה ····

2 Chron. 1.17

וַיּוֹצִיאוּ מִמִּצְרַיִם מֶרְכָּבָה

1 Ki. 10.29   מֶרְכָּבָה מִמִּצְרַיִם ····

11) Coupled words.

2 Chron. 23.7   בְּבֹאוֹ וּבְצֵאתוֹ

2 Ki. 11.8   בְּצֵאתוֹ וּבְבֹאוֹ

2 Chron. 6.20   יוֹמָם וָלַיְלָה

1 Ki. 8.29   לַיְלָה וָיוֹם

2 Chron. 34.30   מִגָּדוֹל וְעַד קָטָן

2 Ki. 23.2   לְמִקָּטֹן וְעַד גָּדוֹל

1 Chron. 21.2   מִבְּאֵר שֶׁבַע וְעַד דָּן

2 Sam. 24.2   מִדָּן וְעַד בְּאֵר שֶׁבַע

§ 79.   Insertion of the subject or apposition thereof.²

a) Subject.

Gen. 21.33 MT   וַיִּטַּע

S   אברהם ····

Gen. 29.23 MT   וַיָּבֹא אֵלֶיהָ

S   יעקב ····

Ex. 15.25 MT   וַיִּצְעַק ··· אֶל יהוה

S   משה ····

Ex. 2.6 MT   וַתַּחְמֹל עָלָיו

S   בת פרעה ····

Lev. 14.37 MT   וְרָאָה

S   הכהן ····

1 Chron. 18.1   וַיִּקַּח

2 Sam. 8.1   דָּוִד ···· ³

1 Chron. 18.10   וַיִּשְׁלַח

2 Sam. 8.10   תֹּעִי ····

1 Chron. 19.1   וַיִּמְלֹךְ

2 Sam. 10.1   חָנוּן ····

2 Chron. 6.12   וַיַּעֲמֹד

1 Ki. 8.22   שְׁלֹמֹה ····

2 Ki. 20.2   וַיַּסֵּב

Isa. 38.2   חִזְקִיָּהוּ ····

2 Sam. 16.23 K   כַּאֲשֶׁר יִשְׁאַל

Q   אִישׁ ····

b) Apposition.

Gen. 25.6 MT   אֲשֶׁר שָׁמַע אַבְרָהָם

S   אביך ····

---

¹ Cf. also 1 Ki. 22.43 — 2 Chron. 20. 32; Isa. 37.2 — 2 Ki. 19.2.

² Cf. my *Septuagintaprobleme* (Stutt-gart 1929), p. 60.

³ Cf. 1 Chron. 18.14 — 2 Sam. 8.15; 1 Chron. 11.18 — 2 Sam. 23.16.

Gen. 48.7	MT	מֵתָה עָלַי רָחֵל	2 Chron. 27.9		בְּעִיר דָּוִיד
	S	אמך ····	2 Ki. 15.38		אָבִיו ····
Gen. 38.13	MT	וַיֻּגַּד לְתָמָר	2 Sam. 10.14		מִפְּנֵי אֲבִישַׁי
	S	כלתו ····	1 Chron. 19.15		אָחִיו ····
Gen. 48.7	MT	בְּבֹאִי מִפַּדָּן	2 Ki. 19.37 K	וְאַדְרַמֶּלֶךְ וְשַׂרְאֶצֶר
	S	ארם ····		Q	בָּנָיו ···· [1]
1 Chron. 19.3		לְחָנוּן			
2 Sam. 10.3		אֲדֹנֶיהֶם ····			

§ 80.   Appositions to ישראל.

a) בני ישראל.[2]

Ex. 3.16	MT	זִקְנֵי ···· יִשְׂרָאֵל	1 Chron. 13.8		וְכָל ···· יִשְׂרָאֵל
	S	···· בני ····	2 Sam. 6.5		···· בֵּית ····
Ex. 12.3	MT	עֲדַת ···· יִשְׂרָאֵל	2 Chron. 11.1		עִם ···· יִשְׂרָאֵל
	S	···· בני ····	1 Ki. 12.21		···· בֵּית ····
Ex. 9.7	MT	מִמִּקְנֵה ···· יִשְׂרָאֵל			
	S	···· בני ····		c) Variae.	
Num. 10.18	MT	מַחֲנֵה ···· רְאוּבֵן	2 Chron. 10.3		וְכָל ···· יִשְׂרָאֵל[4]
	S	···· בני ····	1 Ki. 12.23		···· קָהָל ····
Num. 26.58	MT	מִשְׁפְּחֹת ···· לֵוִי	2 Chron. 11.1		וּבִנְיָמִן
	S	···· בני ····	1 Ki. 12.21		שֵׁבֶט בִּנְיָמִן
2 Chron. 8.7		מִיִּשְׂרָאֵל	1 Chron. 11.1		כָּל ···· יִשְׂרָאֵל
1 Ki. 9.20		מִבְּנֵי יִשְׂרָאֵל	2 Sam. 5.1		···· שִׁבְטֵי ····
1 Chron. 17.5		אֶת ··· יִשְׂרָאֵל[3]			
2 Sam. 7.6		··· בְּנֵי ····			

§ 81.   Insertion of various nouns and particles.

a)   Nouns.

1) Lev. 5.24

MT	מִכֹּל אֲשֶׁר יִשָּׁבַע עָלָיו
S	···· דבר ····

Num. 23.26

MT	כֹּל ···· אֲשֶׁר יְדַבֵּר
S	···· הדבר ····

[1] Cf. Isa. 37.38.

[2] Cf. Josh. 7.1: בבני ישראל; Venice 1515 marg.: בישראל; Josh. 8.27: ישראל; Venice 1515 marg.: בני ישראל.

[3] Cf. Venice 1515: את בני ישראל, marg.: בס״א לית (scil. בני).

[4] Cf. Ex. 12.15: ונכרתה הנפש ההוא מישראל Ex. 12.19: ונכרתה הנפש ההוא מֵעֲדַת ישראל; cf. also our note 1 on page 296.

2) Ex. 15.22
MT   וַיֵּלְכוּ ⋯⋯ שְׁלֹשֶׁת יָמִים
S   ⋯⋯ דרך ⋯⋯

3) Gen. 48.14
MT   וַיִּשְׁלַח ⋯⋯ אֶת יְמִינוֹ
S   יד ⋯⋯ ⋯⋯

4) Gen. 47.16   MT   וְאֶתְּנָה לָכֶם
S   ⋯⋯ לחם

5) Ex. 5.20   MT   מֵאֵת ⋯ פַּרְעֹה
S   ⋯⋯ פני ⋯⋯

6) Gen. 45.23
MT   מִטּוּב ⋯⋯ מִצְרָיִם
S   ⋯⋯ ארץ ⋯⋯ ¹
2 Chron. 5.10   מִמִּצְרָיִם
1 Ki. 8.9   מֵאֶרֶץ מִצְרָיִם ²
2 Sam. 11.1   ⋯⋯ בְּנֵי עַמּוֹן
1 Chron. 20.1   אֶרֶץ ⋯⋯

7) 1 Chron. 13.6
יהוה יוֹשֵׁב הַכְּרוּבִים
2 Sam. 6.2   ⋯⋯ צְבָאוֹת ⋯⋯
1 Chron. 16.2   בְּשֵׁם יהוה
2 Sam. 6.18   ⋯⋯ צְבָאוֹת
2 Ki. 20.16   דְּבַר יהוה
Isa. 39.5   ⋯⋯ צְבָאוֹת ³
2 Ki. 19.31 K   קִנְאַת יהוה
Q   ⋯⋯ צְבָאוֹת

b)   Particles.

1) Deut. 12.22
MT   הַטָּמֵא ⋯⋯ וְהַטָּהוֹר
S   ⋯⋯ בך ⋯⋯
Ex. 13.3 MT   הַיּוֹם אֲשֶׁר יְצָאתֶם
S   בו ⋯⋯
Ex. 20.10
MT   לֹא תַעֲשֶׂה ⋯⋯ כָּל מְלָאכָה
S   ⋯⋯ בו ⋯⋯ ⁴
Ex. 29.33 MT   לְמַלֵּא ⋯ אֶת יָדָם
S   ⋯⋯ בם ⋯⋯
Ex. 37.5 MT   לָשֵׂאת אֶת הָאָרֹן
S   בהם ⋯⋯ ⁵

2) Gen. 21.7   MT   כִּי יָלַדְתִּי
S   ⋯⋯ לו
Ex. 18.21   MT   תֶּחֱזֶה
S   ⋯⋯ לך
Isa. 36.6   הִנֵּה בָטַחְתָּ
2 Ki. 18.21   לָּךְ ⋯⋯
Jer. 50.29   K   אַל יְהִי
Q   ⋯⋯ לָהּ
Num. 31.19 MT   וְאַתֶּם חֲנוּ
S   לכם ⋯⋯

3) Gen. 24.4   MT   כִּי
S   ⋯⋯ אם ⁶
2 Chron. 6.9   כִּי
1 Ki. 8.19   כִּי אם ⁷

---

¹ Cf. similarly: Ex. 6.27; 11.4; 13.3; Deut. 16.12.
² Cf. similarly 1 Ki. 8.16 — 2 Chron. 6.5.
³ Cf. similarly 2 Ki. 19.15 — Isa. 37.16.
⁴ Cf. also Deut. 5.14; 16.16.

⁵ Cf. similarly: Ex. 36.1.
⁶ Cf. Q-K on 2 Ki. 14.6; 2 Sam. 13.33; 15.21; Jer. 39.12; Ruth 3.12; cf. also Jer. 22.12: כִּי, Venice 1515 marg.: כִּי אם.
⁷ Cf. similarly: 2 Chron. 25.4 — 2 Ki. 14.6.

4) Gen. 2.12   MT   טוֹב
       S   •••• מְאֹד

Ex. 8.20   MT   עָרֹב כָּבֵד
       S   מְאֹד ••••

1 Chron. 10.3   וַיָּחֶל
2 Sam. 31.3   מְאֹד •••• [1]
1 Ki. 8.65   קָהָל גָּדוֹל
2 Chron. 7.8   מְאֹד ••••

5) Gen. 47.29   MT   וְעָשִׂיתָ ••• עִמָּדִי
       S   •••• נָא ••••

Ex. 12.3   MT   דַּבְּרוּ
       S   נָא •••• [2]

2 Chron. 6.17   יֵאָמֵן
1 Ki. 8.26   נָא ••••
2 Chron. 18.12   הִנֵּה
1 Ki. 22.13   נָא •••• [3]
2 Ki. 5.18   Q   יִסְלַח
       K   נא ••••

6) Gen. 2.19
       MT   וַיִּצֶר יְהוָה אֱלֹהִים
       S   עוד ••••

Deut. 13.12   MT   וְלֹא יֹסְפוּ
       S   עוד ••••

2 Chron. 10.2   וְהוּא •••• בְּמִצְרַיִם
1 Ki. 12.2   עוֹדֶנּוּ ••••

---

7) Gen. 26.7
       MT   כִּי יָרֵא לֵאמֹר אִשְׁתִּי
       S   הִיא ••••

Gen. 37.33   MT   כְּתֹנֶת בְּנִי
       S   הִיא ••••

Ex. 21.8
       MT   אִם רָעָה •••• בְּעֵינֵי אֲדֹנֶיהָ
       S   הִיא ••••

Ex. 8.16   MT   הִנֵּה •••• יוֹצֵא
       S   •••• הוּא ••••

Gen. 42.28
       MT   וְגַם הִנֵּה •••• בְּאַמְתַּחְתִּי
       S   הוּא ••••

Ex. 28.12
       MT   זִכָּרֹן •••• לִבְנֵי יִשְׂרָאֵל
       S   •••• הִנֵּה ••••

2 Chron. 9.5   אֱמֶת ••• הַדָּבָר
1 Ki. 10.6   •••• הָיָה ••••

1 Chron. 17.24
       וּבֵית דָּוִיד עַבְדְּךָ נָכוֹן לְפָנֶיךָ
2 Sam. 7.26   •••• יִהְיֶה •••• [4]

8) Ex. 32.7
       MT   וַיְדַבֵּר יְהוָה אֶל מֹשֶׁה
       S   לאמר •••• [5]

---

[1] Cf. similarly: 2 Chron. 9.1 — 1 Ki. 10.2.

[2] Cf. also Ex. 14.12.

[3] Cf. also Isa. 37.20 — 2 Ki. 19.19.

[4] Cf. Ex. 28.21: וְהָאֲבָנִים תִּהְיֶיןָ עַל שְׁמֹת בְּנֵי יִשְׂרָאֵל

Ex. 39.14: וְהָאֲבָנִים > עַל שְׁמֹת בְּנֵי יִשְׂרָאֵל ;

Lev. 27.25: עֶשְׂרִים גֵּרָה יִהְיֶה הַשָּׁקֶל

Num. 3.47: עֶשְׂרִים גֵּרָה > הַשָּׁקֶל.

[5] Cf. Ex. 33.1; Num. 27.12. On לאמר as an introductory phrase to the direct speech, see my *Septuagintaprobleme*, p. 60. Instead of לאמר, the form ויאמר may be used, too; cf. 2 Sam. 6.9 — 1 Chron. 13.12; Isa. 38.2, 3 — 2 Ki. 20.2; 2 Ki. 19.15 — Isa. 37.15. Consequently, I am inclined to regard the passage 2 Sam. 5.1: ויאמרו לאמר as a doublet; note that the parallel report 1 Chron. 11.1 reads only: לאמר. See also our notes 2 on page 277 and 3 on page 285.

Num. 5.6			1 Chron. 11.5	וַיֹּאמְרוּ ⋯⋯ לְדָוִיד
MT	דַּבֵּר אֶל בְּנֵי יִשְׂרָאֵל		2 Sam. 5.6	⋯⋯ לֵאמֹר 1
S	⋯⋯ לאמר		2 Sam. 24.12	וְדִבַּרְתָּ אֶל דָּוִד
			1 Chron. 21.10	⋯⋯ לֵאמֹר

E. The Vocabulary

§ 82.   The personal pronoun (B-L § 28d, o; Bergstr. § 2 i).

Gen. 14.23	MT	אֲנִי	Jer. 42.6	K	אנו
	S	אָנֹכִי 2		Q	אֲנַחְנוּ
Gen. 42.11	MT	נַחְנוּ			
	S	אנחנו 3			

§ 83.   Masc. or fem. formation of the noun (B-L § 62z).[4]

Num. 24.9	MT	כָּאֲרִי	Gen. 9.2	MT	וְחִתְּכֶם
	S	כאריה 5		S	וחתתכם
2 Sam. 23.20	Q	הָאֲרִי	Ex. 12.42	MT	לֵיל
	K	האריה 6		S	לילה
1 Ki. 10.20		אֲרָיִים	Prov. 31.18	K	בליל
2 Chron. 9.19		אֲרָיוֹת		Q	בַּלַּיְלָה 8
Lev. 5.23	S	הגזל	Job 31.7	Q	מְאוּם
	MT	הַגְּזֵלָה		K	מאומה
Gen. 48.10	MT	מִזֹּקֶן	1 Chron. 11.7		בַּמְצָד
	S	מזקנה	2 Sam. 5.9		בַּמְצֻדָה
Ex. 30.21	MT	חָק	Gen. 34.12	MT	וּמַתָּן
	S	חקת		S	ומתנה
2 Chron. 34.31		וְחֻקָּיו	2 Ki. 5.4	K	הנער
2 Ki. 23.3		וְאֶת חֻקֹּתָיו 7		Q	הַנַּעֲרָה

1 Cf. 1 Ki. 20.28: אמרו ארם, Venice 1515 marg. adds: לֵאמֹר.

2 Cf. Ex. 22.26; Deut. 32.39; further: 1 Chron. 17.16 — 2 Sam. 7.18; 1 Chron 21.10 — 2 Sam. 24.12; 1 Chron. 21.17 — 2 Sam. 24.17; 2 Chron. 34.27 — 2 Ki. 22.19; also Hos. 7.13: וְאָנֹכִי, Venice 1515 marg.: וַאֲנִי.

3 Cf. Ex. 16.7, 8; Num. 32.32.

4 Cf. p. 124 ff., s.v. ישועה: Hab. 3.13: MT לישועה J — לישע; s.v. נשפה: Jer. 13.16: MT נשף J — נשפה; s.v. עזר: Ps. 46.2: MT עזרה O — עזר; cf. further Ps. 70.6: עֶזְרִי, Venice 1515 marg.: עזרתי.   5 Cf. Num. 23.24.

6 Cf. Lam. 3.10.

7 Cf. Deut. 27.10: MT and S.

8 Cf. Lam. 2.19.

Gen. 27.3	Q	צָיִד	α)	Substantival adjectives.	
	K	צידה	Am. 5.15	Q	רָע
Ps. 18.21		כְּצִדְקִי		K	רעה [4]
2 Sam. 22.21		כְּצִדְקָתִי	Deut. 28.11	S	לטוב
Jer. 31.39	Q	קָו		MT	לְטוֹבָה
	K	קוה [1]			
2 Chron. 8.1		מִקֵּץ	β)	Particles and pronouns.	
1 Ki. 9.10		מִקְצֵה [2]	Gen. 4.9	MT	אֵי
Prov. 27.10	Q	וְרֵעַ		S	איה [5]
	K	ורעה	2 Ki. 19.13		אִיּוֹ
Ps. 96.12		שָׂדַי	Isa. 37.13		אַיֵּה [6]
1 Chron. 16.32		הַשָּׂדֶה [3]	1 Chron. 20.8		אֵל
1 Ki. 7.26		שׁוֹשָׁן	2 Sam. 21.22		אֵלֶּה
2 Chron. 4.5		שׁוֹשַׁנָּה	Gen. 26.3	MT	הָאֵל
				S	האלה [7]
			Gen. 24.65	S	הלז
				MT	הַלָּזֶה [8]

§ 84. Formation by metathesis.

1) Lev. 4.32	MT	כֶּבֶשׂ	2 Chron. 9.24	Q	וּשְׂלָמוֹת	
	S	כשבה		K	ושמלות	
Ex. 12.5	MT	הַכְּבָשִׂים	Deut. 29.4	MT	שַׂלְמֹתֵיכֶם	
	S	הכשבים [9]		S	שמלתיכם	
2) Ex. 22.8	MT	שַׂלְמָה	3) Deut. 28.25	MT	לְזַעֲוָה	
	S	שמלה		S	לזועה [10]	
Ex. 22.25	MT	שַׂלְמַת	4) Prov. 1.27	K	כשאוה	
	S	שמלת		Q	כְּשׁוֹאָה	
Deut. 24.13	MT	בְּשַׂלְמָתוֹ				
	S	בשמלתו				

[1] Cf. 1 Ki. 7.23; Zech. 1.16.
[2] Cf. Gen. 8.3; Deut. 14.28: MT and S.
[3] See B-L § 2v; cf. also K-Q on Hos. 2.22.
[4] Cf. also Jer. 18.10 and Mic. 3.2: K and Q; further: Gen. 44.34; Num. 22.34 and 32.13: MT and S.
[5] Cf. Deut. 32.37.
[6] Cf. K-Q on Jer. 37.19.
[7] Cf. Gen. 19.8, 25; 26.4; Lev. 18.27; Deut. 4.42; 7.22; 19.11.
[8] Cf. Gen. 37.19.
[9] Cf. Num. 15.11.
[10] Cf. Jer. 15.4; 24.9; 29.18; 34.17; Ezek. 23.46: Q and K.

§ 85.   Formation by prefix.

a)   Prefix מ.[1]

Ex. 26.4	MT	בַּחֹבֶרֶת		Num. 3.38	S	הקדש
	S	במחברת			MT	הַמִּקְדָּשׁ
Ex. 21.25	MT	כְּוִיָּה		Ezek. 44.24	K	לשפט
	S	מכוה			Q	לְמִשְׁפָּט
2 Chron. 7.18		מַלְכוּתֶךָ		Ex. 7.4	MT	בִּשְׁפָטִים
1 Ki. 9.5		מַמְלַכְתְּךָ			S	במשפטים [3]
1 Chron. 14.2		מַלְכוּתוֹ				
2 Sam. 5.12		מַמְלַכְתוֹ [2]		b) Prefix ת.		
1 Chron. 11.16		וּנְצִיב		Lev. 25.37	MT	וּבְמַרְבִּית
2 Sam. 23.14		וּמַצָּב			S	ובתרבית
				2 Sam. 10.11		לִישׁוּעָה
				1 Chron. 19.12		לִתְשׁוּעָה

§ 86.   Substantives derived from verbs tertiae ה.[4]

Gen. 3.16	MT	וְהֵרֹנֵךְ	1 Chron. 17.15	הֶחָזוֹן
	S	והריונך	2 Sam. 7.17	הַחִזָּיוֹן

§ 87.   Particles ending in י.

Gen. 9.28	MT	אַחַר	Job 7.1	K	על
	S	אחרי [5]		Q	עֲלֵי
Hos. 9.16	Q	בַּל	1 Ki. 20.41	K	מעל
	K	בלי		Q	מֵעֲלֵי

§ 88.   Formation of theophorous names (B-L § 25c', d'; Bergstr. § 16c).

a)   Ending in יהו or יה.

2 Chron. 10.15	אֲחִיָּהוּ	2 Chron. 29.1	זְכַרְיָהוּ
1 Ki. 12.15	אֲחִיָּה	2 Ki. 18.2	זְכַרְיָה
2 Chron. 25.17	אֲמַצְיָהוּ	2 Chron. 34.18	חִלְקִיָּהוּ
2 Ki. 14.8	אֲמַצְיָה	2 Ki. 22.10	חִלְקִיָּה

[1] Cf. Ex. 12.15: כִּי כָּל אֹכֵל חָמֵץ וְנִכְרְתָה הַנֶּפֶשׁ הַהִוא Ex. 12.19: כִּי כָּל אֹכֵל מַחְמֶצֶת וְנִכְרְתָה הַנֶּפֶשׁ הַהִוא; cf. our note 4 on page 291.

[2] Cf. 1 Chron. 17.11 — 2 Sam. 7.12.

[3] Cf. Ex. 6.6.

[4] Cf. in this connection also: 1 Ki. 10.5: וְעָלָתוֹ — 2 Chron. 9.4: וַעֲלִיָּתוֹ.

[5] Cf. Gen. 10.1, 32; 11.10; 37.17; Lev. 14.36, 43; Num. 6.19; 25.8; further: 2 Ki. 23.3 — 2 Chron. 34.31.

2 Chron. 36.22	יִרְמְיָהוּ	b) By prefix יוֹ or יְהוֹ.	
Ezra 1.1	יִרְמְיָה	2 Chron. 36.2	יוֹאָחָז
2 Chron. 26.1	עֻזִּיָּהוּ	2 Ki. 23.31	יְהוֹאָחָז
2 Ki. 14.21	עֲזַרְיָה	2 Chron. 24.1	יוֹאָשׁ
2 Chron. 22.10	וַעֲתַלְיָהוּ	2 Ki. 12.1	יְהוֹאָשׁ
2 Ki. 11.1	וַעֲתַלְיָה	1 Chron. 10.2	יוֹנָתָן
2 Chron. 18.10	צִדְקִיָּהוּ	1 Sam. 31.2	יְהוֹנָתָן
1 Ki. 22.11	צִדְקִיָּה	2 Ki. 8.21	יוֹרָם
2 Chron. 11.2	שְׁמַעְיָהוּ	2 Chron. 21.9	יְהוֹרָם
1 Ki. 12.22	שְׁמַעְיָה		
2 Sam. 23.30	בְּנָיָהוּ		
1 Chron. 11.31	בְּנָיָה		

CHAPTER THREE

THE COMPOSITE CHARACTER OF THE BIBLE
I. THE HEBREW BIBLE AS EVIDENCE
A. REPETITIONS IN THE BIBLE

§ 1.   Biblical criticism hitherto has been engaged in discovering the sources of the various parts of the Bible and in fixing the chronology of these sources by pointing to the stage in the gradual development of religious ideas and institutions which they exhibit. The dependence of the assumedly younger source upon its older forerunner could thus be demonstrated by listing identical or similar sounding phrases of the older source which found their way into that of a younger date. This approach is theological; I, on the other hand, am concerned solely with the philological aspect of the problems which the Bible offers, and therefore I start from an entirely new angle of observation. I leave the Pentateuch out, at least for the time being, since it has become the bulwark of the theologians, and center my investigations on the historical books of the Bible.

§ 2.   If we find in the prophetic or poetic sections of the Bible repetitions of verses and even groups of verses (as e.g. Jer. 30.10, 11 repeated in 46.27, 28; 30.23, 24 given in 23.19, 20 or 2 Sam. 22=Ps. 18; 1 Chron. 16.8-22=Ps. 105.1-15), it is very hard—nay, even impossible—to assert with certitude just which passage is the genuine one, and which the repetition. How can we even be sure that our terming one occurrence as a "repetition" is correct? It is quite possible that both passages are genuine, and what we call "repetition" is only due to an oversight of the final redactor, who neglected to omit one passage; and who can tell, maybe he was right in doing so! After all, these verses retain their poetic charm in both passages; repetition did them no harm.

B. HISTORICAL EVENTS TOLD TWICE

§ 3.   But this problem of repetitions at once assumes an altogether new aspect when we project it on the narratives in the historical books of the Bible. For events happened but once, and consequently if they are told more than once, they represent a clear case of repetition. There are many aspects to this problem: it can be treated from the viewpoint of the Bible forming a single entity, as accordingly I noted in § oo that 2 Sam. 22 is repeated in Ps. 18 and 1 Chron. 16.8-22 in Ps. 105.1-15; but it can also be treated from another point of view, regarding each historical book as an entity in itself. I shall proceed according to both these aspects; the results of the broader first one will reflect on the redaction of the Bible, while those of the second will shed light on the composition of the individual Biblical books.

§ 4.   The history of the kingdom of Judah (or of the house of David) is narrated twice in the Bible: it is told in the Former Prophets and retold in Chronicles. In mentioning the Former Prophets first and Chronicles in second place, we merely follow the arrangement of the Bible. Approximately 470 verses occur in more or less identical form (on the differences cf. p. 235 ff.) in these two sources; they cannot be regarded as genuine in the Former Prophets and as later repetition in Chronicles, as Biblical scholarship maintains, but are of equal value and rank. But before we take up the discussion of this problem, it is necessary first to give a list of these parallel passages (with supplements in Isaia, cf. p. 500 f.).

C.   THE ANNALS IN TWO RECENSIONS

§ 5.   The narratives in the Former Prophets and the corresponding parallels in the Chronicles.

1 Sam. 31.1-13	1 Chron. 10.1-12	11.1	20.1
2 Sam. 5.1-3	11.1-3		(more or less)
5.6-10	11.4-9	12.30-31	20.2-3
5.5	3.4b	21.18-22	20.4-8
	(more or less)	23.8-39	11.10-41
5.11-25	14.1-16	24.1-4, 9	21.1-5
6.2-11	13.6-14		(more or less)
6.13-16	15.26-29	24.10-25	21.8-26
	(more or less)	1 Ki. 3.4-13 2 Chron.	1.3, 7-
6.17-19	16.1-3		12 (more or less)
7.1-29	17.1-27	5.1a	9.26
8.1-18	18.1-17	7.23-26	4.2-5
10.1-19	19.1-19	7.40-50	4.11-22

```
7.51-8.11  . . . .  5.1-14                                  3-34
8.12-52    . . . .  6.1-40          22.41a,     . . . .  20.31-
8.62-63    . . . .  7.4-5            42-44a     . . . .     33a
8.64-66    . . . .  7.7-10          22.51       . . . .  21.1
9.1-9      . . . .  7.11-22   2 Ki.  8.17-22    . . . .  21.5-
           (more or less)                                  10b
9.10       . . . .  8.1              8.26-29    . . . .  22.2, 3a,
9.17-24    . . . .  8. 5-12                                 4a, 5-6
9.25-28    . . . .  8.13,           11.1-3      . . . .  22.10-12
                    17, 18          11.4-12     . . . .  23.1-11
           (more or less)                      (more or less)
10.1-25    . . . .  9.1-24          11.13-20    . . . .  23.12-21
10.26-29   . . . .  1.14-17         12.1-3      . . . .  24.1-2
10.27, 28a . . . .  9.27,           14.2-3      . . . .  25.1-2
                    28              14.5-6      . . . .  25.3-4
11.41-43   . . . .  9.29-31         14.8-14     . . . .  25.17-24
           (more or less)           14.17-20    . . . .  25.25-28
12.1-19    . . . .  10.1-19         14.21-22    . . . .  26.1-2
12.21-24   . . . .  11.1-4          15.2-3      . . . .  26.3-4
14.21b, 22a. . . .  12.13b,         15.5-7      . . . .  26.21-23
                    14a             15.33-34    . . . .  27.1-2a
14.25-28   . . . .  12.2,           15.36       . . . .  27.7
                    9-11                        (more or less)
14.31      . . . .  12.16           15.38       . . . .  27.9
15.1-27b   . . . .  13.1-2          16.19-20    . . . .  28.26-27
15.7a, 8   . . . .  13.22-23                    (more or less)
15.11      . . . .  14.1            18.2-3      . . . .  29.1-2
15.13-15   . . . .  15.16-18        18.13   Isa. . .  36.1
15.17-22   . . . .  16.1-6          18.17-37    . . . .  36.2-22
15.23-24   . . . .  16.11,          19.1-37     . . . .  37.1-38
                    12a,            20.1-6, 9, 11b . .  38.1-8
                    13a,            20.12-19    . . . .  39.1-8
                    14a;            21.1-9   2 Chron. 33.1-9
                    17.1a           21.18       . . . .  33.20
           (more or less)           21.19a, 20, . . . .  33.21-
22.2, 4-35 . . . .  18.2a,           23-24      . . . .    22a,
```

		24-25	23.30b-31, 33-34	36.1-4
22.1-2	. . . .	34.1-2		(more or less)
22.3-20	. . . .	34.8-28	23.36-37	36.5
		(more or less)	24.1a	36.6a
23.1-3	. . . .	34.29-	24.8-9	36.9
		32a	24.18-19	36.11-
23.22-23	. . . .	35.18-19		12a
		(more or less)		

D. They Cover the History of Judah and Israel

§ 6. The narratives referring to the kingdom of Judah, which are not common to both Former Prophets *and* Chronicles, are indicative for the character of the book in which they occur. Thus, and only thus can the nature of each respective historical book be defined as an entity. For those other passages, which the Former Prophets share with Chronicles, go back to what we term *Annals* (p. 496) and are used by the final redactors of these books merely as the historic background for their ideological amplifications. Though the books of Chronicles limit themselves to the history of the kingdom of Judah, while the Former Prophets deal with both Judah and Israel, I hope to be right in assuming that the original *Annals*, wherefrom both of them got their historic information, were one and the same group of documents. The compiler of the books of the Former Prophets made exhaustive use of them, while in the Chronicles only those parts are utilized which refer to the Southern Kingdom. As proof for this contention I shall demonstrate that certain passages in the Chronicles are understood only in the light of contemporary history of Israel as contained in the *Annals* of the Former Prophets.

1 Chron. 11.3: כִּדְבַר יהוה בְּיַד שְׁמוּאֵל, refers to the narrative 1 Sam. 16.13 f.

2 Chron. 10.15: לְמַעַן הָקִים יהוה אֶת דְּבָרוֹ אֲשֶׁר דִּבֶּר בְּיַד אֲחִיָּהוּ הַשִּׁלוֹנִי; cf. 1 Ki. 11.29 f.

2 Chron. 13.1: בִּשְׁנַת שְׁמוֹנֶה עֶשְׂרֵה לַמֶּלֶךְ יָרָבְעָם; cf. 1 Ki. 15.1.

2 Chron. 21.6: וַיֵּלֶךְ בְּדֶרֶךְ מַלְכֵי יִשְׂרָאֵל כַּאֲשֶׁר עָשׂוּ בֵית אַחְאָב; cf. 2 Ki. 8.18

2 Chron. 22.3: גַּם הוּא הָלַךְ בְּדַרְכֵי בֵית אַחְאָב; cf. 2 Ki. 8.27

2 Chron. 25.25: וַיְחִי אֲמַצְיָהוּ בֶן יוֹאָשׁ מֶלֶךְ יְהוּדָה אַחֲרֵי מוֹת יוֹאָשׁ בֶּן יְהוֹאָחָז מֶלֶךְ יִשְׂרָאֵל חֲמֵשׁ עֶשְׂרֵה שָׁנָה cf. 2 Ki. 14.17.

All these references to contemporary events in Israel are otherwise
unintelligible, since Chronicles pays no attention to the happenings in
Israel.

§ 7.   In § 4 we stated that we consider the *Annals* in both sources
(Former Prophets and Chronicles) as of equal value with regard to their
credence and genuineness. Two examples will suffice to prove our point.
We read in 2 Sam. 7.6: "for I have not dwelt in a house since the day that
I brought up the children of Israel out of Egypt, even to this day, but
have walked in a tent and in a tabernacle." וָאֶהְיֶה מִתְהַלֵּךְ בְּאֹהֶל וּבְמִשְׁכָּן.
In explaining the Lord's objection to the erection of a temple by David,
the verse relates that the Lord had led the life of a nomad (if we may say
so), without a permanent dwelling-place, always וָאֶהְיֶה מִתְהַלֵּךְ בְּאֹהֶל
וּבְמִשְׁכָּן. This cannot be rendered: "but I have walked in a tent and in a
tabernacle," because it does not express the contrast to "I have not dwelt in
a (scil. permanent) house." We must be aware of the fact that the contrast
to which the prophet Nathan points in the name of the Lord, is contained
in the בְּבַיִת as against בְּאֹהֶל וּבְמִשְׁכָּן; in a בַּיִת, a permanent house, you can
"dwell"; but in a movable אֹהֶל (tent) or מִשְׁכָּן (tabernacle) you must needs
lead the life of a nomad. This is expressed in the parallel passage 1 Chron.
17.5: וָאֶהְיֶה מֵאֹהֶל אֶל אֹהֶל וּמִמִּשְׁכָּן "but have [gone] from tent to tent, and
from one tabernacle [to another]." Thus, the contrast is clear and the
picture complete. Another instance is 1 Ki. 8.16 as compared with its
parallel passage 2 Chron. 6.5, 6. We print here the text in full according
to Chronicles, and indicate by brackets what is omitted in Kings, due to a
homoioteleuton: לֹא בָחַרְתִּי בְעִיר מִכֹּל שִׁבְטֵי יִשְׂרָאֵל לִבְנוֹת בַּיִת לִהְיוֹת שְׁמִי שָׁם

[וְלֹא בָחַרְתִּי בְאִישׁ לִהְיוֹת נָגִיד עַל עַמִּי יִשְׂרָאֵל: וָאֶבְחַר בִּירוּשָׁלַם לִהְיוֹת שְׁמִי שָׁם]

וָאֶבְחַר בְּדָוִד לִהְיוֹת עַל עַמִּי יִשְׂרָאֵל

According to Kings, there is no logical connection in the statement.
Thus, Chronicles presents us with a more genuine recension of these verses
than Samuel or Kings do.

E.   Synonyms imply Dialect Differences (Cf. MH p. 133 f.)

§ 8.   By the inclusion of the *Annals* in their two recensions (cf. p. 496),
the Bible has proved itself to be of a composite character. The characteristics of these recensions (cf. pp. 235-277) lost their dialectical colouring
and were later on fused together. The result of this development is that the

language of our Bible exhibits evidence of two different tendencies in its
vocabulary and in its grammar. Cf. MH §§ 145-149.

§ 9.   Here I bring just a few examples of the two distinctly different
trends in the vocabulary:

Gen. 13.18:	(באלני ממרא) וַיֵּשֶׁב –	ib. 20.1:	וַיָּגָר (בגרר)
Gen. 19.26:	(אשתו מאחריו) וַתַּבֵּט –	v. 28:	וַיַּשְׁקֵף (על פני סדם)
Gen. 8.7:	(מעל) הָאָרֶץ –	v. 8:	(מעל פני) הָאֲדָמָה
Gen. 8.14:	(הארץ) יָבְשָׁה –	v. 13:	חָרְבוּ (פני האדמה)
Gen. 31.23:	(אחריו) וַיִּרְדֹּף –	v. 36:	(כי) דָלַקְתָּ (אחרי)
Gen. 3.6:	(ונחמד העץ) לְהַשְׂכִּיל –	ib. 2.9:	(כל עץ נחמד) לְמַרְאֶה
Gen. 5.1:	(אלהים עשה) בִּדְמוּת –	ib. 9.6:	בְּצֶלֶם (אלהים עתה)
Gen. 1.27:	(בצלם אלהים) בָּרָא –	ib. 9.6:	(בצלם אלהים) עָשָׂה
Gen. 6.19:	זָכָר וּנְקֵבָה –	ib. 7.2:	אִישׁ וְאִשְׁתּוֹ
Gen. 6.19:	(... זכר ונקבה) שְׁנַיִם –	ib. 7.9:	שְׁנַיִם שְׁנַיִם (... זכר ונקבה)
Gen. 7.2:	(איש ואשתו) שְׁנַיִם –		שִׁבְעָה שִׁבְעָה (איש ואשתו)
Gen. 25.8:	(זקן) וְשָׂבֵעַ –	ib. 35.29:	(זקן) וּשְׂבַע יָמִים
Gen. 15.4:	(אשר) יֵצֵא מִמֵּעֶיךָ –	Ex. 1.5:	יֹצְאֵי יֶרֶךְ (יעקב)
Ex. 3.16:	(אלהי אבתיכם) נִרְאָה אֵלַי –	v. 18:	(אלהי העבריים) נִקְרָה עָלֵינוּ
Ex. 4.2:	(בידך ...) מַטֶּה –	ib. 12.11:	וּמַקֶּלְכֶם (בידכם)
Ex. 6.12:	(ואני) עֲרַל שְׂפָתָיִם –	ib. 4.10:	כְּבַד פֶּה וּכְבַד לָשׁוֹן (אנכי)
Ex. 12.43:	(כל) בֶּן נֵכָר (לא יאכל בו) –	v. 48:	(וכל) עָרֵל (לא יאכל בו)
Ex. 4.21:	(ואני) אֲחַזֵּק (את לבו) –	ib. 7.3:	(ואני) אַקְשֶׁה (את לב)
Ex. 7.3:	אַקְשֶׁה (את לב) –	ib. 8.11:	וְהַכְבֵּד (את לבו)

Ex. 9.34, 35: וַיֵּכָבֵד לִבּוֹ ... // וַיֶּחֱזַק לב פרעה

Gen. 32.17:	(תשימו) וְרֶוַח –	Josh. 3.4:	(אך) רָחוֹק (יהיה)
Lev. 5.11:	(לא תשיג) וְאִם –	v. 21:	– (נפש) כִּי (תחטא)
	v. 17:		וְאִם (נפש) // כִּי (תחטא)

Ex. 8.26: ;(וַיֵּצֵא מֹשֶׁה מֵעִם פַּרְעֹה   ; ib. 9.29: וַיֹּאמֶר ... מֹשֶׁה כְּצֵאתִי אֶת הָעִיר

ib. 9.33: וַיֵּצֵא מֹשֶׁה מֵעִם פַּרְעֹה // אֶת הָעִיר

Num. 31.28:	אֶחָד נֶפֶשׁ –	v. 30:	אֶחָד אָחֻז
Num. 22.11:	(לכה) קָבָה (לי) –	ib. 23.7:	(לכה) אָרָה (לי)
Num. 22.32:	(זה שלש) רְגָלִים –	ib. 24.10:	(זה שלש) פְּעָמִים

§ 10.   The history of Hebrew grammar is a history of continued
failures (cf. p. 415, § 3) primarily because the grammarians erred in treating

Hebrew as *one* language and brought Hebrew phonology and morphology back to *one* common denominator, regarding the obvious deviations as mere exceptions, instead of seeing in them examples for the other tendency, which runs parallel to the first one; cf. § 25 f.

F. REPETITIONS IN THE SAME BIBLICAL BOOK

§ 11. We shall now take up the discussion of repetitions to be found within the framework of each historical book separately (cf. § 3) and shall divide them into two groups: a) passages which occur twice, and fit well into their context in either place; b) passages which are recorded at their proper place, and reappear again elsewhere, where they are quite obviously out of place. My conclusions will prove of importance in the interpretation of similar phenomena in the Bible.

§ 12. Events told twice in the same historical books, and both times fitting into their context.

Josh. 8.9	Josh. 8.13
וילן יהושע בלילה ההוא בתוך העם	וילך יהושע בלילה ההוא בתוך העמק

On the variant וילך–וילן (ך–ן), cf. p. 487, sub 11, and note 3. The variant העמק–העם presupposes a spelling העמ; cf. p. 490, § 71a, and p. 518.

Josh. 13.14	Josh. 13.33
רק לשבט הלוי לא נתן נחלה אשי יהוה	ולשבט הלוי לא נתן משה נחלה יהוה
אלהי ישראל הוא נחלתו כאשר דבר לו	אלהי ישראל הוא נחלתם כאשר דבר להם

On the addition משה, cf. p. 290, § 79a; on רק, cf. p. 292, sub b. The difference in the number: נחלתו … לו and נחלתם … להם finds its parallel in p. 271, § 49.

Josh. 10.14b, 15	Josh. 10.42b, 43
14 … כי יהוה נלחם לישראל:	42 … כי יהוה אלהי ישראל נלחם לישראל:
15 וישב יהושע וכל ישראל עמו אל	43 וישב יהושע וכל ישראל עמו אל
המחנה הגלגלה:	המחנה הגלגלה:

1 Sam. 14.1	1 Sam. 14.6
ויאמר יונתן בן שאול אל הנער נשא כליו לכה	ויאמר יהונתן אל הנער נשא כליו לכה
ונעברה אל מצב פלשתים	ונעברה אל מצב הערלים

On יהונתן–יונתן, cf. p. 297, sub b; cf. also 2 Sam. 13.3: יונדב with v. 5: יהונדב.

On the addition בן שאול, cf. p. 290, § 79b.

I Sam. 23.19; 24.2	I Sam. 26.1, 2
19 ויעלו זפים אל שאול הגבעתה לאמר הלוא דוד מסתתר עמנו במצדות בחרשה בגבעת החכילה אשר מימין הישמון:	1 ויבאו הזפים אל שאול הגבעתה לאמר הלא דוד מסתתר בגבעת החכילה על פני הישימן:
2 ויקח שאול שלשת אלפים איש בחור מכל ישראל וילך לבקש את דוד ואנשיו	2 ויקם שאול וירד אל מדבר זיף ואתו שלשת אלפים איש בחורי ישראל לבקש את דוד

I Chron. 3,5-8	I Chron, 14.4-7
5 ואלה נולדו לו בירושלם שמעא ושובב ונתן ושלמה ...	4 ואלה שמות הילודים אשר היו לו בירושלם שמוע ושובב נתן ושלמה:
6 ויבחר ואלישמע ואליפלט:	5 ויבחר ואלישוע ואלפלט:
7 ונגה ונפג ויפיע:	6 ונגה ונפג ויפיע:
8 ואלישמע ואלידע ואליפלט	7 ואלישמע ובעלידע ואליפלט:

I Chron. 5.27, 28	I Chron. 6.1, 3
27 בני לוי גרשון קהת ומררי:	1 בני לוי גרשם קהת ומררי:
28 ובני קהת עמרם יצהר וחברון ועזיאל:	3 ובני קהת עמרם ויצהר וחברון ועזיאל:

I Chron. 8.28-38	I Chron. 9.34-44
28 אלה ראשי אבות לתלדותם ראשים אלה ישבו בירושלם:	34 אלה ראשי האבות ללוים לתלדותם ראשים אלה ישבו בירושלם:
29 ובגבעון ישבו אבי גבעון ושם אשתו מעכה:	35 ובגבעון ישבו אבי גבעון יעואל ושם אשתו מעכה:
30 ובנו הבכור עבדון וצור וקיש ובעל ונדב:	36 ובנו הבכור עבדון וצור וקיש ובעל ונר ונדב:
31 וגדור ואחיו וזכר:	37 וגדור ואחיו וזכריה ומקלות:
32 ומקלות הוליד את שמאה ואף המה נגד אחיהם ישבו בירושלם עם אחיהם:	38 ומקלות הוליד את שמאם ואף הם נגד אחיהם ישבו בירושלם עם אחיהם:
33 ונר הוליד את קיש וקיש הוליד את שאול ושאול הוליד את יהונתן ואת מלכי־שוע	39 ונר הוליד את קיש וקיש הוליד את שאול ושאול הוליד את יהונתן ואת מלכי־שוע

Right	Left
ואת אבינדב ואת אשבעל:	ואת אבינדב ואת אשבעל:
40 ובן יהונתן מריב בעל	34 ובן יהונתן מריב בעל
ומרי בעל הוליד את מיכה:	ומריב בעל הוליד את מיכה:
41 ובני מיכה פיתן ומלך ותחרע:	35 ובני מיכה פיתן ומלך ותארע ואחז:
42 ואחז הוליד את יערה	36 ואחז הוליד את יהועדה
ויערה הוליד את עלמת	ויהועדה הוליד את עלמת
ואת עזמות ואת זמרי	ואת עזמות ואת זמרי
וזמרי הוליד את מוצא:	וזמרי הוליד את מוצא:
43 ומוצא הוליד את בנעא	37 ומוצא הוליד את בנעא
ורפיה בנו אלעשה בנו אצל בנו:	רפה בנו אלעשה בנו אצל בנו:
44 ולאצל ששה בנים ואלה שמותם	38 ולאצל ששה בנים ואלה שמותם
עזריקם בכרו וישמעאל	עזריקם בכרו וישמעאל
ושריה ועבדיה וחנן	ושריה ועבדיה וחנן
אלה בני אצל:	כל אלה בני אצל:

2 Chron. 9.25, 27-28

Right	Left
25 ויהי לשלמה ארבעת אלפים	14 ... ויהי לו אלף וארבע מאות רכב
אריות סוסים ומרכבות	
ושנים עשר אלף פרשים	ושנים עשר אלף פרשים
ויניחם בערי הרכב	ויניחם בערי הרכב
ועם המלך בירושלם:	ועם המלך בירושלם:
27 ויתן המלך את הכסף	15 ויתן המלך את הכסף
בירושלם כאבנים	ואת הזהב בירושלם כאבנים
ואת הארזים נתן כשקמים	ואת הארזים נתן כשקמים
אשר בשפלה לרב:	אשר בשפלה לרב:
28 ומוציאים סוסים ממצרים לשלמה	16 ומוצא הסוסים אשר לשלמה ממצרים

2 Chron. 21.5 (left) | 2 Chron. 21.20a (right)

Right	Left
בן שלשים ושתים היה במלכו	בן שלשים ושתים שנה יהורם במלכו
ושמונה שנים מלך בירושלם	ושמונה שנים מלך בירושלם

2 Chron. 27.1 (left) | 2 Chron. 27.8 (right)

Right	Left
בן עשרים וחמש שנה היה במלכו	בן עשרים וחמש שנה יותם במלכו
ושש עשרה שנה מלך בירושלם	ושש עשרה שנה מלך בירושלם

G. REPETITIONS OUT OF PLACE

§ 13. Events narrated at their proper place, and repeated out of place in the same historical book:

2 Sam. 8.6	2 Sam. 8.14
וישם דוד נציבים בארם דמשק	וישם באדום נצבים בכל אדום שם נצביב
ותהי ארם לדוד לעבדים נושאי מנחה	ויהי כל אדום עבדים לדוד
וישע יהוה את דוד בכל אשר הלך:	ויושע יהוה את דוד בכל אשר הלך:

1 Ki. 14.21	1 Ki. 14.31
··· ושם אמו נעמה העמנית:	··· ושם אמו נעמה העמנית ···

1 Ki. 14.30	1 Ki. 15.6
ומלחמה היתה· בין רחבעם	ומלחמה היתה בין רחבעם
ובין ירבעם כל הימים:	ובין ירבעם כל ימי חייו:

1 Ki. 15.16	1 Ki. 15.32
ומלחמה היתה בין אסא	ומלחמה היתה בין אסא
ובין בעשא מלך ישראל כל ימיהם:	ובין בעשא מלך ישראל כל ימיהם:

From v. 27 on, the history of בַּעְשָׁא is taken up. Hence, this reference in v. 32, if genuine, would have been phrased thus: בין בעשא ובין אסא מֶלֶךְ יְהוּדָה.

2 Ki. 8.25	2 Ki. 9.29
בשנת שתים עשרה שנה	ובשנת אחת עשרה שנה
ליורם בן אחאב מלך ישראל	ליורם בן אחאב
מלך אחזיהו בן יהורם מלך יהודה:	מלך אחזיה על יהודה:

2 Ki. 8.29	2 Ki. 9.15a, 16b
וישב יורם המלך להתרפא ביזרעאל	15 וישב יהורם המלך להתרפא ביזרעאל
מן המכים אשר יכהו ארמים ברמה	מן המכים אשר יכהו ארמים
בהלחמו את חזהאל מלך ארם	בהלחמו את חזאל מלך ארם ···
ואחזיהו בן יהורם מלך יהודה	16 ··· ואחזיה מלך יהודה
ירד לראות את יורם ···	ירד לראות את יורם:

2 Ki. 13.12-13	2 Ki. 14.15-16
12 ויתר דברי יואש וכל אשר עשה	15 ויתר דברי יהואש אשר עשה
וגבורתו אשר נלחם עם אמציה	וגבורתו ואשר נלחם עם אמציהו
מלך יהודה	מלך יהודה
הלא הם כתובים על ספר	הלא הם כתובים על ספר
דברי הימים למלכי ישראל:	דברי הימים למלכי ישראל:
13 וישכב יואש עם אבתיו וירבעם ישב	16 וישכב יהואש עם אבתיו
על כסאו	

ויקבר יואש בשמרון עם מלכי ישראל: ויקבר בשמרון עם מלכי ישראל

וימלך ירבעם בנו תחתיו:

Chapter 14 deals with the reign of Amaziah, and not with that of
Jehoash. Furthermore: 14.8-14 give a detailed report of the battle
between these two kings, so that the brief reference in v. 15: ואשר נלחם
עם אמציהו מלך יהודה is quite obviously out of place.

<table>
<tr><td align="center">2 Ki. 17.5-6</td><td align="center">2 Ki. 18.9-11</td></tr>
<tr><td>5 ויעל מלך אשור בכל הארץ ויעל</td><td>9 ··· עלה שלמנאסר מלך אשור על</td></tr>
<tr><td>שמרון</td><td>שמרון</td></tr>
<tr><td>ויצר עליה</td><td>10 ויצר עליה: וילכדה מקצה</td></tr>
<tr><td>שלש שנים:</td><td>שלש שנים</td></tr>
<tr><td>6 בשנת התשיעית להושע</td><td>בשנת ··· תשע להושע מלך ישראל</td></tr>
<tr><td>לכד מלך אשור את שמרון</td><td>נלכדה שמרון:</td></tr>
<tr><td>ויגל את ישראל אשורה</td><td>11 ויגל מלך אשור את ישראל אשורה</td></tr>
<tr><td>וישב אותם בחלח ובחבור</td><td>וינחם בחלח ובחבור</td></tr>
<tr><td>נהר גוזן וערי מדי:</td><td>נהר גוזן וערי מדי:</td></tr>
</table>

On the addition שלמנאסר, cf. p. 290, § 79a; on נלכדה–לכד, cf. p. 251,
§ 18a β; on the addition מלך אשור (v. 11), cf. p. 290, § 79b.

§ 14. The instances which are listed in the two preceding paragraphs
lead to the assumption that the historiographers, who composed the
basic parts of the historical books in our Bible, had at their disposal sources of a fragmentary nature, each probably consisting of a single historic
record, without connection with the rest of the sources. There may have
existed an oral tradition with regard to the arrangement of these *Annals*
or the chronology of the events they recorded. But the very fact that some
of these events are now related out of their proper place (cf. § 13), is proof
enough that such a tradition worked merely as a corrective, and could not
claim absolute mastery. Theoretically, we will have to admit that the
possibility of misplacing an item of the narration is not to be excluded·
For how are we to explain the origin of repetitions? Surely by way of
assuming that a certain part of the *Annals* got into the hands of two
recorders, each responsible for their respective records, listing a number
of events in succession (corresponding to a few verses, in our way of
thinking). When these two separate records were later combined, and

formed a larger unit (comparable to our chapter), this larger unit thus
contained a repetition. In other words: the damage was done, but
nobody was to blame for it.

H. Annals contain Conflicting Data

§ 15.   But is such an explanation as we offered here plausible? Do the
sources of the historical books in our Bible go back to *Annals*, which first
contained separate entries about unrelated facts, which in the course of
time were gradually enlarged until they developed into the *Annals*, which
are the backbone of the historical books? I hope that the following discussion will make this assumption quite plausible. I shall demonstrate
that the *Annals* offer conflicting items in rather close proximity. The
reader must not be misled by the actual distance (measured in verses in
our present-day Bible), between the various events, which we are going to
quote; for only the *Annals'* verses count; the additions of the editors are
of no consequence to us here.

§ 16.   Was there an *interregnum* during the civil war in Israel?

I Ki. 15.9:	··· מלך אָסָא מלך יהודה
I Ki. 15.10:	וְאַרְבָּעִים וְאַחַת שָׁנָה מלך בירושלם ···
I Ki. 16.15:	בִּשְׁנַת עֶשְׂרִים וָשֶׁבַע שָׁנָה לאסא מלך יהודה זִמְרִי שִׁבְעַת יָמִים ···
I Ki. 16.21:	אז יחלק העם ישראל לחצי חצי העם היה אחרי תִבְנִי בן גִּינַת להמליכו והחצי אחרי עָמְרִי
I Ki. 16.22:	ויחזק העם אשר אחרי עמרי ··· וימלך עמרי
I Ki. 16.23:	בשנת שְׁלֹשִׁים וְאַחַת שָׁנָה לאסא מלך יהודה עָמְרִי על עשראל שְׁתֵּים עֶשְׂרֵה שָׁנָה ···
I Ki. 16.28:	וישכב עמרי עם אבתיו ··· וימלך אַחְאָב בנו תחתיו
I Ki. 16.29:	ואחאב בן עמרי מלך על ישראל בִּשְׁנַת שְׁלֹשִׁים וּשְׁמֹנֶה שָׁנָה לאסא מלך יהודה ···

According to 16.23, the civil war between Omri and Tibni must have
resulted in an *interregnum* of four years; for Zimri died in the 27th year
of Asa (16.15), and Omri did not ascend the throne till the 31st year of
Asa (16.23). Now Omri reigned twelve years, until the 38th year of Asa
(16.29); hence he must have ascended the throne twelve years before,
namely in the 27th year of Asa (cf. 16.15), with no *interregnum* between
Zimri and himself. Thus, the narratives in 16.23 and 16.29 exclude one
another.

§ 17.   The reign of Ahaziah the son of Ahab.

1 Ki. 16.29:   ‎... וַיִּמְלֹךְ אַחְאָב בֶּן עָמְרִי עַל יִשְׂרָאֵל בְּשֹׁמְרוֹן עֶשְׂרִים וּשְׁתַּיִם שָׁנָה

1 Ki. 22.41:   ‎וִיהוֹשָׁפָט בֶּן אָסָא מָלַךְ עַל יְהוּדָה בִּשְׁנַת אַרְבַּע לְאַחְאָב מֶלֶךְ יִשְׂרָאֵל

1 Ki. 22.42:   ‎יהושפט ‎... וְעֶשְׂרִים וְחָמֵשׁ שָׁנָה מָלַךְ בִּירוּשָׁלָיִם ‎...

1 Ki. 22.52:   ‎אֲחַזְיָהוּ בֶּן אַחְאָב מָלַךְ עַל יִשְׂרָאֵל בְּשֹׁמְרוֹן בִּשְׁנַת שְׁבַע עֶשְׂרֵה לִיהוֹשָׁפָט מֶלֶךְ
‎יהודה וַיִּמְלֹךְ עַל יִשְׂרָאֵל שְׁנָתָיִם

2 Ki. 1.17:   ‎וַיָּמָת (scil. ‎אחזיה) ‎... וַיִּמְלֹךְ יְהוֹרָם תַּחְתָּיו בִּשְׁנַת שְׁתַּיִם לִיהוֹרָם בֶּן יְהוֹשָׁפָט
‎כִּי לֹא הָיָה לוֹ בֵן

2 Ki. 3.1:   ‎וִיהוֹרָם בֶּן אַחְאָב מָלַךְ עַל יִשְׂרָאֵל בְּשֹׁמְרוֹן בִּשְׁנַת שְׁמֹנֶה עֶשְׂרֵה לִיהוֹשָׁפָט
‎מֶלֶךְ יְהוּדָה וַיִּמְלֹךְ שְׁתֵּים עֶשְׂרֵה שנה

2 Ki. 8.16:   ‎וּבִשְׁנַת חָמֵשׁ לְיוֹרָם בֶּן אַחְאָב מֶלֶךְ יִשְׂרָאֵל ‎... מָלַךְ יְהוֹרָם בֶּן יְהוֹשָׁפָט מֶלֶךְ
‎יהודה

According to 1 Ki. 22.52, at the death of Ahaziah of Israel his contemporary Jehoshaphat of Judah had reigned 17 + 2 = 19 years out of
the 25 years of his reign (22.42); he thus had about 6 years still left to him.
Now, Ahaziah was succeeded by his brother Jehoram, who became king
in the 18th year of Jehoshaphat (2 Ki. 3.1); consequently, the recorder in
2 Ki. 3.1 did not know of Ahaziah's reign of two years, as narrated in
1 Ki. 22.52; for else he would have fixed the ascension of Jehoram on the
20th year of Jehoshaphat. Furthermore, Jehoshaphat outlived Ahab by
18 years (1 Ki. 22.41, 42); in this period, Jehoram reigned in Israel for
twelve years, so that Jehoshaphat outlived him also by about 6 years.
How, then, are we to reconcile this with 2 Ki. 8.16? Even if we consider
the two years of Ahaziah, there still remain (6—2 =) 4 + 5 = 9 years
unaccounted for. Thus, these records contradict one another.

§ 18.   Have we a complete list of the kings of Judah and Israel?

2 Ki. 14.1:   ‎... מָלַךְ אֲמַצְיָהוּ בֶן יוֹאָשׁ מֶלֶךְ יְהוּדָה

2 Ki. 14,2:   ‎... וְעֶשְׂרִים וָתֵשַׁע שָׁנָה מָלַךְ בִּירוּשָׁלָיִם

2 Ki. 14.16:   ‎וַיִּשְׁכַּב יְהוֹאָשׁ עִם אֲבֹתָיו וַיִּקָּבֵר בְּשֹׁמְרוֹן עִם מַלְכֵי יִשְׂרָאֵל וַיִּמְלֹךְ יָרָבְעָם בְּנוֹ
‎תַּחְתָּיו

2 Ki. 14.17:   ‎וַיְחִי אֲמַצְיָהוּ בֶן יוֹאָשׁ מֶלֶךְ יְהוּדָה אַחֲרֵי מוֹת יְהוֹאָשׁ בֶּן יְהוֹאָחָז מֶלֶךְ יִשְׂרָאֵל
‎חֲמֵשׁ עֶשְׂרֵה שָׁנָה

2 Ki. 14.21:   ‎וַיִּקְחוּ כָל עַם יְהוּדָה אֶת עֲזַרְיָה ‎... וַיַּמְלִכוּ אֹתוֹ תַּחַת אָבִיו אֲמַצְיָהוּ

2 Ki. 14.23:   ‎בִּשְׁנַת חֲמֵשׁ עֶשְׂרֵה שָׁנָה לַאֲמַצְיָהוּ בֶן יוֹאָשׁ מֶלֶךְ יְהוּדָה מָלַךְ יָרָבְעָם בֶּן יוֹאָשׁ
‎מֶלֶךְ יִשְׂרָאֵל בְּשֹׁמְרוֹן אַרְבָּעִים וְאַחַת שָׁנָה

2 Ki. 15.1: בִּשְׁנַת עֶשְׂרִים וָשֶׁבַע שָׁנָה לירבעם מלך ישראל מלך עֲזַרְיָה בן אמציה מלך
יהודה

2 Ki. 15.2: ... וַחֲמִשִׁים וּשְׁתַּיִם שָׁנָה מלך בירושלם

2 Ki. 15.8: בִּשְׁנַת שְׁלֹשִׁים וּשְׁמֹנֶה שָׁנָה לעזריהו מלך יהודה מלך זְכַרְיָהוּ בן ירבעם על
ישראל בשמרון ...

According to 14.17 and 14.23, Amaziah reigned for only 15 years synchronistically with Jeroboam (cf. 14.2). But the next king of Judah to be mentioned is Azariah, who became king in the 27th year of Jeroboam (15.1); hence for twelve years (from the 15th to the 27th year) of Jeroboam's rule there is no account of a contemporary king of Judah. And still another difficulty confronts us. According to 14.23, Jeroboam reigned 41 years, of which 27 were gone, when Azariah became king (15.1); he thus was the contemporary of Azariah for his remaining 14 years. But the next king of Israel to be mentioned was enthroned in the 38th year of Azariah (15.8); who, then, was king in Israel in the 24 years between the 14th and the 38th year of Azariah?

§ 19. In order to preclude any possible misunderstanding we wish to emphasize that our discussion in the preceding paragraphs concerns itself exclusively with internal problems of the composition of the Hebrew Bible, and not with the problem of Biblical chronology, the aim of which it is to verify and adjust the discordant indications of the Bible. I have assigned them to different sources without interfering with their data.

I. RECORDS MISPLACED IN ANNALS

§ 20. And now we venture another step ahead in our argument. Since we have proved that events could have been recorded out of their proper place (in addition to being reported at the place where they belong), might it not be likely that in certain Biblical narratives the record was preserved in the wrong place only? Instead of "events narrated at their proper place, and repeated out of place in the same historical book" (cf. § 13), we would thus simply have events narrated out of place, the record in its proper place being missing. Let us illustrate this eventuality. In Josh. 10.1 we read: וַיְהִי כִשְׁמֹעַ אֲדֹנִי צֶדֶק מֶלֶךְ יְרוּשָׁלַם כִּי לָכַד יְהוֹשֻׁעַ אֶת הָעַי וַיַּחֲרִימָהּ — כַּאֲשֶׁר עָשָׂה לִירִיחוֹ וּלְמַלְכָּהּ כֵּן עָשָׂה לָעַי וּלְמַלְכָּהּ — וְכִי הִשְׁלִימוּ יֹשְׁבֵי גִבְעוֹן אֶת יִשְׂרָאֵל וַיִּהְיוּ בְּקִרְבָּם: The words which are between the two hyphens, are obviously out of place here; by eliminating them we get (לְכַד) כִּי ...

וְעָשִׂיתָ לָעַי וּלְמַלְכָּהּ כַּאֲשֶׁר עָשִׂיתָ, וְכִי (הִשְׁלִימוּ), cf. p. 286, § 75. Note Josh. 8.2a: רַק שְׁלָלָהּ וּבְהֶמְתָּהּ תָּבֹזּוּ לָכֶם, and the following (2b): לִירִיחוֹ וּלְמַלְכָּהּ. Hence the words between the hyphens in 10.1 belong after 8.26 and before v. 27.

8.26 וִיהוֹשֻׁעַ לֹא הֵשִׁיב יָדוֹ אֲשֶׁר נָטָה בַּכִּידוֹן עַד אֲשֶׁר הֶחֱרִים אֵת כָּל יֹשְׁבֵי הָעָי:
10.1b כַּאֲשֶׁר עָשָׂה לִירִיחוֹ וּלְמַלְכָּהּ כֵּן עָשָׂה לָעַי וּלְמַלְכָּהּ. 8.27. רַק הַבְּהֵמָה וּשְׁלַל הָעִיר הַהִיא בָּזְזוּ לָהֶם יִשְׂרָאֵל ···

§ 21. In the following cases, too, I find instances of misplacement, and and interpret them in a similar manner.

Judg. 1.16; 4.11 ff.

1.19 ובני קיני חתן משה עלו מעיר התמרים את בני יהודה מדבר יהודה אשר בנגב ערד וילך וישב את העם:

4.11 וחבר הקיני נפרד מקין מבני חבב חתן משה ויט אהלו עד אלון בצענים (בצעננים ק) אשר את קדש:

2 Sam. 4.2, 5-12, 3

4.2 ושני אנשים שרי גדודים היו בן שאול שם האחד בענה ושם השני רכב בני רמון הבארתי מבני בנימן כי גם בארות תחשב על בנימן:

5 וילכו בני רמון הבארתי רכב ובענה ויבאו כחם היום אל בית איש בשת והוא שכב את משכב הצהרים:

v.v. 6-11 in the same order as in the Bible; then

12 ויצו דוד את הנערים ויהרגום ויקצצו את ידיהם ואת רגליהם ויתלו על הברכה בחברון ואת ראש איש בשת לקחו ויקברו בקבר אבנר בחברון:

3 ויברחו דבארתים גתימה ויהיו שם גרים עד היום הזה:

2 Sam. 9.1; 4.4; 9.2 ff.

9.1 ויאמר דוד הכי יש עוד אשר נותר לבית שאול ואעשה עמו חסד בעבור יהונתן:

4.4 וליהונתן בן שאול בן נכה רגלים בן חמש שנים היה בבא שמעת שאול ויהונתן מיזרעאל ותשאהו אמנתו ותנס ויהי בחפזה לנוס ויפל ויפסח ושמו מפיבשת:

9.2 ולבית שאול עבד ושמו ציבא ויקראו לו אל דוד ויאמר המלך אליו האתה ציבא ויאמר עבדך:

1 Ki. 10.10, 13 f.

10 ותתן למלך מאה ועשרים ככר זהב ובשמים הרבה מאד ואבן יקרה לא בא כבשם ההוא עוד לרב אשר נתנה מלכת שבא למלך שלמה:

13 והמלך שלמה נתן למלכת שבא את כל חפצה אשר שאלה מלבד אשר נתן לה כיד המלך שלמה ותפן ותלך לארצה היא ועבדיה:

1 Ki. 9.26-28; 10.11-12

9.26 ואני עשה המלך שלמה בעציון גבר אשר את אלות על שפת ים סוף בארץ אדום:

27 וישלח חירם באני את עבדיו אנשי אניות ידעי הים עם עבדי שלמה:

28 ויבאו אופירה ויקחו משם זהב ארבע מאות ועשרים ככר ויבאו אל המלך שלמה:

10.11 וגם אני חירם אשר נשא זהב מאופיר הביא מאפיר עצי אלמגים הרבה מאד ואבן יקרה:

12 ויעש המלך את עצי האלמגים מסעד לבית יהוה ולבית המלך וכנרות ונבלים לשרים
לא בא כן עצי אלמגים ולא נראה עד היום הזה:

1 Ki. 4.19; 9.23; 5. 7, 6, 8

4.19 גבר בן ארי בארץ גלעד ארץ סיחון מלך האמרי ועג מלך הבשן ונציב אחד אשר
בארץ:

9.23 אלה שרי הנצבים אשר על המלאכה לשלמה חמשים וחמש מאות הרדים בעם העשים
במלאכה:

5.7 וכלכלו הנצבים האלה את המלך שלמה ואת כל הקרב אל שלחן המלך שלמה איש
חדשו לא יעדרו דבר:

5.6 ויהי לשלמה ארבעים אלף ארות סוסים למרכבו ושנים עשר אלף פרשים:

5.8 והשערים והתבן לסוסים ולרכש יבאו אל המקום אשר יהיה שם איש כמשפטו:

§ 22. We now return to the problem of repetitions. So far our discussion has dealt only with narratives which appear twice almost verbatim. But there are narratives appearing once in a style which is easily
recognizable as belonging to the original *Annals* and again in abbreviated
form, giving merely a short abstract.

1 Ki. 16.1-3	1 Ki. 16.7
1 ויהי דבר יהוה אל יהוא בן חני על בעשא לאמר:	וגם ביד יהוא בן חני הנביא דבר יהוה היה אל בעשא ואל ביתו ועל כל הרעה אשר עשה בעיני יהוה להכעיסו במעשה ידיו להיות כבית ירבעם:
2 יען אשר הרימתיך מן העפר ואתנך נגיד על עמי ישראל ותלך בדרך ירבעם ותחטיא את עמי ישראל להכעיסני בחטאתם:	
3 הנני מבעיר אחרי בעשא ואחרי ביתו ונתתי את ביתך כבית ירבעם בן נבט:	

Similarly, 2 Chron. 32 is a digest of the events told in Isa. 36-39, and
2 Chron. 8.17-18 a summary of 1 Ki. 9.26-28.

J. Doublets in the Bible (Cf. MH p. 105 ff.)

§ 23.   Repetitions are narratives of identical events, which are included twice in the same Biblical book. Between the components of the "repetition" (we cannot be sure whether the first or the second narrative is the repetition, except in cases discussed in § 13) there are other narratives. If, however, these components follow one another without a break, and with only slight differences in their wording, we would term them doublets (cf. p. 346, § 7). The components of a doublet need not necessarily be lengthy: groups of words, and even single words, may constitute a component of a doublet. It is even possible that one word only represents both components of a doublet. On p. 273, § 51 I listed examples for the rule that "the emphatic state is indicated by the article or suffix"; e.g. the forms עָרֵיהֶם and הֶעָרִים, which occur in the identical syntactic structure in a parallel passage, reflect the two possibilities for determining the noun עָרִים. When a noun has *both* the prefix and the suffix, it is a doublet. I shall list some doublets in the Bible to illustrate this development and to show how these doublets, having become part of the Bible, influenced Biblical exegesis. The instance in Ex. 23.2 gave rise to a Talmudic discussion, cf. Bab. *Sanhedrin* 3b; but on Josh. 20.6 only the component referring to Num. 35.12 is made the basis of the Talmudic decision in Bab. *Makkoth* 12a, while the other component referring to v. 15 is disregarded.

§ 24.   Doublets in the Hebrew Bible.

הָאָהֳלִי: Josh. 7.21   (composed of הָאֹהֶל and אָהֳלִי)

הָעֲרִכְּךָ: Lev. 27.23   (=הערך+ערכך)

וְהַחְצִיו: Josh. 8.33   (=והחצי+והציו)

הַדָּבְרוֹ: Mic. 1.12   (=הדבר+דברו)

הֲהָרוֹתֶיהָ: 2 Ki. 15.16   (=ההרות+הרותיה)

וַיָּחֶל: Gen. 8.12: combination of וַיִּחֶל and וַיָּחֶל, cf. v. 10

Ex. 38.13:   קֵדְמָה // מִזְרָחָה; id. Num. 2.3

Num. 3.38:   לִפְנֵי הַמִּשְׁכָּן קֵדְמָה // לִפְנֵי אֹהֶל מוֹעֵד מִזְרָחָה

Ex. 37.27:   עַל שְׁתֵּי צַלְעֹתָיו // עַל שְׁנֵי צִדָּיו

Josh. 20.6:   עַד עָמְדוֹ לִפְנֵי הָעֵדָה לַמִּשְׁפָּט // עַד מוֹת הַכֹּהֵן הַגָּדוֹל; cf. Num. 35.12: עד מות and ib. v. 25: עד עמדו לפני העדה למשפט הכהן הגדל

Ex. 23.2: לנטת אחרי רבים and ‏; composed of: לִנְטֹת אַחֲרֵי רַבִּים ‏// לְהַטֹּת
אַחֲרֵי רבִים לְהַטֹת. Translate: *to pervert* [*judgment*] *according
to a multitude.*

Ps. 18.7: וְשַׁוְעָתִי לְפָנָיו תָּבֹא ‏// בְּאָזְנָיו ‏; combination of: ושועתי לפני תבא
and ושועתי תבא באזניו.

Jer. 44.3: לְקַטֵּר ‏// לַעֲבֹד (לֵאלֹהִים אֲחֵרִים)

Jer. 7.24: בְּמֹעֵצוֹת ‏// בִּשְׁרִרוּת (לִבָּם הָרָע) ‏; cf. Mic. 6.16: וַתֵּלְכוּ במעצותם
and Jer. 11.8: וַיֵּלְכוּ … בשרירות

Jer. 1.15: מִשְׁפְּחוֹת ‏// מַמְלְכוֹת (צָפוֹנָה) ‏; cf. 10.25: מִשְׁפָּחוֹת and in the
parallel in Ps. 79.6: מַמְלָכוֹת

Ezek. 6.13: אֶל כָּל גִּבְעָה רָמָה ‏// בְּכָל רָאשֵׁי הֶהָרִים וְתַחַת כָּל עֵץ רַעֲנָן ‏// וְתַחַת כָּל
אֵלָה עֲבֻתָּה

Gen. 29.34: עַתָּה ‏// הַפַּעַם

Num. 16.27: יָצְאוּ ‏// נִצָּבִים

Deut. 14.11: כָּל צִפּוֹר טְהֹרָה תֹּאכֵלוּ ‏//
20: כל עוֹף טָהוֹר תאכלו

1 Sam. 1.26: בִּי אֲדֹנִי ‏// חֵי נַפְשְׁךָ אֲדֹנִי

Jer. 46.9: תֹּפְשֵׂי ‏// דֹּרְכֵי

Hos. 14.8: יָשֻׁבוּ ‏// יֹשְׁבֵי

Am. 5.16: יהוה ‏// … אדני

Prov. 28.2: מֵבִין ‏// יֹדֵעַ

Neh. 10.29: יוֹדֵעַ ‏// מֵבִין

Ex. 30.32: במתכנתה לא תעשו ‏; cf. v. 37: וּבְמַתְכֻּנְתּוֹ לֹא תַעֲשׂוּ ‏// כָּמֹהוּ and
v. 38: אשר יעשה כמוה

1 Sam. 19.20: עֹמֵד ‏// נִצָּב ‏; cf. Isa. 21.8: עֹמֵד and נִצָּב in parallel position.

1 Ki. 8.5: עָלָיו ‏// אִתּוֹ

2 Ki. 18.28: וַיְדַבֵּר ‏// וַיֹּאמֶר ‏; cf. in the parallel narrative Isa. 36.13
only: ויאמר ‏; cf. also 1 Ki. 12.10: תְּדַבֵּר and in the parallel
2 Chron. 10.10: תֹּאמַר ‏; Further: Gen. 42.22; Ex. 5.10,
7.8, 7.14, 7.26, 20.22, 30.34, 31.12, 36.5; Lev. 20.2; Num.
23.30, 26.1, 27.6, 27.12; in all these instances, MT has a
form of אמר, while SAM offers the corresponding form of דבר

Jer. 20.1: פָּקִיד ‏// נָגִיד

Ezek. 12.11: בַּגּוֹלָה ‏// בַּשְּׁבִי

Ps. 78.9: נוֹשְׁקֵי ‏// רוֹמֵי (קָשֶׁת) ‏; cf. 1 Chron. 12.2: נשקי קשת and Jer
4.29: ורמה קשת

Ps. 10.3:	בֵּרֵךְ // נִאֵץ (יהוה); cf. 1 Ki. 21.10: בֵּרַכְתָּ אֱלֹהִים; Ps. 10.13: נִאֵץ רָשָׁע
1 Ki. 21.11:	אֲשֶׁר הַיֹּשְׁבִים
1 Ki. 12.8:	אֲשֶׁר הָעֹמְדִים } cf. p. 285, § 72, note 3
Ezek. 11.1:	הַקַּדְמוֹנִי // הַפֹּונֶה קָדִימָה
Ezek. 2.3:	הַמּוֹרְדִים // אֲשֶׁר מָרְדוּ בִי
Ezek. 6.9:	הַזּוֹנֶה // אֲשֶׁר סָר
Prov. 27.27:	לְלַחְמְךָ // לְלֶחֶם בֵּיתֶךָ
2 Sam. 16.15:	וְכָל הָעָם // אִישׁ יִשְׂרָאֵל
2 Ki. 3.4:	וּמֵאָה // אֶלֶף ;מֵאָה // אֶלֶף
1 Sam. 6.19:	שִׁבְעִים אִישׁ // חֲמִשִּׁים אֶלֶף אִישׁ
Ex. 40.15:	וְהָיְתָה // לִהְיֹת
Ezek. 6.8:	וְהוֹתַרְתִּי // בִּהְיוֹת
2 Ki. 9.25:	בְּחֶלְקַת // שְׂדֵה נָבוֹת; cf. v. 21: בחלקת נבות
Jer. 20.9:	וְנִלְאֵיתִי כַּלְכֵּל // וְלֹא אוּכָל; the components are: ונלאיתי כלכל and כלכל לא אוכל
Jer. 13.17:	וְדָמַע תִּדְמַע // וְתֵרַד עֵינִי דִמְעָה; combination of: ודמע תדמע and תרדנה עיני דמעה; cf. 14.17: ותרד עיני דמעה and עיני.

A confusion of letters is involved in the following cases:

Judg. 10.8:	וירעצו // וירצצו
Judg. 11.10:	יהוה // יהיה; cf. 2 Chron. 36.23: יהוה אלהיו עמו with the parallel Ezra 1.3: יהי אלהיו עמו
Ezek. 12.14:	עזרה // ··· אזרה
Ezek. 6.6:	ונשברו // ונשבתו
Ezek. 23.42:	מובאים // סובאים
Jer. 10.25:	ואכלהו // ויכלהו

A combination of three headings is offered in:

Ps. 88.1:	שִׁיר מִזְמוֹר לִבְנֵי קֹרַח // לַמְנַצֵּחַ עַל מַחֲלַת לְעַנּוֹת // מַשְׂכִּיל לְהֵימָן הָאֶזְרָחִי

K.   CONSTRUCT INFINITIVE WITH SUFFIXES

§ 25.   In § 8 I stated "that the language of our Bible exhibits evidence of two different tendencies in its vocabulary and in its grammar." This assertion is substantiated here with another example, which will be helpful in our interpretation of the Bible. First let us consider the difficulty which the forms of the so-called infinitive construct *ḳal* with suffixes offer to the grammarian.

a) The first radical has *shewâ* (or a *ḥatef*, if it is אהחע), the second ⸗.

אבד	Deut. 28.20:	אָבְדְךָ	הרג	I Sam. 24.11:	לַהֲרָגְךָ
	Josh. 23.13:	אָבְדְכֶם	מרד	Josh. 22.16:	לִמְרָדְכֶם
אכל	Gen. 2.17:	אָכְלְךָ	משח	I Sam. 15.1:	לִמְשָׁחֲךָ
	Gen. 3.5:	אָכְלְכֶם	עזב	I Ki. 18.18:	בַּעֲזָבְכֶם
אמר	Ezek. 35.10:	אָמָרְךָ	עמד	Obad. 11:	עֲמָדְךָ
	Jer. 23.38:	אָמָרְכֶם	רדף	I Sam. 25.29:	לִרְדָפְךָ
אסר	Judg. 15.12:	לְאָסְרְךָ	שמר	Ex. 30.20:	לְשָׁמְרֶךָ

b) The first radical has ⸗, the second *shewâ*.

אכל	Gen. 47.24:	וּלְאָכְלְכֶם	עבר	Deut. 29.11:	לְעָבְרְךָ
אסף	Ex. 23.16:	בְּאָסְפְּךָ		Josh. 4.23:	עָבְרְכֶם
	Lev. 23.39:	בְּאָסְפְּכֶם	שכב	Deut. 6.7:	וּבְשָׁכְבְּךָ
ברח	Gen. 35.1:	בְּבָרְחֲךָ	שפך	Ezek. 9.8:	בְּשָׁפְכְּךָ
מאס	Isa. 30.12:	מָאָסְכֶם	תפש	Josh. 8.8:	כְּתָפְשְׂכֶם
	(cf. Am. 2.4:	מָאֳסָם)	קרב	Deut. 20.2:	כְּקָרְבְכֶם

§ 26.   The verbs listed above represent both sound and weak roots; hence, the nature of the radicals is irrelevant in our quest for an explanation of these different formations. In order to arrive at an understanding of this difficulty, let us extend our investigation to the absolute infinitive and its relation to the imperative (in meaning and form).

L.   INFINITIVE AND IMPERATIVE

§ 27.   The Hebrew grammars differentiate between the infinitive absolute and the infinitive construct; the latter is usually identical in form to the imperative. But not seldom the infinitive absolute is used in the meaning of the imperative:

הָלוֹךְ: 2 Ki. 5.10; Jer. 2.2; 13.1; 17.19

הָפוֹךְ: Prov. 12.7

זָכוֹר: Ex. 13.3, 20.8; Deut. 25.17, 24.9; Josh. 1.13

לָקֹחַ: Deut. 31.26; Ezek. 24.5; Zech. 6.10

נָשֹׁא: Num. 4.2, 21

צָרוֹר: Num. 25.17

רָגוֹם: Num. 15.35

שָׁמֹעַ: Deut. 1.16

שָׁמֹר: Deut. 5.12; 27.1

תָּמֹךְ: Ps. 17.5

This well-known observation leads me to the following conclusion: the infinitive and the imperative are identical in form, and differentiated only by their meaning at a given passage. Thus, שָׁמֹר *and* שָׁמֹר *are two ways of forming the absolute infinitive and the imperative. There is no construct infinitive*; this term is to be discarded.

M.   Two Modi of Hebrew Verbs

§ 28.   On p. 587, § 42 ff. I have shown that "both perfect and imperfect are interchangeably used to indicate present, past or future." On that basis, I shall formulate my views on the Hebrew verb as follows. The Hebrew verb has two *modi*: a) timebound (a finite tense) and b) timeless (infinitive and imperative). Substituting my terminology of suffix-tense (for perfect) and prefix-tense (for imperfect; cf. p. 590 § 48) for what I have called the timebound *modus*, I conclude thus: In order to express actions which are a) timebound, or b) timeless, the Hebrew verb has two parallel forms: A: a) the suffix-tense, and b) the hitherto called absolute infinitive, which in reality is both infinitive and imperative. B: a) the prefix-tense, and b) the so-called construct infinitive, which, likewise, is both, infinitive and imperative. And now we shall proceed to explain these formations: A a) שָׁמַרְתִּי, b) שָׁמֹר; the characteristic vowel is ־ָ=a under the first radical. With suffixes we get forms like those listed in § 25b, where the ־ָ under the first radical is preserved. We now realize that this ־ָ is to be pronounced *ā*; the current pronunciation as *ŏ* (קמץ חטוף) is an obvious error, based on the fact that it is followed by two *shewâs* of which, according to a whim of Hebrew grammarians, the first has to close the preceding syllable with short vowel (as שוא נח); cf. p. 454, Conclusion IV, where we invalidated this Masoretic grammatical law; and see also p. 17, § 11 for similar errors in the present-day pronunciation of Hebrew. Further proof for the pronunciation of this ־ָ as *ā* can be found in the way such forms are vocalized in the Palestinian vocalization; cf. e.g. אָמֹרך (p. ו, VII, line 5), כפתחך (p. כג, II, line 5), עֲנדינו (p. ה, V, line 16); these examples are taken from P. Kahle, *Masoreten des Westens* (1927). As for B: a) אֶשְׁמֹר, b) שְׁמֹר, the characteristic vowel here is ō (*ḥolem*) with the second radical; with suffixes B b) develops into forms like those listed under § 25a, where the second radical has ָ‍ =ŏ. In presenting us with inflected forms like those in § 25a and b, the Hebrew Bible offers a combination of two originally different tendencies.

N. Divine Names (Cf. MH §§ 145-148)

§ 29. Further evidence for the composite linguistic character of our Bible may be found in the use of divine names. In the historic narratives, which occur in the parallel passages of the Former Prophets and Chronicles (cf. § 5), the Former Prophets use the name יהוה, while the Chronicles אלהים. Wherever we find in our Bible the combined use of both divine names as יהוה אלהים or אדני יהוה, we will therefore recognize the presence of a doublet.

Divine Names in Parallel Texts

1) 2 Sam. 5.20:	פרץ יהוה את איבי		2 Sam. 24.10:	ויאמר דוד אל יהוה
1 Chron. 14.11:	··· האלהים ···		1 Chron. 21.8	האלהים ···
2 Sam. 5.24:	כי אז יצא יהוה לפניך		2 Sam. 24.17:	ויאמר דוד אל יהוה
1 Chron. 14.15:···	האלהים ···		1 Chron. 21.17:	האלהים ···
2 Sam. 5.25:	כאשר צוהו יהוה		1 Ki. 7.40:	בית יהוה
1 Chron. 14.16:	האלהים ···		2 Chron. 4.11:	··· האלהים
2 Sam. 6.5:	משחקים לפני יהוה		1 Ki. 7.48:	אשר בית יהוה
1 Chron. 13.8:	האלהים ···		2 Chron. 4.19:	האלהים ···
2 Sam. 6.9:	וירא דוד את יהוה		1 Ki. 7.51:	באצרות בית יהוה
1 Chron. 13.12:	האלהים ···		2 Chron. 5.1:	האלהים ···
2 Sam. 6.9:	ארון יהוה		1 Ki. 8.11:	את בית יהוה
1 Chron. 13.12:	האלהים ···		2 Chron. 5.14:	האלהים ···
2 Sam. 6.11:	וישב ארון יהוה		1 Ki. 8.63:	ויחנכו את בית יהוה
1 Chron. 13.14:	האלהים ···		2 Chron. 7.5:	האלהים ···
2 Sam. 6.17:	ארון יהוה		1 Ki. 12.15:	סבה מעם יהוה
1 Chron. 16.1:	··· האלהים		2 Chron. 10.15:	האלהים ···
2 Sam. 6.17:	עלות לפני יהוה		1 Ki. 15.15:	בית יהוה
1 Chron. 16.1:	האלהים ···		2 Chron. 15.18:	··· האלהים
2 Sam. 7.3:	כי יהוה עמך		2 Ki. 11.3:	ויהי אתה בית יהוה
1 Chron. 17.2:	··· האלהים		2 Chron. 22.12:	האלהים ···

2 Ki. 11.10:	אשר בבית יהוה
2 Chron. 23.9:	... האלהים
2 Ki. 14.14:	הנמצאים בית יהוה
2 Chron. 25.24:	האלהים ...

2)

2 Sam. 7.4:	ויהי דבר יהוה
1 Chron. 17.3:	... אלהים
1 Ki. 3.4:	נראה יהוה
2 Chron. 1.7:	... אלהים
2 Ki. 21.7:	אשר אמר יהוה
2 Chron. 33.7:	... אלהים
2 Ki. 22.4:	כסף המובא בית יהוה
2 Chron. 34.9:	... אלהים
2 Ki. 22.19:	מפני יהוה
2 Chron. 34.27:	... אלהים

3)

2 Sam. 5.19:	וישאל דוד ביהוה
1 Chron. 14.10:	... באלהים
2 Sam. 5.23:	וישאל דוד ביהוה
1 Chron. 14.14:	... באלהים

4)

1 Ki. 22.14:	יאמר יהוה
2 Chron. 18.13:	... אלהי
2 Sam. 23.17:	ויאמר חלילה לי יהוה
1 Chron. 11.19:	... מאלהי
1 Ki. 10.9:	באהבת יהוה את ישראל
2 Chron. 9.8:	... אלהיך ...

5) A graphic error in Samuel finds thus its explanation:

2 Sam. 24.16:	וישלח ידו המלאך
	‪(= וישלח ידוה מלאך‬
	‪= וישלח יהוה מלאך)‬
1 Chron. 21.15:	האלהים מלאך ...

6) Substition of אדני for יהוה:

1 Ki. 22.6:	ויתן אדני
2 Chron. 18.5:	ויתן האלהים

7) The basic sources confused (cf. p. 499 f.):

1 Ki. 12.22:	ויהי דבר האלהים
2 Chron. 11.2:	ויהי דבר יהוה

8) Doublets:

a) In one source only (cf. the two preceding subdivisions 6 and 7):

2 Sam. 5.2:	ויאמר יהוה > לך
1 Chron. 11.2:	ויאמר יהוה אלהיך // לך
2 Sam. 7.25:	ועתה יהוה אלהים //
1 Chron. 17.23:	ועתה יהוה >
2 Ki. 16.2:	בעיני יהוה אלהיו //
2 Chron. 28.1:	בעיני יהוה >
2 Sam. 5.10:	ויהוה // אלהי צבאות עמו
1 Chron. 11.9:	ויהוה > צבאות עמו
2 Sam. 7.19:	ותקטן זאת בעיניך אדני // יהוה
1 Chron. 17.17:	ותקטן זאת בעיניך > אלהים
2 Sam. 7.20:	ואתה ידעת את עבדך אדני //יהוה
1 Chron. 17.18-19:	ואתה את עבדך ידעת > יהוה
2 Sam. 7.28:	ועתה אדני // יהוה
1 Chron. 17.26:	ועתה > יהוה
2 Sam. 7.29:	כי אתה אדני // יהוה
1 Chron. 17.27:	כי אתה > יהוה

b) In both sources:

2 Sam. 7.18:	מי אנכי אדני // יהוה
1 Chron. 17.16:	מי אני יהוה אלהים //
2 Sam. 7.19:	(2°) אדני // יהוה
1 Chron. 17.17:	יהוה // אלהים

II. THE BIBLE OF THE APOSTLES AS EVIDENCE

A. THE PROBLEM

A. THE OLD TESTAMENT AND THE CHRISTIAN MISSION

In the first volume of his monumental work *The Expansion of Christianity in the first three centuries* (New York 1904), Adolf von Harnack devotes a full chapter to the discussion of the role, which the OT played in the propagation of Christianity during the first three centuries of the new era (p. 353). "The OT did exert an influence which brought it (scil. Christianity) to the verge of becoming the religion of a book" (p. 353). It overshadowed even the NT in importance; for "The NT as a whole did not generally play the same role as the OT in the mission and practice of the church" (p. 363).

If we ask for the reason why the OT was kept in so high a regard, we are told: "The OT certainly was a mighty help to the Christian propaganda, and it was in vain that the Jews protested. We have also one positive testimony, in the following passage from Tatian (Orat. XXIX), that for many people *the OT formed the real bridge by which they crossed to Christianity*: 'Some barbarian writings came into my hands, which were too old for Greek ideas and too divine for Greek errors. *These I was led to trust, owing* to . . . . *their foreknowledge of the future*'" (p. 355). Tatian thus admits that, while reading the OT, he became converted to Christianity, since there he found events forestalled which later on actually happened. The necessity of regularly reading in the OT was emphasized by the early Church. See Origen's statement (*Hom. II in Num.*; X, p. 19) that two hours of daily Bible reading could hardly be regarded as sufficient. This and other pertinent passages in Origen's works are indicated in Harnack's *Bible Reading*, 69, note 1. They led Harnack to the following conclusion: "From the OT it could be proved that the appearance and the entire history of Jesus had been previously predicted hundreds and even thousands of years ago; and further, that the founding of the New People which was to be fashioned out of all nations upon earth, had from the very beginning been prophesied and prepared for. *Their own religion appeared, on the basis of this book, to be the religion of a history which was the fulfilment of prophecy*" (pp. 358 f.).

In other words, the missionary preachers, who went out in those early centuries to spread Christianity, believed for themselves and likewise impressed their audiences that they were not teaching a new religion, but that they were conveying the message of the final fulfillment of certain ancient prophecies made to the Hebrews. The NT itself reflects this attitude. When Paul, accompanied by Silas, arrived at Thessalonica, he preached there in the Synagogue, "and three Sabbath days *reasoned with them out of the Scriptures*, opening and alleging, *that Christ must needs have suffered and risen again from the dead*; and that this Jesus, whom I preach unto you, is Christ" (Acts 17.2-3). This procedure was by no means an exceptional one, related for its uniqueness; on the contrary, the introductory phrase "And Paul, *as his manner was*, went in unto them" (Acts 17.2) shows that this was sheer routine with Paul. The very fact that Paul took pains in order to prove from the Scriptures that his was a message of fulfillment, shows that these Scriptures must have been widely known among his listeners. This assumption is corroborated by an explicit statement, referring to the Jewish population of Beroea, which upon hearing Paul's exegesis "searched the Scriptures daily, whether those things were so" (Acts 17.11). The emphasis which the early church thus laid upon its being a religion of fulfillment resulted in stressing the necessity that every Christian acquaint himself thoroughly with the Scriptures. Thus the OT gained wide circulation outside the Jewish communities. Harnack dealt with this particular aspect of early Christian mission among the heathen population in his monograph *Bible Reading in the Early Church* (New York, 1912). "At first primitive Christianity was concerned exclusively with the Scriptures of the *Old* Testament. Even the apologists, when speaking of Scriptures, mean only them" (p. 40, note 1). "The famous passage in the Epistle of Ignatius to the Philadelphians (chap. VIII.): "I have heard some say: '*If I do not find it in the Old Testament I do not believe it in the Gospel*' " — presupposes laymen who knew the Scriptures" (p. 40). "Aristides, the earliest of the apologists, exhorts his heathen readers, after reading his own work to take into their hands and to read the Holy Scriptures themselves. This appeal to the Holy Scriptures runs through all the apologies from the earliest to the latest, and shows that their authors were united in the belief that *the regular way to become a convinced Christian was to read the Holy Scrip-*

tures. In this way Justin, Tatian, and Theophilus expressly say that they themselves became Christians" (p. 42 f.).

B. THE OLD AND NEW TESTAMENT COMBINED
FORM THE BIBLE OF THE CHURCH

On the basis of these statements we may well assume that the missionaries, who set forth to preach the Gospel of Christianity, took along with them a Bible to prove the authenticity of their message. This Bible, which originally consisted of the OT alone, was afterwards extended to include the books of the NT (cf. *Bible Reading*, p. 40, note 1). Thus, finally, the Bible of the Church was complete: it presented the prophecy of the OT, and its fulfillment in the NT. In order to appeal to the prospective Christians and to the newly made converts of heathen origin, both Testaments had to be presented to them in Greek. Whether the Greek of the NT is genuine or a mere translation from an Aramaic original, does not matter in this connection; (the OT in Greek no doubt was merely a translation and still the prophecies contained therein were considered authoritative nevertheless); just the same, no English churchgoer worries over the fact that his Bible after all is only a translation from the Hebrew or Greek. For he turns to his Bible for religious and not for linguistic reasons. And religion he is sure to find here, the same as the early convert to Christianity found in the two parts of his Bible, according to the statements cited above, the prophecy and account of the coming of the Christ.

This procedure of combining the OT and NT into one complete Bible was early adopted by the Church and then retained throughout the centuries. We note, therefore, that even the oldest manuscripts of the Bible in Greek conform with this rule.

C. OLD TESTAMENT QUOTATIONS IN THE NEW TESTAMENT

Thus LXX and NT form a unity, the Bible. And with the statements of Tatian and other early Christian writers, referring to their interrelation as prophecy and fulfillment—as cited above—in mind, we may now attempt to verify some messages of fulfillment as narrated in the NT, on the basis of the pertinent prophecies of the OT. To this end we shall refer in our quotations to the readings of Codex B for both the OT and NT. This Manuscript is admittedly the oldest text-witness which contains almost the entire Bible. Our examination will prove whether or not the underlying text represents a unity.

a. Quotations in the Gospels

1) In Matth. 2.4-6 the incident of the visit of the three wise men is told, which caused Herod considerable embarrassment. The experts whom he consulted told him that the Messiah was to be born in Bethlehem in Juda, and quoted: και συ βηθλεεμ γη ιουδα, ουδαμως ελαχιστη ει εν τοις ηγεμοσιν ιουδα· εκ σου γαρ εξελευσεται ηγουμενος, οστις ποιμανει τον λαον μου ισραηλ. This clearly is a reference to Mic. 5.1, which reads in the OT section of the very same Bible Ms. B as follows: και συ βηθλεεμ οικος εφραθα, ολιγοστος ει του ειναι εν χιλιασιν ιουδα· εξ ου μοι εξελευσεται του ειναι εις αρχοντα του ισραηλ. We are not concerned with the explanation of minor discrepancies: such as εξ ου and εκ σου, where the first is merely a phonetic confusion of the latter; or that ηγεμοσιν and χιλιασιν reflect two different etymologic derivations of the consonants of one and the same basic Hebrew word באלפי, pronounced as בְּאַלְפֵי or בְּאָלְפֵי respectively, which in itself proves that the NT quotation and the LXX on this passage both go back to two independent translations of this verse in Hebrew into Greek (cf. JBL, 1935, 82, paragraph II for similar cases). But quite apart from this we wish to stress the point that the verse in the LXX is entirely different from the one quoted by Matthew; moreover: a reading βηθλεεμ οικος εφραθα could never have been considered as a prophecy for βηθλεεμ της ιουδαιας. The incongruity is too obvious.

2) We continue with Matthew's report. The Virgin Mary with the infant Jesus had to flee to Egypt for their lives, according to a vision which Joseph had. They remained there until the death of Herod, and the whole incident was predetermined by the necessity to fulfill the prophetic statement εξ αιγυπτου εκαλεσα τον υιον μου (verses 14-15). Hence Herod was not acting of his own free evil intention, but was merely an instrument in the hands of the Lord, so that things should happen, which had to happen. We now turn to Hos. 11.1, again in the same Bible manuscript B, in anticipation of finding here the prophecy: οτι νηπιος ισραηλ και εγω ηγαπησα αυτον, και εξ αιγυπτου μετεκαλεσα τα τεκνα αυτου. Here τα τεκνα αυτου, *his* children, clearly refers to ισραηλ mentioned at the beginning of the verse, and no exegesis could twist it round to mean

τον υιον μου, one person out of the multitude of the Israelites, who was in addition *the* son of the Lord.

3) The flight to Egypt infuriated Herod; he took his revenge by killing the innocent infants left in Bethlehem. And even this atrocity was foreseen long ago by Jeremiah in the statement: φωνη εν ραμα ηκουσθη, κλαυθμος και οδυρμος πολυς· ραχηλ κλαιουσα τα τεκνα αυτης, και ουκ ηθελεν παρακληθηναι, οτι ουκ εισιν. (verses 17-18). But in Jer. 31.15 this passage reads: φωνη εν ραμα ηκουσθη, θρηνου και κλαυθμου και οδυρμου· ραχηλ αποκλαιομενη ουκ ηθελεν παυσασθαι επι τοις υιοις αυτης, οτι ουκ εισιν. The passage in Matthew is represented as being a quotation; but though this verse in Matthew shows a great resemblance to that in Jeremiah, it can in no way be considered a direct citation.

4) The great similarity between this Jeremiah verse in the OT section of Codex B and the way it is quoted in the NT part of that Manuscript might lead to an explanation that Matthew at least in this particular case deliberately changed the exact wording of his original, namely the LXX, in order to improve on the Greek style or diction of the passage. But any attempt to explain away in such a fashion the apparent differences between the two sections of the Bible in Greek must end in a complete failure. One more instance, taken from Matthew again, will suffice to clarify this issue: In his record on Jesus healing the sick and obsessed ones on the Sabbath day, in chapter 12, Matthew remarks that these things had to happen again to fulfill the prophecy: ιδου ο παις μου, ον ηρετισα, ο αγαπητος μου, εις ον ευδοκησεν η ψυχη μου· θησω το πνευμα μου επ αυτον, και κρισιν τοις εθνεσιν απαγγελει· ουκ ερισει ουδε κραυγασει, ουδε ακουει τις εν ταις πλατειαις την φωνην αυτου· καλαμον συντετριμμενον ου κατεαξει και λινον τυφομενον ου σβεσει, εως αν εκβαλη εις νικος την κρισιν· και τω ονοματι αυτου εθνη ελπιουσιν. (verses 17-21). It is quite enough to put the corresponding verses Isa. 42.1-4 of the LXX in juxtaposition, in order to be convinced that they cannot be regarded as the original of this quotation: ιακωβ ο παις μου, αντιλημψομαι αυτου· ισραηλ ο εκλεκτος μου, προσεδεξατο αυτον η ψυχη μου· εδωκα το πνευμα μου επ αυτον, κρισιν τοις εθνεσιν εξοισει· ου κεκραξεται ουδε ανησει ουδε ακουσθησεται εξω η φωνη αυτου· καλαμον τεθλασμενον ου συντριψει, και λινον καπνιζομενον ου σβεσει, αλλα εις αληθειαν εξοισει κρισιν· και επι τω ονοματι αυτου εθνη ελπιουσιν. It is quite impossible to regard these two ways of rendering the Hebrew text

of Isa. 42.1-4 into Greek as interdependent; the differences are too many and they interfere in too great a measure with the very structure of the sentences. But, above all other considerations, in the LXX the terms παις and εκλεκτος plainly mean the people of Israel as such, which is referred to by the words ιακωβ and ισραηλ, respectively. How, then, could Matthew see therein an anticipation of Jesus' appearance, thus inferring that Isaiah foresaw his coming and called him "son" and "beloved" of the Lord, and that by this divine providence Jesus was bound to act the way he did, in order to fulfil the words of the prophet? We would consider it poor method to say that Matthew overlooked the references to ιακωβ and ισραηλ, or even—and this would be much worse—purposely suppressed them. *One can not base a theology upon misquotations*! Consequently, there can be no thought of interdependence between the LXX rendering of these verses and their quotation by Matthew.

5)   In order to round up the picture of the life history of Jesus seen as the history of fulfillment, we turn to John for the narrative of the very last incident in his earthly career: Jesus on the cross. For John says that the legs of Jesus were not broken, but his side was pierced by a spear, in order to fulfill the two prophecies: οστουν ου συντριβησεται αυτου, and οψονται εις ον εξεκεντησαν (19.32-37). The first reference is to Ex. 12.46; but this verse reads in the LXX: και οστουν ου συντριψετε απ αυτου. The active construction of the verb makes this verse an ordinance for the Israelites, telling them what they are forbidden to do, while the passive construction in John turns the sentence round to say: what shall not be done to him. Important as the difference in meaning undoubtedly is, it looks insignificant when compared with the second reference to the Scriptures, namely Zech. 12.10 which reads in the Septuagint: και επιβλεψονται προς με ανθ ων κατωρχησαντο. This translation is the result of the LXX's mistakenly reading the Hebrew דקרו as רקדו (metathesis, cf. p. 489, § 70). According to John, the Roman soldier transfixed Jesus with his spear, in order to fulfill an ancient prophecy; εξεκεντησαν is a most suitable expression, indeed, to describe this action. But the corresponding κατωρχησαντο in the LXX indicates "to dance." All the favorite explanations of such discrepancies, that they are free citations, reflect bad memory, etc., fall short of explaining an assumption that John, while reading in his OT κατωρχησαντο, was reminded of the episode of the crucifixion, and quoted the passage as εξεκεντησαν.

b. Classification of the Differences

I hope that these few examples are convincing enough to demonstrate the problem in all its boldness. For a more detailed treatment I must refer to my article *The New Testament and the Septuagint*, which appeared in the Hebrew Quarterly Tarbiz, Jerusalem, VI (1934), 1-29. For the benefit of those interested in the subject, but who are not sufficiently conversant with Hebrew to make free use of that article, I must give here a brief description of its contents. I first went carefully through the entire NT in Greek according to Nestle's editions, which is based upon Codex B, and excerpted all those passages, which are direct quotations from the OT, without paying attention to whether or not an introductory phrase like γεγραπται, η γραφη λεγει, το ρηθεν indicates these passages to be direct quotations. For even in the event of the absence of such a phrase, they definitely go back to the OT and prove to what an extent the speech and thought of the authors of the NT were under the spell of the OT text. The relation of the language of mediaeval Hebrew works (such as שבט יהודה) to that of the Hebrew Bible is not too far fetched a comparison.

This material, which emanates, as I said, from the NT according to Codex B, I then compared with the respective OT passages in Greek in that very same Codex B. After eliminating those instances which I found in full agreement between the NT and OT sections of Codex B, there still remained approximately three hundred passages which appear as quotations in the NT in a wording more or less different from that found in their original places in the OT. With an eye on the basic Hebrew text I tried to group and classify these variants according to the following criteria: i) Greek synonyms. ii) Differences in the exegesis of the same basic Hebrew word. iii) The use of the possessive pronoun. iv) *Waw conjunctivum* in Greek translation. v) The use of the personal pronoun. vi) The use of the article. vii) Collective nouns treated as singulars or plurals. viii. Verb and compound. ix) The use of the Greek tenses and modes. x) Differences in Greek syntax. xi) Addition or omission of Greek particles. xii) Hebrew particles in Greek translation. xiii) Different interpretation of full sentences. xiv) Inner Greek corruptions. xv) Differences resulting from Hebrew *variae lectiones*.

c. These Differences are of Theological Importance

While going through this enumeration of headings, under which the entire material could be listed, the reader might feel doubtful as to whether so strictly linguistic a method is appropriate to the theological nature of the texts involved. For the apostles, one might argue, were primarily concerned to prove their theological ideas, and one should not expect them to pay more than average attention to matters of diction and style. The best refutation of such an objection is to illustrate my procedure by way of examples: Paragraph IV deals with the rendering of Hebrew conjunctive *waw* into the Greek χαι or η. Both reflect the respective meaning of this particle in its various connections. When we read in Ex. 21.15, ומכה אביו ואמו, or ib. verse 17: ומקלל אביו ואמו, it is obvious that the *waw* in ואמו means "or." But when we find Hos. 6.6: כי חסד חפצתי ולא זבח translated in the LXX διοτι ελεος θελω η θυσιαν, while in Matth. 9.13, and 12.7 the verse is quoted as ελεος θελω χαι ου θυσιαν, this difference χαι—η becomes highly significant. According to the conception of the LXX, the Lord merely *prefers* ελεος to sacrifice; this certainly does not exclude the sacrifice as a means to please the Lord, though it is less pleasing than ελεος. But the wording of Matthew plainly *rejects* the sacrifice: What the Lord wants is ελεος *and not sacrifice!*

Paragraph XI lists cases, where particles or similar parts of the speech are added or omitted. So in the case of Isa. 28.16, המאמין לא יחיש, which the LXX translates χαι ο πιστευων ου μη καταισχυνθη: this is quoted in 1 Peter 2.6 and, with here unimportant variants, in Rom. 9.33 as χαι ο πιστευων επ αυτω ου μη καταισχυνθη. Not belief general, but *belief in Jesus as the Christ*, is what Peter preaches: οτι χρηστος ο κυριος, προς ον προσερχομενοι, λιθον ζωντα . . . παρα δε θεω εκλεκτον εντιμον, και αυτοι ως λιθοι ζωντες . . . ανενεγκαι πνευματικας θυσιας ευπροσδεκτους θεω δια ιησου χριστου, διοτι περιεχει εν γραφη. ιδου τιθημι εν σιων λιθον ακρογωνιαιον εκλεκτον εντιμον, και ο πιστευων επ αυτω ου μη καταισχυνθη (verses 3-6). From the point of view of the grammarian, the words επ αυτω represent an addition as compared with the basic Hebrew text, and, therefore, are duly listed in paragraph XI (cf. here similarly p. 292, § 81b 1). But there can be no doubt that Peter found this addition already in the OT in Greek at his disposal, and that he made bona fide theological use of it. It would be too absurd to suspect him of having changed the plain reading of the LXX text by such an insertion, and to base afterwards an entire theology upon this emended text of his own making!

I hope that these two examples are convincing enough and will dispell any such methodological objection as is indicated above.

The result of my examination of the OT quotations in the NT and the respective readings of the LXX section of the same Codex B proves that at as early a period as the time of the compilation of the NT, the OT in Greek must have been published and known in at least two forms, one known to us as the LXX, the other preserved to us in some, at least, of the quotations contained in the NT.

d. Jerome was aware of these difficulties

The apparent discrepancy between some of the OT quotations in the NT and the respective readings of the LXX was noticed in the early Church. Jerome justifies his method of basing his Latin translation upon the Hebrew text and not upon the LXX, though the latter enjoyed great authority as *the* Bible of the Church, by saying: "Quod ut auderem, Origenis me studium provocavit ... maximeque Evangelistarum et Apostolorum auctoritas, in quibus multa de veteri testamento legimus, quae in nostris codicibus [scil. of the LXX] non habentur." (*Biblia Sacra iuxta Latinam Vulgatam versionem, Librum Genesis* ... recensuit D. Henricus Quentin, Romae, 1926. Sancti Hieronymi Presbyteri Praefatio in Pentateuchum, p. 64). But how are we to explain this fact? Did the authors of the NT know of the LXX, and for some reason or other not consider it authoritative enough to be referred to, or were they in ignorance of the very existence of this Greek Version of the OT? Here Jerome is quite positive in his statement: "certe apostoli et evangelistae Septuaginta interpretes noverant" (Praefatio to Chronicles). If this be the case, so we must assume that the authors of the NT had some good reason for deviating from the LXX. Did they arbitrarily revise the text of such passages, where they differ from the LXX, or had they a Greek OT translation at their disposal, which actually contained the passages in question exactly in the same wording as they quoted them? And if so, to which textual form of the OT in Greek shall we give the preference: to the LXX or to those manuscripts, of which the authors of the NT made use? This is, what Jerome has to say on these questions: "sed et evange-listae et dominus quoque noster atque salvator nec non et Paulus apos-tolus multa quasi de veteri testamento proferunt, quae in nostris codicibus [scil. of the LXX] non habentur; super quibus in suis locis plenius disseremus, ex quo perspicuum est illa magis vera esse exemplaria, quae cum novi testamenti auctoritate concordant" (*Quaestiones hebraicae in libro Geneseos*, ed. Paul de Lagarde, Lipsiae 1868, 2 f.). From this statement we learn that in Jerome's days there were still manuscripts of the OT in Greek in existence which offered at the respective places a textual form identical with that in which they appear in NT quotations. No wonder that Jerome is inclined to attribute greater authority to these codices, for the very reason that they uphold the trustworthiness of the NT.

D.   PREVIOUS RESEARCHES IN THIS FIELD

H. B. Swete in his *Introduction to the Old Testament in Greek* (Cambridge 1900), gives the following account of the relation which the NT quotations bear to the Alexandrian version (scil. the LXX). "It may at once be said that every part of the New Testament affords evidence of a knowledge of the Septuagint, and that a great majority of the passages cited from the Old Testament are in general agreement with the Greek version. It is calculated by one writer on the subject (Turpie, *The old Testament in the New*, London 1868, 267) that . . . it departs from the Septuagint in 185 citations; and by another (Grinfield, *Apology for the Septuagint*, 1841, 37) that not more than fifty of the citations materially differ from the Septuagint. On either estimate the Septuagint is the principal source from which the writers of the New Testament derived their Old Testament quotations" (p. 392). "It is necessary to distinguish carefully between the causes which have produced variation. It may be due to a) loose citation, or to b) the substitution of a gloss for the precise words which the writer professes to quote, or to c) a desire to adapt a prophetic context to the circumstances under which it was thought to have been fulfilled, or to d) the fusing together of passages drawn from different contexts" (p. 394). After a discussion of five passages in Matthew, one of which is 2.6 (cf. above C a 1), Swete arrives at the conclusion that "the compiler of the first Gospel has more or less distinctly thrown off the yoke of the Alexandrian version and substituted for it a paraphrase, or an independent rendering from the Hebrew. But our evidence does not encourage the belief that the evangelist used or knew another complete Greek version of the Old Testament or of any particular book" (p. 398).

I hope that on the basis of my preceding expositions I may say that Swete was far from realizing the problem as such, and that all his remarks are consequently to be put into the discard.

E. THE BIBLE OF THE APOSTLES

Now that a translation of OT in Greek, distinct from the LXX, has appeared likely to have existed as the source of Biblical quotations in the NT, a work we may call the "Bible of the Apostles," the object of the present study is to find what of it we can identify. By the term "Bible of the Apostles" we don't mean to imply that the OT in Greek, which the respective authors or compilers of the entire NT used either as a basis for their narratives of events, or while expounding their theology, was a uniform textual type, so that all OT references therein could be made use of in our endeavors to reconstruct this Bible. We shall concern ourselves exclusively with the problem of the source or sources of those OT quotations, which are at a variance with their corresponding LXX passage. This textual type of the OT in Greek, whence they probably were taken, and the nature of which for the time being we still know nothing, we call "Bible of the Apostles." The term is introduced here merely for practical purposes, to serve as a common denominator for the deviations from the LXX text.

B. ORIGEN'S HEXAPLA

A. LAGARDE'S ARCHETYPE THEORY

In our search for the Bible of the Apostles we start with a re-examination of those facts concerning the OT in Greek which seem to be well established and are, therefore, generally agreed upon: we mean the LXX.

During the last sixty years, LXX studies were most deeply influenced by the theories of Paul de Lagarde, which in their turn were based on the following statement of Jerome in his *Praefatio* to Chronicles: "Nunc vero, cum pro varietate regionum diversa ferantur exemplaria . . . Alexandria et Aegyptus in Septuaginta suis Hesychium laudat auctorem;

Constantinopolis usque Antiochiam Luciani martyris exemplaria probat. Mediae inter has provinciae Palaestinos codices legunt, quos ab Origene elaboratos Eusebius et Pamphilius vulgaverunt; totusque orbis hac inter se trifaria varietate compugnat." According to the interpretation of Lagarde, this passage does not indicate that Origen, Lucian, and Hesychius were really "auctores" of respective new translations of the OT; to him they were merely revisers of the one existing text, the LXX, transforming it by additions, omissions or stylistic changes. I have dealt with this "Archetype" theory of Lagarde, and with the editions of texts by Lagarde and Rahlfs, respectively, which are based thereon, in my *Septuagintaprobleme* (Stuttgart, 1929) and in two papers, *The Problems of the Septuagint Recensions* (JBL, 1935, 73-92) and *Probleme einer Edition der Septuaginta* (*Festschrift Paul Kahle*, Leiden, 1935, 39-46). I hope I may say that I have refuted both, the basic theory and the subsequent text editions. I could also prove that Lucian and Hesychius represent two independent translations of the Hebrew Bible into Greek, and not two Greek recensions of one and the same translation according to Lagarde's theory.

Later on we shall have to refer to these results again. But now we wish to turn to Origen and his work. For since Origen ranks first among the three "auctores" whom Jerome mentions, from the point of view of mere chronology his work is of great importance.

B.   THE CURRENT VIEW ON ORIGEN'S WORK

For a summary of the current view on this matter we turn again to H. B. Swete's *Introduction*; for A. Rahlfs, in his survey *History of the Septuagint Text*, pp. xxii-xxxi of his *Septuaginta* (Stuttgart 1935), gives merely an abstract thereof, though he does not indicate Swete as his source. We shall, therefore, quote Swete's pertinent statements verbatim: "Between the years 220 and 250 he gave to the world a succession of commentaries, homilies or notes on nearly all the books of the Old Testament. In the course of these labours, perhaps from the moment that he began to read the Old Testament in the original, he was impressed with the importance of providing the Church with materials for ascertaining the true text and meaning of the original" (p. 60). "To attempt a new version was impracticable. It may be doubted whether Origen possessed the requisite knowledge of Hebrew ... On the other hand, Origen held that Christians must be taught frankly to recognize the divergences between the Septuagint and the current Hebrew text, and the superiority of Aquila and the other later versions, in so far as they were more faithful to the original; it was unfair to the Jew to quote against him passages from the Septuagint, which were wanting in his own Bible, and injurious to the Church herself to withhold from her anything in the Hebrew Bible which the Septuagint did not represent. Acting under these convictions Origen's first step was to collect all existing Greek versions of the Old Testament. He then proceeded to transcribe the versions in parallel columns, and to indicate in the column devoted to the Septuagint the relation in which the old Alexandrian version stood to the current Hebrew text" (p. 61). "The problem before him was to restore the Septuagint to its original purity, i.e. to the Hebraica veritas" (p. 68). "The additions and omissions in the Septuagint presented greater difficulty. Origen was unwilling to remove the former, for they belonged to the version which the Church had sanctioned, and which many Christians regarded as inspired Scripture; but he was equally unwilling to leave them without some mark of editorial disapprobation. Omissions were readily supplied from one of the other versions, namely Aquila or Theodotion, but the new matter interpolated into the Septuagint needed to be carefully distinguished from the genuine work of the Alexandrian translators. Here the genius of Origen found an ally in the system of critical signs which had its origin among the older scholars of Alexandria" (p. 69). "As employed by Origen in the fifth column of the Hexapla, the obelus was prefixed to words or lines which were wanting in the Hebrew, and therefore, from Origen's point of view, of doubtful authority, whilst the asterisk called attention to words or lines wanting in the Septuagint, but present in the Hebrew" (p. 70).

Jerome's explanation of the nature of Origen's work is somewhat different: "Origenis me studium provocavit, qui editioni antiquae translationem Theodotionis miscuit, asterisco et obelo, id est stella et veru, opus omne distinguens, dum aut inlucescere facit quae minus ante fuerat, aut superflua, quaeque iugulat et confodit" (*Praefatio in Pentateuchum*).

Thus Swete (with ample references from statements found in early

works on the subject) and Jerome agree in their definition of the Hexaplaric signs: asterisk signifying an addition, obelus an omission, in the
basic text used for comparison. The basic text was Theodotion's version
according to Jerome, but was the Hebrew Bible according to Swete, or
rather according to the authorities whom he follows.

C.   REFUTATION OF THE CURRENT VIEW

The weak points of this approach to the problem are so obvious that
one wonders how they remained unnoticed: 1) The LXX is a translation
of the Hebrew Bible into Greek and, like all other ancient translations,
no doubt follows slavishly the Hebrew original. If the divergences between the LXX and the Hebrew text as current in the days of Origen
were so great and of such importance that "it was unfair to the Jew to
quote him passages from the LXX, which were wanting in his own Bible,
and injurious to the Church herself to withhold from her anything in the
Hebrew Bible which the Septuagint did not represent," then we must
assume that the Hebrew Bible itself had undergone a corresponding
change and development, from the early phase in which it was known
at about the third century B.C.E., which we possess in the Greek translation of the LXX, to the later phase current in the days of Origen.
2) Now the argument of unfairness to the Jew refers to religious dispu-
tations and implies that the discrepancies between the LXX and the
Hebrew Bible are highly important from the theological point of view,
with the LXX readings proving the case of the Christians. But we saw on
p. 323, sub c how unreliable the LXX is in this very respect. The case
discussed there in subdivision a 2) shows that the Hebrew text with its
reading לִבְנִי could well be taken as foretelling the coming of Jesus, in
keeping with Matthew, while it is just the rendering of this verse as
Septuagint's τα τεκνα αυτου which excludes such an interpretation. The
same holds true of the examples listed there under numbers 4 and 5: The
Hebrew Bible on Isa. 42.1 and Zech. 12.10 offers exactly the same text
which Matthew used in Greek translation for his interpretation in a
christological sense; but the respective LXX readings are decidedly
useless for this purpose. Thus Swete's argument turns against him!
3) Swete has to admit that it "may be doubted whether Origen possessed
the requisite knowledge of Hebrew." How, then, could he "indicate . . .

the relation in which the old Alexandrian version stood to the current Hebrew text," in order "to restore the Septuagint to its original purity, i.e. to the Hebraica veritas?" For such an undertaking more than just an average knowledge of Hebrew is necessary! 4) What is the "Hebraica veritas"? This term is introduced here to explain the "original purity" of the LXX; in this case it is identical with the Hebrew Bible as current in or about the third century B.C.E., and thus materially different from the Hebrew Bible of the days of Origen, since he considers it unfair to fight the Jews with LXX quotations, which they do not possess in their Hebrew Bible (cf. above sub No. 1). But the context of this citation from Swete makes it clear that to him "Hebraic verity" and the Hebrew Bible text of Origen were identical. In other words: Origen aimed at the "restoration" of the LXX in such a way that it might be considered a Greek version of the Hebrew Bible of his own days, thus giving it a form which it had never had before. But a mere glance into the critical apparatus of Kittel's *Biblia Hebraica* with its numerous variant readings from the LXX is enough to convince us of the complete failure of his alleged attempt.

D.   A NEW APPROACH

The main feature of the new evaluation of Origens's work here attempted consists in a complete break with the theories of the past, which are wholly based upon statements found in the works of early Christian writers. Though they lived so many centuries nearer to the time of Origen, they are not reliable as witnesses; for the several generations which separated them from Origen did their part in obscuring the plan and conception of the Hexapla in a mist of tradition. By following their lead, Swete became entangled in inner contradictions, as we have pointed out above.

We shall, therefore, go back to the original sources, and base our conclusions solely on the evidence of Hexaplaric statements themselves. We derive our material from Fridericus Field; *Origenis Hexaplorum quae supersunt* (2 vols., Oxford 1875). His collection has been carefully gone through and I hope that no essential item has been overlooked. What I offer here is not preconceived theories with a few examples to uphold them, and possibly at the same time unconsciously eliminating as immaterial other instances which might well be considered as proof against these theories. I wish to emphasize that while no attempt has been made to bring a complete list of the passages belonging to the various subdivisions—any such attempt would be futile, since from time to time new material comes to light, thus rendering today incomplete the complete list of yesterday—my collection presents no arbitrary selection. I have limited myself to the grouping and classifying of the material. The theories as to how to account for these phenomena thus emerge quite by themselves. In this fashion *we base our conclusions upon the internal evidence of Origen's work alone.*

E.   THE SEPTUAGINT ACCORDING TO THE HEXAPLA

The following paragraphs represent an attempt to arrange in a methodical way the material contained in Field's compilation, so as to allow us to arrive at conclusions regarding the nature of the sources which Origen utilized for the fifth column of his work. While listing the quotations here under the authority of Origen, it should be understood that it is Field to whom belongs the credit of having restored these readings, as well as the responsibility for the exactness of their wording and the correctness of the symbols under which they are brought.

§ 1. Septuagint Quototions of the Hexapla.

The fifth column of the *Hexapla*, which was devoted to the LXX, is being quoted under the following symbols: a. O' or οι O'; b. al ex (= *alia exemplaria*). Both terms refer to Origen's LXX, but reflect two translations, which in their origin were entirely independent from one another. I already brought a few examples to prove this assertion of mine in *Festschrift P. Kahle* on p. 45 f., and wish to add now just a few more: Deut. 27.20: כנף: O': συγκαλυμμα; al ex: ασχημοσυνην. Deut. 5.7: על פני: O': προ προσωπου μου; al ex: πλην εμου. Deut. 19.14: ראשנים: O': οι πατερες σου; al ex: οι προτεροι σου. Num. 13.10: סודי: O': σουδι; al ex: σουρι. Ex. 6.16 and Num. 3.17: גרשון: O': γεδσων; al ex: γηρσων. An interchange of Δ—P has no foundation in Greek palaeography, nor even in Greek phonetics, while a confusion of the corresponding letters ד—ר in the Hebrew alphabet is well attested (cf. p. 482, § 55).

Consequently, the readings quoted under O' and under al ex go back either to two independent translations of the entire Hebrew Bible, or to one genuine translation from the Hebrew and one revision of this Greek translation, which in turn must have been based upon a constant reference to the Hebrew Bible. Thus the interrelation between translation and revision would be comparable to the relation between Jerome's translation of the Hebrew Bible and the *Vetus Latina*. Whether these quotations represent two translations or only one translation and one revision thereof, in either case the Hebrew Bible text has to be presupposed as the basis for the revision and hence for the divergent readings *sub alia exemplaria*; they, therefore, reflect a new and independent translation at least of these Biblical passages.

On passages like Ps. 104.18: לשפנים: O': τοις χοιρογρυλλιοις; al ex: τοις λαγωοις, as indicative of the respective country where such readings could originate, see my article in *Festschrift Kahle*, p. 43 f.

We wish to emphasize that this differentiation between quotations from the fifth column of the *Hexapla* as O' and al ex has no basis in the sources from which they originate, but represent merely a *Notbehelf* of Field which enabled the editor to list both variant readings. While their sources quote them as genuine Hexaplaric LXX, we have just been able to prove that they reflect two independent translations. If this be the case, it is of interest to investigate whether Field's procedure in assigning the quotations to O' and al ex, respectively, is in keeping with the characteristics of these translations (cf. § 9). A few examples will illustrate what we mean: In § 5 I discuss (under a) the rendering of מתוך into Greek; but in Num. 26.62 Field lists the variants vice versa as בתוך בני: O': εν μεσω υιων al ex: εν τοις υιοις. On p. 368 we prove that the asterisktype offers a slavishly literal translation as against the free rendering into readable Greek by O'. This relation appears upset by the way in which Field arranges the readings in Ex. 15.16: קנית: O': ον εκτησω; al ex: ελυτρωσω. Num. 6.19: את נזרו: O': την ευχην αυτου; al ex: την κεφαλην αυτου. Field is similarly inconsistent in Gen. 46.8: הבאים: O': των εισελθοντων; al ex: των εισπορευομενων, compared with Deut 1.8: בא: O': εισπορευθεντες; al ex: εισελθοντες. Consequently we had to be careful in making use of Field's collection. Cf. also § 2.

§ 2. Hexaplaric Symbols.

LXX quotations in the *Hexapla*, both O' and al ex, are often marked with an asterisk or an obelus, the exact form of which differs slightly in the various source-manuscripts. Practical consideration induces us to use ⁕ to indicate the asterisk, and ÷ for the obelus throughout. An × indicates the end of the quotation *sub asterisco* or *sub obelo*, respectively. Both asterisk and obelus may include a) the quotation in full, or b) merely a part of it; cf., e.g., a) Ex. 12.41: ויהי בעצם היום הזה: O': ⁕ και εγενετο εν τη ημερα ταυτη ×. Gen. 46.21: וארד: O': ÷ γηρα δε εγεννησε τον αραδ ×. b) Num. 22.23: ויך בלעם: O': και επαταξε ⁕ Βαλααμ ×. ib. 21.5: הקלקל: O': τω διακενω ÷ τουτω ×. A combination of both symbols in one and the same sentence may occur, too: see e.g. Num. 10.34: וינסו משנאיך מפניך: O': φυγετωσαν ÷ παντες × οι μισουντες σε ⁕ απο προσωπου σου ×. Ex. 14.26: על מצרים: O': ÷ και επικαλυψατω × ⁕ επι × τους αιγυπτιους. Num. 10.31: ידעת חנתנו: O': ησθα ⁕ εν τη παρεμβολη × ÷ μεθ ημων ×.

Since the word or words encircled by asterisk or obelus are part of the full sentence, they must grammatically fit into their context; e.g. Ex. 9.24: בכל ארץ מצרים: O': εν αιγυπτω; al ex: εν ⁕ παση τη γη × αιγυπτου. It is obvious that the words παση τη γη are an addition to the O' reading εν αιγυπτω; but since the sentence thus newly formed is an entity in itself, its Greek language had to be made presentable. Consequently, the original dative αιγυπτω had to be changed into the genitive αιγυπτου. This observation can be varified on numerous passages. Note, e.g., the citation from Ex. 14.26 in this paragraph: we may read και επικαλυψατω τους αιγυπτιους, thus excluding the word επι under asterisk, or even και επικαλυψατω επι τους αιγυπτιους, the full sentence. We realize that in either way the Greek syntax is quite correctly formed, for the compound επικαλυπτω is followed by the object in the accusative, or by a repetition of the particle of composition. This observation will furnish us with a criterion to establish the nature of Origen's critical work.

Those passages, where a Hexaplaric symbol is attested only by the *Syro-Hexaplaris* and not by a genuinely Greek text, are quoted in Field under *Aliter*.

In basing our investigation on the Hexaplaric symbols upon their occurrence in Field's collection of material, the question may be raised as to whether the particular symbol by which he marks a quotation is always reliably attested. A few examples will suffice to demonstrate the seriousness of this problem:

a) The asteriscus. בנות meaning daughter cities appears three times in Josh. 17.11 *sub asterisco*, but in two different translations, according to the two citations: ויבלעם ובנותיה: O': Vacat. ※ και ιεβλααμ και θυγα-τερες αυτης ×. ובנתיה: וישבי עין דר ובנותיה וישבי תענך ובנתיה: O': Vacat. ※ και τους κατοικουντας ενδωρ και τας κωμας αυτης και τους κατοικουντας θααναχ και τας κωμας αυτης ×.

חצר meaning village of the same district: Josh. 19.22: ערים שש עשרה וחצריהן: O': Vacat ※ πολεις εκκαιδεκα και αι κωμαι αυτων ×. Ib. verse 30: ערים עשרים ושתים וחצריהן: O': ※ πολεις εικοσι δυο και αι κωμαι αυτων ×. But ib. verse 38: ערים תשע עשרה וחצריהן: O': ※ πολεις δεκαεννεα και αι επαυλεις αυτων ×.

משפחה: Josh. 19.17: לבני יששכר למשפחותם: O': Vacat. ※ τοις υιοις ισσαχαρ κατα συγγενειας αυτων ×. But ib. verse 32: לבני נפתלי למשפחתם: O': Vacat. ※ τοις υιοις νεφθαλει κατα δημους αυτων ×. Cf. Num. 3.15: למשפחתם: O': κατα δημους αυτων; al ex: κατα δημους αυτων ÷ κατα συγγενειας αυτων ×. Thus, a doublet combines both translations, but assigns συγγενειας to the obelus-text.

This inconsistency in the rendering of Hebrew words into Greek may be taken as an indication that the different sources from which these quotations emanate reflect different recensions of the asterisk text on the passages in question; cf. also Gen. 47.5: ויאמר: O': ※ και ειπε ×; al ex: ※ ειπε δε ×, with JBL, 1935, 90 paragraph XIV 2.

b) The obelus. Anticipating the results reached in p. 364 ff. that readings marked by an obelus do *not* correspond to MT, we note cases like Deut. 9.26: בגדלך: O': εν τη ισχυι σου ÷ τη μεγαλη × (=בכחך הגדול). Ib. 21.9: הישר: O': το καλον ÷ και το αρεστον × (=הטוב והישר). Here, strangely enough, it is exactly the word found in MT which is marked by the obelus.

In the course of the present study we refrained from making any use of such doubtfully marked quotations. Cf. also on p. 368 the list of asteriscized passages without an equivalent in the MT.

§ 3. Asterisk and Obelus Readings originate in Marginal Notes.

In those Hexapla-quotations where the otherwise smooth reading of the context is interrupted by an insertion marked by an asterisk or obelus, the explanation of such a breaking off of the sentence can best be found in an assumption that these insertions were originally meant as marginal notes, which afterwards were erroneously incorporated into the text without their first undergoing the necessary grammatical adjustment, as I pointed out in the preceding paragraph by referring to Ex. 9.24. On the relation of readings *sub asterisco* and *sub obelo* to the Hebrew text which caused these marginal notes, cf. p. 364 ff.

a) Asterisk readings

1) In several instances, the combination of an asterisk insertion together with the Hexaplaric quotation sub O′ results in a translation of the full Hebrew Bible text, each one of these two sources representing a rendition of part of it, which in itself yields quite a good sense. These components now appear to have been put together merely mechanically, since they are not adjusted to the syntax of their context so as to form a unity from the grammatical point of view:

Num. 1.53: על עדת בני ישראל: O′: ※ επι την συναγωγην × εν υιοις ισραηλ. (We should expect: ※ επι την συναγωγην × των υιων ισραηλ.) The underlying Hebrew originals may be explained as על עדת ישראל and על בני ישראל (cf. p. 291, § 80a, c). Note the variation in the use of the particle επι and εν; cf. also the following example.

Josh. 12.2: על שפת נחל ארנון: O′: ※ επι του χειλους × εν τη φαραγγι ※ αρνων ×. On the use of επι and εν see the preceding example. The corresponding Hebrew components are: על שפת ארנון and על נחל ארנון. A correct rendering of these two parts into one sentence would have resulted in: ※ επι του χειλους × της φαραγγος ※ αρνων ×.

Num. 17.6: כל עדת בני ישראל: O′: ※ πασα η συναγωγη × οι υιοι ισραηλ. The Hebrew components are: כל עדת ישראל and בני ישראל. An adjustment of this asterisk-note to the context would lead to: ※ πασα η συναγωγη × των υιων ισραηλ.

2) In other cases the quotation is being interrupted by an insertion, which is a literal translation of the hitherto only freely translated basic Hebrew word. But the inclusion of this insertion should have resulted in a corresponding change of the case of the following noun, an oversight which stamps the insertion as an intrusion from a note on the margin of the page:

Ex. 21.8: ‏אם רעה בעיני אדניה‎: O′: εαν μη ευαρεστηση ※ εν οφθαλμοις ✕ τω
κυριω αυτης. Before εν οφθαλμοις crept into the text, the sentence
was well formed: ευαρεστεω τινι, hence the dative τω κυριω. But now
οφθαλμοις is the nomen regens to τω κυριω; consequently it should
have been changed into του κυριου. Similarly

Josh. 4.10: ‏בתוך הירדן‎: O′: εν ※ μεσω ✕ τω ιορδανη; simply εν τω ιορδανη
is quite correct; but with the asterisk insertion we must insist on εν
※ μεσω ✕ του ιορδανου.

Josh. 12.4: ‏וגבול עוג מלך‎: O′: και ※ ορια ✕ ωγ βασιλευς; should read: και ※
ορια ✕ ωγ βασιλεως.

The government of the possessive pronoun in Greek syntax is a problem, which can not be dealt with here; but a sentence like:

Num. 33.2: ‏מסעיהם למוצאיהם‎: O′: σταθμοι ※ αυτων και ✕ της πορειας αυτων
is not Greek: και can not connect a nominative with a genitive. The
original sentence σταθμοι της πορειας αυτων, with subsequent insertion
of the possessive pronoun αυτων, should have been rearranged to
read: σταθμοι ※ αυτων και ✕ η πορεια αυτων. Similarly.

Josh. 8.2: ‏רק שללה ובהמתה תבזו לכם‎: O′: και την προνομην των κτηνων
προνομευσεις σεαυτω; this translation, too, according to another
source, has been expanded by the inclusion of the possessive pronoun into O′: και την προνομην ※ αυτης και ✕ των κτηνων ※ αυτης ✕
προνομευσεις σεαυτω. A comparison between these two quotations
reveals the thoughtlessness of the procedure; και cannot be used to
connect an accusative with a genitive. A correction of the enlarged
sentence into: και την προνομην ※ αυτης και ✕ τα κτηνη ※ αυτης ✕
προνομευσεις σεαυτω would have removed these difficulties.

3) Further evidence for the originally glossary nature of asterisk
readings can be seen in

Num. 30.11: ‏או אסרה אסר‎: O′: η ο ορισμος; al ex: η ※ ον ωρισατο ✕
ορισμον; it is evident that the proper place for the relative sentence
ον ωρισατο, being dependent on ορισμον, is only after this word, provided it were genuinely part of the full sentence, But being a later
interpolation of a marginal gloss, it was wrongly placed; cf. later in
§ 7 our discussion of the various ways, how Deut. 6.5 is quoted in
the NT.

Num. 28.13: עלה: O': θυσιαν; al ex: ※ ολοκαυτωμα × θυσιαν. We are not concerned at present, whether θυσιαν is an equivalent for a Hebrew עלה or מנחה; but in al ex the addition of the asteriscized word should have resulted in ※ ολοκαυτωμα × θυσιας; cf. the examples listed under 2. Anticipating the results of our investigation in § 5, we wish to call attention to a similar faulty arrangement of words as a result of the inclusion of a marginal note into the text, which is equally being cited under al ex: Num. 3.51: את כסף הפדים: O': τα λυτρα (=הפדים את); al ex: το αργυριον τα λυτρα. The glossary character of το αργυριον is evident from the incongruity of the case of the following τα λυτρα; we would expect: το αργυριον των λυτρων; cf. also § 5 towards the end.

Ex. 20.18: וינעו ויעמדו מרחק: O': ※ και σαλευθεις × εστησαν μακροθεν; the plural in εστησαν necessitates the change of the singular form of the participle σαλευθεις into the same number, too: ※ και σαλευθεντες × εστησαν μακροθεν.

The syntactic congruity of verbs refers not only to their number, but also to their tense. Consequently Jer. 33.9: אשר אנכי עשה: O': α εγω ※ ειμι × ποιησω is an inner contradiction: present and future tense combined! The addition of ειμι is the result of a certain tendency consistently to translate אנכי by εγω ειμι, regardless of the context; cf. § 5d.

Judg. 3.8: ארם נהרים: O': συριας ποταμων has been expanded in other sources to: O': συριας ※ μεσοποταμιας × ποταμων. It is obvious that μεσοποταμιας originally represented another way of rendering ארם נהרים into Greek; it was put just after συριας, probably on account of the fact that both nouns end in ας (genitive).

b) *Obelus readings.*

Judg. 1.36: האמרי: O': του αμορραιου ÷ ο ιδουμαιος. × This combination is a Greek equivalent of MT and האדמי. The connection between the genitive and the following nominative is not clear at all, unless we consider ο ιδουμαιος as a mere gloss. On האדמי as a variant to האמרי, cf. p. 482, § 55 in conjunction with p. 489, § 70.

Jer. 15.1: אל העם הזה: O': προς αυτους. This corresponds to a Hebrew text: אלהם. Other sources bring this verse as: O': προς ÷ αυτους × τον λαον τουτον. Here αυτους impresses me as being a variant to τον λαον τουτον, since no conjunctive particle connects them syntactically. But even if this were the case, the result would be a tautology, since αυτους and τον λαον τουτον refer to the very same persons.

§ 4.   Obelus and O′ Quotations

In order to prove the theory that the readings marked by a so-called Hexaplaric symbol have their origin in marginal notes, from which they later erroneously came into the text itself, I adduced thirteen asteriscized passages, but only two instances with an obelus. This proportion represents more or less accurately the occurrences of these symbols in the material from Origen's *Hexapla* as collected and presented by Field. We are now confronted with the problem, how to explain this apparent anomaly: does Field's collection convey a true picture of the original Hexapla, or is it a mere accident that a comparatively large number of asteriscized readings found their way into the works of Church Fathers and were thus preserved, while obelus readings for some reason or other were neglected from the very beginning? We have no means to solve this problem with certainty; but still there is a great likelihood that even in the original *Hexapla* the number of such obelus readings might have been rather limited. We shall see later that these marginal notes were the result of a comparison of the basic LXX text of the *Hexapla*, which is indicated here by O′, with other Greek codices thereof (cf. § 9 under no. 10). The codex or the codices, the variant readings of which were marked with an obelus, must have belonged to the same textual family as the basic LXX text itself; for, indeed, it often happens that in the tradition concerning *Hexapla* quotations it is uncertain whether to assign them to O′ as such or to an obelus text. A few instances will make this point clear:

a)   The obelus is indicated in the *Syro-Hexaplaris*.

1)   The tradition is uncertain regarding the full quotation:

1 Ki. 8.64: ואת המנחה: O′: και τας θυσιας; Aliter: O′: ÷ και τας θυσιας ×.

1 Ki. 9.9: s.v. מארץ מצרים: O′: (εξ αιγυπτου) εξ οικου δουλειας; Aliter: O′: ÷ εξ οικου δουλειας ×.

1 Ki. 17.22: s.v. וישמע יהוה בקול אליהו: O′: και εγενετο ουτως και ανεβοησε; Aliter: O′: ÷ και εγενετο ουτως και ανεβοησεν ×.

2) Only part of the quotation is involved:

1 Ki. 12.16: **לְאֹהָלֶיךָ יִשְׂרָאֵל**: O′: αποτρεχε ισραηλ εις τα σκηνωματα σου;
Aliter: O′: ÷ αποτρεχε ✕ εις τα σκηνωματα σου ισραηλ.

1 Ki. 18.39: **יהוה הוא האלהים**: O′: αληθως κυριος ο θεος; Aliter: O′: ÷
αληθως ✕ κυριος . . .

1 Ki. 5.32: **העצים והאבנים**: O′: τους λιθους και ξυλα τρια ετη; Aliter: O′: τα
ξυλα και τους λιθους ÷ τρια ετη ✕.

1 Ki. 18.43: **ויבט**: O′: και επεβλεψε το παιδαριον; Aliter: O′: και επεβλεψε
÷ το παιδαριον ✕.

2 Ki. 2.18: **ויאמר אליהם**: O′: και ειπεν ελισαιε; Aliter: O′: και ειπεν ÷
ελισαιε ✕.

b) The obelus can be found in genuine Greek texts.

Gen. 50.18: **וילכו**: O′: και ελθοντες προς αυτον; al ex: και ελθοντες ÷ προς
αυτον ✕.

Ex. 2.6: **בכה**: O′: κλαιον εν τη θιβει; al ex: κλαιον ÷ εν τη θιβει ✕.

Ex. 11.3: **בעיני עבדי פרעה**: O′: και εναντιον φαραω και εναντιον των θεραποντων αυτου; al ex: ÷ και εναντιον φαραω ✕ και εναντιον παντων των
θεραποντων φαραω.

Num. 2.7: **מטה**: O′: και οι παρεμβαλλοντες εχομενοι φυλης; al ex: ÷ και οι
παρεμβαλλοντες εχομενοι ✕ φυλη.

Deut. 15.3: s.v. **ואשר יהיה לך**: O′: παρ αυτω; al ex: ÷ παρ αυτω ✕.

Jer. 35.18: **אשר צוה אתכם**: O′: ενετειλατο αυτοις ο πατηρ αυτων; al ex:
ενετειλατο αυτοις ÷ ο πατηρ αυτων ✕.

Jer. 36.6: **במגלה**: O′: εν τω χαρτιω τουτω; al ex: εν τω χαρτη ÷
τουτω ✕.

Ezek. 24.18: **ותמת אשתי בערב**: O′: ον τροπον ενετειλατο μοι εσπερας; al ex:
÷ ον τροπον ενετειλατο μοι ✕ και απεθανεν η γυνη μου εσπερας.

Ezek. 27.19: s.v. **ויזן**: O′: και οινον; al ex: ÷ και οινον ✕.

Lam. 2.16: **בלענו**: O′: κατεπιομεν αυτην; al ex: κατεπιωμεν ÷ αυτην ✕.

On the relation of the readings marked with an obelus to their Hebrew
text, cf. p. 364 ff.

These examples demonstrate the close affinity between the basic LXX
text of the *Hexapla* and the one quoted *sub obelo*. Henceforth, in speaking
of the obelus group, we shall include the quotations under O′.

§ 5. Asterisk and *Alia Exemplaria* Quotations

In a similar way we can show that readings cited either *sub asterisco* or under the heading *alia exemplaria* (excepting those, which are specifically marked with an obelus, as e.g. the quotations listed above in § 4b) are derived from sources which belonged to one and the same family of Greek textual tradition. We shall demonstrate this relationship by referring to the way, in which certain Hebrew words appear in Greek translation in Hexaplaric quotations *sub asterisco* and *sub alia exemplaria*:

a) מתוך: Ex. 3.2: מתוך הסנה: O′: εκ ⁖ μεσου × του βατου. Bearing in mind our remarks in § 2, we see in this quotation an amplification of the pre-asterisk reading: εκ του βατου. Thus we get two translations: εκ του βατου for O′, and εκ μεσου του βατου for the asterisk type. Compare with these results the way, in which the same Hebrew phrase is rendered in Ex. 3.4: מתוך הסנה: O′: εκ του βατου: al ex: εκ μεσου του βατου.

b) פן: Deut. 6.15, 7.25: פן: O′: μη ⁖ ποτε × ; a combination of μη for O′, and μηποτε for the asterisk-type; cf. Deut 4.16: פן: O′ μη; al ex: μηποτε.

c) הנה: Ex. 16.10: והנה: O′: και ⁖ ιδου × ; the readings: και (for O′) and και ιδου (for the asteriscus) combined; cf. Ex. 14.10: והנה: O′: και; al ex: και ιδου.

d) אנכי: Jer. 33.9: אנכי עשה: O′: εγω ⁖ ειμι × ποιησω; the personal pronoun is thus translated: εγω (by O′) and εγω ειμι (by ⁖), although the fact that אנכי is here followed by a verb in the future tense (ποιησω) should have excluded the insertion of the present ειμι. The same remarkable combination of ειμι with a finite verb in the future tense we can notice in Ruth 2.13: ואנכי לא אהיה: O′: (και ιδου) εγω; al ex: (και) εγω ειμι εσομαι. On אנכי as εγω ειμι in this textual type, cf. also Gen. 50.5: הנה אנכי מת: O′: Vacat. al ex: ιδου εγω ειμι αποθνησκω.

In these instances, the asterisk translation of a Hebrew phrase corresponds to that given elsewhere under al ex; we may, therefore, assume that the sources of asterisk and *alia exemplaria* quotations were members of one and the same group of text-witnesses. In other words, readings listed under al ex are in reality asterisk readings, whose asterisk has been omitted for some reason or other during the long history of text-tradition. On the carelessness of the copyists cf. Jerome's statement quoted here on

p. 360 f., § 10; cf. also the instance from Num. 3.51, brought in § 3a 3 in connection with Num. 28.13.

§ 6.   Origen's Sources

We started in § 1 with the statement that LXX quotations of the fifth column of the *Hexapla* are referred to either sub O′ or sub "al ex." In § 2 we had to add that Origen himself introduced the so-called Hexaplaric symbols in order to indicate the various sources from which certain readings emanated; cf. § 3. It now seems as if Origen based his work upon a collation of four sources, which we would name after the respective authority under which they are quoted: the O′, al ex, asterisk, and obelus texts. But in view of the fact that O′ and obelus form one group (cf. § 4), and al ex and asterisk another (cf. § 5), we arrive at the conclusion that Origen consulted for the purpose of his work representatives (note the plural) of *two Septuagint families*: the obelus group (indicated by O′ and ÷), and the asterisk group (indicated by al ex and by ※).

§ 7. Later Confusions Resulting in Doublets

In § 3 we saw how some asterisk and obelus readings do not fit syntactically into their context—due to the incongruity of the case, number, word order, or the like—and thus suggest a theory that they were originally noted down as a variant on the margin of the respective line, from which they were afterwards erroneously taken into the text itself. In the cases dealt with there, these "variants," as we may call them, represent a Greek rendering of a Hebrew word or phrase, which had otherwise remained without a corresponding translation in the basic Hexaplaric LXX text. This fact can best be explained by assuming that these words or phrases were not contained in the Hebrew original of the basic translation; cf. chapter F, p. 364 ff. With our MT in mind, the variant, therefore, merely supplements the current Greek text.

But there are quite a number of cases where the variants constitute another way of rendering into Greek a Hebrew word or phrase, which already appears in the current Hexaplaric LXX text. The nature of these variants may differ; they are sometimes Greek synonyms, a free translation as compared with the literal one of the basic text, or vice versa, representing a different exegesis of the underlying Hebrew text, etc.

If, by a scribal error, a marginal note of this kind happened to be included in the text, the result is that now a certain Hebrew word or phrase appears therein in two translations; this is termed a doublet.

Before we proceed to classify the doublets and base further conclusions on this phenomenon, it might be deemed advisable to produce an example from a related ancient source in order to show the working process of such copyist's mistakes.

Deut. 6.5: ואהבת את יהוה אלהיך בכל לבבך ובכל נפשך ובכל מאדך is of great theological significance for the NT; Matthew, Mark and Luke quote it; and it is worth while to examine the way in which this verse appears in their respective Gospels: Matth. 22.37 reads: αγαπησεις κυριον τον θεον σου εν ολη τη καρδια σου και εν ολη τη ψυχη σου και εν ολη τη διανοια σου. According to the three items mentioned in the Hebrew text, we have three nouns in Greek, which we would number consecutively as: 1) καρδια, 2) ψυχη, 3) διανοια. But Mark and Luke offer four nouns instead, the arrangement of which is interesting, too. Mk. 12.30: και αγαπησεις κυριον τον θεον σου εξ ολης της καρδιας σου και εξ ολης της ψυχης σου και εξ ολης της διανοιας σου και εξ ολης της ισχυος σου. We will not concern ourselves here with the difference in the use of the particle, which results in a difference of the case for the noun; cf. above p. 327, the classification under XII. It is obvious that ισχυος represents another translation of מאדך and thus forms a doublet to διανοιας according to our definition as given above. The arrangement of the nouns as compared with Matthew, is here: 1, 2, 3, doublet. Let us now consult Luke 10.27: αγαπησεις κυριον τον θεον σου εξ ολης της καρδιας σου και εν ολη τη ψυχη σου και εν ολη τη ισχυι σου και εν ολη τη διανοια σου. The same four nouns as in Mark, but their order is: 1, 2, doublet, 3.

In other words: the doublet ισχυς—the case is merely a matter of adjustment, cf. § 2, and does not matter here—, originally a marginal gloss, was taken into the text by the copyists of Mark and Luke; but the mistake did not produce the same results in these two cases; for each one of the copyists placed the gloss differently. This consideration leads us to the conclusion that in the case of a doublet it would be utterly wrong to assume mechanically that the first reading is the genuine translation or citation, and the second a later addition and therefore the doublet, or vice versa. Only inner criteria will have to be applied in order to solve this question for each case separately; cf. also our note on Ex. 12.5 in § 8, e, β, 1.

§ 8. Classification of the Doublets.

Two vertical strokes like // separate the two components of a doublet.

a) Doublets traceable to their sources.

α) Asyndetic connections.

Gen. 44.28: עד הנה: O′: αχρι νυν; al ex: ετι. The combination of both results in: *alia*: ετι // αχρι νυν.

Deut. 13.18: כאשר נשבע: O′: ον τροπον ωμοσε; al ex: ον τροπον ωμοσεν ÷ κυριος ×; *alia*: καθως ελαλησε κυριος.

These readings asyndetically put together appear in: *alia*: καθως ελα-λησε σοι // ον τροπον ωμοσε κυριος.

Judg. 9. 4: בעל ברית: O′ βααλβεριθ; al ex: βααλ διαθηκης; *alia*: βααλ-βερειθ // διαθηκης.

Lev. 13.2: (ספחת) או בהרת: O′: ((σημασιας)) τηλαυγης; al ex: η τηλαυγης; *alia*: η τηλαυγης // η αυγασμα. Unlike the case of 2 Ki. 1.3 which is dealt with in subdivision β, the particle η is here part of the variant, and not an addition in order to connect the two parts of the doublet. For the source of the reading αυγασμα cf. verse 4: בהרת: O′: τηλ-αυγης; al ex: αυγασμα.

β) Connected by και or η.

Deut. 7.1: רבים (1°): μεγαλα; al ex: πολλα; *alia*: μεγαλα // και πολλα.
Deut. 7.1: רבים (2°): O′: πολλα; al ex: μεγαλα; *alia*: μεγαλα // και πολλα.
2. Ki. 1.3: אלהים: O′: θεον; al ex προφητην; *alia*: θεον // η προφητην.

Cf. JBL 1935, 83, paragraph IV, the instance from Zech. 7.3 where Theodoret similarly connects with η the two readings forming a doublet. See also later under d β our remark on Judg. 5.29. The reading under al ex in Deut. 15.21 proves that και and η were conjunctive particles.

γ) Adjustment of the case of the second noun.

1 Ki. 22.38: את הרכב: O′: το αιμα (free translation); al ex: το αρμα (literal); *alia*: το αιμα // εκ του αρματος. Cf. also later under b β 1 the last two examples.

δ) The source traceable for one reading only.

1) Under alia exemplaria the first translation is quoted.

Ex. 30.8: תמיד: O′: ενδελεχισμου // διαπαντος; al ex: ενδελεχισμου.

Lev. 16.31: שבת שבתון: O′: σαββατα σαββατων // αναπαυσις αυτη; al ex: σαββατα σαββατων. Cf. Lev. 23.3: שבת שבתון: O′: σαββατα αναπαυσις.

Deut. 31.6: עמך: O′: μεθ υμων // εν υμιν; al ex: μεθ υμων. Cf. also Lev. 25.45: עמכם: O′: Vacat. al ex: μεθ υμων; alia: εν υμιν.

Jer. 48.13: מבטחם: O′: ελπιδος αυτων // πεποιθοτες επ αυτοις; al ex: ελπιδος αυτων.

A combination of MT and a variant hereof is represented in 2 Sam. 1.19: על במותיך: O′: υπερ των τεθνηκοτων // επι τα υψη σου; al ex: περι των τεθνηκοτων σου. The first translation equals על מֵתֶיךָ; the second corresponds to MT; cf. also verse 25: על במותיך: O′: επι τα υψη σου.

2) Under alia exemplaria the second translation is quoted.

Ex. 28.3: חכמה: O′: σοφιας // και αισθησεως; al ex: αισθησεως.

Ruth 2.16: וגם של תשלו לה: O′: και βασταζοντες βαστασατε αυτη // καιγε παραβαλλοντες παραβαλειτε αυτη; al ex: καιγε παραβαλλοντες παραβαλειτε αυτη.

3) Both translations combined by asterisk.

Ex. 26.13: בעדף בארך יריעת: O′: εκ του υπερεχοντος των δερρεων // εκ του μηκους των δερρεων; al ex: εκ του υπερεχοντος ※ του μηκους ＜ των δερρεων. The first translation in O′ corresponds to: בעדף יריעת, the second to: בארך יריעת. Under al ex the first translation is quoted, with an asterisk insertion from the second. Thus, the enlarged al ex quotation reflects MT; cf. also later p. 372 § 3.

b) *Doublets in O′-quotations.*

α) Combination of transliteration and translation.

1) Transliteration first.

Judg. 1.11: קרית ספר: O′: καριαθσεφερ // πολις γραμματων.

I Sam. 7.12: אבן העזר: O′: αβενεζερ // λιθος του βοηθου. Cf. ib. sub al ex: αβενεζερ ο σημαινει λιθος του βοηθου.

I Sam. 15.8: החרים: O′: ιεριμ // απεκτεινεν. The spelling ιεριμ is probably a mistake for εριμ; cf. p. 188, § 52.

1 Sam. 23.14: במצדות: O′: εν μασερεμ (sive μασερεθ) // . . . . εν τοις στενοις.
The reading μασερεθ is more likely to be the correct one. On the confusion between ד—ρ (=ר), cf. ch. 00, § 00.

1 Sam. 23.19: במצדות: O′: εν μεσσαρα // εν τοις στενοις. In the Hebrew
original, upon which the transliterated form is based, the text probably read במצודה in the singular; cf. 1 Sam 24.23: על המצודה: O′:
εις την μεσσερα // στενην.

2) Translation first.

1 Sam. 7.4: ואת העשתרת: O′: και τα αλση // ασταρωθ. Cf. verse 3 והעשתרות:
O′: και τα αλση; Αλλος: ασταρωθ.

1 Sam. 21.8: נעצר: O′: συνεχομενος // νεεσσαραν.

Jer. 34.5: והוי אדון: O′: ουαι κυριε // και εως αδου. We have to assume that
the genitive αδου was substituted for αδον, which in turn was taken
to be a Greek word (originally αδων), under the influence of εως.
For a similar case of a misunderstood transliteration treated as a
Greek word, see later 1 Sam. 15.33 in e α on p. 354.

β) Combination of two translations.

1) Asyndetic connection.

Judg. 13.2: ממשפחת: O′: απο δημου // συγγενειας. Cf. ib. 18.2: ממשפחתם:
O′: δημων; al ex: συγγενειων; similarly ib. v. 11.

Judg. 15.5: ועד קמה: O′: και εως σταχυων // ορθων.

1 Sam. 9.21: שבטי: O′: σκηπτρου // φυλης. Cf. ib. 10.19: לשבטיכם: O′:
(κατα τα) σκηπτρα; al ex: φυλας; cf. also ib. verse 20.

1 Sam. 20.35: למועד: O′: καθως εταξατο // εις το μαρτυριον.

Isa. 5.1: בקרן: O′: εν κερατι // εν τοπω.

Isa. 40. 13: ואיש עצתו יודיענו: O′: και τις αυτου συμβουλος εγενετο // ος
συμβιβα αυτον. Cf. 1 Cor. 2.16: τις γαρ εγνω νουν κυριου, ος συμβιβα-
σει αυτον.

Jer. 5.15: לשונו: O′: της φωνης // της γλωσσης αυτου.

Jer. 43.6: את הגברים: O′: τους δυνατους // ανδρας. Cf. ib. 44.20: על הגברים:
O′: τοις δυνατοις.

The following doublets are based upon the formation of two Hebrew
words out of the consonants of the single word as found in the text (cf.
p. 490, § 71):

Judg. 5.8: שְׁעָרִים: O′: πολεις // αρχοντων. A combination of עָרִים and שָׂרִים.

Isa. 24.14: מִיָּם: O′: το υδωρ // της θαλασσης. This corresponds to מִיָּם and
יָם; cf. later e β 1, the example from 1 Ki. 18.44. On the adjustment
of the case of the second noun, cf. above a γ.

2) Connected by και.

Judg. 1.23: וַיָּתִירוּ: O′: και παρενεβαλον // και κατεσκεψαντο.

Isa. 14.2: וְהִתְנַחֲלוּם: O′: και κατακληρονομησουσι // και πληθυνθησονται.

Isa. 24.8: שְׁאוֹן: O′: αυθαδεια // και πλουτος.

Jer. 52.7: הַחֹמֹתַיִם: O′: του τειχους // και του προτειχισματος.

c) *The obelus-text.*

α) Combination of translation and transliteration.

Josh. 5.6: בַּמִּדְבָּר: O′: εν τη ερημω // ÷ τη μαβδαριτιδι ×.

Judg. 20.13: בְּנֵי בְלִיַּעַל: O′: τους ασεβεις // . . . . ÷ τους υιους βελιαλ ×.
Instead of τους ασεβεις read υιους ασεβεις. The doublet is misplaced;
cf. our note on Ex. 12.5 sub e β 1.

It will be noted that in both instances it is the obelus reading, which
offers the Hebrew word in transliteration; cf. below § 9, 5 b.

A variant Hebrew text is reflected in Judg. 1.10: קִרְיַת אַרְבַּע: O′:
καριαθαρβοκ // ÷ σεφερ ×. We have here MT and קִרְיַת סֵפֶר.

β) Combination of two translations.

1) The second translation is sub obelo.

א) Asyndetic connection.

Ex. 25.17: כַּפֹּרֶת: O′: ιλαστηριον // ÷ επιθεμα ×.

Num. 12.12: כַּמֵּת: O′: ωσει ισον θανατω // ÷ ωσει εκτρωμα ×.

Judg. 1.17: וַיַּחֲרִימוּ אוֹתָהּ: O′: και ανεθεματισαν αυτην // ÷ και εξωλοθρευσαν
αυτην ×.

Judg. 1.20: וַיּוֹרֶשׁ מִשָּׁם אֶת שְׁלֹשָׁה בְּנֵי הָעֲנָק: O′: και εκληρονομησεν εκειθεν τας
τρεις πολεις των υιων ενακ // ÷ και εξηρεν εκειθεν τους τρεις υιους ενακ ×.

Judg. 1.27: וְאֶת בְּנוֹתֶיהָ: O′: ουδε τας θυγατερας αυτης // ÷ ουδε το περιοικα
αυτης ×.

Isa. 3.23: הָרְדִידִים: O′: θεριστρα // ÷ κατακλιτα ×.

Lam. 5.10: נִכְמָרוּ: O′: επελιωθη // ÷ συνεσπασθησαν ×.

ב) Connected by και.

Josh. 9.4: ויצטירו: O': επεσιτισαντο // ÷ και ητοιμασαντο ×. The first translation reflects a text ויצטידו; on the confusion between ד—ר cf. p. 482, § 55.

Isa. 3.2: גבור: O': γιγαντα // ÷ και ισχυοντα ×.

Isa. 66.7: והמליטה: O': εξεφυγε // ÷ και ετεκεν. Literal and free translation; cf. above sub a γ, the example from 1 Ki. 22.38.

2) The first translation is sub obelo.

א) Asyndetic connection.

Ex. 15.4: שלשיו: O': ÷ αναβατας × // τριστατας.

Ex. 25.25: זר: O' ÷: στρεπτον × // κυματιον. Cf. also ib. verse 24 sub al ex.

Ex. 27.20: זך: O': ÷ ατρυγον × // καθαρον.

Judg. 20.15: בחור: O': ÷ νεανισκοι × // εκλεκτοι.

Judg. 21.19: ללבונה: O': ÷ του λιβανου × // της λεβωνα.

Lam. 2.20: עללי טפחים אם יהרג: O': ÷ επιφυλλιδα εποιησε μαγειρος φονευθησονται × // νηπια θηλαζοντα μαστους αποκτενεις.

The following two instances have their origin in the two possibilities of pronouncing the consonants of the respective Hebrew word:

Num. 17.2: זרה הלאה: O': ÷ το αλλοτριον τουτο × // σπειρον εκει. Vocalized as זָרָה (and הלאה read as הָאֵלֶּה) and זְרֵה (MT).

1 Ki. 6.1: למלך: O': ÷ βασιλευοντος × // του βασιλεως. This means: לִמְלֹךְ (MT) and לַמֶּלֶךְ. It is noteworthy that in the first example it is the second translation which vocalizes according to MT, while in the second case it is the first one, sub obelo. A similar case reflecting uncertainty of the pronunciation is listed on p. 324, sub a 1; cf. further:

2 Ki. 14.10: לִבְּךָ הִכָּבֵד O': καρδια σου. ενδοξασθητι (=MT); al ex: η καρδια σου η βαρεια // ενδοξασθητι (= הַכָּבֵד and MT); ib. 16.18: הַשַּׁבָּת: της καθεδρας (=הַשֶּׁבֶת); al ex: της καθεδρας // των σαββατων (=הַשַּׁבָּת and MT); 1 Chron. 13.6: שָׁם: O': ονομα αυτου (=MT); al ex: ονομα αυτου // εκει (=MT and שָׁם).

ב) Connected by και.

Gen. 20.4: צדיק: O': ÷ αγνοουν × // και δικαιον.

Ex. 33.5: עדיך: O': ÷ τας στολας των δοξων υμων και × // τον κοσμον. Cf. verse 6, listed on p. 375, sub b.

Deut. 7.15: אשר ידעת‎ :O': ÷ α εωρακας και × // οσα εγνως. Cf. chapter
oo, § 9a, the instance from Gen. 2.9.

Isa. 51.23: מוגיך‎ :O': ÷ των αδικησαντων σε × // και των ταπεινωσαντων σε.
A textual variant is involved in Mich. 5.3: ורעה‎ :O': ÷ και οψεται × //
και ποιμανει. Reflecting וראה‎ and ורעה‎; on the phonetic confusion
between א‎ and ע‎ cf. p. 477, § 37.

γ) The doublet is quoted under al ex.

Num. 3.15: למשפחתם‎ :O': κατα δημους αυτων; als ex: κατα δημους αυτων //
÷ κατα συγγενειας αυτων ×. Cf. above b β 1, the instance from Judg.
13.2.

Ex. 30.10: הכפרים‎ :O': του καθαρισμου; al ex: ÷ του καθαρισμου × // του
εξιλασμου.

Num. 2.3: מזרחה‎ :O': κατα ανατολας; al ex: ÷ κατα νοτον × // κατα
ανατολας.

2 Ki. 1.9: שר חמשים‎ :O': πεντηκονταρχον; al ex: ÷ ηγουμενον × // πεντηκονταρχον.

Jer. 49.3: ספדנה‎ :O': και κοψασθε; al ex: ÷ και επιληπτευσασθε × // και
κοψασθε.

d) *The asterisk-text.*

The doublet is arranged asyndetically, throughout.

α) The first translation is *sub asterisco.*

Deut. 15.8: די מחסרו‎ :O': ⁛ ικανον × // οσον επιδεεται.

Lev. 26.16: בהלה‎ :O': ⁛ σπουδη × // την αποριαν.

Ex. 22.12: עד הטרפה‎ :O': ⁛ μαρτυρα × // επι την θυραν. The asteriscized
reading is based upon the masoretic vocalization עֵד‎; the doublet
presupposes a pronunciation עַד‎.

Ex. 16.4: דבר יום‎ :O': ⁛ ρημα × // το της ημερας. The word-order suggests
an explanation that ρημα was originally a marginal note to το, so as
to conform more closely with the Hebrew word דבר‎; cf. in § 3 a the
instance from Num. 30.11.

β) The second translation is *sub asterisco.*

Lev. 22.18: נדריהם‎ :O': ομολογιαν // ⁛ ευχων × αυτων.

Judg. 5.29: אף היא‎ :O': και αυτη // ⁛ δε ×. Cf. also Gen. 28.8: וירא‎ :O':

ιδων δε // και; this doublet is a combination of και ιδων (cf. the quotation under al ex: και ειδεν) and ιδων δε. Similarly Deut. 15.21: כל מום: O': μωμον; al ex: η // και πας μωμος; cf. on this above under a β the instance from 2 Ki. 1.3, and below under f the instance from Num. 15.6.

Judg. 11.34: יחידה: O': μονογενης αυτω // ※ αγαπητη ×.

Isa. 14.9: לקראת בואך: O': συναντησας σοι // ※ ερχομενου σου ×.

Jer. 27.6: נתתי לו לעבדו: O': εργαζεσθαι αυτω // ※ δεδωκα δουλευειν αυτω ×.

Ezek. 21.24, 25: ברא: דרך תשים: O': επ αρχης οδου διαταξεις // ※ και συ ετοιμασον και διαταξον οδον ×.

e)   Al ex quotations.

α)   Transliteration and translation.

Judg. 8.11: לנבח: O' της ναβαι; al ex: της ναβαι // και εξεναντιας. The translation corresponds to a Hebrew word לנכח; on the confusion between ב—כ cf. p. 483, § 57. The following ναβε in Field is merely a dittography of ναβαι, with a phonetic interchange between αι—ε. Similar cases of dittography are, e.g., Num. 6.3: יזיר: O': αγνισθησεται; al ex: αγνισθησεται ÷ απο οινου × (the words preceding it are: απο οινου και σικερα); Isa. 14.8: ברושים: O': τα ξυλα ÷ του λιβανου × (from the following: η κεδρος του λιβανου).

Judg. 8.33: בעל ברית: O': τω βααλ διαθηκην; al ex: τον βααλβερειθ // εις διαθηκην.

Judg. 9.46: בית אל ברית: O': βαιθηλβεριθ; al ex: οικου // βηθηλ βερειθ. On the change from βαιθ to βηθ cf. p. 124 ff. s.v. בית and חיל.

I Sam. 15.32: מעדנת: O': τρεμων; al ex: εξ αναθωθ // τρεμων. The transliteration interprets the מ as an inseparable preposition, confuses ד with ת (cf. p. 481, § 51) and changes its position by metathesis (cf. p. 489, § 70); thus, a variant Hebrew reading מענתת results.

I Sam 15.33: וישסף: O': και εσφαξε; al ex: και εσφαξε // υιου σασειφ. υιου goes back to a misconception of ουιεσασειφ (cf. p. 185, § 31 in conjunction with § 78c on p. 192) as two words, the first of which is a derivative of υιος; cf. a similar case of a transliteration being mistaken for a Greek word above b α 2, the instance from Jer. 34.5.

β) Combination of two translations.

The arrangement is for the most part asyndetic. The source of one of these translations can be found in an O'-quotation.

1) The O'-translation listed first.

Ex. 12.5: תמים: O': τελειον; al ex: τελειον // . . . . αμωμον. Between these two translations is αρσεν, the Greek equivalent of the following Hebrew word זכר. Thus, αμωμον is inserted in the wrong place; cf. similarly misplaced doublets below under 3 (the instance from Lev. 4.25) and under f (the instances from Josh. 6.5, Num. 15.6 and Isa. 9.5), and above under c α (the instance from Judg. 20.13); see also p. 375, § 9c.

Lev. 1.3: לרצנו: O': δεκτον ※ αυτω ✕; al ex: δεκτον αυτω // εξιλασασθαι.

Judg. 16.16: למות: O': εως του αποθανειν; al ex: εως // εις θανατον.

2 Sam. 3.27: בשלי: O': ενεδρευων; al ex: ενεδρευων // εν παραλογισμω.

Judg. 5.10: צחרות: O': μεσημβριας; al ex: μεσημβριας // και λαμπουσων.

In the following instances the two translations go back to differences in their basic Hebrew texts:

1 Ki. 18.44: מים: O': υδωρ; al ex: υδωρ // απο θαλασσης. Cf. above under b β 1 the instance from Isa. 24.14.

Isa. 2.5: O': και νυν; al ex: και νυν // συ. The underlying Hebrew text, though not to be found in MT, is ואתה—ועתה; on the confusion between א—ע, cf. p. 477, § 37.

Lam. 2.22: כלם: O': παντας; al ex: παντα // συνετελεσεν. O' pronounces the word as: כֻּלָּם, the doublet corresponds to MT; cf. in the following subdivision 2 the example from Isa. 15.6.

2) The O'-translation listed second.

Deut. 32.35: לעת תמוט: O': οταν σφαλη; al ex: εν καιρω // οταν σφαλη.

1 Sam. 1.16: לפני בת בליעל: O': εις θυγατερα λοιμην; al ex: εις προσωπον // εις θυγατερα λοιμην. With the results of § 5 in mind we note that the literal translation of פני and its derivatives is characteristic for the asterisk-group; cf., e.g., Gen. 45.3: מפניו: O': Vacat. ※ απο προσωπου αυτου ✕; Num. 10.35: מפניך: O': ※ απο προσωπου σου ✕.

1 Sam. 16.14: ובעתתו: O': και επνιγεν αυτον; al ex: και συνειχεν αυτον // και επνιγεν αυτον.

Isa. 15.6: כלה: O': εκλειψει; al ex: πας // εκλειψει. Reflecting a pronunciation as כָּלָּה and כָּלָה (MT), respectively; cf. above subdivision 1 the instance from Lam. 2.22.

Lam. 2.22: טפחתי: O': επεκρατησα; al ex: εξεθρεψα // και επεκρατησα.

3) Combination of O'-translation and asterisk-doublet.

Num. 15.11: בכבשים: O': εκ των προβατων; al ex: εκ των προβατων // ÷ εκ των αμνων ×.

Lev. 4.25: ונתן: O': και επιθησει; al ex: και επιθησει // .... ※ και δωσει ×. The doublet is misplaced; cf. above subdivision 1, on Ex. 12.5.

Isa. 1.27: ושביה: O': η αιχμαλωσια αυτης; al ex: η αιχμαλωσια αυτης // και ※ η αποστροφη αυτης ×. The first translation pronounces the word וְשֹׁבְיָהָ; sub asterisco the masoretic vocalization is presupposed.

Jer. 46.20: יפה פיה: O': κεκαλλωπισμενη; al ex: κεκαλλωπισμενη // ※ καλλιστη ×.

A variance in the basic Hebrew word is the underlying reason for:

Jer. 49.22: וידאה: O': οψεται; al ex: οψεται // ※ και επιπτησεται ×. O' read ויראה; sub asterisco the masoretic word is translated. On the confusion between ד — ר cf. p. 482, § 55.

f) Either translation is marked by an Hexaplaric symbol.

Deut. 31.5: ככל המצוה אשר צויתי: O': καθοτι ενετειλαμην; al ex: ÷ καθοτι × // ※ κατα πασαν την εντολην ην × ενετειλαμην. Cf. also Josh. 1.7: ככל התורה אשר: O': ※ κατα παντα τον νομον × // καθοτι. In both instances, sub asterisco MT is translated, whilst the O' quotations reflect a reading כאשר (for המצוה אשר ככל and ככל התורה אשר, respectively).

Josh. 6.5: תחתיה: O': ÷ αυτοματα × // .... ※ υποκατω αυτων ×. The doublet is misplaced; cf. above under e β 1 the instance from Ex. 12.5.

Isa. 9.5: פלא יועץ: O': μεγαλης βουλης ÷ αγγελος × // ※ θαυμαστος συμβουλος ×.

Num. 15.6: או לאיל: O': ÷ και τω κριω .... × // ※ η τω κριω ×. On the difference between και and η cf. our note on Judg. 5.29 above d β. The doublet is misplaced, cf. here on Josh. 6.5.

A difference in the underlying Hebrew texts may be the reason for:

Josh. 10.11: וימתו: O': ※ και απεθανον × // ÷ και εγενοντο ×.

A doublet within the asterisk-quotation occurs in

Isa. 9.5: אבי עד: O': ※ εξουσιαστης // . . . πατηρ του μελλοντος αιωνος ✕.
On the dots indicating that the doublet is wrongly placed, cf. above
on Josh. 6.5.

g) *Doublets in both O' and al ex quotations.*

As a rule, one quotation offers the two doublets of the respective
Hebrew phrase in full, while in the other quotation an effort towards
stylistic adjustment into one Greek sentence is made.

α) The doublet reflects two different Hebrew originals.

Judg. 1.14: ותצנח מעל החמור: O': και εγογγυζεν // και εκραζεν απο του
υποζυγιου; al ex: και εγογγυζεν επανω του υποζυγιου // και εκραζεν απο
του υποζυγιου. The variant in the translation of the particle as επανω
and απο reflects corresponding readings על and מעל in the respective
Hebrew original.

1 Sam. 14.47: לכד המלוכה O': ελαχε του βασιλευειν // κατακληρουται
εργον; al ex: κατακληρουται το εργον // του βασιλευειν. The difference
in the rendering of the Hebrew noun as βασιλευειν and εργον probably
corresponds to the pronunciation of המלכה (in defective spelling) as
המלוכה or המלאכה; cf. p. 562 f., § 1 a (the instance from 2 Sam. 11.1—
1 Chron. 20.1) and p. 564 f., § 3 c.

2 Sam. 19.8: ורעה לך זאת: O': και επιγνωθι σεαυτω // και κακον σοι τουτο;
al ex: και επιγνωθι τουτο σεαυτω // οτι χειρον σοι εσται τουτο. The
reading επιγνωθι reflects a Hebrew word ודעה; κακον equals MT. On
the confusion between ד — ר, cf. p. 482, § 55.

β) One translation is quoted *sub obelo.*

Gen. 15.11: על הפגרים: O': επι τα σωματα // ÷ επι τα διχοτομηματα
αυτων ✕; al ex: επι τα σωματα // τα διχοτομηθεντα.

Ex. 25.24: זר זהב: O': στρεπτα // κυματια χρυσα; al ex: ÷ στρεπτον ✕ //
κυματιον χρυσουν.

Num. 15.19: תרימו תרומה ליהוה: O': αφελειτε αφαιρεμα // αφορισμα κυριω;
al ex: αφελειτε αφαιρεμα τω κυριω // ÷ αφορισμα ✕.

Jer. 51.34: הממני: O': εμερισατο με // κατελαβε με; al ex: ÷ κατελαβε
με ✕ // εμερισατο με.

Lam. 1.12: הוגה: O': φθεγξαμενος εν εμοι // εταπεινωσε με; al ex: εταπεινωσε ÷ με ⨯ // φθεγξαμενος ÷ εν εμοι ⨯.

§ 9. Results of this Classification.

We now sum up the results of our classification of the doublets found
in the Hexaplaric LXX quotations and state:

1)   Doublets occur in O'-quotations as well as in those cited under
the authority of *alia exemplaria*; (cf. § 8b and e).

2)   They consist of a combination of either

a)   a translation and transliteration, or of

b)   two translations of the Hebrew original.

3)   The two translations thus combined represent either

a)   an inner Greek differentiation of vocabulary and style; or

b)   a different interpretation of the same Hebrew text; or

c)   go back to two distinctly different Hebrew originals.

4)   The difference between the two parts of a doublet, be they translation or transliteration, may also originate in an erroneous conception
of the one Hebrew text common to both of them, such as

a)   errors of pronunciation; they might serve as additional proof for
the already established fact (cf. p. 111 f.) that in Origen's day
and even later no uniform and authoritative pronunciation of
Hebrew can have existed, nor consideration for etymology (p. 113)
and context (p. 115 f.);

b)   confusion of letters on account of their resemblance
α)   in script (cf. p. 481, sub B)
β)   in phonetic value (cf. p. 476, § 35-53);

c)   dividing one Hebrew word into two, which leads to the assumption
that in the basic Hebrew text no extra space nor any other indicator was used to separate the words from one another (cf. p. 490,
§ 71).

5)   A so called Hexaplaric symbol may differentiate one reading of
the doublet from the other; if this be the case,

a)   the translation corresponding closer to MT has an asterisk; while

b)   the transliteration is marked by an obelus.

Since according to § 4, obelus and O′ quotations belong to one family, as differentiated from the asterisk-al ex-group (§ 5), we wish to call attention to the following passages, where under O′ a transliteration, and under al ex a translation is quoted: Gen. 18.1: ממרא: O′: τη μαμβρη; al ex: τη υψηλη. Ex. 18.1: מדין: O′: μαδιαμ; al ex: κυριου. Deut. 3.17: הפסגה: O′: την φασγα; al ex: την φαραγγα.

6) The existence of doublets further substantiates our conclusion in § 6 that the Hexapla is based upon two main sources; the examples listed in § 8g show that their number did not exceed two; for the doublets quoted under the authority of O′ are practically identical with those brought as *alia exemplaria*. With our conclusions in § 6 in mind, we would call these sources

a) the obelus group, and
b) the asterisk group.

7) Both groups must be regarded as genuine "LXX," since they are quoted as such and were embodied in the fifth column of the Hexapla, which contained the LXX.

8) The differences in their Hebrew original which they reflect (cf. above 3c and 4) prove that they represent two independent translations of the Hebrew Bible into Greek.

9) While reconstructing their underlying Hebrew texts we realize the futility of any attempt to compromise between them and to unite them on a common basis. On the contrary, we shall have to look for the *two Hebrew Bibles*, each of which shares with the corresponding Greek translation their respective characteristic features and particular readings (cf. p. 364 ff.).

10) The very fact that doublets also represent a combination of Greek synonyms, or otherwise demonstrate the two possibilities of expressing the same Hebrew word or phrase in Greek, is conclusive evidence that Origen made use of Greek Bible texts only, and did not consult the Hebrew Bible of his day (which is the hitherto generally accepted theory, see p. 332 f.). A mere glance into a Hebrew Bible would have convinced him that the Hebrew word in question was already represented in the Greek translation, thus excluding the possibility of combining two

readings of this type into a doublet. On the other hand, while comparing two *Greek* Bibles, one offering, e.g., in 1 Ki. 6.1: του βασιλεως, the other βασιλευοντος, he was right in noting one as a variant (cf. § 3) on the margin, wherefrom it was later included in the text proper. Had Origen known enough Hebrew to verify these readings in the *Hebrew* Bible, he would have noticed that both are based upon one and the same Hebrew word למלך. Thus, Origen's work on the LXX consisted merely in collating Greek manuscripts belonging to one or the other of the two groups of translations (obelus and asterisk group), which in themselves are representatives of different Hebrew Bible types (cf. under no. 9).

The problem before us now is: to search for Hebrew Bible texts, which might justly be considered to reflect the Hebrew prototypes of the aforesaid two Greek Bible types (cf. above under 9). These Greek types were translations; and it may be said of them, too, what I pointed out some time ago with regard to the importance of the Variants in the larger Cambridge LXX edition for the historic development of the Hebrew Bible: "Eine Übersetzung ist die Wiedergabe eines *bestehenden* Textes; also muss der Text jeder Septuaginta-Handschrift zu irgend einer Zeit auch tatsächlich existiert haben und im Umlauf gewesen sein" (*Septuaginta-Probleme*, Stuttgart 1929, 79).

But first we wish to establish beyond doubt the correctness of our assertion that there are only two and not more Greek LXX translations we have to reckon with.

§ 10   Inner Greek Development of Hexaplaric Septuagint-Quotations.

In Field's collection of LXX quotations from the Hexapla, which forms the basis of this study (cf. our statement on p. 335), we sometimes come across passages which are recorded under the authorities of O', *alia exemplaria* and *alia*, respectively; this latter term *alia* is to my knowledge at least in one connection (Ex. 23.18) mentioned even twice. This might be taken as a indication for a corresponding number of independent sources of the fifth column of the Hexapla, namely three or even four translations, as against the two we upheld. However, an examination of quotations of this kind reveals them to be nothing else but later inner Greek developments of the genuine LXX quotations, the number of which does not exceed two. For like every other ancient text, these genuine passages were subject to changes by the hands of subsequent copyists, which, if wittingly made, may have been meant to improve on their language and style, or else were simply the result of the copyists' lack of understanding. In this connection it will be of interest to hear even Jerome complain of such misdeeds by the copyists. In *Epist.*, LXXI, 5 (cited by Harnack, *Bible Reading in the Early Church*, 100, note 2) he writes: "Opuscula mea ad describendum hominibus tuis dedi et descripta vidi in chartaceis codicibus ac frequenter admonui, ut conferrent diligentius et emendarent. ego enim tanta volumina prae frequentia commeantium et peregrinorum turbis relegere non potui . . . . Unde si paragrammata repereris vel minus aliqua descripta sunt, quae sensum legentis impediant, non mihi debes imputare, sed tuis et imperitiae notariorum librariorumque incuriae, qui scribunt non quod inveniunt, sed quod intelligunt, et dum alienos errores emendare nituntur, ostendunt suos." Cf. also above § 2.

This account of the bad experience which Jerome had from having to rely on copyists will help us understand the genesis of certain readings of the Hexapla. We shall illustrate this by a few examples, which we re-arrange in such a way as to demonstrate it beyond doubt that the underlying cause is solely inner Greek corruption and that they are entirely independent of the Hebrew Bible text.

a) *Three Greek readings based upon one translation.*

Ex. 6.22: סתרי: O′: σεγρει al ex: σετρει; *alia*: σεθρει. Considering the fact that ת as a rule is transliterated by θ (cf. p. 177 under ת), which letter could phonetically be confused with τ, thus finally leading to a graphic confusion between Τ and Γ (cf. Thompson, Facs., 3), the chronological arrangement of these readings is just the reverse: σεθρει — σετρει — σεγρει.

Ex. 23.28: וגרשה: O′: και εκβαλεις; al ex: και εκβαλει; *alia:* και εκβαλω. The O′ reading yields no sense, since not Israel but the הצרעה will be used as an instrument for driving the enemy out of the country. For this very reason the reading of *alia* in the first person is a corruption, too. Thus, εκβαλει represents the only genuine Greek translation, εκβαλεις being a graphic error, and εκβαλω an erroneous adjustment to the first person in the preceding verb αποστελω.

Num. 16.3: ויקהלו: O': συνεστησαν; al ex: συνεπεστησαν; *alia*: επισυνεστη-σαν. Compound and decompound, the latter differing in the order of the particles used for its formation.

Deut. 7.1: כי יביאך: O': εαν δε εισαγη; al ex: οταν εισαγαγη; *alia:* εν τω εισαγαγειν. The various possibilities of rendering such conditional sentences in Greek can also be seen from Ex. 6.13: להוציא: al ex: ωστε εξαγαγειν; *alia:* ινα εξαγαγη.

Deut. 28.27: ובעפלים: O': εις την εδραν; al ex: εις τας εδρας; *alia:* εν ταις εδραις. Cf. *Tarbiz*, VI, 16, paragraph 7.

In the same manner the four readings of Ex. 23.18 referred to above can be reduced to two. I bring them first in the same order as they are listed in Field's opus:

Ex. 23.18: זבחי: O': θυμιαματος μου; al ex: θυσιασματος μου; *alia*: αγιασματος μου; *alia*: θυμιασματος μου. I would suggest the following order: θυμιαματος — θυμιασματος — θυσιασματος. It becomes evident that these are merely inner Greek changes, which are in no way influenced by the Hebrew text. The only real variant reading that remains is αγιασματος; no further developments of this reading are recorded by Field.

b)   Three readings representing two genuine variants.

1)   The O' quotation in two forms.

Lev. 4.7: העלה: O': των ολοκαυτωματων; al ex: της καρπωσεως; *alia*: της ολοκαυτωσεως. ολοκαυτωματων and ολοκαυτωσεως are two shades of one and the same rendering; cf. similarly κατακαυμα and κατακαυσις in JBL, 1935, 86, paragraph VIII.

Lev. 9.4: בלולה: O': πεφυραμενην; al ex: αναπεφυραμενην; *alia*: αναπεποιη-μενην. This arrangement indicates that under al ex a compound verb is cited of the O' reading; cf. also JBL, 1935, 87 paragraph IX; *Tarbiz*, VI, 16, paragraph 8.

Deut. 24.14: לא תעשק: O': ουκ απαδικησεις; al ex: ουκ αδικησεις; *alia*: ουκ αποστερησεις. On the relation of the verb αδικησεις to its compound απαδικησεις cf. our remark to the preceding example.

Deut. 32.43: יקום: O': εκδικαται; al ex: εκδικειται; *alia*: εκζητειται Cf. JBL, 1935, 85, s.v. נקם. On εκδικαομαι and εκδικεομαι cf. Walter

Bauer, *Griechisch-Deutsches Wörterbuch zu den Schriften des Neuen Testament*, 1928, Zur Einführung, p. XV.

2)   The al ex quotation in two forms.

The difference consists in a change of the word-order (cf. *Tarbiz*, VI, 19, paragraph 10).

Deut. 22.17: והנה הוא: O': νυν ουτος; al ex: νυν αυτος; *alia*: αυτος νυν.

Deut. 23.10: מחנה: O': παρεμβαλειν; al ex: εις πολεμον παρεμβαλειν; *alia*: παρεμβαλειν εις πολεμον.

Deut. 28.66: לך מנגד: O': απεναντι των οφθαλμων σου; al ex: σοι απεναντι; *alia*: απεναντι σου.

This material shows that while the LXX quotations of the al ex type as a whole are well preserved, those of the O' group were subject to errors and changes by the later copyists. The reason for the different fate of these quotations may be sought in the fact that the O' type gradually became the authoritatiye text, displacing the al ex type, and was therefore more frequently copied.

c)   *Three translations?*

The only instances to my knowledge which might, but not necessarily need, be considered as reflecting three genuine translations, are:

Ex. 4.10: איש דברים: O': ικανος ειμι; al ex: ευλογος ειμι; *alia*: ευλαλος ειμι.

Lev. 22.15: ירימו: O': αφαιρουσι; al ex: αφοριουσι; *alia*: αναφερουσι.

Num. 34.29: לנחל: O': καταμερισαι; al ex: καταμετρησαι; *alia*: κατακληρονομησαι.

Deut. 31.5: לפניכם: O': υμιν; al ex: ενωπιον υμων; *alia*: εις τας χειρας υμων.

I would not attribute too much importance to these four instances; they surely cannot upset the results of our investigation. I am inclined to explain these cases as a Church Fathers' confusion between the fifth column of the *Hexapla* (containing the LXX) and some other column (containing a later Greek Bible translation).

F.　THE HEBREW BIBLE ACCORDING TO THE HEXAPLA

a.　*The Hebrew Original of the obelus-group*

In the course of my studies on Hebrew grammar I became more and more convinced that the Hebrew Pentateuch of the Samaritans does not represent the Bible of the heretic sect of the Samaritans, but was originally another recension of the Hebrew Pentateuch, which might well compare with our MT. Comparing this form of the Hebrew Pentateuch with the obelus readings of the Hexapla, I was surpriced to see how many agreements between both of them could thus be established. In keeping with my policy throughout, I do not aim at completeness in the following list; all I have in mind is to demonstrate the close affinity of the Hebrew and Greek texts. To this end I quote first, as always here, the respective passage of the Hebrew Bible in its Masoretic form:

Gen. 1.14: יהי מארת ברקיע השמים: O': γενηθητωσαν φωστηρες εν τω στε-ρεωματι του ουρανου ÷ εις φαυσιν επι της γης ×; cf. in the Samaritan Pentateuch: יהי מאורות ברקיע השמים להאיר על הארץ.

Gen. 4.8: ויאמר קין אל הבל אחיו: O': και ειπε καιν προς αβελ τον αδελφον αυτου ÷ διελθωμεν εις το πεδιον ×; cf. SAM: ויאמר קין אל הבל אחיו נלכה השדה.

Ex. 4.6: ויוצאה: O': και εξηνεγκε αυτην ÷ εκ του κολπου αυτου ×; cf. SAM: ויציאה מחיקו.

Ex. 8.5: ומבתיך: O': ÷ και απο του λαου σου × και εκ των οικιων υμων; cf. SAM: ומבתיך ומעבדיך ומעמך.

Ex. 12.40: במצרים: O': εν γη αιγυπτω ÷ και εν χανααν ×; cf. SAM: בארץ כנען ובארץ מצרים.

Ex. 22.4: בשדה אחר: O': αγρον ετερον ÷ αποτισει εκ του αγρου αυτου κατα το γεννημα αυτου· εαν δε παντα τον αγρον καταβοσκηση ×; cf. SAM: בשדה אחר שלם ישלם משדהו כתבואתה ואם כל שדה יבעה.

Ex. 26.16: ארך הקרש: O': ποιησεις τον στυλον τον ενα; al ex: ⁒ μηκος × ÷ ποιησεις × τον στυλον ÷ τον ενα ×; cf. SAM: ארך הקרש האחד; on ÷ ποιησεις × cf. verses 10 and 20, where in SAM the verb תעשה is added.

Ex. 33.2: את הכנעני האמרי והחתי והפרזי החוי והיבוסי: O': τον αμορραιον και τον χετταιον και φερεζαιον και γεργεσσαιον και ευαιον και ιεβουσαιον

και χαναναιον; al ex: τον χαναναιον ÷ και ✕ τον αμορραιον και τον
χετταιον και τον φερεζαιον ÷ και τον γεργεσαιον ✕ και τον ευαιον και τον
ιεβουσαιον; cf. SAM: את הכנעני והאמרי והחתי והגרגשי והפרזי והחוי והיבוסי.
Similarly in Ex. 34.11: al ex: ÷ και τον γεργεσαιον ✕ has its
equivalent in the addition of SAM: והגרגשי.

Ex. 35.22: וכומז: O': ÷ και εμπλοκια ✕ και περιδεξια; cf. SAM: עגיל וכומז.

Lev. 19.20: בקרת תהיה: O': επισκοπη εσται ÷ αυτοις ✕; similarly SAM:
בקרת תהיה לו.

Num. 1.44: איש אחד לבית אבתיו היו: Aliter: O': ανηρ εις ÷ κατα φυλην
μιαν, κατα φυλην ✕ εις οικον πατριας αυτων ησαν; cf. SAM: איש אחד
למטה אחד למטה בית אבתם היו.

Deut. 9.28: פן יאמרו הארץ: O': μη ειπωσιν ÷ οι κατοικουντες την γην ✕;
similarly SAM: פן יאמרו עם הארץ.

Deut. 10.11: לפני העם: O': εναντιον του λαου ÷ τουτου ✕; cf. SAM:
לפני העם הזה.

Deut. 14.8: ולא גרה: O': και ÷ ονυχιζει ονυχιστηρας οπλης και τουτο μηρυ-
κισμον ✕ ου μαρυκαται; cf. SAM: ושסע שסע פרסה והוא גרה לא יסר.

Deut. 18.5: לעמד לשרת בשם יהוה: O': παρεσταναι ÷ εναντι κυριου του θεου
✕ λειτουργειν ÷ και ευλογειν ✕ επι τω ονοματι αυτου; cf. SAM: לעמד
לפני יהוה אלהיך לשרתו ולברך בשמו.

The preceding examples show the direct interdependence between the
obelus type and the corresponding textual readings of the Hebrew Pentateuch of the Samaritans. But the relationship between these two Bible
texts can also be demonstrated indirectly by certain characteristics
in the structure of the narrative (*Formgeschichte*), which they have in
common: In Gen. 31.11 ff. Jacob tells Rachel and Lea of a vision which
he had in connection with and approving of his intended return to his
native land: ויאמר אלי מלאך האלהים בחלום יעקב ואמר הנני: ויאמר שא נא עיניך וראה
כל העתדים העלים על הצאן עקדים נקדים וברדים כי ראיתי את כל אשר לבן עשה לך:
אנכי האל בית אל אשר משחת שם מצבה אשר נדרת לי שם נדר עתה קום צא מן הארץ
הזאת ושוב אל ארץ מולדתך. But we search the Bible in vain for the original
narrative of this vision and the time and the place when and where it
happened, in order to confirm Jacob's report. The MT is here of no use; but
the Samaritan Pentateuch brings after Gen. 30.36 such a report, in the
same words as used in both MT and Sam later on in Gen. 31.11-13,

merely changing the first person of ואמר into the third ויאמר so as to fit in the context as the annalists record.

Similarly in Gen. 44.22: Judah argues with Joseph for the release of Benjamin and says: ונאמר אל אדני לא יוכל הנער לעזב את אביו ועזב את אביו ומת. In MT, no record of the original remark of the brothers to this effect is preserved. But here, too, it is the SAM, which on Gen. 42.16 offers this report, again in the same words as SAM and MT have it on Gen. 44.22, with the first person ונאמר changed into the third ויאמרו. Thus, the reader of the Pentateuch in the Samaritan recension is in a position to ascertain that the vision of Jacob and the argument of Judah are not merely made up *ad hoc*, because Jacob and Judah needed them in their respective situation, but are well founded on the preceding records of the objective annalist. In other words: *the historic narrative is now complete*: The vision of the angel leads Jacob to action; the brothers premonition, that Benjamin's departure from his father's house may cause the latter's death, is about to become true.

This characteristic of the SAM has a parallel in the obelus text: In Josh. 6.26 Joshua curses the man, who might attempt to rebuild the city of Jericho, which he had just destroyed. However, his curse did not deter later generations; cf. 1 Ki. 16.34; but the curse became true. Origen on Josh. 6.26 adds *sub obelo* the report of 1 Ki. 16.34.

According to Josh. 16.10 the Canaanites remained as a tributary nation in Gezer in the midst of the Ephraimites עד היום הזה. Origen adds *sub obelo* the passage 1 Ki. 9.16 where the final destruction of Gezer by Pharaoh is reported; the time-limit for "unto this day" is thus given. In these cases the historic narrative of the book of Joshua appears now complete, as far as Biblical sources are concerned.

As similiar cases I wish to note: Num. 14.22, 23: כל האנשים הראים את כבדי ואת אתתי אשר עשיתי במצרים .... אם יראו את הארץ. Here the punishment is pronounced that none of the generation which was redeemed from Egypt shall see the promised land. But the verses 30 and 33 grant mercy to their children, who will be privileged to enter it. Origen limits right from the start the judgment of v. 23 to the adult generation by adding *sub obelo* Deut. 1.39.

Josh. 20.3: here Origen quotes *sub obelo* Num. 35.12. I am under the impression that these additions in the SAM and *sub obelo* in Origen reflect one and the same tendency in narrating Biblical history: to supplement the running narrative from related sources, so as to present the reader with a complete description of the events. (Cf. MH §§ 109-112).

I do not intend to advocate a theory that the Samaritan Pentateuch as it presents itself to us now is *the* Hebrew original of the Greek translation from which citations marked by an obelus in the *Hexapla* emanated. I have already demonstrated that our Samaritan Pentateuch must not be identified with that textual form, under which it was known and pubblished even as late as the days of Jerome; cf. pp. 231 ff. All I mean to say in explaining this coincidence between the quotations *sub obelo* and the actual Hebrew readings of the Samaritan Pentateuch is that the Hebrew Bible, which served as original to that particular type of the LXX which we call the obelus type, belonged to a family of Hebrew Bible tradition, an offspring of which we still possess in the Samaritan Pentateuch.

One more point remains, which has to be clarified: The obelus group of LXX citations is still preserved representing nearly all the books of the OT, while the Samaritan Pentateuch embraces, as the name indicates, merely the Pentateuch. How, then, shall we account for the Hebrew original of the remaining parts of the OT? We shall realize the full importance of this problem if we recall to our minds that the obelus *group* of the Hexaplaric LXX text consist not only of those quotations which are marked by an obelus, but also includes the numerous citations listed under O′ and spread over all the OT; cf. especially the results we arrived at concerning codex B on p. 369 ff. Consequently, we shall have to assume that the Samaritan Hebrew Bible originally included the entire OT. This assumption falls in line with the results I arrived at in my grammatical studies. For the time being I limit myself to the conclusion that the *obelus-group of the LXX according to the Hexapla was a translation into Greek of a Hebrew Bible, which at that time covered all of the OT and of which we still have in the Samaritan Pentateuch a direct offspring in Hebrew.*

b. *The Hebrew Original of the Asterisk Group*

Generally speaking, the readings marked by an asterisk as well as those cited under al. ex. are exact translations into Greek of the respective

Hebrew passages according to the Masoretic text. I wish to demonstrate
the painstaking care which the asterisk type takes in order to give an
exact and literal translation of the MT, by pointing out a few examples,
where such slavishly literal translations *sub asterisco* spoilt the otherwise
readable Greek of the respective sentence, and result in tautology, since
the asteriscized words are already contained in the free renderings
under O':

Gen. 32.14: מן הבא בידו :O': ων εφερεν ⁛ εν χειρι αυτου ⨯.

Gen. 33.1: וישא יעקב עיניו :O': αναβλεψας δε ιακωβ ⁛ τοις οφθαλμοις
αυτου ⨯.

Gen. 34.21: רחבת ידים :O': πλατεια ⁛ εν χερσιν ⨯.

Ex. 18.7: וישאלו איש לרעהו לשלום :O': και ησπασαντο αλληλους ⁛ εις
ειρηνην ⨯.

Deut. 1.7: ובחוף הים :O': και παραλιαν ⁛ θαλασσης ⨯.

Deut. 2.5: עד מדרך כף רגל :O': ουδε βημα ⁛ ιχνους ⨯ ποδος.

Ps. 104.25: ורחב ידים :O': και ευρυχωρος ⁛ χερσιν ⨯ ; cf. Judg. 18.10.

But in view of the fact that some readings of this asterisk type can be
found, which do not have their equivalent in MT, we would prefer to
formulate our statement in a less positive way, and say: it is evident that
the Hebrew Bible used as an original for that Greek translation, quotations
from which are brought in Field's collection of material *sub asterisco* or
under al ex, was most closely related to that textual family of the Hebrew
Bible which is known to us as MT.

It is superfluous to bring examples for the agreement between the
asterisk group and MT; this is the rule, and the reader can convince
himself by opening Field at mere chance. We, therefore, confine ourselves
to prove the existence of exceptions: asterisk readings without a corresponding Hebrew original in our MT; for another possible explanation cf.
p. 339 sub a and b on the reliability of the tradition concerning the
Hexaplaric symbols.

Lev. 22.21: ואיש כי יקריב :O': και ανθρωπος ος αν προσενεγκη ⁛ τα δωρα
αυτου κατα πασαν ομολογιαν αυτων η κατα πασαν αιρεσιν αυτων ⨯ ; cf.
Lev. 22.18.

Josh. 9.24: ונעשה: O': και εποιησαμεν; al ex: ⁕ ως ουχ υπελειφθη εν ημιν πνευμα × και εποιησαμεν; cf. Josh. 2.11.

Josh. 11.14: בני ישראל: O': οι υιοι ισραηλ ⁕ κατα το ρημα κυριου ο ενετειλατο τω ιησου ×; cf. Josh. 8.27.

Josh. 22. 16: כל עדת יהוה: O': πασα η συναγωγη κυριου ⁕ οι υιοι ισραηλ ×; probably on account of verse 12: כל עדת בני ישראל.

Judg. 4.9: ותאמר: O': και ειπε; Aliter: O': και ειπε ⁕ προς αυτον δεββωρα ×; on the addition of the subject cf. my *Septuagintaprobleme*, 60 and here p. 286, § 74c and p. 290, § 79a; further: Gen. 29.12: ויגד יעקב: O': και απηγγειλεν ⁕ ιακωβ ×.

Judg. 4.9: קדשה: O': εκ καδης; Aliter: O': εις κεδες ⁕ της νεφθαλι ×; cf. verse 6.

Judg. 9.54: אשה: O': γυνη; Aliter: O': ⁕ οτι × γυνη; cf. the following passages, where οτι appears *sub asterisco*, corresponding to MT כי: Deut. 15.8: כי פתח: O': ⁕ οτι × ανοιγων; Ps. 116.16: כי אני: O': ⁕ οτι × εγω; Ps. 118.10: כי: O': ⁕ οτι ×.

1 Sam. 20.9: ויאמר יהונתן: O': και ειπεν ιωναθαν ⁕ προς δαυιδ × cf. verses 4, 11 and 12.

1 Ki. 21.29: בימי: O': ⁕ αλλ × εν ταις ημεραις.

2 Ki. 19.16: את דברי: O': ⁕ παντας × τους λογους; cf. in the following passages πας and its derivatives *sub asterisco*, while MT offers the equivalent form of כל: Deut. 4.19; 5.23, 26, 28; 12.2, 21.

Am. 6.8: מתאב: O': ⁕ διοτι × βδελυσσομαι; cf. similarly Zech. 13.5: איש עבד אדמה אנכי: O': ⁕ διοτι ανθρωπος εργαζομενος την γην εγω ειμι ×; thus, *sub asterisco* MT is translated with διοτι as introductory particle.

III. ANCIENT BIBLE VERSIONS AS EVIDENCE

A. THE OLDEST MANUSCRIPTS OF THE BIBLE IN GREEK

A. CODICES B AND A ON THE PENTATEUCH

On p. 227, I showed that "by applying the results of this study to the LXX, we are in a position to differentiate between the various sources, by the combination of which an apparently uniform LXX text arose". I thus made it clear that both codices, B and A, "not only when considered as entities covering the entire Bible, but even on the single Biblical books, go back to different sources.... We thus realize that one of the most significant criteria of the works of those early centuries is their mixed type" (p. 228).

We now wish to substantiate this statement by an examination of the LXX on the Pentateuch, since this part of the LXX represents, according to Jerome's testimony, a more careful translation of the Hebrew text than the rest of it: "accedit ad hoc quod quoque Josephus, qui LXX interpretum proponit historiam, *quinque* tantum ab eis *libros Moysii translatos* refert, quos nos quoque *confitemur plus quam ceteros cum Hebraicis consonare.*" (*Hieronymi quaestiones hebraicae in libro Geneseos* a recognitione Pauli de Lagarde, Lipsia, 1886, 2 f.). We shall base our investigation on Swete's edition. In this edition for the first time the text is taken from Codex B, except for the missing chapters Gen. 1-46.28, where Codex A is being substituted. This combination of the two oldest manuscripts of the LXX on the Pentateuch will be the basis for our examination, too, which will thus shed light upon both of them.

This method of basing the text of the LXX edition on codex B and merely filling the missing chapters according to codex A, has been followed also in subsequent editions: the larger Cambridge edition by Brooke-McLean, and Alfred Rahlfs in his *Septuaginta id est Vetus Testamentum Graece iuxta LXX interpretes*, (Stuttgart 1935). It may be of interest to note here that out of the approximately seventy doublets from the LXX on the Pentateuch alone which we are going to discuss here, only in the following five cases has one component of the doublet been eliminated by Rahlfs from his basic text: Gen. 23.13; Ex. 25.23; Lev. 8.5; Deut. 4.20 and 8.4. Rahlfs does not account for the principles, which have been guiding him in his selection: which one of the two parts of a doublet ro retain and which to reject. But we wish to emphasize that we cannot agree with the results of his selections. In Lev. 8.5, זה הדבר, he preserves τουτο εστιν το ρημα and eliminates τουτο εστι; but in § 9a we are going to prove that "the literal translation of דבר by ρημα is characteristic for the asterisk type of the Hexaplaric LXX"; and since codex B as an entity "shows close affinity to the obelus type" (p. 386), Rahlfs has thus given the preference exactly to the wrong component. In Lev. 15.1 he simply changes the position of και ααρων; he thus obtains, it is true, a smoothly worded verse, but a verse of his own making (cf. § 1). And the remaining more than sixty doublets he left unchallenged at all.

This shows, how far his publication is from a real edition of the LXX!

Our own procedure will be similar to that which we applied in discussing the *Hexapla*; here, too, the existence of doublets proves to be most helpful. By our very method of grouping and classifying them we shall indicate their origin and finally arrive at conclusions as to the nature and the main characteristics of the two genuine texts, in the combination of whose readings our doublets originate. The readings of the basic LXX text (B or A, respectively) of Swete's edition will be quoted here under G.

In order to save space, I refrained as far as feasible from bringing evidence for the separate use of each of these components of the doublets as equivalents of the respective Hebrew words. Such passages can easily be traced with the help of Hatch and Redpath's *Concordance*.

§ 1. The Doublet Originates in a Marginal Note.

This is obvious from the fact that doublets were inserted at a wrong place, where they do not fit into the syntax of the sentence:

Gen. 24.5: אחרי: G: μετ εμου // οπισω. οπισω was noted as a variant to μετα; cf. JBL, 1935, 84, paragraph VI s.v. עם. The two translations in full would be: μετ εμου // οπισω μου; cf. Gen. 24.39: אחרי: G: μετ εμου.

Ex. 28.32: בתוכו: G: εξ αυτου // μεσον. In readable Greek, the inclusion of μεσον, which in itself is an exact rendering of תוך according to the asterisk type of the Hexaplaric LXX (cf. p. 341, § 3a, the instance from Josh. 4.10), would result in εκ μεσου αυτου.

Lev. 15.1: אל משה ואל אהרן לאמר: G: προς μωυσην λεγων // και ααρων. The correct word-order would be: προς μωυσην και ααρων λεγων. Prior to the inclusion of this gloss, the Greek text contained no reference to Aaron.

§ 2. The Sources of the Doublet.

a) The obelus text forms one source.

Gen. 20.4: צדיק: G: αγνοουν // και δικαιον; cf. O': ÷ αγνοουν ✕ και δικαιον.

Ex. 15.4: שלשיו: G: αναβατας // τριστατας; cf. O': ÷ αναβατας ✕ τριστατας; cf. also Ex. 14.7: ושלשם: G: και τριστατας; on the other hand, αναβατης is the equivalent of Hebrew פרש.

Ex. 33.5: עֲדְיְךָ: G: τας στολας των δοξων υμων // και τον κοσμον; cf. O': ÷ τας στολας των δοξων υμων και ⨯ τον κοσμον.

Ex. 25.17: כפרת: G: ιλαστηριον // επιθεμα; cf. O': ιλαστηριον ÷ επιθεμα ⨯.

Num. 15.19: תרומה: G: αφαιρεμα // αφορισμα; cf. al ex: αφαιρεμα τω κυριω ÷ αφορισμαι ⨯. תרומה is translated by G in Num. 15.20: αφαιρεμα, in Ex. 29.28: αφορισμα.

b) *O' and al ex texts combined.*

Ex. 34.15: ליושב: G: τοις ενκαθημενοις // προς αλλοφυλους; cf. O': τοις εγκαθημενοις; al ex: προς αλλοφυλους.

c) *Stylistic adjustment of O' and al ex readings.*

Gen. 15.11: הפגרים: G: τα σωματα // τα διχοτομηματα; cf. O': επι τα σωματα ÷ επι τα διχοτομηματα αυτων ⨯; al ex: επι τα σωματα τα διχοτομηθεντα. Cf. also Lev. 1.8: הנתחים: G: τα διχοτομηματα.

§ 3. The Doublet preserves the Full Source of an Abridged Asterisk-Reading.

Ex. 26.13: בעדף בארך יריעת: G: εκ του υπερεχοντος των δερρεων // εκ του μηκους των δερρεων; cf. al ex: εκ του υπερεχοντος ※ του μηκους ⨯ των δερρεων; see also above p. 349 δ 3.

§ 4. Combination of Literal and Free Translations.

Gen. 3.6: לעינים: G: τοις οφθαλμοις // ιδειν.

Gen. 3.14: גחנך: G: τω στηθει σου // και τη κοιλια; cf. Lev. 11.42: על גחון: G: επι κοιλιας; Ex. 28.30: על לב אהרן G: επι του στηθους ααρων, also free translation.

Gen. 23.13: באזני: G: εις τα ωτα // εναντιον; cf. ib. verse 16: באזני: G: εις τα ωτα; Gen. 44.18: באזני: εναντιον.

Num. 6.7: על ראשו: G: επ αυτω // επι κεφαλης αυτου.

§ 5. Difference in the Exegesis.

Gen. 18.10: כעת: G: κατα τον καιρον τουτον // εις ωρας; cf. ib. 21.22; 38.1: בעת ההיא: G: εν τω καιρω εκεινω; Ex. 9.18: כעת: G: ταυτην την ωραν.

Ex. 27.20: למאור: G: εις φως // καυσαι.

Lev. 26.22: השדה: G: τα αγρια // της γης; an adjective in the nominative and a noun in the genitive; cf. similarly Ex. 1.19: המצרית: O': αιγυπ-του; al ex: αιγυπτιαι; Ps. 104.4: אש להט: G: πυρ φλεγον, quoted in Heb. 1.7 as πυρος φλογα (the context requires the accus.).

Num. 27.14: להקדישני: G: αγιασαι με // ουχ ηγιασατε με. On the interpre-tation of the particle ל as negation (=לא), cf. Gen. 4.15; 30.15: לכן: G: ουχ ουτως.

Ex. 10.5: הנשארת: G: το καταλειφθεν // ο κατελιπεν.

Lev. 14.48: לא פשה: G: ου διαχυσει // ου διαχειται.

§ 6. Combination of Translation and Transliteration.

Cf. JBL, 1935, 83, paragraph III: in both cases listed there, codex B offers a translation of the Hebrew word in question.

Gen. 22.13: בסבך: G: εν φυτω // σαβεκ; cf. ch. 00, s.v. סבך.

Num. 25.15: אמות: G: εθνους // ομμοθ.

Gen. 19.38: בן עמי: G: αμμαν // ο υιος του γενους μου. The transliterator apparently read עמון in his Hebrew text.

§ 7.   The Doublet goes back to a Translator's Mistake.

a) Phonetic confusion.

Gen. 13.14: אתה G: νυν // συ; cf. ib. 26.29: אתה עתה: G: και νυν συ. On the phonetic similarity of א and ע cf. p. 170/71 and p. 174 f. under א and ע; p. 477, § 37.

Gen. 28.18: שָׂם: G: εθηκεν // εκει; cf. Ex. 15.25: שָׁם שָׂם: G: εκει εθετο. On the pronunciation of ש cf. p. 172; see also p. 479, § 44.

Ex. 10.4: ארבה: G: ακριδα // πολλην; this corresponds to MT and הרבה. On the interchangeability of א and ה, due to their pronunciation, cf. p. 170/71 and p. 174 f. under א and ה; p. 476, § 35.

b) Graphic confusion.

Gen. 28.20: אם יהיה: G: εαν η // κυριος. This implies the reading of the Hebrew original once as יהיה (=MT), and once as יהוה; on the con-fusion between י and ו cf. p. 484, § 64.

§ 8.   Translation of Particles.

Lev. 27.18: אחר: G: εσχατον // μετα.

Gen. 38.1: עד: G: εως // προς.

Lev. 27. 18: עד: G: εως // εις.

Deut. 31.6: עמך: G: μεθ υμων // εν υμιν; cf. Lev. 25.45: עמכם: O′: Vacat; al ex: μεθ υμων; *alia*: εν υμιν; cf. also Isa. 53.12: ואת פשעים נמנה: G: και εν τοις ανομοις ελογισθη, which is quoted Luke 22.37 as και μετα ανομων ελογισθη.

9.   Combination of two Translations.

a)   *Asyndetic connection.*

Gen. 2.9: הדעת: G: του ειδεναι // γνωστον; cf. Ex. 22.9: ראה: O′: γνω; al ex: ιδη; Deut. 29.2: ראו: O′: εωρακασιν; al ex: ειδον; Ex. 33.16: יודע: G: γνωστον εσται.

Gen. 48.16: לרב: G: εις πληθος // πολυ.

Ex. 1.9: רב: μεγα // πληθος; cf. Gen. 45.28: רב: G: μεγα; Ex 19.21: רב: G: πληθος.

Ex. 28.6: מעשה חשב: G: εργον υφαντου // ποικιλτου; cf. the rendering of מעשה חשב by G in Ex. 26.1 as εργασια υφαντου; ib. 26.31 as εργον υφαντον; and ib. 28.15 as εργον ποικιλτου.

Ex. 28.33: רמני: G: ωσει εξανθουσης ροας // ροισκους.

Ex. 28.34: פעמן זהב: G: παρα ροισκον χρυσουν // κωδωνα; cf. verse 33 below under b.

Ex. 30.8: תמיד: G: ενδελεχισμου // δια παντος; cf. the translation of תמיד in Ex. 29.42; Num. 28.6: G: ενδελεχισμου; but Ex. 27.20, 28.30: G: δια παντος.

Ex. 35.6: ותולעת שני: G: κοκκινον διπλουν // διανενησμενον; cf. the rendering of this Hebrew phrase by G in Ex. 25.4: κοκκινον διπλουν, and Ex. 28.8: κοκκινου διανενησμενου.

Lev. 8.5: זה הדבר: G: τουτο εστιν το ρημα // τουτο εστιν. The literal translation of דבר by ρημα is characteristic for the asterisk-type of the Hexaplaric Septuagint; cf. Gen. 20.10; Ex. 18.14: הדבר הזה: O′: ※ το ρημα ✕ τουτο; Gen. 37.14; Josh. 21.43: דבר: O′: ※ ρημα ✕.

Deut. 8.4: ורגלך: G: τα υποδηματα σου // οι ποδες σου.

b) *Connected by* και.

Gen. 27.45: אַף: G: τον θυμον // και την οργην; cf. Gen. 49.6: באפם: G: εν τω θυμω αυτων; ib. verse 7: אפם: G: ο θυμος αυτων; but Gen. 39.19: אפו: G: οργη.

Ex. 15.18: לעולם: G: τον αιωνα // και επ αιωνα.

Ex. 22.16: מאן ימאן: G: ανανευων ανανευση // και μη βουληται.

Ex. 28.33: ופעמני זהב: G: το αυτο ειδος ροισκους χρυσους // και κωδωνας; cf. verse 34 above under *a*.

Ex. 33.6: עדים: G: τον κοσμον αυτων // και την περιστολην; cf. verse 5 above p. 352, § 8c β 2 ב.

Lev. 23.40: וערבי: G: και ιτεας // και αγνου κλαδου.

Deut. 3.24: את גדלך: G: την ισχυν σου // και την δυναμιν σου; cf. την ισχυν μου in G Ex. 9.16, quoted in Rom. 9.17 as την δυναμιν μου.

c) *The two translations separated from one another.*

Bearing in mind that doublets originate in marginal glosses, which were included in the text by later copyists (cf. p. 346, § 7), we shall explain the following instances as inclusions at the wrong place; cf. similar mis-placements Lev. 13.37 in § 10 and Ex. 12.5 above on p. 355, § 8 e β 1.

Gen. 15.13: וענו אתם: G: και κακωσουσιν αυτο ... // ... και ταπεινωσουσιν αυτους; cf. Gen. 16.6: ותענה: G: και εκακωσεν αυτην; but ib. verse 9: והתעני: G: και ταπεινωθητι.

Ex. 6.7: לי: G: εμαυτω // ... εμοι.

Ex. 26.3: אשה אל אחתה (1°): G: εξ αλληλων ... // ... η ετερα εκ της ετερας; cf. ib. verse 6: אשה אל אחתה: G: ετεραν τη ετερα.

Ex. 26.12: בעדף ביריעת האהל ··· תסרח: G: το πλεοναζον εν ταις δερρεσιν της σκηνης ... υποκαλυψεις ... // ... το πλεοναζον των δερρεων της σκηνης υποκαλυψεις.

Lev. 17.3, 4: או אשר ישחט מחוץ למחנה: ואל פתח אהל מועד לא הביאו להקריב קרבן ליהוה: G: και ος αν σφαξη εξω της παρεμβολης και επι την θυραν της σκηνης του μαρτυριου μη ενεγκη ωστε ποιησαι αυτο εις ολοκαυτωμα ... // ... και ος αν σφαξη εξω και επι την θυραν της σκηνης του μαρτυριου μη ενεγκη αυτο ωστε προσενεγκαι δωρον κυριου.

Num. 5.8: אליו: G: αυτω ... // ... προς αυτον.

d) Amalgamation of a doublet into one reading.

In the following two cases I am inclined to see a fusion of two genuine translations, which were based upon corresponding Hebrew texts, the characteristic difference of which was their word-order with regard to the particle כל, cf. p. 289, § 78,4. Similar cases of such amalgamations see below in § 10 the instances from Lev. 13.13 and Ex. 25.23.

Gen. 8.9: על פני כל הארץ: G: επι παντι προσωπω πασης της γης. As basic readings I assume: 1. επι προσωπω πασης της γης=MT; 2. επι παντι προσωπω της γης = על כל פני הארץ; cf. Gen. 41.56: על כל פני הארץ: G: επι προσωπου πασης της γης = על פני כל הארץ.

Ex. 10.6: ובתי כל מצרים: G: και πασαι αι οικιαι εν παση γη των αιγυπτιων. I divide this pleonasmus (πασαι ... παση) in: 1) και αι οικιαι εν παση γη των αιγυπτιων = MT; 2) και πασαι αι οικιαι εν τη γη των αιγυπτιων = וכל בתי מצרים. We are here concerned solely with the word-order; hence, the question whether γη των αιγυπτιων really corresponds to MT מצרים, or rather to ארץ מצרים, and whether we should not read τη γη instead of γη (haplography), is at present of no importance.

§ 10.   The Doublet reflects Hebrew Variae Lectiones.

Ex. 8.2: ותעל הצפרדע: G: και ανηγαγεν τους βατραχους // και ανεβιβασθη ο βατραχος. The Hebrew equivalents are: וַיַּעַל הצפרדע (the verb in the *hiph'il*, the noun an object in the accusative) and MT.

Ex. 26.5: אשה אל אחתה: G: αλληλαις // εις εκαστην; this corresponds to: MT and אל אַחַת.

Ex. 28.20: משבצים זהב: G: περικεκαλυμμενα χρυσιω // συνδεδεμενα εν χρυσιω. This is equivalent to מְצֻפִּים זהב and MT.

Lev. 7.3: ואת החלב המכסה את הקרב: G: και παν το στεαρ το κατακαλυπτον τα ενδοσθια // και παν το στεαρ το επι των ενδοσθιων. A combination of ואת כל החלב אשר על הקרב and ואת כל החלב המכסה את הקרב.

Lev. 13.13: וטהר את הנגע: G: και καθαριει αυτον ο ιερευς // την αφην. This is a fusion of two translations: 1) και καθαριει αυτον ο ιερευς = וטהר אתו הכֹּהֵן, and 2) και καθαριει την αφην = MT.

Lev. 13.37: בעיניו: G: επωπιον // ... επι χωρας. The first translation = MT; επι χωρας = תַּחְתָּיו; cf. ib. verse 23: תחתיה: G: κατα χωραν. On the misplacement of the doublet cf. above § 9.

Num. 28.23: הבקר: G: της δια παντος // της πρωινης. The first translation = הַתָּמִיד; the second = MT.

Deut. 4.20: ממצרים: G: εκ γης αιγυπτου // . . . εξ αιγυπτου. A combination of מארץ מצרים and MT.

Ex. 25.23: שלחן עצי שטים: G: τραπεζαν χρυσην // χρυσιου καθαρου. The two genuine translations presumably were: 1) τραπεζαν χρυσην = שלחן זָהָב, and 2) τραπεζαν χρυσιου καθαρου = שלחן זָהָב טָהוֹר; cf. § 9 d.

§ 11. General Results.

Within certain limits the results we arrived at on p. 358 ff., § 9, while summing up the classification of the doublets in the Hexaplaric LXX quotations, hold true for the present groups of Pentateuch-doublets in Codex B and Codex A, too:

1) The doublets represent a combination of

a) a translation and a transliteration (cf. p. 358, § 9 no. 2a), or

b) two translations of the Hebrew original (cf. ib. no. 2b)

2) In one case (Ex. 34.15; cf. § 2b) both sources could be traced, in quotations under O' and al ex, respectively (cf. p. 358, § 8a). In a number of further instances (§ 2a) the obelus text could be established as one of the sources (cf. p. 358, § 8c). Bearing in mind our statement in p. 358, § 9, no. 6, we shall not hesitate to assign the still unidentified translation in § 2a to the asterisk group.

3) When the doublet is formed by the combination of a literal and a free translation (cf. § 4), our remarks in oob concerning the slavishly literal character of the asterisk type of the Hexaplaric LXX furnish us with a clue for assigning the components of these doublets to their respective sources.

4) As transliterations forming one part of a LXX doublet (above no. 1a) we have to consider

a) direct transliterations: Hebrew words which are still preserved in Greek spelling (§ 6); and

b) indirect transliterations: Greek variants, which cannot be explained otherwise than as originating in a phonetic confusion of the basic Hebrew word (§ 7a). The translators must have had the word in question before them in Greek transliteration.

5) While preparing their respective basic Greek texts which form the sources for the doublets, the original translators had their Hebrew originals before them; only thus confusions of letters on the ground of their similarity in the Hebrew alphabet could occur (cf. § 7b, see also p. 358, § 9, no. 4a); the existence of phonetic confusions (cf. § 7a) must, therefore, not be misconstrued as proving a translation upon mere dictation of the Hebrew text.

B.   CODICES B AND A ON JUDGES

In his *Septuaginta Studien*, Erster Teil, Goettingen 1891, Paul de Lagarde writes (p. 3) "Im Jahre 1705 erschien zu Oxford Johann Ernst Grabes *Epistola ad Joannem Millium*, der Professor der Theologie and Principal of Sanct Edmunds Hall war, 'qua ostenditur, libri Judicum genuinam LXX interpretum versionem eam esse, quam ms. codex alexandrinus exhibet, romanam autem editionem, quod ad dictum librum, ab illa prorsus diversam, atque eandem cum hesychiana esse'." Since the Roman edition of the LXX (editio Sixtina, Rome 1587) is based upon codex B (cf. Swete, *Introduction*, p. 181), Grabe's statement means that as far as the book of Judges is concerned, the codices B and A differ so widely from one another that while the latter represents the genuine LXX, codex B must necessarily reflect the recension of Hesychius (cf. p. 331 f.). Grabe indicated the reason, why he considers the text of codex A as the "genuine LXX," and not that of codex B, by saying "libri Judicum versionem τῶν O', quam Origenes in Hexaplis exhibuit, quaque omnes fere Christianorum ecclesiae post iudaicam synagogam olim usae sunt, et orientales hodie utuntur, codice alexandrino contineri deprehendi" (quoted by Lagarde, ib.).

Inspired by Grabe, Lagarde set out to investigate the relationship of the texts which these two manuscripts exhibit on the book of Judges: "Es handelte sich für Grabe, und handelt sich zunächst auch für uns darum, den Text des Alexandrinus und den des Vaticanus, in Siglen A und B, gegen einander abzuschätzen. Diese Abschätzung kann nicht erfolgen, wenn nicht beide Gestaltungen des "Septuaginta"-texts vollständig einander gegenübergestellt werden; die Lesarten des Einen unter dem Abdrucke des Andern anzugeben hilft kaum dem, der sich Jahre lang mit Septuagintastudien beschäftigt hat, Anfängern hilft es gewiss nicht. Es muss auch der Wert der Abschriften jener zwei Gestalten des "Septuaginta"-texts dargelegt werden: darum bessere ich die Fehler und Versehen der Abschreiber in meinem Abdrucke nicht. . . . Es handelt sich darum, den Text von A und B einander gegenüber zu setzen, und diejenigen Zeugen für sie anzuführen, die für den Beweis von Belang sind" (Lagarde, ib. 5).

As a specimen Lagarde published chapters I-V of Judges in such a way that each two pages form a unit: the left page brings the text of A and the right one that of B; both texts are provided with ample critical notes, listing the variant readings of either genuine Greek sources, or of translations based thereon. Thus, the sigla a c d h k p x ל ט indicate the witnesses of the A-text, while b g n ט ק signify the B-group. The chief results of this study are formulated as follows: "Das Vorstehende [scil. the publication of the first five chapters of Judges in the indicated manner] genügt, um folgende Thesen zu stellen: 1) Die im Codex A . . . stehende Übersetzung des Buches der Richter stimmt im Grossen und Ganzen . . . mit dem Texte des Origenes. . . . 2) Codex B liefert nicht Varianten zu A, sondern enthält . . . eine andere Übersetzung des Buches der Richter. Aus B in A, oder aus A in B hinüberkorrigieren darf nur der besonders Kundige und Besonnene" (ib. 71 f.).

Though published more than a century ago, this procedure still enjoys a following. Alfred Rahlfs in his *Septuaginta* (Stuttgart, 1935) gives for the book of Judges the texts of both A and B in full. But a critical re-examination of Lagarde's premises and conclusions will show that what fifty years ago may have been a new and startling theory, has lost its convincing power by now.

In order to arrive at definite conclusions concerning the relation of Codex A to the text of Origen's LXX, we have to bear in mind that our knowledge of the fifth column of Origen's *Hexapla* is based only upon citations. While arranging his large collections according to the order of the books in the OT, Field headed them by the symbol O', or by indicating: *alia exemplaria. Readings under either of these headings must be considered as reflecting Origen's LXX.* They differ from one another to such an extent as to suggest that they go back to two different translations, but this fact does not justify our arbitrarily regarding one of these readings as the "genuine" LXX of Origen, and rejecting the other. On the contrary, the only conclusion to be drawn must be that no "genuine" LXX (in the singular!) existed in Origen's days, but two independent translations of the Bible into Greek, both of which held an equal claim to be called "Septuagint." For the designation of one reading as O' and of the other as merely al ex is not given to them by Origen himself, nor is it to be explained from the nature of their sources; this is only a *Notbehelf* of the editor, and does not imply any difference in their authority as representing Origen's LXX.

With the way thus cleared for understanding Origen's work, we now proceed to an examination of the quotations from the fifth column and their relation to the two codices B and A. We extend our investigation concerning Codex A to include Codex B, too, since we wish to assign to both of them their respective place in the Hexaplaric LXX tradition. All our quotations are taken from the book of Judges in Field's *Hexaplorum quae supersunt*. In parentheses I indicate the symbol of that codex which offers the identical reading in his text.

1.1: ביהוה: O': δια του κυριου (=B); al ex: εν κυριω (=A).

1.1: אל הכנעני ··· בו: O': προς τους χαναναιους ... προς αυτους (=B); al ex: προς τον χαναναιον ... εν αυτω (=A).

1.3: ונלחמה בכנעני: O': και παραταξωμεθα προς τους χαναναιους (=B); al ex: και πολεμησωμεν εν τω χαναναιω (=A, with the only difference that A reads πολεμησω, apparently a haplography before εν).

1.10: לפנים: O': το προτερον (=B); al ex: εμπροσθεν (=A).

1.11: וילך: O': και ανεβησαν (=B); al ex: επορευθησαν (=A).

1.14: בבואה: O': εν τη εισοδω αυτης (=B); al ex: εν τω εισπορευεσθαι αυτην (=A).

1.14: ותצנח מעל החמור: O': και εγογγυζεν και εκραζεν απο του υποζυγιου (=B, with the slight variant: εκραξεν); al ex: και εγογγυζεν επανω του υποζυγιου και εκραζεν απο του υποξυγιου (=A, also with the variant εκραξεν).

1.16: O': ιοθορ (=B); al ex: ιωβαβ (cf. A: ιωαβ).

1.16: חתן O': του γαμβρου (=B); al ex: πενθερου (=A).

1.16: את בני: O': μετα των υιων (=B); al ex: προς τους υιους (=A).

1.17: חרמה: O': αναθεμα (=B); al ex: εξολοθρευσις (=A).

The result is that generally speaking B agrees with the quotations listed under O′, and A with those under al ex. With the conclusions as formulated in p. 358 f., § 6 in mind, we can formulate this result as follows: B reflects the obelus group, and A the asterisk group of the LXX on the book of Judges. Both must, therefore, be considered as reflecting the "genuine" LXX.

In making this statement we wish to emphasize that we do not mean to imply that these codices represent the respective group in all their details. This is a problem which requires a careful and more detailed examination of at least considerable portions of the book of Judges. But since we do not aim at an exhaustive treatment of any of the problems discussed here, we might as well avail ourselves of this opportunity to state that we have reason to believe that the LXX texts as offered in either of these codices are the results of a long history of inner Greek development and adjustment to one another. We wish to demonstrate this assertion with a few examples:

1.6: וירדפו: O′: και κατεδραμον (=B and A); al ex: και κατεδιωξαν.

1.7: ויביאהו: O′: και αγουσιν αυτον (=B and A); al ex: και ηγαγον αυτον.

1.10: קרית ארבע: O′: καριαθαρβοκ ÷ σεφερ × (cf. B: καριαρβοξεφερ; A: καριαρβοκσεφερ); al ex: καριαθαρβοκ εξ εφραιμ.

2.10: נאספו: O′: προσετεθησαν (=B and A); al ex: συνηχθησαν.

2.17: אחרים: O′: ετερων (= B and A): al ex: αλλοτριων.

3.7: את הבעלים: O′: τοις βααλιμ (cf. B: τοις βααλειμ; A: ταις βααλειμ); al ex: τη βααλ.

3.16: גמד: O′: σπιθαμης (=B and A); al ex: δρακος.

In these instances the agreement between B and A in their readings will have to be explained as the result of an adjustment of A to the obelus text of B; for elsewhere A follows the asterisk text of al ex. Consequently, J. E. Grabe's statement "libri Iudicum versionem των O′, quam Origenes in Hexaplis exhibuit, . . . codice alexandrino contineri deprehendi," the correctness of which Lagarde believed to have proven on the basis of his publication of the first five chapters of Judges, becomes now null and void. For in any agreement between O′ and A we shall now see only the resultant of a later development of the text which was originally underlying A. This was achieved by way of eliminating some of the basic characteristics of the text which it had in common with the asterisk group.

This development must have taken place at a time when the obelus type had already gained increased authority at the expense of the asterisk type. We are inclined to see in this adjustment of A to the obelus type an effort to co-ordinate the A text with that textual form which had more or less become *the established text*; and that may also be the reason, why we could thus far discover no traces of a textual adjustment in the other direction, in order to bring about an agreement between B and the asterisk type, as represented by A. The asterisk type had lost ground to the obelus type!

We now return to Lagarde's publication of Judges 1-5 by putting in juxtaposition A and B with their respective critical apparatus. Our contention is that this procedure leads to no end: the texts of the various manuscripts which have been used by Lagarde for the preparation of the two critical apparatus, are already of a mixed type to such an extent that their assignment to either B or A must be considered as highly arbitrary. I will prove this by showing that

1) the critical apparatus on A equals that on B;

2) variant readings on the A text lead up to the respective readings of the B text; and vice versa

3) variants on B lead up to the A text.

a.   The critical apparatus on A lists the same readings as that on B.

A hyphen separates here the symbols used by Lagarde to indicate the textual witnesses for the respective text; on the left side of the hyphen I bring the symbols for the A type; on the right side those for the B type:

1.1:   επηρωτησαν k ℵ — n

1.6:   ελαβοσαν c d p x — b n

1.7:   ηγαγον c d h k p ℵ ∂ — n

1.8:   οι A c d h k p x Euseb: > a — B g n: > b

1.8:   μαχαιρας A — n

1.9:   του A: > a c d h k p x Euseb — B g n: > b

1.10: τον θολμι c d ℵ — g

1.11: beide Male δαβιρ c — b beide Male

1.12: αν > h — g
1.12: vor δωσω+και x — g n

b. Variants on A lead up to the textual readings of B.

1.1: πολεμησαι a c d h k p x ℵ ס = B
1.2: εν τη χειρι k = B
1.3: και παραταξωμεθα προς τους χαναναιους ℵ = B
1.4: εκοψαν x = B
1.4: βεζεκ c d h k p x ℵ = B
1.5: κατελαβον x = B
1.8: ρομφαιας a c d h k p = B
1.9: την ορεινην a p = B
1.10: nach κατοικουντα+εν χεβρων a c d k p x ℵ ס = B
1.10: vor εξ+και εξηλθε χεβρων a d h p ℵ ס = B

c. Variants on B lead up to the textual readings of A.

1.1: προς τον χαναναιον g n = A
1.1: εν αυτω g n = A
1.2: τη > b g n = A
1.3: προς συμεων τον αδελφον g = A
1.3: και γε εγω g = A
1.5: vor φερεζαιον+τον g n = A
1.10: το δε g = A
1.10: χεβρων ην g = A
1.10: επαταξε n = A
1.12: αν b n = A

C. CODICES B AND A ON THE BIBLE

In commenting upon J. E. Grabe's statement concerning the deviation of the LXX text on Judges as offered in Codex A from that in Codex B (see the preceding chapter at the beginning), Lagarde emphasized in a manner which is characteristic for him: "Die vielen Schnüffler mache ich darauf aufmerksam, dass Grabes Ausdruck 'quod ad dictum librum' die Untersuchung auf das Buch der Richter beschränkt. Auch ich rede zunächst nur von dem Buche der Richter" (*Septuaginta Studien*, 3). The question as to whether the results obtained in the discussion of the

book of Judges may be considered generally valid for these two manuscripts, or are applicable to this particular Biblical book only, has thus
been left open. We, therefore, wish to take up this problem now. As a
basis for our discussion we bring a few examples, which are taken at
random from different parts of the Bible:

1) Codex B has the Hexaplaric readings under O'; Codex A those
under al ex:

Hos. 1.2: בהושע: O': εν ωσηε (= B); al ex: προς ωσηε (=A).

Hos. 1.7: בסוסים: O': ουδε εν ιπποις (=B); al ex: praemittit: ουδε εν
αρμασιν (=A).

Hos. 2.25: ורחמתי את לא רחמה: O': και αγαπησω την ουκ ηγαπημενην
(=B); al ex: και ελεησω την ουκ ελεημενην (=A).

Hos. 6.6: ולא זבח: O': η θυσιαν (=B); al ex: και ου θυσιαν (=A).

Hos. 13.3: וכעשן מארבה: O': και ως ατμις απο δακρυων (=B); al ex: και
ως ατμις εκ καπνοδοχης (=A).

This last example is highly instructive. According to the text common
to O' and B, the verse reads: "and like smoke from tears." This is sheer
nonsense! It is quite possible that tears come as a result of smoke, but
never does smoke originate in tears. δακρυων is an obvious error for
ακριδων (cf. the reading noted in Field under *alia*: απο ακριδων), which
goes back to a pronunciation of the basic Hebrew word מארבה as מַאָרְבֶּה;
cf. JBL, 1935, 82, paragraph II. The fact that O' and B share this error
proves their interdependence.

Ezek. 3.5: עמקי שפה וכבדי לשון: O': βαθυγλωσσον (=B); al ex: βαθυ-
χειλον και βαρυγλωσσον (=A).

I Sam. 1.1: צופים: O': σιφα (=B); al ex: σωφιμ (=A).

I Sam. 1.1: ירחם: O': ιερεμεηλ (=B); al ex: ιεροαμ (=A).

I Sam. 1.1: אפרתי: O': εφραιμ (=B); al ex: εφραθαιος (=A).

I Sam. 1.3: האיש ההוא: O': ο ανθρωπος (=B); al ex: ο ανθρωπος εκεινος
(=A).

I Sam. 1.4: ולכל בניה ובנותיה: O': και τοις υιοις αυτης (=B); al ex: και τοις
υιοις αυτης και ταις θυγατρασιν αυτης (=A).

I Sam. 1.13: רק שפתיה: O': και τα χειλη αυτης (=B); al ex: πλην τα χειλη
αυτης (=A).

Ps. 103.2: גמוליו: O': τας αινεσεις (=B); al ex: τας ανταποδοσεις (=A).

Ps. 104.18: לשפנים: O': τοις χοιρογρυλλιοις (=B); al ex: τοις λαγωοις (=A). On the unique importance of this passage cf. *Festschrift Kahle*, 43 ff.

2) Words missing in O' and B, but quoted under al ex and contained in A:

Ezek. 3.9: נתתי מצחך: O': Vacat. (missing in B); al ex: δεδωκα το νικος σου (=A).

Ezek. 6.9: אל הרעות אשר עשו: O': Vacat. (missing in B); al ex: ※ περι των κακιων ων εποιησαν × (=A).

1 Sam. 1.9: ואחרי שתה: O': Vacat. (missing in B); al ex: και μετα το πιειν (=A).

1 Sam. 1.11: לא תשכח את אמתך: O': Vacat. (missing in B); al ex: και μη επιλαθη της δουλης σου (=A).

These examples seem to suggest that the results at which we arrived in the preceding chapter with regard to B and A on Judges, may well be applied in general to the interrelation of these two manuscripts as such. We can not base any final theories on our findings; in order to arrive at well-founded conclusions, we should have to make first a thorough examination of each book separately; and this we did not do. We therefore stress the tentative nature of our suggestion, namely: that after having investigated considerable portions of the Bible we find a striking inter-relation between the obelus type of the Hexaplaric LXX and Codex B on one side, and between the asterisk type and Codex A on the other side. Further examination makes it plausible that here, too, the later adjust-ment of the basic texts of these manuscripts followed a tendency of dis-carding the asterisk type of Codex A, in order to bring it under the influence of the obelus type, by eliminating asterisk readings and sub-stituting readings from the obelus group in their stead. This procedure thus leads to an agreement between the readings under O', B and A, as against the respective al ex readings:

Hos. 1.4: יהוא: O': ιουδα (=B and A); al ex: ιηου.

Hos. 4.4: ועמך: O': ο δε λαος μου (=B and A); al ex: ο δε λαος σου.

Hos. 4.5: עמך: O': μετα σου (=B and A); al ex: μετ αυτου.

Hos. 5.13: לרפא: O': ιασασθαι (=B and A); al ex: ρυσασθαι.

Ezek. 3.18: בעונו: O′: τη αδικια αυτου (=B and A); al ex: τη ανομια αυτου.

Ezek. 4.2: סללה: O′: χαρακα (=B and A); al ex: ταφρον.

In conclusion we may, therefore, say that taking the codices B and A as entities, the divergencies displayed therein largely reflect similar variant readings of the two types of the Hexaplaric LXX; thus, B shows close affinity to the obelus type, and A to the asterisk type. Neither of them can be regarded as representing their respective basic textual type in all its details; the very fact that the text of either manuscript is of a mixed type, precludes any such assumption. But, still, though no absolute classification of these manuscripts is possible, we may say that relatively speaking B has better preserved its original characteristics of the obelus type than A its of the asterisk type, since we saw a tendency of bringing B and A into agreement at the expense of A.

Cautiously as these conclusions are phrased, they are of the utmost significance for the solution of our problem. Until now we had merely evidence for the former existence of an obelus type of the LXX, but no coherent text of it to point to. We could establish certain characteristics of this text, but its very existence was a matter of conjecture, since it was based on fragmentary quotations only. Now we have in Codex B a coherent manuscript, covering nearly all of the Bible, which may rightly be classified as a direct offspring of the obelus type, exhibiting the readings of this type to an extraordinarily large extent.

We are now confronted with the problem: Can we prove in the same or in some similar way the existence of a coherent text of the asterisk type, evidence for which we possess up to now solely in the form of citations? The next chapter will deal with the solution of this problem.

B.   The Church Fathers and Vetus Latina

A.   THE MINOR PROPHETS IN GREEK

What we have attained thus far in our search for coherent Bible texts in Greek as representatives of either of the two Hexaplaric types of the LXX shows that while Codex B might be considered as a witness for the obelus type, the undoubtedly asterisk character underlying Codex A has already undergone too great changes for that MS to be rated a genuine asterisk text now. We therefore turn to the Early Christian writers in the hope of finding some pertinent information in their commentaries on the Bible. It is good to remind ourselves at the very outset that our expectations must not be too high; for the same levelling hand which we noticed at work in Codex A, busy to substitute the more authoritative obelus text for its former asterisk readings, no doubt extended its influence even beyond this manuscript, so as to include Church Father commentaries, too. In those early centuries the Church Fathers' works exercized a great influence in the religious life of Christendom; what good was it, then, to copy such commentaries with references to a Bible text which did not fully agree with the authoritative Bible of the Church? The readings had to be changed, and actually were changed. Corrections of this kind are surely *bona fide* emendations; but the resulting readings are worthless for us. For we realize that any such agreement in the Church Fathers' commentaries with the obelus text might possibly be—though it certainly is not always—the outgrowth of scribal changes. Consequently, we shall value so much higher those deviations from the obelus text in the Church Father literature which obviously escaped the attention of their respective copyists, and remained uncorrected. Evidence of this kind cannot be properly appreciated by merely counting the number of the text-witnesses for a certain reading; but each instance has to be taken *by weight and not by count.*

We have further to bear in mind that, since we established two textual types for the Hexaplaric LXX, we now always need two deviating texts of the same Biblical passage, so as to assign even one of them to the asterisk or obelus type. Now the criteria by which we proceed are very scarce. If we are about to establish the basic type of a given text we must look in Field's Hexapla for quotations from the same Biblical book listed both under O' *and* al ex. A mere O' quotation—as is the vast majority of cases in Field's work—is of no avail; in the agreement between our text and such O' quotations we can not see a proof for the obelus type of our text so long as we have no evidence that the asterisk type had this same passage in a different phrasing. We therefore can base our investigation solely upon a comparison of two divergent readings: be they represented by an O' quotation and a corresponding al ex variant reading, as was our procedure till now, or else by two different coherent texts covering a substantial part of a Biblical book, provided the differences are genuine (cf. our characterizations on p. 358 f., § 9 and p. 377 f., § 11) and not the apparent result of later inner Greek textual development (cf. below under *d*).

We can point to one case which meets with these requirements: the Minor Prophets, as commented upon by Cyril of Alexandria and by Theodoret of Kyros. In an article *"The Problems of the Septuagint Recensions*, JBL, 1935, 73-92, I published the results of an examination of the Greek Bible texts, which served these Fathers as bases for their commentaries. The variant readings are grouped and classified; they prove that these two Fathers used two different Bible texts in Greek, which in turn go back to two independent translations of the Hebrew Minor Prophets into Greek. This is demonstrated by referring to variant readings which cannot be explained otherwise but as reflecting a different approach to the basic Hebrew text. Differences of such a type may be seen in a translation which is based upon a mispronunciation of the Hebrew word or a mistake on account of the similarity in the script of certain Hebrew letters. They may be used as evidence for the fact that the translator was rather poorly equipped for his task, and thus account for so many other errors. But they are, from the viewpoint of the philologian, the most trustworthy evidence for an assertion that this text with all its mistakes is really an independent translation, based upon a Hebrew original, and not a mere stylistic revision of an already existent Greek translation.

We thus have very large portions of the Minor Prophets in Greek in a twofold shape: that of Cyril and that of Theodoret. How do they compare with our division into asterisk and obelus type?

This question can best be answered by referring to the variants themselves. I follow the order of my article in JBL, referring even to the respective headings; but I must leave out those instances for which we have no corresponding citations from the *Hexapla*. The Church Fathers I quote according to Migne's *Patrologia Graeca*; Cyril's commentary (here abbreviated into Cy) appears in vols. 71 and 72; that of Theodoret (here shortened to Th) in volume 81. In Migne's edition, every page is divided into four sections, which are indicated by the letters A, B, C, D. I use these with the page citation.

a. The Hebrew word is incorrectly spelled

Hos. 8.1: אֶל חִכְּךָ שֹׁפָר: O′: εις κολπον αυτων ως γη = Cy (p. 197 B); al ex: επι φαρυγγι αυτων ως γη αβατος ως σαλπιγξ = Th (p. 1592 D).

Al ex contains this reading in addition to the O′ reading; this means that it is a doublet, combining the O′ reading and the Theodoret-text. Hence the text of Th appears to be older and better preserved than that of al ex.

Obad. 16: וְלָעוּ: O′: και καταβησονται = Cy (p. 592 B); al ex: και κατα-πιονται = Th (p. 1716 B).

Hab. 3.12: תִצְעַד: O′: ολιγωσεις = Cy (p. 932 A); al ex: συμπατησεις = Th (p. 1832 B).

b. The Hebrew word is incorrectly vocalized

Hos. 13.3: וּכְעָשָׁן מֵאֲרֻבָּה: O′: και ως ατμις απο δακρυων = Th (p. 1621 D: απο ακριδων); al ex: και ως ατμις εκ καπνοδοχης = Cy (p. 300 D: απο). On the inner Greek corruption of ακριδων as offered by Th, into δακρυων in O′, cf. p. 384, sub 1.

Am. 6.2: עִבְרוּ כַלְנֵה: O′: διαβητε παντες = Cy (p. 513 D); al ex: διαβητε εις χαλανην = Th (p. 1693 B). Here again, al ex has this reading in addition to the O′ reading; cf. our remark above on Hos. 8.1.

Zeph. 1.5: בְּמַלְכָּם: O′: κατα του βασιλεως αυτων = Cy (p. 949 D); κατα του μελχομ = Th (p. 1840 C).

c. Doublets in Theodoret

Zech. 6.7: וַיְבַקֵּשׁ: O′: και επεβλεπον = Cy (p. 88 B); al ex: και εζητουν και επεβλεπον = Th (p. 1905 A).

Zech. 7.3: הַנָּזֵר: O′: το αγιασμα = Cy (p. 100 C); al ex: το αγιασμα η νηστευσω = Th (p. 1908 B/C). The two translations are connected by η; cf. on p. 348 the instance from 2 Ki. 1.3.

d. Greek corruptions in Theodoret

Hos. 4.19: אוֹתָהּ: O′: συ ει = Cy (p. 137 D); al ex: συριει = Th (p. 1576 D). The original translator of συ ει read the Hebrew word as אַתָּה; but no connection can be traced between אותה and συριει (from συριζω = to whistle). It is very likely that the preceding πνευματος misled the copyist to seek in συ ει a verb which expresses some of the doings of the "wind," and thus guessed συριει for it.

Hos. 9.10: כבכורה: O': ως σκοπον = Th (p. 1601 B); al ex: ως συκον = Cy (p. 229 B). Similarly in Nah. 3.12: בכורים is rendered by Theodoret (p. 1805 B/C): σκοπους; how the same mistake could occur in both passages, I am unable to explain.

The last two examples do not count at all when we try to establish the textual types of Cyril's and Theodoret's Bibles. For they do not represent two independent translations (our main requirement), but only one, which appears correctly in one text but corrupt in the other. These corruptions must have been widespread, as becomes evident from the number of texts which have these readings; cf. Field a. 1. Of course, this does not give additional importance to them; they remain corruptions, still. But it proves the interrelation of the texts which have these errors in common.

Similarly the two examples of doublets carry only little weight. They belong to that group which we would term "doublets of which one reading is traceable"; cf. p. 348 and 371. They are the result of a combination of the O' reading (which is identical with Cyril's text) with the reading of another genuine translation, which still remains to be discovered, and which, it may safely be assumed, preserved much better the basic textual type of al ex (i.e. Theodoret's text).

Speaking of doublets, mention must be made of the passages Hos. 8.1 and Am. 6.2 which are listed above. Here Cyril and Theodoret offer different readings, which prove the genuineness of their respective translation. Under al ex a.l. Field quotes readings, which are a combination of these two renderings. These doublets belong to the same type which we discussed on p. 348. They prove that here the texts of Cyril and Theodoret are better preserved than that of al ex, since they still offer the original sources for the doublets of al ex. But they can not be used as evidence to determine the textual type of either of these Church Fathers.

But from the remaining examples it becomes clear that we may assign Cyril's text to the obelus type, and Theodoret's text to the asterisk type. We again emphasize that our conclusions concern themselves only with the basic character of the two texts in question, and do not preclude the existence of sporadic exceptions. Hos. 13.3 seems to be such an exception; but the textual tradition is here confused to such an extent (cf. Field, where Theodoret's reading is listed as a third possibility under *alia*) that we prefer to refrain from commenting on this passage.

Cyril contains all of the Minor Prophets in Greek, Theodoret approximately one-third of the text, but as a more or less coherent text, and not as mere abrupt fragments of sentences, like the quotations in Field's collection. While Cyril is thus a welcome addition to our textual witnesses for the obelus group, we have in Theodoret now the first real text of the asterisk group, covering considerable portions of Biblical books. For further witnesses for the asterisk group we shall have to turn to indirect evidence, namely, the Latin translations of the LXX.

B.   THE LXX IN LATIN

Augustinus in his *De doctrina christiana* 2, 11 (quoted by Friedrich Stummer, *Einführung in die lateinische Bibel*, Paderborn 1928, 51) states that the Latin translations of the Bible—scil. in the period prior to Jerome—were based upon Greek originals: "qui scripturas ex Hebraea lingua in Graecam verterunt, numerari possunt, Latini autem interpretes nullo modo; ut enim cuique primis fidei temporibus in manus venit codex Graecus et aliquantulum facultatis sibi utriusque linguae habere videbatur, ausus est interpretari." This statement clearly refers to those Latin Bible texts which were executed by Christians and meant for Christians, or at least for prospective Christians; the problem raised by D. S. Blondheim in his *Les parlers judéo-romans et la Vetus Latina* (Paris, 1925), whether the Latin speaking Jews of Gaul had a Bible of their own or not, will not concern us here.

Since the Latin Bible translations were based upon Greek originals, they might be used in restoring these originals by retroverting them into Greek. Such a procedure might help us regain an otherwise lost Greek text of the Bible, or at least of portions of it. Accordingly, in MGWJ, 1937, 55-65, I published a translation into Greek of an Old Latin text of the book of Ruth. As a result of this procedure I arrived at the conclusion that "Durch die vorangehende Rückübersetzung erhalten wir *nicht* eine neue griechische *Handschrift* des Buches Ruth — der Gewinn wäre nicht gar so gross, wenn man bedenkt, dass schon Holmes and Parsons, und

später Brooke and McLean 50 Handschriften für ihre Ausgaben kolla-
tionierten! —, sondern eine neue, bisher sonst *unbekannte griechische
Textgestalt* dieses Buches, *die auf eine von der landläufigen Septuaginta
unabhängige Übersetzung des Buches Ruth ins Griechische zurückgeht*"
(ib. 63).

We are thus building upon the foundation laid out by Augustin that
these Old Latin texts go back to respective Greek texts, and reflect only
indirectly a Hebrew text. Can we prove the correctness of Augustin's
statement from the very Latin texts themselves? Inner evidence deserves
more credence than mere tradition handed down by early authors, as we
could see in our analysis of Origen's work on the fifth column of the
Hexapla.

Variant readings, which do or do not coincide with MT, are not conclusive at all. For such variants might just as well be explained as having
their origin in a corresponding Greek prototype of the Latin text, as in a
basic Hebrew text; since they lend themselves to a retroversion into both
languages, it could be argued either way. "Ich glaube nun, dass dies
Problem auf Grund solcher Stellen zu lösen ist, die in ihrem Zu-
sammenhange sinnlos sind, aber durch Vornahme einer kleinen Korrektur
verständlich werden" (MGWJ, 1937, 64). As long as we have to go back
to the Hebrew text in order to explain such a mistake, we shall consider
this Hebrew text to be the direct original of the translation in question.
But in case the Hebrew phrase could by no errors in its pronunciation or
etymology lead to the confusion in the Latin text, while the equivalent
Greek phrase could, we shall see herein a proof of the dependence of the
Latin text upon this Greek text as its basic original. In my article in
MGWJ I demonstrated this by referring to Ruth 3.10: *"ut inires post
iubenes* steht in offenem Widerspruch zu 2.21: *cum puellis meis adiunge te*:
ib. 22: *quod existi cum puellis eius*; und ib. 23: *et adiunxisti te cum puellis
booz*. Was Boaz also in 3.10 im Sinne hatte, war: *ne inires post iubenes*.
Der Fehler erklärt sich aus einer griechischen Vorlage, in der in der
Phrase: του μη πορευθηναι σε das μη ausgefallen war. Das verbleibende
του πορευθηναι σε musste Lat. durch *ut inires* wiedergeben" (ib. 64).

A few more examples will make this point clearer: In Ruth 1.2 this
Latin text reads: *et nomina erat duobus filiis eius*; the subject is a *neutrum
pluralis*, the predicate a singular. This is a grammatical rule in Greek

syntax only, not in Latin; consequently, the translator must have had: και ονοματα ην before him, and imitated this original exactly (cf. similar cases in the Aramaic Bible Version, ZAW, 1927, 279, paragraph XXI). In Ruth 1.11 we read: *redite filie mee ut quid uenistis mecum.* The corresponding Hebrew text has למה תלכנה עמי: future tense. For this speech was delivered *before* Naomi set out to return to Bethlehem in Judaea, and was meant to prevent her daughters-in-law from joining her: Her advice was accepted by Orfa; cf. verse 14: *et osculata est orfa socrum suam et habiit*; but Ruth stood firm in her decision to follow her mother-in-law; cf. verse 16: *ne obuiaberis mici ut relinquam te, ut revertar depost te.* Both women were thus advised in verse 11, *from now on* to part from their mother-in-law; the perfect tense of *uenistis* is, therefore, an apparent mistake for the corresponding future-form. By referring to a Greek original, the explanation is quite simple: ινα τι πορευεσθε was misunderstood in ινα τι επορευεσθε.

Thus inner criteria, as offered by this Latin text itself, substantiate the correctness of Augustin's assertion to the effect that the Vetus Latina is based upon Greek originals. Here the question arises: what textual type did these Greek originals represent? The Vetus Latina is said to originate in the second century C.E., this means about the time of Origen; consequently, the translators had the LXX before them in a twofold form: as the obelus and the asterisk types. Which of them was taken as the basis for their work? This problem is of importance from many points of view: if preference was consistently given by the translators to one and the same Greek type, it may be taken as an indication of its wider circulation and higher authority. In addition: by establishing relation of an interdependence between a Greek type and the Vetus Latina, we might hereafter utilize this Latin translation as a text witness for that Greek type upon which it is based.

Our procedure in such a case, based upon a *comparison of two texts*, is outlined on p. 386 f. We need two parallel Latin texts and corresponding evidence from Origen in order to deal with this problem. Ernest Ranke published under the title *Par Palimpsestorum Wirceburgensium* (Vienna, 1871) fragments of original manuscripts containing Vetus Latina texts, for considerable portions of which he could bring in a parallel column another Old Latin version, referred to as "apud Augustinum, Hieronymum aliosve obvia." Jerome's "Vulgata nova," which Ranke publishes in a third column, does not interest us, since it is based on the Hebrew text. We thus have quite a number of chapters of various Biblical books in two Old Latin translations. A mere cursory examination reveals the existence of many variants between them. Do these variants represent two Latin possibilities of rendering one and the same Greek text into Latin (e.g. synonyms, stylistic polish), or do they reflect two corresponding Greek texts? Here, too, a seemingly hopeless confusion will furnish us with the clue.

Hos. 4.19 צרר רוח אותה: the Vetus Latina according to the Würzburg fragment reads: *haec conuersio spiritus tu es*, thus reading or interpreting אותה as אַתְּ־ *tu es* (we purposely refer first to the Hebrew text as prototype as long as feasible). But the translation in the parallel column has: *turbo spiritus sibilabit* (Ranke, 249). Here the Hebrew word אותה is of no use; for the way from אותה to שרק or נשב is too long! Fortunately, we possess this passage in quotations from both types of the Hexaplaric LXX: cf. p. 389, sub d. Latin *tu es* could never be confused into *sibilabit*; but Greek συ ει into συριει could. Thus, al ex and the second Old Latin text share this mistake, which could originate only in Greek. We may, therefore, say: both the obelus and the asterisk types of the LXX were used as basic texts for retroversion into Latin, the so-called Vetus Latina; and a minute comparison of a given Old Latin text with the extant Greek material of the two LXX types is required, before we assign this Old Latin text to one type or the other.

We shall demonstrate this first on the book of Ruth in the Old Latin version:

a. *Readings both under O' and under alia exemplaria*

1.1: בימי שפט: O': εν τω κρινειν (=B); al ex: εν ταις ημεραις του κρινειν = in diebus iudicis.

1.5: משני ילדיה ומאישה: O': απο του ανδρος αυτης και απο των δυο υιων αυτης (=B); al ex: απο των δυο υιων αυτης και απο του ανδρος αυτης = a duobus filiis suis et a uiro suo.

3.15: ואחזו בה ותאחז בה: O': και εκρατησεν αυτο (=B); al ex: και κρατησον αυτο και εκρατησεν αυτο = et tene eam et tenuit illam.

3.16: ‏ותאמר מי את בתי‎: O': η δε ειπεν αυτη θυγατερ (=B); al ex: η δε ειπε τι εστι θυγατερ = et dixit quid est filia.

3.16: ‏ותגד לה‎: O': και ειπεν αυτη (=B); al ex: και απηγγειλεν αυτη = et indicabit ei.

b. Readings sub asterisco

1.1: ‏ושני בניו‎: O': και οι ⁎ δυο ⨉ υιοι αυτου = et duo filii eius; cf. B: και οι υιοι αυτου.

1.22: ‏כלתה עמה‎: O': η νυμφη αυτης ⁎ μετ αυτης ⨉ = nurus eius cum ea; cf. B: η νυμφη αυτης.

2.23: ‏וקציר החטים‎: O': και ⁎ τον θερισμον ⨉ των πυρων = et messem frumentariam; cf. B: και των πυρων.

3.7: ‏ויאכל בעז וישת‎: O': και εφαγε βοοζ ⁎ και επιε ⨉ = et manducabit booz et bibit; cf. B: και εφαγεν βοος.

3.7: ‏ותשכב‎: O': Vacat. (missing in B, too); al ex: ⁎ και εκοιμηθη ⨉ = et dormibit.

We thus see that this Old Latin text belongs to the asterisk type; the agreement between the Hexaplaric asterisk type and this Old Latin version of Ruth includes: the actual amount of text (which on the other hand is mising in the obelus type), the choice of words, the word-order and the transliteration of Hebrew; on this last item (βοοζ — booz, as against βοος in B), cf. p. 175 under ‏ז‎. By way of retroversion of this Latin text into Greek (MGWJ, 1937, 55 seq.) I restored the asterisk type of the LXX on Ruth, which together with B, representing the obelus type, make a *complete Hexaplaric book of Ruth in Greek.*

We shall now examine the two forms of Old Latin Bible translation as published in Ranke's book, with Field's *Hexapla* at hand, in order to note any interconnection. In parenthesis I indicate the page in Ranke, so as to make easy the locating of the passages. The first quotation in Latin refers to the Wuerzburg fragment; the second to the parallel source, according to Ranke.

a. Hexaplaric readings both under O' and al ex traceable in the Vetus Latina

(p. 181): Ex. 33.19: ‏בשם יהוה‎: nomine meo dms = O': το ονοματι μου· κυριος; nomine Domini = al ex: τω ονοματι κυριου.

(p. 207) Lev. 5.19: אשם אשם: negligentia = O': πλημμελεια; delicto delictum = al ex: πλημμελεια πλημμελησιν.

(p. 241) Hos. 1.2: בהושע: in osee = O': εν ωσηε; ad osee = al ex: προς ωσηε.

(p. 253) Hos. 6.4: מה אעשה לך: quid tibi faciam = O': τι σοι ποιησω; quid faciam tibi = al ex: τι ποιησω σοι.

(p. 253) Hos. 6.6: ולא זבח: quam sacrificium = O': η θυσιαν; et non sacrificium = al ex: και ου θυσιαν.

(p. 321) Lam. 3.23: חדשים לבקרים: et noua in matutinum = O': καινα εις τας πρωιας; renovabit illas sicut lux matutina = al ex: ανακαι-νισον αυτους ως ορθρον πρωιμον.

(p. 335) Ezek. 34.27: את מטות עלם: torquam eorum = O': τον ζυγον αυτων; furcas iugi eorum = al ex: τους κλαιους του ζυγου αυτων.

On the reading: τον ζυγον του κλαιου αυτων, which Field also lists under al ex, cf. G on Ex. 3.2: εν πυρι φλογος, quoted in Acts 7.30 as: εν φλογι πυρος; also G on Jer. 18.6: ο πηλος του κεραμεως, quoted in Rom. 9.21, as: ο κεραμευς του πηλου.

b. Readings *sub asterisco*, traceable with and without the asteriscized words

(p. 258) Isa. 29.7: לילה:—; nocte = O': ※ νυκτος ×.

(p. 261) Isa. 29.13: בפיו:—; cf. O': Vacabat; ore suo = ※ εν τω στοματι αυτου ×.

(p. 296) Jer. 22.28: הוא וזרעו:—; ipse et semen eius = O': ※ αυτος και το σπερμα αυτου ×.

(p. 325) Ezek. 24.9: אוי עיר הדמים:—; cf. O': Vacat.; vae civitas san-guinum = ※ ουαι πολις των αιματων ×.

(p. 332) Ezek. 34.16: ואת השמנה:—; cf. O': Vacat.; et quod pingue est = ※ και το πιον ×.

These observations may, therefore, lead to a conclusion that the Wuerzburg fragment of the Vetus Latina is closely related to the obelus type, while the other evidence for the Vetus Latina is in a similar way dependant on the asterisk type of the LXX. Thus we do not exclude the possibility that either text might at certain passages offer readings which reverse this relationship; for we already noticed that all the texts we had to deal with present themselves as belonging to an already mixed type. A few examples will show that the same is the case with the two Vetus Latina texts under examination:

(p. 177) Ex. 32.24: ואשלכהו : et misi illud = O' : και ερριψα ※ αυτα; et misi.

(p. 183) Ex. 34.7: חסד: et facies misericordiam = al ex: και ποιων ελεος; et misericordiam = O' : και ελεος.

(p. 293) Jer. 22.14: האמר:— ; cf. O' : Vacat;— ; but cf. ※ ο λεγων ×.

(p. 302) Jer. 23.22: מדרכם הרע:— ; —; but cf. ※ εκ της οδου αυτων της πονηρας και ×.

The difficulty which I experienced in trying to find these few instances to prove the mixed type of these two Latin texts, may also be taken as an indication that their basic character as representing the obelus and asterisk types, respectively, is still by far predominant.

We have thus succeeded in proving the existence of the two Hexaplaric LXX types also as coherent Bible texts, represented both in the Greek originals and in their Latin translations. The textual evidence for each one of these types as far as we could now trace them are:

1)   The obelus type: Hexaplaric quotations under O' and *sub obelo*; Codex B of the LXX; Cyril of Alexandria on the Minor Prophets, the Vetus Latina according to the Wuerzburg fragment.

2)   The asterisk type: Hexaplaric quotations under al ex and *sub asterisco*; Codex A of the LXX (to a certain extent only!); Theodoret of Kyros on the Minor Prophets; the book of Ruth according to the Vetus Latina, and one tradition within the Vetus Latina generally.

C.   Conclusions

A.   THE NT AND THE TWO LXX TYPES

The starting point of our investigation was the stressing of the apparent incongruities between certain OT passages as quoted in the NT and the way they are worded at their respective places within the OT itself. These discrepancies resulted from a comparison of both, OT and NT according to one and the same manuscript, Codex B. Our presupposition here was that since this manuscript combines both Testaments into one complete Bible, we should be able to verify easily text-quotations from the OT in the NT, just as cross-references in one volume must refer to passages actually to be found there. But in the course of our re-examination of the ancient sources for our knowledge of the OT in Greek, we realized that there is no basis for the theory of Lagarde of an Archetypal LXX, implying that the OT in Greek was originally known and published in a single uniform type which only later developed into different recensions. On the contrary, we saw that as late as in the days of Origen two different translations of the OT into Greek were known as LXX. In combining their variant readings in the fifth column of his *Hexapla* he indicated the source, from which these variants came, by marking them with an obelus or asterisk, respectively. But the very fact that he incorporated these readings in the fifth column proves that he considered the two translations as genuine LXX.

We said that *as late* as the days of Origen the LXX was so to say the common denominator for two translations. This means that we have evidence to prove the existence of these translations at a period prior to that of Origen. To be exact, we have to limit ourselves to proving the existence of the asterisk type only (the obelus type was well represented throughout the centuries in Codex B; cf. p. 383 ff.); this translation must have been withdrawn from circulation not long after Origen and was then forgotten. We shall do this on the basis of the OT quotations in the NT, which differ from the text offered in Codex B. The number of all these passages combined represents merely a fraction of the total references to the OT as found in the NT, since their vast majority fully agree with Codex B. This in itself is proof that the LXX type of Codex B, which as we said before is the obelus type, originates in a pre-Origenian period, since the authors of the NT quoted from it. But our concern here is only the asterisk type, the former existence of which has to be proven from the NT.

a. OT quotations in the NT identical with readings under al ex

Rom. 9.17: εις αυτο του εξηγειρα σε οπως ενδειξωμαι εν σοι την δυναμιν μου; cf. Ex. 9.16: את כחי: O': την ισχυν μου; al ex: την δυναμιν μου.

Rom. 11.4: κατελειπον εμαυτω επτακισχιλιους ανδρας οιτινες ουκ εκαμψαν γονυ τη βααλ; cf. 1 Ki. 19.18: לא כרעו: O': ουκ ωκλασαν γονυ; al ex: ουκ εκαμψαν γονυ.

Rom. 9.33: ιδου τιθημι εν σιων λιθον προσκομματος και πετραν σκανδαλου και ο πιστευων επ αυτω ου καταισχυνθησεται; cf. Isa. 28.16: המאמין: O': και ο πιστευων; al ex: και ο πιστευων επ αυτω.

Luke. 3.4, 5: φωνη βοωντος ... και εσται τα σκολια εις ευθειαν και αι τραχειαι εις οδους λιας; cf. Isa. 40.4: העקב: O': ÷ παντα × τα σκολια; לבקעה: O': εις πεδια; al ex: εις οδους λειας.

Here the close affinity between the NT and the asterisk type of the OT becomes even more obvious by the fact that the obelus reading ÷ παντα × is not included in this lengthy quotations; cf. similarly Matth. 12.17, 18: ιδου ο παις μου ... ο αγαπητος μου, compared with Isa. 42.1: הן עבדי ... בחירי: O': ÷ ιακωβ × ο παις μου ... ÷ ισραηλ × ο εκλεκτος μου. Here, too, the two words *sub obelo* ÷ ιακωβ × and ÷ ισραηλ × are not contained in the NT quotation; cf. on the importance of this variant reading above p. 325, sub 4.

Rom. 3.10, 16, 17: ουκ εστιν δικαιος ... συντριμμα και ταλαιπωρια εν ταις οδοις αυτων και οδον ειρηνης ουκ εγνωσαν; cf. Isa. 59.8: לא ידעו: O': ουκ οιδασι; al ex: ουκ εγνωσαν.

Matth. 9.13 and 12.7: ελεος θελω και ου θυσιαν; cf. Hos. 6.6: ולא זבח: O': η θυσιαν; al ex: και ου θυσιαν. See the discussion of this passage above p. 328.

Hebr. 12.6: ον γαρ αγαπα κυριος παιδευει; cf. Prov. 3.12: יוכיח: O': ελεγχει; al ex: παιδευει.

Perhaps not quite as convincing as these passages, but still not less important for the establishing of a chronology of the texts involved, is:

Matth. 26.31: παταξω τον ποιμενα και διασκορπισθησονται τα προβατα της ποιμνης; cf. Zech. 13.7: הך את הרעה ותפוצין הצאן: O': παταξατε τους ποιμενας και εκσπασατε τα προβατα; al ex: παταξον τον ποιμενα και διασκορπισθησονται τα προβατα. The agreement between Matthew and al ex in the choice of the verb διασκορπισθησονται (as against εκσπασατε of O') suggests an interdependence of these two texts.

b. NT quotations from the Minor Prophets identical with Theodoret's readings

Matth. 9.13 and 12.7: ελεος θελω και ου θυσιαν; cf. Hos. 6.6 according to Th (p. 1584 C): και ου θυσιαν, while Cy (p. 165 D) has: η θυσιαν. On the variant Th: ελεον — Cy: ελεος cf. JBL, 1935, 86, paragraph VIII.

Luke. 23.30: τοτε αρξονται λεγειν τοις ορεσιν πεσετε εφ ημας και τοις βουνοις καλυψατε ημας; cf. Hos. 10.8 according to Th (p. 1608 A/B); in Cy (p. 248 C) the word-order is changed.

Acts 2.18: καιγε επι τους δουλους μου και επι τας δουλας μου; cf. Joel 3.2 in Th (p. 1653 A), while in Cy (p. 376 C) the second μου is missing.

Heb. 10.38: ο δε δικαιος μου εκ πιστεως ζησεται; cf. Hab. 2.4 according to Th (p. 1820 B); in Cy (p. 869 D) μου is missing.

John 19.37: οψονται εις ον εξεκεντησαν; cf. Zech. 12.10 in Th (p. 1945 A); Cy (p. 221-3) offers here: επιβλεψονται . . . κατωρχησαντο. See the discusion of this passage above p. 326, sub 5.

In these five instances the quotations of the NT are the actual textual readings of Theodoret. This is in keeping with our statement at the end of oo that Theodoret's text belongs basically to the asterisk type. Of course we do not assume that the text preserved these characteristics throughout; the following example (*I could find no more*) will show a confusion of the readings, suggestive of an already mixed type of these texts:

Acts 2.19: και δωσω τερατα εν τω ουρανω ανω και σημεια επι της γης κατω; cf. Joel 3.3 in Cy (p. 381 C); in Th (p. 1653 C) the words ανω, σημεια and κατω are missing.

c. OT quotations in the NT and the Vetus Latina

Matth. 15.7, 8 and similarly Mark 7.6: ο λαος ουτος τοις χειλεσι με τιμα; cf. Isa. 29.13 according to B: ο λαος ουτος . . . εν τοις χειλεσιν αυτων τιμωσιν με. The main difference lies in the treatment of the collective noun λαος as a singular (τιμα in the NT passages), or as a plural (τιμωσιν in B, corresponding to MT כבדוני). The same difference is reflected in the two Old Latin translations of this verse in Isa; cf. Ranke, p. 261: honorant me (pl.) — glorificat me (sing.).

Phil. 2.10, 11: ινα εν τω ονοματι ιησου παν γονυ καμψη . . . και πασα γλωσσα εξομολογησεται. These phrases are borrowed from Isa. 45.23, a passage which reads in B: οτι εμοι καμψει παν γονυ και ομειται πασα γλωσσα. These two readings εξομολογησεται and ομειται are combined into a doublet in one tradition within the Vetus Latina; cf. Ranke, p. 265: et iurauit omnis lingua (=B) — et iurabit et confitebitur omnis lingua (= B and NT).

Matth. 9.13, 12.7: ελεος θελω και ου θυσιαν; cf. Hos. 6.6 in B: ελεος θελω η θυσιαν. Similarly Ranke, p. 253: misericordiam uolo quam sacrificium (=B) — misericordiam volo et non sacrificium (=NT).

In these three instances we are fortunate to have parallel evidence from two Old Latin translations; the fact in itself that they reflect a Greek Bible text according to the NT and the LXX, respectively, proves them to be independent translations, without any inner interdependence.

1 Cor. 5.13: εξαρατε τον πονηρον εξ υμων αυτων is obviously a quotation from Deut. 17.7; cf. B: εξαρεις τον πονηρον εξ υμων αυτων. The plural form of the verb εξαρατε (NT) is evidenced by: auferetis malignum ex uobis ipsis (Ulysse Robert, *Heptateuchi Versio Latina Antiquissima*, Lyon 1900, 13).

Acts 7.30: ωφθη αυτω . . . αγγελος κυριου εν φλογι πυρος; this narrative is based upon Ex. 3.2, which reads in B: ωφθη δε αυτω αγγελος κυριου εν πυρι φλογος. The word-order and construction of this verse according to the NT are corroborated in the Old Latin translation: paruit autem ei angelus domini in *flamma ignis* (Ulysse Robert, *Pentateuchi Versio Latina Antiquissima*, Paris 1881, 167).

On p. 331 we stated that the aim of this investigation was to identify the "Bible of the Apostles"; cf. our definition of this term there. Summing up the results of our discussion in this chapter we may now say that *the "Bible of the Apostles" is identical with the asterisk type of the Hexaplaric LXX*, which thus antedates by centuries the days of Origen.

B. THE FINAL REDACTION OF THE HEBREW BIBLE (Cf. MH pp. 186 ff.)

In the MT of the Hebrew Bible the history of the Kingdom of Judah and the House of David is narrated twice: in the Former Prophets (from 1 Sam. 31 on) and in Chronicles (from 1 Chron. 10 on). We entirely disregard here those paraphrases and other additions of the respective redactors; they are meant to form the "prophetic" background for the narrative of historic events, and reflect in their language and ideology the relatively late period of the compilers of these books. We must concern ourselves solely with the approximately 470 verses of strictly historic character, which we would call the *Annales*, and which are included in almost the identical wording in these two sources. With the slight differences, which show that they are *two recensions of one original*, and which are either differences in dialect (cf. p. 229 ff.)—including differences in the vocabulary, morphology and syntax—or merely the result of scribal errors, I have dealt exhaustively on p. 234 ff., by grouping and classifying them together with related source-material. Here I should like to take up another aspect of this problem. Since these *Annales* are common to both historic sources (the Former Prophets and Chronicles), can we still trace any indication of the period when the one recension was finally assigned to the Former Prophets, while the other was incorporated in Chronicles? In other words: can we fix an approximate date for the final redaction of these Biblical books? Here, too, Origen's *Hexapla* proves very helpful, as the following items will demonstrate. I derive the material from quotations of passages of the Former Prophets which have their parallel in Chronicles, and vice versa; while quoting *one* historic book, Origen's quotation reflects not the recension of this book, but that of the other book. This clearly points to the fact that at the time when Origen's sources, the asterisk and the obelus texts, were composed, a time which may of course have been considerably earlier than his own, the two recensions of the *Annales* were not yet finally assigned to the respective Biblical book; the final redaction of these books must have taken place at a later period. Cf. "Conclusion" on p. 409.

a.   O' Reflects the parallel text instead of MT

a.   O' offers a translation of the variant Parallel Text

§ 1. No Evidence is Preserved of a Translation of MT.

a)   O' on the Former Prophets.

2 Sam. 10.6: בדוד: O': ο λαος δαυιδ. The translator had before him 1 Chron. 19.6: עָם דָּוִיד, which he read: עָם דויד. This difference in the

pronunciation is explained by the fact that the Hebrew Bible at that early period consisted of consonants only, without vowel signs, cf. p. 111 f.

2 Sam. 5.23: הסב אל אחריהם : O': αποστρεφου απ αυτων. Cf. 1 Chron. 14.14: הסב מעליהם.

2 Sam. 8.13: כהנים היו : O': αυλαρχαι ησαν. Cf. 1 Chron. 18.17: הראשנים ליד המלך .

b) O' on Chronicles.

1 Chron. 11.1: ויקבצו : O': και ηλθε. Cf. 2 Sam. 5.1: ויבאו.

1 Chron. 17.5: מאהל אל אהל : O': εν σκηνη. Cf. 2 Sam. 7.6: באהל. For an explanation of the Hebrew variant see p. 479, § 46.

1 Chron. 17.5: וממשכן : O': και εν καλυμματι. Cf. 2 Sam. 7.6: ובמשכן; see also p. 479, § 46.

1 Chron. 17.6: שפטי : O': φυλην. Cf. 2 Sam. 7.7: שבטי. See also p. 480, § 47. Similarly cf. Mic. 4.14: שפט, which appears in Cyril of Alexandria's commentary as φυλας, and which in turn was misunderstood by codex B for πυλας (JBL, 1935, 81).

1 Chron. 21.20: את המלאך. O' τον βασιλεα. Cf. 2 Sam. 24.20: את המלך. See also p. 563, § 1a, especially the instance from 2 Sam. 11.1—1 Chron. 20.1.

§ 2. Under al ex MT is given.

a) O' on the Former Prophets.

2 Sam. 6.11: את עבד אדם ואת כל ביתו : O': ολον τον οικον αβεδδαρα και παντα τα αυτου; al ex: τον αβεδδαρα και ολον τον οικον αυτου. On O' cf. 1 Chron. 13.4: את בית עבד אדם ואת כל אשר לו. Thus, ολον remains without a corresponding equivalent in the Hebrew text. Whether the translator really had את כל בית before him, or whether ολον was merely inserted under the influence of the following παντα, remains in doubt. On ολος as equivalent to כל cf. Deut. 6.22: ובכל ביתו : O': και εν ⁖ ολω ╳ τω οικω αυτου.

2 Sam. 7.21: בעבור דברך : O': και δια τον δουλον σου; al ex: δια τον λογον σου. On O' cf. 1 Chron. 17.19: בעבור עבדך.

1 Ki. 10.29: מרכבה ממצרים : O': εξ αιγυπτου αρμα; al ex: αρματα εξ αιγυπτου. On O' cf. 2 Chron. 1.17: ממצרים מרכבה; see also p. 290, § 78 sub 10.

The difference in the interpretation of מרכבה as a singular or plural reflects a similar divergent conception of collective nouns in the Hebrew text, cf. p. 269, § 48.

b) O' on Chronicles.

1 Chron. 10.1: וינס: O': και εφυγον; al ex: και εφυγεν. On O' cf. 1 Sam. 31.1: וינסו; see also p. 271, § 49 and note 1 there.

1 Chron. 11.4: דויד וכל ישראל: O': ο βασιλευς και ανδρες αυτου; al ex: ο βασιλευς δαυιδ και πας ισραηλ. On O' cf. 2 Sam. 5.6: המלך ואנשיו; al ex reflect a combination of both reports: דויד//המלך; cf. similar cases of doublets under c.

1 Chron. 11.5: ויאמרו ישבי יבוס לדויד: O': ειπαν τω δαυιδ; al ex: ειπαν δε οι κατοικουντες την ιηβους τω δαυιδ. On O' cf. 2 Sam. 5.6: ויאמר לדוד; see also p. 290, § 79a.

1 Chron. 11.23: מדה: O': ορατον; al ex: ευμηκη. On O' cf. 2 Sam. 23.21: מראה: see also p. 482, § 55.

1 Chron. 14.7: ובעלידע: O': και ελιαδε; al ex: και βααλιαδα. On O' cf. 2 Sam. 5.16: ואלידע.

1 Chron. 17.14: והעמדתיהו: O': και πιστωσω αυτον; al ex: και στησω αυτον. On O' cf. 2 Sam. 7.16: ונאמן.

1 Chron. 17.21: הלך: O': ωδηγησεν αυτον; al ex: επορευθη. On O' cf. 2 Sam. 7.23: הָלְכוּ, read as הִלְכוֹ; on the change in the pronunciation involved cf. above p. 402 § 1 a the instance from 2 Sam. 10.6.

2 Chron. 13.2: מיכיהו: O': μααχα; al ex: μιχαια. On O' cf. 1 Ki. 15.2: מעכה.

2 Chron. 15.16: אם אסא המלך: O': την μητερα αυτου; al ex: την μητερα ασα του βασιλεως. On O' cf. 1 Ki. 15.13: אמו.

c) Doublets.

2 Sam. 6.2: להעלות: O': εν αναβασει // του αναγαγειν. The first translation corresponds to 1 Chron. 13.6: בַּעֲלָתָה, interpreted as בְּעֲלִיתָה, cf. p. 296, note 4; του αναγαγειν = MT.

2 Chron. 5.9: מן הארון: O': εκ των αγιων; al ex: απο της κιβωτου // εκ των αγιων. On O' cf. 1 Ki. 8.8: מן הקדש; al ex combines this reading with MT; cf. above in b the instance from 1 Chron. 11.4.

b.   O' omits words and phrases of MT, which are not included in the
Parallel Text

§ 3.   *Sub asterisco* MT is given.

2 Sam. 8.14: שם נצבים: O': Vacat. ⋇ εθηκεν εστηλωμενους ×. Cf. 1 Chron.
18.13.

1 Ki. 12.16: דבר: O': ⋇ λογον ×. Cf. 2 Chron. 10.16; for an explanation
of the Hebrew insertion see p. 291, § 81a 1.

1 Ki. 14.31: ושם אמו נעמה העמנית: O': Vacat. ⋇ και ονομα της μητρος αυτου
νααμα η αμμανιτις ×. Cf. 2 Chron. 12.16.

1 Ki. 22.4: אל מלך ישראל: O': Vacat. ⋇ προς βασιλεα ισραηλ ×. Cf. 2
Chron. 18.3.

1 Ki. 22.15: אליו: O': ⋇ προς αυτον ×. Cf. 2 Chron 18.14; see also p. 286,
§ 74c.

2 Ki. 8.19; לו: O': ⋇ αυτω ×. Cf. 2 Chron. 21.7; see also p. 286, § 74c.

2 Ki. 8.29: ארמים: O': ⋇ οι συροι ×. Cf. 2 Chron. 22.6; see also p. 289,
§ 79a.

2 Ki. 11.17: ובין המלך ובין העם (2°): O': ⋇ και αναμεσον του βασιλεως και
αναμεσον του λαου ×. Cf. 2 Chron. 23.16. The Hebrew text of this Ki.-
passage offers an obvious doublet. Further instances for identifying
Hebrew doublets by means of asterisk quotations in Origen, cf. 2
Sam. 6.3-4: וישאהו מבית אבינדב אשר בגבעה: Deut. 17.5: אשר עשו ‥‥ או
לו חות יאיר בן : בשלום ויתן דמי מלחמה; ib. 4.13: את האשה; 1 Ki. 2.5; מתפסח ועד עזה בכל מלכי עבר הנהר: ib. 5.4: מנשה אשר בגלעד. The
O'-translations of these passages are quoted *sub asterisco* in Field's
Hexapla.

2 Ki. 15.34: עשה (2°): O': ⋇ εποιησεν ×. Cf. 2 Chron. 27.2.

§ 4.   Under al ex MT is given.

1 Sam. 31.11: אליו: O': Vacat. al ex: περι αυτου. On O' cf. 1 Chron. 10.11.

1 Ki. 12.15: דבר יהוה: O': ελαλησεν; al ex: ελαλησεν κυριος. On O' cf. 2
Chron. 10.15.

1 Chron. 13.14: בביתו: O': Vacat. al ex: εν τω οικω αυτου. On O' cf.
2 Sam. 6.11.

1 Chron. 13.14: את בית עבד אדם: O': αβεδδαρα; al ex: τον οικον αβεδδαρα.
On O' cf. 2 Sam. 6.11.

b. O' translates MT, but al ex the parallel text

a. O' on the Former Prophets

2 Sam. 5.21: וַאֲנָשָׁיו: O': και οι ανδρες οι μετ αυτου; al ex: και οι ανδρες αυτου. και ειπε κατακαυσαι αυτους εν πυρι. On al ex cf. 1 Chron. 14.12: וַיֹּאמֶר דָּוִד וַיִּשָּׂרְפוּ בָאֵשׁ; on the difference between the passive construction of the Hebrew verb in Chron. and its active form in al ex, cf. p. 251, § 18a α.

2 Sam. 10.8: פֶּתַח הַשַּׁעַר: O': παρα τη θυρα της πυλης; al ex: παρα τον πυλωνα της πολεως. On al ex cf. 1 Chron. 19.9: פֶּתַח הָעִיר.

2 Sam. 12.31: וַיָּשֶׂם: O': και εθηκεν; al ex: και διεπρισεν. On al ex cf. 1 Chron. 20.3: וַיָּשַׂר; see also p. 481, § 53.

2 Sam. 23.13: אֶל קָצִיר: O': εις κασων; al ex: εις την πετραν. On al ex cf. 1 Chron. 11.15. The rendering εις seems to reflect a Hebrew preposition אֶל; on the interchangeability of עַל and אֶל in Hebrew, cf. p. 288, § 77. O' transliterates the ר in קָצִיר with N (in κασων), cf. p. 481, § 53.

2 Sam. 24.10: אֲשֶׁר עָשִׂיתִי: O': ο εποιησα; al ex: ποιησας το ρημα τουτο. On al ex cf. 1 Chron. 21.8: אֲשֶׁר עָשִׂיתִי אֶת הַדָּבָר הַזֶּה.

2 Sam. 24.17: אָנֹכִי חָטָאתִי וְאָנֹכִי הֶעֱוֵיתִי: O': εγω ειμι ηδικησα; al ex: εγω ημαρτηκα και εγω ειμι ο ποιμην εκακοποιησα. On al ex cf. 1 Chron. 21.17: וְהָרַע הֲרֵעֹתִי, translated as: וְהָרֹעֶה הֲרֵעֹתִי, with dittography of the ה, cf. p. 488, § 69b . As to the difference in the pronunciation of the word in question, cf. our remark on 2 Sam. 10.6 above p. 402, § 1 a. On the difficulty of the Greek construction under O': ειμι with a verb in the aorist tense (ηδικησα), cf. p. 345, § 5d, and the cross-references marked there.

b. O' on Chronicles

1 Chron. 10.11: יָבֵישׁ גִּלְעָד: O': οι κατοικουντες γαλααδ; al ex: οι κατοικουντες ιαβις της γαλααδ. On al ex cf. 1 Sam. 31.11: יֹשְׁבֵי יָבֵישׁ גִּלְעָד. Under O' the Hebrew יבש is obviously translated as ישב or ישבי, cf. p. 269, § 48. On metathesis in the Hebrew Bible see p. 489, § 70.

1 Chron. 11.13: שְׂעוֹרִים: O': κριθων; al ex: φακου. On al ex cf. 2 Sam. 23.11: עֲדָשִׁים. The interrelation between these two Hebrew readings is explained on p. 488, § 69c.

1 Chron. 13.6: שֵׁם: O′: ονομα αυτου; al ex: ονομα αυτου εχει. On al ex cf. 2 Sam. 6.2: שֵׁם שָׁם, read here as: שֵׁם שָׁם. As to the change in the pronunciation, cf. our remark on 2 Sam. 10.6 above § 1 a.

1 Chron. 18.2: ויהיו: O′: και ησαν; al ex: και εγενηθη. On the singular in al ex cf. 2 Sam. 8.2: ותהי. For the difference in the gender of these Hebrew verbal forms, see p. 267, § 45 γ.

2 Chron. 6.9: כי: O′: οτι; al ex: αλλ η. On al ex cf. 1 Ki. 8.19: כי אם; see also p. 292, § 81 b 3.

2 Chron. 7.7: ואת החלבים: O′: και τα στεατα; al ex: και τα στεατα των ειρηνικων. On al ex cf. 1 Ki. 8.64: ואת חלבי השלמים.

2 Chron. 13.2: בת אוריאל מן גבעה: O′: θυγατηρ ουριηλ απο γαβαων; al ex θυγατηρ αβεσσαλωμ. On al ex cf. 1 Ki. 15.2: בת אבשלום.

D. THE BASIC HEBREW BIBLE OF CODEX B

The following examples are derived from the second book of Samuel; only those chapters and verses are represented here which have their parallel in the first book of Chronicles. For chapter 22 in 2 Sam., the parallel is Ps. 18.

5.2: לְנָגִיד: B: εισηγουμενος = נָגִיד = 1 Chron. 11.2.

5.17: מָשְׁחוּ: B: κεχρισται = נִמְשַׁח = 1 Chron. 14.8.

5.19: הֲתִתְּנֵם: B: και παραδωσεις αυτους = וּנְתַתָּם = 1 Chron. 14.10.

5.21: עֲצַבֵּיהֶם: B: τους θεους αυτων = אֱלֹהֵיהֶם = 1 Chron. 14.12.

5.23: אֶל אַחֲרֵיהֶם: B: απ' αυτων = מֵעֲלֵיהֶם = 1 Chron. 14.14.

בְּכָאִים: B: του κλαυθμῶνος = הַבְּכָאִים = 1 Chron. 14.14.

5.25: כֶּן missing in B = 1 Chron. 14.16.

מִגֶּבַע: B: απο Γαβαων = מִגִּבְעוֹן = 1 Chron. 14.16.

6.3,4: חֲדָשָׁה וַיִּשָּׂאֻהוּ מִבֵּית אֲבִינָדָב אֲשֶׁר בַּגִּבְעָה missing in B = 1 Chron. 13.7

6.6: וַיִּשְׁלַח עֻזָּה: B adds: = την χειρα αυτου = אֶת יָדוֹ = 1 Chron. 13.9.

6.9: וַיֹּאמֶר, B: λεγων = לֵאמֹר = 1 Chron. 13.12.

6.10: עַל (עִיר): B: εις = אֶל = 1 Chron. 13.13.

6.11: אֶת עֹבֵד אֱדֹם וְאֶת כָּל בֵּיתוֹ: B: ολον τον οικον Αβεδδαρα και παντα τα αυτου = אֶת כָּל בֵּית עֹבֵד אֱדֹם וְאֶת כָּל אֲשֶׁר לוֹ = 1 Chron. 13.14.

6.16: וְהָיָה: B: και εγενετο = וַיְהִי = 1 Chron. 15.29.

עִיר דָּוִד: B: εως πολεως Δαυειδ = עַד עִיר דוד = 1 Chron. 15.29.

6.19: אַחַת ... אֶחָד ... אַחַת missing in B = 1 Chron. 16.3.

7.5: הַאַתָּה: B: ου συ = לֹא אַתָּה = 1 Chron. 17.4.

7.7: בְּנֵי (ישראל) missing in B = 1 Chron. 17.6.

7.11: וּלְמִן הַיּוֹם: B: απο των ημερων = לְמִיָּמִים = 1 Chron. 17.10.

יהוה (יעשה לך): B: και εσται = וְהָיָה = 1 Chron. 17.11.

7.13: יִבְנֶה: B: οικοδομησει μοι = יבנה לִי = 1 Chron. 17.12.

כִּסֵּא מַמְלַכְתּוֹ: B: τον θρονον αυτον = כִּסְאוֹ = 1 Chron. 17.12.

7.15: לֹא יָסוּר: B: ουκ αποστησω = לֹא אָסִיר = 1 Chron. 17.13.

מֵעָם שָׁאוּל אֲשֶׁר: B: αφ ων = מֵאֲשֶׁר = 1 Chron. 17.13.

7.16: כִּסְאֲךָ: B: και ο θρονος αυτου = וְכִסְאוֹ = 1 Chron. 17.14.

7.19: גַּם missing in B = 1 Chron. 17.17.

אֶל (בית): B: υπερ = עַל = 1 Chron. 17.17.

7.21: דְּבָרְךָ: B: τον δουλον σου = עַבְדְּךָ = 1 Chron. 17.19.

7.22: כְּכֹל (אשר): B: εν πασιν = בְּכֹל = 1 Chron. 17.20.

7.23: כְּיִשְׂרָאֵל: B: Ισραηλ = יִשְׂרָאֵל = 1 Chron. 17.21.

לְעָם: B: λαον = עָם = 1 Chron. 17.21.

וְלָשׂוּם לוֹ: B: του θεσθαι σε = לָשׂוּם לְךָ = 1 Chron. 17.21.

לְאַרְצֶךָ: B: του εκβαλειν = לְגָרֵשׁ = 1 Chron. 17.21.

7.25: הָקֵם: B: πιστωσον = יֵאָמֵן = 1 Chron. 17.23.

7.28: אֶל (עבדך): B: υπερ = עַל = 1 Chron. 17.26.

8.3: הֲדַדְעֶזֶר: B: Αδρααζαρ = הֲדַרְעֶזֶר = 1 Chron. 18.3. Idem v. v. 5, 7, 9, 10, 10.16, 19.

8.4: אֶלֶף: B adds: αρματα = רֶכֶב = 1 Chron. 18.4.

וּשְׁבַע מֵאוֹת: B. και επτα χιλιαδας = וְשִׁבְעַת אֲלָפִים = 1 Chron. 18.4.

8.7: אֶל (עבדי): B: επι = עַל = 1 Chron. 18.7.

8.8: הַרְבֵּה מְאֹד. B adds: εν αυτω εποιησεν Σαλωμων την θαλασσαν την χαλκην και τους στυλους και τους λουτηρας και παντα τα σκευη = בָּהּ עָשָׂה שְׁלֹמֹה אֶת יָם הַנְּחֹשֶׁת וְאֶת הָעַמּוּדִים וְאֵת כָּל הַכֵּלִים = 1 Chron. 18.8.

8.9: תֹּעִי: Θουου = תֹּעוּ = 1 Chron. 18.9.

8.10: יוֹרָם: B: Ιεδδουραν, cf. הֲדוֹרָם: 1 Chron. 18.10.

8.12: מֵאֲרָם: B: εκ της Ιδουμαιας = מֵאֱדוֹם = 1 Chron. 18.11.

8.13: מֵהַכּוֹתוֹ: B: επαταξεν = הַכָּה = 1 Chron. 18.12.

אֲרָם: B: Ιδουμαιαν = אֱדוֹם = 1 Chron. 18.12.

8.14: וַיְהִי: B: και εγενοντο = וַיִּהְיוּ = 1 Chron. 18.13.

8.15: דָּוִד (ויהי) missing in B = 1 Chron. 18.14.

8.18: כֹּהֲנִים: B: αυλαρχαι; cf. הָרִאשׁוֹנִים לְיַד הַמֶּלֶךְ: 1 Chron. 18.17.

10.2: אֶל (אביו): B: περι = עַל = 1 Chron. 19.2.

10.5: וַיַּגִּדוּ לְדָוִד: B adds: υπερ των ανδρων = עַל הָאֲנָשִׁים = I Chron. 19.5.

10.6: בְּדָוִד: B: ο λαος Δαυειδ = עַם דָּוִד; erroneous vocalization of the original: עָם דָּוִד = I Chron. 19.6.

10.17: וַיַּעַרְכוּ אֲרָם לִקְרַאת דָּוִד: B: και παρεταξατο Δαυειδ απεναντι Συριας = וַיַּעֲרֹךְ דָּוִד לִקְרַאת אֲרָם = I Chron. 19.17.

23.8: עַל שְׁמֹנֶה: B praemittit: ουτος εσπασατο την ρομφαιαν αυτου, cf. הוּא עוֹרֵר אֶת חֲנִיתוֹ: I Chron. 11.11.

23.13: וְחַיַּת: B: και ταγμα = וּמַחֲנֶה = I Chron. 11.15.

23.17: מֵעֲשֹׂתִי: B: του ποιησαι = מֵעֲשׂוֹת = I Chron. 11.19.
בְּנַפְשׁוֹתָם: B adds πιομαι = אֶשְׁתֶּה = I Chron. 11.19.

23.21: חֲנִית: B adds: ως ξυλον διαβαθρας = כִּמְנוֹר אֹרְגִים = I Chron. 11.23.

24.12: אֶל דָּוִד: B adds: λεγων = לֵאמֹר = I Chron. 21.10.

24.13: שֶׁבַע: B: τρια = שָׁלוֹשׁ = I Chron. 21.12.

24.14: נִפְּלָה: B: εμπεσουμαι = אֶפְּלָה = I Chron. 21.13.
רַבִּים רַחֲמָיו: B adds: σφοδρα = מְאֹד = I Chron. 21.13.

24.24: עֹלוֹת: B: ολοκαυτωμα = עוֹלָה = I Chron. 21.24.

22.12: חֶשְׁךְ: B adds: αποκρυφης αυτου = סִתְרוֹ = Ps. 18.12.
סֻכּוֹת: B: η σκηνη αυτου = סֻכָּתוֹ = Ps. 18.12.
חֶשְׁרַת: B: σκοτος = חֶשְׁכַת = Ps. 18.12.

22.15: K: ויהמם, Q: וַיָּהֹם: B: και εξεστησεν αυτους = וַיְהֻמֵּם = K = Ps. 18.15.

22.16: יֵגָּלוּ: B: και απεκαλυφθη = וַיִּגָּלוּ = Ps. 18.16.

22.25: כְּבֹרִי: B: κατα την καθαριοτητα των χειρων μου = כְּבֹר יָדַי = Ps. 18.25

22.26: גִּבּוֹר: B: ανδρός = גֶּבֶר = Ps. 18.26.

22.39: וָאֲכַלֵּם missing in B = Ps. 18.39.

22.42: יִשְׁעוּ: B: βοησονται = יְשַׁוְּעוּ = Ps. 18.42.

22.43: אֲרִקָּעֵם missing in B = Ps. 18.43.

Conclusion

The result may be summed up as follows: while translating the second book of Samuel, Codex B very frequently offers a translation of the Hebrew text of the parallel source. This clearly points to the fact that at the time, when the Greek translation underlying Codex B was made, the two recensions of the Hebrew *Annales* were not yet finally assigned to Samuel and Chronicles, respectively, as they appear now. The final redaction of these books must have taken place at a later period.

E. Codex B in Chronicles has Passages from Kings and Vice Versa

Certain narratives, which are contained in the Hebrew Bible in Kings only, but not in Chronicles, appear in Codex B in Chronicles in an obviously new translation (and vice versa). Having no corresponding text in Hebrew, these verses are identified as *a, b, c* (and so on) of the last preceding verse in Brooke-McLean's edition.

2 Ki. 23	2 Ki. 23	2 Chron. 35
24 וְגַם אֶת הָאֹבוֹת	24 και γε τους θελητας	19a και τους ενγαστριμυθους
וְאֶת הַיִּדְּעֹנִים	και τους γνωριστας	και τους γνωστας
וְאֶת הַתְּרָפִים	και τα θεραφειν	και τα θαραφειν
וְאֶת הַגִּלֻּלִים	και τα ειδωλα	και τα ειδωλα
וְאֵת כָּל הַשִּׁקֻּצִים	και παντα τα προσοχθισματα	και τα καρασειμ α ην
אֲשֶׁר נִרְאוּ	τα γεγονοτα	
בְּאֶרֶץ יְהוּדָה	εν γη Ιουδα	εν γη Ιουδα
וּבִירוּשָׁלַ͏ִם	και εν Ιερουσαλημ	και εν Ιερουσαλημ
בִּעֵר יֹאשִׁיָּהוּ	εξηρεν Ιωσειας,	ενεπυρισεν ο βασιλευς Ιωσειας
לְמַעַן הָקִים	ινα στηση	ινα στηση
אֶת דִּבְרֵי הַתּוֹרָה	τους λογους του νομου	τους λογους του νομου
הַכְּתֻבִים עַל הַסֵּפֶר	τους γεγραμμενους επι τω βιβλιω	τους γεγραμμενους επι του βιβλιου
אֲשֶׁר מָצָא	ου ευρεν	ου ευρεν
חִלְקִיָּהוּ הַכֹּהֵן	χελκειας ο ιερευς	χελκειας ο ιερευς
בֵּית יהוה:	εν οικω Κυριου.	εν τω οικω Κυριου.
25 וְכָמֹהוּ לֹא הָיָה	25 ομοιος αυτω ουκ εγενηθη	19b ομοιος αυτω ουκ εγενηθη
לְפָנָיו מֶלֶךְ	εμπροσθεν αυτου βασιλευς	εμπροσθεν αυτου
אֲשֶׁר שָׁב אֶל יהוה	ος επεστρεψεν προς Κυριον	ος επεστρεψεν προς Κυριον
בְּכָל לְבָבוֹ	εν ολη καρδια αυτου	εν ολη καρδια αυτου
וּבְכָל נַפְשׁוֹ	και εν ολη ψυχη αυτου	και εν ολη ψυχη αυτου
וּבְכָל מְאֹדוֹ	και εν ολη ισχυι αυτου	και εν ολη τη ισχυι αυτου
כְּכֹל תּוֹרַת מֹשֶׁה	κατα παντα τον νομον Μωυση,	κατα παντα τον νομον Μωυση.
וְאַחֲרָיו	και μετ αυτον	και μετ αυτον
לֹא קָם כָּמֹהוּ:	ουκ ἀνεστη ομοιος αυτω.	ουκ ανεστη ομοιος.
26 אַךְ לֹא שָׁב יהוה	26 πλην ουκ απεστραφη Κυριος	19c πλην ουκ απεστραφη Κυριος
מֵחֲרוֹן אַפּוֹ הַגָּדוֹל	απο θυμου της οργης αυτου του μεγαλου	απο οργης θυμου αυτου του μεγαλου,
אֲשֶׁר חָרָה אַפּוֹ	ου εθυμωθη οργη αυτου	ου ωργισθη θυμω Κυριος
בִּיהוּדָה	εν τω Ιουδα	εν τω Ιουδα
עַל כָּל הַכְּעָסִים	επι τους παροργισμους	επι παντα τα προσταγματα

אֲשֶׁר הִכְעִיסוֹ	ους παρωργισεν αυτον	α παρωργισεν
מְנַשֶּׁה:	Μανασσης.	Μανασσης.
27 וַיֹּאמֶר יְהוָה	27 και ειπεν Κυριος	19d και ειπεν Κυριος
גַּם אֶת יְהוּדָה	και γε τον Ιουδα	και τον Ιουδαν
אָסִיר מֵעַל פָּנַי	αποστησω απο του προσω-	αποστησω απο προσωπου,
	που αυτου,	
כַּאֲשֶׁר הֲסִרֹתִי	καθως απεστησα	καθως απεστησα
אֶת יִשְׂרָאֵל	τον Ισραηλ,	τον Ισραηλ,
וּמָאַסְתִּי	και απεωσομαι	και απωσαμην
אֶת הָעִיר הַזֹּאת	την πολιν ταυτην	την πολιν
אֲשֶׁר בָּחַרְתִּי	ην εξελεξαμην,	ην εξελεξαμην,
אֶת יְרוּשָׁלַםִ	την Ιερουσαλημ,	την Ιερουσαλημ,
וְאֶת הַבַּיִת	και τον οικον	και τον οικον
אֲשֶׁר אָמַרְתִּי	ου ειπον	ον ειπα
יִהְיֶה שְׁמִי שָׁם:	Εσται το ονομα μου εκει.	Εσται το ονομα μου εκει.

2 Ki. 23	2 Ki. 23	2 Chron. 36
31 וְשֵׁם אִמּוֹ ···	31 . . . . και ονομα τη μητρι	2a και ονομα της μητρος αυτου
	αυτου	
חֲמִיטַל	Αμειται,	Αβειταλ
בַּת יִרְמְיָ֣הוּ	θυγατηρ Ιερεμιου	θυγατηρ Ιερεμιου
מִלִּבְנָה:	εκ Λημνα.	εκ Λοβενα.
32 וַיַּעַשׂ הָרַע	32 και εποιησεν το πονηρον	2b και εποιησεν το πονηρον
בְּעֵינֵי יְהוָה	εν οφθαλμοις Κυριου	ενωπιον Κυριου
כְּכֹל אֲשֶׁר עָשׂוּ	κατα παντα οσα εποιησαν	κατα παντα α εποιησαν
אֲבֹתָיו:	οι πατερες αυτου.	οι πατερες αυτου
33 וַיַּאַסְרֵהוּ	33 και μετεστησεν αυτον	2c και εδησεν αυτον
פַרְעֹה נְכֹה	Φαραω Νεχαω	Φαραω Νεχαω
בְרִבְלָה	εν Αβλαα	εν Δαβλαθα
בְּאֶרֶץ חֲמָת	εν γη Εματ	εν γη Ιεμαθ
מִמְּלֹךְ	του μη βασιλευειν	του μη βασιλευειν
בִּירוּשָׁלָםִ ····	εν Ιερουσαλημ . . .	εν Ιερουσαλημ.

2 Ki. 23	2 Ki. 23	2 Chron. 36
35 וְהַכֶּסֶף וְהַזָּהָב	35 και το αργυριον και το χρυ-	4a και το αργυριον και χρυσιον
	σιον	
נָתַן יְהוֹיָקִים	εδωκεν Ιωακειμ	εδωκεν
לְפַרְעֹה	τω Φαραω.	τω Φαραω.
אַךְ הֶעֱרִיךְ	πλην ετιμογραφησεν	τοτε ηρξατο
אֶת הָאָרֶץ	την γην	η γη φορολογεισθαι,
לָתֵת אֶת הַכֶּסֶף	του δουναι το αργυριον	του δουναι το αργυριον
עַל פִּי פַרְעֹה	επι στοματος Φαραω.	επι στομα Φαραω.

אִישׁ כְּעֶרְכּוֹ	ανηρ κατα την συντιμησιν αυτου	και εκαστος κατα δυναμιν
נָגַשׂ	εδωκαν	απητει
אֶת הַכֶּסֶף וְאֶת הַזָּהָב	το αργυριον και το χρυσιον	το αργυριον και το χρυσιον
אֶת עַם הָאָרֶץ	μετα του λαου της γης,	παρα του λαου της γης,
לָתֵת	δουναι	δουναι
לְפַרְעֹה נְכֹה:	τω Φαραω Νεχαω.	τω Φαραω Νεχαω.

2 Ki. 24	2 Ki. 24	2 Chron. 36
1 בְּיָמָיו עָלָה	1 εν ταις ημεραις αυτου ανεβη Ναβουχοδονοσορ	5a εν ταις ημεραις αυτου ηλθεν Ναβουχοδονοσορ
נְבֻכַדְנֶאצַּר		
מֶלֶךְ בָּבֶל	βασιλευς Βαβυλωνος,	βασιλευς Βαβυλωνος,
וַיְהִי לוֹ יְהוֹיָקִים	και εγενηθη αυτω Ιωακειμ	και ην αυτω
עֶבֶד	δουλος	δουλευων
שָׁלֹשׁ שָׁנִים	τρια ετη,	τρια ετη
וַיָּשָׁב	και απεστρεψεν	
וַיִּמְרָד־בּוֹ:	και ηθετησεν εν αυτω.	και απεστη απ αυτου.
2 וַיְשַׁלַּח יְהוָה בּוֹ	2 και απεστειλεν αυτω	5b και απεστειλεν Κυριος επ αυτω
אֶת גְּדוּדֵי כַשְׂדִּים	τους μονοζωνους των χαλδαιων	τους χαλδαιους
וְאֶת גְּדוּדֵי אֲרָם	και τους μονοζωνους Συριας	και ληστηρια Συρων
וְאֶת גְּדוּדֵי מוֹאָב	και τους μονοζωνους Μωαβ	και ληστηρια Μωαβειτων
וְאֶת גְּדוּדֵי בְנֵי עַמּוֹן	και τους μονοζωνους υιων Αμμων,	και υιων Αμμων και της Σαμαρειας
וַיְשַׁלְּחֵם בִּיהוּדָה	και εξαπεστειλεν αυτους εν τη γη Ιουδα,	
לְהַאֲבִידוֹ	του κατισχυσαι	και απεστησαν μετα τον λογον τουτον
כִּדְבַר יְהוָה	κατα τον λογον Κυριου	κατα τον λογον Κυριου
אֲשֶׁר דִּבֶּר	ον ελαλησεν	
בְּיַד עֲבָדָיו הַנְּבִיאִים:	εν χειρι των δουλων αυτου των προφητων.	εν χειρι των παιδων αυτου των προφητων.
3 אַךְ עַל פִּי יְהוָה	3 πλην επι τον θυμον Κυριου	5c πλην θυμος Κυριου
הָיְתָה בִּיהוּדָה	ην εν τω Ιουδα	ην επι Ιουδαν
לְהָסִיר מֵעַל פָּנָיו	αποστηναι αυτον απο του προσωπου	του αποστηναι αυτον απο προσωπου αυτου
בְּחַטֹּאת מְנַשֶּׁה	εν αμαρτιαις Μανασση	δια Μανασση
כְּכֹל אֲשֶׁר עָשָׂה:	κατα παντα οσα εποιησεν.	εν πασιν οις εποιησεν.
4 וְגַם דַּם הַנָּקִי	4 και γε αιμα αθωον	5d και εν αιματι αθωω
אֲשֶׁר שָׁפַךְ	εξεχεεν	ω εξεχεεν Ιωακειμ ·
וַיְמַלֵּא אֶת יְרוּשָׁלַם	και επλησεν την Ιερουσαλημ	ενεπλησεν την Ιερουσαλημ

דָּם נָקִי	αιματος αθωου.	αιματος αθωου.
וְלֹא אָבָה יהוה	και ουκ ηθελησεν Κυριος	και ουκ ηθελησεν Κυριος
לִסְלֹחַ:	ιλασθῆναι.	εξολεθρευσκι αυτους.

2 Chron. 8	2 Chron. 8	1 Ki. 2
4 וַיִּבֶן	4 και ωκοδομησεν	46d και αυτος ωκοδομησεν
אֶת תַּדְמֹר	την Θοεδομορ	την Θερμαι
בַּמִּדְבָּר …	εν τη ερημω . . .	εν τη ερημω.

2 Chron. 9	2 Chron. 9	1 Ki. 2
26 וַיְהִי מוֹשֵׁל	26 και ην ηγουμενος	46k και ην αρχων
בְּכָל הַמְּלָכִים	παντων των βασιλεων	εν πασιν τοις βασιλευσιν
מִן הַנָּהָר	απο του ποταμου	απο του ποταμου
וְעַד אֶרֶץ פְּלִשְׁתִּים	και εως γης αλλοφυλων	και εως γης αλλοφυλων
וְעַד גְּבוּל	και εως οριων	και εως οριων
מִצְרָיִם:	Αιγυπτου.	Αιγυπτου.

In 2 Sam. 5.14-16, the children of David are listed; with וֶאֱלִיפָלֶט: B: και Ἐλειφααθ, the list is completed. What follows in Codex B is a transliteration (with explainable errors) of the list according to the parallel passage in Chronicles.

1 Chron. 14	1 Chron. 14	2 Sam. 5
4 … שַׁמּוּעַ	4 . . . Σαμαα	16 . . . Σαμαε,
וְשׁוֹבָב	Ισοβοαμ	Ιεσσειβαθ,
נָתָן	Ναθαμ	Ναθαν,
וּשְׁלֹמֹה:	Σαλωμων	Γαλαμααν,
5 וְיִבְחָר	5 και Βααρ	Ιεβααρ,
וֶאֱלִישׁוּעַ	και Εκταε	Θεησους
וְאֶלְפָּלֶט:	και Ελειφαλεθ	Ελφαλατ,
6 וְנֹגַהּ	6 και Ναγεθ	Ναγεδ,
וְנֶפֶג	και Ναφαθ	Ναφεκ,
וְיָפִיעַ:	και Ιανουον	Ιαναθα,
7 וֶאֱלִישָׁמָע	7 και Ελεισαμαε	Λεασαμυς,
וּבְעֶלְיָדָע	και Βαλεδαε	Βααλειμαθ,
וֶאֱלִיפָלֶט:	και Εμφαλετ.	Ελειφααθ.

CHAPTER FOUR

HEBREW GRAMMAR — A HISTORICAL GROWTH

I. VOCALIZATION

A. The Problem and Its History

§ 1. The Basic Laws of Tiberian Grammar.

I) The Tiberian Vocalization System consists of the following vowel-signs which according to the uncontested grammatical theories indicate:

a) Full vowels: ָ ַ ֵ ִ ֶ ֹ ֻ וּ

b) A murmuring vowel: ְ which, according to its function, is differentiated in *shewa quiescens, mobile* and *medium*

c) Composite vowels: ֲ ֱ ֳ

d) *Dagesh*: mainly as *dagesh forte* and *lene*, according to its function.

II) The full vowels are divided in: (α) long vowels and (β) short vowels.

III) A syllable always begins with a consonant. The only exception which B-L § 11a note: "dass *ua* 'und' in der tiberischen Überlieferung in gewissen Fällen zu *u* wurde: וּכְסִיל 'und ein törichter,' וּמִרְמָה 'und Betrug' " reflects a misconception on the part of that grammar. For, while ו as a *mater lectionis* was vocalic, as a *copula* it was originally pronounced as a consonant. Cf. similarly the difference in the pronunciation of ו as a *mater lectionis* in מַצּוֹת (vocalic) and as a consonant in מִצְוֹת.

IV) A syllable is either (α) open, or (β) closed.

V) An open syllable has a long vowel, a closed syllable a short one; except for a stressed syllable, which though closed may have a long vowel.

VI) A syllable is closed (α) by a consonant with *shewa* (in this case the *shewa* is termed: *quiescens*), or (β) by a *dagesh* in the following consonant (which is thus a *dagesh forte*).

VII) The letters א ה ח ע ר do not accept *dagesh*; consequently, a short vowel in an open syllable preceding one of these letters must be lengthened.

VIII)   The laws with regard to the spirantization of the בּ גּ דּ כּ פּ תּ as laid down f.i. by Bergstr. § 18.

§ 2.   The Importance of Rule II.

The division of the vowels into long and short ones is basic for the Tiberian Grammar; the abrogation of this rule would mean the negation of other basic laws, too, since they are closely interwoven into one system: (a) The division of the *shewa* into *shewa mobile* and *shewa quiescens* is determined by the fact whether the vowel of the preceding syllable is long or short: בֵּרְכוּ = בֵּ–רְכוּ but בֵּרְכָיו = בִּרְ–כָיו; כָּבְדָה = כָּ–בְדָה but הֻכְבַּד = הֻכְ–בַּד. These examples prove in addition the interrelation between Rule VIII concerning the בּ גּ דּ כּ פּ תּ and our Rule II.—(b) If in the course of the declension an open syllable becomes closed, or a closed syllable with the stress on it loses the stress, then their long vowel simultaneously changes into the corresponding short one, and vice versa: עִזִּים – עֹז; מַתְכָּנְתּוֹ – מַתְכֹּנֶת; בְּחֶמְלָתוֹ – בְּחֶמְלַת; מִדְבָּרָה – מִדְבָּר; מְדַבֵּר– – מְדַבָּר. — (c) There can be no long vowel two syllables removed from the one with the stress; in such cases as a rule ָ and ֵ are reduced to *shewa* themselves, while in the case of ִ the following *i*-vowel is reduced to *shewa*: רְבָצִים – רֹבֵץ; קְרֵבִים – קָרֵב; שְׁנַת, שָׁנָה and שְׁנָה become; but short vowels are not affected: כְּתָנְתּוֹ; מַלְאָכָיו; מִשְׁמַרְכֶם: here the first vowel remained unchanged though suffixes were added to the nouns.

§ 3.   Inner contradictions.

The history of Hebrew Grammar is a history of endeavors to reconcile the basic laws with one another, and to smooth out the apparent difficulties in their application. E.g., יַבֶּלֶת is a nominal form like נַחֲלַת; the פתח in יַ is short, for which reason a *dagesh* in the following בֶּ closes the syllable. The ח in נַחֲלַת cannot accept a *dagesh*; hence, the פתח in נַ *ought* to have been lengthened, according to Rule VII (§ 1); but in fact it is not lengthened. How, then, are we to explain such discrepancies?

§ 4.   Theories to alleviate such Difficulties.

Three theories were advanced to explain these difficulties, each one from a different angle:

a)   Virtual lengthening (cf. Bergstr. § 28a): according to this theory

the פתח in גְּחֶלֶת is *virtually lengthened*. We thus have two kinds of פתח:
the regular פתח which is short, and another one which is *virtually lengthened*. Needless to say that the same applies to all the short vowels; cf. the
ַ in שֻׁבַּר and רִחַם; the ֶ in וְכֻבַּס and נֶחָמָה.

b)   The validity of Rule VII—argues another theory—is only of
comparatively younger date; originally, the letters א ה ח ע ר were treated
just as all the other sound letters of the alphabet, and only as a later development their ability to be geminated was given up, without consistently
resulting in a lengthening of the preceding vowel: "Geminierte Laryngale
und r wurden vereinfacht. Dabei erhielt immer vor r, oft vor ' und ',
seltener for h und ḥ der vorangehende Vokal Ersatzdehnung, so dass a
zu ā, i zu ē und u zu ō wurde." (B-L § 24q).

c)   These two theories have an hitherto undisputed basic concept in
common: the validity of Rule II: ַ ָ ֶ are of necessity reflecting short
vowels. The problem confronting the grammarian is: how to account for
the missing *dagesh* in the following א ה ח ע ר. The third theory finds the
solution of this problem in the abrogation of Rule II: "Sämtliche Vokalzeichen (ausser Schwa und den Chatefs) (i.e. all the full vowels) können an
sich *lange oder kurze Vokale* bezeichnen: ob ein Vokal lang oder kurz ist,
hängt von der Wortform ab und ist aus der Schreibung zunächst nicht zu
ersehen; tatsächlich allerdings zeigt sich bei Untersuchung der Wort-
formen, dass ָ < a in den allermeisten Fällen lang, ַ fast stets kurz ist.
Einen Anhalt für die Entscheidung bilden die Vokalbuchstaben: plene
geschriebene Vokale sind fast stets lang, defectiv geschriebene in sehr
vielen Fällen kurz." (Bergsträsser § 10d).

§ 5.   The validity of rule VII.

These three attempts to explain how an otherwise short vowel could
remain in an open syllable preceding a laryngal אהחע may create the
impression that such occurrences were rare and represent merely exceptions to our well attested Rule VII. But in reality things are quite
different, as will be seen from the following brief list of verbs *mediae*
אהחע and their vocalization in the various tenses of the pi'el and its
derivatives:

a) *Mediae* א. Vowel-signs used

בּאר: וּבָאֵר–בַּאֵר ;בֵּאֵר

גאל: מְגָאֵל ;וֶאֶגְאָלְךָ

מאן: יְמָאֵן ;מֵאֵן

נאף: תִּנְאַפְנָה–וַיִּנְאֲפוּ ;נִאֲפָה; מְנָאֵף

נאץ: מְנַאֲצֵי–לְמִנְאֲצִי ;נִאֵץ; מֹנָאֵץ ;יְנָאֵץ

נאר: נֵאַרְתָּה–נִאֵר

פאר: יְפָאֵר ;פִּאֲרֵךְ

שאל: יִשְׁאֲלוּ ;וְשָׁאֲלוּ

נחם: נֶחָמָה ;יְנַחֵם ;נִחַם

נחש: יְנַחֵשׁ ;נִחַשְׁתִּי

סחה: וְסִחִיתִי

פחד: מְפַחֵד

צחק: לְצַחֵק

רחם: יְרַחֵם ;רִחַם; רֻחָם

רחף: יְרַחֵף

רחץ: הִתְרָחַצְתִּי ;רָחָץ

רחק: יְרַחֲקוּ ;רִחַק

שחד: שִׁחֲדוּ

שחק: מְשַׂחֵק ;וְשִׂחַקְתִּי

שחר: מְשַׁחֲרֵי ;וְשִׁחֲרוּ

שחת: שַׁחֵת ;שִׁחֵת

b) *Mediae* ה. Vowel-signs used

אהב: מְאַהֲבַי ;תְּאָהֲבוּ

בהל: מְבֹהָלִים ;תְּבַהֵל

טהר: מְטֹהָרָה ;טַהֵר ;וְטִהַר

כהן: יְכַהֵן ;כִּהֵן

להט: תְּלַהֵט ;וְלִהַט

נהג: יְנַהֵג ;נִהַג

נהל: יְנַהֵל ;נֵהַלְתָּ

d) *Mediae* ע. Vowel-signs used

בער: מְבֹעֶרֶת ;יְבַעֵר ;בִּעֵר

בעת: תְּבַעֵת ;בְּעָתַהוּ

כעס: כְּעָסוּנִי

מעט: מֵעֲטוּ

מעך: מֹעֲכוּ

נער: יְנַעֵר ;וְנִעֵר

פעם: וַתִּתְפָּעֶם–לְפַעֲמוֹ

צעק: מְצַעֵק

שער: וְיִשְׂתָּעֵר–וִישָׂעֲרֻהוּ

תעב: יְתָעֵב–תְּתַעֵב ;תְּעֲבוּנִי; לְמְתָעֵב–הַמְתַעֲבִים

c) *Mediae* ח. Vowel-signs used

אחז: מְאַחֵז

אחר: יְאַחֵר ;אִחַר

כחד: אֲכַחֵד ;כִּחֵד

כחש: כַּחֵשׁ ;כִּחֵשׁ

נחל: לְנַחֵל ;נִחַל

The first observation that strikes our eye while we are examining this list is that the cases with *Ersatzdehnung* (i.e., the substitution of ָ and ֵ for ַ and ִ respectively) form a barely noticeable minority, while in the overwhelming majority of instances the verbs *mediae* אהחע are treated as sound verbs. The only difference of importance in the treatment of the verbs *mediae* אהחע as compared with the sound verbs is the absence of the *dagesh* to indicate the gemination of the laryngal. The explanation of this fact seems quite obvious: *The gemination of a letter may, but not necessarily must be indicated by a dagesh.*

It is further noteworthy that ָ and ׳ are not dealt with as a *unit*, corresponding to the other group ַ and ִ; on the contrary: they are used promiscuously. Thus combinations arise like: ַ ָ and ׳; or ִ ִ and ָ ; or ִ and ֵ ; or ַ and ִ ; and—nota bene—in the various formations of one and the same root. In these cases ָ and ַ thus indicate *a*; ֵ and ִ *i*; ֹ and ָ *o*.

§ 6. The role of the *matres lectionis*.

In § 3c a statement by Bergsträsser was quoted with regard to the *matres lectionis* as an aid toward establishing whether the vowel in a given case is long or short. Though this statement is cautiously worded, we still must challenge its applicability. A cursory glance into any reliable Hebrew dictionary or Bible concordance will convince anyone that the *matres lectionis* merely indicate the vowels as such: *a, i,* or *o*; but that "no conclusions can be drawn from our sources as to their quantity or quality" (p. 562, A. The Vowels and their Phonography). Bergsträsser himself considers the *scriptio plena* or *defectiva* not as decisive, but only as an "Anhalt"; the main criterion to him is the "Wortform," i.e. how any given nominal or verbal form *ought* to be spelled according to rules established in his grammar. (And this refers not only to Bergsträsser but to all the grammarians). In other words: The grammarian knows beforehand, how every word has to be spelled; he then approaches the Bible and finds whether the Masoretes were conscientiously discharging their task in copying and preserving the Bible text in such a shape as might be approved of by him (i.e. the grammarian), or whether they were negligent about their work and let spellings occur which do not comply with his (scil. the grammarians) conception of Hebrew. In such cases the Masoretes are sure to get their rebuke: cf. B-L § 49v s.v. הרס, חבש, חמל, חפז, חרש, חשך, חתם, עבד, עבר, עזב, עטף, עמד; ערץ, ib. § 58 p' s.v. ארר, בזז, בלל, גדד, גלל, גרר, דמם, חגג, חנן, מדד, סבב, עזז, פרר, צרר, קבב, תמם, נדד. In these instances the respective *plene* spelling is labelled "späte Pleneschreibung." It might be interesting to investigate just how often a verb *primae laryngalis* or *mediae geminatae* is spelled *defective*, in conformity with B-L's grammatical viewpoint.

§ 7. Bible editions are unreliable.

It is true: grammatical studies do not center around the problem of the *matres lectionis* (though nothing is unimportant in a grammatical system!); but they offer a welcome opportunity to demonstrate this fundamental error which the grammarians make in setting up a theory

first, and then doing their best to explain away the contradicting facts of
the actual Bible text. In a somewhat better position are the respective
editors of the Bible. Being grammarians first and foremost, they have
their preconceived views as to what is correct, and then they emend the
Bible to read accordingly. It is characteristic how this very criticism of
ours is phrased approvingly by Bergsträsser (§ 4b): "Da weiter bei Ben
Chajim (scil. the second Biblia Rabbinica, edited as the first Masoretic
Bible by Jacob ben Chayim, Venice 1524/5) Versehen und Abweichungen
von seinem eigenen massoretischen Material nicht fehlen und die Handschriften und selbständigen Ausgaben vielfach in Einzelheiten vor allem
der Vokalisation und Akzentuation, aber auch der Konsonanten von ihm
abweichen, haben sich besonders S. Baer und D. Ginsburg um die genauere Herstellung des MT bemüht." Under "genauere Herstellung" we
have to understand the removal of readings which run counter to *their*
conception of Hebrew. And when B-L in their "Vorwort," p. vi, state that
"als Bibeltext wurde die Ausgabe von Chr. D. Ginsburg, (London 1894)
zugrunde gelegt," we realize that we are moving in a vicious circle. For in
the course of my investigations in preparing this grammar I came even in
Ginsburg's edition across an astounding number of such premeditated
changes of the same type as pointed out before. Paul Kahle put it rather
mildly when he remarked on that edition that "im wesentlichen den Text
des Jakob ben Hayim druckt ab Chr. D. Ginsburg" (B-L, p. 90). It seems
to me that "essentially" this edition does not represent Jacob ben
Chayim's Bible. A few examples, picked at random, will illustrate characteristic deviations. I put in juxtaposition Ginsburg's reading (left) and
that offered in the Venice 1524/5 edition (right).

The readings from the Venice 1524/5 edition I vocalized only partly
so as to bring the variant into sharp relief:

Gen. 28.18:	ויצק–וַיִּצֹק	Ps. 68.29:	עוֹזָה–עֻזָּה	
Lev. 14.56:	ולשׂאת–וְלַשְׂאֵת	Ps. 5.5:	אַתָּה–אָתָּה	
Deut. 1.25:	דָּבָר–דָּבָר	Ezra 8.30:	משׁקל–מִשְׁקָל	
Ps. 20.6:	נרגנה–נְרַנְּנָה	1 Ki. 1.1:	יֶחַם–יְחַם	
Deut. 1.41:	ותחגרו–וַתַּחְגְּרוּ	Eccl. 2.7:	מקנה–מִקְנֶה	
Ps. 2.1:	יהגו–יֶהְגּוּ	2 Sam. 15.13:	לֵב–לֶב־	
1 Ki. 1.17:	ביהוה–בִּיהוה			

Ps. 10.8:   במארב–בְּמַאֲרָב   Isa. 63.15:   קׇדְשְׁךָ–קׇדְשָׁ,,

Ps. 10.8:   לחטוף–לַחֲטוֹף   2 Ki. 10.19:   בְּעׇקְבָה–בְּעׇקְבָּה

Ps. 10.8:   יחטוף–יַחֲטוֹף

Ex. 15.2:   עֲזִי–עׇזִּי   2 Sam. 14.25:   קׇדְקְדוֹ–קׇדְקְדוֹ

Jer. 31.32:   אכתֶּבנה–אֶכְתֳּבֶנָּה

In order not to get caught in this trap myself, I strictly refrained from referring to any of the current editions of the Masoretic Bible, but relied on Jacob ben Chayim's Bible solely.

§ 8.   The problem still stands.

In denouncing the validity of Rule II while formulating his own solution of the problem of Hebrew phonology, Bergsträsser has got himself entangled in a new difficulty: Granted that "sämtliche Vokalzeichen können an sich *lange oder kurze Vokale* bezeichnen" (cf. § 4c), why, then, this constant change of vowel-signs, when in the course of declension a closed syllable becomes open, and vice versa? Why not say מַתְכֹּנֶת = נֶת–כֹּ–מַת with a long ˙ in כֹּ, while in the closed syllable, but still with ˙ as מַתְכֻּנְתּוֹ = תּוֹ–כֻּנ–מַת explain this ˙ as short? Similarly: בְּחֶמְלָת = לָת–חֶמְ–בְּ with short ˌ and בְּחֶמְלָתוֹ = תוֹ–לָ–חֶמְ–בְּ with long ˌ? This would be strictly in keeping with Bergsträsser's own definition "ob ein Vokal lang oder kurz ist, hängt von der Wortform ab und *ist aus der Schreibung zunächst nicht zu ersehen*"! But the facts speak an entirely different language: It is solely the change in the "Schreibung" of the vowel-signs: whether ˌ or ˏ; . or ˌ; ˌ or ˙ that lead to the basic concept of dividing them into short and long vowels, respectively. What other explanation could be advanced for this change?

Our critical analysis shows that the theories hitherto offered in order to combine the basic laws of the Tiberian Phonology into a system, are a complete failure. The patchwork of modern scholarship is no sufficient support to prevent this basically medieval building from collapsing; cf. MH §§ 2 ff.

§ 9.   A new approach.

Our own method (which has already stood its test in a similar investigation, cf. p. 335 ff.) does not consist in an attempt to reconcile old statements concerning the facts, but in a new and unbiased examination of the facts themselves. We approach this our task unburdened by any preconceived theories, and we risk no ventures at changing the vocalization of the Bible text in order to prove our point by suppressing those instances which contradict it. On the contrary: we let the Bible prove its own point, and limit ourselves to grouping and classifying the evidence from the Bible. *We take nothing for granted*, neither the basic laws, nor even the presuppositions upon which they rest. To mention only one of these presuppositions: In dividing the vowel-signs into three groups (§ 1), we follow their present-day pronunciation; but what are "Die Quellen unserer Kenntnisse (sic! read the singular: Kenntnis) der Aussprache des Hebräischen"? (cf. B-L § 10, chapter C). B-L have to admit that "es liegt auf der Hand, dass uns keine dieser Quellen, weder in bezug auf Zuverlässigkeit noch auf Vollständigkeit, befriedigen kann" (§ 10b'); Bergsträsser (cf. § 4: Quellen) fails even to realize the existence of this problem!

We do hope that the internal evidence of the Bible will prove not only a more suitable basis for a grammatical treatment of Hebrew phonology than the present-day pronunciation of Hebrew by the Jews in the various countries (cf. B-L § 10c), but that the results obtained will be more satisfactory, too.

Our procedure will be to discuss point by point the vowel-signs and the laws governing their application, so as to arrive at certain conclusions with regard to the nature of the vowels themselves which these vowel-signs represent.

B.   The Vowel-Signs and the Vowels

§ 10.   The Tiberian vowel-signs.

The Tiberian Vocalization System employs the following 13 signs: (1) ָ ; (2) ַ ; (3) ֳ ; (4) ׃ ; (5) ֶ ; (6) ׳ ; (7) ֻ ; (8) ׳ ; (9) ׅ ; (10) ֹ ; (11) ֳ ; (12) ֳ ; (13) ׃ (dot within the letter). We shall now investigate the laws governing their application and the vowels which they indicate.

A.   THE DAGESH

For reasons of practical utility an effort is being made here to treat separately—as fas as possible—the so-called *dagesh lene* and *dagesh forte*. This way of arranging our evidence is chosen merely to avoid confusing the student of Hebrew grammar, but does not at all anticipate our acceptance of these grammatical terms and the connotations they carry.

The following classification proves that the *dagesh* is applied inconsistently.

a. *Dagesh Lene*

§ 11.   Construct infinitive with preposition ל.

Num. 4.23: לִצְבֹא	Jer. 11.19: לִטְבֹחַ	Num. 21.4: לִסְבֹב
Isa. 31.4: לִצְבֹּא	Isa. 57.7: לִזְבֹּחַ	Gen. 49.15: לִסְבֹּל
Jer. 47.4: לִשְׁדֹוד	Isa. 33.1: לִבְגֹד	Jer. 1.10: לִנְתֹושׁ
Jer. 16.5: לִסְפֹּוד	Gen. 28.20: לִלְבֹּשׁ	Jer. 51.49: לִנְפֹּל
Chron. 34.10: לִבְדֹּוק	Jer. 1.10: וְלִנְתֹוץ	2 Sam. 7.23: לִפְדֹות
Chron. 16.33: לִשְׁפֹּוט	Jer. 19.11: לִקְבֹּור	2 Sam. 3.34: לִבְכֹּות

§ 12.   Construct infinitive with prepositions ב and כ.

Isa. 30.25: בִּנְפֹּל	Eccl. 12.4: בְּשָׁפַל	2 Sam. 17.9: כִּנְפֹּל
Gen. 35.22: בִּשְׁכֹּן	Ezek. 17.17: בִּשְׁפֹּךְ	Jer. 17.2: כִּזְכֹּר

§ 13.   The identical verb in the construct infinitive with different prepositions.

a)   *Dagesh lene* is inserted throughout.

Gen. 35.22: בִּשְׁכֹּן	Ezek. 17.17: בִּשְׁפֹּךְ	Jer. 17.2: כִּזְכֹּר
Num. 9.22: לִשְׁכֹּן	Ezek. 20.8: לִשְׁפֹּךְ	Gen. 9.16: לִזְכֹּר

b)   Only forms with the preposition ל get the *dagesh*.

Ps. 87.6: בִּכְתֹוב	Isa. 30.25: בִּנְפֹּל	1 Ki. 1.21: כִּשְׁכַב
Deut. 31.24: לִכְתֹּב	Jer. 51.49: לִנְפֹּל	Gen. 34.7: לִשְׁכַּב

§ 14.   Different verbs with different prepositions.

Prov. 29.2: בִּרְבֹות	Ps. 103.11: כִּגְבֹהַּ
Num. 20.5: לִשְׁתֹּות	Isa. 45.1: לְפַתֹּחַ

§ 15.   Construct infinitive with suffixes.

a)   The identical verb with different suffixes.

2 Sam. 10.3: וּלְהָפְכָה	Ruth 3.4: בְּשָׁכְבֹו
Gen. 19.21: הָפְכִּי	Prov. 6.22: בְּשָׁכְבְּךָ

b) Different verbs with identical suffixes.

Ex. 32.34: פָּקְדִי   I Sam. 13.1: בְּמָלְכוֹ   Prov. 28.28: וּבְאָבְדָם

Gen. 19.21: הָפְכִּי   Ex. 12.27: בְּנָגְפוֹ   Hos. 7.6: בְּאָרְבָּם

Job 39.9: עָבְדֶךָ   Jer. 2.17: עָזְבֵךְ   Gen. 19.33: בְּשִׁכְבָהּ

Ezek. 9.8: בְּשָׁפְכְּךָ   Deut. 16.13: בְּאָסְפְּךָ   Ruth 2.7: שִׁבְתָּהּ

c) Different verbs and different suffixes.

     Deut. 11.4: בְּרָדְפָם   Lev. 23.39: בְּאָסְפְּכֶם

§ 16. Imperative.

     Jer. 12.9: אִסְפוּ   Lam. 2.19: שִׁפְכִי

     Jer. 10.17: אִסְפִּי   Isa. 47.2: חֶשְׂפִּי

§ 17. Imperfect (with suffixes).

Jer. 17.11: יַעַזְבֶנּוּ   I Sam. 8.8: וַיַּעַבְדוּ   I Sam. 5.8: וַיַּאַסְפוּ

2 Ki. 10.18: יַעַבְדֶנּוּ   I Sam. 25.12: וַיַּהְפְּכוּ   I Sam. 8.8: וַיַּעַזְבֻנִי

§ 18. Various other verbal forms.

     Deut. 12.14: מְצַוְּךָ   . . . .   ib. 6.2: מְצַוְּךָ

     Isa. 38.18: תוֹדֶךָ   . . . .   v. 19: יוֹדֶךָ

     Prov. 4.6: וְתִשְׁמְרֶךָ   . . . .   Num. 6.24: וְיִשְׁמְרֶךָ

     Judg. 4.22: וְאַרְאֶךָּ   . . . .   Gen. 28.3: וְיִרְבֶּךָ

     Deut. 31.6: יַעַזְבֶךָ   . . . .   Isa. 58.8: יַאַסְפֶךָ

     Jer. 51.30: נָשְׁתָה   . . . .   Isa. 41.17: נָשָׁתָּה

     Deut. 22.21: עָשְׂתָה   . . . .   Gen. 27.17: עָשָׂתָה

§ 19. Misplaced *dagesh* with verbs.

     I Sam. 4.18: כְּהַזְכִּירוֹ   Ps. 122.3: שֶׁחֻבְּרָה

     Ex. 2.3: הַצְּפִינוֹ   Ezek. 22.24: גֻּשְׁמָהּ

§ 20. The noun in the absolute state.

a) The identical noun.

     Isa. 54.12: כַּדְכֹד   Ezek. 42.3: רִצְפָה

     Ezek. 27.16: וְכַדְכֹּד   Isa. 6.6: רִצְפָּה

     Lev. 1.2: קָרְבָּן   Ezra 8.27: לַאֲדַרְכֹנִים

     Ezek. 40.43: הַקָּרְבָן   I Chron. 29.7: וַאֲדַרְכֹּנִים

b)　Different nouns.

Eccl. 11.10: הַיְלָדוּת　　　　　2 Ki. 10.19: בְּעֶקְבָה

1 Sam. 20.30: הַמַּרְדּוּת　　　　Isa. 64.10: לְחָרְבָּה¹

§ 21.　The noun in the absolute state with misplaced *dagesh*.

Ex. 25.8:　　מִקְדָּשׁ　　　　　Ex. 15.17:　　מִקְדָּשׁ

§ 22.　The noun in the construct state singular.

a)　The masculine noun.

Est. 8.6:　　בְּאָבְדָן　　　　Lev. 23.27:　　לְקָרְבַּן

b)　The feminine noun.

Ps. 18.12:　חֶשְׁכַת　　Ex. 16.13:　שְׁכְבַת　　Isa. 58.2:　קִרְבַת

Ps. 22.7:　חֶרְפַּת　　Gen. 28.4:　בִּרְכַּת　　1 Ki. 1.38:　פְּרָדַת

Est. 1.6:　　רִצְפַּת　　　　Deut. 16.10:　נִדְבַת

1 Sam. 9.20:　חֶמְדַת　　　　Prov. 29.25:　חֶרְדַּת

§ 23.　The noun in the singular with suffixes.

a)　The masculine noun.

Ezra 9.3:　　בִּגְדִי　　Dan. 8.18:　עָמְדִי　　Deut. 16.13:　וּמִיִּקְבֶךָ

Isa. 37.24:　רִכְבִּי　　Job 29.4:　חָרְפִּי　　Deut. 13.6:　מִקַּרְבְּךָ

Dan. 10.11:　עָמְדֶךָ　　Gen. 39.12:　בִּגְדוֹ　　2 Chron. 30.16:　עָמְדָם

Isa. 14.3:　מֵעָצְבְּךָ　　Ex. 12.9:　קִרְבּוֹ　　Neh. 9.16:　עָרְפָּם

b)　The feminine noun.

Gen. 27.36:　בִּרְכָתִי　　　　Gen. 49.13:　וְיַרְכָתוֹ

Jer. 12.10:　חֶמְדָתִי　　　　Jer. 5.16:　אַשְׁפָּתוֹ

§ 24.　The noun in the construct state plural.

a)　The masculine noun.

Isa. 55.3:　חַסְדֵי　　Ps. 1.3:　פַּלְגֵי　　Ps. 76.4:　רִשְׁפֵי

Isa. 63.7:　חַסְדֵי　　Ezek. 17.9:　טַרְפֵּי　　Cant. 8.6:　רִשְׁפֵי

Cant. 1.9:　בְּרִכְבֵי　　　　Jona. 2.7:　לְקִצְבֵי

Isa. 5.10:　צִמְדֵי　　　　Josh. 2.6:　בְּפִשְׁתֵי

¹ On *hatef kames* as the earlier form of *kames hatuf* cf. later § 73.

b) The feminine noun.

Josh. 5.2:   חָרְבוֹת   Josh. 4.13:   עַרְבוֹת   Ezek. 40.44:   לִשְׁכוֹת

Josh. 12.3:   אַשְׁדוֹת   I Sam. 2.8:   מֵאַשְׁפּוֹת   Ps. 69.10:   וְחֶרְפּוֹת

c) Both combined.

Isa. 52.9:   חָרְבוֹת   Mic. 7.1:   כְּאָסְפֵּי

§ 25. The noun in the construct state plural with misplaced *dagesh*.

a) The masculine noun.

Ezek. 3.5:   וְכִבְדֵי   Job 21.33:   רִגְבֵי

Gen. 49.27:   עִקְבֵי   Deut. 32.32:   עִנְבֵי

b) The feminine noun.

Ezek. 41.26:   כְּתֵפוֹת   Ex. 27.19:   יִתְדֹת

Prov. 27.25:   עִשְּׂבוֹת   Ps. 89.52:   עִקְבוֹת

§ 26. Dual-forms.

Judg. 7.6:   בִּרְכֵיהֶם   Ex. 26.23:   בַּיַּרְכָתַיִם

Gen. 50.23:   בִּרְכֵּי   Judg. 19.18:   יַרְכְּתֵי

§ 27. Plural-forms (with suffixes).

Deut. 7.24:   מַלְכֵיהֶם   Num. 8.7:   בִּגְדֵיהֶם   Prov. 7.16:   מַרְבַדִּים

Gen. 42.25:   כַּסְפֵּיהֶם   Isa. 41.29:   נְסְכֵּיהֶם   Cant. 5.16:   מַמְתַקִּים

§ 28. The noun in the plural with misplaced *dagesh*.

Neh. 3.1:   דַּלְתֹתָיו   Jonah 4.11:   מִשְׁתֵּים

Isa. 5.28:   קַשְּׁתֹתָיו   Judg. 16.28:   מִשְׁתֵי

b. Dagesh Forte

§ 29. The identical verb in the identical form.

Prov. 31.19:   שִׁלְּחָה   Jer. 34.11:   שִׁלְּחוּ

Ezek. 31.4:   שִׁלְחָה   Ps. 74.7:   שִׁלְחוּ

Ps. 18.3:   וּמְפַלְּטִי   I Chron. 23.5:   מְהַלְלִים

2 Sam. 22.2:   וּמְפַלְטִי   I Chron. 29.13:   וּמְהַלְלִים

§ 30. The identical verb in different forms.

1 Sam. 27.1: לְבַקְשֵׁנִי   Jer. 29.7:   וְהִתְפַּלְלוּ
1 Sam. 27.4: לְבַקְשׁוֹ   Dan. 9.4:   וָאֶתְפַּלְלָה

§ 31. Different verbs in the identical form.

a) Imperfect.

Ezek. 22.26: וַיְחַלְּלוּ   Jer. 6.14:   וַיְרַפְּאוּ   Isa. 10.6:   אֲשַׁלְּחֶנּוּ
Gen. 12.15:   וַיְהַלְּלוּ   Gen. 42.25: וַיְמַלְאוּ   Prov. 23.35: אֲבַקְשֶׁנּוּ

b) Perfect.

Lam. 1.19:   בִּקְשׁוּ   Lam. 4.10:   בִּשְּׁלוּ

c) Participle.

Mal. 1.12:   מְחַלְּלִים   Jer. 23.1:   מְאַבְּדִים   2 Sam. 19.6: הַמְמַלְּטִים
1 Sam. 3.13: מְקַלְלִים   Jer. 38.16: מְבַקְשִׁים   Zeph. 1.9:   הַמְמַלְאִים

§ 32. Nominal forms.

a) Singular.

Gen. 5.29:   וּמֵעִצְּבוֹן   Gen. 3.16:   עִצְּבוֹנֵךְ
Ezek. 21.11: בְּשִׁבְרוֹן   Isa. 57.8:   זִכְרוֹנֵךְ

2 Sam. 7.21: הַגְּדוּלָה   Judg. 18.21: הַכְּבוּדָּה
2 Sam. 19.37: הַגְּמוּלָה   1 Sam. 10.16: הַמְּלוּכָה

b) Plural.

Lev. 23.38:   שַׁבְּתֹת   2 Chron. 26.15: חִשְּׁבֹנוֹת
Cant. 2.7:   בְּאַיְלוֹת   Est. 6.1:   הַזִּכְרֹנוֹת

c) Adjectives.

Prov. 2.15:   עִקְּשִׁים   Isa. 56.10:   אִלְּמִים
Ex. 23.8:   פִּקְחִים   Isa. 56.10:   עִוְרִים

§ 33. Nominal forms with the article.

Eccl. 11.5:   הַמְּלֵאָה   Gen. 41.7:   וְהַמְּלֵאוֹת
Am. 2.13:   הַמְלֵאָה   Isa. 51.20:   הַמְלֵאִים

Lev. 14.56:   וְלַשְּׂאֵת   Ex. 28.34:   הַמְּעִיל
Lev. 13.10:   בַּשְּׂאֵת   Isa. 59.17:   כַּמְעִיל

§ 34. Meaningless *dagesh*.

I Sam. 20.26:	מִקְרֶה	Eccl. 2.15:	יִקְרֵנִי	Isa. 51.16:	וְלִיסֹד
Deut. 23.11:	מִקְרֵה	I Sam. 28.10:	יִקְרֶךָ	2 Chron. 31.7:	לִיסֹד

§ 35. The *mappiḳ* ה.

Num. 5.31:	עֲוֺנָהּ	Isa. 23.18:	וְאֶתְנַנָּהּ
Num. 15.31:	עֲוֺנָהּ	Isa. 23.17:	לְאֶתְנַנָּהּ
Ezek. 24.6:	וְחֶלְאָתָהּ	Jer. 44.19:	לָהּ
Ezek. 24.6:	חֶלְאָתָהּ	Zech. 5.11:	לָהּ

§ 36. General observations.

Throughout this chapter it was deemed advisable to deal with verbal and nominal forms in separate paragraphs. The reason for this procedure is that, inconsistently though the *dagesh* is applied, there is a consistent difference in its application to verbal or nominal forms respectively. While uncertainty prevails with regard to the *dagesh lene* in the syllable following a preposition בכל with verbal forms (cf. §§ 11-14), corresponding *nominal forms never get it*; cf. Cant. 2.9: לִצְבִי; Isa. 13.14: כִּצְבִי; Zeph. 1.5: לִצְבָא; Jonah 2.4: בִּלְבַב; I Ki. 11.4: כִּלְבַב. *Dagesh forte*, on the other hand, is never inserted in the מ of participle forms with the article of the piʻel and its derivatives (cf. § 32); cf. Zeph. 1.9: הַמְמַלְאִים; 2 Chron. 32.31: הַמְשַׁלְּחִים; Gen. 35.17: הַמְיַלֶּדֶת; Ex. 1.17: הַמְיַלְּדֹת. Corresponding nominal forms, beginning with מ, do have the *dagesh forte*: Ex. 25.31: הַמְּנוֹרָה; I Ki. 7.49: הַמְּנֹרוֹת; Deut. 12.9: הַמְּנוּחָה.

It is sometimes impossible to draw the dividing line between *dagesh lene* and *dagesh forte*. This is especially the case, when so-called pausal forms are involved; cf. I Sam. 17.28: יָרַדְתָּ=יָ-רַדְ-תָּ with *dagesh lene* in תּ; but ib. יָרְדְתָּ (on the division into syllables see § 2), the ת has still a *dagesh*! Similarly cf. Ps. 102.5: שָׁכַחְתִּי=שָׁ-כַחְ-תִּי and Ps. 119.61: שָׁכָחְתִּי=שָׁ-כָ-חְתִי; Gen. 26.14: רַבָּה (with *dagesh forte*) but Gen. 18.20: רָבָּה, too; Hos. 6.9: יְרַצְּחוּ and Ps. 62.4: תְּרָצְּחוּ; Ps. 104.35: יִתַּמּוּ and Ps. 102.28: יִתַּמּוּ (note the *dagesh* in מּ!); Lev. 26.39: יִמַּקּוּ ··· יִמַּקּוּ (with *dagesh* in קּ); Deut. 28.43: מַטָּה מָטָּה.

The terms "misplaced *dagesh*" (cf. §§ 19, 21, 25, 28) and "meaningless *dagesh*" (cf. § 34) which we introduced here, have been chosen solely in

order to demonstrate more vividly the inapplicability of Rule VIII in § 1
so as to explain their existence. Cf. also MH § 12.

B.   LARYNGALS WITHOUT A VOWEL

§ 37. Vocalized with *ḥatef* or *shewa*.

a)   Laryngals in medial position without a distinct vowel of their own
have either *shewa* or a *ḥatef* (‑ͅ or ‑ͅ). No rules can be formulated to indicate
just when *shewa* and when a *ḥatef* should be applied. Instances like the
following

Ex. 32.34:	יַחְמָץ	Ezek. 8.8:	וָאֶחְתֹּר	Hos. 7.5:	הֶחֱלוּ
Ex. 12.19:	מַחְמֶצֶת	Ex. 22.1:	בַּמַּחְתֶּרֶת	Ex. 23.25:	מַחֲלָה

might lead to formulating a theory that the laryngals in certain roots are
treated as weak consonant and get a *ḥatef*, while in others they are considered as regular, sound consonants and receive a *shewa*; for in the
examples shown above verb and nominal derivative are treated alike.
But any such theory is without foundation, as will be seen from the
following examples of different treatment of

b)   The identical form.

Gen. 42.24:	וַיֵּאָסֹר	Prov. 16.13:	יֶאֱהָב	Deut. 24.17:	תַחֲבֹל
Gen. 46.29:	וַיֶּאְסֹר	Prov. 15.9:	יֶאֱהָב	Ex. 22.25:	תַחְבֹּל
Num. 30.3:	לֶאְסֹר	Josh. 8.9:	הַמַּאֲרָב	Ps. 46.2:	מַחֲסֶה
Ps. 105.22:	לֶאֱסֹר	Judg. 9.35:	הַמַּאְרָב	Ps. 104.18:	מַחְסֶה

c)   Verb and its derivative noun.

Lam. 3.3:	יַהֲפֹךְ	Judg. 9.5:	נֶחְבָּא
Deut. 29.22:	כְּמַהְפֵּכַת	Isa. 32.2:	כְמַחֲבֵא
Lev. 16.4:	יַחְגֹּר	Isa. 10.7:	יַחְשֹׁב
Isa. 3.24:	מַחֲגֹרֶת	Jer. 18.11:	מַחֲשָׁבָה

d)   Inflected forms of the same root.

Isa. 30.32:	מַעֲבַר	Hos. 9.6:	מַחְמַד
Isa. 10.29:	מַעְבָּרָה	Cant. 5.16:	מַחֲמַדִּים

Isa. 29.15:	בְּמַחְשָׁךְ	Gen. 2.9:	נֶחְמָד	Ezek. 24.22:	תֵעָטוּ
Ps. 88.7:	בְּמַחֲשַׁכִּים	Ps. 19.11:	הַנֶּחֱמָדִים	Ps. 71.13:	יַעְטוּ

In order to solve this problem, we shall take up the discussion of the treatment of laryngals according to their position at the beginning, in the middle, or at the end of a word, with constant reference to respective forms in transliteration (cf. ch. 0) and in the Babylonian vocalization.

§ 38.   The laryngal in final position.

a)   Let us take זָכַר and זָרַח as examples for a sound verb and a verb *tertiae* ח in the perfect. In Greek transliteration they sound: ζαχαρ (cf. p. 178, § 1a) and ζαραε (p. 179, § 1d β), respectively. Dividing them into syllables, we get זָ-כַר=ζα-χαρ and זָ-רַח=ζα-ραε. It thus becomes clear that ε in the second syllable of ζαραε holds the same position as ρ in ζαχαρ. In other words: ε *is the equivalent of the consonantal value of* ח, just as ρ indicates the ר in זכר. We now turn to the imperfect and select here יִגְדֹל and יִזְרַח, again as representing a sound verb and one *tertiae* ח. These forms in transliteration are: *iegdal* (p. 180, § 7b α) and ιεσραε (p. 181, § 7b θ). We again divide them into syllables: יִגְ-דֹל=*ieg-dal* and יִזְ-רַח=ιεσ-ραε. The result is: ε holds the position of *l* as indicator of the third radical. Thus our conclusion is being confirmed: ε stands for the consonantal value of ח. In the very same way we shall now explain יִפְתַּח ιεφθαε (p. 155, s.v. פתח). Similarly, the ε in יָדַע ιαδαε; שָׁמַע σαμαε (p. 123 ff., s.v.) corresponds to the consonantal value of ע.

b)   The results of our findings thus far can be formulated as follows: ח and ע in final position and without a vowel of their own were pronounced like ε. These results are corroborated by the way in which the Babylonian Vocalization proceeds in suchlike cases: cf. e.g. Job 13.9: וְאָגוֹעַ=וָאֶגְוַע; Job 15.8: תִּשְׁמַע=תִּשְׁמֹעַ; Ps. 94.13: רַע=רָֿע (MTK, 31); Job 4.16: אֶשְׁמַע=אֶשְׁמֹֿע; Job 9.29: אֶרְשָׁע=אֶרְשָֿׁע (MdO, 166). Consequently, forms like Ps. 94.1: הוֹפִיעַ=הוֹפִֿיעַ; Ps. 95.2: נָרִיעַ=נָרִֿיעַ; Job 6.7: לִנְגּוֹעַ=לִנְגֹּֿועַ in the Babylonian vocalization, or like זָנוֹחַ=*zanoe*; מִזְבֵּחַ=μασβηη (p. 175, under ח); יָפִיעַ=ιαφιε; שׁוּעַ=*sue* (ib. under ע) in transliteration, must be explained in the same fashion: e, ε or ˔ represent the consonantal value of ח or ע in final position without vowel, and *regardless of the vowel of the preceding syllable*. The so-called *pataḥ furtivum* of the Tiberian vocalization we shall, therefore, explain as a remainder of this old way of pronouncing ח and ע. Its proper place in Hebrew grammar is in the paragraph dealing with the *pronunciation of the alphabet,* and *not* in connection with the *vocalization.*

§ 39.   The laryngal in initial or medial position.

a)   We begin again with forms in transliteration; they are taken from p. 124 ff. and can be traced there s.v.: The imperative-forms קְרָאוּ and חֲזִי in transliteration, divided into syllables, are קְר־אוּ=χερ-ου and חֲזִ־י=εεζ-ου. (I had to divide the monosyllabic חֲזִי, in order to bring into sharp relief its parallel features with קְרָאוּ). In קְר=χερ we have the following order: consonant (קְ=χ), vowel (. =ε) and consonant (ר=ρ). Similarly in חֲ= εεζ: consonant (חֲ=ε), vowel (‚ =ε) and consonant (ז=ζ). The result of this equation is: ה *in initial position*=ε.

As an instance for a laryngal in medial position we take כָּחֲשׁוּ as compared with טָמְנוּ (dividing them into syllables): טָמְ־נוּ=ταμ-νου, and כָּחֲ־שׁוּ=*chae-su.* In the case of the sound verb we have a consonant (ט=τ), vowel (ָ =α) and consonant (מְ=μ). Similarly with the laryngal verb: a consonant (כ=*ch*), vowel (ָ =*a*) and a consonant (חֲ=*e*): ה *in medial position*=*e.* Of nominal forms, קֶשֶׁת and לֶחֶם are both mono-syllabic triconsonantal nouns (ch. o, Grammar, oo). In transliteration: κασθ and λαεμ; the second consonant שׁ=σ, but ה=ε. Similarly we shall explain יְהֶ־מוּ=ιεε-μου as compared with יִבְ־לוּ=ιεβ-λου (ה=ε); הָאֲ־זִי־נוּ= *ee-zi-nu,* as compared with הָרְ־נִי־נוּ=ερ-νι-νου (א=ε). א and ה=ε.

With the number of Hebrew words in transliteration so limited, it is not always possible to find a *tertium comparationis* which is satisfactory in every detail. We must feel content if, at least for the point under discussion, our example is adequate. With this in mind, attention may be called to a few further examples: הֶחֱ־לִיק=εε-λιχ as compared with הֶרְ־עִים= ερ-ιμ (ה=ε); הַחֲ־זֵק=εε-ζεχ as compared with (הַטֶּה=) הַט־טֶה=ετ-τη (ה=ε); נֶאֱ־מָן=νεε-μαν as compared with נִבְ־הָל=νεβ-αλ (א=ε).

b)   In the Babylonian vocalization the sign ⌐ is employed to indicate the consonantal value of the laryngal. We emphasize that corresponding forms of sound roots have no vowel-sign at all: Judg. 16.15: אֲהֵבְתִּיךְ= אֲהַבְתִּיךְ (MdO, 184); Job 36.13: אָסְרָם=אַסְרֵם; Cant. 1.4: אֲהֵבוּךְ=אֲהֵבוּךָ; Ps. 22.2: עֲזַבְתָּנִי=עֲזַבְתַנִי; 2 Chron. 13.11: עֲזַבְתֶּם=עֲזַבְתֶּם; Prov. 31.18: טָעֲמָה=טָעֲמָה; Eccl. 2.10: שָׁאֲלוּ=שָׁאֲלוּ (all instances from MTK, 52);

1 Chron. 29.17: וִידַעְתִּי=וָיֵדַעְתִּי; Deut. 9.23: שְׁמַעְתֶּם=שְׁמֹעְתֶם (MdO, 184);
Isa. 48.6: יְדַעְתֶּם=יְדַעְתֶּם (MdO, 199).

§ 40.   Conclusions.

The Laryngals are transliterated by ε; correspondingly, the Babylonian vocalization has the equivalent sign ـ. In the Tiberian vocalization a *patah* under the laryngals ה and ע in final position is still preserved, the so-called *patah furtivum*, except when the preceding vowel is an *a*. In initial and medial position the Tiberian vocalization uses arbitrarily *patah* or *segol*, both of which correspond to Babylonian ـ, so that this fact might be taken as an indication of the dependence of the Tiberian system upon the Babylonian. In these cases, *patah* or *segol* are not indicating vowels, but solely the consonantal value of the respective laryngal. As corresponding forms of sound roots prove, these laryngals have no vowel of their own. In keeping with the system of the Tiberian vocalization, this absence of a vowel is indicated by a *shewa*. By this combination originate the *hatefs*: ֲ and ֱ. These combined signs (though the components were meant to serve different purposes) were misunderstood for *hatefs* before the introduction of the *dagesh*; hence we find the so-called *dagesh lene* after a laryngal with a *shewa*, but never after a laryngal with a *hatef*.

The tradition as to whether to put a ֲ or ֱ is fluctuating; cf. construct infinitive of אמר in Prov. 25.7: אֲמָר and Ezek. 25.8: אֱמֹר; further in the edition Venice 1515/17: Jer. 13.21: יֶאֱחֵזוּךְ (=MT), marg: יֶאֲחֵזוּךְ; ib. 31.25: הֶקִיצֹתִי (=MT), marg: הֲקִיצֹותִי; Ezek. 11.16: הֲפִיצֹותִים (=MT), marg: הֱפִיצוּ; Ps. 53.6: הֲבִישֹׁותָה, marg: הֱבִישׁ (=MT); 2 Chron. 28.27: הֲבִיאָהוּ, marg: הֱבִיאוּהוּ (=MT).

Hatefs under sound consonants of are a different origin; they represent a combination of the *vowel* ַ and of ְ; cf. e.g., Jer. 31.32: אֶכְתֲּבֶנָּה and Ezra 8.26: וָאֶשְׁקֲלָה. Here two readings are combined: אכתבנה and ואשקלה, with אכתבנה and ואשקלה: imperfect in *a* with preservation of the second vowel, cf. p. 223, A 1; p. 248, § 16. Forms with imperfect both in *o* and *a*, cf. p. 243, note 2, and Mal. 2.15: יְבְגֹּד as compared with ib., verse 10: נִבְגַּד; Mic. 3.11: יִקְסֹמוּ as compared with Ezek. 13.23: תִקְסַמְנָה.

These cases have, therefore, no place in a phonology but belong to that part of Hebrew grammar which deals with the morphology.

The ֱ will be discussed in § 73.

C.   OUR NEW APPROACH BASED UPON THE INDUCTIVE METHOD

§ 41.   Evidence from the Palestinian vocalization.

In § 9 we stated that we are going to base our conclusions with regard to the phonetic value of the vowel-signs solely on internal evidence from the Bible itself. We now wish to illustrate this method of ours with a few examples which, because they are taken from a non-Masoretic source, will serve so much better to clarify the issue. These examples are derived from Biblical passages with Palestinian vocalization which occur in the *piuṭ*-texts published by Paul Kahle in his MdW I. These passages—as well as all further references to Hebrew in Palestinian vocalization in general—can be located there with the help of the index on p. 84/5.

Ps. 139.2:	אַתָּה	Isa. 29.4:	וְהָיָה	Job 10.20:	מְעַט
Jer. 3.32:	אַתָּה	Isa. 32.15:	וְהָיָה	Job 10.20:	מְעַט
Isa. 4.5:	וּבָרָא	Isa. 49.6:	לְהָשִׁיב	Isa. 44.26:	דְּבַר (עַבְדּוֹ)
Hag. 3.6:	רָאָה	Prov. 22.21:	לְהָשִׁיב	Isa. 40.8:	וּדְבַר (אֱלֹהֵינוּ)

We see here two occurrences of either the identical word, a noun in the identical position (construct state), or two verbs of the same class, their *a*-vowels are interchangeably indicated once by the sign ' and once by ˉ. Upon this observation we now base our conclusion: *In the Palestinian vocalization there are two vowel-signs, ' and ˉ, to indicate the identical vowel a. The external shape of the vowel-sign employed in a given case does not lend itself to determine the quality or quantity of the a.*

Projecting this result on the Tiberian vocalization under examination, we state: In case we are able to point to instances where the identical word in the identical position within the syntactic structure of the respective sentence—thus excluding e.g. a comparison between a nominal form in the absolute state and the construct state, or of a form with a *makkeph* and another one, which lacks this sign (pausal-forms are excluded a limine, cf. p. 472, § 29)—is vocalized in two different ways, these two different ways of vocalization are nothing else but the two possibilities of expressing one and the same vowel. Thus, if we should see a word vocalized—under the conditions just mentioned—once with ˳ and another time with ˍ, or with ˍ and ․, ' and ˳ respectively, we would say: ˳ and ˍ both indicate *a*, ˍ and ․ *i*, ˳ and ' *o(u)*; and the way a given word is vocalized (with ˳

or -, .. or ., ˙ or ˎ) does in itself not prove anything as to the quantity or quality of these respective vowels. Their indiscriminate use proves that, at the time of their application to the words in question, they were considered two ways of achieving one and the same goal: the indicating of the respective vowel. Their present-day pronunciation by the Jews in the various countries, which forms the basis of the Hebrew phonology in the current Hebrew grammars (cf. § 9), is of no consequence. This merely reflects the later historic development of the original Hebrew vowels, but in no way the Hebrew vowels themselves.

D. THE VOWEL A: ַ OR ָ

§ 42. Biconsonantal nouns.

Lev. 6.3:	בַּד	Am. 5.11:	בַּר	2 Sam. 13.4:	דַּל
Ex. 28.42:	בָּד	Gen. 45.23:	בָּר	Lev. 19.15:	דל
Isa. 18.4:	טַל	Jer. 41.16:	וְטַף	Ezek. 21.3:	לַח
Cant. 5.2:	טָל	Jer. 40.7:	וְטָף	Ezek. 17.24:	לָח
Ezek. 3.14:	מַר	Num. 22.5:	עַם	Num. 29.36:	פַּר
Jer. 4.18:	מָר	Num. 23.24:	עָם	Num. 23.2:	פָּר
Num. 10.9:	הַצַּר	Ex. 12.38:	רַב	Gen. 41.21:	רַע
Est. 7.4:	הַצָּר	Num. 21.6:	רָב	Deut. 22.19:	רָע
		Gen. 37.34:	שַׂק		
		Lev. 11.32:	שָׂק		

§ 43. Triconsonantal nouns.

Ezek. 26.10:	פָּרַשׁ	Num. 28.10:	שַׁבַּת
Jer. 4.29:	פָּרָשׁ	Isa. 66.23:	שַׁבָּת
Josh. 14.2:	בְּגוֹרַל	Ps. 53.6:	פַּחַד
Num. 26.55:	בְּגוֹרָל	Ps. 53.6:	פָּחַד

§ 44. Verbal forms.

Job. 20.19:	גָּזַל	1 Ki. 3.28:	שָׁפַט
Lev. 5.23:	גָּזָל	1 Sam. 7.17:	שָׁפָט
Gen. 10.25:	יֻלַּד	Gen. 43.12:	הַמּוּשַׁב
Gen. 41.50:	יֻלָּד	Num. 5.8:	הַמּוּשָׁב

§ 45. Before a laryngal.

Deut. 27.8:	בַּאֵר	Jer. 29.23:	וַיְנַאֲפוּ	Jer. 23.17:	לִמְנַאֲצַי
Hab. 2.2:	וּבָאֵר	Hos. 4.13:	תְּנַאַפְנָה	Num. 14.23:	מְנַאֲצַי
Neh. 10.35:	לְבַעֵר	Deut. 23.8:	תְּתַעֵב	Mic. 3.9:	הַמְתַעֲבִים
Isa. 44.15:	לְבָעֵר	Ps. 5.7:	יְתָעֵב	Isa. 49.7:	לִמְתָעֵב
Ex. 21.35:	הַחַי	1 Sam. 16.7:	לַעֵינַיִם	Jer. 1.1.:	בַּעֲנָתוֹת
Gen. 6.19:	הָחַי	Gen. 3.6:	לָעֵינַיִם	Jer. 32.7:	בָּעֲנָתוֹת

§ 46. Various other forms.

	Isa. 42.7:	אַסִיר		Dan. 11.32:	בַּחֲלַקּוֹת
	Ps. 79.11:	אָסִיר		Ps. 73.18:	בַּחֲלָקּוֹת
Ps. 73.9:	שַׁתּוּ	Jer. 13.25:	מְנָת	Zech. 4.10:	בַּז
Ps. 3.7:	שָׁתוּ	Ps. 11.6:	מְנָת	Prov. 11.12:	בָּז

For further evidence of the interchangeability of ֲ and ָ in the Masoretic Bible cf. p. 470, §§ 21 ff.

§ 47. Evidence from the Bible 1515/17.

a)   Zech. 12.8: הַנִּכְשָׁל, marg.: שָׁל (=MT).
       Eccl. 9.2: הַנִּשְׁבָּע (=MT), marg.: הנשבע.

b)   1 Sam. 25.14: וַיָּעַט, marg.: וַיַּעַט (MT: וַיָּעַט).
       Ruth 4.1: וַיָּסַר, marg.: ויסר (=MT).
       Hos. 12.5: וַיִּשָׂר (=MT), marg.: וַיָּשָׂר.

c)   Ezra 3.8: וּשְׁאָר, marg.: וּשְׁאָר (=MT).
       Hos. 6.1: יַךְ, marg.: יַךְ (=MT).

§ 48. Conclusions.

ֲ and ָ are indiscriminately used to indicate the vowel a. Our sources, thus, do not warrant a differentiation between $\bar{a}$ and $\breve{a}$ merely on the basis of the shape of the vowel-sign employed to signify the vowel.

E. THE VOWEL I: ֵ OR ִ

§ 49. Perfect-forms.

| Jer. 20.12: | גָּלִיתִי | Ps. 32.5: | כִּסִּיתִי | Num. 25.11: | כִּלִּיתִי |
| Jer. 49.10: | גִּלֵּיתָ | Ezek. 31.15: | כָּסֵיתִי | Isa. 49.4: | כִּלֵּיתִי |

Ex. 29.35:	צִוִּיתִי	Gen. 49.18:	קִוִּיתִי	Prov. 5.13:	הֲטִיתִי
Lev. 8.31:	צִוֵּיתִי	Isa. 5.4:	קִוֵּיתִי	Judg. 15.16:	הִכֵּיתִי
Ex. 33.1:	הֶעֱלִיתָ	Deut. 27.6:	וְהַעֲלִיתָ	2 Ki. 17.27:	הִגְלִיתֶם
Ex. 32.7:	הֶעֱלֵיתָ	Ex. 40.4:	וְהַעֲלֵיתָ	Ezek. 11.6:	הִרְבֵּיתֶם
		Ezek. 17.19:	הֵפִיר		
		Ezek. 17.16:	הֵפֵר		

§ 50. Participle.

Ps. 68.7:	מוֹצִיא	Ps. 135.7:	מוֹצֵא

§ 51. Imperative.

Jer. 17.18:	הָבִיא	Isa. 43.8:	הוֹצִיא
1 Sam. 20.40:	הָבֵיא	Gen. 19.12:	הוֹצֵא

§ 52. Absolute infinitive.

Isa. 27.9:	הָסִר	Isa. 5.5:	הָסֵר

§ 53. Absolute infinitive equals construct infinitive.

The view held in the current Hebrew grammar that the absolute form of the infinitive of the *hiph'il* has ָ in the last syllable, while the construct form by necessity offers ִ, contrasts with the facts; cf.

Jer. 6.15:	הַכְלִים	Josh. 7.7:	הַעֲבִיר	Hab. 1.13:	וְהַבֵּיט
Prov. 25.8:	בְּהַכְלִים	Ezek. 16.21:	בְּהַעֲבִיר	Jonah 2.5:	לְהַבִּיט

In these cases, both the absolute infinitive and construct infinitive have equally ִ.

Num. 30.13:	הָפֵר	Jer. 7.18:	וְהַסֵּךְ
Lev. 26.44:	לְהָפֵר	Jer. 44.19:	וּלְהַסֵּךְ

Here absolute and construct infinitive both have ֵ.

Isa. 49.8:	לְהַנְחִיל	Prov. 21.11:	וּבְהַשְׂכִּיל	Ps. 106.27:	וּלְהַפִּיל
Deut. 32.8:	בְּהַנְחֵל	Job 34.35:	בְּהַשְׂכֵּיל	Jer. 44.19:	וּלְהַסֵּךְ

Here the construct infinitive is represented both ways, with ִ and ֵ. Vice versa in Ezek. 21.31: הַשְׁפִּיל as compared with Isa. 14.23: הַשְׁמֵד we have forms of the absolute infinitive vocalized with ִ and ֵ, too.

§ 54.   The imperfect unchanged by *waw conjunctivum* or *conversivum*.

a) Isa. 26.17:   תָּחִיל   Prov. 29.4:   יַעֲמִיד
     Zech. 9.5:   וְתָחִיל   Neh. 3.14:   וְיַעֲמִיד

b) Deut. 24.11:   יוֹצִיא   Lev. 4.32:   יָבִיא
     Deut. 4.20:   וַיּוֹצִיא   Neh. 8.2:   וַיָּבִיא

     Deut. 24.4:   תַחֲטִיא   Judg. 20.16:   יַחֲטִא
     I Ki. 16.2:   וַתַּחֲטִיא   2 Ki. 21.11:   וַיַּחֲטִא

§ 55.   The imperfect unchanged by negations לֹא and אַל.

a) Lev. 27.22:   יַקְדִּישׁ   Deut. 4.41:   יַבְדִּיל
     Lev. 27.26:   לֹא יַקְדִּישׁ   Lev. 1.17:   לֹא יַבְדִּיל

     Deut. 28.38:   תּוֹצִיא   Gen. 6.19:   תָּבִיא
     Ex. 12.46:   לֹא תוֹצִיא   Deut. 23.19:   לֹא תָבִיא

b) 2 Ki. 18.32:   יַסִּית   Hab. 1.3:   תַּבִּיט
     2 Chron.   Gen. 19.17   אַל תַּבִּיט
     32.15: וְאַל יַסִּית

לֹא and אַל both indicate the negation of the imperative; cf. Ex. 34.3: אַל יֵרָא ... לֹא יַעֲלֶה; I Ki. 20.8: אַל תִּשְׁמַע וְלֹא תֹאבֶה; cf. also p. 284, § 71. Since the prefixing of לֹא and אַל before a verb in the imperfect does not affect its vocalization, there is no reason why an imperfect-form with ֦ as second vowel should be termed as "Jussive," unless by differentiating between the imperative in the affirmative (scil. the jussive) and in the negative. But this seems highly improbable; for just as both formations, with ֒ and with ֦ do appear in connection with these particles of negation (cf. the following paragraphs), so do they occur even without them, too. Furthermore: the mere external evidence of its vocalization with ֦ alone does not transform an imperfect-form into a jussive; the context is here of primary importance—provided we wish to continue this term "jussive" at all!

§ 56.   I. pers. imperf.

Ex. 10.29:   לֹא אֹסֵף   Ps. 89.34:   לֹא אָפִיר   Neh. 2.20:   וְאָשִׁיב
Deut. 18.16:   לֹא אֹסֵף   Judg. 2.1:   לֹא אָפֵר   Josh. 14.7:   וָאָשֵׁב

§ 57.   2. pers. masc. imperf.

Deut. 23.16: לֹא תַסְגִּיר	Deut. 20.19: לֹא תַשְׁחִית	Josh. 1.8: תַּשְׂכִּיל
Obad 14: וְאַל תַּסְגֵּר	Deut. 9.26: אַל תַּשְׁחֵת	Dan. 9.25: וַתַּשְׁכֵּל
Ps. 35.9: תָּגִיל	Gen. 24.6: תָּשִׁיב	Job 7.12: תָּשִׂים
Isa. 61.10: תָּגֵל	Ps. 90.3: תָּשֵׁב	Job 13.27: וְתָשֵׂם
Gen. 19.17: אַל תַּבִּיט	Deut. 19.14: לֹא תַסִּיג	2 Sam. 15.35: תַּגִּיד
1 Sam. 16.7: אַל תַּבֵּט	Prov. 22.28: אַל תַּסֵּג	Ex. 19.3: וְתַגֵּד

Similarly 3. pers. fem.

Ex. 11.6: לֹא תֹסֵף   Gen. 4.12: לֹא תֹסֵף

§ 58.   3. pers. masc. imperf.

Isa. 56.2: יַחֲזִיק	1 Sam. 20.2: יַסְתִּיר	Isa. 2.20: יַשְׁלִיךְ
Isa. 27.5: יַחֲזֵק	Mic. 3.4: וְיַסְתֵּר	Job 27.22: וְיַשְׁלֵךְ
Job 11.10: וְיַקְהִיל	Zeph. 3.17: יָגִיל	Lev. 4.31: יָסִיר
1 Ki. 8.1: יַקְהֵל	Ps. 14.7: יָגֵל	Job 9.34: יָסֵר
Job 37.11: יָפִיץ	Eccl. 4.10: יָקִים	Ps. 52.9: יָשִׂים
Job 38.24: יָפֵץ	Ps. 107.29: יָקֵם	Ps. 107.33: יָשֵׂם
Lev. 27.10: וְלֹא יָמִיר	Gen. 41.44: לֹא יָרִים	Dan. 11.2: יָעִיר
Ezek. 48.14: וְלֹא יָמֵר	Num. 17.2: וְיָרֵם	Dan. 11.25: וְיָעֵר
Ps. 92.7: יָבִין	Neh. 8.2: וַיָּבִיא	Isa. 21.6: יַגִּיד
Jer. 9.11: וְיָבֵן	Ezek. 40.3: וַיָּבִא	Eccl. 10.20: יַגֵּד
Josh. 6.26: יַצִּיב	Lev. 26.5: יַשִּׂיג	Jer. 32.5: יוֹלִיךְ
Deut. 32.8: יַצֵּב	Ps. 7.6: וְיַשֵּׂג	Deut. 28.36: יוֹלֵךְ

Deut. 25.3: יֹסִיף   Deut. 4.20: וַיּוֹצִיא
Lev. 5.16: יוֹסֵף   Gen. 15.5: וַיּוֹצֵא

§ 59.   Nouns and adverbs.

Ps. 102.1: שִׂיחוֹ	Prov. 5.4: פִּיּוֹת	Isa. 2.4: לְאִתִּים
Am. 4.13: שֵׂחוֹ	Judg. 3.16: פֵּיוֹת	1 Sam. 13.21: וְלָאֵתִים
Judg. 12.4: פְּלִיטֵי		Judg. 5.16: שְׁרִקוֹת
Isa. 66.19: פְּלֵיטִים		Jer. 51.37: וּשְׁרֵקָה
Jer. 51.34: רִיק	Prov. 28.19: רִישׁ	Isa. 46.3: מִנִּי
Deut. 32.47: רֵק	Prov. 13.18: רֵשׁ	Isa. 30.11: מִנִּי

§ 60.　Evidence from the Bible 1515/17.

Jer. 39.5: יְרֵחוֹ, marg.: יְרֵחוֹ (=MT).

Ezek. 11.6: הִרְבֵּיתֶם, marg.: הִרְבֵּיתֶם (=MT).

Neh. 9.23: הִרְבִּיתָ (=MT), marg.: הִרְבֵּיתָ.

I Chron. 19.5: בִּירֵחוֹ (=MT), marg.: בִּירִיחוֹ.

§ 61.　Evidence from the Babylonian vocalization.

The following examples (cf. MTK, 58 and MdO, 189) are made up of verbs *mediae laryngalis* in the perfect of the *pi'el*. In the Tiberian vocalization their respective first radical is vocalized with ., and in the Babylonian vocalization with ˝. A similar phenomenon, involving this time a sound root, is Job 8.11: בִּצָּה which appears in the Babylonian vocalization as בֹּצָּה (MTK, 71). Further evidence against an explanation that the vocalization with ˝ is due to the influence of the laryngals, can be seen in the fact that in the imperfect *ḳal* of *primae laryngalis*, the prefix is vocalized ˙ as is the case with all sound verbs: Lam. 3.3: יַהֲפֹךְ; Job 5.2: יַהֲרֹג; Job 12.14: יַהֲרֹס (MTK, 53); Job 4.15: יַחֲלֹף; Job 9.3: יַחְפֹּץ and many more (MTK, 54). In the imperfect *pi'el*, their first radical is vocalized ⸴, as is the rule with sound verbs: Ps. 102.14: תְּרַחֵם; Eccl. 5.1: יְמַהֵר and תְּבַהֵל (MTK, 59); Deut. 10.6: וַיְכַהֵן; I Sam. 3.17: תְּכַחֵד; Judg. 16.25: וַיְשַׂחֵק; Isa. 51.13: תְּפַחֵד (MdO, 189).

Lam. 2.7:	נֵאֵר = נֹאֵר		Isa. 51.14:	מֹהֵר = מִהַר
			Ex. 40.13:	וּכֹהֵן = וְכִהֵן
			Ex. 40.15:	וּכֹהֲנוּ = וְכִהֲנוּ
I Sam. 3.18:	כֹּחֵד = כִּחֵד		Job 8.18:	וּכֹחֵשׁ = וְכִחֵשׁ
Job 6.10:	כֹּחַדְתִּי = כִּחַדְתִּי		Lam. 2.6:	שֹׁחֵת = שִׁחֵת
Isa. 49.13:	נֹחַם = נִחַם		Job 7.21:	וּשְׁחֹרְתַּנִי = וְשִׁחַרְתַּנִי
I Sam. 15.11:	נֹחַמְתִּי = נִחַמְתִּי			
2 Chron. 19.3:	בֹּעֲרְתָ = בִּעַרְתָ		Job 9.31:	וּתְעֹבוּנִי = וְתִעֲבוּנִי
Ezek. 39.9:	וּבֹעֲרוּ = וּבִעֲרוּ			

§ 62.　Conclusions.

The signs ․ and ˳ are used to indicate the vowel *i*. Merely on the basis of the number of dots in the sign applied to a given word, nothing can be concluded as to the quantity or quality of the vowel.

F.   THE VOWEL O(U): ˙ (AND ָ) OR ָ (וֹ)

§ 63.   The signs ָ and וֹ are interchangeable.

a) Lev. 14.6:   הַשְׁחוּטָה   Deut. 9.1:   וַעֲצֻמִים
   Lev. 14.51:   הַשְׁחֻטָה   Deut. 7.1:   וַעֲצוּמִים

   Ex. 39.13:   בְּמִלֻּאֹתָם   Ex. 39.40:   עַמֻּדֶיהָ
   Ex. 28.20:   בְּמִלּוּאֹתָם   Prov. 9.1:   עַמּוּדֶיהָ

b) Gen. 10.21:   יֻלַּד   Num. 17.20:   תִּלְגֹּות
   Judg. 18.29:   יוּלַּד   Ex. 16.12:   תִּלֻּנֹּת

These examples show that *dagesh* was either inserted (b) or not (a) in the letter following the vowel *u*, regardless of the fact whether this vowel was indicated by ָ or וֹ. Consequently, in cases like

   Prov. 22.14:   עֲמֻקָה   Zech. 1.13:   נִחֻמִים
   Prov. 23.27:   עֲמוּקָה   Hos. 11.8:   נִחוּמָי

we will realize an effort to introduce a difference in the treatment of these signs: ָ to be followed by a *dagesh*, apparently because believed designating a short vowel (cf. Rule VI β in § 1).

The genuinely indiscriminate use of these vowel-signs is also reflected in the Bible 1515/17:

Isa. 5.5:   מְשׂוּכָּתוֹ (=MT), marg.: משׂכתו.
Isa. 55.4:   לְאוּמִּים (=MT), marg.: לאמים.
Jer. 31.33:   כּוּלָּם (=MT), marg.: כלם.

Isa. 59.18:   גְּמֻלֹות (=MT), marg.: גמולות.
Ps. 80.17:   שְׂרָפָה (=MT), marg.: שרופה.

Isa. 16.8:   שְׁלֻחֹתֶיהָ, marg.: שלחתיה (=MT).
Jer. 42.16:   תָּמוּתוּ, marg.:   תָּמֻתוּ (=MT), but
Am. 9.10:   יָמוּתוּ (=MT), marg.: ימתו.

Henceforth, in discussing the vowel-signs of this group ˙ and ָ, the vowel-sign וֹ will implicite be included in ָ (and vice versa).

§ 64.   Imperfect-forms of sound verbs.

2 Sam. 17.16:   תַּעֲבוֹר   Isa. 1.23:   יִשְׁפֹּטוּ   Prov. 2.11:   תִּשְׁמֹר
Ruth 2.8:   תַּעֲבוּרִי   Ex. 18.26:   יִשְׁפּוּטוּ   Prov. 14.3:   תִּשְׁמוּרֵם

§ 65.　Imperfect-forms of verbs *mediae* ו.

Ezek. 5.11:	תָּחוֹס	Job 36.14:	תָּמֹת	Mic. 5.8:	תָּרֹם
Isa. 13.18:	תָּחוּס	Ex. 7.18:	תָּמוּת	Ps. 89.14:	תָּרוּם
Ps. 72.13:	יָחֹס	Num. 24.7:	וְיָרֹם	Deut. 33.6:	יְמֹת (וְאַל)
Jer. 21.7:	יָחוּס	2 Sam. 22.47:	וְיָרֻם	Num. 35.12:	יָמוּת (וְלֹא)

The *waw consecutivum* does not interfere with the way these verbs are vocalized (cf. similarly § 54):

Ps. 46.7: תָּמוּג　as compared with　Prov. 3.11: תָּקֹץ

Am. 9.5: וַתָּמֹג　　　　　　　　　　　　Lev. 20.23: וָאָקֻץ

§ 66.　Infinitive-forms of verbs *mediae* ו.

A number of inifinitives of verbs *mediae* ו occur both, vocalized with ו and וּ. Against any attempt to term such forms with וּ as absolute infinitive, and those with ו as construct infinitive, we are going to prove that the transition of the absolute infinitive into the construct form does not involve a change in the vowel-sign hitherto employed:

a)　Absolute infinitive equals construct infinitive (in the vowel-sign):

1)　Gen. 39.16: בּוֹא; cf. with: Gen. 42.15: בְּבוֹא; Gen. 12.14: כְּבוֹא; Josh.
　　13.5: לְבוֹא; Gen. 24.62: מִבּוֹא.
　　Isa. 24.19: מוֹט; cf. with: Ps. 38.17: בְּמוֹט; Ps. 46.3: וּבְמוֹט; Ps. 66.9:
　　לָמוֹט.

2)　Ezek. 30.16: חוּל; cf. with Judg. 21.21: לָחוּל.
　　Job 5.7: עוּף; cf. with Prov. 26.2: לָעוּף.

Hence, in forms vocalized

b)　Absolute infinitive וּ and construct ו:

Lam. 3.52:	צוּד	Isa. 61.10:	שׂוֹשׂ
Gen. 27.5:	לָצוּד	Deut. 30.9:	לָשׂוֹשׂ

this change from וּ into ו is by no means the result of the change of the absolute form of the infinitive into the construct form, but reflects the two possibilities of vocalizing these verbs, which in these cases accidentally coincide with the absolute infinitive and construct infinitive, respectively. The following paragraphs will corroborate these results.

§ 67. Absolute infinitive of verbs *mediae* ו.

Jer. 44.29:	קוֹם	Deut. 17.15:	שׂוֹם	Dan. 9.5:	וְסוֹר
Ps. 127.2:	קוֹם	Hag. 2.15:	שׂוֹם	Job 28.28:	וְסוּר

§ 68. Construct infinitive of verbs *mediae* ו.

2 Sam. 13.28:	כְּטוֹב	Num. 11.25:	כְּנוֹחַ
Prov. 11.10:	בְּטוֹב	2 Sam. 21.10:	לָנוּחַ
Num. 16.29:	כְּמוֹת	Isa. 7.2:	כְּנוֹעַ
Num. 18.22:	לָמוּת	Jer. 14.10:	לָנוּעַ

§ 69. Absolute infinitive with imperfect of verbs *mediae* ו.

Cant. 8.7:	בּוֹז יָבוּזוּ	Judg. 13.22:	מוֹת נָמוּת	Jer. 44.29:	קוֹם יָקוּמוּ
Isa. 54.15:	גּוֹר יָגוּר	2 Sam. 18.3:	נֹס נָנוּס	Gen. 18.10:	שׁוֹב אָשׁוּב
Isa. 28.28:	אָדוֹשׁ יְדוּשֶׁנּוּ	Isa. 24.20:	נוֹעַ תָּנוּעַ		

§ 70. Nouns with prefix מ, derived from verbs *mediae* ו.

a) Masculine and feminine forms with וֹ.

Ps. 150.4:	וּמָחוֹל	Ps. 71.3:	מָעוֹן
Cant. 7.1:	כְּמֹחֹלַת	Deut. 33.27:	מְעֹנָה

b) Masculine form with וֹ, feminine with וֹ and ו.

Jer. 6.25:	מָגוֹר	Ex. 15.17:	מָכוֹן	Prov. 12.12:	מְצוֹד
Prov. 10.24:	מְגוֹרַת	1 Ki. 7.27:	הַמְּכוֹנָה	Eccl. 9.12:	בִּמְצוֹדָה
Ps. 34.5:	מְגוּרוֹתַי	Zech. 5.11:	מְכֹנָתָהּ	Ezek. 13.21:	לִמְצָדָה

Thus, the vowel-sign employed by these nominal forms is not at all interconnected with the gender of the respective form. Similarly we shall explain the following cases, where consistently the masculine noun is vocalized וֹ and the feminine ו, as a mere coincidence, due to the fact that accidentally these forms happened to be preserved in the Bible:

Ps. 74.16:	מָאוֹר	Gen. 43.21:	הַמָּלוֹן	Gen. 8.9:	מָנוֹחַ
Isa. 11.8:	מְאוּרַת	Isa. 1.8:	כִּמְלוּנָה	Num. 10.33:	מְנוּחָה
Jer. 25.35:	מָנוֹס	1 Sam. 22.2:	מָצוֹק	Deut. 20.20:	מָצוֹר
Isa. 52.12:	וּבִמְנוּסָה	Zeph. 1.15:	וּמְצוּקָה	2 Chron. 14.5:	מְצוּרָה

§ 71.   Various nominal forms with וֹ and וּ.

2 Ki. 12.10:	חֹר	Hab. 3.10:	רוֹם	Ezek. 3.9:	מֵצֹר
Isa. 11.8:	חֻר	Prov. 25.3:	לָרוּם	Ps. 89. 44:	צוּר
Isa. 34.11:	וְיַנְשׁוֹף	Hos. 9.8:	יָקוֹשׁ	Prov. 7.9:	בְּאִישׁוֹן
Lev. 11.17:	הַיַּנְשׁוּף	Ps. 91.3:	יָקוּשׁ	Prov. 20.20	בְּאֶשׁוּן
2 Chron. 9.29:	וּבַחֲזוֹת	Jer. 51.38:	כְּגוֹרֵי	Isa. 52.2:	מוֹסְרֵי
Isa. 21.2:	חָזוּת	Ezek. 19.2:	גּוּרֶיהָ	Job 12.18:	מוּסַר
1 Sam. 11.11:	בְּאַשְׁמֹרֶת	Ex. 15.5:	בִּמְצוֹלֹת	Jer. 41.8:	מַטְמֹנִים
Ps. 63.7:	בְּאַשְׁמֻרוֹת	Mic. 7.19:	בִּמְצֻלוֹת	Isa. 45.3:	וּמַטְמֻנֵי
Eccl. 9.14:	מְצוֹדִים	Ezek. 16.3:	מְכֹרֹתַיִךְ	Isa. 29.7:	וּמְצֹדָתָהּ
Job 19.6:	וּמְצוּדוֹ	Ezek. 21.35:	מְכֻרוֹתַיִךְ	2 Sam. 22.2:	וּמְצֻדָתִי

Similarly Adverbs like:

Deut. 1.1:	מוֹל	1 Sam. 4.7:	אֶתְמוֹל
Deut. 2.19:	מוּל	Isa. 30.33:	מֵאֶתְמוּל

§ 72.   Evidence from non-Masoretic sources.

We refer to our expositions on p. 175, sub וּ; cf. also p. 186, § 40: פַּנּוֹת: φεννωθ with כַּסּוֹת: χεσσουθ (ω—ου). Further in the Bible 1515/17:

Ps. 69.9:   מוּזָר (=MT), marg.:   מוֹזָר
Isa. 27.5:   בְּמָעֻזִּי (=MT), marg.:   מעוזי

§ 73.   ḥatef ḳames (ֳ) and ḳames ḥatuf (ָ).

a)   According to the procedure of the grammarians of the Tiberian School, a holem (ׂ) in a syllable which in the course of the declension either became closed, or which if closed—but with the stress before— lost its stress, immediately was changed into ֳ. In order to avoid any misunderstanding, we once again emphasize the statement made at the end of § 7: that we constantly refer to the readings of the Bible 1524/5 of Jacob ben Chayim; for of all the examples which we are listing here, hardly more than a mere trace has been left in the subsequent "corrected" editions: עֹז becomes Ex. 15.2: עֳזִי; יִפְרֹץ in Ex. 19.24: יִפְרָץ־; similarly Ps. 5.4: אֶעֱרָךְ־לְךָ; קֹדֶשׁ with suffix in Isa. 63.15: קָדְשְׁךָ; יֹגֵף; with suffix in 1 Sam. 26.10: יָגְפֶנּוּ; similarly Num. 35.20: יֶהְדָּפֶנּוּ and Josh. 23.5: יֶהְדָּם;

nominal forms ending in ־ֽ , when in the construct state with *makkef*:
Ex. 30.23: וְקִנְּמָן־; Ex. 21.11: שְׁלָשׁ־; cf. further Ex. 25.40: מָרְאֶה and
2 Ki. 10.19: בְּעָקְבָה. In the majority of these cases the marginal Masora
(the מסורה קטנה) in this Bible of 1524/5 exhibits notes stressing the vocalization with a ָ of the words referred to. I wish to illustrate this with an
example, which upon a re-examination of the cross-references, reveals
the later tendency of the Masoretes to change this ָ into ָ, the so-called
ḳames ḥatuf: In Ex. 15.2 on עָזִּי, the Masora has a note: גׄ. This means: the
word עָזִּי in exactly this vocalization with ָ occurs three times. But the
next time this word actually occurs, in Isa. 12.2, the text reads: עָזִּי and
its masoretic note likewise: גׄ. We see thus the hand of the editor at work;
text and note have both been changed! In order to impress upon the
reader the importance of this observation, I bring here some additional
cases of ָ, picked at random from Jacob ben Chayim's Bible: Gen. 2.23:
לָקֳחָה; 3.5: אֳכָלְכֶם; 3.11: אֳכַל; 14.15: כְּדָרְלָעֹמֶר; 16.13: רֳאִי (Masora:
ל חטף קמץ); 27.19: וְאָכֳלָה; Ex. 19.24: יֶפְרָץ; 28.40: כֻּתֳּנֹת; Lev. 10.5:
בְּכֻתֳּנֹתָם; 14.4: צִפֳּרִים; 22.2: מְקַדְּשִׁי; Num. 3.19: קָהָת; 3.27: הָעָזִּיאֵלִי; 5.10:
קֳדָשָׁיו; 5.15: קָרְבָּנָה; 10.21: הַקְּהָתִים; 11.32: חֳמָרִים; 18.9: קָרְבָּנָם; 18.11:
לְחָק; 23.25: תִּקָּבֶנּוּ; 25.8: קֻבָּתָה; Deut. 6.7: וּבְשָׁכְבְּךָ; 28.35: קָדְקֳדֶךָ; 32.13:
בָּמֳתֵי; Josh. 23.5: יֶהְדֳּפֵם; Judg. 1.13: עָתְנִיאֵל; 1.17: חָרְמָה; 15.12: לְאֶסְרְךָ;
16.28: זָכְרֵנִי; 1 Ki. 8.52: קָרְאָם; 12.10: קָטָנִּי; Isa. 17.5: שִׁבֳּלִים; 18.4:
עָזְּבֵךְ; 2.19: בָּאֳנֵי; Jer. 2.2: דְּמִי; 62.6: יָקֻבֵּנוּ; 62.2: גֶּרְנִי; 21.10: אֵשׁ קֻטָה;
8.22: הַצֳרִי; 30.2: כְּתָב; 49.28: וְשָׁדְדוּ; Ezek. 17.23: אֶשְׁתַּלֶּנּוּ; 23.4: וּקְטָרְתִּי.
Note especially the many instances of a ָ following a ָ. The extent
of the changes effected prior to the submitting of this Bible to the press
can be seen by an even cursory comparison with the Bible 1515/17:
Here as a rule, the vowel *o* in a closed syllable is indicated by ָ; cf. e.g.:
מְלָכִי, מֶלְכָה, חֳנֵּי, שְׁפָטֵנִי, אָזְנֶךָ, אָרְחוֹת, שֳרָשָׁם, חֳכְמָה, to mention but a few.
In this connection it is interesting to note that the *naḳdan*, who was
responsible for the vocalization of the Bible 1515/17, held a view, even
on the division of words into syllables, different from that of Jacob ben
Chayim; cf. his text

1 Sam. 3.11: שִׁמְעוֹ (=MT), marg.: שֶׁ
Ezek. 28.9: הֹרֶגֶךָ (=MT), marg.: הָרֹגֶךָ

The masoretic vocalization of these words with ־ֽ presupposes their division into syllables as שׁ–מֵעוּ and ה–רגך, while the marginal reading in the Bible 1515/17 reflects שׁמ–עוּ and הר–גך. I am inclined to assume that similarly Jer. 46.7: (מימיו) יִתְגָּעֲשׁוּ might originally have been vocalized with גּ as: יִתְגָּֽעֲשׁוּ; cf. v. 8: (מים) יִתְגָּֽעֲשׁוּ.

b)   With the results of our discussion in § 64 ff. in mind, we shall now demonstrate the interrelation of the vowel-signs ˙ and ֫ as well as ֯ and ֫. We stress the point that the ֫ we are concerned with here is an original ֳ which due to a later conception of the grammarians was changed into ֫, but which is utterly different from the ֫ as discussed in § 42 f.:

1)   Isa. 3.12: אֹרְחֹתֶיךָ as compared with Job 13.27: אָרְחֹתָי and Venice 1515: אֲרְחֹתָי.

   Ezek. 35.10: אֹמרֹךֽ (MdO, 188) = אֲמָרֽךָ, and Venice 1515 marg.: אֲמָרֽךָ.
   1 Sam. 15.7: למשֹׁחֹךֽ = לִמְשָׁחֶךָ, and Venice 1515 marg.: לִמְשָׁחֶךָ.

The omission of the ֫ in the ֳ in these cases by the Masora reflects a period when ֳ was already considered to form together with ֱ and ֲ (cf. § 37 ff.) one group, the so-called hatefs. In case such a hatef was followed immediately after by a simple shewa, then one of the components of the hatef was omitted; cf. 1 Sam. 4.19: נֶהְפְּכוּ with Ps. 78.57: נֶהֶפְכוּ; 2 Sam. 10.11: יֶחֶזְקוּ with Isa. 28.22: יֶחְזְקוּ; Hos. 11.11: יֶחֶרְדוּ with Ezek. 26.18: יֶחְרְדוּ; Ps. 5.12: וְיַעְלְצוּ with the variant from the Soncino edition (1488) as noted by Ginsburg: וְיַעֲלְצוּ. Similarly: Job 9.27: אֶעֶזְבָה with Num. 21.22: אֶעְבְּרָה; Num. 32.27: יַעֲברוּ with 1 Sam. 14.1: וְנַעְבְּרָה.

2) Isa. 37.18: אָמְנָם Deut. 5.21: גְּדֹלוֹ Mic. 2.10: טָמְאָה
   Gen. 18.13: אָמְנָם Ps. 150.2: גְּדֹלוֹ Judg. 13.7 טָמְאָה

   Isa. 12.2:   עָזִּי   Lev. 2.1:   קָרְבַּן
   Isa. 49.5:   עָזִּי   Neh. 10.35:   קָרְבַּן

§ 74.   Conclusions.

The vowel-signs וֹ ו ֯, ֳ and ֫ represent various ways of indicating one and the same vowel o(u). The fact in itself that ˙ and ֳ (֫) could be used interchangeably, excludes any theory that they signify long and short o, respectively.

G.   THE VOWEL-SIGN SEGOL (ֶ)

In order to identify the vowel which this sign ֶ was meant to indicate, we first turn to the Palestinian and Babylonian vocalizations to see what vowel-signs they use for vocalizing a syllable which has ֶ in the Tiberian system. The vocalic value in the respective vocalization system of the equivalent Palestinian and Babylonian vowel-signs thus established will be fixed by our inductive method.

§ 75.   The Palestinian equivalent of ֶ.

a)   Palestinian ׳ : corresponds to Tiberian ֶ.

Deut. 26.15:	אָרֶץ = אֵרֶ׳ץ	Ps. 12.7:	כֶּסֶף = כֹסֹ׳ף
Isa. 66.3:	כֶּלֶב = כֹלֹ׳ב	Isa. 49.6:	עֶבֶד = עֹבֹ׳ד
Ps. 39.14:	בְטֶרֶם = בֹטֹ׳רם	Isa. 66.17:	וְהַשֶּׁקֶץ = והשׁ׳קץ

b)   The vocalic value of ׳ : equals Tiberian ֵ.

Jer. 25.30:	הָאֵלֶה = הָאֵ׳לה	Isa. 60.11:	וּמַלְכֵיהֶם = ומלכי׳הם
Deut. 32.2:	עֵשֶׂב = עֹ׳שׂב	Jer. 3.22:	מְשׁוּבֹתֵיכֶם = משׁובֹתי׳כם
Hos. 2.17:	עֵמֶק = עֹ׳מק	Jonah 1.5:	מֵעֲלֵיהֶם = מעלי׳הם
	Ps. 39.14:		וְאֵינֶנִּי = ואי׳נֹני

In these words the two vowel-signs ֶ : ֵ occur in their Tiberian vocalization, while the Palestinian system has ׳ : ׳. This sign corresponds to Tiberian ֵ; cf. 1 Ki. 8.20: וָאֵשֶׁב = ואשׁ׳ב; Jer. 30.18: יֵשַׁב = ישׁ׳ב. We therefore conclude that the vowel which in the Palestinian vocalization was indicated by ׳, had two equivalents in the Tiberian system, ֵ and ֶ. Whether this implies a break of the vowel into two shades will be discussed later on.

§ 76.   The Babylonian equivalent of ֶ.

a)   Babylonian ⟂ corresponds to Tiberian ֶ.

Jer. 6.26:	אֵבֶל = אֹבֹ֞ל	Isa. 50.1:	סֵפֶר = סֹפֹ֞ר	Job 5.9:	חֵקֶר = חֹקֹ֞ר
Jer. 22.28:	חֵפֶץ = חֹפֹ֞ץ	Deut. 10.9:	חֵלֶק = חֹלֹ֞ק	Joel 4.2:	עֵמֶק = עֹמֹ֞ק

These examples are taken from MdO, 195.

b)   The vocalic value of ֱ equals Tiberian ֶ.

This fact is so obvious to anyone who has even only a chance acquaintance with Hebrew Bible texts in the Babylonian vocalization that we consider it superfluous to bring examples for it.

Summing up the results obtained thus far: that ֱ corresponds phonetically to ֶ (according to the evidence from the Palestinian system) and (or) ֲ (as the *naḳdan* of the Babylonian system heard it) we may safely assume that ֱ as a vowel formed the phonetic transition from ֲ to ֶ. We shall now proceed to apply this our inductive method to the Tiberian vocalization itself in our search to fit ֱ into the system of vowels.

§ 77.   The vowel-signs ֱ and ֶ interchangeably used in the Tiberian system.

a)   Verbs of sound roots.

1)   Imperative.

Isa. 58.1:	הָרֵם	2 Ki. 5.23:	הוֹאֶל
2 Ki. 6.7:	הָרֵם	2 Ki. 6.3:	הוֹאֵל

2)   Imperfect with אל.

Ps. 132.10:	תָּשֵׁב	1 Sam. 22.15:	יָשֵׂם	Ex. 8.25:	יֹסֵף
1 Ki. 2.20:	תָּשֵׁב	1 Sam. 9.20:	תָּשֵׂם	Ex. 10.28:	תֹּסֶף

3)   Imperfect *niph'al*.

Isa. 62.4:	יֵאָמֵר	Jer. 48.44:	יִלָּכֵד
Isa. 4.3:	יֵאָמֶר	Eccl. 7.26:	יִלָּכֶד
Ex. 5.18:	יִנָּתֵן	2 Ki. 10.19:	יִפָּקֵד
Lev. 24.20:	יִנָּתֶן	Prov. 19.23:	יִפָּקֶד

4)   Imperfect with *waw consecutivum*.

Num. 11.30:	וַיֵּאָסֵף	Gen. 24.67:	וַיִּנָּחֵם
Gen. 25.8:	וַיֵּאָסֶף	Gen. 6.6:	וַיִּנָּחֶם
Ezra 8.23:	וַיֵּעָתֵר	Gen. 47.11:	וַיּוֹשֵׁב
2 Chron. 33.13:	וַיֵּעָתֶר	2 Ki. 17.6:	וַיּוֹשֶׁב

5)   *Inf. constr.*

Ex. 17.10:	לְהִלָּחֵם	Ex. 32.6:	לְצַחֵק
Num. 22.11:	לְהִלָּחֶם	Gen. 39.14:	לְצַחֶק

6) Perfect.

    Lev. 5.21:   וְכִחֵשׁ   Lev. 5.22:   וְכִחֶשׁ

b) Verbs *tertiae* ה.

1) Imperfect.

    Ex. 22.22:   תְּעַנֶּה   Dan. 1.13:   תֵּרָאֶה
    Gen. 31.50:   תְּעַנֶּה   Ps. 35.17:   תֵּרָאֶה

Similary

    Gen. 24.39:   תֵּלֵךְ   Jer. 48.2:   תֵּלֵךְ

With a Particle of Negation.

    Jer. 17.17:   אַל תִּהְיֵה   2 Sam. 13.12: אַל תַּעֲשֵׂה
    Ex. 22.24:   לֹא תִהְיֶה   Ex. 20.4:   לֹא תַעֲשֶׂה

2) Participle *ḳal*.

Isa. 64.5:   וְעֹשֵׂה   Gen. 14.19:   קֹנֵה   Ps. 64.9:   רֹאֶה
Ps. 86.10:   וְעֹשֵׂה   Prov. 15.32:   קֹנֶה   Jer. 20.12:   רֹאֶה

    Similarly:

    Ps. 119.162:   כְּמוֹצֵא   Eccl. 7.26:   וְחוֹטֵא
    Eccl. 7.26:   וּמוֹצֵא   Eccl. 9.18:   וְחוֹטֶא

3) Participle *hiph'il*.

Ex. 21.12:   מַכֵּה Isa. 66.3:   מַעֲלֵה   Lev. 11.42:   מַרְבֵּה
Ex. 2.11:   מַכֶּה Jer. 33.18:   מַעֲלֶה   Prov. 28.8:   מַרְבֶּה

4) Similar nominal formations.

    Isa. 60.21:   מַעֲשֵׂה   Gen. 26.14:   וּמִקְנֵה
    Isa. 3.24:   מַעֲשֶׂה   Eccl. 2.7:   מִקְנֶה

Consequently, there is no justification for assigning such forms in ֵ to the absolute and those in ֶ to the construct state. Solely the word's position in the structure of the sentence ought to be decisive; cf. also 1 Ki. 10.28: מִקְוֵה (absol.) and Lev. 11.36: מִקְוֵה־ (constr.) both equally vocalized.

c)   Bisyllabic nouns.

1)   Nouns of sound roots.

Ezek. 16.34:	הֵפֵךְ	Isa. 56.12:	יֶתֶר	Ps. 49.14:	כֶּסֶל
Ezek. 16.34:	לְהֵפֵךְ	Dan. 8.9:	יֶתֶר	Eccl. 7.25:	כֶּסֶל
1 Sam. 10.5:	נֵבֶל	Num. 30.14:	נֶדֶר	Ex. 30.9:	וְנִסְךְּ
Ps. 71.22:	נֵבֶל	Lev. 22.21:	נֶדֶר	Gen. 35.14:	נֶסֶךְ

1 Ki. 10.25:	וְנֶשֶׁק	Ezek. 8.3:	סֵמֶל
2 Chron. 9.24:	נֶשֶׁק	2 Chron. 33.7:	הַסֵּמֶל

Am. 6.6:	שֵׁבֶר	Ps. 32.6:	לְשֵׁטֶף	Ps. 111.10:	שֵׂכֶל
Lev. 21.19:	שֵׁבֶר	Nah. 1.4:	וּבְשֶׁטֶף	1 Sam. 25.3:	שֵׂכֶל

2)   Nouns *tertiae laryngalis*.

Ps. 49.20:	נֵצַח	2 Sam. 16.13:	בְּצֵלַע
Jer. 15.18:	נֵצַח	Ex. 26.20:	וּלְצֵלַע
Ps. 119.130:	פֵּתַח	Ps. 20.7:	יֵשַׁע
Gen. 38.14:	בִּפְתַח	Isa. 45.8:	יֵשַׁע

d)   Monosyllabic nouns.

1)   Absolute state.

Zech. 14.4:	גֵּיא	Isa. 40.4:	גֵּיא

2)   Construct state.

1 Sam. 22.20:	בֶּן־	2 Sam. 24.10:	לֵב־	Gen. 19.22:	שֵׁם־
1 Sam. 22.20:	בֶּן־	2 Sam. 15.13:	לֵב־	Gen. 16.15:	שֵׁם־
		1 Sam. 14.4:	שֵׁן־	Ruth 3.15:	שֵׁשׁ־
		Job 39.28:	שֵׁן־	Prov. 6.16:	שֵׁשׁ־

Similarly with *makkeph*:

Gen. 16.2:	הִנֵּה־	Gen. 19.2:	הִנֵּה

§ 78.   Evidence from the Bible 1515/17.

1)   Eccl. 5.7:   וְגֵזֶל, marg.:   וגֵזֶל (=MT).

Ps. 90.9:   הֶגֶה, marg.:   הֶגֶה (=MT).

2 Sam. 8.2:   הַחֵבֶל, marg.:   הַחֶבֶל (=MT),

Ps. 81.7:   מִסֵּבֶל (=MT), marg.:   מִסֵּבֶל.

Ps. 32.6:   לְשֵׁטֶף (=MT), marg.:   לְשֵׁטֶף.

2) Ezek. 3.7:   מֵצַח (=MT), marg.: מֶצַח.
    Ps. 109.19:   וּלְמֵזַח (=MT), marg.: מֶזַח.

3) Zech. 9.5:   תֵּרָא, marg.: תֵּרֶא (=MT).
    Job 29.3:   אֵלֵךְ, marg.: אֵלֶךְ (=MT).
    Isa. 33.21: תֵּלֵךְ (=MT), marg.: תלֶךְ.
    Job 27.8:   יֵשֶׁל (=MT), marg.: יֵשֵׁל.

4) 1 Ki. 18.1: הֵרָאֵה (=MT), marg.: הֵרָאֶה.
    Jer. 25.29: הִנָּקֵה (=MT), marg.: קֶה.

5) Jer. 51.15: עֹשֵׂה, marg.: עֹשֶׂה (=MT).
    2 Sam. 5.8: מַכֵּה, marg.: מַכֶּה (=MT).

6) Jer. 17.18: וּמִשְׁנֵה (=MT), marg.: שׁנֶה.
    Est. 1.9:   מִשְׁתֵּה (=MT), marg.: משׁתֶה.

7) 1 Sam. 25.25: כֵּן־ (=MT), marg.: כֶּן.
    2 Sam. 9.12:   בֵּן־, marg.: בֶּן (=MT).

§ 79.   The vowel-signs ֵ and ֶ

With the results of our investigation in § 49 ff. in mind: that the vowel-signs ֵ and ֶ were interchangeable, we shall now try to find out, how ֶ fits into this scheme:

Ps. 147.15:   אִמְרָתוֹ   Gen. 41.43:   בְּמִרְכֶּבֶת   Ps. 150.5:   בְּצִלְצְלֵי
Lam. 2.17:   אֶמְרָתוֹ   Gen. 46.29:   מֶרְכַּבְתּוֹ   2 Sam. 6.5:   וּבְצֶלְצְלִים

A similar uncertainty as to the use of ֶ or ֵ is noticeable in some other nominal formations, too; from the root רכב the noun is formed: Lev. 15.9: הַמֶּרְכָּב, but from the root רמס: Isa. 10.6: מִרְמָס; the absolute forms עֵגֶל and עֵמֶק with suffixes become Hos. 8.5: עֶגְלֵךְ and Jer. 49.4: עִמְקֵךְ; the construct state pluralis of חֶבֶל and חֵקֶר is: Hos. 13.13: חֲבָלֵי, and Judg. 5.16: חִקְרֵי.

Further traces of this uncertainty may be found in the Bible 1515/17 also:

Am. 6.6:   מִרְזַח (= MT), marg.: מֶרְזַח.
Jer. 29.4: הִגְלֵיתִי (= MT), marg.: הֶגְלתִי.

§ 80.　The vowel-signs ֞ and ֔.

a) Ps. 40.5: מִבְטַחוֹ　Isa. 20.5: מַבָּטָם　Num. 4.9: מַלְקָחֶיהָ

　　Prov. 21.22: מִבְטָחָהּ　Zech. 9.5: מֶבָּטָה　Isa. 6.6: בְּמֶלְקָחַיִם

　　　Joel 2.5:　מַרְכָּבוֹת　　Isa. 33.17: מֶרְחַקִּים

　　　2 Sam. 15.1: מֶרְכָּבָה　　Zech. 10.9: וּבְמֶרְחַקִּים

Cf. also Josh. 10.2: הַמַּמְלָכָה (from the root מלך) with Mic. 4.8: הַמֶּמְשָׁלָה
(from משל).

b) Judg. 16.5:　נְתָּן‎־　Gen. 41.7:　וַיִּיקַץ　Lam. 3.2:　וַיֹּלַךְ

　　Num. 22.18:　יִתֶּן‎־　Gen. 9.24:　וַיִּיקֶץ　Jer. 52.26:　וַיֹּלֶךְ

　　Job 40.32: אַל תּוֹסַף　Lam. 3.48:　תֵּרַד　Judg. 19.20: אַל תָּלַן

　　Deut. 3.26: אַל תּוֹסֶף　2 Ki. 1.10:　תֵּרֶד　2 Sam. 17.16: אַל תָּלֶן

§ 81.　Conclusions.

The vowel-sign ֞ may be classified as reflecting a variation of the
vowel indicated by ֔. Our attempt to establish an interrelation between
֞ and ֔ (cf. § 79) which would be only the self-understood outcome of
such close an inter-connection between ֞ and ֔, on one side, and between
֞ and ֔ on the other side, proved to be futile. As an explanation of this
result we are inclined to suggest a theory that ֞ was introduced as a vowel-
sign at a comparatively later time when ֔ had already branched off ֔ and
had become a separate vowel: e. As a step further to bridge over the still
existing gap between the i-sound and the a-sound, came the new vowel
indicated by ֞. Thus the connection between ֞ and ֔ finds its explanation,
too. Graphically expressed, the interrelation between the vowels i and a
originally was ֔ ֔ (these two being identical then) and ֔, but later developed into: ֔ ֞ ֔; cf. Lev. 5.1: יַגִּיד — Gen. 9.22: וַיַּגֵּד — Judg. 14.17:
וַיַּגֶּד‎־; Deut. 18.15: יָקִים — 1 Sam. 1.23: יָקֶם — Ex. 40.18: וַיָּקֶם with § 80b.

H.　ARE THE VOWELS I AND A DIRECTLY INTERRELATED?

The present status of this problem is summed up by Bergsträsser § 26b:
"Sogenannte *Verdünnung* des *a*: In unbetonter geschlossener Silbe ist *a*
unter gewissen nicht mehr bestimmbaren Bedingungen zu *i* geworden;
infolge mannigfacher Ausgleichungen ist in manchen Formklassen *i*,
in anderen *a* durchgedrungen, während anderwärts gleichartige Formen

teils *i*, teils *a* haben." In other words: certain forms have the vowel *a*, while others have an *i* instead; and since these forms with *a* or *i* belong to the very same group, no satisfactory theory could be advanced till now so as to explain this uncertainty of vocalization. Before we attempt to solve the problem, we wish to present it in a clear way. The very way in which we arrange and group the material, will illustrate the futility of any theory hitherto advanced. Our examples consist of nouns with the preformative מ and demonstrate the two possibilities of vocalizing it: מַ and מִ.

a. The identical noun

§ 82.   Plural-forms.

Jer. 10.4:	בְּמַסְמְרוֹת	Isa. 41.7:	בְּמַסְמְרִים
2 Chron. 3.9:	לְמִסְמְרוֹת	1 Chron. 22.3:	לַמִּסְמְרִים

§ 83.   Masculine and feminine forms.

Isa. 24.22:	מַסְגֵּר	Isa. 3.1:	מַשְׁעֵן
Ex. 25.25:	מִסְגֶּרֶת	Isa. 36.6:	מִשְׁעֶנֶת

The change from the masc. form to the fem. is in no way interconnected with this change from מַ to מִ; cf. Lev. 25.14: מִמְכָּר and ib. verse 42: מִמְכֶּרֶת.

§ 84.   Inflected forms.

Neh. 8.10:	מַשְׁמַנִּים	Cant. 5.5:	הַמַּנְעוּל
Isa. 10.16:	בְּמִשְׁמַנָּיו	Deut. 33.25:	מִנְעָלֶךָ

The suffix has no influence upon the vocalization of the prefix; cf. Neh. 3.3: מַנְעוּלָיו.

Ezek. 27.24:	בְּמַכְלֻלִים	Ps. 141.10:	בְּמַכְמֹרָיו
Ezek. 38.4:	מִכְלוֹל	Isa. 19.8:	מִכְמֹרֶת

b. Different nouns

§ 85.   Nouns derived from verbs *primae* ח or ר.

Gen. 12.11:	מַרְאֶה	Ex. 23.25:	מַחֲלָה	Lev. 2.7:	מַרְחֶשֶׁת
Gen. 47.4:	מִרְעֶה	Judg. 6.4:	מִחְיָה	Gen. 41.43:	בְּמִרְכֶּבֶת

§ 86.   Nouns derived from verbs *tertiae* ה.

Gen. 13.10:	מַשְׁקֶה	Ex. 35.25:	מַטְוֶה
Gen. 43.12:	מִשְׁגֶּה	Prov. 26.28:	מִדְחֶה
Ex. 34.33:	מַסְוֶה	Deut. 28.60:	מַדְוֶה
Jer. 15.7:	בְּמִזְרֶה	Jer. 14.8:	מִקְוֶה

Similarly with additional primae נ:

Lev. 26.21:	מַכָּה	2 Ki. 4.10:	מִטָּה

§ 87.   Nouns with *o* as second vowel.

Ex. 12.7:	הַמַּשְׁקוֹף	Ps. 69.27:	מַכְאוֹב
Ezek. 4.10:	בְּמִשְׁקוֹל	Ezek. 7.19:	מִכְשׁוֹל
Gen. 43.23:	מַטְמוֹן	Zech. 10.1:	מַלְקוֹשׁ
Isa. 4.6:	וּלְמִסְתּוֹר	Ps. 3.1:	מִזְמוֹר

§ 88.   Nouns with *i* as second vowel.

Isa. 14.21:	מַטְבֵּחַ	Isa. 24.22:	מַסְגֵּר	2 Ki. 19.3:	מַשְׁבֵּר
Gen. 8.20:	מִזְבֵּחַ	Eccl. 9.15:	מִסְכֵּן	Gen. 50.10:	מִסְפֵּד

§ 89.   Nouns with *a* as second vowel.

Judg. 3.31:	בְּמַלְמַד	Judg. 5.11:	מַשְׁאַבִּים
Lev. 25.25:	מִמְכַּר	2 Sam. 22.19:	מִשְׁעָן

§ 90.   Inflected forms.

1 Sam. 4.18:	מַפְרַקְתּוֹ	2 Sam. 12.31:	וּבְמַגְזְרוֹת	Joel 4.10:	וּמִזְמָרֹתֵיהֶם
Judg. 5.17:	מִפְרָצָיו	Jer. 34.5:	וּבְמִשְׂרְפוֹת	Ex. 27.3:	וּמִזְלְגֹתָיו
Gen. 27.4:	מַטְעַמִּים	Isa. 19.2:	מַמְלָכָה	Cant. 5.16:	מַמְתַקִּים
Dan. 11.43	בְּמִכְמַנֵּי	Gen. 14.2:	מִלְחָמָה	1 Chron. 26.6:	הַמִּמְשָׁלִים

§ 91.   Construct state of the singular.

2 Ki. 8.15:	הַמַּכְבֵּר	Isa. 3.1:	מַשְׁעֵן
Ex. 35.16:	מִכְבָּר	Isa. 3.1:	מִשְׁעֵן־
Ex. 27.4:	מִכְבָּר	2 Sam. 22.19:	מִשְׁעָן

These examples show two possibilities of forming nouns with the prefix מ: with the second vowel *i* or *a*. It is obvious that מִכְבָּר and מִשְׁעֵן־ form

the construct state to the absolute nouns מִכְבָּר and מִשְׁעָן, respectively.
Similarly in:

Isa. 22.22:	מַפְתֵּחַ	Zeph. 2.15:	מַרְבֵּץ
Prov. 8.6:	וּמִפְתַּח	Ezek. 25.5:	לְמִרְבַּץ־
Jer. 16.5:	מַרְזֵחַ	2 Ki. 19.3:	מַשְׁבֵּר
Am. 6.7:	מִרְזַח	Hos. 13.13:	בְּמִשְׁבַּר

Here the absolute form of the respective nouns with the second vowel *a*
is not preserved; its former existence is attested by the construct state.
These words should consequently not be listed in the Hebrew dictionaries
under one and the same heading as *stat. absol.* and *constr.* thereof.

§ 92.   Evidence from the Palestinian and Babylonian vocalization.

An examination of the extensive lists of nominal formations with the
prefix מ in MTK, 70 and MdO, 197 f., reveals the correctness of Kahle's
assertion (MTK, 69) that "bei den babylonischen Juden (scil. in Hebrew
according to the Babylonian vocalization) hat sich das *a* bei der ersten
Silbe in der Regel erhalten." In the Palestinian vocalization, on the other
hand, this prefix מ as a rule has the vowel *i*. In the following list I put
in juxtaposition the different ways in which the same Hebrew word is
vocalized according to the Palestinian (PV) and Babylonian system (BV):

PV:				BV:		
PV:	Am. 5.9:	מִבצָּר	—	BV:	2 Chron. 17.19:	הַמֻּבצָּר
	Cant. 5.13:	מִגדלוֹת	—		Cant. 4.4:	מֻגדָּל
	Isa. 32.15:	מִדבָּר	—		Deut. 9.28:	מֻדבָּר
	Ps. 9.8:	למֻשׁפָּט	—		Prov. 1.3:	מֻשׁפָּט
	Jer. 51.20:	מִלחָמֹה	—		Prov. 20.19:	מֻלחֹמֹה
	Ps. 26.8:	מִשׁכָּן	—		Prov. 26.8:	מֻשׁכָּן

§ 93.   Conclusions.

The prefix מ in nominal forms is vocalized מַ in some cases, and מִ in
others. As the classification of these forms (in §§ 82-91) and the external
evidence from the Palestinian and Babylonian vocalization prove, nouns
vocalized מַ and those vocalized מִ represent formations which were independent of one another. Thus the theory about a "Verdünnung" of
a into *i* is without basis.

C. General Conclusions (Cf. also MH § 86)

As a result of our researches we now arrive at the following conclusions which represent an attempt to establish the main characteristics of Hebrew phonology prior to the Masoretic activities towards unification and standardization of the basic texts into the Masoretic Bible, as has been demonstrated in § 1.

I)   Hebrew originally had three vowels: *a, i, o(u)*; cf. p. 562, § 1 ff. and note 1, there.

II)   The phonography (τ or $\_$ for *a*; $\_$ or $.$ for *i*; $'$ or $\,$ for *o*) does not indicate any differentiation of these basic three vowels as to quantity or quality; cf. §§ 42-48, 49-62, 63-74.

III)   A syllable may therefore be either open or closed, regardless of the graphic form of the vowel-sign which is used to indicate its vowel.

IV)   The division of the *shewa* into *shewa quiescens* and *shewa mobile*, which is based on the assumption that the vowel of the preceding syllable necessarily is either short (*shewa quiescens*) or long (*shewa mobile*), is invalid for pre-Masoretic Hebrew.

V)   *Dagesh lene* is younger than the misconception of $\_$ and $\_$ as *ḥatefs* (cf. § 39). It is inconsistently put (cf. here §§ 11-27). Consequently, the terming of a *shewa* before a בגדכפת without *dagesh lene* as *shewa medium* has no foundation; cf. MH § 3.

VI)   A consonant with *shewa* may as well be deemed the close of the preceding syllable, as the beginning of the next one; cf. above Rule IV. The *dagesh forte* to substitute for such a consonant with *shewa* (cf. § 1, Rule VIβ) is based on the assumption that the vowel of the preceding open syllable is short and consequently must be closed. This assumption is inconsistent with our Rules I-III (above); thus *dagesh forte* is merely an innovation of the Masoretes.

VII)   The Hebrew alphabet consisted of 22 sound consonants. The singling out of the letters אהחער for special treatment is only Masoretic: a) the combination of the laryngals אהחע with the liquid ר is strange; ר belongs together with ל. — b) on the inability of these letters to accept *dagesh forte*, which results in the lengthening of the preceding short vowel

in an open syllable, cf. above Rules VI and II; also § 5. — c) on the vocalization of the אהחע with *hatefs*, cf. §§ 37-40. — d) as to the vocalization
of the prefix in the imperfect *ḳal* with ֱ or ֲ before a אהחע, while otherwise the prefix is vocalized with ֶ (e.g.: יַחשׁב, יֶהגה, as compared with
יִשׁמר): ֱ and ֲ represent here *one* vowel, corresponding to the ⸜ in the
Babylonian vocalization. Thus the original vowel *a* was preserved under
the influence of the fact that the consonantal value of the laryngals was
equally ⸜; cf. § 40.

VIII)   Since the phonography did not differentiate between long and
short vowels (cf. above Rule II), a vowel in an open syllable remained,
even though in the course of the declension this vowel became two syllables
removed from the stressed one (cf. § 2b); cf. p. 215, sub a) the statement: "I am inclined to consider as the most characteristic feature
of the pronunciation of Hebrew, as reflected in the transliterations, the
fact that the vocalization of the noun does not undergo any changes —
except in the latter period—when suffixes are added to it, or when the
noun is being put in the plural." (Note the many examples!) In
addition to the instances from the Palestinian vocalization which are
listed on p. 224, B under 6, 8 and 10, I now wish to call attention to:
Isa. 40.8: וּדבּר (אינו); ib. 44.26: דּבּר (עבדו); Ps. 26.8: וּמקוֹם (משכן); Jer.
30.18: שׁבוֹת (אהלי יעקב); Isa. 44.26: וְעֹצת (מלאכיו): these are cases of nouns
in the construct state with preservation of their first vowel. Similarly in
the Tiberian vocalization: Jer. 3.23: הָמוֹן (הרים) as compared with the
marginal reading in the Bible 1515/17: הֲמוֹן.

IX)   The differentiation of the *dagesh* as *dagesh lene* and *dagesh forte*
is based on the assumption that in either case the *dagesh* fulfills a different
function. This assumption has no basis in pre-Masoretic Hebrew: we
have direct evidence to the contrary in the transliterations (cf. p. 174 f.
under the letters בגדכפת) and in a Tannaitic tradition contained in
a statement in b. Berakoth 15b (attention to which has been called
by Paul Kahle in the Marti-Festschrift, Giessen 1925, p. 171). Consequently, in dealing with the *dagesh* as an innovation of the Masoretes
(cf. above Rules V and VI), we shall consider the terming of a *dagesh*
in question as *forte* or *lene* irrelevant. Cf. also MH §§ 45-46.

X)   The rules for the insertion of the *dagesh* (cf. our definition of *dagesh* in the preceding Rule IX) according to the Tiberian vocalization may be formulated thus: *Dagesh* was inserted as a means by which to indicate that the vowel-sign of the preceding syllable indicates a short vowel. Of the 22 letters of the Hebrew alphabet a) one half (=11: וטילמנסצקש) get it, when the preceding syllable is open; b) one quarter (=6: בגדכפת) always; and c) one quarter (=5: אהחער) never. Only after the Masoretes had introduced the division of the Hebrew vowels into long and short, according to the external form of the vowel-signs used, did it become necessary to emphasize this division by the innovation of the *dagesh*. Cf. p. 124 ff., s.v. גל: γαλειμ B — γαλλειμ A; s.v. לחש: αλωης B — αλλωης A; s.v. קוץ: ακως B — ακκως A; s.v. קטן: ακαταν B — ακκαταν A.

XI)   The terms context-forms and pausal-forms of nouns and verbs are based on a misconception. The accentuation of a nominal or verbal form does not influence its vocalization; cf. p. 469 ff., § 21 ff.

a)   The so-called pausal-forms of verbs are in reality verbal forms with preservation of the second vowel; cf. p. 249, note 1, and the cross-reference there.

b)   Pausal-forms of nouns are in reality another form of the noun in the absolute state and represent a different class of the root in question, as compared with ts so-called context-form. Cf. the following examples (taken from MdO, MTK, and here p. 124 ff. respectively):

1)   בֶּגֶד: *kitl*-form: Gen. 39.12: בְּגְדוֹ; but *katl*-form: Ezek. 18.7: בָּגֶד and Ex. 40.13: בֹּגְדִי.

בֶּטֶן: *kitl*: Num. 5.21: בִּטְנֵי; but *katl*: Gen. 30.2: בָּטֶן and בֹּטְנִי, βατνε.

קֶבֶר: *kitl*: Jer. 20.17: קִבְרִי; but *katl*: Gen. 23.9: קָבֶר and Jer. 20.17: קֹברִי.

קֶצֶף: *kitl*: Isa. 60.10: בְּקִצְפִּי; but *katl*: Eccl. 5.16: וָקֶצֶף and Ps. 102.11: קָצֹפָּךְ.

שֵׁבֶט: *kitl*: Prov. 13.24: שִׁבְטוֹ; but *katl*: Ex. 28.21: שָׁבֶט and βσαβτ.

שֵׂכֶל: *kitl*: Dan. 8.25: שִׂכְלוֹ; but *katl*: Job 17.4: מִשָּׂכֶל and Dan. 8.25: שֹׂכְלוֹ.

שֶׁמֶשׁ: *kitl*: Jer. 15.9: שִׁמְשָׁה; but *katl*: Eccl. 1.3: הַשָּׁמֶשׁ and χσαμς.

2)   חֶסֶד: *kitl*: εσδι, חֹסְדִי; but *katl*: חָסֶד and חַסְדִי.

דֶּרֶךְ: *kitl*: δερχι, דרכִי; but *katl*: דָּרֶךְ and דַּרְכִּי.

נֶפֶשׁ: *kitl*: νεφσι; but *katl*: נָפֶשׁ and נַפְשִׁי.

Similarly: מֶלֶךְ is a *kitl*-form, cf. μελχει, מלכיה, melchechem, μελχαμ; the *katl*-form is not preserved in the absolute state, but only with suffixes, cf. מַלְכִּי etc. The forms with suffixes according to the Tiberian vocalization are thus taken either from the *kitl*- (cf. under 1) or from the *katl*-group (cf. under 2).

XII)   Thus in the so-called *nomina segolata* the Masoretic Bible exhibits, in the combination of the so-called context- and pausal-forms with the forms with suffixes, a mixture of nominal forms which originally belonged to two different classes: *katl* and *kitl*. The nominal formations with prefix מ represent a similar mixture, according to the vocalization of this prefix as מַ (conform with the Babylonian system) or as מֶ (as in the Palestinian vocalization; cf. § 92). *The composite character of Masoretic Hebrew is thus established.*

II.   ACCENTS AND THEIR FUNCTIONS

A.   INDICATING STRESS

A.   ACCENTS AND STRESS

§ 1.   According to the current theory, presented as valid beyond question in all Hebrew grammars, the accents serve a threefold purpose: they are musical notations, they indicate the stressed syllable in the word, and they determine the syntactic position of the word within the verse, thus being also marks of punctuation. E.g.: "In allen Fällen richtet sich der musikalische Vortrag des Textes streng nach der logischen Gliederung des Satzes. . . . So kommt es, dass die Akzente zugleich eine Art von Interpunktionszeichen bilden. . . . dass sie die Sinneinschnitte innerhalb der Verse und die engere oder weniger enge Zusammengehörigkeit der einzelnen Worte des Verses erkennen lassen. . . . Indem die Akzente auf die Drucksilbe des Wortes gesetzt werden, erfüllen sie zugleich eine dritte Aufgabe, sie deuten den Wortdruck an" (B-L § 9m-n).

§ 2.   But the accents were not introduced to accomplish this threefold task from the very first: "Es ist nicht anzunehmen, dass die Akzente von Anfang an diese dreifache Aufgabe gehabt haben" (B-L § 9 o). This can be seen from a study of Hebrew Bible texts with the Babylonian vocalization: "In der einfachen babylonischen Punktation, wie sie im Berliner

Ms. or. qu. 680 und den ihm verwandten Handschriften. . . . vorliegt, haben die Akzente mit dem Wortdruck nichts zu tun. Sie stehen lediglich über dem Worte, nicht über der Drucksilbe desselben" (B-L § 9b). In short: In our Tiberian system, the accents are attached to the syllable which carries the stress; but in the Babylonian vocalization, the accents are indiscriminately put, and thus belong to the word rather than to the respective syllable.

§ 3.   But we may ask: Does not this way of putting the problem represent a case of *petitio principii*? How do we know which syllable in a given word is stressed? The answer is given "indem die Akzente auf die Drucksilbe des Wortes gesetzt werden." In other words: the presence of an accent is the only evidence of this syllable being the stressed one. And since in manuscripts with the Babylonian vocalization the accent is not found exactly where the Tiberian accentuators put it later, the accents do not indicate the stressed syllable! I consider it more in keeping with the historical-critical approach to formulate these very findings differently. Whatever practical purpose the accents originally served—whether merely the indication of the melody, or also of the interpunctuation—they marked only entire words, not syllables. Consequently, in the Babylonian vocalization they are not always to be found in the same place of a word. But the Tiberian system shows a tendency toward consistency in the choice of the accented syllable. The readers of the Bible thus got into the habit of cantillating the accented syllable, which was therefore regarded as the stressed syllable. This explains the un-Semitic way of stressing the last syllable in Hebrew: it dates back only to the Middle Ages.

§ 4.   My contention that there is a tendency toward stressing the last syllable (but not absolute consistency), finds support in a phenomenon, which grammarians term נָסוֹג אָחוֹר, and which is explained in the following words:

B.   THE נָסוֹג אָחוֹר

"Der Rhythmus verträgt bei lebhafter Sprechweise (Allegrotempo) nicht zwei stärkere Drucksilben nebeneinander. Der eine Druck muss entweder geschwächt oder auf eine entferntere Silbe versetzt werden. Diese für alle Sprachen geltende Tatsache haben die Punktatoren sehr oft beobachtet.

Der normale, dem isolierten Worte zukommende Druck wird zu diesem Zwecke nach einer der folgenden Regeln verändert:

1) Das vorhergehende (ultimabetonte) Wort verliert seinen Hauptdruck und verbindet sich mit dem folgenden unter *einem* Wortakzent; in dem so entstandenen Wortkomplex entwickelt sich ein Nebendruck nach den bei einfachen Wörtern geltenden Regeln: יִמְשָׁל־בָּךְ ··· Gen. 3.16, אֶמְצָא־חֵן ··· Gen. 33.15.

2) Der Hauptdruck des vorhergehenden Wortes wird auf die Paenultima verschoben, oder, wenn diese Schwa enthält, auf die Antepaenultima: וַיֵּצֵא קַיִן Gen. 4.16, תֹּאכַל לֶחֶם .... Die jüdischen Grammatiker nannten den aus rhythmischen Gründen zurückgeworfenen Druck נָסוֹג אָחוֹר "zurückweichend." (B-L § 13n-p)."

§ 5. But even a cursory examination of the Bible will provide us with innumerable instances militating against the validity of the theory underlying the term נָסוֹג אָחוֹר: cases of two consecutive words, the second of which is either a monosyllable, or stressed on its first syllable, while the first word has, on the last syllable, what grammarians term a conjunctive accent (cf. § 10 f.); thus are "zwei stärkere Drucksilben nebeneinander."

Gen. 3.19:	עָפָר אַתָּה	Deut. 12.4:	תַּעֲשׂוּן כֵּן
Gen. 47.3:	רֹעֵה צֹאן	Deut. 12.6:	וַהֲבֵאתֶם שָׁמָּה
(cf. 46.34:	רֹעֵה צֹאן)	Deut. 15.7:	נָתַן לָךְ;
Num. 33.19:	בְּרִמֹּן פֶּרֶץ;		cf. 18.14: נָתַן לָךְ
ib. v. 20:	מֵרִמֹּן פֶּרֶץ	Deut. 15.10:	בְּתִתְּךָ לוֹ
Num. 33.35:	בְּעֶצְיֹן גֶּבֶר;	Deut. 15 21:	יִהְיֶה בּוֹ
ib. v. 36:	מֵעֶצְיֹן גֶּבֶר	Deut. 18.16:	אֶרְאֶה עוֹד
Num. 33.45:	בְּדִיבֹן גָּד;	Deut. 19.2:	תַּבְדִּיל לָךְ;
ib. v. 46:	מִדִּיבֹן גָּד		ib. v. 7: תַּבְדִּיל לָךְ
Deut. 1.16:	וּשְׁפַטְתֶּם צֶדֶק	Deut. 19.4:	יָנוּס שָׁמָּה
Deut. 1.17:	לֵאלֹהִים הוּא	Deut. 24.3:	לְקָחָהּ לוֹ
Deut. 2.9:	תִּתְגָּר בָּם;	Judg. 1.15:	וְנָתַתָּה לִי גֻּלֹּת מָיִם
ib. v. 19:	תִּתְגָּר בָּם	Judg. 2.14:	יָכְלוּ עוֹד
Deut. 2.31:	הָחֵל רָשׁ	Judg. 2.21:	לְהוֹרִישׁ אִישׁ
Deut. 7.25:	תְּ֯בַ֯קֵ֯שׁ בּוֹ; וְלָקַחְתָּ לָךְ	Judg. 2.22:	הַשֹּׁמְרִים הֵם; נַסּוֹת בָּם

Judg. 3.1:	לְנַסּוֹת בָּם	I Sam. 16.3:	וּמְשַׁחְתָּ לִי
Judg. 3.25:	נֹפֵל אַרְצָה	I Sam. 17.34:	וְנָשָׂא שֶׂה
Judg. 3.31:	מֵאוֹת אִישׁ	I Sam. 17.36:	כִּי חֵרֵף
Judg. 4.22:	נֹפֵל מֵת	I Sam. 22.13:	בְּתִתְּךָ לוֹ
Judg. 15.11:	מֹשְׁלִים בָּנוּ	2 Sam. 15.19:	נָכְרִי אַתָּה
Judg. 15.12:	תִּפְגְּעוּן בִּי	I Ki. 18.7:	הַאַתָּה זֶה
I Sam. 10.5:	כְּבֹאֲךָ שָׁם		

C. WORDS WITH TWO ACCENTS

§ 6. But there is no need for us to look for two consecutive words, to disprove the idea of נָסוֹג אָחוֹר. How are grammarians to account for two consecutive syllables, in one and the same word, both carrying accents?

Num. 20.2:	וַ יָּ ק הַ לֹ וּ	Num. 17.23:	וַיָּצֵץ
Num. 23.27:	אֶ קֳ חָ דֹּ	Isa. 66.3:	מְבָרֵךְ
Num. 24.7:	מִדָּלְיוֹ	Deut. 1.14:	וַתַּאמְרוּ
Num. 24.14:	אִיעָצְךָ	Deut. 1.25:	וַיַּאמְרוּ
Num. 31.13:	וַיֵּצְאוּ	Deut. 1.45:	בְּקֹלְכֶם
Num. 33.8:	וַיֵּלְכוּ	Deut. 2.25:	וְיִרְאָתְךָ
Deut. 6.11:	וּבָתִּים	Deut. 4.9:	מִלְּבָבְךָ
Deut. 7.13:	דְּגָנְךָ	Deut. 6.15:	וְהִשְׁמִידְךָ
Deut. 8.4:	שִׂמְלָתְךָ	Deut. 7.10:	לְשֹׂנְאוֹ
Deut. 8.15:	הַמּוֹלִיךָ	Deut. 7.17:	בִּלְבָבְךָ
Deut. 8.16:	הַמַּאֲכִלְךָ	Deut. 9.14:	אוֹתְךָ
Deut. 16.1:	הוֹצִיאֲךָ	Deut. 9.26:	וְנַחֲלָתְךָ
Deut. 16.16:	זְכוּרְךָ	Deut. 14.28:	תְּבוּאָתְךָ
Deut. 25.19:	אֹיְבֶיךָ	Deut. 15.7:	יָדְךָ
Deut. 28.1:	וּנְתָנְךָ	Deut. 15.14:	מִצֹּאנְךָ
Gen. 28.2:	פַּדֶּנָה; v. 7: פַּדֶּנָה	Deut. 19.8:	גְּבֻלְךָ

§ 7. We thus have cases of words with two accents. These accents cannot be taken as implying stress, as will be seen from the following instances:

Num. 20.29:	הָעֵדָה	Deut. 7.7:	הָעַמִּים (1°)
Num. 22.23:	הָאָתוֹן (2°)	Deut. 11.9:	הָאֲדָמָה
Num. 22.35:	הָאֲנָשִׁים	Gen. 2.19:	הָאָדָם (1°)
Deut. 3.9:	וְהָאֱמֹרִי	Gen. 10.3:	וְהַחֲמֹר

Deut. 20.15:	הֶעָרִים		Num. 8.6:	הַלְוִיִּם
Deut. 21.16:	הָאֲהוּבָה		Deut. 10.2:	הַדְּבָרִים
Deut. 22.6:	הָאֶפְרֹחִים		Ex. 32.16:	וְהַלֻּחֹת
Deut. 29.19:	הָאֵלֶּה		Lev. 7.8:	וְהַכֹּהֵן
Deut. 30.3:	הָעַמִּים		Lev. 7.19:	וְהַבָּשָׂר (2°)
Num. 22.37:	הַאֻמְנָם		Deut. 4.49:	הָעֲרָבָה
Num. 20.12:	לְהַקְדִּישֵׁנִי		1 Ki. 1.37:	מִכִּסֵּא
Gen. 17.25:	בְּהִמֹּלוֹ		Lev. 7.37:	וְלַמִּלּוּאִים
Num. 8.9:	וְהִקְהַלְתָּ		Judg. 1.6:	וַיְקַצְּצוּ
Gen. 37.36:	וְהַמְּדָנִים		1 Ki. 18.26:	וַיְפַסְּחוּ
Deut. 29.21:	וְהַנָּכְרִי			

In these examples, the first accent is attached to a preformative, which no reasonable grammarian can call the stressed syllable of the word. *Hence, there exists no interrelation between accent and stress.*

§ 8.   Words with two accents are quite a common feature in the Hebrew Bible. The following examples are picked at random, and arranged according to the combination of accents, which they represent:

a) Gen. 37.7:	אֲלֻמֹּתֵיכֶם		Deut. 12.3:	מַצֵּבֹתָם
Num. 29.39:	וּלְמִנְחֹתֵיכֶם		Deut. 12.6:	מַעְשְׂרֹתֵיכֶם
Num. 31.10:	בְּמוֹשְׁבֹתָם		Deut. 12.6:	וְנִדְבֹתֵיכֶם
Num. 33.4:	וּבֵאלֹהֵיהֶם		Deut. 12.12:	וּבְנֹתֵיכֶם
Num. 35.2:	סְבִיבֹתֵיהֶם		Deut. 16.7:	וְאָכַלְתָּ
Deut. 1.16:	שֹׁפְטֵיכֶם		Deut. 16.12:	וְזָכַרְתָּ
Deut. 2.11:	וְהָאֵמִים		Deut. 19.17:	וְהַשֹּׁפְטִים
Deut. 3.19:	בְּעָרֵיכֶם		b) Num. 28.26:	בְּהַקְרִיבְכֶם
Deut. 3.26:	לְמַעַנְכֶם		Num. 31.6:	פִּינְחָס
Deut. 6.5:	וְאָהַבְתָּ		Num. 33.52:	וְהוֹרַשְׁתֶּם
Deut. 7.8:	לַאֲבֹתֵיכֶם		Deut. 1.8:	לַאֲבֹתֵיכֶם
Deut. 7.9:	וְיָדַעְתָּ		Josh. 2.1:	וַיֵּלְכוּ
Deut. 7.13:	וַאֲהֵבְךָ		Josh. 5.11:	וַיֹּאכְלוּ
Deut. 8.6:	וְשָׁמַרְתָּ		Josh. 6.5:	וְנָפְלָה
Deut. 10.1:	כָּרִאשֹׁנִים		Judg. 9.6:	וַיַּאַסְפוּ
Deut. 10.10:	הָרִאשֹׁנִים		1 Sam. 4.18:	אֲחֹרַנִּית
Deut. 11.1:	וְאָהַבְתָּ		1 Sam. 7.11:	וַיֵּצְאוּ

1 Sam. 8.16:	שִׁפְחֹתֵיכֶם	Deut. 26.4:	וְהִנִּיחֹו
1 Sam. 19.11:	אֵינְךָ	Deut. 26.10:	וְהִשְׁתַּחֲוִיתָ
2 Sam. 2.30:	וַיִּפְקְדוּ	Deut. 29.28:	הַנִּסְתָּרֹות
1 Ki. 8.30:	וְשָׁמַעְתָּ	Gen. 35.1:	בְּבָרְחֲךָ
c) Num. 28.20:	וּמִנְחָתָם	Gen. 37.24:	וַיִּקָּחֻהוּ
Num. 33.52:	וְאִבַּדְתֶּם	Ex. 33.8:	וְנִצְּבוּ

D. CONCLUSION

§ 9. In the foregoing paragraphs I believe to have finally disposed of the current theory that the accent serves to indicate the stressed syllable. The numerous cases of words with two accents cannot be explained as representing two stressed syllables; for how, then, would we account for the fact that the identical words occur elsewhere with one accent only? We might well ask: what is the reason for this change in the pronunciation of these syllables? Why are they stressed in one passage, and not so in another? Moreover, how could we possibly explain the stressing of a preformative? Accentuation and stress were originally not connected. The only function which grammarians throughout the ages have attributed to the accents, and which remains unshaken by these reaserches, is that of musical notation. Cantillation takes no heed of pronunciation in normal speech; we recite Homer disregarding the way we would pronounce, connect, and separate the words in Greek prose. I have to admit (much though I deplore the fact) that I am entirely unmusical, and thus incompetent to deal with the problem of the value of the accents as notation of the melody—an unsolved mystery anyhow.

B. INTERPUNCTUATION

A. CONJUNCTIVE AND DISJUNCTIVE ACCENTS

§ 10. We now take up the discussion of the third function attributed to the accents: their use for interpunctuation. The accents are divided in disjunctive and conjunctive. I fail to see what the criterion for this division is. We might consider it a mere duplication of effort to provide the Bible text with disjunctive *and* conjunctive accents; either one of them would be sufficient, since the absence of e.g. a disjunctive accent would implicitly connect the word with the following one, and thus make it superfluous to add a conjunctive accent. But it might be argued that the Eastern mind works differently, and while Western languages use only separating signs of interpunctuation, Hebrew may make use of both disconnecting and connecting accents. Even the frequency of their appearance is no valid argument; why not grant Hebrew the right to be a language of frequent stops and disconnected words? Modern Biblical exegesis, of course, often connects words which carry disjunctive accents, and *vice versa*; but the fact that we prefer this new exegesis does not imply that the exegesis presupposed by the accentuation is wrong (cf. p. 2, § 4). This problem can be solved by internal evidence only: a) The construct state owes its Hebrew name סְמִיכוּת to the fact that the nouns constituting it are closely interconnected. Consequently, it is with the مضاف of a construct state (cf. p. 602, § 64) that we expect a conjunctive accent. b) Certain groups of words occur more than once in the Bible. We may, without projecting our mentality upon the Bible, expect to find a uniform accent regularly. Whatever type of accent they carry, disjunctive or conjunctive, it should be used with consistency. In the following paragraphs examples will be listed according to these two tests of the current theory.

B. THIS DIVISION UNTENABLE

§ 11.   The identical group of words, once with conjunctive and once with disjunctive accents:

וּבַיּוֹם השמיני׃	Lev. 15.29	בְּעַרְבֹת מואב׃	Num. 33.50
וּבַיּוֹם השמיני׃	Lev. 12.3	בְּעַרְבֹת מואב׃	Num. 33.49
מִחוּץ למחנה׃	Lev. 16.27	מִבֵּית לפרכת׃	Lev. 16.12
מִחוּץ למחנה׃	Lev. 17.3	מִבֵּית לפרכת׃	Lev. 16.2
מִקְרָאֵי קדש׃	Lev. 23.37	מוֹעֲדֵי יהוה׃	Lev. 23.4
מִקְרָאֵי קדש׃	Lev. 23.4	מוֹעֲדֵי יהוה׃	Lev. 23.44
יִטְמָא עד הערב׃	Lev. 15.19	אֶת־דְּבָרֵנוּ זֶה׃	Josh. 2.20
יִטְמָא עד הערב׃	Lev. 15.23	את־דְּבָרֵנוּ זה׃	Josh. 2.14

§ 12.   The مضاف in a construct state with disjunctive accent.

a) טפחא׃

		Lev. 15.26:	כְּטֻמְאַת נדתה
Lev. 7.35:	מֵאִשֵּׁי יהוה	Lev. 15.30:	מִזּוֹב טמאתה
Lev. 7.32:	מִזִּבְחֵי שלמיכם	Lev. 16.16:	בְּתוֹךְ טמאתם
Lev. 8.22:	אֵיל המלאים	Lev. 16.31:	חֻקַּת עולם
Lev. 8.33:	יְמֵי מלאיכם	Lev. 23.14:	קׇרְבַּן אלהיכם
Lev. 14.57:	תּוֹרַת הצרעת	Lev. 26.30:	פִּגְרֵי גלוליכם

b) תביר: d) זקף קטן:

Gen. 37.19:   בַּעַל הַחֲלֹמוֹת   Lev. 16.1:   מוֹת שני בני אהרן

Num. 4.25:   וּמִכְסֵה הַתַּחַשׁ   Num. 4.25:   מָסַךְ פתח אהל מועד

Num. 11.11:   מַשָּׂא כל העם הזה   Num. 4.45:   פְּקוּדֵי משפחת בני מררי

Num. 14.19:   לַעֲוֹן העם הזה   Ezek. 45.19:   מְזוּזֹת שער החצר

Gen. 40.20:   רֹאשׁ שר האפים

Num. 1.16:   רָאשֵׁי אלפי ישראל   e) זקף גדול:
                                           Ex. 39.24:   רִמּוֹנֵי תכלת

c) רביע: Num. 31.30:   שֹׁמְרֵי משמרת

Lev. 7.15:   וּבְשַׂר זבח תודת שלמיו   Num. 31.36:   חֵלֶק היצאים בצבא

Num. 4.41:   פְּקוּדֵי משפחת בני גרשן Num. 3.48:   פְּדוּיֵי העדפים

Num. 24.16:   נְאֻם שמע אמרי אל   Num. 4.42:   וּפְקוּדֵי משפחת בני אהרן

                                           Num. 24.4:   נְאֻם שמע אמרי אל

                                           Deut. 4.17:   תַּבְנִית כל בהמה

§ 13.   Inconspicuous little particles appear with important disjunctive accents.

וְאֵת: Ex. 35.17   מִפְּנֵי: Judg. 5.5

מֵאֵת: 2 Sam. 21.12   מִבַּלְעֲדֵי: Josh. 22.19

אַךְ: Num. 31.23   וְאַף: Lev. 26.40

וּבֵין: Judg. 4.17   יַעַן: Deut. 1.36

אַחֲרֵי: Josh. 9.16   וְגַם: 2 Sam. 19.41

לִפְנֵי: Ex. 40.6

§ 14.   The טפחא is a disjunctive accent of high ranking; how, then, are we to reconcile with it the fact that it occurs in the middle of a word, which also carries another accent; cf. Jer. 2.31: מַאֲפֵלְיָה; Ezek. 10.13: לָאוֹפַנִּים; Num. 15.21: לְדֹרֹתֵיכֶם; Hos. 11.6: מִמֹּעֲצוֹתֵיהֶם? In these cases, the טפחא is in the very same position as e.g. the מונח in 2 Sam. 12.25: יְדִידְיָה; why term מונח a conjunctive, and טפחא a disjunctive accent?

§ 15.   Some of the examples discussed in § 12 f. represent series of construct states. But this is no reason for separating the مضاف by a disjunctive accent. For there is ample evidence for the corresponding use of a series of conjunctive accents.

Num. 32.29:   אִם־יַעַבְרוּ בְנֵי־גָד וּבְנֵי־   Deut. 31.17:   וְחָרָה אַפִּי בוֹ ביום

              רְאוּבֵן   Josh. 3.13:   כְּנוֹחַ כַּפּוֹת רַגְלֵי הכהנים

Judg. 19.9:   וַיֹּאמֶר לוֹ חֹתְנוֹ אֲבִי   Lev. 8.10:   וְאֶת־כָּל־אֲשֶׁר־בּוֹ
                            הנערה   2 Sam. 6.12:   וְאֶת־כָּל־אֲשֶׁר־לוֹ

I Ki. 6.1:   וַיְהִי בִשְׁמוֹנִים שָׁנָה וְאַרְבַּע   2 Sam. 15.2:   אֲשֶׁר־יִהְיֶה־לּוֹ־רִיב
                       מֵאוֹת שנה   I Ki. 8.6:   אֶת־כָּל־אֲשֶׁר־לָהּ

I Ki. 8.1:   אָז יַקְהֵל שְׁלֹמֹה אֶת־זִקְנֵי
                ישראל

§ 16.   On the basis of our discussion from § 10 on we arrive at the conclusion that *any assumption of the accents' use for interpunctuation does not correspond to the facts. Thus, the accents have no importance whatsoever in our endeavor to interpret the Bible*; just as the hexameter is irrelevant for the understanding of the text in Homer (cf. § 9). Cf. also MH § 85c.

§ 17.   Our investigation in this chapter concerned itself with the importance of the accentuation for the interpretation of the Bible, and the result was negative: there exists no interrelation between accentuation and interpretation. Of course, the study of the rise and development of the accentuation will continue to form part of the study of the Bible. With this in mind, we wish to say that we are inclined to see in the accentuation the confluence of various and contradictory tendencies, which have hitherto either escaped detection, or have at least not been clearly recognized as contradictory.

C.   THE ROLE OF THE *makkef*

§ 18.   In § 30 we are going to quote several passages from Bauer-Leander's grammar to prove that these outstanding scholars did not make up their minds as to the exact definition of a *makkef*: is it "Hauptdruck," "Nebendruck," or "Drucklosigkeit?". But one thing is beyond question: the *makkef* is an accent. Consequently, if we find a word with *makkef* carrying also an accent, or—as we would rather put it—carrying another accent, we will call this a doublet, reflecting not only two different accentuators, but also two different systems of accentuation:

Gen. 7.8:   וּמִן־הבהמה   Deut. 17.8:   אֶל־המקום
Gen. 17.17:   וְאָם־שרה   Deut. 32.46:   לְכָל־הדברים
Num. 10.14:   וְעַל־צבאו   I Sam. 7.14:   וְאֶת־גבולן
Deut. 15.10:   בְּכָל־מעשך

The words involved here are monosyllables, and thus cannot have two accents. The two accent signs are doublets. I shall similarly explain as doublets cases like the following:

Gen. 41.12:	וַנְסַפֶּר־לוֹ	Judg. 7.20:	וּבְיָד־יְמִינָם
Gen. 18.18:	וְנִבְרְכוּ־בוֹ	I Sam. 8.3:	וַיִּקְחוּ־שֹׁחַד
Josh. 2.23:	וַיְסַפְּרוּ־לוֹ	I Sam. 19.18:	וַיַּגֶּד־לוֹ
	Num. 9.17:	וְאַחֲרֵי־כֵן	

D.   THE ROLE OF THE פסיק

§ 19.   As an outright combination of contradictory accents we consider cases, where a conjunctive accent is followed by פסיק. The term לגרמיה, which the ancient grammarians invented for this hybrid, confuses the issue: for we have here before us not *one* accent לגרמיה, but *two* distinct and utterly different accents, one of which the grammarians term conjunctive, while the other indicates by its very shape that it is disjunctive. In connection with מונח, the פסיק occurs very frequently; I, therefore, list only instances where other accents are involved:

a) מירכא :

Num. 11.25:	יְהֹוָה /	2 Sam. 10.14:	עַמּוֹן /
	id. Judg. 2.18; 20.	2 Sam. 14.26:	יָמִים /
	35	2 Sam. 24.3:	הֵהֵם /
Num. 6.20:	הַכֹּהֵן /	I Ki. 11.36:	הַיָּמִים /
2 Sam. 24.16:	הַמַּלְאָךְ /	I Ki. 7.24:	לִשְׂפָתוֹ /
I Ki. 2.30:	וַיֹּאמֶר /	I Ki. 7.29:	אֲרָיוֹת /
		Deut. 4.32:	אֱלֹהִים /
b) דרגא:		I Sam. 18.10:	רָעָה /
I Sam. 20.21:	קָחֶנּוּ /		
I Sam. 25.14:	מַלְאָכִים /	d) אזלא:	
	id. 2 Sam. 3.12	Judg. 20.25:	בִנְיָמִן /
2 Sam. 7.24:	יִשְׂרָאֵל /	I Sam. 18.10:	אֱלֹהִים /
Isa. 5.19:	יְמַהֵר /	I Sam. 24.11:	יְהֹוָה /
		I Ki. 12.32:	יוֹם /
c) שופר מהפך:		I Ki. 13.11:	הָאֱלֹהִים /
I Sam. 19.9:	יְהֹוָה /		
I Sam. 20.12:	כָּעֵת /	e) תלישא:	
I Sam. 24.11:	הַיּוֹם /	I Sam. 12.3:	שׁוֹר /
2 Sam. 2.1:	בַּיהֹוָה /	I Ki. 21.2:	לֵאמֹר /

f) Different accents in one and
the same verse.

2 Ki. 7.1:

כֹּה / אמר יהוה כָּעֵת / מחר

2 Ki. 10.6:

סֵפֶר / שנית · · · וּלקְלִי / אתם

2 Ki. 18.14:

אַשּׁוּר / לָכִישָׁה / לֵאמֹר /

2 Ki. 19.4:

אֶת / כל · · · אַשּׁוּר /

2 Ki. 25.4:

הַמִּלְחָמֶה / הלילה דרך שַׁעַר /

Isa. 24.3:

הִבֹּוק / תבוק הארץ וְהִבֹּוז /

E. *Dagesh lene* AND ACCENTUATION

§ 20. And now we return to a discussion of the problem, which we
have only very briefly indicated at the beginning of the chapter (§ 10):
Is there any evidence to justify the division of the accents into disjunctive
and conjunctive accents? In MH § 68 I have stated that "the only existing
criterion to divide the accents . . . is the fact whether (in case the first word
ends in a open syllable) the following word has or has not a *dagesh lene*."

The following examples will, we hope, remove the last semblance of
justification for our continued use of this terminology and the division
it implies:

Ex. 15.11:	(מִי) כָמֹכָה · · · (מִי) כָּמֹכָה		
Josh. 15.1:	(מִפְּנֵי) בְנֵי · · · (מִפְּנֵי) בְּנֵי		
1 Sam. 29.4:	(שָׂרֵי) פְלִשְׁתִּים · · · (שָׂרֵי) פְּלִשְׁתִּים		
1 Ki. 16.21:	(אַחֲרֵי) תִבְנִי	— v. 22:	(אַחֲרֵי) תִבְנִי
Gen. 11.8:	(עַל פְּנֵי) כָל	— v. 9:	(עַל פְּנֵי) כָּל
2 Sam. 15.36:	(שְׁנֵי) בְנֵיהֶם	— 21.8:	(שְׁנֵי) בְּנֵי
Gen. 30.15:	(דּוּדָאֵי) בְנֵךְ	— v. 14:	(מדּוּדָאֵי) בְּנֵךְ
Ex. 5.19:	(שֹׁטְרֵי) בְנֵי	— v. 14:	(שֹׁטְרֵי) בְּנֵי
Judg. 9.2:	(בְּאָזְנֵי) כָל	— v. 3:	(בְּאָזְנֵי) כָּל
2 Sam. 3.36:	(בְעֵינֵי) כָל	— v 19:	(וּבְעֵינֵי) כָּל
Num. 22.36:	(כִּי) בָא	— 21.1:	(כִּי) בָּא
Josh. 7.1:	(זַבְדִּי) בֶן	— v. 18:	(זַבְדִּי) בֶּן
Ex. 2.23:	(וַיְהִי) בַיָּמִים	— v. 11:	(וַיְהִי) בַּיָּמִים
Josh. 6.20:	(וַיְהִי) כשְׁמֹעַ	— 5.1:	(וַיְהִי) כִּשְׁמֹעַ
Josh. 17.7:	(וַיְהִי) גְבוּל	— 16.5:	(וַיְהִי) גְּבוּל
1 Ki. 16.1:	(וַיְהִי) דְבַר	— 13.21:	(וַיְהִי) דְּבַר

Num. 15.35:	(אֹתוֹ) בָּאֲבָנִים — v. 36:	(אֹתוֹ) בָּאֲבָנִים
Gen. 36.22:	(וַיִּהְיוּ) בְּנֵי — v. 11:	(וַיִּהְיוּ) בְּנֵי
Josh. 15.7:	(וְהָיָה) תֹצְאֹתָיו — v. 11:	(וְהָיוּ) תֹצְאוֹת
Josh. 18.14:	(וְהָיָה) תֹצְאֹתָיו — v. 12:	(וְהָיוּ) תֹצְאֹתָיו
Josh. 15.63:	(יָכְלוּ) בְּנֵי — 17.12:	(יָכְלוּ) בְּנֵי
Josh. 22.11:	(וַיִּשְׁמְעוּ) בְּנֵי — v. 12:	(וַיִּשְׁמְעוּ) בְּנֵי
1 Sam. 11.19:	(וַיֹּאמְרוּ) כָל — v. 1:	(וַיֹּאמְרוּ) כָל
2 Sam. 2.32:	(וַיֵּלְכוּ) כָל — v. 29:	(וַיֵּלְכוּ) כָל
1 Ki. 1.38:	(וּבְנָיֵהוּ) בֶּן — v. 44:	(וּבְנָיֵהוּ) בֶּן
1 Ki. 2.29:	(בְּנָיֵהוּ) בֶּן — v. 34:	(בְּנָיֵהוּ) בֶּן
Gen. 36.28:	(אֵלֶּה) בְּנֵי — v. 27:	(אֵלֶּה) בְּנֵי
Num. 10.20:	(מַטֵּה) בְּנֵי — v. 19:	(מַטֵּה) בְּנֵי
Josh. 13.15:	(לְמַטֵּה) בְּנֵי — 15.1:	(לְמַטֵּה) בְּנֵי
1 Sam. 17.43:	(אַתָּה) בָא — v. 45:	(אַתָּה) בָא
2 Sam. 13.5:	(תָּבוֹא נָא) תָמָר — v. 6:	(תָּבוֹא נָא) תָמָר
2 Ki. 12.5:	(יוּבָא) בֵית — v. 17:	(יוּבָא) בֵית
1 Ki. 15.6:	(הָיְתָה) בֵּין — v. 7:	(הָיְתָה) בֵּין
Jer. 3.14:	(שׁוּבוּ) בָנִים (שׁוֹבָבִים) — v. 22:	(שׁוּבוּ) בָנִים (שׁוֹבְבִים)
Jer. 11.4:	(שִׁמְעוּ) בְּקוֹלִי — v. 7:	(שִׁמְעוּ) בְּקוֹלִי
Ezek. 21.3:	(לֹא) תִכְבֶּה — v. 4:	(לֹא) תִכְבֶּה
Ezek. 26.19:	(כִּי) כֹה (אָמַר אֲדֹנָי יהוה) — 29.13:	(כִּי) כֹה (אָמַר אֲדֹנָי יהוה)
Zeph. 1.10:	(וְהָיָה) בַיּוֹם — v. 8:	(וְהָיָה) בַיּוֹם
Hos. 2.5:	(וְשַׂמְתִּיהָ) כַמִּדְבָּר (וְשַׁתִּהָ) כְּאֶרֶץ	
Joel 4.19:	(לִשְׁמָמָה) תִהְיֶה ⋯ (שְׁמָמָה) תִהְיֶה	
Mic. 1.5:	(מִי) פֶשַׁע ⋯ (וּמִי) בָּמוֹת	
Ezek. 14.6:	(לִדְרֹשׁ לוֹ) בִי ⋯ (נַעֲנָה לוֹ) בִי	
Ex. 29.39:	(תַּעֲשֶׂה) בַּבֹּקֶר ⋯ (תַּעֲשֶׂה) בֵּין	
Num. 15.3:	(אוֹ) בִנְדָבָה (אוֹ) בְּמוֹעֲדֵיכֶם	
1 Ki. 7.25:	(וּשְׁלֹשָׁה) פֹנִים ⋯ (וּשְׁלֹשָׁה) פֹנִים	
Lev. 12.8:	(שְׁתֵּי) תֹרִים (אוֹ שְׁנֵי) בְּנֵי	
1 Sam. 26.12:	(כִּי) כֻלָּם ⋯ (כִּי) תַרְדֵּמַת	
2 Sam. 3.9:	(כִּי) כַּאֲשֶׁר ⋯ (כִּי) כֵן	

2 Sam. 5.2:	(אַתָּה) תִרְעֶה ··· (וְאַתָּה) תִהְיֶה	
I Ki. 5.23:	(וְאַתָּה) תִשָּׂא (וְאַתָּה) תַּעֲשֶׂה	
2 Sam. 12.9:	(הִכִּיתָ) בַחֶרֶב ··· (הָרַגְתָּ) בְּחֶרֶב	
I Sam. 28.4:	(וַיַּחֲנוּ) בְשׁוּנֵם ··· (וַיַּחֲנוּ) בַּגִּלְבֹּעַ	
I Sam. 31.12:	(וַיָּקוּמוּ) כָל ··· (וַיֵּלְכוּ) כָל	
2 Sam. 10.6:	(וַיִּרְאוּ) בְנֵי ··· (וַיִּשְׁלְחוּ) בְנֵי	

Gen. 39.15:	(וַיְהִי) כְשָׁמְעוֹ — v. 13:	(וַיְהִי) כִּרְאוֹתָהּ
Josh. 8.25:	(וַיְהִי) כָל — v. 24:	(וַיְהִי) כְּכַלּוֹת
I Sam. 4.1:	(וַיְהִי) דְבַר — v. 5:	(וַיְהִי) כְּבוֹא
I Sam. 14.25:	(וַיְהִי) דְבַשׁ — 15.10:	(וַיְהִי) דְבַר
I Sam. 18.14:	(וַיְהִי) דָוִד — v. 19:	(וַיְהִי) בְּעֵת
I Sam. 25.37:	(וַיְהִי) בַבֹּקֶר — v. 2:	(וַיְהִי) בְּגֹז
2 Sam. 11.14:	(וַיְהִי) בַבֹּקֶר — v. 16:	(וַיְהִי) בְּשְׁמֹר
Num. 11.12:	(כִּי) תֹאמַר — v. 18:	(כִּי) בְכִיתֶם
Deut. 15.8:	(כִּי) פָתֹחַ — v. 16:	(כִּי) בְּגִלָל
Judg. 11.12:	(כִּי) בָאתָ — v. 16:	(כִּי) בַּעֲלוֹתָם
I Sam. 20.3:	(כִּי) כְפֶשַׂע — v. 8:	(כִּי) בִּבְרִית
Num. 32.9:	(לְבִלְתִּי) בֹא — v. 12:	(בִּלְתִּי) כָלֵב
I Ki. 18.26:	(וַיִּקְרְאוּ) בְשֵׁם — v. 28:	(וַיִּקְרְאוּ) בְקוֹל
2 Ki. 11.18:	(וַיָּבֹאוּ) כָל — v. 19:	(וַיָּבֹאוּ) דֶּרֶךְ
Josh. 18.14:	(עַל פְּנֵי) בֵית — v. 16:	(עַל פְּנֵי) גֵּי
Judg. 4.15:	(לִפְנֵי) בָרָק — v. 23:	(לִפְנֵי) בְּנֵי
I Sam. 24.5:	(אַחֲרֵי) כֵן — v. 14:	(אַחֲרֵי) כֶּלֶב
2 Ki. 9.26:	(דְּמֵי) בָנָיו — v. 7:	(וּדְמֵי) כָל
2 Sam. 14.18:	(אַל נָא) תְכַחֲדִי — v. 17:	(יִהְיֶה נָּא) דְבַר
2 Ki. 2.6:	(נָא) פֹה — v. 9:	(נָא) פִי
Judg. 6.10:	(לֹא) תִירְאוּ — v. 23:	(לֹא) תָמוּת

C. Affecting Vocalization

In the current Hebrew grammars it is taken for granted that amongst the factors which influence the vocalization, the accent plays an important role: according to its being conjunctive or disjunctive, the word thus accentuated changes from the context- to the pausal-form (cf. Bergsträsser § 29a). We shall prove the fallacy of this axiom by showing that both the so-called context-form and the so-called pausal-form are used in connection with the very same accents:

§ 21.   The סוֹף פָּסוּק.

1 Ki. 4.6:	הַמַּס	Jer. 52.24:	הַסַּף
1 Ki. 5.28:	הַמַּס	2 Ki. 25.18:	הַסַּף
Neh. 5.14:	אָכַלְתִּי	Ps. 78.10:	לָלֶכֶת
Gen. 31.38:	אָכַלְתִּי	Eccl. 1.7:	לָלֶכֶת

§ 22.   The אתנח.

Isa. 33.11:	קַשׁ	Job 3.4:	מִמַּעַל	Job 3.9:	וָאַיִן
Joel 2.5:	קַשׁ	Job 31.2:	מִמַּעַל	Prov. 14.6:	וָאַיִן
Ps. 66.12:	וּבַמַּיִם	Prov. 23.5:	כְנָפַיִם	Ps. 148.1:	הַשָּׁמַיִם
Neh. 13.2:	וּבַמַּיִם	Isa. 18.1:	כְנָפַיִם	Ps. 148.4:	הַשָּׁמַיִם
Ps. 27.2:	חַיַּי	Ps. 69.4:	עֵינָי	Ps. 31.14:	עָלַי
Ps. 7.6:	חַיַּי	Ps. 77.5:	עֵינָי	Ps. 86.13:	עָלַי
Ps. 129.1:	מִנְּעוּרַי	Ps. 142.7:	מֵרֹדְפָי	Job 9.22:	אָמַרְתִּי
Ps. 129.2:	מִנְּעוּרַי	Ps. 35.3:	רֹדְפָי	Ps. 40.11:	אָמַרְתִּי
Ps. 35.15:	יָדַעְתִּי	Ps. 2.7:	אַתָּה	Job 41.8:	יִגַּשׁוּ
Hos. 8.4:	יָדַעְתִּי	Ps. 5.5:	אַתָּה	Ex. 24.2:	יִגַּשׁוּ
Ps. 35.20:	אֶרֶץ	Ps. 50.23:	דֶּרֶךְ	Ps. 68.14:	בַּכֶּסֶף
Ps. 37.22:	אֶרֶץ	Ps. 89.42:	דֶּרֶךְ	Deut. 21.14:	בַּכֶּסֶף
Ps. 14.4:	לֶחֶם	Ps. 35.19:	שֶׁקֶר	Ps. 45.6:	יִפְּלוּ
Prov. 12.11:	לֶחֶם	Prov. 6.17:	שֶׁקֶר	Ezek. 32.20:	יִפְּלוּ

Ps. 119.65:	עַבְדֶּךָ	Judg. 13.14:	תֹּאכַל
Ps. 119.84:	עַבְדֶּךָ	2 Sam. 22.9:	תֹּאכַל

§ 23.   סוֹף פָּסוּק and אתנח.

These two accents rank equally high and may, therefore, be combined in our discussion.

Prov. 30.16:	מָיִם	Ps. 35.1:	יְרִיבַי	Job 42.6:	וְנִחַמְתִּי
Prov. 25.21:	מָיִם	Jer. 18.19:	יְרִיבַי	Zech. 8.14:	נִחַמְתִּי

Ps. 26.1:	הָלַכְתִּי	Josh. 1.6:	וֶאֱמָץ	Ezek. 19.4:	נִתְפַּשׂ
Judg. 4.8:	וְהָלַכְתִּי	Josh. 1.18:	וֶאֱמָץ	Ezek. 19.8:	נִתְפַּשׂ
Mic. 6.10:	רֶשַׁע	Ps. 48.5:	נוֹעֲדוּ	Ps. 18.13:	עָבְרוּ
Eccl. 3.16:	הָרֶשַׁע	Am. 3.3:	נוֹעָדוּ	Ps. 42.8:	עָבְרוּ

§ 24. The זקף קטן.

Jonah 3.6:	שַׂק	Deut. 31.12:	וְהַטַּף	Jer. 46.6:	הַקַּל
Am. 8.10:	שָׂק	Jer. 40.7:	וָטָף	Am. 2.14:	מִקָּל
Lev. 18.19:	תִקְרַב	Gen. 32.12:	וְהִכֵּנִי	2 Ki. 13.12:	נִלְחַם
Lev. 18.14:	תִקְרָב	1 Sam. 17.9:	וְהִכַּנִי	2 Ki. 14.28:	נִלְחָם
Gen. 1.10:	אֶרֶץ	Josh. 10.33:	גֶּזֶר	Isa. 49.6:	עֶבֶד
Deut. 32.13:	אָרֶץ	1 Ki. 9.17:	גָּזֶר	Gen. 44.10:	עָבֶד
Ex. 28.7:	אֶבֶן	1 Ki. 7.38:	הָאַחַת	2 Ki. 2.7:	הָלְכוּ
Gen. 11.3:	לְאָבֶן	1 Ki. 7.17:	הָאֶחָת	Jer. 50.6:	הָלָכוּ
Ex. 40.37:	יִסְעוּ	2 Sam. 2.13:	יָצְאוּ	2 Chron. 30.11:	נִכְנְעוּ
Num. 2.17:	יִסָּעוּ	Josh. 2.5:	יָצָאוּ	2 Chron. 12.7:	נִכְנָעוּ
1 Sam. 1.16:	אֲמָתְךָ	Isa. 64.3:	זוּלָתְךָ	Ex. 23.33:	בְּאַרְצְךָ
1 Sam. 1.11:	אֲמָתֶךָ	2 Sam. 7.22:	זוּלָתֶךָ	Deut. 2.27:	בְּאַרְצֶךָ
		Jer. 12.12:	אֹכְלָה		
		Isa. 33.14:	אוֹכֵלָה		

It is worth-while noting that זקף קטן is here never affixed to a letter with a *shewa* (but to the following one with a full vowel), while אתנח, though being considered as of much higher disjunctive value, frequently appeared thus in §§ 22 and 23.

§ 25. The טפחא.

Ex. 12.38:	רַב	Mic. 5.7:	וְטָרָף	1 Ki. 5.19:	הַבַּיִת
Num. 21.6:	רָב	Hos. 6.1:	טָרָף	1 Ki. 5.31:	הַבָּיִת
2 Chron. 17.17:	חַיִל	2 Chron. 7.15:	וְאָזְנַי	Num. 9.6:	הַפֶּסַח
2 Chron. 25.6:	חָיִל	Isa. 5.9:	בְּאָזְנָי	Num. 9.2:	הַפָּסַח
		Gen. 7.1:	בֵּיתְךָ		
		Deut. 6.9:	בֵּיתֶךָ		

§ 26. The רביע.

Ps. 22.30:	אֶרֶץ	Job 14.14:	גֶּבֶר
Ps. 44.4:	אָרֶץ	Ps. 128.4:	גֶּבֶר
Judg. 7.5:	הַכֶּלֶב	Job 29.11:	רָאֲתָה
Ps. 59.7:	כַּכֶּלֶב	Isa. 64.3:	רָאֲתָה

§ 27. The עולה ויורד.

Ps. 42.12:	עָלַי
Ps. 43.5:	עָלַי

§ 28. Conjunctive accents.

a) מונח.

Deut. 28.22:	יַכְּכָה	Isa. 58.1:	הָרֵם
Jer. 40.15:	יַכְּכָה	2 Ki. 6.7:	הָרֵם

b) מירכא.

Ps. 82.4:	דַל	Ex. 21.12:	מַכֵּה
Ps. 82.3:	דָל	Ex. 2.11:	מַכֵּה

c) אזלא.

Gen. 32.33:	יֹאכְלוּ	Cant. 3.4:	כִּמְעַט
Isa. 65.13:	יֹאכֵלוּ	2 Chron. 12.7:	כִּמְעָט

§ 29. Conclusions.

The vocalization of a word is independent of the kind of an accent it carries. We shall, therefore, disregard the accentuation henceforth and pay attention solely to the position of the words in question within the syntactic structure of the respective sentences, where they are found.

Here I wish to bring a few additional examples, so as to do away finally with the arbitrary terms of "pausal-forms" and "context forms," respectively.

הַבַּיָת:	Gen. 19.4	שְׁמְךָ:	Gen. 32.29	עִמְךָ:	Gen. 33.15
בָּיִת:	Gen. 17.27	שְׁמֶךָ:	Gen. 32.30	עִמָּךְ:	Gen. 29.25
עָז:	Num. 21.24	לִקְרָאתְךָ:	Gen. 32.7	מַטְּךָ:	Ex. 8.12
עָז:	Gen. 49.7	לִקְרָאתֶךָ:	Ex. 4.14	בְּמַטְּךָ:	Ex. 8.1

תֹּאכְלוּ: Lev. 7.16   וּלְעַמְּךָ: Ex. 8.5   וְעַמְּךָ: Ex. 33.16

תֹּאכֵלוּ: Ex. 12.15   וּבְעַמֶּ֣ךָ: Ex. 7.28   וְעַמֶּ֣ךָ: Ex. 33.16

תִּקְרָב: Lev. 18.19   תִּשְׁמְרוּ: Lev. 26.3   עֶרְכְּךָ: Lev. 27.7

תִּקְרְב: Lev. 18.14   תִּשְׁמֹרוּ: Lev. 26.2   מֵעֶרְכֶּ֣ךָ: Lev. 27.8

§ 30. The accent is credited with yet another function: according to the Hebrew grammars, the reduction to *shewâ* of the first vowel of a مضاف is due to the fact that its accent changes either position or character: the "Hauptdruck" becomes "Nebendruck": "Diese Reduktion (scil. 'kurze Vokale in offener Silbe vor Nebendrucksilbe wurden zu Schwa reduziert', cf. ib. under n') erfolgte auch vor dem Nebendruck auf dem *Status constructus*, welcher Nebendruck durch Schwächung des dem isolierten Worte zukommenden Hauptdrucks entstanden ist: *dabàr* > דְּבַר 'Wort'; *zaqìn* > זְקַן 'Greis' ..." (B-L § 26 o'). But what is a "Nebendruck"? Here, Bauer-Leander get hopelessly confused: "... meist kleine Worte, die ... nur mit Nebendruck zu lesen waren, durch ein Zeichen mit dem folgenden den Hauptdruck tragenden Wort verbunden. Dies Zeichen ... führt den Namen *Maqqef*" (B-L § 9g'). This means: the *makkef* is an indicator of a "Nebendruck"; cf. also: "... zur Andeutung eines Nebendrucks wird ... ein Zeichen gebraucht, das ... *Meteg* genannt wird" (B-L § 9h'): another indicator of a "Nebendruck". But entirely differently later on: "Der Nebendruck des *Status constructus* wird (in tiberischer Überlieferung) in der Regel durch einen *konjunktiven Akzent* ausgedrückt, ... seltener durch *Metheg+Maqqef*. ... Die Drucklosigkeit des *Status constructus* wird, wie gewöhnlich, durch ein *Maqqef* nach dem Worte ausgedrückt" (B-L § 64c). According to this definition, the *makkef* indicates entire "Drucklosigkeit" (note: "wie gewöhnlich"); but *makkef* plus *meteg* or—more frequently—a conjunctive accent denote "Nebendruck". While we have full sympathy for the earnest endeavors of these scholars to bring system and method into the confusion of the accents, we still must warn against such arbitrary procedure. All of a sudden the conjunctive accents are reduced to indicate mere "Nebendruck"! And what about the disjunctive accents in the indentical position with a مضاف (cf. § 12)? Do they, too, indicate "Nebendruck"? Hence it is not the accent used that matters in our differentiation between "Hauptdruck" and "Nebendruck" (since both, conjunctive and disjunctive accents alike are used with a مضاف, which is not allowed but a mere "Nebendruck" by Bauer-Leander), but solely the prescience of the grammarian and his preconceived theories are of importance (cf. p. 418, § 6).

§ 31.   But it is useless to worry about the meaning of the terms "Hauptdruck" and "Nebendruck", or over their indicators. For these terms are not based upon the observation of facts (cf. p. 2 f., § 5 f.)—or should we rather say that the Bible displays the utmost indifference to the demands of these learned grammarians? To put it bluntly: the vocalization of the مضاف (according to the Tiberian system) is in no way dependent on the accent; disjunctive or conjunctive accents or even *makkef* exhibit no influence on the retention of the vowel or its reduction to *shewâ* (cf. p. 614, § 84a: two ways of forming the absolute noun).

a) (הָרִים) הֲמוֹן: Jer. 3.23   מָקוֹם (מְנוּחָתִי): Isa. 66.1
    (עָרִיצִים) הֲמוֹן: Isa. 29.5   מְקוֹם (אֶהֱלָךְ): Isa. 54.2
    גְּאוֹן (שִׂבְעַת לֶחֶם): Ezek. 16.49   בָּקָר (רֵעִי): 1 Ki. 5.3
    גְּאוֹן (זֵדִים): Isa. 13.11   בָּקָר (זֶבַח הַשְּׁלָמִים): Num. 7.88

b) חָכְמַת חֲכָמָיו: Isa. 29.14   וּלְשִׂמְחַת לְבָבִי: Jer. 15.16
    חָכְמַת וָדָעַת: Isa. 33.6   כְּשִׂמְחָה בַקָּצִיר: Isa. 9.2

    מְזוּזַת הַבַּיִת: Ezek. 45.19
    מְזוּזַת רְבָעָה: Ezek. 41.21

c) מִדְבָּר (וְצִיָּה): Isa. 35.1   נָוֶה (שַׁאֲנָן): Isa. 33.20
    מִדְבָּר (שְׁמָמָה): Joel 2.3   נָוֶה (תַנִּים): Isa. 34.13

d) דְּבַר (יהוה): Ex. 9.20   שְׁלַל אֹיְבֶיךָ: Deut. 20.14
    דְּבַר־יהוה: Gen. 15.4   שְׁלַל־אֹיְבֵיכֶם: Josh. 22.8

    שְׂכַר שָׂכִיר: Deut. 15.18   וּרְחַב לֵבָב: Ps. 101.5
    שְׂכַר־שָׂכִיר: Mal. 3.5   וּרְחַב־לֵב: Prov. 21.4

    וּגְבַהּ קוֹמָה: Ezek. 31.3
    גְּבַהּ־לֵב: Prov. 16.5

Jer. 19.9:   בְּשַׂר בניהם ואת בְּשַׂר בנתיהם ואיש בְּשַׂר־רעהו · · ·
Isa. 35.2:   כְּבוֹד הלבנון · · · כְּבוֹד־יהוה

§ 32.   In this connection we wish to call to the attention of students of Hebrew grammar that even another grammatical law, which aims at

establishing an interrelation between the stress and the change to *shewâ*
of a vowel, is—at least in its present general form—equally untenable.
On p. 415, § 2c I stated as basic for the Tiberian grammar that "there can
be no long vowel [=open syllable] two syllables removed from the one with
the stress." In the following list of exceptions to this rule, the examples
carry the accent mostly on the last syllable. And the few cases where the
accent is on the *paenultima* (like: הַשְׁפֵלָה) are in contradiction with the
laws of accentuation (הַשָּׁפְלָה is no pausal form!), and represent an attempt
to justify the preservation of the first vowel. In view of the conclusion
at which we arrived in § 9 (that accent and stress are not interrelated)
I would like to term the following list: cases of preservation of the first
vowel.

§ 33.   Cases of inflected forms with preservation of the first vowel:

תּוֹלָעִים: Ex. 16.20	בְּכוֹכָעִים: Jer. 46.4	כּוֹכָבִים: Gen. 37.9
שׁוֹבָבִים: Jer. 3.14	וְאָהֳלִים: 2 Ki. 7.10	עוֹלָמִים: 1 Ki. 8.13
נוֹעָצִים: 1 Ki. 12.6	הַנּוֹתָרִים: Lev. 10.12	הַנּוֹעָדִים: 1 Ki. 8.5
כְּמוֹצָאֵי: Ezek. 12.4	מִתְשָׁבֵי: 1 Ki. 17.1	בְּחֹתָמוֹ: 1 Ki. 21.8
לְאֹהָלָיו: 1 Ki. 12.16	מוֹרָשֵׁיהֶם: Obad 17	עוֹלָמוֹ: Eccl. 12.5
גּוֹרָלוֹת: Lev. 16.8	שׁוֹפָרוֹת: Judg. 7.16	אֹצָרוֹת: Jer. 51.13
כֹּתָרֹת: 1 Ki. 7.16	הַנּוֹתָרֹת: Gen. 30.36	
פָּרָשִׁים: 1 Ki. 10.26		but: חֳרָשִׁים: 1 Chron. 4.14
לְחָרָשִׁים: 2 Ki. 22.6;	סָרָבִים: Ezek. 2.6	לְחָרָשֵׁי: 2 Ki. 12.12
סָרִיסִים: 2 Ki. 20.18	בְּרִיחִים: Isa. 43.14	פָּרִיצִים: Ezek. 7.22
שָׂרִיגִם: Gen. 40.10	וְעָרִיצִים: Ps. 54.5	עָרִיצֵי: Ezek. 30.11
but:	פְּקִדִים: Gen. 41.34	וְהַשְּׂרִידִים: Josh. 10.20
סְדִינִים: Judg. 14.12	וּשְׂעִירִים: Isa. 13.21	
מוֹסֵרוֹת: Jer. 27.2		בְּחָרְבָה: 2 Ki. 2.8
הָרֵכָבִים: Jer. 35.3	נָכוֹנוּ: Prov. 19.29 but: נְכוֹנָה: Ps. 5.10
הַשְׁפֵלָה: Ezek. 21.31	בֹּגֵדָה: Jer. 3.8	בָּגוֹדָה: Jer. 3.7
נָכוֹנָה: I Ki. 2.46;	הָאָשֵׁרִי: Judg. 1.32	חָרוּצִים: Prov. 10.4

§ 34.   Cases of مضاف with preservation of the first vowel (cf. p. 612,
§ 83 1).

רְעוֹת מַרְאֶה: Gen. 41.3; but: יְפוֹת מראה ib. v. 2
לְשׁוֹן נָכְרִיָּה: Prov. 6.24 (parallel רָע (מֵאֵשֶׁת

מִלָּשׁוֹן רְמִיָּה: Ps. 120.2 (parallel מִשְׁפַּת שֶׁקֶר)

מִצְּפוֹן חַנָּתוֹן: Josh. 19.14

הֲמוֹן הָרִים: Jer. 3.23

קָרוּעַ כֻּתָּנְתּוֹ (construct state; for if it were an adjective, it would be קְרוּעָה): 2 Sam. 15.32

שְׁנֵי – (שָׁנִים); שָׂרֵי – (שָׂרִים) ;but :

יְפַת – (יָפָה); but: רָמַת – (רָמָה)

דְּגַת – (דָּגָה); but: פְּרָת – (פְּרָה)

חֲלָל רָשָׁע: Ezek. 21.30 is construct state; cf. plural v. 34 חַלְלֵי רְשָׁעִים (p. 619, § 89)

מְלֵא (הַגּוֹצָה): Ezek. 17.3; but: טְמֵא (שְׂפָתַיִם): Isa. 6.5

גֹּבַהּ (רוּחַ): Prov. 16.18; but: גְּבֹהַּ (קוֹמָתוֹ): 1 Sam. 16.7

III. THE CONSONANTAL TEXT

A. THE PHONETIC VALUE OF THE LETTERS (Cf. MH pp. 95 ff.)

Due to the similarity of their phonetic value, certain letters could be misunderstood for one another, thus leading to scribal errors. They can be grouped as follows [1] (cf. also p. 234 the paragraph headed by: The Sources):

A. THE GUTTURALS א ה ח ע [2]

§ 35.   א – ה. [3]

Gen. 21.24	MT	אֶשָּׁבֵעַ	Ex. 2.9	MT	וְהֵנִיקִהוּ
	S	השבע		S	ואינקהו
Gen. 14.23	MT	הֶעֱשַׁרְתִּי			
	S	אעשרתי	a) Proper names (B-L § 62x). [4]		
Gen. 19.29	MT	הַהֲפֵכָה	Gen. 8.4	MT	אֲרָרָט
	S	האפכה		S	הררט
Gen. 41.25	MT	הִגִּיד	Gen. 10.27	MT	הֲדוֹרָם
	S	אגיד		S	אדורם

[1] Only the consonants matter; the vocalization is here immaterial; cf. p. 105.

[2] Cf. p. 170/71 and 173 f. sub א, ה, ח, ע.

[3] Cf. Gen. 34.1: MT ותצא — Var K; ib. 29.19: MT שבה — Var K שבא; ib. 33.15: MT אציגה — Var K אציגא.

[4] Cf. also p. 563, § 1b.

2 Chron. 10.18	הֲדֹרָם		
I Ki. 12.18	אֲדֹרָם	b) Various forms.	
2 Chron. 22.5	הָרַמִּים	Jer. 52.15	הֶאָמוֹן
2 Ki. 8.28	אֲרַמִּים	2 Ki. 25.11	הֶהָמוֹן
I Chron. 11.35	הַהֲרָרִי	2 Sam. 6.9	אֵיךְ
2 Sam. 23.33	הָאֲרָרִי	I Chron. 13.12	הֵיךְ

§ 36. ח – א.

2 Ki. 17.21	Q	וַיַּדַּח	I Chron. 9.41	וְתַחְרֵעַ
	K	וידא	I Chron. 8.35	וְתַאְרֵעַ
Lev. 11.16	MT	הַשַּׁחַף		
	S	השאף		

§ 37. ע – א. [1]

Gen. 23.18	MT	בָּאֵי	Ex. 4.12	MT	עִם
	S	בעי		S	אם
Ex. 22.29	MT	אִמּוֹ	I Ki. 1.18	MT	(2/) וְעַתָּה
	S	עמו		Seb	ואתה

§ 38. ח – ה. [2]

Prov. 20.21	Q	מְבֹהֶלֶת	Gen. 2.14	MT	חִדֶּקֶל
	K	מבחלת		S	הדקל
Cant. 1.17	Q	רָהִיטֵנוּ	Gen. 25.9	MT	צֹחַר
	K	רחיטנו		S	צהר

§ 39. ה – ע. [3]

Gen. 27.19	MT	שְׁבָה	Ex. 4.7	MT	שָׁבָה
	S	שבע		S	שבע

---

[1] Cf. Gen. 29.7: MT רעו — Var K ראו; ib. 41.2: MT ותרעינה — Var K ותראינה; ib. 9.12: MT אות — Var K עות.

[2] Cf. p. 109 f.: Gen. 14.5: MT בהם — Jerome: בחם; also Gen. 4.20: MT אהל — Var K אחל; ib. 29.3: MT והשיבו — Var K וחשיבו; ib. 11.31: MT ויקח — Var K ויקה. The interchange between ה and ח could be explained as a graphic error, too. But then we would have to assume that these confusions were committed at a time when the Bible was already written in the Square Alphabet; and I am most anxious to avoid here, as far as possible, a discussion of the interrelation between the change in the Hebrew Alphabet and the textual errors of the Bible, which may and may not have been the result thereof.

[3] Cf. Jer. 48.28: MT ערים — Var K הרים.

| Lev. 13.6 | MT | פָּשָׂה | Num. 24.6 | MT | נָטַע |
| | S | פשע | | S | נטה |

§ 40. ע – ח.[1]

Gen. 10.22	MT	עוּץ	2 Ki. 20.13		וַיִּשְׁמַע
	S	חוץ	Isa. 39.2		וַיִּשְׂמַח[2]
Ex. 28.26	MT	עֵבֶר	1 Sam. 17.7	Q	וְעֵץ
	S	חבר		K	וחץ

B. THE SIBILANTS ז ס צ שׁ[3]

§ 41. ז – צ.[4]

Ex. 15.5	MT	בִּמְצוֹלֹת	Ezek. 45.8	K	וְהָאָרֶץ
	S	במזלות		Q	והארז
Num. 22.39	MT	חֻצוֹת			
	S	חיזות			

§ 42. שׂ – ס.[5]

a) Gen. 1.21	MT	הָרֹמֶשֶׂת	Num. 15.29	MT	יִשְׂרָאֵל
	S	הרמסת		S	יסראל
Gen. 27.31	MT	וַיַּעַשׂ	b) Isa. 17.14	Q	שׁוֹסֵנוּ
	S	ויעס		K	שושנו
Gen. 40.9	MT	שַׂר	Isa. 10.13	Q	שׁוֹסֵתִי
	S	סר		K	שושתי
Gen. 42.25	MT	שַׂקּוּ			
	S	סקו			

[1] Cf. Gen. 12.15: MT ותקח — Var K ותקע; Jer. 16.6: MT יקרח — Var K יקרע; cf. also Paul Kahle in ZAW 1921, p. 235: "Dass ח und ע in der Aussprache zusammengefallen sein müssen, geht daraus hervor, dass mehrfach Wörter, die auf diese Konsonanten ausgehen, miteinander reimen." See also MdWI, p. 47.

[2] On the interchange שׂ – שׁ, cf. § 44.

[3] Cf. p. 172.

[4] The possibility of regional difference in the pronunciation must be taken into consideration; cf. Ps. 96.12: יַעֲלֹז — 1 Chron. 16.32: יַעֲלֹץ; Ex. 2.23: MT ויזעקו — S ויצעקו; Gen. 18.20: MT זעקת — S צעקת (B-L § 2v).

[5] Cf. Job 17.7: Venice 1515 מְכַּעַס, marg.: מכעש; ibid. 20.22: שְׁפְקוֹ, Venice 1515 marg. ספקו; further: Gen. 6.11: MT חמס — Var K חמש; ib. 9.2: MT תרמש — Var K תרמס; ib. 40.3: MT במשמר — Var K במסמר.

§ 43. ש – צ.[1]

Num .16.30	MT	וּפָצְתָה	1 Chron. 18.3		לְהַצִּיב
	S	ופשתה	2 Sam. 8.3		לְהָשִׁיב

§ 44. ש – שׂ.[2]

2 Ki. 20.13	וַיִּשְׁמַע	Ezek. 30.18	Ma חָשַׁךְ
Isa. 39.2	וַיִּשְׂמַח[3]		Md חָשַׂךְ

C. THE LABIALS ב ו מ פ

§ 45. ב – ו.[4]

Ex. 12.29	MT	הַשְּׁבִי
	S	השוי
Gen. 25.8	MT	וַיִּגְוַע
	S	ויגבע
Gen. 8.12	MT	הַיּוֹנָה
	S	היבנה

a) ב – יו.

Jer. 29.22	Q	וּכְאָחִיו
	K	וכאחב

§ 46. ב – מ.[5]

Num. 12.8	MT	וּתְמֻנַת	Ezra 1.1		מִפִּי
	S	ותבונת	2 Chron. 36.22		בְּפִי
1 Chron. 20.4		מִילִידֵי	2 Chron. 25.23		מִשַּׁעַר
2 Sam. 21.18		בִּילִידֵי	2 Ki. 14.13		בְּשַׁעַר[6]
2 Chron. 10.2		מִמִּצְרָיִם	2 Ki. 23.33	Q	מִמְּלֹךְ
1 Ki. 12.2		בְּמִצְרָיִם		K	ב.לך
2 Sam. 5.13		מִירוּשָׁלַםִ	Josh. 3.16	Q	מֵאָדָם
1 Chron. 14.3		בִּירוּשָׁלַםִ		K	באדם

[1] Cf. also 1 Chron. 16.16: לְיִצְחָק —
Ps. 105.9: לְיִשְׂחָק (B-L § 2v; Bergstr.
§ 14 f.); for explanation cf. our note 4
on p. 478. Cf. further Gen. 21.33: MT
אשל — Var K אצל; ib. 24.63: MT
וישא — Var K ויצא; ib. 43.4: MT משלח
— Var K מצלח.

[2] Cf. Jer. 36.9: Venice 1515 תַּשִּׂיאוּ;
marg.: תַּשִּׁיאוּ; Ps. 89.23: יַשִּׂיא, Venice
1515 marg.: ישׁיא; Ps. 50.23: Ven. 1515:
וְשָׂם, marg.: וְשָׁם. See also p. 172 and
p. 230.

[3] On the change between ע–ח, cf. § 40.
[4] Cf. Gen. 7.16: MT צוה — Var K
צבא; Jer. 42.14: MT וללחם — Var K
בללחם; Gen. 22.13: MT בסבך — Var K
בסוך; cf. also p. 125, s.v. אָן.
[5] Cf. Gen. 33.10: MT מידי — Var K
בידי; Jer. 4.8: MT שב — Var K שם;
ib. 23.18: MT הקשיב — Var K הקשים;
further: Ezek. 14.9: מתוך, Venice 1515
marg.: בתוך.
[6] Cf. Md-Ma on 2 Ki. 14.13.

Josh. 22.7	K	מעבר				
	Q	בְּעֵבֶר	a) Proper names.			
Josh. 24.15	Q	מֵעֵבֶר	Isa. 39.1			מְרֹאדַךְ
	K	בעבר	2 Ki. 20.12			בְּרֹאדַךְ
2 Ki. 12.10	Q	מִיָּמִין	2 Ki. 5.12	Q		אֲמָנָה
	K	בימין		K		אבנה
Job 34.14	Ma	יָשִׂים				
	Md	וישיב 1				

§ 47.   ‏פ – ב‎. [2]

Gen. 31.35	MT	וַיְחַפֵּשׂ	Gen. 31.40	MT	חֹרֶב
	S	ויחבש		S	חרף
Gen. 31.49	MT	וְהַמִּצְפָּה	Ex. 32.22	MT	בְּרָע
	S	והמצבה		S	פרוע [3]
Ex. 15.10	MT	נָשַׁפְתָּ	1 Chron. 19.16		וְשׁוֹפַךְ
	S	נשבת	2 Sam. 10.16		וְשׁוֹבַךְ
Num. 3.6	MT	לִפְנֵי	1 Chron. 17.6		שֹׁפְטֵי
	S	לבני	2 Sam. 7.7		שִׁבְטֵי
Deut. 33.3	MT	אַף	Ps. 80.3	MT	לִפְנֵי
	S	אב		Seb	לבני [4]

§ 48.   ‏פ – מ‎.

Isa. 37.27		וּשְׁדָמָה	Isa. 65.4	Q	וּמְרַק
2 Ki. 19.26		וּשְׁדָפָה		K	ופרק

D.   THE PALATALS — VELARS ‏ג כ ק‎

§ 49.   ‏כ – ג‎. [5]

Gen. 14.23	MT	שְׂרוֹךְ	Lev. 11.19	MT	הַדּוּכִיפַת
	S	שרוג		S	הדגיפת
Gen. 21.23	MT	וּלְנֶכְדִּי			
	S	ולנגדי			

---

[1] On the interchange between ‏שׂ‎ and ‏שׁ‎ involved hereby, cf. § 44.

[2] Cf. Gen. 31.35: MT ‏ויחפש‎ — Var K ‏ויחבש‎; ib. 48.4: MT ‏מפרך‎ — Var K ‏מברך‎; Jer. 15.9: MT ‏השבעה‎ — Var K ‏השפעה‎.

[3] On the spelling with or without the mater lectionis ‏ו‎, cf. p. 564, § 3.

[4] Cf. K-Q on Prov. 4.3 and Seb-MT on Job 19.17.

[5] Cf. Jer. 3.2: MT ‏שגלת‎ — Var K ‏שכלת‎.

§ 50.   כ – ק.¹

| Deut. 15.7 | MT | תִּקְפֹּץ |
| | S | תכפץ |

E.   THE DENTALS ט ד ת

§ 51.   ד – ת.²

Ex. 31.10	MT	הַשָּׂרָד	Gen. 10.3	MT	וְרִיפַת
	S	השרת		S	ריפד
Ezek. 22.4	Q	עַד	Isa. 66.17	Q	אַחַת
	K	עת		K	אחד

§ 52.   ט – ת.³

Gen. 15.10	MT	בִּתְרוֹ	Deut. 12.3	MT	וְנִתַּצְתֶּם
	S	בטרו		S	ונתצתם
Gen. 19.26	MT	וַתַּבֵּט			
	S	ותביט			

F.   THE LIQUIDS ל מ נ ר

§ 53.   ר – ל; נ – מ; ר – מ; ר – נ.⁴

Isa. 37.24	מְרוֹם	Ps. 18.33	וַיִּתֵּן
2 Ki. 19.23	מְלוֹן	2 Sam. 22.33	וַיַּתֵּר
2 Sam. 12.31	וַיָּשֶׂם		
1 Chron. 20.3	וַיָּשַׂר		

B.   THE GRAPHIC FORM OF THE LETTERS (Cf. MH p. 100 f.)

Certain letters could, on account of their resemblance in script, be confused with one another; the result was an obvious mistake in the

---

¹ Cf. Gen. 23.15: MT שקל — Var K שכל; ib. 42.33: MT קחו — Var K כחו; ib. 33.4: MT ויבכו — Var K ויבקו; cf. also p. 176, sub כ.

² Cf. Gen. 22.2: MT אחד — Var K אחת; Jer. 49.1: MT גד — Var K גת; ib. 8.7: MT עת — Var K עד. Cf. also p. 174, sub ד, and p. 226, sub ת.

³ Cf. Gen. 4.7: MT לפתח — Var K לפטח; Ex. 7.4: MT בשפטים — Var K בשפתים; Gen. 33.14: MT לאטי — Var K לאתי.

⁴ Cf. Gen. 8.1: MT רוח — Var K לוח; ib. 3.24: MT וישכן — Var K וישכם; Jer. 6.27: MT ובחנת — Var K ובחרת; Gen. 27.41 וישטם — ib. 26.21: שטנה.

spelling of a given word. Scribal errors of this kind can be classified as follows:[1]

A.　THE GROUP ב ד ר

§ 54.　.ר – ב

Gen. 11.29	MT	אַבְרָם		Num. 9.19	MT	מִשְׁמֶרֶת
	S	אררם			S	משמבת
Gen. 13.8	MT	אַבְרָם		Num. 15.16	MT	וְלַגֵּר
	S	אבבם			S	ולגב
Gen. 25.27	MT	וְיַעֲקֹב		Num. 16.30	MT	יִבְרָא
	S	ויעקר			S	יבבא
Lev. 6.5	MT	(2°) בַּבֹּקֶר		1 Ki. 22.32		וַיָּסֻרוּ
	S	בבקב		2 Chron. 18.31		וַיָּסֹבּוּ
Lev. 16.18	MT	הַמִּזְבֵּחַ		Ezek. 3.15	Q	וָאֵשֵׁב
	S	המזרח			K	ואשר
Num. 3.5	MT	וַיְדַבֵּר				
	S	וידרר				

§ 55.　[2].ר – ד

Gen. 13.6	MT	יַחְדָּו		Jer. 2.20	Q	אֶעֱבוֹר
	S	יחרו			K	אעבוד
Gen. 14.14	MT	וַיָּרֶק		Jer. 31.40	Q	הַשְּׁדֵמוֹת
	S	וידק			K	השרמות
Gen. 22.13	MT	אַחַר		Prov. 19.19	Q	גְּדָל
	S	אחד			K	גרל
Deut. 1.22	MT	וְיַחְפְּרוּ		Ezek. 6.14	Md	דִּבְלָתָה
	S	ויחפדו			Ma	רבלתה
Deut. 28.49	MT	יִדְאֶה				
	S	יראה		a)　Proper names.		
Ps. 18.43		אֲרִיקֵם		Gen. 10.4	MT	וְדֹדָנִים
2 Sam. 22.43		אֲדִקֵּם			S	ורודנים
Ps. 18.11		וַיֵּדֶא		Gen. 14.2	MT	וְשֶׁמְאֵבֶר
2 Sam. 22.11		וַיֵּרָא			S	ושמאבד

---

[1] Cf. p. 476, note 1.

[2] Cf. Gen. 4.2: MT לָלֶדֶת — Var K לָלֶרֶת; ib. 31.53: MT בפחד — Var K בפחר; ib. 49.26: MT נזיר — Var K נזיד; further Ps. 54.5: זָרִים, Venice 1515 marg.: זֵדִים.

Num. 2.14	MT	רְעוּאֵל	2 Sam. 8.3		הֲדַדְעֶזֶר
	S	דעואל	1 Chron. 18.3		הדדעזר¹
Gen. 10.4		וְדֹדָנִים	2 Ki. 16.6	Q	וַאֲדוֹמִים
1 Chron. 1.7		וְרוֹדָנִים		K	וארומים
Gen. 36.26		חֶמְדָּן			
1 Chron. 1.41		חַמְרָן			

§ 56.   ד – ב.²

2 Sam. 23.29	חֵלֶב	Josh. 15.47	K	הגבול
1 Chron. 11.30	חֵלֶד		Q	הַגָּדוֹל

B.   THE GROUP ב כ ר

§ 57.   ב – כ.³

2 Sam. 7.22		כְּכֹל	Isa. 63.6	K	וַאֲשַׁכְּרֵם
1 Chron. 17.20		בְּכֹל		Q	ואשברם
2 Sam. 24.19		כִּדְבַר	Hos. 13.9	Q	בְּעֶזְרֶךָ
1 Chron. 21.19		בִּדְבַר		K	כעזרך
1 Ki. 22.20		בְּכֹה	Prov. 21.29	Q	יָבִין
2 Chron. 18.19		כָּכָה		K	יכין
2 Sam. 12.31	Q	בַּמַּלְבֵּן	Job 21.13	Q	יְכַלּוּ
	K	במלכן		K	יבלו
2 Ki. 3.24	Q	וַיַּכּוּ ⋯ וְהַכּוֹת			
	K	ויבו ⋯ והבות			

§ 58.   ר – כ.

Gen. 31.15	MT	מְכָרָנוּ	Ps. 18.12	חֶשְׁכַּת
	S	מככנו	2 Sam. 22.12	חַשְׁרַת

C.   THE GROUP ב כ נ פ

§ 59.   ב – נ.⁴

Jer. 33.3	K	וּבְצֻרוֹת
	Q	ונצורות

¹ Cf. vv. 5, 7, 8 in these parallel chapters.

² Cf. Judg. 20.34: מנגד; Venice 1515 marg.: מנגב.

³ Cf. Gen. 31.25: MT לבן — Var K לכן; Jer. 2.15: MT מבלי — Var K מכלי;

Gen. 43.22: MT אכל — Var K אבל. Only obvious graphic errors are dealt with in this paragraph. On the stylistic difference in the use of the prepositions כ and ב, cf. § 67 on p. 283.

⁴ Cf. Jer. 27.18: MT נא — Var. K בא.

§ 60.   נ – כ.[1]

Gen. 3.2	MT	הַנָּחָשׁ	2 Ki. 14.10		הַכֵּה
	S	הכחש	2 Chron. 25.19		הֵנָּה

§ 61.   כ – פ.

2 Sam. 24.13		נַסֹךְ[2]
1 Chron. 21.12		נִסְפֶּה

§ 62.   נ – פ.

2 Sam. 23.35		פַּעֲרַי
1 Chron. 11.37		נַעֲרַי

D.   THE GROUP הוי

§ 63.   ו – ה.

Ex. 34.31	MT	וַיָּשֻׁבוּ	Gen. 17.21	MT	הָאַחֶרֶת
	S	וישבה		S	ואחרת
Gen. 1.16	MT	וַיַּעַשׂ ··· וְאֶת	Gen. 22.9	MT	הָעֵצִים
	S	היעש ··· האת		S	ועצים
Gen. 7.12, 17	MT	וַיְהִי	Gen. 25.12	MT	הַמִּצְרִית
	S	היהי		S	ומצרית
Gen. 7.23	MT	וַיִּשָּׁאֶר	Ex. 1.10	MT	תִקְרֶאנָה
	S	הישאר		S	תקראנו
Gen. 14.13	MT	וַיַּגֵּד	Ex. 15.1	MT	אָשִׁירָה
	S	היגד		S	אשירו
Gen. 19.2	MT	וַיֹּאמֶר	1 Ki. 10.8		הַשֹּׁמְעִים
	S	היאמר	2 Chron. 9.7		וְשֹׁמְעִים
Gen. 22.24	MT	וְאֶת	2 Sam. 7.23		הָלְכוּ אֱלֹהִים
	S	האת	1 Chron. 17.21		הָלַךְ הָאֱלֹהִים[3]

§ 64.   י – ו.[4]

1 Sam. 22.17	Q	אָבוּ	2 Sam. 22.51	Q	מִגְדּוֹל
	K	אבי		K	מגדיל

---

[1] Cf. Jer. 43.11: MT והכה — Var K והנה.

[2] Lege נסכה; cf. § 41α on p. 265.

[3] Cf. also § 71.

[4] Cf. Codex Petropolitanus, Isa. 14.18: בביתו; further p. 125 ff., s.v. הגית: Ps. 49.4: MT והגות O והגית; s.v. חדל: Ps. 49.9: MT וחדל O יחדל; s.v. כון: Am. 4.12: MT הכון J הכין; s.v. עזר: Ps. 46.6: MT יעזרה O ועזרה.

Jer. 48.18	Q	וּשְׁבִי			
	K	ישבי	a) Proper names.		
Zech. 14.6	Q	וְקִפָּאוֹן	1 Sam. 25.18	Q	אֲבִיגַיִל
	K	יקפאון		K	אבוגיל
Job 10.17	Q	וְצָבָא	Gen. 10.27	MT	אוּזָל
	K	יצבא		S	איזל
2 Ki. 17.13	Q	נְבִיאֵי	Gen. 36.22		וְהֵימָם
	K	נביאו	1 Chron. 1.39		וְהוֹמָם
Isa. 47.13	Q	הֹבְרֵי	Gen. 36.27		וַעֲקָן
	K	הברו	1 Chron. 1.42		יַעֲקָן
Isa. 52.2	Q	מוֹסְרֵי	1 Ki. 10.11		חִירָם
	K	מוסרו	2 Chron. 9.10		חוּרָם
Isa. 60.21	Q	מַטָּעַי	2 Ki. 23.31	Q	חֲמוּטַל
	K	מטעו		K	¹חמיטל
Jer. 48.31	Q	יֶהְגֶּה	2 Sam. 21.16	Q	וְיִשְׁבִּי
	K	והגה		K	וישבו
Jer. 49.12	Q	יִשְׁתּוּ	Gen. 10.28		עוֹבָל
	K	ושתו	1 Chron. 1.22		²עֵיבָל
Ps. 10.10	Q	יִדְכֶּה	Jer. 40.8	Q	עֵיפַי
	K	ודכה		K	עופי
Ps. 102.24	Q	כֹּחִי	Gen. 36.39		פָּעוּ
	K	כחו	1 Chron. 1.50		פָּעִי
Ps. 108.7	Q	וַעֲנֵנִי	Gen. 36.11		צְפוֹ
	K	וענני	1 Chron. 1.36		צְפִי
Ps. 119.79	Q	וְיֹדְעֵי	1 Ki. 16.34		וּבִשְׂגוּב
	K	וידעו		K	ובשגיב
Prov. 11.3	Q	יְשָׁדֵּם	1 Ki. 14.25	Q	שִׁישַׁק
	K	ושדם		K	שושק
Prov. 17.27	Q	יְקַר	Gen. 36.23		שְׁפוֹ
	K	וקר	1 Chron. 1.40		שְׁפִי
Prov. 31.4	Q	אֵי	2 Sam. 8.9		תֹּעִי
	K	או	1 Chron. 18.9		תֹּעוּ

¹ Cf. similarly 2 Ki. 24.18; Jer. 52.1.   ² Cf. MT-S on Gen. 10.28.

§ 65.   ה – י.¹

a) Ex. 3.13 MT אָנֹכִי   Josh. 18.24 Q הָעַמּוֹנָה
             S אנכה   K העמוני

Ex. 28.26 MT שְׁתֵּי   2 Sam. 16.10 Q כֹּה
            S שתה   K כי

Lev. 10.19 MT אֹתִי   Gen. 31.31 MT כִּי
            S אתה   S כה

Lev. 13.52 MT הֻשְׁתִּי   2 Sam. 23.18 Q הַשְּׁלֹשָׁה
            S השתה   K השלשי

Lev. 26.12 MT וְהִתְהַלַּכְתִּי Mic. 6.5 Q מַה
            S והתהלכתה   K מי

b) Lev. 23.19 MT שָׁנָה
             S שני

E. VARIOUS OTHER CONFUSIONS (Cf. MH § 179)

§ 66. 1) ת – א.²

Gen. 4.12 MT תֵּת
          S את   5) ך – ד.³

Gen. 19.32 MT אָבִינוּ   1 Sam. 4.13 Q יַד
           S תבינו   K יך

    2) ג – ו.   6) ה – ם.⁴

2 Sam. 23.36 יִגְאָל   1 Chron. 8.32 שִׁמְאָה
1 Chron. 11.38 יוֹאֵל   1 Chron. 9.38 שִׁמְאָם

    3) ג – ז.   1 Ki. 14.31 אֲבִים

Ezek. 25.7 Q לְבַז   2 Chron. 12.16 אֲבִיָּה
          K לבג   2 Ki. 11.3 אַתָּה

    4) ד – ו.   2 Chron. 22.12 אַתָּם

1 Ki. 12.33 Q מִלְבּוֹ   Isa. 30.32 Q בָּם
          K מלבד   K בה

---

¹ Cf. also p. 245, § 10.
² Cf. Gen. 15.5: MT אם — Var K תם; ib. 31.27: MT נחבאת — Var K נחבתת.
³ Cf. Gen. 4.1: MT ותלד — Var K ותלך.
⁴ Cf. Gen. 9.11: MT יהיה — Var K יהים; ib. 12.10: MT מצרימה — Var K מצרימם; Jer. 38.5: MT הנה — Var K הנם.

Prov. 20.16; 27.13	Q	נָכְרִיָה
	K	נכרים
Isa. 6.13	MT	בָּם
	Seb	בה

7) ז – ן.¹

Isa. 44.14	Q	אָרֶן
	K	ארז
Jer. 39.13	Q	וּבוּשַׁזְבָּן
	K	ונבושזבז
Prov. 16.28	Q	וְנִרְגָּן
	K	ונרגז

8) ח – ת.²

| Eccl. 12.6 | Q | יֵרָתֵק |
| | K | ירחק |

9) ט – שׁ.

| 1 Sam. 14.32 | Q | וַיַּעַט |
| | K | ויעש |

10) י – צ.

Gen. 25.29	MT	וַיָּזֶד
	S	וצוד
Lev. 13.23	MT	הַשְׂחִין
	S	השחצן

11) ך – ן³

| Gen. 47.15 | MT | כְּנַעַן |
| | S | כנעך |

12) ס – כ.

| 1 Ki. 7.40 | | הַכִּירוֹת |
| 2 Chron. 4.11 | | הַסִּירוֹת |

13) ך – ף.

| Gen. 27.13 | MT | אַךְ |
| | S | אף |

14) מ – ת.⁴

| Gen. 4.5 | MT | מִנְחָתוֹ |
| | S | מנחמו |

15) ק – ר.⁵

| Num. 11.12 | MT | תֹאמַר |
| | S | תאמק |

16) ה – ר.

1 Ki. 7.43		עָשֶׂר ... עֲשָׂרָה
2 Chron. 4.14		עָשָׂה ... עָשָׂה
1 Ki. 22.49	Q	עָשָׂה
	K	עשר

17) ן – ט.

| 2 Sam. 23.26 | | הַפַּלְטִי |
| 1 Chron. 11.27 | | הַפְּלוֹנִי |

18) גו – ם.

2 Ki. 22.4		וְיַתֵּם
2 Chron. 34.9		וְיִתְּנוּ
Josh. 5.1	Q	עָבְרָם
	K	עברנו

---

¹ Cf. Codex Petropolitanus: Isa. 9.14: זקן; ib. 23.11: הרגיז and כנען.

² Cf. Gen. 7.23: MT וימחו — Var K וימתו.

³ Cf. Josh. 8.9: וַיֵּלֶן יהושע בלילה ההוא בתוך העם. Josh. 8.13: וַיֵּלֶךְ יהושע בלילה ההוא בתוך העמק.

cf. also Jer. 9.6, 18: MT אִיךְ — Var K אִין.

⁴ Cf. Gen. 42.9, 26; MT את—Var K אם.

⁵ Cf. Judg. 5.15: בפלגות ראובן גדלים חקקי לב. Judg. 5.16: בפלגות ראובן גדלים חקרי לב; cf. also Gen. 7.17: MT ותרם — Var K ותקם.

§ 67.   Confusion of groups of letters.

2 Sam. 23.27	מִבֻּנַּי	2 Sam. 23.30	הִדַּי
I Chron. 11.29	סִבְּכַי ¹	I Chron. 11.32	חוּרַי
2 Sam. 23.36	הַגָּדִי	2 Sam. 23.33	שָׁרָר
I Chron. 11.38	² הַגְרִי	I Chron. 11.35	³ שָׂכָר
2 Sam. 23.35	הַחֶרְדִּי	I Ki. 23.2	וְהַנְּבִיאִים
I Chron. 11.27	הַחֲרוֹרִי	2 Chron. 34.30	⁴ וְהַלְוִיִּם

The following classes of textual confusion can also be assigned to the oversight of the copyists:

§ 68.   Haplography (Bergsträsser § 20e).

Ezek. 7.21	Q (וַהֲסִבֹּתִי) וְחִלְּלוּהוּ	2 Sam. 7.12	כִּי יִמְלְאוּ
	K וחללוה	I Chron. 17.11	⁵ כִּי מָלְאוּ
2 Ki. 20.18	Q (והיו) יֻקְחוּ	2 Sam. 22.15 K	ויהמם
	K יקח	Q	וַיְהֻם

§ 69.   Dittography.

a)   Words.

2 Ki. 11.1	K	(אֲחַזְיָהוּ) וראתה
	Q	רָאָתָה

Ezek. 48.16	K	חֲמֵשׁ חמש
	Q	>
Jer. 51.3	K	אֶל יִדְרֹךְ יִדְרֹךְ
	Q	>

Ezek. 44.3	K	(וַיְבִיאֵנִי) יצאו
	Q	יֵצֵא
Ezek. 46.6	K	(1°) תְּמִימִם
	Q	תמים

b)   Letters. ⁶

2 Ki. 9.33	K (וַיִּשְׁמְטוּהָ) שמטוהו
	Q שְׁמְטוּהָ

c)   With confusion of letters.

2 Ki. 19.23	K	⁷ ברכב (רִכְבִּי)
	Q	בְּרֹב

---

¹ Cf. Jer. 20.8: MT ולקלס — Var. K
ולקלם.
² Cf. §§ 38 and 55.
³ Cf. §§ 44 and 58.
⁴ Cf. §§ 45 and 53.

⁵ For another possible explanation, cf. § 17a on p. 250.
⁶ Cf. Gen. 42.26: MT שברם על — Var
K שברם מעל.
⁷ = Isa. 37.24; on כ—ב cf. § 57.

§ 70. Metathesis (Bergsträsser § 20d). [1] (Cf. MH § 179, sub 4).

Gen. 23.9	MT	קֶבֶר	2 Sam. 22.46		וְיַחְגְּרוּ
	S	קרב	Ps. 18.46		וְיַחְרְגוּ
Gen. 28.20	MT	יַעֲקֹב	2 Ki. 19.29		סָחִישׁ
	S	יעבק	Isa. 37.30		שָׁחִיס
Gen. 47.19	MT	וְהָאֲדָמָה	2 Ki. 20.12		חִזְקִיָּהוּ
	S	והאמדה	Isa. 39.1		וַיֶּחֱזַק
Lev. 13.21	MT	שִׁבְעַת	1 Sam. 27.8	Q	וְהַגִּזְרִי
	S	בשעת		K	והגרזי
Num. 1.38	MT	מִבֶּן	2 Sam. 15.28;	Q	בְּעַרְבוֹת
	S	מנב	17.16	K	בעברות
Num. 4.6	MT	בֶּגֶד	2 Sam. 20.14	Q	וַיִּקָּהֲלוּ
	S	בדג		K	ויקלהו
Num. 7.29	MT	בֶּן	1 Ki. 7.45	Q	הָאֵלֶּה
	S	נב		K	האהל
Num. 21.11	MT	בַּמִּדְבָּר	Isa. 38.11	Q	חָדֶל
	S	במדרב		K	חלד [2]
Deut. 12.17	MT	לֶאֱכֹל	Ezek. 17.7	Q	כנפה
	S	לאלך		K	כָּפְנָה
2 Sam. 23.31		הַבַּרְחָמִי	Ezek. 42.16	Q	מֵאוֹת
1 Chron. 11.33		הַבַּחֲרוּמִי		K	אמות
1 Ki. 8.7		וַיָּסֹכּוּ	Eccl. 9.4	Q	יְחֻבַּר
2 Chron. 5.8		וַיְכַסּוּ		K	יבחר
1 Ki. 10.11		אַלְמֻגִּים			
2 Chron. 9.10		אַלְגּוּמִים			

a) With confusion of one letter.

Josh. 21.20	גּוֹרָלָם
1 Chron. 6.51	גְּבוּלָם [3]
2 Sam. 21.18	וַתְּהִי עוֹד
1 Chron. 20.4	וַתַּעֲמֹד [4]

2 Sam. 22.12	סֻכּוֹת
Ps. 18.12	סֻכָּתוֹ
2 Sam. 22.13	בָּעֲרוּ
Ps. 18.13	עָבְרוּ

[1] Cf. Gen. 27.11: MT שעיר — Var K עשיר; ib. 35.17: MT בהקשתה — Var K בהשקתה; ib. 47.14: MT וילקט — Var K ויקלט.

[2] For another possible explanation of this variant, cf. § 84 on p. 295.

[3] ר–ב, cf. § 54.

[4] מ–ה, cf. § 66 6; on the spelling with or without the matres lectionis, cf. p. 564, §§ 2 and 3.

2 Sam. 23.12	וַיַּעַשׂ	2 Sam. 23.11	עֲדָשִׁים
I Chron. 11.14	¹וַיּוֹשַׁע	I Chron. 11.13	³שְׂעוֹרִים
b) With confusion of two		2 Ki. 8.21	צָעִירָה
letters.		2 Chron. 21.9	⁴עִם שָׂרָיו
2 Sam. 6.5	עֲצֵי בְרוֹשִׁים		
I Chron. 13.8	²עֹז וּבְשִׁירִים		

§ 71. Division of words. (Cf. MH § 178).

2 Sam. 5.2	Q	הָיִיתָ הַמּוֹצִיא		Isa. 9.6	Q	לְמַרְבֵּה
	K	הייתה מוציא			K	לם רבה
I Ki. 20.33	Q	וַיַּחְלְטוּ הֲמִמֶּנּוּ		Job 38.1	Q	מִן הַסְּעָרָה
	K	ויחלטוה ממנו			K	⁵מנהסערה
Jer. 8.4	Q	(אִם) ישובו לא (יָשׁוּב)		Job 40.6	Q	מִן סְעָרָה
	K	יָשׁוּב וְלֹא			K	מנסערה
Ezek. 42.9	Q	וּמְתַחַת הַלְּשָׁכוֹת				
	K	ומתחתה לשכות		b) Resulting in haplography.		
Job 38.12	Q	יִדַּעְתָּ הַשַּׁחַר		Jer. 18.3	Q	וְהִנֵּה הוּא
	K	ידעתה שחר			K	והנהו
a) Involving the final letters				Ezek. 8.6	Q	מָה הֵם
ם and ן.					K	מהם
2 Sam. 21.12	Q	שָׁמָּה פְלִשְׁתִּים		Ps. 123.4	Q	לִגְאֵי יוֹנִים
	K	שם הפלשתים			K	לגאיונים

IV. THE MASORAH AND THE EDITING OF THE BIBLE

A. INTRODUCTION

A. THE MASORETIC BIBLE

The first quarter of the sixteenth century or—to be more exact—the decade from 1515 to 1525 witnessed the publication of two almost equally elaborate editions of the entire Hebrew Bible by one and the same publishing house: Daniel Bomberg in Venice put out the so-called Rabbinic

---

¹ שׂ–שׁ, cf. § 44; on the possibility of the defective spelling of ויושע cf. the instance from 2 Sam. 8.6 on p. 564 § 3a.

² ז–צ, cf. § 41; י–ו, cf. § 64.

³ ר–ד, cf. § 55; שׂ–שׁ, cf. § 44.

⁴ ם–ס, cf. § 66 6; שׂ–שׁ, cf. § 43.

⁵ Cf. I Chron. 27.12: Venice 1515: לָבֶן יְמִינִי, marg.: לְבֶן־יְמִינִי.

Bible in its first edition in the years 1515/17, and a comparatively short time afterwards, in 1524/5, the second edition. All subsequent Bible editions up to our own days were based—or at least claimed to be—cf. p. 418 f., § 7, — upon the second *Biblia Rabbinica*, while the first edition survived merely in well equipped museums and in first class libraries. The reason for the different fates that befell Bomberg's two Bible editions lies in the fact that the second edition was *essentially* different from the first and was published with the express claim of representing the only reliable and trustworthy text of the Hebrew Bible, namely the Masoretic Text.

By the strange workings of fate, Bomberg had met, after the publication of his first Bible edition, Jacob ben Chayim, had given him a job as proofreader in his printing plant, and was finally persuaded by him (though Jacob ben Chayim in his *Introduction* puts it to the effect that it was Bomberg, who took the initiative)—quoting Jacob ben Chayim verbatim— להדפיס כֹּל באופן זה שיהיה עם פירושים ותרגום· ומסרה גדולה וקטנה· וקריין ולא כתבן· וכתבן ולא קריין· ומלאים וחסרים· וכולהו דקדוקי ספרי· ובתר הכי המסרה הגדולה כדרך הערוך· למען ירוץ קורא בה למצוא מבוקשו (see Jacob ben Chayim's *Introduction* towards the beginning. There the text has וקריין וכתבן, which we corrected into וקריין ולא כתבן, cf. the parallel וכתבן ולא קריין, and the later references to this point in the *Introduction*; cf. also the statement in Ned. 37b, to be quoted and discussed shortly, which corroborates our emendation).

This brief outline contains the basic features of the new Bible edition; they were meant to raise its standard from the level of *a* Bible edition to the authority of *the* Bible edition, i. e. the Masoretic Bible. These characteristics are: (1) the inclusion of the מסרה in its two forms, as מסרה גדולה and מסרה קטנה; (2) marginal notes indicating קריין ולא כתבן and כתבן ולא קריין; (3) exactness in the use of the *matres lectionis*, expressed by the terms מלאים and חסרים; and (4) כולהו דקדוקי ספרי. I purposely retained here the original terminology of Jacob ben Chayim, without even attempting to translate or paraphrase it. For any such procedure would subconsciously prejudice us to connect a certain and historically established meaning with each term. We, on the other hand, aim at a new and unbiased investigation of the original meaning of these ancient terms.

In discussing, in his *Introduction*, the importance of these features for the establishment of a correct Bible text, Jacob ben Chayim does not follow the order in which he first listed them. While postponing the enumeration of the many and variegated difficulties in editing the מסרה גדולה וקטנה till the very end, he loses no time in taking up the discussion of the terms concerning קרי וכתיב (number 2 in the list above), in order to clarify their origin and meaning. To this end he first deals with the various theories advanced by scholars of preceding generations, demonstrating their weak points and inadequacies. On the ruins of these shattered theories he then "solves" the problem, not by formulating a new theory of his own, but by plainly denying us the right to apply our reason and judgment to its solution: (scil. of כל אלו התרוצים (השר דון יצחק אברבנאל הם מסברה· ואנן לית לן כי אם תלמודא דילן· אשר קבלנו עלינו· כי לבן של ראשונים כפתחו של אולם· והם אמת ודבריהם אמת. Instead of arguing, Jacob ben Chayim thus merely refers us to the statement in Ned. 37b, where these terms together with references to other Masoretic activities are classed as הלכה למשה מסיני. Now, whatever הלכה למשה מסיני may mean, one thing is surely implied herein: no human argument can prevail against it!

This way of proving his point no doubt fully appealed to Jacob ben Chayim's contemporaries, and even to later generations. Yet one cannot but wonder how Christian D. Ginsburg could base his *Introduction to the Masoretico-critical edition of the Hebrew Bible* which appeared in the year 1897, on Jacob ben Chayim's *Introduction*, without even as much as attempting to analyze critically Jacob ben Chayim's presentation of the problems connected with the Masora, and asking whether arguments, which sounded quite convincing in the early sixteenth century, still hold true in our days of historical-critical approach.

B. A NEW APPROACH

In taking up now the discussion of the problems of the Masora in the same order in which Jacob ben Chayim refers to them, we wish to emphasize, at the very beginning, that we concern ourselves solely with the problems as such and the possibility of their solution, but not with the history of dealing with these problems. To such an extent is the very starting point of all previous researches in this field outdated and obsolete,

and to such an extent have the ancient arguments used as proof pro and
con for the respective theories lost their weight and power in our own
age that, interesting though their study may be to the historian, they
have nothing to offer to the philologian. We, therefore, turn instead right
to *the sources and concentrate on their interpretation*, with our view un-
obstructed by the débris of decayed theories which were based upon late
Masoretic compilations.

B.   THE MASORETIC ACTIVITIES

A.   THE PROBLEM OF כתיב AND קרי

1.   *The Talmudic Statement*

The first reference to the terms כתיב and קרי can be found in Ned. 37b,
a statement which has been referred to already by Jacob ben Chayim. It
reads: אמר רב יצחק מקרא סופרים ועיטור סופרים· וקריין ולא כתיבן· וכתיבן ולא
קריין· הלכה למשה מסיני. The statement continues by giving examples for
each one of the categories mentioned. We postpone the examples for the
terms מקרא סופרים and עיטור סופרים for a later discussion, and proceed to
קריין ולא כתיבן: פרת דבלכתו· איש דכאשר ישאל איש בדבר האלהים· באים דנבנתה·
לה דפליטה· את דההגד הגד· אלי דהגרן· אלי דהשערים· אלין קריין ולא כתבן· וכתבן
ולא קריין: נא דיסלח· זאת דהמצוה· ידרך דהדורך· חמש דפאת נגב· אם דכי גואל
Thus the Talmud explains the term קריין ולא כתיבן by pointing out the
following examples: (1) פרת in connection with the verb בלכתו; (2) איש
in the verse כאשר ישאל איש בדבר האלהים; (3) באים in connection with נבנתה;
(4) לה in connection with פליטה; (5) את in connection with הגד הגד; (6) אלי
in connection with הגרן; and (7) אלי in connection with השערים. These
words represent cases of קריין ולא כתבן. As to the counterpart of this
term, namely the term כתבן ולא קריין, the Talmud again offers the
explanation by way of listing examples. They are the instances of: (1) נא
in connection with יסלח; (2) זאת in connection with המצוה; (3) ידרך in
connection with הדורך; (4) חמש in connection with פאת נגב; and (5) אם in
connection with כי גואל.

2.   *Identification of the Examples of the Talmud*

In commenting upon this Talmudic statement, רבנו ניסים remarks s.v.
את דההגד הגד: ברות· ויען בעז ויאמר לה הגד הגד לי את אשר עשית את חמותך· האי את

קרי ולא כתיב· מיהו בספרים שלנו קרי וכתיב· ואף במסרה לא מדכר ליה בהנך דקריין
ולא כתיבן. He identifies the example את דהגד הגד (cf. above number 5 in the
list of the קריין ולא כתיבן) with Ruth 2.11, but voices his amazement at
the fact that the Talmud considers the את here as קרי ולא כתיב, while his
Bible copy exhibited it as just as regular a word of the text (כתיב and קרי
identical) as any other word. We on our part are puzzled, too;
for in our Bible text את does not occur here at all, neither as קרי nor
as כתיב.

On זאת דהמצוה (cf. above number 2 in the list of the כתבן ולא קריין), Rashi
remarks: כתיב בירמיה. But רבנו ניסים under the same heading says: בסדר
ואתחנן· כך מצאתי כתוב· ולא נמצא בספרים שלנו. Rashi's indication that this
passage is to be found in Jeremiah, is rather vague; and R. Nissim's
remark is even by far less satisfactory: he saw a note giving the weekly
portion ואתחנן (Deut. 3.23-7.11) as the location of this passage, but could
not locate it there himself.

The oldest Hebrew Bible manuscript in existence, which exhibits a
reference to the terms now under discussion, is the Codex Petropolitanus
(written in 916/7 C.E.). In practically identical Masoretic notes on Jer.
39.12 and Ezek. 48.16 it states: חד מן ח מלין דכתבין ולא קריין· וסימנך: אם
במקום· אם אמנון· אם כאשר· אם גאל· נא יייי· את אשר· ידרך הדרך· חמש דנגב. We see
that here the five examples of the Talmud have increased in number and
become eight. But, to our dismay, we notice that, of the five original
examples of the Talmud, only four (nos. 1, 3, 4 and 5 of our list above)
survived and were incorporated in this Masoretic note; זאת דהמצוה (above
number 2) has been displaced by את אשר; and three more new items
make their appearance, which offer the word אם as a common feature
(אם כאשר and אם אמנון, אם במקום).

The discrepancy in the number and choice of instances between the
Talmudic statement and the Masoretic note in the Codex Petropolitanus
might be explained by assuming that either source intended merely to
examplify the term, but did not aim at presenting us with a complete list
of such cases. Of course, the fact that the Codex Petropolitanus explicitly
limits the number of cases to eight seems to exclude such an explanation.
But an even more startling fact remains unaccounted for: that of the 12
instances mentioned in the Talmud, R. Nissim already found himself
unable to locate two. This reflects in a strange way on the attention which

post-Talmudic Jewry paid to a phenomenon which the Talmud itself characterized as הלכה למשה מסיני.

3. *The Solution of the Problem*

The identification of the remaining ten Talmudic instances could easily be ascertained with the help of a concordance. So e.g. פרת דבלכתו (cf. above number 1 in the list of the קריין ולא כתיבן) was identified as referring to 2 Sam 8.3, where our Bible text reads: בְּלֶכְתּוֹ להשיב ידו בנהר ; a Masoretic note here informs us that the open space with the vowel-signs , , is reserved for the word פרת, which is קרי ולא כתיב. We thus have פרת in connection with the verb בלכתו, as the Talmud stipulates it. Simple and convincing though this identification sounds, we have grave objections against it: The Talmudic assertion is centuries older than the Masoretic note on 2 Sam. 8.3 and than the invention of the vowel-signs. In Talmudic days there were no , , to keep the space open for the oral insertion of an unwritten word, and also no Masoretic note to instruct the reader what word to insert. Hence, vocalization and Masoretic note must not be brought up as arguments in our search for the locating of the passage פרת דבלכתו.

The historic events as narrated in 2 Sam. 8 are once again retold in 1 Chron. 18. With the differences in the choice of words, the morphology and syntax between these two narratives of identical events I have dealt exhaustively in ch. 0. We now compare the *consonantal text* of verse three in these sources: 2 Sam. 8.3 reads בְּלֶכְתּוֹ להשיב ידו בנהר ; 1 Chron. 18.3 reads: בְּלֶכְתּוֹ להציב ידו בנהר פְּרָת. (On the variant להציב – להשיב cf. p. 479, § 43). And now let us interpret the Talmudic statement on the basis of this parallel passage: The Talmud states that קרי ולא כתיב is פרת דבלכתו; actually we find that פרת in connection with the verb בלכתו is offered by Chron., but not by Sam. We may formulate our findings by way of an equation: According to the Bible, פרת in connection with בלכתו is offered in Chron., but not in Sam.; according to the Talmud, פרת in connection with בלכתו is offered in קרי, but not in כתיב. The conclusion is: *Chron. represents the* קרי*-text, and Sam. the* כתיב*-text.* And while stating that פרת דבלכתו is קרי ולא כתיב, the Talmud meant to indicate: in connection with the verb בלכתו, Chronicles has the noun פרת, while Samuel does not have it. The Biblical passage 2 Sam. 8.3 would, therefore, have to be read as: בלכתו

לְהָשִׁיב יָדוֹ בַּנָּהָר (and not vocalized בִּנְהָר). The noun הַנָּהָר (with the article) instead of נְהַר פְּרָת, is often used to describe the Euphrates; cf. Ex. 23.31: וַיִּשְׁלַח Num. 22.5: וְשַׁתִּי אֶת גְּבֻלְךָ מִיַּם סוּף וְעַד יָם פְּלִשְׁתִּים וּמִמִּדְבָּר עַד הַנָּהָר; מַלְאָכִים אֶל בִּלְעָם פְּתוֹרָה אֲשֶׁר עַל הַנָּהָר Deut. 11.24: מִן הַנָּהָר נְהַר פְּרָת; cf. similarly the use of הַיְאֹר for the Nile.

Formulating our findings on a broader basis, we now state: The history of the kingdom of Judah is told twice in our Bible: in the Former Prophets (from 1 Sam. 31 on) and in Chronicles (from 1 Chron. 10 on). We disregard as later additions the paraphrases and interpolations of the original strictly historic narrative, which occupies approximetely 470 verses in more or less identical form (cf. ch. 0) in each of the parallel sources. The Talmud—or the ancient source whence the Talmud derived its information—designated with כתיב *that recension of historic narrative, which is now included in the Former Prophets*, while קרי *was applied to the other recension, which Chronicles now exhibits*. The problem as to whether the Talmud has the terms כתיב and קרי from his ancient source, or whether they already represent a confusion of a later generation, when the original meaning of the genuine symbols had been forgotten and was subsequently replaced by a later popular explanation (cf. similarly תֹא: originally for תרגום ארמי, later explained as: תרגום אונקלוס; or תֹי: originally meaning: תרגום ירושלמי, later misunderstood as: תרגום יונתן) is irrelevant for our investigation. On the connotation which these terms כתיב and קרי carry in the mediaeval Masoretic terminology, cf. §§ 6-8, 12c and 17c in C.

4. The Solution Tested on Parallel Historic Narratives

a. Samuel, Kings, and Chronicles

If our contention be correct that the historic *Annales* in the recension of the Former Prophets are meant by כתיב, and in that of Chronicles by קרי, then we should be able to verify it on more examples than just the one of פרת דבלכתו, which the Talmud mentions. Theoretically reasoning we would say: whenever a Masoretic note appears on a word in a verse of the Former Prophets, which belongs to these *Annales* (that means: the Bible offers this verse twice; in the Former Prophets and in the respective parallel passage in Chronicles), stating that the spelling of the text represents the כתיב, while the קרי has it differently, we should expect the parallel passage in Chronicles to offer this word in exactly the same way as the Masoretic note stipulates for the קְרִי. This theoretical demand is fully corroborated by the facts. In order to prove this highly essential point I shall list all the passages in the *Annales* (as defined above) which have Masoretic notes regarding the כתיב and קרי, with constant reference to the textual reading of the parallel passage. The material is derived from both Bible editions, the *Biblia Hebraica* ed. Kittel-Kahle and Jacob ben Chayim's second edition of the *Biblia Rabbinica*. As a rule they agree in their application of the terms כתיב and קרי, so that I do not have to bring their sigla. Only when such a Masoretic note has but one of these Bible editions as a basis, do I put its symbol to indicate the source. I consistently vocalize the קְרִי-word:

2 Sam. 5.2:   K מוציא
               Q הַמּוֹצִיא = 1 Chron. 11.2

2 Sam. 5.2:   K והמבי
               Q וְהַמֵּבִיא = 1 Chron. 11.2

2 Sam. 5.24:   K בשמעך
               Q כְּשָׁמְעֲךָ = 1 Chron. 14.15

2 Sam. 8.3 as compared with 1 Chron. 18.3, cf. above p. 495.

2 Sam. 21.21: K שמעי
               Q (Ven) שִׁמְעָא = 1 Chron. 20.7; the Q (BHKK) is: שִׁמְעָה; cf. p. 563, § 1 b.

2 Sam. 23.8:   K אחד
               Q אֶחָת = 1 Chron. 11.11

2 Sam. 23.9:   K ואחרו
               Q וְאַחֲרָיו = 1 Chron. 11.12

2 Sam. 23.9:   K דדי
               Q דֹדוֹ = 1 Chron. 11.12; the spelling in Chron. is plene (דודו), cf. ch. 0, § 00.

2 Sam. 23.9:   K גברים
               Q הַגִּבֹּרִים = 1 Chron. 11.12

2 Sam. 23.13: K שלשים
               Q שְׁלֹשָׁה = 1 Chron. 11.15; the spelling in Chron. is plene (שלושה), cf. p. 564, § 3.

2 Sam. 23.15,　　K מבאר

16, 20:　　Q (Ven) מִבֹּר = 1 Chron. 11.17, 18, 22; the spelling in Chron. is plene (מבור), cf. p. 564, § 3.

2 Sam. 23.18:　　K השלשי

　　Q הַשְּׁלֹשָׁה = 1 Chron. 11.20 the spelling in Chron. is plene (השלושה), cf. p. 564, § 3.

2 Sam. 23.20:　　K חי

　　Q חַיִל = 1 Chron. 11.22

2 Sam. 23.20:　　K האריה

　　Q הָאֲרִי = 1 Chron. 11.22

2 Sam. 23.21:　　K אשר

　　Q אִישׁ = 1 Chron. 11.23

2 Sam. 23.37　　K נשאי

　　Q נֹשֵׂא = 1 Chron. 11.39

2 Sam. 24.14:　　K רחמו

　　Q רַחֲמָיו = 1 Chron. 21.13

2 Sam. 24.22:　　K בעינו

　　Q בְּעֵינָיו = 1 Chron. 21.23

1 Ki. 7.23:　　K וקוה

　　Q וְקָו = 2 Chron. 4.2

1 Ki. 8.26:　　K דבריך

　　Q דְּבָרְךָ = 2 Chron. 6.17

1 Ki. 8.48:　　K בנית

　　Q (BHKK) בָּנִיתִי = 2 Chron. 6.38; the Masoretic note in Ven: בנית קׄ· יֹב חסׄ יׄ בסוף תיבו וקרי shows that בנית קׄ is a misprint for בניתי קׄ, too. (Cf. later p. 537, § 13).

1 Ki. 9.9:　　K וישתחו

　　Q וַיִּשְׁתַּחֲווּ = 2 Chron. 7.22

1 Ki. 9.18:　　K תמר

　　Q תַּדְמֹר = 2 Chron. 8.4

1 Ki. 10.5:　　K משרתו

　　Q מְשָׁרְתָיו = 2 Chron. 9.4

1 Ki. 12.3:　　K ויבאו

　　Q (BHKK) וַיָּבֹא = 2 Chron. 10.3

1 Ki. 12.7:　　K וידבר

　　Q וַיְדַבְּרוּ = 2 Chron. 10.7

1 Ki. 12.12:   K ויבו

            Q וַיָּבֹא = 2 Chron. 10.12

1 Ki. 12.21:   K ויבאו

            Q וַיָּבֹא = 2 Chron. 11.1

1 Ki. 14.25:   K שושק

            Q שִׁישַׁק = 2 Chron. 12.2

1 Ki. 22.13:   K דבריך

            Q דְּבָרְךָ = 2 Chron. 18.12

2 Ki. 8.17:   K שנה

            Q שָׁנִים = 2 Chron. 21.5

2 Ki. 11.1:   K וראתה

            Q רָאֲתָה = 2 Chron. 22.10

2 Ki. 11.2:   K הממותתים

            Q הַמּוּמָתִים = 2 Chron. 22.11

2 Ki. 11.4,   K המאיות

  10, 15:   Q הַמֵּאוֹת = 2 Chron. 23.1, 9, 14

2 Ki. 11.18:   K מזבחתו

            Q מִזְבְּחֹתָיו = 2 Chron. 23.17

2 Ki. 14.2:   K יהועדין

            Q יְהוֹעַדָּן = 2 Chron. 25.1

2 Ki. 14.12:   K לאהלו

            Q לְאֹהָלָיו = 2 Chron. 25.22

vice-versa:

1 Chron. 14.1:   K חִירָם = 2 Sam. 5.11

            Q חוּרָם; thus, the reading of the parallel passage in the
            Former Prophets is termed here כתיב in Chron.

The only exceptions are the following three instances, in which Chronicles exhibits textual readings which are termed כתיב in the Former Prophets:

2 Sam. 10.9:   K בְּיִשְׂרָאֵל = 1 Chron. 19.10
            Q יִשְׂרָאֵל

2 Sam. 23.35:   K חֶצְרוֹ = 1 Chron. 11.37
            Q חֶצְרַי

2 Ki. 22.5:   K בְּבֵית = 2 Chron. 34.10
            Q בֵּית.

These cases may be taken as an indication of the fact that the form in which the original *Annales* appear in the Hebrew Bible, represents an already mixed type. This explanation is further substantiated by a few cases, in which the Masoretic note concerning כתיב and קרי occurs in the Chronicles passage, while it is the corresponding parallel verse in the Former Prophets, which exhibits the קרי-reading as its text:

I Chron. 11.20: K ולא
                 Q וְלוֹ = 2 Sam. 23.18
I Chron. 14.10: K פלשתיים
                 Q (BHKK) תִּים (= פְּלִשְׁתִּים) = 2 Sam. 5.19
I Chron. 18.10: K לשאול
                 Q (BHKK) לִשְׁאָל = 2 Sam. 8.10
2 Chron. 18.8:   K מיכהו
                 Q מִיכָיְהוּ = I Ki. 22.8
2 Chron. 18.33: K ידיך
                 Q (BHKK) יָדְךָ =I Ki. 22.34
2 Chron. 25.17: K לך
                 Q (BHKK) לְכָה = 2 Ki. 14.8
2 Chron. 26.21: K החפשות
                 Q הַחָפְשִׁית = 2 Ki. 15.5

b.   2 Ki. 18-20 and Isa. 36-39

The incidents told in 2 Ki. 18.13, 17-37; 19.1-37; 20.1-6, 9, 11b-19 are narrated again in Isa. 36.1-22; 37.1-38; 38.1-8; 39.1-8. In 2 Chron. 32 we have merely a short abstract of these narratives, which can in no way be considered as a parallel to the reports of 2 Ki. We find ourselves thus confronted with a new problem: what place does the narrative in Isa. occupy in comparison with that of 2 Ki.? An examination of the relation of this text to the Masoretic notes on 2 Ki. concerning כתיב and קרי will furnish us with a clue towards the solution of this problem:

2 Ki. 19.23:   K ברכב
                 Q בְּרֹב = Isa. 37.24
2 Ki. 19.23:   K קצה
                 Q (Ven) קִצּוֹ = Isa. 37.24
2 Ki. 19.31:   K vacant
                 Q צְבָאוֹת (קרי ולא כתיב) = Isa. 37.32

2 Ki. 19.37:   K vacant

                Q בָּנָיו (קרי ולא כתיב) = Isa. 37.38

2 Ki. 20.18:   K יקח

                Q יְקָחוּ = Isa. 39.7

There is only one instance, in which Isa. offers a Masoretic note of כתיב and קרי; and here the parallel in 2 Ki. has the קרי-reading:

Isa. 37.30:   K ואכול

             Q וְאִכְלוּ = 2 Ki. 19.29

I would not lay too much stress on the evidence of this instance. I feel by no means sure that this Masoretic note is based upon sound tradition. For it is quite possible that we have here rather a confusion of the sources similar to the case of 2 Ki. 20.13 and its parallel Isa. 39.2, where BHKK and Ven differ as to where the Masoretic note rightly belongs:

BHKK: Isa. 39.2:   K נכתה

                Q נְכֹתוֹ; but 2 Ki. 20.13 merely

                נְכֹתֹה without any Masoretic note.

Ven: 2 Ki. 20.13:   K נכתה

                Q נְכֹותוֹ; but Isa. 39.2 merely

                נְכֹתֹה without a Masoretic note.

We may, therefore, sum up the result of our investigation by stating that *the reports in Isa. 36-39 are of the* קרי *type and that consequently their proper place would be within the framework of Chronicles.*

5. *The Hebrew Bible in Two Recensions*

Our investigation has led us to the relization that in the ancient source from which the Talmudic statement in Ned. 37b emanated, כתיב and קרי (or whatever form these symbols originally had) were used to indicate variants between the two recensions of historic narrative as contained in the Former Prophets (כתיב) and Chronicles (קרי). An apparent gap in the narrative of Chronicles could be filled by pointing to the chapters 36-39 in Isa.

The Masoretic notes on כתיב and קרי do in no way represent an exhaustive list of these differences between the two recensions. I refer to p. 235 ff. for an adequate treatment of this problem: identification of the variants and their explanation by way of grouping and classification. The preceding investigation furnishes the methodical justification of my procedure there in basing it upon the three parallel sources as defined in the introductory remarks (p. 234). The fact that we possess Masoretic notes on כתיב and קרי for all Biblical books, while the parallel passages of our Hebrew Bible are limited mainly to the narration of certain historic events, may be taken as evidence that, originally, considerably larger portions of the Bible were transmitted in two recensions, but were subsequently withdrawn in the course of redactional developments. The fate of the parallel recension of the Pentateuch makes our explanation plausible: It is not much more than two centuries since the Hebrew Pentateuch of the Samaritans was discovered and became available to scholarship. This text represents—as demonstrated on p. 235 ff. parallel recension of our Masoretic Pentateuch, which prior to this discovery was all we had of the Pentateuch in Hebrew. I already proved that "we shall have to assume that the Samaritan Hebrew Bible originally included the entire Old Testament" (p. 367). It now becomes clear that *the three sources in two recensions, upon which* p. 234 ff., *is based, are in reality three fragments of one and the same genuine source, consisting of major portions of the Hebrew Bible in two recensions.*

These two recensions differed from one another in very many details. These variants are dealt with on p. 235 f., they reflect differences in the vocabulary, morphology, and syntax. According to the results obtained there, the basic sources can be divided into two groups; the members of each group have certain linguistic or dialectic phenomena in common, as against the members of the other group. Of course, no division can claim to be correct in each and every detail, since we possess the basic texts only in a later form, which is of an already mixed type; but in general I hope to be correct. Recension A is represented by: 1) the Masoretic Pentateuch; 2) the parallel passages in Chronicles, and 3) קרי-readings. Recension B is evidenced by: 1) the Samaritan Pentateuch; 2) the parallel passages in Samuel and Kings; and 3) כתיב-readings.

In support of these results, I should now like to refer to the conclusions I arrived at on p. 336 ff. with regard to the sources of the Old Testament in Greek. I could prove there the previous existence of two independent Greek Bible translations of the Septuagint-type, which in turn were based upon two different Hebrew Bibles. As far as the Pentateuch in Greek is concerned, these two different Hebrew *Vorlagen* may be identified as more or less represented by the Masoretic and Samaritan Pentateuch, respectively (cf. especially p. 364 ff., and the concluding remarks on p. 397). In other words, the Hebrew Bible—or at least very considerable portions thereof—was originally known in two recensions, which in their turn even served as bases for two respective translations into Greek.

On the *terminus ad quem*, how long these recensions continued their separate existence, and at what approximate period we might fix the time of their final merger into the one Hebrew Bible (which in certain parallel chapters still preserves the original two-recensional character), cf. p. 401 ff.

6. *The Examples of the Talmud Re-interpreted*

I am under the impression that the instances which the Talmud lists in Ned. 37b in order to explain the terms כתיב and קרי do not represent just casual variants, but were deliberately chosen so as to illustrate some of the characteristic differences between the two types or recensions of the original Hebrew Bible:

פרת דבלכתו reflects the use of הַנָּהָר or נְהַר פְּרָת for the Euphrates; cf. p. 496.

איש דכאשר ישאל איש בדבר האלהים: the indefinite pronoun "one" (German: man) is expressed in Hebrew by איש or merely by the 3rd person of the predicative verb; cf. Ex. 10.23: ולא קמו איש מתחתיו with ib. verse 5: ולא יוכל לראת את הארץ. In terming this use of איש as קרי ולא כתיב, the Talmud—according to our interpretation—wishes to indicate that Recension A has it, but not Recension B. On p. 364 ff. in conjunction with p. 397, I proved the close interconnection between the Samaritan Pentateuch and the obelus-type, and between the Masoretic Pentateuch and the asterisk-type of the Septuagint. With the results of our discussion in the preceding paragraph in mind, we may claim the asterisk-type for Recension A, and the obelus-type for Recension B. And now we can illustrate the Talmudic example under discussion by way of reference to Origen's Hexapla. We note here the following instances, which have this particular use of אִישׁ in common with the passages, which the Talmud quotes:

Deut. 28.54: הָאִישׁ הָרַךְ :O′: ※ ο ανηρ ✕ ο απαλος;

2 Ki. 18.31: וּשְׁתוּ אִישׁ :O′: και πιεται ※ ανηρ;

Isa. 36.6: אֲשֶׁר יִסָּמֵךְ אִישׁ עָלָיו :O′: ως αν επιστηρισθη ※ ανηρ ✕ επ αυτην.

In these cases, אִישׁ signifies "someone"; its Greek equivalent ανηρ is quoted *sub asterisco*, which means: it was added on the evidence of a Septuagint text which was based upon a Hebrew Bible of the Recension A-type. This shows that the usage of אִישׁ in this meaning is typical for Recension A, in accordance with our interpretation of the Talmud.

אֶת דהגד הגד: *the use of the nota accusativi* אֶת *to indicate the verbal object is termed* קרי ולא כתיב. I must confess that the examples which I listed on p. 288, § 76 lead to the assumption of the contrary, namely that the use of אֶת is characteristic of Recension B (and not A). It is, therefore, perhaps significant that the example אֶת דהגד הגד, which the Talmud quotes, finds no support in the reading of our Bible (cf. also רבנו ניסים's remark, quoted here on p. 493 f.). Similarly אלי דהגרן and אלי דהשערים: the use of אל with verbs of speech (with reference to תאמרי in Ruth 3.5, and אמר ib. verse 17) is termed קרי ולא כתיב. But on p. 286, § 74c, we could show it to be a characteristic feature of Recension B. Whether the Talmud erroneously listed these instances under the wrong heading, I dare not assert, though the number of examples listed under קריין ולא כתיבן, seven, seems to suggest that the last two are not genuine; the preceding term עיטור סופרים and the following term כתבן ולא קריין have only five examples each. The Munich Ms. reads אֶת דהשעורי׳ (instead of אלי דהשערים). However, it is enough for me to have so plainly pointed to the only existing difficulty in the application of my theory.

נא דיסלח: the addition of the particle נא to stress the meaning of supplication (referring to 2 Ki. 5.18) is termed כתיב ולא קרי. In our own terminology we would call it: characteristic of Recension B (as against A); cf. p. 293, § 81 b 5, where this one example finds further support in an additional number of similar cases listed there.

זאת דהמצוה: whether or not the article includes the meaning of a demonstrative pronoun. The reference can not be located (cf. the quotations from רש״י and רבנו ניסים on p. 494), but its implication is clear: המצוה הזאת or המצוה; the choice of the noun מצוה is obviously irrelevant. The use of the demonstrative pronoun in addition to the article is termed כתיב ולא קרי, hence: typical for Recension B. Cf. p. 273, § 52, where I could list further evidence for this characteristic feature of Recension B.

אם דכי גואל: the use of כי אם or simply כי in the meaning "but" (with reference to Ruth 3.12) is termed כתיב ולא קרי, i.e. particular for Recension B. Cf. p. 292, § 81b 3 and the notes 6 and 7 thereon, where this assertion finds further substantiation.

As to the examples of the Masoretic note in the Codex Petropolitanus, which we quoted above p. 494, they contain in addition to Ruth 3.12 (which is cited there as אם גאל) three more instances of this characteristic difference: אם במקום (2 Sam. 15.21), אם אמנך (2 Sam. 13.33) and אם כאשר (Jer. 39.12). In these cases, אם is preceded by כי.

The cases of ידרך דהדורך (Jer. 51.3) and חמש דפאת נגב (Ezek. 48.16) are merely examples for dittography; cf. p. 488, § 69.

Of a similar nature—examplifying the interchangeability of certain letters—is the כתיב and קרי referred to in Sanh. 20a: דרש רבא׳ מאי דכתיב: ויבא כל העם להכרות את דוד? כתיב להכרות וקרינן להברות! בתחלה להכרותו ולבסוף להברותו. Here the verse 2 Sam. 3.35 is expounded in a midrashic way, which is based upon the observation that the text has a כתיב the reading להכרות, and as קרי the word להברות instead. While our Bible, which goes back to Jacob ben Chayim's edition (cf. p. 490 f.), offers להברות without any Masoretic note thereon, the first Rabbinic Bible, Venice 1515/7, has here as text-reading actually להכרות and as marginal note להברות. Thus, the textual basis for the statement of the Talmud is fully substantiated; for the fact that the Venice 1515/7 edition brings להברות merely as a marginal note, without classing it as קרי, can not be used as an argument against this evidence, since this edition lists the marginal notes anonymously throughout and does not use the term קרי in order to differentiate between them. Now, the only difference between these two readings, which the Talmud styles כתיב and קרי respectively, is the interchange between כ and ב; cf. p. 483, § 57. Consequently, this case reflects, like the two cases from Ned. 37b mentioned last, merely the paleographic condition of the Bible manuscripts of those days, and is of no consequence for the solution of the problem of כתיב and קרי now under investigation.

For a similar case in the Talmud, where the explanation of a Bible verse is based on an interchange between כ and ב as compared with our Bible, cf. Ber. 7b: רב הונא רמי: כתיב לענותו· וכתיב לכלותו? בתחלה לענותו· ולבסוף לכלותו. "R. Huna tried to reconcile the difference in the expression which the Bible uses with regard to the future of Israel. In 2 Sam. 7.10 it is written: 'and the children of wickedness shall not *afflict it* any more'; but in the parallel narrative 1 Chron. 17.9 the word *destroy it* is written instead. This reflects the evil intentions of these children of wickedness towards Israel: first they aim only at affliction, but finally at complete destruction of Israel." The basis of this explanation is the reading לכלותו in the passage 1 Chron. 17.9. But our Bible has לְבַלֹתוֹ here, and thus cannot have been the *Vorlage* of the Talmud. On the interchangeability of the letters כ and ב, cf. p. 483, § 57.

Phonetic confusions, too, sometimes play a role in such midrashic explanations of the Talmud; cf. Sanh. 103a: אמר רבי יוחנן משום רבי שמעון בר יוחאי· מאי דכתיב: ויתפלל אליו ויחתר לו? ויעתר לו מיבעי ליה! מלמד שעשה לו הקב״ה כמין מחתרת ברקיע· כדי לקבלו בתשובה מפני מדת הדין. "R. Johanan said on the authority of R. Simeon b. Johai: What is meant by: "and he prayed unto Him and an opening was made for him" (2 Chron. 33.13)? Should not "and was entreated of Him" rather have been written?—This teaches that the Holy One blessed be He made for him a kind of opening in the Heavens in order to accept him with his repentance, on account of the Attribute of Justice, which was against it." This is based on a reading ויחתר; but our Bible actually offers ויעתר which—according to the Talmud—*should* have been written there! On the interchange between ח and ע due to the similarity of their phonetic value, cf. p. 478, § 40.

B.　THE PROBLEM OF מלאים וחסרים

7.　*The Talmudic Statement*

The uncertainty in matters of spelling Hebrew words: whether and when to apply the vowel-letters to indicate the respective vowel, finds its clear expression in Ḳid. 30a (cf. the parallels in Rabbinic literature in Higger's מסכת סופרים, chapter IX, section 2): לפיכך נקראו ראשונים סופרים·

שהיו סופרים כל האותיות שבתורה· שהיו אומרים: ואי'ו דגָּחוֹן חצין של אותיות של ספר
תורה ··· בעי רב יוסף: ואי'ו דגָּחוֹן מהאי גיסא או מהאי גיסא? אמרו ליה: ליתי ספר
תורה ולימנינהו! מי לא אמר רבה בר בר חנה: לא זזו משם עד שהביאו ספר תורה ומנאום?
אמר להון: אינהו בקיאי בחסירות ויתרות· אנןלא בקיאין. "The early scholars were
called *soferim* (cf. I Chron. 2.55), because they used to count all the letters
of the Torah. Thus they said: The *waw* in גָּחוֹן (Lev. 11.42) marks half the
letters of the Torah .... R. Joseph propounded: Does the *waw* in גָּחוֹן
belong to the first half or the second? Said the scholars to him: Let a
Scroll of the Torah be brought, and we will count them! Did not Rabbah
b. Bar Ḥanah say (on a similar occasion): They did not stir from there
until a Scroll of the Torah was brought and they counted them? Answered
he to the scholars: *They were thoroughly versed in the defective and plene
spellings, but we are not.*"

This general statement is being corroborated by Talmudic references
to the spelling of specific words. In Ket. 5a we read: השיב בבלי אחד· ורבי
חייא שמו: ויבשת ידיו יצרו· ידו כתיב. "Here a Babylonian scholar interrupted
the discourse (of a Palestinian colleague) and his name was R. Ḥiyya by
referring to the verse Ps. 95.5, where God's hands are spoken of (in connection with the creation) as a plural: ידיו. He got the reply: the actual
spelling of the word in question in the text is defective: ידו, thus implying
a singular." This statement contrasts with the *plene*-spelling in our Bible!

The Palestinian Talmud, too, contains evidence for this fact that at that
early period, the spelling differed from the one which our Bible has
adopted; cf. Yer. Ber. VII, 11c: מה מקיימין רבנן טעמא דרבי יוסי הגלילי?
במקהלות· בכל קהילה וקהילה· אמר רבי חנינא בריה דרבי אבהו: במקהלת כתיב
"How will the Rabbis explain the argument of R. Josse ha-Gelili? The
answer is: The plural במקהלות (Ps. 68.27) has collective meaning, em-
bracing the multitude of single communities. To this R. Ḥanina the son
of R. Abahu replied: Your supposition is wrong, because the word is
spelled *defective* as במקהלת (thus implying a singular)." But our Bible has
the word in *plene* spelling!

The controversy in the Talmud, whether יש אם למקרא or יש אם למסרת:
whether we are guided in our conclusions by the pronunciation (מקרא) or
the spelling (מסרת) of a given word in the Bible, sheds light on our problem, too; cf. Sanh. 4a: רבי ורבי יהודה בן רועץ ובית שמאי ורבי שמעון ורבי
עקיבא· כולהו סבירא להו: יש אם למקרא ··· בית שמאי דתנן ··· ואמר רב הונא: מאי

טעמא דבית שמאי? קרנות· קרנות· קרנות· הרי כאן שש ··· ובית הלל אומר: קרנות· קרנת·
קרנת· הרי כאן ארבע. "Rabbi and R. Judah b. Ro'ez, the Shammaites,
R. Simeon and R. Akiba, all hold that the pronunciation of the word is
determinant in Biblical exposition ... R. Huna said: What basis in the
Bible text have the Shammaites for their opinion? The answer is: The
word קרנות, meaning horns of the altar, occurs three times in the context
(Lev. 4.25, 30, 34) and, being pronounced *ḳarnoth*, as a plural, each
occurrence implies two sprinklings; that makes six altogether ... But the
Hillelites argue from the way the word in question is spelled: twice
defective, implying only one sprinkling each, and once *plene*; this makes
four sprinklings altogether." This reference to the spelling of the word is
in open contrast with our Bible, where all three occurrences appear in
defective spelling.

Similarly we read in Sanh. 4b: ודכולי עלמא יש אם למקרא? והתניא: לטטפת·
לטטפת· לטטפות· הרי_כאן ארבע· דברי רבי ישמעאל. "But do all, indeed, regard
the pronunciation of the word as determinant? Has it not been taught:
The word for "frontlets" occurs three times in the Torah, twice in *defective*
spelling, implying only one section each, and once *plene*, thus indicating
altogether the four sections, into which the phylacteries are to be
divided." The word occurs Ex. 13.16; Deut. 6.8 and Deut. 11.18. The
controversy here refers to the spelling of the ending of the word: whether
plene ות, thus necessitating us to see in it a plural-form, or *defective* ת,
classing it as a singular. Against this statement of R. Ismael cf. our Bible,
where the word is spelled in all three instances with a *defective* ending ת.

8. *Rashi and Tosaphot*

In the Talmudic statement quoted last, R. Ismael does not explain
which of the three occurrences of לטטפת is spelled *plene*, and which
defective. In commenting upon this passage, Rashi identifies them by
saying: בפרשת שמע ובפרשת כי יביאך כתיב לטטפת חסר וי"ו· אבל בפרשת והיה
אם שמוע כתיב לטוטפות מלא· הרי כאן ד' בתים לתפילין של ראש. "In Deut. 6 and
in Ex. 13 the word is spelled לטטפת, *defective*, implying a singular; but
in Deut. 11 that word appears *plene* as לטוטפות, thus indicating a plural.
Hence we derive the law of the four divisions for the frontlet." We thus
see that in this particular controversial instance, Rashi's Bible had
preserved the same reading as that which we have to surmise for the

Talmudic period. But already his grandson's Bible exhibited in this passage the reading of our own Bible (as against Talmud and Rashi); cf. ·תוספות דה לטטפת לטטפת לטוטפות: תימא· דלא כתיב וי״ו בין פ״ה לתי״ו בכולהו "R. Ismael's conclusion is surprising, since in none of the three passages is there a *waw* between the פ and ת (to indicate the *plene* spelling of the ending)."

Even more outspoken in underlining the apparent discrepancy between Biblical quotations in the Talmud and the respective text-readings in their proper places in the Bible itself, is another marginal gloss on Shab. 55b. Here the Talmud asserts: והכתיב מעבירים? אמר רב הונא בריה דרב יהושע: מעבירם כתיב. "But it is written (I Sam. 2.24): 'ye (scil. plural) cause the Lord's people to transgress'? To this replied R. Huna the son of R. Joshua: It is written: 'he (singular) causes them to transgress'." The interpretation of R. Huna is based upon the spelling of the word. According to his assertion which arose no contradiction, the spelling of the ending is defective (merely ם, and not ים), and implies that the subject is in the singular. The Tosaphot avail themselves of this opportunity of an obvious difference between the Bible text itself and the quotation in the Talmud, to point out another similar case: cf. תוספות דה מעבירם כתיב: השׂ שלנו חולק על הספרים שלנו· שכתוב בהם מעבירים· וכן מציגו בירושלמי בשמשון: והוא שפט את ישראל ארבעים שנה· מלמד שהיו פלשתים יראים ממנו עשרים שנה אחר מותו כמו בחייו· ובכל הספרים שלנו כתיב: עשרים שנה. "The Talmud text disagrees with our Bible text which offers the reading מעבירים (in I Sam. 2.24), implying a plural. Similarly we find a discrepancy between the Palestinian Talmud text and our Bible text in the case of Samson. The Palestinian Talmud quotes Judg. 16.31 as: 'And he judged Israel forty years.' The apparent contradiction between this indication and that of Judg. 15.20, where Samson's period of rule is given as twenty years, is explained in this fashion: hence the Philistines dreaded him for twenty years after his death just as in his lifetime. But our Bible text has both in Judg. 16.31 and 15.20 equally 'twenty years'." Thus the Talmudic interpretation finds, according to the Tosaphot, no basis in these readings. Though, strictly speaking, this variant, forty-twenty, does not belong in our present discussion of *plene* and *defective* spelling, I still should like to remark that though the way the Talmud quotes Judg. 16.31 is without foundation in *our* Bible, it most likely was well based in the Bible of those days. Cf. similar uncertainties of transmission concerning the numbers forty and twenty: The verses 2 Ki. 8.26 and 2 Chron. 22.2 are identical; but in 2 Ki. the age of Aḥazia is given as: בן־עשרים ושתים, while in 2 Chron. it is: בן־ארבעים ושתים. Furthermore: according to 1 Sam. 4.18 the period of Eli's judgeship is given as: ארבעים שנה; but Origen *ad loc.* is quoted by Field as translating: εικοσιν ετη.

In the preceding discussion of Sanh. 4b, we found Tosaphot's Bible agreeing with our own text, as against the way these words were quoted in the Talmud. This does not yet mean that the Bible in the days of Tosaphot and in ours is the same. It is enough to refer to Men. 43b in order to exclude any such assumption: תוספות דֹה שואל מעמך: פירש רבנו תם דהוי מלא· ויש מאה אותיות בפסוק. ''R. Tam explains this Talmudic passage by pointing out the fact that in Deut. 10.12 the word שואל is spelled *plene*, thus bringing the number of letters in this verse up to hundred.'' But our Bible has שאל in *defective* spelling! Had R. Tam had this our Bible before him, then he would certainly have looked for another possible explanation of this Talmudic passage.

We now return to Rashi (cf. p. 508): On Gen. 25.6 Rashi comments on דֹה הפלגשם: חסר כתיב· שלא היתה אלא פלגש אחת· היא הגר· היא קטורה. ''The ending of the Hebrew term for concubines is in *defective* spelling, thus indicating a singular; for Abraham had only one concubine, Hagar and Keturah being two names for one and the same person.'' But in our Bible the ending is spelled *plene*: הפילגשים, and clearly signifies a plural.

A similar case is that of Num. 7.1 on דֹה ויהי ביום כלות משה: כלת כתיב· יום הקמת המשכן היו ישראל ככלה הנכנסת לחופה. ''The Hebrew equivalent for 'made an end (finished)' appears in *defective* spelling and thus resembles the Hebrew word for 'bride'; for on the day when the tabernacle was set up, Israel was like a bride, ready to enter the canopy.'' Not only does our Bible offer the word in question in a *plene* spelling, but in addition to it there is a Masoretic note on it saying: ל ומל: this word occurs only here and is spelled *plene*!

A ritual still in common use in Israel is involved in Deut. 6.9. Here Rashi remarks on דֹה מזוזות ביתיך: מזוזת כתיב· שאין צריך אלא אחת. ''The ending of the Hebrew word for 'doorposts' is spelled *defective*, implying a singular; accordingly, one *mezuzah* is enough.'' But our Bible exhibits מזוזות, with a *plene* spelling of the ending; and this implies a plural!

C.   THE PROBLEMS OF כולהו דקדוקי ספרי

9. *The Division into Verses* (Cf. MH p. 156 f.)

The statement in Ķid. 30a, parts of which we cited above on p. 506/7 in
order to inaugurate our investigation of the problem of spelling, contains
also remarks of basic importance with regard to the way of dividing the
Bible text into verses. For the sake of clarity of presentation, the
repetition of the introductory phrases is unavoidable: לפיכך נקראו ראשונים
סופרים· שהיו סופרים כל האותיות שבתורה· שהיו אומרים: ··· וְהִתְגַּלַּח [חציין] של
פסוקים [של ספר תורה] ··· וְהוּא רַחוּם יְכַפֵּר עָוֹן חציו דפסוקים [של תהלים] ··· בעי
רב יוסף: וְהִתְגַּלַּח מהאי גיסא או מהאי גיסא? פסוקי ליתו למניוה! בפסוקי נמי לא בקיאינן
"The early scholars were called *soferim*, bcause they used to count
all the letters of the Torah. Thus they said: ··· והתגלח (Lev. 13.33) marks
half of the verses of the Torah ··· והוא רחום יכפר עון (Ps. 78.38) half
of the verses of the Psalms . . . R. Josef propounded: Does והתגלח belong
to the first half or the second? Said the scholars to him: For the verses
at least we can bring a Scroll of the Torah and count them! But the answer
was: *In the division of verses we are not certain, either.*"

In passing we wish to point out that according to a Masoretic note Lev.
8.8 is the middle verse of the Pentateuch; from Lev. 8.8 till ib. 13.33 there
are 160 verses, too many to be ascribed only to faulty counting. According to מסכת סופרים ed. Higger, chapter IX, section 2, the middle
verse begins with וישחט; on the location of this verse cf. Higger's note *a. l.*

The expression לא בקיאינן "we are not certain" with regard to the
division into verses in the Talmudic statement just quoted seems to imply
that no fixed and generally recognized division of the text into verses was
known at that period. Different schools may have followed their own
respective stylistic taste in subdividing scriptural portions into verses. In
Meg. 22a we have positive evidence for this explanation of ours: רב אמר:
··· כל פסוקא דלא פסקיה משה· אנן לא פסקינן ליה· ושמואל אמר: פסקינן ליה
"Rab said: . . . Any verse which Moses had not divided, we do not divide;
but Samuel said: we do divide it." The reference to Moses as authority in
matters of division into verses merely seeks to claim greater antiquity for
a certain system of division; cf. the terming of the Masoretic activities
הלכה למשה מסיני in the Talmudic passage quoted here above, p. 493.

Further support for our interpretation of the implication of the

expression לא בקיאינן may be found in a statement in Ḳid. 30a (following
the statement cited above and referred to): כי אתא רב אחא בר אדא אמר:
במערבא פסקי ליה להאי קרא לתלתא פסוקי: ויאמר ה׳ אל משה הנה אנכי בא אליך בעב
הענן. "When R. Aḥa b. Adda came (from Palestine to Babylon), he said:
In the west (scil. Palestine) *the one verse Ex.* 19.9 *is divided into three verses.*"

Was the verse Ex. 19.9 the only instance, in which the Palestinians
differed so widely from the Babylonians on this point? Or is Ex. 19.9
merely referred to as one example (but by no means the only one!) to
illustrate the immediately preceding assertion בפסוקי נמי לא בקיאינן" in the
division of verses we are not certain, either"? We are inclined to favor this
second alternative, in support of which even another Talmudic statement
may be cited, which follows right after the one quoted last. It reads (cf.
Higger's אוצר הברייתות, Vol. V, p. 561, par. 281): תנו רבנן: חמשה אלפים
ושמונה מאות ושמונים ושמונה פסוקים הוו פסוקי ספר תורה· יתר עליו תהלים שמונה·
חסר ממנו דברי הימים שמונה. "Our Rabbis taught: There are 5888 verses in
the Torah; the Psalms exceed this number by 8, while Chronicles are less
by 8." These three Biblical books were selected for a comparison in the
number of their verses for an obvious reason: because they provided the
Talmud with an example for a play on the number 8: we have 5888,
5888+8 and 5888—8. Hence, there can be no room for any doubt in the
exactness of the tradition concerning the numbers given.

Let us now compare these numbers with the respective indications
of the Masora on our Bible. In parenthesis I bring the number according
to the Talmud: Pentateuch: 5845 (5888); Psalms: 2527 (5896); Chronicles: 1656 (5880). We discard the discrepancy concerning the number
of the verses of the Pentateuch, since the difference is insignificant. But
the proportion of the numbers as given by the Masora to those of the
Talmud is for the Psalms approximately 1 : 2, and for Chronicles almost
1 : 4. This can surely not be attributed to a mistake in counting, but
positively *reflects a difference in the respective system of division, with one
system (Masora) favoring larger sentences (verses), while the other (Talmud)
preferred short ones.*

In the light of these results we shall now be able to interpret the Tosaphot on Meg. 22a: דה׳ אין מתחילין בפרשה פחות משלשה פסוקים: גזירה משום
הנכנסין· שלא יטעו לומר שאותו שקרא לפניו לא קרא אלא שני פסוקים· וקשה על מנהג
שלנו· שאנו קורין בפרשת ויחל בתעניות· והראשון מתחיל שם· והוא לסוף שני פסוקים

מפרשה שלמעלה· וכן המפטיר ביו״ט בחוה״מ דפסח· שמתחיל מוהקרבתם· שהוא לסוף שני פסוקים מראש הפרשה. "In reading from the Torah at services we do not read less than three verses together at the beginning of a section. This is done out of apprehension that late comers might err in assuming that someone who was called up first read only two verses from the Torah. Now the difficulty arises with rgeard to our custom: On public fast days we read the section beginning with ויחל (Ex. 32.11). The first person to be called up starts there, though only two verses separate it from the preceding section. Similarly he who is called up as *"maftir"* on the intermediate days of the Passover-festival begins his reading of the Torah with והקרבתם (Num. 28.19), and this, too, is only two verses removed from the beginning of the section." In comparing this statement with our Bible we find that Ex. 32.11 is four verses removed from the beginning of the section (Ex. 32.7), and Num. 28.19 three verses (Num. 28.16). Had Tosaphot had any knowledge of these facts, then no question וקשה על מנהג שלנו would have been asked, since only three verses' distance from the section are required by the law. The continuity of the narrative in these sections excludes any explanation that according to Tosaphot the sectional division of these passages must have been a different one. We thus see that the two verses, according to the division of Tosaphot, correspond to our four or three verses, respectively. This means a proportion of $1 : 1^1/_2$ or even $1 : 2$.

The very same proportional difference in the methods applied in dividing the verses can be demonstrated on the basis of our Bible also, by way of internal evidence. Certain genealogic or historic material appears twice in our Bible; but its division into verses follows different stylistic rules or taste.

1) One verse in Chron. corresponds to $1^1/_2$ verses elsewhere:

1 Chron. 1.17 = Gen. 10.22, 23b	1 Chron. 17.13 = 2 Sam. 7.14a, 15
1 Chron. 1.30 = Gen. 25.14, 15a	2 Chron. 13.2 = 1 Ki. 15.2, 7b
1 Chron. 1.40 = Gen. 36.23, 24a	2 Chron. 24.1 = 2 Ki. 12.1, 2b
1 Chron. 16.29 = Ps. 96.8, 9a	

2) One verse in Chron. corresponds to two verses elsewhere:

1 Chron. 1.42 = Gen. 36.27, 28	1 Chron. 1.43 = Gen. 36.31, 32

I Chron.   6.42 = Josh. 21.13, 14   I Chron.   17.1 = 2 Sam. 7.1, 2

I Chron. 10.12 = I Sam. 31.12, 13   2 Chron.   9.1 = I Ki. 10.1, 2

3) One third of a verse in Chron. corresponds to a full verse elsewhere:

I Chron. 2.3c = Gen. 38.7

4) One and a half-verse in Chron. correspond to one verse elsewhere:

I Chron. 21.11a, 12 = 2 Sam. 24.13   2 Chron. 7.8, 9b = I Ki. 8.65

10.   *The Division into Sections*

While discussing the Tosaphot in Meg. 22b with regard to the division
into verses, we emphasized that the continuity of the narrative in the
passages referred to by Tosaphot makes it impossible to suggest a different
sectional division as the solution of the difficulty (p. 513). We thus
admitted that but for the logical interconnection of the verses under
discussion, we might have questioned the correctness of the tradition
concerning the sectional division in our Bible. In doing so, we would be in
a position to refer to the authority of a Talmudic statement which plainly
upsets the Masoretic division into sections; the resulting discrepancy
becomes even more striking by the elaborate working out of the details
involved in the comment of Tosaphot. We refer to Pes. 117a (cf. also
Higger's מסכת סופרים, chapter XX, section 7 and his Introduction p. 33):
אמר רב חסדא: הללויה סוף פירקא· רבה בר רב הונא אמר: הללויה ריש פירקא· אמר
רב חסדא: חזינא להו לתילי דבי רב חנין בר רב· דכתיב בהו הללויה באמצע פירקא·
אלמא מספקא ליה· אמר רב חנין בר רב: הכל מודים בתהלת ה' יְדַבֶּר פִּי וִיבָרֵךְ כָּל בָּשָׂר
שֵׁם קָדְשׁוֹ לְעוֹלָם וָעֶד· הללויה דבתריה ריש פירקא· רָשָׁע יִרְאֶה וְכָעָס שִׁנָּיו יַחֲרֹק וְנָמָס
תַּאֲוַת רְשָׁעִים תֹּאבֵד· הללויה דבתריה ריש פירקא· וְשֶׁעוֹמְדִים בְּבֵית ה' הללויה דבתריה
ריש פירקא. "R. Ḥisda said: "Hallelujah" marks the end of a chapter;
Rabba b. R. Huna said: "Hallelujah" marks the beginning of a chapter.
R. Ḥisda observed: I saw that in the copies of the Psalms used in the
college of R. Ḥanin b. Rab, "Hallelujah" was written in the middle of a
chapter, *which proves that he was in doubt.* — R. Ḥanin b. Rab said: All
agree that in the case of Ps. 145.21, the "Hallelujah" which follows it is
the beginning of the next Psalm (Ps. 146.1); in Ps. 112.10, the "Hallelujah" which follows it commences the next Psalm (Ps. 113.1); and also
in the passage "Ye that stand in the house of the Lord" (Ps. 135.2), the

following "Hallelujah" commences the next Psalm (Ps. 135.3)." A mere
glance at our identification of the quotations of the Talmud, which we
bring in parenthesis, shows that in the Psalms of the Talmud, the very
same verse which forms Ps. 135.3 according to our Bible, marked the
beginning of a new Psalm. Thus, R. Ḥanin b. Rab's doubts as to the
division of the Psalms into sections were well founded.

We now turn to Tosaphot's comment: דה הכי גרסינן: שעומדים בבית ה׳
בחצרות בית אלהינו· הללויה דבתריה ריש פירקא· ולא גרסינן: העומדים בבית ה׳
בלילות· דאם כן הוה ליה למינקט: יברכך ה׳ מציון· שזהו פסוק למעלה מהללויה· ולא
הוה ליה למנקט שלשה פסוקים למעלה· לכך נראה דגרסינן כדפרישית· ולפי זה אנו
צריכין לומר בו: הללויה הללו את שם ה׳ הללו עבדי ה׳ שעומדים בבית ה׳ וגומר שלמעלה
מזה אינו תחלת המזמור· דלא יתכן שיהיה המזמור שני פסוקים· ועוד דאמרינן במדרש:
קמ״ז מזמורים יש בספר תהלים כנגד שנות יעקב· אלא הוא סופו של שיר המעלות הנה
ברכו וגומר· ואתי שפיר דקאמרינן לקמן: רב אחא בר יעקב דמתחיל הלל הגדול מכי
יעקב בחר לו יה· דהוי תחילת המזמור· דבענין אחר לא יתכן שהיה מתחיל הלל מאמצע
המזמור. "The Talmud's last quotation refers to Ps. 135.2 and to the following "Hallelujah" of ib. verse 3; but not to Ps. 134.1, a verse which
highly resembles our verse of Ps. 135.2. Had the Talmud thought of citing
Ps. 134, it would not have quoted the verse 1 of Ps. 134, but verse 3 there;
for it is this verse 3 which is immediately followed by "Hallelujah"
(namely Ps. 135.1), while verse 1 of Ps. 134 is three verses ahead of the
next "Hallelujah" (namely Ps. 135.1; between Ps. 134.1 and 135.1 are
three verses). Hence it is evident that the Talmud had Ps. 135.2 in mind.
As a result of this observation we shall say that the verses Ps. 135.1-2
which precede the "Hallelujah," are not the beginning of a Psalm, since
in this case the Psalm would consist of two verses only (for "Hallelujah"
in verse 3 marks already the beginning of a new Psalm), and this would be
in itself an anomaly, and would in addition upset the established number
of Psalms which is 147 in accordance with the life-span of the Patriarch
Jacob. It thus follows that Ps. 135.1-2 form the end of Ps. 134. This also
explains why R. Aḥa b. Jacob, as stated later on, began the Great Hallel
with the verse Ps. 135.4 (since the verses 1-2 of Ps. 135 thus belong to Ps.
134, and verse 3 of this Ps. 135 is merely the introduction of the Pslam, as
indicated by הללויה, the Psalm really commences with what is in our
Bible verse 4 thereof). He surely would not have started the Great Hallel
in the middle of a Psalm! But according to our interpretation, the

"Hallelujah" in Ps. 135.3 marks the beginning of a new Psalm, of which Ps. 135.4 is the first verse."

Again we wish to stress the importance of our indicating the location of Biblical passages in Tosaphot's quotations; by this procedure we have brought into sharp relief the divergences in the division of the Psalms according to Tosaphot as against our Bible. In addition, we desire to point out that Tosaphot's argument: no Psalm consists of two verses only, is further proof of our thesis, since in our Bible Ps. 117 has only two verses. As to the number of Psalms which the Tosaphot give (on the basis of the Midrash) as 147—while we have 150—I refer to A. Z. Schwarz' Catalogue of the Hebrew manuscripts of the *Nationalbibliothek* (formerly: *k. k. Hofbibliothek*) in Vienna (published in 1925): In the manuscript no. 5 (described on p. 6 of the Catalogue) the number of Psalms is 147. This number is achieved by the following deviations from the practice of our Bible: Pss. 9 and 10 form only one Psalm in this manuscript; similarly Pss. 70 and 71, Pss. 114 and 115. Ps. 113 of the manuscript corresponds to our Ps. 117-118.4 and consists thus not of two verses only (but of six verses), in accordance with the assertion of the Tosaphot: דלא יתכן שיהיה המזמור שני פסוקים.

11. *The Extraordinary Points* (נקודות)

That by putting a dot above a letter, the scribe meant to indicate that this letter was written by mistake and should, therefore, be erased, is too well known a fact to dwell on here; cf. במדבר רבה, פרשה ג, סוף הפרשה: ויש אומרים: למה נקוד? אלא כך אמר עזרא: אם יבוא אליהו ויאמר: למה כתבת אותן? אומר לו: כבר נקדתי עליהם. ואם יאמר לי: יפה כתבת! כבר אמחוק נקודותיהם מעליהם This passage not only explains the origin of the points as meaning *delendum*, but also gives the reason why subsequent scribes did not take the hint and leave these letters out, instead of copying them with their dots above. For, in doing so, they secured for themselves the possibility of an honorable retreat: in case later scholars were of the opinion that the letter thus stigmatized did by right belong to the word, they could still save it by deleting the point. In the language of our own period we would put the thought thus: A word with one or more letters with such points on them represents a combination of two words: one consisting of all the letters written, and another formed by the free letters only.

We shall now discuss from this our point of view the words with such dots in the same order as they are listed in מסכת סופרים ed. Higger, chapter VI, section 3; there the parallel Rabbinic sources are mentioned, too:

1) Gen. 16.5: יִשְׁפּוֹט ה' בִּינִי וּבֵינֶיךָ: a combination of וּבֵינֶיךָ and וּבֵינֵךְ. The *mater lectionis* י merely indicates the vowel, but not the number (sing. or plur.) of the suffix; cf. p. 261, § 35.

2) Gen. 18.9: וַיֹּאמְרוּ אֵלָיו; against this way of putting the points already Mueller in his edition, p. 87, suggested the order וֹאִי, namely: וַיֹּאמְרוּ אֵלָיו. This results in the readings: וַיֹּאמֶר לוֹ and וַיֹּאמְרוּ אֵלָיו; cf. p. 285, § 74. Note also the singular וַיֹּאמֶר in the following verse 10.

3) Gen. 19.33: וְלֹא יָדַע בְּשִׁכְבָהּ וּבְקוּמָהּ; hence *plene* spelling וּבְקוּמָהּ or *defective* וּבְקֻמָהּ; cf. p. 565, § 3c.

4) Gen. 33.4: וַיִּפֹּל עַל צַוָּארָיו וַיִּשָּׁקֵהוּ: a textual difference.

5) Gen. 37.12: וַיֵּלְכוּ אֶחָיו לִרְעוֹת אֶת צֹאן אֲבִיהֶם: on the use of the *nota accusativi* אֵת cf. p. 288, § 76.

6) Num. 3.39: כָּל פְּקוּדֵי הַלְוִיִּם אֲשֶׁר פָּקַד מֹשֶׁה וְאַהֲרֹן: a textual difference; cf. ib. verse 14: the command was issued to Moses alone.

7) Num. 9.10: אוֹ בְדֶרֶךְ רְחֹקָה; this leads to: רְחוֹקָה and (or) רָחוֹק. The gender of דֶרֶךְ is given as masc. or fem.; cf. p. 267, § 45, especially note 4 there.

8) Num. 21.30: וַנַּשִּׁים עַד נֹפַח אֲשֶׁר; the two readings are: אֲשֶׁר and אֵשׁ; cf. πῦρ in the Septuagint, and אֵשׁ in the Hebrew Pentateuch of the Samaritans.

9) Num. 29.15: וְעִשָּׂרוֹן עִשָּׂרוֹן; but according to the parallel Rabbinic source in במדבר רבה, the passage Num. 28.21 is meant: עִשָּׂרוֹן עִשָּׂרוֹן: "a tenth" in a distributive sense can thus be expressed either by the repetition of the term, or by the simple term: עִשָּׂרוֹן עִשָּׂרוֹן or עִשָּׂרוֹן; cf. similarly Gen. 7.2: שְׁנַיִם with Sam.: שְׁנַיִם שְׁנַיִם; ib. verse 16: זָכָר וּנְקֵבָה with Sam.: זָכָר וּנְקֵבָה זָכָר וּנְקֵבָה; Num. 4.19: אִישׁ אִישׁ with Sam.: אִישׁ; 1 Chron. 21.3: כָּהֵם with 2 Sam. 24.3: כָּהֵם וְכָהֵם; 2 Chron. 4.18: מְאֹד with 1 Ki. 7.47: מְאֹד מְאֹד. Cf. here p. 635, § 112 sub a and b.

10) Deut. 29.28: הַנִּסְתָּרֹת לַה' אֱלֹהֵינוּ וְהַנִּגְלֹת לָנוּ וּלְבָנֵינוּ עַד עוֹלָם: The ע in עַד leaves the ד without support; I, therefore, believe that the dot over the ע originates in a confusion of the Masoretic note עד

meaning "up to" (עד עד עולם) with the text-word עד. We now get
two sentences: the one as spelled above, and the other reading:
הנסרות לה אלהינו והנגלות עד עולם.

12.   *The Final Letters*

In Meg. 2b we read the following assertion: ואמר רבי ירמיה ואיתימא רבי
חייא בר אבא: מנצפ״ך צופים אמרום. "R. Jeremiah—or you may also say:
R. Ḥiyya b. Abba—also said: The alternative forms of the letters
MNZPK were prescribed by the Watchmen."

This rather brief statement is found in a clearer and more elaborate
form in Yer. Meg. I, 9: כל האותיות הכפולים באל״ף בי״ת כותב הראשונים בתחילת
התיבה ובאמצע התיבה· ואת האחרונים בסופה· ואם שינה פסל· משום רבי מתיה בן חרש
אמרו: מנצפ״ך הלכה למשה מסיני ··· אנשי ירושלים היו כותבין ירושלים ירושלימה·
ולא היו מקפידין· ודכותה: צפון צפונה· תימן תימנה. "With regard to all the
letters of the alphabet which appear in alternative forms, one writes the
first forms at the beginning of a word and in the middle of a word, and
the later forms at the end [of a word]. A deviation from this rule makes
the Torah unfit for religious use. It is said on the authority of R. Matyah
b. Ḥeres: The alternative forms of the letters MNZPK are הלכה למשה
מסיני ... People of Jerusalem were in the habit of writing ירושלים and
ירושלימה without differentiating; similarly: צפון and צפונה; תימן and
תימנה." In quoting the text and in the translation I followed the way the
words are spelled in the Krotoschin edition. The result is only too obvious:
the second part of the quotation seems entirely out of place here. The
statement deals with the final letters, but suddenly shifts over to what
appears to be an indifference of the inhabitants of Jerusalem towards the
use or omission of the ה *euphonicum* (on this new term, instead of the misleading term ה *locativum* hitherto applied, cf. p. 277, §§ 60 ff.). But we can
not fail to observe that the examples chosen end either in ם or ן. We,
therefore, suggest seeing in the second part of the statement the continuation of rules for the scribe concerning the final letters, allowing
for an exception of the foregoing general assertion ואם שינה פסל, in keeping
with the custom prevalent in Jerusalem. We should like to repeat this
second part, both in the original and in translation, in order to adjust the
spelling of the words in question to our interpretation: אנשי ירושלים היו
כותבין ירושלים· ירושלימה· ולא היו מקפידין· ‪ו‬דכותה: צפון צפונה· תימן תימנה

"People of Jerusalem were in the habit of writing מ and נ, both in medial
and final position, and did not differentiate;" with the statement in this
revised form cf. p. 490, § 71a, where additional cases are listed in which מ
and נ are employed in final positions (according to the כתיב); cf. also the
next paragraph passim.

D. THE EVIDENCE OF THE OLDEST HEBREW BIBLE MS. ON RECORD

Abraham Epstein in an article "Biblische Textkritik bei den Rabbinen"
(*Chwolson-Festschrift*, Berlin 1899, pp. 42 seq.), called attention to a list
of variant readings of an ancient Pentateuch manuscript, the Codex
Severus, as compared with the readings of the accepted text of those days.
This list is contained in several manuscripts of the בראשית רבה, and was
presented by Epstein in the article just mentioned on the basis of a
comparison of all the sources which were available to him. Originally,
this list must have had a wide circulation; Epstein proves that even
Ḳimḥi quoted it. It is headed by the following introductory remarks:
אלין פסוקיא דהוו כתיבין בספר אורייתא דאשתכח ברומא· והות גנוזה וסתומה בכנישתא
דסוירוס· בשינוי אותיות ותיבות. We shall follow here the order in which Epstein
lists these variants, and accept the readings which he establishes. But the
interpretation which we are going to offer, will be based on the results at
which we arrived in our independent researches on Biblical philology. A
hyphen divides the readings of the Codex Severus (right) from those of
the Bible text then in authority (left):

Gen. 1.31: מות – (טוב) מאד; cf. p. 226.

Gen. 3.21: אור – (כתנות) עור; cf. p. 477, § 37.

Gen. 18.21: הכצעקתם – הכצעקתה; cf. p. 486, § 66, 6.

Gen. 25.33: מכרתו – (את) בכרתו; cf. p. 479, § 46; on the nominal form of
the variant spelling מכירתו, cf. p. 257, § 27α.

Gen. 27.2: יום מותי – יום מותי; cf. p. 490, § 71α, and here the preceding
paragraph.

Gen. 27.27: סדה – (כריח) שדה; cf. p. 478, § 42; cf. also Baba Batra 9a the
quotation of Isa. 58.7 as: הלא פרוש לרעב לחמך· בשי׳׳ן כתיב (but in the
Bible: פְּרֹס).

Gen. 36.5, 14: יעיש – יעוש; cf. p. 484, § 64.

Gen. 36.12: בנ עדה – בן עדה; cf. p. 490, § 71α, and here the preceding
paragraph.

Gen. 43.15: מצרים – מצרימה; cf. p. 282, § 65c. It is noteworthy that our Bible exhibits here מצרים. This shows that the Bible text which served as basic text for the comparison with the Codex Severus, can not be identified with our Bible.

Gen. 48.7: שם – שמ; cf. p. 490, § 71α, and here the preceding paragraph.

Gen. 46.8: מצרימה – מצרים; cf. p. 282, § 65c.

Ex. 12.37: מרעמסס – מרעמס; cf. p. 488, § 68.

Lev. 4.34: מדם – מדמ; cf. p. 490, § 71α, and here the preceding paragraph.

Lev. 14.10: תמימה – תמימים; cf. p. 486, § 66, 6.

Num. 4.3: הבא – (כל) בא; cf. p. 272, § 50b.

Num. 36.1: בן יוסף – בני יוסף; cf. p. 488, § 68.

Deut. 1.26: אביתמ – אביתם; cf. p. 490, § 71α, and here the preceding paragraph.

Deut. 3.20: המ – הם; cf. p. 490, § 71α, and here the preceding paragraph.

Deut. 22.6: האבנים – הבנים; cf. p. 562, § 1a.

Deut. 32.25: אף איהם – אפאיהם; cf. p. 490, § 71.

C. THE MASORA PARVA (מסרה קטנה) EXAMINED IN THE SOURCES

A. THE CODEX PETROPOLITANUS

§ 1. The Masora Originates in Masoretic Lists.

It seems most plausible that the original sources of the marginal Masoretic notes (Masora parva) in our manuscript have been Masoretic compilations in the form of lists. They contained uncommon phenomena in the spelling or the pronunciation of certain Hebrew words, grouping them according to these unusual features which they exhibit:

Jer. 7.32: יאמר: חֲיֵ· כנמרד· היום· עוד· בספר· כעת· ולציון·
                                     לעם הזה· עוד· התפת· שוע· עזובה· שֹנ בתֹ·
                                                  מספר· שֹנ בתֹ·

This list offers references to 14 instances only and is, therefore, incomplete; for חֹי states that the word occurs 18 times. The Tiberian vowel-signs ִ ְ ֵ under חֹי are an addition, presumably from another source, since the genuine vocalization of the Masora to this manuscript applies the Babylonian system; cf. § 5. The addition of the vocalization ִ ְ ֵ results in a disagreement between the list and MT; for יאמר in connection with כנמרד (Gen. 10.9), בספר (Num. 21.14), and ולציון (Ps. 87.5) is vocalized יֵאָמַר in MT. But of by far greater importance for us here is the fact that, incomplete though this list is, it contains a reference to התפת as item number 9; and התפת refers to the very same verse, Jer. 7.32, where this note is found. The Masorete substantiated his statement הֹי by adding the catchwords of the list, the heading of which was הֹי.

The following examples are similarly excerpts of lists; we indicate the respective headings by extra spacing:

Hos. 1.2: זנה‬   זנֹה ל׃ אלֹה׃ נדמֹה׃ פנֹה׃ כהֹה׃ הלין דכֹת הי בֹס מלתא וֹק וֹא

After remarking that זנה occurs only here in this spelling, the Masoretic note mentions four more verbs of the *tertiae* ה group in the absolute infinitive which are spelled with ה at the end; this ה serves as *mater lectionis* for the vowel *o* which elsewhere is indicated by *waw*.

Ezek. 40.4: הראותכה‬   ל מלֹ׃ בֹ׃ את כחֹי׃ הראותך כֹת׃ הלין׃ הראותכה׃
והוא מן כֹ מלין דכֹת הי בסוף תיֹב

The brief note מל ל׃: the word does not occur any more in this *plene* spelling, is followed by an elaborate statement: Twice this verbal form occurs in the Bible: in Ex. 9.16 ending in ך, but here in כה; and this is one of the twenty words which have (in connection with כ) a ה as *mater lectionis* in final position.

Ezek. 37.22: יהיה‬   יו קֹ׃ והוא מן יֹד מלין הי כֹת בסוֹף וו קֹ

The structure of this note closely follows the pattern which we described in the preceding example: First a short remark on the word under consideration (יו קֹ); and then an abstract of the pertinent list: this is one of the 14 cases, in which ה is written but *waw* (as *mater lectionis* for *u*) is heard in the pronunciation.

In the examples which we discussed till now, the respective Masoretic notes at least take cognizance of the somewhat peculiar spelling or pronunciation of a given word. The Masoretic lists which are quoted—in full or merely by their headings—in this connection, show further instances of the same grammatical phenomenon. But our assertion that such Masoretic lists were the original basis of all marginal Masoretic notes will become even more convincing, when we turn to the following examples:

Isa. 48.15: אני‬   מן זֹ מלין גֹ.גֹ אתין בהון

This is one of the seven triliteral words (which are repeated).

Isa. 57.1: הצדיק: מן כֹּט הפסוקין דסופיהון כרישיהון

There are 29 verses, in which the first and the last word are identical; this is one of them.

Isa. 10.13: כאביר: אֹ לֹ קֹ· מן מֹח דנֹס אֹ בימצע תיב ולא קרֹ

There are in all 48 cases in which (like here) א is spelled in medial position, but not pronounced.

It seems that the Masorete had a number of Masoretic lists in front of him. He must have felt that somehow he had to dispose of them and make their contents available to those who might use the manuscript.

§ 2.   The text contradicts the Masoretic note.

In many instances, where the marginal Masoretic note points to some detail of the spelling or pronunciation of the word in question, this statement is in open contradiction to the actual text of the manuscript. This proves that the compilers of the Masoretic lists, whence these notes emanate, had as *Vorlage* the Hebrew Bible in a different textual type before them, and that this fact had remained unnoticed by the copyist of the marginal Masora in our manuscript:

Ezek. 37.3: ל מֹל ובתרין יוֹ״ד :התחינה

The Masoretic note asserts that nowhere else but here does this word occur in *plene* spelling, namely with two י. Still, the text offers a *defective* spelling, exhibiting only one י.

Jer. 27.3: לא כֹת הי וֹק :המלאכים

Though the letter ה does not appear in the spelling, it is nevertheless heard in the pronunciation. But the text offers ה in the spelling, too.

Jer. 5.22: בֹ חֹס :האותי

This word occurs twice, and both times its spelling is *defective*. But our text is quite obviously *plene*.

§ 3.   The text was revised so as to conform with the Masora.

Difficulties of a typographical nature make it impossible for us to reproduce in print the way how the scribal changes discussed in this paragraph are accomplished in the manuscript.

a) By eliminating a contradicting vowel-letter.

Isa. 10.16: חס כת‎ :כבודו

The original reading כבודו in *plene* spelling was changed into כבדו by putting a circle round the first *waw*, so as to conform with the Masoretic note which states that the spelling of the word is *defective*. A circle around a letter indicates that this letter was erroneously written, and, hence, should be deleted. Similar instances for this procedure are:

Isa. 10.17: חס כת‎ :וקדושו

Isa. 24.16: חס כת‎ :זמירות

Jer. 32.41: חס יוד קד‎ :להיטיב

This formula indicates wherein the defectivity of the spelling consists: the first ' is missing.

Ezek. 37.7: חס יוד קדמ‎ :גידים

Ezek. 13.20: קד וו חס‎ :מצודדות

b) By adding or changing a vowel-letter.

Jer. 44.8: יא דכת ביוד‎ :במעשה

The first hand wrote here במעשה. The reviser found herein an open contradiction to the Masoretic note: that this word is one of the eleven occurrences in a spelling with '. Consequently he drew a line through the ה in such a manner that a ' actually resulted above the line.

Isa. 3.2: ו מל‎ :שׁ'פט

The Masoretic note: that this passage is one of six, in which the word occurs in *plene* spelling (as שופט), has induced the reviser to add a ו in the space between the letters פ and שׁ. The graphic picture which the word now offers, makes it evident that the reviser accomplished his task prior to the vocalizer, since the vowel ˙ is added to the ו (שׁׄוֹפֵט).

Jer. 26.6: ה ל ק‎ :הזאתה

The Masoretic note remarks: the letter ה appears merely in the spelling, but not in the pronunciation of the word. The word as written down by the first hand (הזאת), actually has a ה in the initial position. But the reviser evidently realized that this ה, being the article, has its place in the pronunciation of the word, and therefore added a final ה. This fact here combined with our observation on the preceding example may lead to the assumption that the reviser and the vocalizer were one and the same person.

Ezek. 11.6: ל ק ׃ומלאת'ם ז

The reviser must have had a model codex in front of him, while going through this manuscript. For how else could he have known that the Masoretic note refers to י as an indicator of the vowel *i* and not of the preceding vowel *ē*?

§ 4. The Masora based upon different sources.

Thus far, our examples demonstrate contradictions between the text and its marginal Masoretic notes. Consequently, the *Vorlagen* of the Masoretic notes must have been drawn up on the basis of a different textual type of the Bible. Now the question arises: Do they all spring from one and the same source, or were these *Vorlagen* merely a compilation of Masoretic material, originating in and based upon various textual types of the Bible? In other words: are the Masoretic notes consistent within themselves, and do their cross-references agree with one another, so as to corroborate the manuscript's Masoretic statements?

One example will bring clarity into this problem: The word מנוחתו occurs twice in the Bible: in Isa. 11.10 and Zech. 9.1. In Isa. 11.10 the manuscript reads: ב חס ודמשק ׃מנוחתו. We see that the scribe wrote the word *plene*, but the reviser eliminated the first vowel-letter ו (by inserting a circle, cf. § 3a), in accordance with the Masoretic note which says: this word occurs twice in the Bible, both times in *defective* spelling, the second instance being in connection with the noun ודמשק. This is a cross-reference to Zech. 9.1. But here the manuscript offers: מנחתו ׃חס ל. According to this note, the instance here is the only one, in which the word occurs in *defective* spelling (note the contradiction between ב חס and ל חס!). Hence, in the Bible upon which this second Masoretic note is based, the Isa.-passage must have been spelled *plene*; cf. the original of that spelling by the scribe of our manuscript as מנוחתו!

This internal disagreement between the *Masoretic notes* themselves proves that they do not form a unity reflecting only one Bible text with all the peculiarities of its spelling, but that they *reflect a variety of sources.*

§ 5.   The terminology.

While discussing the instance from Jer. 7.32 (in § 1) we stated that the Tiberian vowel-signs ָ , ָ are an addition from another source, since the basic character of the manuscript is Babylonian. In order to prove the correctness of this assertion, I wish to refer to a few cases, in which it is even more obvious that their Tiberian vowel-signs were added later, since they result in a doublet:

Isa. 44.15:   בָ קֹמ :וישתחו

This note originally read: בֹ קֹמ : twice וישתחו is vocalized with קמץ. The addition of ָ under the בֹ made קֹמ superfluous; as it stands now, the note offers a doublet.

Jer. 10.8:   יֹבֹ פֹת :מוסר

The components of this doublet are: יֹבֹ פֹת and יָֹבֹ. It is noteworthy that the text has a *ḳameṣ*; on the discrepancy between text and Masoretic note cf. § 2.

Isa. 19.20:   הָ בתרין קֹמ :ורב
A combination of הֹ בתרין קֹמ and הָ.

Our regarding these Tiberian vowel-signs as later additions by no means implies that they were added to our manuscript at a later period. It is quite feasible that the Masorete of our manuscript found them already in his sources. This would lead us to the assumption that these sources already were of a mixed type. There is nothing startling in such an assumption; we even have additional proof for it in the fact that one and the same grammatical phenomenon is described in this Masora by different terms:

Isa. 3.2:   ו מֹל :שֹופֹט
Isa. 10.13:   נבוותי כֹת :נבנֹותי

The fact that the vowel *o* is indicated by *waw* as a *mater lectionis* is termed once: מלא, and once: כתיב.

Isa. 28.2: חֹס כֹּת :וֹאמץ

Jer. 13.2: שים ק :וֹאשם

In either case the Masora dwells on the fact that the vowel *i* is spelled without a *mater lectionis*. It is quite clear that קרי here cannot mean: read (as against the speclling of the word), since there can be no doubt as to the pronunciation of וֹאשם, no matter whether with or without י. We do not wish to press this point, we merely argue: As a rule, the terms כתיב and קרי are used to exclude one another. Thus, חֹס כֹּת :וֹאמץ implies: but the קרי is with י. On the other hand, שים ק :וֹאשם means: but the כתיב is without the י. Now, if the terminology were uniform, we would have either:

חֹס כֹּת :וֹאמץ and חֹס כֹּת :וֹאשם; or

מיץ ק :וֹאמץ and שים ק :וֹאשם.

But, as it stands, these Masoretic notes reflect a different terminology, and this implies: different sources of origin.

This result is being corroborated by the doublet in:

Jer. 2.9:   עוד קי· // יֹב דכֹת חֹס :עד

This Masoretic note is a combination of עוד ק and יֹב דכֹת חֹס into one note. Thus, the terms קרי and כתיב חסר, מלא and כתיב are inter-changeably used here.

§ 6.   The terms קרי and לא קרי and their equivalent in other Masoretic sources.

a)   The term קרי. We have thus far realized that the Masoretic notes in our manuscript go back to different sources, and employ a different terminology for the very same phenomena. Our interest is now focussed on the term קרי. Does this term possess a *unique* significance of its own, or is it merely one of the *several* possibilities of terming certain phenomena? To this end we shall compare a few passages exhibiting this term in our manuscript, with the respective Masoretic notes in BHKK and Ven, which aim at the establishing of the very identical readings. We thus base our investigation on three sources, which are independent of one another:

Isa. 3.8: עיני ק :עֵינֵי; cf. BHKK and Ven: ל חס :עֵנֵי
Jer. 13.2: שִׂים ק :ואשם; cf. BHKK and Ven: ג חס :ואשם

These examples uphold our findings at the end of the preceding paragraph that קרי and חסר are interchangeably used.

Isa. 10.33: פורה ק :פארה; cf. פארה: BHKK: א כֹֽת :ל; Ven: ל
Jer. 30.16: שוסיך ק :שאסיך; cf. שאסיך: BHKK: ל   ; Ven: א ויתיר ל

Here קרי is interchangeably used with the terms כתיב (אלף) and יתיר (אלף), respectively. Note that in the first instance it is BHKK, and in the second instance Ven, which exhibit this term, cf. also later bβ.

b)   The term לא קרי.

α)   Often, when the Masorete wished to indicate that a letter, though contained in the spelling of the text, should not be pronounced, he remarked on it: this letter to be לא קרי. The same result is achieved in BHKK and Ven by a somewhat different procedure: here the remaining letters of the word in question are termed קרי. The difference in the Masoretic practice consists therein that our manuscript directs the reader by לא קרי: what to omit, while in BHKK and Ven the reader is told by קרי: what to retain.

1)   Jer. 4.5: ותקעו: ו ל ק; cf. BHKK and Ven: תקעו ק :ותקעו
     Jer. 8.1: ויציאו: ו ל ק; cf. BHKK and Ven: יציאו ק :ויציאו
     (in Ven both the text and the Masoretic note are spelled *plene*: יוציאו ק :ויוציאו).

2)   Jer. 2.33: למדתי: י ל ק ; cf. BHKK and Ven: למדת ק :למדתי
     Jer. 3.4: קראתי: י ל ק ; cf. BHKK and Ven: קראת ק :קראתי
     Jer. 4.30: ואתי: י ל ק ; cf. BHKK and Ven: ואת ק

3)   Jer. 3.7: ותראה: ה ל ק; cf. BHKK and Ven: ותרא ק :ותראה

β)   With the results of our discussions in §§ 5 and 6 in mind: that קרי does not signify a term of unique importance, but is interchangeably used with such other terms as חסר and יתיר, the following instances find their explanation:

Jer. 1.5: אצורך: ו ל ק; cf. אצורך: BHKK: אצרך ק; Ven: ל ומל
Jer. 5.7: אסלוח: ו ל ק; cf. אסלוח: Ven: אסלח ק; BHKK: ו יתיר

§ 7.   Each Masoretic source has קרי-readings of its own.

a)   Readings termed קרי in our manuscript only.   On a number of passages, in which the textual reading of our manuscript agrees with that of BHKK and Ven, there is a marked disagreement in the respective Masoretic notes. The marginal Masora on our manuscript exhibits a textual variant termed קרי, but in the other sources which are made use of here for comparison (BHKK and Ven) the Masora merely emphasizes the characteristic feature of the spelling of the text, thus endowing it with additional authority, and—possibly— silently rejecting as incorrect the very קרי-reading of our manuscript:

Isa. 41.18: שפיים :שפאים ק; cf. BHKK and Ven: שפיים :מל ג׃

The note מלא refers to the spelling of the ending יים with two *yod*; in our manuscript the additional א of the קרי is *mater lectionis* for the vowel *a* in פ, cf. ch. o, § ooa.

Isa. 25.6: ממחים :ממוחאים ק; cf. ממחים: BHKK: חס ל, Ven: ל

The term חסר (in BHKK) may indicate the absence of *waw* as *mater lectionis* for *u*, or even the spelling of the ending ים with only one *yod*; cf. the preceding example, where יים is termed מלא. The note לית is—as always—an abbreviateon for לית כתיב כן: the word does not occur any more in this spelling; cf. also:

Isa. 30.5: הביש :הבאיש ק; cf. BHKK and Ven: הבאיש :כת כן ל

Here, too, לית כתיב כן upholds the spelling of the word as offered in the text.

Isa. 53.4: חלינו :לאי ק; cf. חלינו: Ven: ל; BHKK: no note.

This example shares with the first two instances a certain tendency of the קרי-readings to make use of א as *mater lectionis* for the vowel *a*. But our manuscript is far from being consistent in this point, as the following example will show:

Jer. 40.1: באזקים :א ל ק; cf. BHKK and Ven: באזקים :ל

While the note אלף לא קרי eliminates this vowel-letter from the קרי-reading of our manuscript, the לית in the other sources represents an effort to preserve it.

b) Readings termed קרי in other sources.

Isa. 28.15: שוט; cf. BHKK and Ven: שוט ק :שיט

Isa. 47.13: הברי; cf. BHKK and Ven: הברי ק :הברו

Isa. 57.19: ניב; cf. BHKK and Ven: ניב ק :נוב

Isa. 60.21: מטעי; cf. BHKK and Ven: מטעי ק :מטעו

§ 8.   Readings of the text termed קרי.

Marginal Masoretic notes sometimes offer two different readings,
terming one כתיב and the other קרי. A comparison of these variants with
the actual word in the text reveals it to be identical with the form termed
קרי in the Masoretic note.

We arrange the material according to the parallel evidence from
BHKK and Ven on the words under consideration:

a) BHKK and Ven have the identical textual reading, but no
Masoretic note to it.

Isa. 18.2, 7: קו קו :חד כת ובתרין קר. The כתיב is as one word, but the קרי
          as two.

Isa. 22.18: צניף כת צנוף ק :צנוף

Jer. 4.30: יך כת וך ק :בפוך

Jer. 22.14: י כת ו ן ק :וספון

Jer. 26.24: בני כת בן ק :בן

Jer. 29.7: הגילתי כת הגליתי ק :הגליתי

b) BHKK and Ven have the same Masoretic קרי note on the presupposed כתיב text.

Jer. 2.27: תני כת תנו ק :ילדתנו ק :ילדתני; cf. BHKK and Ven: ילדתני

Jer. 8.6: רצות כת רוצת ק :במרוצתם ק :במרוצתם; cf. BHKK and Ven: במרוצתם·
          במרוצתם ק

Jer. 13.20: אי כת או ק :שאו ק; cf. BHKK and Ven: שאי ק :שאו

Jer. 13.20: אי כת או ק :וראו; cf. BHKK and Ven: וראי ק :וראו

Jer. 17.10: כו כת כיו ק :כדרכיו; cf. BHKK and Ven: כדרכו ק :כדרכיו

Jer. 21.12: הם כת כם ק :מעלליכם; cf. BHKK and Ven: מעלליהם·
          מעלליכם ק

Jer. 32.4: נו כת ניו ק :עיניו ק :עיניו. cf. BHKK: עינו ק :עיניו. Ven has here עיניו as
          reading of the text; but cf. there the preceding ועיניו ק :ועינו

Jer. 49.30: עליכם קֹ: הם כֹֿת כם קֹ: עליכם; cf. BHKK and Ven: עליהם קֹ: עליהם

Ezek. 46.19: תם כֹֿת תים קֹ: בירכתים; cf. BHKK and Ven: בירכתם: בירכתים קֹ

c)   BHKK and Ven offer the presupposed כתיב text, with Masoretic notes upholding these readings.

Hos. 4.6: ואמאסאך כך כֹת ולא קֹ א תלתא: ואמאסך. The word is spelled in the כתיב with three א, but the third א is omitted in the קרי; cf. ואמאסאך: BHKK: יתיר אֿ; Ven: יתיר אֿ // ל וכתֿי כן. The note in Ven is a doublet; cf. later § 17c, 23.

Zech. 8.20: עד כֹת עוד קֹ: עוד; cf. עד: BHKK: יֹב חֹט; Ven: יֹד חֹט. The same difference יֹד – יֹב occurs also in the note on עד in Hos. 12.10.

d)   Various other cases.

Jer. 48.21: מי כֹת מו קֹ: מופעת. This identification of the reading with *yod* as כתיב, and that with *waw* as קרי is reversed in BHKK and Ven: מיפעת קֹ: מופעת.

Jer. 32.19: אדם כֹת האדם קֹ: האדם. But BHKK and Ven have as text אדם, i.e. the presupposed כתיב, without any Masoretic note. Similarly in:

Jer. 28.13: מוטת כֹת: מטות. This כתיב form is the text-reading of BHKK and Ven: ל כתיב כן: מוטת. But in:

Isa. 27.6: ופ קֹ: יפרח, it is the קרי form, which is the text-reading in BHKK and Ven: ופרח, with no note to it.

B.   THE MS. 19A OF THE PUBLIC LIBRARY IN LENINGRAD
(According to the *Biblia Hebraica* ed. Kittel-Kahle)

§ 9.   Errors are not considered.

No conclusions will be based in this study upon such discrepancies between the text and the Masora, which can best be explained as scribal (or printer's) mistakes. The human eye is not infallible!

Isa. 47.7: וּגְבֶרֶת: לֹ; mistake for: לֹ. The word does not occur any more in this vocalization with ָ.

Isa. 51.2: וַאֲבָרְכַהוּ: לֹ; mistake for: לֹ.

Isa. 53.7: יוּבָל: בֹ זקף; mistake for: בֹ זקף. Cf. ib. verse 11: יִשְׂבָּע: בֹ זקף קמצ. The second occurrence of יוּבָל is Hos. 10.6.

Ps. 136.1: אילו כֹו פסוקים כנגד; mistake for: כֹו. This Psalm has only 26 verses.

Ezek. 39.9: ל בְּקֶשֶׁת; mistake for: בׁ. Cf. Hos. 1.7: בׁ בְּקֶשֶׁת.

§ 10. The Masora originates in Masoretic lists (cf. § 1).

Gen. 50.9: ז פסוק בתור: גם גם ומלה חדה ביניהֿ :גם

1 Sam. 18.5: כֹא פסוק: וגם ובתרֹ תלת מלין :וגם

Ezek. 5.13: ו פסוק: בם בם :בם

Judg. 12.4: בׁ פסוק אית בהון: בתוך בתוך :בתוך

2 Sam. 19.7: בׁ פסוק אית בהון: כי כי כי כי :כי; cf. the identical note on Josh. 17.18. In both instances the context excludes an error of mis-spelling כי into וכי.

Esth. 3.13: כֹו פסוק אית בהון אלפֿ בית. This is obviously the heading of a list; it has been rephrased in Isa. 5.25 and Zech. 6.11 to read: אית בפסוק אלף בית.

Num. 7.20: בֹכ פסוק דלי בהון לא ו ולא יׁ :כף

Lev. 13.9: יֹא פסוק ראש נון וסוף נון :נגע

1 Sam. 20.29: הׁ פסוק דאית בהון חמש מלין מן בׁ אתין :על

1 Sam. 13.19: אמרו קֿ· ז פסוקין: שבעה מכה· ושבעה מכה· ומציעי כֹת :אמר
There are 7 verses consisting of 15 words each, the middle word of which has a Masoretic note referring to כתיב and קרי.

§ 11. The text contradicts the Masora.

a) The Masoretic cross-references reflect a different textual type of the Hebrew Bible.

1 Sam. 18.10: כְּיוֹם :יׁ; but Isa. 9.3: כְּיוֹם :יֹא. The text of BHKK offers the word כְּיוֹם ten times only, but according to the text of Ven, it occurs eleven times; for Ezek. 30.9 which reads in BHKK: כְּיוֹם, has כְּיוֹם in Ven. Hence, both notes יׁ and יֹא are correct in themselves, but refer to two textual types as represented by BHKK and Ven re-pectively.

The following cases are to be explained in a similar way:

2 Ki. 18.31: בׁ חד מל :בורו. The word occurs twice, once in *plene* spelling. But Isa. 36.16: בורו is plene, too! And the Masora remarks on it:

ל מל: it does no more occur מלא, thus presupposing that in 2 Ki. 18.31 the word is in *defective* spelling.

Neh. 7.4: ב׳ חד מל׳ וגדולה. But in the other passage, where this word occurs, namely Eccl. 9.13, it is *plene*, too: וגדולה.

2 Ki. 23.29: כראתו: ב׳ חד חס; cf. in the other passage, 2 Ki. 6.21: כראתו, which is equally חסר and the Masoretic note there: ב׳ חס plainly states that this word is both times spelled *defective*.

Similarly:

Zech. 9.1: מנחתו: ב׳ חד חס; but Isa. 11.10: מנחתו: ב׳ חס. Cf. our discussion of this word in connection with Codex Petropolitanus in § 4.

Ex. 19.13: סקול: ב׳ חד מל׳ וחד חס; cf. the other passage referred to: Ex. 21.28: סקול, equally in *plene* spelling.

Ex. 14.14: תחרישון: ב׳ חד מל׳ וא׳ חס׳, as compared with the *plene* spelling in Job 13.5: תחרישון.

Eccl. 11.3: שיפול: ב׳ חד מל׳ וחד חס; but ib. 4.10 equally: שיפול.

Ps. 64.5: לירות: ב׳ חד חס; but ib. 11.2: לירות.

Ezra 9.12: שלמם: ב׳ חד חס; but Deut. 23.7: שלמם.

b) The Masora contradicts its own catchword.

Ex. 16.7: תלינו: קרי י׳. But the text actually has a *yod*! (Cf. Lev. 13.20: הוא: קרי י׳, where the text offers a *waw*). Our Masoretic note presupposes a textual type like that of Ven; cf. there: תלונו (with *waw*): תלינו ק (with *yod*).

Similarly reflecting the Ven textual type:

Ezra 10.44: נָשְׂאוּ: נשאו ק; cf. Ven, where the text נשאי (with *yod*) has this Masoretic note: נשאו ק.

Ps. 99.6: קֹרְאָים: ל׳ יתיר א׳. The vocalization shows that the אלף is not superfluous, but on the contrary belongs to the root; cf. Neh. 5.7: נשאים: יתיר א׳. Hence, our Masoretic note was meant for Ven, where the word is vocalized: קֹרְאים.

The following examples are to be explained in the same way as based upon a different type of the Bible text:

2 Ki. 10.5: ל וחס: נַמְלִיךְ

Jer. 2.17: ל וחס: מוֹלִיכֵךְ

Esth. 2.3:   ל וחס :תַּמְרוּקֵיהֶן

1 Chron. 9.40:   ל וחדה מלה :וּמְרִי־בַעַל

Ex. 17.16: ה מלין מן ב אתין :כֵּסְיָה. This presupposes a division of כסיה
into two words of two letters each: כֵּס־יָה, against the text offered
here.

§ 12.   The terminology (cf. § 5).

Throughout this Masora two distinctly different terminologies are in
use. Since the Masora goes back to Masoretic lists (cf. § 10), it is very
plausible that in these various Masoretic terms we have the original
headings of those lists before us. Sometimes one item is indicated by a
combination of two terms, thus forming a doublet.

a)   General terms.

1)   Gen. 3.24:   כול אורית חס :הַכְּרֻבִים

     Gen. 3.17:   ב מל בתור :צִוִּיתִיךָ

Similarly we find the Pentateuch referred to as אוריתא and תורה,
respectively, in an otherwise identical note:

     Lev. 22.16:   לט מל באור :אוֹתָם

     Lev. 23.43:   לט מל בתור :אוֹתָם

2)   1 Chron. 25.4:   ל שם אנש :הוֹתִיר

     1 Chron. 25.28:   ל שום גבר :לְהוֹתִיר

3)   1 Chron. 11.31:   ל וכל לשון ארמית כות :אִיתַי

     Dan. 2.10:   ל בלשון תרג :יוּכַל

4)   Num. 32.42:   ג לא מפק ה :לָהּ

     Ruth 2.14:   ג רפ :לָהּ

b)   Vocalization and accentuation.

5)   The *ḳameṣ* is indicated by קמצא or ָ :

     Ex. 15.2: ג קמצ :עָזִּי   Josh. 3.5: ג קמצ :הִתְקַדָּשׁוּ

     Ex. 27.16: ָ :מְסָךְ   Josh. 2.15: בָּ :יוֹשֶׁבֶת

The combination of both terms results in a doublet:

Esth. 1.5: הָ קמ׳ :קָטָן; the components are: הָ קמ and הָ.

If two *ḳameṣ* come in succession, the Masora indicates it by קמצין דסמיכין or ָ ָ :

Eccl. 4.3:   ב קמצ דסמ :הָרָע

Eccl. 1.7:   לָ ָ :לָלֶכֶת

Combined with the indication of the accentuation (זקפא), the Masoretic note on *ḳameṣ* is phrased thus:

Lam. 3.53:   ל זק קמ :חַיָּי

Lam. 3.35:   לָ זק :גֶּבֶר

6) The *pataḥ* is indicated by פתחא or ַ :

Judg. 16.5:   ב פתח :פַּתִּי   Prov. 1.8:   יב פת :מוּסַר

Judg. 19.11:   לָ :רַד   Prov. 1.3:   יַב :מוּסַר

In connection with the accentuation (אתנחתא), we get:

Ps. 107.35:   ג באתנח פת :מַיִם

Ps. 137.6:   לָ :יְרוּשָׁלֵַם

7) The *segol* is indicated by מנוקד בתלת or ֶ :

1 Chron. 15.1:   ב מנוקדים בתלת :וַיֶּט

2 Chron. 18.15:   גֶ :כַּמֶּה

8) In case the identical word is vocalized sometimes with *ḳameṣ* and some other times with *pataḥ*, the Masora indicates it thus:

Ps. 78.50:   ז ו פת וא קמ :חָשַׂךְ: the word occurs all in all seven times; six times it is vocalized with פתח, and once with קמץ.

Ps. 72.7:   דב וב :יִפְרַח: occurs four times; twice ָ , and twice ַ .

9) The אתנחתא is indicated:

Ps. 35.20:   דָ באתנח :אֶרֶץ

Prov. 30.21:   לֶ :אֶרֶץ

10) A doublet in connection with the indication of the גרישא appears in:

Ps. 78.17:   לָ גריש :לַמְרוֹת; the components are: לָ גריש and לָ ; cf. Ps. 104.3:   לָ :הַמְקָרֶה.

c)   Details of spelling.

11) The fact that a certain letter remains silent in the pronunciation of the word is indicated by the terms קרי and יתיר:

Eccl. 6.10: שתקוף ק שֶׁהַתַּקִּיף   2 Chron. 13.14: מחצרים ק מַחְצְצְרִים

Eccl. 10.3: ל יתיר ה כְּשֶׁהַסָּכָל   2 Chron. 29.28: יתיר צ מַחְצְצְרִים

Ps. 119.147: לדברך ק לְדַבָרֶיךָ   2 Ki. 16.17: את ק וְאֶת

Ps. 119.161: יתיר י וּמִדְּבָרֶיךָ   Neh. 9.17: יתיר ו וָחֶסֶד

Esth. 8.7: ביהודים ק בַּיְּהוּדִיים   Judg. 9.12: מלכי ק מָלוֹכִי

Esth. 4.7: יתיר י בַּיְּהוּדִיים   1 Sam. 28.8: יתיר ו קָסֳמִי

Jer. 3.4: קראת ק קָרָאתִי   1 Chron. 18.10: לשאל ק לִשְׁאוֹל

Jer. 3.5: יתיר י דִּבַּרְתִּי   Prov. 22.8: יתיר ו יְקְצוֹר

Prov. 28.16: שנא ק שֹׂנֵא

Prov. 8.35: יתיר י מָצָאִי

The combination of both terms results in a doublet:

Isa. 26.20: יתיר י // דלתך ק דְּלָתֶיךָ

2 Chron. 34.22: יתיר ו // תקהת ק תֻּוקְהַת

Ezek. 47.8: ונרפו ק ל ויתיר א וְנִרְפְּאוּ

12) The omission of a letter of the root from the spelling is indicated by קרי and חסר:

2 Ki. 21.29: אביא ק אָבִי

Mic. 1.15: ב׳ חֹס א אָבִי

The ב׳ (=twice) in the Masoretic note on the Micah passage refers to 2 Ki. 21.29; accordingly, this occurrence is classed as חסר, too.

A combination of both terms leads to a doublet in:

Jer. 32.35: החטיא ק // ב׳ חֹס הַחֲטִי

13) The spelling of the nominal suffix of the 3. pers. sing. masc. with ה is annotated on with: קרי and כתיב or כתיב כן:

Ps. 42.9: שירו ק שִׁירֹה

2 Ki. 20.13: ב׳ כת כן נְכֹתֹה

Jer. 2.3: ב׳ כת ה תְּבוּאָתֹה

Both terms are combined into a doublet in:

Ezek. 48.21: בתוכו ק // ב׳ כת ה בְּתוֹכֹה

14) The use of א to indicate the vowel *a* in medial position is termed מלא and כתיב:

2 Sam. 12.1:‎ רָאש׃‎ גׄ מל‎

Prov. 10.4:‎ רָאש׃‎ גׄ כתׄ א‎

15) The spelling of the nominal plur. ending as ם without the vowel-letter *yod* is termed חסר‎ and כתיב כן‎:

Num. 6.5:‎ הַיָּמׄם׃‎ בׄ חסׄ‎

Num. 7.10:‎ הַנְּשִׂיאׄם׃‎ דׄ כתׄ כן‎

Both terms are combined to a doublet in:

Gen. 17.20:‎ נְשִׂיאׄם‎ כתׄ כן //‎ דׄ חסׄ בתורׄ‎

d)   The term חד‎.

16) It refers to the very passage, in which the Masoretic note belongs to (meaning: this one):

Ezek. 38.7:‎ הִכֹּן׃‎ בׄ חד חסׄ‎   Ps. 78.28:‎ לְמִשְׁכְּנֹתָיו׃‎ בׄ חד חסׄ‎

Am. 4.12:‎ הִכּוֹן׃‎ בׄ חד מלׄ‎   Ps. 132.7:‎ לְמִשְׁכְּנוֹתָיו׃‎ בׄ חד מלׄ‎

Dan. 12.4:‎ יְשׁטְטוּ׃‎ בׄ חד חסׄ‎

Am. 8.12:‎ יְשׁוֹטְטוּ׃‎ בׄ חד מלׄ‎

Similarly in Ps. 112.10:‎ וְכָעַס‎ בׄ חד קמׄ‎, and Isa. 28.28:‎ וְהָמַם׃‎ בׄ חד פתׄ‎, the term חד‎ refers to these passages, since their respective other occurrence (as indicated by בׄ‎) is vocalized: Eccl. 5.16:‎ וְכָעַס‎ (with *patah*) and Deut. 7.23:‎ וְהָמָם‎ (with *kames*).

17) It refers to the other occurrence of the word in question (the cross-reference):

Dan. 10.12:‎ בִּדְבָרֶיךָ׃‎ בׄ חד חסׄ‎

Ps. 119.42:‎ בִּדְבָרֶךָ׃‎ בׄ חד מלׄ‎

Jer. 23.15:‎ וְהִשְׁקִיתִים‎ בׄ חד מלׄ‎ refers to Jer. 9.14:‎ וְהִשְׁקִיתִים‎.

Ps. 139.23:‎ שַׂרְעַפָּי׃‎ בׄ חד פתׄ‎ refers to Ps. 94.19:‎ שַׂרְעַפַּי‎.

Ps. 60.4:‎ רְפָה׃‎ בׄ חד כתׄ א‎ refers to Num. 12.13:‎ רְפָא‎.

e)   The identical note on passages in a different spelling.

This uncertainty of the meaning of the term חד‎: whether it refers to the word under consideration or to the cross-reference, may best be explained as a result of the fact that these Masoretic notes originate in different sets of Masoretic lists headed by בׄ חד מלׄ‎ and בׄ חד חסׄ‎, respectively. The later Masorete, in utilizing these lists so as to adorn a Bible manuscript and thus give it additional authority by making it "Masoretic," added his notes to whatever passage he changed to come across. Little did he concern himself over the implication of the term חד; to him, חד was merely a word, and not a scientific term with a well-defined connotation.

In order to establish beyond doubt the fact that these Masoretic notes were not meant to serve any practical purpose (as e.g. to direct the scribe or reviser), but that they represent merely annotations from Masoretic lists with corresponding headings, we wish to call attention to the following examples: According to our interpretation they go back to lists, the headings of which were complete. They indicated how often the word under consideration occurs in any spelling, e.g. מלא *and* חסר, *and not*, as heretofore, bringing only one indication: מלא *or* חסר, thus leaving it to us to guess at the other missing item:

I Sam. 26.21: וֹ חד כת ֹס ואֹ שׁ :הִסְכַּלְתִּי

Ps. 119.99: וֹ חד כתֹ שׁ וחד כתֹ ֹס :הִשְׂכַּלְתִּי

Here we might be tempted to explain חד in the first part of each note as referring to the same passage (cf. above under 16), and the second part of each note (ואֹ שׁ and וחד כתֹ ֹס) as later additions, since they are self-understood. But how then could we account for the identical notes in the very identical arrangement in cases like:

Lev. 14.6: וֹ חד מל וחד חֹס :הַשְּׁחָטָה

Lev. 14.51: וֹ חד מל וחד חֹס :הַשְּׁחוּטָה

Ex. 9.4: וֹ חד כתֹ אֹ וחד כתֹ הֹ :וְהִפְלָה

Deut. 28.59: וֹ חד כתֹ אֹ וחד כתֹ הֹ :וְהִפְלָא

Nothing but utmost confusion could have been the outcome, if any scribe or reviser would have felt inclined to follow the lead of such directions. They were truly never meant to "guide" them!

C.   THE BIBLIA RABBINICA, VENICE 1524/5

§ 13.   Printer's mistakes not considered (cf. § 9).

Num. 23.19: וְהִנֵּה הוֹלִיד בֵּן יַעֲשֶׂה: בֵּ. This is a reference to Ezek. 18.14. In both instances the word is vocalized יַעֲשֶׂה; hence, בֵּ is a misprint for בְֵּ.

Jer. 12.3: בְּ:תִּרְאֵנִי; misprint for בְּ; cf. Job 10.18.

Isa. 49.2: לְחֵץ:וחד ל; refers to Lam. 3.12: לַחֵץ:ל וא לְחֵץ; consequently, our note is a misprint for: ל וחד לַחֵץ.

Prov. 17.17: וְאָח:ל וחד וָאַח; misprint for: וָאָח וחד ל; cf. Eccl. 4.8: וָאָח:
ל וא וְאח.

Ezra 10.8: יָחֳרָם:ג בּ וא; misprint for: ג בּ וא; cf. Ex. 22.19: יָחֳרָם:
ג ב פתחי ודין קמ.

Judg. 5.18: מְרוֹמֵי:ג ב מל וא חס; mistake for: ג ב חס וא מל; cf. Prov. 9.3,
14: מְרֹמֵי:ג חד מל.

1 Ki. 7.36: וּמִסְגְּרֹתֶיהָ:ומסגרתיה ק; misprint for: מסגרתיה ק, without the
waw.

2 Ki. 24.14: עֲשֶׂרֶה:עשרה ק; mistake for: עשרת ק.

Num. 7.60: The lengthy Masoretic note beginning with לגלגלתם is merely
a reprinting of the identical note on Num. 1.22: s.v. לְגֻלְגְּלֹתָם, and
is here out of place.

2 Sam. 2.5, 6: וְגַם אָנֹכִי:בְּרָכִים: בלי משיח :תלתיהון נמסרו לעיל בדף שמתחיל
בשמן• יען כי נשמטו מפה בהדפסה. On the indicated page these Masoretic
notes are not to be found in the Masora Parva, but they are
included in the Masora Magna.

Lev. 23.17: תָּבִיאוּ:חד מן ד אלפין דגשין; but actually the א has no *dagesh*.

Gen. 11.32: בְּחָרָן:נון הפוכה; but the text has a regular *nun*.

Josh. 14.11: כְּכֹחִי:ל והוא מן אב רבתי; but the text has a normal sized כ.

§ 14.   The Masora originated in Masoretic lists (cf. §§ 1 and 10).

Gen. 2.14: חִדֶּקֶל:ל וא חדקל• אב מן חד חד• חד פתח וחד קמץ• דלוג. Here פתח
obviously means *segol*, unless we assume that this list is of Babylonian
origin, where ◡ served as the equivalent for both ◡ and ◡.

Gen. 32.12: וְהִכֵּנִי:אב מן חד חד• חד פתח וחד קמץ• דלוג

Gen. 13.9: אָם:ז• פסו דאית בהון אם ואם באמצע פסו; cf. on Gen. 31.52:
אָם:פסו אם ואם מצעו פסו בתורה 'י; and on Gen. 24.49: אָם:י פסו בתור
וירמיה אם ואם מצעו פסוק

Gen. 35.5: וַיִּסָּעוּ:ב א רפ וא סֹפ• והוא חד מן כ זוגין א רפ וא סֹפ

Gen. 23.16: עֶפְרוֹן:ט פסו מן ב מלין• קדמ מל תני חס

Gen. 17.24: בְּהִמֹּלוֹ:ב זוגין• קדמא לא נסב את תנין נסב את

Gen. 49.20: וְהוּא:חד מן ג פסו מן ז מלין• ג מכא וג מכא• והוא באמצ

1 Sam. 26.23: יהוה:ג פסו רישי וסופי אזכרה

Isa. 18.13: ל פסו ריש וסוף זי״ן :זֶה

Lev. 23.42: יֹא פסוקים רישיהון וסופיהון חד :בַּסֻּכֹּת

Ex. 21.29: יֹד פסו אית בסופיהון וגם ותרין מלין בתרוהי :וְגַם

Num. 36.8: גֹ פסוקי אית בהון פֹ אתין :וְכָל

Gen. 26.6: חד מן יֹד פסו כתובי מן גֹ מלין :יִצְחָק

Gen. 24.23: שיטה מן כֹו דכל חד וחד לית דכו :לָלִין. Cf. in Codex Petropolitanus, fol. 130b, the Masoretic list headed by: שיטה כל חד וחד לית דכו.

§ 15. Rabbinic sources utilized.

Gen. 18.5: הֹ מלי עטור סופרי :אַחַר; cf. Ned. 37b.

Num. 29.15: וְעִשָּׂרֹון :חד מן יֹ נקודות בתורה; cf. מסכת סופרים ed. Higger, chapter VI, section גֹ (p. 166).

Gen. 33.4: וַיִּשָּׁקֵהוּ :טֹו מלין נקדו בקרי; cf. the parallel Rabbinic sources listed in Higger's מסכת סופרים, p. 166.

Gen. 18.22: עֹודֶנּוּ :יֹח מלין תקון סופרים; cf. מדרש תנחומא ed. Warsaw on Ex. 15.7; cf. also on Deut. 23.24: מֹוצָא :תיקון סופרי בֹיֹח שמו בריש הדף בספר מוגה· ויש גמגום· ועיין בהגהה במיימוני בהלכות סֹ״ת.

Gen. 49.7: קָשָׁתָה :לֹ· הֹ פסוקים בתור שאין להם הכרע; cf. Yoma 55a; cf. also on Deut. 31.16: וָקָם :הֹ פסו שאין להם הכרע· אי מהאי גיסא אי מהאי גיסא· וסֹי אוטיבו שבטיא ליהושע בנהורא דמשה.

§ 16. The text contradicts the Masora (cf. §§ 2 and 11).

a) The Masoretic cross-references reflect a different textual type of the Hebrew Bible.

Hab. 3.19: בָּמֹותַי :גֹ חד חֹס and Ps. 18.34: בָּמֹותָי :גֹ חד מֹל, go both back to different texts; cf. BHKK, Ps. 18.34: בָּמֹתָי in *defective* spelling.

Num. 14.27: תְּלֻנֹּות :בֹ כתיב כן בתור· שמעתי את; this refers to the passage Ex. 16.12: תְּלֻנֹּת :בֹ כתיב כן.

Josh. 2.16: שֻׁב :בֹ חֹס· אשוב אליך; but Gen. 18.10 referred to here, has שׁוב in *plene* spelling.

2 Sam. 7.18: הֲבִיאֹתַנִי :בֹ חד חֹס וחד מֹל· דין חֹס; cf. the Masoretic note on the second occurrence of this word 1 Chron. 17,16: הֲבִיאֹתַנִי :בֹ וחֹס ו: occurs twice without a *waw*!

2 Sam. 19.6: הֹובַשְׁתָּ :בֹ חד מֹל וחד חֹס; cf. the identical spelling in Ps. 74.15: הֹובַשְׁתָ :בֹ בתרי ליֹש.

I Ki. 20.31: ב׳ חד מל וחד חס· אם יד תהיה מל :בְּרֹאשֵׁנוּ; but the passage referred to, Josh. 2.19, reads equally: ב׳ וחבלים :בְּרֹאשֵׁנוּ.

Jer. 38.22: ב׳ חד מל וחד חס :שְׁלָמֵךְ. Since the spelling of the word here is חסר, we expect the מלא spelling in the other instance; but cf. Obad 7: ב׳ חד מל :שְׁלָמֶךָ!

Ezek. 39.3: ב׳ חד חס :שְׂמֹאלְךָ; but cf. the identical spelling 2 Sam. 2.21.

Ps. 11.2: ב׳ חד חס :לִירוֹת and Ps. 64.5: ב׳ חד מל :לִירֹת exclude one another. The same is true of:

Ps. 78. 28: ב׳ חד מל :לְמִשְׁכְּנוֹתָיו and Ps. 132.7: ב׳ א׳ חס :לְמִשְׁכְּנֹתָיו.

Ps. 76.12: ב׳ חד מל :יוֹבִילוּ; but cf. Ps. 68.30: יוֹבִילוּ.

Ps. 106.8: ד׳ חד חס :וַיּוֹשִׁיעֵם; but cf. the *plene* spelling in all the three other occurrences, too: 2 Ki. 14.27; Judg. 3.9; Ps. 106.10.

Job 40.13: ג׳ חד מל :חֲבֹשׁ; Ezek. 24.17: ג׳ ב׳ חס וא׳ מל :חֲבוֹשׁ; and the third occurrence Isa. 30.26: ג׳ :חֲבֹשׁ make it clear that Job and Ezek. with their plene spelling exclude one another.

b)   The Masora contradicts its own catchword.

Isa. 2.15: בָּ׳ ויעזקהו :מִגְדָּל presupposes a vocalization מִגְדָּל, cf. Isa. 5.2: בָּ׳ ועל כל :מִגְדָּל. The Masoretic notes on these passages refer to one another.

Isa. 26.20: ז׳ מל :יַעֲבוֹר; but cf. the way the word is vocalized in Isa. 40.27: ז׳ מל :יַעֲבֹר.

Josh. 19.8: ל׳ כתיב א׳ :רָמַת, presupposes a spelling ראמת, cf. BHKK.

Josh. 19.49: דאורייתא חס דיהושע מל :לִגְבוּלֹתֶיהָ; cf. BHKK: לגבולתיה.

I Sam. 4.7: ד׳ חס בנבי :שִׁלְשׁוֹם; cf. BHKK: שלשם.

Isa. 59.19: ל׳ וחס :נוֹסָסָה.

Jer. 8.5: ב׳ חס :בַּתַּרְמִית.

Jer. 8.9: ב׳ חס דחס :הֹבִישׁוּ; cf. ib. verse 12: ב׳ חס דחס :הֵבִשׁוּ.

Judg. 1.3: ל׳ ומל :בְּגֹרָלֶךְ; cf. BHKK: בגורלך.

Judg. 9.37: ב׳ מל :יֹרְדִים; cf. BHKK: יורדים.

Isa. 59.19: ה׳ ד׳ מל ודין חס :וְיִירְאוּ.

§ 17.   The terminology (cf. §§ 5 and 12).

a)   General terms.

1) Gen. 18.33: כל אורי׳ חס :לִמְקֹמוֹ   כל אוריי׳ חס :וּשְׁמֹנֶה Gen. 5.7:

Gen. 19.22: ל׳ חס בתו׳ :בֹּאֲךָ   כל התורה חס :הַכְּרֻבִים Gen. 3.24:

2) Deut. 32.4: הַצּוּר: ל צדי רבתי
   Deut. 32.6: הַלַיהוה: ה גדולה

Both terms appear combined in a doublet:

Lev. 13.33: וְהִתְגַּלָּח: מאותיות גדולות // ג רבתי

3) The various terms for small letters are contained in the following doublets:

Num. 25.12: שָׁלוֹם: והיא חד מאב מאותיות קטנות // ו זוטא
Gen. 27.46: קַצְתִּי: מן אב מאותיו קטנות // קוף זעיר

4) Ex. 35.34: וּלְהוֹרֹת: ב חס וי׳׳ו בתרא
   Lev. 10.11: וּלְהוֹרֹת: ב וחס ו תניין

5) Ezek. 7.22: פָּרִיצִים: ב חד חס
   Jer. 32.29: נַגּוֹתֵיהֶם: ב א חס

b) Vocalization and accentuation.

6) Gen. 32.27: בֵּרַכְתָּנִי: ל קמץ   Gen. 27.39: מֵעָל: ג קמׄ
   Gen. 24.19: אֶשְׁאָב: לֹ   Gen. 17.12: בָּיִת: דָ

7) Gen. 16.13: רֳאִי: ל חטף קמץ   Jer. 49.28: וְשָׁדְדוּ: ל חטף
   Ex. 30.23: וְקִנְּמָן: לֹ   Ezek. 16.33: וַתִּשְׁחֳדִי: לֹ

8) Isa. 27.12: לְאַחַד: ז פתח
   Isa. 28.28: גִּלְגַּל: לֹ

9) Lev. 16.13: עֲנַן: ד חטפין פתחין
   Isa. 44.13: יְתָאֲרֵהוּ: לֹ

10) Deut. 5.10: וְעֹשֶׂה: ג בספר בסגול   1 Ki. 16.24: מֵאֵת: ל סגול
    Deut. 10.18: עֹשֶׂה: גֵ   Ex. 13.2: קַדֶּשׁ: ל רֹפ
    Isa. 8.7: מַעֲלֵה: ח סגול
    Isa. 19.4: קָשֶׁה: הֵ

11) Lev. 18.15: תְּגַלֵּה: כל חסופי בצרי   1 Ki. 10.25: וְנֵשֶׁק: ג צירי בליש
    Ex. 15.11: עֹשֵׂה: חֵ   1 Ki. 10.1: שֵׁמַע: הֵ

12) Gen. 41.43: בְּמִרְכֶּבֶת: ל בנקודה אחת
    1 Sam. 29.3: נָפְלוֹ: ל וכד אחרי נפלו

13) 2 Sam. 6.23: מוֹתָהּ: ל מל פום· וחד קבוץ פום :וכעת מותה
    Isa. 32.14: נֻטַּשׁ: לֹ

14) Num. 10.9: הַצֵּר׃ קמץ וב פתח ל   Gen. 43.12: הַמּוּשָׁב׃ קמ ואׁ פתׁ אׁ בׁ

Num. 23.10: וּמִסְפָּר׃ וד לֹ   Gen. 47.19: תֵשָׁם׃ ואׁ אׁ בׁ

Gen. 27.33: וָאֲבָרֲכֵהוּ׃ פת ואׁ קמׁ ל   Gen. 1.10: לַיַּבָּשָׁה׃ ל וחד ל

Isa. 51.2: וַאֲבָרֲכֵהוּ׃ ואׁ אׁ בׁ

15) Two different vowel-signs coming in succession are indicated by:

Gen. 33.5: חָנַן׃ ופת קמׁ ל

Gen. 41.57: חָזַ‎ _ ׃ הָ

The variety of sources whence these notes emanate, leads to a corresponding difference in the annotations on the identical word: Num. 5.7: אָשֵׁם׃ פתחין ב refers to the second vowel only; but Lev. 5.19: אָשֵׁם׃ בָּ _ reflects both vowel-signs.

16) The vocalization of *waw* with verbal forms as copular or as consecutive *waw* is indicated by referring to the following consonant: whether or not it carries a *dagesh*:

Isa. 50.2: וְתָמֹת׃ דגש וחד רפי ל

Ex. 28.28: וְיִרְכְּסוּ׃ וירכסו וחד רפי ל

17) Hos. 2.6: אֲרַחֵם׃ באתנחת פתחי יאׁ

1 Ki. 3.6: אֱלֹהָי׃ _ ˄ במׂבׁ דכו אסׂף וכל קמץ חׂ

c) Details of spelling.

18) The terms קרי and יתיר interchangeably used:

1 Ki. 22.13: דְּבָרֶיךָ׃ ק דברך   Jer. 2.33: לִמַּדְתְּי׃ ק למדת

1 Ki. 18.36: וּבִדְבָרֶיךָ׃ יו״ד יתיר   Jer. 13.21: לִמַּדְתְּי׃ יו״ד יתיר

1 Ki. 1.27: עֲבָדֶיךָ׃ ק עבדך   Jer. 18.10: הָרָעָה׃ ק הרע

Ps. 16.10: חֲסִידֶיךָ׃ יו״ד יתיר   Prov. 27.10: וְרֵעֲךָ׃ הׁ יתיר

Both terms combined result in a doublet:

Prov. 15.14: וּפְנֵי׃ נון יתיר // ק ופי

19) The terms קרי and חסר; קרי and מלא:

α) Job 5.18: וְיָדָו׃ ק וידיו

Lev. 16.21: יָדָו׃ חׂ הׁ

Both terms appear together in the doublet:

Ezek. 43.26: יָדָו׃ חׂ הׁ // ק ידיו

1 Sam. 18.22: עבדיו ק׃ עֲבָדָו; the equivalent term חסר is to be found in the doublet Jer. 22,4: וַעֲבָדָו ב׳ חס // ועבדיו ק.

Similarly: 1 Ki. 6.38: מִשְׁפָּטַו׃ ב׳ חס // משפטיו ק.

β) 2 Sam. 23.16: מבר ק׃ מִבֹּאר; the equivalent term מלא occurs in the doublet ib. verse 15: מבר ק // ג מל אלף מִבֹּאר. The third occurrence of the word in this spelling referred to here, is ib. verse 20: הבר ק׃ הַבֹּאר.

Nah. 1.3:   וגדל ק׃ וּגְדָול
Ps. 145.8:   ב׳ חד מל׃ וּגְדָול

The term חד proves that this note belongs to a different textual type of the Bible, in which one of these two passages had the word in *defective* spelling; cf. BHKK on Ps. 145.8: וּגְדָל ב׳ חד מל.

20) The terms קרי and כתיב or כתיב כן׃

α) Ex. 22.26: כסותו ק׃ כְּסוּתֹה   Josh. 15.48: כו ק׃ וְשֹוֹכֹה
Gen. 9.21: ד כתיב כן אָהֳלֹה   2 Sam. 9.4: י כתיב כן אִיפֹה

β) The equivalent term can now be traced in a doublet only.

2 Ki. 14.13: ויבא ק׃ וַיָּבֹאוּ; cf. both terms in: 2 Ki. 12.21: ויבא ק // ג כֹב וַיָּבֹאוּ.

Jer. 31.39: וקו ק // ג כֹב וְקָוֶה; cf. 1 Ki. 7.23: קו ק׃ קָוֶה
Ezek. 16.36: נתת ק // ב׳ כֹב נָתַתְּי; cf. ib. verse 18: נתת ק׃ נָתַתְּי
Ps. 140.13: ידעתי ק // ב כֹב יָדַעְתָּ; cf. Job 42.2: ידעתי ק׃ יָדַעְתָּ

γ) The components of the doublets cannot be traced separately.

Josh. 11.16:   ל וֹכֹב // תו ק׃ וּשְׁפֵלָתֹה
1 Ki. 14.2:   ה כתי י // את ק׃ אַתְּי
Josh. 3.4:   ניו ק // ב׳ כתי כן׃ וּבֵינָו
1 Sam. 24.19:   ואתה ק // ו כֹב׃ וְאַתְּ
Isa. 9.2:   לו ק // טֹו כֹב׃ לֹא

21) The terms חסר and כתיב כן.

The fact that the plural of יד in connection with the suffix of the 3. pers. masc. sing. appears in the *defective* spelling ידו, is termed. as follows:

Ex. 32.19:　　דיו ק̇ // ה̇ כֹכ :מִיָּדָו

Lev. 9.22:　　ידיו ק̇ // ה̇ כתיב ידו וקרינן ידיו :יָדָו

Ezek. 43.26:　　ידיו ק̇ // ה̇ חס̇ :יָדָו

Hence, the terms חסר and כתיב כן are interchangeably used in order
to indicate one and the same spelling. They go back to different lists;
cf. Deut. 32.35: ל̇ וכתֹ̇ כן· ובסֹא נמסר ל̇ חס דחֹס :עֵתְדת.

22) The terms יתיר and מלא.

Josh. 18.20: יתיר ו̇　:וְגְבֹול	Josh. 6.3: יתיר יו̇"ד :הַקֵּיף
Isa. 11.3: ג̇ מל̇ :יִשְׁפֹּוט	1 Ki. 9.25: ל̇ מל̇ :וְהַקְטִיר
Ps. 89.29: יתיר וי̇"ו :אֶשְׁמֹור	
Isa. 26.20: ז̇ מל̇ :יַעֲבֹור	

23) The terms כתיב and יתיר.

2 Sam. 11.1: יתיר א̇ :הַמְּלָאכִים	Jer. 30.16: ל̇ ויתיר א̇ :שֹׁאסַיִךְ
2 Sam. 12.1: ג̇ כתיב אלף :רָאש	1 Ki. 4.11: ד̇ כתֹ̇ א̇ :דֹּאר
2 Sam. 11.24: יתיר אלף :הַמֹּורִאים	
Isa. 30.5: ל̇ כתיב כן :הֹבְאֹיש	

A combination of both terms results in a doublet:

Hos. 4.6:　　ל̇ וכתֹ̇ כן // יתיר א̇ :וְאֶמְאָסְאָךְ

Josh. 21.32:　　ג̇ כֹכ // יתיר א̇ :דֹּאר

24) The terms כתיב and מלא.

The absence of a *waw* to signify the vowel *o* is termed as follows:

1 Ki. 8.18:　　ב̇ חד כתֹ̇ הטיבות :הֲטִיבֹת

Ezek. 16.7:　　ב̇ א̇ מל̇ :נָכֹנוּ

25) The terms כתיב and כתיב כן.

2 Sam. 12.1: ג̇ כתיב אלף :רָאש	Lev. 21.6: ט̇ כתֹ̇ יו̇"ד :אֹשֵּׁי
Prov. 10.4: ג̇ כתיב כן :רָאש	Lev. 21.21: ט̇ כתֹ̇ כן :אֹשֵּׁי

2 Sam. 9.4: י̇ כתֹ̇ כן :אֵיפֹה; both terms combined: 1 Sam. 19.22:
י̇ כתֹ̇ כן // בה̇"א :אֵיפֹה

Judg. 21.19: ח̇ כתֹ̇ וי̇"ו בסוף :בְּשִׁלֹו; both terms: 1 Sam. 3.21: בְּשִׁלֹו:
ח̇ כֹכ // בוי̇"ו

26) The terms חסר and כתיב כן.

I Ki. 21.9: בֹ חס וי״ו :וְהָשִׁיבוּ   Gen. 17.20: ד חֹס י בתֹרֹ בתוֹ :וְשִׂיאָם

I Ki. 21.12: ב כֹב ובענין :וְהָשִׁיבוּ   Gen. 25.16: ד כֹב בתורֹ :וְשִׂיאָם

Lev. 5.16: ג חֹס יו״ד תניין :חֲמִישִׁתוֹ; the equivalent term in the doublet:

Lev. 27.13: ג כֹב וו חֹס יו״ד תניין :חֲמִישִׁתוֹ

Ezek. 16.43: ה כתֹ כן :תּוֹעֲבֹתָיִךְ; the equivalent term in the doublet:

Ezek. 5.11: ה כֹב וֹ חֹס בתֹרֹ :תּוֹעֲבֹתָיִךְ

Both terms appear combined in doublets:

Deut. 17.8: ל כֹב // חֹס וי״ו :רִיבֹת

Mic. 4.3: ג כֹב // חֹס וי״ו :עֲצָמִים

Jer. 2.17: ל וכֹב // חֹס י :מוֹלִכֵךְ

Jer. 2.18: ל כֹב // חֹס י :שָׁחֹר

Deut. 1.32: ל וכֹב // חֹס יו״ד בתֹרֹ :מַאֲמִינִם

Deut. 4.13: ה כֹב בתורֹ // חֹס וי״ו קדמֹ :לֻחוֹת

Jer. 6.20: ב כֹב // חֹס וי״ו קדמֹ :עֹלוֹתֵיכֶם

27) Specification of the vowel-letter referred to.

From the Masoretic note on the passage Josh. 22.27: :דֹרוֹתֵינוּ
ב ובענין· חד מלֹ וחד חֹס דחֹס· ובסֹא נמסר: חד מלֹ וי״ו קדמֹ וחד חֹס דחֹס: we
learn that while the terms in general use מלֹ or חֹס had no reference
as to which vowel-letter was meant by this remark, certain manuscripts were more specific in their terminology. Cf. the following
examples:

α) Lev. 14.4: כל חֹס וי״ו קדמֹ :טָהֹרוֹת

    I Ki. 7.2: ב חֹס וי״ו קדמֹ :וּכְרֻתוֹת

    I Sam. 1.20: ל וחֹס וי״ו קדמֹ :לִתְקֻפוֹת

β) Lev. 14.37: ל וחֹס וי״ו בתֹרֹ :שְׁקַעֲרוּרֹת

γ) Lev. 23.17: ל ומלֹ וֹ קדמֹ :מִמּוֹשְׁבֹתֵיכֶם

δ) Jer. 33.11: חֹס יו״ד קדמֹ :מְבִאִים

ε) I Sam. 20.13: ב חֹס יו״ד בתֹרֹ :יֵיטֵב

    2 Ki. 4.44: ב חֹס יו״ד בתֹרֹ :וַיּוֹתִרוּ

d) The term חד refers to the cross-reference.

Ezek. 33.25: ב חד מלֹ :וְעֵינְכֶם   Hos. 5.13: ב חד מלֹ :לִרְפֹּא

Mal. 1.5: ב חד חֹס :וְעֵינֵיכֶם   Eccl. 3.3: ב חד חֹס :לִרְפֹּוא

Ps. 39.11:   בֹ חד כתי א :כָלִיתִי   Ps. 51.10:   בֹ חד כתי א :דִּכִּיתָ

Ps. 119.101:   בֹ חד כתי י :כָּלִאתִי   Ps. 89.11:   בֹ חד כתי יו"ד :דִּכִּאתָ

Hab. 1.5: בֹ חד פת :יְסֻפַּר refers to Ps. 22.31: יְסֻפַּר.

Job 21.4: בֹ חד קמץ :תִּקְצַר refers to Num. 11.23: תִקְצָר.

With our finding (above under a 5) in mind that חד and אחד are interchangeably used, cf. also:

Ezek. 16.7: נָכֹנוּ : בֹ א מל; cf. Prov. 19.29: נָכוֹנוּ.

Lev. 14.6: הַשְּׁחוּטָה :ל חס וא מל; cf. Lev. 14.51: הַשְּׁחֻטָה.

Of the usage of the term חד to indicate the very passage under observation (cf. § 12 d 16), I came across these two instances only:

Hab. 1.16: בֹ חד חס :בְּרִאָה; the cross-reference Num. 16.30: בְּרִיאָה is in *plene* spelling.

Mic. 1.4: גֹ חד קמץ :בְּמוֹרָד; cf. Josh. 10.11 and Jer. 48.5: בְּמוֹרַד with *patah*.

e)   The identical notes on passages in a different spelling (cf. § 12 e).

Jer. 32.8:   גֹ בֹ חס וא מל :דּוֹדִי

Jer. 32.9:   גֹ בֹ חס וא מל :דֹּדִי

2 Sam. 15.27:   בֹ חד מל וחד חס :הֲרוֹאֶה

Ezek. 8.6:   בֹ חד מל וחד חס :הֲרֹאֶה

2 Chron. 6.25:   בֹ א חס וא מל :וַהֲשֵׁיבוֹתָם

1 Ki. 8.34:   בֹ חד חס וחד מל :וַהֲשֵׁבֹתָם

2 Sam. 22.30:   דֹ גֹ מל וא חס :אָרוּץ

Ps. 18.30:   דֹ גֹ מל וא חס :אָרֻץ

f)   The term דין.

Ps. 78.43:   גֹ דין מל :וּמוֹפְתָיו   Lev. 15.19:   בֹ דין חס :זֹבָהּ

Ex. 15.11:   בֹ ודין חס :בָּאֵלִם   Ezek. 47.22:   בֹ דין חס :הוֹלִדוּ

The use of the term דין in conjunction with חד results in a doublet; cf. Lev. 13.45: בֹ חד חס :פָּרֻעַ; this note refers (according to subdivision d) to the second occurrence, namely Ex. 32.25 where we actually find פָּרֻעַ in *defective* spelling. On this second passage the Masora notes: בֹ א מל ודין חס. This is obviously a combination of בֹ א מל (referring to Lev. 13.45) and בֹ ודין חס. Similarly we shall have to explain as doublets the following instances:

Ezek. 40.4: הַרְאוֹתְכָה‎: מל ודין // חס חד ב‎

Jer. 5.22: הַאוֹתִי‎: מל דין // חס א ב‎

Ex. 22.19: יָחֳרָם‎: קמֹ ודין // פתחי ב ג‎

On Ezek. 3.17: וְהִזְהַרְתָּ‎ the Masora remarks: מל וא חס ב ג.‎ This might be considered merely as an amplification of an original note: חס ב ג;‎ for now it is self-understood that the one remaining instance is in *plene* spelling. However, as the note reads, it does not clearly indicate the way how the instance under consideration (Ezek. 3.17) is spelled. Clarity is achieved by employing the term דין;‎ cf. Ex. 18.20: וְהִזְהַרְתָּה‎: וא חס ב ג‎ מל דין מל.‎ Compare the note on Ezek. 3.17 with that on Ex. 18.20, and it becomes at once evident that in Ex. 18.20 we have a doublet: מל וא //‎ ודין מל.‎ A similar case is Lev. 25.45: הוֹלִידוּ‎: מל ודין // מל וא חס א ב;‎ cf. Ezek. 47.22: הוֹלִדוּ‎: חס דין ב.‎ We have thus demonstrated the separate use of each component and their combination into a doublet. Consequently we shall regard as doublets Masoretic notes as the following:

2 Sam. 2.12: גִּבְעוֹנָה‎: מל דין // מל וחד חס חד ב‎

Ex. 38.18: וְקוֹמָה‎: מל דין // חס וחד מל חד ב‎

Ex. 28.20: בְּמִלּוּאֹתָם‎: מל דין // חס וחד מל חד ב‎

Ex. 7.12: מַטֹּתָם‎: מל ודין // מל וחד חס חד ב‎

2 Sam. 7.18: הֲבִיאֹתַנִי‎: חס דין // מל וחד חס חד ב‎

1 Sam. 17.24: בִּרְאוֹתָם‎: הוא ודין // מל וא חס ב ג‎

Isa. 50.1: כְּרִיתוּת‎: דין והוא // מל וא חס ב‎

2 Sam. 19.42: וַיַּעַבְרוּ‎: דין והוא // חס וא מל ג ד‎

Ex. 32.10: וַאֲכַלֵּם‎: פתח דין // קמץ וחד פתח חד ב‎

Lev. 14.51: הַשְּׁחוּטָה‎: מל דין // חס קדמֹ ב‎

In a similar way, the Masoretic note on 1 Ki. 12.27: וַהֲרָגֵנִי‎: חס וחד מל חד ב‎ was expanded into a doublet on Gen. 20.11: וַהֲרָגוּנִי‎: חס וחד מל חד ב‎ דרחבעם חס.‎ For the separate use of the second component cf. similarly Gen. 24.10: טוב‎: דמשק ב,‎ a reference to 2 Ki. 8.9. Consequently, 1 Sam. 28.6: בָּאוּרִים‎: על כן באורים חס // חס וחד מל חד ב‎ is a doublet, too; the cross-reference is to Isa. 24.15. The apparent anomaly in the note: על כן באורים חס‎ (while באורים‎ is quoted in *plene* spelling!) reflects only carelessness of the scribe or printer; cf. similarly on Deut. 32.47: וּבַדָּבָר הַזֶּה‎

the Masoretic note בֿ אינכם מאמינים, which refers to Deut. 1.32 where the
word occurs in *defective* spelling: מַאֲמִינָם: בתרֿ חס יוֿ׳׳ד // וכֿכֿ לֿ.

D.   Jacob ben Chayim as Editor

A.   The Masoretic Text is Eclectically Established

Jacob ben Chayim does not follow any manuscript or authority in every
detail, but uses his own judgment. Though a Spanish manuscript served
him as a basis for his work, he nevertheless deviates from it occasionally;
cf. on Gen. 19.13. In Num. 5.27 he accepts the vocalization of Ben Asher,
but in Jer. 25.29 he follows Ben Naphtali. Similarly he sometimes exhibits
the readings of the מערבאי in his text, and on other occasions those of the
מדנחאי. He thus proceeds according to the eclectic method. But we are
at a complete loss, when searching for the underlying principles.

§ 18.   Authorities quoted for doubtful readings.

a)   Referring to the spelling-text.

Gen. 19.13: אֶת הַמָּקוֹם: המקום אל נמצא עליו נסמך אשר אספמיא ובספר

Gen. 25.14: וְדוּמָה: בעל אומֿ וכן בהֿ׳׳א דומה עליו: נסמך אשר אספמיא ובספר
באלף דומא נמצא: ספרי וברוב המסורֿ

Gen. 27.3: צֵידָה: בסוף הֿ כתיֿ תיבין כֿאֿ מן חד והיא נחמןֿ דרב פלוגת אבל יתירֿ הֿ
קרי ולא תיבותֿ

Ps. 105.22: שָׂרָיו: קֿ שריו כתיֿ שרו בבֿרֿ אידי רב דעת לפי

Deut. 32.6: הֲלַיהוה: לסֿפריֿ לחוד יֿ׳׳י לחוד הל לחוד לנהרדעיֿ לחודֿ יֿ׳׳י לחוד הֿ לסוראיֿ
מלתא חדא אחרי

b)   Referring to the vocalization-text.

Gen. 26.35: וַתְּהֶיֵין: דינו וכן שמשון החֿר ובשם אספמיא בספרי נמצא כן

Gen. 18.15: וַתְּכַחֵשׁ: שהוא אמר: מלונדרש משה והרֿ׳׳ר בפתחֿ מנקדים הנקדנים כל
לכחש רגילה היתה שלא לפי בקמץֿ

Num. 7.85: הַקְּעָרָה: הֲקְעָרָה יוסףֿ רב ופליג לֿ

Ezek. 18.11: אָכָל: ומסר פתוחֿ כתבו זרקא יוסף רֿ אבל קמוץֿ מצאתיו ספרים בקצת
פומיה קמץ אכל דלא פומיהֿ פתח דאכיל עליו:

Lev. 4.35: וּיֹסַר חֵלֶב: כאשר מפריֿ׳׳ז גרשם רבינו ונקד שכתב אחד בחומש נמצא כן
מונחים ובֿ אזלא יוסר

c)   Differences between Ben Asher and Ben Naphtali.

Ex. 21.19:   פלוגתא דבן אשר ובן נפתלי· דין אליבא דבן אשר :וְהִתְהַלֵּךְ

Num. 5.27:   לבן אשר כן ניקודו :הַמְאָרֲרִים

Jer. 25.29:   לבן נפתלי :אֲשֶׁר־נִקְרָא

d)   מדינחאי and מערבאי.

α)   The text exhibits the מדינחאי-reading:

1 Ki. 16.1:   ל· למערבאי: אל בעשא :עַל־בַּעְשָׁא

1 Ki. 3.20:   למערבאי מל· למדנחאי ב חס: ולבי ער· ודין :יְשֵׁנָה

1 Ki. 3.12:   למדנחאי חס :כִּדְבָרֶךָ

β) The text exhibits the מערבאי-reading:

1 Sam. 1.3:   למערבאי חס· למדנחאי מל :וּפִנְחָס

2 Sam. 6.23:   למדנחאי כתי ולד :יָלֶד

Jer. 34.2:   (סֹא יכניהו :יְכָנְיָה § 22γ :cf) למדנחאי: צדקיה :צִדְקִיָּהוּ

Mic. 6.5:   מדינחאי: מי כתי· מה קרי :מַה

Isa. 3.17:   ל· מדינחאי פַתהן :פָּתְהֵן

§ 19.   The Masoretic tradition at variance.

Cf. Jacob ben Chayim's statement in his *Introduction*: וּבמקומות
שמצאתי הפרש בין ספרי המסרה· זה אומר בכה· וזה אומר בכה· הבאתי
דעות שניהם

Ex. 16.13:   ב· וכב· יבסֹא נמסר: ל מל השליו :הַשְּׂלָו

Ex. 26.5:   דין חס תנין מל· ובמסר אחרת נמסר: ב· וכתי כן :מַקְבִּילֹת

Judg. 10.6:   ל מל· ובסֹא נמסר: ב מל :עֲבָדוּהוּ

Judg. 19.17:   סֹא נמסר עליו: ב חס בליש :בִּרְחֹוב

1 Sam. 1.28:   ל· ובסֹא נמס: ל וחס :הִשְׁאִלְתִּיהוּ

Isa. 31.4:   ל· סֹא נמסר: ב :וּמֵהֲמֹונָם

Jer. 6.19:   ב מל· סֹא: ל מל :מַחְשְׁבֹותָם

Jer. 29.11:   ל חס· סֹא: ב חס :הַמַּחֲשָׁבֹת

Ex. 4.12:   ל ומל· ובסֹא: והורתיך· ונמסר עליו: ל וכב· :וְהֹורֵיתִיךָ

Gen. 36.7:   ד ג חס ו· ודין מל· ויֹס· דין חס וא'ו :מְגוּרֵיהֶם

2 Sam. 17.14:   חס· ופלוגתא עליה· אית סיפרי דמסֹר נמסר: טֹו חס· ואית :(2°) אַבְשָׁלֹם
סיפרי נמסר: יד חס· ואין מונין זה מן המנין

Josh. 21.11:   כול כן: חס יו''ד· ובסֹא זקן ומדוייק: כול חס י בֹמֹב· חברון לבנה :מִגְרָשֶׁהָ

Gen. 49.21:   חד מן ה̇ מל̇(!)· ובסْא̇ נמסר עליו: ד̇ חס̇· וכן הוא בתיקון סֹת̇ חס̇   :הַנֹּתֵן
   ובֿרוב הספרים

Gen. 26.22:   כן כתוב· ובתיקון סֹת̇ ראיתי: רחבת חס̇· ומוגה חס̇   :רְחֹבֿות

Josh. 8.12:   כן כתי̇ וקרי מכח מסֹה̇   :לָעַיר

2 Sam. 14.21:   עשית ק̇· ובֿרוב הספרים בדקתי ולא מצאתי זה קרי וכתי̇ כי   :עָשִׂיתָי
   אם אחד מני אלף

Isa. 38.14:   בקצת ספרי̇ כתי̇ כסיס וקרי̇ כסוס· אמנם לא מצאתיו שנמנה עם   :כְּסוּס
   אֹת̇ הכתובֿי יו̇̇ד באמצע תיבות וק̇ וי̇̇ו

Ps. 24.4:   נפשי ק̇· ותימא דלא נמנה במסורה גדולה מאינון דכתיבֿין וי̇̇ו   :נַפְשׁו
   בסוף תיבות וקריין יו̇̇ד

§ 20.   Masora and text-tradition at variance.

On Prov. 23.5: עָשֹׁה the marginal Masora states: עיין במסֹר̇ רבֿת̇ בערך עשו
מה דקשה. In the Masora *finalis* referred to we read s.v. עשו: ד̇ כֹב̇· וסימ̇ נמסר
בירמיה סֹי̇ כֹב̇· ועיין שם מה דאקשין (we re-arranged here the somewhat
confused word-order of the statement). In a note on the passage Jer. 22.4
referred to, the problem is clearly formulated: עשו: ד̇ כתיבֿ ו בסוף̇· וסימ̇:
דרכך ומעלליך· כי אם הטיב תטיבו· כי אם עשו תעשו את הדבר הזה· ואתנהו ביד איל גוים·
ויש ספרים נמסר: בזנותך אחר גוים· במקום: אם עשו תעשו· דסיפֿרא· ובדקתי אֹכֹ בֿספרים
מדוייקים ומצאתיו בה̇̇א· ותמיה לי: אם כן למה לא נמנה עם אותם ד̇ עשה שהם כתובֿים
בה̇̇א ואם נאמר: שהוא בוי̇̇ו· אם כן נשבש כל הספרים המדוייקים· שבכלם נמסר על כל
אחד מהד̇ עשו: ד̇ כתי̇ וי̇̇ו· וגם ספרי המסֹר̇· ועוד תמיה לי: למה נמנה הסכלת עשו דאורייתא
עם הד̇ כתיבֿ ה̇· מאחר שהוא בוי̇̇ו· ונמסר עליו: לית כתיבֿ וי̇̇ו· ימנה אותו עם אותם שהם
בוי̇̇ו· .The word עשו occurs ··בוי̇̇ו· ונתקשיתי בהאי עניינא טובֿא· ולא ידֿענא מה למימר ביה
four times in this spelling, with *waw* as final letter. These passages are:
Jer. 4.18; ib. 7.5; ib. 22.4 and Ezek. 31.11. In some manuscripts the
Masora substitutes Ezek. 23.30 for Jer. 22.4 of our list. I, therefore,
examined manuscripts which are reputed as correct, and found the
instance Ezek. 23.30 spelled with ה. But now I wonder. Since Ezek. 23.30
is spelled עשה with ה, why is this passage not enumerated together with
the four other occurrences of עשה in this spelling with ה? (According to
our Bible, עשה with ה at the end occurs eight times!). This argument might
be taken as a proof that in Ezek. 23.30 עשו should be spelled, with *waw*.
But if so, then all those manuscripts which are reputed as correct turn
out to be incorrect, for in all of them there occurs a Masoretic note on
each of the four passages (mentioned above) stating: עשו occurs 4 times

with ו. The same is true of the Masoretic compilations. There is even another fact that puzzles me: why is עשו in the passage Gen. 31.28 enumerated among the four occurrences of עשה with ה? This passage is not only spelled with ו in the text, but also has a Masoretic note saying: this is the only occurrence of this form (construct infinitive) with ו! Let the Masora enumerate this passage together with the other instances of spelling עשו with *waw*! I did much hard thinking on this subject. Still I do not know how to explain it."

§ 21.   The text is made to conform with the Masora.

Whenever feasible the reading of the text is selected—or revised—in such a manner as to conform to the respective Masoretic list:

Gen. 25.25:   אַדְמוֹנִי: איתי ראיתי בתיקון ס״ת · וכן ראיתי בתיקון מלא· ולפי המסורה מלא· וכן ראיתי ברוב הספרי חס׳

Gen. 26.25:   אָהֳלֹה: בתיקון ס׳ת וגם בספרי מדוייקי ראיתי· אהלו· בו· אבל בעל המסר

אומר אהלה· בה״א· ויש חילוק גם במסרי· שיש קצת ספרי

שאינם מונין זה בחשבון

Gen. 46.3:   מֵרְדָה מִצְרָיְמָה: ובתיקון סופרים ראיתי· מרדה מצרים· אבל בעל המסור

אומר· מרדה מצרימה

Jer. 21.6:   וְאֶת הָאָדָם: ל· ובקצת ספרי כתי· את האדם· וטעות· כי הוא נמנה במסר

רבת עם אותם ואת· דלית להון זוגא

Ezek. 22.18:   בֶּן אָדָם: בהרבה ספרים הוא בזקף· וטעות· כי אינו ממנין הל״א שמונה

המסרה בטע׳ זקף

Ezek. 39.28:   אֶל אַדְמָתָם: יפה וכך דינו· כי לא נמנה במסר כי אם ד· על אדמתם בסיפ׳

וזה לא נמנה בכללם· ומטעי ביה ספרי

Ezek. 45.10:   יְהִי: כן דינו· כי בקצת ספרי מצאתיו· יהיה· ובמקצת· יהי· וטעות· כי לא

נמנה עם אותם דחס ה׳ בסוף תיבות וקרי· אלא דינו· יהי הכתיב והקרי

Ps. 88.10:   בְּכָל יוֹם: ג· וראיתי בספר מדוייק כתוב· בכל עת· ולולי המסורה הייתי

מגיה כך

Ps. 144.2:   תַחְתָּי: רש״י פי׳ כי בספר מוגה ועליו מסורה שהיה לו· היה כתוב תחתי·

וקרי תחתיו· ונ׳׳ל כי הוא טעות· שבמסר רבת לא נמנו כי אם י״ב· חס וי״ו

בסוף תיבות וקריין· ובדקתי בד׳ ובה׳ ספרי מסר ואינ׳ מונים כי אם י״ב·

וזה לא נמנה עמהם

Prov. 4.15:   וַעֲבֹר: בקצת ספרי כתו׳ יעבור· וקרי ועבור· אמנם לפי דעת בעלי המסרה

לא יתכן· כי לא נמנו כי אם כ׳ב דכתי׳ יו״ד בריש תיבות וקרי׳ וי״ו·

וזה לא נמנה עמהם

Ex. 14.25:   נִלְחָם: כל׳ בקמ׳· כי לא נמנה במסור במספר הי׳׳ב פתח׳

Josh. 21.35: יש ספרי מוגה בהם: וממטה ראובן את בצר וגו ובכל הספ המדוייקים הישנים
לא נמצא· ועיין בפי הקמחי· וגם במסֹר עיין· כי כשמונה כ״ח את· לא
נמצא בכללן· וזו ראיה גדולה

The only instances I am aware of, in which Jacob ben Chayim wittingly
deviates from what he considers to be implied by the Masora, are the two
following passages, in one of which he yields to the authority of Ḳimḥi:

Gen. 16.12: כן בכל הספרים· אבל לפי המסורה לא יכול להיות ובתיקון :וְעַל פְּנֵי
ס״ת ראיתי: על פני

Ezek. 43.26: יכפרו קֹ· אמנם בקצת ספרים מדוייקים ישנ׳ מצאתי שהכת והקרי: :וְכִפְּרוּ
יכפרו· וגם המסרה מוכחת כן· כי לא נמנה עם אות שהם כתובים וי״ו
בריש תיבות וקרי יו״ד· לולי שראיתי לרד״ק בפירושיו שאמר:
שהכת וכפרו· והקרי יכפרו

§ 22.   The selecting of a reading in the absence of Masora.

In all of those numerous cases, in which Jacob ben Chayim found himself confronted with the problem of selecting his reading among the
variants offered in the source-manuscripts which he consulted, and where
no Masoretic note was at hand to guide him in his choice, he seems not
to have followed any fixed rules as to which manuscript deserves greater
credence in every detail, but decided each case on its own merits, according
to his judgment. In a note he records the variant reading which he rejected:

Ex. 19.4: חלוקים הספרים· ויש הרבה ספרי· במצרים· ובספרים מדוייקֹ :לְמִצְרָיִם
גם בקצת סֹת מדוייקים נמצא: למצרים

Ezek. 29.2: כן דינו לדעת הקמחי· ובספרים מדוייקים ישנים מצאתי כתו כלה :כָּלָה
בחולם

1 Ki. 20.20: וינס ארם בספרים מדוייקים וישנים :וַיָּנֻסוּ אֲרָם

Josh. 24.26: ל חס׳ ובסֹא מדוייק מלא :וַיְּקִמֶהָ

1 Sam. 23.4: בקצת ספרים חס׳ ובס מוגה מל :קְעִילָה

Jer. 22.2: סֹא שמעו· ובס מוגה: שמע :שְׁמַע

Job 15.17: בסֹפ מוגה דגש :אֲחַוְּךָ

Judg. 9.35: כן בסֹפ מוגה :הַמַּאְרָב

Jer. 9.22: כן בסֹפ מוגה: (3°) אַל

Jer. 13.7: כן בס מוגה :לֹא

Jer. 51.46: כן בסֹפ מוגה: (1°) מִשֵּׁל

Ezek. 46.6:   כן בסיפ מוגה ויפה :בָּקָר תְּמִימָם

Ps. 109.18:   כן בסֹפֿ מוגה :וְהַשֶּׁמֶן

In these cases Jacob ben Chayim decided according to the evidence of the ספר מוגה; but in other instances he rejected this evidence:

Isa. 15.2:   בסֹפֿ מוגה: ודיבן כתֿי :וְדִיבוֹן

Jer. 44.8:   בספר מוגה: להם :לָכֶם

Ezek. 14.23:   בספר מוגה: לה :בָּה

Job 9.8:   ובספר מוגה: במתי עב :בָּמֳתֵי יָם

Josh. 19.34:   סֹאֿ מוגה: אזנו :אַזְנוֹת

Josh. 9.21:   סֹאֿ ישׁן מצאתיו מוגה: אלהם :לָהֶם

Josh. 19.15:   ל· סֹאֿ ויראלה בריש :וְיִדְאֲלָה

Isa. 34.16:   סֹאֿ ואשה :אִשָּׁה

Jer. 6.27:   סֹאֿ לבם :דַּרְכָּם

Jer. 9.15:   סֹאֿ ידעום :יָדָעוּ

Jer. 14.14:   סֹאֿ לכם :לָהֶם

Jer. 24.1:   (למדנחאי צדקיה :צִדְקִיָּהוּ :18dβ § .cf) סֹאֿ יכניהו :יְכָנְיָה

Ezek. 23.5:   סֹאֿ וַתַעְנָב :וַתַּעְגַּב

Ezek. 36.4:   ל· סֹאֿ השממות :הַשֹּׁמֵמוֹת

Isa. 51.5:   סֹאֿ חֹסֿ :זְרֹעִי

Josh. 8.21:   מצאנו בספר ישׁן: העיר :הָעִי

Isa. 63.15:   ברוב הספרים חֹסֿ :מִזְּבֻל

Ezek. 40.4:   ל· וכֿכֿ· ובקצת ספרֿי חֹסֿ ה בתרֿ :הֲבָאתָה

Gen. 36.7:   ישׁ ספרים חסר :רְכוּשָׁם

Isa. 27.4:   ל· ויֹסֿ שׁי״ן בחטף קמץ :אֶפְשְׂעָה

I Sam. 25.22:   ישׁ ספרים: אור :עַד הַבֹּקֶר

Lev. 10.12:   כ ספר ירושׁ· ובסֹאֿ נמצא:וְאֶל אלעזר :וְאֶל אֶלְעָזָר

E. Conclusions

A. HOW TO EDIT THE BIBLE

§ 23.   The problem.

1)   The Hebrew Bible is the basic source for our knowledge of Hebrew grammar. In this relationship between Bible and grammar, the Bible occupies the first place, being of primary importance, while the grammar can best be described by the Talmudic term of a תולדה דידה (an offspring

thereof). Thus, a reliable Bible text is an indispensable prerequisite for all grammatical researches; but on the other hand: no grammatical theories must be permitted to influence in any way the shaping of the Bible text. For else, the grammar based upon such a Bible text would merely demonstrate to what extent our own preconceived grammatical theories were actually applied in the editing of the aforesaid Bible, instead of revealing any genuinely Hebrew grammatical laws.

2) It is lamentable that this fundamental consideration has obviously not been the guiding principle of the Bible editions hitherto published:

a) The Bible editions which at present are in common use, as those published by S. Baer, C. D. Gindsburg, R. Kittel (first and second edition of his *Biblia Hebraica*) and M. Letteris, are based upon Jacob ben Chayim's first Masoretic Bible. Though they claim to be faithful reproductions thereof, they very frequently changed the vocalization in its many aspects (cf. p. 418, § 7) as well as the accentuation, so as to make their text the better conform with what they considered "correct" Hebrew grammar, but which we would more adequately term as *their* respective conception of Hebrew grammar. The many differences which exist between these editions—all of which claim to be *carefully revised according to the Masora*—reflect solely the corresponding differences in the grammatical views held by the respective editors. Cf. the post-script of the *"Neu revidirte und verbesserte"* Bible edition, published in מנצא תרנ״ד under the auspices of the "Jewish Orthodox Bible Institute in Germany", which reads: הוגה על פי המראה אשר ראיתי בספרי דפוס קדמונים ועל משפט דקדוק הלשון. It goes without saying that our scientific Hebrew grammars, being based upon one or the other of these Bible editions, are basically valueless.

b) Jacob ben Chayim's Bible is, according to his own statement in his *Introduction*, a revision of the then extant Bible texts: ואחר שראיתי בספרי המסרה והתבוננתי בהם· ראיתים מבולבלים בתכלית ומשובשים· עד שאין בהם בית אשר אין שם מת ··· וכשראיתי כל זה ··· הייתי מתקנם על נכון· ובמקומות שמצאתי הפרש בין ספרי המסרה: זה אומר בכה וזה אומר בכה· הבאתי דעות שניהם ··· ובמקומות שהיה קשה לי על לשון ספר אחד מהמסרה· שלא הייתי מוצא כדבריו ברוב הספרים· ובמסרה אחרת באופן אחר· ולא היה קשה· ובמקומות שהיה קשה מדידה אדידיה ··· הייתי חוקר עד שהייתי מוצא האמת לעניות דעתי ··· והשם יודע כמה טורח עבדתי על זה In establishing his text, Jacob ben Chayim proceeded according to what might be called the eclectic method—provided we consent to call his procedure a method. Thus, some times he follows Ben Naftali, but on some other occasions he gives Ben Asher the preference; on two occasions he refers to Spanish codices as שאנו נסמכין עליהם, but elsewhere he frequently adopts the reading found in ברוב הספרים as against that of במקצת ספרים. Jacob ben Chayim thus used his own judgment in chosing one and discarding another reading.

c) Amongst the many authorities, which Jacob ben Chayim quotes by name in order either to accept or to reject their readings, Ben Asher and Ben Naftali rank very high as Masoretic scholars. But even their work as editors of the Bible was of the same type as has just been characterized for the later generations, namely: basing their editions on preconceived grammatical theories. At least for Ben Asher's work we have explicit evidence for this rôle of his, in a colophon to ms. Adler 1701 of our Seminary Library, which reads: הכל על תקון הספר הידוע במצרים· שהוא כולל כל ספרים· שהגיהן בן אשר ודקדק בן אשר שנים רבות. In other words: The fame of the well-known Egyptian codex (הספר הידוע במצרים) rests on the fact that Ben Asher spent many years of his life (שנים רבות) in correcting it (שהגיהן) and revising every detail (ודקדק). By this procedure, an otherwise common Bible ms. became an authoritative Model Codex. But in order to correct and carefully revise the ms., Ben Asher must have worked out beforehand his own grammatical laws as to what is correct in Hebrew, and what is not. These laws he then painstakingly applied to the ms., which thus became a Model Codex, since Ben Asher's reputation as a grammarian imbued it with authority. But the relationship between Bible and grammar was thus reversed: for the Bible of Ben Asher was an offspring of his grammar!

3) Thus, Bible editors till now made the fundamental error to approach their task as grammarians, anxious to eliminate and correct what in their eyes plainly were "errors." By this procedure they achieved that grammatical studies finally became hopelessly entangled in inner contradictions, resulting from the attempts to put on a common denominator different Hebrew forms, which in reality represent the remnants of the many hands which had been at work editing the Bible throughout the generations.

4)   In order to free ourselves from these many layers of editorial debris, we have to search for such Bible texts, the readings of which do not exhibit systematic revisions of this kind. We emphasize: "systematic" revisions; because it would be too much to hope to find texts which entirely escaped such editorial changes. But inconsistency in their application will permit us to arrive at general conclusions as to the characteristics of their genuine *Vorlage*. We, therefore, turn to *incunabula* and old Bible manuscripts, which up to now have been entirely disregarded by grammarians and Bible editors alike, since the text they present was considered utterly incorrect.

§ 24.   The basic Bible text.

As specimina for our new approach we first publish, both in facsimile reproduction and in trans two pages from the famous *Codex Reuchlinianus* (written in 1105) in Karlsruhe, and one page from a very rare *Spanish incunabulum* of our Seminary Library.

The transcription aims at faithfully reproducing all the details of the vocalization. However, a few external changes in the position of certain vowel-signs in the *Codex Reuchlinianus* had to be introduced in order to simplify their reproduction in print. Thus, we indicate *ḳamez* here by , , while the Ms. has – ; ו in final position is vocalized ‏וּ‎ in the Ms., but here ‏וֹ‎; instead of ‏ה‎ and ‏ה‎ of the Ms. we print ‏ח‎ and ‏ה‎, respectively; the *dagesh* in ‏א‎ and ‏ר‎ we put above these letters: ‏אֿ‎ and ‏רֿ‎, instead of ‏א‎ and ‏ה‎, as the Ms. presents.

Codex Reuchlinianus

(Landesbibliothek, Karlsruhe)

Fol. 83b

I Sam. 30.27-31.9:

27   לַאֲשֶׁר בְּבֵי֯תְאֵל וְלַאֲשֶׁר בְּרָמֹת נֶגֶב וְלַאֲשֶׁר בְּיַתִּיר:

28   וְלַאֲשֶׁר בַּעֲרֹעֵר וְלַאֲשֶׁר בְּשִׂפְמֹות וְלַאֲשֶׁר בְּאֶשְׁתְּמֹעַ:

29   וְלַאֲשֶׁר בְּרָכָל וְלַאֲשֶׁר בְּעָרֵי הַיְרַחְמְאֵלִי וְלַאֲשֶׁר בְּעָרֵי הַקֵּנִי׃

30 וְלַאֲשֶׁר בְּחָרְמָה וְלַאֲשֶׁר בְּבֹר עָשָׁן וְלַאֲשֶׁר בַּעֲתָךְ׃

31 וְלַאֲשֶׁר בְּחֶבְרוֹן וּלְכָל הַמְּקוֹמוֹת אֲשֶׁר הִתְהַלֶּךְ שָׁם דָּוִד הוּא וַאֲנָשָׁיו׃

1 וּפְלִשְׁתִּים נִלְחָמִים בְּיִשְׂרָאֵל וַיָּנֻסוּ אַנְשֵׁי יִשְׂרָאֵל מִפְּנֵי פְלִשְׁתִּים וַיִּפְּלוּ חֲלָלִים בְּהַר הַגִּלְבֹּעַ׃

2 וַיַּדְבְּקוּ פְלִשְׁתִּים אֶת שָׁאוּל וְאֶת בָּנָיו וַיַּכּוּ פְלִשְׁתִּים אֶת יְהוֹנָתָן וְאֶת אֲבִינָדָב וְאֶת מַלְכִּישׁוּעַ בְּנֵי שָׁאוּל׃

3 וַתִּכְבַּד הַמִּלְחָמָה עַל שָׁאוּל וַיִּמְצָאֻהוּ הַמּוֹרִים אֲנָשִׁים בַּקָּשֶׁת וַיָּחֶל מְאֹד מֵהַמּוֹרִים׃

4 וַיֹּאמֶר שָׁאוּל לְנֹשֵׂא כֵלָיו שְׁלֹף חַרְבְּךָ וְדָקְרֵנִי בָהּ פֶּן יָבֹאוּ הָעֲרֵלִים הָאֵלֶּה וּדְקָרֻנִי וְהִתְעַלְּלוּ בִי וְלֹא אָבָה נֹשֵׂא כֵלָיו כִּי יָרֵא מְאֹד וַיִּקַּח שָׁאוּל אֶת הַחֶרֶב וַיִּפֹּל עָלֶיהָ׃

5 וַיַּרְא נֹשֵׂא כֵלָיו כִּי מֵת שָׁאוּל וַיִּפֹּל גַּם הוּא עַל חַרְבּוֹ וַיָּמָת עִמּוֹ׃

6 וַיָּמָת שָׁאוּל וּשְׁלֹשֶׁת בָּנָיו וְנֹשֵׂא כֵלָיו וְגַם כָּל אֲנָשָׁיו בַּיּוֹם הַהוּא יַחְדָּו׃

7 וַיִּרְאוּ אַנְשֵׁי יִשְׂרָאֵל אֲשֶׁר בְּעֵבֶר הָעֵמֶק וַאֲשֶׁר בְּעֵבֶר הַיַּרְדֵּן כִּי נָסוּ אַנְשֵׁי יִשְׂרָאֵל וְכִי מֵתוּ שָׁאוּל וּבָנָיו וַיַּעַזְבוּ אֶת הֶעָרִים וַיָּנֻסוּ וַיָּבֹאוּ פְלִשְׁתִּים וַיֵּשְׁבוּ בָּהֶן׃

8 וַיְהִי מִמָּחֳרָת וַיָּבֹאוּ פְלִשְׁתִּים לְפַשֵּׁט אֶת הַחֲלָלִים וַיִּמְצְאוּ אֶת שָׁאוּל וְאֶת שְׁלֹשֶׁת בָּנָיו נֹפְלִים בְּהַר הַגִּלְבֹּעַ׃

9 וַיִּכְרְתוּ אֶת רֹאשׁוֹ וַיַּפְשִׁיטוּ אֶת כֵּלָיו וַיְשַׁלְּחוּ בְאֶרֶץ פְלִשְׁתִּים סָבִיב לְבַשֵּׂר בֵּית עֲצַבֵּיהֶם וְאֶת הָעָם׃

Fol. 382b

Mal. 3.19-24:

19 כִּי הִנֵּה הַיּוֹם בָּא בֹּעֵר כַּתַּנּוּר וְהָיוּ כָל זֵדִים וְכָל עֹשֵׂי רִשְׁעָה קַשׁ וְלִהַט אֹתָם הַיּוֹם הַבָּא אָמַר יְהוָה צְבָאוֹת אֲשֶׁר לֹא יַעֲזֹב לָהֶם שֹׁרֶשׁ וְעָנָף׃

20 וְזָרְחָה לָכֶם יִרְאֵי שְׁמִי שֶׁמֶשׁ צְדָקָה וּמַרְפֵּא בִּכְנָפֶיהָ וִיצָאתֶם וּפִשְׁתֶּם כְּעֶגְלֵי מַרְבֵּק׃

21 וְעַסּוֹתֶם רְשָׁעִים כִּי יִהְיוּ אֵפֶר תַּחַת כַּפּוֹת רַגְלֵיכֶם בַּיּוֹם אֲשֶׁר אֲנִי עֹשֶׂה אָמַר יְהוָה צְבָאוֹת׃

22 זִכְרוּ תּוֹרַת מֹשֶׁה עַבְדִּי אֲשֶׁר צִוִּיתִי אוֹתוֹ בְחֹרֵב עַל כָּל יִשְׂרָאֵל חֻקִּים וּמִשְׁפָּטִים׃

23 הִנֵּה אָנֹכִי שֹׁלֵחַ לָכֶם אֵת אֵלִיָּה הַנָּבִיא לִפְנֵי בּוֹא יוֹם יְהוָה הַגָּדוֹל וְהַנּוֹרָא׃

24 וְהֵשִׁיב לֵב אָבוֹת עַל בָּנִים וְלֵב בָּנִים עַל אֲבוֹתָם פֶּן אָבוֹא וְהִכֵּיתִי אֶת הָאָרֶץ חֵרֶם׃

23 הִנֵּה אָנֹכִי שֹׁלֵחַ לָכֶם

Pentateuch with Targum

Spanish Incunabulum (Library, Jewish Theological Seminary, shelf mark 72050)

Deut. 29.2-19:

הַגְּדֹלִים הָהֵם:

3 וְלֹא נָתַן יְהוָה לָכֶם לֵב לָדַעַת וְעֵינַיִם לִרְאוֹת וְאָזְנַיִם לִשְׁמֹעַ עַד הַיּוֹם הַזֶּה:

4 וָאוֹלֵךְ אֶתְכֶם אַרְבָּעִים שָׁנָה בַּמִּדְבָּר לֹא בָלוּ שַׂלְמֹתֵיכֶם מֵעֲלֵיכֶם וְנַעַלְךָ לֹא בָלְתָה מֵעַל רַגְלֶךָ:

5 לֶחֶם לֹא אֲכַלְתֶּם וְיַיִן וְשֵׁכָר לֹא שְׁתִיתֶם לְמַעַן תֵּדְעוּ כִּי אֲנִי יְהוָה אֱלֹהֵיכֶם:

6 וַתָּבֹאוּ אֶל הַמָּקוֹם הַזֶּה וַיֵּצֵא סִיחֹן מֶלֶךְ חֶשְׁבּוֹן וְעוֹג מֶלֶךְ הַבָּשָׁן לִקְרָאתֵנוּ לַמִּלְחָמָה וַנַּכֵּם:

7 וַנִּקַּח אֶת אַרְצָם וַנִּתְּנָה לְנַחֲלָה לָרֹאוּבֵנִי וְלַגָּדִי וְלַחֲצִי שֵׁבֶט הַמְנַשִּׁי:

8 וּשְׁמַרְתֶּם אֶת דִּבְרֵי הַבְּרִית הַזֹּאת וַעֲשִׂיתֶם אֹתָם לְמַעַן תַּשְׂכִּילוּ אֵת כָּל אֲשֶׁר תַּעֲשׂוּן:

9 אַתֶּם נִצָּבִים הַיּוֹם כֻּלְּכֶם לִפְנֵי יְהוָה אֱלֹהֵיכֶם רָאשֵׁיכֶם שִׁבְטֵיכֶם זִקְנֵיכֶם וְשֹׁטְרֵיכֶם כֹּל אִישׁ יִשְׂרָאֵל:

10 טַפְּכֶם נְשֵׁיכֶם וְגֵרְךָ אֲשֶׁר בְּקֶרֶב מַחֲנֶיךָ מֵחֹטֵב עֵצֶיךָ עַד שֹׁאֵב מֵימֶיךָ:

11 לְעָבְרְךָ בִּבְרִית יְהוָה אֱלֹהֶיךָ וּבְאָלָתוֹ אֲשֶׁר יְהוָה אֱלֹהֶיךָ כֹּרֵת עִמְּךָ הַיּוֹם:

12 לְמַעַן הָקִים אֹתְךָ הַיּוֹם לוֹ לְעָם וְהוּא יִהְיֶה לְּךָ לֵאלֹהִים כַּאֲשֶׁר דִּבֶּר לָךְ וְכַאֲשֶׁר נִשְׁבַּע לַאֲבֹתֶיךָ לְאַבְרָהָם לְיִצְחָק וּלְיַעֲקֹב:

13 וְלֹא אִתְּכֶם לְבַדְּכֶם אָנֹכִי כֹּרֵת אֶת הַבְּרִית הַזֹּאת וְאֶת הָאָלָה הַזֹּאת:

14 כִּי אֶת אֲשֶׁר יֶשְׁנוֹ פֹּה עִמָּנוּ עֹמֵד הַיּוֹם לִפְנֵי יְהוָה אֱלֹהֵינוּ וְאֵת אֲשֶׁר אֵינֶנּוּ פֹּה עִמָּנוּ הַיּוֹם:

15 כִּי אַתֶּם יְדַעְתֶּם אֵת אֲשֶׁר יָשַׁבְנוּ בְּאֶרֶץ מִצְרָיִם וְאֵת אֲשֶׁר עָבַרְנוּ בְּקֶרֶב הַגּוֹיִם אֲשֶׁר עֲבַרְתֶּם:

16 וַתִּרְאוּ אֶת שִׁקּוּצֵיהֶם וְאֵת גִּלֻּלֵיהֶם עֵץ וָאֶבֶן כֶּסֶף וְזָהָב אֲשֶׁר עִמָּהֶם:

17 פֶּן יֵשׁ בָּכֶם אִישׁ אוֹ אִשָּׁה אוֹ מִשְׁפָּחָה אוֹ שֵׁבֶט אֲשֶׁר לְבָבוֹ פֹנֶה הַיּוֹם מֵעִם יְהוָה אֱלֹהֵינוּ לָלֶכֶת לַעֲבֹד אֶת אֱלֹהֵי הַגּוֹיִם הָהֵם פֶּן יֵשׁ בָּכֶם שֹׁרֶשׁ פֹּרֶה רֹאשׁ וְלַעֲנָה:

18 וְהָיָה בְּשָׁמְעוֹ אֶת דִּבְרֵי הָאָלָה הַזֹּאת וְהִתְבָּרֵךְ בִּלְבָבוֹ לֵאמֹר שָׁלוֹם יִהְיֶה לִּי כִּי בִּשְׁרִרוּת לִבִּי אֵלֵךְ לְמַעַן סְפוֹת הָרָוָה אֶת הַצְּמֵאָה:

19 לֹא יֹאבֶה יְהוָה סְלֹחַ לוֹ כִּי אָז ·········· וְקִנְאָתוֹ בָּאִישׁ הַהוּא וְרָבְצָה בּוֹ כָּל הָאָלָה ······· וּמָחָה יְהוָה אֶת שְׁמוֹ מִתַּחַת הַשָּׁמָיִם:

§ 25.   The significance of these specimens.

a)   In order to fully appreciate the importance of these texts for Hebrew grammar, it is essential that we free ourselves from the established grammatical views as expressed in the current works on this subject. For it is not our aim to compare the vocalization of any given word in these texts with that of the so-called Masoretic text and note deviations. Such an approach would imply our silent admission of the validity of the Masoretic grammatical laws even for our texts, though they may not have been punctiliously enough observed here. We on the other hand decline to commit ourselves *a priori* neither to admitting, nor to denying it. Solely the way how the vowel-signs are applied in the texts themselves, shall decide this problem (cf. p. 420, § 9).

b)   *Dagesh* and *raphe*.

1)   The *Codex Reuchlinianus* applies *dagesh* indiscriminately to almost all the letters of the alphabet (the sole exceptions being ח and ע), regardless of the position of the letter (whether at the beginning, in the middle or at the end of a word) and of the nature of the preceding vowel-sign (whether ָ or ַ ; ָ or ָ ; ' or ְ). Those letters of a word, which for no apparent reason at all have no *dagesh*, get a *raphe* instead. But neither α) *dagesh* nor β) *raphe* follow any rules; they are irregularly put:

α)   I Sam. 30.31: הוּא   I Sam. 31.7: אַנְשֵׁי (1°)
              31.5: הוּא   אַנְשֵׁי (2°)

β)   I Sam. 31.5: וַיָּמָת   I Sam. 31.7: וַיָּבֹאוּ
                6: וַיָּמָת   8: וַיָּבאוּ

      I Sam. 31.8: וְאֵת   Mal. 3.19: כָּל
                9: וְאֶת   22: כָּל

The complete disregard of the Masoretic laws concerning *dagesh* and *raphe* is further evidenced by the fact that these signs are used here γ) interchangeably or even δ) combined:

γ)   I Sam. 31.4: לְנֹשֵׂא   I Sam. 31.6: וּשְׁלֹשֶׁת
                    נֹשֵׂא   8: שְׁלֹשֶׁת
      Cf. also I Sam. 30.27: וְלַאֲשֶׁר with verse 28: וְלַאֲשֶׁר.

δ)   I Sam. 31.6: שָׁאוּל   Mal. 3.23: הַנָּבִיא

2) The *Spanish incunabulum* has only very, very rarely a *dagesh* or *raphe*. But the inconsistency of their application becomes clear, when we consider the following cases:

α) Gen. 41.5:   שִׁבֳּלִים   Gen. 41.4:   וְהַבְּרִיאֹת

          6:    שִׁבֳּלִים   20:   הַבְּרִיאֹת

    Gen. 41.4:   הַפָּרוֹת

          20:    הַפָּרוֹת (2°)

β) Gen. 41.37:   עֲבָדָיו   Deut. 30.2:   אֱלֹהֶיךָ

          38:    עֲבָדָיו   1:   אֱלֹהֶיךָ

    Deut. 29.4:   בָלוּ (לֹא)   Deut. 29.13:   הַזֹּאת (1°)

                    בָלְתָה (לֹא)   הַזֹּאת (2°)

c) The vowel *a* is indicated by the indiscriminate use of ֲ and ַ.

1) In the *Codex Reuchlinianus*.

I Sam. 31.3:   הַמּוֹרִים   I Sam. 30.31:   וַאֲנָשָׁיו

                מֵהָמּוֹרִים   31.6:   אֲנָשָׁיו

I Sam. 31.1:   הַגִּלְבֹּעַ   I Sam. 31.5:   גַּם

          8:    הָגִּלְבֹּעַ   6:   וְגָם

I Sam. 31.1:   יִשְׂרָאֵל   Mal. 3.23:   אָנֹכִי

Mal. 3.22:   יִשְׂרָאֵל   אָנֹכִי

2) In the *Spanish incunabulum*.

Gen. 41.5:   שֶׁבַע   Gen. 41.14:   פַּרְעֹה

          6:    שֶׁבָע   16:   פַּרְעֹה

Gen. 41.18:   בַּשַׂר   Gen. 41.4:   הַפָּרוֹת

          19:    בְשָׂר   20:   הָפָּרוֹת (1°)

Gen. 41.21:   קִרְבֶּנָה (1°)   Gen. 41.17:   בַּחֲלֹמִי

                קִרְבֶנָה (2°)   22:   בָחֲלֹמִי

Gen. 41.31:   הַשָׂבַע   Gen. 41.35:   כָּל

          34:    הַשָׂבַע   37:   כָל

Deut. 29.11:   הַיּוֹם   Deut. 30.3:   אֱלֹהֶיךָ (1°)

          12:    הָיּוֹם   אֱלֹהֶיךָ (2°)

Deut. 29.22:   יְהֹוָה

          30.1:   יְהֹוָה

d) Similarly ָ and ֳ are interchangeably used.

1) In the *Codex Reuchlianus*.

1 Sam. 31.4: כֵּלָיו (1°)   Mal. 3.19:   אֲשֶׁר

כֵּלָיו (2°)   22:   אֲשֶׁר

2) In the *Spanish incunabulum*.

Gen. 41.26: הֵנָּה   Lev. 11.4:   גֵּרָה

27: הֵנָּה   5:   גֵּרָה

Deut. 29.26: הַזֶּה

27: הַזֶּה

e) The material at our disposal, especially from the so highly important *Codex Reuchlinianus*, is very limited; the two pages which form
the basis for our discussion are all we possess. There are abundant indications that an examination of the entire ms. would reveal startling
results; cf. e.g. 1) the absence of *paṭaḥ furtivum* as evidenced by forms like
שָׁלַח ,מַלְכִּישׁוּעַ ,הַגִּלְבֹּעַ ,בְּאֶשְׁתָּמֹעַ (bis); 2) the vocalization of *waw* in final
position with *shewa*, as f.i.: אֲנַשָּׁיו ,יַחְדָּו. בָּנָיו ,כֵּלָיו; 3) the fact that *ḥolem*
is affixed to the consonant to which it belongs, and not to the following
mater lectionis waw, thus resulting in a two-ways vocalization of the word:
first by the *mater lectionis waw* (cf. p. 564, § 3), and subsequently by
ḥolem, e.g. כַּפֹּת ,הַיֹּום ,הַמֹּורִים; הַמְּקֹומֹות.

§ 26. Towards a new Bible edition.

The results at which we arrived in the foregoing paragraph, incomplete
though they are due to the scarcity of material, are of the utmost importance for the New Edition of the Hebrew Bible, which we plan to
publish. No matter whether we adopt the procedure of the *Codex Reuchlinianus* and use *dagesh* indiscriminately throughout, or whether we follow
the lead of the *Spanish incunabulum* and put the *dagesh* into the discard
altogether, the final outcome remains the same: the *dagesh* has outlived
its existence! It ceases to be a *dagesh*, i.e. a *crux grammaticarum* (cf.
p. 422, §§ 11 ff.), and is reduced to its original insignificance of a mere dot,
inserted at random in curved letters for the sole purpose of their beauti-
fication.

Since ָ and ֳ are promiscuously used, and there is not the slightest
semblance of evidence that they were meant to indicate two distinct

vowels, there could be no objection from the scholarly point of view to simplify matters by substituting one single vowel-sign for both of them. The same procedure is herewith advocated with regard to ֓ and ֘, which are used interchangeably, too.

I emphasize: these are merely temporary and incomplete results; and a thorough examination of the hitherto neglected "incorrect" manuscripts in the old European libraries will no doubt round up and bring to a conclusion this *tendency towards simplification*, which *is based solely on a careful study and an unbiased interpretation of old texts*, the soundest bases a philologian can think of. In conclusion I wish to state that the results outlined here fully substantiate the "General Conclusions" (p. 454 ff.), which were formulated after an examination of the laws of Masoretic Hebrew Phonology, and at a time, when the basic texts of this investigation here still were *terra incognita* to me.

V.　THE HISTORICAL APPROACH TO HEBREW GRAMMAR

A.　THE VOWELS AND THEIR PHONOGRAPHY (Cf. MH § 47 ff.)

As evidenced by the textual variations listed here, Hebrew had three vowels: a, i, o. No conclusions can be drawn from our sources as to their quantity or quality. (Cf. also p. 234 the paragraph headed by: The Sources).

A.　VOCALIZATION BY THE LETTERS א ה ו י [1]

§ 1.　The vowel *a* is indicated.

a)　In medial position by א.

Gen. 18.11	MT	(אֹרַח) כַּנָּשִׁים	Ex. 23.31	MT	וְשַׁתִּי
	S	כאנשים		S	ושאתי
Num. 31.35	MT	הַנָּשִׁים	Deut. 23.25	MT	קָמַת ··· בְּקָמַת
	S	האנשים		S	קאמת ··· בקאמת
Gen. 37.7	MT	קָמָה	Deut. 28.7	MT	הַקָּמִים
	S	קאמה		S	הקאמים

---

[1] On the three basic vowels of Hebrew, a, i, o, cf. also p. 216, sub b. Correspondingly, Hebrew has *three* vowel letters; for ה is a substitute either for י (cf. p. 245, § 10 and p. 256, § 25), or for א (cf. p. 246, § 12 and p. 256, § 24).

Josh. 21.36		רָמֹת	Jer. 40.4	Q	הַזִּקִים
I Chron. 6.65		רָאמוֹת		K	האזקים

Josh. 21.36 — רָמֹת
I Chron. 6.65 — רָאמוֹת

Josh. 21.30 — מִשְׁאָל
I Chron. 6.59 — מָשָׁל

Isa. 37.12 — בִּתְלַשָּׂר
2 Ki. 19.12 — בִּתְלָאשָּׂר

2 Sam. 11.1 — הַמַּלְאָכִים
I Chron. 20.1 — הַמְּלָכִים

Judg. 4.21   Q   בַּלָּט
              K   בלאט

Judg. 9.41   Q   בָּרוּמָה
              K   בארומה

2 Sam. 10.17 Q   חֶלְאָמָה
              K   חלאמה

2 Sam. 12.1   Q   רָשׁ
              K   ¹ ראש

2 Sam. 12.4   Q   הָרָשׁ
              K   הראש

2 Sam. 23.33 Q   הָרָרִי
              K   האררי

Isa. 10.13   Q   כַּבִּיר
              K   כאביר

Isa. 27.8   Q   בְּסַסְאָה
              K   בסאסאה

Isa. 33.20   Q   נָוֶה
              K   נאוה

Jer. 40.1   Q   בַּזִּקִים
              K   באזקים

Jer. 40.4   Q   הַזִּקִים
              K   האזקים

Ezek. 27.26   Q   הַשָּׁטִים ²
              K   השאטים

Hos. 10.14   Q   וְקָם
              K   וקאם

Joel 2.6   Q   פרור
              K   ³ פָּארוּר

Hag. 2.2   Q   שַׁלְתִּיאֵל
              K   שאלתיאל

α) Omission of the root
    letter א. ⁴

Ps. 18.40 — וַתְּאַזְּרֵנִי
2 Sam. 22.40 — וַתַּזְּרֵנִי

2 Ki. 7.1, 16 Q   וְסָאתַיִם
               K   וסתים

Jer. 29.22   Q   וּכְאַחְאָב
               K   וכאחב

b) In final position by א or ה. ⁵

Gen. 10.7 — וְסַבְתָּה וְרַעְמָה
I Chron. 1.9 — וְסַבְתָּא וְרַעְמָא

2 Sam. 21.18 — הָרָפָה
I Chron. 20.4 — הָרָפָא

2 Ki. 15.33 — יְרוּשָׁא
2 Chron. 27.1 — יְרוּשָׁה

2 Ki. 18.18 — וְשֶׁבְנָה
Isa. 36.3 — וְשֶׁבְנָא

Ezek. 36.5   Q   כלה
               K   כָּלָא

¹ Cf. similarly Prov. 10.4.
² Cf. also ib. 28.24, 26.
³ Cf. similarly Nah. 2.11.
⁴ Cf. 1 Sam. 25.8: בָּנוּ, Venice 1515
marg.: באנו; 1 Ki. 12.12: וַיְבֹּ, Venice 1515 marg.: ויבא.
⁵ Cf. also p. 476, § 35α.

| 2 Ki. 17.24 | Md | וּמְעַנָּא | | Ezek. 27.31 | Md | קָרְחָא |
| | Ma | ומעוה | | | Ma | קרחה |

§ 2. The vowel *i* is indicated by י.

a) Corresponding to *i* (ִ).

| 2 Sam. 5.22 | וַיִּסְפּוּ | | Ezek. 7.22 | Md | פרצים |
| 1 Chron. 14.13 | וַיְסִיפוּ | | | Ma | פָּרִיצִים |

b) Corresponding to *e* (ֵ or ֶ). ²

| 2 Sam. 6.3 | וַיַּרְכִּבוּ | | Ex. 1.16 | MT | בְּיַלֶּדְכֶן ⋯ וּרְאִיתֶן |
| 1 Chron. 13.7 | וַיַּרְכִּיבוּ | | | S | בילדכין ⋯ וראיתין |

| 2 Sam. 6.9 | וַיִּרָא ¹ | | Ex. 1.18 | MT | עֲשִׂיתֶן |
| 1 Chron. 13.12 | וַיִּירָא | | | S | עשיתין |

| 2 Sam. 6.17 | וַיַּצִּגוּ ⋯ וַיָּבֵאוּ | | Ex. 2.18 | MT | מִהַרְתֶּן |
| 1 Chron. 16.1 | וַיַּצִּיגוּ⋯ וַיָּבִיאוּ | | | S | מהרתין |

| 2 Sam. 7.9 | וְעָשֶׂתִי | | Ex. 2.20 | MT | עֲזַבְתֶּן |
| 1 Chron. 17.8 | וְעָשִׂיתִי | | | S | עזבתין |

| 2 Sam. 23.23 | וַיְשִׂמֵהוּ | | 1 Ki. 8.1 | | יַקְהֵל |
| 1 Chron. 11.25 | וַיְשִׂימֵהוּ | | 2 Chron. 5.2 | | יַקְהִיל |

| 1 Ki. 8.40 | יִרָאוּךָ | | Jer. 42.20 | Q | הִתְעֵיתֶם |
| 2 Chron. 6.31 | יִירָאוּךָ | | | K | התעתים |

| Ezek. 6.6 | Q | תשמנה | | Ezek. 11.6 | Q | וּמִלֵּאתֶם |
| | K | תִּישָׁמְנָה | | | K | ומלאתים |

| Ezek. 7.7 | Md | הצפרה | | Ezek. 32.7 | Q | וכסתי |
| | Ma | הַצְּפִירָה | | | K | וְכִסֵּיתִי |

§ 3. The vowel *o* is indicated by ו.

a) Corresponding to ֹ.

| 1 Sam. 31.13 | עַצְמֹתֵיהֶם | | 2 Sam. 23.17 | הַגִּבֹרִים |
| 1 Chron. 10.12 | עַצְמוֹתֵיהֶם | | 1 Chron. 11.19 | הַגִּבּוֹרִים |

| 2 Sam. 8.6 | וַיֹּשַׁע | | 2 Sam. 23.18 | בַּשְּׁלֹשָׁה |
| 1 Chron. 18.6 | וַיּוֹשַׁע | | 1 Chron. 11.20 | בַּשְּׁלוֹשָׁה |

---

¹ Cf. Gen. 8.10: וַיָּחֶל עוֹד שבעה ימים
　　Gen. 8.12: וַיִּיָּחֶל עוֹד שבעת ימים
² Cf. p. 264, §40; further: אִתִּים 1 Sam. 13.21 and אִתִּים Isa. 2.4; stat. constr.

בְּאֵרֹת Gen. 26.18 and בְּאֵרֹת ib. 14.10; הַגֹּלָם Jer. 20.4 and הַגֹּלָם 1 Chron. 8.7; also Jer. 29.4, 7; הִגְלֵיתִי, Venice 1515 marg.: הִגְלֵתִי.

1 Sam. 31.4		יָבוֹאוּ	Ezek. 27.15	Q		וְהָבְנִים
1 Chron. 10.4		יָבֹאוּ		K		והובנים
Ezek. 17.6	Q	פֹּארוֹת	Ezek. 34.25	Q		בִּיעָרִים
	K	פֹּארת		K		ביערים

b) Corresponding to ◌ָ.

c) Corresponding to ◌ֶ. [1]

Jer. 27.20	Q	יְכָנְיָה	1 Sam. 31.13			וַיָּצֻמוּ
	K	יכוניה	1 Chron. 10.12			וַיָּצוּמוּ
Jer. 33.8	Q	לְכָל	2 Sam. 5.6			הַיְבָסִי
	K	לכול	1 Chron. 11.4			הַיְבוּסִי
Josh. 15.63	Q	יָכְלוּ	2 Sam. 6.2			הַכְּרֻבִים
	K	יוכלו	1 Chron. 13.6			הַכְּרוּבִים
Ezek. 23.42	Q	סָבָאִים				
	K	סובאים				

§ 4. The diphthong *au* is indicated.

a) By י (B-L § 17z). [2]

Zech. 7.1	Q	בכסליו	Ezek. 9.4	Q		תָּיו
	K	בְּכִסְלֵו		K		תו
Cant. 2.11	Q	הַסְּתָיו	1 Sam. 21.14	Q		וַיְתָיו
	K	הסתו		K		ויתו
Num. 12.3	Q	עָנָיו				
	K	ענו		b) By וי or יו. [4]		
Ps. 105.40	Q	שְׁלָיו	Jer. 48.30	Q		בַּדָּיו
	K	שלו		K		בדוי [5]
Ex. 16.13	Q	הַשְּׂלָיו [3]	Ex. 16.13	MT		הַשְּׂלָיו
	K	השלו		S		השלוי [6]

[1] Cf. p. 175, sub ◌ and p. 136 s.v. זרע:
Ps. 18.35: MT זְרוֹעֹתַי — O זְרוּעֹתַי; cf.
also Jer. 13.14: Ma אָחוּס — Md אָחוּס;
further: 2 Sam. 5.14: הַיְלָדִים — 1
Chron. 14.4: הַיְלוּדִים; Gesenius-Buhl's
Dictionary s.v. אֲמָנָה, אָמְנָם and אַשְׁמוּרָה
and אַשְׁמֹרֶת; גָּדְלוּ Deut. 5.21 and גָּדְלוּ
Ps. 150.2; Isa. 54.15: גּוּר יָגוּר.

[2] Cf. p. 124 ff., s.v. צו sau; קו cau;
שוא σαυ; and p. 211, § 133, sub 1; see also
p. 263, § 37.
[3] Cf. also Num. 11.32.
[4] Cf. p. 211, § 133, sub 2.
[5] Cf. Ma-Md on Job 18.13.
[6] Cf. similarly Num. 11.32.

§ 5. The diphthong *ai* is indicated.

a) By אי (B-L § 21g; Bergsträsser § 15g).

| Isa. 53.4 | Q | חלאינו | Isa. 41.18 | Q | שפאים |
| | K | חֲלָיֵנוּ | | K | שְׁפָיִים 3 |

| Ps. 104.12 | Q | עֳפָיִם | b) | By י (B-L § 2v and § 63b |
| | K | עפאים | | on צהרים). 4 |

| Judg. 13.18 | Q | פֶּלִי | Isa. 36.2 | Q | ירושלימה |
| | K | פלאי | | K | יְרוּשָׁלֵמָה |

| Ps. 139.6 | Q | פְּלִיאָה | Ezek. 46.19 | Q | בַיַרְכָּתַיִם |
| | K | פלאיה | | K | בירכתם |

| Hos. 11.8 | Q | כִּצְבוֹיִם 1 | Ezek. 25.9 | Q | וְקִרְיָתָיְמָה |
| | K | כצבאים | | K | וקריתמה |

| Ex. 12.37 | MT | רַגְלִי | 2 Sam. 21.9 | K | שבעתים |
| | S | רגלאי 2 | | Q | שְׁבַעְתָּם |

B. VOCALIZATION THROUGH VOWEL-LETTERS

§ 6. In the present study I wish to demonstrate how much we gain, in our understanding of the Bible, by discarding *superimposed* grammatical rules and relying instead on a grammar and a syntax *evinced* by the Bible itself. In other words I interpret the Bible by means gained from the Bible itself.

The *matres lectionis* ו and י

a. General Observations

§ 7. Two vowels involved.

1) The two extremes: *plene* and *defective* spelling.

| מֶטְבֵי: Prov. 30.29 | נְפֹצֹתֶם: Ezek. 20.41 | וּמֹלְדתַיִךְ: Ezek. 16.3 |
| מיטיבי: Prov. 30.29 | נפוצותם: Ezek. 20.34 | וּמולדותיך: Ezek. 16.4 |

| דֹּרתֵינוּ: Josh. 22.28 | חֲלִפֹת: Judg. 14.12 |
| דורותינו: Josh. 22.27 | חליפות: Judg. 14.13 |

---

1 Cf. p. 155, s.v. צבי sabai; see also B-L § 21h.

2 Cf. also Num. 11.21.

3 Cf. similarly ib. 49.9; Jer. 3.21.

4 Cf. 1 Sam. 9.4: שַׂעֲלִים, Venice 1515 marg.: שעלִים; cf. also p. 127, s.v. איתן a and b, and the cross-references there.

2) Either vowel can be indicated by a *mater lectionis*.

אֵדֹת: Gen. 21.25   מֹטוֹת: Jer. 28.13   לֻחוֹת: Deut. 9.11

אדת: Gen. 21.11   מוטת: Jer. 28.13   לוחת: Deut. 9.9

וְעֵירֹם: Ezek. 18.7   וְהַחֹנִם: Num. 2.12   שְׁדֻפוֹת: Gen. 41.23

וערום: Ezek. 18.16   והחנים: Num. 2.5   שדופת: Gen. 41.6

3) The gradual transition from *plene* to *defective* spelling.

הַחִצֹנָה: Ezek. 42.9   קְבֻרֹתֶהָ: Ezek. 32.25   חֲמִשֻׁתוֹ: Lev. 27.27

החצונה: Ezek. 42.8   קברתיה: Ezek. 32.23   חמישתו: Lev. 27.13

החיצונה: Ezek. 42.14   קברותיה: Ezek. 32.26   חמישיתו: Lev. 27.31

b. The Verb [1]

a. Ḳal

§ 8. Infinitive.

a) Regular verbs.

הָלֹךְ: Jer. 35.13   אָכֹל: Isa. 22.13   לֶאֱכֹל : 2 Sam. 13.11

הלוך: Jer. 35.2   אכול: Isa. 22.13   לאכול : 2 Sam. 13.9

b) *Mediae waw.*

מֻשָׁט: Job 2.2   וּבְקֻמָהּ: Gen. 19.35   לָבֹא: Jer. 42.15

משוט: Job 1.7   ובקומה: Gen. 19.33   לבוא: Jer. 42.17

c) *Tertiae he.*

לִזְנֹת: Lev. 20.6   לַעֲשֹׂת: Ex. 35.32   לִשְׁתֹּת: Ex. 7.24

לזנות: Lev. 20.5   לעשות: Ex. 35.33   לשתות: Ex. 7.24

בִּבְנֹתְכֶם: Josh. 22.19

בבנותכם: Josh. 22.16

§ 9. Imperfect.

a) Regular verbs.

אֶשְׁפֹּט: Ezek. 11.11   הֲתִשְׁפֹּט: Ezek. 20.4

אשפוט: Ezek. 11.10   התשפוט: Ezek. 20.4

---

[1] Irrespective of their roots, verbs are listed in this chapter under the heading of "regular verbs," if the variant of *plene* and *defective* spelling occurs in their sound part. Hence, הָאוֹסִף–הָאֹסֵף is listed as sound (§ 12a), but יוֹסֵף–יֹסֵף as *primae yod* (§ 12b).

b) *Primae yod.*

וְיִיטַב: Judg. 19.6   וַיִּצֶר: Gen. 2.19   וַיִּרְאוּ: 1 Sam. 17.11
וייטב: Judg. 19.9   וייצר: Gen. 2.7   וייראו: 1 Sam. 17.24

Similarly: Cf. also perfect:

תֵּעָשֶׂה: Ex. 35.2   בָּנִתִי: 1 Ki. 8.44:
תיעשה: Ex. 25.31   בניתי: 1 Ki. 8.43

c) *Mediae waw.*

אָרְצָה: 2 Sam. 18.22   יָסֹר: 2 Ki. 4.8   תָּמֻתוּ: Jer. 42.16
ארוצה: 2 Sam. 18.19   יסור: 2 Ki. 4.10   תמותו: Jer. 42.22

יָבְזוּ: Cant. 8.1   יָקֻמוּ: 2 Sam. 2.14   וַיָּנֻסוּ: 2 Ki. 7.7
יבוזו: Cant. 8.7   יקומו: 2 Sam. 2.14   וינוסו: 2 Ki. 7.7

וַיָּקֻמוּ: 2 Ki. 7.5   תָּבֹא: 2 Sam. 13.5   וַיָּבֹא: 2 Ki. 9.34
ויקומו: 2 Ki. 7.7   תבוא: 2 Sam. 13.6   ויבוא: 2 Ki. 9.30

וַיָּבֹאוּ: 2 Ki. 11.18
ויבואו: 2 Ki. 11.19

§ 10. Imperative.

Mediae waw.

שֵׁב: 1 Ki. 18.43   שֻׁבִי: Jer. 31.20   שֻׁבוּ: Gen. 43.2
שוב: 1 Ki. 19.15   שובי: Jer. 31.20   שובו: Hen. 43.13

Similarly:

אֹרוּ: Judg. 5.23
אורו: Judg. 5.23

§ 11. Participle.

א) Active.

a) Regular verbs.

יֹשֵׁב: Num. 13.19   יֹצֵא: 2 Sam. 16.5   שֹׁטֵף: Ezek. 13.13
יושב: Num. 13.19   יוצא: 2 Sam. 16.5   שוטף: Ezek. 13.11

הַסֹּבֵב: Gen. 2.11   הַשֹּׁפֵט: Judg. 2.18   הַקֹּצְרִים: Ruth 2.3
הסובב: Gen. 2.13   השופט: Judg. 2.18   הקוצרים: Ruth 2.5

יֹשֶׁבֶת: Jer. 48.18   יֹשְׁבֵי: Jer. 51.35   יֹרְדֵי: Ezek. 32.29
יושבת: Jer. 48.19   יושבי: Jer. 51.24   יורדי: Ezek. 32.29

ב) Passive.

a) Regular verbs.

לְבַשׁ: Ezek. 10.2   שְׁלָפָה: Num. 22.31   חָרָצִים: Prov. 13.4

לבוש: Ezek. 9.11   שלופה: Num. 22.23   חרוצים: Prov. 12.24

    הַשְּׁחָטָה: Lev. 14.6   הַקְּרָאִים: 1 Sam. 9.13

    השחוטה: Lev. 14.51   הקרואים: 1 Sam. 9.22

b. Hiph'il

§ 12. Imperfect.

a) Regular verbs.

אֶרְגָּעָה: Jer. 50.44   הָאוֹסֵף: Judg. 20.28   יַקְדִּשׁ: Lev. 27.14

ארגיעה: Jer. 49.19   האוסיף: Judg. 20.23   יקדיש: Lev. 27.16

       וַיַּגִּדוּ: 2 Ki. 7.15

       ויגידו: 2 Ki. 7.11

b) *Primae yod.*

יֹסֵף: Lev. 5.24   יְעִידֶנִּי: Jer. 49.19   וַיֹּסֶף: Num. 22.25

יוסף: Lev. 5.16   יועדני: Jer. 50.44   ויוסף: Num. 22.26

וַיִּרַשׁ: Judg. 1.19   וַיֹּשַׁע: 2 Sam. 8.6   וַתֹּרֶד: Gen. 24.18

ויורש: Judg. 1.20   ויושע: 2 Sam. 8.14   ותורד: Gen. 24.46

c) *Mediae waw.*

יָבֵא: Num. 6.10   יְבִאֲךָ: Ex. 13.11   וַיָּבֵא: Ezek. 40.1

יביא: Num. 6.13   יביאך: Ex. 13.5   ויביא: Ezek. 40.3

וַיְבִאֵנִי: Ezek. 40.48   וַיְמִתֵהוּ: 1 Ki. 13.26   וַהֲקִמֹתִי: Jer. 23.5

ויביאני: Ezek. 40.32   וימיתהו: 1 Ki. 13.24   והקימתי: Jer. 23.4

§ 13. Perfect.

a) Regular verbs.

הִקְרִב: Num. 7.19   וְהֶחֱרִשׁ: Num. 30.12   הֶעְמִקוּ: Jer. 49.8

הקריב: Num. 7.18   והחריש: Num. 30.5   העמיקו: Jer. 49.30

b) *Primae yod.*

הֹלִד: 1 Chron. 5.30   הֹבִישׁ: Joel 1.12   וְהֹשִׁיבוּ: 1 Ki. 21.9

הוליד: 1 Chron. 5.30   הוביש: Joel 1.10   והושיבו: 1 Ki. 21.10

       וְהִפְרֵתִי: Gen. 17.6

       והפריתי: Gen. 17.20

c) *Mediae waw.*

הֲסִרֹתִי: 2 Sam. 7.15

הסירתי: 2 Sam. 7.15

Similarly in infinitive forms:

וְהַסֵּךְ: Jer. 44.18   הַקֵּף: Josh. 6.11

והסיך: Jer. 44.17   הקיף: Josh. 6.3

§ 14. Various forms of *med. gem.*

וַהֲשִׁמֹּתִי: Lev. 26.32   הַטֹּחַ: Lev. 14.48   לְהִמֹּל: Gen. 34.15

והשמותי: Lev. 26.31   הטוח: Lev. 14.43   להמול: Gen. 34.17

c) Verbs with suffixes.

§ 15. 3. pers. plur.

שַׁלְחָנִי: Gen. 24.54   וּשְׂרָפָהּ: Jer. 37.8   וְהִשִּׂיגֻךָ: Deut. 28.2

שלחוני: Gen. 24.56   ושרפוה: Jer. 38.18   והשיגוך: Deut. 28.15

c. *The Noun*

§ 16. The vowel *i* is indicated by *yod.*

a) Nouns with two *i*-vowels.

הַנִּבְאִים: 1 Ki. 22.12   הַנְּפִלִים: Num. 13.33   הַצְּמִדִים: Gen. 24.30

הנביאים: 1 Ki. 22.10   הנפילים: Num. 13.33   והצמידים: Gen. 24.47

נְצִבִים: 2 Sam. 8.14   בִּילְדֵי: 2 Sam. 21.18   וּבִנְבָאֵי: Jer. 23.14

נציבים: 2 Sam. 8.6   בילידי: 2 Sam. 21.16   ובנביאי: Jer. 23.23

חֲמִשִׁת: Lev. 27.19   וְהַשְּׁלִשִׁית: Ezek. 5.2   שְׁלִשִׁים: Ezek. 23.23

חמישית: Lev. 27.15   והשלישית: Ezek. 5.12   שלישים: Ezek. 23.15

b) *i* in final position.

וְהַשְּׁלִשֶׁת: 2 Sam. 18.2   וּמִמַּחֲצַת: Num. 31.30

והשלשית: 2 Sam. 18.2   וממחצית: Num. 31.42

c) *i* in initial or medial position.

עֶרֹם: Ezek. 16.7   לְנֻדָה: Lam. 1.17   פִּלֶגֶשׁ: 2 Sam. 3.7

עירם: Ezek. 16.22   לנידה: Lam. 1.8   פילגש: 2 Sam. 3.7

הַצְּפֹרָה: Ezek. 7.10   חֲלִפוֹת: 2 Ki. 5.22

הצפירה: Ezek. 7.7   חליפות: 2 Ki. 5.5

d)   Nouns with suffixes.

מִקְנֵהֶם: Gen. 47.17   נְשִׂיאֵהֶם: Num. 17.17   עֲרֹסֹתֵכֶם: Num. 15.20
מקניהם: Gen. 47.17   נשיאיהם: Num. 17.21   ערסתיכם: Num. 15.21

מַחֲנֶךָ: Deut. 23.15
מחניך: Deut. 23.15

§ 17.   The vowels o and u are indicated by *waw*.

a)   o in initial position.

חֹמָה: Ex. 14.29   עֹרֹת: Ex. 39.34   תֹּלְדֹת: Gen. 25.12
חומה: Ex. 14.22   עורת: Ex. 39.34   תולדת: Gen. 25.19

אֹצְרוֹת: 1 Ki. 14.26   מִשְׁבֹּתֵיכֶם: Lev. 23.14   הַדֹּב: 1 Sam. 17.37
אוצרות: 1 Ki. 14.26   מושבתיכם: Lev. 23.3   הדוב: 1 Sam. 17.36

הַיֹּבֵל: Lev. 25.40   וּמֹרֶה: Deut. 21.20   לְעֹלָה: Josh. 22.29
היובל: Lev. 25.28   ומורה: Deut. 21.18   לעולה: Josh. 22.28

b)   o in final position.

הַגָּדֹל: Num. 34.7   קֹדֶשׁ: Lev. 21.8   שָׁלֹם: 1 Sam. 16.4
הגדול: Num. 34.6   קדוש: Lev. 21.8   שלום: 1 Sam. 16.5

שְׁאֹל: 1 Ki. 2.6   בְּכֹר: Num. 3.41   הַבְּכֹר: Gen. 48.18
שאול: 1 Ki. 2.9   בכור: Num. 3.41   הבכור: Gen. 48.14

בַּחֲלֹם: Gen. 31.24   אֶשְׁכֹּל: Num. 13.23   הָרֹאשֹׁן: Ex. 12.15
בחלום: Gen. 31.11   אשכול: Num. 13.24   הראשון: Ex. 12.16

גִּבֹּר: Gen. 10.9   גִּבֹּרִים: 2 Sam. 1.25   הַכִּיֹּר: Ex. 39.39
גבור: Gen. 10.9   גבורים: 2 Sam. 1.27   הכיור: Ex. 38.8

צִפֹּר: Num. 22.10   הַצִּפֹּר: Lev. 14.6   מִמְּקֹמוֹ: Judg. 20.33
צפור: Num. 22.4   הצפור: Lev. 14.5   ממקומו: Judg. 20.33

c)   Feminine forms.

בְּשֹׂרָה: 2 Sam. 18.20   הַטָּהֳרָה: Gen. 8.20   הַמְּכֹנָה: 1 Ki. 7.35
בשורה: 2 Sam. 18.25   הטהורה: Gen. 7.8   המכונה: 1 Ki. 7.35

הַמְּנֹרָה: Ex. 25.33   הַקִּיצֹנָה: Ex. 36.17
המנורה: Ex. 25.31   הקיצונה: Ex. 36.11

d)   Forms with the vowel *u*.

הַגְּבֻל: Num. 34.11	וּבְעַמֻּד: Num. 14.14	הָעַמֻּדִים: Ex. 38.12
הגבול: Num. 34.18	ובעמוד: Num. 14.14	העמודים: Ex. 38.11
גְּבֻלְךָ: Num. 20.17	טֻרִים: 1 Ki. 7.20	הַכְּרֻבִים: Ezek. 10.18
גבולך: Num. 20.16	טורים: 1 Ki. 7.18	הכרובים: Ezek. 10.19
שְׁמֻעָה: Jer. 49.23	הָעֻדֻת: Ex. 26.34	הֹלֶדֶת: Ezek. 16.5
שמועה: Jer. 49.14	העדות: Ex. 26.33	הולדת: Ezek. 16.4

§ 18.   Feminine plural ending.

וְאֶצְבְּעֹת: 2 Sam. 21.20	הָאֲתֹנֹת: 1 Sam. 9.3	הָאֹת: Ex. 4.17
ואצבעות: 2 Sam. 21.20	האתנות: 1 Sam. 9.3	האתות: Ex. 4.9
הַדַּקֹּת: Gen. 41.24	חַלֹּת: Lev. 7.12	בַּחֲצֹצְרֹת: Num. 10.9
הדקות: Gen. 41.7	חלות: Lev. 7.12	בחצצרות: Num. 10.8
הַטֹּבֹת: Gen. 41.26	טַבְּעֹת: Ex. 28.28	יְפֹת: Gen. 41.4
הטבות: Gen. 41.24	טבעות: Ex. 28.27	יפות: Gen. 41.2
יְקָרֹת: 1 Ki. 7.9	יְשׁוּעֹת: Ps. 42.12	הַכְּלָיֹת: Lev. 3.4
יקרות: 1 Ki. 7.10	ישועות: Ps. 42.6	הכליות: Lev. 3.4
מֵאֹת: Gen. 23.15	מִזְבְּחֹת: 2 Ki. 21.4	הַנֵּרֹת: Num. 8.2
מאות: Gen. 23.16	מזבחות: 2 Ki. 21.5	הנרות: Num. 8.2
מַצֹּת: Ex. 13.6	סְבִיבֹת: Num. 11.24	סִבְלֹת: Ex. 6.6
מצות: Ex. 13.7	סביבות: Num. 11.31	סבלות: Ex. 6.7
סֻכֹּת: Gen. 33.17	הָעִבְרִיֹּת: Ex. 1.15	הָעֲגָלֹת: Num. 7.8
סכות: Gen. 33.17	העבריות: Ex. 1.16	העגלות: Num. 7.7
עֹלֹת: Gen. 41.2	וְעַשְׁתְּרֹת: Deut. 28.18	צִדְקֹת: Judg. 5.11
עלות: Gen. 41.3	ועשתרות: Deiit. 28.4	צדקות: Judg. 5.11
קֹלֹת: 1 Sam. 12.18	קַרְנֹת: Lev. 4.18	רָעֹת: Jer. 44.9
קלות: 1 Sam. 12.17	קרנות: Lev. 4.7	רעות: Jer. 44.9

שָׁבֻעֹת: Deut. 16.9	שֵׁמֹת: Num. 1.26
שבעות: Deut. 16.9	שמות: Num. 1.24

§ 19.   The noun with suffixes.

אַרְמְנֹתֶיהָ: Am. 1.10	בְּחוּרֹתֶיךָ: Eccl. 12.1	תּוֹעֲבֹתַיִךְ: Ezek. 16.51
אמרנותיה: Am. 1.14	בחורותיך: Eccl. 11.9	תועבותיך: Ezek. 16.51

Similarly:

לְמִטְעַמֹּתָיו: Prov. 23.6   אֲחֹתִי: 2 Sam. 13.5

למטעמותיו: Prov. 23.3   אחותי: 2 Sam. 13.6

§ 20. Masculine plural ending.

הַחַרְטָמֻּם: Ex. 8.15   הַנּוֹתָרִם: Lev. 10.16

החרטמים: Ex. 8.14   הנותרים: Lev. 10.12

§ 21. Proper names.

a) The vowel *i*.

אֲחִטוּב: 1 Sam. 22.9   בִּנְיָמִן: 1 Sam. 13.16   דָּוִד: 1 Ki. 3.7

אחיטוב: 1 Sam. 22.11   בנימין: 1 Sam. 13.2   דויד: 1 Ki. 3.14

יָבֵשׁ: 2 Ki. 5.13   קְעִלָה: 1 Sam. 23.5   בְּרְפִידִם: Ex. 17.8

יביש: 2 Ki. 5.14   קעילה: 1 Sam. 23.5   ברפידים: Ex. 17.1

                תַּחְפְּנֵס: 1 Ki. 11.20

                תחפנים: 1 Ki. 11.20

b) The vowel *o*.

אַבְשָׁלֹם: 2 Sam. 17.9   אֹן: Gen. 41.45   גֹּב: 2 Sam. 21.18

אבשלום: 2 Sam. 17.7   און: Gen. 41.50   בגוב: 2 Sam. 21.19

גֵּרְשֹׁם: 1 Chron. 6.1   דְּבֹרָה: Judg. 4.14   סִיחֹן: Num. 21.26

גרשום: 1 Chron. 6.2   דבורה: Judg. 4.9   סיחון: Num. 21.27

צֹר: Ezek. 27.2   שֹׂכֹה: 1 Sam. 17.1   הַתְּקֹעִית: 2 Sam. 14.4

צור: Ezek. 27.3   שוכה: 1 Sam. 17.1   התקועית: 2 Sam. 14.9

c) The vowel *u*.

צְרֻיָה: 2 Sam. 16.10   שָׁלֻם: 2 Ki. 5.10   הַשֻּׁנַמִּית: 2 Ki. 2.22

צרויה: 2 Sam. 16.9   שלום: 2 Ki. 5.13   השונמית: 2 Ki. 2.17

§ 22. Particles.

לֹא: 1 Ki. 5.25   הֲלֹא: 1 Ki. 1.13   לְלֹא: Isa. 65.1

לוא: 1 Ki. 5.17   הלוא: 1 Ki. 1.11   ללוא: Isa. 65.1

אֹתָךְ: Ezek. 16.5   אֹתוֹ: Ps. 101.5   אֹתָם: 2 Ki. 10.8

אותך: Ezek. 16.4   אותו: Ps. 101.5   אותם: 2 Ki. 10.6

אֲלֵהֶם: Gen. 37.22	אֲלֵהֶן: Ex. 1.19	כָּמֹנִי: 2 Ki. 3.7
אליהם: Gen. 37.13	אליהן: Ex. 1.17	כמוני: 1 Ki. 22.4
עֵד: Gen. 8.32	בַּעֲבֻר: Gen. 27.10	בָּאַחֲרֹנָה: 1 Sam. 29.2
עוד: Gen. 8.21	בעבור: Gen. 27.4	באחרונה: 2 Sam. 2.26

כִּתְמֹל שִׁלְשֹׁם: Gen. 31.5	
כתמול שלשום: Gen. 31.2	

§ 23.   Numerals.

שָׁלֹשׁ: Num. 22.33	שְׁלֹשָׁה: Ezek. 48.32	הַשְּׁלִשִׁי: Ex. 19.11
שלוש: Num. 22.32	שלושה: Ezek. 48.31	השלישי: Ex. 19.11
הַחֲמִשִׁי: Zech. 7.3	הַשְּׁבִעִי: Ex. 12.15	הַתִּשְׁעִי: Jer. 36.9
החמישי: Zech. 8.19	השביעי: Ex. 12.16	התשיעי: Jer. 36.33

Conclusions

§ 24.   The *matres lectionis* represent the first attempt towards vocalization of the consonantal text; cf. p. 562, §§ 1 ff. After the invention of vowel signs to indicate vowels, the *matres lectionis* were gradually, but never consistently withdrawn. Our examples are taken either from one and the same verse, or else from two verses in very close proximity. They prove that the presence or absence of a *mater lectionis* is quite irrelevant in our quest to establish the quantity of a vowel; cf. p. 418, § 6.

§ 25.   The letters ו and י were in the same fashion eliminated even in cases, where—according to the theories current in Hebrew grammar—they represent a root-letter; cf. § 8b; § 9b, c; § 10; § 12b, c; § 13b, c. These theories work under the tacit assumption that in such cases (as referred to above) the *plene* spelling is the correct way of rendering the words in question, while the *defective* spelling is erroneous. In other words, these theories were formulated independently from, and with no regard for, the actual spelling in the Bible. This is a fundamental error; for in the relationship between Bible and grammar, the Bible unquestionably ranks first; cf. p. 418, §§ 6 and 7, and p. 553, § 23. Hence, the grammatical theories will have to be revised, and adjusted to the facts as found in the Bible. We should not proceed arbitrarily by recognizing one way of spelling only, merely because it agrees with our theories, to the exclusion of divergent spellings, which make these theories untenable. We shall

draw our conclusions from the actual spelling, in the following manner:
the preservation of the letters ו and י after a vowel-sign of the *o* and *i*
group (= =; = =) is solely due to the inconsistency in eliminating
vowel-letters, but is in itself no evidence of their being root-letters.

§ 26.   Equally untenable is the explanation of the current Hebrew
grammar that the letter י in nominal forms with personal suffixes is meant
to differentiate between the noun in the plural (spelled with י) and in the
singular (spelled with no י). The following examples will demonstrate that
here, too, the י is merely a vowel-letter, and does not indicate the number
of the noun (cf. p. 261, § 35 ff.).

a)   Gen. 12.3:   מְבָרְכֶיךָ וּמְקַלֶּלְךָ
     Num. 24.9:   מְבָרֲכֶיךָ בָּרוּךְ וְאֹרֲרֶיךָ אָרוּר
     Deut. 21.10:   עַל אֹיְבֶיךָ וּנְתָנוֹ
     Deut. 23.15:   מַחֲנֶךָ · · · וְהָיָה מַחֲנֶיךָ
     Deut. 28.48:   אֶת אֹיְבֶיךָ אֲשֶׁר יְשַׁלְּחֶנּוּ
     Judg. 13.12:   יָבֹא דְבָרֶיךָ
     1 Sam. 19.4:   וְכִי מַעֲשָׂיו טוֹב
     2 Sam. 12.11:   וְנָתַתִּי לְרֵעֶיךָ וְשָׁכַב
     2 Sam. 24.13:   לִפְנֵי צָרֶיךָ וְהוּא רֹדְפֶךָ
     Isa. 30.20:   וְלֹא יִכָּנֵף עוֹד מוֹרֶיךָ
     Ezek. 35.11   מִשַּׁאֲתֶיךָ
     Ps. 66.3:   מַה נּוֹרָא מַעֲשֶׂיךָ
     Eccl. 12.1:   בּוֹרְאֶיךָ

b)   Deut. 3.24:   וְכִגְבוּרֹתֶךָ
     1 Ki. 8.29:   לִהְיוֹת עֵינֶךָ פְּתֻחוֹת
     Jer. 38.22:   הָטְבְּעוּ · · · רַגְלֶךָ

§ 27.   The material upon which these conclusions are based, is derived
from Jacob ben Chayim's First Masoretic Bible. But no matter what
good manuscripts we substitute for Jacob ben Chayim, the result will
remain the same, though the examples probably will have to be taken
from different Biblical passages. Owing to the inconsistency in the elimination of the vowel letters, it happens that a word which is spelled *plene*
in Jacob ben Chayim, appears in *defective* spelling in another Bible text,
and *vice versa*. A cursory examination of the critical apparatus in Ken-

nicott's Bible, a disproportionately large part of which consists of such differences in *plene* and *defective* spellings, will prove the correctness of our assertion.

§ 28.   These observations are of fundamental importance for the preparation of a new edition of the Hebrew Bible. A thorough examination of all Bible manuscripts is an indispensable pre-requisite for this undertaking. But we now realize that no matter how many Bible manuscripts we will have at our disposal for our work, we shall have to select a single one as the basis of our edition, and follow its readings in every detail. Any attempt to base a Bible edition upon all the texts available, selecting and rejecting the different readings, would mean only the proceed in accordance with purely subjective theories.

§ 29.   א as *mater lectionis* for *a*.

a)   Names of persons.

2 Ki. 16.7:	פִּלֶסֶר	1 Chron. 5.26:	פִּלְנֶסֶר	Jer. 34.1:	וּנְבוּכַדְנֶצַּר
2 Ki. 16.10:	פִּלְאֶסֶר	1 Chron. 5.6:	פִּלְנְאֶסֶר	Jer. 39.5:	נְבוּכַדְנֶאצַּר
	Jer. 29.22	וּכְאָחָב		Hag. 1.12:	שַׁלְתִּיאֵל
	Jer. 29.21:	אַחְאָב		Hag. 1.1:	שְׁאַלְתִּיאֵל

D)   Names of places.

1 Sam. 31.10:	בֵּית שָׁן	1 Chron. 11.13:	בְּפַס דַּמִּים
Josh. 17.11:	בֵּית שְׁאָן	1 Sam. 17.1:	בְּאֶפֶס דַּמִּים
Ezek. 43.15:	וְהַהַרְאֵל	2 Sam. 10.16:	חֵילָם
Ezek. 43.15:	וּמֵהַאֲרְאֵיל	2 Sam. 10.17:	חֶלְאמָה

c)   Various other parts of speech.

Jonah 2.1:	דָּג	2 Sam. 12.3:	וְלָרָשׁ	Prov. 1.22:	פְּתָיִם
Neh. 13.16:	דָּאג	2 Sam. 12.4:	הָרָאשׁ	Prov. 1.4:	לִפְתָאיִם
Ezek. 27.26:	הַשָּׁטִים	Prov. 6.17:	רָמוֹת	Ex. 26.24:	תַּמִּים
Ezek. 28.24:	הַשָּׁאטִים	Prov. 24.7:	רָאמוֹת	Ex. 26.24:	תֹּאמָם
1 Sam. 18.22:	בַּלָט	Job 31.26:	יָהֵל	"when it shined"
Judg. 4.21:	בַּלָּאט	Job 25.5:	יַאֲהִיל	"hath [no] brightness"

	Isa. 27.8:	בְּסַאסְאָה	Joel 2.6:	פָּארוּר

d) The article.

Num. 14.6:   הַתָּרִים

Num. 21.1:   הָאֲתָרִים   Num. 11.4:   וְהָאסַפְסֻף

Jer. 40.4:   הָאזִקִּים

e) Preposition בּ.

Isa. 45.14:   בַּזִּקִּים

Jer. 40.1:   בָּאזִקִּים   Judg. 9.41:   בָּארוּמָה

Conclusions

§ 30.   Proper names are very instructive; for regardless of their spellings (with or without an א), there can have been but one way to pronounce them. But at a later period, when the function of the א as a vowel-
letter was no longer remembered, the vocalizers accounted for its presence by putting vowel-signs underneath it. This trend continued till
our own days. For we were all taught to read in Num. 11.4 (quoted under
d): וְהָאסַפְסֻף. How unsound the vocalization is, may be seen from cases
like תַּמִּים and תֹּאֲמִים; it is obvious that they represent one and the same
word in *defective* and *plene* spelling, respectively; cf. p. 562, § 1. A similar
discrepancy between the vocalization and the spelling is offered in cases
like: ראשׁ, צֹאן, נֹאד. Cf. MH §§ 48-52.

§ 31.   There are at least indications left that ה, too, was used as vowel-
letter for *a*; cf. Ex. 7.11: בְּלַהֲטֵיהֶם with ib. v. 22: בְּלָטֵיהֶם; Ps. 29.7:
לַהֲבוֹת with Ex. 3.2: בְּלַבַּת. Similar cases of elimination of the vowel-letter
ה are: Ex. 4.2: מַזֶּה; Isa. 3.15: מַלְּכֶם. Consequently, I am inclined to
regard merely as *plene* spelling cases like: בְּהַדְּרֵךְ: Neh. 9.19; בְּהַשָּׁמַיִם:
Ps. 36.6; כְּהֶחְכָּם: Eccl. 8.1 (originally pronounced כְּהֶחָכָם, cf. p. 217,
sub d); כְּהַחֲלֹנוֹת: Ezek. 40.25; כְּהַיּוֹם: Gen. 39.11; לְהַגְּדוּד: 2 Chron.
25.10; וּלְהַגֵּרִים: Ezek. 47.22; לְהַחוֹמָה: Neh. 12.38; לְהַמִּזְבֵּחַ: 2 Chron. 29.27;
לְהָעָם: 2 Chron. 10.7; וּלְהַקַּרְדֻּמִּים: 1 Sam. 13.21; לְהָרָפָה: 2 Sam. 21.20.

B. THE VERB—ITS TENSES AND ROOTS

§ 32.   In order to arrive at a better understanding of the Hebrew verb,
we must first clarify the verbal forms with the so-called *waw consecutivum*.
We start our discussion with the definition of the *waw consecutivum* as

given by G. R. Driver in his monograph *Problems of the Hebrew Verbal System*, adding in brackets some other usage listed in modern grammars.

"The principal peculiarity of the Hebrew verbal system is the construction with consecutive *waw*, which raises the whole problem of the Semitic tenses in its acutest form. Put briefly, the essence of this idiom is that a perfect tense might be continued [or preceded] by an imperfect introduced by consecutive *waw*, and inversely an imperfect tense might be continued [or preceded] by consecutive *waw* introducing a perfect [in either case, perfect and imperfect indicate synchronistic events; similarly, an imperative might be continued by a perfect tense with consecutive *waw*]. This *waw* is recognized by the fact that before the imperfect tense it was vocalized *wa-* and generally required the doubling of the following prefix (where this was possible) or else the lengthening of its vowel (in compensation for the doubling), while the verb was accented on the first instead of the last syllable (where this was possible); with the perfect tense the conjunction was either *wᵉ-* or *û-*, while the accent fell on the final instead of any other syllable (where this was possible). Thus *qámtā wattḗlek* (not *wᵉhālāktā*) means 'thou didst arise and go' (with the imperfect for the perfect tense) and *tāqúm wᵉhàlaktấ* (not *wᵉtēlḗk*) means 'thou shalt arise and go' (with the perfect for the imperfect tense). Thus the tenses seem to be inverted" (p. 85).

One important point must be immediately rectified. Driver was not correct when he said the *waw consecutivum* is "recognized" by the way it is vocalized. On the contrary, with a verb in the perfect there is no difference between *waw consecutivum* and *conjunctivum* in the vocalization. It is solely the syntactic usage of the *waw* which makes it a *waw consecutivum*; the vocalization results from the meaning. In our diagnosis of the *waw consecutivum* we must not confuse the symptom with the function. It is not the vocalization which matters, but the context.

The last sentence in the passage quoted from Driver is courageously phrased: "Thus the tenses seem to be inverted." For the very notion of *waw consecutivum* has as a presupposition the assumption that Hebrew perfect is otherwise used to indicate past events, and Hebrew imperfect future happenings. And it is solely due to this *waw* that the tenses, which they supposedly ordinarily represent, all of a sudden become inverted.

A.   THE VOCALIZATION OF THE PREPOSITION וַ

a.   With Verbs

§ 33.   *Waw consecutivum* with imperfect-forms, vocalized וְ.

In their *critical apparatus*, the editors of the various Biblical books in
Kittel's *Biblia Hebraica*, 2nd ed. (Leipzig 1913) [1] have in almost all of
the cases listed here suggested a correction of the vocalization וְ into וַ
with subsequent *dagesh* (before an א: וַ is changed into וָ). They thus took
it for a fact that these *waws* are consecutive. We, therefore, forego
proving this fact at each case, and limit ourselves to making it clear at
the few instances only, which are not identified as such in the *Biblia
Hebraica*.

Judg. 6.9:	וָאֲגָרֵשׁ	Isa. 47.9:	וְתָבֹאנָה
Judg. 20.6:	וָאֲנַתְּחֶהָ וָאֲשַׁלְּחֶהָ.		(following: בָּאוּ)
	(In *Biblica Hebraica*	Isa. 48.3:	וָאַשְׁמִיעֵם
	the text is emended	Isa. 49.5:	וְאֶכָּבֵד
	to read וָ··· וְ···)	Isa. 49.8:	וְאֶצָּרְךָ וְאֶתֶּנְךָ
2 Sam. 1.10:	וַאֲמֹתְתֵהוּ	Isa. 51.2:	וַאֲבָרְכֵהוּ וְאַרְבֵּהוּ
2 Ki. 19.23:	וְאֶכְרֹת ··· וְאָבוֹאָה	Isa. 57.17:	וָאַכֵּהוּ ··· וְאֶקְצֹף
2 Ki. 19.24:	וְאַחֲרִב	Isa. 57.18:	וְאֶרְפָּאֵהוּ וְאַנְחֵהוּ וַאֲשַׁלֵּם
2 Ki. 19.25:	וּתְהִי		(preceding: רָאִיתִי)
Isa. 8.2:	וְאָעִידָה	Isa. 63.3:	··· וְאֶדְרְכֵם ··· וְאֶרְמְסֵם
Isa. 10.13:	וְאָסִיר ··· וְאוֹרִיד		וְיֵז
Isa. 37.24:	וְאֶכְרֹת ··· וְאָבוֹא	Isa. 63.5:	וְאַבִּיט ··· וְאֶשְׁתּוֹמֵם
Isa. 37.25:	וְאַחֲרִב	Isa. 63.6:	וְאָבוּס ··· וַאֲשַׁכְּרֵם ···
Isa. 37.26:	וּתְהִי		וְאוֹרִיד
Isa. 41.5:	וַיִּירָאוּ	Jer. 3.19:	וְאֶתֵּן (following: וָאֹמַר)
	(preceding: רָאוּ)	Jer. 23.18:	וְיֵרֶא וְיִשְׁמַע
Isa. 41.28:	וְאֵרֶא	Ezek. 16.10:	וָאַכַּסֵּךְ (preceding:
Isa. 42.6:	וְאֶחֱזַק ··· וְאֶצָּרְךָ וְאֶתֶּנְךָ		··· וָאֶנְעֲלֵךְ ··· וָאַלְבִּשֵׁךְ
Isa. 43.4:	וְאֶתֵּן		(וָאֲחַבְּשֵׁךְ)
Isa. 43.9:	וְיֵאָסְפוּ	Ezek. 22.30:	וָאֲבַקֵּשׁ. (In *Biblia*
	(preceding: נִקְבְּצוּ)		*Hebraica* the text is
Isa. 43.28:	וָאֲחַלֵּל ··· וְאֶתְּנָה		corrected in וַאֲבַקֵּשׁ)

[1] The 3rd edition, Stuttgart 1929 ff., does not present Jacob ben Chayim's
text, which forms the basis of our researches.

Ezek. 31.11:   וָאֶתְּנֵהוּ   Job 3.11:   וָאֶגְוָע

Hos. 4.19:   (preceding: צָרַר) וְיֵבֹשׁוּ   (preceding: יָצָאתִי)

Hos. 11.4:   וָאַט   Job 3.13:   וְאֶשְׁקוֹט

Mic. 6.16:   וְיִשְׁתַּמֵּר   (preceding: שָׁכַבְתִּי)

Zech. 8.10:   וַאֲשַׁלַּח   Job 30.26:   וָאֲיַחֲלָה

§ 34.   *Waw conjunctivum* with imperfect-forms vocalized וְ.

Gen. 37.7:   וַתִּשְׁתַּחֲוֶיןָ (preceding: תְּסֻבֶּינָה)

Num. 8.18:   וָאֶקַּח (cf. ib. v. 6: קַח, and the following description of the
induction ceremonies to be performed; hence ואקח and
ואתנה (v. 19) refer: hereafter).

Num. 8.19:   וָאֶתְּנָה

Deut. 2.12:   וַיִּשְׁמִידוּם (preceding: יִירָשׁוּם)

Deut. 17.3:   וַיִּשְׁתַּחוּ ··· וַיֵּלֶךְ וַיַּעֲבֹד (cf. v. 2: יַעֲשֶׂה ··· יִמְצֵא)

Deut. 32.13:   וַיִּנְקֵהוּ ··· וַיֹּאכַל (all the verbs from v. 8 on are in the imperfect)

Josh. 9.21:   וַיִּהְיוּ (cf. v. 20: נַעֲשֶׂה; v. 21: יִחְיוּ; v. 23: עֶבֶד מִכֶּם יִכָּרֵת וְלֹא
וְחֹטְבֵי עֵצִים)

Judg. 2.1:   וָאֹמַר ··· וָאָבִיא (preceding: אַעֲלֶה)

Judg. 6.4:   וַיַּחֲנוּ ··· וַיַּשְׁחִיתוּ (cf. following: יַשְׁאִירוּ וְלֹא)

Judg. 6.5:   וַיָּבֹאוּ (preceding: יַעֲלוּ)

Judg. 12.5:   וַיֹּאמֶר ··· וַיֹּאמְרוּ (preceding: אֶעֱבֹרָה ··· יֹאמְרוּ)

I Sam. 1.7:   וַתִּבְכֶּה (preceding: תַּכְעִסֶנָה; following: תֹאכַל)

I Sam. 2.16:   וַיֹּאמֶר (a frequently recurring happening is narrated)

I Sam. 2.29:   וַתְּכַבֵּד (preceding: תִבְעֲטוּ)

I Sam. 13.20:   וַיֵּרְדוּ (cf. v. 19: יַעֲשׂוּ ··· יִמְצֵא; this event happened frequently)

I Sam. 27.9:   וַיָּשָׁב וַיָּבֹא (cf. preceding note)

I Sam. 28.17:   וַיַּעַשׂ ··· וַיִּקְרַע ··· וַיִּתְּנָה (these events were going to happen
in the future only)

2 Sam. 12.3:   וַתְּהִי (preceding: תֹאכַל ··· תִּשְׁתֶּה ··· תִּשְׁכָּב)

2 Sam. 22.38:   וָאַשְׁמִידֵם (preceding: אֶרְדְּפָה; following: אָשׁוּב)

2 Sam. 22.39:   וַיִּפְּלוּ ··· וָאֲכַלֵּם וָאֶמְחָצֵם (cf. יְקוּמוּן)

2 Sam. 22.40:   וַתַּזְרֵנִי (following: תַּכְרִיעַ)

2 Sam. 22.44:   וַתְּפַלְּטֵנִי (following: תִּשְׁמְרֵנִי)

I Ki. 3.16:   וַתָּבֹאנָה (preceding: תֵּעָמֹדְנָה)

1 Ki. 21.6: וָאֹמַר (preceding: אֲדַבֵּר)

2 Ki. 20.7: וַיֶּחִי‏ · · · וַיָּשִׂימוּ וַיִּקְחוּ; cf. the parallel report in Isa. 38.21: וְיֶחִי · · · וְיִמְרְחוּ · · · יִשְׂאוּ

Isa. 5.15: וַיִּשְׁפַּל · · · וַיִּשַׁח (following: תִּשְׁפַּלְנָה)

Isa. 6.4: וַיִּנָּעוּ (following: יִמָּלֵא)

Isa. 9.10: וַיְשַׂגֵּב (following: יְסַכְסֵךְ)

Isa. 29.21: וַיַּטּוּ (preceding: יְקֹשׁוּן)

Isa. 31.1: וַיִּבְטְחוּ (preceding: יִשָׁעֵנוּ)

Isa. 42.25: וַתְּבְעַר (following: יָשִׂים)

Isa. 44.12: וַיִּפְעָלֵהוּ (preceding: יִצְרֵהוּ)

Isa. 44.13: וַיַּעֲשֵׂהוּ (preceding: יְתָאֲרֵהוּ · · · יַעֲשֵׂהוּ · · · יְתָאֲרֵהוּ)

Isa. 44.15: וַיִּשְׁתָּחוּ (preceding: יִפְעַל)

Isa. 57.20: וַיְגָרְשׁוּ (preceding: יוּכָל)

Jer. 5.22: וַיִּתְגָּעֲשׁוּ (following: יוּכָלוּ)

Jer. 38.9: וַיָּמָת ("he is like to die")

Jer. 52.7: וַיֵּצְאוּ (preceding: יִבְרְחוּ)

Hos. 2.15: וַתַּעַד (preceding: תַּקְטִיר)

Hos. 8.10: וַיָּחֵלּוּ (preceding: יִתְּנוּ · · · אֲקַבְּצֵם)

Hos. 8.13: וַיֹּאכֵלוּ (preceding: יִזְבְּחוּ)

Hos. 11.4: וְאֶהְיֶה (preceding: אֶמְשְׁכֵם; following: וְאַט)

Hos. 13.7: וָאֱהִי (cf. v. 8: אֶבְקָעֵם · · · וְאֶקְרַע · · · וְאֶפְגְּשֵׁם · · · וְאֹכְלֵם)

Hab. 1.3: וַיְהִי (following: יִשָּׂא; cf. also preceding: תַּבִּיט · · · תַּרְאֵנִי)

Hab. 1.9: וַיֶּאֱסֹף (preceding: יָבוֹא)

Hab. 1.10: וַיִּלְכְּדָהּ · · · וַיִּצְבֹּר (preceding: יִשְׂחָק · · · יִתְקַלָּס)

Zech. 7.14: וַיָּשִׂימוּ (cf. v. 13: יִקְרָאוּ · · · אֶשְׁמָע; v. 14: וְאֶסָעֲרֵם)

Ps. 7.16: וַיִּפֹּל (following: יִפְעָל)

Ps. 18.20: וַיּוֹצִיאֵנִי (following: יְחַלְּצֵנִי)

Ps. 18.40: וַתְּאַזְּרֵנִי (following: תַּכְרִיעַ)

Ps. 42.6: וַתֶּהֱמִי (preceding: תִּשְׁתּוֹחֲחִי)

Ps. 52.9: וַיִּבְטַח (preceding: יָשִׂים)

Ps. 55.6: וַתְּכַסֵּנִי (preceding: יָבֹא)

Ps. 55.18: וַיִּשְׁמַע (preceding: אָשִׂיחָה וְאֶהֱמֶה)

Ps. 59.16: וַיָּלִינוּ (preceding: יִשְׂבְּעוּ)

Ps. 78.15: וַיַּשְׁקְ (preceding: יְבַקַּע)

Ps. 78.36: וַיְפַתּוּהוּ (following: יְכַזְּבוּ)

Ps. 78. 45: וַתַּשְׁחִיתֵם · · · וַיֹּאכְלֵם (preceding: יְשַׁלַּח)

Ps. 78.46:   וַיִּתֵּן (cf. v. 47: יַהֲרֹג)
Ps. 78.48:   וַיַּסְגֵּר (cf. v. 49: יְשַׁלַּח)
Ps. 78.72:   וַיִּרְעֵם (following: יַנְחֵם)
Ps. 80.9:   וַתִּטָּעֶהָ (preceding: תַּסִּיעַ)
Ps. 94.7:   וַיֹּאמְרוּ · · · יְרַצֵּחוּ (cf. v. 6: יַהֲרֹגוּ)
Ps. 104.32:   וַתִּרְעָד (cf. parallel: יִגַּע · · · וְיֶעֱשָׁנוּ)
Ps. 106.17:   וַתְּכַס · · · וַתִּבְלַע (preceding: תִּפְתַּח)
Ps. 106.18:   וַתִּבְעַר (following: תְּלַהֵט)
Ps. 106.19:   וַיִּשְׁתַּחֲווּ (preceding: יַעֲשׂוּ)
Prov. 24.32:   וָאֶחֱזֶה (following: אָשִׁית)
Job 3.21:   וַיַּחְפְּרֻהוּ (preceding: הַמְחַכִּים; cf. v. 22: יִשִׂישׂוּ · · · הַשְּׂמֵחִים)
2 Chron. 24.20: וַיַּעֲזֹב (cf. preceding parallel: תַּצְלִיחוּ)

§ 35.   *Waw consecutivum* with perfect-forms voçalized וְ.

וְשָׁב: Isa. 6.10; cf. also: וְשָׁב: Isa.
29.17

וְקָם: Prov. 24.16; cf. also: וְקָם:
Deut. 31.16

וְרָב: Isa. 19.20; on the root, cf.
1 Sam. 25.39: אֲשֶׁר רָב אֶת
רִיב חֶרְפָּתִי

וָמֵת: Gen. 44.9; cf. also: וּמֵת:
Ex. 21.20

וְחַי: Gen. 3.22; cf. also וְחִי:
2 Sam. 12.22

וְחָיָה: Ex. 1.16; cf. also: וְחָיָה:
Ezek. 33.11

וָמֵתָה: Deut. 22.21

וָמַתָּה: Ezek. 28.8

וְבָשְׁתְּ: Ezek. 16.63
וְסַכְתְּ: Ruth 3.3
וָמַתִּי: Gen. 19.19
וְשָׁבוּ: Zech. 10.9; cf. also: וְשָׁבוּ:
Ex. 13.17
וְקָמוּ: Isa. 49.7; cf. also: וְקָמוּ:
Gen. 41.30
וְחַתּוּ: Jer. 50.36; cf. also: וְחַתּוּ:
Isa. 20.5
וָמֵתוּ: Gen. 33.13; cf. also: וּמֵתוּ:
Lev. 22.9
וָבֹשׁוּ: Isa. 20.5; cf. also: וּבֹשׁוּ:
Isa. 19.9
וְרֹבּוּ: Gen. 49.23
וָמַתְנוּ: 2 Ki. 7.4

§ 36.   *Waw conjunctivum* with various verbal forms vocalized וְ.

a)   Perfect.

וְחָתָּה: Jer. 48.1
וְשָׁבְתִּי: 1 Sam. 12.2
וְבָאוּ: Eccl. 8.10

וְבֹשׁוּ: Isa. 37.27; cf. also: יֵבֹשׁוּ:
Isa. 19.9

b)   Infinitive.

וְנָבֹא: 1 Ki. 3.7; cf. also: וּבֹא: וְשׁוֹב: Gen. 8.7; cf. also: וְשׁוֹב:
Jer. 17.27   Jer. 3.1

c)   Imperative.

וְנָבֹא: 1 Ki. 22.30; cf. also: וּבֹא: וְדֹמִי: Jer. 47.6
Esth. 5.14   וָדוֹשִׁי: Mic. 4.13
וְבֹאָה: 1 Sam. 20.21   וּבֹאוּ: Joel 4.11; cf. also: וּבֹאוּ:
וְלֵךְ: 2 Ki. 4.29; cf. also: וְלֵךְ:   Jer. 49.14
2 Ki. 8.8   וָחֹתּוּ: Isa. 8.9
וְצֵאָה: Judg. 9.29   וָשֵׁעוּ: Isa. 29.9
וָמֻת: Job 2.9; cf. also: וּמֻת: Deut.   וְקוֹשּׁוּ: Zeph. 2.1
32.50   וָלֵכוּ: Gen. 42.33; cf. also: וְלֵכָה:
וְרֵד: 1 Ki. 18.44   1 Sam. 23.27
וְשׁוּב: Prov. 3.28; cf. also: וְשׁוּב: וְשׁוּבוּ: Ex. 32.27; cf. also: וְשׁוּבוּ:
Gen. 31.13   Josh. 18.8
וְגֹחִי: Mic. 4.10

b.   With Other Parts of Speech

§ 37.   *Waw conjunctivum* vocalized וְ

1)   Man and his family.

אָב וָאֵם: Ezek. 22.7   זָקֵן וָנַעַר: Jer. 51.22
בֵּן וָאָח: Eccl. 4.8   Similarly:
וְנִין וָנֶכֶד: Isa. 14.22   שָׁדַיִם וָרָחַם: Gen. 49.25
וְנָשִׁים וָטָף: Jer. 40.7   כְּלָיוֹת וָלֵב: Jer. 11.20

2)   Food.

בָּר וָלֶחֶם: Gen. 45.23   יַיִן וָקַיִץ: Jer. 40.12
לֶחֶם וָמַיִם: 2 Ki. 6.22   סֹלֶת וָשֶׁמֶן: Ezek. 16.19
לֶחֶם וָיַיִן: Judg. 19.19

3)   Cattle and beast.

בְּהֵמָה וָרֶמֶשׂ: Gen. 1.24   וְעֵגֶל וָכֶבֶשׂ: Lev. 9.3
בְּהֵמוֹת וָעוֹף: Jer. 12.4   פַּר וָאַיִל: Num. 23.2
בָּקָר וָצֹאן: Lev. 27.32   וְשׁוֹר וָאַיִל: Lev. 9.4
וְכֶשֶׂב וָעֵז: Lev. 7.23   וְשׁוֹר וָשֶׂה: Lev. 22.23

וְשֶׂה וָשׁוֹר: Judg. 6.4   לָבִיא וָלַיִשׁ: Isa. 30.6

וּפָרָה וָדֹב: Isa. 11.7

4) Phenomena of nature.

יוֹמָם וָלַיְלָה: Jer. 16.13   שָׁרָב וָשָׁמֶשׁ: Isa. 49.10

לַיְלָה וָיוֹם: Isa. 27.3   וְקֹר וָחֹם: Gen. 8.22

בֹּקֶר וָעֶרֶב: Ps. 65.9   וְקַיִץ וָחֹרֶף: Gen. 8.22

שָׁמַיִם וָאָרֶץ: Jer. 51.48   נֶפֶץ וָזֶרֶם: Isa. 30.30

5) Pronouns.

אֲנִי וְאַתָּה: 2 Ki. 9.25   לִי וָלָךְ: 1 Ki. 17.18

אֲנִי וָהוּא: Gen. 41.11   לָכֶם וָלָנוּ: Ezra 4.3

אַתָּה וָהֵם: Num. 16.16   Similarly:

דִיא וָהוּא: 1 Ki. 17.15   בַּיהוה וָבָךְ: Num. 21.7

6) Numerals.

שֵׁשׁ וָשֵׁשׁ: 2 Sam. 21.20   תִּשְׁעִים וָתֵשַׁע: Gen. 17.24

עֶשְׂרִים וָשֵׁשׁ: 1 Ki. 16.8   מֵאָה וָעֶשֶׂר: Gen. 50.22

עֶשְׂרִים וָשֶׁבַע: 1 Ki. 16.15   חֲמִשָּׁה וָאָלֶף: 1 Ki. 5.12

7) Proper names.

חָם וָיֶפֶת: Gen. 10.1   נַחַת וָזֶרַח: Gen. 36.13

וְגֶתֶר וָמַשׁ: Gen. 10.23   וְשֵׁלָה וָפֶרֶץ וָזֶרַח: Gen. 46.12

עֵיפָה וָעֵפֶר: Gen. 25.4   קֹרַח וָנֶפֶג: Ex. 6.21

8) Synonyms.

a) Alliterations.

חוֹמוֹת וָחֵל: Isa. 26.1   שָׁמִיר וָשַׁיִת: Isa. 7.24

שֹׁד וָשֶׁבֶר: Isa. 59.7   פַּחַד וָפַחַת וָפָח: Isa. 24.17

וְדֶבֶר וָדָם: Ezek. 5.17   דּוֹר וָדוֹר: Isa. 13.20

אֶבֶן וָאָבֶן: Deut. 25.13

b) Various nouns.

עֵץ וָאֶבֶן: Deut. 4.28   חָמָס וָשֹׁד: Jer. 20.8

גָּפְרִית וָמֶלַח: Deut. 29.22   רָעָב וָדֶבֶר: Ezek. 7.15

רֶפֶשׁ וָטִיט: Isa. 57.20   עָפָר וָאֵפֶר: Gen. 18.27

זָהָב וָכֶסֶף: Ex. 35.5   כַּפְתּוֹר וָפֶרַח: Ex. 25.33

יָד וָשֵׁם: Isa. 56.5

בְּכִי וָנֶהִי: Jer. 9.9

חָח וָנֶזֶם: Ex. 35.22

קִינִים וָהֶגֶה וָהִי: Ezek. 2.10

רָעָה וָפֶשַׁע: I Sam. 24.12

חֶרְפָּה וָבוּז: Ps. 119.22

אֵימָתָה וָפַחַד: Ex. 15.16

כִּנּוֹר וָנֶבֶל: Isa. 5.12

חָכְמַת וָדַעַת: Isa. 33.6

צְדָקוֹת וָעֹז: Isa. 45.25

סוּס וָרֶכֶב: Deut. 20.1

רֶכֶב וָסוּס: Isa. 43.17

קָמוֹשׂ וָחוֹחַ: Isa. 34.13

בְּשׁוּבָה וָנַחַת: Isa. 30.15

שֵׁשׁ וָמֶשִׁי: Ezek. 16.13

הוֹן וָעֹשֶׁר: Ps. 112.3

אֱלֹהִים וָמֶלֶךְ: I Ki. 21.10

שִׂמְחָה וָגִיל: Isa. 16.10

עֹפֶל וָבַחַן: Isa. 32.14

מַסְלוּל וָדֶרֶךְ: Isa. 35.8

עוֹלָה וָזֶבַח: Jer. 7.22

שָׂדֶה וָכֶרֶם: Num. 16.14

לְקָנֶה וָגֹמֶא: Isa. 35.7

וְשָׂדֶה וָזֶרַע: Jer. 35.9

9) Adjectives

גָּדוֹל וָרָם: Deut. 1.28

גָּדוֹל וָרָב: Deut. 2.10

עָצוּם וָרָב: Deut. 9.14

טוֹב וָרָע: Deut. 1.39

שְׁלֵמָה וָצֶדֶק: Deut. 25.15

רַע וָמָר: Jer. 2.19

בָּחוּר וָטוֹב: I Sam. 9.2

10) Particles.

כֹּה וָכֹה: Ex. 2.12

מִי וָמִי: Ex. 10.8

אָנֶה וָאָנָה: 2 Ki. 5.25

הֵנָּה וָהֵנָּה: I Ki. 20.40

יֵשׁ וָיֵשׁ: 2 Ki. 10.15

11) Adverbs.

a) Two adverbs.

תֹהוּ וָבֹהוּ: Gen. 1.2

מֵאֶפֶס וָתֹהוּ: Isa. 40.17

הֶבֶל וָרִיק: Isa. 30.7

הַפְלֵא וָפֶלֶא: Isa. 29.14

הַשְׁקֵט וָבֶטַח: Isa. 32.17

b) An adverb connected with a sentence.

מִמְּךָ וָהֵנָּה: I Sam. 20.21

מִמְּךָ וָהָלְאָה: I Sam. 20.22

חֹדֶשׁ וָמַעְלָה: Num. 3.15

אֲשֶׁר צִוָּה יהוה וָהָלְאָה: Num. 15.23

מִקִּיר הָעִיר וָחוּצָה: Num. 35.4

הֶחָצֵר הַפְּנִימִית וָבָיְתָה: Ezek. 44.17

Similarly:

וְאַמָּה וָחֵצִי: Ex. 25.10

אַמָּה וָטֹפַח: Ezek. 40.5

שֵׁשׁ אַמּוֹת וָזֶרֶת: I Sam. 17.4

Noteworthy:

צָפֹנָה וָנֶגְבָּה וָקֵדְמָה וָיָמָּה: Gen. 13.14

12) Verbs.

יָצוֹא וָשׁוֹב: Gen. 8.7   רָצוֹא וָשׁוֹב: Ezek. 1.14

קְחוּ וָלֵכוּ: Gen. 42.33   עוּשׁוּ וָבָאוּ: Joel 4.11

הִקָּבְצוּ וָבֹאוּ: Isa. 45.20   עֹבֵר וָשָׁב: Ezek. 35.7

יוֹצֵא וָבָא: 1 Sam. 18.16   הוֹלֵךְ וָרָב: 2 Sam. 15.12

וְגָדֵל וָטוֹב: 1 Sam. 2.26   צֵאת וָבֹא: 1 Ki. 3.7

Conclusions

§ 38.   The preposition ו in connection with verbal forms can be vocalized with ־ָ, ־ַ or ־ְ. With the results of our discussion in ch. 0, §§ 00-00
in mind: that ־ַ and ־ָ were interchangeably used to indicate the vowel *a*,
we shall now say: that the *waw* was vocalized either with *sheva* or with
the vowel *a*; cf. p. 219 sub 3, p. 225 sub B 12 and p. 192, § 78 f.

§ 39.   The assumption of current Hebrew grammars that these two
ways of vocalizing the *waw* with verbal forms correspond to the two
functions of the *waw* (the *waw consecutivum* with imperfect-forms being
vocalized with *a*, but with perfect-forms with *sheva*, like the *waw conjunctivum* with any verbal form) finds no support in the actual vocalization
of the Bible. On the contrary, the vocalization of the *waw* with verbal
forms with *sheva* or *a* shows no regard for the difference in the tenses,
whether perfect or imperfect, and is equally indifferent to the function
which the grammar ascribes to the variousoc currences; cf. p. 192, § 78
and here § 50.

§ 40.   The preposition ו connecting two monosyllabic words or segolates is vocalized with *a*; in all other cases, the preposition ו is vocalized
with *sheva*; so e.g., in all cases where the *waw* does not connect two words,
but the two sentences to which these two words belong. Compare e.g.,
1 Ki. 17.18: לִי וָלָךְ with ib. verse 13: לִי וְלָךְ; Isa. 35.8: מַסְלוּל וָדֶרֶךְ וְדֶרֶךְ;
Esth. 8.11: בְּכָל עִיר וָעִיר with Jer. 48.8: כָּל עִיר וְעִיר. The only exceptions
I am aware of are: Judg. 5.8: מָגֵן אִם יֵרָאֶה וָרֹמַח (a poetical passage, however; מָגֵן and וָרֹמַח syntactically belong together), and Isa. 26.19 (though
vocalized with *a*, וָאָרֶץ is really not connected with the preceding טַלֶּךָ).

§ 41.   The term *pretonic ḳameṣ* which Hebrew grammars use for cases
discussed in §§ 35-37, is meaningless and should be discarded. It merely
states the fact that these forms are vocalized with *ḳameṣ*, but does not

explain why one and the same word, with its stress unchanged, has the preopsition *waw* sometimes vocalized with *a*, and some other times with *sheva* (cf. § 40). This proves that there is no connection between the stress (tone) and the *ḳameṣ*, the *ḳameṣ* being dependent only on the syntactical position of the word in question.

B. THE USE OF THE TENSES (cf. p. 250, § 17)

§ 42. Perfect and imperfect interchangeably used.

Lev. 4.31: וְאֵת כָּל חֶלְבָּהּ יָסִיר כַּאֲשֶׁר הוּסַר חֵלֶב

Lev. 4.35: ואת כל חלבה יסיר כאשר יוסר חלב

Lev. 11.5: כִּי מַעֲלֵה גֵרָה הוּא וּפַרְסָה לֹא יַפְרִיס טָמֵא הוּא לָכֶם

Lev. 11.6: כי מעלת גרה הוא ופרסה לא הפריסה טמאה הוא לכם

Lev. 17.4: אֲשֶׁר יִשְׁחָט; cf. v. 3: וְאֶל פֶּתַח אֹהֶל מוֹעֵד לֹא הֱבִיאוֹ

Lev. 17.9: אֲשֶׁר יַעֲלֶה; cf. v. 8: וְאֶל פתח אהל מועד לא יְבִיאֶנּוּ

Deut. 2.25: אָחֵל תֵּת; cf. v. 24: הָחֵל רָשׁ

Deut. 2.31: הַחִלֹּתִי תת; cf. ib.: הָחֵל רָשׁ

Ps. 22.32: (לְעַם) נוֹלָד: "that shall be born"

Ps. 78.6: (בָּנִים) יִוָּלֵדוּ: "that should be born"

§ 43. Perfect continued by imperfect in the same verse.

Num. 9.15: כִּסָּה · · · · יִהְיֶה: "covered ... there was"; cf. v. 16: יִהְיֶה · · · · יְכַסֶּנּוּ

Judg. 5.6: חָדְלוּ · · · · יֵלְכוּ: "ceased ... walked"

1 Sam. 3.2: הֵחֵלּוּ · · · · לֹא יוּכַל: "had begun ... he could not"; cf. 4.15: ולא יָכוֹל

1 Sam. 3.7: טֶרֶם יָדַע · · · · וְטֶרֶם יִגָּלֶה: "did not yet know ... was ... yet revealed"

2 Sam. 1.22: לֹא נָשׂוֹג · · · · לֹא תָשׁוּב: "turned not ... returned not"

2 Sam. 22.5: אֲפָפוּנִי · · · · יְבַעֲתֻנִי: "compassed me ... assailed me"

2 Sam. 22.9: עָלָה · · · · תֹּאכֵל: "arose up ... did devour"

2 Ki. 20.14: אָמְרוּ · · · · יָבֹאוּ: "said ... came"; id. Isa. 39.3

Isa. 9.17: בָּעֲרָה · · · · תֹּאכֵל: "burneth ... devoureth"

Isa. 30.4: הָיוּ · · · · יַגִּיעוּ: "are ... are come"

Isa. 33.7: צָעֲקוּ · · · · יִבְכָּיוּן: "cry ... weep"

Isa. 44.13: נָטָה · · · · יְתָאֲרֵהוּ: "stretcheth out ... marketh it out"

Isa. 44.16: שָׂרַף · · · יֹאכֵל: "he burneth . . . he eateth"

Isa. 44.19: אָפִיתִי · · · אֶצְלֶה: "I have baked . . . I have roasted"

Isa. 51.6: נִמְלָחוּ · · · תִּבְלֶה: "shall vanish away . . . shall wax old"

Isa. 51.14: מִהַר · · · וְלֹא יָמוּת: "he . . . shall speedily . . . and he shall not go down"

Isa. 52.8: נָשְׂאוּ · · · יְרַנֵּנוּ: "they lift up . . . they sing"

Isa. 53.12: נָשָׂא · · · יַפְגִּיעַ: "he bore . . . made intercession"

Isa. 58.3: צַמְנוּ וְלֹא רָאִיתָ; cf. parallel: עִנִּינוּ · · · וְלֹא תֵדָע

Isa. 59.5: בִּקֵּעוּ · · · יֶאֱרֹגוּ: "they hatch . . . and weave"

Isa. 59.9: רָחַק · · · וְלֹא תַשִּׂיגֵנוּ: "is . . . far . . . doth not . . . overtake us"

Isa. 59.14: וְהֻסַּג · · · תַּעֲמֹד: "is turned away . . . standeth"

Isa. 61.10: הִלְבִּישַׁנִי · · · יְעָטָנִי: "he hath clothed me . . . he hath covered me"

Jer. 5.31: נִבְּאוּ · · · יִרְדּוּ: "prophesy . . . bear rule"

Jer. 12.3: יְדַעְתָּנִי תִּרְאֵנִי: "thou . . . knowest me, thou seest me"

Jer. 15.6: נָטַשְׁתְּ · · · תֵּלֵכִי: "thou hast cast . . . off . . . thou art gone"

Jer. 31.32: נָתַתִּי · · · אֶכְתֳּבֶנָּה: "I will put . . . will I write it"

Ezek. 18.6: (לֹא) טִמֵּא · · · (לֹא) יִקְרָב: "hath defiled . . . hath come near"

Ezek. 18.12: גָּזֵל · · · לֹא יָשִׁיב: "hath taken . . . hath not restored"

Am. 4.9: הִכֵּתִי · · · יֹאכַל: "I have smitten . . . hath . . . devoured"

Hab. 1.2: שִׁוַּעְתִּי וְלֹא תִשְׁמָע: "shall I cry, and thou wilt not hear"

Ps. 18.41: נָתַתָּה · · · אַצְמִיתֵם: "thou hast . . . made . . . I did cut off"

Ps. 69.33: רָאוּ · · · יִשְׂמָחוּ: "shall see it and be glad"

Ps. 73.6: עֲנָקַתְמוֹ · · · יַעֲטָף: "is as a chain . . . covereth"

Ps. 77.18: נָתְנוּ · · · יִתְהַלָּכוּ: "sent out . . . went abroad"

Ps. 81.6: לֹא יָדַעְתִּי אֶשְׁמָע: "I knew not did I hear"

Ps. 81.7: הֲסִירוֹתִי · · · תַּעֲבֹרְנָה: "I removed . . . were freed"

Ps. 82.5: לֹא יָדְעוּ וְלֹא יָבִינוּ: "they know not, neither do they understand"

Prov. 7.21: הִטַּתּוּ · · · תַּדִּיחֶנּוּ: "she causeth him to yield . . . she enticeth him away"

Job 4.3: יִסַּרְתָּ · · · תְּחַזֵּק: "thou hast instructed . . . thou hast strengthened"

§ 44.   Imperfect continued by perfect in the same verse.

Lev. 6.21: תְּבֻשַּׁל · · · בֻּשָּׁלָה: "it is sodden . . . it be sodden"

1 Sam. 27.11: עָשָׂה · · · · יְחַיֶּה "left ... alive ... did"

2 Sam. 2.28: וְלֹא יָסְפוּ · · · · וְלֹא יִרְדְּפוּ: "pursued ... no more, neither (fought they) any more"

2 Sam. 22.42: וְלֹא עָנָם · · · · יִשְׁעוּ: "they looked ... he answered them not"

Isa. 24.14: צָהֲלוּ · · · · יָרֹנּוּ: "they sing ... they shout"

Isa. 30.19: עָנֶךָ · · · · יָחְנְךָ: "he will ... be gracious ... he will answer"

Isa. 45.4: אֲכַנְּךָ וְלֹא יְדַעְתָּנִי: "I have surnamed thee, though thou hast not known me"; cf. also v. 5: אֲאַזֶּרְךָ וְלֹא יְדַעְתָּנִי

Jer. 2.15: נָתְנוּ (קוֹלָם) · · · · יִשְׁאֲגוּ: "have roared ... let ... resound"

Jer. 6.16: לֹא יָדָעוּ · · · · לֹא יֵבוֹשׁוּ: "they are not at all ashamed, neither know they"

Ezek. 9.10: נָתַתִּי · · · · אֶחְמֹל: "will I have pity, but I will bring"

Ezek. 18.9: שָׁמָר · · · · יְהַלֵּךְ: "hath walked ... hath kept"

Ezek. 31.13: הָיוּ · · · · יִשְׁכְּנוּ: "do dwell ... are"

Ezek. 33.15: הָלַךְ · · · · יְשַׁלֵּם: "give back ... walk"

Ezek. 33.27: יָמוּתוּ · · · · נְתַתִּיו · · · · יִפֹּלוּ: "shall fall ... will I give ... shall die"

Hos. 7.1: יָבוֹא פָּשַׁט: "enterth in ... maketh a raid"

Zech. 14.18: לֹא תַעֲלֶה וְלֹא בָאָה: "go not up, and come not"

Ps. 38.12: עָמָדוּ · · · · יַעֲמֹדוּ: "stand ... stand"

Ps. 44.12: זֵרִיתָנוּ · · · · תִּתְּנֵנוּ: "thou hast given us ... hast scattered us"

Prov. 1.22: חָמְדוּ · · · · תֶּאֱהָבוּ: "will ye love ... will delight"

Lam. 2.1: הִשְׁלִיךְ · · · · יָעִיב: "hath ... covered with a cloud ... hath cast down"

§ 45.   Imperfect with the meaning of a past tense.

Gen. 2.6: וְאֵד יַעֲלֶה: "but there *went up* a mist"

Gen. 2.19: וְכֹל אֲשֶׁר יִקְרָא לוֹ הָאָדָם: and whatever the man *called*

Gen. 18.19: לְמַעַן אֲשֶׁר יְצַוֶּה אֶת בָּנָיו: because he *commanded* his children

Gen. 19.4: טֶרֶם יִשְׁכָּבוּ: "before they *lay* down"

Gen. 24.45: טֶרֶם אֲכַלֶּה: "before I *had done*"; cf. v. 15: טֶרֶם כִּלָּה (perf.)

Gen. 27.33: בְּטֶרֶם תָּבוֹא: "before thou *camest*"

Gen. 30.42: לֹא יָשִׂים: "he *put* them not in"

Gen. 37.18: וּבְטֶרֶם יִקְרַב אֲלֵיהֶם: "and before he *came* near unto them"

Gen. 41.50: בְּטֶרֶם תָּבוֹא שְׁנַת הָרָעָב: "before the year of famine *came*"

Gen. 43.7: הֲיָדוֹעַ נֵדַע: "*could* we in any wise know"

Gen. 48.17: כִּי יָשִׁית אָבִיו יַד יְמִינוֹ: that his father *laid* his right hand

Ex. 1.12: וְכַאֲשֶׁר יְעַנּוּ אֹתוֹ כֵּן יִרְבֶּה וְכֵן יִפְרֹץ: "but the more they *afflicted* them, the more they *multiplied* and the more they *spread* abroad"

Ex. 1.19: בְּטֶרֶם תָּבוֹא אֲלֵהֶן הַמְיַלֶּדֶת: ere the midwife *came* unto them

Ex. 12.34: טֶרֶם יֶחְמָץ: "before it *was* leavened"

Ex. 15.1: אָז יָשִׁיר מֹשֶׁה: "then *sang* Moses"; the particle אָז does not influence the tense; cf. I Ki. 11.7: אָז יִבְנֶה with ib. 9.24: אָז בָּנָה

Ex. 17.11: כַּאֲשֶׁר יָרִים מֹשֶׁה יָדוֹ · · · וְכַאֲשֶׁר יָנִיחַ יָדוֹ: "when Moses *held* up his hand . . . and when he *let* down his hand"

Ex. 19.19: מֹשֶׁה יְדַבֵּר וְהָאֱלֹהִים יַעֲנֶנּוּ: "Moses *spoke* and God *answered* him"

Ex. 21.29: וְלֹא יִשְׁמְרֶנּוּ: "and he *hath* not *kept* it in"

Ex. 33.7: כָּל מְבַקֵּשׁ יהוה יֵצֵא: "every one that sought the Lord *went* out"

Ex. 33.8: יָקוּמוּ כָּל הָעָם: "all the people *rose* up"

Ex. 33.9: יֵרֵד עַמּוּד הֶעָנָן: "the pillar of cloud *descended*"

Ex. 33.11: לֹא יָמִישׁ מִתּוֹךְ הָאֹהֶל: "*departed* not out of the Tent"

Ex. 34.34: יָסִיר · · · אֵת אֲשֶׁר יְצֻוֶּה: "he *took* off . . . which he *was* commanded"

Lev. 5.24: מִכֹּל אֲשֶׁר יִשָּׁבַע עָלָיו: "about which he *hath sworn* falsely"

Lev. 6.3: אֲשֶׁר תֹּאכַל הָאֵשׁ: "whereto the fire *hath consumed*"

Num. 9.16: כֵּן יִהְיֶה תָמִיד הֶעָנָן יְכַסֶּנּוּ: "so it *was* always the cloud *covered it*"

Num. 9.17: וְאַחֲרֵי כֵן יִסְעוּ · · · יִשְׁכָּן שָׁם · · · שָׁם יַחֲנוּ: "then after that . . . *journeyed* . . . where *abode* . . . there... *encamped*"

Num. 9.18: יִסְעוּ · · · יַחֲנוּ · · · יִשְׁכֹּן · · · יַחֲנוּ: "*journeyed* . . . *encamped* . . . *abode* . . . *encamped*"

Num. 9.19: וְלֹא יִסָּעוּ: "and *journeyed* not"

Num. 9.20: יִהְיֶה · · · יַחֲנוּ · · · יִסָּעוּ: "*was* . . . *encamped* . . . *journeyed*"

Num. 9.21: וְיֵשׁ אֲשֶׁר יִהְיֶה: "and sometimes . . . *was*"

Num. 9.22: יַחֲנוּ · · · וְלֹא יִסָּעוּ · · · יִסָּעוּ: "*encamped*, and *journeyed* not . . . they *journeyed*"

Num. 11.5: אֲשֶׁר נֹאכַל בְּמִצְרַיִם: "which we *were* wont to eat in Egypt"

Num. 11.9: יֵרֵד הַמָּן עָלָיו: "the manna *fell* upon it"

Num. 11.33: טֶרֶם יִכָּרֵת: "ere it *was chewed*"

Num. 23.7: מִן אֲרָם יַנְחֵנִי בָלָק: from Aram Balak *brought me*

Num. 35.26: אֲשֶׁר יָנוּס שָׁמָּה: whither he *fled*

Duet. 2.11: וְהַמּאָבִים יִקְרְאוּ לָהֶם: but the Moabites *called* them

Deut. 2.12: וּבְנֵי עֵשָׂו יִירָשׁוּם: "but the children of Esau *succeeded* them"

Deut. 4.41: אָז יַבְדִּיל מֹשֶׁה: "then Moses *separated*"

Deut. 21.4: אֲשֶׁר לֹא יֵעָבֵד בּוֹ וְלֹא יִזָּרֵעַ: which *has* neither *been plowed* nor *sown*

Deut. 23.16: אֲשֶׁר יִנָּצֵל אֵלֶיךָ: that *has escaped* unto thee

Deut. 31.21: בְּטֶרֶם אֲבִיאֶנּוּ "before I *have brought* them"

§ 46. Perfect with the meaning of a future tense.

Gen. 9.13: אֶת קַשְׁתִּי נָתַתִּי בֶּעָנָן: I *shall set* My bow in the cloud

Gen. 23.11: הַשָּׂדֶה נָתַתִּי לָךְ: the field I *will give* thee

Ex. 10.3: עַד מָתַי מֵאַנְתָּ: "how long *wilt* thou refuse"

Ex. 16.28: עַד אָנָה מֵאַנְתֶּם: how long *will* you refuse

Lev. 25.28: וְאִם לֹא מָצְאָה יָדוֹ: but if he *will* not *have* sufficient means

Lev. 25.45: אֲשֶׁר הוֹלִידוּ בְּאַרְצְכֶם: which they *will beget* in your land

Lev. 25.49: אוֹ הִשִּׂיגָה יָדוֹ: or *should* he wax rich

Lev. 26.44: לֹא מְאַסְתִּים וְלֹא גְעַלְתִּים: "I *will* not reject them, neither *will* I abhor them"

Num. 8.16: לָקַחְתִּי אֹתָם לִי: I *will take* them unto Me; cf. v. 15: יָבֹאוּ

Deut. 3.2: כִּי בְיָדְךָ נָתַתִּי אֹתוֹ: for I *will deliver* him into thy hand.

Conclusions

§ 47. Both perfect and imperfect are interchangeably used to indicate present, past or future (cf. § 42). Hence, there is no logical justification whatsoever for retaining the established, but meaningless terms of perfect and imperfect. Moreover, they are in reality a handicap in our endeavor to understand the meaning and the functions of the tenses thus designated. Unwittingly we are prejudiced, and connect with perfect and imperfect the implication of certain well-defined *tempora*. The grammars have then to invent new rules and list exceptions to these rules in order to account for the vast number of occurrences diverging from our notion of "perfect" and "imperfect" tenses.

§ 48. We, therefore, suggest a neutral, timeless terminology which is based solely on morphological characteristics and which does not explicitly indicate any definite time at all: *suffix tense* (instead of perfect), and *prefix tense* (for imperfect).

§ 49.   Each of these tenses (the suffix tense and the prefix tense) may indicate any and every time. Thus, they do not complement one another in order to form a complete verbal conjugation expressing past and future, respectively, but they run parallel to one another, representing two possibilities of expressing one and the same time. The difference that existed between the suffix tense and the prefix tense was not of temporal, but rather of a dialectic character; cf. p. 250, § 17. The combined use of both tenses, which runs through our Biblical literature, is further evidence for our assertion that the language of our Bible is of a mixed type (cf. p. 501 f.).

§ 50.   The term *waw consecutivum*, which the grammar had to invent in order to explain the use of an imperfect with the meaning of a perfect, and *vice versa*, thus becomes obsolete. Neither the vocalization (cf. § 39), nor the function (cf. § 47) justify the differentiation of the preposition ו into *waw conjunctivum* and *consecutivum*.

§ 51.   We shall, therefore, now assert that e.g., יִשְׁמֹר and שָׁמַר are two entirely different and independent grammatical formations of the triliteral root שמר, and should not be listed in our dictionaries under the same catchword as imperfect and perfect, respectively. With verbs of sound triliteral root the difference in the treatment as proposed here may seem to be more of a purely academic nature, and of no consequence from the practical point of view. For it may be deemed to matter little, whether we follow the current procedure, or change it according to our suggestion and list שמר twice: once with the suffix tense, and once with the prefix tense. But the import of our suggestion becomes at once clear, when we turn to the verbs of weak roots.

§ 52.   To all outward appearance, the forms יִפֹּל, יִצֹּק and יִסֹּב belong to one and the same group of verbal formations; the same is true of e.g. יִגַּח and יִקַּח. But in view of the fact that our Bible offers the so-called perfect forms of these verbs as נָפַל, יָצַק and סָבַב, or נָגַח and לָקַח respectively, and with the hitherto unchallenged axiom in mind that perfect and imperfect by necessity belong together as the two tenses of one verb, our dictionaries list יִפֹּל under the rubric נפל, but יִצֹק under יָצַק, and יִסֹב under סָבַב; similarly: יִגַּח under נֶגַח, but יִקַּח under לָקַח. And our grammars had to invent far-fetched theories of *verba primae nun* (cf. § 54)—a term unknown even in Arabic grammar—which include, strangely enough, the verb לקח (cf. B-L § 52 p) as well as of *verba primae yod* and *mediae geminatae* (cf. § 58), so as to explain these so-called imperfect-forms as derived from what supposedly are their perfect-forms. By accepting our suggestion, all this mental effort appears futile and unnecessary. For now we have: s.v. נפל: the suffix tense: נָפַלְתִּי; s.v. יצק: the suffix tense: וְיָצַקְתָּ; s.v. לקח: the suffix tense: לָקַחְתִּי; all these are sound triliteral verbs. But s.v. פל we list the prefix tense: אֶפֹּל; s.v. צק: the prefix tense: יִצֹּק; s.v. קח: the prefix tense: אֶקַּח; these are weak verbs of biliteral root.

§ 53.   We thus arrive at a division of the verbs into triliteral and biliteral roots, which of course do not correspond to the suffix tense and prefix tense, respectively, as might be inferred by our examples נָפַל - יִפֹּל; יָצַק – יִצֹק; יִקַּח – לָקַח in § 52, as will be seen below § 58b. Hitherto, the verbs of biliteral roots were considered triconsonantal weak verbs. Their triliterality was achieved by the assumption of the original existence of a third radical, which however had disappeared in the course of the conjugation; for this reason these roots were considered to be weak. Cf. B-L § 39e: "Schwache Verba, d.h. Verba, bei denen irgendein Stammkonsonant in gewissen Formen entweder einem anderen Laute assimiliert oder auch elidiert wird." But we, on the other hand, cannot help seeing in this procedure of the grammarians a scholastic schematization, which is an anachronism in our age. Moreover, the current theories are based on an arbitrary selection of the linguistic material offered in the Bible; those instances which disprove them, are either entirely overlooked, or else relegated to footnotes with the headings: "exceptions," or "but." In discussing first the so-called *verba primae nun*, we shall demonstrate how untenable these theories are in the light of the material available in the Bible.

§ 54.   The so-called *verba primae nun* serve as common denominator for verbs, which according to their formations and conjugations belong to altogether different groups, but are listed in our grammars and dictionaries under one and the same catchword. For the sake of practical expediency, we follow as far as possible the current terminology in our presentation of the material.

a)   Infinitive-forms.

נגע: Josh. 9.19:   לִנְגֹּעַ; but 2 Sam. 14.10: לָגַעַת
נטע: Isa. 51.16:   לִנְטֹעַ; but Eccl. 3.2:   לָטַעַת
נשא: Gen. 4.13:   מִנְּשֹׂא; but Gen. 36.7:   לָשֵׂאת
נתן: Num. 20.21:   נְתֹן; but Deut. 2.25:   תֵּת

b)   Imperfect-forms.

נגש: Isa. 58.3:   תִּנְגֹּשׂוּ; but Deut. 15.3:   תִּגֹּשׂ
נדף: Ps. 68.3:   תִּנְדֹּף; but Ps. 1.4:   תִּדְּפֶנּוּ
נחת: Ps. 38.3:   וַתִּנְחַת; but Prov. 17.10:   תֵּחַת
נטר: Jer. 3.5:   הֲיִנְטוֹר; but Ps. 103.9:   יִטּוֹר
נצר: Ps. 140.2:   תִּנְצְרֵנִי; but Ps. 32.7:   תִּצְּרֵנִי

c)   The close interconnection between imperfect and imperative can be seen from the following examples, all of which are identified as *primae nun* according to the current theories.

נגש: impf.: Ex. 24.14:   יִגַּשׁ;   imp.: 2 Sam. 1.15: גַּשׁ
נסע: impf.: Ex. 40.36:   יִסְעוּ;   imp.: Deut. 2.24: סְעוּ
נפח: impf.: Gen. 2.7:   וַיִּפַּח;   imp.: Ezek. 37.9: וּפְחִי
נשא: impf.: Gen. 18.24:   תִּשָּׂא;   imp.: Gen. 13.14: שָׂא
נגע: impf.: Lev. 5.2:   תִּגַּע;   imp.: Ps. 144.5: גַּע

d)   Consequently, the imperfect- and imperative-forms listed now reflect different roots, against the current theories.

נפל: impf.: Num. 6.12:   יִפְּלוּ;   imp.: Hos. 10.8:   נִפְלוּ
נצר: impf.: Isa. 26.3:   תִּצֹּר;   imp.: Ps. 34.14:   נְצֹר
נקם: impf.: Lev. 19.18:   תִּקֹּם;   imp.: Num. 31.2:   נְקֹם

The foregoing material leads to the following conclusion: The verbs which actually are *primae nun* (i.e., whose first radical is *nun*) are sound triliteral verbs; there is no justification in separating them from all the other triliteral verbs, and treat them in a special chapter. What the grammars list as characteristics of the *verba primae nun* (the elision of the *nun*), is nothing else but the result of their erroneous identification of biliteral verbs with similar sounding triliteral verbs. It is obvious that e.g.

לָטַעַת is a formation like לָדַעַת, but utterly different from לִנְטֹעַ, and can, therefore, not be considered as derived from the root נטע, just as there is no thought of deriving לָדַעַת from a root נדע.

§ 55. The verbs *tertiae* א *and* ה form one group only, the א and ה being merely vowel-letters; cf. p. 246, § 12 and the cross references indicated there in note 11. The uncertainty as to which vowel-letter should be applied, is the underlying cause for the following variants:

דכא:	Ps. 89.11:	דִּכְּאתָ; but Ps. 51.10:	דִּכִּיתָ
כלא:	Ps. 119.101:	כָּלִאתִי; but Ps. 39.11:	כָּלִיתִי
	Hag. 1.10:	כָּלְאוּ; but 1 Sam. 6.10:	כָּלוּ
מלא:	Ezek. 8.17:	מָלְאוּ; but Ezek. 28.16:	מָלוּ
נבא:	Jer. 28.6:	נִבֵּאתָ; but Jer. 26.9:	נִבֵּיתָ
פלא:	Deut. 28.59:	וְהִפְלָא; but Ex. 9.4:	וְהִפְלָה
קרה and קרא:	Gen. 44.38:	וּקְרָאָהוּ; but Gen. 44.29:	וְקָרָהוּ
	Ex. 5.3:	נִקְרָא; but Ex. 3.18:	נִקְרָה
רפא:	Hos. 14.5:	אֶרְפָּא; but Jer. 3.22:	אֶרְפָּה
	Num. 12.13:	רְפָא; but Ps. 60.4:	רְפָה
	Jer. 14.19:	מַרְפֵּא; but Jer. 8.15:	מַרְפֵּה

For outright combination of verbal forms of *tertiae* ה and א, cf.

a) 2 Sam. 1.6: נָקְרֹא נִקְרֵיתִי   Ezek. 8.3: הַקִּנְאָה הַמַּקְנֶה
Jer. 23.39: וְנָשִׁיתִי אֶתְכֶם נָשֹׁא

b) Judg. 8.1: קְרֹאות; cf. 1 Sam. 3.6: קְרָא
Lev. 12.6: וּבִמְלֹאת
Prov. 8.13: שְׂנֹאת; cf. Gen. 37.5: שְׂנֹא
2 Sam. 21.2: בְּקַנֹּאתוֹ; cf. Num. 25.11: בְּקַנְאוֹ
Zech. 13.4: בְּהִנָּבְאֹתוֹ; cf. ib. verse 3: בְּהִנָּבְאוֹ

§ 56. Similarly, verbs of the *various groups of weak roots* are indiscriminately used, if they have the two sound root-consonants in common. All references to verbal roots in the following examples are according to the theories current in Hebrew grammar with regard to the derivations of the respective verbal forms from supposedly triliteral roots (cf. § 53):

a) Ex. 23.22: וְצַרְתִּי אֶת צֹרְרֶיךָ: "then I will be an enemy unto thine enemies"; play on the roots צור and צרר.

Jud. 2.14:   בְּיַד שֹׁסִים וַיָּשֹׁסּוּ: "into the hands of spoilers that spoiled them"; play on the roots שסה and שסס.

Jer. 48.9:   כִּי נָצֹא תֵּצֵא: for away she must fly; play on the roots נצא and יצא.

Nah. 2.2:   נָצוֹר מְצוּרָה: laying siege with siege works; play on the roots נצר and צור.

Jer. 42.10:   שׁוֹב תֵּשְׁבוּ: absolute infinitive with finite verb; play on the roots שוב and ישב.

b) 2 Sam. 19.6: הוֹבַשְׁתָּ: "thou hast shamed"; ab בוש = יבש

Gen. 2.25:   יִתְבֹּשָׁשׁוּ: "and were not ashamed"; ab בוש = בשש

Judg. 3.25:   בּוֹשׁ: (they tarried) exceedingly; ab בוש = בשש

Ps. 23.6:   וְשַׁבְתִּי: "and I shall dwell"; ab שוב = ישב

Jer. 31.17:   מִתְנוֹדֵד: "bemoaning himself"; ab נוד = נדד; cf. Isa. 51.19: מִי יָנוּד לָךְ; but cf. Ps. 64.9: יִתְנוֹדְדוּ: "they shake the head," ab נדד.

Nah. 2.5:   יְרוֹצֵצוּ: "they run"; ab רוץ = רצץ; but cf. Judg. 10.8: וַיְרֹצְצוּ: "and they crushed," ab רצץ

2 Sam. 5.23:   הָסֵב: "make a circuit"; ab סוב = סבב.

Jer. 9.9:   נָדְדוּ הָלָכוּ; cf. ib. 50.3: נָדוּ הָלָכוּ; ab נדד and נוד, respectively.

Jer. 4.31:   כְּחוֹלָה: "of a woman in travail"; ab חיל = חלה; but cf. Ezek. 34.4: הַחוֹלָה: "the weak"; ab חלה.

Ps. 40.14:   רְצֵה: hasten; ab רוץ = רצה; but cf. Ps. 119.108: רְצֵה ab רצה.

I Sam. 14.24:   וַיֹּאֶל: "he adjured"; ab אלה = יאל; but cf. ib. 17.39: וַיֹּאֶל: "and he essayed"; ab יאל.

Jer. 7.21:   סְפוּ: "add"; ab ספה = יסף.

Ex. 5.7:   תֹאסִפוּן: "ye shall no more (give)": ab אסף = יסף.

I Sam. 18.29:   וַיֹּאסֶף: "he was more (afraid)": ab אסף = יסף.

2 Sam. 6.1:   וַיֹּסֶף: "gathered": ab יסף = אסף; but cf. I Sam. 19.21: וַיֹּסֶף: "and again (he sent)": ab יסף.

Ps. 104.29:   תֹּסֵף: "thou withdrawest"; ab יסף = אסף; but cf. Deut. 13.1: תֹסֵף: "thou shalt (not) add"; ab יסף.

Ex. 23.21:   תַּמֵּר: "be not rebellious": ab מרה = נמר.

I Sam. 13.11:   נָפַץ; Gen. 9.19: נָפְצָה: ab נפץ; but cf. Gen. 11.4: נָפוּץ and I Sam. 13.8: וַיָּפֶץ: ab פוץ.

Gen. 17.11:   וּנְמַלְתֶּם ab נמל; but cf. ib. 17.23: וַיָּמָל: ab מול.

2 Sam. 18.18: וַיַּצֶּב: ab נצב; but cf. ib. 21.5: מֵהִתְיַצֵּב: ab יצב

Gen. 45.11: תִּוָּרֵשׁ; 1 Sam. 2.6: מוֹרִישׁ: ab ירש = רוש

§ 57. a) While presenting the material in the preceding paragraphs, we had to employ the terminology exhibited in the current grammars, so as to be understood by the student of Hebrew philology unfamiliar with our new terminology. But in doing so we have shown the weakness of the current theory concerning the verbal system. Let us take up for discussion the first five examples in § 56. It is obvious that each one of these phrases represents a play on words; וְצַרְתִּי · · · צֹרְרֶיךָ not only look alike in script, but also sound alike in speech. But the grammar assigns one word to the root צור, and the other to צרר, i.e., two utterly different verbal roots; the same is true of the remaining four examples. But just as the preceding וְאָיַבְתִּי · · · אֹיְבֶיךָ, so does even וְצַרְתִּי · · · צֹרְרֶיךָ represent—to use the established terminology—perfect and participle of one and the same verb; similarly שָׂסִים וַיָּשֹׁסּוּ is participle and imperfect of the identical verb. Grammar being logical explanation of the language by means of grouping and classifying the facts, if we find certain grammatical rules in contradiction with logic and common sense, then there is something wrong with these grammatical rules.

b) Let us now take up the discussion of the second group of examples listed in § 56. Grammatically they are derived from one root, but according to their meaning in their context, two different roots must be postulated. Thus the accepted grammatical rules bid us derive הוֹבַשְׁתָּ from יבש; in Ps. 74.15: "thou driest up ever-flowing rivers" yields good sense. But in 2 Sam. 19.6 this meaning does not fit the context, and a form of the root בוש is expected here: "thou hast shamed this day the faces of all thy servants." We therefore say הוֹבַשְׁתָּ is ab יבש = בוש. We arrive at the general conclusion that the verbs, which hitherto were termed weak verbs belonging to different groups (cf. § 53), are in reality biconsonantal verbs. Thus, צור and צרר are both of the root צר; שסה and שסס are really שס; יבש and בוש should be בש. In their conjugations they follow different patterns.

§ 58. a) In the light of our findings in the preceding paragraphs, and with the results of our previous researches in mind, we now wish to offer our own new interpretation of those verbal formations, which hitherto have been explained as representing the various groups of weak roots (cf. § 53). At the very outset we shall bear in mind that the presence or absence of a vowel-letter is quite irrelevant, (cf. § 25); also, that the insertion or omission of a *dagesh* cannot be considered significant (cf. p. 422, §§ 11-36; and p. 455 under X; p. 559, § 25b) being due to Masoretic schematization; and finally, that ⟨ָ⟩ and ⟨ַ⟩ were originally used indiscriminately to indicate one and the same vowel (cf. p. 434, §§ 49-62); on the sign ⟨ֶ⟩ as merely a variation of ⟨ַ⟩, cf. p. 445, §§ 75 ff.

In the interest of unbiased objectivity towards the current theory, we adopt at first the terminology and examples of Bauer-Leander's Hebrew grammar: 1) verbs *primae nun*: נָקַם, נָשַׁק, נָתַן; B-L include in this group also לָקַח (cf. B-L § 52p: "Durch Angleichung an נָתַן assimilierte sich das *l* von לָקַח 'nehmen' im Aorist Qal an den 2. Stammkonsonanten"); 2) verbs *primae ו* and *י*: יָנַק, יָלַד, יָדַע; 3) verbs *mediae י* and *ו*: לִין, בּוֹשׁ, קוּם; 4) verbs *mediae geminatae*: קָלַל, סָבַב.

b)   And now we proceed according to our own terminology (cf. § 48):

α)   The *suffix-tense*: The verbs belonging to group 1 and 2 are of sound triconsonantal root; the verbs of group 3 and 4 are biconsonantal: קַמְתִּי (ab קם), לַנְתִּי (ab לן) are forms in *a*; בּוֹשְׁתִּי (ab בשׁ) is a form in *o* (cf. triconsonantal יָכֹלְתִּי); סַבּוֹתִי (ab סב) and קַלּוֹתִי (ab קל) have *o* in the second syllable. It is worth while noting here that the real *mediae geminatae*, i.e., verbs of triconsonantal root with the second and third radical identical, are sound verbs; cf. ab זָמַם the suffix-tense: זַמַּמְתִּי. The form זַמֹּתִי is derived from the root זם.

β)   The *prefix-tense*: All the verbs listed in the four groups above are of biconsonantal root. They can be grouped as follows, according to their characteristic vowel:

א)   Prefix-tense in *a*: אִינַק (ab נק), אֵדַע (ab דע), אֵקַל (ab קל), אֶקַּח (ab קח), אֶשַּׁק (ab שק)

ב)   Prefix-tense in *i*: אֵלֵד (ab לד), אֶתֵּן (ab תן), אָלִין (ab לן)

ג)   Prefix-tense in *o*: אָסֹב (ab סב), אָקֹם (ab קם), אָאוֹר (ab אר)—אָקוּם (ab קם) (Cf. MH § 160).

c)   Of course, objections might be voiced against this treatment of verbs which supposedly belong to different groups of weak roots, by referring us to their so-called derived stems. For, according to the current Hebrew grammar, the weak root-letter may appear in one form or another in the derived stems; thus e.g. the י of the *primae yod* turns into ו in the *hiph'il*, the ו of the *mediae waw* into י in the *pi'el*. But here, the grammar confuses the two functions of the letters ו and י: as consonants and as vowel-letters. The י in the *primae yod* is a consonant, but the ו in the *hiph'il* a vowel-letter; the ו in the *mediae waw* is a vowel-letter, but the י in the *pi'el* a consonant. As consonants, ו and י are as sound as any other consonant of the Hebrew alphabet. But as vowel-letters, their presence or even absence is irrelevant for the establishment of the root; cf. § 25. Finally, the so-called derived stems are not verbal stems, but independent verbal conjugations; cf. p. 14 (end of paragraph 7).

§ 59. How shall we explain the differing vocalization (mainly by *a*, or *o*) of the prefix-tense? First I wish to stress that forms with the characteristic vowel *a* are quite frequent. Here is a tentative list of such verbs, which includes only sound verbs where the middle consonant (which matters) is sound. *Mediae gutturalis* are therefore disregarded here.

אבל:	Jer. 4.28:	תֶּאֱבָל	חרף:	Isa. 18.6:	תֶּחֱרָף
אטר:	Ps. 69.16:	תֶּאְטַר	חרץ:	Ex. 11.7:	יֶחֱרַץ
אנף:	Ps. 2.12:	יֶאֱנַף	חרש:	Mic. 7.16:	תֶּחֱרַשְׁנָה
אשם:	Hos. 14.1:	תֶּאְשַׁם	חשך:	Ex. 10.14:	וַתֶּחְשַׁךְ
גבר:	1 Sam. 2.9:	יִגְבַּר	כבד:	Ex. 5.9:	תִּכְבַּד
גדל:	1 Sam. 3.19:	וַיִּגְדַּל	לבש:	Lev. 6.3:	יִלְבַּשׁ
גזר:	Job 22.28:	וְתִגְזָר	למד:	Deut. 14.23:	תִּלְמַד
דבק:	Deut. 13.18:	יִדְבַּק	ערב:	Ps. 104.34:	יֶעֱרַב
דלק:	Ps. 10.2:	יִדְלַק	עשן:	Ps. 104.32:	וְיֶעֱשָׁנוּ
זקן:	2 Chron. 24.15:	וַיִּזְקַן	צדק:	Ezek. 16.52:	תִּצְדַּקְנָה
חדל:	Deut. 15.1:	יֶחְדַּל	קדש:	Deut. 22.9:	תִּקְדָּשׁ
חזק:	2 Sam. 10.11:	תֶּחֱזַק	קטן:	2 Sam. 7.19:	וַתִּקְטַן
חכם:	Prov. 9.9:	וְיֶחְכַּם	קרב:	Lev. 22.3:	יִקְרַב
חלש:	Job 14.10:	וְיֶחֱלָשׁ	רבץ:	Num. 22.27:	וַתִּרְבַּץ
חנן:	Am. 5.15:	יֶחֱנַן	רגז:	1 Sam. 14.15:	וַתִּרְגַּז
חנף:	Jer. 3.1:	תֶּחֱנַף	רטב:	Job 24.8:	יִרְטָבוּ
חרב:	Isa. 19.5:	יֶחֱרָב	רכב:	Hos. 14.4:	נִרְכָּב
חרד:	Ex. 19.16:	וַיֶּחֱרַד	רקב:	Isa. 40.20:	יִרְקָב

שכב: Gen. 28.11: וַיִּשְׁכַּב   שכל: Gen. 27.45: אֶשְׁכַּל

שכח: Hos. 4.6: אֶשְׁכַּח   שפל: Isa. 2.9: וַיִּשְׁפַּל

The key to the explanation I find in cases like the following, where the identical verb appears in formations with *a* and *o*, and even also with *i*.

Mal. 2.10: נִבְגַּד — ib. 2.15: יִבְגֹּד

Prov. 16.10: יִמְעַל — Lev. 5.15: תִּמְעֹל

Lev. 26.34: תִּשְׁבַּת — ib. v. 35: תִּשְׁבֹּת

Ezek. 13.23: תִקְסַמְנָה — Mic. 3.11: יִקְסֹמוּ

Gen. 28.20: וַיִּדַּר — 1 Sam. 1.11: וַתִּדֹּר

Num. 21.4: וַתִּקְצַר — Prov. 10.27: תִּקְצֹרְנָה

Ezek. 1.9: יְסַבּוּ — Zech. 14.10: יְסֹוב

2 Ki. 4.41: צַק — Num. 5.15: יְצֹק

2 Sam. 1.15: גַּשׁ — Gen. 19.9: גֶּשׁ — Josh. 3.9: גֹּשׁוּ

I explain these different formations used as dialectic differences, and the occurrence of both (or even all three) formations with the identical verb as the result of the Dialekt-Mischung: the confluence of Judaean and Israelitish Hebrew in order to form Biblical Hebrew. Cf. MH §§ 189 and 210; cf. also here p. 243, note 2.

C. The Noun and its Construct State

A. Prefatory Remarks

§ 60. Considerations of practical expediency make it advisable to employ the terminology of Western philology. But at the same time we urge the discriminating student of Hebrew philology to bear in mind that these terms, which were coined according to the pattern of Latin and subsequently taken over by Western philology in general, are not at all suited for a Semitic language like Hebrew. So it is misleading to speak of "particles" in Hebrew. For it is characteristic of particles that though they themselves are indeclinable, they do influence the case of the following noun or pronoun. In Hebrew, on the other hand, these words are declinable themselves, but have no influence whatsoever on the structure of the following word. Furthermore, we fail to see any valid reason why the identical suffixes, when attached to a noun are translated as possessive pronouns, but when joined to a so-called particle are rendered as personal pronoun in the dative or accusative. This, of course, is merely a result of the inadequacy of a Western language to retain all the implications of the Hebrew original in a translation. It is, therefore, well to remind ourselves of this limitation and to realize that these so-called "particles" in Hebrew are in fact nouns, and ought to be translated as such; e.g. אֶל = direction, אֵלַי = my direction; אֶת = accompaniment, אִתִּי = my accompaniment; תַּחַת = basis, תַּחְתַּי = my basis; עַד = destination, עָדַי = my destination; עַל = direction or location, עָלַי = my direction or location; אֵצֶל = proximity; etc.

§ 61.   The construct state occupies a key-position in our endeavor to understand the Hebrew noun. Before we attempt a solution of these problems, it is well to review what the current Hebrew grammars have to say in this connection. In Bauer-Leander we read as follows: "Das letzte Wort einer syntaktisch zusammengehörigen Wortgruppe erhielt im Hebräischen, wie im Semitischen überhaupt, einen stärkeren Druck als die vorhergehenden. Infolgedessen zeigen viele Wörter in dieser Stellung einen anderen Typus als sonst" (B-L § 13a). "Beim Nomen bewirkt die oben besprochene Eigenart des Satzakzentes die Entstehung verschiedener Formen für verschiedene *Status*. Wenn nämlich ein Nomen besonders nahe an das Folgende angeschlossen wird, wie namentlich das Regens an sein Genetiv-attribut, erhält es einen schwächeren Druck als sonst und gerät infolgedessen oft unter den Einfluss anderer Gesetze . . . Die unabhängige Stellung nennt man *Status absolutus*, die vom Folgenden abhängige *Status constructus*" (ib. § 13k). "Ein Nomen tritt in den Status constructus, wenn es in nahe syntaktische Verbindung gestellt wird mit einem folgenden: 1) *Substantiv*, das den Charakter eines Genetivattributs hat: חֲמַת אָחִיךָ 'der Zorn deines Bruders' Gen. 27.44; 2) *Präpositionsausdruck*: חֹסֵי בוֹ 'die bei ihm Zuflucht Suchenden' Nah. 1.7; אַחַד מִמֶּנּוּ 'einer von uns' Gen. 3.22; 3) *ganzen Satz*: מְקוֹם אֲשֶׁר יוֹסֵף אָסוּר שָׁם 'der Ort, wo J. Gefangener war' Gen. 40.3; קִרְיַת חָנָה דָוִד 'die Stadt, wo D. Lager schlug' Jes. 29.1" (ib. § 64g). And this is all!

The Construct State

§ 62.   Any word which under given circumstances can be treated as a substantive (i.e. by being determined by the article or personal suffixes), is to be regarded as a noun. This term thus includes: a) substantives, adjectives and numerals; b) particles and prepositions (see §§ 85 and 86).

§ 63.   According to the construction of their context, adjectives and numerals may be found in substantival position (cf. Lev. 27.32: הָעֲשִׂירִי), and—*vice versa*—substantives in adjectival position (cf. 2 Ki. 25.18: כֹּהֵן הָרֹאשׁ not *priest of the head* but *headpriest*; see § 67).

§ 64.   A construct state consists of two nouns (cf. § 62), which syntactically form a unity. The first noun we term مضاف, the second *nomen regens*.

§ 65.   The connotation of the construct state depends on the *regens*. As a rule, the *regens* is a substantive (cf. also § 68) and can (cf. § 63) have substantival or adjectival meaning.

§ 66.   If the *regens* has substantival meaning, then the construct state denotes: 1) *genetivus objectivus*: Gen. 20.11: יִרְאַת אֱלֹהִים; 2) *genetivus subjectivus*: Gen. 10.10: רֵאשִׁית מַמְלַכְתּוֹ; 3) *genetivus possessivus*: Jer. 1.15: שַׁעֲרֵי יְרוּשָׁלַם; 4) *ablativus instrumenti* (when the مضاف is an adjective): 1 Sam. 16.7: גְּבֹהַּ קוֹמָתוֹ.

§ 67.   But if the *regens* has adjectival meaning, then the construct state denotes an attribute: Jer. 1.18: וּלְעַמּוּד בַּרְזֶל וּלְחֹמוֹת נְחֹשֶׁת; 2 Sam. 7.2: בְּבֵית אֲרָזִים.

§ 68.   There are, however, quite a number of instances in which the *regens* is an adjective, pronoun or numeral. They have adjectival meaning and thus belong to the same category as discussed in § 67, but are used here in substantival position. The fact that in each of these cases the respective substantive has no article, is evidence that it is considered a مضاف to the following *regens*.

1)			
שֶׁמֶן הַטּוֹב:	2 Ki. 20.13	הָרִים הַגְּבֹהִים:	Ps. 104.18
דֶּרֶךְ הַטּוֹב:	Jer. 6.16	גְּבָעוֹת הַגִּבְהוֹת:	Jer. 17.2
וְקָנֶה הַטּוֹב:	Jer. 6.20	שַׁעַר הַפְּנִימִית:	Ezek. 8.3
בְּדֶרֶךְ הַטּוֹבָה וְהַיְשָׁרָה:	1 Sam. 12.23	שַׁעַר הַיְשָׁנָה:	Neh. 3.6
פָּרֹת הַטֹּבֹת:	Gen. 41.26	שַׁעַר הָעֶלְיוֹן:	2 Chron. 23.20
בּוֹר הַגָּדוֹל:	1 Sam. 19.22	חָצֵר הָאַחֶרֶת:	1 Ki. 7.8
חָלָל הַגָּדוֹל:	Ezek. 21.19	חָצֵר הַחִצוֹנָה:	Ezek. 40.31
הַר הַגָּדוֹל:	Zech. 4.7	נֶפֶשׁ הַחַיָּה:	Gen. 9.10
אָבֵל הַגְּדוֹלָה:	1 Sam. 6.18	רוּחַ הָרָעָה:	1 Sam. 16.23
וְחָצֵר הַגְּדוֹלָה:	1 Ki. 7.12	אֶבֶן הַזֹּחֶלֶת:	1 Ki. 1.19

סֵפֶר הַגָּלוּי :Jer. 32.14   וְאִישׁ הַיִּשְׂרְאֵלִי :Lev. 24.10

מִפְּלִשְׁתִּים הָעֲרֵלִים :Judg. 14.3

a)   It is sometimes hard to tell, whether a given noun is a substantive with adjectival meaning, or an adjective in substantival position; cf.

Deut. 21.8:   דָּם נָקִי   Deut. 19.10:   דַּם נָקִי

Deut. 21.9:   הַדָּם הַנָּקִי   Deut. 19.13:   דַּם הַנָּקִי

both combined in one and the same verse: 2 Ki. 24.4: דַּם הַנָּקִי · · · דָּם נָקִי

Ezek. 9.2:   וְאִישׁ · · · לָבֻשׁ בַּדִּים

Ezek. 9.3:   הָאִישׁ הַלָּבֻשׁ הַבַּדִּים

Ezek. 9.10:   הָאִישׁ לְבֻשׁ הַבַּדִּים

see also under 3a.

2)   דְּבַשׁ הַזֶּה :1 Sam. 14.29   עָרִים הָאֵלֶּה :Josh. 17.9

לֶחֶם הַזֶּה :1 Sam. 17.17   כִּבְשֹׂת הָאֵלֶּה :Gen. 21.28

יוֹם הַהוּא :Mic. 7.11

The different ways in treating a pronoun are reflected in

שְׁלֹשׁ אֵלֶּה :Ex. 21.11 compared with: הַשָּׁלֹשׁ הָאֵלֶּה :Deut. 19.9

3)   יוֹם הַשְּׁלִישִׁי :Lev. 19.6   מָבוֹא הַשְּׁלִישִׁי :Jer. 38.14

יוֹם הַשִּׁשִּׁי :Gen. 1.31   חֹדֶשׁ הַתְּשִׁיעִי :Ezra 10.9

יוֹם הַשְּׁבִיעִי :Ex. 12.15   מִיּוֹם הָרִאשֹׁן :Ex. 12.15

יוֹם הָאֶחָד וְעֶשְׂרִים :Ex. 12.18   וּמִיּוֹם הַשְּׁמִינִי :Lev. 22.27

וּפַר הַשֵּׁנִי :Judg. 6.25

In such cases, where the prepositions ב כ ל are used, they are vocalized by the Masora with *a*; e.g. בַּיּוֹם הָרִאשֹׁן :Num. 7.12; בַּיּוֹם הַשְּׁמִינִי :ib. verse 54. This *a* does not necessarily imply the article, cf. §§ 99 ff.

a)   The uncertainty of grammatical treatment discussed under 1a is reflected with numerals, too; cf.

בִּשְׁנַת הָרְבִיעִית :Jer. 46.2   שְׁנַת הַשְּׁבִיעִית :Ezra 7.8

בַּשָּׁנָה הָרְבִיעִית :2 Ki. 18.9   הַשָּׁנָה הַשְּׁבִיעִית :Neh. 10.32

בִּשְׁנַת הַתְּשִׁיעִית :Ki. 17.6

בַּשָּׁנָה הַתְּשִׁיעִית :Jer. 39.1

Similar cases of adjectives in substantival position as *nomina regentia* are:

בִּרְכַּת טוֹב :Prov. 24.25   עֵין יָמִין :1 Sam. 11.2

בִּרְכוֹת טוֹב :Ps. 21.4   אֵשֶׁת רָע :Prov. 6.24

All cases under discussion here have one characteristic facture in common: one of the two nouns has adjectival meaning.

B. THE NOUN WITH ADJECTIVAL MEANING INTERCHANGEABLY
IN FIRST OR SECOND PLACE

§ 69.   This noun in the absolute state. Correctly identified as such by JPS:

Gen. 43.12:   וְכֶסֶף מִשְׁנֶה ⎱
Gen. 43.15:   וּמִשְׁנֶה כֶּסֶף ⎰   "and . . . double money"

Gen. 49.32:   מִקְנֵה הַשָּׂדֶה :   "The field . . . which was purchased"
Lev. 27.22:   שְׂדֵה מִקְנָתוֹ :   "a field which he hath bought"

Ex. 9.9:   פֹּרֵחַ אֲבַעְבֻּעֹת ⎱
Ex. 9.10:   אֲבַעְבֻּעֹת פֹּרֵחַ ⎰   "breaking forth with blains"

Ex. 30.23:   בְּשָׂמִים רֹאשׁ ⎱
Cant. 4.14:   רָאשֵׁי בְשָׂמִים ⎰   "the chief spices"

But in many other similar cases, JPS was misled by the changed position of the words:

Ezek. 22.18:   סִיגִים כֶּסֶף :   "dross of silver"
Prov. 26.23:   כֶּסֶף סִיגִים :   erroneously: "silver dross"

Josh. 22.4:   אֶרֶץ אֲחֻזַּתְכֶם :   "the land of your possession"
Lev. 27.24:   אֲחֻזַּת הָאָרֶץ :   erroneously: "the possession of the land"

Isa. 8.9:   מֶרְחַקֵּי אָרֶץ :   "far countries"
Isa. 33.17:   אֶרֶץ מֶרְחַקִּים :   erroneously: "a land stretching afar"

Num. 32.32:   אֲחֻזַּת נַחֲלָתֵנוּ :   "the possession of our inheritance"
Num. 35.2:   מִנַּחֲלַת אֲחֻזָּתָם :   erroneously: "of the inheritance of their possession"

Josh. 5.2:   חַרְבוֹת צֻרִים :   "knives of flint"
Ps. 89.44:   צוּר חַרְבּוֹ :   erroneously: "the edge of his sword"

§ 70.   The first or second noun, interchangeably, has a pronominal suffix.

Num. 25.12:   בְּרִיתִי שָׁלוֹם ⎱
Isa. 54.10:   וּבְרִית שְׁלוֹמִי ⎰   *the covenant of My peace.*

Isa. 22.18:   מַרְכְּבוֹת כְּבוֹדֶךָ ⎱
Hab. 3.8:   מַרְכְּבֹתֶיךָ יְשׁוּעָה ⎰   *the chariots of Thy victory.*

§ 71. The second noun has a pronominal suffix.

Ps. 79.1: הֵיכַל קָדְשֶׁךָ: "Thy holy temple."
Ps. 65.5: קְדֹשׁ הֵיכָלֶךָ:
    Not: "The holy place of Thy temple."
    But: *Thy holy temple.*

Neh. 9.5: שֵׁם כְּבוֹדֶךָ: "Thy glorious Name."
Ps. 79.9: כְּבוֹד שְׁמֶךָ:
    Not: "the glory of Thy name."
    But: *Thy glorious name.*

Isa. 44.12: בִּזְרוֹעַ כֹּחוֹ: "with his strong arm."
Ps. 111.6: כֹּחַ מַעֲשָׂיו:
    Not: "the power of His works."
    But: *His powerful works.*

Ps. 12.4: שִׂפְתֵי חֲלָקוֹת: "flattering lips."
Prov. 7.21: בְּחֵלֶק שְׂפָתֶיהָ:
    Not: "With the blandishment of her lips."
    But: *with her blandishing lips.*

C.   THE SECOND NOUN HAS ADJECTIVAL MEANING

§ 72. This noun in the absolute state.

a)   Correctly identified as such by JPS.

Ex. 28.2:   בִּגְדֵי קֹדֶשׁ: "holy garments."
1 Sam. 21.5: לֶחֶם חֹל: "common bread."
1 Sam. 21.7: לֶחֶם חֹם: "hot bread."
1 Ki. 20.31: מַלְכֵי חֶסֶד: "merciful kings."
Isa. 61.4:   עָרֵי חֹרֶב: "waste cities."
Ezek. 23.6:   בַּחוּרֵי חֶמֶד: "handsome young men."
Ezek. 25.17: בְּתוֹכְחוֹת חֵמָה: "with furious rebukes."
Zech. 7.14:   אֶרֶץ חֶמְדָה: "pleasant land."

b)   But instances like the following are of the same character.

Lev. 10.17: בִּמְקוֹם הַקֹּדֶשׁ:
    Not: "in the place of the sanctuary."
    But: *in the holy place*; identical in meaning with ib. 24.9: בִּמְקוֹם קָדֹשׁ.

Isa. 28.1: עֲטֶרֶת גֵּאוּת׃

   Not: "the crown of pride."

   But: *the proud crown*; cf. parallel the adjective נָבֵל.

Ps. 107.4: עִיר מוֹשָׁב׃

   Not: "city of habitation."

   But: *inhabited city*.

Prov. 3.17: דַּרְכֵי נֹעַם׃

   Not: "ways of pleasantness."

   But: *pleasant ways*.

§ 73.   This noun has a pronominal suffix.

   a)   Correctly identified as such by JPS.

1)   Isa. 41.10:   בִּימִין צִדְקִי: "with My victorious right hand."

      Jer. 12.10:   חֶלְקַת חֶמְדָּתִי: "My pleasant portion."

2)   Isa. 52.1:   בִּגְדֵי תִפְאַרְתֵּךְ: "thy beautiful garments."

      Isa. 64.9:   עָרֵי קָדְשֶׁךָ: "Thy holy cities."

      Jer. 5.17:   עָרֵי מִבְצָרֶיךָ: "thy fortified cities."

      Ezek. 16.18:   בִּגְדֵי רִקְמָתֵךְ: "thy richly woven garments."

3)   Isa. 44.12:   בִּזְרוֹעַ כֹּחוֹ: "with his strong arm."

      Isa. 63.10:   רוּחַ קָדְשׁוֹ: "His holy spirit."

      Prov. 10.15:   קִרְיַת עֻזּוֹ: "his strong city."

   b)   But instances like the following are of the same character.

1)   Hab. 1.12: אֱלֹהַי קְדֹשִׁי׃

      Not: my God, my Holy One (= אֱלֹהַי קדשי).

      But: *my holy God*.

   Ps. 4.2: אֱלֹהֵי צִדְקִי׃

      Not: "O God of my righteousness."

      But: *my righteous God*.

   Ps. 43.2: אֱלֹהֵי מָעוּזִּי׃

      Not: "the God of my strength."

      But: *my mighty God*; cf. ib. 31.5: כי אתה מעוזי; hence מעוזי is an attribute of God and does not refer to man.

   Ps. 59.18: אֱלֹהֵי חַסְדִּי׃

      Not: "the God of my mercy."

      But: *my merciful God*.

2) Isa. 49.19: וְאֶרֶץ הֲרִסֻתֵךְ:

   Not: "And thy land that hath been destroyed."

   But: *And thy destroyed land.*

   Isa. 49.20: בְּנֵי שִׁכֻּלָיִךְ:

   Not: "The children of thy bereavement."

   But: *thy children, o bereaved one*; cf. v. 21.

   Mic. 1.16: בְּנֵי תַעֲנוּגָיִךְ:

   Not: "the children of thy delight."

   But: *thy delightful* (or: *dandled*) *children.*

3) Lev. 26.19: גְּאוֹן עֻזְּכֶם:

   Not: "the pride of your power."

   But: *your mighty pride.*

D.   THE FIRST NOUN HAS ADJECTIVAL MEANING

§ 74.   Correctly idenified as such by JPS.

a)   The second noun in the absolute state.

Gen. 3.24:   לַהַט הַחֶרֶב: "the flaming sword."
Num. 17.3:   רִקֻּעֵי פַחִים: "beaten plates."
I Sam. 17.40: חַלֻּקֵי אֲבָנִים: "smooth stones."
Isa. 8.11:   בְּחֶזְקַת הַיָּד: "with a strong hand."
Isa. 28.11:   בְּלַעֲגֵי שָׂפָה: "with stammering lips."

b)   The second noun has a pronominal suffix.

Ps. 20.7:   יֵשַׁע יְמִינוֹ: "His saving right hand."

§ 75.   But instances like the following are of the same character.

a)   The second noun in the absolute state.

Ex. 13.3: בְּחֹזֶק יָד:

Not: "by strength of hand."

But: *with a strong hand*; cf. v. 9: בְּיָד חֲזָקָה.

Lev. 7.21: בְּטֻמְאַת אָדָם:

Not: "the uncleanness of man."

But: *an unclean man*; cf. the entire context.

Num. 19.17: שְׂרֵפַת הַחַטָּאת:

   Not: "the burning of the purification."

   But: *the burned purification*; in v. 6: שְׂרֵפַת הַפָּרָה, the heifer is still "burning"; but here he is already "burned" to ashes.

Isa. 10.16: כִּיקֹד אֵשׁ:

   Not: "like the burning of fire."

   But: *like a burning fire* (= Isa. 65.5: אֵשׁ יֹקֶדֶת).

Isa. 51.13: חֲמַת הַמֵּצִיק:

   Not: "the fury of the oppressor."

   But: *the furious oppressor*; cf. the following כַּאֲשֶׁר כּוֹנֵן: "as he maketh ready", thus referring to המציק.

Joel 2.5: לַהַב אֵשׁ:

   Not: "a flame of fire."

   But: *a flaming fire* (= Isa. 4.5: אֵשׁ לֶהָבָה).

   b)   The second noun has a pronominal suffix.

Ex. 15.16: בִּגְדֹל זְרוֹעֲךָ:

   Not: "By the greatness of Thine arm" (= בְּגָדֵל זרועך).

   But: *By Thy great arm.*

1 Sam. 16.7: גְּבֹהַּ קוֹמָתוֹ:

   Not: "the height of his stature" (= גֹבַה קומתו).

   But: *his high stature.*

Hos. 13.8: סְגוֹר לִבָּם:

   Not: "the enclosure of their heart."

   But: *their shut-up heart.*

Gen. 27.16: חֶלְקַת צַוָּארָיו:

   Not: "the smooth of his neck."

   But: *his smooth neck.*

Isa. 1.16: רֹעַ מַעַלְלֵיכֶם:

   Not: "the evil of your doings."

   But: *your evil doings* (= Zech. 1.4: וּמַעַלְלֵיכֶם הָרָעִים).

Jer. 16.18: בְּנִבְלַת שִׁקּוּצֵיהֶם:

   Not: "with the carcasses of their detestable things" (= בְּנִבְלַת שקוציהם).

   But: *with their detestable abominations.*

§ 76.   The مضاف and *nomen regens* in interchanged position.

Deut. 22.14: עֲלִילֹת דְּבָרִים: "wanton charges."

Deut. 23.15: עֶרְוַת דָּבָר: "unseemly thing."

Deut. 31.16: נֵכַר הָאָרֶץ: *of strange lands.*

Isa. 16.2: קֵן מְשֻׁלָּח: *driven out from (its) nest;* cf. Prov. 27.8: כְּצִפּוֹר נוֹדֶדֶת מִן קִנָּהּ.

Isa. 35.4: גְּמוּל אֱלֹהִים: *the God of recompense.*

Jer. 6.30: כֶּסֶף נִמְאָס: *refuse of silver.*

Ezek. 24.17: מֵתִים אֵבֶל: "mourning for the dead."

§ 77.   The مضاف (in changed position) has an Inseparable Particle.

a) ב: Ex. 19.9: בְּעַב הֶעָנָן: "in a thick cloud"; cf. v. 16: וְעָנָן כָּבֵד.

Josh. 2.6: בְּפִשְׁתֵּי הָעֵץ: "with the stalks of flax."

2 Chron. 16.14: בְּמִרְקַחַת מַעֲשֶׂה: "by the perfumer's art."

1 Sam. 14.27: בְּיַעֲרַת הַדְּבָשׁ: *in the honey of the forest;* cf. v. 26. On the difference in the gender between הַיַּעַר (v. 26) and בְּיַעֲרַת cf. ooo.

1 Ki. 8.37: בְּאֶרֶץ שְׁעָרָיו: *in the cities of their land.*

Am. 8.9: בְּיוֹם אוֹר: *in broad daylight.*

Mic. 2.5: חֶבֶל בְּגוֹרָל: *(none that cast) a lot for a portion.*

Ps. 88.7: בִּבוֹר תַּחְתִּיּוֹת: *in the depth of the dungeon.*

Prov. 31.13: בְּחֵפֶץ כַּפֶּיהָ: *a (choice) thing with her hands.*

b) כ: Isa. 44.13: כְּתִפְאֶרֶת אָדָם: *like a beautiful man;* cf. Ps. 22.7: חֶרְפַּת אָדָם: *a despicable man.*

Prov. 5.4: כְּחֶרֶב פִּיּוֹת: *as the edges of a sword.*

Hos. 4.4: כִּמְרִיבֵי כֹהֵן: *like fighting priests.*

Job. 3.5: כִּמְרִירֵי יוֹם: *like black days.*

Deut. 23.25: כְּנַפְשְׁךָ שָׂבְעֶךָ: *to the satisfaction of thy soul.*

c) מ: Deut. 15.7: מֵאַחַד אַחֶיךָ: "one of thy brethren."

Deut. 32.13: מֵחַלְמִישׁ צוּר: "of the flinty rock."

Ps. 81.7: מִסֵּבֶל שִׁכְמוֹ: *the burden from his shoulder,* cf. Isa. 14.25.

Lam. 3.55: מִבּוֹר תַּחְתִּיּוֹת: *from the depth of the dungeon.*

Job 31.16: מֵחֵפֶץ דַּלִּים: *a (choice) thing from the needy.*

The مضاف (in changed position) has a pronominal suffix.

Gen. 37.2:   דִּבָּתָם רָעָה: *the report of their wickedness.*
Num. 12.6:   נְבִיאֲכֶם יהוה (אם יהיה): *a prophet of the Lord among you.*
Isa. 31.7:   יְדֵיכֶם חֵטְא: *your sinful hands.*
Isa. 35.4:   אֱלֹהֵיכֶם נָקָם: *the God of your vengeance.*
Hab. 3.8:   מַרְכְּבֹתֶיךָ יְשׁוּעָה: *the chariots of Thy salvation* (or: *victory*).
Ezra 2.62:   כְּתָבָם הַמִּתְיַחֲשִׂים: *the register of their genealogy.*

Similarly:

Gen. 3.15:   יְשׁוּפְךָ רֹאשׁ: "shall bruise thy head."
Gen. 3.15:   תְּשׁוּפֶנּוּ עָקֵב: "shall bruise their heel."
Ezek. 25.6:   שָׁאטְךָ בְּנֶפֶשׁ: "with the disdain of thy soul".

§ 78.   Both مضاف and *nomen regens* (in either position) have a pronominal suffix.

Gen. 9.5:   דִּמְכֶם לְנַפְשֹׁתֵיכֶם: *the blood of your lives.*
Gen. 37.27:   אָחִינוּ בְשָׂרֵנוּ: *our onw brother* (as against אָח = kinsfolk).
Deut. 18.15:   מִקִּרְבְּךָ מֵאַחֶיךָ: *from amongst thy brethren.*
Deut. 23.25:   כְּנַפְשְׁךָ שָׂבְעֶךָ: *to the satisfaction of thy soul.*
Deut. 29.9:   רָאשֵׁיכֶם שִׁבְטֵיכֶם: *the heads of your tribes.*

§ 79.   The *nomen regens* has an Inseparable Particle.

Gen. 18.11:   אֹרַח כַּנָּשִׁים: "after the manner of women."
Prov. 19.12:   נַהַם כַּכְּפִיר: "as the roaring of a lion."

§ 80.   Construct State as an attribute (to substantive with a pronominal suffix).

Gen. 44.2:   גְּבִיעִי גְּבִיעַ הַכֶּסֶף: *my silver goblet.*
Deut. 3.11:   עַרְשׂוֹ עֶרֶשׂ בַּרְזֶל: *his iron bedstead.*
2 Ki. 25.30:   וַאֲרֻחָתוֹ אֲרֻחַת תָּמִיד: *And his complete provision* (or: *allowance*).

Similarly:

Gen. 42.25:   כַּסְפֵּיהֶם אִישׁ (ולהשיב) = כֶּסֶף אִישׁ כספיהם; cf. ib. 43.21 and
               כֶּסֶף אִישׁ :44.1.

§ 81.   Two Construct States combined.

a)   One مضاف (in medial position).

Gen. 49.3:   כֹּחִי וְרֵאשִׁית אוֹנִי : *the first-fruits of my might and strength.*

Deut. 30.20:   חַיֶּיךָ וְאֹרֶךְ יָמֶיךָ : *the length of thy life and days.*

Isa. 7.20:   (אֶת) הָרֹאשׁ וְשַׂעַר הָרַגְלַיִם : *the hair of the head and the feet.*

Isa. 51.3:   תּוֹדָה וְקוֹל זִמְרָה : *the voice of thanksgiving and song.*

Isa. 53.3:   אִישׁ מַכְאֹבוֹת וִידוּעַ חֹלִי : *a man, familiar with pain and disease.*

Jer. 30.19:   תּוֹדָה וְקוֹל מְשַׂחֲקִים : *the voice of thanksgiving and making merry.*

Zech. 8. 16:   אֱמֶת וּמִשְׁפַּט שָׁלוֹם : *"the judgement of truth and peace."*

b)   Two مضاف (in initial and medial position, respectively).

Ezek. 31.16:   מִבְחַר וְטוֹב לְבָנוֹן

Mal. 3.3:   מְצָרֵף וּמְטַהֵר כֶּסֶף

Dan. 1.4:   סֵפֶר וּלְשׁוֹן כַּשְׂדִּים

c)   Two مضاف (in initial and final position, respectively).

α)   Lev. 22.10:   תּוֹשַׁב כֹּהֵן וְשָׂכִיר : *a tenant of a priest or (his) hired servant.*

     Isa. 11.2:   (רוּחַ) דַּעַת וְיִרְאַת יהוה : *of knowledge and fear of the Lord.*

β)   Gen. 4.4:   מִבְּכֹרוֹת צֹאנוֹ וּמֵחֶלְבֵהֶן

     Gen. 40.1:   מַשְׁקֵה מֶלֶךְ מִצְרַיִם וְהָאֹפֶה

     Deut. 22.15:   אֲבִי הַנַּעֲרָה וְאִמָּהּ

d)   One مضاف with several *nomina regentia.*

     Ex. 10.2:   בְּאָזְנֵי בִנְךָ וּבֶן בִּנְךָ

     Ex. 14.24:   בְּעַמּוּד אֵשׁ וְעָנָן ; cf. v. 19 : עַמּוּד הֶעָנָן

     Ex. 32.2:   בְּאָזְנֵי נְשֵׁיכֶם בְּנֵיכֶם וּבְנֹתֵיכֶם

     Num. 16.27:   מִשְׁכַּן קֹרַח דָּתָן וַאֲבִירָם

     Mal. 3.5:   שְׂכַר שָׂכִיר אַלְמָנָה וְיָתוֹם

e)   A مضاف to each *nomen regens.*

     Gen. 19.16:   וּבְיַד אשתו וּבְיַד שתי בנתיו

     Gen. 37.14:   את שְׁלוֹם אחיך וְאת שְׁלוֹם הצאן

     Ex. 5.21:   בְּעֵינֵי פרעה וּבְעֵינֵי עבדיו

     Lev. 7.24:   וְחֵלֶב נבלה וְחֵלֶב טרפה

     Lev. 8.27:   עַל כַּפֵּי אהרן וְעַל כַּפֵּי בניו

     Num. 18.17:   בְּכוֹר שור או בְכוֹר כשב או בְכוֹר עז

     Deut. 21.18:   בְּקוֹל אביו וּבְקוֹל אמו

Deut. 23.20:   נֶשֶׁךְ כסף נֶשֶׁךְ אכל נֶשֶׁךְ כל דבר

2 Ki. 14.26:   וְאֶפֶס עצור וְאֶפֶס עזוב

2 Sam. 8.10:   כְּלֵי כסף וּכְלֵי זהב וּכְלֵי נחשת

1 Chron. 18.10: כְּלֵי זהב וכסף ונחשת

§ 82..   Different Cases of Construct State.

In the instances listed in § 68 the vocalization of the respective nouns remained unchanged, though they were in the position of مضاف in a construct state; cf. similarly p. 217, sub c and p. 224, sub B 4, p. 260, § 34 and p. 455, sub VIII. We now realize that it is not the way a word is vocalized, but its syntactical position which makes it a مضاف in a construct state. The change in the vocalization, which we notice in the Tiberian system, is merely a result of being in the position as مضاف, but by no means an indispensable prerequisite. The vocalizer may have overlooked the close syntactical interconnection between two nouns, and have left the vocalization unaltered; but they form a construct state, nevertheless. On the other hand, an erroneous interpretation (no matter whether by the vocalizer himself, or by later grammarians) of the position of a given word as مضاف does not make it really one. With an eye on the vocalization, we shall now differentiate between *cases of construct state a) in reality* (though the vocalization does not indicate it), and *b) in semblance* (where the vocalization was falsely interpreted as implying it).

§ 83.   Construct State in Reality.

1)   The مضاف is a masculine noun in the singular.

1 Ki. 5.3:   בָּקָר רְעִי

Ezek. 16.49:   גָּאוֹן שִׂבְעַת לֶחֶם

Isa. 22.22:   מַפְתֵּחַ בֵּית דָּוִד

Ps. 60.5:   יַיִן תַּרְעֵלָה

Jer. 3.23:   הָמוֹן הָרִים

Ps. 66.2:   כְּבוֹד תְּהִלָּתוֹ (cf. parallel: כְּבוֹד שְׁמוֹ)

1 Chron. 19.8:   צָבָא הַגִּבּוֹרִים

2)   The مضاف is a feminine noun in the singular.

Lev. 6.13:   מִנְחָה תָּמִיד (cf. v. 14: מִנְחַת פִּתִּים; Num. 28.6: עֹלַת תָּמִיד)

Judg. 7.8:   צֵדָה הָעָם

Ps. 45.5:   וְעַנְוָה צֶדֶק (cf. parallel: דְּבַר אֱמֶת)

Isa. 25.1:   אֱמוּנָה אֹמֶן

Prov. 13.12:   מַחֲלָה לֵב

Isa. 42.25:   חֵמָה אַפּוֹ

Isa. 66.15:   בְּחֵמָה אַפּוֹ

3)   The مضاف is a masculine noun in the plural.

Ex. 28.17:   טוּרִים אָבֶן (ארבעה)(אַרְבָּעָה); cf. ib. 39.10: טוּרֵי אבן

Josh. 7.4:   אֲלָפִים אִישׁ (כשלשת)(כִּשְׁלֹשֶׁת); cf. Ex. 32.28: אַלְפֵי אִישׁ

Judg. 4.6:   אֲלָפִים אִישׁ (עשרת)(עֲשֶׂרֶת); cf. ib. v. 10: אַלְפֵי אִישׁ

1 Ki. 7.12:   טוּרִים גָּזִית (שלשה)(שְׁלֹשָׁה); cf. ib. 6.36: טוּרֵי גָזִית

1 Ki. 7.42:   טוּרִים רִמֹּנִים (שְׁנֵי)

1 Ki. 22.27:   וּמַיִם לַחַץ

Ezek. 47.4:   מַיִם בִּרְכָּיִם; cf. parallel: מֵי מָתְנָיִם

Zech. 1.13:   דְּבָרִים נִחֻמִים

Ex. 30.23:   בְּשָׂמִים רֹאשׁ

2 Ki. 3.4:   אֵילִים צָמֶר

Jer. 10.10:   אֱלֹהִים אֱמֶת

Ezek. 22.18:   סִגִים כֶּסֶף

1 Chron. 15.19:   בִּמְצִלְתַּיִם נְחֹשֶׁת

Am. 3.15:   בָּתִּים רַבִּים: *the houses of the great*

Ps. 81.2:   לֵאלֹהִים עוּזֵּנוּ: *unto the God of Our Strength*

Prov. 23.29:   פְּצָעִים חִנָּם: *undeserved wounds*

4)   The مضاف is a numeral.

Deut. 17.6:   שְׁנַיִם עֵדִים; cf. ib. 19.15: שְׁנֵי עדים

Judg. 11.37:   שְׁנַיִם חֳדָשִׁים; cf. ib. v. 38: שְׁנֵי חדשים

1 Sam. 25.18:   וּשְׁנַיִם נִבְלֵי יַיִן; but cf. ib. 30.5: וּשְׁתֵּי נְשֵׁי דָוִד; Ex. 28.9:
שְׁתֵּי אַבְנֵי שֹׁהַם

Ezek. 41.24:   וּשְׁתַּיִם דְּלָתוֹת · · · · וּשְׁתֵּי דְלָתוֹת

Josh. 4.3:   שְׁתֵּים עֶשְׂרֵה אֲבָנִים; cf. ib. v. 8: שְׁתֵּי עשרה אבנים

Ex. 39.14:   לִשְׁנַיִם עָשָׂר שָׁבֶט; cf. ib. 28.21: לִשְׁנֵי עָשָׂר שבט

Josh. 4.2:   שְׁנַיִם עָשָׂר אֲנָשִׁים; cf. ib. 3.12: שְׁנֵי עשר איש

§ 84.   *Construct State in Semblance*: There are a number of nominal forms which are erroneously interpreted as representing the مضاف of a construct state formation with either no *regens* at all, or else an entire sentence taking the place of the *regens* (cf. B-L § 64g3). The reason for identifying these nouns as مضاف is that in their present form they seem to have already undergone the changes which are characteristic for a مضاف according to the Tiberian Vocalization System: a) In the case of a masculine noun this means that there is a vowel which appears to be the result of the reduction of a genuine vowel to be found in what supposedly is its absolute form; b) with a femine noun it is the ending in ת, while there exists a parallel form ending in ה which assumedly is its absolute form.

a) The masculine noun. Working under the silent supposition that צְפוֹן by necessity is the construct state form to the absolute form צָפוֹן, and similarly מְקוֹם to מָקוֹם, עֵין to עָיִן, בֵּית to בַּיִת, grammars and dictionaries alike consider as construct forms cases like: מִצְפוֹן לְבֵית הָעֲרָבָה :Josh. 15.6; מְקוֹם אֲשֶׁר :Gen. 39.20; בַּעֲוֹן אֲשֶׁר יָדַע :1 Sam. 3.13; מִבֵּית לְאוּלָם :1 Ki. 7.8. But against this procedure of taking the vocalization as the only criterion, it is well to consider instances like: מִצְפוֹן לְשַׁעַר הַמִּזְבֵּחַ :Ezek. 8.5; אֲרוֹן אֶחָד: 2 Ki. 12.10; מִבַּית לִדְבִיר :1 Ki. 6.16. Here we have either the supposedly absolute form in the identical syntactical position, or an analogous form (אֲרוֹן cf. with בַּעֲוֹן) which by reason of its context must be taken as the absolute form. We will, therefore, discard the mere external evidence of the vocalization, and shall base our conclusions on the position of the words in question in the syntactical structure of the context. Accordingly, the instances referred to represent another way of forming the absolute state of the respective nouns. We thus get formations like צָפוֹן and צְפוֹן, עָיִן and עֵין, מָקוֹם and מְקוֹם as the absolute state; cf. p. 199 ff. (Triconsonantal Nouns), §§ 91-92, 94-95, 97 and 98. In the examples listed there, the characteristic vowel is in the second syllable, while the first syllable of nouns belonging to one and the same class can be vocalized with *a* or *e*. On the forms בַּיִת and בֵּית as absolute state cf. p. 130, s.v. בית and p. 137 s.v. חיל.

b) The feminine noun. With our preceding discussion in mind, we shall no longer regard as construct state the following feminine nouns: שְׂפַת לֹא יָדַעְתִּי :Ps. 81.6 (not: the speech of him, whom I do not know, but: a speech, which I do not know); שִׁפְעַת אֲנִי רֹאֶה :2 Ki. 9.17; וּשְׁכֻרַת וְלֹא מִיָּיִן: Isa. 51.21; קִרְיַת חָנָה דָוִד :Isa. 29.1. But we will conclude that שָׂפָה and שְׂפַת, שְׁפָעָה and שִׁפְעַת, שִׁכְרָה and שְׁכֻרַת, קִרְיָה and קִרְיַת are all forms of the absolute state. In a number of instances, feminine nouns ending in ת or ה occur in the very same syntactic connection, so that there can be no justification in assigning the forms in ה and ת to the absolute and construct state, respectively.

It will be noticed that the vocalization of the forms ending in ת is inconsistent: the *paṭaḥ* in forms like שִׂמְחַת, מְזוּזַת, יִתְרַת, חָכְמַת strikingly contrasts with the *ḳames* in עֶזְרַת, נַחֲלַת, זִמְרָת. Similarly, שְׂפַת has hitherto been explained as construct state to שָׂפָה, with reduction of the first syllable to *sheva*, according to a basic law of Tiberian grammar (cf. p. 415, § 2c); but while שְׁנַת (as compared with שֵׁנָה) has retained the *ḳames* in the second syllable, it was changed into *paṭaḥ* in שְׂפַת. On the interchangeability between *ḳames* and *paṭaḥ* in Masoretic Hebrew cf. p. 433, §§ 42 ff.

אִשָּׁה: Job 14.1:	יְלוּד אִשָּׁה	מַמְלָכָה: Ezek. 17.14:
אֵשֶׁת: Ps. 58.9:	נֵפֶל אֵשֶׁת	לִהְיוֹת מַמְלָכָה שְׁפָלָה
דֵּעָה: Jer. 3.15:	דֵּעָה וְהַשְׂכֵּיל	מַמְלֶכֶת: Mic. 4.8: מַמְלֶכֶת לְבַת יְרוּשָׁלָם
דַּעַת: Isa. 11.2:	דַּעַת וְיִרְאַת יהוה	נַחֲלָה: Ps. 135.12: נַחֲלָה לְיִשְׂרָאֵל
זִמְרָה: Isa. 51.3:	וְקוֹל זִמְרָה	נַחֲלָת: Ps. 16.6: אַף נַחֲלָת שָׁפְרָה עָלַי
זִמְרָת: Ex. 15.2:	עָזִּי וְזִמְרָת יָהּ	עֲצָרָה: 2 Ki. 10.20: קַדְּשׁוּ עֲצָרָה
חֲטָאָה: Gen. 20.9:	חֲטָאָה גְדֹלָה	עֲצֶרֶת: Num. 29.35:
חַטָּאת: Gen. 4.7:	חַטָּאת רֹבֵץ	עֲצֶרֶת תִּהְיֶה לָכֶם
חַיָּה: Ezek. 33.27:	לַחַיָּה נְתַתִּיו	שֵׁנָה: Prov. 6.4: אַל תִּתֵּן שֵׁנָה לְעֵינֶיךָ
חַיַּת: Ps. 74.19:	אַל תִּתֵּן לְחַיַּת	שְׁנַת: Ps. 132.4: אִם אֶתֵּן שְׁנַת לְעֵינָי
חָכְמָה: Prov. 23.23:	חָכְמָה וּמוּסָר	תּוֹכֵחָה: Hos. 5.9: בְּיוֹם תּוֹכֵחָה
חָכְמַת: Isa. 33.6:	חָכְמַת וָדַעַת	תּוֹכַחַת: Prov. 10.17: וְעֹזֵב תּוֹכַחַת
יַבָּשָׁה: Ex. 14.22: בְּתוֹךְ הַיָּם בַּיַּבָּשָׁה		תּוֹלֵעָה: Job 25.6: וּבֶן אָדָם תּוֹלֵעָה
יַבֶּשֶׁת: Ex. 4.9: וַיִּהְיוּ לְדָם בַּיַּבָּשֶׁת		תּוֹלַעַת: Ps. 22.7: תּוֹלַעַת וְלֹא אִישׁ
יִתְרָה: Isa. 15.7: עַל כֵּן יִתְרָה עָשָׂה		תִּפְאָרָה: Isa. 28.5: וְלִצְפִירַת תִּפְאָרָה
יִתְרַת: Jer. 48.36: עַל כֵּן יִתְרַת עָשָׂה		תִּפְאֶרֶת: Isa. 62.3: עֲטֶרֶת תִּפְאֶרֶת
מְזוּזָה: Ex. 21.6:	אֶל הַמְּזוּזָה	יְשׁוּעָה: Ps. 119.155:
מְזוּזַת: Ezek. 41.21:	מְזוּזַת רְבָעָה	רָחוֹק מֵרְשָׁעִים יְשׁוּעָה
מַחֲשָׁבָה: Jer. 49.30:		יְשׁוּעָתָה: Ps. 3.3: אֵין יְשׁוּעָתָה לִי
וְחָשַׁב עֲלֵיהֶם מַחֲשָׁבָה		צָרָה: Ps. 81.8: בַּצָּרָה קָרָאתָ
מַחֲשֶׁבֶת: Ezek. 38.10: וְחָשַׁבְתָּ מַחֲשֶׁבֶת		צָרָתָה: Ps. 120.1: בַּצָּרָתָה לִי
מִלְחָמָה: Hos. 10.14:	בְּיוֹם מִלְחָמָה	מַכָּה: Jer. 14.17: מַכָּה נַחְלָה מְאֹד
מִלְחֶמֶת: 1 Sam. 13.22:	בְּיוֹם מִלְחֶמֶת	מַכַּת: Isa. 14.6: מַכַּת בִּלְתִּי סָרָה

מֶמְשָׁלָה : Mic. 4.8:	הַמֶּמְשָׁלָה הָרִאשֹׁנָה	שִׂמְחָה : Ps. 4.8:	נָתַתָּה שִׂמְחָה בְלִבִּי
מֶמְשֶׁלֶת : Ps. 136.8:	לְמֶמְשֶׁלֶת בַּיּוֹם	שִׂמְחַת : Isa. 9.2:	כְּשִׂמְחַת בַּקָּצִיר
מַצֵּבָה : Hos. 3.4:	וְאֵין מַצֵּבָה	עֶזְרָה : Ps. 46.2:	עֶזְרָה בְצָרוֹת
מַצֶּבֶת : Isa. 6.13:	מַצֶּבֶת בָּם	עֶזְרַת : Ps. 60.13:	עֶזְרַת מִצָּר

c)   Numerals ending in ה and ת

Gen. 23.1:	מֵאָה שָׁנָה	2 Ki. 15.8:	שִׁשָּׁה חֳדָשִׁים
Gen. 25.7:	מְאַת שנה	1 Ki. 11.16:	שֵׁשֶׁת חדשים
Judg. 20.44:	שְׁמֹנָה עָשָׂר אֶלֶף	Ezek. 46.4:	שִׁשָּׁה כְבָשִׂים
Judg. 20.25:	שְׁמֹנַת עשר אלף	Ezek. 46.6:	וְשֵׁשֶׁת כבשים
2 Sam. 18.3:	עֲשָׂרָה אֲלָפִים	1 Sam. 30.12:	שְׁלֹשָׁה יָמִים
Judg. 1.4:	עֲשֶׂרֶת אלפים	2 Sam. 20.4:	שְׁלֹשֶׁת ימים
Lev. 27.7:	עֲשָׂרָה שְׁקָלִים	2 Sam. 2.18:	שְׁלֹשָׁה בְנֵי (צְרוּיָה)
Lev. 27.5:	עֲשֶׂרֶת שקלים	1 Sam. 17.13:	שְׁלֹשֶׁת בני (יִשַׁי)
1 Ki. 11.31:	עֲשָׂרָה הַשְּׁבָטִים	Deut. 22.19:	מֵאָה כֶסֶף
1 Ki. 11.35:	עֲשֶׂרֶת השבטים	Ex. 38.25:	מְאַת כִּכָּר
Num. 23.1:	שִׁבְעָה פָרִים	2 Sam. 9.10:	חֲמִשָּׁה עָשָׂר בָּנִים
Ezek. 45.23:	שִׁבְעַת פרים	2 Sam. 19.18:	וַחֲמֵשֶׁת עָשָׂר בָּנָיו
Num. 28.27:	שִׁבְעָה כְבָשִׂים		
Lev. 23.18:	שִׁבְעַת כבשים		

The following forms have been misunderstood by the vocalizers of the Hebrew Bible as representing the absolute and construct state, respectively; hence they vocalized accordingly:

Ezek. 40.30: חָמֵשׁ אַמּוֹת; but ib. v. 7: חָמֵשׁ אמות

Vocalizations like שֶׁבַע עֶשְׂרֵה, חָמֵשׁ עֶשְׂרֵה, שְׁלֹשׁ עֶשְׂרֵה must not be regarded as reflecting construct states, as becomes evident when compared with their respective masculine equivalents: שִׁבְעָה עָשָׂר, חֲמִשָּׁה עָשָׂר, שְׁלֹשָׁה עָשָׂר. Similarly, אַחַד in אַחַד עָשָׂר is the absolute (and not construct) form; cf. 1 Sam. 16.18: אֶחָד מֵהַנְּעָרִים with ib. 9.3: אַחַד מֵהַנְּעָרִים; 2 Ki. 7.13: אֶחָד מֵעֲבָדָיו with ib. 6.12: אַחַד מֵעֲבָדָיו; also: 2 Sam. 17.22: אַחַד לֹא נֶעְדָּר.

§ 85.   According to our definition of the term *noun* in § 62b the following instances represent regular cases of construct state:

Ps. 5.12:	חוֹסֵי בָךְ	Ezek. 32.15:	יוֹשְׁבֵי בָהּ
Ps. 2.12:	חוֹסֵי בוֹ	Isa. 30.18:	חוֹכֵי לוֹ

Jer. 33.22:	מְשָׁרְתֵי אֹתִי	Isa. 9.1:	יֹשְׁבֵי בָּאָרֶץ
Ezek. 13.2:	לִנְבִיאֵי מִלִּבָּם	Gen. 5.13:	בָּאָרֶץ לֹא לָהֶם
2 Sam. 16.21:	יְדֵי כָּל אֲשֶׁר אִתָּךְ	Num. 16.5:	חֲמוֹר אֶחָד מֵהֶם
Ezek. 44.30:	בִּכּוּרֵי כֹל	Gen. 29.27:	שְׁבֻעַ זֹאת
Ezek. 44.30:	תְּרוּמַת כֹּל	1 Ki. 2.31:	דְּמֵי חִנָּם
Num. 23.3:	וּדְבַר מַה	Gen. 3.7:	עֵינֵי שְׁנֵיהֶם
Jer. 8.9:	וְחָכְמַת מַה	Gen. 9.23:	שְׁכֶם שְׁנֵיהֶם
Isa. 28.9:	גְּמוּלֵי מֵחָלָב	Ex. 22.8:	דְּבַר שְׁנֵיהֶם
Isa. 28.9:	עַתִּיקֵי מִשָּׁדָיִם	1 Sam. 17.58:	בֶּן מִי
Isa. 5.11:	מַשְׁכִּימֵי בַבֹּקֶר	Gen. 24. 23:	בַּת מִי
Isa. 5.11:	מְאַחֲרֵי בַנֶּשֶׁף	1 Sam. 12.3:	וַחֲמוֹר מִי

§ 86. A participle preceding a construct state and in close syntactical connection with it, may be used either in the absolute or even in the construct form; cf. p. 260, § 34b, the example from Num. 3.38, where MT has שֹׁמְרִים (מִשְׁמֶרֶת הַקֹּדֶשׁ), while the Samaritan Pentateuch offers שמרי instead. With our definition of the term *noun* in mind (§ 62b), we shall thus explain the following cases as series of construct states:

Jud. 5.10:	יֹשְׁבֵי עַל מִדִּין	Judg. 5.10:	וְהֹלְכֵי עַל דֶּרֶךְ
Isa. 32.20:	זֹרְעֵי עַל כָּל מָיִם	Ezek. 38.12:	יֹשְׁבֵי עַל טַבּוּר הָאָרֶץ

§ 87. A construct state formation (both مضاف and *regens* together) can grammatically be treated either: a) as an entity, equal to one word only, or b) as a combination of two individual words, each of which is subject to grammatical laws of its own. We base this assertion upon the observation of certain grammatical phenomena; they shall be discussed in the following §§ 88-91. On our thesis that this different treatment reflects dialectic differences, cf. p. 501 ff.

§ 88. *The determined construct state*: The determination is indicated by the article ה. But there is a difference noticeable in the application of the article: it is either prefixed to the *regens* only (cf. § 87a), or to both nouns, مضاف and *regens* (cf. § 87b). The first procedure is by far the rule in the Biblical literature. We therefore limit ourselves to proving the treatment of a construct state as a combination of two distinct words (cf. § 87b) by listing cases in which both nouns are determined, grouping the material according to the characteristic features of the respective *regens*.

a) The *regens* is a proper name.

הַמֶּלֶךְ אַשּׁוּר:	Isa. 36.8	הָאָרֶץ כְּנָעַן:	Num. 34.2
הַמֶּלֶךְ בָּבֶל:	2 Ki. 25.11	הַבּוֹר מַלְכִּיָּהוּ:	Jer. 38.6
הַמִּזְבֵּחַ בֵּית אֵל:	2 Ki. 23.17	הַשֵּׁבֶט הַמְנַשֶּׁה:	Josh. 13.7
וְהָאָרֶץ הַגִּבְלִי:	Josh. 13.5	הָאָרֶץ מִרְתַיִם:	Jer. 50.21
הָעָם יִשְׂרָאֵל:	Josh. 8.33	הָאֶבֶן הָאָזֶל:	1 Sam. 20.19
הַצָּבָא יִשְׂרָאֵל:	2 Sam. 20.23	הָאֶבֶן הָעָזֶר:	1 Sam. 4.1

b) The *regens* has adjectival meaning (cf. § 67).

הָאֶבֶן הַבְּדִיל:	Zech. 4.10	הַכֹּהֵן הָרֹאשׁ:	2 Chron. 31.10
הָעֲבֹתֹת הַזָּהָב:	Ex. 39.17	הָאֶבֶן הָרֹאשָׁה:	Zech. 4.7
הַבָּקָר הַנְּחֹשֶׁת:	2 Ki. 16.17	הָעָם הַמִּלְחָמָה:	Josh. 8.11
הַמִּזְבֵּחַ הַנְּחֹשֶׁת:	2 Ki. 16.14	הַלִּשְׁכוֹת הַקֹּדֶשׁ:	Ezek. 46.19
הַשַּׁעַר הַדָּרוֹם:	Ezek. 40.28	הַצָּבָא הַגִּבֹּרִים:	2 Sam. 10.7
הַשַּׁעַר הַצָּפוֹנָה:	Ezek. 40.40		

c) The *regens* is descriptive.

הַיְתַד הָאָרֶג:	Judg. 16.14	הָאָדָם הַמַּעֲלָה:	1 Chron. 17.17
הָעָם הָאָרֶץ:	Ezek. 45.16	הַפָּר הַחַטָּאת:	Ezek. 43.21
הַמַּמְלָכוֹת הָאָרֶץ:	Jer. 25.26	הָאָרוֹן הַבְּרִית:	Josh. 3.14
הַתּוֹעֲבֹת הַגּוֹיִם:	1 Ki. 14.24	הַמִּסְגְּרוֹת הַמְּכֹנוֹת:	2 Ki. 16.17
הָעֵמֶק הַפְּגָרִים:	Jer. 31.39	הַסֵּפֶר הַמִּקְנָה:	Jer. 32.12
הַשָּׁר הַמַּשָּׂא:	1 Chron. 15.27	הַיַּחַשׂ הָעוֹלִים:	Neh. 7.5
הַנַּעַר הַנָּבִיא:	2 Ki. 9.4	הַלַּעַג הַשַּׁאֲנַנִּים:	Ps. 123.4
הַיַּיִן הַחֵמָה:	Jer. 25.15		

d) The *regens* is a determined construct state.

הָאָרוֹן בְּרִית יהוה:	Josh. 3.17
הָאוֹצָרוֹת בֵּית הָאֱלֹהִים:	1 Chron. 9.26
הַגַּג עֲלִיַּת אָחָז:	2 Ki. 23.12
הַקֶּבֶר אִישׁ הָאֱלֹהִים:	2 Ki. 23.17

e) The *regens* a noun with suffixes.

הָאָרֶץ בָּשְׁתָּם:	Zeph. 3.19	(לְמִן) הַיּוֹם הִוָּסְדָה:	Ex. 9.18

Similarly: (לְמִן) הַיּוֹם לֶכֶת: 2 Sam. 19.25

§ 89. *The plural of a construct state*: It can be formed in three ways: a) the مضاف is put in the plural, with the *regens* remaining unchanged

(cf. § 87a), b) the *nomen regens* alone is put in the plur. with the مضاف remaining unchanged or c) both nouns are put in the plural (cf. § 87b):

a)   בֶּן גִּלְעָד: Num. 27.1   שַׂר צָבָא: 2 Sam. 2.8

          בְּנֵי גִלְעָד: Num. 26.30   וּלְשָׂרֵי הַצָּבָא: 1 Ki. 1.25

     מִבְּנֵי גִלְעָדִים: 2 Ki. 15.25   שָׂרֵי צְבָאוֹת: Deut. 20.9

       מֶלֶךְ הָאָרֶץ: 1 Sam. 21.12   עַם הָאָרֶץ: Lev. 20.2

        מַלְכֵי הָאָרֶץ: Josh. 12.7   מֵעַמֵּי הָאָרֶץ: Ezra 10.2

    מַלְכֵי הָאֲרָצוֹת: Ezra 9.7   עַמֵּי הָאֲרָצוֹת: Ezra 9.11

         שַׂר הַחַיִל: 2 Sam. 24.2   גִּבּוֹר חַיִל: Judg. 11.1

       שָׂרֵי הַחַיִל: 2 Ki. 9.5   גִּבּוֹרֵי חָיִל: 1 Chron. 7.9

    שָׂרֵי הַחֲיָלִים: 1 Ki. 15.20   גִּבּוֹרֵי חֲיָלִים: 1 Chron. 7.7

b)   בְּנֵי עֲנָק: Deut. 9.2   לֻחֹת אֶבֶן: Ex. 31.18

      בְּנֵי עֲנָקִים: Deut. 9.2   לֻחֹת אֲבָנִים: Ex. 34.1

       שָׂרֵי הַחַיִל: 2 Ki. 9.5   עָרֵי מְצוּרָה: 2 Chron. 14.5

    שָׂרֵי הַחֲיָלִים: 1 Ki. 15.20   עָרֵי הַמְּצֵרוֹת: 2 Chron. 12.4

c)   רֹאשׁ הָהָר: Ex. 19.20   שַׂר אֶלֶף: 1 Sam. 18.13

     רָאשֵׁי הֶהָרִים: Gen. 8.5   שָׂרֵי אֲלָפִים: Ex. 18.21

        שַׂר גְּדוּד: 1 Ki. 11.24   גּוּר אַרְיֵה: Gen. 49.9

     שָׂרֵי גְדוּדִים: 2 Sam. 4.2   כְּגוֹרֵי אֲרָיוֹת: Jer. 51.38

        אִישׁ מִדָּה: 1 Chron. 11.23   תְּרוּמַת הַקֹּדֶשׁ: Ezek. 45.6

      אַנְשֵׁי מִדּוֹת: Num. 13.32   תְּרוּמֹת הַקֳּדָשִׁים: Num. 18.19

d)   בְּרֹאשׁ הֶהָרִים: Isa. 2.2   רֹאשׁ הַפָּרִים: Num. 8.12

    רֹאשׁ הָעַמּוּדִים: 1 Ki. 7.17   מֵרֹאשׁ צֻרִים: Num. 23.9

e)   חֲכַם לֵב: Ex. 31.6   לְעִיר מִבְצָר: Jer. 1.18

        חַכְמֵי לֵב: Ex. 28.3   עָרֵי הַמִּבְצָר: Jer. 4.5

         מַטֵּה עֹז: Ezek. 19.14

        מַטּוֹת עֹז: Ezek. 19.11

§ 90. *Construct state in adjectival position*: A substantive which is
followed by a construct state in adjectival position can be treated in two
ways: either the substantive remains unchanged, thus indicating that the
following construct state formation is from the grammatical point of view
nothing more than one adjective (cf. § 87a), or it is put in the construct

state, too, and treated as another مضاف to the following *regens* (cf. § 87b).

בְּרִיחִם עֲצֵי שִׁטִּים:	Ex. 26.26	אֲנָשִׁים בְּנֵי בְלִיַּעַל:	Deut. 13.14
בְּרִיחֵי עֲצֵי שִׁטִּים:	Ex. 36.31	אַנְשֵׁי בְנֵי בְלִיַּעַל:	Judg. 19.22
אִשָּׁה יְפַת מַרְאֶה:	Gen. 12.11	אִשָּׁה קְשַׁת רוּחַ:	1 Sam. 1.15
אֵשֶׁת יְפַת תֹּאַר:	Deut. 21.11	אֵשֶׁת בַּעֲלַת אוֹב:	1 Sam. 28.7

but cf. § 84b.

§ 91. *Construct state with adjective or apposition* (cf. p. 268, § 45 β): The same grammatical attitude towards a construct state formation as described in the preceding three paragraphs is reflected in the gender and number of an adjective or apposition to a construct state. They agree either a) with the *regens*, or b) with the مضاف. With our statement in § 87 in mind, we shall now say that according to a) the construct state is regarded an entity, while according to b) the adjective or apposition follows the gender and number of the مضاف, to which they logically refer. Consequently, we shall exclude from our discussion instances of agreement in gender and number with the *regens*, to which the adjective or apposition logically belong since they are irrelevant.

1) פַּר אֶחָד בֶּן בָּקָר:	Num. 7.15	בְּנֵי אַהֲרֹן הַכֹּהֲנִים:	Lev. 1.5
פַּר בֶּן בָּקָר אֶחָד:	Num. 15.24	בְּנֵי אַהֲרֹן הַכֹּהֵן:	Lev. 1.7
יְשַׁעְיָהוּ הַנָּבִיא בֶן אָמוֹץ:	2 Ki. 19.2	בְּסֵפֶר הַתּוֹרָה הַזֶּה:	Deut. 29.20
יְשַׁעְיָהוּ בֶן אָמוֹץ הַנָּבִיא:	2 Ki. 20.1	בְּסֵפֶר הַתּוֹרָה הַזֹּאת:	Deut. 28.61
2) שַׂר חֲמִשִּׁים אַחֵר:	2 Ki. 1.11	סֵפֶר הַבְּרִית הַזֶּה:	2 Ki. 23.21
שַׂר חֲמִשִּׁים שְׁלִשִׁים:	2 Ki. 1.13	דִּבְרֵי הַבְּרִית הַזֹּאת:	2 Ki. 23.3
וְעֹלַת הַתָּמִיד וּמִנְחָתָהּ:	Num. 29.6	צֶלַע הַמִּשְׁכָּן הַשֵּׁנִית:	Ex. 26.27
עֹלַת הַתָּמִיד וּמִנְחָתוֹ:	Num. 28.31	צֶלַע הַמִּשְׁכָּן הָאֶחָד:	Ex. 26.26
אֵשֶׁת נָבָל הַכַּרְמְלִית:	1 Sam. 27.3	וּרְקִיק מַצָּה אֶחָד:	Num. 6.19
אֵשֶׁת נָבָל הַכַּרְמְלִי:	1 Sam. 30.5	וּלְשׁוֹן זָהָב אֶחָד:	Josh. 7.21

3) In the following three instances, the adjective reflects the gender and number of the *regens*, though logically it refers to the مضاف:

אַדְמַת הַכֹּהֲנִים לְבַדָּם:	Gen. 47.26	לֶחֶם הַפָּנִים הַמּוּסָרִים:	1 Sam. 21.7
קֶשֶׁת גִּבֹּרִים חַתִּים:	1 Sam. 2.4		

4) Similar cases of illogical adjustment:

Josh. 8.29: גַּל אֲבָנִים גָּדוֹל is not "a great heap of stones," but: a heap of great stones; for גָּדוֹל refers to אֲבָנִים; cf. ib. 10.27, where a similar event is narrated: אֲבָנִים גְּדֹלוֹת.

Isa. 29.13: מִצְוַת אֲנָשִׁים מְלֻמָּדָה; here מְלֻמָּדָה logically belongs to אֲנָשִׁים: the commandment of learned men. But in

Isa. 2.11: עֵינֵי גַּבְהוּת אָדָם שָׁפֵל; the verb refers to עֵינֵי (plur.): the lofty looks of man shall be brought down.

Deut. 21.6: (וְכָל זִקְנֵי הָעִיר הַהִוא) הַקְּרֹבִים: *which is nearest unto the slain man*

1 Sam. 4.6: קוֹל הַתְּרוּעָה הַגְּדוֹלָה הַזֹּאת: *this great noise of shouting*

Jer. 50.9: קְהַל גּוֹיִם גְּדֹלִים: *a great assembly of nations*

Job. 29.10: קוֹל נְגִידִים נֶחְבָּאוּ: "the voice of the nobles was hushed"

§ 92. The Number of a Noun with a Numeral (cf. p. 269, § 48).

a) The identical noun with the identical numeral.

1 Sam. 30.10:	מָאתַיִם אִישׁ	Lev. 27.4:	שְׁלֹשִׁים שָׁקֶל
1 Sam. 30.21:	מאתים הָאֲנָשִׁים	Ex. 21.32:	שלשים שְׁקָלִים
Ezek. 40.23:	מֵאָה אַמָּה	Ex. 26.18:	עֶשְׂרִים קֶרֶשׁ
Ezek. 40.27:	מאה אמֹת	Ex. 36.23:	עשרים קְרָשִׁים
Josh. 13.30:	שִׁשִּׁים עִיר	Ex. 26.19:	עֶשְׂרִים הַקֶּרֶשׁ
1 Ki. 4.13:	ששים עָרִים	Ex. 36.24:	עשרים הַקְּרָשִׁים
2 Ki. 2.17:	חֲמִשִּׁים אִישׁ	1 Sam. 14.14:	כְּעֶשְׂרִים אִישׁ
2 Ki. 2.16:	חמשים אֲנָשִׁים	2 Sam. 3.20:	עשרים אֲנָשִׁים
Ezek. 42.7:	חֲמִשִּׁים אַמָּה	2 Sam. 5.5:	שְׁלֹשִׁים וְשָׁלֹשׁ שָׁנָה
Ezek. 42.2:	חמשים אמֹת	1 Ki. 2.11:	שלשים ושלש שָׁנִים
Lev. 27.3:	חֲמִשִּׁים שָׁקֶל	Ex. 39.14:	לִשְׁנֵים עָשָׂר שָׁבֶט
Josh. 7.21:	חמשים שְׁקָלִים	Ex. 24.4:	לשנים עשר שְׁבָטֵי
Judg. 14.19:	שְׁלֹשִׁים אִישׁ	Ezek. 40.25:	חָמֵשׁ וְעֶשְׂרִים אַמָּה
Jer. 38.10:	שלשים אֲנָשִׁים	Ezek. 40.29:	עֶשְׂרִים וְחָמֵשׁ אַמּוֹת
		cf. ib. 8.16:	כְּעֶשְׂרִים וַחֲמִשָּׁה אִישׁ
Num. 1.44:	שְׁנֵים עָשָׂר אִישׁ	2 Ki. 22.1:	שְׁמֹנֶה שָׁנָה
Deut. 1.23:	שְׁנֵים עָשָׂר אֲנָשִׁים	Judg. 3.8:	שמנה שָׁנִים

b)   Different nouns with the identical numeral.

Ezek. 40.14:	שְׁשִׁים אַמָּה	1 Ki. 9.11:	עֶשְׂרִים עִיר
Cant. 3.7:	ששים גִּבֹּרִים	2 Sam. 9.10:	ועשרים עֲבָדִים
Judg. 9.2:	שִׁבְעִים אִישׁ		
Judg. 1.7:	שבעים מְלָכִים;	2 Ki. 10.14:	אַרְבָּעִים וּשְׁנַיִם אִישׁ
cf. 1 Ki. 20.1:	וּשְׁלֹשִׁים וּשְׁנַיִם מֶלֶךְ	2 Ki. 2.24:	ארבעים וּשְׁנֵי יְלָדִים

cf. § 83 4) where, no matter whether שְׁנַיִם or שְׁנֵי is used, the noun is in the plural.

Lev. 27.7:	חֲמִשָּׁה עָשָׂר שָׁקֶל	Ex. 24.4:	וּשְׁתֵּים עֶשְׂרֵה מַצֵּבָה
2 Sam. 9.10:	חמשה עשר בָּנִים	Josh. 4.3:	שתים עשרה אֲבָנִים

In conclusion, a noun may be either put in the plural, or even used in its singular form as a *nomen collectivum*, irrespective of the numeral (whether above or below 10 or 20), with which it is syntactically connected.

D.   Prepositions and Particles—Their Application and Vocalization

A.   the preposition ה

(Indicating the determinate state or a question)

§ 93.   Questions may, but not necessarily need be introduced by ה *interrogativum*.

Gen. 27.24:	אַתָּה זֶה בְּנִי עֵשָׂו	2 Sam. 18.29:	שָׁלוֹם לַנַּעַר לְאַבְשָׁלוֹם
Gen. 27.21:	הַאַתָּה זֶה בְּנִי עֵשָׂו	2 Sam. 18.32:	הֲשָׁלוֹם לַנַּעַר לְאַבְשָׁלוֹם
1 Sam. 16.4:	שָׁלֹם בֹּאֶךָ	Ezek. 17.9:	תִּצְלָח
1 Ki. 2.13:	הֲשָׁלוֹם בֹּאֶךָ	Ezek. 17.10:	הֲתִצְלָח

§ 94.   Questions syntactically resemble assertions; it is the context that matters.

1 Sam. 11.12: שָׁאוּל יִמְלֹךְ עָלֵינוּ: "shall Saul reign over us?"

1 Sam. 14.30: כִּי עַתָּה לֹא רָבְתָה מַכָּה בַּפְּלִשְׁתִּים: "had there not been then a much greater slaughter among the Philistines?"

1 Sam. 14.43: הִנְנִי אָמוּת: shall I now die?

1 Sam. 21.16: חֲסַר מְשֻׁגָּעִים אָנִי: "do I lack madmen?"

1 Sam. 22.15: הַיּוֹם הַחִלֹּתִי לִשְׁאָל לוֹ בֵּאלֹהִים: "have I to-day begun to inquire of God for him?"

1 Sam. 30.8: אֶרְדֹּף אַחֲרֵי הַגְּדוּד הַזֶּה: "shall I pursue after this troop?"

2 Sam. 19.23: הַיּוֹם יוּמַת אִישׁ בְּיִשְׂרָאֵל: "shall there any man be put to death this day in Israel?"

1 Ki. 1.24: ··· אַתָּה אָמַרְתָּ "hast thou said .... ?"

1 Ki. 21.7: אַתָּה עַתָּה תַּעֲשֶׂה מְלוּכָה: "dost thou now govern?"

Isa. 1.18: כַּשֶּׁלֶג יַלְבִּינוּ ··· כַּצֶּמֶר יִהְיוּ: shall they be as white as snow ... shall they be as wool?

Jer. 2.18: לִשְׁתּוֹת מֵי שִׁחוֹר ··· לִשְׁתּוֹת מֵי נָהָר: "to drink the waters of Shihor ... to drink the waters of the River?"

Ezek.15.5: וְנַעֲשָׂה עוֹד לִמְלָאכָה: "shall it yet be meet for any work?" cf. v. 4: הֲיִצְלַח לִמְלָאכָה

Ezek. 17.15: וְנִמְלָט: "chall he ... yet escape?" cf. preceding: הֲיִמָּלֵט

Ezek. 20.31: וַאֲנִי אִדָּרֵשׁ לָכֶם: "shall I then be inquired of by you?"

Hos. 4.14: לֹא אֶפְקֹד ···: shall I not punish .... ?

Hos. 4.16: עַתָּה יִרְעֵם יהוה כְּכֶבֶשׂ בַּמֶּרְחָב: "now shall the Lord feed them as a lamb in a large place?"

Hos. 7.13: וְאָנֹכִי אֶפְדֵּם: "shall I then redeem them?"

Jonah 4.11: וַאֲנִי לֹא אָחוּס עַל נִינְוֵה: "and shall I not have pity on Nineveh?"

Ps. 74.1: לָנֶצַח יֶעְשַׁן אַפְּךָ בְּצֹאן מַרְעִיתֶךָ: "doth Thine anger smoke for ever against the flock of Thy pasture?"

Cant. 3.3: אֵת שֶׁאָהֲבָה נַפְשִׁי רְאִיתֶם: "saw ye him whom my soul loveth?"

95. ה *interrogativum* and ה of the article are both equally vocalized (under 1-6, instances of ה *interrogativum* are listed first):

1) Num. 11.12: הֶאָנֹכִי
   2 Sam. 19.43: הֶאָכוֹל
   Ezek. 28.9: הֶאָמֹר; cf. Mic. 2.7: הֶאָמוּר, article
   Ps. 77.9: הֶאָפֵס
   Job 34.31: הֶאָמַר
2) Gen. 19.9: הָאֶחָד: does one come merely to sojourn, and plays the judge? (cf. Jacob ben Chayim's Masoretic note on Gen. 30.2 s.v. התחת)
   Gen. 42.16: הָאֱמֶת; cf. 32.11: הָאֲמֶת, article
   Num. 16.22: הָאִישׁ; cf. v. 7: הָאִישׁ, article
   Deut. 20.19: הָאָדָם; cf. 8.3: דָאָדָם, article

Judg. 6.31:   הָאַתֶּם

Judg. 12.5:   הָאֶפְרָתִי

3)   Gen. 24.5:   הֶהָשֵׁב; cf. Josh. 10.24: הֶהָלְכוּא, article

Jer. 26.19:   הֲהָמֵת; cf. 1 Ki. 20.13: הֶהָמוֹן, article

Joel 1.2:   הֶהָיְתָה; cf. 1 Ki. 18.30: הֶהָרוּס, article

4)   Num. 13.18:   הֶחָזָק; cf. Josh. 11.17: הֶחָלָק, article

Judg. 9.9:   הֶחֳדַלְתִּי

Ezek. 18.23:   הֶחָפֹץ; cf. 1 Ki. 13.33: הֶחָפֵץ, article

Eccl. 2.19:   הֶחָכָם; cf. v. 16: הֶחָכָם, article

Job 13.25:   הֶעָלֶה; cf. Jer. 8.13: וְהֶעָלֶה, article

Eccl. 3.21:   הָעֹלָה; cf. Judg. 21.19: הָעֹלָה, article

Job 26.5:   הָרְפָאִים; cf. Gen. 15.20: הָרְפָאִים, article

5)   Gen. 30.15:   הַמְעַט; cf. Num. 35.8: הַמְעַט, article

Gen. 18.17:   הַמְכַסֶּה; cf. Lev. 3.3: הַמְכַסֶּה, article

1 Sam. 15.22:   הַחֵפֶץ; cf. Eccl. 5.7: הַחֵפֶץ, article

Num. 23.19:   הַהוּא; cf. 14.1: הַהוּא, article

2 Sam. 10.3:   הַמְכַבֵּד; cf. 14.10: הַמְדַבֵּר, article

Gen. 24.21:   הַהִצְלִיחַ; cf. 1 Chron. 26.28: הַהִקְדִּישׁ, article

6)   Ezek. 20.30   הַבַּדֶּרֶךְ

Num. 13.19:   הַבְּמַחֲנִים

Job. 23.6:   הַבְּרָב (כֹּחַ); cf. 22.13: הַבְעַד

Isa. 27.7:   הַכְּמַכַּת

2 Sam. 3.33:   הַכְּמוֹת

Gen. 17.17:   הַלְּבֶן; cf. Ex. 2.14: הַלְהָרְגֵנִי

Joel 4.4:   הַגְּמוּל

2 Ki. 8.13:   הַכֶּלֶב; cf. 1 Sam. 17.43: הֲכֶלֶב (interrogat.); 2 Sam.
                      16.9: הַכֶּלֶב (article)

Gen. 37.32:   הַכְּתֹנֶת; cf. Ex. 28.39: הַכְּתֹנֶת (article)

Jer. 23.36:   הַמַּשָּׂא; cf. Isa. 22.25: הַמַּשָּׂא (article)

Jer. 48.27:   הַשְּׂחֹק

2 Ki. 9.22:   הַשָּׁלוֹם (2°); cf. ib. הֲשָׁלוֹם (interrogat.); Jer. 25.37:
                      הַשָּׁלוֹם (article)

Am. 5.25:   הַזְּבָחִים; cf. 2 Sam. 15.12: הַזְּבָחִים (article)

Ezek. 13.18:   הַנְּפָשׁוֹת; cf. ib. v. 20: הַנְּפָשׁוֹת (article)

Ezek. 18.29:   הַדְּרָכִי; cf. v. 25: הֲדַרְכַי

Gen. 18.21:   הַכְּצַעֲקָתָה; cf. 34.31: הַכְזוֹנָה

Num. 13.20:   הַשְּׁמֵנָה; cf. Ezek. 34.16: הַשְּׁמֵנָה (article)

Eccl. 3.21:   הַיֹּרֶדֶת

Lev. 10.19:   הַיִּיטַב

2 Ki. 6.32:   הֲרְאִיתֶם

7)   2 Sam. 5.6:   הַעִוְרִים   Isa. 42.18:   וְהַעִוְרִים

Zeph. 1.17:   כַּעִוְרִים   Isa. 65.11:   הַעֹרְכִים

Zech. 12.4:   בַּעִוָּרוֹן   Ezek. 22.7:   בַּעֹשֶׁק

Prov. 2.13:   הַעֹזְבִים   Prov. 24.5:   בַּעֹז

Prov. 2.17:   הַעֹזֶבֶת   Prov. 22.26:   בַּעֹרְבִים

Isa. 51.23:   לַעֹבְרִים

§ 96.   Verbal forms with the preposition ה; only their context proves the function of the preposition, whether it is determinating or questioning. These examples here are all of them determinating, regardless of their vocalization.

Josh. 10.24   הֶחָלְכוּא   1 Chron. 29.17:   הַנִּמְצְאוּ

Ezra. 10.14   הַהֹשִׁיב   2 Chron. 29.36:   הַהֵכִין

Ezra. 10.17   הַהֹשִׁיבוּ   1 Ki. 16.31:   (וַיְהִי) הֲנָקֵל

Ezra. 8.25   הַהֵרִימוּ   Ps. 94.9:   הֲנֹטַע (אֹזֶן)

1 Chron. 26.28:   הַהִקְדִּישׁ   Ps. 94.10:   הֲיֹסֵר (גּוֹיִם)

§ 97.   There was no difference in the pronunciation of the preposition ה, whether in the function of an article, or in that of an interrogative particle. The context excluded the possibility of confusion. It is solely due to Masoretic schematization that the tendency became prevalent to differentiate between the two functions of the preposition by way of vocalization (cf. B-L § 31 and § 80g-j).

§ 98.   The treatment of the letter ר: In connection with ה interrog., the ר is treated like any other consonant; cf. Num. 12.2: הֲרַק; ib. 13.18: הֲרָפֶה; Judg. 11.25: הֲרוֹב; 1 Ki. 21.29: הֲרָאִיתָ; similarly cf. Gen. 39.15: הֲרִימֹתִי (as compared with Deut. 4.26: הַעִידֹתִי and 1 Sam. 15.13: הֲקִימֹתִי).

B.   THE PREPOSITIONS ל, כ, ב

§ 99.   Promiscuously vocalized with שוא and פתח.

a.   Nouns.

1)   Isa. 14.6:   בְּעֶבְרָה ··· בְּאַף: "in wrath ... in anger"

Isa. 16.5:   בַּחֶסֶד ··· בֶּאֱמֶת: "through mercy ... in truth"

Isa. 33.15:   בְּרָע · · · · בְּשֹׁחַד : "of bribes . . . upon evil"

Hab. 3.8:   בַּנְּהָרִים · · · · הֲבִנְהָרִים : "against the rivers . . . against the rivers"

Ps. 6.6:   בִּשְׁאוֹל · · · · בַּמָּוֶת : "in death . . . in the nether-world"

Ps. 31.11:   בַּאֲנָחָה · · · · בְּיָגוֹן : "in sorrow . . . in sighing"

2)   Isa. 38.14:   כַּיּוֹנָה · · · · כְּסוּס : "like a swallow . . . as a dove"

Isa. 41.2:   כְּקַשׁ · · · · כֶּעָפָר : "as the dust . . . as the stubble"

Isa. 53.7:   וּכְרָחֵל · · · · כַּשֶּׂה : "as a lamb . . . and as a sheep"

Isa. 61.11:   וּכְגַנָּה · · · · כָאָרֶץ : "as the earth . . . and as the garden"

Isa. 62.1:   כְּלַפִּיד · · · · כַנֹּגַהּ : "as brightness . . . as a torch"

Jer. 23.29:   וּכְפַטִּישׁ · · · · כָאֵשׁ : "like as fire . . . and like a hammer"

Jer. 50.11:   כָּאַבִּרִים · · · · כְּעֶגְלָה : "as a heifer . . . as strong horses"

Hos. 2.5:   כְּאֶרֶץ · · · · כַמִּדְבָּר : "as a wilderness . . . like a land"

Hos. 6.3:   כְּמַלְקוֹשׁ · · · · כְּגֶשֶׁם : "as the rain, as the latter rain"

Mic. 1.4:   כְּמַיִם · · · · כַּדּוֹנַג : "as wax . . . as waters"

Ps. 89.37, 38:   כְּיָרֵחַ · · · · כַשֶּׁמֶשׁ : "as the sun . . . as the moon"

Ps. 102.12:   כָּעֵשֶׂב · · · · כְּצֵל : "like a shadow . . . like grass"

Job 14.2:   כַּצֵּל · · · · כְּצִיץ : "like a flower . . . as a shadow"

Cant. 8.6:   כִשְׁאוֹל · · · · כַמָּוֶת : "as death . . . as the grave"

3)   Gen. 11.3:   לַחֹמֶר · · · · לְאָבֶן : "for stone . . . for mortar"

2 Sam. 12.2, 3:   וְלָרָשׁ · · · · לְעָשִׁיר : "the rich man . . . but the poor man"

Isa. 25.2:   לְמַפֵּלָה · · · · לַגָּל : "a heap . . . a ruin"

Isa. 42.16:   לְמִישׁוֹר · · · · לָאוֹר : "light . . . plain"

Isa. 43.6:   וּלְתֵימָן · · · · לַצָּפוֹן : "to the north . . . and to the south"

Isa. 59.9:   לִנְגֹהוֹת · · · · לָאוֹר : "for light . . . for brightness"

Isa. 59.11:   לִישׁוּעָה · · · · לַמִּשְׁפָּט : "for right . . . for salvation"

Isa. 60.22:   לְגוֹי · · · · לָאֶלֶף : "a thousand . . . a nation"

Jer. 10.23:   לְאִישׁ · · · · לָאָדָם : "man's (way) . . . in man"

Jer. 49.32:   לְשָׁלָל · · · · לָבַז : "a booty . . . a spoil"

Hab. 2.19:   לְאֶבֶן · · · · לָעֵץ : "to the wood . . . to the stone"

4)   Isa. 40.23:   כַּתֹּהוּ · · · · לְאָיִן : "to nothing . . . as a thing of nought"

Isa. 42.17:   לְמַסֵּכָה · · · · בַּפָּסֶל : "in graven images . . . unto molten images"

b.   Pronouns.

Gen. 42.15:   בָּזֹאת (תִּבָּחֵנוּ)

Mal. 3.10:   (וּבְחָנוּנִי נָא) בָּזֹאת

Jer. 9.23:   (כִּי) בְּאֵלֶּה (חָפַצְתִּי)

1 Sam. 16.10:   (לֹא בָחַר יהוה) בָּאֵלֶּה

Gen. 45.23:   (וּלְאָבִיו שָׁלַח) כָּזֹאת

Judg. 8.8:   (וַיְדַבֵּר אֲלֵיהֶם) כָּזֹאת

Job. 16.2:   (שָׁמַעְתִּי) כְאֵלֶּה (רַבּוֹת)

Jer. 18.13:   (מִי שָׁמַע) כָּאֵלֶּה

Gen. 2.23:   לְזֹאת (יִקָּרֵא אִשָּׁה)

Isa. 30.7:   (לָכֵן קָרָאתִי) לָזֹאת

1 Chron. 26.12:   לְאֵלֶּה (מַחְלְקוֹת הַשֹּׁעֲרִים)

Num. 26.53:   לָאֵלֶּה (תֵּחָלֵק הָאָרֶץ)

§ 100.   The vocalization with שׁוא has a determinate meaning.

Gen. 38.25:   לָאִישׁ: "by the man"

Gen. 40.4:   בְּמִשְׁמָר: "in ward"; cf. Num. 15.34: בַּמִּשְׁמָר "in ward"

2 Sam. 3.20:   וְלָאֲנָשִׁים: "and the men"

1 Ki. 12.32:   לָעֲגָלִים: "unto the calves"

2 Ki. 4.40:   לָאֲנָשִׁים: "for the men"

§ 101.   Vocalization with פתח with a noun plus suffix.

Isa. 24.2:   כַּגְּבִרְתָּהּ

Prov. 16.4:   לַמַּעֲנֵהוּ

Ezek. 43.7:   בְּמוֹתָם; cf. Lev. 11.32: בְּמֹתָם

Ezra 10.17:   בְּכֹל אֲנָשִׁים

§ 102.   Vocalization with פתח has indeterminate meaning:

1)   Gen. 13.2:   בַּמִּקְנֶה בַּכֶּסֶף וּבַזָּהָב: "in cattle, in silver, and in gold"

Gen. 15.1:   בַּמַּחֲזֶה: "in a vision"

Gen. 19.11:   בַּסַּנְוֵרִים: "with blindness"

Gen. 19.30:   בַּמְּעָרָה: "in a cave"

Ex. 2.3:   בַּחֵמָר וּבַזָּפֶת: "with slime and with pitch"

Lev. 26.26:   בַּמִּשְׁקָל: "by weight"

Deut. 27.2:   בַּשִּׂיד: "with plaster"

1 Sam. 17.43:   בַּמַּקְלוֹת; (cf. v. 45: בְּחֶרֶב) "with staves"

2 Sam. 11.11: בַּסֻּכּוֹת: "in booths"

1 Ki. 1.1: בַּבְּגָדִים: "with clothes"

2 Ki. 10.7: בַּדּוּדִים: "in baskets"

2 Ki. 19.2: בַּשַּׂקִּים: "with sackcloth"

Isa. 15.3: בְּבֶכִי ("weeping profusely")

Isa. 18.5: בַּמַּזְמֵרוֹת: "with pruning-hooks"

Isa. 24.9: בַּשִּׁיר "with a song"

Isa. 43.24: בְכֶסֶף: "with money"

Isa. 45.16: בִּכְלִמָּה: "in confusion"

Isa. 54.11: בַּפּוּךְ · · · בַּסַּפִּירִים: "in fair colours . . . with sapphires"

Zeph. 1.12: בַּנֵּרוֹת: "with lamps"

Ex. 3.2: בָּאֵשׁ: "with fire"

Num. 10.13: בָּרִאשֹׁנָה: "(their) first (journey)"

2 Sam. 16.6: בָּאֲבָנִים: "stones"

2 Sam. 16.13: בֶּעָפָר: "dust"

2) Ex. 15.10: כַּעוֹפֶרֶת: "as lead"

1 Ki. 22.17: כַּצֹּאן: "as sheep"

2 Ki. 3.22: כַּדָּם: "as blood"

Isa. 13.8: כַּיּוֹלֵדָה: "as a woman in travail"

Isa. 14.17: כַּמִּדְבָּר: "as a wilderness"

Isa. 16.11: כַּכִּנּוֹר: "like a harp"

Isa. 19.16: כַּנָּשִׁים: "like unto women"

Isa. 51.6: כַּבֶּגֶד: "like a garment"

Isa. 51.6: כְּעָשָׁן: "like smoke"

Isa. 16.2: כָּעוֹף: "as birds"

3) Gen. 41.55: לַלֶּחֶם: "for bread"

Ex. 17.3: לַמַּיִם: "for water"

Num. 14.34: לַשָּׁנָה: "for . . . a year"

Josh. 18.4: לַשֵּׁבֶט: "for each tribe"

Isa. 49.11: לַדֶּרֶךְ: "a way"

Isa. 65.23: לַבֶּהָלָה: "for terror"

Am. 2.1: לַשִּׂיד: "into lime"

4) Gen. 1.6: (וַיְהִי) לְמָיִם); but Josh. 7.5: (בֵּין מַיִם) לְמָיִם

Ex. 32.27: (מִשַּׁעַר הֶחָצֵר) לְשַׁעַר; but ib. 38.15: (מִשַּׁעַר) לְשַׁעַר

2 Ki. 10.21: (פֶּה) לָפֶּה; but Ex. 4.16: לְפֶה (יִהְיֶה לְךָ)

Isa. 28.13: (קַו) לָקָו; but ib. v. 17: לְקָו (וְשַׂמְתִּי מִשְׁפָּט)

Isa. 34.10: (מִדּוֹר) לָדוֹר; but ib. v. 17: לְדוֹר (וָדוֹר)

Ezek. 34.17: (בֵּין שֶׂה) לָשֶׂה

Prov. 11.21: (יָד) לְיָד

Deut. 17.8: (בֵּין דָּם) לְדָם

Deut. 17.8: (בֵּין דִּין) לְדִין

Ex. 16.3: (בְּאָכְלֵנוּ לֶחֶם) לָשׂבַע; but Prov. 13.25: (צַדִּיק אֹכֵל) לְשׂבַע

Ex. 24.10: (וּכְעֶצֶם הַשָּׁמַיִם) לָטֹהַר

Lev. 25.19: (וִישַׁבְתֶּם) לָבֶטַח

Num. 9.10: (לֹא יִטְמָא) לְנֶפֶשׁ; but Lev. 21.1: (טָמֵא) לְנֶפֶשׁ

Num. 14.3: (לָבַז יִהְיֶה); but 2 Ki. 21.14: (וְהָיוּ) לְבַז

Deut. 20.11: (וַיַּעַלֵם שְׁלֹמֹה) לָמַס; but 2 Chron. 8.8: (יִהְיוּ לְךָ) לָמַס

Deut. 14.1: (קָרְחָה בֵּין עֵינֵיכֶם) לָמֵת; but ib. 26.14: (וְלֹא נָתַתִּי מִמֶּנּוּ) לְמֵת

Isa. 1.14: (הָיוּ עָלַי) לָטֹרַח

Isa. 25.8: (בִּלַּע הַמָּוֶת) לָנֶצַח

Num. 2.31: (יִסָּעוּ) לָאַחֲרֹנָה

Gen. 28.19: (שֵׁם הָעִיר) לָרִאשֹׁנָה

Isa. 65.23: (לֹא יִגְעוּ) לָרִיק; but ib. 49.4: (יָגַעְתִּי) לְרִיק

Deut. 1.10: (כְּכוֹכְבֵי הַשָּׁמַיִם) לָרֹב

Gen. 41.19: (בְּכָל אֶרֶץ מִצְרַיִם) לָרֹעַ

Isa. 30.8: (עַד עוֹלָם) לָעַד

Gen. 45.22: (נָתַן) לָאִישׁ; but ib. 34.14: (לָתֵת אֶת אֲחֹתֵנוּ) לְאִישׁ

Isa. 42.15: (וְשַׂמְתִּי נְהָרוֹת) לָאִיִּים; but Dan. 11.18: (וַיָּשֵׂם פָּנָיו) לְאִיִּים

§ 103. The prepositions ב, כ, ל can thus be vocalized either with *a* (ָ or ַ), or with *sheva*. The explanation of the current Hebrew grammars (cf. B-L § 25w) that the vocalization with *a* implies the article is untenable in the light of the actual facts; cf. also p. 218 sub e and p. 224 sub B 5 and 11; cf. further the transliteration of these prepositions in connection with verbal forms, where there can be no thought of an article: p. 184 f., §§ 25, 40g, 64b.

C. VARIOUS OTHER PREPOSITIONS

§ 104. The preposition ב indicates the direction

Gen. 31.33: וַיָּבֹא בְּאֹהֶל · · · בְּאֹהֶל · · · וַיָּבֹא : "and ... went *into* ... and entered *into* ..."

Gen. 37.20:   וַיַּשְׁלִכוּ אֹתוֹ בְּאַחַד הַבֹּרוֹת: "and cast him *into* one of the pits";
cf. v. 22: הַשְׁלִיכוּ · · · אֶל הַבּוֹר

Gen. 40.13:   וְנָתַתָּ כוֹס פַּרְעֹה בְּיָדוֹ: "and thou shalt give Pharao's cup *into* his hand"

Ex. 7.28:   וּבָאוּ בְּבֵיתֶךָ: "and come *into* thy house"

Lev. 16.22:   וְשִׁלַּח אֶת הַשָּׂעִיר בַּמִּדְבָּר: and he shall send the goat away *into* the wilderness (cf. v. 21: וְשִׁלַּח · · · הַמִּדְבָּרָה)

Lev. 26.41:   וְהֵבֵאתִי אֹתָם בְּאֶרֶץ: "and (I will) bring them *into* the land"

Num. 22.23:   וַתֵּלֶךְ בַּשָּׂדֶה: "and went *into* the field"

Judg. 7.9:   וְיָרַדְתָּ בַּמַּחֲנֶה; cf. v. 10: רֵד · · · אֶל הַמַּחֲנֶה and v. 11: רֵד בַּמַּחֲנֶה

Judg. 7.19:   וַיָּבֹא · · · בִּקְצֵה: "and came *unto* the outermost part"

1 Sam. 1.7:   עֲלֹתָהּ בְּבֵית יהוה: "when she went up *to* the house of the Lord"

1 Sam. 9.5:   בָּאוּ בְּאֶרֶץ: "they were come *to* the land"

1 Sam. 9.14:   בָּאִים בְּתוֹךְ הָעִיר: "they came *within* the city"

1 Sam. 14.25:   וַיָּבֹא · · · אֶל הַיַּעַר: "came *into* the forest"; cf. v. 26: בָּאוּ בַיַּעַר

2 Ki. 2.16:   וַיַּשְׁלִכֵהוּ בְּאַחַד הֶהָרִים אוֹ בְּאַחַת · · ·: "and cast him *upon* some mountain or *into* some . . ."

2 Ki. 6.23:   לָבוֹא בְּאֶרֶץ: "came . . . *into* the land"

Am. 9.2:   אִם יַחְתְּרוּ בִשְׁאוֹל: "though they dig *into* the netherworld"

Zech. 9.4:   וְהִכָּה בַיָּם חֵילָהּ: "and He will smite her power *into* the sea"

Ps. 61.3:   בְּצוּר · · · תַּנְחֵנִי: "lead me *to* a rock"

Ps. 63.10:   יָבֹאוּ בְּתַחְתִּיּוֹת: "shall go *into* the nethermost parts"

Ex. 9.14:   שֹׁלֵחַ · · · אֶל לִבְּךָ וּבַעֲבָדֶיךָ

Ex. 15.26:   שַׂמְתִּי בְמִצְרַיִם לֹא אָשִׂים עָלֶיךָ

1 Ki. 2.44:   וְהֵשִׁיב · · · בְּרֹאשֶׁךָ

1 Ki. 2.32:   וְהֵשִׁיב · · · עַל רֹאשׁוֹ

§ 105.   The ה euphonicum (cf. p. 277, § 60 ff.).

a)   בְּאָבֵלָה: 2 Sam. 20.15 (cf. ib. v. 18: בְּאָבֵל: "in Abel"

בְּאֶפְרָתָה: Ps. 132.6: "in Ephrath"

בְּיָבֵשָׁה: 1 Sam. 31.13 (cf. 1 Chron. 10.12: בְּיָבֵשׁ): "in Jabesh"

בְּיַהְצָה: Judg. 11.20 (cf. Isa. 15.4: יַהַץ): "in Jahaz"

בְּרִבְלָתָה: Jer. 52.10 (cf. 2 Ki. 25.21: בְּרִבְלָה): "in Riblah"

בְּתִמְנָתָה: Judg. 14.1: "to Timnah"

לִדְבִרָה: Josh. 10.39 (cf. ib. 13.26: לִדְבִר): "to Debir"

מִבָּבֶלָה: Jer. 27.16 (cf. ib. 28.6: מִבָּבֶל): "from Babylon"

מִיָּנוֹחָה: Josh. 16.7 (cf. 2 Ki. 15.29: יָנוֹחַ): "from Janoah"

מֵעֶגְלוֹנָה: Josh. 10.36 (cf. ib. v. 3: עֶגְלוֹן): "from Eglon"

הַגָּלִילָה: 2 Ki. 15.29 (cf. 1 Ki. 9.11: הַגָּלִיל): "Galilee'

(עַד) אֲפֵקָה: Josh. 13.4 (cf. ib. 12.18: אֲפֵק): "unto Aphek"

וְיַהְצָה: Josh. 13.18 (cf. Isa. 15.4: יַהַץ): "and Jahaz"

וְתִמְנָתָה: Josh. 19.43 (cf. ib. 15.10; תִּמְנָה): "and Timnah"

b)　בַּנֶּגְבָּה: Josh. 15.21 (cf. Num. 13.17: בַּנֶּגֶב)

לַיָּמָּה: Josh. 19.11 (cf. Deut. 30.13: לַיָּם)

לִפְנִימָה: Ezek. 40.16

לִשְׁאוֹלָה: Ps. 9.18 (cf. ib. 16.10: לִשְׁאוֹל)

מִבַּיְתָה: 1 Ki. 6.15 (cf. ib.: מִבַּיִת)

מִפְּנִימָה: 1 Ki. 6.21

מִצָּפוֹנָה: Josh. 15.10 (cf. ib. 16.6: מִצָּפוֹן)

הַיָּמָּה: Josh. 15.12 (cf. ib. 17.10: הַיָּם)

הַצָּפוֹנָה: Ezek. 8.14 (cf. 1.4: הַצָּפוֹן)

הַקָּדִימָה: Ezek. 40.6 (cf. ib. v. 10: הַקָּדִים)

(מֵאֶרֶץ צָפֹנָה): Jer. 23.8 (cf. ib. 3.18: מֵאֶרֶץ צָפוֹן))

c)　וָאֶתְּנָה: Judg. 6.9

וָאֹמְרָה: Judg. 6.10

וָאוֹשִׁיעָה: Judg. 10.12

וָאֶקְרָאֶה: 1 Sam. 28.15

§ 106.　The Particles אל and על:

Num. 4.19:　　וְשָׂמוּ · · · עַל עֲבֹדָתוֹ וְאֶל מַשָּׂאוֹ

Judg. 6.39:　　וַיְהִי נָא חֹרֶב אֶל הַגִּזָּה · · · וְעַל כָּל הָאָרֶץ; cf. v. 40: וַיְהִי חֹרֶב אֶל

· · · הַגִּזָּה · · · וְעַל כֹּל · · ·

1 Sam. 20.25:　וַיֵּשֶׁב · · · עַל מוֹשָׁבוֹ · · · אֶל מוֹשַׁב · · ·

1 Sam. 25.17:　כָּלְתָה הָרָעָה אֶל אֲדֹנֵינוּ וְעַל כָּל בֵּיתוֹ

1 Sam. 25.25:　אַל נָא יָשִׂים · · · אֶת לִבּוֹ אֶל אִישׁ · · · עַל נָבָל

1 Sam. 27.10:　פְּשַׁטְתֶּם · · · עַל נֶגֶב · · · וְעַל נֶגֶב · · · וְאֶל נֶגֶב

2 Sam. 2.9:　　וַיַּמְלִכֵהוּ אֶל הַגִּלְעָד · · · וְאֶל · · · וְאֶל · · · וְעַל · · · וְעַל · · · וְעַל

2 Sam. 3.29:　　יָחֻלוּ עַל רֹאשׁ · · · וְאֶל כָּל בֵּית

2 Sam. 6.10:　　לְהָסִיר אֵלָיו · · · עַל עִיר דָּוִד

2 Sam. 24.4:　(וַיֶּחֱזַק דְּבַר הַמֶּלֶךְ) אֶל יוֹאָב וְעַל שָׂרֵי הֶחָיִל

1 Ki. 6.8:　　יַעֲלוּ עַל הַתִּיכֹנָה וּמִן · · · אֶל

2 Ki. 18.27:　　הַעַל אֲדֹנֶיךָ וְאֵלֶיךָ שְׁלָחַנִי

2 Ki. 22.16:	הִנְנִי מֵבִיא רָעָה אֶל הַמָּקוֹם הַזֶּה וְעַל יֹשְׁבָיו
Isa. 22.15:	בֹּא אֶל הַסֹּכֵן הַזֶּה עַל שֶׁבְנָא
Isa. 36.10:	עָלִיתִי עַל הָאָרֶץ הַזֹּאת · · · עֲלֵה אֶל הָאָרֶץ הזאת
Isa. 36.12:	הַאֶל אֲדֹנֶיךָ וְאֵלֶיךָ שְׁלָחַנִי · · · הֲלֹא עַל הָאֲנָשִׁים
Jer. 7.20:	נִתֶּכֶת אֶל הַמָּקוֹם הַזֶּה עַל הָאָדָם וְעַל · · ·
Jer. 11.2:	וְדִבַּרְתֶּם אֶל אִישׁ · · · וְעַל יֹשְׁבֵי · · ·
Jer. 18.11:	אֱמָר נָא אֶל אִישׁ · · · וְעַל יוֹשְׁבֵי · · ·
Jer. 19.15:	הִנְנִי מֵבִיא אֶל הָעִיר הַזֹּאת וְעַל כָּל עָרֶיהָ
Jer. 23.35:	תֹאמְרוּ אִישׁ עַל רֵעֵהוּ וְאִישׁ אֶל אָחִיו
Jer. 25.2:	דִּבֶּר · · · עַל כָּל · · · וְאֶל כָּל · · ·
Jer. 26.15:	אַתֶּם נֹתְנִים עֲלֵיכֶם וְאֶל הָעִיר הַזֹּאת
Jer. 27.19:	כֹּה אָמַר · · · אֶל הָעַמֻּדִים וְעַל הַיָּם
Jer. 28.8:	וַיִּנָּבְאוּ אֶל אֲרָצוֹת · · · וְעַל מַמְלָכוֹת
Jer. 31.11:	וְנָהֲרוּ אֶל טוּב יהוה עַל דָּגָן וְעַל · · ·
Jer. 33.14:	אֲשֶׁר דִּבַּרְתִּי אֶל בֵּית · · · וְעַל בֵּית
Jer. 34.7:	נִלְחָמִים עַל יְרוּשָׁלַם וְעַל · · · אֶל לָכִישׁ וְאֶל · · ·
Jer. 36.31:	וְהֵבֵאתִי עֲלֵיהֶם וְעַל יֹשְׁבֵי · · · וְאֶל אִישׁ
Jer. 44.20:	וַיֹּאמֶר · · · אֶל כָּל הָעָם עַל הַגְּבָרִים וְעַל · · ·
Jer. 46.25:	הִנְנִי פוֹקֵד אֶל אָמוֹן · · · וְעַל פַּרְעֹה
Jer. 50.35:	חֶרֶב עַל כַּשְׂדִּים · · · וְאֶל יֹשְׁבֵי בָבֶל
Jer. 51.1:	הִנְנִי מֵעִיר עַל בָּבֶל וְאֶל יֹשְׁבֵי · · ·
Ezek. 21.12:	עַל מָה אַתָּה נֶאֱנָח וְאָמַרְתָּ אֶל שְׁמוּעָה
Ezek. 22.13:	הִכֵּיתִי כַפִּי אֶל בִּצְעֵךְ · · · וְעַל דָּמֵךְ
Ezek. 23.5:	וַתַּעְגַּב עַל מְאַהֲבֶיהָ אֶל אַשּׁוּר
Ezek. 23.42:	וַיִּתְּנוּ צְמִידִים אֶל יְדֵיהֶן וַעֲטֶרֶת · · · עַל רָאשֵׁיהֶן
Ezek. 38.12:	לְהָשִׁיב יָדְךָ עַל חֳרָבוֹת · · · וְאֶל עַם
Ps. 42.2:	כְּאַיָּל תַּעֲרֹג עַל אֲפִיקֵי מָיִם כֵּן נַפְשִׁי תַעֲרֹג אֵלֶיךָ
Ps. 79.6:	שְׁפֹךְ חֲמָתְךָ אֶל הַגּוֹיִם · · · וְעַל מַמְלָכוֹת
Ps. 90.16:	יֵרָאֶה אֶל עֲבָדֶיךָ פָעֳלֶךָ וַהֲדָרְךָ עַל בְּנֵיהֶם
Eccl. 12.7:	וְיָשֹׁב הֶעָפָר עַל הָאָרֶץ · · · וְהָרוּחַ תָּשׁוּב אֶל הָאֱלֹהִים
2 Chron. 32.19:	וַיְדַבְּרוּ אֶל אֱלֹהֵי · · · כְּעַל אֱלֹהֵי

Josh. 19.50:	עַל פִּי יהוה נָתְנוּ	1 Sam. 14.10:	עֲלוּ עָלֵינוּ
Josh. 21.3:	וַיִּתְּנוּ · · · אֶל פִּי יהוה	1 Sam. 14.12:	עֲלוּ אֵלֵינוּ
1 Sam. 14.1:	וְנַעְבְּרָה אֶל מַצַּב פְּלִשְׁתִּים	1 Sam. 14.33:	לֶאֱכֹל עַל הַדָּם
1 Sam. 14.4:	לַעֲבֹר עַל מצב פלשתים	1 Sam. 14.34:	לֶאֱכֹל אֶל הַדָּם

I Sam. 22.8:	הֵקִים · · · עָלַי לְאֹרֵב	Jer. 35.13:	לִשְׁמֹעַ אֶל דְּבָרַי
I Sam. 22.13:	לָקוּם אֵלַי לארב	Jer. 35.18:	שְׁמַעְתֶּם עַל מִצְוֹת
I Sam. 26.15:	לֹא שָׁמַרְתָּ אֶל אֲדֹנֶיךָ	Jer. 36.2:	מְגִלַּת סֵפֶר וְכָתַבְתָּ אֵלֶיהָ
I Sam. 26.16:	לֹא שְׁמַרְתֶּם עַל אֲדֹנֵיכֶם	Jer. 36.28:	מְגִלָּה אַחֶרֶת וּכְתֹב עָלֶיהָ
2 Sam. 7.25:	דִּבַּרְתָּ עַל עַבְדְּךָ	Jer. 37.13:	אֶל הַכַּשְׂדִּים אַתָּה נֹפֵל
2 Sam. 7.28:	וַתְּדַבֵּר אֶל עַבְדְּךָ	Jer. 37.14:	אֵינֶנִּי נֹפֵל עַל הַכַּשְׂדִּים
I Ki. 16.13:	אֶל כָּל חַטֹּאות · · · אֲשֶׁר חָטְאוּ	Ezek. 11.10:	עַל גְּבוּל יִשְׂרָאֵל אֶשְׁפּוֹט אֶתְכֶם
I Ki. 16.19:	עַל חַטֹּאתָיו אֲשֶׁר חָטָא	Ezek. 11.11:	אֶל גבול ישראל אשפט אתכם
2 Ki. 8.3:	לִצְעֹק · · · אֶל בֵּיתָהּ וְאֶל שָׂדֶה	Ezek. 12.6:	עַל כָּתֵף תִּשָּׂא
2 Ki. 8.5:	צֹעֶקֶת · · · עַל ביתה וְעַל שדה	Ezek. 12.12:	אֶל כָּתֵף יִשָּׂא
2 Ki. 9.3:	וְיָצַקְתָּ עַל רֹאשׁוֹ	Ezek. 14.3:	הֶעֱלוּ גִלּוּלֵיהֶם עַל לִבָּם
2 Ki. 9.6:	וַיִּצֹק · · · אֶל ראשו	Ezek. 14.4:	יַעֲלֶה אֶת גִּלּוּלָיו אֶל לִבּוֹ
2 Ki. 18.20:	עַל מִי בָטַחְתָּ	Ezek. 18.6:	אֶל הֶהָרִים לֹא אָכָל
2 Ki. 18.22:	אֶל · · · בְּטַחְנוּ	Ezek. 18.15:	עַל ההרים לא אכל
Isa. 17.7:	יִשְׁעֶה הָאָדָם עַל עֹשֵׂהוּ	Ezek. 28.21:	בֶּן אָדָם שִׂים פָּנֶיךָ אֶל צִידוֹן
Isa. 17.8:	וְלֹא יִשְׁעֶה אֶל הַמִּזְבְּחוֹת	Ezek. 29.2:	בן אדם שים פניך עַל פַּרְעֹה
Isa. 29.11:	יִתְּנוּ אֹתוֹ אֶל יוֹדֵעַ סֵפֶר	Am. 7.15:	לֵךְ הִנָּבֵא אֶל עַמִּי יִשְׂרָאֵל
Isa. 29.12:	וְנִתַּן · · · עַל אֲשֶׁר לֹא יָדַע סֵפֶר	Am. 7.16:	לֹא תִנָּבֵא עַל יִשְׂרָאֵל
Isa. 56.3:	בֶּן הַנֵּכָר הַנִּלְוָה אֶל יהוה	Job 1.11:	אִם לֹא עַל פָּנֶיךָ יְבָרְכֶךָּ
Isa. 56.6:	וּבְנֵי הַנֵּכָר הַנִּלְוִים עַל יהוה	Job 2.5:	אם לא אֶל פניך יברכך

§ 107. The particles אל and על are used promiscuously (cf. p. 288, § 77). Any differentiation in their meaning is without any foundation in the Bible, and must be considered as arbitrary. The practice adopted by commentators to amend the Bible text even on the evidence of Ms. readings to the end that אל shall stand for "toward" and על "upon" or "against," works on the *presupposition* that these are the real meanings of these words. An objective examination will reveal that any and every Ms. uses them promiscuoulsy, though they may differ in their readings in any given passage.

D. THE GOVERNMENT OF PARTICLES (Cf. MH §§ 193-195)

§ 108. The particle לֹא.

a) Lev. 19.12:   וְלֹא תִשָּׁבְעוּ בִשְׁמִי לַשֶּׁקֶר וְחִלַּלְתָּ אֶת שֵׁם אֱלֹהֶיךָ

Num. 16.14: אַף לֹא אֶל אֶרֶץ זָבַת חָלָב וּדְבַשׁ הֲבִיאֹתָנוּ וַתִּתֶּן לָנוּ

Deut. 7.25:   לֹא תַחְמֹד כֶּסֶף וְזָהָב עֲלֵיהֶם וְלָקַחְתָּ לָךְ

Deut. 7.26:   וְלֹא תָבִיא תוֹעֵבָה אֶל בֵּיתְךָ וְהָיִיתָ חֵרֶם כָּמֹהוּ

Ezek. 11.11: הִיא לֹא תִהְיֶה לָכֶם לְסִיר וְאַתֶּם תִּהְיוּ בְתוֹכָהּ לְבָשָׂר

Am. 8.8:   הַעַל זֹאת לֹא תִרְגַּז הָאָרֶץ וְאָבַל כָּל יוֹשֵׁב בָּהּ

Ezek. 13.5:   לֹא עֲלִיתֶם בַּפְּרָצוֹת וַתִּגְדְּרוּ גָדֵר

Ps. 9.19:   כִּי לֹא לָנֶצַח יִשָּׁכַח אֶבְיוֹן תִּקְוַת עֲנִיִּים תֹּאבַד לָעַד

Ps. 44.19:   לֹא נָסוֹג אָחוֹר לִבֵּנוּ וַתֵּט אֲשֻׁרֵינוּ מִנִּי אָרְחֶךָ

Job 9.32:   לֹא אִישׁ כָּמוֹנִי אֶעֱנֶנּוּ נָבוֹא יַחְדָּו בַּמִּשְׁפָּט

Job 22.11:   אוֹ חֹשֶׁךְ לֹא תִרְאֶה וְשִׁפְעַת מַיִם תְּכַסֶּךָּ

Job 30.25:   אִם לֹא בָכִיתִי לִקְשֵׁה יוֹם עָגְמָה נַפְשִׁי לָאֶבְיוֹן

Job 32.9:   לֹא רַבִּים יֶחְכָּמוּ וּזְקֵנִים יָבִינוּ מִשְׁפָּט

Prov. 30.3:   וְלֹא לָמַדְתִּי חָכְמָה וְדַעַת קְדֹשִׁים אֵדָע

b) Isa. 59.1:   לֹא קָצְרָה יַד יְהוָה מֵהוֹשִׁיעַ וְלֹא כָבְדָה אָזְנוֹ מִשְּׁמוֹעַ

Ps. 16.10:   כִּי לֹא תַעֲזֹב נַפְשִׁי · · · · לֹא תִתֵּן חֲסִידְךָ

Job 5.6:   כִּי לֹא יֵצֵא מֵעָפָר אָוֶן וּמֵאֲדָמָה לֹא יִצְמַח עָמָל

Deut. 1.42: נַעֲלֶה וְנִלְחַמְנוּ: cf. v. 41 ;לֹא תַעֲלוּ וְלֹא תִלָּחֲמוּ

§ 109. The particle אַל.

a) 1 Sam. 2.3: אַל תַּרְבּוּ תְדַבְּרוּ גְּבֹהָה · · · · יֵצֵא עָתָק

Jer. 17.21:   וְאַל תִּשְׂאוּ מַשָּׂא בְּיוֹם הַשַּׁבָּת וַהֲבֵאתֶם בְּשַׁעֲרֵי

Ps. 35.19:   אַל יִשְׂמְחוּ לִי אֹיְבַי שֶׁקֶר שֹׂנְאַי חִנָּם יִקְרְצוּ עָיִן

Ps. 75.6:   אַל תָּרִימוּ לַמָּרוֹם קַרְנְכֶם תְּדַבְּרוּ בְצַוָּאר עָתָק

Ps. 143.7:   אַל תַּסְתֵּר פָּנֶיךָ מִמֶּנִּי וְנִמְשַׁלְתִּי עִם יֹרְדֵי בוֹר

b) Ps. 6.2:   אַל בְּקִצְפֶּךָ; cf. Ps. 38.2: אַל בְּאַפְּךָ תוֹכִיחֵנִי וְאַל בַּחֲמָתְךָ תִיסְּרֵנִי
                                           תוֹכִיחֵנִי וּבַחֲמָתְךָ תְיַסְּרֵנִי

§ 110. Various other Particles.

a) Hab. 1.3:   לָמָּה תַרְאֵנִי אָוֶן וְעָמָל תַּבִּיט

Hab. 1.13:   לָמָּה תַבִּיט בּוֹגְדִים תַּחֲרִישׁ בְּבַלַּע רָשָׁע צַדִּיק

Ps. 2.1:   לָמָּה רָגְשׁוּ גוֹיִם וּלְאֻמִּים יֶהְגּוּ רִיק

Ps. 10.1:   לָמָה יְהוָה תַּעֲמֹד בְּרָחוֹק תַּעְלִים לְעִתּוֹת בַּצָּרָה

Ps. 88.15: לָמָה יהוה תזנח נפשי תַסְתִּיר פניך ממני

Lam. 5.20: לָמָּה לנצח תשכחנו תַּעַזְבֵנוּ לארך ימים

Ps. 8.5: מָה אנוש כי תזכרנו וּבֶן אָדָם כי תפקדנו

Ps. 114.5: מַה לך הים כי תנוס הַיַּרְדֵּן תסב לאחור

Isa. 40.13: מִי תכן את רוח יהוה וְאִישׁ עצתו יודיענו

Isa. 41.4: מִי פעל ועשה קָרָא הדרות מראש

Hos. 2.5: פֶּן אפשיטנה ערמה וְהַצַּגְתִּיהָ כיום הולדה

Ps. 13.5: פֶּן יאמר איבי יכלתיו צָרַי יגילו

b) Ps. 15.1: מִי יגור באהלך מִי ישכן בהר קדשך

Ps. 12.2: כִּי גמר חסיד כי פסו אמונים

Ps. 13.2: עַד אָנָה יהוה תשכחני נצח עַד אָנָה תסתיר

Ps. 16.4: בַּל אסיך נסכיהם מדם וּבַל אשא את שמותם

Isa. 59.4: אֵין קרא בצדק וְאֵין נשפט באמונה

§ 111. The ה interrogativum.

a) Job 38.16: הֲבָאתָ עד נבכי ים וּבְחֵקֶר תהום התהלכת

Job 39.11: הֲתִבְטַח בו כי רב כחו וְתַעֲזֹב אליו יגיעך

b) 1 Sam. 14.37: הַאֵרֵד אחרי פלשתים הַתִתְּנֵם ביד

2 Sam. 5.19: הַאֶעֱלֶה אל פלשתים הַתִתְּנֵם בידי; cf. 1 Chron. 14.10:

הַאֶעֱלֶה ‧‧‧ וּנְתַתָּם

Job 39.19: הֲתִתֵּן לסוס גבורה הַתַלְבִּישׁ צוארו

Ruth 1.13: הֲלָהֵן תשברנה ‧‧‧ הֲלָהֵן תעגנה

§ 112. Distributive Expressions.

a) Gen. 6.14: קְנִים תעשה את התבה

Gen. 6.19: שְׁנַיִם מכל תביא אל התבה

Gen. 7.2: שְׁנַיִם איש ואשתו

Num. 1.44: (שנים עשר איש) אִישׁ אֶחָד לבית אבתיו

Deut. 1.23: (שנים עשר אנשים) אִישׁ אֶחָד לשבט

Josh. 18.4: (הבו לכם) שְׁלֹשָׁה אֲנָשִׁים לשבט

b) Gen. 7.2: תקח לך שִׁבְעָה שִׁבְעָה

Gen. 32.17: ויתן ביד עבדיו עֵדֶר עֵדֶר לבדו

Gen. 39.10: כדברה אל יוסף יוֹם יוֹם

Ex. 8.10: ויצברו אתם חֳמָרִם חֳמָרִם

Ex. 16.21: וילקטו אתו בַּבֹּקֶר בַּבֹּקֶר

c) Gen. 7.9:   שְׁנַיִם שְׁנַיִם בָּאוּ

     Ex. 23.30:   מְעַט מְעַט אֲגָרְשֶׁנּוּ

     Num. 1.4:   אִישׁ אִישׁ לַמַּטֶּה

     Num. 3.47:   חֲמֵשֶׁת חֲמֵשֶׁת שְׁקָלִים

     Num. 7.86:   עֲשָׂרָה עֲשָׂרָה הַכַּף

     Num. 17.17:   מַטֶּה מַטֶּה לְבֵית אָב

     Num. 29.10:   עִשָּׂרוֹן עִשָּׂרוֹן לַכֶּבֶשׂ הָאֶחָד

d) Ex. 17.12:   תָּמְכוּ בְיָדָיו מִזֶּה אֶחָד וּמִזֶּה אֶחָד

     Lev. 24.8:   בְּיוֹם הַשַּׁבָּת בְּיוֹם הַשַּׁבָּת יַעַרְכֶנּוּ לִפְנֵי יְהוָה

     Num. 13.2:   אִישׁ אֶחָד אִישׁ אֶחָד לְמַטֵּה אֲבֹתָיו

     Num. 14.34:   יוֹם לַשָּׁנָה יוֹם לַשָּׁנָה תִּשְׂאוּ אֶת עֲוֹנֹתֵיכֶם

     Num. 34.18:   וְנָשִׂיא אֶחָד נָשִׂיא אֶחָד מִמַּטֶּה תִּקְחוּ

e) Num. 7.11:   נָשִׂיא אֶחָד לַיּוֹם נָשִׂיא אֶחָד לַיּוֹם יַקְרִיבוּ אֶת קָרְבָּנָם

     Num. 17.21:   וַיִּתְּנוּ אֵלָיו · · · מַטֶּה לְנָשִׂיא אֶחָד מַטֶּה לְנָשִׂיא אֶחָד לְבֵית אֲבֹתָם

f) Ex. 25.19:   כְּרוּב אֶחָד מִקָּצָה מִזֶּה וּכְרוּב אֶחָד מִקָּצָה מִזֶּה

     Ex. 26.21:   שְׁנֵי אֲדָנִים תַּחַת הַקֶּרֶשׁ הָאֶחָד וּשְׁנֵי אֲדָנִים תַּחַת הַקֶּרֶשׁ הָאֶחָד

     Ex. 25.12:   וּשְׁתֵּי טַבָּעֹת עַל צַלְעוֹ הָאֶחָת וּשְׁתֵּי טַבָּעֹת עַל צַלְעוֹ הַשֵּׁנִית

     Ex. 25.33:   שְׁלֹשָׁה גְבִעִים מְשֻׁקָּדִים בַּקָּנֶה הָאֶחָד כַּפְתֹּר וָפֶרַח וּשְׁלֹשָׁה גְבִעִים מְשֻׁקָּדִים בַּקָּנֶה הָאֶחָד כַּפְתֹּר וָפֶרַח

     Ex. 26.19:   שְׁנֵי אֲדָנִים תַּחַת הַקֶּרֶשׁ הָאֶחָד לִשְׁתֵּי יְדֹתָיו וּשְׁנֵי אֲדָנִים תַּחַת הַקֶּרֶשׁ הָאֶחָד לִשְׁתֵּי יְדֹתָיו

g) Ex. 25.35:   וְכַפְתֹּר תַּחַת שְׁנֵי הַקָּנִים מִמֶּנָּה וְכַפְתֹּר תַּחַת שְׁנֵי הַקָּנִים מִמֶּנָּה תַּחַת שְׁנֵי הַקָּנִים מִמֶּנָּה

CHAPTER FIVE

TOWARDS A NEW EXEGESIS OF THE BIBLE

We started our discussion (on p. 31, § 23) with the statement that "the study of Hebrew philology leads up to and climaxes in the understanding of the Hebrew Bible." Any change in our philological conception of Hebrew must *ipso facto* result in a corresponding change in our interpretation of the Bible, as the following examples will show clearly. I hope they offer not merely a new, but also a better interpretation of the various passages. I almost entirely refrained from referring to the previous interpretations, which I consider unsatisfactory. In the first place, all of us accept or reject suggested interpretations instinctively, through personal intangible feelings and convictions. No reasoning can prevail against inner predilections and inclinations. In the second place, lengthy "Auseinandersetzungen" are unnecessary for experts, and obscure to the novice. It is not the aim of this study to supplant current text-books.

Gen. 1.1: בְּרֵאשִׁית is determined; cf. p. 627, § 100 and Judg. 21.19: לִמְסִלָּה הָעֹלָה.

Gen. 1.14: לְאֹתֹת וּלְמוֹעֲדִים: *signs* (or: *indicators*) *of seasons* (or: *fixed times*)

Gen. 2.3: re-arrange: כִּי בוֹ שָׁבַת אֱלֹהִים לַעֲשׂוֹת מִכָּל מְלַאכְתּוֹ אֲשֶׁר בָּרָא.

Gen. 3.18: וְאָכַלְתָּ: read: וְאָכַל; namely: the קוֹץ וְדַרְדַּר *shall eat up the vegetation of the field.* Nowhere is עשב השדה, which provides food for man (cf. 1.29), used as a curse.

Gen. 4.13: גָּדוֹל עֲוֺנִי מִנְּשֹׂא: *Is my sin too great for forgiveness?*

Gen. 7.13: וּשְׁלֹשֶׁת נְשֵׁי בָנָיו = ונשי שלשת בניו (*and the wives of his three sons*).

Gen. 9.6: בָּאָדָם דָּמוֹ יִשָּׁפֵךְ: *of that man* (scil: the murderer) *shall his blood be shed.*

Gen. 12.2: וְהֶיֵה (בְּרָכָה): vocalize: וְהָיָה: *and it* (scil.: thy name) *shall be* (or: *become*) *a blessing*; cf. 48.20.

Gen. 14.15: וַיֵּחָלֵק (עליהם לילה); cf. Jer. 37.12: לַחֲלֹק (משם בתוך העם): *to slip through.*

Gen. 15.12: אֵימָה חֲשֵׁכָה גְדֹלָה: *a great dark* (or: *oppressive*) *fear*

Gen. 17.17: וְאִם שָׂרָה הֲבַת: "... Sarah, that is ninety years old" fails to render the הֲ in הבת; hence: *and as for Sarah, can a ninety years old woman bear children?*

Gen. 19.9: הָאֶחָד בָּא לָגוּר: *does one come merely to sojourn, and plays the judge?* Cf. p. 623, § 95.

Gen. 21.6: צְחֹק עָשָׂה לִי אֱלֹהִים: *The Lord hath made me the laughing-stock.* On the case of לִי (accusative), cf. 1 Sam. 3.13: כִּי מְקַלְלִים לָהֶם בָּנָיו: *that his children misbehave themselves.*

Gen. 22.14: בְּהַר is determined: *on this mountain.*

Gen. 29.34: הַפַּעַם // עַתָּה form a doublet (cf. p. 314, § 24); cf. v. 32: כִּי עַתָּה and v. 35: הַפַּעַם. The fact that the Hebrew text offers a doublet could be indicated in the translation by using different type for the components.

Gen. 30.38: re-arrange: בְּשִׁקְתוֹת הַמַּיִם לְנֹכַח הַצֹּאן אֲשֶׁר תָּבֹאןָ לִשְׁתּוֹת
וַיֵּחַמְנָה הַצֹּאן בְּבֹאָן לִשְׁתּוֹת

Gen. 31.18: וינהג את כל מקנהו ואת כל רְכֻשׁוֹ אֲשֶׁר רָכָשׁ // מִקְנֵה קִנְיָנוֹ אֲשֶׁר רָכָשׁ: a doublet.

Gen. 31.26: כִּשְׁבֻיוֹת חָרֶב: *like prisoners of a war.*

Gen. 31.27: וְלֹא (הגדת לי): vocalize: וְלֹא; cf. 1 Sam. 13.13.

Gen. 31.31: כִּי יָרֵאתִי // כִּי אָמַרְתִּי: a doublet; cf. 20.11 and 26.9: כִּי אָמַרְתִּי.

Gen. 38.27: The spelling תְאוֹמִים reflects the two possibilities of pronouncing the word: with the vowel *o*, cf. 25.24; תוֹמִים; and with the vowel *a*, cf. Ex. 26.24: תאמים (cf. p. 576, §§ 29 f.; also the vocalization of תַּמִּים in Ex. 26.24). On one word representing a doublet, cf. p. 314, § 24 (the first six examples).

Gen. 41.34: וְחִמֵּשׁ: "and take up the fifth part" conveys no meaning at all in the context. Furthermore: no indication is given as to who was intended to do this task (whatsoever it may have been): Pharaoh himself, being the subject to the preceding verb וְיַפְקֵד, or his appointees (cf. the plural וְיִקְבְּצוּ in v. 35), in which case the singular of וְחִמֵּשׁ offers a difficulty. I, therefore, suggest to vocalize the word as inf. וְחַמֵּשׁ (cf. p. 276, § 58) and to translate: *and to mobilize,* or: *inventorize.*

Gen. 43.18: וַיִּרְאוּ (הָאֲנָשִׁים): *And when the men saw that they were brought into Joseph's house;* ab √ראה, the second *yod* being *mater lectionis,* cf. p. 567, § 9b. On the structure of the verse, cf. Gen. 50.15: וַיִּרְאוּ אֲחֵי יוֹסֵף כִּי מֵת אֲבִיהֶם וַיֹּאמְרוּ.

Gen. 43.29: יְחֻנְּךָ; originally *יָחֹנְךָ, with reduction of the second vowel to שוא, cf. p. 415, § 2c. Hence, the first ḳames (ָ) was *a*, and still has to be pronounced *a*. For if we reduce it to *o* in the pronunciation, then we would have to restore the ḥolem to the second syllable; cf. on Jer. 18.3. (Cf. p. 318, § 28 for similar errors in our present-day pronunciation of Hebrew). Cf. also MH § 62, sub c.

Gen. 47.3: רֹעֵה (צֹאן עֲבָדֶיךָ) is plural; cf. p. 256, § 25 and note 2 there. Similarly: Gen. 3.7: עָלֵה תְאֵנָה; Mal. 3.19: עֹשֵׂה רִשְׁעָה; Ezra 3.9: עֹשֵׂה הַמְּלָאכָה; and especially 2 Chron. 34.10: עֹשֵׂי ··· עֹשֵׂה הַמְּלָאכָה.

Gen. 47.29: שִׂים נָא יָדְךָ תַּחַת יְרֵכִי is identical in meaning with הִשָּׁבְעָה לִי; hence וְעָשִׂיתָ עִמָּדִי חֶסֶד וֶאֱמֶת is: *that you will deal kindly und truly with me.*

Ex. 3.8: וָאֵרֵד (לְהַצִּילוֹ): *and I am resolved to deliver them*; cf. ارود; cf. in similar connection v. 17: וָאֹמַר אַעֲלֶה אֶתְכֶם.

Ex. 5.3: (פֶּן) יִפְגָּעֵנוּ (בדבר): *lest He plague us*; cf. פָּגַע.

Ex. 12.4: מֹשֶׂה (וְאִם יִמְעַט הַבַּיִת מִהְיֹת): *And if the household be too little (in number) for a lamb-unit*: The dagesh in שׂ is meaningless, cf. p. 427, § 34; מֹשֶׂה is a nominal form with prefix מ to שֶׂה, just like הַמִּנְהָרוֹת Judg. 6.2 (to נָהָר), מֶחְקְרֵי Ps. 95.4 (to חֵקֶר), הַמִּקְרֶה Judg. 3.20 (to קָרָה), וּמִשְׁמַן Isa. 17.4 (to שָׁמֵן). Cf. MH § 12.

Ex. 14.30: וַיַּרְא יִשְׂרָאֵל אֶת מִצְרַיִם מֵת עַל שְׂפַת הַיָּם = וירא ישראל על שפת הים את מצרים מת (*And Israel, [safe] on the seashore, saw the Egyptians dying [in the sea]*).

Ex. 20.3: אֱלֹהִים אֲחֵרִים is not: "other gods", but: *another god*. The context implies a singular; cf. 1 Sam. 6.20: הָאֱלֹהִים הַקָּדוֹשׁ הַזֶּה with Josh. 24.19: כִּי אֱלֹהִים קְדֹשִׁים הוּא; also: Ex. 32.8: אֵלֶּה אֱלֹהֶיךָ ··· אֲשֶׁר הֶעֱלוּךָ with Neh. 9.18: זֶה אֱלֹהֶיךָ אֲשֶׁר הֶעֶלְךָ.

Ex. 20.5: תָעָבְדֵם (וְלֹא); originally *תַעַבְדֵם–תַּעֲבָדֵם (cf. p. 415, § 2c). Thus, the vocalization תָעָ proves the interchangeable use of ָ and ֲ; cf. p. 433, §§ 42 ff.

Ex. 25.37: וְהֵאִיר ··· (וְעָשִׂיתָ ··· וְהֶעֱלָה). The two verbs are in the identical number and person, but refer to different subjects. I suggest to vocalize וְהַעֲלֵה ··· וְהָאִיר as inf. (cf. p. 276, § 58).

Ex. 30.23: בְּשָׂמִים רֹאשׁ is construct state; (cf. p. 613, § 83 3).

Ex. 30.25: רֹקַח (מַעֲשֵׂה רוֹקֵחַ) מִרְקַחַת // רֹקַח is a doublet; cf. v. 35: מַעֲשֵׂה רֹקֵחַ.

Ex. 32.35: עַל אשר עָשׂוּ אֶת הָעֵגֶל אשר עָשָׂה אהרן: "because they made the calf, which Aaron made" is not clear: who was responsible for the making of the calf? And how could the Israelites "make" the calf, after Aaron had done it? In a hitherto unpublished paper (cf. PAAJR, vol. VI p. 2), Dr. Julian Morgenstern interpreted the root עשה in passages like 2 Ki. 17.29: וַיִּהְיוּ עֹשִׂים; ib. v. 30: וְאַנְשֵׁי בָבֶל עָשׂוּ, as meaning: to worship. Hence, our passage should be rendered as: *because they had worshipped the calf, which Aaron had made*; cf. also Targum Onkelos.

Lev. 12.2: אִשָּׁה כִּי תַזְרִיעַ: *If thou shalt inseminate a woman*. On the syntax cf. Lev. 19.19: שָׂדְךָ לֹא תִזְרַע.

Lev. 25.49: מִשְׁאֵר (בשרו) is a nominal form with prefix מ to שאר (cf. on Ex. 12.4): *or his kinsman*.

Num. 11.4: וְהָאסַפְסוּף is onomatopoetic, reflecting the hissing sound of a mob-gathering (סֹף, סף); hence translate: *the riffraff*.

Num. 11.25: (וַיִּתְנַבְּאוּ וְלֹא יָסָפוּ): *they prophesied and did not stop*; ab √יסף = סוּף, cf. p. 595, § 56.

Num. 15.21: (ערסתיכם) מֵרֵאשִׁית is a nominal form with prefix מ to רֵאשִׁית; cf. in the identical meaning v. 20: (רֵאשִׁית ((ערסתכם.

Num. 16.27: יָצְאוּ // נִצָּבִים is a doublet (cf. p. 314, § 24); "came out and stood" is evading the difficulty at issue; for it implies that they first "came out" and subsequently "stood", while the tenses in Hebrew point to a reversed order.

Num. 33.2: מוֹצָאֵיהֶם is an inflected form with preservation of the first vowel (cf. p. 475, § 33).

Deut. 4.16: פֶּסֶל תְּמוּנַת כָּל סֶמֶל תַּבְנִית זָכָר; vocalize כֹּל (תמונת); then סֶמֶל and תַּבְנִית form a doublet; cf. v.v. 23 and 25.

Deut. 5.19: (קוֹל גָּדוֹל וְלֹא) יָסָף: *a great voice that did not stop*; cf. on Num. 11.25.

Deut. 14.11, 20: כָּל עוֹף טָהוֹר תֹּאכֵלוּ (v. 11) and כָּל צִפּוֹר טְהֹרָה תֹּאכֵלוּ (v. 20) form a doublet (cf. p. 314, § 24).

Deut. 21.6: (וכל זקני העיר ההוא) הַקְּרֹבִים (אל החלל): "And all the elders of that city, who are nearest unto the slain man". Is it thinkable that amongst "the elders of that city" are some "who are nearest", and consequently others who are farthest "unto the slain man"? But הַקְּרֹבִים refers to הָעִיר (cf. p. 620, § 91): *which is nearest unto the slain man*.

Deut. 20.10: ‏לְשָׁלוֹם‎ (‏···וקראת···וְתִקְרַב אֶל עִיר לְהִלָּחֵם‎): An agressive war, as described in the following verses, does not begin with "proclaiming peace". The context allows for ‏שָׁלוֹם‎ (and its derivate ‏תשלים‎ v. 12) only one meaning: *surrender*.

Josh. 6.1: ‏סֹגֶרֶת וּמְסֻגֶּרֶת‎ (‏וִירִיחוֹ‎): *Jericho was completely shut up*. ‏סֹגֶרֶת‎ is perfect, ‏וּמְסֻגֶּרֶת‎ participle; on the interchangebility of ‏ֻ‎ and ‏ֹ‎, cf. p. 439, § 64 f.; cf. also: ‏יְרֵחָם‎ Prov. 28.13 with ‏יְרֻחָם‎ 1 Sam. 1.1; ‏מוּתָה‎ 1 Sam. 4.20 with ‏מוֹתָה‎ 2 Sam. 6.23; ‏מִפְּדוּת‎ Isa. 50.2 (inf. construct, cf. parallel ‏לְהַצִּיל‎), instead of ‏מִפְדוֹת‎; 1 Ki. 7.19: ‏שׁוּשַׁן‎ with ‏שׁוֹשָׁן‎ v. 22.

Josh. 6.8: ‏וַיְהִי כֶּאֱמֹר יְהוֹשֻׁעַ אֶל הָעָם‎: *And it came to pass just as Joshua had spoken to the people*.

Josh. 8.29: ‏גַּל אֲבָנִים גָּדוֹל‎ is not "a great heap of stones," but: a heap of great stones; for ‏גָּדוֹל‎ refers to ‏אֲבָנִים‎; cf. ib. 10.27, where a similar event is narrated: ‏אֲבָנִים גְּדֹלוֹת‎.

Judg. 3.26: ‏הִתְמַהְמְהָם‎: an onomatopoetic verb, emphasizing the slow progress of the action taken by Eglon's servants (‏מה, מה‎) (cf. our pooh-pooh).

Judg. 4.20: ‏עֲמֹד‎ (‏וַיֹּאמֶר אֵלֶיהָ‎): imper. fem.; hence vocalize ‏עֲמֹד‎; cf. Prov. 17.26: ‏עֲנוֹשׁ‎: absolute infinitive, instead of ‏עָנוֹשׁ‎; cf. p. 317, § 27.

Judg. 5.10: ‏מִדִּין‎ (‏יֹשְׁבֵי עַל‎): *ye that sit on judgment*. ‏מִדִּין‎ is a prefix ‏מ‎-form of ‏דִּין‎; cf. on Ex. 12.4 and also Isa. 10.2. Cf. MH § 12c.

Judg. 8.18: ‏אֵיפֹה‎ (‏הָאֲנָשִׁים‎) ‏וַיֹּאמְרוּ כָּמוֹךָ כְמוֹהֶם···‎: *How were the men*; read ‏אֵיכָה‎ (‏כ–פ‎; cf. p. 484, § 61). Note the answer: "As thou art, so were they"; hence the question must refer to the appearance.

Judg. 9.31: ‏וְהִנָּם‎) ‏צָרִים‎ (‏אֶת הָעִיר עָלֶיךָ‎): *and behold, they make the city (dwellers) hostile against thee*. ‏צָרִים‎ is a demoninative verb, ab ‏צָר‎: to make an enemy.

Judg. 9.54: re-arrange: ‏וַיִּקְרָא אֶל הַנַּעַר נֹשֵׂא כֵלָיו מְהֵרָה שְׁלֹף לוֹ וַיֹּאמֶר חַרְבְּךָ‎: *Draw hastily thy sword*.

Judg. 11.9: ‏אָנֹכִי אֶהְיֶה לָכֶם לְרֹאשׁ‎: *Will I be your head* (or: *leader*)?

Judg. 11.27: ‏יִשְׁפֹּט יהוה הַשֹּׁפֵט‎. is a doublet, composed of: ‏יִשְׁפֹּט יהוה‎ (cf. Gen. 16.5 and 1 Sam. 24.12) and ‏יהוה הַשֹּׁפֵט‎.

Judg. 16.18: re-arrange: ‏עֲלוּ כִּי הַפַּעַם הִגִּיד לִי אֶת כָּל לִבּוֹ‎: *Come up, for this time he hath told me all his heart*.

Judg. 21.22: ‏כִּי לֹא לָקַחְנוּ‎ (‏אִישׁ אִשְׁתּוֹ‎) ‏בַּמִּלְחָמָה‎: *Have we not taken ... in battle*? A rhetoric question. On the structure (with no *he interrogativum*), cf. p. 622, §§ 93 and 94.

(כִּי) לֹא אַתֶּם נְתַתֶּם לָהֶם: *for if you had given them unto them*; vocalize לֹא.

I Sam. 1.6: וְכָעֲסָתָה ‧‧‧ כַּעַס: finite verb with noun (and not infinitive), cf. Ezek. 32.10: שַׂעַר ‧‧‧ יִשְׂעֲרוּ.

I Sam. 1.26: חֵי נַפְשְׁךָ אֲדֹנִי // בִּי אֲדֹנִי is a doublet (cf. p. 314, § 24 f.); cf. I Ki. 3.17: בִּי אֲדֹנִי, and 2 Sam. 14.19: חֵי נַפְשְׁךָ אֲדֹנִי.

I Sam. 2.29: מֵרֵאשִׁית: cf. on Num. 15.21.

I Sam. 3.13: cf. on Gen. 21.6.

I Sam. 4.6: קוֹל הַתְּרוּעָה הַגְּדוֹלָה הַזֹּאת: *this great noise of shouting*; הגדולה הזאת refer to קוֹל; cf. on Deut. 21.6.

I Sam. 4.11: נִלְקָח: *was captured*; cf. מַלְקוֹחַ.

I Sam. 4.14: אֶת קוֹל הַצְּעָקָה: *the loud wailing*.

קוֹל הֶהָמוֹן הַזֶּה: *this loud excitement*; cf. 14.19: וְהֶהָמוֹן with ib. v. 20: מְהוּמָה, where both words are used in the identical meaning.

I Sam. 6.7: re-arrange and read: וְעַתָּה עֲשׂוּ עֲגָלָה חֲדָשָׁה אַחַת וּקְחוּ שְׁתֵּי פָרוֹת עָלוֹת: *prepare you a new cart, and take two milch kine.*

I Sam. 9.6: (אוּלַי יַגִּיד לָנוּ אֶת דַּרְכֵּנוּ אֲשֶׁר) הָלָכְנוּ: future-meaning, cf. p. 591, § 46: *the way wherein we should walk*; for their experience in the past, they need no man of God to inquire of him.

I Sam. 13.13: לֹא(שָׁמַרְתָּ): vocalize: לֹא.

I Sam. 14.29: אֹרוּ (עֵינַי). Cf. p. 32, § 24.

I Sam. 14.43: הִנְנִי אָמוּת: shall I now die? Cf. p. 622, § 94.

I Sam. 15.23: כִּי חַטַּאת: connect: כְּחַטַּאת; cf. Ezek. 7.4: כִּי דרכיך with ib. v. 9: כִּדרכיך.

I Sam. 20.23: עַד עוֹלָם. This agreement was to remain a secret for not more than one day only (unlike עד עולם in v. 42, where the lifespans of זרעי and זרעך are included in the covenant); hence I would vocalize it as עֵד עָלֻם: *The Lord is a hidden* (or: *unseen*) *witness between me and thee*; cf. Gen. 51.50: אין איש עמנו ראה אלהים עֵד בֵּינִי וּבֵינֶךָ.

I Sam. 20.38: מְהֵרָה is imper.; cf. on Ps. 31.3.

I Sam. 21.14: וַיְשַׁוּ is a verb *tertiae waw*, cf. p. 246, § 11; cf. also 2 Sam. 14.6: וַיַּכּוּ, and on the Mesha inscription line 5: ויענו and line 6: אענו.

I Sam. 25.6: לְחָי is the absolute form of the plural (=לחיים), cf. p. 39, § 34 f.: *Hail*.

1 Sam. 25.8: לַעֲבָדֶיךָ וּלְבִנְךָ לְדָוִד: *unto thy servant and son David*; cf. 2 Ki. 16.7: עבדך ובנך אני; cf. p. 261, § 35 Aa.

1 Sam. 25.30: כְּכֹל אֲשֶׁר דִּבֶּר אֶת הַטּוֹבָה עָלֶיךָ; re-arrange: ככל // את הטובה אשר דבר עליך; on the doublet (ככל–את), cf. p. 314, § 24.

1 Sam. 25.39: (חָשַׂךְ)מֵרָעָה: vocalize: מֵרֵעָה: *He Hath kept back His servant from doing evil.*

2 Sam. 1.19: re-arrange: (הצבי ישראל) אֵיךְ נָפְלוּ גִבּוֹרִים עַל בָּמוֹתֶיךָ חָלָל.

2 Sam. 2.16: (חֶלְקַת) הַצָּרִים, ab √צור=צרר: *the portion of the enemies*; cf. p. 595, § 56.

2 Sam. 6.3, 4: By printing the verses in this order:

3: וירכבו את ארון האלהים אל עגלה

חדשה וישאהו מבית אבינדב אשר בגבעה

ועזא ואחיו בני אבינדב נהגים את העגלה

4: חדשה וישאהו מבית אבינדב אשר בגבעה

we not only realize that from חדשה (2°) in v. 3 till בגבעה in v. 4 is a dittography (cf. p. 488, § 69), but get in addition an important indi- cator as to the length of the lines in the original manuscript, in a copy of which this error occurred. The dittography corresponds exactly to one third of the remainder of v. 3; the copyist thus erroneously copied again the line before the last one (aberration of the eye); cf. also MH §§ 173 and 174.

2 Sam. 15.27: הֲרוֹאֶה is an assertion (and not a question), cf. p. 623, § 95: *Seer!* אַתָּה is to be connected with the following שֻׁבָה הָעִיר בְּשָׁלוֹם: *you return into the city in peace!*

2 Sam. 15.34: וְאָמַרְתָּ לְאַבְשָׁלוֹם עַבְדְּךָ אֲנִי הַמֶּלֶךְ אֶהְיֶה עֶבֶד אָבִיךָ וַאֲנִי מֵאָז וְעַתָּה; re-arrange, connect and read: ואמרת לאבשלום אֲנִי אֶהְיֶה וַאֲנִי עַבְדְּךָ; cf. 16.19: עַבְדְּךָ הַמֶּלֶךְ עֶבֶד אָבִיךָ אֲנִי מֵאָז וְעַתָּה אֲנִי עַבְדְּךָ; למי אני אעבד הלא לפני בנו כאשר עבדתי לפני אביך כן אהיה לפניך.

2 Sam. 18.14: לֹא כֵן (אֹחִילָה לְפָנֶיךָ); read: לָאכֵן: *Therefore I'll start before you do*; cf. לָכֵן Gen. 4.15, originally לֹא כֵן and thus translated by the Septuagint; לָכֵן Gen. 30.15, originally לאכן, misunderstood by the Septuagint as לֹא כֵן. On א as *mater lectionis*, cf. p. 562, § 1 and p. 576, § 29.

2 Sam. 19.33: בְּשִׂיבָתוֹ, the *yod* is merely a *mater lectionis* (cf. p. 564, § 2 and p. 570, § 16 ff.) (= בְּשִׂבְתּוֹ) and has misled the vocalizer.

2 Sam. 20.13: הֵגָּה; on the vocalization with ֵ (and not הַגֵּה), cf. on Isa. 30.14.

1 Ki. 1.5: מִתְנַשֵּׂא: *does as if he were The* (scil.: ruling) *Prince*; cf. Num. 16.3: תִּתְנַשְּׂאוּ (from נָשִׂיא) and ib. v. 13: תִּשְׂתָּרֵר (from שַׂר).

1 Ki. 3.11: הָבִין is a noun (=5.9: תְּבוּנָה); cf. similarly Job 6.25: הוֹכֵחַ and ib. v. 26: הֲלְהוֹכַח.

1 Ki. 3.28: כִּי רָאוּ ··· וַיִּרְאוּ; play on the roots ירא and ראה, cf. p. 595, § 56 f. Similarly 1 Ki. 8.48: וְשָׁבוּ אֵלֶיךָ ··· שָׁבוּ אֹתָם; play on √ שׁוב and √ שׁבה; cf. also on Jer. 25.5.

1 Ki. 8.37: בְּשַׁעֲרֵי שְׁעָרָיו (=בְּאֶרֶץ אַרְצוֹ; cf. on Prov. 31.13): *in the cities of their land.*

1 Ki. 12.5: Divide: לכו עד שלשה ימים ושובו אלי: *Depart* (*now*): *after three days come again to me.*

1 Ki. 14.15: מַכְעִיסִים refers as an attributive adjective to the preceding noun אֲשֵׁרֵיהֶם: *because they have made their Asherim that anger the Lord.* On this construction (אשריהם הַמַּכְעִיסִים =), cf. similarly Hag. 1.4: בְּבָתֵּיכֶם סְפוּנִים: "in your ceiled houses"; Gen. 42.19: אֲחִיכֶם אֶחָד.

1 Ki. 18.43: re-arrange: וַיֹּאמֶר שֶׁבַע פְּעָמִים שֻׁב: *And seven times he said* (*unto him*): *go again.*

2 Ki. 2.9: פִּי שְׁנַיִם: *two parts* (or: *thirds*) *of thy spirit*; cf. Zech. 13.8: פִּי שְׁנַיִם ··· וְהַשְּׁלִשִׁית.

2 Ki. 3.4: אֵילִים צָמֶר is a construct state (cf. p. 613, § 83 sub 3).

2 Ki. 5.2: וּגְדוּדֵי אֲרָם יָצְאוּ (=וַאֲרָם יָצְאוּ; cf. 6.23, 13.20): *And the bands of the Arameans had gone out.*

2 Ki. 11.2: הַמּוּמָתִים בַּחֲדָר; re-arrange: הַמּוּמָתִים אֹתוֹ וְאֵת מֵנִקְתּוֹ בַּחֲדַר הַמִּטּוֹת; הַמִּטּוֹת אֹתוֹ וְאֶת מֵנִקְתּוֹ. The slaying took place in the bed-chamber; as a hiding-place served the בֵּית יהוה (v. 3).

2 Ki. 12.9: (ולבלתי) קָחַת (כסף), (לבלתי), as compared with Jer. 17.23: קָחַת (מוסר), is a case of reduction of the first vowel (originally: קַחַת) to שׁוא (in קְחַת); cf. similarly 2 Ki. 23.11: נָתַן (מלך), from נָתָן; Judg. 16.28: נָקָם (אחת משתי עיני), from נָקָם. The vocalization of the words under consideration with ָ or ַ, respectively, is irrelevant (cf. p. 433, § 42 ff.).

2 Ki. 13.20: בָּא שָׁנָה; read: בַּאשָׁנָה, cf. 19.29: הַשָּׁנָה (=השנה הזאת); cf. p. 273, § 52. א is *mater lectionis*, cf. on 2 Sam. 18.14.

2 Ki. 18.26, 28: יְהוּדִית: *in the Judaean* (*language*); cf. p. 229 ff.

Isa. 1.4: זֶרַע מְרֵעִים is parallel to בָּנִים מַשְׁחִיתִים, and hence cannot be considered a construct state ("A seed of evil-doers"), but must be ex-

plained as a collective noun with its asjective in the plural (cf. p. 271,
§ 49): *An evil-doing seed.*

Isa. 1.7: שְׁמָמָה (ארצכם) is a verb, 3 pers. perf. (=שָׁמְמָה): "Your country
is desolate"; but later on: וּשְׁמָמָה is a noun: *And a desolation like the
destruction (wrought by) strangers.*

Isa. 1.18: כַּצֶּמֶר יַלְבִּינוּ · · · כַּשֶּׁלֶג: shall they be as white as snow . . .
shall they be as wool? (Cf. p. 623, § 94).

Isa. 1.20: חֶרֶב (תְּאֻכְּלוּ): *drought*; cf. Deut. 28.22: וּבַחֶרֶב. Note also the
antithesis in Lev. 26.5: ואכלתם להמכם לָשֹׂבַע and ib. v. 19: ונתתי את
שמיכם כַּבַּרְזֶל, implying drougnt. In our verse, תאכלו is now to be
vocalized as an active verb (תֹּאכֵלוּ).

Isa. 1.23: וְחַבְרֵי גַּנָּבִים: "And companions to thieves" reflects only indirectly and, therefore, feebly on the princes themselves. Hence I see
in וחברי the plural to חֶבֶר: *And gangs* (or: *bands*) *of thieves.*

Isa. 1.27: וְשָׁבֶיהָ: *and her inhabitants*; ab √שׁוב=ישׁב; cf. p. 595, § 56.

Isa. 1.31: וּפֹעֲלוֹ, from פֹּעַל – פֹּעֳלוֹ* – פֹּעֳלוֹ* – פָּעֳלוֹ – till finally פָּעֳלוֹ; cf.
Ps. 111.3; id. Jer. 22.13; Isa. 52.14.

Isa. 2.3: מִדְּרָכָיו (וְיוֹרֵנוּ); nominal form with prefix מ to דֶּרֶךְ; cf. on Ex.
12.4: *and He will teach us His ways.*

Isa. 2.12: וְשָׁפֵל (ועל כל נשא); perhaps: ונשף, the masculine form to וְנִשְׁפָּה
(cf. on Jer. 13.16). נשא is used in connection with גבעות, and נשפה
with הר (cf. 13.2), thus referring to both of them, as mentioned
in v. 2 and v. 14.

Isa. 2.18: וְהָאֱלִילִים כָּלִיל יַחֲלֹף: *And the idols are like the night that passes
away;* כָּלִיל=כַּלֵּיל (cf. 15.1), cf. p. 433, § 42 f. (for ־ and ־) and § 49 f.
(for ־ and ־).

Isa. 3.9: Correct and divide וְחַטָּאתָם כִּסְדֹם הִגִּידוּ לֹא כִחֵדוּ: *And their sin in
the manner of Sodom, they declare it (openly), they hide it not.*

Isa. 3.12: מְאַשְּׁרֶיךָ is parallel to וְדֶרֶךְ (hence: מַדְרֶכֶךָ?), and מַתְעִים to
אֹרְחֹתֶיךָ בִּלֵּעוּ: *And those that guide thee, confuse* (or: *entangle*)*thy paths.*

Isa. 5.13: צָחֵה (צמא) is plural; cf. the parallel מְתֵי (רעב) (cf. p. 256, § 25 and
note 2 there).

Isa. 7.6: וּנְקִיצֶנָּה: denominative verb, from קֵץ: *and let us finish it up.*
JPS: "and vex it", corresponds to a correction into וּנְצִיקֶנָּה; cf.
Kittel's *Biblia Hebraica.*

Isa. 7.11: שְׁאָלָה (=שׁאלה); cf. on Jonah 1.6.

Isa. 9.14: (זָקֵן) וּנְשׂוּא (פָּנִים): the וּ is merely euphonic, so as to separate the two *nun* from one another (זקן נ(שוא; cf. the parallel וְנָבִיא מוֹרֶה שֶׁקֶר. Hence translate: *The respected elder.*

Isa. 10.1: וּמְכַתְּבִים עָמָל כִּתֵּבוּ. The כתבו finds its parallel in הַחֹקְקִים; and ומכתבים עמל is parallel to חִקְקֵי אָוֶן. Hence, ומכתבים עמל is a construct state, cf. p. 613, § 83, and perhaps to be vocalized as וּמְכַתְבִים עמל (cf. Ex. 32.16: וְהַמִּכְתָּב מִכְתַּב אֱלֹהִים הוּא): *and that write writings of iniquity.*

Isa. 10.2: (לְהַטּוֹת) מִדִּין (דַּלִּים): *To pervert the judgment of the needy.* On מדין, cf. on Judg. 5.10.

Isa. 10.5: וּמַטֶּה הוּא בְיָדָם זַעְמִי; re-arrange: ומטה זעמי הוא בידם: *In whose hand is the staff of Mine indignation.*

Isa. 10.15: (כְּהָרִים מַטֶּה) לֹא עֵץ; read: לָאֵץ: *As if a staff* (or: *rod*) *should lift up a tree;* on א as *mater lectionis,* cf. on 2 Sam. 18.14.

Isa. 11.13: וְצֹרְרֵי יְהוּדָה: *And the Judaeans that harass* (or: *the harassing Judaeans*); just as in the preceding and parallel קִנְאַת אֶפְרַיִם it is Ephraim who does the envying; cf. also the end of the verse: וִיהוּדָה לֹא יָצֹר אֶת אֶפְרָיִם: *And Judah shall not harass Ephraim.* Thus, in the first instance יְהוּדָה is in adjectival position, cf. p. 605, § 72.

Isa. 13.20, 21: וְרָבְצוּ····יַרְבִּצוּ; cf. p. 9, § 7a s.v. רבץ.

Isa. 14.1: (עַל אַדְמָתָם) וְהִנִּיחָם ab √נוח=נוח, cf. p. 595, § 56: *and He will let them rest on their land.*

Isa. 14.2: וּלְקָחוּם; read: וְלָקְחוּ: *And they* (scil. Israel) *shall take peoples and bring them to their place.* It is ill fitting into this picture of the rehabilitation of Israel, to translate: "And the peoples shall take them," scil. Israel. The addition of ם was probably caused by the fact that the four following words end in this letter, too.

Isa. 14.11: (הוּרַד) שְׁאוֹל (גְּאוֹנֶךָ); parallel to שאול is הֵמְיַת; therefore I read: שְׁאוֹן: *The uproar of thy pomp is brought down;* cf. p. 481, § 53.

Isa. 17.13: re-arrange: וְגָעַר בּוֹ מִמֶּרְחָק וְנָס: *And He will roar at them from far off, and they shall flee.*

Isa. 19.11: חַכְמֵי יֹעֲצֵי פַרְעֹה עֵצָה נִבְעָרָה; re-arrange: חכמי פרעה יעצי עצה נבערה: *the wise men of Pharao (are) counsellors of senseless counsel.*

(בֶּן) חֲכָמִים (אֲנִי); note the parallel: (בֶּן) מַלְכֵי (קֶדֶם). I, therefore, derive מלכי from the Aramaic root מלך: to counsel: *the son of ancient counsellors;* cf. on Jer. 10.7.

Isa. 21.17: וּמִסְפַּר קֶשֶׁת גִּבּוֹרֵי בְנֵי קֵדָר יִמְעָטוּ ;re-arrange: מספר קשת שאר: גבורי בני קדר ימעטו: *And the number of bows of the residue of the mighty men of the children of Kedar shall be diminished*; on the plural ימעטו, cf. p. 620, § 91 sub 3.

Isa. 22.11: (ולא) הִבַּטְתֶּם ··· (לא) רְאִיתֶם: *And ye did not rely* (cf. ib. 20.5: מַבָּטָם and 20.6: מַבָּטֵנוּ) ...*neither* ... *did ye fear* (יִרָא=רָאָה).

Isa. 22.18: Connect צְנֵפָה כַדּוּר (construct state, cf. p. 612, § 83): *tossing like a ball.*

Isa. 24.22: Connect אֲסֵפָה אַסִּיר (construct state, cf. p. 612, § 83): *And as prisoners are gathered shall they be gathered in the dungeon.*

Isa. 25.12: re-arrange: הִשְׁפִּיל לָאָרֶץ הִגִּיעַ עַד עָפָר: *He will lay low to the ground, bring to the dust*; cf. 26.5.

Isa. 26.10: בְּאֶרֶץ (נְכֹחוֹת יְעַוֵּל): *Uprightness he turns into wrong in the land* (continue: *therefore shall he not behold the majesty of the Lord*). Thus, בְּאֶרֶץ is determined; cf. Isa. 65.17: וְאֶרֶץ חֲדָשָׁה and Jer. 17.4: בְּאֶרֶץ לֹא יָדַעְתָּ, where אֶרֶץ and בְּאֶרֶץ are indetermined.

Isa. 29.3: re-arrange: וְצַרְתִּי עָלַיִךְ מְצֻרָת וַהֲקִימֹתִ עָלַיִךְ מָצָב.

Isa. 30.10: נְכֹחוֹת, from הוֹכִיחַ: *reproves* or: *rebukes*; cf. as contrast the parallel חֲלָקוֹת.

Isa. 30.14: כָּתוּת is inf. (=כָּתוֹת); on the interchange of ו and ֹ, cf. p. 175 under ו, and p. 439, § 63 ff.

Isa. 30.16: נָנוּס (עַל סוּס): *high upon horses will we be* (נֵס=נוּס).

Isa. 31.7: יְדֵיכֶם חֵטְא: *your sinful hands*; cf. on 1 Ki. 14.15 and Isa. 35.4.

Isa. 32.6: לְהָרִיק נֶפֶשׁ רָעֵב וּמַשְׁקֶה צָמֵא יַחְסִיר: "To make empty the soul of the hungry." But the soul of the hungry is actually empty, and need not and cannot be made empty. Hence: *To keep empty the soul of the hungry, And to withhold the drink of the thirsty*; as contrast cf. Ps. 107.9.

Isa. 35.4: אֱלֹהֵיכֶם נָקָם (יָבֹא): *The God of your vengeance*, or: *your vengeful God*. On the grammatical structure, cf. Hab. 3.8: מַרְכְּבֹתֶיךָ יְשׁוּעָה; here, too, the suffix refers to the *nomen regens* (cf. p. 602, § 64). גְּמוּל אֱלֹהִים (=אלהים גמול), is a construct state (cf. p. 612, § 83): *The God of recompense* (He will come).

Isa. 40.10: בְּחָזָק is a noun, the masc. form to Judg. 4.3: בְּחָזְקָה (cf. p. 22, § 20): *with might*. Similarly: Ps. 111.18: וְיָשָׁר. Cf. MH § 159.

Isa. 41.4: קֹרֵא still refers to מִי: *(Who) calleth the generations.*

Isa. 44.11: חֲבֵרָיו (הן כל): *(all) who assemble it.*

Isa. 44.13: כְּתִפְאֶרֶת אָדָם: *like a beautiful man*; cf. here on Ps. 22.7 and 39.9.

Isa. 44.23: הָאָרֶץ מִתַּחַת is identical in meaning with Isa. 51.6: תַּחְתִּיּוֹת אָרֶץ *the earth beneath*; cf. Isa. 8.9: מֶרְחַקֵּי אָרֶץ with ib. 33.17: אֶרֶץ מַרְחַקִּים, both identical in meaning with Isa. 39.3: מֵאֶרֶץ רְחוֹקָה.

Isa. 45.9: חֶרֶשׂ אֶת חַרְשֵׂי אֲדָמָה: *A clod with the ploughman.* Note the preceding and following stichi, where the futility of a rebellion of the creation against the creator is described. On the interchangeability of שׂ – שׁ, cf. p. 177, sub שׁ and p. 479, § 44.

Isa. 45.15: מִסְתַּתֵּר (אֵל); denominative verb, from סֵתֶר, cf. Ps. 91.1: *Thou art a protecting God*; cf. the parallel מוֹשִׁיעַ. Similarly in Isa. 28.15: נִסְתָּרְנוּ: *do we find protection.*

Isa. 50.2: מִפְּדוּת is inf. (=מִפְּדוֹת); cf. on Isa. 30.14.

Isa. 50.4: לְשׁוֹן לִמּוּדִים: *a wise tongue*; cf. p. 605, § 72.

Isa. 51.3: re-arrange: קוֹל תּוֹדָה וְזִמְרָה: *The voice of thanksgiving and song.* Cf. p. 611, § 81a.

Isa. 52.14: וְתָאֲרוֹ (=וְתָאֳרוֹ cf. 1 Sam. 28.14); cf. on Isa. 1.31. On the opposite development, cf. Isa. 30.12: מָאָסְכֶם, from the original form מָאֹסְכֶם.

Isa. 53.3: נִבְזֶה וַחֲדַל אִישִׁים (=אִישׁ נִבְזֶה וְחָדֵל): *A man, despised and short-lived*; cf. Ps. 89.48: זָכָר אֲנִי מֶה חָלֶד=זכר מה חלד אני (חדל=חלד; cf. Ps. 39.5: מֶה חָדֵל אָנִי).

אִישׁ מַכְאֹבוֹת וִידוּעַ חֹלִי (=איש ידוע מכאבות וחלי): *A man, familiar with pain and disease*; on ידוע, cf. Ruth 2.1: מוֹדָע: "kinsman."

Isa. 53.5: מִפְּשָׁעֵנוּ is plural; cf. p. 261, § 35 ff.

Jer. 2.25: מִיָּחֵף is a noun (יָחֵף); cf. the parallel מִצִּמְאָה.

Jer. 3.6: וַתִּזְנִי=ותזנה, cf. the spelling of the final ה (as י) of the verbs *tertiae he* in the Samaritan Pentateuch; cf. also p. 245, § 10.

Jer. 3.23: מִגְּבָעוֹת (אָכֵן לַשֶּׁקֶר); a nominal form with prefix מ to גבע (or גבעה), cf. on Ex. 12.4.

Jer. 4.1: אִם תָּשׁוּב ···· אֵלַי תָּשׁוּב: *If thou wilt return, O Israel, Saith the Lord, unto Me, (then) shalt thou stay on (in the land)*; תשוב (1°) is ab √שׁוּב; תשוב (2°) ab √שׁוּב=ישב, cf. parallel וְלֹא תָנוּד; cf. p. 595, § 56.

Jer. 4.24: הִתְקַלְקְלוּ is an onomatopoetic verb, imitating the roaring noise (perhaps: *reverberate*), hence, the parallel רֹעֲשִׁים is not :"they trembled," but: *they are tempestuous.*

Jer. 5.6: זְאֵב עֲרָבוֹת is plural to *זאב ערבה; another way of forming the plural of this construct state is זְאֵבֵי עֶרֶב Zeph. 3.3; cf. p. 619, § 89; on עֶרֶב – עֲרָבוֹת, cf. p. 22, § 20.

Jer. 5.10: (עֲלוּ בְשָׁרוֹתֶיהָ (וְשַׁחֵתוּ וְכָלָה אַל תַּעֲשׂוּ). Walls or ramparts have no shoots; furthermore: as soon as a breach has been effected, they have lost their defensive value; what, then, does וכלה אל תעשו mean? Therefore read: בְּשָׂדוֹתֶיהָ: *Enter their fields*. (שׂ – שׁ, cf. on Isa. 45.9; ד – ר, cf. p. 482, § 55).

Jer. 6.30: כֶּסֶף נִמְאָס. The process of refining as described in v. 29 results in a separation of the refuse from the valuable metal, the silver. "Refuse silver" is therefore an illogical translation; for the metal obtained is either refuse or silver, but not both together. Hence, כסף נמאס corresponds to נִמְאָס כֶּסֶף (cf. p. 609, § 76): *Refuse of silver*; cf. Isa. 16.2: (מְשֻׁלָּח קֵן) קֵן מְשֻׁלָּח: *driven out from (their) nest*.

Jer. 7.10: נִצַּלְנוּ has the meaning of a future tense, cf. p. 591, § 46: *we shall be delivered*. Cf. also on 1 Sam. 9.6.

Jer. 8.4: אִם יָשׁוּב וְלֹא יָשׁוּב: *Doth one slide back and not return?* ישוב (1°) is ab √שוב=שבב; ישוב (2°) ab √שוב; cf. v. 5: שובבה‧‧‧לשוב (cf. p. 595, § 56).

Jer. 8.10: לְיוֹרְשִׁים: to those who will dispossess (them); cf. 49.2: וְיָרַשׁ ישראל את יֹרְשָׁיו.

Jer. 8.14: (וְנִדְּמֶה (שָׁם ab √דמה=דמם (cf. p. 595, § 56): *and let us resign ourselves there*; cf. Ps. 37.7: דּוֹם לַיהוָה.

Jer. 10.2: (כִּי יֵחַתּוּ (=כאשר): *as the nations are dismayed at them*.

Jer. 10.5: (כְּתֹמֶר מִקְשָׁה (הֵמָּה): *Like a pillar of beaten work are they*; cf. Ex. 35.31 where מקשה (likewise) refers to זהב טהור.

Jer. 10.7: (וּבְכָל מַלְכוּתָם): *in all their councils*; from the Aramaic root מלך; cf. the parallel חַכְמֵי הַגּוֹיִם; cf. on Isa. 19.11.

Jer. 10.8: מוּסַר עֵץ הֶבֶל (or הבלים) הוּא re-arrange: מוּסַר הַבָּלִים עֵץ הוּא: *The instruction of a tree is sheer vanity*; cf. v. 3: כִּי חֻקּוֹת הָעַמִּים הֶבֶל הוּא.

Jer. 10.10: (ויהוה) אֱלֹהִים אֱמֶת is construct state, cf. p. 613, § 83. It corresponds in meaning to (יִשָּׁבַע) בֵּאלֹהֵי אָמֵן Isa. 65.16.

Jer. 11.10: עֲוֹנֹת אֲבוֹתָם הָרִאשֹׁנִים *the original iniquities of their fathers*; cf. p. 621, § 91, sub 4.

Jer. 13.16: (עַל) הָרֵי נָשֶׁף: *upon the high mountains*; cf. the singular עַל הַר נֶשֶׁף Isa. 13.2. Cf. on Nah. 1.8.

Jer. 13.22: (עֲקֵבָיִךְ) (נֶחְמְסוּ (· · ·) (נִגְלוּ)); read נחמו, from the Aramaic root חמא: *became visible, appeared*; cf. v. 26: וְנִרְאָה קְלוֹנֵךְ.

Jer. 13.27: עַד מָתַי לֹא תִטְהֲרִי אַחֲרֵי מָתַי עוֹד: *For* re-arrange: לֹא תִטְהֲרִי אַחֲרֵי; *how long wilt thou not purify thyself after me.*

Jer. 14.18: תַּחֲלוּאֵי · · · · חַלְלֵי; play on the roots חלל and חלה; cf. p. 595, § 56.

Jer. 14.21: (שְׁמֶךָ) לְמַעַן; vocalize: לִמְעֹן: *the dwelling-place of Thy name*; cf. the parallel כִּסֵּא כְבוֹדֶךָ; cf. also Jer. 25.30: וּמִמְּעוֹן קָדְשׁוֹ.

Jer. 15.8: הִפְלַתִּי עָלֶיהָ פִּתְאֹם עִיר וּבֶהָלוֹת; re-arrange: הפלתי על העיר פתאם בהלות: *I caused terrors to fall suddenly upon the city.*

Jer. 15.18: נֶצַח: *overpowering.*

Jer. 17.12: Divide: כִּסֵּא כָבוֹד מָרוֹם מֵרֹאשׁוֹן מְקוֹם מִקְדָּשֵׁנוּ: *A high throne of glory, Is our chief holy place.* מראשון is a nominal form with prefix מ to ראשון.

Jer. 17.26: מְבִאִים עוֹלָה · · · · וּמְבִאֵי תוֹדָה; cf. p. 617, § 86.

Jer. 18.3: הָאָבְנָיִם; cf. p. 125, s.v. אבן: *abanim*; hence, originally this form was *הָאָבְנָיִם, which became (according to p. 415, § 2c) הָאָבְנָיִם (with reduction of the second ḳames to שוא); but the first ḳames retained its vocalic value of *a*, cf. on Gen. 43.29. But הָאָבְנָיִם Ex. 1.16 originates from a misunderstood הָאֲבָנִים (so already quoted by Ibn Ezra); cf. p. 520, the example Deut. 22.6. On the structure cf. Isa. 17.7: וְעֵינָיו אֶל קְדוֹשׁ יִשְׂרָאֵל תִּרְאֶינָה. Thus, אָבְנָיִם as a catchword in our dictionaries is an obvious error.

Jer. 18.21: הַרֻגֵי מָוֶת: "slain of death" is a tautology; cf. 2 Ki. 4.40: מָוֶת בַּסִּיר and translate: *plague-ridden.*

Jer. 18.23: תִּמְחֶה=(אַל) תֶּמְחִי; cf. on 3.6.

Jer. 23.1: מְאַבְּדִים is here causative: *that let wander*, or: *cause to get lost*; cf. 50.6: צֹאן אֹבְדוֹת. Similarly Eccl. 3.6: (וְעֵת) לְאַבֵּד as contrasted with לְבַקֵּשׁ.

Jer. 23.3: הִדַּחְתִּי; read: הִדַּחְתֶּם, cf. v. 2: וַתַּדְחוּם.

Jer. 23.8: וְיָשְׁבוּ עַל אַדְמָתָם: *and they shall return to their land*; cf. on Ezek. 37.25.

Jer. 23.23: מִקָּרֹב and מֵרָחֹק are nominal formations with prefix מ to קָרֹב and רָחֹק, respectively; cf. on Prov. 7.19.

הָאֱלֹהֵי מִקְרֹב ··· אֱלֹהֵי מֵרָחֹק; construct state, cf. p. 616, § 85. Similarly:
יֹשְׁבֵי בְצִלּוֹ ··· מֵאַחֲרֵי בַנֶּשֶׁף ; Ex. 44.30; בְּכוּרֵי כֹל Isa. 5.11; מַשְׁכִּימֵי בַבֹּקֶר ··· מֵאַחֲרֵי בַנֶּשֶׁף
Hos. 14.8; מִסְפַּר כֻּלָּם Job 1.5.

Jer. 23.28: (יְדַבֵּר) דְּבָרִי אֱמֶת: *let him speak My faithful word*; on אֱמֶת in
adjectival meaning, cf. 14.13: שְׁלוֹם אֱמֶת: "assured peace."

Jer. 23.31: (לְשׁוֹנָם) הַלֹּקְחִים; read: הַחֹלְקִים or הַמַּחֲלִקִים: *that make smooth
their tongues*; cf. Ps. 5.10: לְשׁוֹנָם יַחֲלִיקוּן.

Jer. 23.39: וְנָשִׁיתִי אֶתְכֶם נָשֹׁא: *I will utterly forget you*; cf. p. 173 and here
on Hos. 1.6.

Jer. 25.5: שׁוּבוּ ··· וּשְׁבוּ; play on the roots שׁוב and ישב; cf. on 1 Ki. 3.28.

Jer. 29.12: וַהֲלַכְתֶּם; read: וְהָלַכְתִּי: *And ye shall call upon Me, and I
will go.*

Jer. 31.9: וּבְתַחֲנוּנִים: *and with (a show of) mercy*; cf. Zech. 12.10: רוּחַ חֵן
וְתַחֲנוּנִים.

Jer. 31.13: יַחְדָּו: vocalize: יֶחֱדוּ (cf. parallel תִּשְׂמַח): *shall rejoice.*

Jer. 31.19: (כִּי אַחֲרֵי) שׁוּבִי (נִחַמְתִּי): *For after sliding back I repented*; ab
שׁוב√=שבב; cf. p. 595, § 56. With all due reserve I would suggest to
read the following (וְאַחֲרֵי) הִוָּדְעִי as: הָרֵעִי: *And after doing evil I smote
upon my thigh*. The parallelism comes thus out quite fine (ר - ד,
cf. p. 482, § 55).

Jer. 33.3: (גְּדֹלוֹת) וּבְצֻרוֹת: *great and withholden things*; cf. Gen. 11.6:
לֹא יִבָּצֵר מֵהֶם כֹּל.

Jer. 42.12: (אֶתְכֶם) וְהֵשִׁיב אֶל אַדְמַתְכֶם: *and he will let you dwell upon your
land*. At that time, they still were in Palestine, and only the continuation of their stay there was problematic. והשיב is ab ישב=שוב√
(cf. p. 595, § 56); cf. v. 10: שׁוֹב תֵּשְׁבוּ. On אל (=על) meaning: upon,
cf. p. 631, § 106.

Jer. 43.3: (אֹתָנוּ) לְהָמִית אֹתָנוּ וּלְהַגְלוֹת: *or carry us away captives*. On this
meaning of the *waw*, cf. p. 328; also Jer. 44.28: מִמֶּנִּי וּמֵהֶם.

Jer. 44.6: וַתִּתַּךְ חֲמָתִי וְאַפִּי וַתִּבְעַר; re-arrange: ותך חמתי ואפי תבער: *And
My fury was poured forth, and Mine anger was kindled.*

Jer. 49.4: (מַה תִּתְהַלְלִי) בָּעֲמָקִים זָב עִמְקֵךְ; read: בָּעֵמֶק כָּזַב עמקך: *Wherefore
gloriest thou in the valley, thy valley will fail thee*. On this use of כזב
cf. כחש in the phrase כִּחֵשׁ מַעֲשֵׂה זַיִת Hab. 3.17. Valleys were most
important; cf. Isa. 22.7: מִבְחַר עֲמָקַיִךְ.

Jer. 50.9: קְהַל גּוֹיִם גְּדֹלִים: *a great assembly of nations* (cf. p. 621, § 91).

Jer. 50.17: שֶׂה פְזוּרָה is collective ("a" sheep cannot be "scattered"!), and should be translated as a plural.

Jer. 50.19: וְשׁוֹבַבְתִּי: *and I will let* (Israel) *return*; but Ezek. 38.4: וְשׁוֹבַבְתִּיךָ: *I will seize* (or: *apprehend*) *you*; cf. also ib. 39.27: בְּשׁוֹבְבִי: "when I have brought (them) back" (שוב – שבה – ישב – שבב). Cf. p. 595, § 56.

Jer. 52.28, 30: יְהוּדִים: *Judaeans*; id. Est. 2.5: אִישׁ יְהוּדִי: *a Judaean*.

Ezek. 2.4: וְהַבָּנִים קְשֵׁי פָנִים וְחִזְקֵי לֵב אֲנִי שׁוֹלֵחַ אוֹתְךָ אֲלֵיהֶם; re-arrange: והבנים אני שולח אותך אליהם קשי פנים וחזקי לב: *And the children unto whom I send thee are brazen-faced and stiff-hearted.*

Ezek. 3.3: בִּטְנְךָ תַאֲכֵל: "cause thy belly to eat"; but the "belly" does not "eat". Therefore: *feed thy belly.*

Ezek. 3.6: אִם לֹא אֲלֵיהֶם שְׁלַחְתִּיךָ; אם and לא exclude one another. Here is a doublet: אם אליהם שלחתיך and לא אליהם שלחתיך are combined in the text; cf. p. 314, § 24.

Ezek. 3.20: re-arrange the entire verse thus: וּבְשׁוּב צַדִּיק מִצִּדְקוֹ וְנָתַתִּי מִכְשׁוֹל לְפָנָיו וְעָשָׂה עָוֶל הוּא צַדִּיק (from v. 21) יָמוּת בְּחַטָּאתוֹ יָמוּת וְלֹא תִזָּכַרְןָ צִדְקֹתָיו אֲשֶׁר עָשָׂה וְדָמוֹ מִיָּדְךָ אֲבַקֵּשׁ כִּי לֹא הִזְהַרְתּוֹ: *Again, when a righteous man doth turn from his righteousness, so I will lay a stumbling-block before him and he will commit iniquity; the same righteous man shall die, because of his sin shall he die, and his righteous deeds which he hath done shall not be remembered; but his blood will I require at thy hand, because thou hast not given him warning.* Thus, crime and punishment for both, the backsliding righteous man and the negligent prophet, are clearly defined.

Ezek. 4.13: יֹאכְלוּ · · · אֶת) לַחְמָם טָמֵא): *their unclean bread.* On the construction (טָמֵא, and not הַטָּמֵא), cf. on I Ki. 14.15. טמא cannot be explained as referring to בני ישראל, since both verbs, יאכלו (preceding) and אדיחם (following) treat it as a plural; and in v. 14 the prophet emphasizes that no prohibited *food* had hitherto come into his mouth. Cf. also Hos. 9.3: ובאשור טמא יאכלו: "And they shall eat unclean food in Assyria."

Ezek. 5.3: וְלָקַחְתָּ מִשָּׁם מְעַט) בְּמִסְפָּר): how can one take "a few hairs by number"? But cf. v. 1: תַּעַר (· · · קַח לְךָ) "a razor"; this word is rendered מספר by the Targum. Hence במספר in v. 3 is to be explained as an Aramaism, and translated: *Thou shalt also take thereof a few with a razor.*

Ezek. 5.15: וְהָיְתָה חֶרְפָּה וּגְדוּפָה; read: וְהָיִיתָ חֶרְפָּה וגדפה (or וְהָיִיתָ): *Thou shalt be reproached and taunted.*

Ezek. 6.12: (וְהַנִּשְׁאָר) וְהַנָּצוּר: *and he that remaineth and is hid;* cf. Isa. 48.6: וּנְצֻרוֹת וְלֹא יְדַעְתָּם.

Ezek. 6.13: אֶל כָּל גִּבְעָה רָמָה בְּכֹל רָאשֵׁי הֶהָרִים וְתַחַת כָּל עֵץ רַעֲנָן וְתַחַת כָּל אֵלָה עֲבֻתָּה; re-arrange and divide the components of this doublet: אל כל גבעה רמה ותחת כל עץ רענן // בכל ראשי ההרים ותחת כל אלה עבתה; cf. p. 314, § 24.

Ezek. 7.3: עַתָּה (הַקֵּץ עָלַיִךְ); read: אָתָא: *The end hath come upon thee,* cf. vv. 2 and 6: בָּא הַקֵּץ. On the interchange between א – ע, cf. p. 477, § 37.

Ezek. 7.6: הֵקִיץ: denominative verb, from קֵץ: *it endeth.*

Ezek. 7.16: וּפָלְטוּ פְּלִיטֵיהֶם: *And some shall escape among them.* On the construction and meaning of the suffix, cf. Num. 12.6: אִם יִהְיֶה נְבִיאֲכֶם יהוה: *if there be a prophet of the Lord among you.* For another grammatical construction of the suffix in the identical meaning, cf. Josh. 10.20: וְהַשְּׂרִידִים שָׂרְדוּ מֵהֶם: *and (only) remnant were left of them.*

Ezek. 7.24: (גּוֹיִם) רָעֵי: from the root רעע=רעה (cf. p. 595, § 56): *destroyers of nations.*

Ezek. 8.2: re-arrange: וָאֶרְאֶה וְהִנֵּה דְמוּת כְּמַרְאֵה אֵשׁ מִמָּתְנָיו וּלְמַטָּה כְּמַרְאֵה אֵשׁ וּמִמָּתְנָיו וּלְמַעְלָה · · · .

Ezek. 13.6: מֶחֱזוּ; vocalize: חָזוּ שָׁוְא וְקֶסֶם כָּזָב; cf. v. 7: · · · חָזוּ שָׁוְא וְקֶסֶם כָּזָב וּמִקְסָם.

Ezek. 16.50: (כַּאֲשֶׁר) רָאִיתִי is 2 pers. fem. (cf. p. 236, § 2): *as thou hast seen.*

Ezek. 22.3: עִיר שֹׁפֶכֶת דָּם בְּתוֹכָהּ לָבוֹא עִתָּהּ וְעָשְׂתָה גִלּוּלִים; read and divide: עִיר שפכת דם בתוכה לָבִיא עַתָּה עָשְׂתָה גלולים: *O city that sheddeth blood, In whose midst is a lion* (cf. 19.2 ff.), *Now she makes idols.* On the interchange between י – ו, cf. p. 484, § 64.

Ezek. 22.18: סִגִים כֶּסֶף is construct state; cf. p. 613, § 83.

Ezek. 25.6: (יַעַן) מַחְאֲךָ (יָד) וְרַקְעֲךָ (בְּרֶגֶל): construct inf. with suffixes. Such forms are vocalized with ֳ under the first radical as a rule; but here they appear with ֲ. This is additional proof for the correctness of our theory (cf. p. 318, § 28) that originally this ֲ indicated the vowel *a.*

שָׁאטְךָ בְּנֶפֶשׁ: "with the disdain of thy soul"; the suffix is appended to the مضاف (cf. p. 602, § 64).

Ezek. 28.2: מוֹשַׁב אֱלֹהִים יָשַׁבְתִּי: *I sit like a god, In the heart of the seas.*

Ezek. 28.25: (עַל אַדְמָתָם) וְיָשְׁבוּ: *and they shall return unto their land;* ab √ישב=שׁוּב (cf. p. 595, § 56); cf. preceding בְּקַבְּצִי, and following (v. 26): וְיָשְׁבוּ עָלֶיהָ: *and they shall dwell thereon* (scil. after having returned).

Ezek. 30.12: חָרְבָה: noun to the verb חָרֵב; with preservation of the first vowel (cf. p. 475, § 33).

וּמָכַרְתִּי אֶת הָאָרֶץ בְּיַד) רָעִים: *And I will give the land over into the hands of destroyers;* ab √רעה=רעע; cf. Ps. 2.9: תְּרֹעֵם בְּשֵׁבֶט בַּרְזֶל (cf. p. 595, § 56).

Ezek. 35.12: נָאֲצוֹתֶיךָ is an inflected form with preservation of the first vowel (cf. p. 475, § 33).

Ezek. 36.35: הֶחֱרֵבוֹת (וְהֶעָרִים); originally *הֶחֱרָבוֹת: preservation of the first vowel (cf. p. 475, § 33). The הָ was then changed into הֶ, so as to indicate a short vowel.

Ezek. 37.23: מוֹשְׁבֹתֵיהֶם: *their backsliding* (שבב=ישב).

Ezek. 37.25: וְיָשְׁבוּ עַל הָאָרֶץ: *And they will return to the land;* cf. v. 21: וקבצתי ···והבאתי and v. 25: וישבו עליה.

Ezek. 41.7: (וְרָחֲבָה) וְנָסְבָה is *kal* √נסב; cf. p. 256, § 26, note 7. Tne masculine form is וְנָסַב: Num. 34.4; plural וְנָסַבּוּ (with preservation of the second vowel, cf. p. 223 f., sub A1 and B3): Josh. 7.9.

Ezek. 43.2: (וְהָאָרֶץ) הֵאִירָה: denominative verb, from אוֹר: *and the earth became bright with His glory.* But Ps. 31.17: הָאִירָה is causative: "Make to shine."

Hos. 1.6: כִּי נָשֹׂא אֶשָּׂא לָהֶם: *But I shall utterly forget them;* cf. on Jer. 23.39. On the interchange between שׂ – שׁ, cf. p. 172 and p. 479, § 44.

Hos. 1.9: לֹא אֶהְיֶה לָכֶם: *And I am not your* אהיה; cf. Ex. 3.14: אֶהְיֶה שלחני; ואמרתי ללא עמי עמי aliaכם; cf. also here 2.25 (referring to our verse): אתה והוא יאמר אֱלֹהָי.

Hos. 2.4: כִּי הִיא לֹא אִשְׁתִּי וְאָנֹכִי לֹא אִישָׁהּ: *For is she not My wife, and am I not her husband?* (cf. p. 622, §§ 93 and 94). An exclamation and not a statement. For if the verse is taken as a statement, then the terming of the incriminated acts as "adultories" is not justified, since this refers to a married woman's transgressions only. וְתָסֵר: *So let her put away.*

Hos. 3.1: רֵעַ is the husband or lover; cf. Cant. 1.9, 15: רַעְיָתִי, parallel to

כַּלָּה in Cant. 4.12: *beloved of her husband and yet an adulteress.* Hence the comparison כְּאַהֲבַת יהוה; for the Lord's love is compared to that of a husband, cf. 2.21: וְאֵרַשְׂתִּיךְ.

וְהֵם פֹּנִים: *yet they turn.*

Hos. 3.1: (וְאֹהֲבֵי אֲשִׁישֵׁי) עֲנָבִים; read עֲנָבִים: *and delight in cakes of love;* cf. Ezek. 33.32: כְּשִׁיר עֲגָבִ׳ם.

Hos. 3.2: the betrothal.

Hos. 3.3: תֵּשְׁבִי לִי: *thou shalt wait for me.*

וְגַם אֲנִי אֵלַיִךְ: *and so will even I (wait) for you.* In the simile: the Lord waits for Israel's return and does not choose another people, while Israel rebels against him.

Hos. 4.4: כִּמְרִיבֵי כֹהֵן (=מריבים; cf. p. 609, § 77b): *like fighting priests;* cf. Job 3.5: כִּמְרִירֵי יוֹם: *black days.*

Hos. 4.14: לֹא אֶפְקֹד: shall I not punish . . . .? Cf. p. 623, § 94.

Hos. 4.18: סָר סָבְאָם is one word (parallel to מָגִנֶּיהָ), with confusion of ר – ב; the same is אָהֲבוּ הֵבוּ (one word). Similarly Mic. 2.4: נְהִי נִהְיָה and ib. 7.11: יִרְחַק חֹק.

Hos. 5.5: וְעָנָה גְאוֹן יִשְׂרָאֵל בְּפָנָיו: *And He will crush Israel's pride in His wrath* (or: *anguish*); cf. Ruth 1.21: ויהוה עָנָה בִי and 1 Sam. 1.18: וּפָנֶיהָ לֹא הָיוּ לָהּ עוֹד.

Hos. 5.9: בְּשִׁבְטֵי יִשְׂרָאֵל הוֹדַעְתִּי נֶאֱמָנָה: *With My rod I taught Israel surely* (or: *truly*); cf. 4.14: בַּשֵּׁבֶט יכו על הלחי, and Judg. 8.16: וַיֹּדַע בהם.

Hos. 8.5: (עֶגְלֵךְ) שֹׁמְרוֹן זָנַח: *Cast off thy calf, O Samaria!;* imperative (=זְנַח) cf. p. 317, § 27; cf. the reverse case Gen. 43.16: וּטְבֹחַ (imperative).

Hos. 9.3: (אֶפְרַיִם מִצְרַיִם) וְשָׁב: *but Ephraim shall dwell in Egypt;* ab √שׁוב= ישׁב; cf. preceding לֹא יֵשְׁבוּ (cf. p. 595, § 56).

Hos. 11.11: וְהוֹשַׁבְתִּים: from שׁוב=ישׁב (cf. p. 595, § 56): *And I will bring them back to their houses.*

Hos. 12.7: (וְאַתָּה בֵּאלֹהֶיךָ) תָּשׁוּב: *And in thy God shalt thou find rest;* cf. Isa. 30.15: בשובה ונחת.

Hos. 13.15: יַפְרִיא: denominative verb, from פֶּרֶא: *to run wild about.*

Hos. 14.8: יֵשְׁבֵי // יָשֻׁבוּ is a doublet (cf. p. 314, § 24); on the interchange between ו and י, cf. p. 484, § 64); vocalize: יֵשְׁבוּ; cf. following יְחַיּוּ.

Joel 1.7: וְהִשְׁלִיךְ: denominative verb, from Isa. 6.13: שַׁלֶּכֶת: *and hath cast down its leaves.*

Joel 1.8: "...like a virgin ... for the husband...". The comparison is: the virgin never had a husband, and so the גפן and תאנה had no fruit, either; cf. v. 11: עַל חטה וְעַל שערה, implying: *for the absence of* חטה and שערה.

Joel 1.12: רִמּוֹן (גַּם תָּמָר וְתַפּוּחַ): perhaps: רמו: *even the palmtree and apple-tree deceived*; cf. Hos. 9.2: וְתִירוֹשׁ יְכַחֶשׁ בה; Hab. 3.17: כְּחֵשׁ מעשה זית.

Joel 2.5: כְּקוֹל מַרְכָּבוֹת: "like the noise ... do they leap"; but "noise" does not "leap"; therefore: *like noisome chariots* (cf. on Ps. 22.7).

Joel 4.8: לִשְׁבָאִים: *as captives*; plur. to שְׁבִי; cf. 1 Chron. 12.9: וְכִצְבָאִים, plur. to צְבִי; Prov. 8.5: פְּתָאִים, plur .to פֶּתִי ib. 9.4.

Am. 1.3: (לֹא) אֲשִׁיבֶנּוּ: *I shall not let them dwell in peace*; ab √ישׁב=שׁוּב; cf. Isa. 30.15: בְּשׁוּבָה וָנַחַת (cf. p. 595, § 56).

Am. 2.14: (כֹּחוֹ) יְאַמֵּץ (לֹא); vocalize יֶאֱמָץ: *And the strong, his might shall not be powerful*; cf. v. 16: וְאַמִּיץ לבו בגבורים ערום ינוס ביום ההוא.

Am. 3.6: (אִם תִּהְיֶה) רָעָה (בְּעִיר): *Shall a commotion be in the city*; ab √רעה; לָמָה תָּרִיעִי רֵעַ; (תְּרוּעָה): commotion, shouting; cf. Mic. 4.9: =רוע (cf. תְּרוּעָה): commotion, shouting; cf. Mic. 4.9; cf. on Ps. 107.26 (cf. p. 595, § 56).

Am. 3.15: בָּתִּים רַבִּים is construct state, cf. p. 613, § 83: *the houses of the great*; cf. parallel בָּתֵּי הַשֵּׁן; cf. also 2 Ki. 25.9: בֵּית גָּדוֹל and Jer. 52.13: בֵּית הַגָּדוֹל; further: Jer. 39.13: וְכָל רַבֵּי מֶלֶךְ בָּבֶל.

Am. 4.2: (נִשְׁבַּע אדני יהוה) בְּקָדְשׁוֹ: *The Lord God hath sworn in His sanctuary* (scil. His dwelling-place; cf. Hab. 2.20: ויהוה בהיכל קדשו; Ps. 60.8: אלהים דבר בקדשו); cf. also in Jonah 2.5: נגרשתי מִנֶּגֶד עֵינֶיךָ with following אַךְ אוֹסִיף לְהַבִּיט אל הֵיכַל קָדְשֶׁךָ.

Am. 4.5: וְקַטֵּר מֵחָמֵץ תּוֹדָה קְרָאוּ; divide: וְקַטֵּר מֵחָמֵץ תּוֹדָה וְקִרְאוּ נְדָבוֹת הַשְׁמִיעוּ: *And offer a sacrifice of that which is leavened, proclaim thanksgiving, make public freewill-offerings*.

Am. 5.16: אֲדֹנָי (אלהי צבאות) // יהוה is a doublet (cf. p. 320, § 29 under 6 and 8).

Am. 5.16: וְיוֹדְעֵי נֶהִי; re-arrange: וּמִסְפֵּד אֶל מִסְפֵּד אֶל יוֹדְעֵי נֶהִי: *and those skilful of wailing* (scil.: *call*) *to lamentation*; the predicate is still: וְקִרְאוּ.

Am. 6.10: (דּוֹדוֹ) וּמְסָרְפוֹ; perhaps: וּמַסְפְּדוֹ (or: pi'el): *his friend and mourner*. Cf. Jer. 16.1: לֹא יִקָּבְרוּ ולֹא יִסָּפְדוּ להם; also ib. 22.18/19; ספד is almost regularly found in connection with death and burial. On the interchange between ר and ד, cf. p. 482, § 55.

Am. 6.12: הַיְרָצוּן בַּסֶּלַע סוּסִים; perhaps הַיַרְצוּן סֶלַע בַּסּוּסִים; *Does one reap rocks with horses, or plow* (them) *with oxen?* Om the construction of the -בְ (appended to סלע, while referring to סוסים), cf. on Prov. 31.13.

Am. 8.9: (וְהַחֲשַׁכְתִּי לָאָרֶץ) בְּיוֹם אוֹר; re-arrange: בְּאוֹר יוֹם: *And I will darken the earth in broad daylight*; cf. parallel בַּצָּהֳרָיִם, and Mic. 2.1: בְּאוֹר הַבֹּקֶר.

Obad 7: לַחְמְךָ; vocalize: לֹחֲמֶךָ; cf. Prov. 23.1: כי תשב לִלְחוֹם את מושל; translate: *They that dine with thee.*

Obad 16: (וְשָׁתוּ) וְלָעוּ (cf. Prov. 23.2: בְּלֹעֶךָ): *They shall drink and get choked*; cf. following: וְהָיוּ כְּלֹא הָיוּ.

Obad 17: וְיָרְשׁוּ (... את) מוֹרָשֵׁיהֶם: *And the house of Jacob shall disinherit those who disinherited* (or: *displaced*) *them*; cf. on Jer. 8.10.

Jonah 1.6: נִרְדָּם is inf. (=נִרְדֹּם). Similar cases of interchange between -ָ and -ֹ, cf. Zeph. 2.9: יָבֹזּוּם (=יבוזום), Isa. 7.11: שְׁאָלָה (=שאלה), Nah. 1.2: קַנּוֹא (=קנּא).

Jonah 1.14: אל נא נאבדה בנפש האיש הזה implies that Jonah was guilty and they were ready to cast him into the sea; but with ואל תתן עלינו דם נקיא they admit that they were not at all certain of Jonah's guilt, but were apprehensive lest they throw an innocent man into the water. Hence עלינו is perhaps a euphemism (תקון סופרים) for עָלֶיךָ, and דם נקיא refering to themselves, who would otherwise perish (note the ending of the verse: כי אתה יהוה כאשר חפצת עשית).

Jonah 2.7: (הָאָרֶץ) בְּרִחֶיהָ; perhaps: בְּרִיחָה: *The earth is barred unto me for ever.*

Mic. 2.1: וּפֹעֲלֵי (רָע); plur. to פֹּעַל (=וּפָעֳלֵי): *and acts of evil*; cf. Isa. 59.6: מַעֲשֵׂה אָוֶן וּפֹעַל חָמָס.

Mic. 2.4: (שָׂדֵינוּ יְחַלֵּק) לְשׁוֹבֵב: *To the captors doth he divide our fields*; ab שׁוּב√=שבה; cf. p. 595, § 56.

Mic. 2.4: יְחַלֵּק: denominative verb, from חֵלֶק (cf. in this same verse!): *he apportions.*

Mic. 2.8: (מֵעֹבְרִים בֶּטַח) שׁוּבֵי (מִלְחָמָה): *From them that pass by securely* (scil.: *you make*) *prisoners of war*; ab שׁוּב√=שבה; cf. ch. 0, § 00.

Mic. 2.9: מִבֵּית תַּעֲנֻגֶיהָ: *from the houses of their delight*; namely: the houses, where they experienced delight. "Pleasant houses" reflects on the architecture or interior furnishing of the houses, but not on the personal experiences of their inhabitants.

Mic. 2.10: טָמְאָה is a noun (=טֻמְאָה; cf. p. 444, § 74).

Mic. 2.11: divide and read: שֶׁקֶר וְכָזָב   לוּ אִישׁ הֹלֵךְ רוּחַ; on the expression
הֹלֵךְ רוּחַ, cf. Hos. 12.2: רֹעֶה רוּחַ.

Mic. 3.4: הֵרֵעוּ: denominative verb, from רָעָה: *their doings are evil*.

Mic. 3.6: וְחָשְׁכָה is a noun, the fem. form to חֹשֶׁךְ (cf. p. 22 f., § 20).

Mic. 3.10: בֹּנֶה is plural (cf. p. 256, § 25 and note 2 there); cf. the plural in
preceding v. 9: הַמְתַעֲבִים ···· יְעַקֵּשׁוּ.

Mic. 3.11: יוֹרוּ: *decide* (or: *make decisions*); cf. Hag. 2.11 f.

Mic. 3.12: שָׂדֶה תֵחָרֵשׁ: *shall be plowed into a field*; namely, by destroying
the buildings. עִיִּין: "heaps," scil. of stones.

Mic. 4.6: וַאֲשֶׁר הֲרֵעֹתִי; perhaps וַאֲאַשֵּׁר הָרֵעַ, cf. Num. 14.33: ובניכם יהיו
רֹעִים במדבר: *And I will put right* (or: *on the right way*) *those that are
going astray*; cf. Isa. 9.15: ויהיו מְאַשְּׁרֵי העם הזה מתעים.

Mic. 4.13: וְהַחֲרַמְתִּי is 2. pers. fem. Cf. p. 236, § 2.

Mic. 4.14: (תִּתְגֹּדְדִי) בַּת גְּדוּד; probably one word: בְּתַגְדוּד: nominal formation with prefix ת to גדוד; cf. Ezek. 27.6: בַּת אֲשֻׁרִים, which according
to the Targum, is one word, too: בתאשרים.

Mic. 5.4-5: וְרָעוּ ···· רֹעִים; play on the roots רעה and רעע; cf. p. 595, § 56.

Mic. 5.7: עָבָר (אֲשֶׁר אִם): *Who, if he be enraged*; cf. עֶבְרָה.

Mic. 7.3: עַל הָרַע כַּפַּיִם לְהֵיטִיב הַשַּׂר שָׁאֵל; if it is not too daring, I would
suggest: לְהָרַע וּלְהֵיטִיב כֹּפֶר הַשַּׂר שָׁאֵל: *To do evil or act kindly, ransom
asketh the prince*; cf. Am. 5.12: צֹרְרֵי צדיק לקחי כֹפֶר; Jer. 10.5:
לֹא יָרֵעוּ וגם הֵיטֵיב אין אותם.

Mic. 7.11: (יוֹם הַהוּא) יִרְחַק חֹק; verb formed by reduplication: רחקחק, "to
be not far off"; cf. Hos. 4.18: אָהֲבוּ הֵבוּ ab אהבהב; similarly: Mic. 2.4:
וְהִתַּמֵּהוּ תְּמֵהַּ ab נהנה (cf. parallel מָשָׁל ···· (יִשָּׂא); (וְנָהָה) נְהִי נִהְיָה; Hab. 1.5:
ab תמהמה; cf. on Hos. 4.18.

Nah. 1.8: וּבְשֶׁטֶף עֹבֵר: *And with a flood of wrath*; cf. v. 6: לִפְנֵי זַעְמוֹ. עבר is
the masculine equivalent to עֶבְרָה; cf. p. 22 f., § 20; cf. also: Jer. 13.16:
הָרֵי נָשֶׁף, plural to הַר נִשְׁפֶּה Isa. 13.2; Zeph. 3.3: זְאֵבֵי עֶרֶב as compared
with זְאֵב עֲרָבוֹת Jer. 5.6.

Nah. 3.1: הוֹי עִיר דָּמִים כֻּלָּהּ כַּחַשׁ פֶּרֶק מְלֵאָה לֹא יָמִישׁ טָרֶף; re-arrange and
read: הוֹי עִיר דָּמִים כֻּלָּהּ כַּחַשׁ פֶּרֶק מִלֵּאָה לֹא יָמִישׁ טָרֶף: *Woe to the bloody
city, All lies and crushing, From her throat departeth not prey*. On the
interchange between ע – א, cf. p. 477, § 37.

Nah. 3.17: כְּגוֹב גֹּבָי is one word: a noun formed by reduplication (cf.

on Mic. 7.11). On the absolute form of the plur. ending in בֶ֫יךָ, cf. p. 39, § 34 f.

Hab. 1.3: תַּבִּיט has here causative meaning: *And lettest me behold*; cf. the parallel תַּרְאֵנִי: "dost Thou show me." Similarly, Zech. 3.9: וּמַשְׁתִּי has transitive, ib. 14.4: וּמָשׁ intransitive meaning; Isa. 28.19: הָבִין (שְׁמוּעָה): "to understand," but ib. v. 9: יָבִין (שְׁמוּעָה): "shall one make to understand" (causative).

Hab. 1.4: לָנֶ֫צַח: *victorious*; cf. on Ps. 13.2.

מַכְתִּיר: denominative verb, from כֶּ֫תֶר or כֹּתֶ֫רֶת: *to be the head of, superior* or *above of*.

Hab. 2.6: וּמְלִיצָה (חִידוֹת): perhaps to read: יַמְלִיצָה (cf. the parallel יִשָּׂאוּ; on the ending הָ֫ cf. p. 237, § 3): a denominative verb, from מְלִיצָה (cf. Prov. 1.6): *Figure out riddles*.

Hab. 3.8: מַרְכְּבֹתֶ֫יךָ יְשׁוּעָה: "Thy chariots of victory" would correspond to a Hebrew text מרכבתיך מרכבת ישועה, cf. Isa. 59.7: מַחְשְׁבוֹתֵיהֶם מַחְשְׁבוֹת אָ֫וֶן; a noun with suffixes cannot be مضاف in a construct state. Therefore: *the chariots of Thy victory*. Cf. p. 610, § 77.

Zeph. 2.4: יְגָרְשׁוּהָ (אַשְׁדּוֹד · · ·); perhaps to read: יְשָׁדּוּהָ: *Ashdod, at the noonday they shall despoil her* (on the interchange ר – ד, cf. p. 482, § 55).

Zeph. 3.20: The י in שְׁבוּתֵיכֶם is merely *mater lectionis* (cf. p. 570, § 16).

Zech. 12.10: וְתַחֲנוּנִים (חֵן): nominal formation with prefix ת to חֵן; similarly: Ezra 9.8: תְּחִנָּה; cf. on Mic. 4.14; also Isa. 29.2: תַּאֲנִיָּה וַאֲנִיָּה. Hence: *of grace and of kindness*.

Zech. 13.6: מְאַהֲבָי (בֵּית): the absolute state of the plur., cf. p. 39, § 34 f.: *in the house of love*.

Mal. 3.17: הָעֹבֵד; read: הָעֹבֵר (cf. p. 482 f., §§ 55 and 57): Though Israel troubled the Lord, still, He spares them as His children. Filial duties are termed כַּבֵּד and יָרֵא; only God expects Israel to עָבַד him, cf. v. 18.

Mal. 3.19: עֹשֵׂה (רִשְׁעָה) is plural; cf. preceding זֵדִים. Cf. on Mic. 3.10.

Ps. 1.6: וְדֶ֫רֶךְ רְשָׁעִים תֹּאבֵד: *But the way of the wicked is destruction*; cf. on Prov. 10.28.

Ps. 4.7: מִי יַרְאֵ֫נוּ טוֹב: *Will He let us see the good?* מִי (=הַאִם) is an Aramaism; cf. Am. 7.2: מִי יָקוּם יַעֲקֹב: Will Jacob (be able to) stand? This explanation of the Amos-passage I heard from my late brother Jakob in the name of Professor Jakob Barth.

Ps. 10.6: לֹא אֶשָּׁר בְּרָע: *I shall not face adversity.* (לְדֹר וָדֹר); re-arrange: אֲשֶׁר לֹא בְרָע;

Ps. 10.13-14: רָעָתָם (cf. p. 477 f., § 37 and p. 486, § 66, sub 6): *Thou wilt not search out their wickedness.* (לֹא תִדְרֹשׁ) רָאִתָה; read:

Ps. 10.17: תַּחַן: *Thy ear will listen to the supplication of their heart.* (לִבָּם) תָּכִין; read:

Ps. 10.18: רָע (cf. p. 482, § 55): *That the wicked man no more crush a (humble) man (away) from the land.* (בַּל יֹסִיף) עוֹד; read

Ps. 11.4: יהוה בְּהֵיכַל קָדְשׁוֹ: *The Lord, His sanctuary is in the temple*; cf. parallel יהוה בַּשָּׁמַיִם כִּסְאוֹ. On בְּהֵיכַל as determined form, cf. on Gen. 1.1.

Ps. 13.2: נֶצַח cannot mean "for ever", since verse a and b offer עַד אָנָה "how long" as a question. Hence: *Wilt Thou utterly forget me*; cf. on Jer. 15.18 and Hab. 1.4.

Ps. 22.7: חֶרְפַּת אָדָם: *a repulsive man*; the opposite is תִּפְאֶרֶת אָדָם Isa. 44.13: a beautiful man. On the grammatical structure, cf. אֵשֶׁת זְנוּנִים Hos. 1.2, meaning: אֵשָּׁה זוֹנָה; אֵשֶׁת לֵדָה Jer. 13.21, meaning: אֵשָּׁה יוֹלֵדֶת; צִיצַת נֹבֵל Isa. 28.4, meaning: צִיצָה נֹבֶלֶת; אֵשֶׁת רָע Prov. 6.24, meaning: אֵשָּׁה רָעָה; צֶמַח צְדָקָה Jer. 33.15 identical in meaning with צֶמַח צַדִּיק Jer. 23.6.

Ps. 23.3: (נַפְשִׁי) יְשׁוֹבֵב: *He grants rest* (or: *calms down*) *my soul,* cf. Isa. 30.15: בשובה ונחת.

Ps. 26.7: לַשְׁמִעַ בְּקוֹל תּוֹדָה: *To make thanksgiving be heard with (loud) voice*; cf. on 66.8.

Ps. 31.3: מְהֵרָה is an imperative, cf. preceding הַטֵּה and following הֱיֵה (=1 Sam. 23.27: מַהֲרָה): *Make haste to deliver me.* No לְ has to be added to הַצִּילֵנִי; cf. 68.19: מַהֵר עֲנֵנִי.

Ps. 39.9: חֶרְפַּת נָבָל: *Make me not a repulsive (or despicable) base*; cf. on 22.7.

Ps. 40.14: רְצֵה (יהוה לְהַצִּילֵנִי): *Hasten, O Lord, to deliver me*; ab √רצה= רוץ, cf. parallel חוּשָׁה; cf. 595, § 56.

Ps. 46.5: מִשְׁכְּנֵי קְדֹשׁ עֶלְיוֹן; re-arrange: מִשְׁכְּנֵי עֶלְיוֹן; on the plural מִשְׁכְּנֵי cf. מִקְדְּשֵׁי בֵּית יהוה Jer. 51.51.

Ps. 54.3: תְּדִינֵנִי: *shield* (or: *protect*) *me*; cf. ib. 68.6: (אלמנות) וְדַיָּן: *protector.*

Ps. 55.22: חָלְקוּ מַחֲמָאֹת פִּיו: *Smooth are the blandishments of his mouth*; מַחֲמָאֹת is a nominal form with prefix מ to חֶמְאָה, cf. on Ex. 12.4.

Ps. 63.2: (בְּאֶרֶץ צִיָּה) וְעָיֵף is a construct state; עָיֵף is a noun; cf. on Jer. 2.25.

Ps. 66.8: וְהַשְׁמִיעוּ קוֹל תְּהִלָּתוֹ: *And make His praise be heard with (loud) voice*; cf. on 26.7. Note also here v. 17: אֵלָיו פִּי קָרָאתִי: "I cried unto Him with my mouth"; v. 19: הִקְשִׁיב בְּקוֹל תְּפִלָּתִי: "He hath attended to the voice of my prayer."

Ps. 66.20: תְּפִלָּתִי (וְחַסְדּוֹ) is probably dittography from v. 19; a prayer cannot be "removed" or "turned away" (הֵסִיר); the verb refers solely to חַסְדּוֹ: "his mercy" or "grace'.'

Ps. 69.24: (וּמָתְנֵיהֶם) תָּמִיד הַמְעַד; read: תַּמְעִיד הַמְעַד: *And make their loins utterly to totter.*

Ps. 81.2: (הַרְנִינוּ) לֵאלֹהִים עוּזֵּנוּ: *Sing aloud unto the God of Our Strength*; לֵאלֹהִים עוּזֵּנוּ is a construct state, like the parallel לֵאלֹהֵי יַעֲקֹב, cf. p. 613, § 83.

Ps. 81.6: שְׂפַת לֹא יָדַעְתִּי אֶשְׁמָע: *A speech, which I did not know, did I hear*; cf. p. 614, § 84b.

Ps. 81.17: (וַיַּאֲכִילֵהוּ) מֵחֵלֶב (חִטָּה); cf. 147.14: חֵלֶב חִטִּים יַשְׂבִּיעֵךְ; hence, מֵחֵלֶב is a nominal form with prefix מ to חֵלֶב; cf. on Ex. 12.4.

Ps. 90.12: הוֹדִיעֵנִי יהוה קִצִּי וּמִדַּת יָמַי מַה הִיא; cf. 39.5: לִמְנוֹת (יָמֵינוּ כֵּן הוֹדַע). Hence read here: לִמְנָת: *Make known the measure of our days* (namely: for how long we are going to live). On the structure with ל, cf. Isa. 26,7: כִּי לַיהוה מָגִנֵּנוּ; Jer. 30.12: אָנוּשׁ לְשִׁבְרֵךְ; Ps. 89.19: אֹרַח לַצַּדִּיק; וְלִקְדֹשׁ יִשְׂרָאֵל מַלְכֵּנוּ; cf. on Ps. 93.5. On the spelling with *waw*, cf. Ezek. 34.25: בַּיְּעוּרִים.

Ps. 91.15: וַאֲכַבְּדֵהוּ: *and I will make him rich*, cf. Gen. 13.2: וְאַבְרָהָם כָּבֵד מְאֹד בַּמִּקְנֶה בַּכֶּסֶף וּבַזָּהָב.

Ps. 93.5: (לְבֵיתְךָ) נַאֲוָה (קֹדֶשׁ); vocalize נָאוֶה: *Thine house is a holy dwelling-place*; cf. 2 Sam. 15.25: נָוֵהוּ referring to the sanctuary. The א is *mater lectionis*, cf. p. 563, § 1a (especially the example from Isa. 33.20), and p. 576, § 29. On the structure with ל (in לְבֵיתְךָ), cf. Jer. 19.13: לְכָל הַבָּתִּים "even all the houses," and above on Ps. 90.12.

Ps. 102.25: בְּדוֹר דּוֹרִים is one word: a noun formed by reduplication; cf. on Nah. 3.17.

Ps. 105.6: בְּחִירָיו is sing. (cf. p. 263, § 37) and refers to יעקב cf. Isa. 42.1: עַבְדִּי · · · בְּחִירִי, to which Origen adds *sub obelo*: Ιακωβ . . . Ισραηλ; cf. 1 Chron. 16.13, where the text actually has יַעֲקֹב · · · עבדו יִשְׂרָאֵל

Isa. 45.4: ‏יעקב עבדי וישראל בחרתי בו‏. cf. also Isa. 44.1: ‏בחיריו‏;
‏עבדי יעקב וישראל בחירי‏. Translate: *The children of Jacob, His chosen one.*

Ps. 106.3: ‏עֹשֵׂה (צְדָקָה)‏ is parallel to ‏שֹׁמְרֵי (מִשְׁפָּט)‏ and hence plural[1]; cf. on
Mic. 3.10.

Ps. 107.26: ‏(נַפְשָׁם) בְּרָעָה (תִּתְמוֹגָג)‏: *Their soul melted away in the uproar (of
the waves)*; cf. on Am. 3.6.

Ps. 109.24: ‏וּבְשָׂרִי כָּחַשׁ מִשָּׁמֶן‏; re-arrange and read: ‏וּמִשְׁמַן בְּשָׂרִי כָּחַשׁ‏: *And
the fatness of my flesh hath waxen lean*; cf. Isa. 17.4: ‏וּמִשְׁמַן בְּשָׂרוֹ יֵרָזֶה‏.

Ps. 119.32: ‏(דֶּרֶךְ מִצְוֹתֶיךָ) אָרוּץ‏: *I choose the way of Thy commandments*;
‏אָרוּץ‏ ab √‏רוּץ‏=‏רצה‏, cf. on Ps. 40.14.

Ps. 119.50: ‏נֶחָמָתִי‏ is an inflected form with preservation of the first vowel,
cf. on Ezek. 35.12.

Ps. 119.83: ‏(בְּקִיטוֹר) כְּנֹאד‏; vocalize: ‏כְּנֶאְד‏: *For I am become (for weakness)
like one who is moving with the smoke.* On the ‏א‏ as *mater lectionis*,
cf. on 93.5.

Ps. 137.3: ‏(צִיּוֹן) מִשִּׁיר‏: *Sing us the song of Zion*; ‏מִשִּׁיר‏ is a nominal form
with prefix ‏מ‏ to ‏שִׁיר‏; cf. on Ex. 12.4.

Ps. 141.3: ‏שָׁמְרָה‏ is a noun (=‏מִשְׁמָר‏); cf. on Mic. 3.6 and 2.10.

Ps. 141.10: ‏אָנֹכִי עַד אֶעֱבוֹר‏; re-arrange: ‏עַד אֶעֱבוֹר אָנֹכִי‏: *Let the wicked
altogether fall into the nets, while I pass by [safely].*

Prov. 1.3: divide thus: ‏לָקַחַת מוּסָר   הַשְׂכֵּל צֶדֶק   וּמִשְׁפָּט מֵישָׁרִים‏. *To receive
instruction, be wise in justice, and judge rightly.* Now, ‏וּמִשְׁפָּט‏
may be explained as (Aramaic) infinitive; cf. Jer. 46.5: ‏וּמָנוֹס נָסוּ‏;
Ezek. 36.5: ‏לְמַעַן מִגְרָשָׁהּ‏ (ab √‏גרש‏); Prov. 12.12: ‏מְצוֹד‏ (ab √‏צוד‏).
Cf. MH § 13d.

Prov. 1.16: ‏(כִּי רַגְלֵיהֶם) לָרַע (יָרוּצוּ)‏: *For their feet run to do evil*; ‏לְהָרַע‏=‏לָרַע‏;
cf. 24.17: ‏וּבְהִכָּשְׁלוֹ‏=‏וּבְכָּשְׁלוֹ‏.

Prov. 1.32: ‏(פְּתָיִם) מְשׁוּבַת‏ is parallel to ‏(כְּסִילִים) וְשַׁלְוַת‏; hence cf. Isa. 30.15:
‏בשובה ונחת‏ and translate: *carelessness.*

Prov. 2.9: Connect: ‏וּמִשְׁפָּט מֵישָׁרִים‏: *and rightful judgment*; cf. on 1.3.

Prov. 4.7: ‏וּבְכָל קִנְיָנְךָ קְנֵה בִינָה‏: *and whensoever you acquire (anything),
acquire* (or: *let it be*) *understanding.*

Prov. 5.23: ‏וּבְרֹב אִוַּלְתּוֹ יִשְׁגֶּה‏: *And for the greatness of his folly, (in which)
he erred*; cf. p. 589, § 45.

Prov. 6.34: ‏קִנְאָה‏ is a verb (=‏קָנְאָה‏): *For jealous is a man's rage.*

Prov. 7.19: ‏מֵרָחוֹק‏ is a noun (=‏מֶרְחָק‏); cf. also Isa. 22.3: ‏מֵרָחוֹק בָּרָחוּ‏,

where מֵרָחוֹק indicates the direction, whereto they fled. Cf. on Jer. 23.23.

Prov. 7.21: (הִטַּתּוּ בְּרֹב) לִקְחָהּ; read: חֶלְקָהּ (cf. p. 489, § 70): *With the abundance of her smooth (speech) she causeth him to yield.*

Prov. 7.22: פִּתְאֹם is adverb to פֶּתִי: *foolishly* (or: *unthinking*).

Prov. 7.22: וּכְעֶכֶס אֶל מוּסַר אֱוִיל; re-arrange: וּכְאֱוִיל מוּסַר אֶל עֶכֶס: *And like a fool, fettered to an anklet.* מוּסָר is ab √אסר=יסר; cf. p. 595, § 56.

Prov. 8.6: נְגִידִים is a derivation of נֶגֶד: *the obvious, apparent.*

Prov. 8.23: (מֵרֹאשׁ) מִקַּדְמֵי (אָרֶץ): *Even from before the beginnings of the earth.* מִקַּדְמֵי is a nominal form with prefix מ to קֶדֶם; cf. on Ex. 12.4.

Prov. 10.3: (וְהַוַּת רְשָׁעִים יֶהְדֹּף); read: וְחַיַּת (cf. p. 477, § 38 and p. 484, § 64): *But the life of the wicked He thrusteth away*; cf. Job 33.20, where חַיָּתוֹ is parallel to וְנַפְשׁוֹ (like here).

Prov. 10.4: רָאשׁ עֹשֶׂה כַף רְמִיָּה; re-arrange: כַּף רְמִיָּה עֹשָׂה רָאשׁ: *A cheatful hand maketh poor (but a diligent hand maketh rich).* On the adjectival meaning of חָרוּצִים (in the construct state וְיַד חָרוּצִים), cf. p. 602, § 67.

Prov. 10.14: (וּפִי אֱוִיל מְחִתָּה) קְרֹבָה; vocalize: קִרְבָּה (cf. p. 265, § 43): *But the mouth of the fool, ruin is within it*; cf. Ps. 5.10: קִרְבָּם הַוּוֹת.

Prov. 10.25: כַּעֲבוֹר סוּפָה וְאֵין רָשָׁע: *Like a whirlwind that passes and is no more, is the wicked.* On the vocalization וְאֵין cf. Ezek. 1.27: בֵּית (לָהּ); אֵין כָּמֹהוּ Isa. 36.2: (כָּבֵד) בְּחַיִל; and also Jer. 30.7: מֵאַיִן כָּמֹהוּ with Job 1.8: אֵין כָּמֹהוּ.

Prov. 10.28: תּאֹבֵד is a noun with prefix ת: *The expectation of the wicked is destruction*; cf. similarly 11.23: תִּקְוַת רְשָׁעִים עֶבְרָה (a noun, too). On the meaning of תּאֹבֵד cf. אֲבַדּוֹן; on the formation cf. Judg. 14.4: תּאֲנָה, which according to the Babylonian tradition (cf. *Biblia Hebraica* ed. Kittel-Kahle) is vocalized תּאֲנָה.

Prov. 12.7: הָפוֹךְ רְשָׁעִים וְאֵינָם: *Turn round, and the wicked are no more* (=הָפוֹךְ וּרְשָׁעִים אֵינָם).

Prov. 15.20: בּוֹזֶה אִמּוֹ: *puts his mother to shame*; cf. parallel יְשַׂמַּח אָב; cf. p. 7, § 7a.

Prov. 15.28: (יַבִּיעַ) רָעוֹת; read דֵּעוֹת (cf. p. 482, § 55): *But the mouth of the wicked poureth forth opinions*; cf. parallel יֶהְגֶּה לַעֲנוֹת.

Prov. 15.30: מְאוֹר עֵינַיִם: *Radiant eyes give joy to the heart.* On the structure מְאוֹר עֵינַיִם (as meaning עֵינַיִם מְאִירוֹת), cf. עָרֵי הַמִּבְצָר Josh. 10.20 identical with וְעָרִים · · · בְּצֻרוֹת ib. 14.12; cf. also Prov. 16.15: בְּאוֹר פְּנֵי מֶלֶךְ חַיִּים: *In the radiance of the king's countenance is life.*

Prov. 16.6: (וּבְיִרְאַת יהוה) סוּר מֵרָע: *And in the fear of God is* (or *lies*) *the chastisement of an evil-doer*; ab √סוּר=יסר, cf. Ps. 118.18; cf. p. 595, § 56.

Prov. 17.17: וְאָח לְצָרָה יִוָּלֵד: *A friend is a lover all the time, And a brother in coming adversity*. On the form יִוָּלֵד (masculine, thus illogically referring to אָח), cf. p. 621, § 91, sub 4.

Prov. 17.26: (לְהַכּוֹת נְדִיבִים) עַל (יֹשֶׁר); read: אַל (cf. p. 477, § 37): *To strike the noble is not just*; on לֹא · · · אַל, cf. p. 15, § 9.

Prov. 18.4: נַחַל נֹבֵעַ מְקוֹר חָכְמָה; re-arrange: חכמה מקור נחל נבע: *Wisdom welleth with a flowing brook*; מקור is participle *hiph'il*, cf. Jer. 6.7: הֵקֵרָה רָעָתָה.

Prov. 18.10: בּוֹ יָרוּץ צַדִּיק וְנִשְׂגָּב: *The righteous chooses it, and is saved*. יָרוּץ is ab √רצה=רוּץ (cf. p. 595, § 56); on וְנִשְׂגָּב cf. the noun מִשְׂגָּב in phrases like כִּי הָיִיתָ מִשְׂגָּב לִי וּמָנוֹס בְּיוֹם צַר לִי Ps. 9.10; וַיְהִי יהוה מִשְׂגָּב לַדָּךְ Ps. 59.17.

Prov. 18.15: (וְאֹזֶן חֲכָמִים) תְּבַקֶּשׁ (דָעַת); read: תַּקְשֵׁב (cf. p. 489, § 70): *And the ear of the wise hearkens to knowledge*.

Prov. 18.19: אָח נִפְשָׁע מִקִּרְיַת עֹז (וּמִדְיָנִים כִּבְרִיחַ אַרְמוֹן); re-arrange and read: נֶפֶשׁ אָח כְּקִרְיַת עֹז: *A brother's soul is like a mighty city; But contentions are like the bars to the fortified castle* (scil. to open it to the enemy).

Prov. 20.6: רָב אָדָם יִקְרָא (אִישׁ חַסְדּוֹ): re-arrange and vocalize: אדם רב יִקָּרֵא: *A great man is called* (*his*) *benefactor*.

Prov. 20.8: מְזָרֶה is a nominal form with prefix מ to זָר: *abomination*.

Prov. 22.3: (עָרוּם רָאָה) רָעָה (וְנִסְתָּר): *A prudent man seeth a commotion, and hideth himself*; on רָעָה cf. on Am. 3.6.

Prov. 23.3: וְהוּא לֶחֶם כְּזָבִים: To what word does וְהוּא refer? Certainly not to לְמַטְעַמּוֹתָיו! Vocalize: וְהוּא לֹחֵם כְּזָבִים: *Be thou not desirous of his dainties, while he is feeding* (*thee*) *lies*; cf. v. 1.

Prov. 23.7: כִּי בְנַפְשׁוֹ כְּמוֹ שָׁעַר בְּנַפְשׁוֹ כֵּן הוּא: rearrange: כִּי כְּמוֹ רָשָׁע כֵּן הוּא *For inwardly, he is like a wicked man*; cf. p. 489, § 70.

Prov. 23.23: חָכְמָה (וּמוּסָר וּבִינָה): imperative with euphonic ה (cf. p. 279, § 60c): וְחָכְמָה מוּסָר וּבִינָה: *And be wise with instruction and understanding*.

Prov. 23.28: תּוֹסִיף; from the root אסף=יסף (cf. p. 595, § 56): *gathers in* or: *collects*; cf. Ps. 104. 29: תֹּסֵף רוּחָם; vice versa: Ex. 5.7: (לֹא) תֹאסִפוּן, from יסף=אסף.

Prov. 23.29: פְּצָעִים חִנָּם is construct state: *undeserved wounds*; cf. 26.2: קִלְלַת חִנָּם: *undeserved curse*.

Prov. 24.25: בִּרְכַּת טוֹב is equivalent to בְּרָכָה טוֹבָה; cf. on Ps. 22.7 (cf. p. 603, § 68, sub 3a).

Prov. 26.17: connect: כֶּלֶב עֹבֵר: *a stray dog*.

Prov. 26.18: כְּמִתְלַהְלֵהַּ; read: כְּמִהַתֵּל; cf. v. 19: הֲלֹא מְשַׂחֵק אָנִי.

Prov. 26.21: לַחֲרְחַר (רִיב) is onomatopoetic, imitating the growling guttural sounds accompanying a dog-fight (חר חר).

Prov. 27.12: עָרוּם רָאָה רָעָה נִסְתָּר; cf. on 22.3.

Prov. 27.17: (וְאִישׁ) יַחַד (פְּנֵי רֵעֵהוּ): *And a man gladdeneth his friend's countenance*. Play on √חדד and √חדה; cf. p. 595, § 56; "to make sharp" means "to make shining"; cf. Ezek. 21.14, 15.

Prov. 27.19: הַפָּנִים (לַפָּנִים); vocalize: הַפָּנִים: *Like water that floweth onward*.

Prov. 27.21: וְאִישׁ לְפִי מַהֲלָלוֹ; re-arrange: וּפִיו לְמַהֲלַל אִישׁ (or: וּפֶה): *And the mouth is for a man's praise*.

Prov. 27.26: וּמְחִיר שָׂדֶה עַתּוּדִים (=ומחיר עתודים שדה): *And the sale of goats is (for) a field*.

Prov. 28.2: רַבִּים; vocalize: רָבִים: *their princes fight*. מֵבִין ‖ יֹדֵעַ is a doublet (cf. p. 315, § 24); cf. similarly Neh. 10.29: כָּל יוֹדֵעַ מֵבִין. כֵּן (יַאֲרִיךְ): *right prevails*; cf. Gen. 42.11: כֵּנִים אֲנַחְנוּ.

Prov. 28.5: אַנְשֵׁי רָע (corresponding to אֲנָשִׁים רָעִים); cf. on Ps. 22.7 and p. 602 f., § 68.

Prov. 28.6: מֵעִקֵּשׁ דְּרָכַיִם וְהוּא עָשִׁיר (=מעשיר והוא עקש דרכים): *Than the rich, who is perverse in his ways*.

Prov. 28.12: וּבְקוּם רְשָׁעִים יֵחָפֵשׂ (אָדָם); read: חֶרְפַּת; cf. parallel רַבָּה תִפְאָרֶת and our note on Ps. 22.7: *But when the wicked rise, there is shame for men*.

Prov. 28.13: מְכַסֶּה פְשָׁעָיו לֹא יַצְלִיחַ: *He who covereth up his transgressions shall not succeed (in it)*.

Prov. 29.2: בִּרְבוֹת (צדיקים): *when righteous men rule*; cf. Jer. 39.13: שָׂרֵי. with ib. v. 3: וכל רַבֵּי מֶלֶךְ בָּבֶל.

Prov. 29.10: וִישָׁרִים יְבַקְשׁוּ נַפְשׁוֹ (=ויבקשו נפש ישרים): *and seek the life of the upright*.

Prov. 31.13: (וַתַּעַשׂ) בְּחֵפֶץ כַּפֶּיהָ (=חפץ בכפיה); cf. 19.12: נַהַם כַּכְּפִיר=

כְּחֶרֶב פִּיּוֹת Josh. 2.6: בְּפִשְׁתֵּי הָעֵץ=בעצי הפשתה; Prov. 5.4: ; כנהם כפיר
=כפיות חרב): *And maketh a (choice) thing with her hands.*

Job 3.5: כִּמְרִירֵי יוֹם; cf. on Hos. 4.4.

Lam. 1.8: לְנִדָּה is identical in meaning with מָנוֹד (scil. ראש); cf. Ps. 44.15:
משל בגוים מנוד ראש בלאמים: *shaking (of the head).* "Unclean" here is
meaningless, since the גוים did not observe the laws of "clean" and
"unclean".

Lam. 1.9: הִגְדִּיל is a denominative verb, from גדול: *For the enemy is
great,* cf. v.16: כי גבר אויב.

Ezra 2.62: כְּתָבָם הַמִּתְיַחֲשִׂים: *their genealogical register.* The مضاف (cf. p. 602,
§ 64) has the suffix; cf. on Isa. 31.7. Cf. also Ezra 8.1: וְהִתְיַחְשָׂם:
"the genealogy of them."

Ezra 9.3: מִשְׂעַר (ראשׁי): nominal formation with prefix מ to שַׂעַר (cf. on
Ex. 12.4).

Neh. 2.16: (וּלְיֶתֶר) עֹשֵׂה (הַמְּלָאכָה) is plur.; cf. on Mic. 3.10.

1 Chron. 4.10: וְעָשִׂיתָ מֵרָעָה לְבִלְתִּי עָצְבִּי: vocalize: וְעָשִׂתִי מרעה לְבִלְתִּי עצבי:
then I shall do (or: act) evil toward Belthi my idol; מרעה is a nominal
form with prefix מ to רעה; cf. on Ezra 9.3. On the vocalization of
עצבי (with עָ), cf. p. 30 f., § 21.

INDEX OF SUBJECT MATTERS

II. TWO HEBREW DIALECTS COMBINED FORM BIBLICAL HEBREW

I. PRE-MASORETIC PRONUNCIATION OF HEBREW

III. THE COMPOSITE CHARACTER OF THE BIBLE

I. THE HEBREW BIBLE AS EVIDENCE

II. THE BIBLE OF THE APOSTLES AS EVIDENCE

V. TOWARDS A NEW EXEGESIS OF THE BIBLE

INDEX OF BIBLICAL PASSAGES

THE MAKING OF THE
PACEMAKER

Celebrating a Lifesaving Invention

Wilson Greatbatch
Inventor of the Pacemaker

Foreword by Seymour Furman, M.D.
Professor of Surgery and Medicine, Albert Einstein College of Medicine

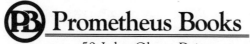 **Prometheus Books**
59 John Glenn Drive
Amherst, New York 14228-2197

Published 2000 by Prometheus Books

Inquiries should be addressed to
Prometheus Books
59 John Glenn Drive
Amherst, New York 14228-2197
VOICE: 716-691-0133, ext. 207
FAX: 716-564-2711
WWW.PROMETHEUSBOOKS.COM

04 03 02 01 00   5 4 3 2 1

Library of Congress Cataloging-in-Publication Data

Greatbatch, Wilson.
    The making of the pacemaker : celebrating a lifesaving invention / Wilson
Greatbatch.
        p. cm.
    Includes bibliographical references and index.
    ISBN 1-57392-806-2 (cloth : alk. paper)
    1. Cardiac pacemakers—History. I. Title.

RC684.P3 G69 2000
617.4'120645'09—dc21   00-023296
                                                                CIP

Printed in the United States of America on acid-free paper

This book is dedicated to Eleanor,
my loving and long-suffering wife
of fifty-six years,
and to
Warren Dee, John Leslie,
Kenneth Alan, Anne Katherine,
and Peter Neville (1958–1998).